Economics

Third Edition

David Begg

*Professor of Economics
Birkbeck College
University of London*

and

Stanley Fischer
Rudiger Dornbusch

*Professors of Economics
Massachusetts Institute of Technology*

McGRAW-HILL BOOK COMPANY

London · New York · St Louis · San Francisco · Auckland
Bogotá · Caracas · Hamburg · Lisbon · Madrid · Mexico
Milan · Montreal · New Delhi · Panama · Paris · San Juan
São Paulo · Singapore · Sydney · Tokyo · Toronto

For

Honora, Mary, and Robin

Published by
McGRAW-HILL Book Company Europe
Shoppenhangers Road, Maidenhead, Berkshire SL6 2QL, England
Telephone: 0628 23432   Fax: 0628 770224

British Library Cataloguing in Publication Data
Begg, David K. H.
Economics.
1. Economics
I. Title   II. Fischer, Stanley   III. Dornbusch, Rudiger
IV. Fischer, Stanley, *Economics*
330

ISBN 0-07-707245-6

3 4 5 MAT 9 4 3 2

Filmset by Mid-County Press, London.
Printed and bound in Great Britain by M. & A. Thomson Litho, Glasgow

Contents

Chapter 9
Perfect Competition and Pure Monopoly: The Limiting Cases of Market Structure

Chapter 10
Market Structure and Imperfect Competition

Chapter 11
The Analysis of Factor Markets: Labour

Suggested Outlines for a Shortened Course

Third Option: An Introduction to Macroeconomics

Preface

Students take up economics for different reasons. Some students are preparing for a career in business, some wish a deeper understanding of government policy, and some are concerned about the plight of the poor or the unemployed. Our guiding principle in writing this book has been to provide a self-contained introductory textbook which shows that economics is a live subject offering powerful insights about the world in which we live.

Two ideas have governed the level and range of material that we discuss. The first is that there is an essential, simple, usable body of economics that has to be learned in any introductory economics course. The second is that modern economics is more interesting and more readily applicable to analysis of the real world than traditional approaches suggest.

The Core Chapters

In the introductory chapters and in the core of both the microeconomics and macroeconomics parts of the book, the material covered is fundamental. We deal immediately with the tools economists use and we confront some common criticisms of economics and economists. In microeconomics we then provide an overview of supply and demand before analysing these forces in greater depth. This leads naturally on to market structure, factor markets, and an important section on welfare economics and government policy. In macroeconomics we start with national income accounting and go on to aggregate demand, fiscal policy, money and banking, government policy, and international trade and payments.

Even in these core chapters, we go beyond the standard introduction to the process of economic reasoning and the development of simple theories. Theories should be confronted with the relevant facts and can be used to discuss policy options. Our discussion emphasizes a blend of theory, applications, and policy analysis that brings economics across as the live social science that it is. Our examples use actual facts and figures about the UK and many other countries.

Beyond the Core

In two distinct senses, our discussion goes beyond the material often covered in traditional introductory economics courses. First, we discuss many topical applications of the standard theoretical framework. Here the intention is both to reinforce the material that has already been learned and to maintain the motivation for mastering theoretical analysis in order to apply it to relevant problems that people actually face today. In microeconomics we discuss human capital, discrimination, competition policy, the problems of industry, and the role of the government in resource allocation. In macroeconomics we examine practical difficulties in controlling the money supply, the relation between deficits, money and inflation, and the nature of unemployment. We show that the international dimensions can completely alter the consequences of domestic policies. And we have a whole section on the world economy.

Second, we believe in introducing students immediately to the latest ideas in economics. If these can be conveyed simply, why force students to use traditional approaches in cases where we no longer believe them to be helpful or realistic? Thus in microeconomics we discuss signalling and education, moral hazard and insurance, and the modern analysis of cartels and OPEC. In macroeconomics we discuss information, new theories of unemployment, supply side economics, rational expectations, and theories of speculation and exchange rate determination.

Economics for the Nineties

Our aim is to allow students to understand the economic environment in the nineties. Most of our examples, applications, and extensions are drawn from the real world. We equip students with the theoretical framework to understand today's discussion of tomorrow's problems. Among the issues we treat extensively are government deficits and inflation, the limits to Keynesian and monetarist economics, the prospects for unemployment, the costs of inflation, the economics of discrimination by race and sex, the role of the public sector, the new protectionism, and the future of European integration.

Level of Exposition

We cover the essential principles of economics slowly and thoroughly, starting from square one. Chapter 2 provides a self-contained introduction to the tools of economics that we use. We do not rely on algebra. There are very few equations in this book. Even where we discuss topics usually considered rather difficult – for example, aggregate supply – we keep the exposition at a level appropriate for a beginning student.

To the Student

It takes many years to become a complete economist with a professional's command of the subject. Most of you probably have no wish to become professional economists. Fortunately, the basic issues studied by economists, the framework of analysis, and many of the conclusions can be understood very quickly in an introductory course. Our emphasis on applications is designed to convince you that the economics you are learning is about the real world. It is not just a set of textbook exercises.

There is an old complaint that economists never agree about anything. This complaint is simply wrong. The press, taxi drivers, and politicians love to talk about topics on which there is disagreement. It would be boring television if the participants on a panel discussion held identical views. Producers of TV programmes search for economists who will disagree about some things. But economics is not a field in which there is always an argument for everything. There *are* answers to many questions. One of the aims of the book is to show where economists agree, and on what, and for what reason, they sometimes disagree. In choosing applications in this book, and especially in a policy discussion, we have tried to develop this perspective.

How to Study

There is a world of difference between reading about economics and· actually *doing* and understanding economics. The aim of the book

is *not* to tell you what economics is about. Rather, we hope the book will enable you both to learn how to use economics and to understand how to attack and analyse problems.

To *do* economics you have to learn actively. Reading is not enough. You should be questioning the text. When the book says 'clearly', ask yourself 'why'. When the text makes three points, check back to the first when you get to the third. Above all, when the text applies a previous piece of analysis, follow the application with care. When a line is drawn one way, ask 'why'. See if it can be drawn differently. Do the problems.

Be on guard against our attempts to make the text clear. Each paragraph may be easy reading, but you also have to keep check on how the paragraphs add up to a complete picture. At the end of each section ask yourself what you have learned. And to make sure, you may wish to jump ahead to the summary at the end of the chapter.

Workbook

The main text is accompanied by a third edition of the *Workbook* written by Peter Smith. The *Workbook* takes you step by step through the analysis of each chapter and provides many questions, exercises and solutions that enable you to learn actively the material of each chapter. Sample pages from the *Workbook* immediately follow the Test Quiz. These pages give a 'taster' of the *Workbook* and its contents. The *Workbook* is the best way to check that you have really mastered the economics you have learned.

David Begg
Stanley Fischer
Rudiger Dornbusch

Acknowledgements to First Edition

In the Preface to their original US edition of *Economics*, Stanley Fischer and Rudiger Dornbusch acknowledge with thanks the advice and suggestions offered by colleagues, students, and friends throughout the world. In completely rewriting the text for this edition, I, too, have drawn extensively on the advice and experience of teachers and students, and I thank them all.

Special thanks are due to Mike Artis, Nick Crafts, Steve Nickell and George Yarrow who offered suggestions on particular areas, and to Peter Smith and Susie Symes with whom I discussed the book at every stage. The McGraw-Hill team provided incredible support – sometimes it seemed that the whole company was working on just this one book – but Liz Nemecek deserves a special mention. As cajoler, consoler, and when necessary courier, she remained patient and cheerful even when we were all working under considerable pressure.

Acknowledgements to Second Edition

In preparing the Second Edition I have drawn extensively on the experience of teachers and students in using the First Edition. I owe a particular debt to my undergraduates at Worcester College Oxford, to the Tutors and members of the Oxford University Business Summer School, and to the many school teachers who discussed the use of the book in the classroom.

I thank Nick Crafts, Susie Symes and John Vickers for specific suggestions and Peter Smith who read the entire manuscript and made numerous improvements. At McGraw-Hill, my editor Maggie Pickering provided constant encouragement and assistance, and Liz Nemecek supervised the production with her usual efficiency.

Acknowledgements to Third Edition

As usual, I have benefited enormously from Peter Smith's eagle eye, and the efforts of what seems like the whole of McGraw-Hill (UK). Personally, as well as professionally, my deepest thanks go to Roger Horton.

David Begg

Test Quiz

Before you even look at this book, try the quiz below. Tick the answers you think are correct. When you have worked through the book, try the quiz again and compare your answers.

1 Economics is the study of:
   (a) how to produce the most goods for the most people.
   (b) how society decides what, how, and for whom to produce.
   (c) how to avoid waste and inefficiency.

2 (a) By encouraging customers, lower food prices raise revenues of farmers.
   (b) By discouraging customers, higher oil prices reduce revenues to oil producers.
   (c) Neither of the above.

3 (a) Higher income tax rates are a disincentive to work.
   (b) Higher income tax rates are an incentive to work.
   (c) Income tax rates have only a small effect on the incentive to work.

4 Nationalized industries that are efficient:
   (a) might still make losses.
   (b) should at least break even.
   (c) should lose money only on activities providing a wider social service.

5 An increase in the proportion of income saved:
   (a) tends to increase output since investment rises.
   (b) tends to reduce output since consumer spending falls.
   (c) tends to increase inflation since the money supply rises.

6 (a) Inflation makes people worse off because goods become more expensive.
   (b) Inflation makes a country uncompetitive in international markets.
   (c) A high but constant rate of inflation need not be a major problem.

7 An exchange rate devaluation improves a country's international competitiveness:
   (a) only after a few years.
   (b) only for a few years.
   (c) only if interest rates are simultaneously reduced.

8 It is well known that economists cannot forecast changes in stock market prices. This shows:
   (a) that economics works.
   (b) that economics pays insufficient attention to real world problems.
   (c) neither of the above.

focus upon the detailed aspects—for instance, by analysing the decisions taken by individual agents about particular commodities. Such analysis falls within the province of microeconomics. Alternatively, we may choose to gain a broader perspective by focusing upon the interactions in the economy at large—which takes us into macroeconomics. As our journey continues, we look first at the decisions made by individuals (microeconomics) before broadening the perspective to refocus upon macroeconomics.

IMPORTANT CONCEPTS AND TECHNICAL TERMS

Match each lettered concept with the appropriate numbered phrase:

(a) Scarce resource
(b) Law of diminishing returns
(c) Market
(d) Gross national product
(e) Distribution of income
(f) Positive economics
(g) Free markets
(h) Microeconomics
(i) Production possibility frontier
(j) Unemployment rate
(k) Opportunity cost
(l) Macroeconomics
(m) Mixed economy
(n) Aggregate price level
(o) Normative economics
(p) Command economy

1   The branch of economics offering a detailed treatment of individual decisions about particular commodities.
2   Economic statements offering prescriptions or recommendations based on personal value judgements.
3   An economy in which the government and private sector interact in solving economic problems.
4   The way in which income (in a country or in the world) is divided between different groups or individuals.
5   The process by which households' decisions about consumption of alternative goods, firms' decisions about what and how to produce, and workers' decisions about how much and for whom to work are all reconciled by adjustments of prices.
6   The quantity of other goods that must be sacrificed in order to obtain another unit of a particular good.
7   Markets in which governments do not intervene.
8   A resource for which the demand at a zero price would exceed the available supply.
9   The branch of economics emphasizing the interactions in the economy as a whole.
10 The value of all goods and services produced in the economy in a given period such as a year.

11 The percentage of the labour force without a job.
12 A measure of the average level of prices of goods and services in the economy, relative to their prices at some fixed date in the past.
13 A curve which shows, for each level of the output of one good, the maximum amount of the other good that can be produced.
14 The situation in which, as more workers are employed in an industry, each additional worker adds less to total industry output than the previous additional worker added.
15 A society where the government makes all decisions about production and consumption.
16 Economic statements dealing with objective or scientific explanations of the working of the economy.

EXERCISES

1   A tribe living on a tropical island includes five workers whose time is devoted either to gathering coconuts or to collecting turtle eggs. Regardless of how many other workers are engaged in the same occupation, a worker may gather either 20 coconuts or 10 turtle eggs in a day.
    (a) Draw the production possibility frontier for coconuts and turtle eggs.
    (b) Suppose that a new climbing technique is invented making the harvesting of coconuts easier. Each worker can now gather 28 coconuts in a day. Draw the new production possibility frontier.

2   Figure 1.1 shows a society's production possibility frontier for cameras and watches.
    (a) Identify each of the following combinations of the two goods as being either efficient, inefficient, or unattainable:

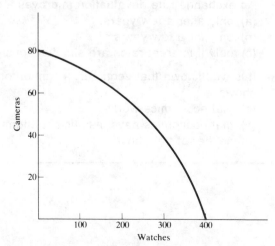

FIGURE 1.1 The production possibility frontier

Note: These pages have been reproduced smaller than the actual size of *Economics Workbook* (Third Edition) by Peter Smith and David Begg, published by McGraw-Hill and available from bookshops.

   (*i*) 60 cameras and 200 watches.
   (*ii*) 60 watches and 80 cameras.
   (*iii*) 300 watches and 35 cameras.
   (*iv*) 300 watches and 40 cameras.
   (*v*) 58 cameras and 250 watches.

(*b*) Suppose the society is producing 300 watches and 40 cameras, but wishes to produce an additional 20 cameras. How much output of watches must be sacrificed to enable these extra cameras to be made?

(*c*) How much output of watches would need to be given up to enable a further 20 cameras (i.e., 80 in all) to be produced?

(*d*) Explain the difference in the shape of the frontier in Figure 1.1 as compared with the ones you drew in exercise 1.

3 Figure 1.2 illustrates a production possibility boundary for an economy. If the economy is in recession, which of the four combinations of goods (*A, B, C,* or *D*) would be produced?

(Associated Examining Board GCE A level
Economics Paper 1, June 1988)

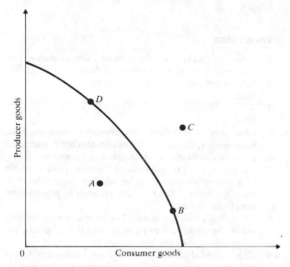

FIGURE 1.2

4 Which of the following statements are *normative*, and which are *positive*?

(*a*) The price of oil more than tripled between 1973 and 1974.

(*b*) In 1984, the poor countries of the world received less than their fair share of world income.

(*c*) The world distribution of income is too unjust, with poor countries having 61 per cent of the world's population, but receiving only 6 per cent of world income.

(*d*) In the early 1980s, most Western economies faced sharp rises in the aggregate unemployment rate.

(*e*) The UK government ought to introduce policies to reduce the unemployment rate.

(*f*) Smoking is antisocial and should be discouraged.

(*g*) The imposition of higher taxes on tobacco will discourage smoking.

(*h*) The economy of Hong Kong is closer to a free market system than that of Albania.

5 Which of the following statements are the concern of microeconomics and which of macroeconomics?

(*a*) Along with other Western economies, the UK faced a sharp rise in the unemployment rate in the early 1980s.

(*b*) The imposition of higher taxes on tobacco will discourage smoking.

(*c*) Unemployment among building labourers rose sharply in the early 1980s.

(*d*) An increase in a society's aggregate income is likely to be reflected in higher consumer spending.

(*e*) A worker who has received a pay rise is likely to buy more luxury goods.

(*f*) A firm will invest in a machine if the expected rate of return is sufficiently high.

(*g*) High interest rates in an economy may be expected to discourage aggregate investment.

(*h*) The level of gross national product in the UK is higher this year than in 1981.

6 Figure 1.3 shows society's choice between social

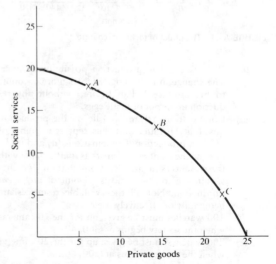

FIGURE 1.3 Society's choice between social services and private goods

ANSWERS AND COMMENTS FOR CHAPTER 1

Please note Where questions are reproduced from A level examinations, the examination boards bear no responsibility for the answers provided in this volume, which are the sole responsibility of the authors.

Important Concepts and Technical Terms

1	*h*	7	*g*	12	*n*
2	*o*	8	*a*	13	*i*
3	*m*	9	*l*	14	*b*
4	*e*	10	*d*	15	*p*
5	*c*	11	*j*	16	*f*
6	*k*				

Exercises

1 (a) The straight line PPF_a in Figure A1.1 represents the production possibility frontier for this society.

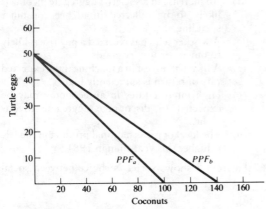

FIGURE A1.1 The effect of technical change

(b) PPF_b is the new production possibility frontier. The change in technology enables more coconuts to be 'produced' than before, without any reduction in output of turtle eggs.

2 (a) Combinations (*i*) and (*iv*) lie on the production possibility frontier and thus represent points of *efficient* production. Combinations (*ii*) and (*v*) lie outside the frontier and are thus *unattainable* with the resources available. Combination (*iii*) lies within the frontier, and is a point of *inefficient* production. Not all the available resources are being fully or effectively used.

(b) 100 watches must be given up for the 20 cameras when the society begins at (300, 40).

(c) 200 watches must be given up for the 20 cameras when the society begins at (200, 60).

(d) The difference in shape results from the law of diminishing returns. On the tropical island, the amounts produced by a worker did not vary according to whether other workers were engaged in the same activity. In the cameras and watches case, this is not so: as more workers are used to produce cameras, the additional output produced falls. This is explained in Section 1–2 of the main text.

3 A.

4 (*a*), (*d*), (*g*), and (*h*) are positive statements, containing objective descriptions of economies and the way they work. (*b*), (*e*), and (*f*) are normative statements which rely upon value judgements for their validity. Statement (*c*) contains elements of both: it includes a (positive) statement of fact about the distribution of world population and income but also rests on a (normative) value judgement that this was 'too unjust'.

5 (*a*), (*d*), (*g*), and (*h*) deal with economy-wide issues, and are thus the concern of macroeconomics. (*b*), (*c*), (*e*), and (*f*) are devoted to more detailed microeconomic issues.

6 (*a*) C. (*b*) A. (*c*) B.

7 Only (*a*) would be untrue for a *pure* command economy. Remember, though, that no such 'pure' command economy actually exists.

8 (*d*).

True/False

1 False: the claim of economics to be a science rests not on its subject matter, but upon its methods of analysis.

2 False: see Section 1–1 of the main text.

3 True.

4 True.

5 True.

6 False: while being closer to a command economy than many others, the Soviet Union tolerates the existence of some private markets, for instance in agriculture.

7 Sorry, this was a trick question! This is another example of a normative statement, which rests on a subjective value judgement. As a result, it can never be proven to be either true or false.

8 False: don't forget services! The production of services may be more difficult to measure than that of goods, but is important none the less.

9 True: many disagreements between economists reflect differences in beliefs and values (normative statements), rather than differences of opinion about objective analysis.

Questions for Thought

1 *Hint* It is rare that an economic issue involves only one of the three basic questions.

2 *Hint* So far, we have only considered an economy in a single time period. Here, the production of one of the goods directly affects what can be produced in the future.

3 D.

1

Introduction

1

Economics and the Economy

Every group of people must solve three basic problems of daily living: *what* goods and services to produce, *how* to produce these goods and services, and *for whom* to produce these goods and services.

Economics is the study of how society decides what, how, and for whom to produce.

By goods we mean physical commodities such as steel, cars, and strawberries. By services we mean activities such as massages or live theatre performances which can be consumed or enjoyed only at the instant they are produced. In exceptional circumstances, society may find that some of the questions about what, how, and for whom to produce have already been answered; until the arrival of Man Friday, Robinson Crusoe need not worry about the 'for whom' question. In general, however, society must answer all three questions.

By emphasizing the role of society, our definition places economics within the social sciences, the sciences that study and explain human behaviour. The subject matter of economics is that part of human behaviour which relates to the production, exchange, and use of goods and services. The central economic problem for society is how to reconcile the conflict between people's virtually limitless desires for goods and services, and the scarcity of resources (labour, machinery, and raw materials) with which these goods and services can be produced. In answering the questions what, how, and for whom to produce, economics explains how scarce resources are allocated between competing claims on their use.

Because economics is about human behaviour, you may be surprised that we describe it as a science rather than a subject within the arts or humanities. This reflects the way economists analyse problems, not the subject matter of economics. Economists aim to develop theories of human behaviour and to

test them against the facts. In Chapter 2 we discuss the tools economists use and explain the sense in which this approach is scientific. This does not mean that economics ignores people as individuals. Moreover, good economics retains an element of art, for it is only by having a feel for how people actually behave that economists can focus their analysis on the right issues. Before examining the tools of the trade, it is helpful to have a clearer understanding of the problems in which economists are interested.

1-1 Two Economic Issues

Trying to understand what economics is about by studying definitions is like trying to learn to swim by reading an instruction manual. Formal analysis makes sense only once you have some practical experience. In this section we discuss two economic issues to show how society allocates scarce resources between competing uses. In each case we see the importance of the questions what, how, and for whom to produce.

The Oil Price Shocks

Oil and its derivatives provide fuel for heating, transport, and machinery, and are basic inputs for petrochemicals and many household products ranging from plastic utensils to polyester clothing. From the beginning of this century until 1973 the use of oil increased steadily. Economic activity was organized on the assumption of cheap and abundant oil.

In 1973–74 there was an abrupt change. The main oil-producing nations belong to OPEC – the Organization of Petroleum Exporting Countries. OPEC decided in 1973 to raise the price for which their oil was sold. OPEC thought that cutbacks in the quantity demanded would be small since most other nations were very dependent on oil and had few commodities available as potential substitutes for oil. Thus OPEC correctly anticipated that a substantial price increase would lead to only a small reduction in sales volume. It would be very profitable for OPEC members.

Figure 1-1 shows the price of oil from 1971 to 1989. Between 1973 and 1974 the price of oil *tripled*, from $2.90 to $9 per barrel. After a more gradual rise between 1974 and 1978 there was another sharp increase between 1978 and 1980, from $12 to $30 per barrel. The dramatic price increases of 1973–74 and 1978–80 have become known as the OPEC *oil price shocks*.

Much of this book teaches you that people respond to prices. When the price of some commodity increases, consumers will try to use less of it but producers will want to sell more of it. These responses, guided by prices, are part of the process by which most Western societies determine what, how, and for whom to produce.

Consider first *how* the economy produces

goods and services. When, as in the 1970s, the price of oil increases sixfold, every firm will try to reduce its use of oil-based products. Chemical firms will develop artificial substitutes for petroleum inputs; airlines will look for more fuel-efficient aircraft; electricity will be produced from more coal-fired generators. Higher oil prices make the economy produce in a way that uses less oil.

How does the oil price increase affect *what* is being produced? Firms and households reduce their use of oil-intensive products which are now more expensive. Households switch to gas-fired central heating and buy smaller cars. Commuters form car-pools or move closer to the city. High prices not only choke off the demand for oil-related commodities; they also encourage consumers to purchase substitute commodities. Higher demand for these commodities bids up their price and encourages their production. Designers produce smaller cars, architects contemplate solar energy, and research laboratories develop alternatives to petroleum in chemical production.

The *for whom* question in this example has a clear answer. OPEC revenues from oil sales increased from $35 billion in 1973 to nearly $300 billion in 1980. Much of their increased revenue was spent on goods produced in the industrialized Western nations. In contrast, oil-importing nations had to give up more of their own production in exchange for the oil imports that they required. In terms of goods as a whole, the rise in oil prices raised the buying power of OPEC and reduced the buying power of oil-importing countries such as Germany and Japan. The world economy was producing more for OPEC and less for Germany and Japan.

In 1986 there was a sharp fall in world oil prices. Try working out for yourself what effect this should have had on what goods the world economy produces, how they are produced, and for whom they are produced.

The OPEC oil price shocks example illustrates how society allocates scarce resources between competing uses.

A *scarce resource* is one for which the demand at a zero price would exceed the available supply.

We can think of oil as having become more scarce in economic terms when its price rose.

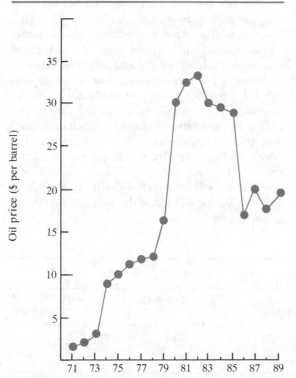

Figure 1-1 THE PRICE OF OIL 1971–89. (*Source: IMF, International Financial Statistics.*)

Income Distribution

The second economic issue concerns the distribution of income. You and your family have an annual income which allows you to enjoy various goods and services, live in a particular neighbourhood, and maintain a certain standard of living. Your standard of living will include what you think of as the necessities of life – food, shelter, health, education – but also something beyond, such as recreation. Your income will be less than some of your neighbours but more than that of some other people, both in this country and abroad.

Nations also have different levels of income. A nation's income, or national income, is the sum of the incomes of all the people living in that country. World income is the sum of all countries' incomes or the sum of the incomes earned by all the people in the world. We want to look now at the distribution of world income and national incomes to ask who in the world gets what share of these incomes.

The *distribution of income* (in a country or in the world) tells us how income is divided between different groups or individuals.

As we will show, income distribution is closely linked to the what, how, and for whom questions.

Table 1-1 reports the percentage of world population that lives in different groups of countries. About 60 per cent of the world's population live in poor countries, the three largest of which are India, China, and Indonesia. A little over a quarter live in middle-income countries, a group including Thailand, Brazil, Mexico, and Hungary. A group comprising the Persian gulf oil countries, Saudi Arabia, Kuwait, Oman, and the United Arab Emirates, accounts for less than 1 per cent of the world's population. The rich industrial countries, including the United States, Western Europe, Canada, and Japan, account for 16 per cent of world population. We want to examine how incomes differ between these groups of countries.

Income per person, calculated by dividing the total income of a group of countries by the population of that group, provides an approximate indication of the standard of living within that group of countries. The first row of Table 1-1 shows income per person for each group. In poor countries the average income per person is only £180 *per year*, or just 50p *per day*. In the rich industrial countries income is £9015 *per person per year*, over *fifty* times larger. These are striking differences. They are differences not between the poorest person in the world and the richest but between the average person in a country such as India and an average person in a country such as the UK or the United States.

The last row in Table 1-1 makes the same point in a different way. More than half the world's population, living in the poor countries, receives only 6 per cent of total world income. The 16 per cent of world population living in the industrial countries, including the UK, receives nearly 80 per cent of the world income. These income differences raise a number of questions both for society and for economists.

Table 1-1 sheds light on our three fundamental questions. *For whom* does the world economy produce? Essentially, for the 16 per cent of its population living in the rich industrial countries. This answer about for whom the goods and services are produced also suggests the answer to *what* is produced. World population will be directed chiefly to the goods and services consumed in the rich industrialized countries.

Table 1-1 World population and income in the late 1980s

	POOR COUNTRIES	MIDDLE-INCOME COUNTRIES	GULF OIL COUNTRIES	INDUSTRIAL COUNTRIES
Income per head (£)	180	1130	8000	9015
% of world population	61	22.6	0.4	16.0
% of world income	6	14	1	79

Note: Data exclude Soviet Union and several Eastern bloc countries.
Source: World Bank, *World Development Report, 1989.*

Why are there such large differences in incomes between groups? This relates to the question of *how* goods are produced. In the poor countries there is very little machinery relative to the size of the population, and the proportion of the population with professional and technical training is also small. In an industrialized country a worker may use power-driven earth-moving equipment to accomplish a task that is undertaken in a poor country by many more workers equipped only with shovels. Workers in poor countries are much less productive because they work under highly unfavourable conditions.

Income is unequally distributed within each country as well as between countries. In Brazil, the richest 20 per cent of families receive 67 per cent of Brazil's national income. In countries such as Yugoslavia and Denmark, the richest 20 per cent of families receive less than 40 per cent of national income. In countries such as the UK and the United States, the top 20 per cent of families receive a smaller share of national income than in countries such as Brazil but a larger share of national income than in countries such as Denmark or Yugoslavia.

In part, these differences can be attributed to factors we have already discussed. The provision of state education in socialist Yugoslavia reduces the disparity in the training and education its workers receive compared with countries in which expensive education must be privately purchased. However, when examining the income distribution *within* a country we must take account of two additional factors, which can largely be neglected when discussing differences in income per person *between* countries.

First, individual incomes come not just from working but also from ownership of assets (land, buildings, corporate equity) which earn rent, interest payments, and dividends. In comparing national incomes (in total or per person) it does not matter which members of the population own these assets and earn this income; in assessing the distribution of incomes within a country, it does matter. In countries such as Brazil, ownership of land and factories is concentrated in the hands of a small group. In Yugoslavia, where factories are owned by their workers through the state, a more equal distribution of wealth removes a major source of very unequal income distribution.

Second, acting through their governments, societies can decide whether or not to take steps to change the distribution of income. A state-owned economy aims to produce a fair degree of equality of income and wealth. In an economy of private ownership, wealth and power may become concentrated in the hands of a few rich families. Between these extremes, the government may levy taxes to alter the income distribution that would otherwise have emerged in a private ownership economy. One reason why Denmark has a more equal income distribution than Brazil is that Denmark levies high taxes on high incomes to reduce the buying power of the rich, and levies high taxes on inheritances to reduce the concentration of wealth in the hands of a few families.

The degree to which income is unequally distributed within a country will directly affect the question of for whom goods and services are produced, but it will also affect what goods are produced. In Brazil, where income is unequally distributed, many people work as domestic servants, chauffeurs, and maids. In Denmark, where income is much more evenly distributed, few people can afford to hire servants.

1-2 Scarcity and the Competing Use of Resources

Consider a hypothetical economy in which there are two types of good, food and films. There are four workers in the economy. A worker can produce in either the food industry or the film industry.

Table 1-2 shows how much of each good can be produced per week. The answer depends on how the workers are allocated between the two industries. In each industry, the more workers

Table 1-2 Production possibilities

FOOD EMPLOYMENT	OUTPUT	FILMS EMPLOYMENT	OUTPUT
4	25	0	0
3	22	1	9
2	17	2	17
1	10	3	24
0	0	4	30

there are, the greater is the total output of the good produced. We have assumed that production in each industry satisfies the *law of diminishing returns*. Each additional worker adds less to total industry output than the previous additional worker added. For example, consider the film industry. Beginning from the position of no workers and no output, the first worker employed increases output by 9 units per week. Adding a second worker raises film output only by 8 units per week, taking total film output to 17 units per week. Adding a third worker increases output by only 7 units per week, and the addition of yet more workers leads to even smaller increases in film output.

What lies behind the law of diminishing returns? We have implicitly assumed that workers in the film industry have at their disposal a fixed total amount of cameras, studios, and other equipment. The first worker has sole use of all these facilities. When a second worker is added, the two workers must share these facilities. The addition of further workers reduces equipment per worker to even lower levels. Thus, output per worker in the film industry falls as employment in the film industry rises. One worker produces 9 units per week, two workers average only $8\frac{1}{2}$ units per week, and three workers average only 8 units per week. A similar story applies in the food industry. Both industries exhibit diminishing returns as additional workers are added.

Table 1-2 shows the possible combinations of food and film output that can be produced in the hypothetical economy if all workers are employed. By transferring workers from one industry to the other, the economy can produce more of one good, but only at the expense of producing less of the other good. We say that there is a *trade-off* between food production and film production. In moving down the rows of Table 1-2, society is trading off food for films.

In Figure 1-2 we illustrate the maximum combinations of food and film output that the economy can produce. The point A corresponds to the first row of numbers in Table 1-2, where food output is 25 units and film output is zero. The point B corresponds to the second row of numbers in Table 1-2, with 22 units of food output and 9 units of film output. The points C, D, and E correspond to the last three rows of Table 1-2. The curve joining points A to E

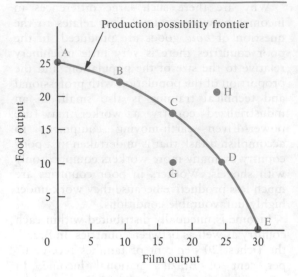

Figure 1-2 THE PRODUCTION POSSIBILITY FRONTIER. The production possibility frontier shows the maximum combinations of output that the economy can produce using all available resources. The frontier represents a trade-off; more of one commodity implies less of the other. Points such as H lying above the frontier are unattainable. They require more resource inputs than the economy has available. Points such as G inside the frontier are inefficient. By fully utilizing available resource inputs the economy could expand output and produce on the frontier.

in Figure 1-2 is called the 'production possibility frontier'.

The *production possibility frontier* shows, for each level of the output of one good, the maximum amount of the other good that can be produced.

Notice the way the frontier bends round. Mathematically, we say that the curve is *concave* to the origin. It curves around the point given by zero production of both goods. This is because of the law of diminishing returns. Movements from A to B to C each involve the transfer of one worker from the food industry to the film industry, and each transfer reduces output per person in the film industry but increases output per person in the food industry. With each transfer we get less additional film output and have to give up increasing amounts of food output.

The *opportunity cost* of a good is the quantity of other goods which must be sacrificed to obtain another unit of that good.

In Figure 1-2 suppose we begin at point A with 25 units of food but no films. Moving from A to B, we gain 9 films but give up 3 units of food. Thus, 3 units of food is the opportunity cost of producing the first 9 films. The slope of the production possibility frontier tells us the opportunity cost: how much of one good we have to sacrifice to make more of another.

To explain why the curve through the points A to E is called a 'frontier', let us think about the point G in Figure 1-2. Society is then producing 10 units of food and 17 units of films. This is a *feasible* combination. From Table 1-2 it can be seen that this requires one person in the food industry and two in the film industry. But with only three people working, society has spare resources because the fourth person is not being employed. G is *not* a point on the production possibility frontier because it is possible to produce more of one good without sacrificing output of the other good. Putting the extra person to work in the food industry would take us to the point C, yielding 7 extra units of food for the same film output. Putting the extra person to work in the film industry would take us to the point D, with 7 extra units of films but no loss of food output.

The production possibility frontier shows the points at which society is producing *efficiently*. More output of one good can be obtained only by sacrificing output of the other good. Points such as G, which lie inside the frontier, are *inefficient* because society is wasting resources. More output of one good would not require less output of the other.

Points that lie outside the production possibility frontier, such as the point H in Figure 1-2, are said to be *unattainable*. It would be nice to have even more food and films but, given the amount of labour available, it is simply impossible to produce this output combination. Scarcity of resources limits society to a choice of points that lie inside or on the production possibility frontier. Society has to accept that its resources are scarce and make choices about how to allocate these scarce resources between competing uses.

Given that people like food and films, society should want to produce efficiently. To select a point inside the production possibility frontier is to sacrifice output unnecessarily. Society's problem is therefore to make a choice between the different points that lie on the production

possibility frontier. In so doing, it decides *what* to produce. Depending on society's preferences between food and films, it might choose any point on the production possibility frontier. However, in choosing a particular point, society will also be choosing *how* to produce. It will then be necessary to refer back to Table 1-2 to determine how many workers must be allocated to each of the industries to produce the desired output combination. As yet, our example is too simple to show *for whom* society produces. To answer that question, we need more information than the position on the production possibility frontier.

How does society decide where to produce on the production possibility frontier? One possibility is that the government decides. In Figure 1-3 we show a production possibility frontier where the two goods are private goods (motor-cars, lawnmowers, holidays) and social services (police, education, road sweeping). Through the political process a society might decide which point on this frontier to select. A 'big government' country like Sweden might choose a point such as B, where output of social services is high relative to the output of private

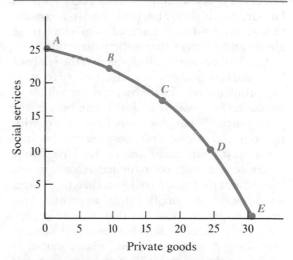

Figure 1-3 SOCIETY'S CHOICE BETWEEN SOCIAL SERVICES AND PRIVATE GOODS. This production possibility frontier shows the choices society faces between social services and private goods. This choice is made through the political process. A big-government country, like Sweden, chooses a point like B, with a lot of social services and not many private goods. A country like Japan chooses a point like D, where the output of private goods is large and that of social services small.

goods. A country like Japan might choose a point such as *D*, where priorities were reversed.

That is one way of allocating scarce resources. But in most Western economies, the most important process that determines what, how, and for whom goods are produced is the operation of *markets*.

1-3 The Role of the Market

Markets bring together buyers and sellers of goods and services. In some cases, such as a local fruit stall, buyers and sellers meet physically. In other cases, such as the stock market, business can be transacted over the telephone, almost by remote control. We need not go into these details. Instead, we use a general definition of markets.

> A *market* is a shorthand expression for the process by which households' decisions about consumption of alternative goods, firms' decisions about what and how to produce, and workers' decisions about how much and for whom to work are all reconciled by adjustment of *prices*.

Prices of goods, and of resources, such as labour, machinery and land, adjust to ensure that scarce resources are used to produce these goods and services that society demands.

Much of economics is devoted to the study of how markets and prices enable society to solve the problems of what, how, and for whom to produce. Suppose you buy a hamburger for your lunch. What does this have to do with markets and prices? You chose the café because it was fast, convenient and cheap. Given your desire to eat, and your limited resources, the low hamburger price told you that this was a good way to satisfy your appetite. You probably prefer steak but that is more expensive. The price of steak is high enough to ensure that society answers the 'for whom' question about lunchtime steaks in favour of someone else.

Now think about the seller's viewpoint. The café owner is in the business because, given the price of hamburger meat, the rent and the wages that must be paid, it is still possible to sell hamburgers at a profit. If rents were higher, it might be more profitable to sell hamburgers in a cheaper area or to switch to luxury lunches for rich executives on expense accounts. The student behind the counter is working there because it is a suitable part-time job which pays a bit of money. If the wage were much lower it would hardly be worth working at all. Conversely, the job is unskilled and there are plenty of students looking for such work, so owners of cafés do not have to offer very high wages.

Prices are guiding your decision to buy a hamburger, the owner's decision to sell hamburgers, and the student's decision to take the job. Society is allocating resources – meat, buildings, and labour – into hamburger production through the price system. If nobody liked hamburgers, the owner could not sell enough at a price that covered the cost of running the café and society would devote no resources to hamburger production. People's desire to eat hamburgers guides resources into hamburger production. However, if cattle contracted a disease, thereby reducing the economy's ability to produce meat products, competition to purchase more scarce supplies of beef would bid up the price of beef, hamburger producers would be forced to raise prices, and consumers would buy more cheese sandwiches for lunch. Adjustments in prices would encourage society to reallocate resources to reflect the increased scarcity of cattle.

The Command Economy

To highlight the role of markets and prices, we now ask how resources might be allocated if markets did not exist. One example is a command economy.

> A *command economy* is a society where the government makes all decisions about production and consumption. A government planning office decides what will be produced, how it will be produced, and for whom it will be produced. Detailed instructions are then issued to households, firms, and workers.

Such planning is a very complicated task, and there is no complete command economy where all allocation decisions are undertaken in this way. However, in many countries, for example those in the Soviet bloc, there was a large measure of central direction and planning. The state owned factories and land, and made the most important decisions about what people should consume, how goods should be produced, and how much people should work.

To appreciate the immensity of this task, imagine that you had to run by command the city in which you live. Think of the food, clothing, and housing allocation decisions you would have to make. How would you decide who should get what and the process by which these goods and services would be produced? Of course these decisions are being made every day in your own city, but chiefly through the allocative mechanism of markets and prices.

The Invisible Hand

Markets in which governments do not intervene are called *free markets*.

Individuals in free markets pursue their own interests, trying to do as well for themselves as they can without any government assistance or interference. The idea that such a system could solve the what, how, and for whom problems is one of the oldest themes in economics, dating back to Adam Smith, the famous Scottish philosopher–economist whose book *The Wealth of Nations* (1776) remains a classic. Smith argued that individuals pursuing their self-interest would be led 'as by an invisible hand' to do things that are in the interests of society as a whole.

Suppose you wish to become a millionaire. You play around with new ideas and invent a new good, perhaps the television, the motor car or the hand calculator. Although motivated by our own self-interest, you make society better off by creating new jobs and opportunities. You have moved society's production possibility frontier outwards – the same resources now make more or better goods – and become a millionaire in the process. Smith argued that the pursuit of self-interest, *without any central direction,* could produce a coherent society making sensible allocative decisions.

This remarkable insight has been studied at length by modern economists. In later chapters, we discuss in greater detail the circumstances in which the invisible hand works well. We also show that there are circumstances in which it does not lead society to allocate resources efficiently. Some government intervention may then be justified.

The Mixed Economy

The free market allows individuals to pursue their self-interest without any government restrictions. The command economy allows little scope for individual economic freedom since most decisions are taken centrally by the government. Between these two extremes lies the mixed economy.

In a *mixed economy* the government and private sector interact in solving economic problems. The government controls a significant share of output through taxation, transfer payments, and the provision of goods and services such as defence and the police force. It also regulates the extent to which individuals may pursue their own self-interest.

In a mixed economy the government may also be a producer of private goods such as steel or motor cars. Examples of this in the UK include the nationalized industries such as railways and coal.

Most countries are mixed economies, though some are close to command economies and others are much nearer the free market economy. Figure 1-4 illustrates this point. Even the Soviet Union allows consumers some choice over the goods they buy. Private agricultural markets co-exist with centrally organized 'collectives'. Conversely, even countries such as the United States which espouse more enthusiastically the free market approach, still have substantial levels of government activity in the

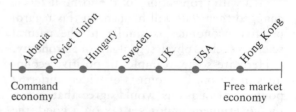

Figure 1-4   DEGREES OF MARKET ORIENTATION.   The role of the market in allocating resources differs vastly between countries. At one extreme, in the command economy resources are allocated by central government planning. At the other extreme, in the free market economy there is virtually no government regulation of the consumption, production, and exchange of goods. In between lies the mixed economy, where market forces play a large role but the government intervenes extensively.

provision of public goods and services, the redistribution of income through taxes and transfer payments, and the regulation of markets.

1.4 Positive and Normative Economics

In studying economics it is important to distinguish two branches of the subject. The first is known as 'positive economics', the second as 'normative economics'.

> *Positive economics* deals with objective or scientific explanations of the working of the economy.

The aim of positive economics is to explain how society makes decisions about consumption, production, and exchange of goods. The purpose of this investigation is twofold: to satisfy our curiosity about why the economy works as it does, and to have some basis for predicting how the economy will respond to changes in circumstances. Normative economics is very different.

> *Normative economics* offers prescriptions or recommendations based on personal value judgements.

In positive economics, we hope to act as detached scientists. Whatever our political persuasion, whatever our view about what we would like to happen or what we would regard as 'a good thing', in the first instance we have to be concerned with how the world actually works. At this stage, there is no scope for personal value judgements. We are concerned with propositions of the form: if *this* is changed then *that* will happen. In this regard, positive economics is similar to the natural sciences such as physics, geology, or astronomy.

Here are some examples of positive economics in action. Economists of widely differing political persuasions would agree that, when the government imposes a tax on a good, the price of that good will rise. The normative question of whether this price rise is desirable is entirely distinct. Many propositions in positive economics would command widespread agreement among professional economists.

Of course, as in any other science, there are unresolved questions where disagreement remains. These disagreements are at the frontiers of economics. Research in progress will resolve some of these issues but new issues will arise and provide scope for further research.

Although competent and comprehensive research can in principle resolve many of the outstanding issues in positive economics, no corresponding claim can be made about the resolution of disagreement in normative economics. Normative economics is based on subjective value judgements, not on the search for any objective truth. The following statement combines positive and normative economics: 'The elderly have very high medical expenses compared with the rest of the population, and the government should subsidize health bills of the aged.' The first part of the proposition – the claim that the aged have relatively high medical bills – is a statement in positive economics. It is a statement about how the world works, and we can imagine a research programme that could determine whether or not it is correct. Broadly speaking, this assertion happens to be correct. The second part of the proposition – the recommendation about what the government should do – could never be 'proved' to be correct or false by any scientific research investigation. It is simply a subjective value judgement based on the feelings of the person making the statement. Many people might happen to share this subjective judgement. But other people might reasonably disagree. You might believe that it is more important to devote society's scarce resources to improving the environment.

There is no way that economics can be used to show that one of these normative judgements is correct and the other is wrong. It all depends on the preferences or priorities of the individual or the society that has to make this choice. But we can use positive economics to spell out the detailed implications of making the choice one way or the other. For example, we might be able to show that failure to subsidize the medical bills of the elderly leads middle-aged people to seek a lot of unnecessary medical check-ups in an attempt to detect diseases before their treatment becomes expensive. Society might have to devote a great deal of resources to providing check-up facilities, leaving less resources available than had been supposed to devote to improving the environment. Positive economics can be used to clarify the menu of options from which society must eventually make its normative choice.

Most economists have normative views and some economists are vociferous champions of particular normative recommendations. However, this *advocacy role* about what society should do must be distinguished from the role of the economist as an expert about the likely consequences of pursuing any course of action. In the latter case, the professional economist is offering expert advice on positive economics. However, in a democracy economists have no monopoly on pure value judgements merely because they happen to be economists. Scrupulous economists clearly distinguish their role as an expert adviser on positive economics from their status merely as involved private citizens in arguing for particular normative choices.

1-5 Microeconomics and Macroeconomics

Many economists specialize in a particular branch of the subject. Labour economics deals with problem of the labour market as viewed by firms, workers, and society as a whole. Urban economics deals with city problems: land use, transport, congestion, and housing. However, we need not classify branches of economics according to the area of economic life in which we ask the standard questions what, how, and for whom. We can also classify branches of economics according to the approach or methodology that is used. The very broad division of approaches into microeconomic and macroeconomic cuts across the large number of subject groupings cited above.

Microeconomic analysis offers a detailed treatment of individual decisions about particular commodities.

For example, we might study why individual households prefer cars to bicycles and how producers decide whether to produce cars or bicycles. We can then aggregate the behaviour of all households and all firms to discuss total car purchases and total car production. Within a market economy we can discuss the market for cars. Comparing this with the market for bicycles, we may be able to explain the relative price of cars and bicycles and the relative output of these two goods. The

sophisticated branch of microeconomics known as *general equilibrium theory* extends this approach to its logical conclusion. It studies simultaneously every market for every commodity. From this it is hoped that we can understand the complete pattern of consumption, production, and exchange in the whole economy at a point in time.

If you think this sounds very complicated you are correct. It is. For many purposes, the analysis becomes so complicated that we tend to lose track of the phenomena in which we were interested. The interesting task for economics, a task that retains an element of art in economic science, is to devise judicious simplifications which keep the analysis manageable without distorting reality too much. It is here that microeconomists and macroeconomists proceed down different avenues. Microeconomists tend to offer a detailed treatment of one aspect of economic behaviour but ignore interactions with the rest of the economy in order to preserve the simplicity of the analysis. A microeconomic analysis of miners' wages would emphasize the characteristics of miners and the ability of mine owners to pay. It would largely neglect the chain of indirect effects to which a rise in miners' wages might give rise. For example, car workers might use the precedent of the miners' pay increase to secure higher wages in the car industry, thus being able to afford larger houses which burned more coal in heating systems. When microeconomic analysis ignores such indirectly induced effects it is said to be *partial analysis*.

In some instances, indirect effects may not be too important and it will make sense for economists to devote their efforts to very detailed analyses of particular industries or activities. In other circumstances, the indirect effects are too important to be swept under the carpet and an alternative simplification must be found.

Macroeconomics emphasizes the interactions in the economy as a whole. It deliberately simplifies the individual building blocks of the analysis in order to retain a manageable analysis of the complete interaction of the economy.

For example, macroeconomists typically do not worry about the breakdown of consumer goods into cars, bicycles, televisions, and calculators.

They prefer to treat them all as a single bundle called 'consumer goods' because they are more interested in studying the interaction between households' purchases of consumer goods and firms' decisions about purchases of machinery and buildings.

Because these macroeconomic concepts are intended to refer to the economy as a whole, they tend to receive more coverage on television and in the newspapers than microeconomic concepts, which are chiefly of interest to those who belong to the specific group in question. To give an idea of the building blocks of macroeconomics, we introduce three concepts which you have probably read about in the newspapers or seen discussed on television.

> *Gross domestic product* (GDP) is the value of all goods and services produced in the economy in a given period such as a year.

GDP is the basic measure of the total output of goods and services in the economy.

> The *aggregate price level* is a measure of the average level of prices of goods and services in the economy, relative to their prices at some fixed date in the past.

There is no reason why the prices of different goods should always move in line with one another. The aggregate price level tells us what is happening to prices on average. When the price level is rising, we say that the economy is experiencing *inflation*.

> The *unemployment rate* is the percentage of the labour force without a job.

By the labour force we mean those people of working age who in principle would like to work if a suitable job were available. Some of the landed gentry are of working age but have no intention of looking for work. They are not in the labour force and should not be counted as unemployed.

Already we can see two themes of modern macroeconomic analysis. Society reveals, both through statements by individuals and by the policy pronouncements of politicians who must submit themselves for re-election by the people, that it does not like inflation and unemployment. Yet for most of the 1970s economic interactions within and between national economies led to substantial inflation rates. In the 1980s, most Western economies faced sharp

rises in the aggregate unemployment rate. Macroeconomists wish to understand how interactions within the economy can lead to these outcomes and whether government policy can make any difference.

Getting the Most Out of This Chapter

At the end of each chapter in the book you will find a summary of the main points of the chapter. There is also a problem set for you to work through to check that you have understood the chapter. We suggest you always do the problems. The last problem in each chapter lists a number of fallacies. You should always be able to use the material in the chapter to show why these statements are incorrect.

Summary

1   Economics analyses what, how, and for whom society produces. The central economic problem is to reconcile the conflict between people's virtually unlimited demands with society's limited ability to produce goods and services to fulfil these demands.

2   The production possibility frontier shows the maximum amount of one good that can be produced for each given level of output of the other good. It depicts the trade-off or menu of choices that society must make in deciding what to produce. Resources are scarce and points outside the frontier are unattainable. It is inefficient to produce within the frontier. By moving on to the frontier, society could have more of some good without having less of any other good.

3   Industrial Western countries rely extensively on markets to allocate resources. The market is the process by which production and consumption decisions are co-ordinated through adjustments in prices. The role of prices is central to this definition.

4   In a command economy, decisions on what, how, and for whom are made in a central planning office. No economy relies entirely on command, but there is extensive planning in many Soviet bloc countries.

5   A free market economy has no government intervention. Resources are allocated entirely

through markets in which individuals pursue their own self-interest. Adam Smith argued that an invisible hand would nevertheless allocate resources efficiently.

6   Modern economies in the West are mixed, relying mainly on the market but with a large dose of government intervention. The optimal level of government intervention remains a subject of controversy.

7   Positive economics studies how the economy actually behaves. Normative economics makes prescriptions about what should be done. The two should be kept separate as far as possible. Given sufficient research, economists should eventually agree on issues in positive economics. Normative economics involves subjective value judgements. There is no reason why economists should agree about normative statements.

8   Microeconomics offers a detailed analysis of particular activities in the economy. For simplicity, it may neglect some interactions with the rest of the economy. Macroeconomics emphasizes these interactions at the cost of simplifying the individual building blocks.

Key Terms

Scarcity
Income distribution
Production possibility frontier
Opportunity cost
Efficiency
Diminishing returns
Trade-off
The free market
The command economy
The mixed economy
Positive and normative economics
Microeconomics and macroeconomics
Gross domestic product
Inflation
Unemployment rate

Problems

1   (a) Suppose you live by yourself on an island. Which of the problems, what, how, and for whom would you not have to solve? (b) How are these three problems settled within your own family?

2   There are five workers in an economy. Each worker can make either four cakes or three shirts per day. Output per worker is independent of the number of other workers in the same industry. (a) Draw society's production possibility frontier. (b) How many cakes could society produce if it was willing to do without shirts? (c) Indicate the points in your diagram that show inefficient organization of production. (d) Why are points outside the frontier unattainable?

3   The Soviet Union relies on prices to allocate production among different consumers. Central planners determine production targets but then put output in shops, fix prices, and give workers a certain amount of money to spend. Why not plan everything including the allocation of particular goods to particular people?

4   Suppose society decides to abolish higher education. Students have to find jobs immediately. Pretend there are no jobs available. How should wages and prices adjust so that the invisible hand will ensure that those who wants jobs can find them?

5   Which of the following statements are positive and which are normative? Explain. (a) The rate of inflation has fallen below 10 per cent per annum. (b) Because inflation has fallen the government should now expand its activity. (c) The level of income is higher in the UK than in the Soviet Union. (d) People in the UK are happier than people in the Soviet Union. (e) People should not be encouraged to drink and taxes must be kept high on alcoholic beverages.

6   Which of the following statements refer to microeconomics and which refer to macroeconomics? (a) The inflation rate is lower than in the 1970s. (b) Food prices have fallen this month. (c) Favourable weather conditions will mean a good harvest this year. (d) Unemployment in the London area is lower than the national average. (e) The oil price shock in 1973–74 led to a great deal of inflation and unemployment in the UK.

7   Common Fallacies   Show why the following statements are incorrect: (a) Since some economists are right-wing and others left-wing, this proves that economics can be used to justify anything we like. (b) There is no such thing as a free lunch. To get more of one thing you have to give up something else. (c) Economics is all about money and greed. It has no relevance in discussing a true socialist state. (d) The price of oil rose because people suddenly realized that world oil supplies were running out and should be conserved.

2

The Tools of Economic Analysis

It is more fun to play tennis if you know how to serve, and felling trees is much easier with a chain saw. Every activity or academic discipline involves a basic set of tools. The tools may be tangible, like the dentist's drill, or intangible, like the ability to serve in tennis. In this chapter the emphasis is on mastering the tools of the trade. To analyse economic issues we use both *models* and *data*.

A *model* or theory makes a series of simplifying assumptions from which it deduced how people will behave. It is a deliberate simplification of reality.

Models are frameworks for organizing the way we think about a problem. They simplify by omitting some details of the real world to concentrate on the essentials. From this manageable picture of reality we develop our analysis of how the economy works.

An economist uses a model in the way a traveller uses a map. A map of London misses out many features of the real world – traffic lights, roundabouts, the exact width of streets – but if you study it carefully you can get a good picture of how the traffic is likely to flow and what will be the best route to take. This simplified picture is easy to follow, yet helps you understand real-world behaviour when you must drive through the city in the rush hour.

The data or facts interact with models in two ways. First, the data help us quantify the relationships to which our theoretical models draw attention. It may be insufficient to work out that all bridges across the Thames are likely to be congested. To choose the best route we need to know how long we would have to queue at each bridge. We need some facts. The model is useful because it tells us which facts are likely to be the most important. Bridges are more likely to be congested than six-lane motorways.

Second, the data help us to *test* our models. Like all careful scientists, economists must check that their theories square with the relevant facts. Here the crucial word is *relevant*. It is this that prevents a chimpanzee or a computer sifting through all the facts in the world to establish the single definitively correct theory. For example, it turns out that the number of Scottish dysentery deaths is closely related to the actual inflation rate in the UK over many decades. Is this a factual coincidence or the key to a theory of inflation in the UK? The facts alert us to the need to ponder this question, but we can make a decision only by recourse to logical reasoning.

In this instance, since we can find no theoretical or logical connection, we regard the close factual relationship between Scottish dysentery deaths and UK inflation as a coincidence that should be ignored. Without any logical underpinning, the empirical connection will break down sooner or later. Paying attention to this spurious relationship in the data neither increases our understanding of the economy nor increases our confidence in predicting the future.

The blend of models and data is thus a subtle one. The data may alert us to logical relationships we had previously overlooked. And whatever theory we wish to maintain should certainly be checked against the facts. But only theoretical reasoning can guide an intelligent assessment of what evidence should be regarded as being of reasonable relevance.

To introduce the tools of the trade we begin with the representation of the economic data. Then we show how an economist might approach the development of a theoretical model of an economic relationship. Finally, we discuss how actual data might be used to test the theory that has been developed.

2.1 Economic Data

Initially we focus on the data or facts. How

Table 2-1 The price of silver in 1988
(US cents/troy ounce)

SEPT.	OCT.	NOV.	DEC.
637	629	628	611

Source: IMF, *International Financial Statistics.*

might we reorganize their presentation to help us think about an economic problem?

Time Series Data

Table 2-1 reports a time series of average monthly silver prices.

> A *time series* is a sequence of measurements of a variable at different points in time.

It shows how a variable changes over time. This information may be presented in tables or charts. A chart is simply a diagrammatic representation of a table.

Figure 2-1 *plots* the data shown in Table 2-1. Each point in the figure corresponds to an entry in the table. Point A shows graphically that in September 1988 the price of silver was 637 cents per troy ounce. For each point in the figure, we first locate the month on the horizontal axis then move vertically upward until we reach the corresponding price. The series of points or dots in Figure 2-1 contains exactly the same information as the row of numbers in Table 2-1.

However, charts or diagrams must be interpreted with care. The eye is easily misled by simple changes in the presentation of the data. Figure 2-2 plots the same time series as Figure 2-1 but adopts a much larger scale on the vertical axis. The monthly silver price now *seems* to show much more movement. Diagrams can be manipulated in suggestive ways even to

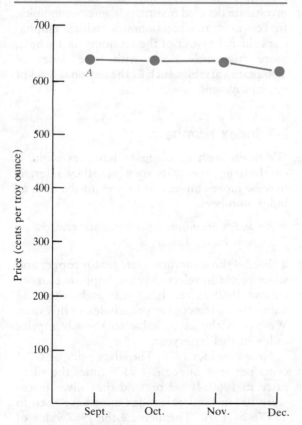

Figure 2-1   THE MONTHLY PRICE OF SILVER IN 1988 (US cents/troy ounce).   The figure plots the data shown in Table 2-1.

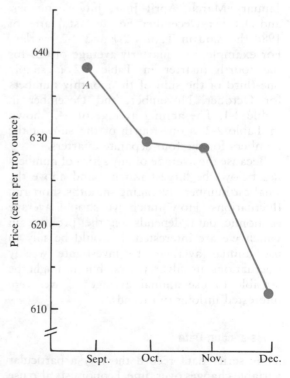

Figure 2-2   THE PRICE OF SILVER IN 1988. The figure contains exactly the same information as Figure 2-1. However, the vertical scale is increased. The price now seems to vary much more than it does in Figure 2-1.

Table 2-2 THE price of silver in 1988
(US cents/troy ounce)

ANNUAL AVERAGE	QUARTERLY AVERAGES			
	I	II	III	IV
647	623	674	669	623

Source: IMF, *International Financial Statistics.*

Table 2-3 UK unemployment by age group, 1988
(thousands of workers unemployed)

18–19	20–24	25–34	35–44	45–54	55–59	60+
178	428	321	400	317	421	46

Source: Department of Employment *Gazette.*

the point of being misleading, a point well understood in advertising and politics.[1] For most purposes daily data contain too much detail. It would be tedious to work with a table of daily prices over 10 or 20 years. Averages over a month, over a quarter (three months), or over a whole year may then be the best way to present data even though daily data have been collected.

Table 2-2 presents quarterly averages for silver prices in 1988. By the four quarters of the year we mean the four three-month periods January–March, April–June, July–September, and October–December. For the last quarter of 1988 the data in Tables 2-1 and 2-2 overlap. For example, the quarterly average of 623 for the fourth quarter in Table 2-2 is simply one-third of the sum of the monthly numbers for October, November, and December in Table 2-1. The annual average of 647 shown in Table 2-2 is one-fourth of the sum of the numbers for the four separate quarters.

Because the average of any series of numbers lies below the largest number and above the smallest number, averaging smooths short-run fluctuations. How much we should average economic data depends on the problem in which we are interested. It would be silly to use annual averages to investigate weekly fluctuations in silver prices, but it might be sensible to use annual averages if we were interested in long-run trends.

Cross-section Data

Time series data record the way a particular variable changes over time. Economists also use cross-section data.

Cross-section data record at a point in time the way an economic variable differs across different individuals or groups of individuals.

Table 2-3 shows a cross section of thousands of people unemployed in different age groups in 1988. Such data might be used to examine whether young workers, who are eligible for the Youth Training Scheme, are consequently less likely to be unemployed than older workers. Because cross-section data disaggregate data by some characteristic like age, region, or industry, they tend to be used to investigate detailed questions in microeconomics. In contrast, macroeconomics, which emphasizes the behaviour of the economy as a whole, more frequently deals with time series of aggregate variables such as the national level of unemployment.

2-2 Index Numbers

We often wish to compare numbers without emphasizing the units to which they refer. It may be more convenient to present the data as index numbers.

An *index number* expresses data relative to a given base value.

Table 2-4 shows annual averages for copper and silver prices in selected years. Suppose that we choose 1960 as the base year and assign the value 100 to the copper price index in this year. We assign the same value to the silver price index in this base year.

Now consider 1970. The silver price of 177.1 cents per troy ounce is 1.9376 times the silver price in 1960. If we pretend that silver prices were 100 in 1960, this index must have risen to 193.76 by 1970. To calculate the 1987 value of the silver price index, we divide the 1987 silver price of 700.9 cents per troy ounce by the 1960 price of 91.40 cents per troy ounce to obtain

[1] See Darrell Huff and Irving Geis, *How to Lie With Statistics,* W. W. Norton, New York.

Table 2-4 Prices of silver and copper
(US cents per troy ounce of silver or per pound of
copper)

	1960	1970	1987
Silver price	91.40	177.10	700.9
Copper price	32.05	57.67	81.1
Silver index (1960 = 100)	100	193.76	766.85
Copper index (1960 = 100)	100	179.94	253.28

Source: IMF, *International Financial Statistics.*

Table 2-5 Price indices for silver, copper, and metals
(1960 = 100, silver share = 0.2, copper share = 0.8)

	1960	1970	1987
Silver	100.0	193.76	766.85
Copper	100.0	179.94	253.28
Metals	100.0	182.7	355.99

Source: Calculated from Table 2-4.

7.6685. Multiplying this by the starting value of 100 for the index in 1960, we obtain 766.85, as shown in Table 2-4. The price index for copper is calculated in the same way, dividing each price by the 1960 price and multiplying the answer by 100.

Now check that you understand this procedure. In 1981 average silver prices were 1052.1 cents per troy ounce and average copper prices 83.99 cents per pound. What were the values of the silver and copper price indices? (Answer: 1151.09 and 262.06.) Looking at the last two rows of Table 2-4, it is now immediately apparent that between 1960 and 1987 the price of silver increased sixfold while the price of copper only doubled. The first two rows of the table contain the same information, but it cannot be interpreted so quickly.

Index Number as Averages

Suppose we now wish to know about movements in the price of metals as a whole. The prices of individual metals do not necessarily change in the same way. To derive a single measure of metals prices we have to look at an *average* of different metal prices.

Suppose copper and silver are the only two metals. To construct an index of all metal prices, we must make a single time series out of the two time series shown in the bottom two rows of Table 2-4. We give the price index of each metal a weight or share in the new index for metals as a whole. The weight should reflect the purpose for which the index is being constructed. If it is to be used to summarize what firms must pay for metal inputs, the weights should reflect the relative use of silver

and copper as industrial inputs. Since copper is much more widely used than silver, we might decide to assign a weight of 0.8 to copper and 0.2 to silver. The weights are always chosen to add up to unity.

Table 2-5 shows how the metal price index, the *weighted average* of the indices for silver and copper, changes over time. In the base year 1960, the metals index is 100, being $(0.2 \times 100) + (0.8 \times 100)$. By 1970 the index has risen to 182.7, since this equals $(0.8 \times 179.94) + (0.2 \times 193.76)$. By 1987 the index stands at 355.99.

The metals index is a weighted average of silver and copper prices and must therefore lie between the indices for the two separate metals. The weights determine whether the metals index more closely resembles the behaviour of copper prices or the behaviour of silver prices.

The Retail Price Index and Other Indices

In the UK the most famous price index is the *retail price index* (RPI). Announced monthly, and closely watched by the news media and economic commentators, the RPI is an index of the prices of goods purchased by a typical household. It includes everything from food and housing to entertainment. The RPI is used to measure changes in the cost of living, the money that must be spent to purchase the typical bundle of goods consumed by a representative household. The percentage increase in the RPI over 12 months, comparing, say, its value in September 1991, with its value in September 1990, is the most widespread definition of the *inflation rate* in the UK.

The RPI is constructed in two stages. First, index numbers are calculated for each of the main categories of commodities purchased by households. For example, the index of food prices averages the price of individual foods such as coffee, bread, and milk. Again, the

Table 2-6 Weights used in the RPI

ITEM	WEIGHT
Food	0.167
Housing	0.157
Motoring	0.127
Alcohol	0.076
Clothing and footwear	0.074
Household goods	0.073
Fuel and light	0.061
Leisure goods	0.047
Catering	0.046
Household services	0.044
Personal goods and services	0.038
Tobacco	0.038
Leisure services	0.030
Other	0.022

Source: Department of Employment Gazette.

Table 2-7 Unit labour costs in UK manufacturing (1980 = 100 for all indices)

	UNIT LABOUR COSTS	RETAIL PRICES	REAL UNIT LABOUR COSTS
1970	100.0	100.0	100.0
1974	143.4	148.7	96.4
1978	252.3	269.0	93.8
1982	405.7	438.6	92.5
1986	462.6	528.2	87.6

Source: CSO, Economic Trends.

relative weights reflect the relative importance of the different commodities. Then the RPI is constructed by taking a weighted average of the different commodity groupings. Table 2-6 shows the weights used and the main commodity groupings. A 10 per cent rise in food prices will change the RPI more than a 10 per cent rise in tobacco prices because food has a much larger weight than tobacco.

Other examples of indices are the index of wages in manufacturing, a weighted average of wages in different manufacturing industries, and the Financial Times 30-share index, a weighted average of the share prices of 30 of Britain's largest companies. Nor need the use of index numbers be confined to the prices of goods, labour, or corporate shares. The index of industrial production is a weighted average of the quantity of goods produced by British industry. However, the procedure by which index numbers are calculated is always the same. We choose a base date and set the index equal to 100 at that date. Where the index refers to more than one commodity, we have to choose weights by which to average across the different commodities that the index describes.

2-3 Nominal and Real Variables

Table 2-7 shows data on wages and salaries per unit of output, or unit labour costs, over the last two decades in UK manufacturing. The first column shows that unit labour costs

increased more than fourfold between 1970 and 1986.

The index is constructed from data measured in pounds. We cannot say whether an increase in the value of this index made firms worse off until we know what was happening to the prices of goods that firms sold. The second column of Table 2-7 shows the behaviour of the RPI over the same period. Because of inflation – increases in the general price of goods – the fourfold increase in unit labour costs between 1970 and 1986 must be set against increases in firms' revenue from higher prices for their products. For this reason, we distinguish nominal and real costs.

Costs measured in pounds, or indices based on such data, are said to be nominal costs. Real costs are calculated by adjusting nominal costs for changes in the price level.

The third column of Table 2-7 calculates an index for real unit labour costs. Each number in the first column is divided by the corresponding number in the second column then multiplied by 100. From the third column of Table 2-7 we see that real unit labour costs actually fell during the period, because of a large rise in labour productivity.

Only when inflation is zero will nominal and real indices move in the same way. This distinction between nominal and real values is widely used in economics and is especially important when the economy is experiencing high rates of inflation.

Real or Relative Prices

The distinction between nominal and real variables applies to all variables whose unit of measurement is so many pounds per unit. It does not apply to units of output, such as 4000 washing machines per annum, which relate to physical quantities. Whatever the inflation rate, 4000 washing machines is 4000 washing machines. However, we do not know whether £100 is a large or a small number until we know the general price level for goods.

The argument carries over to prices themselves. The nominal price of silver has risen considerably since 1970. We can calculate an index of the *real price of silver* by dividing an index of nominal silver prices by the retail price index and multiplying by 100.

Real prices provide an indicator of economic scarcity. They show whether the price of some commodity is rising more rapidly than prices of goods in general. For this reason real prices are sometimes called *relative prices*, just as real wage rates tell us what is happening to the price of labour relative to the price of goods in general.

Consider the price of televisions over the last 20 years. Television prices, as measured in pounds, have risen very slowly. The RPI has risen much more quickly. Thus, the real price of televisions has actually fallen. Advances in technology have reduced the cost of producing televisions. The real price, measuring economic scarcity, has fallen. Because the real price has fallen, many more households are now able to afford a television. Nominal earnings have risen much more rapidly than the nominal price of televisions. This example reinforces our claim that it may be very misleading to base our analysis on nominal values of variables.

The Purchasing Power of Money

When the price of goods rises, we say that the purchasing power of money falls because £1 buys fewer goods.

> The *purchasing power of money* is an index of the quantity of goods that can be bought for £1.

The distinction between real and nominal variables is sometimes expressed by saying that real variables measure nominal variables as if the purchasing power of money had been constant. Another way to express this idea is to say that we distinguish between measure-

ments of nominal variables in *current* pounds and real variables in *constant* pounds.

Look again at Table 2-7. The first column is an index of unit labour costs in current pounds. It is based on numbers describing actual costs in pounds. We can think of the third column as an index of costs in *1970 pounds*, a particular example of the idea of measuring variables in constant pounds. Measuring variables in constant pounds (here, 1970 pounds) is designed to adjust for changes in the general price level. It is just another way of saying that variables are measured in real terms.

2-4 Measuring Changes in Economic Variables

The 1984 miners' strike reduced UK coal output from 89 m tonnes in 1983 to 28 m tonnes in 1984. By the *absolute change* in annual coal production between 1983 and 1984, we mean the second number minus the first number. The absolute change was −61 million tonnes per annum. The minus sign tells us that production *fell* between 1983 and 1984.

By the *percentage change* in annual coal production, we mean the absolute change divided by the first number and multiplied by 100. Thus, the percentage change in coal production between 1983 and 1984 is given by

$$\left(\frac{28 - 89}{89} \right) \times 100\% = \frac{-6100}{89}\% = -68.5\%$$

Whereas absolute changes must specify units (e.g., million tonnes of coal per annum), percentage changes are *unit-free*. For many purposes it is more convenient to present data on changes in the form of percentage changes.

When we study time series data over long periods such as a decade, we do not want to know just the percentage or absolute change between the initial date and the final date.

> The *growth rate* of a variable is the percentage change per period (typically per year).

Negative growth rates simply show percentage falls. Economists usually take *economic growth* to mean the percentage annual change in the national income of a country or a group of countries.

2-5 Economic Models

Now for an example of economics in action. In the early 1980s there was a controversy over the 'Fares Fair' policy of cutting bus and tube fares in London. Some people thought low fares would increase passengers and bring in extra revenue for London Transport, which runs the bus and tube services. Others thought that low fares would lead to disastrous losses. Eventually the matter was referred to the courts. Suppose you had been a consultant brought in to analyse the relationship between tube fares and revenue from running the tube: how would you have analysed the problem?

To organize our thinking, or – as economists describe it – to build a model, we require a simplified picture of reality which picks out the most important elements of the problem. We begin with the simple equation

Total fare collection
= fare × number of passengers   (1)

In this stark form, equation (1) emphasizes, and thus organizes our thoughts around, two factors: the fare and the number of passengers. London Transport directly controls the fare, but can influence the number of passengers only through the fare that is set. (Cleaner stations and better service might also encourage passengers, but we neglect these effects for the moment.)

It might be argued that the number of passengers is determined by habit, convenience, and tradition, and is therefore completely unresponsive to changes in fares. This is *not* the view or model of traveller behaviour that an economist would initially adopt. It is possible to travel by car, bus, taxi, or tube, and decisions about the mode of transport are likely to be sensitive to the relative costs of the competing alternatives. Thus in equation (1) we must not view the number of passengers as fixed but develop a 'theory' or 'model' (we use these terms interchangeably) of what determines the number of passengers. We must model the *demand* for tube journeys.

In later chapters we study the theory of demand in detail. Applying a little common sense, we can probably work out the most important elements straight away. First, the fare itself matters. Other things equal, higher tube fares reduce the quantity of tube journeys demanded. Of course what matters is the price of the tube relative to the price of other means of transport – cars, buses, and taxis. If their prices remain constant, lower tube fares will encourage tube passengers. Rises in the price of these other means of transport will also encourage tube passengers even though tube fares remain unaltered.

We now have a bare-bones model of the demand for tube journeys. We summarize this model in the formal statement:

Quantity of tube journeys demanded
= *f*(tube fare, taxi fare, petrol price,
**   bus fare, . . .)   (2)**

This statement reads as follows. The quantity of tube fares 'depends on', or 'is a function of', the tube fare, the taxi fare, petrol prices, bus fares, and some other things. The notation $f(\ )$ is just a shorthand for 'depends on all the things listed inside the brackets'. In equation (2) we have named explicitly the most important determinants of the demand for tube journeys. The row of dots reminds us that we have omitted some possible determinants of the demand for tube journeys in an effort to simplify our analysis. For example, tube demand probably depends on the temperature. It gets very uncomfortable in the underground when it is very hot. Since the purpose of our model is to study *changes* in the number of tube passengers, it will probably be all right to neglect the weather provided weather conditions are broadly the same every year.

To answer our original question, it is not sufficient to know the factors on which the demand for tube journeys depends. We need to know *how* the number of passengers varies with each of the factors we have identified in our model. Other things equal, we assume that an increase in tube fares will reduce tube passengers and that an increase in the price of any of the competing modes of transport will increase tube passengers. To make real progress, we shall somehow have to quantify each of these separate effects. Then, given predictions for bus and taxi fares and the price of petrol, we would be able to use our model to predict the number of tube passengers who would want to travel at each possible tube fare that might be set by London Transport. Multiplying the fare per journey by the predicted corresponding number of journeys demanded at this fare, we could then predict London Transport revenue given any decision about the level of tube fares.

Writing down a model is a safe way of forcing ourselves to look for all the relevant effects, to worry about which effects must be taken into account and which are minor and can probably be ignored in answering the question we have set ourselves. Without writing down a model, we might have forgotten about the influence of bus fares on tube journeys, an omission that might have led to serious errors in trying to understand and forecast revenue raised from tube fares.

Models in Perspective

From equations (1) and (2) we can summarize our model of total revenue collected by London Transport from tube fares as

tube revenue

$$= \textbf{tube fare} \times \textbf{number of passengers}$$
$$= \textbf{tube fare} \times f(\textbf{tube fare, taxi fare,}$$
$$\textbf{petrol price, bus fare, . . .)} \qquad (3)$$

Your natural reaction may be to ask what all the fuss is about. Given five minutes thought, you would probably have organized your approach along similar lines. That is precisely the correct reaction. Models are simply devices for ensuring that we think clearly about a particular problem. Clear thinking requires some simplification. The real world is too complicated for us to think about everything at once. Nor can we offer any precise guidelines about how far a model should deliberately simplify reality. Learning to use models is more of an art than a science. Too much simplicity will lead to the omission of a crucial factor in the analysis. Too much complexity and the analysis gets bogged down: even if we can use the model to answer the question at hand, we lose any feel for why the answer is turning out as it is.

Sometimes we can use the data to guide us about which factors are crucial and which are not. On other occasions, as in our example with tube fares, it is not enough to understand the forces at work. We need to quantify them. For both these reasons, we turn now to the interaction of economic models and economic data.

2-6 Economic Models and Economic Data

Equation (3) is our model of the factors determining revenue from tube fares. Had we concluded that higher fares are accompanied by more journeys we might have been able to offer a purely theoretical answer to the questions we posed for ourselves: raising the fare raises the revenue. But, in organizing our thinking, we have concluded that, other things equal, higher tube fares will be accompanied by fewer passengers. Theory alone cannot answer our question. Whether or not higher tube fares raise or lower total revenue depends entirely on the *empirical* or factual issue of how many passengers are discouraged by higher fares.

Nevertheless, our model has been of some use. It tells us that the key fact we have to discover is how many passengers are put off by higher fares alone, holding constant the price of all other means of transport. Knowledge of this fact will allow us to calculate whether higher or lower fares are better for revenue.

Empirical Evidence

We shall have to conduct some empirical research to establish the facts. In *experimental* sciences, including for example many branches of physics and chemistry, it is possible to conduct controlled experiments in a laboratory, varying one factor at a time while holding constant all the other relevant factors. Like astronomy, economics is primarily a *non-experimental* science. Just as astronomers cannot suspend planetary motion to examine the relation between the earth and the sun in isolation, so economists can rarely suspend the laws of economic activity to conduct controlled experiments.

Thus most empirical research in economics must deal with data collected over periods in which many of the relevant factors were simultaneously changing. The problem is how to disentangle the separate influences on observed behaviour. We approach this in two stages. First, we proceed by examining the relationship of interest – the dependence of journeys on fares – neglecting the possibility that other relevant factors were changing. Then we indicate how economists deal with the

Table 2-8 Fares and passengers on the London underground, 1973–87

YEAR	(1) FARE PER PASSENGER KILOMETRE (pence)	(2) RPI (1985 = 100)	(3) REAL FARE PER PASSENGER KILOMETRE (1987 pence)	(4) PASSENGER KILOMETRES (billions)	(5) REAL REVENUE (£ million, 1987 prices)
1973	1.5	25.1	6.5	5.2	338
1974	1.5	29.1	5.6	5.1	286
1975	2.0	36.1	5.9	4.8	283
1976	2.8	42.1	7.1	4.4	312
1977	3.3	48.8	7.4	4.3	318
1978	3.9	52.8	8.0	4.5	360
1979	4.6	59.9	8.2	4.5	369
1980	6.0	70.7	9.0	4.3	387
1981	6.1	79.1	8.3	4.1	340
1982	7.6	85.9	9.4	3.7	348
1983	6.4	89.8	7.7	4.4	339
1984	5.5	94.3	6.3	5.2	327
1985	5.6	100.0	6.0	5.9	354
1986	5.8	103.4	6.1	6.2	378
1987	6.2	107.7	6.2	6.3	391

Sources: Department of Transport, *Transport Statistics Great Britain, 1973–83;* CSO, *Monthly Digest of Statistics.*

harder problem in which variations in these other factors are simultaneously included in the analysis.

Table 2-8 presents data on tube fares and passengers collected by the Department of Transport. Column (1) shows the tube fare per passenger kilometre. Although this rises from 1.5 pence in 1973 to 6.2 pence in 1987, we know from previous sections of this chapter that the general price level rose steadily throughout this period. In times of inflation it is *real* tube fares, not nominal tube fares, that will influence behaviour. Column (2) shows the behaviour of the retail price index over the period. Thus we can construct an index of real tube fares, as shown in column (3). Each number in column (3) is the corresponding number in column (1) divided by the corresponding number in column (2) and multiplied by 107.7. For example, in 1983 we take 6.4 pence, divided by 89.8, the value of the RPI in that year, and multiply by 107.7 to obtain 7.7.Column (3) shows what happened to real tube fares by expressing tube fares in 1987 pence, or removing from nominal tube fares the increase that can be attributed solely to general inflation since 1973.

Because of inflation, shown by the increase in the RPI in column (2), the increase in nominal tube fares shown in column (1) implies a much

smaller increase in real tube fares in column (3). Nevertheless real tube fares did rise steadily until the early 1980s. Our model suggests that such fare increases should tend to reduce the demand for tube journeys.

Column (4) shows a measure of tube demand corresponding to the fares data we have shown in previous columns. Passenger usage in billions of passenger kilometres travelled per annum seems to fall as real tube fares rise over the period. This is certainly suggestive, but our model reminds us that we really need to know what was happening to prices of other transport before we can claim that the rise in real tube fares *caused* the decline in passenger use.

Scatter Diagrams

It is often convenient to present evidence such as that given in Table 2-8 in a *scatter diagram* such as Figure 2-3. A scatter diagram shows how two variables are related. Along the vertical axis we measure the units of column (3), 1987 pence per passenger kilometre. Along the horizontal axis we measure the units of column (4), passenger kilometres in billions per annum. We now plot the points representing data in columns (3) and (4) of Table 2-8.

Consider the data for 1973. We find the height on the vertical axis corresponding to 6.5

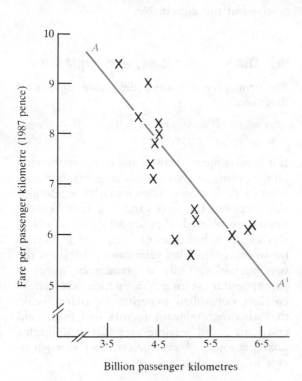

Figure 2-3 SCATTER DIAGRAM OF FARES AND PASSENGERS. This diagram shows the relationship between tube fares and passenger use between 1973 and 1987. Higher real fares tend to reduce passenger use.

1987 pence. At this height we move horizontally along a distance corresponding to the quantity 5.2 billion passenger kilometres. At this point we put a cross. We now repeat this procedure for every other year. Each cross in the diagram corresponds to a row of the table and shows both the price (column (3)) and quantity (column (4)) for that year. The scatter diagram shows the crosses, one for each of the years between 1973 and 1987.

It is easier to interpret the scatter diagram than the same information in table form. Figure 2-3 suggests that, on average, higher real tube fares are associated with lower passenger use. However, the relationship is not exact. The crosses in Figure 2-3 do not lie along any smooth line or curve. We have drawn in line AA' which might describe the average relation between fares and usage. Why do some crosses lie to the left of this line and others to the

right of it? This is precisely what our model suggests we ought to expect. Perhaps if the real prices of all other transport had remained constant, we would have observed crosses *on* our line. When real bus and taxi fares are high they will stimulate extra demand for the tube, leading to crosses to the right of the line AA' where tube demand is unusually high. Conversely, when real bus and taxi fares are abnormally low they will attract passengers away from the tube, whatever the tube fare, leading to crosses to the left of the line AA'. Using our theoretical model, we would predict that the degree of dispersion of the crosses around the line AA' will depend on the degree of variation in real taxi fares, real bus fares, and real petrol prices. We could examine data on these prices and see whether our explanation is correct. If real prices of other transport remained constant over the entire period, something else must be causing the dispersion of the crosses around AA'. We would then discover that our model had omitted something important.

Nevertheless, most of the points in Figure 2-3 lie quite close to the line AA', which probably gives a reasonable indication of the effect of tube fares on passenger use. We can get an approximate answer to our original question by proceeding as if changes in real tube fares had been the only cause of changes in passenger use.

Table 2-8 also examines the relation between the real tube fare and real revenue that London Transport obtains from selling tube tickets. Real revenue is simply the real fare per passenger kilometre multiplied by the number of passenger kilometres travelled. The last column of Table 2-8 is obtained by multiplying together data in columns 3 and 4 of Table 2-8. For example, for 1973 we multiply 6.5 pence per passenger kilometre by 5.2 billion passenger kilometres to obtain £338 million revenue. For 1974 we multiply 5.6 pence per passenger kilometre by 5.1 billion passenger kilometres to obtain £286 million revenue. This is a figure for *real* revenue, since it is measured at 1987 prices which already correct for inflation between 1973 and 1974.

The years of lowest real revenue coincide with the years in which the real tube fare was lowest. To the extent that we are prepared to neglect the other factors identified in our model

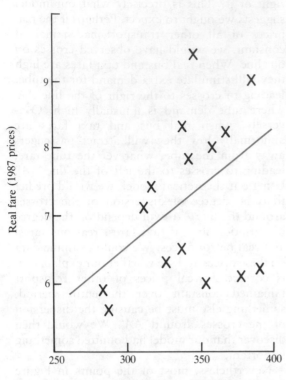

Figure 2-4 SCATTER DIAGRAM OF REAL TUBE FARES AND REAL REVENUES. This diagram shows the relation between real tube fares and real revenue over the period 1973–87. Higher fares are associated with higher revenue.

of passenger use and pretend that changes in real fares were the only cause of changes in use, Table 2-8 offers a clear answer to our original question. Raising real tube fares reduces passenger use, but not sufficiently to compensate for the fact that fares are higher. Revenue, being fares times passenger use, rises in real terms when the real fares are increased.

Figure 2-4 plots the data of Table 2-8 in a scatter diagram. As in Figure 2-3, we could draw a line through these crosses to capture the average relation between fares and revenue in the 1970s. Such a line would slope up, indicating that higher fares were associated with higher revenue.

How confident can we be that we have found the right answer to our question? Only if other determinants of passenger usage remained constant can we infer that higher tube fares cause higher revenue. Until we investigate

whether or not other determinants of passenger demand changed, our analysis so far is suggestive but not conclusive.

2-7 Diagrams, Lines, and Equations

We now give a formal definition of scatter diagrams.

> A *scatter diagram* plots *pairs* of values simultaneously observed for two different variables.

If it is possible to draw a line or curve through all the points or crosses, this suggests, but does not prove, that there is an underlying relationship between the two variables. If, when the points are plotted, they lie all over the place, this suggests, but does not prove, that there is no strong underlying relationship between the two variables. Only if economics were an experimental science, in which we could conduct controlled experiments guaranteeing that all other relevant factors had been held constant, could we interpret scatter diagrams unambiguously. Nevertheless, they often provide helpful clues.

Fitting Lines through Scatter Diagrams

In Figure 2-3 we drew the line *AA'* through the collection or scatter of points we had plotted. The line depicted the average relation between fares and tube usage during the period 1973–87. We could use the line to make more precise statements than we have offered so far. By looking at the *slope* of the line, how much usage changes each time we raise the fare 0.1 pence, we could quantify the average relation between fares and usage.

Given a particular scatter of points, as in Figure 2-3, how do we decide where to draw the line, given that it cannot fit all the points exactly?

Econometrics is the branch of economics devoted to measuring relationships using economic data. The details need not concern us here, but the idea is simple enough. Having plotted the points describing the data, a computer works out where to draw the line to minimize the dispersion of points around the line. The fitted line quantifies average relationships in the data just as our line in Figure 2-3.

After some practice, most people get used to working with two-dimensional diagrams such as Figures 2-3 and 2-4. A few gifted souls can even draw diagrams in three dimensions. Fortunately, computers can work in 10 or 20 dimensions at once, even though we cannot imagine what this looks like.

And therein lies the answer to the problem of trying to hold other things constant. The computer can measure the tube fare on one axis, the bus fare on another, petrol prices on a third, traffic congestion on a fourth, and tube revenue on a fifth, plot all these variables at the same time, and fit or work out the average relation between tube revenue and each of these influences when they are simultaneously considered. Although this is technically quite difficult, conceptually it is simply an extension of fitting lines through scatter diagrams such as Figure 2-3. By disentangling separate influences from data where many different factors are all moving at once, econometricians can conduct empirical economic research even though economics is not an experimental science like physics. In later chapters we report the results of some econometric research, but we never use anything more complicated than two-dimensional diagrams in the text.

Reading Diagrams

Since we do use diagrams in the text, it is important to make sure you know how to read a diagram or understand what it says. In Figure 2-5 we show a hypothetical relationship between two variables labelled P for price and Q for quantity. The diagram plots $Q = f(P)$ which in words means that quantity Q is a function of price P. Knowing the value of P allows us to work out the corresponding value of Q. The notation $f(P)$ merely tells us that we need to know values of P to make statements about Q. The diagram is a special case of this general idea. In Figure 2-5 Q is a *positive* function of P. By this we mean that higher values of P are associated with higher values of Q. Because there are units on the horizontal and vertical axes, the diagram also implies that Q is a particular function of P. The diagram tells us exactly what value of Q is implied by a particular value of P, not merely that Q is higher when P is higher.

When, as in Figure 2-5, the function can be

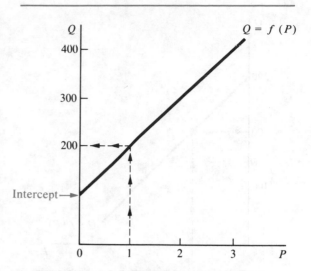

Figure 2-5 A POSITIVE LINEAR RELATIONSHIP BETWEEN TWO VARIABLES, P AND Q. The diagram shows a straight line or linear relation between the two variables P and Q. The schedule $Q = f(P)$ describes the relation between P and Q. The statement $Q = f(P)$ says that to every value of P, say $P = 1$, there corresponds a particular value of Q that can be read off the schedule. For example, with $P = 1$ we can read off the value $Q = 200$.

represented as a straight line, only two pieces of information are needed to allow us to draw in the complete relationship between Q and P. We need to know the *intercept* and the *slope*. The intercept is the height at which the line crosses the vertical axis. In Figure 2-5 this occurs at $Q = 100$. It is the value of Q when $P = 0$.

There are many lines that we might have drawn in Figure 2-5, all beginning at the same point, $Q = 100$ and $P = 0$. The other characteristic is the *slope* of the line, measuring its steepness. The slope tells us how much Q (the variable on the vertical axis) changes each time we increase P (the variable on the horizontal axis) by one unit. In Figure 2-5, the slope is 100. By defintion, a straight line has a constant slope. Q increases by 100 whether we move from a price of 1 to 2 or from 2 to 3 or from 3 to 4.

We have already said that Figure 2-5 displays a *positive* relation between Q and P. In a diagram, the fact that higher P values are associated with higher Q values is shown by a line that slopes *up* as we move to the right. We say the line has a positive slope. Figure 2-6

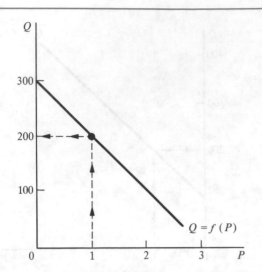

Figure 2-6   A NEGATIVE LINEAR RELATIONSHIP BETWEEN TWO VARIABLES P AND Q.   For each P we can read off from the negative linear relationship $Q = f(P)$ the corresponding value of Q. When $P = 1$ then $Q = 200$. The intercept (300) and the slope (-100) together determine the exact position of the line $Q = f(P)$.

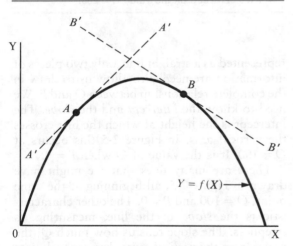

Figure 2-7   A NONLINEAR RELATIONSHIP BETWEEN X AND Y.   For each value of X the nonlinear function $Y = f(X)$ still allows us to determine the corresponding value of Y. The slope of a nonlinear function is not constant. At the point A the function $Y = f(X)$ has the same positive slope as the line $A'A'$, but at B the function $Y = f(X)$ has the same negative slope as the line $B'B'$.

shows a case where Q is a *negative* function of P. Higher P values now imply smaller Q values. The line has a negative slope.

Relationships in economics need not be

straight lines, or what we call linear relationships. Figure 2-7 shows a nonlinear relationship between two variables Y and X. Notice that the slope keeps changing. Each time we increase X by one unit we obtain a different increase (or decrease) in Y. Such a relationship might characterize the relationship between the rate of income tax X and total revenue from income tax Y. When the tax rate is zero, no revenue is raised. When the tax rate is 100 per cent nobody bothers to work and revenue is again zero. Beginning from a zero tax rate, increases in tax rates first raise then lower total tax revenue. Diagrams are useful in economics because they can display in a simple way the essence of real-life problems.

2-8 A Final Look at the Problem of 'Other Things Equal'

Diagrams are especially useful for thinking about the relationship between two variables when it is known that other things can be held constant. A diagram might help London Transport think about the effects of changing tube fares if it is known that bus fares and petrol prices will be pegged for the next 12 months. This is quite a different matter from using two-dimensional diagrams to analyse data without first checking that other relevant factors did indeed remain constant over that period.

Had we been unscrupulous consultants for a transport authority wishing to justify a fare increase, we might have tried to present Figures 2-3 and 2-4 as strong evidence that higher tube fares would raise revenue and end losses in operating the service. In discussing these diagrams, we warned you of the danger of assuming other things equal, and suggested that it would require an econometric study, which could examine simultaneously the effect of separate influences on passenger use and tube revenues, before conscientious economists could justify any conclusion about the facts.

Looking again at Table 2-8, real revenue increased every year from 1975 to 1980. So did real fares. It is tempting to draw the conclusion that higher fares cause higher revenue. A more careful economist would try to check the validity of the implicit 'other things equal' assumption behind this conclusion. In fact, real

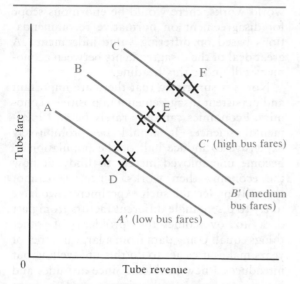

Figure 2-8 AN ALTERNATIVE EXPLANATION OF THE DATA. The scatter of points seems to show a positive relation between tube fares and tube revenue. This figure shows an alternative explanation. Other things equal, higher tube fares lead to lower tube revenue. When bus fares are low, *AA'* shows the relation between tube fares and revenue. At higher bus fares, *BB'* shows the negative relation between tube fares and tube revenue. *BB'* lies to the right of *AA'*. Higher bus fares lead to more tube passengers and tube revenue at any particular tube fare. At even higher bus fares, *CC'* shows the negative relation between tube fares and revenue. Steadily rising bus fares could lead to the scatter of points observed even though, for any given level of bus fares, higher tube fares reduce tube revenue.

bus fares increased by 34 per cent between 1975 and 1980. It is just possible that the true relation between tube fares and tube revenue is the one shown in Figure 2-8.

When real bus fares are held constant at a low level, the relation between real tube fares and real tube revenue is given by *AA'*. Unlike our previous interpretation of the data, if Figure 2-8 is correct, higher tube fares *reduce* tube revenue because passenger usage is very sensitive to the level of tube fares. Higher fares deter a large number of passengers.

For a higher level of bus fares, *BB'* describes the relation between tube fares and revenue. Other things equal, higher tube fares again reduce revenue. The line *BB'* lies to the right of the line *AA'* because higher bus fares lead to greater tube use, and hence more revenue, at each and every possible level of tube fares.

Even higher real bus fares lead to the relation *CC'* between tube fares and tube revenue.

We can see now that there are two competing explanations of the data on tube fares and revenue in the 1970s. Other transport costs did not remain constant over the period. If tube usage is sensitive to tube fares but not sensitive to other transport costs, Figure 2-4 is the correct interpretation of the data, and higher tube fares lead to higher tube revenues. However, if as in Figure 2-8 tube usage is sensitive to changes in other transport costs, higher real bus fares (and higher real petrol prices) might have led to shifts to the right in a *downsloping* relation between tube fares and tube revenue. The scatter points in Figure 2-4 may in fact be describing points such as *D*, *E* and *F* in Figure 2-8.

These different interpretations have completely different policy implications for London Transport. If, other things equal, higher tube fares increase revenue, fares should be raised to eliminate an operating deficit. However, if Figure 2-8 is the correct interpretation, for any given level of bus fares and petrol prices it requires lower fares to increase revenue. Two-dimensional diagrams cannot resolve this ambiguity. It requires a full econometric study, which simultaneously examines the effect on tube revenue of tube fares, bus fares, petrol prices, and any other variables that our model suggests are relevant.

2-9 Theories and Evidence

We can now summarize the way in which economists approach the analysis of a particular problem. There are three distinct stages. First, a phenomenon is observed or contemplated and the problem is formulated. By armchair reasoning or a cursory inspection of the data, it is recognized that tube fares have something to do with tube revenues. We want to understand what this relationship is and why it exists.

The second stage is to develop a theory or model that captures the essence of the phenomenon. By thinking about the decision about which type of transport to use, we identify the factors relevant to tube usage and hence tube revenue.

The third stage is to *test* the predictions of the theory by confronting it with economic data.

An econometric examination of the data can be used to quantify the factors the model emphasizes. In particular, we can see if on average these factors work in the direction our model suggests. Indeed, we can go further. By including in our econometric investigation some additional factors that we deliberately left out of our model in the quest for simplicity, we can check that these additional influences were of sufficiently small quantitative importance that it was legitimate to leave them out of the analysis.

Suppose we confront our theory with the data and conclude that the two seem compatible. We then say that we *do not reject* our theory. When our model is rejected we have to start again. However, when our model is not rejected by the data, this does not guarantee that we have found the correct model. There may be a completely different model which has escaped our attention and which would also be compatible with our particular collection of data. As time elapses, we will acquire new data. We can also use data from other countries. The more we confront our model with different collections of data and find that it is still not rejected, the more confidence we shall have that we have discovered the correct explanation of the economic behaviour in which we are interested.

2-10 Some Popular Criticisms of Economics and Economists

In this chapter we have introduced the toolkit used by economists. You may have some nagging doubts about some of these techniques or about the whole approach. Even if you yourself are persuaded that we have outlined a sensible approach to the study of economic problems, you may soon find yourself at a party wondering how to justify this approach to a sceptic. We conclude this chapter by discussing some of the popular criticisms of economics and economists.

Economics is a non-subject. It is well known that no two economists ever agree It is important to distinguish positive economics and normative economics. In Chapter 1 we pointed out that, even if all economists agreed on a positive economic analysis of how the

world works, there would be enormous scope for disagreement on normative recommendations based on differing value judgements. A great deal of the disagreements between economists fall under this heading.

Nor is it surprising that there are important and persistent disagreements in positive economics. Economics can only rarely be an experimental science. It would be prohibitively expensive to induce half of the population to become unemployed merely to find out how the economy then works. Since we cannot typically undertake such experiments, we have to try to disentangle different factors from past data to overcome the problem of other things equal. Using data from a large number of years makes it easier to do this unravelling but introduces a new problem. Since attitudes and institutions are slowly changing, data from many years ago may no longer be relevant to current behaviour. The problems we confront are difficult ones and we simply have to do the best we can.

Finally, it would be a mistake to suppose that there are not serious disagreements between physicists or doctors or engineers. These may be less apparent than disagreements between economists. Most ordinary citizens do not pretend to know much about physics; everybody thinks he or she knows a bit about the problems that economists study.

Models in economics are hopelessly simple. They have nothing to do with reality A model is a deliberate simplification to help us think more clearly. A good model simplifies a lot but does not distort reality too much. It is successful in capturing the main features of the problem. The test of a good model is not how simple it is, but how much of observed behaviour it is capable of explaining.

Sometimes we can get a long way with a very simple model. You will see examples of such models in later chapters. On other occasions, the behaviour we wish to describe is genuinely complex and a simple model may be insufficient. Where a more realistic model would take us beyond the scope of this book, we will nevertheless introduce a simple model to allow us to begin to understand the elements of the problem.

People are not as mercenary as economists

make out. Prices, incomes, and profit are not the mean determinants of behaviour We can certainly think of decisions where this is a fair comment. Marriage is typically though not exclusively determined by non-economic considerations. Economists believe that most of the phenomena they study, such as the decision about whether to travel by bus or tube, are determined primarily by economic incentives. This is very different from asserting that only economic incentives matter.

In Figure 2-8 we saw that changes in bus fares would shift the line describing the relation between tube fares and tube revenue. A successful advertising campaign by bus operators would have the same effect. So too would a change in social attitudes as, for example, if it become the 'done thing' to take the bus. Economists recognize that knowledge of politics, sociology, and psychology would be necessary to provide a more complete description of human behaviour. These are all factors that economists subsume under the heading of 'other things equal'. Economics emphasizes the effect of economic incentives. Social attitudes change only slowly and for many purposes may be treated as being held constant. However, if an economist were told, or discovered, that there had been an important change in social attitudes, it would be straightforward to include this in the analysis.

People are human beings. You cannot reduce their actions to scientific laws Physicists accept that molecules behave randomly but that it is possible to construct and test theories based on average or systematic behaviour. Economists take the same view about people. We shall never be able to explain actions based on whim or because you got out of bed on the wrong side. However, random differences in behaviour tend to cancel out on average. We may be able to describe average behaviour with a lot more certainty.

If behaviour shows no systematic tendencies – tendencies to do the same thing when confronted by the same situation – there is really nothing to discuss. The past will be no guide to the future and every decision is a one-off decision. Not only is this view unconstructive, but it is not usually supported by the data. In the last resort the economic theories that survive are those that are consistently com-patible with the data. The more random is human behaviour, the less will be the systematic element about which we can form theories and use to make predictions. Nevertheless, we must always do the best we can. It is better to be able to say something about behaviour than nothing at all. Sometimes, as you will shortly discover, we can say rather a lot about behaviour.

Summary

1   There is a continuing interplay between models and facts in the study of economic relationships and problems. A model is a simplified framework for organizing the way we think about a problem.

2   Data or facts are essential for two reasons. They suggest relationships which we should aim to explain. Having formulated our theories, we can also use data to test our hypotheses and to quantify the effects that they imply.

3   Tables present data in a form that is easily understood. Time series data are values of a given variable at different points in time. Cross-section data refer to the same point in time but to different values of the same variable across different people.

4   Index numbers express data relative to some given base value.

5   Many index numbers refer to averages of many variables. The retail price index summarizes changes in the prices of all goods bought by households. It weights the price of each good by its importance in the budget of a typical household.

6   The annual percentage change in the retail price index is the usual measure of inflation, the rate at which prices in general are changing.

7   Nominal or current price variables refer to values at the prices ruling when the variable was measured. Real or constant price variables adjust nominal variables for changes in the general level of prices. They are inflation-adjusted measures.

8   Scatter diagrams show the relationship between two variables plotted in the diagram. It is possible to fit a line through these points to summarize the average relationship between

the two variables. Econometricians use computers to fit average relationships between many variables simultaneously. In principle, this allows us to get round the other-things-equal problem which always applies in two dimensions.

9   Analytical diagrams are often useful in building a model. They show relationships between two variables holding other things equal. If we wish to change one of these other things, we have to shift the line or curve we have shown in our diagram.

10   To understand how the economy works we need both theory and facts. We need theory to know what facts to look for: there are too many facts for the facts alone to tell us the correct answer. Facts without theory are useless, but theory without facts remains an unsupported assertion. We need both.

Key Terms

Model
Data
Time series data
Cross-section data
Index numbers
Retail price index (RPI)
Inflation rate
Nominal and real variables
Real or relative prices
Current and constant prices
Purchasing power of money
Percentage change
Growth rate
Function
Scatter diagram
Econometrics
Other things equal
Testing an economic model

Problems

1   Use the data of Table 2-7 to plot a scatter diagram of the relation between the index of unit labour costs and the retail price index.

2   The accompanying table shows total consumption (spending by households) and total income received by households in the UK, both in £ billion at 1980 prices. (a) Plot the scatter diagram showing consumption on the vertical axis and income on the horizontal axis. (b) Sketch in a fitted line through

	INCOME	CONSUMPTION
1979	159.1	137.6
1980	161.2	137.0
1981	157.3	136.6
1982	157.9	137.6
1983	161.6	142.9
1984	165.3	147.7
1985	169.2	153.3
1986	175.0	162.5
1987	180.8	170.9

Source: CSO, *Economic Trends.*

these points. (c) Can you use this to suggest a relation between consumption and income of households? Does this make sense?

3   Draw a diagram showing the variable X measured in pounds on the vertical axis and the variable Y

				YEAR			
	1	2	3	4	5	6	7
Y	40	33	29	56	81	19	20
X	5	7	9	3	1	11	10

measured in tons on the horizontal axis. (a) Plot the scatter diagram. (b) Is the relation between the two variables positive or negative? (c) Would it be better to fit a straight line or a curve through these points?

4   You have been employed by the police research department to study whether the level of crime is affected by the percentage of people unemployed. (a) How would you test this idea? What data would you want? (b) What other-things-equal problems would you want to bear in mind?

5   The following table gives the RPI and an index of energy prices showing the behaviour of prices for coal, gas and electricity, oil and petrol.

	1971	1973	1975	1977
RPI	100.0	115.7	166.7	223.8
Energy index	100.0	110.8	172.8	248.3

	1979	1981	1985	1987
RPI	276.5	366.3	463.3	499.0
Energy index	293.6	445.4	574.1	478.2

Source: CSO, *Monthly Digest of Statistics.*

(a)Calculate an index of the real price of energy (1971 = 100). (b) Measuring different years along the horizontal axis, plot the three time series: the RPI, the energy price index, and the real energy price index. (c) Why do you think real energy prices behaved in this way? (d) In Figure 2-8 we showed how changes in real bus fares might have influenced the relation between real tube fares and real tube revenue. Real energy prices affect the cost of private motoring. Did changes in real energy prices tend to reinforce or to offset the effect of changes in real bus fares on the relation between tube fares and tube revenue?

6 Common Fallacies Show why the following statements are incorrect: (a) The purpose of a theory is to allow you to ignore the facts. (b) Economics cannot claim to be a science since it is incapable of controlled laboratory experiments. (c) If you look hard enough at the facts you will inevitably discover the correct theory. (d) People are people not machines. They have feelings and act haphazardly. It is misguided and even insulting to reduce their actions to scientific laws.

3

Demand, Supply, and the Market

Society has to find *some* way of deciding what, how, and for whom to produce. In Chapter 1 we said that Western economies rely heavily on markets and prices to allocate resources between competing uses. We now examine markets in greater detail. The ideas discussed in this chapter are central to economic analysis and must be mastered by anyone who wishes to understand how our own society solves the basic economic problems.

The framework of analysis is very general. It can be applied to the market for motor cars, labour, haircuts, or even footballers. In each case, the interplay between *demand* (the behaviour of buyers) and *supply* (the behaviour of sellers) determines the quantity of the good that is produced and the price at which it is bought and sold.

3-1 The Market

In Chapter 1 we defined markets in a very general way as arrangements through which prices guide resource allocation. We now adopt a narrower definition.

A *market* is a set of arrangements by which buyers and sellers are in contact to exchange goods or services.

Some markets (shops and fruit stalls) physically bring together the buyer and the seller. Other markets (the London Stock Exchange) operate chiefly through intermediaries (stockbrokers) who transact business on behalf of clients. In supermarkets, sellers choose the price, stock the shelves, and leave customers to choose whether or not to make a purchase. Antique auctions force buyers to bid against each other with the seller taking a passive role.

Although superficially different, these markets perform the same economic function. They determine prices that ensure that the quantity people wish to buy equals the quantity people wish to sell. Price and quantity cannot be considered separately. In establishing that the price of a Rolls-Royce is ten times the price of a small Ford, the market for motor cars simultaneously ensures that production and sales of small Fords will greatly exceed the production and sale of Rolls-Royces. These prices guide society in choosing what, how, and for whom to purchase.

To understand this process more fully, we require a model of a typical market. The essential features on which such a model must concentrate are demand, the behaviour of buyers, and supply, the behaviour of sellers. It will then be possible to study the interaction of these forces to see how a market works in practice.

3-2 Demand, Supply, and Equilibrium

Demand is the quantity of a good buyers wish to purchase at each conceivable price.

Thus demand is not a particular quantity, such as six bars of chocolate, but rather a full description of the quantity of chocolate the buyer would purchase at each and every price which might be charged. The first column of Table 3-1 shows a range of prices for bars of chocolate. The second column shows the quantities that might be demanded at these prices. Even when chocolate is free, only a finite amount will be wanted. People get sick from eating too much chocolate. As the price of chocolate rises, the quantity demanded falls, other things equal. We have assumed that nobody will buy any chocolate when the price is more than £0.40 per bar. Taken together, columns (1) and (2) describe the demand for chocolate as a function of its price.

Supply is the quantity of a good sellers wish to sell at each conceivable price.

Table 3-1 The demand for and supply of chocolate

(1) PRICE (£/bar)	(2) DEMAND (million bars/year)	(3) SUPPLY (million bars/year)
0.00	200	0
0.10	160	0
0.20	120	40
0.30	80	80
0.40	40	120
0.50	0	160

Again, supply is not a particular quantity but a complete description of the quantity that sellers would like to sell at each and every possible price. The third column of Table 3-1 shows how much chocolate sellers wish to sell at each price. Chocolate cannot be produced for nothing. Nobody would wish to supply if they receive a zero price. In our example, it takes a price of at least £0.20 per bar before there is any incentive to supply chocolate. At higher prices it becomes increasingly lucrative to supply chocolate bars and there is a corresponding increase in the quantity of bars that would be supplied. Taken together, columns (1) and (3) describe the supply of chocolate bars as a function of their price.

Notice the distinction between *demand* and the *quantity demanded*. Demand describes the behaviour of buyers at every price. At a particular price such as £0.30, there is a particular quantity demanded, namely 80 million bars/year. The term 'quantity demanded' makes sense only in relation to a particular price. A similar distinction applies to *supply* and *quantity supplied*.

In everyday language, we would say that when the demand for football tickets exceeds their supply some people will not get into the ground. Economists must be more precise. At the price charged for tickets, the quantity demanded exceeded the quantity supplied. Although the size of the ground sets an upper limit on the quantity of tickets that can be supplied, a higher ticket price would have reduced the quantity demanded, perhaps leaving empty space in the ground. Yet there has been no change in demand, the schedule describing how many people want admission at each possible ticket price. The quantity demanded has changed because the price has changed.

As in our discussion of tube fares in the previous chapter, we must recognize that the demand schedule relating price and quantity demanded and the supply schedule relating price and quantity supplied are each constructed on the assumption of 'other things equal'. In the demand for tube tickets, the 'other things' were the cost of alternative modes of transport. In the demand for football tickets, one of the 'other things' that is important is whether or not the game is being shown on television. If it is, the quantity of tickets demanded at each and every price will be lower than if the game is not televised. To understand how a market works, we must first explain why demand and supply are what they are. (Is the game on television? Has the ground capacity been extended by building a new stand?) Then we must examine how the price adjusts to balance the quantities supplied and demanded, given the underlying supply and demand schedules relating quantity to price.

Let us think again about the market for chocolate described in Table 3-1. Other things equal, *the lower the price of chocolate, the higher the quantity demanded*. Other things equal, *the higher the price of chocolate, the higher the quantity supplied*. A campaign by dentists warning of the effect of chocolate on tooth decay, or a fall in household incomes, would change the 'other things' relevant to the demand for chocolate. Either of these changes would reduce the demand for chocolate, reducing the quantities demanded at each price. Cheaper cocoa beans, or technical advances in packaging chocolate bars, would change the 'other things' relevant to the supply of chocolate bars. They would tend to increase the supply of chocolate bars, increasing the quantity supplied at each possible price.

The Market and the Equilibrium Price

For the moment, we assume that all these other things remain constant. We wish to combine the behaviour of buyers and sellers described in Table 3-1 to model how the market for chocolate bars would actually work. At low prices, the quantity demanded exceeds the quantity supplied but the reverse is true at high prices. At some intermediate price, which we call the 'equilibrium price', the quantity demanded just equals the quantity supplied.

The *equilibrium price* clears the market for chocolate. It is the price at which the quantity supplied equals the quantity demanded.

Table 3-1 shows that the equilibrium price for chocolate bars is £0.30: 80 million bars per year is the quantity buyers wish to buy and sellers wish to sell at this price. We call 80 million bars per year the *equilibrium quantity*. At prices below £0.30, the quantity demanded exceeds the quantity supplied and some buyers will be frustrated. There is a shortage, what we call *excess demand*. From our previous discussion, you will realize that when economists say there is excess demand they are using a convenient shorthand for the more complicated expression: the quantity demanded exceeds the quantity supplied *at this price*.

Conversely, at any price above £0.30, the quantity supplied exceeds the quantity demanded. Sellers will be left with unsold stock. To describe this surplus, economists use the shorthand *excess supply*, it being understood that this means excess in the quantity supplied *at this price*. Only at £0.30, the equilibrium price, does the quantity demanded equal the quantity supplied. At the equilibrium the market clears and people can buy or sell as much as they want at the equilibrium price.

Will the market for chocolate bars automatically be in equilibrium? If so, what mechanism brings this about? Suppose the price of chocolate is initially £0.50, higher than the equilibrium price. Producers wish to sell 160 million bars per year but nobody wishes to buy at this price. To recoup the money spent in producing chocolate, sellers will have to cut the price to clear their stock. Cutting the price to £0.40 has two effects. It increases the quantity demanded to 40 million bars per year and it reduces the quantity producers wish to supply to 120 million bars per year. Both effects work to reduce the excess supply. The process of price-cutting will continue until the equilibrium price of £0.30 is reached and excess supply has been eliminated. At this price the market clears.

When the initial price lies below the equilibrium price the process works in reverse. At a price of £0.20, the quantity demanded is 120 million bars per year but the quantity supplied is only 40 million bars per year. Sellers will quickly run out of stock and realize they could

have charged higher prices. This incentive to raise prices to ration scarce stocks will continue until the equilibrium price is reached, excess demand is eliminated, and the market clears.

At any particular instant, the market price may not be the equilibrium price. If not, there will be either excess supply or excess demand, depending on whether the price lies above or below the equilibrium price. But these forces themselves provide the incentive to change prices towards the equilibrium price. In this sense, markets are self-correcting.

Later in this book, we shall see that some of the most important issues in economics turn on how quickly prices adjust to restore equilibrium in particular markets. When prices are very flexible, as for example on the stock exchange, where prices can change several times a minute, it may be realistic to simplify the analysis by supposing that the market is always in equilibrium. When prices are less flexible, as for example in many labour markets, where firms and workers negotiate a wage contract that remains in force for a whole year, it may be misleading to simplify by assuming that the market is always in equilibrium. If anything happens during the year to change the equilibrium wage rate, the market may not be able to adjust immediately. We shall then have to study explicitly how the market behaves when it is not in equilibrium.

3-3 Demand and Supply Curves

Table 3-1 shows demand and supply conditions in the chocolate market and allows us to find the equilibrium price and quantity. It is convenient to approach the same problem diagrammatically using demand and supply curves.

The *demand curve* shows the relation between price and quantity demanded, holding other things constant. In Figure 3-1 we measure on the vertical axis prices of chocolate bars. Corresponding quantities demanded in millions of bars per year are measured on the horizontal axis. The demand curve plots the data in the first two columns of Table 3-1. The point A shows that 160 million bars per year are demanded at a price of £0.10. The point B shows that 120 million bars per year are demanded at a price of £0.20. Plotting all the

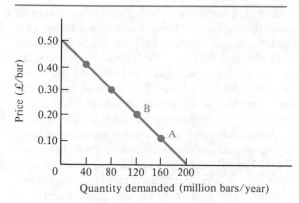

Figure 3-1 THE DEMAND CURVE FOR CHOCOLATE BARS. The demand curve shows the negative relation between price and quantity demanded, holding other things equal. The vertical axis measures the price of chocolate bars and the horizontal axis measures the quantity demanded. The diagram plots the points in the first two columns of Table 3-1. Point *A* shows that 160 million bars per year are demanded at £0.10. Point *B* shows that 120 million bars per year are demanded at £0.20. Plotting all the points and joining them up, we obtain the demand curve.

points and joining them up, we obtain the demand curve. In our example, this curve happens to be a straight line. As expected, it has a negative slope showing that larger quantities are demanded at lower prices.

The *supply curve* shows the relation between price and quantity supplied, holding other things constant. In Figure 3-2 we plot the supply information given by columns (1) and (3) of Table 3-1. Again we join up the different data points.

In Figure 3-3, we show the demand curve, labelled *DD*, and the supply curve, labelled *SS*, in the same diagram. We can now re-examine our analysis of excess supply, excess demand, and equilibrium. Consider a particular price as represented by a height on the vertical axis. At a price below the equilibrium price, the horizontal distance between the supply curve and the demand curve at this height shows the excess demand at this price. For example, at £0.20 the quantity supplied is 40 million bars per year, the quantity demanded 120 million bars per year, and the distance *AB* represents the excess demand of 80 million bars per year. Conversely, at a price above the equilibrium price there is excess supply. At £0.40, 40 million bars per year are demanded, 120 million bars

per year are supplied and the horizontal distance *FG* measures the excess supply of 80 million bars per year at this price.

Suppose the price is £0.40. Only 40 million

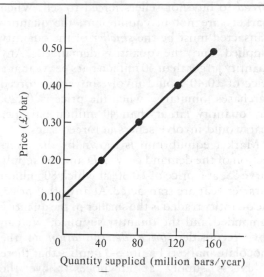

Figure 3-2 THE SUPPLY CURVE FOR CHOCOLATE BARS. The supply curve shows the positive relation between the price and quantity supplied, holding other things equal. The diagram plots the points in the first and third columns of Table 3-1.

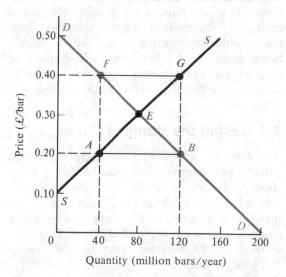

Figure 3-3 THE MARKET FOR CHOCOLATE BARS. Market equilibrium occurs at the point *E*. At prices below the equilibrium price there is an excess demand: *AB* shows the excess demand at the price £0.20. At prices above the equilibrium price there is excess supply: *FG* shows the excess supply at the price £0.40.

bars per year are sold even though sellers would like to sell 120 million bars per year. How do we know that it is sellers not buyers who are frustrated when their wishes differ? Participation in a market is voluntary. Buyers are not *forced* to buy nor sellers forced to sell. When markets are not in equilibrium, the quantity transacted must be the *smaller* of the quantity supplied and the quantity demanded. Any quantity larger than 40 million bars per year at a price of £0.40 would involve buyers in forced purchases. Similarly, when the price is £0.20, any quantity larger than 40 million bars per year would involve sellers in forced sales.

Market equilibrium is shown by the intersection of the demand curve *DD* and the supply curve *SS*, at a price of £0.30, at which 80 million bars per year are transacted. At any other price, the quantity traded is the smaller of the quantity demanded and the quantity supplied. We can now reconsider *price determination* in the chocolate market. Figure 3-3 implies that there is excess supply at all prices above the equilibrium price of £0.30. Sellers react to unsold stocks by cutting prices. Only when prices have been reduced to the equilibrium price will excess supply be eliminated. The equilibrium position is shown by the point *E*. Conversely, at prices below £0.30 there is excess demand, which bids up the price of chocolate, gradually eliminating excess demand until the equilibrium point *E* is reached. In equilibrium buyers and sellers can trade as much as they wish at the equilibrium price and there is no incentive for any further price changes.

3-4 Behind the Demand Curve

The demand curve depicts the relation between price and quantity demanded *holding other things constant*. What are those 'other things'? The other things relevant to demand curves can usually be grouped under three headings: the price of related goods, the income of consumers (buyers), and consumer tastes or preferences. We look at each of these in turn.

The Price of Related Goods

In Chapter 2 we discussed the demand for tube travel. We saw that a rise in bus fares or petrol prices would increase the quantity of tube travel demanded at each possible price. In everyday language, we think of buses and private cars as *substitutes* for the tube. Loosely speaking, this means that a journey may be made by bus or car instead of by tube. Similarly, everyday language suggests that petrol and cars are *complements* because you cannot use a car without also using petrol. A rise in the price of petrol tends to reduce the demand for cars.

How do these ideas about substitutes and complements relate to the demand for chocolate bars? Clearly, other sweets (mint drops and jelly babies) are substitutes for chocolate. We expect an increase in the price of other sweets to increase the quantity of chocolate demanded at each possible chocolate price, as people substitute away from other sweets towards chocolate. If people buy chocolate to eat at the cinema, films would be a complement for bars of chocolate. A rise in the price of cinema tickets would reduce the demand for chocolate since fewer people will go to the cinema. Nevertheless, it is difficult to think of a lot of goods that are complements for chocolate. This suggests, correctly, that most of the time goods are substitutes for each other. Complementarity, while present in many instances, is usually a more specific feature (record players and records, coffee and milk, shoes and shoelaces).

Consumer Incomes

The second category of 'other things equal' when we draw a particular demand curve is consumer income. When incomes rise, the demand for most goods increases. Typically, consumers buy more of everything. However, there are exceptions.

> A *normal good* is a good for which demand increases when incomes rise. An *inferior good* is a good for which demand falls when incomes rise.

As their name suggests, most goods are normal goods. An example of an inferior good might be cheap but nasty cuts of meat. As household incomes rise, households spend absolutely less on cheap cuts and more on better cuts of meat such as steaks. Inferior goods are typically cheap but low-quality goods which people would prefer not to buy if they could afford to spend a little more.

Tastes

The third category of things held constant along a particular demand curve is consumer tastes or preferences. In part, these are shaped by convenience, custom, and social attitudes. When the Beatles and the Rolling Stones first became popular, the demand for haircuts suddenly fell. The fashion for the mini-skirt reduced the demand for textile material. More recently, the emphasis on health and fitness has increased the demand for jogging equipment, health foods, and sports facilities while reducing the demand for cream cakes, butter, and cigarettes.

3-5 Shifts in the Demand Curve

We are now in a position to distinguish between movements along a given demand curve and shifts in the demand curve itself. In Figure 3-1 we drew the demand curve for chocolate bars for a given level of the three underlying factors: the price of related goods, incomes, and tastes. Movements along the demand curve isolate the effects of chocolate prices on quantity demanded holding other things equal. Changes in any of these three factors will change the demand for chocolate. Table 3-2 illustrates the effect of a rise in the price of a substitute for chocolate, say ice cream, which leads people to demand more chocolate and less ice cream. At

Table 3-2 Ice cream prices and chocolate demand

PRICE OF CHOCOLATE ((£/bar)	DEMAND FOR CHOCOLATE	
	LOW ICE CREAM PRICE (m. bars/year)	HIGH ICE CREAM PRICE (m. bars/year)
0.00	200	280
0.10	160	240
0.20	120	200
0.30	80	160
0.40	40	120
0.50	0	80

each chocolate price there is a larger quantity of chocolate demanded when ice cream prices are high, since people substitute chocolate for ice cream. In Figure 3-4 we show the same change in ice cream prices leading to a *shift* in the demand curve from DD to D'D'. The entire demand curve shifts to the right since a higher quantity is demanded at each price.

Changes in the price of ice cream have no effect on the incentives to supply chocolate bars: at each price suppliers will wish to supply the same quantity of chocolate as before. The increase in demand, or rightward shift in the demand curve, changes the equilibrium price and quantity in the chocolate market. Equilibrium has changed from the point E to the point E'. The new equilibrium price is £0.40 and the new equilibrium quantity is 120 million

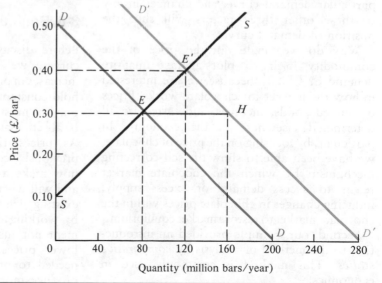

Figure 3-4 ICE CREAM PRICES AND CHOCOLATE DEMAND. At low ice cream prices, the demand curve for chocolate is DD and the market equilibrium occurs at the point E. Higher ice cream prices raise the demand for chocolate, shifting the demand curve to D'D'. At the former equilibrium price there is now excess demand EH, which gradually bids up the price of chocolate until the new equilibrium is reached at E'.

bars per year. A glance back at Table 3-1 will confirm this.

We can even sketch how the chocolate market makes the transition from the old equilibrium at E to the new equilibrium at E'. Consider the instant when ice cream prices rise. The demand curve for chocolate shifts from DD to $D'D'$. Until the price changes from £0.30 there is no excess demand EH at this price: 160 million bars per year are now demanded but only 80 million bars per year are supplied. This excess demand puts upward pressure on prices which gradually rise to the new equilibrium price of £0.40, choking the quantity demanded back from 160 million bars per year to 120 million bars per year and providing the incentive to increase the quantity supplied from 80 million bars per year to 120 million bars per year.

We can draw two general lessons from this example. First, the quantity of chocolate demanded depends on four things: its own price, prices of related goods, incomes, and tastes. We could choose to draw a two-dimensional diagram showing the relation between quantity of chocolate demanded and any one of these four factors. The other three factors would then become the 'other things equal' for this particular diagram. In drawing demand curves, we always choose to single out the price of the commodity itself (here the price of chocolate bars) to put in the diagram with quantity demanded. The other three factors become the 'other things equal' for drawing a particular demand curve, and changes in any of these other three factors will shift the position of demand curves.

Why do we single out the price of the commodity itself to plot against quantity demanded? Chiefly because we are interested in how the market for chocolate works. Prices of related goods, incomes, and tastes are all determined elsewhere in the economy. In particular, by focusing on the price of chocolate, we have been able to show the self-correcting mechanism by which the chocolate market reacts to excess demand or excess supply, inducing changes in chocolate prices within the chocolate market to restore market equilibrium.

Second, our example provided an introduction to the method of analysis by *comparative statics*. This method is commonly used in economics.

In *comparative static analysis* we change one of the 'other things equal' categories and examine the effect on equilibrium price and quantity.

The analysis is comparative because it compares the old and new equilibrium positions, and it is static because it compares only the two equilibrium positions. In each equilibrium, prices and quantities are unchanging. Comparative static analysis is not interested in the dynamic path by which the economy moves from one equilibrium to the other, only in the point from which it began and the point at which it ends up.

Figure 3-4 may also be used to analyse the effect of a change in one of the 'other things equal' which reduces the demand for chocolate. Suppose the demand curve is initially $D'D'$ and the market begins in equilibrium at the point E'. Let there be a change that reduces the demand for chocolate to DD. This change might be a fall in the price of a chocolate substitute such as ice cream, a fall in consumer incomes, or a change in tastes away from liking chocolate. When the demand curve shifts left to DD, showing less chocolate demanded at each price, the new equilibrium will be given at the point E. At the original price of £0.40 there will be excess supply, which will gradually bid prices down to the new equilibrium price of £0.30. When the demand curve shifts to the left, there is a fall in both the equilibrium price and the equilibrium quantity.

3-6 Behind the Supply Curve

Before discussing changes that shift supply curves, we discuss in greater detail why increases in price increase the quantity supplied, hold constant all other factors. At low prices, only the most efficient chocolate producers will be able to make any profits producing chocolate. As prices rise, producers who could not previously compete will find that they can now make a profit in the chocolate business and will wish to supply. Moreover, previously existing firms may be able to expand output by working overtime, or buying fancy equipment not justified when selling chocolate at lower prices. In general, higher prices are needed to provide an incentive for firms to produce more chocolate. Other things equal, supply curves slope upward as we move to the right.

Just as we investigated the 'other things equal' along a demand curve, we now examine three categories of 'other things equal' along a supply curve. These categories are: technology available to producers, the cost of inputs (labour, machines, fuel, and raw materials), and government regulation. Along any particular supply curve, all of these are held constant. A change in any of these categories will shift the supply curve by changing the amount producers wish to supply at each price.

Technology

A supply curve is drawn for a given technology. An improvement in technology will shift the supply curve to the right since producers will be willing to supply a larger quantity than previously at each price. An improvement in cocoa refining makes it possible to produce more chocolate for any given total cost. So do improvements in mass production packaging techniques. Faster shipping and better refrigeration may lead to less wastage in spoiled cocoa beans. Each of these technological advances enables firms to supply more at each price.

As a determinant of supply, technology must be interpreted very broadly. It embraces all know-how about production methods, not merely the state of available machinery. In agriculture, the development of disease-resistant seeds is a technological advance. Improved weather forecasting might enable better timing of planting and harvesting. A technological advance is any idea that allows more output from the same inputs as before. Using the terminology of Chapter 1, a technological advance shifts the production possibility frontier outwards.

Input Costs

A particular supply curve is drawn for a given level of input prices. A reduction in input prices (lower wages, lower fuel costs) will induce firms to supply more output at each price, shifting the supply curve to the right. Higher input prices make production less attractive and shift the supply curve to the left. For example, if a late frost destroys much of the cocoa crop, the ensuing scarcity will bid up the price of cocoa

beans. Chocolate producers will then wish to supply less chocolate at each price than previously.

Government Regulation

In discussing technology we spoke only of technological advances. Once people have discovered a better production method they are unlikely subsequently to forget it. Government regulations can sometimes be viewed as imposing a technological change that is *adverse* for producers. If so, the effect of regulations will be to shift the supply curve to the left, reducing quantity supplied at each price.

More stringent safety regulations prevent chocolate producers using the most productive process because it is quite dangerous to workers. Anti-pollution devices may raise the cost of making cars, and regulations to protect the environment may make it unprofitable for firms to extract surface mineral deposits which could have been cheaply quarried but whose extraction now requires expensive landscaping. Whenever government regulations prevent producers from selecting the production methods they would otherwise have chosen, the effect of these regulations is to shift the supply curve to the left.

3-7 Shifts in the Supply Curve

Along a given supply curve we hold constant technology, the prices of inputs, and the extent of government regulation. We now undertake a comparative static analysis of what happens when a change in one of these 'other things equal' categories leads to a reduction in supply. Suppose, for example, that an increase in the stringency of safety legislation makes it more expensive to produce chocolate bars in highly mechanized factories. In Figure 3-5 we show a shift to the left in the supply curve from SS to $S'S'$. If we wish to know only the direction, but not the magnitude, of the change in equilibrium price and quantity, it is not necessary to put scale units on the horizontal and vertical axis. Equilibrium shifts from the point E to the point E'. Thus equilibrium price rises but equilibrium quantity falls when the supply curve shifts to the left. Conversely, a supply curve shift to the right can be analysed

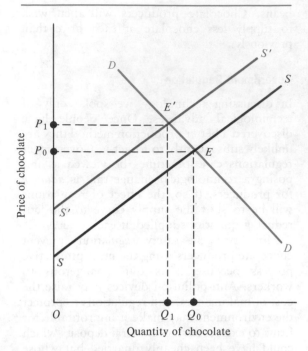

Figure 3-5 THE EFFECT OF A REDUCTION IN THE SUPPLY OF CHOCOLATE. The supply curve initially is *SS* and market equilibrium is at *E*. A reduction in the supply of chocolate shifts the supply curve to the left and is shown by the new supply curve *S'S'*. The new equilibrium at *E'* has a higher equilibrium price and a lower equilibrium quantity than the old equilibrium at *E*.

by supposing the supply curve is initially *S'S'* and the market is in equilibrium at the point *E'*. A change that increases supply will shift the supply curve to the right, say to the position shown by the supply curve *SS*. The new equilibrium will be at the point *E*. Thus an increase in supply leads to a higher equilibrium quantity and lower equilibrium price.

3-8 The Pope and the Price of Fish

Hypothetical examples are all very well, but it is reassuring to learn that demand and supply analysis works in practice. We report an interesting example based on research by Frederick Bell.[1] Until 1966 Roman Catholics were not allowed to eat meat on Fridays and tended to eat fish instead. In 1966 the Pope said that henceforth Catholics could eat

[1] Frederick W. Bell, 'The Pope and the Price of Fish', *American Economic Review*, December 1968.

meat on Friday. What do you think happened to the average weekly price of fish and average weekly quantity of fish consumed?

In 1966 we should expect the demand curve for fish to shift to the left as in Figure 3-6. Some Catholics who had previously been forced to eat fish no doubt preferred to eat meat and would substitute meat for Friday fish when allowed to do so. This is a simple example of the effect of a change in tastes on the demand curve. Our model predicts that the demand curve should shift from *DD* to *D'D'*, leading to a fall in the equilibrium price and quantity of fish as equilibrium shifts from the point *E* to the point *E'*.

Using data on fish prices and quantities of fish sales in the United States before and after 1966, Bell shows that this is precisely what happened.

3-9 Free Markets and Price Controls

Free markets allow prices to be determined purely by the forces of supply and demand.

Government actions may shift demand and supply curves, as when changes in safety

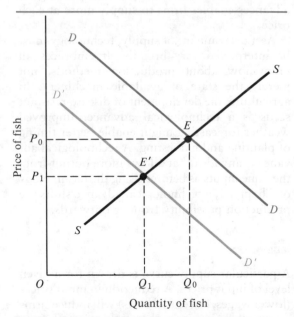

Figure 3-6 THE POPE AND THE PRICE OF FISH. Allowing Catholics to eat meat on Fridays leads to a change in tastes for fish. The demand curve shifts from *DD* to *D'D'* and the equilibrium moves from *E* to *E'*. The equilibrium price and quantity of fish fall.

legislation shift the supply curve, but the government makes no attempt to regulate prices directly. If prices are sufficiently flexible, the pressure of excess supply or excess demand will quickly bid prices in a free market to their equilibrium level. Markets will not be free when effective price controls exist.

> *Price controls* are government rules or laws that forbid the adjustment of prices to clear markets.

Price controls may be *floor* prices (minimum prices) or *ceiling* prices (maximum prices).

Price ceilings make it illegal for sellers to charge more than a specific maximum price and are typically introduced when a shortage of a commodity threatens to raise its price by a substantial amount. High prices are the device by which a free market rations goods in scarce supply. Although high prices are one way to solve the allocation problem, ensuring that only a small quantity of the scarce commodity will be demanded, they may lead to a solution that society believes to be unfair, a normative value judgement. For example, high food prices may lead to considerable hardship among the poor. Faced with a national food shortage, a government might prefer to impose a price ceiling on food so that poor people can continue to buy adequate quantities of food.

In Figure 3-7 we show the market for food. Perhaps war has disrupted imports of food. The supply curve lies far to the left and the free market equilibrium price P_0 is very high. Instead of allowing free market equilibrium at the point E, the government imposes a price ceiling at P_1. The quantity sold is then Q_1 and excess demand is given by the distance AB. The price ceiling creates a shortage of supply relative to demand by holding food prices below their equilibrium level.[2]

The ceiling price P_1 allows some of the poor to buy food they could not otherwise have afforded. However, it has reduced total food supplied from Q_0 to Q_1. Furthermore, since there is excess demand AB at the ceiling price, some form of rationing must be used to decide which potential buyers are actually supplied.

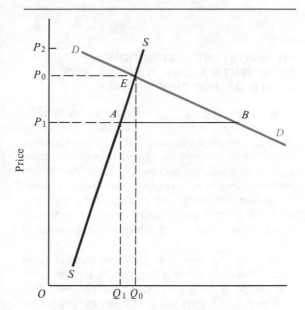

Figure 3-7 THE EFFECT OF A PRICE CEILING. Since supply is scarce, the supply curve *SS* lies well to the left. Free market equilibrium occurs at the point *E*. The high price P_0 chokes off quantity demanded to ration scarce supply. A price ceiling at P_1 succeeds in holding down the price but leads to excess demand *AB*. It also reduces quantity supplied from Q_0 to Q_1. A price ceiling at P_2 is irrelevant since the free market equilibrium at *E* can still be attained.

This rationing system could be highly arbitrary. Food suppliers may reserve supplies for their friends, not necessarily the poor. Indeed, suppliers may even accept bribes from those who can afford to pay to jump the queue. We should then say a 'black market' had developed. Holding down the price of food might not help the poor after all. For this reason, the imposition of ceiling prices may be accompanied by government-organized rationing by quota, as in the UK during the Second World War, to ensure that available supply is shared out fairly, independently of ability to pay.

Where price controls are maintained for many years they may have further repercussions. Many countries, including the UK, have imposed rent controls limiting the rent a landlord can charge tenants for accommodation. Intended to provide cheap housing for the poor, such legislation may have perverse effects,

---

[2] Notice that a price ceiling imposed at P_2 above the equilibrium price would simply be irrelevant. The free market equilibrium at E could still be attained and the price control would make no difference.

BOX 3-1

AN IMPORTANT DISTINCTION: MOVEMENTS ALONG A CURVE AND SHIFTS OF THE CURVE ITSELF

In everyday language we refer to an increase in demand without distinguishing between *shifts* in the demand curve and *movements along* a given demand curve. The accompanying figure shows that, from the point A on the demand curve DD two quite different 'increases in demand' are possible. One is an increase in the quantity demanded, moving along the curve from A to B. Such an increase in quantity demanded results from consumer adjustment to a reduction in price.

The second is a shift in the entire demand curve from DD to $D'D'$. At the going price P_0 the consumer used to purchase Q_0 but now purchases Q_1. This shift in demand is the response to an increase in the price of a substitute good (decrease in the price of a complement good), an increase in income, or a change of tastes.

The distinction between the two kinds of demand change is very important. Movement along the demand curve represents consumer adjustment to changes in the market price. Shifts in demand, by contrast, represent adjustment to outside factors (other prices, income, tastes) and lead in turn to changes in the equilibrium price and quantity.

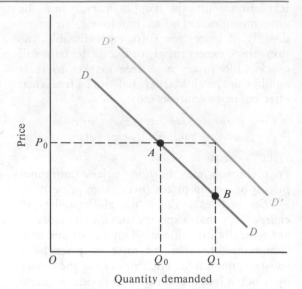

Quantity demanded

The same distinction between movements along a schedule and shifts in the schedule applies on the supply side. Sellers adjust to higher prices by moving along the supply curve. But changes in input prices, technology, or regulation shift the supply curve.

Other things equal, changes in price move us along demand and supply curves. 'Other things equal' is an important reminder that the price of a good is only one determinant of demand and supply. When other determinants change, they lead to shifts in the schedules.

---

as Figure 3-8 illustrates. When the legislation is first introduced, the supply curve SS may be very steep. Existing landlords cannot quickly put their accommodation to other uses. Hence a reduction in rents may scarcely diminish the quantity of rental housing supplied. In the short run the total quantity supplied at the ceiling rent R_1 is only a little less than the free market equilibrium quantity Q_0. As time elapses, however, some landlords will respond to lower rents by converting their property for their own use or for sale to purchasers who wish to own their own home. After some time, the supply curve will become flatter, reaching the position $S'S'$. The rent control R_1 now leads to a large reduction to Q_2 in the quantity of rental accommodation supplied. Shortages increase, and less and less housing is available for the poor who cannot afford to buy their own houses.

Indeed, this problem may be exacerbated by inflation. Rent ceilings are usually fixed in nominal terms – so many pounds per week. If rent ceilings are not raised in line with inflation, real rents fall. This has the same effect as a reduction in nominal rent ceilings when there is no inflation. It is as if rent ceilings had been reduced to R_2 in Figure 3-8. Quantity supplied falls yet further and shortages or excess demand increase still further. Countries such as the UK, which had rent ceilings for many years and failed to raise nominal ceilings in line with inflation, saw the steady erosion of the supply of rental accommodation as private landlords have quit the business.

Price controls need not have these consequences. We could raise ceiling prices in line with inflation to maintain their real value, and devise fair rationing systems to cope with shortages and excess demand. What should be

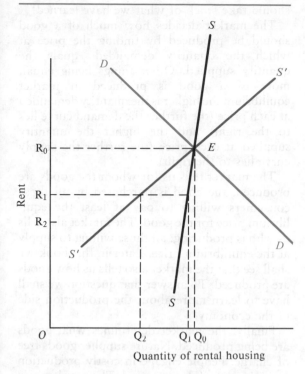

Figure 3-8   THE EFFECT OF A RENT CEILING.
Given the demand curve DD and the supply curve
SS, free market equilibrium occurs at E. If a rent
ceiling at R_1 is introduced, initially the quantity
supplied falls only from Q_0 to Q_1. Over time, quantity
supplied becomes more sensitive to rent and the
supply curve rotates to $S'S'$. Rent control now
induces a much larger decrease in quantity
supplied, which falls to Q_2.

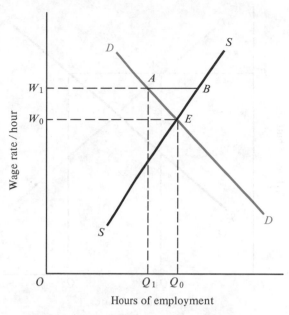

Figure 3-9   THE EFFECT OF A MINIMUM
WAGE.   The demand curve for hours DD and the
supply curve of hours SS imply free market
equilibrium at the point E. A legal minimum wage at
W_1 raises hourly wages for those who remain
employed but reduces the quantity of hours of
employment available from Q_0 to Q_1.

recognized is the severe administrative burden
of operating such a system of controls, both in
deciding when and by how much to change
the nominal ceiling price and in ensuring that
the rationing system works fairly, for it is
clearly open to abuse. Only when it is known
how a particular system will operate in practice
will it be possible to allow society to make a
sensible choice between the equilibrium that a
free market would determine and the allocations
that a controlled market would imply.

Whereas the aim of a ceiling price is to reduce
the price for consumers, the aim of a floor price
is to raise the price for producers or suppliers.
One example of a floor price is a national
minimum wage rate per hour, which raises the
wage rate received by suppliers of labour.
Figure 3-9 shows the demand curve and supply
curve for labour. At higher wage rates, buyers
of labour (firms) demand less labour but

suppliers of labour (households) wish to sell
more labour. The free market equilibrium is at
the point E, where the wage rate is W_0. A
minimum wage below W_0 will be irrelevant
since the free market equilibrium can still be
attained. Suppose, in an effort to help workers,
the government imposes a minimum wage at
W_1. Firms will demand the quantity Q_1 and
there will be excess supply AB. The lucky
workers who manage to sell as much labour as
they wish will be better off than before, but
some workers may be worse off since total
number of hours worked has fallen from Q_0
to Q_1.

Many countries set floor prices for agricultural products. Figure 3-10 shows a floor price
P_1 for butter. In previous examples we have
assumed that the quantity traded would be the
smaller of quantity supplied and quantity
demanded at the controlled price since private
individuals cannot be forced to participate in
a market. There is however another possibility:
the government may intervene not only to set
the control price but also to buy or sell

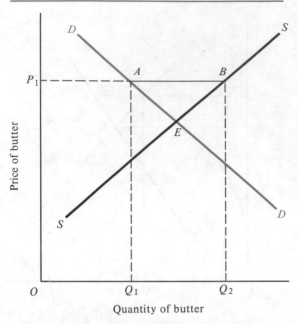

Figure 3-10 A FLOOR PRICE FOR BUTTER.
At the floor price P_1 individuals wish to supply Q_2
units of butter but demand only Q_1 units. In the
absence of government purchases of butter only Q_1
will be traded. By buying up the excess supply AB,
the government can satisfy both suppliers and
consumers at the price P_1.

quantities of the good to supplement private
purchases and sales.

At the floor price P_1 private individuals
demand Q_1 but supply Q_2. In the absence of
government sales or purchases the quantity
traded will be Q_1, the smaller of Q_1 and Q_2.
However, the government may agree to purchase the excess supply AB so that neither
private suppliers nor private demanders need
be frustrated. Because European butter prices
are set above the free market equilibrium price
as part of the Common Agricultural Policy,
European governments have been forced to
purchase massive stocks of butter which would
otherwise have been unsold at the controlled
price. Hence the famous 'butter mountain'.

3-10 What, How, and For Whom

The free market is one way for society to solve
the basic economic questions what, how, and
for whom to produce. In this chapter we have
begun to see how the market allocates scarce
resources among competing uses, and we

should take stock of what we have learned.

The market decides how much of a good
should be produced by finding the price at
which the quantity demanded equals the
quantity supplied. Other things being equal,
more of a good is produced in market
equilibrium the higher is the quantity demanded
at each price (the further the demand curve lies
to the right) and the higher the quantity
supplied at each price (the further the supply
curve lies to the right).

The market tells us for whom the goods are
produced: the good is purchased by all those
consumers willing to pay at least the equilibrium price for the good. The market also tells
us who is producing: all those willing to supply
at the equilibrium price. Later in this book we
shall see that the market also tells us how goods
are produced. To answer that question we shall
have to learn more about the production side
of the economy.

Finally, the market determines what goods
are being produced. Nature supplies goods free
of charge. People engage in costly production
activities only if they are paid. The supply curve
tells us how much has to be paid to bring forth
quantities of supply. Figure 3-11 shows an
example of a good that will not be produced.
The highest price, P_1, that consumers are
prepared to pay is still insufficient to persuade
producers to produce.

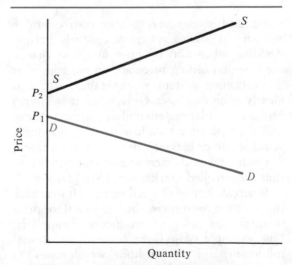

**Figure 3-11 A GOOD THAT WILL NOT BE
PRODUCED.** Even P_1, the highest price consumers
will pay, is lower than P_2, the minimum price
producers require to produce any of this good.

BOX 3-2

ANATOMY OF PRICE AND QUANTITY CHANGES

The accompanying figure shows data for the real price of timber in the UK and for the quantity of timber produced. Economists are frequently confronted with such data and asked to interpret them. How can we tell what was happening in the UK timber market? Was it a shift in demand, in supply, or in both that caused the low real price and low quantity in 1981–82?

The timber market is a free market. It is probably reasonable to suppose that all the observations represent *equilibrium* prices and quantities. Thus each observation can be viewed as the intersection of a demand and a supply curve. Next, we ask what changes in the 'other things equal' determinants of supply and demand may have led to shifts in supply and demand curves and hence to changes in equilibrium price and quantity. Is it possible that all shifts are supply curve shifts? Try drawing a diagram with a given demand curve and a shifting supply curve. The equilibrium points you will trace out all lie on the given demand curve. If only supply shifts we expect a negative relation between price and quantity. We must rule out this explanation since the data shows that low prices tend to be associated with low quantities.

Suppose the supply curve is fixed but the demand curve shifts. The equilibrium points then all lie on the supply curve and exhibit a positive relation between price and quantity. That fits the data much better.

Of course, in practice there will be shifts in both demand and supply curves. The points in the scatter diagram suggest large fluctuations in the demand curve but relatively small shifts in the supply curve. Try drawing this for yourself. Over this period, demand shifts are much more important in the UK timber market than the supply shifts. In 1980 the demand curve shifted to the left, and it did so again in 1981. This led to falls in both equilibrium price and equilibrium quantity in those years. After 1982, the demand curve shifted to the right again.

Having made a diagnosis, we now attempt to gather corroborating evidence. The volume of construction activity is an important determinant of the demand

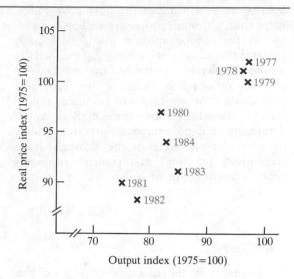

Output index (1975=100)

for timber. An index of UK construction output (1975 = 100) shows that, from an average level of 101.5 for the period 1977–79, construction output fell to 95.9 in 1980 and 84.9 in 1981. This recession in the building industry led to a leftward shift in the demand for timber.

Examining price and quantity data, it is sometimes difficult to disentangle supply shifts and demand shifts. Given only the data from 1977–79, it would have been much harder to be confident that we could interpret the data correctly. Our example really has two lessons. By plotting a scatter diagram it may become evident that the points essentially lie along either a supply curve or a demand curve, suggesting it was the other curve that was shifting. However, we should then bring our economic theory to bear in the search for corroborating evidence. Supply and demand have determinants that differ. Timber supply (the supply curve, *not* the equilibrium quantity supplied) has nothing to do with housing construction, whereas timber demand (the whole demand curve) has nothing to do with forest fires. Because we have an economic theory of what shifts supply or demand curves, we may be able to bring to bear independent evidence (housing starts and forest fires) to interpret the data even where the scatter diagram does not have any obvious pattern at first sight.

We have seen too that society may not like the answers the market provides. Free markets do *not* provide enough food for everyone to go without hunger, or enough medical care to treat all the sick. They provide food and medical care for those willing and *able to pay* the equilibrium price. Society may adopt the normative judgement that the poor should be able to enjoy more food and medical care than the free market provides them with.

Society may also adopt the normative judgement that, although people are willing and able to pay for pornography, it would be socially better if this activity were banned. Few societies allow completely unrestricted free markets for all commodities. It is because society frequently decides that the allocation of resources should not be the allocation a free market would determine that governments intervene widely to alter the market outcome through direct regulation, taxation, and transfer payments such as unemployment benefit.

Summary

1   Demand is the quantity of a good that buyers wish to buy at each price. Other things equal, the lower the price, the higher the quantity demanded. This relation between price and quantity demanded can be graphically depicted as a demand curve. Demand curves slope downwards.

2   Supply is the quantity of a good sellers wish to sell at each price. Other things equal, the higher the price, the higher the quantity. The supply curve shows graphically the relation between price and quantity supplied. Supply curves slope upwards.

3   The market clears, or is in equilibrium, when the price equates the quantity supplied and the quantity demanded. At this point supply and demand curves intersect or cross. At prices below the equilibrium price there is excess demand (shortage), which itself tends to raise the price. At prices above the equilibrium price there is excess supply (surplus), which itself tends to reduce the price. In a free market, deviations from the equilibrium price tend to be self-correcting.

4   Along a given demand curve, the other things assumed equal are the prices of related goods, consumer incomes, and tastes or habits.

5   An increase in the price of a substitute good (or decrease in the price of a complement good) will raise the quantity demanded at each price. An increase in consumer income will increase demand for the good if the good is a normal good but decrease demand for the good if it is an inferior good.

6   Along a given supply curve the other things assumed constant are technology, the price of inputs, and the degree of government regulation. An improvement in technology, or a reduction in input prices, will increase the quantity supplied at each price.

7   Any factor inducing an increase in demand shifts the demand curve to the right, increasing equilibrium price and equilibrium quantity. A decrease in demand (leftward shift of the demand curve) reduces both equilibrium price and equilibrium quantity. Any factor increasing supply shifts the supply curve to the right, increasing equilibrium quantity but reducing equilibrium price. Reductions in supply (leftward shift of the supply curve) reduce equilibrium quantity but increase equilibrium price.

8   To be effective, a price ceiling must be imposed below the free market equilibrium price. It will then reduce the quantity supplied and lead to excess demand unless the government itself provides the extra quantity required. An effective price floor must be imposed above the free market equilibrium price. It will then reduce the quantity demanded unless the government adds its own demand to that of the private sector.

Key Terms

Demand and supply
Quantity demanded and quantity supplied
Movement along the demand curve or supply curve
Shifts in the demand curve or supply curve
Equilibrium price and quantity
Excess demand (shortage) and excess supply (surplus)
Normal and inferior goods
Complements and substitutes
Price ceilings and price floors
Free market

Problems

1   Hypothetical supply and demand data for toasters are shown below. Plot the supply curve and demand curve and find the equilibrium price and quantity.

Supply and demand for toasters

PRICE (£)	QUANTITY DEMANDED (millions)	QUANTITY SUPPLIED (millions)
10	10	3
12	9	4
14	8	5
16	7	6
18	6	7
20	5	8

2 In the sample example, what is the excess supply or demand (*a*) when price is £12? (*b*) when price is £20?

3 Describe the price movements induced by the positions described in parts (*a*) and (*b*) of the previous question. Be as precise as you can.

4 What happens to the demand curve for toasters when the price of bread rises? Show in a supply–demand diagram how the equilibrium price and quantity of toasters change.

5 How is the demand curve for toasters affected by the invention of the toaster oven, which to many people seems like a new and better way of toasting? What effect would this have on the equilibrium quantity of toasters bought and sold, and on the price of toasters? Why?

6 Goods with snob value, such as mink coats and gold cigarette lighters, may be demanded only because they are expensive. Does the demand curve for such goods slope downwards?

7 Returning to the toaster data, suppose that the quantity supplied at each price rises by 1 million. Calculate the new equilibrium price and quantity. Does the equilibrium quantity sold increase by more or less than 1 million, that is by more or less than the increase in the quantity supplied at each price? Why?

8 (*a*) Suppose that cold weather makes it more difficult to catch fish. What happens to the supply curve for fish? What happens to price and quantity? (*b*) Suppose that the cold weather also reduces the demand for fish, because people do not go shopping. Show what happens to the demand curve for fish. (*c*) What happens to the quantity of fish bought and sold when the cold weather sets in? (*d*) Can you say what happens to the price of fish?

9 Show, using demand and supply schedules, how an increase in income would affect the demand curve for a product that is inferior. What happens to price and quantity?

10 (*A much harder question. If you can do this you have really understood this chapter.*) Using the toaster data, suppose a tax of £1 per toaster is now imposed directly on firms supplying toasters. Thus if a seller charges £16, the seller gets £15 and the government £1. What happens to the quantity of toasters sold when the tax is imposed? What happens to the price that consumers pay? (*Hint:* There is now a gap between the price consumers pay and the net price sellers receive. If you measure the price to the consumer on the vertical axis, does either the demand curve or the supply curve shift? If so, by how much?)

11 Common Fallacies (*a*) Manchester United is a more famous football club than Sunderland. United will always have greater success in filling their stadium. (*b*) The European 'butter mountain' illustrates the success of the Common Agricultural Policy. It shows how productivity can be improved when farmers are inspired by the European ideal. (*c*) Holding down rents ensures plenty of cheap housing for the poor.

4

Government in the Mixed Economy

Most resources in Western economies are allocated through markets in which individuals and privately owned firms trade with other individuals or firms. However, governments also play a major role. They set the legal rules; in the marketplace they buy goods and services, from paper clips to aircraft carriers; they produce some services, such as defence; and they make payments such as social security benefits. In financing themselves through taxation and borrowing, governments exert a major influence on prices, interest rates, and production.

Governments in modern industrial economies collect between one-quarter and one-half of GNP in taxes each year and typically spend a little more than they receive in taxes. Because governments play so large a part in economic life, to understand the operation of a modern economy we have to understand not only how markets work but also how government affects the operation of the economy.

This chapter addresses three basic questions about the government's role in economic life. What do governments *actually do*? How can governments *in principle* improve the allocation of resources in the economy? How do governments *decide* what to do? Our aim here is to develop an overview of the role of government as a basis for our continuing discussion of government policy in later chapters.

4-1 What Do Governments Do?

Table 4-2 shows how the scale of government activity has grown steadily over the last century. It now ranges from a third of national income in Japan to two-thirds of national income in Sweden. What do governments actually do?

Create Laws, Rules, and Regulations

Governments determine the legal framework that sets the basic rules for the ownership of property and the operation of markets. If the legal framework outlaws private ownership of businesses, the economy is socialist; if businesses are owned by individuals and operated for private profit, the economy is capitalist.[1] Even in the most capitalist economies, there are limits to the rights of ownership. Not everyone can own a gun, for instance. Nor are people entirely free to use their property as they please; it is usually illegal to build a factory on land in a residential area.

In addition, governments at all levels *regulate* economic behaviour, setting detailed rules for the operation of businesses. Regulations include planning permission (how land can be used and where businesses can locate), health and safety regulations, and attempts to prevent some types of business, such as the sale of heroin. Some regulations apply to all businesses; examples include laws against fraud and laws that prohibit competitors from agreeing to fix prices. Some regulations apply only to certain industries, such as requirements that barbers and doctors have appropriate training.

Buy and Sell Goods and Services

Governments buy and produce many goods and services, such as defence, education, parks, and roads, which they provide to firms and households. Most of these goods, such as defence and education, are provided to users free of direct charge. Some, such as local bus rides and government publications, are paid for directly by the user.

Governments, like private firms, must decide what to buy and what to produce themselves.

---

[1] The extent of private ownership is always a matter of degree, however. Governments own some businesses even in the most capitalist economies; some farms are private in even the most socialist economies.

Table 4-1 Government activity as a percentage of national income in the mid-1980s

	UK	USA	GERMANY	SWEDEN
Goods and services bought	24.1	19.9	21.2	30.4
Debt interest	3.5	2.5	2.2	3.1
Other transfer payments	19.2	14.5	20.6	30.3
Total spending	46.8	36.9	44.0	63.8
Tax revenue	44.1	33.6	42.9	60.0
Deficit	2.7	3.3	1.1	3.8

Source: OECD *National Accounts.*

For instance, governments typically buy computers but write the programs they need to operate them. In order to do this, governments must act as buyers in the markets for the services of computer programmers.

Governments also produce and sell goods. In some countries, the phone company is government-owned; in most countries, the government owns and operates urban transport such as buses and the underground.

Make Transfer Payments

Governments also make transfer payments, such as social security and unemployment benefits, to individuals.

Transfer payments are payments for which no current direct economic service is provided in return.

A fireman's salary is not a transfer payment; a social security cheque is, as are unemployment benefits and interest payments on government borrowing.

Government spending is the sum of government purchases of goods and services and transfer payments. Table 4-1 gives a breakdown of government and welfare activity for several countries. The scale of government activity is much bigger in a country like Sweden than in a country such as the United States.

Impose Taxes

Governments pay for the goods they buy and for the transfer payments they make by levying taxes or by borrowing. Taxes raised at national level, such as income tax or VAT, are usually supplemented by local taxes assessed on property values or household size.

Spending, Taxes, and Deficits Table 4-2 shows that the scale of government activity has risen over a long period. For much of this time, governments have been reluctant to meet this extra cost in full by raising taxes. They have run *budget deficits* financed by borrowing. Budget deficits add to the government's debt. Table 4-3 shows how government debt has changed over the 1980s. Only in the UK has the debt income ratio fallen during the 1980s.

Table 4-2 Government spending as percentage of national income

	1880	1929	1960	1985
Japan	11	19	18	33
USA	8	10	28	37
Germany	10	31	32	47
UK	10	24	32	48
France	15	19	35	52
Sweden	6	8	31	65

Source: World Bank, *World Development Report,* 1988.

Table 4-3 Government debt as a percentage of national income, 1980–89

	1980	1989
USA	37.9	51.2
Japan	52.0	65.1
Germany	32.5	43.8
France	37.3	43.8
Italy	58.5	96.7
UK	54.6	40.1
Sweden	44.8	53.0
Netherlands	45.9	82.5
Ireland	78.0	132.2

Source: OECD, *Economic Outlook, 1989.*

In countries like Italy and Ireland it has now grown to very high levels indeed. In later chapters we shall address several questions. Will government spending continue to increase? Should it? Can government debt be allowed to increase indefinitely?

Try to Stabilize the Economy

Every market economy suffers from business cycles.

> The *business cycle* consists of fluctuations of total production, or GDP, accompanied by fluctuations in the level of unemployment and the rate of inflation.

Governments, through their control of taxes and government spending and through their ability to control the quantity of money in the economy, often attempt to modify fluctuations in the business cycle. The national government may reduce taxes in a recession in the hope that people will increase spending and thus raise the GDP. The central bank (in the UK the Bank of England), which controls the quantity of money, may increase the quantity of money more rapidly in a recession to help bring the economy out of the recession. When inflation is high, the central bank may reduce the rate of money growth with the aim of reducing inflation.

These are macroeconomic policies through which the government attempts to *stabilize* the economy, keeping it as close as possible to full employment with low inflation. We return to this issue when we study macroeconomics in Part 4.

Affect the Allocation of Resources

By spending and taxing, the government of course plays a major part in allocating resources in the economy. In terms of what, how, and for whom, government chooses much of *what* gets produced, from defence expenditures to education to its support for the arts. It affects *how* goods are produced through regulation and through the legal system. It affects *for whom* goods are produced through its taxes and transfers, which take income away from some people and give it to others.

Beyond these direct effects, the government also affects the allocation of resources indirectly through taxes (and subsidies, which are negative taxes) on the price and level of production in individual markets. When government taxes a good, such as cigarettes, it generally reduces the quantity of that good produced; when it subsidizes a good, such as milk, it generally increases the quantity of the good produced.

The power to tax is thus the power to affect the allocation of the economy's resources, or to change what gets produced. By taxing cigarettes, the government can reduce the amount of cigarettes smoked and thereby improve health. By taxing income earned from work, the government affects the amount of time people want to work. Because they affect the allocation of resources indirectly, through their effects on relative prices, as well as directly, taxes loom large in the workings of the market system and have a profound effect on the way society allocates its scarce resources.

4-2 What Should Governments Do?

Why should governments intervene in a market economy? Adam Smith, the father of economics, argued in his 1776 classic, *The Wealth of Nations*, that people pursuing their own interests are led as if by 'an invisible hand' to promote the interests of society. If there is an invisible hand, if markets allocate resources efficiently so that consumers' wants are satisfied at minimum cost, why should governments intervene in the economy at all?

In this section we discuss theoretical justifications for government intervention in a market economy. The general argument for government intervention is *market failure*. Sometimes markets do not allocate resources efficiently, and government intervention may improve economic performance. Economic theory identifies six broad types of market failure, which we describe below.

Very few economists dispute the idea that the government could in theory improve the allocation of resources by correcting market failures, but many dispute the idea that government in fact improves the allocation of resources. Conservative economists, including Nobel Prize winners Milton Friedman of the Hoover Institution and James Buchanan of George Mason University, argue that in practice the government is even more likely to fail

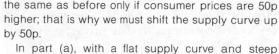

BOX 4-1

WHO REALLY PAYS THE TAX?

Suppose cigarettes cost £1 a packet in the absence of a cigarette tax, and the government imposes a tax of 50p per packet. Do cigarette smokers end up paying the tax, or is it borne by manufacturers of cigarettes? It all depends on how much of the tax cigarette producers can pass on to the consumer. We now show that this depends on the slopes of the supply and demand curve.

In parts (a) and (b) of the figure we plot the (after-tax) price to the consumer on the vertical axis. *DD'* shows the demand curve, which depends on the price to cigarette smokers (consumers). Since the price received by the producer is the consumer price minus the 50p tax per packet, the effect of levying the tax is to *shift* the supply curve from *SS* to *SS'* in both diagrams. Each possible quantity supplied depends on the price received by the producer, which will be

the same as before only if consumer prices are 50p higher; that is why we must shift the supply curve up by 50p.

In part (a), with a flat supply curve and steep demand curve, the tax is borne mainly by cigarette consumers. Point *B* is nearly 50p higher than point *A*. Since demand is inelastic, producers can pass on most of the tax in higher prices. Supply is elastic, so any significant drop in the price received by producers would lead to a large drop in the quantity produced. Consumers pay £1.45 and producers get £0.95 a packet. In part (b), with a flat demand curve and a steep supply curve, most of the tax is borne by cigarette producers. Demand is elastic, so attempts to pass on the tax in higher prices quickly lead to a drop in the quantity of cigarettes sold. Supply is inelastic, and firms produce nearly as many cigarettes even though the price they receive (after tax) has fallen nearly 50p, from point *A* to point *C*. Consumers pay £1.05 and producers get £0.55 a packet.

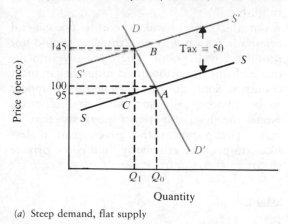

(a) Steep demand, flat supply

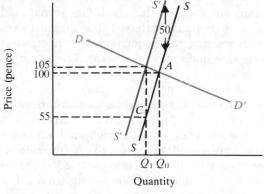

(b) Flat demand, steep supply

to allocate resources efficiently than are markets. We take up their arguments in Part 3, but first we discuss the six reasons why government intervention may, at least in principle, improve the allocation of resources.

The Business Cycle

The business cycle has many external causes, from wars or oil price changes to bursts of new inventions. Government policies also affect the business cycle. Increases in taxes and reductions in government spending generally reduce GNP; increases in the money stock increase GNP and prices. Government policy can make the business cycle worse, lengthening recessions

and creating inflation, or it can reduce economic fluctuations.

There are major controversies in macroeconomics over whether and to what extent the government can stabilize the economy. Obviously, the government cannot control the economy perfectly or we would not have severe recessions and inflation. But since the government does control a large share of total spending and the quantity of money, it must make its decisions with their effect on the business cycle in mind. And it does: taxes may be cut when the economy is in a recession, and the growth rate of money may be reduced when the inflation rate is too high or be increased when the economy is in a recession.

Public Goods

Most of the goods supplied by businesses and demanded by consumers are private goods.

> A *private good* is a good that, if consumed by one person, cannot be consumed by another.

Ice cream is a private good. When you eat your ice cream cone, your friend doesn't get to consume it. Your clothes are also private goods. When you wear them, everyone else is precluded from wearing them at the same time.

But there are goods we can all consume simultaneously, without anyone's consumption reducing anyone else's. These are called public goods.

> A *public good* is a good that, even if it is consumed by one person, is still available for consumption by others.

Clean air is a public good. So is national defence, or public safety. If the armed forces are protecting the country from danger, your being safe in no way prevents anyone else from being safe.

It is no coincidence that most public goods are not provided in private markets. Because of the *free-rider* problem, private markets have trouble ensuring that the right amount of a public good will be produced. A free-rider is someone who gets to consume a good that is costly to produce without paying for it. The free-rider problem applies particularly to public goods because, if anyone were to buy the good, it would then be available for everyone else to consume.

For instance, suppose a market were set up for national defence. Even if each of us felt that we needed defence, we would not have the right incentives to buy our share of defence. Since the amount of national defence I will have is the same as the amount everyone else has, I have a strong incentive to wait for someone else to buy it rather than contribute my fair share. I will have a free ride on everyone else's purchases. But of course, if everyone is waiting for someone else to buy national defence, there will be no defence.

To get around the free-rider problem, the country has to find some way of deciding *together* how much to spend on defence. Governments are set up to make such *collective* decisions. Many of the goods provided by the government are in fact public goods. National defence and police services are certainly public goods. National parks are a mixed case, since the views in the parks are a public good, at least until congestion sets in, but use of the eating facilities is not.

It may seem from this discussion that the government *should* produce public goods and *should not* produce any other goods. Neither conclusion is correct. The government does not have to produce public goods; it only has to specify how much of each should be produced. It may rely on private contractors to do the actual production, as it does, say, with regard to defence equipment. Indeed, it used to be common for countries to have private contractors provide armies on a commercial basis. It is increasingly common for municipalities to hire private contractors to remove the rubbish.

On the other hand, there is no general economic reason why governments should not produce private goods. There are government-owned firms or nationalized industries in most countries. Some government enterprises appear to be commercially successful and efficient. None the less, experience suggests that in many circumstances the government is less likely to produce efficiently than is the private sector.

Externalities

Markets work well when the price of a good equals society's cost of producing that good and when the value of the good to the buyer is equal to the benefit of the good to society. However, the costs and benefits of production are sometimes not fully reflected in market prices.

Consider the problem of pollution. A firm produces chemicals and discharges the waste into a lake. The discharge pollutes the local water supply, kills fish and birds, and creates an offensive smell. These adverse side-effects represent costs to society of producing the chemical, and they should accordingly be reflected in its market price – but they may not. Unless the chemical company is charged for the damages caused by its pollution, the market price of its output will understate the true cost of production to society. In this case there is an externality in the production of the chemical.

An *externality* exists when the production or consumption of a good directly affects businesses or consumers not involved in buying and selling it and when those spillover effects are not fully reflected in market prices.

Externalities are not all negative. The home-owner who repaints her house provides spill-over benefits for the neighbours; they no longer have to look at a peeling or dilapidated house. In all externalities, there exists something that affects firms' costs or consumers' welfare (such as pollution or views of newly painted houses) but is not traded in a market. Economists often speak of externalities as caused by 'missing markets'.

When externalities are present, market prices do not reflect all the social costs and benefits of the production of a good. Government intervention may improve the functioning of the economy, for example by requiring firms to treat their waste products in certain ways before dumping them. Since externalities involve missing markets, they can also be handled in principle by market-type solutions. The government might charge firms (an estimate of) the damages their pollution causes, or might permit a certain amount of total pollution and allow firms to buy and sell rights to pollute.

The presence of externalities can provide the justification for a number of government activities besides pollution control. Examples range from control of broadcasting (inter-ference is an externality) to various restrictions on land use.

Information-related Problems

Unless firms and consumers are well informed, they may take actions that are not in their own interests. Unless decisions are made on the basis of good information, markets will not work well. But in a free market economy, particularly a modern, complex free market economy, firms and consumers are not likely to be well informed about the consequences of all their decisions.

Private markets may not produce the right kinds and amounts of information. Firms have little incentive to study the long-term health hazards to which their workers are exposed,

and if there were no penalties for fraud, producers of unsafe goods would have every incentive to conceal the flaws in their products. Furthermore, modern economies are so complex that few individuals can digest and evaluate all the information necessary to make fully in-formed decisions all the time. It may be efficient to have the government process some complex information on behalf of its citizens.

Governments have long recognized a need to protect poorly informed consumers from actions they would regret. Laws against fraud have been around for centuries. Modern governments generally regulate working conditions, inspect and grade foods, regulate the design and safety of consumer products, and require that certain products (such as foods and dangerous chemi-cals) have informative labels.

Monopoly and Market Power

Competitive markets generally work well, but markets where either buyers or sellers can manipulate prices generally do not. In parti-cular, too little output will be produced and price will be too high in a market where a single sellers controls supply.

A *monopolist* is the single seller of a good or service.

Monopolists can earn high profits by restricting the quantity sold and raising the price. Because they are the only sellers, they have no fear of being undercut by competitors – and consumers end up paying more than they should.

Some monopolies are almost unavoidable. Most public utilities (gas and electricity, for example) are potential monopolies. The govern-ment can regulate such companies by controlling the prices they are allowed to charge, or it may elect to supply the products involved itself. Other monopolies may be artificial, brought about through manipulation by firms. Here governments intervene with competition laws, seeking to make competition more vigorous and to prevent monopolies or other attempts to control supply.

Any buyer or seller who has the ability to affect market price significantly is described as having *market power* or *monopoly power*. Government intervention to limit market power, for instance by preventing firms with market power from charging high prices, can improve the allocation of resources.

Income Redistribution and Merit Goods

The distribution of income that is generated by free markets has no ethical claim to being just or fair. Depending on who starts out with what resources, private markets can produce many different final distributions – different 'for whoms' – of resources and welfare. Private markets may produce a distribution in which the top 1 per cent of income-earners receive 40 per cent of total income in the economy, or they may produce an even distribution of income. Either way, government may want to intervene to affect the distribution of income, by taxing some and giving to others.

In practice, modern governments engage in large-scale redistribution of income. The share of transfers in government spending has increased all over the world in the period since 1960. Government spending on transfer payments, shown in Table 4-1, represents government redistribution of income – towards the elderly (through social security), the unemployed (through unemployment benefits), farmers (through price supports), and other beneficiaries. The rapid growth of transfer spending has been a source of controversy, with critics arguing that many government welfare programmes have harmed the people they were designed to help.

There is a difference between government intervention to affect the distribution of income and intervention to ensure the right level of production of public goods or to make market prices reflect externalities. In the latter cases the government is taking actions that at least in principle can make everyone in society better off. But when the government intervenes to affect the income distribution, it makes some people better off by making others worse off.

Governments are concerned not just with the distribution of income, but also with the consumption of particular goods and services.

> *Merit goods* are goods that society thinks people should consume or receive, no matter what their incomes are.

Merit goods typically include health, education, shelter, and food. Thus we – society – might think that everyone should have adequate housing and take steps to provide it. Is there an economic justification for government intervention in regard to merit goods? In a sense there always is, because the sight of someone who is homeless creates an externality, making everyone else unhappy. By providing housing or shelter for those who would otherwise be on the streets, the government make the rest of us feel better.

Society's concern over merit goods is closely related to its concern over the distribution of income. The difference in the case of merit goods is that society wants to ensure an individual's consumption of *particular* goods rather than goods in general. Some of the goods provided by the government (such as health and education) are merit goods.

With merit goods, as with public goods, government concern with consumption does not justify government production. Economic theory justifies policies that ensure that individuals consume the specified amounts of merit goods. It does *not* say that the government should produce these goods itself, nor does it say exactly how the government should intervene.

One way would simply be to require that the right amounts of the goods be consumed. In the case of education, everyone has to go to school up to a certain age. But nobody has to go to a state school; any accredited school will do. In the case of housing, the government can build low-income houses and rent them at a subsidized rate, provide rent supplements, or simply specify minimum housing standards.

The most difficult question that has to be answered in discussing both merit goods and the distribution of income is how society or the government decides who should get what. Any one person can have a perfectly sensible viewpoint on these issues – for instance, that the more even the distribution of income the better, that the distribution of income we have is best, that people who work harder should be rewarded, that people who need more should get more, or that everyone should have decent housing and no one should starve. Translating these different opinions into a consistent view that is taken by the government and implemented in taxation and transfer policy is the impossible task of politics.

Recap

The discussion in this section provides some theoretical justification for government intervention in a market economy. However, governments do not make their tax and spending decisions on the basis of what economists say their role should be. Only by a huge stretch of the imagination could we say that in fact all government purchases of goods and services are purchases of public goods or merit goods, or that interventions in any particular market are designed only to remove externalities. It would take even more imagination to see government intervention that affects the distribution of income as resulting from a consistent view of the optimal distribution. We now discuss the mechanisms that democratic societies use to make their actual decisions about taxation and government spending.

4-3 How Do Governments Decide?

The motivations economists ascribe to individuals and firms are simple. Firms are in business to make profits for their owners. Individuals are assumed to choose those combinations of goods that make them best off. These simple assumptions permit economists to explain most consumer and business decision-making.

Government decision-making cannot be explained so simply. Voters express their preferences by electing governments whose job is to make the basic decisions on spending and taxing, pass new laws, and establish new regulatory programmes. Thus, by voting, the electorate gets to express its preferences among alternative policy packages, though not on each issue.

The people who run the government – elected officials and civil servants – are not mere ciphers who simply do the bidding of society. They have their own objectives, in some sense trying like everyone else to maximize their own well-being. They may maximize their own well-being by doing what they believe is good for the public, or they may have much narrower goals, such as getting re-elected or advancing up the hierarchy. A well designed system is one in which the people who run the government are led to pursue the interests of society as they pursue their own goals, just as the invisible hand in competitive markets leads individuals pursuing their own interest to pursue society's interests.

Voting

If everyone were identical and of one mind, public decision-making would be easy. The most important problem that society solves through the political process is how to reconcile different views and different interests. In this section we discuss two features of majority voting. The first is the *paradox of voting*, which concerns cases where majority voting will lead to inconsistent decision-making. The second is the *median voter result*, which shows how public choice will tend to avoid extreme outcomes.

The Paradox of Voting   Table 4-4 shows how voters 1, 2, and 3 rank three possible outcomes A, B, and C. For example, voter 1 likes A best, then B, then C. Let the group choose by *majority vote* between outcomes A and B. Voters 1 and 3 prefer A to B so the group will prefer A to B by two votes to one. Similarly, the group will vote two to one for outcome B rather than C. Since A is preferred to B, and B preferred to C, you might expect the group to prefer A to C. But the first and third columns of Table 4-4 imply that the group would choose C rather than A by two votes to one. When individual preferences are as depicted in Table 4-4 majority voting will choose A over B, B over C, and C over A. *Consistent* decision-making will not be possible under majority voting.

This is a serious problem. Society cannot necessarily rely on majority voting to lead to consistent decision-making.[2] It also means that

Table 4-4 The paradox of voting

VOTER	EACH VOTER'S RANKING OF OUTCOMES A, B, AND C		
	A	B	C
1	1	2	3
2	3	1	2
3	2	3	1

[2] Professor Kenneth Arrow of Stanford University won the Nobel Prize in economics in part for his work on this problem. Since each individual acting alone would make consistent choices, Arrow showed that to guarantee consistent decisions in public choice it would be necessary to allow one person alone (a dictator!) to make decisions. The proof is based on the paradox of voting.

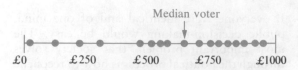

Figure 4-1   THE MEDIAN VOTER.   Each dot represents the preferred expenditure of each of 17 voters. The outcome under majority voting will be the level preferred by the median voter. Everybody to the left will prefer the median voter's position to any higher spending level. Everybody to the right will prefer it to any lower spending level. The median voter's position is the only position that cannot be outvoted against some alternative. Hence it will be chosen.

the decisions taken by society may well depend on the order in which it votes on them.

The Median Voter   Majority voting does not always lead to inconsistent public choice. Figure 4-1 shows for 17 voters how much between £0 and £1000 each would like to spend on the police. Each dot represents an individual voter's preferred amount.

We also assume that each voter will vote for a spending level close to his or her own preferred amount rather than for one that is further away. A voter who wants to spend £250 will prefer £300 to £400 and will prefer £200 to £100. Each person has *single-peaked* preferences, being happier with an outcome the closer it is to the peak or preferred level as judged by that individual.

Now suppose there is a vote on how much to spend on the police. A proposal to spend £0 would be defeated by 16 votes to 1. Only the voter represented by the left-hand dot in Figure 4-1 would vote for £0 rather than £100. As we move to the right we get more people voting for any particular proposal. Figure 4-1 emphasizes the special position of the median voter. With 17 voters, the median voter is the person who wants to spend the ninth-highest amount on the police. There are 8 voters wanting to spend more and 8 wanting to spend less. The median voter is the person in the middle on this particular issue.

What is special about the median voter? Suppose the vote is between the amount the median voter wants to spend and some higher amount. The 8 people wanting less than either will vote for the median voter's proposal, and

so will the median voter. There will be a majority against higher expenditure. By an identical argument there will be a 9–8 majority against lower expenditure when the alternative is the amount wanted by the median voter. Hence the median voter's preferred outcome will be the one that is chosen by majority voting.

Thus, majority voting works when each individual has single-peaked preferences. The paradox of voting arises in Table 4-4 precisely because preferences are not single-peaked. Suppose outcome A is low expenditure, B is moderate expenditure, and C is high expenditure on the police. Voter 1 prefers low to moderate and moderate to high. Voter 1 has single-peaked preferences. So does voter 2, whose peak is at moderate expenditure. But voter 3 prefers high to low and low to moderate expenditure, even though moderate expenditure is closer than low expenditure to the best outcome of high expenditure. Voter 3 does not have single-peaked preferences.

This is why majority voting is likely to get into trouble when individual preferences are not single-peaked. In contrast, with single-peaked preferences the outcome is likely to be that most preferred by the median voter. Consistent public choice under majority voting on particular issues is more likely the more each voter feels that the next best thing is an outcome close to that voter's preferred outcome. On issues where voters feel they must make an all-or-nothing choice between very different alternatives, intermediate positions are a complete waste of time. The failure of preferences to be single-peaked may result in inconsistent public choices.

Legislators

When preferences are single-peaked the median voter models helps us to understand how society makes decisions on particular issues, especially if there is a referendum on the issue. But the process of making decisions through legislative compromises is much more complicated. Decisions are not made issue by issue. There may be a trading of votes between different issues so that an individual gets a package that is preferred. *Logrolling* is one example.

Table 4-5 shows two issues, A and B, and

Table 4-5 Logrolling

PERSON	A	B
1	−4	−1
2	−3	4
3	6	−1

three legislators, 1, 2, and 3. The value in pounds of each outcome to each individual is shown. These values are merely illustrative measures of how much each individual stands to gain or lose under each outcome. Suppose each person votes for a proposal only if the outcome is positive. Person 1 votes against A and B, person 2 against A but for B, and person 3 for A but against B. Both issues would be defeated on a majority vote.

Now suppose persons 2 and 3 do a deal and vote together. Suppose they decide to vote for A, which person 3 wants, and for B, which person 2 wants. Person 2 will make a net gain of +£1, gaining £4 since B passes, and losing only £3 when A passes. Person 3 gains a total of £5, gaining £6 since A passes and only losing £1 when B passes. By forming a coalition they do better than they would have done under independent majority voting, when neither A nor B would have passed.

This kind of model helps us understand some behaviour by politicians, but they are subject to many other forces. They want to do good, to be powerful, to be popular, and above all to be re-relected. Even if society as a whole has consistent goals, it does not follow that politicians will act so as to reflect those goals as faithfully as possible.

Civil Servants

Civil servants influence public decision-making and its execution in two ways. They offer advice and expertise, which influence the government in deciding how laws and policies should be framed. They are also responsible for carrying out the enacted laws and stated policies and may have some discretion in how far and how fast to put into practice the directives with which they have been issued.

Civil servants also have vested interests. Those at the defence ministry are likely to try to persuade the government to expand defence

activities. Those in education will press for higher spending on education. Although the final responsibility must be taken by elected politicians, governments sometimes argue that civil servants are quite skilled in obstructing policies that the civil servants do not like.

The main point of this section is that the process through which governments make spending and taxing decisions does not magically and automatically translate society's wishes into the appropriate action. Indeed, as the paradox of voting shows, it may be impossible for society always to express consistent aims. The simple view that the government acts to maximize the public good is a convenient one on which we frequently fall back. But a complete understanding of how public choices are made, and could possibly be made, requires an extension of the ideas we have briefly examined in this section.

Summary

1   Governments play a major role in modern mixed economies. The scale of their activities is between a third and two-thirds of national income.

2   The role of government extends beyond purchasing goods and services, raising taxes, and making transfer payments. Governments also set the legal framework, regulate economic activity, and attempt to stabilize the business cycle.

3   Taxes affect the allocation of resources. Taxing a good raises the price to the buyers and lowers the price to the seller, thereby reducing the output of the good.

4   Government intervention in the economy can be justified on economic grounds by market failure. Stabilizing the business cycle, deciding on the amount of public goods, responding to externalities, correcting informational problems, preventing the exercise of market power, and creating a socially desirable distribution of income and merit goods are all economic grounds for a government role in the economy.

5   Government decisions should represent the interests of society, but society's true preferences may be hard to ascertain. A democratic society votes for legislators who make decisions

that are carried out by civil servants under the supervision of the government.

6 Unless individual preferences are single-peaked, majority voting can lead to inconsistent public choices. With single-peaked preferences, majority voting will lead to consistent results. Society will tend to choose according to the median voter on any issue. Legislative decisions may reflect complex deals and vote-trading on different issues. There is no simple relation between the final choices of public servants and the underlying preferences of the voters who make up society.

Key Terms

Transfer payment
Business cycle
Market failure
Public and private goods
Free riders
Externalities
Monopoly
Merit goods
Public choice
Paradox of voting
Single-peaked preferences
Median voter
Logrolling

Problems

1 Which of the following items of government spending reflect (a) provision of public goods, (b) concern with merit goods, (c) concern with income distribution: (i) police patrols, (ii) old age pensions, (iii) unemployment benefit, (iv) free state primary schools?

2 Which of the following are public goods: (a) clean streets, (b) ambulance services, (c) the postal service? Discuss alternative ways of providing these services.

3 Give an example of a good where the tax is mainly passed on to the consumer, and a good where it is largely borne by the producer. Why is this?

4 Name the two goods or services you buy from a monopolist. Should the government regulate the price? Does it?

5 Why should the European Commission seek to enforce tough standards reducing pollution of rivers by nitrates used as fertilizers in farming?

6 An individual usually manages to make consistent choices. Why is it harder for governments?

7 Common Fallacies Show why the following statements are incorrect: (a) My tax bill is £100; that is how much worse off the tax has made me. (b) Public goods are whatever the public sector provides. (c) Free markets always allocate resources efficiently. (d) Majority voting makes public decisions reflect society's wishes.

2

Positive Microeconomics

5

The Effect of Price and Income on Demand Quantities

In Chapter 3 we learned to use demand curves to show the effect of the price of a good on the quantity demanded. We saw also that changes in income, or in the price of related goods, would shift demand curves, altering the quantity demanded at each price. In this chapter we examine these effects in more detail. Then, to get behind these demand relations, in the next chapter we build a model of the decision problem facing consumers who must choose how to spend their income on different goods.

In Chapter 2 we discussed the effect of tube fares on tube revenue. Other things equal, higher tube fares reduce the quantity of tube journeys demanded. If the quantity demanded is very sensitive to the price, higher fares discourage so many passengers that total revenue from tickets falls. However, if the quantity demanded is relatively insensitive to the price, higher fares more than compensate for reduced volume, and the total revenue increases.

In this chapter we introduced the concept of the *price elasticity of demand*, a measure of the sensitivity of the quantity demanded to the price. The price elasticity of demand is a key piece of information in many economic problems such as the pricing decision about tube fares that we studied in Chapter 2.

We now adopt a different example to develop the theory of demand. Suppose you are the owner of a football club. Before the season begins you have to set the price of football tickets for the season. Your sole aim is to maximize your revenue from ticket sales so you can afford to buy some better plays next season. Should you set a ticket price that will ensure that the ground is full? It all depends on the sensitivity of ticket sales to ticket prices. If the quantity demanded is insensitive to the price,

it will require a very low price to fill the ground and total revenue will collapse. If, however, small reductions in ticket prices lead to large increases in the quantity of tickets demanded, it makes much more sense to charge a price that will fill the ground. Higher sales volume will more than compensate for the lower ticket price. Without undertaking some empirical research to find out the price elasticity of demand for football tickets, you cannot make a sensible pricing decision.

The demand for football tickets depends also on the price of related goods. Lower admission prices for race courses, cinemas, and other ways of spending Saturday afternoon will reduce the demand for football tickets. The *cross price elasticity of demand* measures the sensitivity of the quantity demanded of one good to changes in the price of a related good. We illustrate the use of this concept later in the chapter.

The demand curve for football tickets will also be shifted by changes in consumer incomes. If people become richer they can afford more football tickets whatever the price. The *income elasticity of demand* measures the sensitivity of the quantity demanded to changes in consumer incomes. Goods for which demand grows quickly as incomes rise will have better growth prospects in an expanding economy than goods for which demand increases more slowly with income. Investors and businesses will be interested in differences in the income elasticity of demand for different goods.

5-1 The Price Responsiveness of Demand

The downward slope of the demand curve shows that quantity demanded increases as the price of a good falls. Frequently we need to know by how much the quantity demanded will increase. Table 5-1 presents some hypothetical numbers for the relation between ticket price and quantity demanded, other things equal. Figure 5-1 plots the demand curve, which happens to be a straight line in this example.

How should we measure the responsiveness of the quantity of tickets demanded to the price of tickets? One obvious measure is the *slope* of the demand curve. Each price cut of £1 leads to 8000 extra ticket sales per game. Suppose, however, that we wish to compare the price responsiveness of football ticket sales with the price responsiveness of the quantity of cars demanded: clearly, £1 is a trivial cut in the price of a car and will have a negligible effect on the quantity of cars demanded.

In Chapter 2 we argued that when commodities are measured in different units it is often best to examine the percentage change, which is unit-free. This suggests that we think about the effect of a 1 per cent price cut on the quantity of cars and football tickets demanded. Similarly, it is not the absolute number of cars or tickets we should examine but the percentage change in quantity demanded.

> The *price elasticity of demand* is the percentage change in the quantity of a good demanded divided by the corresponding percentage change in its price.

Although we shall shortly introduce other demand elasticities – the cross price elasticity and the income elasticity – the (own) price elasticity is perhaps the most frequently used of the three. Whenever economists speak of *the* demand elasticity they mean the price elasticity of demand as we have defined it above.

If a 1 per cent increase reduces the quantity demanded by 2 per cent, the demand elasticity is

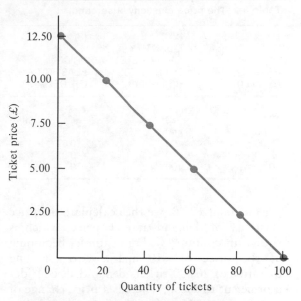

Figure 5-1 THE DEMAND FOR FOOTBALL TICKETS. For given prices of related goods and consumer incomes, higher ticket prices reduce the quantity of tickets demanded.

−2. Because the quantity *falls* 2 per cent, we express this as a change of −2 per cent, then divide by the price change of 1 per cent (a price rise) to obtain −2. If a price fall of 4 per cent increases the quantity demanded by 2 per cent, the demand elasticity is $-\frac{1}{2}$, since the quantity change of 2 per cent is divided by the price change of −4 per cent. Since demand curves slope down, we are either dividing a positive percentage change in quantity (a quantity rise) by a negative percentage change in price (a price fall), or dividing a negative percentage change in quantity (a quantity fall) by a positive percentage change in price (a price rise). The price elasticity of demand tells us about movements along a demand curve and the demand elasticity must be a negative number.[1]

We now investigate the price elasticity of demand for football tickets. Table 5-2 reproduces in columns (1) and (2) the demand data from Table 5-1. By considering the effect of

Table 5-1 The demand for football tickets

PRICE (£/ticket)	QUANTITY OF TICKETS DEMANDED (thousands)
12.50	0
10.00	20
7.50	40
5.00	60
2.50	80
0	100

[1] For further brevity, economists sometimes omit the minus sign. It is easier to say the demand elasticity is 2 than to say it is −2. Whenever the price elasticity of demand is expressed as a positive number, it should be understood (unless there is an explicit warning to the contrary) that a minus sign should be added. Otherwise, we should be implying that demand curves slope upwards, a rare but not unknown phenomenon.

Table 5-2 The price elasticity of demand

(1) PRICE (£/ticket)	(2) QUANTITY OF TICKETS DEMANDED (thousands)	(3) PRICE ELASTICITY OF DEMAND
12.50	0	$-\infty$
10.00	20	-4
7.50	40	-1.5
5.00	60	-0.67
2.50	80	-0.25
0	100	0

price cuts of £2.50, we then calculate the price elasticity of demand at each price, which is shown in column (3). For example, beginning at the price of £10 and a corresponding quantity of 20 000 tickets demanded, consider a price cut to £7.50. There is a price change of -25%, from £10 to £7.50, and a corresponding change in quantity demanded of 100%, from 20 000 to 40 000 tickets. The demand elasticity at £10 is thus $(100/-25) = -4$. Other elasticities are calculated in the same way, dividing the percentage change in quantity by the corresponding percentage change in price. Notice that when we begin from the price of £12.50 the demand elasticity is minus infinity. This is because the percentage change in quantity demanded is $(20 - 0)/0$. Any positive number divided by zero yields plus infinity. When we then divide by the -20 per cent change in price, from £12.50 to £10.00, we obtain minus infinity as the demand elasticity at this price.

We say that the demand elasticity is *high* when it is a large negative number. The quantity demanded is then very sensitive to the price. We say the demand elasticity is *low* when it is a small negative number and the quantity demanded is relatively insensitive to the price. 'High' or 'low' thus refer to the magnitude of the elasticity ignoring the minus sign. The demand elasticity falls when it becomes a smaller negative number and quantity demanded becomes less sensitive to the price.

Although the demand curve for football tickets is a straight line with constant slope – along its entire length a £1 cut in price always leads to 8000 extra ticket sales – Table 5-2 shows that the demand elasticity falls as we move down the demand curve from higher

prices to lower prices. At high prices, £1 is a small percentage change in the price but 8000 tickets is a large percentage change in the quantity demanded. Conversely, at low prices £1 is a large percentage change in the price but 8000 is a small percentage change in the quantity. When the demand curve is a straight line, the price elasticity falls steadily as we move down the demand curve.[2]

It is possible to construct curved demand schedules (still of course sloping downwards all the time) along which the price elasticity of demand remains constant. Generally, however, the price elasticity changes as we move along demand curves, and we expect the elasticity to be high at high prices and low at low prices.[3]

Because the demand curve is a straight line in this example, we get the same size of quantity response (20 000 tickets) whether we raise or lower the price by £2.50. That is why it does not matter whether we use price rises or price cuts to calculate the demand elasticity. When, as in Figure 5-2, the demand curve is not a straight line we encounter a minor difficulty. Beginning at point A where the price is P_0, moves to points B and C represent percentage price changes of equal magnitude but opposite sign. Figure 5-2 makes clear that the size of quantity response (from Q_0 to either Q_1 or Q_2) differs for price rises and price falls when the demand curve is not a straight line.

When dealing with nonlinear demand curves, economists resolve this ambiguity about the definition of price elasticity of demand by defining it with respect to *very small* changes in price. If we move only a short distance to either side of the point A, the demand curve hardly has time to bend round. Over the very short distance corresponding to a small percentage price rise or fall, the demand curve is as near a straight line as makes no difference.

---

[2] This conclusion stems from the fact that both price and quantity change as we move down a demand curve. There are two special cases of linear demand curves where this is not true. A horizontal or infinitely elastic demand curve has an elasticity of $-\infty$ at all points since the *price* never changes. A vertical or completely inelastic demand curve has an elasticity of zero at all points since the *quantity* never changes.

[3] You may be puzzled about the elasticity at a zero price. Raising the price to £2.50 induces a change in quantity of -20 per cent. The change in price is $(2.50 - 0)/0$ per cent, which is ∞ per cent. However, any number divided by infinity yields zero. Hence the demand elasticity is $(-20/\infty) = 0$ at this price.

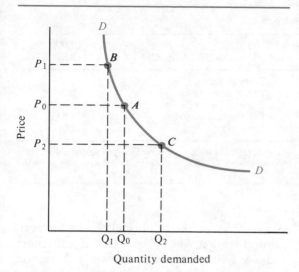

Figure 5-2 A NONLINEAR DEMAND CURVE
DD. When the demand curve *DD* is nonlinear, price rises and price cuts of equal size lead to quantity changes that differ in size. Beginning from the point *A*, a price rise leads to a smaller reduction in quantity than the quantity increase induced by an equivalent price cut.

With this amendment we can continue to use the old definition.

Elastic and Inelastic Demand

Although elasticity typically falls as we move down the demand curve, an important dividing line occurs at the demand elasticity of -1.

> Demand is *elastic* if the price elasticity is more negative than -1. Demand is *inelastic* if the price elasticity lies between -1 and 0.

In Table 5-2 demand is elastic at all prices of £7.50 and above and inelastic at all prices of £5.00 and below. If the demand elasticity is exactly -1, we say that demand is *unit-elastic*.

Later in this section we show that a cut in prices raises revenue from football ticket sales if demand for football tickets is elastic but lowers revenue if demand is inelastic. Whether or not demand is elastic is the key piece of information required in setting tube fares in the example of Chapter 2 and in setting the price of football tickets in the example we are currently studying.

Although the price elasticity of demand typically changes as we move along demand curves, economists frequently talk of goods with high or low demand elasticities. For example, they will say that the demand for oil is price-inelastic (price changes have only a small effect on quantity demanded) but the demand for foreign holidays is price-elastic (price changes have a large effect on quantity demanded). Such statements implicitly refer to parts of the demand curve corresponding to prices that are typically charged for these goods or services.

The Determinants of Price Elasticity

What determines whether the price elasticity of demand for a good is high (say, -5) or low (say, -0.5)? Ultimately the answer must be sought in consumer tastes. If it is considered socially essential to own a television, higher television prices may have little effect on quantity demanded. If televisions are considered a frivolous luxury, the demand elasticity will be much higher. Psychologists and sociologists may be able to explain more fully than economists why tastes are as they are. Nevertheless, as economists, we can identify some considerations likely to affect consumer responses to changes in the price of a good. *The most important consideration is the ease with which consumers can substitute another good that fulfils approximately the same function.*

Consider two extreme cases. Suppose first that the price of all cigarettes is raised 1 per cent. Do you expect the quantity of cigarettes demanded to fall by 5 per cent or by 0.5 per cent? Probably the latter. People who can easily quit smoking have already done so. In contrast, suppose the price of one particular brand of cigarettes is increased by 1 per cent, all other brand prices remaining unchanged. We should now expect a much larger quantity response from buyers. Consumers will switch away from the more expensive brand to other brands that basically fulfil the same function of nicotine provision. For a particular cigarette brand the demand elasticity could be quite high.

Ease of substitution implies a high demand elasticity for a particular good. In fact, our example suggests a general rule. The more narrowly we define a commodity (a particular brand of cigarette rather than cigarettes in general, or oil rather than energy as a whole), the larger will be the price elasticity of demand.

Table 5-3 Estimates of price elasticities of demand in the UK

GOOD (GENERAL CATEGORY)	DEMAND ELASTICITY	GOOD (NARROWER CATEGORY)	DEMAND ELASTICITY
Fuel and light	−0.47	Dairy produce	−0.05
Food	−0.52	Bread and cereals	−0.22
Alcohol	−0.83	Entertainment	−1.40
Durables	−0.89	Expenditure abroad	−1.63
Services	−1.02	Catering	−2.61

Source: The left-hand column is taken from John Muellbauer, 'Testing the Barten Model of Household Composition Effects and the Cost of Children', *Economic Journal*, September, 1977, Table 7. The right-hand column is taken from Angus Deaton, 'The Measurement of Income and Price Elasticities', *European Economic Review*, Volume 6, 1975.

Measuring Price Elasticities

To illustrate these general principles we report estimates of price elasticities of demand in Table 5-3. The table confirms that the demand for general categories of basic commodities, such as fuel, food, or even household durable goods, is inelastic. As a category, only services such as haircuts, the theatre, and sauna baths, have an elastic demand. Households simply do not have much scope to alter the broad pattern of their purchases.

In contrast, there is a much wider variation in the demand elasticities for narrower definitions of commodities. Even then, the demand for some commodities, such as dairy produce, is very inelastic. However, particular kinds of services such as entertainment and catering have a much more elastic demand.

Using Price Elasticities

Price elasticities of demand are useful in calculating the price rise required to eliminate a shortage (excess demand) or the price fall required to eliminate a surplus (excess supply). One important source of surpluses and shortages is shifts in the supply curve. Harvest failures (and bumper crops) are a central feature of many agricultural markets. Because the demand elasticity for many agricultural products is very low, harvest failures produce very large increases in the price of food. Conversely, bumper crops induce very large falls in food prices. When demand is very inelastic, shifts in the supply curve lead to large fluctuations in price but have little effect on equilibrium quantities.

Figure 5-3(a) illustrates this point. We can interpret SS as the supply curve in an agricultural market when there is a harvest failure and $S'S'$ as the supply curve when there is a bumper crop. These extremes lead the equilibrium price to fluctuate between P_1 (harvest failure) and P_2 (bumper crop) but induce little fluctuation in the corresponding equilibrium quantities. Contrast this with Figure 5-3(b), which shows the effect of similar supply shifts in a market with very elastic demand. Price fluctuations are much smaller but quantity fluctuations are now much larger. Knowing the demand elasticity of a good helps us understand why some markets exhibit volatile quantities but stable prices, while other markets exhibit volatile prices but stable quantities.

5-2 Price, Quantity Demanded, and Total Expenditure

Other things equal, the demand curve shows how much consumers of a good wish to purchase at each price. At each price, total spending by consumers will be the price multiplied by the quantity demanded. We now discuss the relation between total spending and price and show the relevance of the price elasticity of demand.

In Figure 5-4 we show how total spending changes as price changes. We consider three cases. In case A, we begin at the point A with price P_A and quantity demanded Q_A. Total spending is given by $P_A \times Q_A$ or the area of the rectangle $OP_A A Q_A$. We then examine a price cut to P_B at which consumers demand Q_B. Total spending is now $P_B \times Q_B$ or the area of the rectangle $OP_B B Q_B$. What is the change in total

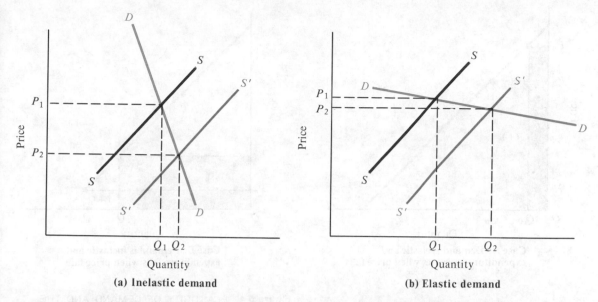

Figure 5-3   THE EFFECT OF DEMAND ELASTICITY ON EQUILIBRIUM PRICE AND QUANTITY FLUCTUATIONS.   In each case, the supply curve fluctuates between *SS* and *S'S'*. In case (a) demand is inelastic, and supply shifts lead to large changes in equilibrium price but little change in equilibrium quantity. In case (b) demand is elastic, and the same supply shift now leads to large changes in equilibrium quantity but little change in equilibrium price.

spending when prices are reduced from P_A to P_B? Spending falls by the grey shaded area marked $(-)$ but rises by the green shaded area marked $(+)$. In case A the $(+)$ area exceeds the $(-)$ area and total spending increases. In the elastic range of the demand curve (towards the upper end) a cut in price raises the quantity demanded by more than sufficient to offset the lower price. Total spending increases.

Case B examines the lower end of the demand curve where demand is inelastic. Although the price cut raises the quantity demanded, the increase in quantity is insufficient to compensate for the lower price. The $(+)$ area is smaller than the $(-)$ area. Total spending falls. If price cuts increase total spend at high prices where the demand elasticity is high and reduce total spending at low prices where the demand elasticity is low, you might guess that at some intermediate price a price cut will leave total spending unaltered. Case C shows this possibility. The higher quantity demanded exactly compensates for the lower price.

Let us return to our definition of total spending, which we write formally as

Total spending = price × quantity demanded

If quantity demanded rises 1 per cent when the price falls 1 per cent, total spending will remain unaltered. In fact, case C depicts the point on the demand curve at which the price elasticity of demand is -1 (a 1 per cent change in quantity divided by a -1 per cent change in price). If demand is elastic, a demand elasticity that is more negative than -1, as in case A, a 1 per cent price cut leads to an increase in quantity by *more* than 1 per cent. Hence total spending rises. Conversely, when demand is inelastic, a demand elasticity lying between 0 and -1, as in case B, a 1 per cent price cut leads to an increase in quantity by *less* than 1 per cent. Hence total spending falls. These results are summarized in Table 5-4.

The Price of Football Tickets

We are now required to advise the owner of the football club on the ticket price that will maximize spending on football tickets and thus the owner's revenue. Table 5-5 shows again the demand data of Tables 5-1 and 5-2. For reasons that will shortly become apparent, we also show the quantity of tickets demanded at a

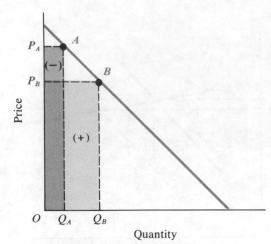

Case A: Demand is elastic and expenditure increases when price falls

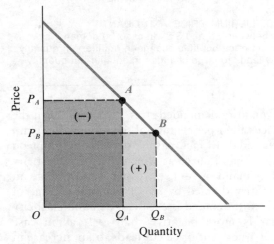

Case C: Demand is unit-elastic and expenditure is constant

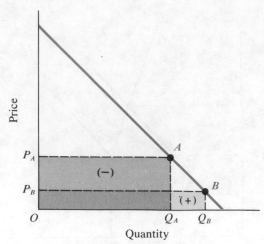

Case B: Demand is inelastic and expenditure falls when price falls

Figure 5-4 ELASTICITY OF DEMAND AND THE EFFECT OF PRICE CHANGES ON EXPENDITURE. When the price is reduced from P_A to P_B, expenditure changes from OP_AAQ_A to OP_BBQ_B. Thus expenditure rises when demand is elastic (case A), falls when demand is inelastic (case B), and remains unchanged when demand is unit-elastic (case C).

price of £6.25 per ticket. At this price the demand elasticity is -1. A 20 per cent price change (of £1.25) induces a 20 per cent change in the quantity demanded (of $-10\,000$ tickets per game). Column (4) shows total spending on football tickets at each price.

Beginning from the highest price of £12.50, which completely deters football supporters, the table shows that successive price cuts first increase total spending on tickets then reduce total spending. Table 5-4 explains why. When the price is high, demand is elastic: price reductions increase total spending. When demand is unit-elastic, at the price of £6.25, we reach a turning point. Above this price, price cuts have steadily increased total spending. Once we get below this price, further price cuts reduce total spending. We can thus draw two conclusions. First, as we imagine moving down the demand curve, total spending is instantaneously unchanging as we move through the price £6.25 at which demand is unit-elastic. Second, and of more importance, *spending and revenue reach a maximum at the point of unit-elastic demand*. This theoretical idea, and the empirical knowledge that this occurs at the price of £6.25 per ticket, are the pieces of information the football club owners needs to know.

Table 5-4 Demand elasticities and changes in spending

CHANGES IN TOTAL SPENDING INDUCED BY	PRICE ELASTICITY OF DEMAND		
	ELASTIC (e.g. -3)	UNIT-ELASTIC (-1)	INELASTIC (e.g. -0.3)
Price increase	Fall	Unchanged	Rise
Price reduction	Rise	Unchanged	Fall

Table 5-5 The price elasticity of demand and total spending on football tickets

(1) PRICE (£/ticket)	(2) QUANTITY DEMANDED (thousands/game)	(3) PRICE ELASTICITY OF DEMAND	(4) TOTAL SPENDING (£ thousand)
12.50	0	$-\infty$	0
10.00	20	-4	200
7.50	40	-1.5	300
6.25	50	-1	312.5
5.00	60	-0.67	300
2.50	80	-0.25	200
0	100	0	0

5-3 Further Applications of the Price Elasticity of Demand

Tube Fares

The relation between demand elasticities and total spending summarized in Table 5-4 can equally be applied to the problem of setting tube fares discussed in Chapter 2. If we know the demand elasticity, then we know in which direction to change fares in order to increase spending on tube tickets.

Suppose the underground is running at a deficit. After some empirical research it is concluded that the price elasticity of demand for tube journeys is -1.4. Demand is elastic. After all, potential tube users have many substitution possibilities. A rise in tube fares will reduce the quantity of journeys demanded but will also reduce total spending on tube fares. In this example it would be quite misguided to raise fares in an effort to increase tube revenues. A policy of cutting tube fares is needed. Conversely, if the demand elasticity is -0.7, raising tube fares will improve revenue.

The First Oil Price Shock

Perhaps the most dramatic illustration of the relation between demand elasticity and total spending is the oil price shock of 1973–74 discussed in Chapter 1. By collectively restricting oil supplies, OPEC induced a quadrupling of the equilibrium price of oil in 1973–74.

We now know that increases in price raise consumer spending and hence seller revenues when demand is inelastic. And demand for oil was *very* inelastic. Estimates of the demand elasticity for oil in the mid-1970s were around -0.1. Oil users had little immediate prospects

of substituting other commodities for oil in its many uses: fuel for cars and aeroplanes, fuel for heating and for oil-fired power stations generating electricity, inputs for petrochemical processes. A small restriction in total supply produced a large rise in the equilibrium price and vast revenue gains for OPEC members.

The Coffee Frost

In 1977 a frost in Brazil, the world's largest supplier of coffee, led to a sharp reduction in the supply of coffee. Coffee prices rose significantly. The implication for total spending on coffee and the revenues of coffee producers depends on the elasticity of demand for coffee. If demand is inelastic, spending and revenue will increase when prices rise. Table 5-6 gives data for 1976–78 for the United States, the world's most important consumer of coffee. Even adjusting for general inflation, the US price of coffee rose from $2.01 per pound in 1976 to $3.20 per pound in 1977, falling back to $2.40 per pound in 1978. Although the quantity demanded fell in 1977, the table shows that total spending on coffee *rose* in that year. Far from hurting coffee producers, the frost actually made them better off.

Table 5-6 The market for coffee in the United States

	1976	1977	1978
Price ($/lb)*	2.01	3.20	2.40
Quantity (lbs)*	12.8	9.4	10.9
Total spending (price × quantity)	25.7	30.0	26.2

* Prices are in 1976 US dollars. Quantities are in pounds of coffee per head per year consumed in the United States.
Source: Statistical Abstract of the United States, 1980.

The demand for coffee turns out to be inelastic, although armchair reasoning might suggest an abundance of substitutes – tea, soft drinks, and beer. This example emphasizes the importance of consumer tastes. If buyers refuse to abandon coffee drinking it is useless to point out that a blend of tea and Coca-Cola contains as much caffeine as the average cup of coffee.

Farmers and Bad Harvests

The example of coffee illustrates a general result. When demand is inelastic farmers may earn more revenue from a bad harvest than from a good one. As we pointed out earlier in Figure 5-3(a), when the supply curve shifts to the left it requires a large increase in price to eliminate excess demand if demand is inelastic. And price increases *raise* consumer spending and producer revenues when demand is inelastic. Nor is it surprising that the demand elasticity is low for many agricultural commodities such as coffee, milk, and wheat. These commodities are part of the staple diet of most households and eating habits are slow to change, even when prices of these commodities change.

If bad harvests raise farmers' revenues and good harvests lead to a collapse in agricultural prices and hence farmers' revenue, you may now be wondering why farmers do not get together like OPEC to restrict their supply in order to increase revenues in the face of inelastic demand. If so, you are beginning to think like an economist. If it were very easy to organize such collusion between farmers we would expect to see this done more often. Later in this book we discuss the difficulties that arise in trying to maintain a co-operative policy to restrict supply.

When demand is inelastic, suppliers *taken together* will be better off if supply can be reduced. However, if one farmer has a fire that destroys part of the crop but all other farmers' crops are unaffected, the unlucky farmer will definitely be worse off (unless fully insured). The reduction in a single farmer's output, unlike the reduction of all farmer's outputs simultaneously, will have only a negligible effect on supply. Market price will be unaffected and the unlucky farmer will simply be selling less output at the price that would have prevailed in any case. This illustrates a very important lesson in economics.

What is true for the individual is not necessarily true for everyone together, and what is true for everyone together does not necessarily hold for the individual.

As in our example about cigarettes earlier in the chapter, the individual producer faces a demand that is very elastic – consumers can easily switch to the output of similar farmers – even though the demand for the crop as a whole is very inelastic.

5-4 The Long Run and the Short Run

The price elasticity of demand for a good is not independent of the length of time that consumers have to adjust their spending patterns when prices change. The dramatic oil price rise of 1973–74 caught many households owning a new but fuel-inefficient car. The households' immediate response to higher oil prices may have been to *plan* to buy a smaller car with greater fuel economy, but some households were unable to buy smaller cars immediately. In the *short-run*, they were stuck with their large-fuel-consumption cars. Unless they could rearrange their life-styles to make less use of a car, these households simply had to pay the higher petrol prices. That is precisely why the demand for petrol was so inelastic.

Over a longer period, however, consumers had time to sell their cars and buy cars with better fuel economy, or to move from the distant suburbs closer to their place of work in the city centre. Over this longer period, they were able to reduce the quantity of petrol demanded much more than they could initially.

The price elasticity of demand is lower in the short run than in the long run when there is more scope for substitution of other goods. This result is very general. For example, even if addicted smokers cannot reduce their consumption of cigarettes in response to a rise in the price of cigarettes, fewer young people will start smoking if the price is high and gradually the number of smokers in the population will fall.

How Long is the Long Run?

The *long run* is the period necessary for complete adjustments to a price change. Its

Table 5-7 Adjustment in energy demand to the oil price shock of 1973–74

	7 MAJOR INDUSTRIAL COUNTRIES	JAPAN
% change by 1976		
In quantity	−3.7	−0.3
In real price	32.7	79.6
Demand elasticity*	−0.11	0
% change by 1981		
In quantity	−14.0	−19.1
In real price	82.4	176.1
Demand elasticity*	−0.17	0.11

* Although demand elasticities refer to movements along a demand curve holding income constant, income levels have changed in all these countries since 1973. The quantity data, and the demand elasticities calculated thereby, refer to quantity of energy divided by total income in the corresponding countries to crudely correct for the effect of changing incomes on energy demand.
Source: OECD Economic Outlook, 1981.

length depends on the type of adjustments consumers wish to make. Demand responses to a change in the price of chocolate should be completed within a few months, but full adjustment to changes in the price of oil or cigarettes may take several years. The short run refers to the period immediately after prices change and before long-term adjustment can occur.

Table 5-7 shows actual data on energy demand for a group of seven major industrial countries – the UK, United States, France, West Germany, Holland, Canada, and Japan. Behaviour in Japan is so striking that it is shown separately. The first part compares quantity and price data (adjusted for inflation) in 1976 with the corresponding data for 1973. It gives us some idea of the short-run response to the OPEC oil price shock of 1973–74 which quickly led to general increases in energy prices. The second part shows equivalent data for 1981, giving an idea of longer-run responses.

Table 5-7 makes two points clearly. First, the demand elasticity for energy increased once oil users had time to adjust. Second, even in the longer run, the demand for energy remains very inelastic. Even eight years may be insufficient to design and produce smaller cars to reduce household demand for petrol, to design and build factories with better insulation so that firms may reduce their demand for heating

fuel, or to design and bring on stream chemical process plant capable of using synthetic inputs to replace hydrocarbons derived from oil.

5-5 The Cross-Elasticity of Demand

The price elasticity of demand tells us about movements along a given demand curve holding constant all determinants of demand except the price of the good itself. To complete the analysis of demand behaviour, we now hold constant the own price of the good and examine the effect of variations in the prices of related goods. In the next section we examine the effect of changes in consumer income.

The cross-elasticity tells us the effect on the quantity demanded of the good *i* when the price of *another* good, good *j*, is changed. As before, we use percentage changes.

The *cross price elasticity of demand* for good *i* with respect to changes in the price of good *j* is the percentage change in the quantity of good *i* demanded, divided by the corresponding percentage change in the price of good *j*.

The cross-elasticity may be positive or negative. The cross-elasticity is positive if a rise in the price of good *j* increases the quantity demanded of good *i*. Suppose good *i* is tea and good *j* is coffee. We expect an increase in the price of coffee to raise the demand for tea. The cross-elasticity of tea with respect to coffee is positive. Cross price elasticities tend to be positive when two goods are substitutes and negatives when two goods are complements. We expect a rise in the price of petrol to reduce the demand for cars because petrol and cars are complements.

Table 5-8 shows estimates for the UK. Own price elasticities for food, clothing and footwear, and travel and communication are given down the diagonal of the table, from top left (the own price elasticity of demand for food) to bottom right (the price elasticity of demand for travel and communication). Off-diagonal entries in the table show cross price elasticities of demand. Thus, for example, −0.12 is the cross price elasticity of demand for food with respect to travel and communications. A 1 per cent increase in the price of travel and communication reduces the quantity of food demanded by 0.12 per cent.

The own price elasticities for the three goods

Table 5-8 Cross price and own price elasticities of demand in the UK

PERCENTAGE CHANGE IN QUANTITY DEMANDED OF	WITH RESPECT TO A 1% PRICE CHANGE IN:		
	FOOD	CLOTHING AND FOOTWEAR	TRAVEL AND COMMUNICATION
Food	−0.37	−0.03	−0.12
Clothing and footwear	0.19	−0.30	−0.23
Travel and communication	0.42	−0.01	−0.61

Source: Angus Deaton, 'The Analysis of Consumer Demand in the UK 1900–70', Econometrica, March 1974, Table 1.

lie between −0.30 (clothing and footwear) and −0.61 (travel and communication), much as we might have expected from our previous discussion of price elasticities of demand for broad categories of basic commodities. Nor should we be surprised that for all three goods the quantity demanded is more sensitive to changes in the own price of the good than to changes in the price of any other good.

The largest cross price elasticity is for the demand for travel and communication with respect to food. Higher food prices *increase* the quantity of travel and communication demanded. Perhaps households make more extensive shopping expeditions in search of supermarkets offering special discounts on meat. However, an increase in the price of travel and communications *reduces* the demand for food since the cross price elasticity is −0.12. Perhaps the decline in passengers on trains and aeroplanes reduces the number of people who eat between meals.

5-6 The Effect of Income on Demand

Finally, holding constant the own price of a good and the prices of related goods, we examine the response of the quantity demanded to changes in consumer incomes. For the moment we neglect the possibility of saving. Thus a rise in the income of consumers will typically be matched by an equivalent increase in total consumer spending.

In Chapter 3 we pointed out that higher consumer incomes will tend to increase the quantity demanded for most goods. However, demand quantities will typically increase by different amounts as incomes rise. Thus the pattern of consumer spending on different goods depends on the level of consumer incomes. We define the budget share of a good as the fraction of total consumer spending for which it accounts.

The *budget share* of a good is its price multiplied by the quantity demanded, divided by total consumer spending or income.

Table 5-9 reports the share of consumer spending in the UK devoted to food and to services (personal and leisure activities such as eating out and going to the theatre) between 1977 and 1987. The first column shows that real consumer spending (and incomes) have risen over the decade. Column (2) shows that the budget share of food has fallen over the decade, whereas column (3) shows that the budget share of serves has risen. Since the real price of both food and services has remained fairly constant over the decade, it seems plausible to attribute these changes in budget share primarily to changes in real consumer incomes. To investigate this question further, we must now develop a measure of the response of quantity demanded to changes in income. By analogy with our previous measures of demand responsiveness, we now define the income elasticity of demand.

The *income elasticity of demand* for a good is the percentage change in quantity demanded divided by the corresponding percentage change in income.

Since our strategy for analysing demand has been to consider varying one determinant at a time, the income elasticity of demand measures the effect on quantity demanded when incomes are changed but the own price of the good and the prices of related goods are held constant.

Table 5-9 Budget shares of food and wines and services in the UK, 1977–87

	(1) REAL CONSUMER SPENDING (£ billion, 1985 prices)	(2) (3) BUDGET SHARE (%) OF:	
		FOOD	SERVICES
1977	176	16.2	25.3
1980	194	15.4	26.4
1984	208	14.2	26.9
1987	238	13.3	29.4

Source: CSO, UK National Accounts.

Normal, Inferior, and Luxury Goods

The income elasticity of demand measures how far the demand curve shifts horizontally when incomes change. Figure 5-5 shows two possible shifts caused by a given percentage increase in income. The income elasticity is larger if the given rise in income shifts the demand curve from *DD* to *D"D"* than if the same income rise shifts the demand curve only from *DD* to *D'D'*. When an income rise shifts the demand curve to the left, the income elasticity of demand is a negative number, indicating that higher incomes are associated with smaller quantities demanded at any given prices.

In Chapter 3 we distinguished *normal* goods, for which demand increases as income rises, and *inferior* goods, for which demand falls as income rises. We can now define normal and inferior goods in terms of their income elasticities of demand.

> A *normal* good has a positive income elasticity of demand. An *inferior* good has a negative income elasticity of demand.

It is also useful to distinguish luxury goods and necessities.

> A *luxury* good has an income elasticity that is larger than one. A *necessity* has an income elasticity that is less than one.

All inferior goods are necessities, since their income elasticities of demand are negative. However, necessities also include normal goods whose income elasticity of demand lies between zero and one.

These definitions also tell us what will happen to budget shares when incomes are changed but prices remain unaltered. The budget share of inferior goods must fall as

incomes rise. Higher incomes (budgets) are associated with lower quantities demanded at constant prices. Conversely, the budget share of luxuries must rise when income rises. Because the income elasticity of demand for luxuries exceeds one, a 1 per cent rise in income increases quantity demanded (and hence total spending on luxury goods) by more than 1 per cent. Rises in income will *reduce* the budget share of normal goods that are necessities. Although income rises increase the quantity demanded, a 1 per cent income rise leads to a rise in

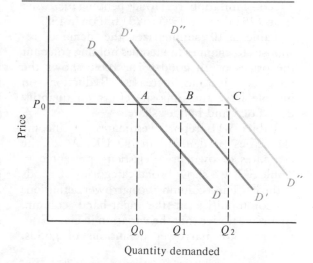

Figure 5-5 INCOME ELASTICITY AND SHIFTS IN THE DEMAND CURVE. Beginning at the Point *A* on the demand curve *DD*, the income elasticity measures the horizontal shift in the demand curve when income rises 1 per cent. At the given price *P*₀, a shift to the point *B* on the demand curve *D'D'* reflects a lower income elasticity than a shift to the point *C* on the demand curve *D"D"*. Leftward shifts in the demand curve when income rises would indicate a negative income elasticity.

quantity demanded by less than 1 per cent, so the budget share must fall.

Inferior goods tend to be low-quality goods for which there exist higher-quality, but more expensive, substitutes. Poor people satisfy their needs for meat and clothing by buying low-quality cuts of meat and nylon shirts. As their incomes rise, they switch to nicer cuts of meat (steak) and more comfortable shirts (cotton). Rising incomes lead to an absolute decline in the demand for cheap cuts of meat and nylon shirts.

Luxury goods tend to be high-quality goods for which there exist lower-quality, but quite adequate, substitutes: Mercedes cars rather than small Fords, foreign rather than domestic holidays. Necessities that are normal goods lie between these two extremes. As incomes rise, the quantity of food demanded will rise but only a little. Most people still enjoy fairly simple home cooking even when the their incomes rise. Looking back at Table 5-9, we see that services are luxuries whose budget share increased as UK incomes rose after 1977. Food cannot be a luxury, since its budget share fell as incomes rose, but it is not an inferior good either. At constant (1985) prices which adjust for the effects of inflation, real food spending *increased* from £29 billion in 1985 to £31 billion in 1987.

Table 5-10 summarizes the demand responses to changes in incomes holding constant the prices of all goods. The table shows the effect of income increases. Reductions in income have the opposite effect on quantity demanded and budget share.

Table 5-11 reports estimates of income elasticities of demand in the UK. As in the estimates of own price elasticity presented in Table 5-3, we show broad categories of goods in the left-hand column and narrower definitions of commodities in the right-hand column. Again we notice that the variation in elasticities is larger for narrower definitions of goods.

Higher incomes have much more effect on the way in which households eat (more steak, less bread) than on the amount they eat in total. As we suggested earlier, food is a normal good but not a luxury. The income elasticity of 0.45 confirms this. The right-hand column indicates that, within the food budget, increases in income lead to a switch towards vegetables (whose income elasticity is higher than the income elasticity for food as a whole) and away from bread, for which the quantity demanded declines. Richer households can afford to eat lots of salads in order to avoid getting fat. Poorer people need large quantities of bread to ward off the pangs of hunger. Notice that tobacco (chiefly cigarettes) is not only a necessity but even an inferior good. Although strictly inessential for physical survival, tobacco has the largest budget share among the poorer people. Richer people get their kicks in other (more expensive) ways.

Using Income Elasticities of Demand

Income elasticities are key pieces of information in forecasting the pattern of consumer demand as the economy grows and people become richer. Suppose we think that on average incomes will grow at 3 per cent per annum for the next five years. Given the estimates of Table 5-11, a 15 per cent change in incomes will reduce the demand for tobacco by 7.5 per cent (even if tobacco taxes are not raised) but will increase the demand for wines and spirits by 39 per cent. The growth prospects for these two industries are very different. These forecasts will affect decisions by firms about whether or not to build new factories, projections by governments of tax revenue from cigarettes and alcohol (the former will fall if tax rates per packet remain unchanged but the latter will rise sharply if taxes per bottle remain unchanged), and calculations by British Rail about the

Table 5-10 Summary of demand responses to a 1 per cent increase in income

TYPE OF GOOD	INCOME ELASTICITY	CHANGE IN QUANTITY DEMANDED	CHANGE IN BUDGET SHARE	EXAMPLE
Normal	Positive	Increases		
Luxury	Larger than 1	Increases by more than 1%	Increases	Yachts
Necessity	Between 0 and 1	Increases by less than 1%	Falls	Food
Inferior	Negative	Falls	Falls	Bread

Table 5-11 Estimates of income elasticities of demand in the UK

BROAD CATEGORIES OF GOODS	INCOME ELASTICITY OF DEMAND	NARROWER CATEGORIES OF GOODS	INCOME ELASTICITY OF DEMAND
Tobacco	−0.50	Coal	−2.02
Fuel and light	0.30	Bread and cereals	−0.50
Food	0.45	Dairy produce	0.53
Alcohol	1.14	Vegetables	0.87
Clothing	1.23	Travel abroad	1.14
Durables	1.47	Recreational goods	1.99
Services	1.75	Wines and spirits	2.60

Source: as in Table 5-3.

balance of smoking and non-smoking carriages that should be provided.

Later in this book we shall see that these considerations apply not only within national economies but in trade between nations. As Third World countries become richer, their demand for luxuries such as the familiar household durables, televisions, washing machines, and cars will rise rapidly. If the British government wants to improve the export performance of the UK, it may make more sense to subsidize new firms in these industries rather than to subsidize the dairy industry, where demand prospects are much worse.

5-7 The Effect of Inflation on Demand

We have now introduced elasticities to measure the response of quantity demanded to separate variations in three factors – the own price, the price of related goods, and income. In Chapter 2 we distinguished *nominal* variables, measured in the prices of the day, and *real* variables, which make adjustments for inflation when comparing measurements at different dates. You may have noticed that the examples in this chapter that discuss actual numbers for the UK and other economies refer to real·prices (Table 5-7) and real incomes (Table 5-9). We conclude this chapter by examining the effect of inflation on demand behaviour.

Suppose all nominal variables double. Every good costs twice as much, wage rates are twice as high, rents charged by landlords and dividends paid by firms double in money terms. Whatever bundle of goods could previously be purchased out of income can still be purchased.

Goods cost twice as much but incomes are twice as high. If meat used to cost twice as much as bread it still costs twice as much. In fact, nothing at all has really changed. Demand behaviour will be unaltered by a doubling of the nominal value of *all* prices and *all* forms of income.

How do we reconcile this assertion with the idea that demand elasticities measure changes in quantity demanded as prices change? Remember that each of the elasticities (own price, cross price, and income) measured the effect of changing that variable holding constant all other determinants of demand. When all prices and all incomes are simultaneously changing, the definitions of elasticities warn us that it is incorrect simply to examine the effect of one variable, such as the own price, on quantity demanded. We can decompose the change in quantity demanded into three components: the effect of changes in the own price alone, plus the effect of changes in price of other goods alone, plus the effect of changing incomes. When all nominal variables change by the same proportion, the sum of these three effects turns out to be exactly zero.

In examining economic data we can pursue one of two strategies. The first is to undertake a complete econometric analysis which is capable of simultaneously capturing the three distinct effects. However, a simpler strategy will sometimes suffice. Let us think again about the definition of elasticities. If we hold income and the price of all other goods constant, the own price elasticity tells us the effect of changes in the price of a good that affect its real or relative price compared with other goods. Similarly, holding constant the prices of all goods, the income elasticity tells us the effect of changes in money income that affect its real purchasing power, the quantity of goods that it will purchase. The definitions of elasticities make sense not because they refer to nominal variables but because their 'other things equal' assumptions make nominal and real changes coincide. Own price and cross price elasticities tell us about the effects of changes in real or relative prices. Income elasticities tell us about the effects of changes in real income.

With this insight, we can see how to amend our analysis to handle economies that are experiencing inflation, where the nominal values of most prices and incomes are rising over time. We can see now why doubling all prices has no effect on demand: it affects neither real income nor relative prices. We can also see how it may be possible to examine data in a simple way without resorting to a full econometric analysis. If an economy is experiencing inflation, prices are certainly changing. We may be able to get round the 'other things equal' problem simply by measuring all nominal variables in real terms. In Table 5-7 we examined the dramatic changes in oil prices. In real terms, changes in incomes or other prices are small relative to the change in real oil prices, though nominal incomes and prices of other goods changed a lot in the 1970s. By working in real terms, we may increase the relevance of the 'other things equal' assumption to the point at which we can essentially explain changes in oil quantity demanded by looking only at real oil prices.

Similarly, in Table 5-9 we looked at the effect of real income on budget shares. We picked two commodities (food and services) whose real price had remained fairly constant. Again, by working in real terms we may make the 'other things equal' assumption sufficiently relevant that a simple examination of the relationship between two variables tells most of the story.

We can thus restate the central theme of our analysis of demand behaviour. *Price elasticities measure the response of quantity demanded to changes in the relative price of goods. Income elasticities measure the response of quantity demanded to changes in the real value or purchasing power of income.*

Summary

1   Unless otherwise specified, the elasticity of demand refers to the own price elasticity of demand. It measures the sensitivity of quantity demanded to changes in the own price of a good, holding constant the prices of other goods and income. Demand elasticities are negative since demand curves slope down. In general, the demand elasticity changes as we move along a given demand curve. Along a straight line demand curve, elasticity falls as price falls.

2   Demand is elastic if the price elasticity is more negative than -1 (for example -2). Price cuts then increase total spending on the good. Demand is inelastic if the demand elasticity lies between -1 and 0. Price cuts then reduce total spending on the good. When demand is unit-elastic the demand elasticity is -1 and price changes have no effect on total spending on the good.

3   The demand elasticity depends on how long customers have to make adjustments to a price change. In the short run the substitution possibilities may be limited. Demand elasticities will typically rise (become more negative) with the length of time allowed for adjustment. The time required for complete adjustment will vary from good to good.

4   The cross price elasticity of demand measures the sensitivity of quantity demanded of one good to changes in the price of a related good. Positive cross-elasticities tend to imply that goods are substitutes. Negative cross-elasticities tend to imply that goods are complements.

5   The income elasticity of demand measures the sensitivity of quantity demanded to changes in income, holding constant the prices of all goods.

6   Inferior goods have negative income elasticities of demand. Higher incomes reduce the quantity demanded and the budget share of such goods. Luxury goods have income elasticities larger than 1. Higher incomes raise the quantity demanded and the budget share of such goods.

7   Goods that are not inferior are called normal goods and have positive income elasticities of demand. Goods that are not luxuries are called necessities and have income elasticities less than 1. All inferior goods are necessities, but normal goods are necessities only if they are not luxuries.

8 Doubling all nominal variables should have no effect on demand since it alters neither the real value (purchasing power) of incomes nor the relative prices of goods. In examining data from economies experiencing inflation it is often best to look at real prices and real incomes which measure prices and incomes adjusted for the rate of inflation.

Key Terms

Price elasticity of demand
Cross price elasticity of demand
Income elasticity of demand
Short-run and long-run adjustments
Budget shares
Luxuries and necessities
Normal and inferior goods
Elastic, inelastic, and unit-elastic demand
Substitutes and complements
Real prices and real incomes

Problems

1 You own a fruit stall, and have 100 baskets of strawberries that must be sold immediately, regardless of the price. Your supply curve of strawberries is vertical. From past experience in the fruit business you know that the demand curve for strawberries slopes down and that you can sell exactly 100 baskets if you charge £1 per basket. (a) Draw a supply and demand diagram showing market equilibrium. (b) You believe that the elasticity of demand for strawberries at £1 per basket is −0.5. You suddenly discover that 10 of your baskets are rotten and cannot be sold. Draw the new supply curve and show what happens to the equilibrium price of strawberries. What is the new equilibrium price?

2 Consider the following goods: (a) milk, dental services, beer; (b) chocolate, chickens, train journeys;

(c) theatre trips, tennis clubs, films. For each of the three categories, state whether you expect demand to be elastic or inelastic. Then rank the elasticities within each category. Explain your answer.

3 Where along a straight line demand curve does consumer spending reach a maximum? Explain why. What use is this information to the owner of a football club?

4 The following table shows price and income elasticities for vegetables and catering services. For each good, explain whether it is a luxury or a necessity, and whether demand is elastic or inelastic.

	PRICE ELASTICITY	INCOME ELASTICITY
Vegetables	−0.17	0.87
Catering services	−2.61	1.64

5 In 1974 UK households spent £1.3 m on bread and cereals and in 1989 they spent nearly £5 m on bread and cereals, yet bread is supposed to be an inferior good. How do you account for this?

6 (*Harder question.*) Suppose the price of oil falls. Think about the market for coal. How will the oil price fall affect the demand curve for coal (a) in the short run? (b) in the long run? What will happen to the price of each substitute for oil as a result of the fall in oil prices?

7 Common Fallacies Show why the following statements are incorrect: (a) Because cigarettes are a necessity the government can raise the tax on cigarettes (and hence cigarette prices) as much as it likes. Tax revenues from cigarettes will always increase when the tax rate is raised. (b) Farming is a risky business. Farmers should take out insurance against bad weather which could lead to a huge reduction in all their crops. (c) Higher levels of consumer income must be good news for producers.

6

The Theory of Consumer Choice

In previous chapters we have learned to use demand curves to represent consumer behaviour. In this chapter we go behind demand curves by building a model of consumer choice. It explains how buyers reconcile what they would like to do, as described by their tastes or preferences, and what the market will allow them to do, as described by their incomes and the prices of different goods. The model allows us to predict how consumers will respond to changes in market conditions. It helps to make sense of the price and income elasticities examined in Chapter 5.

6-1 The Theory of Consumer Choice

The model has four elements which describe both the consumer and the market environment:

1   The consumer's income
2   The prices at which goods can be bought
3   The consumer's tastes, which rank different bundles of goods by the satisfaction they yield
4   The behavioural assumption that consumers do the best they can for themselves. Of the affordable consumption bundles, the consumer picks the bundle that maximizes her own satisfaction.

Each of these elements in the model requires detailed discussion.

The Budget Constraint

Together, elements (1) and (2) define the consumer's budget constraint.

The *budget constraint* describes the different bundles that the consumer can afford.

Which bundles are feasible, or can be afforded, depends on two factors: the consumer's income and the prices of different goods.

Consider a student with a weekly budget (income, allowance, or grant) of £50 which can be spent on meals or films.[1] Each model costs £5 and each film £10. What combination of meals and films can she afford? Completely going without films, she can spend £50 on 10 meals at £5 each. Completely going without meals, she can buy 5 cinema tickets at £10 each. Between these two extremes lies a range of combinations of meals and films that together cost exactly £50. These combinations are called the budget constraint.

The budget constraint shows the *maximum* affordable quantity of one good given the quantity of the other good being purchased.[2] Table 6-1 shows the budget constraint for the student. Each row shows an affordable consumption bundle. Row 4 shows that 6 meals (costing £30) and 2 films (costing £20) use up all available income. Other rows are calculated in the same way.

Table 6-1 shows the *trade-off* between meals and films. Higher quantities of meals require lower quantities of films. For a given income, the budget constraint shows how much of one good must be sacrificed to obtain larger quantities of the other good. It is because there is a trade-off that she must *choose between* meals and films.

The Budget Line

It is useful to depict the budget constraint of Table 6-1 as a *budget line*. Plotting the data of Table 6-1, the budget line in Figure 6-1 again shows the maximum combinations of meals and films that the student can purchase out of available income.

---

[1] When there are more than two goods, we can think of 'films' as standing for 'all goods other than meals'.

[2] We assume that all income is spent on goods. There is no saving. We defer analysis of the important choice between spending and saving until later.

Table 6-1 Affordable consumption baskets

QUANTITY OF MEALS (Q_M)	SPENDING ON MEALS (£5 × Q_M)	QUANTITY OF FILMS (Q_F)	SPENDING ON FILMS (£10 × Q_F)
0	0	5	50
2	10	4	40
4	20	3	30
6	30	2	20
8	40	1	10
10	50	0	0

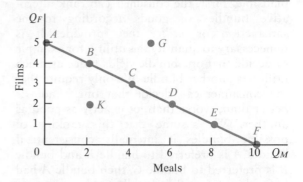

Figure 6-1 THE BUDGET LINE. The budget line shows the maximum combinations of goods that the consumer can afford, given income and the prevailing prices. Points such as B and C, on the budget line AF, use up the entire consumer budget. Points such as G, above the budget line, are unaffordable. Points such as K, inside the budget line, would allow additional consumption.

The position of the budget line is determined by its end points *A* and *F*, which have a simple economic interpretation. Point *A* shows the maximum quantity of films (5) that the budget will purchase if the student does without meals: £50 buys at most 5 tickets at £10 each. Point *F* shows that £50 buys at most 10 meals at £5 each if she goes without films. The budget line joins up points *A* and *F*. Intermediate points such as *B* and *C* show more balanced purchases of meals and films.

The slope of the budget line indicates how many meals must be sacrificed to get another film. Moving from point *F* to point *E* reduces the quantity of meals from 10 to 8 but increases the quantity of films from 0 to 1. This trade-off between meals and films is constant along the budget line. Giving up two meals always provides the extra £10 to buy an additional cinema ticket.

We now see the crucial role of prices. It is because film tickets cost twice as much as meals that two meals must be sacrificed to purchase another film ticket. *The slope of the budget line depends only on the ratio of the prices of the two goods.* The slope of a line is the change in the vertical distance divided by the corresponding change in the horizontal distance. In Figure 6-1 the slope of the budget line is $-\frac{1}{2}$. A positive change of 1 film must be divided by the corresponding negative change of −2 meals.

This example illustrates the general rule

Slope of the budget line $= -P_H/P_V$ (1)

where P_H is the price of the good on the horizontal axis and P_V is the price of the good on the vertical axis. In our example, the price of meals P_H is £5 and the price of films P_V is £10. Formula (1) confirms that the slope of the budget line is $-\frac{1}{2}$ and the minus sign reminds us that there is a trade-off. We have to *give up* one good to get more of the other good.

Thus, the two end-points of the budget line (here, *A* and *F*) show how much of each good the budget will buy if the other good is not purchased at all. The slope of the budget line joining these end-points, depends only on the *relative* prices of the two goods.

Any point above the budget line (such as *G* in Figure 6-1) is unaffordable. The budget line shows the maximum quantity of one good that can be afforded, given the quantity purchased of the other good and given the budget available for spending. Given an income of £50, the point *G* is out of reach since it requires £25 to buy 5 meals and £50 to buy 5 cinema tickets. Points such as *K*, which lie inside the budget line, leave some income unspent. Only on the budget line is there a trade-off where the student must choose *between* films and meals.

Tastes[3]

The budget line summarizes the market environment (income and prices) of the consumer. We now consider the consumer's *tastes*. We make three assumptions that seem rather

---
[3] The Appendix to this chapter presents an alternative approach to tastes based on measurable utility. It is less satisfactory, but you may find it easier.

plausible. First, the consumer can rank alternative bundles of goods according to the satisfaction or *utility* they provide. It is unnecessary to quantify this utility, for example to decide that one bundle yields twice as much utility as another bundle. We only require that the consumer can decide that one bundle is better than, worse than, or exactly as good as another. We assume that this ranking of possible bundles is internally consistent: if bundle A is preferred to bundle B and bundle B is preferred to bundle C, then bundle A had better be preferred to bundle C.

Second, we assume that *the consumer prefers more to less*. If bundle B offers more films but the same number of meals as bundle K we assume that bundle B is preferred. How do we handle things like pollution, which are not goods but 'bads'? Consumers do not prefer more pollution to less. We get round this problem by redefining commodities so that the assumption will be satisfied. We can analyse tastes for clean water rather than for polluted water. More clean water is better, other things equal.

Figure 6-2 examines the implications of these assumptions about tastes. Each point shows a particular consumption bundle of meals and films. For the moment we ignore whether or not these bundles are affordable. We are interested only in tastes themselves. We begin at the bundle shown by the point a. Since more is preferred to less, any point such as c to the north-east of a is preferred to a. Point c offers more of *both* goods than a. Conversely, points to the south-west of a offer less of both goods than a. Point a is preferred to points such as b.

Without knowing the consumer's exact tastes we cannot be sure how points in the other two regions (north-west and south-east) will compare with a. At points such as d or e the consumer has more of one good but less of the other good than at a. Someone who really likes food might prefer e to a, but an avid film buff would prefer d to a. Others might be indifferent between d, a, and e, ranking them equal in terms of the utility they provide.

We now introduce the concept of the marginal rate of substitution of meals for films.

The *marginal rate of substitution* of meals for films is the quantity of films the consumer

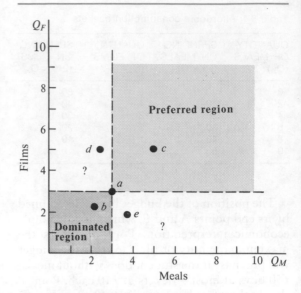

Figure 6-2 CONSUMER RANKING OF ALTERNATIVE CONSUMPTION BUNDLES. The consumer evaluates alternative consumption bundles, which are identified by points a, b, c, d, and e. With respect to point a, any point to the north-east is preferred and any point to the south-west is dominated by a. Points such as d or e in the other two regions may or may not be preferred to a, depending on the consumer's tastes.

must sacrifice to increase the quantity of meals by one unit *without changing total utility.*

Since consumers prefer more to less, an additional meal tends to increase utility. To hold utility constant, when one meal is added the consumer must simultaneously sacrifice some quantity of the other good (films). The marginal rate of substitution tells us how many films the consumer could exchange for an additional meal without changing total utility.

Suppose the student begins with 5 films and no meals. Having already seen 4 films that week, she probably does not enjoy the fifth film very much. With no meals, she is *very* hungry. The utility of this bundle is low: being so hungry, she cannot really enjoy the films anyway. For the same amount of utility she could give up a lot of films for a little food.

Suppose instead that the student is consuming a large number of meals but seeing few films. She will be reluctant to sacrifice much cinema attendance to gain yet another meal. It makes sense to sacrifice abundant films for scarce meals. Conversely, when the ratio of films to meals is already low, it does not make sense to sacrifice scarce films for yet more meals.

Economists believe that this common-sense reasoning about tastes or preferences is very robust. It will hold in a wide range of circumstances. Indeed, it is sufficiently plausible that it can become a general principle, the third assumption we need to make about consumer tastes. It is called the assumption of a diminishing marginal rate of substitution.

> Consumer tastes exhibit a *diminishing marginal rate of substitution* when, to hold utility constant, diminishing quantities of one good must be sacrificed to obtain successive equal increases in the quantity of the other good.

For example, our student might be equally happy with bundle $X = (6$ films, 0 meals), bundle $Y = (3$ films, 1 meal), and bundle $Z = (2$ films, 2 meals). Beginning from bundle X, a move to Y sacrifices 3 films for 1 meal, but a further move from Y to Z sacrifices only 1 film for 1 extra meal. Such tastes satisfy the assumption of a diminishing marginal rate of substitution.

These three assumptions – that consumers prefer more to less, can rank alternative bundles according to the utility provided, and have tastes satisfying a diminishing marginal rate of substitution – are all we shall require. It is now convenient to show how tastes can be represented as *indifference curves*.

Representing Tastes as Indifference Curves

If we join up all the many points the student likes equally, we obtain an indifference curve.

> An *indifference curve* shows all the consumption bundles which yield the same utility.

Figure 6-3 shows three indifference curves labelled U_1U_1, U_2U_2, and U_3U_3.

Every point on U_2U_2 yields the same utility. Point C offers a lot of meals and few films, and point A offers many films but few meals. Because the consumer prefers more to less, *indifference curves must slope downwards*. Since more meals tend to increase utility, some films must simultaneously be sacrificed to hold utility constant.

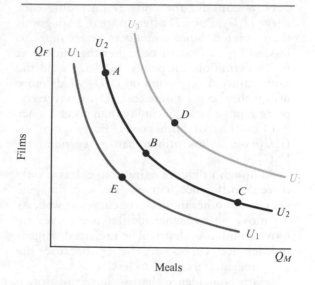

Figure 6-3 REPRESENTING CONSUMER TASTES BY INDIFFERENCE CURVES. Along each indifference curves, such as U_2U_2, consumer utility is constant. Since more is preferred to less, any point on a higher indifference curve, such as U_3U_3, is preferred to any point on a lower indifference curve. Indifference curves must slope downwards. Otherwise the consumer would have more of both goods and would be better off. Diminishing marginal rates of substitution imply that each indifference curve becomes flatter as we move along it to the right.

The slope of each indifference curves gets steadily flatter as we move to the right. This follows immediately from the assumption of a diminishing marginal rate of substitution. At point A, where films are relatively abundant compared with meals, the consumer will sacrifice a lot of films to gain a little more food. At the point B, where films are less abundant relative to meals, she will sacrifice a smaller quantity of films to gain the same additional quantity of meals. And at the point C she now has so many meals that hardly any films will be sacrificed for additional meals. In fact, we now recognize that the marginal rate of substitution of meals for films is simply the slope of the indifference curve at the point from which we begin. These two properties of a single indifference curve – its downward slope and its steady flattening as we move to the right – follow directly from the assumptions that consumers prefer more to less and that their tastes satisfy the assumption of diminishing marginal rates of substitution.

Now consider the point D on indifference curve U_3U_3. Point D offers more of both goods than point B. Since consumers prefer more to less, utility at D must be higher than utility at B. By definition, all points on U_3U_3 yield the same utility. Every point on U_3U_3 yields more utility than every point on U_2U_2. Conversely, point E must yield less utility than point B since it offers less of both goods. Every point on U_1U_1 yields less utility than every point on U_2U_2.

Although in Figure 6-3 we have drawn only three indifference curves, we can imagine drawing in other indifference curves as well. As we move on to higher indifference curves we move to bundles that will be preferred. Higher indifference curves are better because the consumer prefers more to less.

Is it a coincidence that we have not drawn any indifference curves that cross each other? It is not: indifference curves cannot cross. Figure 6-4 shows why. Suppose the indifference curves UU and U'U' were to intersect. Since X and Y lie on the same indifference curve UU, the consumer is indifferent between these

points. But Y and Z both lie on the indifference curve U'U'. Hence the consumer is indifferent between Y and Z. Together these imply that the consumer is indifferent between X and Z. But this is impossible, since the consumer gets more of both goods at Z than at X. Hence intersecting indifference curves would violate our assumption that consumers prefer more to less. Our assumptions about consumer tastes rule out intersecting indifference curves.

We can represent the tastes of any consumer by drawing the complete *map* of indifferent curves. Figure 6-5 shows the indifference map for two consumers with different tastes. In each case, moves to a higher indifference curve imply an increase in utility. In Figure 6-5(a) we show the indifference map for a glutton who is always prepared to give up a lot of films to gain a little extra food. Figure 6-5(b) shows the indifference map for a weight-watching film buff, who will give up large quantities of food to increase the quantity of films by even a small amount. Both indifference maps are valid: they satisfy our three basic assumptions about consumer tastes. Our theory is sufficiently general to cope with extreme kinds of preferences as well as with more typical preferences which lie in between.

Utility Maximization and Choice

The budget line describes the affordable bundles given the consumer's market environment (the budget for spending and the price of different goods). The indifference map shows the tastes of the consumer. To complete the model, we assume that *the consumer chooses the affordable bundle that maximizes his or her utility*.

The consumer cannot afford points that lie above the budget line, and will never choose points that lie below the budget line where it is possible to purchase more of one good without sacrificing any of the other good.

Thus we know the consumer will select a point on the budget line. To determine which point on the budget line maximizes utility we need to think about the consumer's tastes. We expect our glutton to pick a point with more meals and less films than the point our film buff will select. We begin by showing in general how to use indifference curves to determine the bundle the consumer will choose. Then we confirm that our model of consumer choice

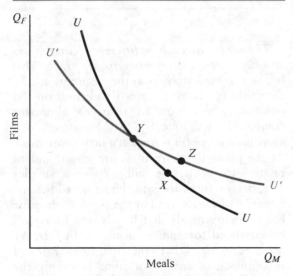

Figure 6-4 INDIFFERENCE CURVES CANNOT INTERSECT. If indifference curves intersected, the consumer would be indifferent between X and Y on the indifference curve UU, and between Y and Z on the indifference curve U'U', and hence indifferent between X and Z. Since Z offers more of both goods than X, this violates the assumption that consumers prefer more to less. Indifference curves cannot intersect.

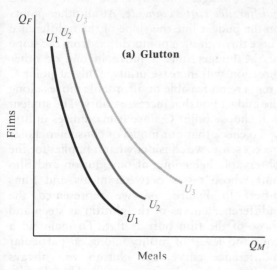
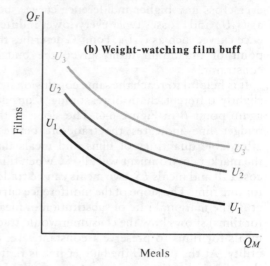

Figure 6-5 REPRESENTING DIFFERENCES IN TASTES. To hold utility constant along a particular indifference curve, a glutton will give up a large quantity of films for extra meals but a weight-watching film buff will give up very few films for the same increase in meals.

can capture the different behaviour of the glutton and the film buff.

Figure 6-6 again shows the budget line AF for the student who has £50 to spend on films at £10 each and meals at £5 each. The indifference curves U_1U_1, U_2U_2, and U_3U_3 are part of the indifference map describing her tastes.

Since U_3U_3 lies everywhere above the budget line AF, all points on U_3U_3 are unattainable, however much the student would like to obtain this amount of utility. Suppose she considers the attainable point B on the indifference curve U_1U_1. This will certainly be preferred to the point A, which must lie on a lower indifference curve (since indifferent curves cannot intersect, the indifference curve through A must lie everywhere below the indifference curve U_1U_1). Similarly, F must lie on a lower indifference curve than E and she prefers E to F.

However, she will chose neither the point B nor the point E. By moving to the point C she can reach a higher indifference curve and obtain more utility, so C is the point that the student will choose. Any other affordable point on the budget line will be on a lower indifference curve. The assumption that consumers choose the bundle that maximizes their utility given the affordable possibilities described by the budget line thus has the following simple

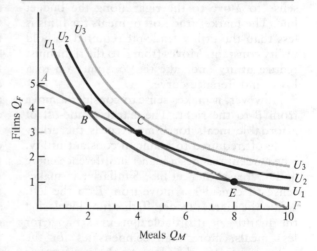

Figure 6-6 CONSUMER CHOICE IN ACTION.
Points above the budget line AF are unaffordable. The consumer cannot reach the indifference curve U_3U_3. Points such as B and E are affordable but only allow the consumer to reach the indifference curve U_1U_1. The consumer will choose the point C to reach the highest possible indifference curve U_2U_2. At the chosen point C, the indifference curve and the budget line just touch and their slopes are equal.

implication: *the chosen bundle will be the point at which an indifference curve just touches the budget line.* Mathematicians would say that the budget line is *a tangent* to the indifference curve

U_2U_2 at the point C. The budget line does not ever cross any higher indifference curve, such as U_3U_3 and crosses twice every lower indifference curve, such as U_1U_1. Point C describes the point of maximum utility given the budget constraint.

It is helpful to reach the same conclusion by a slightly different chain of reasoning. Consider again point B in Figure 6-6. The slope of the budget line indicates the trade-off between affordable quantities of films and meals that the market environment will allow. When films cost £10 and meals £5, two meals can be traded for one film. The slope of the indifference curve at B (the marginal rate of substitution of meals for films) shows how the consumer would trade meals for films to preserve a constant level of utility. At the point B the budget line is flatter than the indifference curve. Moves to the left would take the student on to a lower indifference curve because the market trade-off is less than the required utility trade-off. Similarly, beginning at the point E it cannot make sense to move to the right along the budget line. The market trade-off of meals for films is less than the utility trade-off required to hold utility constant. Moves from E to the right must reduce utility and take the consumer on to a lower indifference curve.

However, it makes sense to consider a move from B to the right. The market trade-off of affordable meals for films exceeds the utility trade-off required to maintain constant utility. The student reaches a higher indifference curve and increases her utility. Similarly, it makes sense to consider a move from E to the left. Again the market trade-off, this time increasing the quantity of affordable films in exchange for less meals, more than compensates for the utility trade-off, the slope of the indifference curve, required to maintain utility at a constant level. Moves from E leftwards along the budget line increase utility and allow her to reach a higher indifference curve.

In fact, we can make a general principle out of these examples. Wherever the budget line *crosses* an indifference curve, a move along the budget line in one direction will increase utility since the market trade-off is better than the utility trade-off required to maintain constant utility.

Viewed in these terms, *the point C, which maximizes utility, is the point at which the slope of the budget line and the slope of the indifference curve coincide*. At all other points on the budget line the slope of the indifference curve through such points differs from the slope of the budget line: a move in one or other direction will increase utility. Only at point C are there no feasible or affordable moves along the budget line that increase utility. The student will choose point C since it maximizes utility.

To check that our model of consumer choice makes sense, we consider what it implies for the observable behaviour of our glutton and film buff whose tastes between meals and films differ. In Figure 6-5 we represented the indifference curves of the glutton as steep and those of the film buff as flat. To maintain a constant level of utility along a particular indifference curve, the glutton will always sacrifice a lot of films for more food but the film buff will hardly sacrifice any films for a lot more food.

In Figure 6-7 we give these two students the same budget line. They have the same income and face the same prices for food and films. Only their tastes differ. Figure 6-7(a) shows that the chosen point C for the glutton occurs at a combination of a lot of meals but few films. Figure 6-7(b) confirms that the film buff will choose a point C with many more films but much less food. The theory of consumer choice based on individual utility maximization successfully translates differences in tastes into differences in revealed or observable demands for the two goods.

Each student will choose a point C at which their marginal rate of substitution equals the slope of the budget line, which depends only on the relative price of films and meals. Because the glutton has a strong preference for food (steep indifference curves), the chosen point must lie far to the right to give the indifference curve a long time to flatten out. Because the film buff has flat indifference curves, the chosen point must lie well to the left before indifference curves can become flatter than the budget line.

6-2 Adjustment to Income Changes

In the previous chapter we introduced the concept of the income elasticity of demand to describe, other things equal, the response of

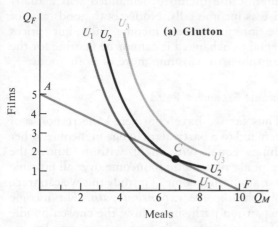

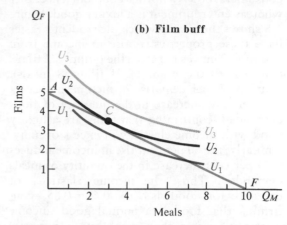

Figure 6-7 THE EFFECT OF TASTES ON CONSUMER CHOICE. Both students face the same budget line
AF and choose the point *C*, maximizing utility where the indifference curve is tangent to the budget line.
The glutton has steep indifference curves and must consume a lot of meals before the diminishing marginal rate of
substitution flattens the indifference curve sufficiently. The film buff has flat indifference curves and the point
of tangency occurs much further to the left. Thus the glutton chooses more meals but fewer films than the film
buff.

quantity demanded to changes in consumer
incomes. Now we can use our model of
consumer choice to analyse this response
in greater detail.

For given tastes and prices, Figure 6-8 shows
the adjustment to a change in income. The
student has an income of £50, faces the budget
line *AF*, and chooses the point *C* at which utility
is maximized. Now suppose her income rises
from £50 to £80. Prices of meals and films
remain unchanged at £5 and £10 respectively.
With higher income, she can afford more of
one or both of the goods. The budget
line shifts outwards from *AF* to *A'F'*. To find
the exact position of this new line we have to
calculate the purchasing power of the new
income in terms of the two goods. Again we
calculate the end points at which all income is
spent on a single good. The point *A'* shows
that at most £80 buys 8 films at £10 each. The
point *F'* shows that £80 buys at most 16
meals at £5 each. Joining these points yields
the new budget line *A'F'*. Since the slope of a
budget line depends only on the relative prices
of the two goods, which remain unchanged, the
new budget line *A'F'* is parallel to the old budget
line *AF*.

Which point on *A'F'* will the student choose?
She will choose the point *C'* at which the new
budget line is tangent to the highest attainable

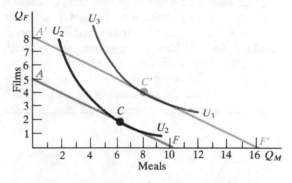

Figure 6-8 THE EFFECT OF AN INCREASE
IN CONSUMER INCOME. An increase in consumer
income from £50 to £80 induces a parallel shift in the
budget line from *AF* to *A'F'*. The new end points *A'*
and *F'* reflect the increase in purchasing power if
only one good is purchased. The slope remains
unaltered since prices have not changed. At the
higher income the consumer chooses *C'*. Since both
goods are normal, higher income raises the quantity
of each good demanded but the percentage increase
in film quantity is larger since its income elasticity is
higher.

indifference curve. However, the position of
this point *C'* depends on the map of indifference
curves that describe her tastes.

The empirical evidence examined in the
previous chapters suggests that for most

consumers food is a normal good but a necessity whereas entertainment is a luxury good. Figure 6-8 shows the case in which the student's tastes have these properties. A rise in income from £50 to £80 moves her from the point C (2 films, 6 meals) to the point C' (4 films, 8 meals). Thus, a 60 per cent rise in income induces a 100 per cent increase in the quantity of films demanded, confirming that films are a luxury good with income elasticity in excess of unity. Similarly, the 60 per cent rise in income induces a 33 per cent increase in the quantity of meals demanded. Thus, the income elasticity of demand for food is $(0.33/0.6) = 0.55$, confirming that food is a normal good (income elasticity greater than zero) but a necessity (income elasticity less than unity).

In contrast, Figure 6-9 illustrates the case in which the student's tastes make food an inferior good, for which the quantity demanded declines as income rises. At the point C' on the budget line A'F' fewer meals are demanded than at the point C on the budget line AF, corresponding to the lower income.

The effects of a fall in income are, of course, exactly the opposite. The budget line shifts inwards but remains parallel to the original budget line. When both goods are normal, lower consumer income reduces the quantity demanded for both goods. If one good is

inferior the quantity demanded will actually rise as income falls. Notice both goods cannot be inferior: when income falls but prices remain unchanged it cannot be feasible for the consumer to consume more of both goods.

Income Expansion Paths

Thus far we have considered the response of demand to a particular change in income, other things equal. We might wish to know the response of demand to income over all possible variations in income. To study this we can trace out the *income expansion path*. The income expansion path shows how the chosen bundle of goods varies with consumer income levels.

Look again at Figure 6-8. The budget lines AF and A'F' correspond to incomes of £50 and £80 respectively. With yet higher incomes we could draw more budget lines, parallel to AF and A'F' but higher up. We could then find the points on these new budget lines which the consumer would choose at these higher income levels. Joining up the chosen points (C and C' in Figure 6-8) and these new points (say C'' and C'''), we obtain the income expansion path. Try drawing it for yourself.

6-3 Adjustment to Price Changes

Having studied the effects of changing tastes and changing income on quantity demanded, we now isolate the effect of a price change. Relying on common sense, in Chapter 5 we argued that an increase in the price of a good will reduce the quantity demanded, other things equal. The own price elasticity of demand measures this response, and will be larger the easier it is to substitute towards goods whose prices have not risen.

We also introduced the cross-elasticity of demand to measure the response of the quantity demanded of one good to a change in the price of another good. An increase in the price of good j tends to increase the quantity demanded of good i when the two goods are substitutes but tends to reduce the quantity demanded of good i when the two goods are complements. The empirical evidence in favour of all these propositions was presented in Tables 5-3 and 5-8.

Are those propositions invariably true, or did

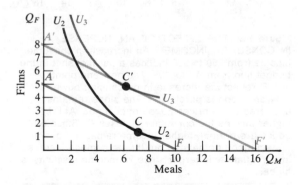

Figure 6-9 AN INCREASE IN INCOME REDUCES DEMAND FOR THE INFERIOR GOOD. Again, income is increased from £50 to £80 and there is a parallel shift in the budget line from AF to A'F'. If meals were an inferior good, the quantity demanded would fall as income rose. The consumer then moves from C to C' when income rises.

the evidence we examined just happen to confirm our common-sense reasoning? To answer this question we now offer a more formal analysis based on the model of consumer choice we have now developed.

Price Changes and the Budget Line

In Figure 6-10 we draw the budget line AF for a consumer with an income of £50 facing prices of £10 and £5 for films and meals respectively. Now suppose that meal prices increase to £10. Since the price of films remains unaltered, £50 still buys 10 films when all income is spent on films. The point A must lie on the new budget line as well as the old budget line. But when all income is spent on meals, £50 buys only 5 meals at £10 each instead of the 10 meals it used to buy at £5 each. Thus the other extreme point on the budget line shifts from F to F' when meal prices double. As usual, we join up these end-points to obtain the new budget line AF'. Thus the effect of an increase in meal prices is to *rotate* the budget line inwards around the point A, at which no meals are bought and meal prices are irrelevant.

Except at the point A itself, at the higher meal

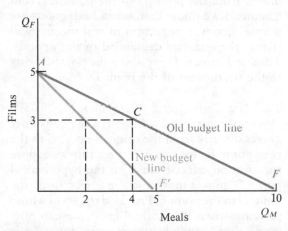

Figure 6-10   AN INCREASE IN MEAL PRICES. The consumer begins at the point C on the budget line AF. Doubling meal prices halves the amount that can be spent on meals when no films are bought. The point F shifts to F'. The budget line rotates around the point A at which no meals are bought. Along the new budget line the consumer can no longer afford the original consumption bundle C. Consumption of one or both commodities must be reduced.

prices the consumer can now afford fewer meals for any given number of films purchased, or fewer films for any given number of meals. The new budget line AF' lies inside the old budget line AF. The consumption bundles lying between AF' and AF are no longer affordable at the higher price of meals. In particular, the chosen point on the old budget line is no longer affordable unless it happened to be the extreme point A. This analysis shows how a price increase makes the consumer worse off by reducing consumption opportunities out of a fixed money income. The consumer's standard of living will fall.

To check that you understand, try drawing diagrams to illustrate the effect on the budget line of: (1) a reduction in the price of meals (*hint:* Figure 6-10 can be used. How?); (2) an increase in the price of films (*hint:* around which point does the budget line rotate?).

Substitution and Income Effects

Our model of consumer choice is based on the interaction of affordable opportunities represented by the budget line, and tastes represented by indifference curves. To analyse the effect of price changes on the actual quantity of goods demanded, we must now study how rotations of the budget line affect the highest indifference curve that the consumer can reach.

An increase in the price of meals has two distinct effects on the budget line in Figure 6-10. First, the budget line becomes steeper, reflecting the increase in the relative price of meals. To obtain an additional meal a larger quantity of films must now be sacrificed. Second, in general the budget line AF' lies inside the original budget line AF. The purchasing power of a given money income has been reduced by the price increase. Economists therefore break up the effect of a price increase into these two distinct effects: the change in the relative prices of the two goods, and the reduction in the purchasing power of the given money income.

The *substitution effect* of a price change is the adjustment of demand to the relative price change alone. The *income effect* of a price change is the adjustment of demand to the change in real income alone.

In Figure 6-11 we show how substitution and income effects may be used to organize the way

Figure 6-11 INCOME AND SUBSTITUTION
EFFECTS OF AN INCREASE IN MEAL
PRICES. Higher meal prices rotate the
budget line from AF to AF'. The consumer
moves from the point C to the point E. This
move can be decomposed into a pure
substitution effect, from C to D, the
response to relative price changes at the
old standard of living, plus a pure income
effect, from D to E, the response to a fall in
real income at constant relative prices. The
substitution effect must reduce the quantity
of meals demanded. The income effect also
reduces the quantity of meals demanded
provided meals are a normal good. Under
these circumstances, price increases
reduce the quantity demanded and demand
curves slope downwards.

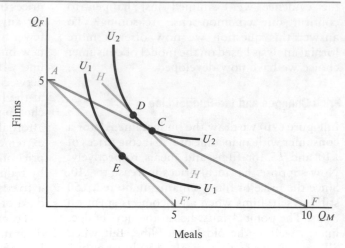

we think about the response of demand quantities to an increase in the price of meals. At the original prices the consumer faces the budget line AF and chooses the point C to reach the highest possible indifference curve U_2U_2. At the higher meal price the budget line rotates to AF' and the consumer chooses the point E to reach U_1U_1, the highest indifference curve now possible. In this example, the doubling of meal prices reduces the quantity of meals demanded and the quantity of films demanded.

The Substitution Effect   To isolate the effect of relative prices alone, imagine drawing the *hypothetical* budget line HH, parallel to AF' but tangent to the original indifference curve U_2U_2. Because HH is a parallel to the new budget line AF', its slope reflects the new relative prices of films and meals after the price of meals has risen. Because HH is tangent to the old indifference curve U_2U_2, it allows the consumer to attain the original level of utility and standard of living that, by definition, is constant along U_2U_2.

If confronted with the hypothetical budget line HH the consumer would choose the point D. The move from C to D captures the pure substitution effect, the adjustment of demand to relative prices when income is adjusted to maintain the old standard of living in the face of the new higher prices. *The substitution effect of an increase in the price of meals unambiguously reduces the quantity of meals*

demanded. This result is perfectly general.[4] As meals become relatively more expensive, the consumer has an incentive to switch towards films, which have become relatively cheaper.

The Income Effect   To isolate the effect of the reduction in real income, holding relative prices constant, consider now the parallel shift in the budget line from the hypothetical position HH to the actual new position AF'. The consumer moves from the point D to the point E. From Chapter 5 we know that, when both goods are normal goods, a reduction in real income will reduce the quantity demanded of both goods. Thus in Figure 6-11 we show the point E lying to the south-west of the point D.

The Net Effect of a Price Increase on the Quantity Demanded   Although the consumer moves directly from the original point C to the new point E, we can interpret this as a pure substitution effect from C to the hypothetical point D plus a pure income effect from the point D to the point E. Provided the good whose price has risen is a normal good, we can now prove that demand curves slope downwards as we asserted in Chapter 5.

The substitution effect from C to D neces-

---

[4] With only two goods, substitution away from meals must imply substitution towards films. However, when there are more than two goods, we cannot be sure that the substitution effects will tend to increase the quantity demanded for all other goods. We discuss this shortly under the heading 'Complements and Substitutes'.

Figure 6-12   A PRICE INCREASE
INCREASES THE QUANTITY OF A
GIFFEN GOOD DEMANDED.   The price
increase rotates the budget line from *AF* to
AF'. The substitution effect, from *C* to *D*,
reduces the quantity of the inferior good
demanded. Since the good is inferior, the
income effect, from *D* to *E*, increases the
quantity of the inferior good demanded. For
a Giffen good, the income effect dominates
and *E* lies to the right of *C*. In practice, the
income effect for inferior goods is less
strong and the point *E*, although to the
right of *D*, usually lies to the left of *C* so
that the quantity demanded falls as the
price of the inferior good rises.

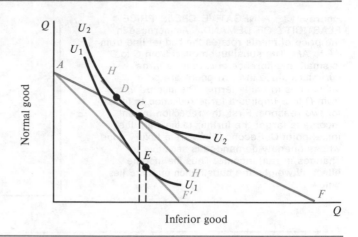

sarily reduces the quantity of meals demanded.
When the price of meals rises, the budget line
becomes steeper and we must move along U_2U_2
to the left to find the point at which it is tangent
to *HH*. Similarly, the income effect must further
reduce the quantity of meals demanded provided meals are a normal good. The point *E*
must lie to the left of the point *D*.

Inferior Goods   Although the substitution
effect is guaranteed to reduce the quantity of
meals demanded when the price of meals
increases, the income effect will go in the
opposite direction when we examine a good
that is inferior. Then reductions in real income
increase the quantity demanded. We can even
imagine a perverse case in which this effect
is so strong that price rises actually increase the
quantity of that good demanded. Demand
curves then slope *upwards*! This possibility is
illustrated in Figure 6-12. An increase in the
price of the inferior good rotates the budget
line from *AF* to *AF'*. The substitution effect,
from *C* to *D*, tends to reduce the quantity of
the inferior good demanded, but this is
outweighed by the income effect, from *D* to *E*.
Since the point *E* lies to the right of the point
C, the net effect of the increase in price of the
inferior good has been to increase the quantity
demanded. Economists refer to such goods as
'Giffen goods', after a nineteenth century
economist who claimed that increases in the
price of bread increased the quantity of bread
demanded by the poor.

Even though a good is an inferior good it

need not be a Giffen good. It requires a very
strong income effect – here an increase in
demand in response to real income reductions
– to offset the substitution effect, which must
be negative. When goods are inferior, theoretical reasoning alone cannot establish which
affect will dominate. We have to look at the
empirical evidence. After many decades of
empirical research, economists are convinced
that the possibility of Giffen goods is largely a
theoretical *curiosum*. In practice, goods are
rarely sufficiently inferior that the income effect
can reverse the substitution effect.

Thus, as an empirical judgement, economists
have concluded that for inferior goods, the
substitution effect outweighs the income effect
and demand curves will slope downwards as
price is increased. For the much more common
case in which goods are normal, having a
positive income elasticity of demand, the
income and substitution effects both act to
reduce the quantity demanded, as in Figure
6-11. The proposition that demand curves slope
downwards can then be established by theoretical reasoning alone.

Cross Price Elasticities of Demand

We now investigate the effect of an increase in
the price of one good on the quantity of another
good demanded. In Chapter 5 we suggested that
cross price elasticities might be negative or
positive, and we now illustrate these two
possibilities, highlighting the different roles
played by substitution and income effects.

Figure 6-13 illustrates the case where the

Figure 6-13 A NEGATIVE CROSS PRICE
ELASTICITY OF DEMAND. An increase in
the price of meals rotates the budget line from
AF to *AF'*. The substitution effect from *C* to *D*
is small. Indifference curves have large
curvature since the two goods are poor
substitutes in utility terms. The income effect
from *D* to *E* implies a large reduction in films
for two reasons. First, the reduction in real
income is larger the further to the right the
initial point *C*. Second, films are a luxury good
whose quantity demanded is sensitive to
changes in real income. Thus the income
effect outweighs the substitution effect. *E* lies
below *C*.

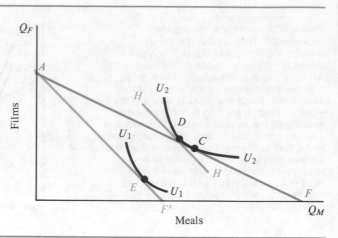

cross price elasticity is negative. A rise in the price of meals leads to a reduction in the quantity of films demanded. Figure 6-13 has three properties. First, the two goods are poor substitutes. Indifference curves are very curved. Moving away from balanced combinations of the two goods requires very large additional quantities of one good to compensate for small losses of the other good if a constant level of utility is to be preserved. When the price of meals is increased, the substitution effect towards films is very small. Moving leftwards along U_2U_2, we quickly attain the slope required to match the new relative prices of the two goods. The substitution effect from *C* to *D* adds little to the quantity of films demanded.

Second, films have a high income elasticity of demand. They are a luxury good. Hence the income effect, the move from *D* to *E* in response to the parallel downward shift in the budget line from *HH* to *AF'*, leads to a large reduction in the quantity of films demanded.

Finally, the point *C* lies well to the right on the original budget line *AF*. Meal expenditure takes up a large part of consumer budgets. Hence changes in meal prices lead to large changes in the purchasing power of consumer income. Not only is the quantity of films demanded very responsive to given changes in consumer real income, but in addition a given increase in meal prices has a large effect on consumer real income because meals are a large part of consumer budgets.

These last two effects lead to a large income effect, which reduces the quantity of films demanded. Because the substitution effect in

favour of films is small, the net effect is a reduction in the quantity of films demanded. An increase in meal prices reduces the quantity of films demanded. The cross price elasticity of demand is negative.

Figure 6-14 illustrates the opposite case, in which the cross price elasticity is positive. We now suppose the consumer is choosing between bread and other food and examine the effect of an increase in the price of bread. First, there are quite good substitutes for bread, for example potatoes. To preserve a given level of utility consumers do not require large additional amounts of one good to depart from balanced combinations of the two goods. Indifference curves have much less curvature than in Figure 6-13.

Second, other food has a relatively low income elasticity of demand. To the extent that higher bread prices reduce real consumer income, this has a relatively small income effect acting to reduce the quantity of other food demanded. Third, since bread forms a relatively small share in consumer budgets, the increase in bread prices has a relatively small effect in reducing consumer purchasing power. Comparing Figures 6-13 and 6-14, the parallel shift from *HH* to *AF'* is much smaller in the latter.

These last two effects mean that there is only a small income effect acting to reduce the quantity of other food demanded. In contrast, the substitution effect in favour of other food is large. Hence a rise in bread prices increases the quantity of other food demanded. The cross price elasticity is positive. This positive effect would be even stronger if 'other food' were an

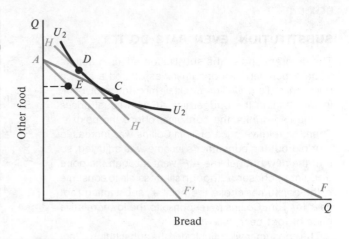

Figure 6-14 A POSITIVE CROSS PRICE ELASTICITY OF DEMAND. An increase in the price of bread rotates the budget line from *AF* to *AF'*. The substitution effect from *C* to *D* is large. Indifference curves have little curvature since the two goods are good substitutes in utility terms. The income effect from *D* to *E* is relatively small because the income elasticity of demand for other food is low and because the reduction in real income is small since bread forms a small share of the consumer budget. The substitution effect outweighs the income effect. *E* lies above *C*.

inferior good. The income effect would then act to increase the quantity of other food demanded, thereby reinforcing the substitution effects in this direction.

Table 6-2 summarizes the implications of our model of consumer choice for the demand response to a price change.

6-4 The Market Demand Curve

We have now established the foundations for the proposition that individual demand curves slope downwards. For the rest of this book we assume that this proposition is correct. We consider now what this implies for the market demand curve.

The market demand curve is the sum of the demand curves of all individuals in that market. It is obtained by asking, at each price, how much each person demands. By adding the quantities demanded by all consumers at that price we obtain the total quantity demanded at each price, the market demand curve. Since, as price is reduced, each person increases the

quantity demanded, the total quantity demanded must also increase as price falls. The market demand curve also slopes downwards.

We sometimes say that the market demand curve is the *horizontal addition of individual demand curves*. With prices on the vertical axis, we must add together individual quantities demanded at the same price. Figure 6-15 illustrates this idea for two consumers.

6-5 Complements and Substitutes

We have now given many illustrations of how income and substitution effects may be used to understand the consequences of a price change. Whatever the direction of the income effect, when there are only two goods the substitution effect is always unambiguous. The pure relative price effect leads the consumer to substitute away from the good whose relative price has risen towards the good whose relative price has fallen. In this sense, abstracting from income effects, goods are necessarily substitutes for one another in a two-good world.

Table 6-2 The effect of an increase in the price of good I on the quantity demanded of goods I and J

GOOD	TYPE	SUBSTITUTION EFFECT	INCOME EFFECT	TOTAL EFFECT
I	Normal	Negative	Negative	Negative
	Inferior	Negative	Positive	Ambiguous (usually negative)
J	Normal	Positive	Negative	Ambiguous
	Inferior	Positive	Positive	Positive

BOX 6-1

SUBSTITUTION: EVEN RATS DO IT

The diagram shows the substitution effect in action. In an experiment, a consumer was offered a choice between a Tom Collins cocktail mix and root beer. Initially, facing the budget line *AF* with equal prices for the two drinks, the consumer chose the point *e*. Then the relative price of Tom Collins was increased fourfold but the consumer's income was adjusted, so that the new budget line *A'F'* went through the point *e* originally chosen. Although still possible to consume *e*, the consumer chose the point *e'*, substituting root beer for Tom Collins in response to the lower relative price of root beer.

The consumer who illustrated the substitution effect so well was a white male albino rat. The budget line was the number of times he was required to push on two levers to get the two kinds of drink. Each push gave the rat some quantity of one drink but the quantity per push changed with the price of the drink. The experiment is reported in a paper by Professor John Kagel and others, 'Experimental Studies of

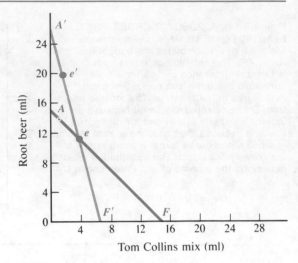

Consumer Demand Behaviour Using Laboratory Animals' (*Economic Inquiry*, March 1975).

The authors report one other fascinating finding. When large changes were made in relative prices, there were 'severe disruptions' in the rat's consumer choice behaviour. Many humans feel the same way.

When there are more than two goods we must recognize the possibility that some goods are consumed jointly – pipes and pipe tobacco, bread and cheese, electric cookers and electricity. We therefore have to recognize the possibility of *complementarity*.

When there are many goods it is still possible

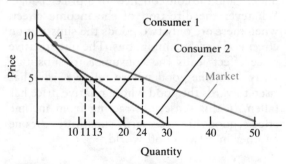

Figure 6-15 INDIVIDUAL DEMAND CURVES AND THE MARKET DEMAND CURVE. The market demand curve is the horizontal sum of individual demand curves. For example, if the price is £5, the quantity demanded by consumer 1 is 11 units, and the quantity demanded by consumer 2 is 13 units. The total quantity demanded in the market at £5 is thus 24 units, as shown on the market demand curve. The market demand curve is kinked at point A, the price at which consumer 2 first comes into the market.

to prove that there will be a substitution effect *away* from the goods whose relative price has risen. However, it is not necessarily true that there is a substitution *towards* all other goods. Consumers will tend to substitute *away* from goods consumed jointly with the good whose price has risen.

Suppose the price of pipes rises. What will happen to the demand for pipe tobacco? (We ignore the income effect since expenditure on pipes is a tiny fraction of household budgets, so real incomes are only slightly reduced. Since pipes and pipe tobacco are used jointly, we expect the demand for pipe tobacco will fall along with the quantity of pipes demanded. The demand curve for pipe tobacco shifts to the left in response to the increase in pipe prices.

Whenever goods are complements, an increase in the price of one good will reduce the demand for the complement both through the substitution effect (substituting away from the higher priced activity) and of course through the income effect (provided goods are normal).

6-6 Transfers in Kind

A transfer is a payment, usually by the government, for which no corresponding service is provided by the recipient. Social security payments are an example. Wages are not: the recipient is providing labour services in exchange for wages.

Although some transfers are in cash, some are *in kind*. For example, the poor may be given food stamps entitling them to buy food, but only food. The stamps cannot be spent on films or petrol. In this section we use the model of consumer choice to ask whether an in-kind transfer payment is preferred by the consumer to a cash transfer payment of equivalent monetary value.

The consumer has £100 to spend on food or films, each costing £10 per unit. Figure 6-16 shows the budget line AF. Now suppose in addition the government issues the consumer with food stamps worth four food units. For any point on the old budget line AF the consumer can now have an additional four units of food by using the food stamps. Moving horizontally to the right a distance of four food units we obtain the new budget line BF'. To remind ourselves that food stamps cannot be used for buying films, we can think of the new budget line as ABF', reminding ourselves

that the consumer can still consume at most 10 films.

Suppose the consumer had originally chosen point e on the old budget line AF. Since both goods are normal, the parallel shift in the budget line to ABF' – effectively, an increase in real income – will lead the consumer to choose a point to the north-east of e. This is precisely the point the consumer would have chosen had the transfer been in cash. When food costs £10 per unit, the cash-equivalent of four food units is £40, shifting the budget line to $A'F'$. Thus, if the consumer begins at e it makes no difference whether the transfer is in cash or in kind.

Suppose, however, that the consumer had begun at point e'. With a cash payment, the consumer might have wished to move to point c on the budget line $A'F'$. The transfer in kind, by restricting the consumer to the budget line ABF', prevents the consumer reaching the preferred point c. Perhaps instead the consumer moves to the point B, which can be reached. The point B must yield the consumer less utility than point c: when the consumer was given a cash payment and could choose either, c was preferred to B.

Cash transfers allow consumers to spend the extra income in any way that they desire. Transfers in kind may limit the consumer's option. Where they do, the increase in consumer utility will be less than under a cash transfer of the same monetary value.

Yet transfers in kind are politically popular. The electorate wants to know that money raised in taxation is being wisely spent. Some who favour transfers in kind will argue that the poor really do not know how to spend their money wisely and may spend cash transfers on 'undesirable' goods such as alcohol or entertainment rather than on 'desirable' goods such as food or housing.

One view says that people can best choose for themselves, whereas the other says that people may not act in their own best interests. This issue is not merely one of economics but also of philosophy, involving wider questions such as liberty and paternalism. In so far as people are capable of judging their own self-interest, economic analysis is clear: people will be better off, or at least no worse off, if they are given transfers in cash rather than in kind.

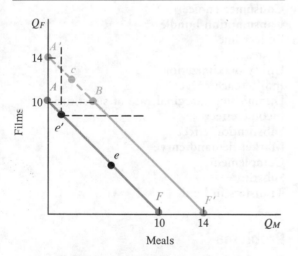

Figure 6-16 TRANSFERS IN CASH AND IN KIND. A food transfer in kind may leave the consumer less satisfied than a cash transfer of the same value. A consumer beginning at e' might wish to spend less than the full in-kind allowance on food, moving to a point such as c. The budget line $A'BF'$ is available under a cash transfer. The in-kind transfer restricts the budget line to ABF', ruling out points $A'B'$.

Summary

1 The theory of demand is based on the assumption that the consumer, given the budget constraint, seeks to reach the maximum possible level of utility.

2 The budget line shows the maximum affordable quantity of one good for each given quantity of the other good. The position of the budget line is determined by income and prices alone. Its slope reflects only relative prices.

3 Because the consumer prefers more to less, he or she will always select a point on the budget line. The consumer has a problem of choice. Along the budget line, more of one good can be obtained only by sacrificing some of the other good.

4 Consumer tastes can be represented by a map of non-intersecting indifference curves. Along each indifference curve, utility is constant. Higher indifference curves are preferred to lower indifference curves. Since the consumer prefers more to less, indifference curves must slope downwards. To preserve a given level of utility, increases in the quantity of one good must be offset by reductions in the quantity of the other good.

5 Indifference curves reflect the principle of a diminishing marginal rate of substitution. Their slope becomes flatter as we move along them to the right. To preserve utility, consumers will sacrifice ever smaller amounts of one good to obtain successive unit increases in the amount of the other good.

6 Utility-maximizing consumers choose the consumption bundle at which the highest reachable indifference curve is just tangent to the budget line. At this point the market trade-off between goods, the slope of the budget line, just matches the utility trade-off between goods, the slope of the indifference curve.

7 At constant prices, an increase in income leads to a parallel outward shift in the budget line. If goods are normal, the quantity demanded will increase.

8 A change in the price of one good rotates the budget line around the point at which none of that good is purchased. Such a price change has an income effect and a substitution effect. The income effect of a price increase is to reduce the quantity demanded for all normal goods. The substitution effect, induced by relative price movements alone, leads consumers to substitute away from the good whose relative price has increased.

9 In a two-good world, the goods are necessarily substitutes. The substitution effect is unambiguous. With many goods, the pure substitution effect of a price increase will also reduce the demand for goods that are complementary to the good whose price has risen.

10 A rise in the price of a good must lower its quantity demanded if the good is a normal good. For inferior goods, the income effect operates in the opposite direction but empirically never seems to dominate the substitution effect in this case. Demand curves slope downwards.

11 The market demand curve is the horizontal sum of individual demand curves, at each price adding together the individual quantities demanded.

12 Consumers prefer to receive transfers in cash rather than in kind, if the two transfers have the same monetary value. A transfer in kind may restrict the choices a consumer can make.

Key Terms

Consumer choice
Consumption bundle
Budget line
Tastes
Utility maximization
Indifference curves
Diminishing marginal rate of substitution
Income effect
Substitution effect
Market demand curve
Complement
Substitute
Transfers in kind

Problems

1 A consumer's income is £50. Food costs £5 per unit and films cost £2 per unit. (*a*) Draw the budget line. Choose a point *e* for the optimal initial consumption bundle. (*b*) Suppose now the price of food falls to £2.50. Draw the new budget line and indicate what can be said about the new consumption point if both goods are normal. Label the new consumption point *e'*. (*c*) Suppose the price of films

also falls to £1. Draw the new budget line and indicate where the consumer now chooses. Label this point e''. (d) How does e'' differ from e? Explain your answer.

2 The own price elasticity of demand for food is negative. The demand for food is inelastic. An increase in food prices raises spending on food. Hence higher food prices imply that less is spent on all other goods and that the quantity demanded of each of these other goods must fall. Discuss carefully these statements and identify any that you think might be wrong.

3 Suppose films are normal but transport is inferior. Draw the income expansion path for films and transport as incomes rise.

4 'If an increase in the price of drinks raises the demand for chocolate, an increase in the price of chocolate must increase the demand for drinks.' Is this true?

5 Suppose Londoners have a given income. They consume a large variety of goods, including petrol and weekend trips to the countryside (a three-hour drive). Now let the price of petrol double. (a) What is the effect on the demand for weekend trips to the countryside? Discuss both the income and substitution effects. (b) Use a demand and supply diagram to show what happens to the price of hotel rooms in the countryside at weekends. (c) Suppose there is a holiday place closer to London. What happens to the demand for hotel rooms there?

6 Common Fallacies Show why the following statements are incorrect: (a) The average consumer has never heard of an indifference curve or a budget line. Consumers don't choose the point on the budget line which is tangent to the highest possible indifference curve. (b) If inflation leads to a doubling of all incomes and prices, the budget line will shift and consumers will reduce quantities of each good demanded. (c) If in (b) consumers demand the same quantities as before, this proves that income effects can be neglected.

Appendix: Consumer Choice with Measurable Utility

We developed the theory of consumer choice under the very general assumption that consumers could rank or order different bundles according to the utility or satisfaction they gave. Saying bundle A gave higher utility than bundle B just meant that the consumer preferred A to B. Nothing we said required the consumer to

decide *by how much* A was preferred to B. Higher indifference curves were better, but we did not need to know how much better.

In the nineteenth century, some economists believed that utility levels could actually be measured. It was as if each consumer had a *utility meter* measuring his happiness. The further to the right the needle on his utility meter, the happier he was. The units on this meter were traditionally marked off in *utils*. Nowadays this seems a bit strange: are you 2.9 times as happy if you get an extra week's holiday?

Nevertheless, analysing consumer choice when utility *is* measurable in this way is quite interesting, even though we have been able to derive all the main propositions in the text without this additional assumption. The (rather robot-like) individual whose utility can be exactly calibrated in utils we shall call Fred.

Fred goes to rock concerts and eats hamburgers. His utility depends on the bundle of hamburgers and concerts he consumes. For a given consumption of one of these goods, he prefers more of the other to less. His utility goes up; he gets more utils.

> The *marginal utility* of a good is the increase in total utility obtained by consuming one more unit of that good, for given consumption of other goods.

Thus, if Fred gets 67 utils of utility from consuming 10 hamburgers and 1 rock concert, and 70 utils of utility from 11 hamburgers but still 1 rock concert, his marginal utility of the eleventh hamburger is $(70 - 67 = 3)$ utils.

Fred was hardly going hungry. He had 10 hamburgers at his only concert. He cannot have got much from an extra one; indeed, he got only an extra 3 utils. In contrast, if Fred had only 2 hamburgers at one concert (say, giving him 20 utils), he might rather have enjoyed one more hamburger (say, taking his utils to 27). The marginal utility of that extra hamburger is $(27 - 20 = 7)$ utils. Fred's tastes obey the law of diminishing marginal utility.

> A consumer has *diminishing marginal utility* from a good if each extra unit consumed adds successively less to total utility.

Figure 6-A1 plots Fred's marginal utility of hamburgers. He gets fewer *extra* utils from extra consumption of hamburgers, the more he

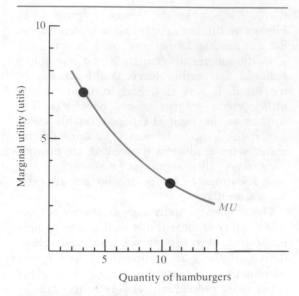

Figure 6-A1 MARGINAL UTILITY. *MU* shows marginal utility, the amount by which total utils increase when consumption increases one unit. Diminishing marginal utility means that *MU* falls as quantity rises.

is already consuming; we show this as the downward-sloping schedule *MU*.

Fred has a given income to spend. Once we know the prices of rock concerts and hamburgers, we can work out his budget line. How does Fred choose the affordable point on this line at which to consume? He maximizes his utility.

Suppose the price of hamburgers in pounds is P_H and the price of concerts is P_C. Thus, if MU_H is the marginal utility Fred gets from another hamburger, he gets an extra number of utils equal to MU_H/P_H for each extra pound spent on hamburgers. And he gets an extra MU_C/P_C for each extra pound spent on concerts.

Suppose MU_H/P_H is bigger than MU_C/P_C. An extra pound spent on hamburgers increases Fred's utility more than an extra pound spent on concerts. More importantly, if Fred spends one *extra* pound on hamburgers and one *less* pound on concerts his total utils will rise: he gains more from hamburgers than he loses from concerts. He can increase utility *without spending more*. He will always want to transfer spending towards the good that yields more marginal utility per pound spent. It is easy to see how Fred maximizes his utility. He

spends all his income (he is *on* rather than *inside* his budget line), and he adjusts his spending between hamburgers and concerts until

$$MU_H/P_H = MU_C/P_C \qquad (A1)$$

Only when this condition holds can Fred not rearrange the division of his total spending to increase his utility.[5]

> The consumer maximizes utility by choosing the consumption bundle which satisfies the budget constraint and for which the ratio of marginal utility to price is the same for every good.

Given Fred's *utility function* (the meter from which we read off utils depending on the quantities of hamburgers and concerts Fred consumes), the prices P_H and P_C for hamburgers and concerts, and his income, we can now derive Fred's demand curves for hamburgers and concerts.

Deriving Demand Curves

Suppose the price of hamburgers falls. For given hamburger consumption, MU_H/P_H has risen because hamburger prices have fallen. MU_H/P_H now exceeds MU_C/P_C for concerts. This violates equation (A1). To maximize utility, Fred will have to change the quantities he demands.

If Fred buys *more* hamburgers when the price *falls*, the law of diminishing marginal utility implies that MU_H will fall as Fred increases the quantity of hamburgers demanded in response to their cheaper price. MU_H/P_H moves towards MU_C/P_C, as required by equation (A1). We call this the *substitution effect* of the relative change in the price of hamburgers and concerts. On its own, the substitution effect suggests that *demand curves slope down*: when the price of hamburgers falls, the quantity demanded increases.

---

[5] Equation (A1) implies $MU_H/MU_C = P_H/P_C$. Multiplying both sides by (-1), the right-hand side is simply the slope of the budget line, which we know depends only on relative prices. The left-hand side is simply the marginal rate of substitution: if the marginal utility of one hamburger is 2 and of one concert is 4, then $-MU_H/MU_C = -\frac{1}{2}$. Equivalently, we can exchange 1 hamburger for $\frac{1}{2}$ a concert without altering total utility, which is precisely what the marginal rate of substitution measures. Hence equation (A1) is equivalent to saying that the slope of the indifference curve, measured by the marginal rate of substitution, must equal the slope of the budget line. This is precisely the tangency condition we derived in the text without the use of measurable utility!

BOX 6-2

MARGINAL UTILITY AND THE WATER DIAMOND PARADOX

Nineteenth-century economists were puzzled as to why the price of water, essential for survival, was so much lower than that for decorative diamonds. One answer is that diamonds are scarcer than water. Yet consumers clearly get more total utility from water (without it they die) than from diamonds. The concept of marginal utility solves the problem.

Equation (A2) tells us that consumers keep buying a good until the ratio of its *marginal* utility to price equals that for other goods. *At the margin*, the last litre of water we drink or use in the shower gives very little extra utility. At the margin, the last diamond still makes a big difference. People are willing to pay more for extra diamonds than for extra water.

In terms of a figure like Figure 6-A1, the marginal utility schedule MU is *very* high for the first few drops of water. Not dying is worth lots of utils. But most of us are a long way down this schedule, using lots of water to the point where its marginal value to us has become quite low.

However we must be careful; a second effect is at work. Cheaper hamburger prices increase the purchasing power of Fred's given money income. We need to think about the effect of this on Fred's marginal utility. Suppose first that hamburgers are a normal good; Fred wants more when the purchasing power of his income rises. We can think of higher income as shifting Fred's marginal utility schedule upwards in Figure 6-A2.

This *income effect* means that Fred finds that MU_H/P_H rises not only because P_H falls but also because, with a higher marginal utility schedule for hamburgers, MU_H rises at any particular level of hamburger consumption. Fred will have to increase his hamburger demand yet further to slide down the higher schedule (diminishing marginal utility) to restore MU_H/P_H to equality with MU_C/P_C. Thus, for normal goods the income effect reinforces the substitution effect. Demand curves must slope down.

Suppose however that hamburgers are an inferior good. In Figure 6-A2 we could show this as a downward shift in the marginal utility schedule when the purchasing power of Fred's income increases. At his original consumption bundle, it is now possible that MU_H has fallen a lot; specifically, it could have fallen more than P_H the price of hamburgers. If so, Fred will have to *reduce* his hamburger consumption in order to increase its marginal utility and restore MU_H/P_H to equality with MU_C/P_C as utility maximization requires.

Thus, for inferior goods the income effect goes in the opposite direction to the substitution effect. If the income effect is powerful enough, it could win out. Lower hamburger prices would then reduce the quantity of hamburgers demanded. Demand curves would slope upwards! As we discuss in the text, we call such goods Giffen goods. In practice they are rarely if ever found. It is safe to assume that demand curves slope down in practice.

Modern economists are pretty sniffy about measurable utility, preferring the more general indifference curve analysis we used in the text. But indifference curves seem a bit tricky the first time you meet them, and you need to practice using them before you get comfortable with them. In contrast, measurable utility and the simple idea of diminishing marginal utility allows an easier introduction to the basic properties of demand curves and consumer choice we have developed in this chapter.

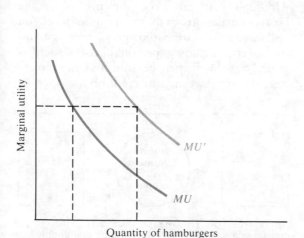

Figure 6-A2 AN INCREASE IN THE PURCHASING POWER OF INCOME. If hamburgers are a normal good, higher income shifts the marginal utility schedule upwards. The quantity demand must increase if marginal utility is to remain unaltered.

7

Business Organization and Behaviour

Having analysed demand in the last two chapters, we turn now to supply. How do firms decide how much to produce and offer for sale? Can a single theory of supply describe the behaviour of a wide range of different producers, from giant companies such as ICI and Shell to the self-employed ice cream vendor with a van?

For each possible output level a firm will wish to know the answer to two questions: how much will it *cost* to produce this output and how much *revenue* will be earned by selling it. For each output level, production costs depend on technology that determines how many inputs are needed to produce this output, and on input prices that determine what the firm will have to pay for these inputs. The revenue obtained from selling output depends on the demand curve faced by the firm. The demand curve determines the price for which any given output quantity can be sold and hence the revenue that the firm will earn. Figure 7-1 emphasizes that it is the interaction of costs and revenues that determines how much output firms wish to supply.

Profits are the excess of revenues over costs. The key to the theory of supply is the assumption that all firms have the same objective: to make as much profit as possible. By examining how revenues and costs change with the level of output produced and sold, the firm can select the output level which maximizes its profits. To understand how firms make output decisions we must therefore analyse the determination of revenues and costs.

We introduce two essential concepts in the theory of supply, *marginal cost* and *marginal revenue*. Although later chapters give a more detailed analysis, these concepts form the framework for the economist's approach to supply. Finally, because the assumption of profit maximization forms the cornerstone of

this approach, we discuss the plausibility of this assumption and examine alternative views of what firms' aims might be.

7-1 Business Organization

In the UK businesses are self-employed sole traders, partnerships, or companies. Self-employment increased throughout the 1980s and sole traders are by far the commonest type of business organization, though each sole trader operates on a relatively small scale. Partnerships operate on a larger scale and companies are larger still. The largest companies have sales measured in billions of pounds.

A *sole trader* is a business owned by a single individual who is fully entitled to the income or revenue of the business and is fully responsible for any losses the business suffers. You might open a health food shop, renting the premises and paying someone to stand at the till. Although you can keep the profits, if the business makes losses that you cannot meet you will have to declare bankruptcy. Your remaining assets, including personal assets such as your house, will then be sold and the money shared out between your creditors.

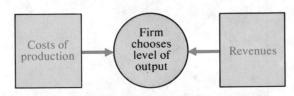

Figure 7-1 THE THEORY OF SUPPLY. Firms' decisions about how much to produce and supply depend both on the costs of production and on the revenues they receive from selling the output. This is the essence of the theory of supply. For the rest of this chapter and in the next chapter we fill in the details of this picture.

However, your health food shop may prosper. You need money to expand, to buy bigger stocks, better premises, a delivery van, and office furniture. To raise all this money, you may decide to go into partnership with some other people.

A *partnership* is a business arrangement in which two or more people jointly own a business, sharing the profits and being jointly responsible for any losses. Not all the partners need to be active. Some may have put up some money for a share of the profits but take no active part in running the business. Some large partnerships, such as famous law and accounting firms, may have over a hundred partners, usually all taking an active interest in the business.

Nevertheless, partnerships still have *unlimited liability*. In the last resort, the owners' personal assets must be sold to cover losses that cannot otherwise be met. This is one reason why firms where trust is involved – for example, firms of solicitors or accountants – are partnerships. It is a signal to the customers that the people running the business are willing to put their own personal wealth behind the firm's obligations.

Any business needs some financial capital, money to start the business and finance its growth, paying for stocks, machinery, or advertising before the corresponding revenue is earned. Firms of lawyers, accountants, or doctors, businesses that rely primarily on human expertise, need relatively little money for such purposes. The necessary funds can be raised from the partners and, possibly, by a loan from the bank. Businesses that require large initial expenditure on machinery, or are growing very rapidly, may need much larger amounts of initial funds. Because of legal complications, it may not make sense to take on an enormous number of partners. Instead, it makes sense to form a company.

A *company* is an organization legally allowed to produce and trade. Unlike a partnership, it has a legal existence distinct from that of its owners. Ownership is divided among shareholders. The original shareholders are the people who started the business, but now they have sold shares of the profits to outsiders. By selling these entitlements to share in the profits, the business has been able to raise new funds.

For *public companies* these shares can be resold on the *stock exchange* to anyone prepared to pay the going price. Trading on the stock exchange, reported in most daily newspapers, is primarily the sale and resale of existing shares in public companies. However, even the largest company occasionally needs to issue additional new shares to raise money for especially large projects.

To buy into a company, a shareholder must purchase shares on the stock exchange at the equilibrium share price, which just balances buyers and sellers of the company's shares on that particular day. In return for this initial outlay, shareholders earn a return in two ways. First, the company makes regular *dividend* payments, paying out to shareholders that part of the profits that the firm does not wish to re-invest in the business. Second, the shareholders may make *capital gains* (or losses). If you buy ICI shares for £600 each and then everyone decides ICI profits and dividends will be unexpectedly high, you may be able to resell the shares for £650, making a capital gain of £50 per share on the transactions.

The shareholders of a company have *limited liability*. The most they can lose is the money they originally spent buying shares. Unlike sole traders and partners, shareholders cannot be forced to sell their personal possessions when the business cannot pay. At worst, the shares merely become worthless.

Companies are run by boards of directors. The board of directors makes decisions about how the firm is run but must submit an annual report to the shareholders. At the annual meeting the shareholders can vote to sack the directors, each shareholder having as many votes as the number of shares owned.

Companies are the main form of organization of big businesses.

7-2 Revenues, Costs, and Profits

A firm's *revenue* is the amount it earns by selling goods or services in a given period such as a year. The firm's *costs* are the expenses incurred in producing goods or services during the period. *Profits* are the excess of revenues over costs.

Although these ideas are simple, in practice the calculation of revenues, costs, and profits for a large business is complicated. Otherwise we

Figure 7-2
Rent-a-Person
Income Statement
Year Ending 31 December 1990

Revenue	£1 000 000
(100 000 hours, £10/hour)	
Deduct expenses (costs)	
Wages	£700 000
Advertising	50 000
Office rent	50 000
Other expenses	100 000
	£900 000
Profits before tax	£100 000
Taxes paid	25 000
Profits after tax	£75 000

would not need so many accountants. We begin with a simple example.

Rent-a-Person is a firm that hires people whom it then rents out to other firms that need temporary workers. Rent-a-Person charges £10 per hour per worker but pays its workers only £7 per hour. During 1990 it rented 100 000 hours of labour. Business expenses, including leasing an office, buying advertising space, and paying telephone bills, came to £200 000. Figure 7-2 shows the *income statement* or *profit-and-loss account* for 1990. Profits or net income before taxes were £100 000. Taxes came to £25 000. Rent-a-Person's after-tax profits in 1990 were £75 000.

Now we can discuss some of the complications in calculating profits.

Outstanding Bills

People do not always pay their bills immediately. At the end of 1990, Rent-a-Person has not been paid for all the workers it hired out during the year. On the other hand, it has not paid its telephone bill for December. From an economic viewpoint, the right definition of revenues and costs relates to the activities carried out during the year whether or not payments have yet been made.

This distinction between economic revenues and costs and actual receipts and payments raises the important concept of cash flow.

A firm's *cash flow* is the net amount of money actually received during the period.

Profitable firms may still have a poor cash flow, for example when customers are slow to pay their bills.

Part of the problem of running a business is that cash flow at the beginning is bound to be slow. Set-up costs must be incurred before revenues start to flow in. That is why firms need financial capital to start the business. If the business prospers, revenues will build up and eventually there will be a healthy cash inflow.

Capital and Depreciation

Physical capital is the machinery, equipment, and buildings used in production.

Rent-a-Person owns little physical capital. Instead, it rents office space, typewriters, and desks. In practice, businesses frequently buy physical capital. Economists use 'capital' to denote goods not entirely used up in the production process during the period. Buildings and lorries are capital because they can be used again in the next year. Electricity is not a capital good because it is used up entirely during the period. Economists also use the terms 'durable goods' or 'physical assets' to describe capital goods.

How should the cost of a capital good such as typewriters be treated in calculating profits and costs? The essential idea is that it is the cost of *using* rather than *buying* a piece of capital equipment that should be treated as part of the firm's costs within the year. If Rent-a-Person leases all its capital equipment, its costs include merely the rentals paid in leasing capital goods.

Suppose however that Rent-a-Person buys eight typewriters at the beginning of the year for £1000 each. It should *not count* £8000 as the cost of typewriters in calculating costs and profits for that year. Rather, the cost should be calculated as the reduction in the value of the typewriters over the year. Suppose the wear-and-tear on the typewriters over the year has reduced their value from £1000 to £700 each. The economic cost of the use of eight typewriters over the year is £2400 (8 × £300). This amount of depreciation is the cost during the year.[1]

---

[1] There is a *second* economic cost – the interest payments on the money used to buy the typewriters – which we discuss shortly.

Depreciation is the loss in value resulting from the use of machinery during the period.

The cost *during the period* of using a capital good is the depreciation or loss of value of that good, not its purchase price.

The existence of depreciation again leads to a difference between economic profits and cash flow. When a capital good is first purchased there is a large cash outflow, much larger than the depreciation cost of using the good during the first year. Profits may be high but cash flow low. However, in subsequent years the firm makes no further cash outlay, having already paid for the capital goods, but must still calculate depreciation as an economic cost since the resale value of goods is reduced still further. Cash flow will now be higher than economic profit.

The consequence of treating depreciation rather than purchase price as the true economic cost is thus to spread the initial cost over the life of the capital goods; but that is not the reason for undertaking the calculation in this way. Rent-a-Person could always have sold its typewriters for £5600 after one year, restricting its costs to £2400. The fact that the firm chose to keep them for re-use in the next year indicates that the latter strategy is even more profitable. Hence the true economic cost of *using* the typewriters in the first year can be at most £2400.

Inventories

Inventories are goods held in stock by the firm for future sales.

If production were instantaneous, firms could produce to meet orders as they arose. In fact, production takes time. Firms will hold inventories to meet future demand.

Suppose at the beginning of 1990, the Rover Group has a stock of 100 000 cars completed and available for sale. During the year it produces 1 million new cars and sells 950 000. By the end of the year its inventories of finished cars have risen to 150 000. How does this complicate the profit calculation? Revenues accrue from the sale of 950 000 cars. Should costs be based on sales of 950 000 cars or the 1 million actually made?

The answer is that costs should relate to the 950 000 cars actually sold. The 50 000 cars added to stocks are like capital the firm made for itself, available for sale in the following period. There was a cash outflow to pay for the manufacture of 1 million cars but part of this cash outflow was for the purchase of inventories which will provide cash revenue the following year without requiring any cash outlay on production.

Borrowing

Firms usually borrow to finance their set-up and expansion costs, buying capital goods, solicitors' fees for the paperwork in registering the company, and so on. There is interest to be paid on the money borrowed. This interest is part of the cost of doing business and should be counted as part of the costs.

The Balance Sheet

The income statement or profit-and-loss account of Figure 7-2 tells us about the flow of money during a given year. We also paint a picture of the position the firm has reached as a result of all its past trading operations. The *balance sheet*, a sheet listing the assets the firm owns and the liabilities for which it is responsible, gives such a picture at a point in time, for example at the year end.

Figure 7-3 is a balance sheet for Snark International on 31 December 1990.

Assets are what the firm owns.

The assets are shown on the left. Snark has some cash in the bank, is owed money by customers which is entered as 'accounts receivable', and has large inventories in its warehouses. It owns a factory which originally cost £250 000 but is now worth only £200 000 because of depreciation. Its other equipment, listed together, has also depreciated and is now worth £180 000. The total value of Snark assets is £590 000.

Liabilities are what the firm owes.

The liabilities are shown on the right. They include unpaid bills and salaries, the mortgage on the factory, and a bank load for short-term cash needs. The total value of debts is £350 000. The *net worth* of Snark International is £240 000, the excess of its assets over its liabilities.

Figure 7-3

Snark International
Balance Sheet
31 December 1990

ASSETS		LIABILITIES	
Cash	£40 000	Accounts payable	£90 000
Accounts receivable	70 000	Salaries payable	50 000
Inventories	100 000	Mortgage from insurance company	150 000
Factory building (original value £250 000)	200 000	Bank loan	60 000
Other equipment (original value £300 000)	180 000		350 000
		Net worth	240 000
	590 000		590 000

We have shown the net worth on the liabilities side. Because the firm is owned by the shareholders, the net worth is really owed to them; it is a liability of the firm to the shareholders.

You wish to make a take-over bid for Snark International. Should you offer £240 000, the net worth of the company? Probably not. Snark International is a live company with good prospects for future growth and a proven record. You are bidding not merely for its physical and financial assets minus liabilities but also for the firm as a going concern. You will also get its reputation, customer loyalty and a host of intangibles which economists call *goodwill*. If Snark is a sound company it will be worth bidding more than £240 000.

Alternatively, you may feel that Snark's accountants have undervalued the resale value of its assets. If you can buy the company for close to £240 000 you might make a profit selling off the separate pieces of equipment and buildings, a practice known as 'asset-stripping'.

Earnings

Finally, we must consider what the firm does with its profits after taxes. It can pay them out to shareholders as dividends, or keep them in the firm as retained earnings.

Retained earnings are the part of after-tax profits that is ploughed back into the business rather than paid out to shareholders as dividends.

Retained earnings affect the balance sheet. If they are kept as cash or used to purchase new equipment, they increase the asset side of the balance sheet. Alternatively, they may be used to reduce the firm's liabilities, for example by repaying the bank loan. Either way, the firm's net worth is increased.

Opportunity Cost and Accounting Costs

The income statement and the balance sheet of a company provide a useful guide to how that company is doing. We have already hinted that economists and accountants do not always take the same view of costs and profits. Whereas the accountant is chiefly interested in describing the actual receipts and payments of a company, the economist is chiefly interested in the role of costs and profits as determinants of the firm's supply decision, the allocation of resources to particular activities. Accounting methods can be seriously misleading in two ways.

Economists identify the cost of using a resource not as the payment actually made but as its opportunity cost.

Opportunity cost is the amount lost by not using the resource (labour or capital) in its best alternative use.

To show that this is the right measure of costs, given the questions economists wish to study, we give two examples.

Any persons working in their own businesses should take into account the cost of their own labour time spent in the business. A self-employed sole trader might draw up an income statement such as Figure 7-2, find that profits were £20 000 per annum, and conclude that this business was a good thing. But this conclusion neglects the opportunity cost of the individual's labour, the money that could have been earned by working elsewhere. If that individual could have earned a salary of £25 000 working for someone else, being self-employed is actually *losing* the person £5000 per annum even though the business is making an accounting profit of £20 000. If we wish to understand the incentives that the market provides to guide people towards particular occupations, we must use the economic concept of opportunity cost, not the accounting concept of actual payments. Including the opportunity cost of £25 000 in the income statement would quickly convince the individual that the business was not such a good idea.

The second place where opportunity cost must be counted is with respect to capital. Somebody has put up the money to start the business. In calculating accounting profits, no cost is attached to the use of owned (as opposed to borrowed) financial capital. This financial capital could have been used elsewhere, in an interest-bearing bank account or perhaps to buy shares in a different company. The opportunity cost of that financial capital is included in the *economic* costs of the business but not its accounting costs. For example, if the owners could have earned a return of 10 per cent elsewhere, the opportunity cost of their funds is 10 per cent times the money they put up. If, after deducting this cost, the business still makes a profit, economists call this 'supernormal profit'.

> *Supernormal profit* is the profit over and above the return which the owners could have earned by lending their money elsewhere at the market rate of interest.

Supernormal profits provide the true economic indicator of how well the owners are doing by tying up their funds in the business. Supernormal profits, not accounting profits, are the measure that will explain the incentive to shift resources into or out of a business.

These are the two most important adjustments between accounting and economic notions of costs and profits. In other cases there may be minor differences – for example, since it is hard to calculate the resale value of a second-

ACCOUNTING COSTS: INCOME STATEMENT	
Revenues	£80 000
Costs	50 000
Accounting profit	£30 000

OPPORTUNITY COSTS: INCOME STATEMENT		
Revenues		£80 000
Costs:		
Accounting costs	£50 000	
Cost of owner's time	25 000	
Opportunity cost of financial capital (£30 000) used in firm, at 10%	3 000	78 000
Economic profit (supernormal)		£ 2 000

Figure 7-4   ACCOUNTING AND OPPORTUNITY COSTS: TWO IMPORTANT ADJUSTMENTS. Economic costs represent the opportunity costs of resources used in production. Accounting costs include most economic costs but are likely to omit costs of the owner's time and the opportunity cost of financial capital used in the firm. Economic (supernormal) profit deducts the right measure of economic costs from revenues.

hand factory, economic and accounting approaches to depreciation may vary slightly. In many cases the two approaches are the same – for example, the wages paid by farmers to students for help in picking crops are not only an accounting cost but an economic cost. Without making these payments, farmers would not have been able to attract temporary student labour resources to the activity of crop picking.

Figure 7-4 summarizes the two most important adjustments that must be made to accounting costs and profits to get economic measures of costs and profits.

7-3 Firms and Profit Maximization

Firms are in business to make money. Economists assume that firms make supply and output decisions so as to make as much money as possible, in other words to *maximize profits*.

Some economists and business executives question the assumption that firms have the sole aim of maximizing profits. For example, in the last section we described a self-employed individual making £20 000 per annum who could have made £25 000 per annum in a different job. Individuals who like to be their own boss may happily exchange the extra £5000 for the additional independence. Such a business is maximizing not the net income but the total satisfaction of its owner.

Ownership and Control

A more significant reason to question the assumption of profit maximization is that large firms are not run by their owners. A large company is run by a salaried board of directors and by the managers this board appoints. Although at the annual meeting the shareholders have the opportunity to dismiss the board, in practice this happens rarely. The directors are the experts with the information; it is hard for the shareholders, even in bad times, to be sure that different directors would raise the profitability of the company.

Economists call this a separation of ownership and control. Although the shareholders clearly want the maximum possible profit, the directors who actually make the decisions have the opportunity to pursue different objectives. Do the managers and directors have an incentive to act other than in the interests of the shareholders?

Managers' salaries are usually higher the larger is the firm. Some economists have argued that this leads managers to aim for size and growth rather than the maximum possible profit. For example, such managers might spend large sums on advertising even though this secured only a relatively small addition to total sales.

Nevertheless, there are two reasons why the assumption of profit maximization is a good place from which to begin. Even if the shareholders cannot recognize that profits are lower than they might be, other firms with experience in the industry may catch on faster. If profits are low, share prices will be low. By mounting a take-over, another company can buy the shares cheaply, sack the existing managers, restore profit-maximizing policies, and make a handsome capital gain as the share prices then rise once the stock market perceives the improvement in profits.

Alternatively, being aware of the opportunity for managerial discretion, shareholders may try to ensure that the interests of the managers and the shareholders coincide. By giving senior managers a quantity of shares that is small relative to the total number of shares but large relative to managerial salaries, shareholders can try to ensure that senior managers care about profits as much as other shareholders do.

For these reasons, the assumption that firms try to maximize profits is more robust than might first be imagined. We now use this assumption to develop the theory of supply.

7-4 The Firm's Production Decisions: An Overview

We begin by focusing on how much output should be produced. Many details are left for later chapters, but the really important ideas of marginal cost and marginal revenue are introduced here.

Imagine a firm that makes snarks. Of the many ways to make snarks, some use a lot of labour and few machines, others a lot of machines but little labour. Not only does the firm know the different techniques for making snarks, it also knows the wage rate for a skilled snark lathe operator and the rental on a snark lathe. The firm also knows its demand curve – how much it would earn by selling different quantities of snarks at each possible price.

The objective is to maximize profits by choosing the best level of output to produce. Changing the output level will affect both the costs of production and the revenues obtained from sales. We now show how production costs and demand conditions interact to determine the level of output chosen by a profit-maximizing firm.

Cost Minimization

Any firm that is maximizing profits will certainly want to be producing its chosen output level at the minimum possible cost. Otherwise, by producing the same output level at lower cost it could increase profits. Thus a profit-maximizing firm must be producing its output at minimum cost.

The Total Cost Curve

Knowing the available production methods and the costs of hiring labour and machinery, the firm's managers can calculate the lower cost at which each level of output can be produced.

To make a few snarks per annum it is probably cheapest to use some workers but hardly any machinery. To make more snarks, it probably makes sense to use more machinery per worker.

Table 7-1 shows the minimum costs at which each output level can be produced. The firm incurs a cost of £10 even when no output is produced.[2] This cost includes the expenses of being in business at all – running an office, renting a telephone, and so on. Thereafter, costs rise with the level of production. The costs shown in the table include the opportunity costs of all resources used in production. Total costs of production are higher the more is produced, but costs need to rise smoothly as the level of output increases. At intermediate levels of output, such as 4 or 5 units per week, costs rise quite slowly as output rises. At high

---

[2] Imagine the numbers in Table 7-1 are in thousands. To keep things simpler, we have left out the thousands.

Table 7-1 Total costs of production

OUTPUT (goods produced/week)	TOTAL COSTS (£/week)
0	10
1	25
2	36
3	44
4	51
5	59
6	69
7	81
8	95
9	111
10	129

levels of output, such as 9 units per week, costs rise sharply as output increases. For example, at high levels of output the firm may have to pay the workers extra money to work at weekends.

Total Revenue

Information on costs is not sufficient to assess profits. The firm must also think about its revenue, which depends on the demand for its product.

Table 7-2 shows the demand curve facing the firm. At a price of £21 it can sell only one snark. The lower the price, the more snarks it can sell: its demand curve slopes down. Given the prices at which each quantity can be sold, in Table 7-2 we calculate the firm's total revenue from selling different quantities of snarks per week. Total revenue is just price times quantity, as shown in the third column.

The fourth column shows the total cost of producing each output level. The last column shows weekly profits, the difference between revenues and costs. At low levels of output, profits are negative. At the highest level of output, 10 units per week, profits are again negative. At intermediate levels of output, the firm is making profits.

The highest level of profits is £27 per week and the corresponding output level is 6 snarks per week. To maximize profits the firm produces 6 snarks per week. At £16 each, this brings in £96 in total revenue. Costs of production, properly calculated to include the opportunity cost of all resources used, are

---

Table 7-2 Revenues, costs, and profits

(1) OUTPUT (goods produced/week)	(2) PRICE RECEIVED PER UNIT (£)	(3) TOTAL REVENUE (PRICE × OUTPUT) (£/week)	(4) TOTAL COSTS (FROM TABLE 7-2) (£/week)	(5) PROFITS (TOTAL REVENUE MINUS TOTAL COSTS)
0	—	0	10	−10
1	21	21	25	− 4
2	20	40	36	4
3	19	57	44	13
4	18	72	51	21
5	17	85	59	26
6	16	96	69	27
7	15	105	81	24
8	14	112	95	17
9	13	117	111	6
10	12	120	129	− 9

£69 per week, leaving a profit of £27 per week. The level of output and profits chosen by the firm are shown in green in Table 7-2.

Maximizing profit is *not* the same as maximizing revenue. By selling 10 snarks a week the firm could earn £120, but its costs would be £129. As we shall see in the next section, making the last few snarks is very expensive and brings in very little extra revenue. It is actually much more profitable to make a few less.

To sum up, the firm calculates the level of profit associated with each possible output level. To do this, it must know both the revenue received at each output level and the cost of producing each output level. From revenues and costs it calculates profit at each output level, and selects the level of output that maximizes total economic profit.

7-5 Marginal Cost and Marginal Revenue

It is helpful to view the same problem from a different angle. At each output level we now ask whether the firm should increase output still further. Suppose the firm produces 3 snarks and considers moving to 4 snarks. From Table 7-2, we reproduce the relevant cost and revenue data in Table 7-3. Increasing output from 3 to 4 snarks will raise total cost from £44 to £51, a £7 increase in total cost. Revenue will increase from £57 to £72, an increase of £15 in total revenue. Increasing output from 3 to 4 snarks adds more to revenue than costs. Profit will rise by £8 (£15 of extra revenue less £7 of extra costs). Having decided that it is profitable to increase production from 3 to 4 snarks, we can repeat the exercise, asking whether it is profitable to move from 4 to 5, and if so whether it is profitable to move from 5 to 6, and so on.

This approach – examining how the produc-tion of 1 more unit of output will affect profits – focuses on the marginal cost and marginal revenue of producing one more unit.

Marginal cost is the increase in total cost when output is increased by 1 unit. *Marginal revenue* is the increase in total revenue when output is increased by 1 unit.

The crucial point is that, so long as marginal revenue exceeds marginal costs, the firm should increase its level of output. Why? Because producing and selling 1 more unit is adding more to total revenue than to total cost, thereby increasing total profit.

Conversely, if marginal cost exceeds mar-ginal revenue, the extra unit of output reduces total profit. Thus we can use marginal cost and marginal revenue to calculate the output level that maximizes profit. So long as marginal revenue exceeds marginal cost, keep increasing output. As soon as marginal revenue falls short of marginal cost, stop increasing output. To clarify this argument, we look more closely at marginal revenue and marginal cost.

Marginal Cost

Table 7-4 uses Table 7-1 to calculate the marginal cost of producing each extra unit of output. Increasing production from 0 to 1 snark increases total costs from £10 to £25. The marginal cost of the first unit is £15. In Table 7-4 we show the marginal cost on a line between 0 and 1 snark to make clear that it is the cost of increasing output from 0 to 1 snark. All other marginal costs in the table are calculated in the same way. For example, the marginal cost of increasing output from 6 to 7 snarks is £12 (£81 − £69).

The marginal cost of increasing output by 1 unit at each output level is shown in Figure 7-5(b), taken directly from Table 7-4. But it can also be calculated from Figure 7-5(a) taken from Table 7-2. In Figure 7-5(a) we show the total

Table 7-3 Effects of output changes on costs and revenues

OUTPUT (snarks/week)	TOTAL COST (£/week)	COST INCREASE (£/week)	TOTAL REVENUE (£/week)	REVENUE INCREASE (£/week)
3	44		57	
4	51	7	72	15

Table 7-4 Total and marginal costs of production

OUTPUT (snarks/week)	TOTAL COST (£/week)	MARGINAL COST (£/week)
0	10	
1	25	15
2	36	11
3	44	8
4	51	7
5	59	8
6	69	10
7	81	12
8	95	14
9	111	16
10	129	18

cost of producing each output level. Marginal cost is the amount total cost rises when output is increased 1 unit. For example, going from 0 to 1 unit, total costs rise by £15, shown by the shaded area *ABCD*. The shaded area just shows the marginal cost of producing 1 more unit. Thus Figure 7-5(b) could be taken from Figure 7-5(a) as well as Table 7-2.

Either way, we see that marginal cost is high when output is low but also when output is high. Marginal cost is lowest for the production of the fourth unit, which adds only £7 to total costs.

Why do marginal costs start high, then fall, then rise again? The answer depends mainly on the different production techniques for making snarks. At low output levels, the firm is probably using simple techniques. As output rises more sophisticated machines can be used, which make extra units of output quite cheaply. Automated production lines make additional units cheaply but are prohibitively expensive at very small output levels. As output rises still further, the difficulties of managing a large firm begin to emerge. More office staff, who do not directly make snarks, are needed just to keep track of the business. Increased output is now expensive and marginal costs become higher.

The relation of marginal costs to output will vary from firm to firm. In a coal mine that is nearly worked out, marginal costs will rise steeply with additional output. In mass production industries that can be easily managed, marginal costs may have the pattern of Figure 7-6, starting out high but declining to a constant level. Higher levels of output are obtained

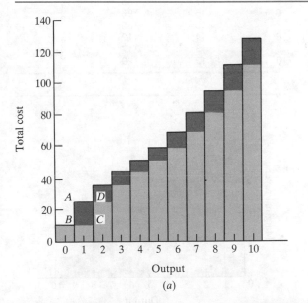

(a)

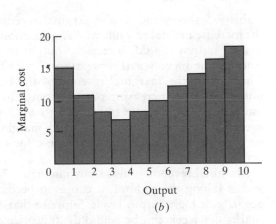

(b)

Figure 7-5 TOTAL AND MARGINAL COSTS OF PRODUCTION. Part (a) shows total costs of production for each level of output. The shaded parts show the amount by which total costs go up when the level of output increases by 1 unit. Thus, total costs rise from 10 to 25 when output increases from 0 to 1 unit. This increase in total costs, at each level of output, is the marginal cost of increasing output by 1 unit. The marginal costs are shown in part (b), which uses a larger vertical scale. But it can be seen that the pattern of marginal costs are shown in part (b) is precisely that shown in part (a): marginal costs are first high and decreasing; then they reach a minimum and start increasing again.

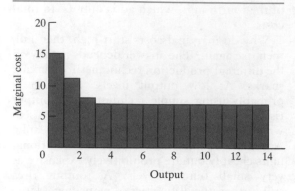

Figure 7-6   MARGINAL COSTS: A DIFFERENT PATTERN. In Figure 7-5, marginal costs first decline output increases, but then begin to increase. A different possibility is that marginal costs at first decline, as it becomes possible to use more efficient methods of production with a larger output. But then marginal costs become constant: any further increases in output can be produced at the same addition to cost per unit (in the figure, the marginal cost is 7 for all units of output beyond 3). Which pattern actually applies in practice depends mainly on the techniques of production available to the firm. The pattern of marginal costs will vary from firm to firm and industry to industry.

merely by adding a second production line identical to the first. In the next chapter we examine evidence on the shape of cost curves in practice.

Marginal Revenue

Table 7-5 shows the firm's marginal revenue, the increase in total revenue when an additional unit of output is sold. Increasing output from 0 to 1 unit increases revenue from 0 to £21. Thus £21 is the marginal revenue of the first unit. Similarly, increasing output from 7 to 8 units increases revenue from £105 to £112 so marginal revenue is £7. Total and marginal revenue depend on the demand curve for the firm's product.

Marginal revenue is also shown in Figure 7-7 and is falling throughout. It can even become negative at high output levels. Suppose that 11 snarks per week can be sold only at a price of £10 each. Total revenue would then be £110 per week. Table 7-5 implies that the marginal revenue from moving from 10 to 11 snarks per week would be −£10 per week.

To understand how marginal revenue changes with output, we must keep track of two

separate effects, which we show in the following equation

$$
\begin{aligned}
\text{Marginal} \atop \text{revenue} &= \text{change in total revenue from} \\
& \quad \text{selling 1 more unit of output} \\
&= \text{(additional revenue earned on} \\
& \quad \text{last unit alone)} \\
& \quad - \text{(revenue lost by selling existing} \\
& \qquad \text{output at a lower price)} \quad \textbf{(1)}
\end{aligned}
$$

Demand curves slope down. To sell more output, the price must be cut. Selling an additional unit of output at this lower price is the first component of marginal revenue in equation (1). However, we must also take account of the fact that, in selling additional

Table 7-5 Price, total revenue and marginal revenue

OUTPUT (snarks/week)	PRICE RECEIVED (£/snark)	TOTAL REVENUE (£/week)	MARGINAL REVENUE (£/week)
0	—	0	
1	21	21	21
2	20	40	19
3	19	57	17
4	18	72	15
5	17	85	13
6	16	96	11
7	15	105	9
8	14	112	7
9	13	117	5
10	12	120	3

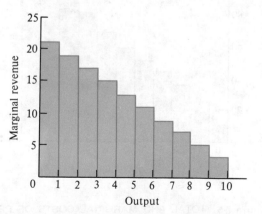

Figure 7-7   MARGINAL REVENUE. Marginal revenue is the increase in the firm's revenue resulting from an increase in sales by one unit. In this diagram, the firm can sell more output only by reducing its price. Marginal revenue therefore declines as output rises.

output, we bid down the price for which *all* previous units of output can be sold. This effect acts to reduce the additional revenue obtained from selling an extra unit of output.

In Table 7-5 the firm can sell 5 snarks at £17 each or 6 snarks at £16 each. Increasing output from 5 to 6, the firm earns £16 from selling the extra snark at £16, but it also loses £5 by cutting the price £1 on the 5 snarks it was already selling. Marginal revenue is thus £11.

Marginal revenue falls steadily for two reasons. First, because demand curves slope down, the last unit itself must be sold at a lower price the higher is output. Second, successive price reductions reduce the revenue earned from existing units of output. When the firm's demand curve slopes down, we have thus established two propositions.

(i) Marginal revenue falls as output rises.
(ii) Marginal revenue must be less than the price for which the last unit is sold. From this we must subtract the effect of lower prices on revenue earned from previous units of output.

The shape of the marginal revenue curve depends only on the shape of the firm's demand curve. Having studied the case where the demand curve slopes down, and having agreed in Chapter 6 to neglect the possibility that demand curves slope upwards, we must study only one further possibility. A small firm in a huge market may be able to sell as much output as it wishes without affecting the existing market price. A single wheat farmer's output may be insignificant relative to the total supply of wheat. Although the market demand curve for wheat slopes down, the individual farmer can sell wheat without bidding down the market price. For the individual farmer, the demand curve is horizontal at the equilibrium price of wheat. Each extra unit of output by the individual farmer earns the same marginal revenue, the wheat price itself. In terms of equation (1), the first term is constant and the second term, 'revenue lost on existing units', is zero. The marginal revenue schedule for such a firm is shown in Figure 7-8.

Using Marginal Revenue and Marginal Cost to Determine the Level of Output

Combining marginal cost and marginal revenue schedules, Table 7-6 examines the level of

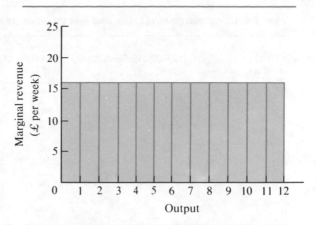

Figure 7-8 MARGINAL REVENUE: AN ALTERNATIVE PATTERN. In this figure the firm has the same marginal revenue however much it sells. This means it can sell goods at the existing market price without having to cut price. The existing price is £16. The firm will have constant marginal revenue if its output is very small relative to total amount sold in the market.

output that maximizes the firm's profits. If marginal revenue exceeds marginal cost, a 1-unit increase in output will increase profits. The last column shows that this reasoning will lead the firm to produce at least 6 units of output.

Suppose the firm now considers increasing output from 6 to 7 units. Marginal revenue is £9 and marginal cost £12, so profits would fall by £3. Output should *not* be expanded to 7 units. Similar reasoning rules out expansion to any output level above 6 units. Wherever marginal cost exceeds marginal revenue the firm will save money by reducing output. It saves more by giving up the marginal cost that it loses by giving up the marginal revenue.

The firm should expand up to 6 units of output but no further. This is the output level that maximizes profits, as we know already from Table 7-2.

Total Cost and Revenue versus Marginal Cost and Revenue

Table 7-2, based on total cost and total revenue, and Table 7-6, based on marginal cost and revenue, are different ways of examining the same problem. Economists use marginal analysis more frequently because it suggests a useful way of thinking about the decision problem

Table 7-6 Using marginal revenue and marginal cost to determine output

OUTPUT (units/wk)	MARGINAL REVENUE (£/wk)	MARGINAL COST (£/wk)	MARGINAL REVENUE MINUS MARGINAL COST (£/wk)	OUTPUT DECISION
0				
1	21	15	6	Increase
2	19	11	8	Increase
3	17	8	9	Increase
4	15	7	8	Increase
5	13	8	5	Increase
6	11	10	1	Increase
7	9	12	− 3	Decrease
8	7	14	− 7	Decrease
9	5	16	−11	Decrease
10	3	18	−15	Decrease

faced by firms or consumers. Is there a small change that could make the firm (or the consumer) better off? If so, the current position cannot be the best possible one and changes should be made.

Marginal analysis should be subjected to one very important check. It may miss an all-or-nothing choice. For example, suppose that marginal revenue exceeds marginal cost up to an output level of 6 units but thereafter marginal revenue is less than marginal cost. This suggests that 6 units should be produced. Producing 6 units is certainly better than producing any other output level. However, if the firm incurs large costs whether or not it produces (for example a vastly overpaid managing director), the profit earned from producing 6 units may not cover these fixed costs. Conditional on paying these fixed costs, an output level of 6 units is then the loss-minimizing output level. However, the firm might do better to shut down altogether. We examine this issue in greater detail in the next chapter.[3]

In summary, a profit-maximizing firm should expand output so long as marginal revenue exceeds marginal cost but should stop expansion as soon as marginal cost exceeds marginal revenue. This rule guides the firm to the best positive level of output. If the firm is not making

profits even in this position, it might do better to close down altogether.

7-6 Marginal Cost and Marginal Revenue Curves: $MC = MR$

Thus far we have assumed that the firm can produce only an integer number of goods, such as 0, 1 or 7, rather than a quantity such as 1.5 or 6.7. In most cases output is not confined to integer levels, for two reasons. First, for goods such as wheat or milk, there is no reason to think that only 1 bushel or 1 gallon units can be sold. The firm can sell in odd amounts. Second, even for goods such as cars, which are necessarily sold in whole units, the firm may be selling 75 cars every four weeks, or 18.75 cars per week. Thus it is convenient to imagine that firms can vary production levels and sales almost continuously.

If so, we can draw smooth marginal cost (MC) and marginal revenue (MR) schedules as in Figure 7-9. Profits are maximized where the two schedules cross, at the point E. The output level Q_1 maximizes profits (or minimizes losses). At smaller outputs, MR exceeds MC and expansion will increase profits (or reduce losses).

To the right of Q_1, MC exceeds MR. Expansion adds more to costs than revenue and contraction saves more in costs than it loses in revenue. The profit incentive to increase output to the left of Q_1 and to reduce output to the right of Q_1 is shown by the arrows in Figure 7-9. This incentive guides the firm to choose

---

[3] Readers familiar with mathematical calculus will recognize that choosing output to set marginal revenue equal to marginal cost ensures that marginal profit equals zero. Although necessary for a local maximum of profits with respect to output, this condition does not guarantee positive profits.

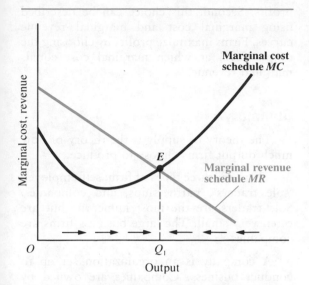

Figure 7-9 MARGINAL COST AND MARGINAL REVENUE DETERMINE THE FIRM'S OUTPUT LEVEL. The marginal cost and marginal revenue schedules or curves are shown changing smoothly here. The firm's optimal level of output is Q_1, the output level at which marginal revenue is equal to marginal cost. Anywhere to the left of Q_1, marginal revenue is larger than marginal cost and the firm should increase output, as shown by the arrows. Where output is greater than Q_1, marginal revenue is less than marginal cost and profits are increased by reducing output. This is shown by the arrows pointing to the left for output levels above Q_1. Once again, if the firm is losing money at Q_1 it has to check whether it might be better not to produce at all than to produce Q_1.

the output level Q_1, provided the firm should be in business at all. At Q_1 marginal revenue is exactly equal to marginal cost.

Table 7-7 summarizes the conditions for determining the output level that maximizes profits.

The Effect of Changing Cost on Output

Suppose the firm agrees to pay a higher wage rate or faces a price increase for a raw material.

At each output level, marginal costs will rise. Figure 7-10 illustrates this change by an upward shift from MC to MC'. Choosing output to set $MC = MR$, the firm now produces at E'. Higher marginal costs reduce profit-maximizing output from Q_1 to Q_2.

The Effect of a Shift in the Demand Curve on Output

Suppose that the firm's demand curve and marginal revenue curve shift upwards. At each output level, price and marginal revenue are higher than before. In Figure 7-11 the MR curve shifts out to MR', inducing the firm to move from E to E''. Higher demand has led the firm to expand output from Q_1 to Q_3.

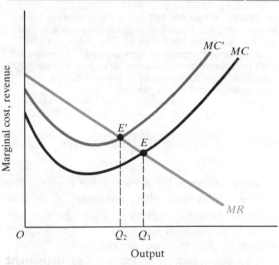

Figure 7-10 AN INCREASE IN MARGINAL COST REDUCES OUTPUT. The marginal cost curve shifts up from MC to MC' as a result of an increase in the costs of using a factor of production: for instance, the wage may have risen. This upward shift moves the intersection of MC and MR curves from E to E' and results in a lower level of output. Output falls from Q_1 to Q_2. Thus, when the firm's costs rise, it decides to produce less.

Table 7-7 Determining the firm's output level

MARGINAL CONDITION	DECISION	CHECK
$MR > MC$	Increase output	
$MR < MC$	Cut output	
$MR = MC$	Optimal output	If positive profits, produce this output level. If not, consider closing down for a while or going out of business altogether

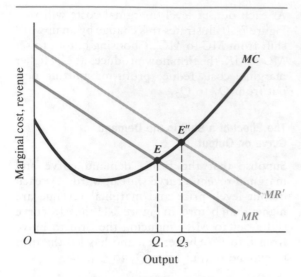

Figure 7-11   AN UPWARD SHIFT OF THE MARGINAL REVENUE CURVE INCREASES OUTPUT.   When the *MR* curve shifts upward from *MR* to *MR'*, the intersection point between *MR* and *MC* curves shifts from *E* to *E''*. The firm's optimal level of output increases from Q_1 to Q_3. The upward shift in the marginal revenue curve could result, for instance, from an increase in the number of customers in the firm's market.

Do Firms Know Their Marginal Cost and Revenue Curves?

By now you may be wondering if firms in the real world know their marginal cost and marginal revenue curves, let alone go through some sophisticated calculations to make sure output is chosen to equate the two.

It is important to grasp that such thought experiments by firms are not necessary for the relevance of our model of supply. What we have shown is that if, by luck, hunch, or judgement, a manager succeeds in maximizing the firm's profits, then marginal cost and marginal revenue will *necessarily* be equal. What we have been doing is to develop a formal analysis by which we can keep track of the hunches of smart managers who get things right on average and survive in a tough business world.

In this chapter we have presented only an overview of cost and revenue conditions. Although later chapters will fill in the picture, we already have the basis for a theory of how much output firms choose to supply. First, firms choose the output level that will maximize

profits. Second, this choice can be described using marginal cost and marginal revenue curves. Firms maximize profits by choosing the output level at which marginal cost equals marginal revenue.

Summary

1   The theory of supply is the theory of how much output firms choose to produce.

2   There are three types of firm: self-employed 'sole traders', partnerships, and companies. Sole traders are the most numerous but are often very small. The large business firms are companies.

3   A company is an organization set up to conduct business. Companies are owned by their shareholders but run by managers responsible to the board of directors.

4   Shareholders have limited liability. Partners and sole traders have unlimited liability.

5   Revenue is what the firm earns from sales. Costs are the expenses incurred in producing and selling. Profits are the excess of revenue over costs.

6   Costs should include opportunity costs of all resources used in production. Opportunity cost is the amount an input could obtain in its next highest paying use. In particular, economic costs include the cost of the owner's time and effort in running a business. Economic costs also include the opportunity cost of financial capital used in the firm. Supernormal profit is the pure profit accruing to the owners after allowing for all these costs.

7   Firms are assumed to aim to maximize profits. Even though the firm is run by its managers, not its owners, profit maximization is a useful assumption in understanding the firm's behaviour. Firms that make losses cannot continue in business indefinitely.

8   In aiming to maximize profits, firms necessarily produce each output level as cheaply as possible. Profit maximization implies minimization of costs for each output level.

9   Firms choose the optimal output level to maximize total economic profits. This decision can be described equivalently by examining marginal cost and marginal revenue. Marginal

cost is the increase in total cost when one more unit is produced. Marginal revenue is the corresponding change in total revenue and depends on the demand curve for the firm's product. Profits are maximized at the output at which marginal cost equals marginal revenue. If profits are negative at this output, the firm should close down if this allows smaller losses.

10   An upward shift in the marginal cost curve reduces output. An upward shift in the marginal revenue curve increases output.

11   It is unnecessary for firms to calculate their marginal cost and marginal revenue curves. Setting *MC* equal to *MR* is merely a device that economists use to mimic the hunches of smart firms who correctly judge, by whatever means, the profit-maximizing level of output.

Key Terms

Sole trader
Partnership
Company
Shareholder
Limited liability
Dividends
Capital gains
Retained earnings
Depreciation
Balance sheet
Income statement
Cash flow
Opportunity cost
Total costs
Total revenue
Marginal cost
Marginal revenue

Problems

1   (a) What are the main advantages of a company over a large partnership as a way of doing business? (b) List five companies whose products you buy. (c) Do you buy goods or services from any partnerships or sole traders? Say which goods and firms.

2   How would each of the following affect the income statement for Rent-a-Person presented in Figure 7-2? (a) Rent-a-Person still owes £70 000 to the people it rented out during the year. (b) Instead of renting an office, the company owns its office. (c) During the year Rent-a-Person was paid by one of the people who owed it money at the end of 1989.

3   (a) Suppose that Rent-a-Person is run by a hard-working owner, who would be paid £40 000 per year in a management job in another firm. Suppose also that she has invested £200 000 of her own in the company, on which she could earn 12 per cent elsewhere. What are the economic profits earned by Rent-a-Person? (Use Figure 7-2.) (b) What is the general principle underlying the adjustments made to accounting costs?

4   (a) Suppose that Snark International borrows another £50 000 from the bank and increases its inventory holdings. Show how its balance sheet is affected. (Refer back to Figure 7-3.) (b) Explain how the interest paid on the loan would appear in the income statement of Snark International.

5   (a) Do you think firms aim to maximize profits? Explain. (b) Do you think firms *should* aim to maximize profits, or should they rather have a social conscience and do things like support charities, the arts, and political campaigns? Explain.

6   In Table 7-2, assume that total costs of producing each level of output are higher by £40 than the costs shown in the fourth column of the table. What level of output should the firm produce? Explain. (You can work out the answer using the table — no need to draw graphs.)

7   Suppose that a firm that has the same costs as those shown in Table 7-4 can sell as much output as it wants at a price of £13. (a) Draw *MR* and *MC* curves. (b) Show the level of output that the firm will produce.

8   Table 7-2 shows the level of output produced by a firm. (a) What price is it charging? (b) Is price above, below, or equal to marginal revenue? Explain why, using equation (1).

9   Common Fallacies Show why the following statements are incorrect: (a) Firms which show an accounting profit must be thriving. (b) Firms do not know their marginal costs. It is unreasonable to base the theory of supply on the assumption that firms set marginal revenue equal to marginal cost. (c) The way to make the most profit is to sell as much output as possible.

8

Developing the Theory of Supply: Costs and Production

Firms don't always close down when they start losing money. Sometimes they expect things to get better again. They may expect demand to increase, or they may think that, given time, they can reduce their production costs enough to get back into profit. This chapter takes a closer look at costs and their influence on the output that firms wish to produce.

In Chapter 7 we introduced the theory of supply by showing that firms would choose the output at which marginal cost equals marginal revenue. This would maximize profits (or minimize losses). If profits were positive, the firm would indeed produce this output level. If profits were negative, it would check whether losses could be reduced by not producing at all.

In this chapter we distinguish between the *short-run* and the *long-run* output decisions of firms. No firm will stay in business if it expects to make losses for ever. We show how and why cost curves differ in the short run, when the firm cannot fully react to changes in conditions, and the long run in which the firm can fully adjust to changes in demand or cost conditions.

In fact, we have to consider the short-run and long-run versions of three different cost curves: total cost; marginal cost, which of course can be derived from changes in total cost; and average cost, or total cost divided by total output. As we shall see, average cost is relevant to the decision of whether or not to stay in business.

Figure 8-1 summarizes the material of this chapter. The new material is all on the cost side of the diagram. Because there are so many different cost curves, you may find all this confusing at first. It will be useful to keep checking back to Figure 8-1. We start at the left of Figure 8-1 by introducing the *production function*, which describes the firm's technology.

8-1 Inputs and Output

An *input* (or *factor of production*) is any good or service used to produce output.

The firm's inputs include labour, machinery, buildings, raw materials, and energy. The term 'input' covers everything from senior management to bandages used in the firm's first-aid room.

The firm uses these inputs to produce output. Suppose our firm uses inputs to make snarks. This is an engineering and management problem. The recipe for making snarks is largely outside the field of economics and is a matter of technology and on-the-job experience. The economist takes the recipe as given, subject to one important qualification: *no waste*. We explain this qualification in discussing the *production function*.

The Production Function

The *production function* specifies the maximum output that can be produced from any given amount of inputs.

The production function summarizes the *technically efficient* methods of combining inputs to produce output. A production method is technically inefficient if, to produce a given output, it uses more of some inputs and no less of other inputs than some other method that could make the same output. Since profit-maximizing firms will not be interested in wasteful or inefficient production methods, we can restrict our attention to those that are technically efficient.

For example, method A produces 1 snark from 2 hours of labour and 1 hour of machine time. Method B produces 1 snark from 2 hours

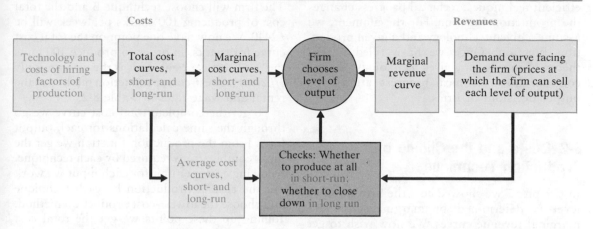

Figure 8-1   THE COMPLETE THEORY OF SUPPLY.   This diagram extends the analysis of Chapter 7 in two ways. First, short- and long-run cost curves and output decisions are carefully distinguished. Second, we go behind the total cost curve to show how the firm chooses the lowest cost way of producing each level of output, given the technology available to it and the costs of hiring factors of production.

of labour and 2 hours of machine time. Method B is less efficient than method A since it uses more machine time but the same amount of labour to produce the same output as method A. Method B is not one of the production methods summarized in the production function.

Table 8-1 summarizes the technically efficient production techniques listed by the production function. The first two rows of the table show two different ways to produce 100 snarks: the firm can use 4 machines and 4 workers, or 2 machines and 6 workers. Beginning from the latter, the third row shows the effect of adding an extra worker. Output rises 6 snarks per week. The last row shows that doubling both the inputs in the second row also doubles the output, though this need not necessarily be so. For example, overcrowding a small factory can slow people down.

Table 8-1 could be enlarged to include other combinations of labour and capital that are also technically efficient. How does the firm discover its production function, the complete set of technically efficient production techniques? In part, it will ask its engineers, designers, and time-and-motion experts. In part, it may experiment with different techniques and observe the results. Fortunately, the firm does not need to know its complete set of options in detail. If labour is very expensive relative to other inputs, techniques that are very labour-intensive are unlikely to be cost-minimizing and

Table 8-1 The production function gives the output levels produced by different quantities of inputs

OUTPUT LEVEL (snarks/wk)	CAPITAL INPUT (no. of machines*)	LABOUR INPUT (no. of workers*)
100	4	4
100	2	6
106	2	7
200	4	12

* Machines and labour are each used 40 hours per week.

will be disregarded. The firm can then pay more attention to discovering the complete set of techniques that use relatively little labour.

Before turning to a detailed analysis of this choice of technique, we summarize the terms we have used so far. A *technique* is a particular method of combining inputs to make output. *Technology* is the list of all known techniques. The production function is the list of all techniques that are technically efficient. By *technical progress* economists mean an invention or improvement in organization that allows a given output to be produced with fewer inputs than before. A technique that used to be technically efficient has been rendered inefficient by the technical advance that has introduced a new, more productive production technique. By changing the set of technically efficient techniques, technical progress changes the production function. For the moment, we assume a given technology and a given production function. Once we have filled in the theory of supply for a given technology, we can consider how technical progress affects the output decisions of firms.

8-2 Costs and the Choice of Production Technique

In Chapter 7 we showed how the firm's output level is determined by marginal cost and marginal revenue curves. We now wish to get behind the marginal cost curve and the total cost curve from which it is derived.

Minimizing Costs: The Choice of Technique

The production function relates volumes of inputs to volume of output. However, costs are calculated in value terms. To make the transition from the production function to a cost curve we need to introduce the price that the firm pays for inputs.

We return to Table 8-1 and consider the lowest-cost way to produce 100 snarks per week. To simplify the calculations, we assume that there are only two technically efficient techniques, those described in the first two rows of Table 8-1, which are reproduced in the first two columns of Table 8-2 and labelled techniques A and B. Either technique can be used to make 100 snarks per week. The firm knows the cost of renting a machine (£320 per week) and of hiring labour (£300 per week). From the production function the firm knows the quantities of labour and capital required to make 100 snarks per week using each technique. Table 8-2 shows that the total cost of this output is £2480 per week using technique A and £2440 per week using technique B.

The firm will choose technique B and the total cost of producing 100 snarks per week will be £2440. We now have one point on the total cost curve for snarks: in order to produce 100 units the total cost is £2440. This is the *economically efficient* (lowest-cost) production method at the rental and wage rates in Table 8-2.

To get the complete total cost curve we go through the same calculations for each output level. From the production function we get the input combinations required by each technique. Knowing costs per unit for each input we work out the cost of production by each technique and choose the lowest-cost production method. Joining up these points we get the total cost curve, which may embody switching from one production technique to another at different output levels. From the total cost curve we calculate the marginal cost curve – the increase in total costs at each output level as output is increased by one more unit.

Factor Intensity

When a technique uses a lot of capital and relatively little labour we say that it is 'capital-intensive'. Conversely, a technique using a lot of labour but relatively little capital is said to be 'labour-intensive'. In Table 8-2, technique A is more capital-intensive and less labour-intensive than technique B. The ratio of the units of capital input to labour input is 1 (= 4/4) in technique A but only 1/3 (= 2/6) in technique B.

Changes in Factor Prices and the Choice of Technique

At the factor prices (costs per input unit) in Table 8-2, the firm chooses the more labour-intensive technique because it is cheaper. Suppose the wage rate rises from £300 to £340 per week: labour has become more expensive but the rental on capital remains unchanged.

Table 8-2 Choosing the lowest-cost production technique

	CAPITAL INPUT	LABOUR INPUT	RENTAL RATE PER MACHINE (£/wk)	WAGE RATE (£/wk)	CAPITAL COST (£/wk)	LABOUR COST (£/wk)	TOTAL COST (£/wk)
Technique A	4	4	320	300	1280	1200	2480
Technique B	2	6	320	300	640	1800	2440

Table 8-3 The effect of an increase in the wage rate

	CAPITAL INPUT	LABOUR INPUT	RENTAL RATE (£/wk)	WAGE RATE (£/wk)	CAPITAL COST (£/wk)	LABOUR COST (£/wk)	TOTAL COST (£/wk)
Technique A	4	4	320	340	1280	1360	2640
Technique B	2	6	320	340	640	2040	2680

The *relative price* of labour has risen.

We ask two questions. First, what happens to the total cost of producing 100 snarks per week? Second, is there any change in the preferred production technique? Table 8-3 recalculates the costs of production at the new factor prices. Because both techniques use some labour, the total cost of producing 100 snarks by technique A has risen and the total cost of producing 100 snarks using technique B has risen. Even though the firm selects the cheaper technique, the lowest-cost way to produce 100 snarks is now higher. Repeating this argument for all other output levels, this implies that the total cost curve for snark production shifts *upwards* at each output level when the wage rate (or the price of any other input) rises.

In this particular example, the change in the relative price of inputs also leads the firm to switch production techniques for producing 100 snarks. Table 8-2 showed that before the wage increase the firm used technique B with 6 workers and 2 machines. After the wage increase, the higher price of labour relative to capital leads the firm to substitute capital for labour. Technique A is now a cheaper way to produce 100 snarks. Labour use has been reduced from 6 to 4 workers and machine use has been increased from 2 to 4 machines.

8-3 Long-run Total, Marginal, and Average Costs

Faced with an upward shift in its demand and marginal revenue curves, a firm will want to expand production, as we explained in the previous chapter. However, adjustment takes time. In the short run, perhaps the first few months, the firm can get its existing workforce to do overtime. Over a longer period it may be cheaper to build a new factory and increase capacity.

The *long run* is the period long enough for the firm to adjust *all* its inputs to a change in conditions.

In the long run the firm can vary its factory size, switch techniques of production, hire new workers and negotiate new contracts with suppliers of raw materials.

The *short run* is the period in which the firm can make only *partial* adjustment of its inputs to a change in conditions.

The firm may have the flexibility to vary the shift length almost immediately. Hiring or firing workers takes longer, and it might be several years before a new factory is designed, built, and fully operational.

In this section we deal with long-run cost curves, describing production costs when the firm is able to make all the adjustments it desires.

The *long-run total cost curve* describes the minimum cost of producing each output level when the firm is able to adjust all inputs optimally.

Total and Marginal Costs in the Long Run

Table 8-4 shows long-run total costs (LTC) and long-run marginal costs (LMC) of producing each output level. LTC reflects the lowest-cost method of producing each output level and is shown in the second column of the table. Since there is always an option to close down entirely, the LTC of producing zero output is zero. LTC describes the eventual costs after any adjustments such as redundancy payments have been made.

Table 8-4 also shows the LMC of production. These represent the increase in LTC at each output level if output is permanently raised by one unit.

LTC must rise with output. It must cost more

Table 8-4 Long-run costs

(1) OUTPUT (goods/wk)	(2) TOTAL COST (£/wk)	(3) MARGINAL COST (£/wk)	(4) AVE. COST (£/wk)
0	0	—	—
1	30	30	30
2	54	24	27
3	74	20	24.67
4	91	17	22.75
5	107	16	21.40
6	126	19	21.00
7	149	23	21.29
8	176	27	22.00
9	207	31	23.00
10	243	36	24.30

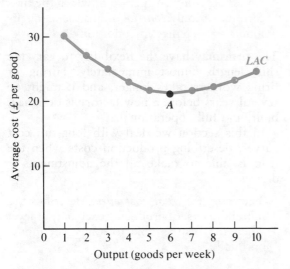

Figure 8-2 THE LONG-RUN AVERAGE COST CURVE (*LAC*).   This long-run average cost curve *LAC* plots the data in the last column of Table 8-4. The *LAC* curve has the typical U-shape. The minimum average cost of production is at point *A*, with output level of 6 and average cost of £21.

Long-run Average Costs

To answer these questions it is convenient to examine the cost per unit of output or the average cost of production.

The *average cost of production* is the total cost divided by the level of output.

The last column of Table 8-4 shows long-run average cost (*LAC*). *LAC* is *LTC* divided by output.

The *LAC* data of Table 8-4 are plotted in Figure 8-2. Average cost starts out high – £30 per unit for the first unit – then fall as low as £21 per unit when output is 6. Therefore average costs rise, reaching £24.30 at an output of 10. This common pattern of average costs is called the U-shaped average cost curve. To see why the U-shaped average cost curve is common in practice we introduce the concept of 'returns to scale'.

8-4 Economies and Diseconomies of Scale

There are *economies of scale* (or *increasing returns to scale*) when long-run average costs decrease as output rises. There are *constant returns to scale* when long-run average costs are constant as output rises. There are *diseconomies of scale* (or *decreasing returns to scale*) when long-run average costs increase as output rises.

In these definitions scale refers to the size of the firm as measured by its output. The three cases are illustrated in Figure 8-3.

In Figure 8-2 the U-shaped average cost curve has increasing returns to scale up to the point *A*, where average cost is lowest. At higher output levels there are decreasing returns to scale. Why should there be economies of scale at low output levels but diseconomies of scale at high output levels?

We draw a cost curve for given input prices. Hence changes in average costs as we move along the *LAC* curve cannot be explained by changes in factor prices. (We have already seen that changes in factor prices *shift* cost curves.) The relationship between average costs and output as we move along the *LAC* curve must be explained by the relation between physical quantities of inputs and output summarized in the production function. At given factor prices, does the firm use more or fewer inputs per unit of output as output rises? This is a

to produce more output than less. How fast do total costs increase without output? Is there any advantage in size in the sense that large firms can produce goods at a lower unit cost than small firms? Might it be a disadvantage to be large?

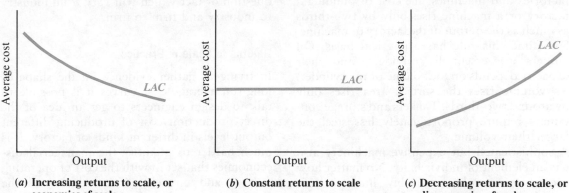

(*a*) **Increasing returns to scale, or economies of scale**   (*b*) **Constant returns to scale**   (*c*) **Decreasing returns to scale, or diseconomies of scale**

Figure 8-3   RETURNS TO SCALE AND LONG-RUN AVERAGE COST CURVE. The three long-run average cost *LAC* curves show the relationship between returns to scale and the shape of the *LAC* curve. When *LAC* is declining, average costs of production fall as output increases and there are economies of scale. When *LAC* is increasing, average costs of production increase with higher output, and there are decreasing returns to scale. The intermediate case, where average costs are constant, has constant returns to scale.

technological question about the most efficient production techniques. Thus the discussion of economies or diseconomies of scale indirectly refers back to the production function although we discuss the issue in terms of the average cost curve.

Economies of Scale

There are three reasons for economies of scale. The first is *indivisibilities* in the production process, some minimum quantity of inputs required by the firm to be in business at all whether or not output is produced. These are sometimes called *fixed costs*, because they do not vary with the output level. To be in business a firm requires a manager, a telephone, an accountant, a market research survey. These costs are indivisible in the sense that the firm cannot have half a manager and half a telephone merely because it wishes to operate at low output levels. Beginning from small output levels, these costs do not initially increase with output. The manager can organize three workers as easily as two. As yet there is no need for a second telephone and the accounts take no longer. There are economies of scale because these fixed costs can be spread over more units of output as output is increased, thereby reducing average cost per unit of output. However, as the firm expands further it will have to hire more managers and

telephones and these economies of scale die away. The average cost curve stops falling.

The second reason for economies of scale is *specialization*. A sole trader must undertake all the different tasks of the business. As the firm expands and takes on more workers, each worker can concentrate on a single task and handle it more efficiently. Adam Smith, the father of economics, emphasized the gains from specialization in *The Wealth of Nations* (1776). His example (he calls it a 'very trifling manufacture') is the pin industry:

> A workman not educated to this business . . . could scarce . . . make one pin a day, and certainly could not make twenty. But in the way in which this business is now carried on, . . . it is divided into a number of branches. . . . One man draws out the wire, another straightens it, a third cuts, a fourth points it. . . .

There were 18 stages in making a pin, and Smith estimated average output per worker at 4800 pins per day. The economies of scale from specialization in this case are impressive. Similar benefits from specialization occur in assembly line work, for example in the motor car industry.

The third reason for economies of scale is closely related. Large scale is often needed to take advantage of better machinery. Engineers have a rule of two-thirds that applies to many factories and machines: the cost of building a factory or a machine rises only by two-thirds as much as the output of the factory or machine. Sometime this rule has a physical basis. Oil tankers are essentially cylinders, and their capacity depends on the volume of the cylinder. As volume rises the surface area rises only by around two-thirds. Tankers and storage containers require proportionately less steel the larger their volume.

Sophisticated but expensive machinery also has an element of indivisibility. No matter how productive a robot assembly line is, it is pointless to install one to make five cars a week. Average costs would be enormous. However, at high output levels the machinery cost can be spread over a large number of units of output and this production technique may produce so many cars that average costs are low.

Diseconomies of Scale

With such powerful reasons for economies of scale, why does the U-shaped average cost curve turn upward again as diseconomies of scale set in? Notice first that the second and third reasons for economies of scale are much more prevalent in manufacturing than in service industries such as restaurants and laundries.

The main reason for diseconomies of scale is that management becomes more difficult as the firm becomes larger. These are described as *managerial diseconomies of scale*. Large companies need many layers of management, which themselves have to be managed. The company becomes bureaucratic, co-ordination problems arise, and average costs *may* begin to rise.

Geographical factors may also explain diseconomies of scale. If the first factory is located in the best site, perhaps to minimize the cost of transporting goods to the market, the site of a second factory will necessarily be less advantageous. To take a different example, in extracting coal from a mine, a firm will extract the easiest coal first. To produce a higher output, deeper coal seams will have to be worked and these will be more expensive.

The shape of the average cost curve thus depends on two things: how long the economies of scale persist, and how quickly the diseconomies of scale occur as output is increased. The balance of these two forces is an empirical question of fact which will vary from industry to industry and firm to firm.

Returns to Scale in Practice

In trying to gather evidence on the shape of long-run average cost curves it is possible to talk to design engineers to get an idea of the direct production cost of producing different output levels in different kinds of factory. It is much harder to quantify the managerial diseconomies that set in with the cost of operating a large and unwieldy firm. Almost all the empirical research focuses only on the direct production cost of different output levels. Because it ignores managerial diseconomies of scale it overestimates the falling range of average cost curves. In practice, average cost curves start rising sooner than the following estimates suggest.

Figure 8-4 shows data on average costs for firms in the cement industry in the United States and for firms in the brewing industry in the UK. Average costs fall steadily as output increases. Even at large output levels, the forces inducing economies of scale dominate the forces inducing diseconomies of scale. Many studies of costs in manufacturing industry confirm this pattern of falling average costs as output rises.[1]

For such firms the typical pattern of the *LAC* curve is that of Figure 8-3(a). At low output levels, average costs fall rapidly. As output rises, average costs fall but more slowly. Economists have tried to measure the output level at which further economies of scale become unimportant for the individual firm, the point at which the average cost curve first becomes horizontal. This output level is called the *minimum efficient scale (MES)*.

Table 8-5 contains some estimates of the MES for firms operating in different industries in the UK and the United States. The first column gives an idea of how steeply average costs fall before minimum efficient scale is reached. It shows how much higher average

---

[1] C. F. Pratten, *Economies of Scale in Manufacturing Industry*, Cambridge University Press, 1971, presents data for 25 industries including steel, bread, soap, oil, socks, and newspapers. F. M. Scherer, *Industrial Market Structure and Economic Performance* (2nd ed.), Rank McNally, 1980, pp. 81–118, has an excellent description of the relationship between average cost and output in practice.

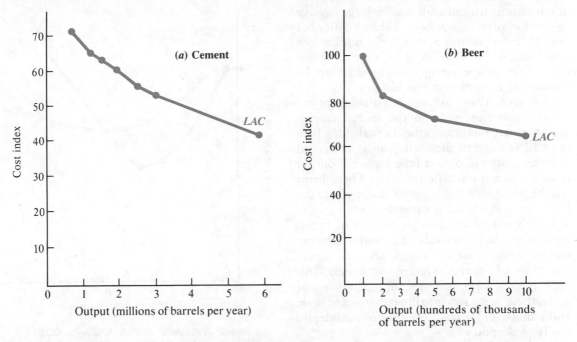

Figure 8-4 AVERAGE COST CURVES IN THE LONG RUN. The figure shows long-run average cost curves for cement and beer drawing. In both cases, average cost falls as the level of output rises. (Sources: Cement data are from Mark E. McBride, 'The Nature and Source of Economies of Scale in Cement Production', in *Southern Economic Journal*, July 1981, pp. 105–115. Brewing data from C. F. Pratten, *Economies of Scale in Manufacturing Industry*, Cambridge University Press, 1971, page 75.)

Table 8-5 Minimum efficient scale for selected industries in the UK and the USA

INDUSTRY	% INCREASE IN AVERAGE COSTS AT $\frac{1}{3}$ MES	MES AS % OF MARKET IN	
		UK	USA
Cement	26.0	6.1	1.7
Steel	11.0	15.4	2.6
Glass bottles	11.0	9.0	1.5
Bearings	8.0	4.4	1.4
Fabrics	7.6	1.8	0.2
Refrigerators	6.5	83.3	14.1
Petroleum refining	4.8	11.6	1.9
Paints	4.4	10.2	1.4
Cigarettes	2.2	30.3	6.5
Shoes	1.5	0.6	0.2

Source: F. M. Scherer *et al., The Economics of Multiplant Operation* Harvard University Press, 1975, Tables 3.11 and 3.15.

costs are when output is one-third of the output at minimum efficient scale. The second and third columns show the *MES* output level relative to the output of the industry as a whole. This provides a benchmark of the importance of economies of scale to firms in each industry. Since firms in the UK and the United States essentially have access to the same technical know-how, differences between the second and third columns primarily reflect differences in the size of the industry in the two countries rather than differences in the *MES* output level for an individual firm.

These figures suggest that in heavy manufacturing industries economies of scale are substantial. At low outputs, average costs are much higher than at minimum efficient scale. We would expect similar effects in aircraft and motor car manufacture, which have very large fixed costs for research and development of new models and which can take advantage of highly automated assembly lines if output is sufficiently high. Yet in a large country such as the United States, minimum efficient scale for an individual firm occurs at an output that is small relative to the industry as a whole. Most firms will be producing on a relatively flat part of their averge cost curve with few economies of scale still to be exploited.

In smaller countries such as the UK, the point of minimum efficient scale may be large relative to the industry as a whole. Table 8-5 implies that if there is more than one refrigerator manufacturer in the UK it is impossible for every firm in the refrigerator industry to be producing at minimum efficient scale.

However, Table 8-5 suggests that there are many industries, even in the manufacturing sector, where minimum efficient scale for a firm is small relative to the market as a whole and average costs are only a little higher if output is below minimum efficient scale. These firms will be producing in an output range where the *LAC* curve is almost horizontal.

Finally, there are a large number of firms, especially those outside the manufacturing sector, whose cost conditions are well represented by a U-shaped average cost curve. With only limited opportunities for economies of scale, these firms run into diseconomies of scale and rising average costs even at quite moderate levels of output.

We begin by discussing the output decision of a firm with a U-shaped average cost curve. Then we show how this analysis must be amended when firms face significant economies of scale. In later chapters which discuss the structure of different types of industry it will be important to remember which shape of average cost curve we think of relevance for the industry we are studying.

8-5 Average Cost and Marginal Cost

In Table 8-4 we showed long-run marginal costs (*LMC*) and long-run average costs (*LAC*). We now want to connect these two cost measures whose behaviour is closely related.

The last two columns of Table 8-4 are plotted in Figure 8-5. At each output *LAC* is simply total cost divided by that output level. However, marginal costs are incurred by moving from one output level to another so we plot *LMC* at points halfway between the corresponding output levels. For example the *LMC* of £30 for the first output unit is plotted at the output level half way between 0 and 1.

Two facts stand out from the table and diagram.

1   *LAC* is falling when *LMC* is less than *LAC*,

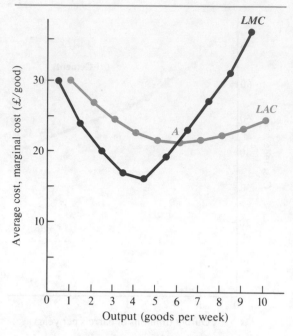

Figure 8-5 AVERAGE AND MARGINAL COST CURVES.   These cost data are plotted from Table 8-4. There are two special features of the relationship between the marginal cost curve (*LMC*) and the average cost curve (*LAC*). First, *LAC* is declining whenever *LMC* is below *LAC*, and rising whenever *LMC* is above *LAC*. Second, the *LMC* curve cuts the *LAC* curve at the minimum point of the *LAC* curve – in other words, at the point where output is produced at lowest unit cost.

and rising when *LMC* is greater than *LAC*.
2   *LAC* is at a minimum at the output level at which *LAC* and *LMC* cross.

Neither of these facts is an accident. The relation between average and marginal is a matter of arithmetic, as relevant for football as for production costs. A footballer who has scored 3 goals in 3 games is averaging 1 goal per game. To score 2 goals in the next game, implying 5 goals from 4 games, would raise the average to 1.25 goals per game. In the fourth game the marginal score is 2 goals, the increase in total goals from 3 to 5. Because the marginal score exceeds the average score in previous games, the extra game must drag up the average.

The same relation holds for production costs. When the marginal cost of the next unit exceeds the average cost of the existing units, making the next unit must drag up average cost. Conversely, when the marginal cost of the next unit lies below the average cost of existing units, an extra unit of production drags down average costs. When marginal and average cost are equal, adding a unit leaves average cost unchanged. This explains fact 1.

Fact 2 follows from fact 1. In Figure 8-5 average and marginal cost curves cross at the point A, which must be the point of minimum average cost. Why? To the left of A, LMC lies below LAC so average cost is still falling. To the right of A, LMC lies above LAC so average cost is rising. Hence the point A must be the output level at which average costs are at a minimum.

As in the football example, this relation rests purely on arithmetic. Although Figure 8-5 refers to long-run average and marginal cost, the same reasoning will hold when we discuss short-run average and marginal cost in section 8-7. With a U-shaped average cost curve, the marginal cost curve lies below the average cost curve to the left of minimum average costs but above the average cost curve to the right of minimum average cost. The marginal cost curve crosses the average cost curve from below at the point of minimum average cost.

Table 8-6 summarizes this important relationship. It is true both for the relationship between LMC and LAC and for the relationship between short-run average cost (SAC) and short-run marginal cost (SMC).

Table 8-6 Marginal and average cost

	$MC < AC$	$MC = AC$	$MC > AC$
AC is:	falling	minimum	rising

8-6 The Firm's Long-run Output Decision

We can now analyse the firm's long-run output decision. Figure 8-6 shows smooth LAC and LMC curves for a firm not restricted to produce integer units of output. It also shows the marginal revenue (MR) curve. From Chapter 7 we already know that the output level of maximum profit or minimum loss occurs at B, the output at which marginal revenue equals marginal cost. The firm then has to check whether it makes profits or losses at this output. It should not stay in business if it makes losses for ever.

Total profits are average profits per unit of output multiplied by the number of units of output. Hence total profits are positive only if average profits per unit of output exceed zero. Average profits are average revenue per unit minus average cost per unit. But average revenue per unit is simply the price for which each output unit is sold. Hence *if long-run average costs at B exceed the price for*

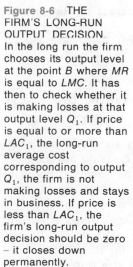

Figure 8-6 THE FIRM'S LONG-RUN OUTPUT DECISION. In the long run the firm chooses its output level at the point B where MR is equal to LMC. It has then to check whether it is making losses at that output level Q_1. If price is equal to or more than LAC_1, the long-run average cost corresponding to output Q_1, the firm is not making losses and stays in business. If price is less than LAC_1, the firm's long-run output decision should be zero – it closes down permanently.

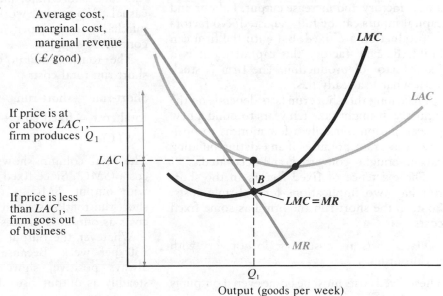

Average cost, marginal cost, marginal revenue ($£$/good)

If price is at or above LAC_1, firm produces Q_1

If price is less than LAC_1, firm goes out of business

LAC_1

B

$LMC = MR$

MR

Q_1

Output (goods per week)

which the output Q_1 can be sold, the firm is making losses even in the long run and should close down. If, at this output, price equals *LAC*, the firm just covers its costs and breaks even. And if price exceeds *LAC* at this output, the firm is making long-run profits and should happily remain in business.

Notice that this is a two-stage argument. First we use the *marginal condition* ($LMC = MR$) to find the profit maximizing or loss minimizing output provided the firm stays in business, *then* we use the *average condition* (the comparison of *LAC* at this output with the price or average revenue received) to determine whether the profit maximizing or loss minimizing output in fact yields profits and hence allows the firm to stay in business in the long run. If even the best output from the firm's viewpoint yields losses, then the firm should close down.

8-7 Short-run Cost Curves and Diminishing Marginal Returns

The short run is the period in which the firm cannot fully adjust to a change in conditions. In the short run the firm has some fixed factors of production.

A *fixed factor of production* is a factor whose input level cannot be varied.

A rise in demand for the firm's output can shift its marginal revenue curve outwards. In the long run it may be profit-maximizing to build a new factory and increase output. Labour and capital inputs can be fully adjusted. No factors of production are fixed. But until the firm can build the new factory this capital input is a fixed factor of production. The firm is stuck with what it already has.

How long this short run lasts depends on the industry. It might take ten years to build a new power station but only a few months to open new restaurant premises if an existing building can be bought, converted, and decorated.

The existence of fixed factors in the short run has two implications for a firm's costs. First, in the short run the firm has some fixed costs.

Fixed costs are costs that do not vary with output levels.

These fixed costs must be borne even if output is zero. If the firm cannot quickly add to or dispose of its existing factory, it must still pay depreciation on the building and meet the interest cost of the money it originally borrowed to buy the factory.

Second, because in the short run the firm cannot make all the adjustments it would like, its short-run costs of production must be different from its long-run production costs, and must be higher. When adjustment eventually becomes possible, the firm has an incentive to make this adjustment only if it can get on to a lower cost curve by doing so. We now study these short-run costs in more detail.

Short-run Fixed and Variable Costs of Production

Table 8-7 presents data on short-run costs. The second column shows the fixed costs, which are independent of the output level. The third column shows the variable costs.

Variable costs are costs that change as output changes.

Variable costs are the costs of hiring variable (non-fixed) factors of production, typically labour and raw materials. Although firms may have long-term contracts with workers and material suppliers, which tend to reduce the speed at which adjustment of these factors can be accomplished, in practice most firms retain important elements of flexibility through overtime and short time, hiring or non-hiring of casual and part-time workers, and raw material purchases in the open market to supplement contracted supplies.

The fourth column of Table 8-7 shows short-run total costs

Short-run   short-run   short-run
total cost = fixed cost + variable cost   (1)
  (*STC*)   (*SFC*)   (*SVC*)

The final column shows short-run marginal costs (*SMC*). Since fixed costs do not increase with output, *SMC* is the increase both in short-run total costs and in short-run variable costs as output is increased by 1 unit.

Whatever the output level, fixed costs are £30 per week. Because marginal costs are always positive, short-run total costs rise steadily as output rises. Extra output adds to

Table 8-7 Short-run costs of production

(1) OUTPUT (goods/wk)	(2) (SFC) SHORT-RUN FIXED COST (£/wk)	(3) (SVC) SHORT-RUN VARIABLE COST (£/wk)	(4) (STC) SHORT-RUN TOTAL COST (£/wk)	(5) (SMC) SHORT-RUN MARGINAL COST (£/wk)
0	30	0	30	
1	30	22	52	22
2	30	38	68	16
3	30	48	78	10
4	30	61	91	13
5	30	79	109	18
6	30	102	132	23
7	30	131	161	29
8	30	166	196	35
9	30	207	237	41
10	30	255	285	48

total cost, and adds more the higher is the marginal cost. Looking at the last column of Table 8-7 we see that, as output increases, marginal costs first fall then rise again. The short-run marginal cost curve has the same general shape as the long-run marginal cost curve shown in Figure 8-7, but for a very different reason.

In the long run the firm can vary all factors freely. As output expands, it may become cost-minimizing to install a sophisticated assembly line which then allows extra output to be produced quite cheaply. Then diseconomies of scale set in and marginal costs of further output increases start to rise again.

The short-run marginal cost curve assumes that there is at least one fixed factor, probably capital. We cannot explain the shape of the SMC by switches to different machinery and production techniques. Suppose there are only two inputs in the short run, fixed capital and variable labour. To change output as we move along the short-run marginal cost curve, the firm must be adding ever-increasing amounts of labour to a given amount of plant and machinery. It is here we must seek the explanation for the shape of the short-run marginal curve.

The Marginal Product of Labour and Diminishing Marginal Productivity

Table 8-8 shows how output increases as variable labour input is added to the fixed quantity of capital. With no workers, the firm

Table 8-8 Total and marginal products of labour

LABOUR INPUT (workers/wk)	OUTPUT (goods/wk)	MARGINAL PRODUCT OF LABOUR (goods/wk)
0	0	
1	0.8	0.8
2	1.8	1.0
3	3.1	1.3
4	4.3	1.2
5	5.4	1.1
6	6.3	0.9
7	6.3	0.7
8	7.5	0.5
9	7.8	0.3

produces no output. The first unit of labour increases output by 0.8 units.

> The *marginal product* of a variable factor (in this example, labour) is the increase in output obtained by adding 1 unit of the variable factor, holding constant the input of all other factors (in this example the fixed factor, capital).

The first unit of labour has a marginal product of 0.8 units. The third unit of labour has a marginal product of 1.3 units since output increases from 1.8 units with 2 labour units to 3.1 with 3 labour units.

At low levels of output and labour input, the first worker has a whole factory to work with and has to do too many jobs to produce very much. A second worker helps, and a third helps even more. Suppose the factory has three machines and the three workers are each specializing in fully running one of the factory's machines. The marginal product of the fourth worker is lower. With only three machines, the fourth worker gets to use one only when one of the other workers is having a rest. There is even less useful machine work for the fifth worker to do. The marginal product of that worker is still lower. In fact, beyond a labour input of 3, the marginal product of each additional worker decreases steadily as the number of workers is increased. When this happens we say that there are diminishing returns to labour.

> Holding all factors constant except one, *the law of diminishing returns* says that, beyond some level of the variable input, further increases in the variable input lead to a steadily decreasing marginal product of that input.

This is a law about technology. Adding ever-increasing numbers of workers to a fixed quantity of machinery gets less and less useful.

The ninth worker's main role in production is to get coffee for the others operating the machines. This contributes to output but not a great deal. Figure 8-7 summarizes our discussion of marginal productivity. If capital happened to be the variable factor and labour the fixed factor, a similar argument would obtain. Adding more and more machines to a given labour force might initially lead to large increases in output but would quickly encounter diminishing returns as machines became under-utilized. Thus the schedule in Figure 8-7 showing the marginal product of labour when labour is the variable factor could equally well describe the behaviour of the marginal product of capital when capital is the variable factor.[2]

Before we show the relevance of marginal products for short-run marginal cost, notice that this concept is *not* the everyday meaning of 'productivity' which refers to the *average*

---

[2] Notice that economists use *diminishing* returns to describe the addition of one variable factor to other fixed factors in the short run, but *decreasing* returns to describe diseconomies of scale when *all* factors are freely varied in the long run.

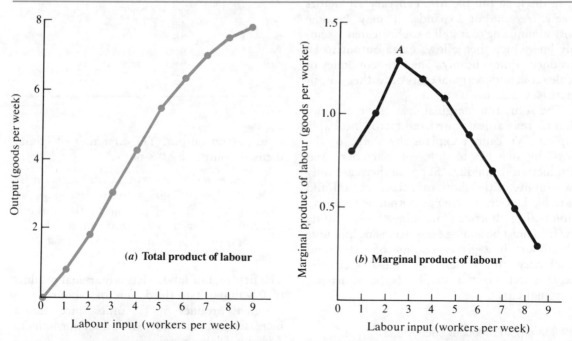

Figure 8-7 THE PRODUCTIVITY OF LABOUR AND DIMINISHING MARGINAL RETURNS. The data plotted are from Table 8-8. The total product of labour increases as the input of labour is increased. But the marginal product of labour first increases and then decreases. Beyond point A in part (b) the marginal product of labour is decreasing, or there are diminishing marginal returns to labour. This is because more and more workers are being put to work with the same stock of machines.

product. For example, the average product of labour, what is most commonly meant by 'productivity', is output divided by total labour input. Of course, the same old arithmetic holds good. If the marginal product of labour lies above the average product, the addition of another worker will raise the average product and 'productivity'. When diminishing returns set in, the marginal product will quickly fall below the average product and the latter will fall if further workers are added. If you do not see why this must be true, try calculating output per unit of labour input as an extra column in Table 8-8.

Finally, as usual, we must distinguish between movements along a curve and shifts in a curve. The marginal product curve is drawn for given levels of the other factors. For a higher given level of the fixed factors, the marginal product curve would be higher. With more machinery to work with, an extra worker will generally be able to produce more extra output than previously. The numbers in Table 8-8 and the height of the marginal product curve in Figure 8-7 depend on the amount of fixed factors with which the firm began.

Short-run Marginal Costs

We can now explain why Table 8-7 shows that, as output is increased, short-run marginal costs first fall then rise. Every worker costs the firm the same wage. While the marginal product of labour is increasing, each worker adds more to

output than the previous workers. Hence the extra cost of making extra output is falling. *SMC* is falling so long as the marginal product of labour is rising.

Once diminishing returns to labour set in, the marginal product of labour falls and *SMC* starts to rise again. It takes successively more workers to make each extra unit of output.

Thus the shape of the short-run marginal cost curve and hence the short-run total cost curve is determined by the shape of the marginal product curve in Figure 8-7, which in turn depends on the technology facing the firm.

Short-run Average Costs

Table 8-9 shows short-run *average* cost data corresponding to Table 8-7.

Short-run average fixed cost (SAFC) equals short-run fixed cost (SFC) divided by output. Short-run average variable cost (SAVC) equals SVC divided by output and short-run average total cost (SATC) equals STC divided by output.

Each number in Table 8-9 is obtained by dividing the corresponding number in Table 8-7 by the output level. (The first row is omitted: dividing by zero output does not make sense.) The table also shows short-run marginal costs, taken from Table 8-7.

Figure 8-8 plots the three short-run average cost measures from Table 8-9. It is no accident

Table 8-9 Short-run average costs of production

OUTPUT (goods/wk)	(*SAFC*) SHORT-RUN AVERAGE FIXED COST (£/good)	(*SAFC*) SHORT-RUN AVERAGE VARIABLE COST (£/good)	(*SATC*) SHORT-RUN AVERAGE TOTAL COST (£/good)	(*SMC*) SHORT-RUN MARGINAL COST (£/good)
0	—	—	—	
1	30.00	22.00	52.00	22
2	15.00	19.00	34.00	16
3	10.00	16.00	26.00	10
4	7.50	15.25	22.75	13
5	6.00	15.80	21.80	18
6	5.00	17.00	22.00	23
7	4.29	18.71	23.00	29
8	3.75	20.75	24.50	35
9	3.33	23.00	26.33	41
10	3.00	25.50	28.50	48

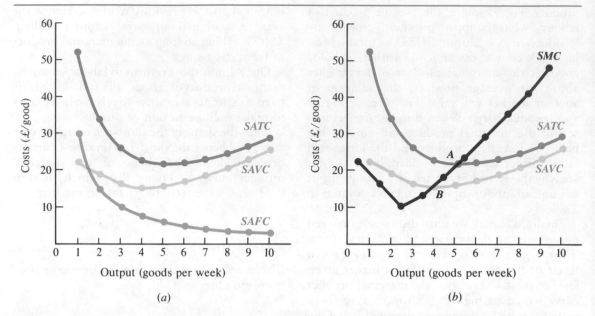

Figure 8-8 SHORT-RUN AVERAGE COST AND MARGINAL COST CURVES.   These diagrams plot the data of Table 8-9. They are shown in two separate figures to avoid clutter. Part (a) shows the relationship between short-run average fixed, variable, and total costs. *SATC* is equal to *SAFC* plus *SAVC*. The shape of the *SATC* curve is a result of the shapes of its two components. When both *SAVC* and *SAFV* are declining, so is *SATC*. When *SAVC* starts rising, the shape of *SATC* depends on whether *SAVC* is rising more rapidly than *SAFC* is falling. In part (b) the relationship between marginal and average cost curves established for the long-run applies also to the short-run curves. The *SMC* curve goes through the minimum points of both the *SAVC* curve, at *B*, and the *SATC* curve, at *A*.

that

$$
\begin{array}{ccc}
\textbf{Short-run} & \textbf{short-run} & \textbf{short-run} \\
\textbf{average} & \textbf{average} & \textbf{average} \\
\textbf{total cost} = & \textbf{fixed cost} + & \textbf{variable cost} \qquad (2) \\
\textbf{(SATC)} & \textbf{(SAFC)} & \textbf{(SAVC)}
\end{array}
$$

This follows from dividing each term in equation (1) by the output level.

Look first at Figure 8-8(b). We already understand the shape of the *SMC* curve that follows from the behaviour of marginal labour productivity. The usual arithmetical relation between marginal and average explains why *SMC* passes through the lowest point *A* on the short-run average total cost curve. To the left of this point, *SMC* lies below *SATC* and is dragging it down as output expands. To the right of *A* the converse holds. That explains the shape of the *SATC* curve in Figure 8-8.

Variable costs are the difference between total costs and fixed costs. Since fixed costs do not change with output, marginal costs also show how much total *variable* costs are

changing. The same arithmetic relation between marginal costs and average *variable* costs must hold and the usual reasoning implies that *SMC* goes through the lowest point *B* on *SAVC*. To the left of *B*, *SMC* lies below *SAVC* and *SAVC* must be falling. To the right of *B*, *SAVC* must be rising. Finally, since average total costs exceed average variable costs by average fixed costs, *SAVC* must lie below *SATC*. Hence point *B* must lie to the left of point *A*. That explains the shape of *SAVC* and its relation to *SATC* in Figure 8-8(b).

In Figure 8-8(a), *SAFC* falls steadily because the same total fixed cost (what firms call 'overheads') is being spread over ever larger output levels, thereby reducing average fixed costs. The reasoning of Figure 8-8(b) is easily confirmed in Figure 8-8(a). Carrying over from Figure 8-8(b) the *SATC* and *SAVC* curves we can check that, at each output level, *SATC = SAVC + SAFC* as in equation (2) above.

By now any reasonable person is asking two questions: how can anyone remember all these curves, and what use are they? To answer the 'how' question, go back to Figure 8-1, which shows the three basic costs: total, marginal, and average. We must distinguish between the short and long run, and between fixed and variable costs. With these distinctions we generate all the cost curves we have examined.

The second question is more important. We make these distinctions not to exercise the mind but because they are necessary to understand the firm's output decision. We have already used long-run cost curves to analyse the firm's long-run output decision. Now we use short-run cost curves to analyse the firm's output decision in the short run.

8-8 The Firm's Output Decision in the Short Run

Figure 8-9 illustrates the firm's choice of output in the short run. Since fixed factors cannot be varied in the short run, it is *short-run* marginal cost that must be set equal to marginal revenue

to determine the output level Q_1 which maximizes profits or minimizes losses.

Next, the firm decides whether or not to stay in business in the short run. Again, profits are positive at the output Q_1 if the price p at which this output can be sold covers average total costs. It is the short-run measure $SATC_1$ at this output that is relevant. If p exceeds $SATC_1$, the firm is making profits in the short run and should certainly produce Q_1.

Suppose p is less than $SATC_1$. The firm is losing money because p does not cover costs. In the long run the firm closes down if it keeps losing money, but there the difference between the long run and the short run appears. Even at zero output the firm must pay the fixed costs in the short run. The firm needs to know whether losses are bigger if it produces at Q_1 or produces zero.

If revenue exceeds variable cost the firm is earning something towards paying its overheads. Thus the firm will produce Q_1 provided revenues exceed variable costs even though Q_1 may involve losses. The firm produces Q_1 if p exceeds $SAVC_1$. If not, it produces zero.

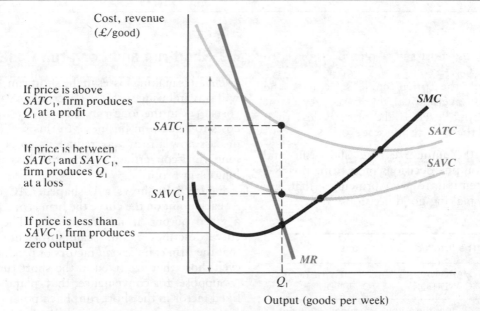

Figure 8-9 THE FIRM'S SHORT-RUN OUTPUT DECISION.   The firm sets output at level Q_1, at which short-run marginal cost (*SMC*) is equal to marginal revenue. Then it has to check whether it should produce at all. If price is above $SATC_1$, the level of short-run average total cost at output level Q_1, then the firm is making a profit and should certainly produce Q_1. If price falls between $SATC_1$ and $SAVC_1$, then the firm is partly covering its fixed costs, even though it is losing money. It should still produce output Q_1. Only if the price is below $SAVC_1$ should the firm produce zero. At those prices, the firm is not even covering its variable costs, and it therefore does better to produce zero and not incur the variable costs.

MARGINAL CONDITIONS AND SUNK COSTS

The analysis of supply illustrates two principles of good decision-making which are frequently encountered in economics and in other aspects of life. The first is the *marginal principle*. If the best position has been reached, there cannot be even a small change that improves things. In deciding how much to produce, the firm keeps examining the effect on profits when output is increased or decreased by 1 unit. If profits can be increased by such a change, the change is made. When no further improvement is possible, the point of maximum profits has been found. To decide how many hours to study, you should assess the extra costs and benefits of studying another hour. If the benefits outweigh the costs, consider studying yet another hour. When you reach the point at which the two are equal, you have found the best position.

Of course it is also necessary to examine the big picture. Not only does the firm have to set marginal cost equal to marginal revenue; it must check that it is not better to close down completely. Similarly, the marginal principle will guide you to the best number

of hours for which to study economics, but you must look at the big picture to assess whether you should be studying economics in the first place.

The second general principle is that *sunk costs are sunk*. If certain costs have already been incurred and cannot be affected by your decision, ignore them. They should not influence your future decisions. In deciding how much to produce in the short run, the firm ignores its fixed costs which must be incurred anyway. It finds the best output using the marginal principle, then examines whether the price at which this output can be sold will cover its variable costs in the short run, the costs that still can be affected by the decision the firm is making now. You have read nearly eight chapters of this book: should you keep reading? The answer depends entirely on the costs and benefits you will get from the *rest* of the book, not on the time you have already spent.

The *sunk cost fallacy* is the view that sunk costs matter. It may seem a pity to abandon a project on which a lot of money has already been invested. Poker players call this throwing good money after bad. If you do not think it will be worth reading the next ten chapters in their own right, you should not do it merely because you have put a lot of effort into the first eight chapters. Bygones should be bygones.

The firm's short-run output decision is to produce Q_1, the output at which $MR = SMC$, provided the price at least equals the short-run average variable cost $(SAVC_1)$ at that output level. If the price is less than $SAVC_1$ the firm produces zero.

Table 8-10 summarizes the short-run and long-run output decisions of a firm. Box 8-1 draws attention to two principles that are central to making good decisions.

Table 8-10 The firm's output decisions

	MARGINAL CONDITION	CHECK WHETHER TO PRODUCE
Short-run decision	Choose the output level at which $MR = SMC$	Produce this output unless price lower than $SAVC$. If it is, produce zero.
Long-run decision	Choose the output level at which $MR = LMC$	Produce this output unless price is lower than LAC. If it is, produce zero.

8-9 Short-run and Long-run Costs

Even if it is making losses in the short run, a firm will stay in business if it is covering its variable costs. Yet in the long run it must cover all its costs to remain in business. In this section we discuss how a firm may reduce its costs in the long run, converting a short-run loss into a long-term profit.

Figure 8-10 shows a U-shaped LAC curve. At each point on the curve the firm is producing a given output at minimum cost. The LAC curve describes a time scale sufficiently long that the firm can vary *all* factors of production, even those that are fixed in the short run.

Suppose, for convenience, that 'plant' is the fixed factor in the short run. Each point on the LAC curve involves a particular quantity of plant. Holding constant this quantity, of plant, we can draw the short-run average total cost curve for this plant size. Thus, the $SATC_1$ curve corresponds to the plant size at point A on the LAC curve and the $SATC_2$ and $SATC_3$ curves correspond to the plant size at points B and C

Figure 8-10 THE LONG-RUN AVERAGE COST CURVE *LAC*. Suppose the plant size is fixed in the short run. For each plant size we obtain a particular *SATC* curve. But in the long run even plant size is variable. To construct the *LAC* curve we select at each output the plant size which gives the lowest *SATC* at this output. Thus points such as *A*, *B*, *C*, and *D* lie on the *LAC* curve. Notice the *LAC* curve does *not* pass through the lowest point on each *SATC* curve. For example, the plant size corresponding to $SATC_1$ happens to give the lowest average cost of producing Q_1 even in the long run but Q_2 is the minimum average cost at which this plant could produce since it is the lowest point on $SATC_1$. Nevertheless, it is even cheaper to produce the output Q_2 by employing the plant size corresponding to $SATC_2$. Thus the *LAC* curve shows the minimum average cost way to produce a given output when all factors can be varied *not* the minimum average cost at which a given plant can produce.

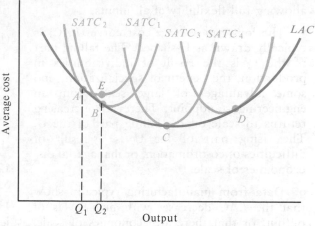

on the *LAC* curve. In fact, we could draw an *SATC* curve corresponding to the plant size at each point on the *LAC* curve.

By definition, the *LAC* curve describes the minimum-cost way to produce each output when all factors can be freely varied. Thus, point *B* describes the minimum average cost way to produce an output Q_2. Hence it *must* be more costly to produce Q_2 using the wrong quantity of plant, the quantity corresponding to point *E*. For the plant size at *A*, $SATC_1$ shows the cost of producing each output including Q_2. Hence $SATC_1$ must lie *above* *LAC* at every point except *A*, the output level for which this plant size happens to be best.

This argument can be repeated for any other plant size. Hence $SATC_3$ and $SATC_4$ corresponding respectively to the fixed plant size at *C* and at *D*, must lie above *LAC* except at points *C* and *D* themselves. In the long run the firm can vary all its factors and will generally be able to produce a particular output more cheaply than in the short run, when it is stuck with the quantities of fixed factors it was using previously. A firm that is currently suffering losses because demand has fallen will be able to look forward to future profits after it has had time to build a plant that is more suitable to its new level of output.

Summary

1   This chapter develops the distinction be-

tween short-run and long-run cost curves and output decisions. The long-run is a period over which the firm can fully adjust all its inputs to a change in conditions. The short run is a period in which the firm cannot fully adjust all its inputs to changed conditions. In particular, in the short run the firm is not able to change the quantity of fixed factors, such as plant and equipment, that it is using. The length of calendar time corresponding to the long run varies from industry to industry.

2   The production function specifies the maximum amount of output that can be produced using any given quantities of inputs. The inputs are machines, raw materials, labour, and any other factors of production. The production function summarizes the technical possibilities open to the firm.

3   The total cost curve is derived from the production function, for given wages and rental rates of factors of production. The long-run total cost curve is obtained by finding, for each level of output, the method of production that minimizes costs when all inputs are fully flexible. When the relative price of using a factor of production rises, the firms substitutes away from that factor in its choice of production techniques. For instance, if the wage rate rises, the firm tends to use more machines and less labour.

4   Average cost is equal to total cost divided by output. The long-run average cost curve is

derived from the long-run total cost curve, allowing full flexibility of all inputs.

5   The long-run average cost curve (*LAC*) is typically drawn as U-shaped. The falling part of the U is the result of indivisibilities in production, the benefit of specialization, and some advantages of large scale from an engineering standpoint. There are increasing returns to scale on the falling part of the U. The rising part of the U is a result of difficulties of co-ordination, or managerial diseconomies of scale.

6   Data from manufacturing typically show that the *LAC* decreases with high levels of output, or that there are economies of scale. For some industries the economies of scale become small at levels of output that are only a small percentage of total industry output.

7   When marginal cost is below average cost, average cost is falling. When marginal cost is above average cost, average cost is rising. Average and marginal cost are equal only at the lowest point on the average cost curve.

8   In the long run the firm produces at the point where long-run marginal cost (*LMC*) equals *MR* provided price is not less than the level of long-run average cost at that level of output. If price is less than long-run average cost, the firm goes out of business.

9   In the short run the firm cannot adjust some of its inputs. But it still has to pay for them. It has short-run fixed costs (*SFC*) of production. Other factors of production, like labour, are variable in the short run. The cost of using the variable factors is short-run variable cost (*SVC*). Short-run total costs (*STC*) are equal to *SFC* plus *SVC*.

10   The short-run marginal cost curve (*SMC*) reflects the marginal product of the variable factor holding other factors fixed. Usually we think of labour as variable, but capital as fixed in the short run. When very little labour is being used, the plant is too big for labour to produce much. Increasing labour input leads to large rises in output and *SMC* falls. Once machinery is fully manned, each extra worker adds progressively less to output and *SMC* begins to rise.

11   Short-run average total costs (*SATC*) are equal to short-run total costs (*STC*) divided by output. *SATC* is equal to short-run average fixed costs (*SAFC*) plus short-run average variable costs (*SAVC*). The *SATC* curve is U-shaped. The falling part of the U results both from declining *SAFC* as the fixed costs are spread over more units of output and from declining *SAVC* at low levels of output. The *SATC* continues to fall after *SAVC* begins to increase, but eventually increasing *SAVC* outweighs declining *SAFC* and the *SATC* curve slopes up.

12   The *SMC* curve cuts both the *SATC* and *SAVC* curves at their minimum points.

13   The firm sets output in the short run at the level at which *SMC* is equal to *MR*. It produces that level of output so long as price is not less than short-run average *variable* cost. In the short run the firm is willing to produce at a loss provided it is recovering at least part of its fixed costs.

14   The *LAC* curve is always below the *SATC* curve, except at the point where the two coincide. This implies that a firm is certain to have higher profits in the long run than in the short run if it is currently producing with a plant size that is not best from the viewpoint of the long run. A firm may be producing with plant size that is inappropriate (with regard to the long run) if it has recently faced a change in demand or cost conditions.

Key Terms

Inputs and outputs
Technology
Production function
Long run
Short run
Long-run total cost curve
Long-run marginal cost (LMC) curve
Long-run average cost (LAC) curve
Returns to scale
Economies of scale
Diseconomies of scale
Constant returns to scale
Fixed factors
Variable factors
Choice of production technique
Factor intensity
Technical efficiency
Short-run fixed costs (AFC)

Short-run variable costs (SVC)
Short-run total costs (STC)
Marginal product of labour
Law of diminishing returns
Short-run marginal costs (SMC)
Short-run average fixed costs (SAFC)
Short-run average variable costs (SAVC)
Short-run average total costs (SATC)
Sunk cost fallacy
Marginal principle

Problems

1 (*a*) What information does the production function provide? (*b*) Explain why the production function does not provide enough information for anyone actually to run a firm.

2 (*a*) What are economies of scale and why might they exist? Discuss the evidence and say to what types of firms this applies. (*b*) The following table shows how output changes as inputs change. Assume the wage rate is £5 and the rental rate of capital is £2. Calculate the lowest-cost (economically most efficient) method of producing, 4, 8, and 12 units of output. (*c*) Do you have increasing, constant, or decreasing returns to scale between those output levels? Which applies where?

CAPITAL INPUT	LABOUR INPUT	OUTPUT
4	5	4
2	6	4
7	10	8
4	12	8
11	15	12
8	16	12

3 (*a*) For each output level in the above table, say which technique of production is more capital intensive. (*b*) Does the firm switch towards or away from more capital-intensive techniques as output rises?

4 Suppose the rental rate of capital in question 2 rose to £3. (*a*) Would the firm change its method of production for any levels of output? Say which, if any. (*b*) How do the firm's total and average costs change when the rental rate of capital rises?

5 (*a*) Calculate the marginal and average costs for each level of output from the following total cost data. (*b*) Show how marginal and average costs are related. (*c*) Are these short-run or long-run cost curves? Explain how you can tell.

OUTPUT	0	1	2	3	4	5	6	7	8	9
TOTAL COST (£)		12	27	40	51	60	70	80	91	104	120

6 (*a*) Why does a firm have fixed costs of production in the short run? (*b*) Explain the typical shape of *SAFC*, *SAVC*, and *SATC* curves. (*c*) Why does the law of diminishing marginal productivity have anything to do with short-run cost curves?

7 (*a*) Explain why it might make sense for a firm to produce goods that it can only sell at a loss. (*b*) Can it keep on doing this for ever? Explain.

8 Common Fallacies Show why the following statements are incorrect: (*a*) Firms which make losses are lame ducks who should be closed down at once. (*b*) The long-run average cost curve passes through the lowest point on each short-run average cost curve. (*c*) Larger firms can always produce more cheaply than smaller firms.

9

Perfect Competition and Pure Monopoly: The Limiting Cases of Market Structure

An industry is the set of all firms making the same product. The output of an industry is the sum of the outputs of its individual firms. Yet different industries have very different numbers of firms. Intercity train services in the UK are produced by British Rail, which we call a *nationalized industry* because it is owned and run by the state. However, some sole suppliers are private firms. Until recently almost all car windscreens in the UK were made by the Pilkington glass company. Until its patent expired, IBM was the sole supplier of golfball typewriters. In contrast, the UK has over 200 000 farms and 30 000 grocers.

How can we analyse how price and output are determined for an industry as a whole? Some hints were offered in Chapter 3. Since then we have refined our analysis of demand in Chapters 5 and 6 and our analysis of the output supply decision of the individual firm in Chapters 7 and 8. We now combine the supply decisions of the individual firms to derive the industry supply curve and examine its interaction with the market demand curve to determine price and output for the industry as a whole.

How is this analysis affected by the size and number of firms in an industry? Why indeed do some industries have many firms but others only one? These are questions about *market structure*.

The structure of a market is a description of the behaviour of buyers and sellers in that market.

In the next chapter we develop a general theory of market structure, showing how demand and cost conditions together determine the number of firms and their behaviour. First it is useful to establish two benchmark cases, the opposite extremes between which all other types of market structure must lie. These limiting cases are *perfect competition* on the one hand and *monopoly* or *monopsony* on the other hand.

A *perfectly competitive* market is one in which both buyers and sellers believe that their own buying or selling decisions have no effect on the market price. A *monopolist* is the only seller or potential seller of the good in that industry. A *monopsonist* is the only buyer or potential buyer of the good in that industry.

In this and the following chapter we are interested primarily in the relationship between the number of sellers and the behaviour of sellers. For the moment we neglect the possibility of monopsony. We assume that there are many buyers whose individual downward-sloping demand curves can be aggregated to yield the market demand curve. We take up the possibility of monopsony in Chapter 11 when discussing the market not for outputs but for inputs such as labour. At present we assume that the demand side of the market is competitive, and we contrast the limiting cases on the supply side.

The economist's definition of perfect competition is different from the meaning of competition in everyday usage. The economist means that each individual, recognizing that his own quantities supplied or demanded are trivial relative to the market as a whole, acts on the assumption that his actions will have no effect on the market price. This assumption is built into our model of consumer choice in Chapter 6. Each consumer constructs a budget line on the assumption that market prices are *given* and unaffected by the quantities he chooses. Changes in *market* conditions, applying to all firms and consumers, change the equilibrium price and hence individual quantities demanded, but each individual neglects any feedback from his own actions to market price.

This concept of competition, which we now extend to firms, differs from everyday usage. Ford and Renault are fighting each other vigorously for the European car market, but an economist would not call them perfectly competitive. Each commands such a large share of the total market that changes in their quantities supplied affect the market price. Each must take account of this in deciding how much to supply. They cannot regard themselves as *pricetakers*. Only under perfect competition can individuals make decisions that treat the price as independent of their own actions.

9-1 Perfect Competition

A perfectly competitive industry, in which everyone believes that their own actions have no effect on market price, must have many buyers and many sellers. Agricultural markets are a good example. In London the New Covent Garden fruit market confronts many buyers with many sellers. Neither buyers nor sellers believe their own actions affect the market price.

Firms in a perfectly competitive industry face a flat or horizontal demand curve as shown in Figure 9-1. No matter how much the firm sells it gets exactly the market price. If it tries to charge a price in excess of P_0 it will not sell any output: buyers will go to one of the other firms whose product is just as good. Since the firm can sell as much as it wants at P_0, there is no point contemplating a price lower than P_0. The individual firm's demand curve is *DD*.

This horizontal demand curve for its product is the crucial feature of a perfectly competitive firm. For this to be a plausible description of the demand curve facing the firm, we really need to have in mind an industry with four characteristics. First, there must be a large number of firms in the industry so that each is trivial relative to the industry as a whole. Second, the firms must be making a reasonably standard product, such as wheat or potatoes. Even if the car industry had a large number of firms it would not be sensible to view it as a

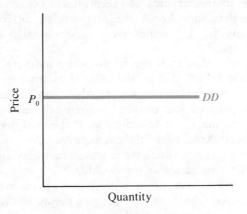

The competitive firm's demand curve

Figure 9-1   THE COMPETITIVE FIRM'S DEMAND CURVE.   A competitive firm can sell as much as it wants at the market price P_0. Its demand curve *DD* is horizontal at this price.

competitive industry. A Ford Sierra is not a perfect substitute for a Vauxhall Cavalier. The more imperfect they are as substitutes, the more it will make sense to view Ford as the sole supplier of Sierras and Vauxhall as the sole supplier of Cavaliers. Each producer will then cease to be trivial relative to the relevant market and will no longer be able to act as a price-taker.

This example alerts us to the problem of which goods can be grouped together within the same market or industry. We return to this issue in the next chapter. For the moment we can evade this issue. In a perfectly competitive industry all firms must be making essentially the same product, *for which they must all charge the same price.*

Even if all firms in an industry made *homogeneous* or identical goods each firm might have some discretion over the price it charged if buyers have imperfect information about the quality or characteristics of the products of different firms in the industry. If you don't know much about cars you may *think* that a 1970 Ford Cortina being sold for £1000 must be in a *better* condition than a 1970 Ford Cortina being sold for £500. Hence, if no firm in a competitive industry can affect the price for which it sells its output, it is not sufficient that all firms are selling a homogeneous product. We must also assume that buyers have almost perfect information about the characteristics of the products being sold so that they know the products of different firms in a competitive industry really are identical.

Why don't all the firms in the industry do what OPEC did in 1973–74? If existing firms collectively restrict supply, they can increase the price of their output by moving the industry up its market demand curve. If the analysis of price-taking perfectly competitive firms is to have any relevance we must explain why such collective action is impossible.

One answer is that, with so many firms in the industry, the costs of organizing themselves into a cohesive group might be prohibitive. Think of all the committee meetings that would be needed. Managers might spend more time negotiating with other firms than organizing production. Nevertheless, if the market demand curve is very inelastic, the potential increase in revenue from such co-operation could be enormous, as OPEC discovered. We need a more profound answer to rule out co-operation.

Thus the fourth crucial characteristic of a perfectly competitive industry is *free entry and exit*. Even if existing firms could organize themselves to restrict total supply and drive up the market price, the consequent increase in revenues and profits would simply attract new firms into the industry, thereby increasing total supply again and driving the price back down. Conversely, as we shall shortly see, when firms in a competitive industry are losing money, some firms will close down and, by reducing the number of firms remaining in the industry, reduce the total supply and drive the price up, thereby allowing the remaining firms to survive.

To sum up, each firm in a competitive industry faces a horizontal demand curve for its product at the going market price. To be a reasonable description of the demand conditions facing a firm, the industry must have four characteristics: (1) many firms, each trivial relative to the industry as a whole; (2) a standardized or homogeneous product, so that it is legitimate to examine the industry as a whole rather than a series of sub-industries each with many fewer firms; (3) perfect customer information about product quality so that buyers recognize that the identical products of different firms really are the same; and (4) free entry and exit so there is no incentive for existing firms to collude.[1]

9-2 The Firm's Supply Decision under Perfect Competition

In Chapter 8 we developed a general theory of the supply decision of the individual firm in the short run and in the long run. First, the firm uses the marginal condition ($MC = MR$) to find the best positive level of output; then it uses the average condition to check whether the price for which this output could be sold covers the relevant measure of average cost.

This general theory must hold for the special case of perfectly competitive firms. *The special feature of perfect competition is the relationship between marginal revenue and price.* The competitive firm faces a horizontal demand curve as in Figure 9-1. Unlike the more general case, in which the firm faces a downward-sloping demand curve, the competitive firm does *not* bid down the price as it sells more units of output. Since there is no effect on the revenue from existing output, the marginal revenue from an additional unit of output is simply the price received.

This special feature of a perfectly competitive firm has far-reaching consequences. It is so important we show this feature as equation (1):

$$\text{(\textbf{Marginal revenue})} \quad MR = P \text{ (price)} \qquad \text{(1)}$$

The Firm's Short-run Supply Curve

Figure 9-2 shows again the short-run cost curves – marginal cost SMC, average total cost $SATC$, and average variable cost $SAVC$ – from Chapter 8. From equation (1) the marginal condition for the best level of positive output now implies

$$SMC = MR = P \qquad \text{(2)}$$

Suppose the firm faces a horizontal demand curve at the price P_4 in Figure 9-2. Equation (2) implies that the firm chooses the output level Q_4 to reach the point D, at which price equals marginal cost.

---

[1] Many factors may inhibit entry and exit. IBM's patent prevented other firms entering the golfball typewriter industry. Until 1980 de Beers controlled virtually all diamond mines in the non-communist world, preventing new firms entering the diamond industry. In many countries doctors and lawyers, acting through their professional bodies, have restricted entry to the medical and legal professions. Governments may also urge firms *not* to exit from an industry in which they provide a lot of jobs.

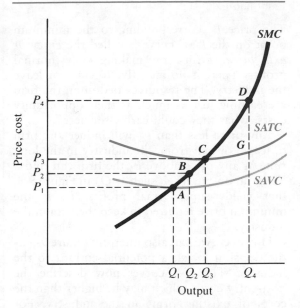

Figure 9-2   SHORT-RUN SUPPLY DECISIONS
OF THE PERFECTLT COMPETITIVE FIRM.
The perfectly competitive firm produces at that level
of output at which price is equal to marginal cost,
provided it makes more profit by producing some
output than none at all. The firm's short-run supply
curve is the *SMC* curve above the point *A*, the
shutdown point below which the firm cannot cover
average variable costs *SAVC* in the short run.

Next, the firm checks whether it would rather shut down in the short run. From Chapter 8 we know that it will shut down only if the price P_4 at which output can be sold fails to cover short-run variable costs of producing this output. In Figure 9-2 P_4 exceeds *SAVC* at the output level Q_4. Not only does the firm wish to produce this output, it also makes profits in the short run. The point *D* lies above the point *G*, the short-run average total cost (including overheads) of producing Q_4.

Suppose the firm had faced a different price. In the short run the firm should produce positive output for any price above P_1. Any price below P_1 lies below the minimum point on the *SAVC* curve and the firm cannot find an output at which price covers *SAVC*. Given any price such as P_2, above P_1, the firm produces Q_2, the output at which price equals marginal cost.

The curve showing the quantity the firm wants to produce at each price is the firm's *supply curve.*

The short-run supply curve is thus the *SMC* curve above point *A*, the point at which the *SMC* curve crosses the lowest point on the *SAVC* curve.

Between points *A* and *C* (prices P_1 and P_3) the firm will be making short-run losses, since price is less than average total cost. But it will be recouping some of its overheads. At any price above P_3, the point at which the *SMC* curve crosses the lowest point on the *SATC* curve, the firm is making short-run profits. For example, at the price P_4 the profit per unit of output is the distance *DG*, the difference between price and average total cost per unit of output. Remember that these profits are economic or supernormal profits after allowing for the economic costs, including the opportunity costs of the owners' financial capital and work effort, summarized in the *SAVC* and *SATC* curves.

The price P_1 is called the *shutdown price*, the price below which the firm reduces its losses by choosing not to produce at all.

The Firm's Long-run Supply Curve

The same principles apply in deriving the long-run supply curve of the perfectly competitive firm. Figure 9-3 shows the firm's average and marginal costs in the long run. Remember that the long-run marginal cost curve *LMC* will be flatter than the *SMC* curve since the firm can freely adjust all factors of production only in the long run.

Facing a price P_4, the marginal condition leads the firm to choose the long-run output level Q_4 at the point *D*. Again we must check whether it is better to shut down than to produce this output. In the long run, shutting down means leaving the industry altogether.

In the long run the firm exits from the industry only if price fails to cover long-run average cost *LAC* at the best positive output level. At the price P_2 the marginal condition leads to the point *B* in Figure 9-3, but the firm is losing money and should leave the industry in the long run.

Thus the firm's *long-run supply curve*, the schedule relating output supplied to price in the long run, is the portion of the *LMC* curve to the right of point *C* corresponding to the price P_3. At any price below P_3 the firm can find no positive output at which price covers *LAC*. At

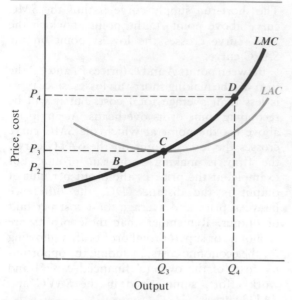

Figure 9-3 LONG-RUN SUPPLY DECISIONS OF THE PERFECTLY COMPETITIVE FIRM. The perfectly competitive firm produces at that level of output at which P is equal to marginal cost, provided it make more profit by producing some output than none at all. It therefore chooses points on the LMC curve. At any price above P_3 the firm makes profits because price is above long-run average cost (LAC). At any price below P_3, such as P_2, the firm makes losses because price is below long-run average cost. It therefore will not produce any output at prices below P_3. The long-run supply curve is the LMC curve above point C.

the price P_3 the firm would produce Q_3 and just break even after paying all its economic costs. The firm would be making only normal profits.[2]

When economic profits are zero we say the firm is making *normal profits*. Its accounting profits just pay the opportunity cost of the owner's money and time.

[2] The firm's behaviour in the short run and in the long run is rather like the behaviour of a good poker player. In the short run the poker player is dealt a particular hand and plays the hand if it is likely to be profitable. If not, the player temporarily shuts down by throwing in the hand. Over time the player gets new hands just as a firm can gradually rearrange its factors of production. When the poker player realizes that, whatever the cards, the long-run outlook is bad because other players are better, the player should leave the game altogether. Similarly, if a firm realizes that, however it adjusts its factors of production, it is going to make losses in the long run, it should leave the industry.

Entry and Exit

The price P_3 corresponding to the minimum point on the LAC curve is called the *entry or exit price*. Firms are making only normal profits. There is no incentive to enter or leave the industry. The resources tied up in the firm are earning just as much as their opportunity costs, what they could earn elsewhere.

Any price less than P_3 will induce the firm to leave, or exit from, the industry in the long run. At any price above P_3 the firm can find a long-run output level, such as Q_4 in Figure 9-3, that yields supernormal profits. P_3 is the minimum price required to keep the firm in the industry.

However, we can also interpret Figure 9-3 as the decision facing a potential entrant to the industry. The cost curves now describe the post-entry costs, which may be higher than the costs of existing firms in the industry. For example, if existing firms have all the best locations, new entrants may have to build factories further away from the market and incur higher transport costs. Nevertheless, P_3, the price that just covers the lowest average cost at which the entrant could produce, is the critical point at which entry becomes attractive. Any price above P_3 yields supernormal profits and means that the return on the owners' time and money will be higher than their opportunity costs, the highest return that these resources could earn elsewhere in the economy.

The Long-run and Short-run Supply Decisions of the Competitive Firm

Figure 9-4 summarizes the preceding discussion. For each level of fixed factors there exists a different SMC curve and short-run supply curve ($SRSS$). The long-run supply curve ($LRSS$) is flatter than $SRSS$ because extra factor flexibility in the long run makes the LMC curve flatter than the SMC curve. The $SRSS$ curve starts from a lower shutdown price because in the short run the firm will produce if it can cover average variable costs. In the long run all costs are variable and must be covered if the firm is to remain in the industry. In either case, the competitive firm's supply curve is the part of the marginal cost curve above the point at which it is better to produce no output at all. Table 9-1 sets out this principle.

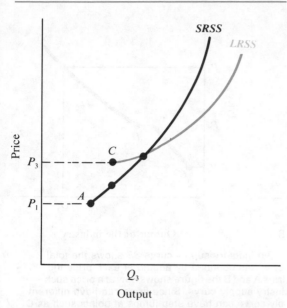

Figure 9-4 SHORT- AND LONG-RUN SUPPLY CURVES OF THE COMPETITIVE FIRM. Taken from the two previous figures, the short-run supply curve is the firm's *SMC* curve above *A* and the long-run supply curve *LRSS* is the firm's *LMC* curve above *C*. P_1 is the shutdown price in the short run and P_3 the entry and exit price in the long run. If the firm happens to begin with the stock of fixed factors it would choose at the lowest point on its *LAC* curve, then *C* will actually lie on the *SRSS* curve.

Table 9-1 The supply decision of the perfectly competitive firm

MARGINAL CONDITION	AVERAGE CONDITION	
	SHORT-RUN	LONG-RUN
Produce output where $P = MC$	If $P < SAVC$ shut down temporarily	If $P < LAC$ leave industry

9-3 The Industry Supply Curves

A competitive industry ,comprises many firms. In the short run two things are fixed: the quantity of fixed factors employed by each firm in the industry, and the number of firms in the industry. In the long run, each firm can vary all its factors of production, but the number of firms can also change through entry and exit from the industry.

The Short-run Industry Supply Curve

Just as we can add individual demand curves by buyers to obtain the market demand curve, we can add the individual supply curves of firms to obtain the industry supply curve. Figure 9-5 shows how. Whether we are discussing the short or the long run, at each price we add together the quantities supplied by each firm to obtain the total quantity supplied at that price.

In the short run the number of firms in the industry is given. Suppose there are two firms, A and B. Each firm's short-run supply curve is the part of its *SMC* curve above its shutdown price. Figure 9-5 assumes that firm A has a lower shutdown price than firm B, Firm A has a lower *SAVC* curve, perhaps because of a more favourable geographical location or superior technical know-how. Each firm's supply curve is horizontal at the shutdown price. At a lower price, no output is supplied.

At each price, the industry supply Q is the sum of Q^A, the supply of firm A, and Q^B, the supply of firm B. Thus at the price P_3, $Q_3 - Q_3^A + Q_3^B$. The industry supply curve is the horizontal sum of the separate supply curves. Notice the industry supply curve is discontinuous at the price P_2. Between P_1 and P_2 only the lower-cost firm A is producing. At P_2 suddenly firm B starts to produce as well.

When there are many firms, each with a different shutdown price, there are a large number of very small discontinuities as we move up the industry supply curve. In fact, since each firm in a competitive industry is trivial relative to the total, the industry supply curve is effectively smooth.

Comparing Short- and Long-run Industry Supply Curves

Figure 9-5 may also be used to derive the long-run industry supply curve. For each firm the individual supply curve is the portion of the *LMC* curve above the firm's entry and exit price. However, unlike the short run, the number of firms in the industry is no longer fixed. Not only can existing firms leave the industry, but also new firms can enter. Instead of horizontally aggregating at each price the quantities supplied by the existing firms in industry, we must horizontally aggregate the quantities supplied by existing firms *and firms that might potentially enter the industry*.

At a price below P_2 in Figure 9-5 firm B will

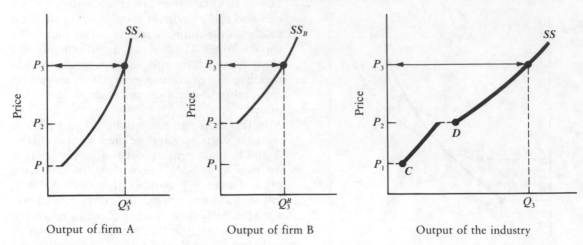

Figure 9-5 DERIVING THE INDUSTRY SUPPLY CURVE. The industry supply curve *SS* shows the total quantity supplied at each price by all the firms in the industry. It is obtained by adding at each price the quantity supplied by each firm in the industry. With only two firms A and B the figure shows how at a price such as P_3 we add Q_3^A and Q_3^B to obtain the output Q_3 on the industry supply curve. Since firms can have different shutdown prices or entry and exit prices, the industry supply curve can have step jumps at points such as *C* and *D* where an extra firm starts production. However, with many firms in the industry, each trivial relative to the industry as a whole, the step jumps in the industry supply curve when another firm starts production are so small that we can effectively think of the upward sloping industry supply curve as smooth.

not be in the industry in the long run. As we contemplate prices above P_2 we must recognize that firm B *will* wish to enter the industry in the long run. As the market price rises, the total industry supply rises in the long run for two distinct reasons: each existing firm will move up its long-run supply curve, and new firms will find it profitable to enter the industry.

Conversely, at lower prices, the higher-cost firms will begin to lose money and will decide to leave the industry. Entry and exit in the long run play a role analogous to shutdown in the short run. In the long run, entry and exit affect the number of producing firms whose output must be horizontally aggregated to obtain the industry supply. In the short run, although the number of firms in the industry is given, the fraction that is producing rather than being temporarily shut down is not. Again, the industry supply curve is the horizontal sum of the outputs of those actually producing at the given market price.

Figure 9-6 illustrates what these arguments imply about the relation between short- and long-run industry supply curves. The long-run supply curve is flatter for two reasons: each firm can vary its factors more appropriately in

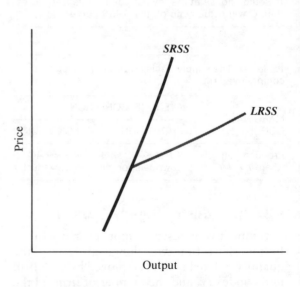

Figure 9-6 SHORT- AND LONG-RUN INDUSTRY SUPPLY CURVES. The long-run industry supply curve *LRSS* is flatter than the short-run industry supply curve *SRSS*. Each firm has a flatter supply curve in the long run because inputs can be varied more appropriately than in the short run. The *LRSS* curve also reflects changes in the number of firms in the long run as firms enter or exit from the industry.

the long run and has a flatter supply curve (Figure 9-4); and higher prices attract additional firms into the industry, causing industry output to rise by more than the additional output supplied by the firms previously in the industry.

Conversely, when the price falls firms initially move down their (relatively steep) short-run supply curves. Provided short-run average variable costs are covered firms will continue to produce and may not reduce output very much. In the long run each firm will reduce output further since all factors of production can now be varied. In addition some firms will leave the industry since they are no longer covering long-run average costs. Thus, in response to a price reduction, industry output will fall by more in the long run than it does in the short run.

The Marginal Firm   Suppose there is a large number of firms, each making the same product for sale at the same price but having slightly different cost curves. Figure 9-7 shows the cost curves for two firms, a low-cost firm A and a

high-cost firm B. Some firms have costs lying between those of A and B and others have even higher costs than B.

The long run is the period in which all adjustment – both in factors and in number of firms – has been completed. There is no further entry and exit. Suppose the long-run price is P^* in Figure 9-7. The low-cost firm A is producing Q_A and making healthy profits, since P^* exceeds LAC at the output Q_A. Slightly higher-cost firms are making slightly less profit. Firm B is the last firm that can survive in the industry. It is just breaking even producing Q_B. It is the *marginal firm* in the industry. A slight price fall would force it to leave the industry.

All firms with higher costs than firm B cannot compete in the industry if the long-run price is P^*. Suppose one potential entrant has an LAC curve whose lowest point is only slightly above P^*. It is the *marginal firm* waiting to enter the industry. If anything causes P^* to rise a little, this marginal firm will enter the industry.

The Horizontal Long-run Industry Supply Curve

Each firm has a rising LMC curve and hence a rising long-run supply curve. The industry supply curve is somewhat flatter. Higher prices not merely induce existing firms to produce more; they also induce new firms to enter the industry. In the extreme case the industry long-run supply curve is horizontal. This case occurs when all existing firms and potential entrants have *identical cost* curves. This is illustrated in Figure 9-8. Each firm has the same LAC curve and will supply along the part of its LMC curve that is not below C. Any supply curve shows the minimum price required to elicit a certain quantity of output. Below P^* no firm will wish to supply. Although it takes a price above P^* to persuade each individual firm to produce more than Q_1, no higher price than P^* is required to expand industry output.

Consider any price such as P_2 above P^*. Each firm produces Q_2 and makes supernormal profits since point D lies above point E. Since potential entrants face the same cost curves, there would be a flood of new firms entering the industry. In fact, we would say that the output of the industry would be infinite.

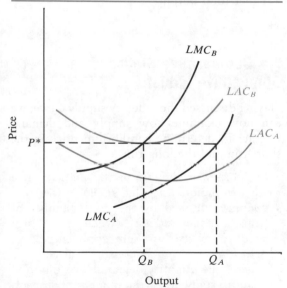

Figure 9-7   THE MARGINAL FIRM IN THE INDUSTRY.   Suppose firms have different cost curves. Firm A, the lowest-cost firm in the industry, has long-run average costs LAC_A and marginal costs LMC_A. Firm B faces much higher costs LAC_B and LMC_B. Other firms have intermediate costs. At the price P^* firm A produces Q_A and makes profits. Firm B produces Q_B and just breaks even. Firm B is the marginal firm in the industry, the highest-cost producer that can remain in the industry in the long run.

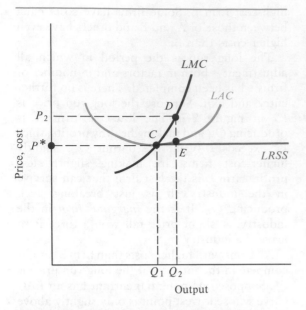

Figure 9-8   THE HORIZONTAL LONG-RUN INDUSTRY SUPPLY CURVE. When all existing firms and potential entrants have identical costs, industry output can be expanded without offering a price higher than P^* to induce firms to move up their LMC curves. P^* is the price at which entrants can survive in the industry in the long run. The long-run industry supply curve $LRSS$ is the horizontal line $LRSS$ at P^*. Industry output can be indefinitely expanded at this price by increasing the number of firms that each produce Q_1.

There would be an infinite number of firms each producing Q_2. A similar argument applies for any price in excess of P^*, the price that just covers minimum average costs at the output Q_1.

Hence, for any finite output, the industry supply curve is horizontal in the long run at the price P^*. It is not necessary to offer a higher price to bribe existing firms to move up their individual supply curves. Industry output can be expanded by the entry of new firms alone. At any price below P^* no output will be produced. In Figure 9-8 we show the long-run industry supply curve $LRSS$ as a horizontal line at the price P^*. Moving along this line, we are simply adding more and more firms each producing Q_1.

There are two reasons why the general case of a rising long-run industry supply curve is much more likely than the special case of a horizontal long-run supply curve for a competitive industry. First, it is unlikely that every firm and potential firm in the industry has identical

cost curves. For example, some firms are likely to have better managers or a more favourable location for producing the industry's product. When firms have different costs there cannot be unlimited expansion of industry output at a constant price. Existing firms face rising marginal costs, and high-cost firms, presently excluded from the industry, require higher prices before it is profitable to enter the industry and contribute to supply.

Second, even if all firms face the same cost curves, the industry long-run supply curve may not be horizontal. We draw a cost curve for given technology *and* given input prices. Although each firm is small relative to the total and can affect neither output prices nor input prices when it acts alone, the collective expansion of output by all firms may bid up input prices. If so, it requires a higher output price to allow an increase in industry output that will bid up input prices and shift the cost curves for each individual firm upwards. Thus in general we expect the long-run supply curve of the industry to be rising. It requires a higher price to call forth a higher total output.

9-4 Comparative Statics for a Competitive Industry

Having discussed the industry supply curve, we can now examine how supply and demand interact to determine equilibrium price in the short run and the long run.

In *short-run equilibrium* the market price equates the quantity demanded to the total quantity supplied by the *given* number of firms in the industry when each firm produces on its short-run supply curve.

In *long-run equilibrium* the market price equates the quantity demanded to the total quantity supplied by the number of firms in the industry when each firm produces on its long-run supply curve. Since firms can freely enter or exit from the industry, the marginal firm must make only normal profits so that there is no further incentive for entry or exit.

We now examine equilibrium in a competitive industry and apply the method of comparative static analysis introduced in Chapter 3.

Comparative statics examines how equilibrium changes when there is a change, for example, in demand or cost conditions.

The Effect of an Increase in Costs

First we discuss the effect of an increase in costs that hits all firms. Perhaps there has been an increase in the price of a raw material, or in the wage rate which must be paid to workers in the industry. For simplicity, we discuss the case in which all firms face the same costs and the long-run supply curve of the industry is horizontal. The same general principles carry over to the case in which the industry supply curve slopes upwards in the long run.

Figure 9-9 summarizes the implications of our analysis of a competitive industry. The industry faces the downward-sloping demand curve DD. Initially, the long-run supply curve is $LRSS_1$ and the market clears at the price P_1^* and the total output Q_1^*. The short-run industry supply curve is $SRSS_1$. The market is in both short-run and long-run equilibrium.

The left-hand figure shows what is going on at the level of the firm. Each firm is producing

q_1^* at the lowest point on its average cost curve LAC_1. This point must also be the lowest point on its $SATC$ curve and hence also lies on its SMC curve, though the initial position of these two curves is not shown in Figure 9-9. If there are N_1 firms in the industry, total output Q_1^* is N_1 times the individual firm's output q_1^*.

Now suppose there is an increase in input prices that raises costs for all firms. LAC_2 is the new long-run average cost curve for a firm. In the short run the firm has some fixed factors. $SATC_2$ and $SAVC_2$ depict average total and average variable costs at this level of fixed factors. Short-run marginal costs SMC_2 pass through the lowest point of both these curves. The part of SMC_2 lying above $SAVC_2$ is the firm's short-run supply curve. In the short run the number of firms in the industry remains fixed.

Horizontally adding these short-run supply curves for the given number of firms, we obtain the new industry short-run supply curve $SRSS_2$. The new short-run equilibrium occurs at P_2, where $SRSS_2$ crosses the demand curve. Each firm sets P_2 equal to SMC_2 and produces an output q_2. Together the N_1 firms produce Q_2.

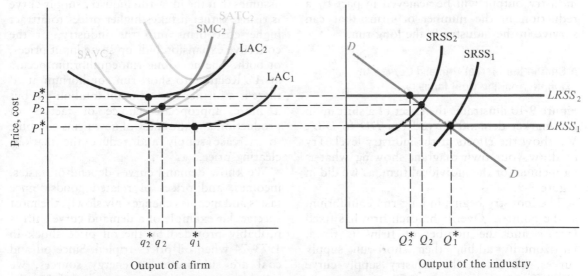

Figure 9-9   THE EFFECT OF A COST INCREASE ON A COMPETITIVE INDUSTRY.   The industry begins in long-run equilibrium producing Q_1^* at a price P_1^*. Each identical firm produces q_1^* at the lowest point on LAC_1. The long-run supply curve $LRSS_1$ is horizontal at P_1^*. When costs increase, firms have fixed factors and the number of firms is given in the short run. Each firm produces q_2 where the short-run equilibrium price P_2 equals SMC_2. Together these firms produce Q_2. Since firms are losing money, in the long run some firms leave the industry. The new long-run supply curve $LRSS_2$ for the industry is horizontal at P_2^*, the minimum point on each firm's new long-run average cost curve LAC_2. In the long run each firm produces q_2^*. Industry output is Q_2^*.

Firms are now covering their variable costs but not their fixed costs at the price P_2. They are losing money.

As time elapses two things happen: fixed factors can be varied, and firms can leave the industry. Long-run equilibrium occurs at the price P_2^* since the new long-run industry supply curve $LRSS_2$ is horizontal at P_2^*, which just covers minimum long-run average costs. Each firm produces q_2^* and the number of firms contracts to N_2 such that Q_2^* equals q_2^* times N_2.

Figure 9-9 makes two points about the change in the long-run equilibrium position. First, the rise in average costs is eventually passed on to the consumer in higher prices. In long-run equilibrium the marginal firm (here, all firms, since they are identical) must make only normal profits to prevent an incentive for further entry or exit. To allow normal profits, prices must rise to cover the increase in minimum average costs.

Second, since higher prices reduce the total quantity demanded, industry output must fall. Unless the rise in costs takes a strange form which greatly reduces the minimum average cost output for each individual firm (so that q_2^* lies well to the left of q_1^*), the reduction in total industry output will be achieved in part by a reduction in the number of firms that can survive in the industry in the long run.

A Shift in the Market Demand Curve: An Example from the Coal Industry

Figure 9-10 illustrates the effect of a shift up in the market demand curve from DD to $D'D'$. We show the effects at the industry level. Try to draw your own diagram showing what is happening for the individual firm, as we did in Figure 9-9.

The industry begins in long-run equilibrium at the point A. Overnight, each firm has fixed factors and the number of firms is fixed. Horizontally adding their short-run supply curves, we obtain the industry supply curve $SRSS$. The new short-run equilibrium occurs at the point A'. When demand first increases it requires a large price rise to persuade individual firms to move up their steep short-run supply curves with given fixed factors.

In the long run, firms can adjust all factors and move on to their flatter long-run supply

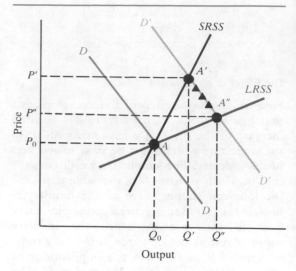

Figure 9-10   A SHIFT IN DEMAND IN A COMPETITIVE INDUSTRY.   The industry begins in long-run equilibrium at A. When the demand curve shifts from DD to $D'D'$ the new short-run equilibrium occurs at A'. As fixed factors are gradually adjusted and new firms enter the industry, equilibrium gradually moves from A' towards A'', the new long-run equilibrium.

curves. In addition, supernormal profits attract extra firms into the industry. Figure 9-10 assumes that the long-run industry supply curve is rising. Either it takes higher prices to attract higher-cost firms into the industry, or the collective expansion bids up some input prices, or both. The new long-run equilibrium occurs at A''. Relative to short-run equilibrium at A' there is a further expansion of total output but a more appropriate choice of factors of production and the entry of new firms combine to increase supply and reduce the market-clearing price.

We know demand curves depend on tastes, incomes, and prices of related goods. Since tastes and incomes change only slowly, the most spectacular example of a demand curve shift is probably provided by the oil price shock in 1973–74 when oil prices tripled. Since oil and coal are substitutes as energy sources, we should expect a large outward shift in the demand for coal.

In many European countries the coal industry is at least partially regulated by the government. The best example of a competitive coal industry is the case of the United States.

How did higher oil prices affect the US coal

Table 9-2 The coal industry in the United States

YEARS	REAL PRICE*	OUTPUT
1970–73	100	100
1974–77	152	112
1978–80	145	129

YEAR	REAL PRICE	NUMBER OF FIRMS	WORKERS
1972	102	3365	155 000
1977	147	5275	242 000

* Index for 1970–73 = 100
Sources: *Survey of Current Business* (various issues), and *Statistical Abstract of the United States*, 1981.

industry? Table 9-2 presents some statistics for the 1970s which confirm the prediction of Figure 9-10. In 1974–77, immediately following the oil price shock, there was a 52 per cent rise in the real price of coal but only a modest 12 per cent rise in production of coal. This matches the move from A to A' in Figure 9-10.

For the period 1978–80 output rises a lot but the real price falls back, as the move from A' to A" predicts. Table 9-2 confirms that firms were being attracted into the industry as the theory implies. These additional firms provide a substantial amount of the increase in total output. Many of these new coal mines were quite small relative to the large mines previously in operation. We see from Table 9-2 that the addition of these new smaller mines actually reduced average output per mine. Only at the higher prices could these small, higher-cost mines survive in the coal industry.

Thus the messages of Figure 9-10 are confirmed. When demand increases there must eventually be a rise in the price. This price rise has three effects which act to restore long-run equilibrium. First, by moving consumers up the demand curve, the price rise partly mitigates the increase in quantity demanded. Second, the price rise induces existing firms to expand along their long-run supply curves and produce more output. Finally, the price rise entices new firms into the industry.

In the short run the price *overshoots* its long-run position. In Figure 9-10 the point A' lies above the point A". Consumers may well complain about the large price increase in the short run, especially since firms in the industry

are temporarily making large profits. But these profits fulfil an important role in the adjustment process, for they act as the signal to potential entrants that this is an industry that can profitably be entered. Entry helps increase long-run supply and mitigate the initial price increase. As entry takes place and existing firms also manage to adjust their previously fixed factors, the industry gradually moves from A' to A" in Figure 9-10. Eventually, the extra output competes away the supernormal profits by bidding the price down, and the industry comes to rest at A", its new long-run equilibrium position.

9-5 Competition in World Markets

Changes in conditions in domestic markets are often the result of events in other countries. The fall in world oil prices in 1986 quickly led British producers of North Sea oil to follow suit. Wool prices in the European Community change when there is a drought in Australia, one of the world's largest wool suppliers. We now discuss how competitive markets in different countries are linked together and show why shifts in foreign supply or demand curves affect domestic markets.

When a commodity is internationally traded, its price in one country cannot be independent of its price in another country. In the extreme case, the 'Law of One Price' will hold.

If there were no obstacles to trade and no transport costs, the *Law of One Price* implies that the price of a given commodity will be the same all over the world.

Without trade barriers and transport costs, suppliers would always wish to sell in the market with the highest price but consumers would always wish to purchase in the market with the lowest price. The commodity could be simultaneously traded in two different countries only if its price were the same in both markets.[3]

In practice, transport costs and trade restrictions such as tariffs (taxes levied only on

---

[3] In the early 1980s the UK price and German price of BMW cars was so different that UK consumers found it profitable to fly to Germany, buy a BMW for Deutschmarks, and drive it home. Such examples are the exception, not the rule.

BOX 9-1

THE ELASTICITY OF SUPPLY

The elasticity of supply measures the responsiveness of the quantity supplied to a change in the price of that commodity. As with elasticity of demand, we use percentage changes.

Supply elasticity =

(% change in quantity supplied)/(% change in price)

Because supply curves slope upwards, the elasticity of supply is *positive*. As we move along a supply curve, positive price changes are associated with positive output changes. The more elastic is supply the larger the percentage increase in quantity supplied in response to a given percentage change in price. Thus, elastic supply curves are relatively flat and inelastic supply curves relatively steep.

Unlike the special case of unit-elastic demand, the case in which a price change leaves revenue unchanged, a supply elasticity of unity has no

special significance. Since price and quantity move in the same direction as we move along a supply curve, higher prices are always associated with higher revenue whatever the supply elasticity.

The diagram shows a typical supply curve SS with a positive supply elasticity and also shows the two limiting cases. The vertical supply curve S'S' has a zero supply elasticity. A given percentage change in price is associated with a zero percentage change in quantity supplied. The horizontal supply curve S"S" has an infinite supply elasticity. Any price increase above the price P* would lead to an infinite increase in quantity supplied.

The elasticity of supply is crucial in telling us how much the equilibrium price and quantity will change when there is a shift in demand. The diagram shows that a demand shift from DD to D'D' leads to higher price rises and lower quantity rises the more inelastic is supply.

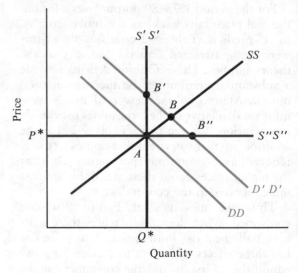

SUPPLY ELASTICITIES   Along the supply curve SS the supply elasticity is positive. Higher price is associated with higher output. The vertical supply curve S'S' has a zero supply elasticity. Higher prices lead to a zero change in output. The supply curve S"S" has an infinite supply elasticity. Any price increase above P* leads to an infinite increase in quantity supplied. Beginning from equilibrium A, a demand shift from DD to D'D' leads to a new equilibrium at B', B, or B" depending on the elasticity of supply. The more inelastic is supply the more the demand increase leads to higher prices rather than higher quantities. In the extreme cases, the move from A to B' reflects only a price increase and the move from A to B" reflects only a quantity increase.

imports) allow international differences in the price of a commodity. Nevertheless, unless these costs and restrictions are prohibitive, international competition will ensure that prices of the same good in different countries generally move together.

We now show how international trade affects competitive markets. To highlight this issue, we assume transport costs and trade restrictions are negligible. Producers and consumers throughout the world are essentially part of a unified world market for the commodity.

Equilibrium in the Domestic Market

Figure 9-11 shows the domestic supply curve SS and the domestic demand curve DD for such a commodity. Suppose first that there is no international trade, perhaps because the domestic country has enormous tariffs in imports. The domestic market will be in equilibrium at the point A, at which price is P^* and quantity is Q^*.

Now suppose tariffs are abolished and transport costs are negligible. There is a world supply curve, which horizontally aggregates the supply curve of each country, and a world demand curve, which horizontally aggregates the demand curve of each country. Together these determine a world equilibrium price for the commodity. Suppose the domestic country is small relative to the world and must take the world price as given.

One of three things can happen, and Figure 9-11 illustrates each of these cases. Suppose, first, that the world equilibrium price is P^*, exactly the price that would have cleared the domestic market in isolation. Point A continues to describe equilibrium in the domestic market. The Law of One Price is satisfied. Consumers cannot buy the good more cheaply abroad and producers cannot sell the good at a higher foreign price. Domestic supply exactly caters for domestic demand and the domestic country neither imports nor exports the good.

Now suppose the given world price is P_1^*. If domestic suppliers attempt to charge a higher price domestic consumers will simply import the good and pay P_1^*. But domestic suppliers will produce at Q_1 since they can always export the good if domestic consumers will not buy it. Hence the domestic market is in equilibrium at the price P_1^*, at which producers supply Q_1, consumers demand Q_1', and the quantity $(Q_1' - Q_1)$, corresponding to the horizontal distance between C and C', is imported from abroad. Conversely, if the given world price is P_2^*, domestic consumers will demand the quantity Q_1 but domestic producers will supply Q_1'. The quantity $(Q_1' - Q_1)$ corresponding to the horizontal distance between B and B' will now be exported to consumers abroad.

The Effect of Changes in World Conditions on the Domestic Market

When our industries compete in world markets, a change in the world price, reflecting a shift in the world supply curve or the world demand curve, will affect the domestic market. Figure 9-11 may be used to show why.

Suppose a drought in Australia reduces the world supply of wool. The world price of wool rises. Suppose originally the world price was P_1^* in Figure 9-11. British farmers were producing Q_1 but clothing manufacturers in Britain were additionally importing $(Q_1' - Q_1)$ since their total quantity demanded was Q_1'. The Australian drought raises the world price above P_1^* and this has two effects. First, it reduces the quantity of wool demanded by British clothing manufacturers. Second, it allows British farmers to charge higher prices and move up their supply curve, expanding output and attracting new resources into the farming industry.

Since the domestic quantity demanded has declined but the domestic quantity supplied has increased, the higher world price of wool has led to a fall in imports. Indeed, if the world

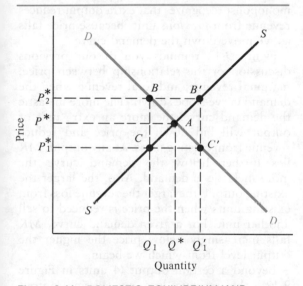

Figure 9-11 DOMESTIC EQUILIBRIUM AND WORLD PRICES. DD and SS show the domestic supply and demand curves for a commodity competitively traded in world markets. In the absence of trade, domestic equilibrium occurs at A. When trade is possible at the world price P^*, equilibrium occurs at A. When trade is possible at the given world price P_1^*, domestic producers supply Q_1 and domestic consumers demand Q_1'. The excess demand (the horizontal distance between C and C') is met from imports. Conversely, when world prices are P_2^*, domestic producers supply Q_1', domestic consumers demand Q_1, and the excess supply (the horizontal distance between B and B') is exported.

price rises sufficiently, Figure 9-11 implies that the UK would become a net exporter of wool.

This brief look at international trade, which we examine in greater detail in Chapter 32, also reminds us that the relevant definition of the market or the industry may be a good deal wider than that of the domestic economy. When transport costs are low and trade restrictions unimportant, it is in the *world* market that we must seek the forces that determine the equilibrium price of a good.

9-6 Pure Monopoly: The Opposite Limiting Case

The perfectly competitive firm is too small to worry about the effect of its own output decision on industry supply. It can sell much as it wants at the market price. Before setting out a general theory of market structure, we discuss the opposite limiting case on the supply side, the case of pure monopoly.

A monopolist is the sole supplier and potential supplier of the industry's product. The firm and the industry coincide. The sole national supplier need not be a monopolist if the good or service is internationally traded. The Post Office is the sole supplier of UK stamps and is a monopolist. British Steel, although effectively the sole UK steel supplier, is not a monopolist since it must compete with imports. Some monopolists are nationalized industries. The state makes price and output decisions and may not aim primarily to maximize profits. The behaviour of national-ized industries will be discussed in Chapter 18.

Here we are concerned with the decisions of a private profit-maximizing monopolist. Bricks are so heavy that huge transport costs effectively insulate national markets from one another. Since 1968 the London Brick Company has been the sole UK supplier of fletton bricks. Based on a particular clay, these bricks enjoy a substantial cost advantage over all other bricks because their higher carbon content greatly reduces the cost of firing the clay. Other examples of *private* monopolists can be given (e.g., Rank Xerox copiers until the 1970s), but the analysis of this section has a wider significance. In many countries there is currently a programme to 'privatize' state-run monopolies. The analysis in the remainder of this chapter illustrates how

we might expect such industries to behave when they are restored to private ownership.

9-7 Profit-maximizing Output for a Monopolist

To maximize profits a firm chooses the output at which marginal revenue MR equals marginal cost MC (SMC in the short run and LMC in the long run). The firm then checks that it is covering average costs ($SAVC$ in the short run and LAC in the long run).

The special feature of a competitive firm is that MR equals price. Selling an extra unit of output does not bid down the price and reduce the revenue earned on previous units. The price at which the extra unit is sold *is* the change in total revenue.

In contrast, the monopolist's demand curve *is* the industry demand curve, which slopes down. This implies MR is less than the price at which the extra unit of output is sold. The monopolist recognizes that extra output reduces revenue from *previous* units because price falls as we move down the demand curve.

Figure 9-12 reminds you of our previous discussion of the relationship between price, marginal revenue, and total revenue when the demand curve slopes down. The more inelastic the demand curve, the more an extra unit of output will bid down the price and reduce revenue from existing units. At any output, MR lies further below the demand curve the more inelastic is demand. Also, the larger the existing output, the larger the revenue loss from existing units when the price is reduced to sell another unit. For a given demand curve, MR falls increasingly below price the higher the output level from which we begin.

Beyond a certain output (4 units in Figure 9-12), the revenue loss on existing output exceeds the revenue gain from the extra unit itself. Marginal revenue becomes negative. Hence Figure 9-12 shows total revenue starting to fall at this output. Further expansion reduces total revenue.

On the cost side, there is only one producer, and the discussion of the cost curves for a single firm in Chapter 8 carries over directly. The monopolist has the usual cost curves, average and marginal, short-run and long-run. For simplicity we discuss only the long-run curves.

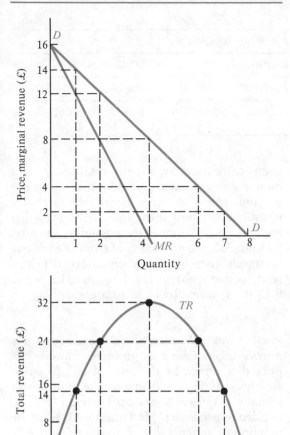

Figure 9-12 DEMAND, TOTAL REVENUE AND MARGINAL REVENUE. Total revenue (TR) equals price times quantity. From the demand curve DD we can plot the TR curve at each quantity. Maximum TR occurs at £32, when 4 units are sold for £8 each. Marginal revenue (MR) shows how TR changes when quantity is increased a small amount. MR lies below the demand curve DD. From the price received for the extra unit we must subtract the loss in revenue from existing units as the price is bid down. This effect is larger the higher is existing output and the more inelastic is the demand curve. At a particular output, the MR curve lies further below DD the larger is output and the more inelastic the demand curve. Beyond an output of 4 units, MR is negative and further expansion reduces total revenue.

The following analysis is easily supplemented by inclusion of short-run cost curves to explain how a monopolist makes the transition from one long-run equilibrium to another when demand or cost conditions alter.

There is one other crucial aspect of our definition of monopoly. Not only is a monopoly the sole existing supplier, it need take no account of new entrants to the industry. When existing suppliers take account of the threat of new firms entering the industry they are *not* monopolists. The behaviour of such firms forms the basis of the next chapter. Without anticipating that discussion of when entry will or will not be possible, we simply assume for the moment that the monopolist need not take any account of potential entry. Imagine that the firm is the sole legal licensee (the Post Office), the sole patent holder (Rank Xerox), or simply has an enormous cost advantage over its nearest rival (the London Brick Company).

Profit-maximizing Output

In Chapter 7 we showed why setting MR equal to MC would lead to the profit-maximizing level of positive output. When MR exceeds MC, an additional unit of output will add more to revenue than to costs and will increase profits. When MC exceeds MR, the last unit has added more to costs than to revenue. Profits would be increased by cutting back output. When MR equals MC output is at the profit-maximizing or loss-minimizing level, given that the firm produces anything at all.

Then the monopolist must check whether at this output the price (or average revenue) covers average variable costs in the short run and average total costs in the long run. If not, the monopolist should shut down in the short run and leave the industry in the long run. In the latter case, the industry will probably cease to exist. Table 9-3 summarizes the criteria by which a profit-maximizing monopolist decides how much to produce.

Figure 9-13 shows the average cost curve AC with its usual U-shape. The marginal cost curve MC passes through the lowest point on the AC curve. The marginal revenue curve MR lies below the down-sloping demand curve DD. Setting $MR = MC$, the monopolist chooses the output level Q_1. However, to find the price for which Q_1 units can be sold we must look at the demand curve DD. The monopolist sells Q_1 units of output at a price P_1 per unit. Profit per unit is given by $P_1 - AC_1$, price minus average cost when Q_1 is produced. Total

Table 9-3 Monopolist's criteria for maximizing profits

MARGINAL CONDITION			AVERAGE CONDITION			
			SHORT-RUN		LONG-RUN	
$MR > MC$	$MR = MC$	$MR < MC$	$P \geqslant SAVC$	$P < SAVC$	$P \geqslant LAC$	$P < LAC$
OUTPUT DECISION	Raise	Optimal	Lower	Produce	Shut down	Stay	Exit

profits are given by the shaded area $(P_1 - AC_1) \times Q_1$.

Even though we are studying the long run, the monopolist continues to make these *supernormal* profits. They are sometimes called *monopoly* profits. They are pure profit after making all cost deductions for the opportunity cost of the owners' time and money. Unlike the competitive industry, supernormal profits of a monopolist are not eliminated in the long run by the entry of new firms. An industry is a monopoly only if the sole existing supplier need take no account of the possibility of entry. By ruling out the possibility of entry, we remove the mechanism by which supernormal profits tend to disappear in the long run. In Figure 9-13 the monopolist is on to a good thing for ever.

Price-setting Whereas the competitive firm is a *price-taker*, taking as given the equilibrium price determined by the interaction of market supply and market demand, the monopolist actually sets prices and is a *price-setter*. Having decided to produce Q_1 in Figure 9-13, what the monopolist actually does is to quote a price P_1 knowing that customers will then demand exactly Q_1 units of output.

Elasticity and Marginal Revenue In Chapter 5 we saw that when the (own-price) elasticity of demand lies between 0 and -1 demand is inelastic and an increase in output will reduce total revenue. Marginal revenue is negative. In percentage terms, the fall in price exceeds the rise in quantity. All outputs to the right of Q_2 in Figure 9-13 have negative MR. The demand curve is inelastic at quantities above Q_2. At quantities below Q_2 the demand curve is elastic. Higher output leads to higher revenue.

The monopolist sets MC equal to MR. Since MC must be positive, so must MR. The chosen output must lie to the left of Q_2. Hence, we say that *a monopolist will never produce on the inelastic part of the demand curve.*

Price, Marginal Cost, and Monopoly Power At any output, price exceeds the monopolist's marginal revenue since the demand curve slopes down. Hence, in setting MR equal to MC the

Figure 9-13 THE MONOPOLY EQUILIBRIUM: $MC = MR$. Applying the usual marginal condition, a profit-maximizing monopolist produces the output level Q_1 at which marginal cost MC equals marginal revenue MR. Then it must check that price covers average cost. In this figure, Q_1 can be sold at a price P_1 in excess of average costs AC_1. Monopoly profits are the shaded areas $(P_1 - AC_1) \times Q_1$.

monopolist sets a price that *exceeds* marginal cost. In contrast, a competitive firm always *equates* price and marginal cost, since its price is also its marginal revenue. This suggests that we might view the excess of price over marginal cost as a measure of *monopoly power*. The competitive firm cannot raise price above marginal cost and has no monopoly power.

Comparative Statics for a Monopolist

Figure 9-13 may also be used to analyse the effect of changes in costs or demand. Suppose there is a change in costs, for example an increase in input prices, which shifts the MC and AC curves upwards. The higher MC curve must cross the MR curve at a lower level of output. Provided the monopolist can sell this output at a price that covers average costs, the effect of the cost increase must be to reduce output. Since the demand curve slopes down, this reduction in output will be accompanied by an increase in the equilibrium price.

Now suppose for the original cost curves shown in Figure 9-13 that there is an outward shift in demand and marginal revenue curves. MR must now cross MC at a higher level of output. Thus an increase in demand leads the monopolist to increase output as we should expect.

9-8 Output and Price under Monopoly and Competition

We now compare a perfectly competitive industry with a monopoly. For this comparison to be of interest the two industries must face the same demand and cost conditions. We are interested in how the *same* industry would behave if it were organized first as a competitive industry then as a monopoly.

Clearly this is a tricky comparison. In the next chapter we develop a theory of market structure that aims to explain why some industries are competitive but others are monopolies. If this theory has any content, can it be legitimate to assume that the same industry could be competitive or monopolized? The answer turns out to be yes in some circumstances but no in other circumstances. We now distinguish these two cases.

Comparing a Competitive Industry and a Multi-plant Monopolist

Consider a competitive industry in which all firms and potential entrants have the same cost curves. From our earlier discussion of the horizontal *LRSS* curve for a competitive industry we know this case can be analysed using Figure 9-14.

Facing the demand curve DD, the industry is in long-run equilibrium at A where the price is P_1 and total output is Q_1. The industry *LRSS* curve is horizontal at P_1, the lowest point on the *LAC* curve of each firm. Any other price would eventually lead to infinite entry or exit from the industry. We can regard *LRSS* as the industry's long-run marginal cost curve LMC_1 of expanding output by enticing new firms into the industry.

Each firm is producing at the lowest point on its *LAC* curve and breaking even. This point is also the lowest point on the firm's *SATC* curve for the level of factors it now has. Since marginal cost curves pass through the point of minimum average costs, each firm is also on its *SMC* and *LMC* curves. Horizontally adding

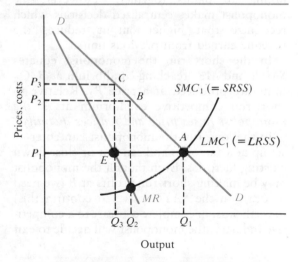

Figure 9-14   A MONOPOLIST PRODUCES A LOWER OUTPUT AT A HIGHER PRICE.   Long-run equilibrium in a competitive industry occurs at A. Total output is Q_1 and the price P_1. On taking over the industry, a monopolist sets MR equal to SMC_1, restricting output to Q_2 and increasing price to P_2. In the long run the monopolist sets MR equal to LMC_1, reducing output to Q_3 and increasing the price again to P_3. There are no entrants to compete away supernormal profits P_3CEP_1 by increasing the industry output.

these SMC curves, the supply curves of each firm in the short run, we obtain $SRSS$, the short-run industry supply curve. We can regard this as the industry's short-run marginal cost curve SMC_1 of expanding output from existing firms with temporarily fixed factors. Since $SRSS$ crosses the demand curve at P_1, the industry is both in short-run and long-run equilibrium.

Beginning from this position, suppose the competitive industry became a monopoly. The monopolist takes over each plant (firm) but makes centralizing pricing and output decisions. For example, in 1967 the UK steel industry was nationalized. British Steel bought out all the private steel producers and had a legal monopoly on UK steel production. If we could ignore international trade in steel and assume that British Steel were instructed to maximize profits, how would the monopolization of the steel industry affect pricing and output decisions?

Overnight the monopolist still has the same number of factories (ex-firms) as in the competitive industry. Since the firm and the industry now coincide, SMC_1 remains the short-run marginal cost curve for the monopolist taking all plants together.[4] However, the monopolist makes centralized decisions which recognize that higher output reduces the revenue earned from previous units.

In the short run the monopolist equates SMC_1 and MR, reaching equilibrium at B. Q_2 units are produced at a price P_2. Relative to short-run competitive equilibrium at A, *the monopolist raises price and reduces quantity.*

In the long run the monopolist can enter or set up new factories and can exit or close down existing factories. Even though the monopolist may be making short-run profits at B (we need to draw in the $SATC$ curve to confirm this) nevertheless, in complete contrast to a competitive industry, the monopolist will decide to exit

or retire some factories from the industry in the long run.

The monopolist wants to cut back output to force up the price. Yet in the long run it makes sense to operate each factory at the lowest point on its LAC curve. To reduce total output some factories must be retired. In the long run the monopolist sets LMC_1 equal to MR and reaches the equilibrium position C. *Price has risen yet further to P_3 and output has fallen to Q_3.* Long-run supernormal profits are given by the area P_3CEP_1 since P_1 remains the long-run average cost when all plants are producing at the lowest point on their LAC curve.

Although it is the recognition that MR is less than price that provides the incentive for a monopolist to produce less than a competitive industry and charge a higher price, in this example it is the legal prohibition on entry by competitors that allows the monopolist to succeed in the long run. In a competitive industry supernormal profits are competed away by the new entrants that they attract to the industry. That is why we have insisted that the absence of entry is intrinsic to the model of monopoly we have developed.

The Social Cost of Monopoly   Should society mind that a monopolist restricts output and drives price above marginal cost? This is not an issue in positive economics, the description of actual behaviour, but rather an issue in normative economics, which deals in recommendations and policy prescriptions. We deal with such questions at length in Part 3 of this book.

At this point we merely sketch how that argument might go. The marginal cost measures the resources used to make the last unit of the good. Since consumers voluntarily buy the good, the price of the good must measure the marginal benefit to consumers of buying the last unit of the good. If the marginal benefit were higher than the price, consumers would buy even more at that price. If the marginal benefit were less than the price, consumers would not demand that last unit at that price.

Society should want to equate the marginal cost of the good and its marginal benefit. If marginal cost is less than marginal benefit, society will be better off with more of the good. Whereas a competitive industry automatically

---

[4] In a competitive industry each firm equates the given price to its own marginal cost. Hence firms produce at the same marginal cost. Thus we horizontally add individual SMC curves (i.e. at the same price) to get the industry SMC curve. A multi-plant monopolist need not equate MC across all plants but will always find it profitable to do so. Why? If marginal costs in two plants differed, the monopolist could always produce the same total output more cheaply by producing an extra unit in the low MC plant and one less unit in the high MC plant. Thus the SMC_1 curve for the monopolist across all plants remains the horizontal sum of the SMC curves for individual plants, as in a competitive industry.

sets marginal cost equal to price (equal to presumed marginal consumer benefit) monopoly does not. It sets marginal cost less than price and, by implication, produces less of the good than society might wish. Whether this simple argument is generally correct is one of the issues we explore in Part 3.

Comparing a Single-plant Monopolist with a Competitive Industry

In the previous example we examined a multi-plant monopolist who took over a large number of previously competitive firms. Now we examine a monopolist meeting the entire industry demand from a single plant. This is most plausible when there are large economies of scale. There are huge costs in setting up a national telephone network. Yet the cost of connecting a marginal subscriber is low once the network has been set up.

Monopolies enjoying huge economies of scale – falling *LAC* curves over the entire range of output – are called *natural monopolies*. As we shall see in the next chapter, large scale-economies may explain why there is a sole supplier who need not worry about entry. Smaller new entrants would be at a prohibitive cost disadvantage.

Figure 9-15 illustrates the long-run equilibrium for a natural monopoly. In the long run the natural monopoly faces average and marginal cost curves *LAC* and *LMC*. Given the position of the demand curve, long-run average cost is declining over the entire range of outputs that might be demanded. The monopoly produces at *LMC* equal to *MR*, selling an output Q_1 for a price P_1. At this output, price exceeds *LAC*. The monopoly makes supernormal profits and is happy to remain in business.

It does not make sense to compare this equilibrium with how the industry would behave if it were competitive. With such economies of scale, there should be only one firm in the industry. *LAC* is the cost curve for each possible firm. If there were only one firm, it would be crazy not to recognize that its output decisions affected price. If it were stupid enough to try to set price equal to *LMC* it would reach the point *B*, conclude that it was not covering average costs, and leave the industry.[5] If a lot of small firms produced a small fraction

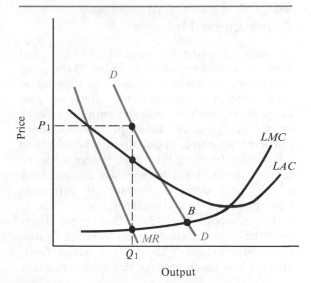

Figure 9-15 A NATURAL MONOPOLY WITH ECONOMIES OF SCALE. The *LAC* curve is falling throughout the relevant range of output levels. Economies of scale are large relative to the market size. The monopoly produces Q_1 at a price P_1 and makes profits. If it tried to behave like a price-taking competitive firm it would produce at *B* where price equals *LMC* and make losses. By recognizing the effect of output on price the single firm monopoly can do much better. This industry cannot support a lot of small firms. Each would have very high average costs at low output. This cannot be a competitive industry.

each of total demand, their average costs would be enormous. A single large firm could undercut them and wipe them out. This industry must have a sole supplier, and that natural monopoly will maximize profits only by recognizing that its marginal revenue is not its price.

It is this insight that we develop in the next chapter to provide a general theory of market structure. Turning to the normative issue, society may still be interested in forcing the monopolist to produce at a price closer to marginal cost. In the extreme case, society might order the monopoly to price at marginal cost, produce at the point *B*, make losses, and receive a government subsidy. We return to this issue in Part 3 when discussing nationalized industries and more general forms of government regulations of monopolies.

[5] From Chapter 8 we know that marginal cost lies below average cost at all points left of the point of minimum average cost. Since the *LAC* curve is still falling in Figure 9-15 it must lie above *LMC*. Pricing at marginal cost *must* yield losses at point *B*.

9-9 The Absence of a Supply Curve under Monopoly

A competitive firm sets price equal to marginal cost if it supplies at all. If we know its marginal cost curve we know how much it supplies at each price. Aggregating across firms, we also know how much the industry supplies at each price. We can draw the supply curve without knowing anything about the market demand curve. Confronting the supply curve with the market demand curve, we then analyse how supply and demand interact to determine equilibrium price and quantity.

The monopolist recognizes that output affects marginal cost and marginal revenue simultaneously. Figure 9-16 shows a given LMC curve. How much will the monopolist produce

at the price P_1? It all depends on demand and marginal revenue. When demand is DD and the corresponding marginal revenue MR, the monopolist produces Q_1 and charges a price P_1. However, when demand is $D'D'$ and marginal revenue MR', the monopolist produces Q_2 but still charges P_1.

The monopolist does not have a supply curve independent of demand conditions. What we can say is that the monopolist simultaneously examines demand (hence marginal revenue) and cost (hence marginal cost) when deciding how much to produce and what to charge.

Discriminating Monopoly

Thus far we have assumed that all consumers must be charged the same price, although this price will depend on the level of output and the position of the demand curve. Unlike a competitive industry, where competition between firms prevents any individual firm charging more than its competitors, a monopolist may be able to charge different prices to different customers. This will be especially attractive when it is possible to identify different types of customer whose demand curves are quite distinct.

Consider an airline monopolizing flights between London and Rome. It has business customers whose demand curve is very inelastic. They have to fly, and the plane fare is a trivial expense for their companies. For this group, demand and marginal revenue curves are very steep.

The airline also carries tourists whose demand curve is much more elastic. If flights to Rome get too expensive tourists can holiday in Athens instead. Tourists have much flatter demand and marginal revenue curves.

Recall why the marginal revenue curve lies below the demand curve. Adding an extra unit of output and sales bids down the price for which existing output can be sold and reduces revenue from existing units of output. The more inelastic is the demand curve the more the marginal revenue curve must lie below the demand curve because the higher will be the reduction in revenue from existing output units.

Suppose the airline charges tourists and business travellers the same price. From the separate demand curves we can read off at each

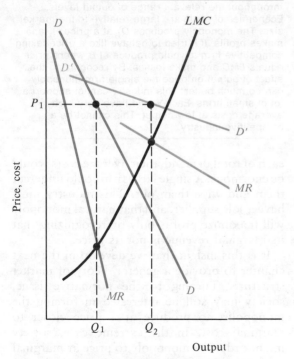

Figure 9-16 ABSENCE OF A SUPPLY CURVE UNDER MONOPOLY. Given the demand curve DD and the corresponding marginal revenue curve MR, the monopolist produces Q_1 at a price P_1. However, facing $D'D'$ and MR', the monopolist produces Q_2 at a price P_1. Knowing the price, we cannot uniquely infer the quantity supplied unless we also know demand and marginal revenue. Because the monopolist knows that output affects both marginal cost and marginal revenue, the two must be considered simultaneously.

price the number of each type of traveller and add these to obtain the total number of travellers at each price. However since the demand curve of business travellers is less elastic, the marginal revenue obtained from the last business traveller must be lower than the marginal revenue obtained from the last tourist.

Whatever the total number of passengers (and hence total cost of carrying them), the airline is carrying the wrong *mix* between tourists and business travellers. Since the marginal revenue from the last tourist exceeds the marginal revenue from the last business traveller the airline would gain revenue without adding to cost by carrying the same number of passengers but carrying more of the group with the higher marginal revenue and less of the group with the lower marginal revenue. And it will pay to keep changing the mix until the marginal revenue of the two groups is equated.

To do this, the airline must charge the two groups *different* prices. Since tourist demand is elastic the airline wants to charge tourists a low fare to increase tourist revenues. Since business demand is inelastic the airline want to charge business travellers a high fare to increase business revenue.

Profit-maximizing output will satisfy two separate conditions. First, business travellers with inelastic demand will pay a fare sufficiently higher than tourists with elastic demand that the marginal revenue from the two separate groups is equated. Then there is no incentive to rearrange the mix by altering the price differential between the two groups. Second, the general level of prices and the total number of passengers will be determined to equate the marginal cost of carrying passengers to both these marginal revenues. This ensures that the airline operates on the most profitable scale as well as with the most profitable mix.

When a producer charges different customers different prices we say that the producer *price discriminates*. There are many examples of this in the real world. Air fares per mile between London and Brussels, almost exclusively an expense account business trip, are among the highest in Europe, but package holidays are much cheaper. British Rail charges rush-hour commuters a higher fare than midday shoppers whose demand for trips to the city is much more elastic. Expensive doctors in private practice frequently charge lower prices to less

well-off patients but charge very high prices to the very rich whose demand for the best medical care is very inelastic.

It is no accident that many of the best examples of price discrimination refer to services which must be consumed on the spot rather than to goods which can be resold. Price discrimination in a standardized commodity is unlikely to work. The group buying at the lower price have an incentive to resell to the group paying the higher price thus undercutting the monopolist's attempt to charge some customers a higher price. Effective price discrimination is feasible only when the submarkets can be isolated from one another to prevent resale of the product from one group to another.

What does price discrimination have to do with the absence of a supply curve under monopoly? Figure 9-17 illustrates this most clearly for the case of *perfect price discrimination* where we assume that it is actually possible to

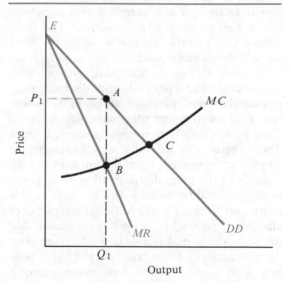

Figure 9-17   PERFECT PRICE DISCRIMINATION.
Charging all customers the same price the monopolist will produce at B where $MC = MR$. If each output unit can be sold for a different price, the revenue from existing units is not reduced by cutting the price to sell another unit. The demand curve DD is the marginal revenue curve and the perfectly discriminating monopolist will produce at C. Output is higher and profits are higher. By price discrimination the monopolist gains an extra revenue EP_1A from selling Q_1 but also increases output beyond this level making a marginal profit of ABC in expanding from A to C.

charge each and every customer a different price for the same good.

Suppose first that the monopolist charges every customer the same price. Given the demand curve DD we obtain the usual marginal revenue curve MR which lies below DD precisely because to sell more output the monopolist must reduce the price not only on the extra unit of output but also on all existing units. The profit-maximizing output is Q_1 where MR equals MC and the corresponding price is P_1.

Now suppose the monopolist can perfectly price discriminate, charging a different price for each unit of output sold. The very first can be sold for a price E. Having sold this output to the highest bidder, the customer most desperate for the good, the next unit can be sold to the next highest bidder and so on. As we move down the demand curve DD we can read off the price for which each extra unit can be sold. However, in reducing the price to sell that extra unit, the monopolist no longer reduces revenue from previously sold units. *Hence the demand curve is the marginal revenue curve under perfect price discrimination.* The marginal revenue of the last unit is simply the price for which it can be sold.

Treating DD as the marginal revenue curve we conclude that a perfectly price discriminating monopolist will produce at point C where marginal revenue and marginal cost are equal. Two points follow immediately. First, if price discrimination is possible it is profitable to employ it. In moving from the uniform pricing point A to the price discriminating point C the monopolist adds the area ABC to profits. This represents the excess of additional revenue over additional cost when output is increased. But the monopolist makes a second gain from price discrimination. Even the output Q_1 now brings in more revenue than under uniform pricing. The monopolist also gains the area EP_1A by being able to charge different prices on the first Q_1 units of output rather than the single price P_1. In practice, when firms call in economic consultants one of the main ways these consultants manage to increase the profits of the firm is by devising new ways in which the firm can price discriminate.

Second, whether or not the firm is able to price discriminate affects the output it will choose to produce even if demand and cost conditions remain unaltered. Earlier in this section we said there was no unique supply curve relating output to price for a monopolist. We also had to know the elasticity of the demand curve and hence how far marginal revenue would lie below the price. Figure 9-17 shows it is not even sufficient to know the total demand curve facing a firm. In addition we need to know whether the market can be segmented enough to allow price discrimination. Uniform and discriminatory pricing will lead to very different outputs because they affect the marginal revenue obtained from any given total demand curve facing a monopolist.

9-10 Monopoly and Technical Change

In Section 9-8 we compared the behaviour of a monopoly and a perfectly competitive industry. When such a comparison was meaningful we discovered two things: (1) a monopoly will tend to restrict output and drive up prices; and (2) in consequence a monopoly will tend to make economic profits in the short run, and need not fear the erosion of these profits by entrants in the long run.

Joseph Schumpeter (1883–1950) argued that this comparison might be misleading because it ignores the possibility of technical advances, which reduce costs and may allow price reductions and output expansion. If banks are unwilling to lend money for risky research projects, a large monopolist with steady profits may find it much easier to fund internally the research and development (R & D) necessary to make cost-saving breakthroughs. Second, and completely distinct, a monopolist may have a greater *incentive* to undertake R & D.

In a competitive industry a firm with a technical advantage has only a temporary opportunity to earn high profits to recoup its research expenses. Imitation by existing firms and new entrants gradually compete away any supernormal profits. In contrast, by shifting down all its cost curves, a monopoly may be able to enjoy higher supernormal profits for ever. Schumpeter argued that these two forces – greater resources available for R & D and a higher potential return on any successful venture – tend to make monopolies more innovative than competitive industries. Taking a dynamic long-run view, rather than a snapshot static picture, monopolists tend to enjoy lower cost curves which lead them to charge lower prices thereby increasing the quantity demanded.

This argument has some substance. Very small firms typically do little R & D, whereas many of the largest firms have excellent research departments. Many small firms complain about the problem of trying to raise bank loans for risky research projects. Nevertheless, the Schumpeter argument may overstate the case in two respects.

Most Western economies operate a *patent* system. Inventors of new processes acquire a temporary legal monopoly of the process for a fixed period. By temporarily excluding entry and imitation the patent laws increase the incentive to conduct R & D without establishing a monopoly in the long run. Over the patent life the inventor can charge a higher price and make handsome profits. Eventually the patent expires and competition from other firms leads to higher output and lower prices. The real price of copiers and micro computers fell significantly when the original patents of Xerox and IBM expired.

The patent laws can provide an R & D incentive even in industries that are not permanent monopolies. Nor does the empirical evidence show unusually high R & D expenditure in industries that are monopolies. What the evidence does show is that small firms do little research. But above a certain size of firm there is no further correlation between the size of the firm and its research expenditure.

Summary

1 In a competitive industry each buyer and seller acts as a price-taker, believing that individual actions have no effect on the market price. Competitive supply is most plausible when a large number of firms make a standard product under conditions of free entry and exit from the industry, and customers can easily verify that the products of different firms really are the same.

2 For a competitive firm, marginal revenue and price coincide. Output is chosen to equate price to marginal cost. The firm's supply curve is its *SMC* curve above *SAVC*. At any lower price the firm temporarily shuts down. In the long run, the firm's supply curve is its *LMC* curve above its *LAC* curve. At any lower price the firm eventually leaves the industry.

3 Adding at each price the quantities supplied by each firm, we obtain the industry supply curve. It is flatter in the long run both because each firm can fully adjust all factors and because the number of firms in the industry can vary. In the extreme case where all potential and existing firms have identical costs, the long-run industry supply curve is horizontal at the price corresponding to the lowest point on each firm's *LAC* curve.

4 An increase in demand leads to a large price increase but only a small increase in quantity. The existing firms move up their steep *SMC* curves. Price exceeds average costs and the ensuing profits attract new entrants. In the long run output increases still further but the price falls back. In the long-run equilibrium the marginal firm makes only normal profits and there is no further change in the number of firms in the industry.

5 An increase in costs for all firms reduces the industry's output and increases the price. In the long run the marginal firm must break even. A higher price is required to match the increase in its average costs.

6 Markets for the same good in different countries will be closely linked if transport costs are small and there are no trade restrictions. In a competitive world market each country takes the world price of the commodity as given. Discrepancies between domestic supply and domestic demand are met through imports or exports. Foreign trade transmits foreign shocks to the domestic economy but acts as a shock absorber for domestic shocks.

7 A pure monopoly is the only seller or potential seller of a good and need not worry about entry even in the long run. Though rare in practice, this case offers an important benchmark against which to compare less extreme forms of monopoly power.

8 A profit-maximizing monopolist has a supply rule: choose output to set *MC* equal to *MR*, but not a supply curve uniquely relating price and output. The relation between price

and marginal revenue depends on the demand curve.

9 Where a monopoly and a competitive industry can meaningfully be compared, the monopolist produces a smaller output at a higher price. However, natural monopolies with large economies of scale could not exist as competitive industries.

10 A discriminating monopolist charges different prices to different customers. To equate the marginal revenue from different groups, groups with an inelastic demand must pay a higher price. Successful price discrimination requires that customers cannot trade the product among themselves.

11 Monopolies may have more internal resources available for research and may have a higher incentive for cost-saving research because the profits from technical advances will not be eroded by entry. Although small firms do not undertake much expensive research, it appears that the patent laws provide adequate incentives for medium- and larger-sized firms. There is no evidence that an industry has to be a monopoly to undertake cost-saving research.

Key Terms

Market structure
Perfect competition
Shutdown price
Entry and exit
Marginal firm
Law of One Price
Monopoly
Supernormal profits
Monopoly power
Social cost of monopoly
Natural monopoly
Discriminating monopoly
Technical change through R & D

Problems

1 Draw a diagram such as Figure 9-9 showing the position of a competitive firm and the industry in long-run equilibrium. Suppose this is the wool industry. The development of artificial fibres reduces the demand for wool by the clothing industry. Show what happens in the short run and the long run if all sheep farmers have identical costs. What happens if there are high-cost and low-cost sheep farmers?

2 Suppose the wheat crop is hit by a drought. Explain the adjustment in the price of wheat in the short run and the long run. How is the price of bread affected in the short run and the long run?

3 A country can trade at given world prices. Draw the domestic supply and demand curves. Show a price that would make the country an importer of the good. The government now taxes imports adding to their price in the domestic market. Show what happens to the quantities demanded and supplied in the domestic market. What happens to the quantity of imports?

4 The table shows the demand curve facing a monopolist who produces at a constant marginal cost of £5.

Price (£)	9	8	7	6	5	4	3	2	1	0
Quantity	0	1	2	3	4	5	6	7	8	9

Calculate the monopolist's marginal revenue curve. What is the equilibrium output? What is the equilibrium price? What would be the equilibrium price and output for a competitive industry? Explain in words why the monopolist produces a lower output and charges a higher price.

5 Now suppose that, in addition to the constant marginal cost of £5, the monopolist has a fixed cost of £2. What difference does this make to the monopolist's output, price, and profits? Why do we get this answer?

6 The Association of University Teachers of Economics in the UK has different membership rates for students, university lecturers, and professional economists working outside universities. Why do you think the AUTE pursues this policy?

7 Common Fallacies Show why the following statements are incorrect: (a) Since competitive firms break even in the long run there can be no incentive to be a competitive firm. (b) Monopolists always make profits. (c) By introducing a law to break up every monopoly into smaller companies society could always obtain more output at a lower price. (d) Perfect competition is possible only if all firms face the same cost curves.

10

Market Structure and Imperfect Competition

Perfect competition and pure monopoly are useful benchmarks of the extreme kinds of market structure, but in reality most markets lie somewhere in between these two extremes. In nearly half the 800 major product categories in UK manufacturing 70 per cent of the market is shared by the five largest firms in the industry. The car industry and the brewing industry are obvious examples.

What determines the structure of a particular market between these two extremes: why are there 10 000 florists in the UK but only a handful of chemical producers? And how does the structure of a particular industry affect the behaviour of its constituent firms?

A perfectly competitive firm faces a horizontal demand curve at the going market price. It is a price-taker. Any other type of firm faces a downward sloping demand curve for its product and is called an *imperfectly competitive* firm.

> An *imperfectly competitive firm* cannot sell as much as it wants at the going price. It must recognize that its demand curve slopes down and that its output price will depend on the quantity of goods produced and sold.

In the extreme case of pure monopoly the downward-sloping demand curve for the firm is the industry demand curve itself. We now distinguish two intermediate cases of an imperfectly competitive market structure, an *oligopoly* and a *monopolistically competitive* industry.

> An *oligopoly* is an industry with only a few producers, each recognizing that its own price depends not merely on its own output but also on the actions of its important competitors in the industry. An industry with *monopolistic competition* has many sellers producing products that are close substitutes

for one another. Each firm has only a limited ability to affect its output price.

In most countries the car industry is a good example of an oligopoly. The price the Rover Group can charge for its cars depends not only on its own production levels and sales, but also on the decisions taken by major competitors such as Ford and Vauxhall. The corner grocer's shop is a good example of a monopolistic competitor. Its output is a subtle package of physical goods such as jars of coffee, personal service and extra convenience for those customers who live nearby. It can charge a few pence more for a jar of coffee than the supermarket in the main shopping area some distance away. But, if prices are higher by more than a few pence, even shoppers who live nearby will make the trip to the supermarket.

As with most definitions, the lines between these types of market structure are a little blurred. A major reason is the ambiguity about the relevant definition of the market. Is British Rail a monopoly in railways or an oligopolist in transport? Similarly, when a country trades in a competitive world market, even the sole domestic producer may have little influence on market price. We can never fully remove these ambiguities, but Table 10-1 shows some things to bear in mind as we proceed through this chapter. Notice that the table includes the ease with which new firms can enter the industry. This has a crucial bearing on the ability of existing firms to maintain high prices and supernormal profits in the long run.

10-1 Why Market Structures Differ

We have already drawn attention to the influence of government legislation on market

Table 10-1 Market structure

| | | IMPERFECT COMPETITION | | |
CHARACTERISTIC	PERFECT COMPETITION	MONOPOLISTIC COMPETITION	OLIGOPOLY	MONOPOLY
Number of firms	Many	Many	Few	One
Ability to affect price	None	Limited	Some	Considerable
Entry barriers	None	None	Some	Complete
Example	Fruit stalls	Corner grocer	Cars	Post office

structure. Nationalized industries, for example coal and rail, are legal monopolies; they are the sole licensed producers. Patent laws may confer temporary monopoly on producers of a new process. Ownership of a raw material may also confer monopoly status on a single producer. Having noted these interesting special cases, we now develop a general theory of how the economic factors of demand and cost interact to determine the likely structure of a particular industry.

The car industry is not an oligopoly one day but perfectly competitive the next. It is in long-run influences that we must seek the causes of different market structures. Similarly,

although a particular firm may have a temporary advantage in technical know-how or workforce skill, in the long run one firm can hire another's workers and learn its technical secrets. In the long run all firms or potential entrants to an industry essentially have access to the same cost curves.

Figure 10-1 shows the demand curve DD for the output of an industry. Suppose first that in the long run all firms and potential entrants face the average cost curve LAC_1. At the price P_1, free entry and exit ensures that each firm produces q_1. Given the demand curve DD, the industry output is Q_1 and the industry can support N_1 firms where $N_1 = Q_1/q_1$. If q_1, the

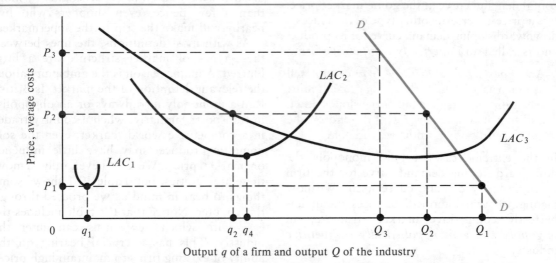

Output q of a firm and output Q of the industry

Figure 10-1   DEMAND, COSTS, AND MARKET STRUCTURE. *DD* is the industry demand curve. In a competitive industry, minimum efficient scale occurs at an output level q_1 when firms have average cost curves LAC_1. The industry can support a very large number of firms whose total output is Q_1 at the price P_1. When LAC_3 describes average costs, the industry will be a natural monopoly. When a single firm produces the entire industry output, no other firm can break into the market and make a profit. For intermediate positions such as LAC_2 the industry can support a few firms in the long run, and no single firm can profitably meet the entire demand. The industry will be an oligopoly.

minimum average cost output on LAC_1, lies sufficiently far to the left relative to DD, then N_1 will be a very large number of firms. Each firm will have a trivial effect on industry supply and market price. We have discovered a perfectly competitive industry.

Now suppose that each firm has the cost curve LAC_3. Economies of scale are very large relative to the market size. The lowest point on LAC_3 occurs at an output large relative to the demand curve DD. Suppose initially there are two producers each producing q_2. Market output Q_2 is twice as large. The market clears at P_2 and both firms break even. However, if one firms expands a little its average costs will fall. It will also bid the price down. With lower average costs, that firm will survive and the other firm will lose money. The firm that expands will gobble up the whole market, undercut its competitor, and eventually drive the other firm out of business.

We have discovered an industry that is a natural monopoly. Suppose that Q_3 is the output at which its marginal cost and marginal revenue coincide. The price is P_3 and the natural monopoly makes supernormal profits. Yet there is no room in the industry for other firms with access to the same LAC_3 curve. A new entrant needs a large output to get average costs down. Extra output on this scale would so depress the price that both firms would make losses. The potential entrant is powerless to break in. The natural monopolist can completely disregard the threat of entry.

Finally, we show the LAC_2 curve with more economies of scale than a competitive industry but fewer than a natural monopoly. This industry will support at least two firms enjoying economies of scale near the lowest point of their LAC_2 curves. It will be an oligopoly. Attempts to expand either firm's output beyond q_4 quickly encounter decreasing returns to scale and prevent it from expanding to drive its competitor out of business.

In Chapter 8 we introduced the notion of the minimum efficient scale.

> The *minimum efficient scale* is the output at which a firm's long-run average cost curve stops falling.

We now see that the crucial determinant of market structure is the output at minimum efficient scale relative to the size of the total

Table 10-2 Demand, costs, and market structure

MINIMUM EFFICIENT SCALE RELATIVE TO MARKET SIZE		
TINY	INTERMEDIATE	LARGE
Perfect competition	Oligopoly	Natural monopoly

market as represented by the demand curve. Table 10-2 summarizes our discussion. It is the interaction of market size and the output at minimum efficient scale that matters. When the demand curve shifts to the left, an industry previously supporting many firms may have room for only a few. Similarly, an increase in fixed costs which increases the output at minimum efficient scale will reduce the number of producers. In the 1950s there were a large number of European aircraft manufacturers. Today, the research and development costs of a major commercial airliner are enormous. Apart from the co-operative European venture Airbus Industrie, subsidized by European governments, only the American giants Boeing, Lockheed, and McDonnell-Douglas survive.

Monopolistic competition lies midway between oligopoly and perfect competition. But it is the fact that monopolistic competitors all supply slightly different products, such as the location in which you do your shopping, that makes them special.

Evidence on Market Structure

The larger the minimum efficient scale relative to the market size, the fewer will be the number of plants – and probably the number of firms – in the industry. What is the number of plants (NP) operating at minimum efficient scale that the current market size could allow? In Chapter 8 we discussed how economists have tried to estimate the minimum efficient scale for plants in different industries. By looking at the total quantity of consumption of a product we can estimate the market size. Hence we can construct estimates of NP for each industry.

How do we measure how many firms there are in an industry? Even industries that essentially have only a few very large firms may have some small firms on the fringe. The number of firms in the industry tells us nothing about their size or importance. It might be a misleading indicator of the essential structure of the industry. For this reason, economists use the N-firm concentration ratio to measure the number of important firms in the industry.

> The N-*firm concentration ratio* is the market share of the largest N firms in the industry.

Thus the 3-firm concentration ratio tells us the percentage of the total market supplied by the largest three firms in the industry. If there are basically only three firms that matter, they will supply almost 100 per cent of the total market for the product. If the industry is perfectly competitive, the largest three firms will still account for only a tiny share of the total market for the product.

Table 10-3 looks at the evidence for the UK, France, and Germany. CR is the 3-firm concentration ratio, the market share of the top three firms. NP is the number of plants at minimum efficient scale which the market size would allow. Nothing guarantees that all plants are being operated at minimum efficient scale. Nevertheless, if our theory of market structure is correct, industries with large economies of scale relative to the market size – a very low value of NP – should exhibit a large CR. Such industries should have only a few important firms. Conversely, where NP is very high, economies of scale are relatively unimportant and the largest three firms should control a much smaller market share. CR should be much lower.

Table 10-3 confirms that our theory of market structure is compatible with the facts. In industries such as refrigerator and cigarette manufacture there is room for only very few

plants operating at minimum efficient scale, and these industries exhibit high degrees of concentration. The largest three firms control almost the whole market. Economies of scale are still substantial in industries such as brewing and petroleum refining and the top three firms control around half the market. Industries such as shoe manufacture quickly encounter rising average cost curves; they have room for a large number of factories operating at minimum efficient scale, and consequently are much closer to competitive industries. The top three firms in shoe manufacturing control less than one-fifth of the market.

10-2 Monopolistic Competition

The essence of oligopoly is interdependence. Large firms must guess what their large rivals are up to. Before turning to this exciting branch of economic analysis, however, we begin with a simpler case.

The theory of monopolistic competition[1] envisages a large number of quite small firms so that each firm can neglect the possibility that its own decisions provoke any adjustment in other firms' behaviour. We also assume free entry and exit from the industry in the long run. In these respects the framework resembles our earlier discussion of *perfect* competition. What distinguishes monopolistic competition is that each firm faces a *downward*-sloping demand curve.

[1] This theory was independently invented in the early 1930s by E. H. Chamberlin in the United States and by Joan Robinson in Britain.

Table 10-3 Concentration and scale economies in three European countries

INDUSTRY	UK		FRANCE		GERMANY	
	CR	NP	CR	NP	CR	NP
Refrigerators	65	1	100	2	72	3
Cigarettes	94	3	100	2	94	3
Petroleum refining	79	8	60	7	47	9
Brewing	47	11	63	5	17	16
Fabrics	28	57	23	57	16	52
Shoes	17	165	13	128	20	197

CR = % market share of 3 largest firms; NP = market size divided by output of minimum efficient scale.
Source: F. M. Scherer *et al., The Economics of Multiplant Operation,* Harvard University Press, 1975, and F. M. Scherer, *Industrial Market Structure and Economic Performance,* Rand McNally, 1980.

Monopolistic competition describes an industry in which each firm can influence its market share to some extent by changing its price relative to its competitors. Its demand curve is not horizontal because different firms' products are only limited substitutes. We have given one example, the location of corner grocers. A lower price attracts some customers from another shop, but each shop will always have some local customers for whom the convenience of a nearby shop is more important than a few pence on the price of a jar of coffee.

Monopolistically competitive industries exhibit *product differentiation*. For corner grocers this differentiation is based on location, but in other cases it is based on brand loyalty. The special features of a particular restaurant or hairdresser may allow that firm to charge a slightly different price from other producers in the industry without losing all its customers.

Although brand loyalty and product differentiation may also be important in many other industries these need not be monopolistically competitive. Brand loyalty limits the substitution between Ford and Vauxhall in the car industry but, with so few producers, the key feature of the industry remains the oligopolistic interdependence of the decisions of different firms. Monopolistic competition requires not merely product differentiation,

but also limited opportunities for economies of scale so that there are a great many producers who can largely neglect their interdependence with any particular rival. Hence many of the best examples of monopolistic competition are service industries where economies of scale are small.

The industry demand curve shows the total industry output which would be demanded at each price if every firm in the industry charged that price. The market share of each firm depends on the number of firms in the industry and on the price it charges. For a given number of firms, a shift in the industry demand curve will shift the demand curve for the output of each individual firm. For a given industry demand curve, an increase (decrease) in the number of firms in the industry will shift the demand curve of each firm to the left (right) as its market share falls (rises). But each firm faces a downward-sloping demand curve. For a given industry demand curve, number of firms, and price charged by all other firms, a particular firm can increase its market share to some extent by charging a lower price and inducing some consumers to switch to its particular product.

Figure 10-2 shows the supply decision of a firm. Given its own demand curve DD and marginal revenue curve MR the firm produces

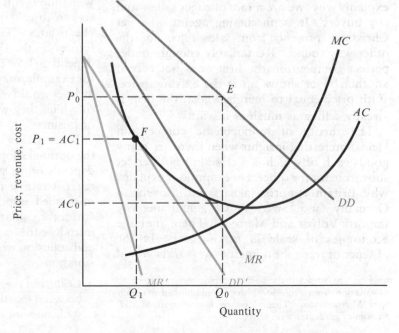

Figure 10-2 EQUILIBRIUM FOR A MONOPOLISTIC COMPETITOR. In the short run the monopolistic competitor faces the demand curve DD and sets MC equal to MR to produce Q_0 at a price P_0. Profits are $Q_0 \times (P_0 - AC_0)$. Profits attract new entrants and shift each firm's demand curve to the left. When the demand curve reaches DD' we reach the long-run tangency equilibrium at F. The firm sets MC equal to MR' to produce Q_1 at which P_1 equals AC_1. Firms are breaking even and there is no further entry.

Q_0 at a price P_0 making short-run profits equal to $Q_0 \times (P_0 - AC_0)$. In the long run these profits attract new entrants, who dilute the market share of each firm in the industry, shifting their demand curves to the left. Entry stops when each firm's demand curve has shifted so far to the left that price equals average cost and firms are just breaking even. In Figure 10-2 this occurs when demand has shifted to DD' and the firm produces Q_1 at a price P_1 to reach the tangency equilibrium at F.

> In monopolistic competition the long-run *tangency equilibrium* occurs where each firm's demand curve is tangent to (just touches) its AC curve at the output level at which MC equals MR. Each firm is maximizing profits but just breaking even. There is no further entry or exit.

Notice two things about the firm's long-run equilibrium at F. First, the firm is *not* producing at minimum average cost. It has excess capacity. It could reduce average costs by further expansion. However, its marginal revenue would be so low this would not be profitable. Second, the firm retains some monopoly power because of the special feature of its particular brand or location. Price exceeds marginal cost.

This second observation helps explain why firms are usually eager for new customers prepared to buy additional output at the *existing* price. In Robert Bishop's phrase, it explains why 'we are a race of eager sellers and coy buyers'. It is purchasing agents who get Christmas presents from sales reps, not the other way round.[2] Remarkably enough, under perfect competition the firm does not care if another buyer shows up at the existing price. With price equal to marginal cost, the firm is already selling as much as it wants.

The theory of monopolistic competition yields interesting insights when there are many goods each of which is a close but not perfect substitute for the other. For example, it explains why Britain exports Jaguars and Rovers to Germany and Sweden but simultaneously imports Volvos and Mercedes. There are large economies of scale in making cars. In the absence of trade the domestic car market would have room for only a few varieties. Producing a large number of brands at low output would enormously raise average costs. International trade allows each country to specialize in a few types of car and produce a much larger output of that brand than the home market alone could support. By swapping these cars between countries, consumers get a wider choice while each individual producer enjoys economies of scale, holding prices down.

10-3 Oligopoly and Interdependence

Under perfect competition or monopolistic competition, there are so many firms in the industry that no single firm need worry about the effect of its own actions on rival firms. However, the very essence of an oligopolistic industry is the need for each firm to consider how its own actions will affect the decisions of its relatively few competitors.

Although in the last chapter we used a hypothetical example of a *monopoly* airline, in practice of course airlines are oligopolists. Even on the popular transatlantic routes, British Airways, Air France, and TWA have significant market shares, and the position of each of their demand curves depends crucially on how their rivals behave and can be induced to behave. In contemplating a cut-price deal, each airline needs to consider whether or not other airlines will follow suit. Similarly, when new airlines try to break into the market by offering cheap fares – Laker in the 1970s and People's Express in the 1980s – these entrants' prospects depend on how existing airlines respond. Laker, for example, may have miscalculated how other airlines would react, failing to foresee the extent to which they would cut prices to drive it out of business.

What makes oligopoly so fascinating is that the optimal supply decision of a particular firm depends on its guess about how its rivals will react. Exciting recent developments in economics shed important insight into what constitutes a smart guess. First, however, we introduce the basic tension between competition and collusion which lies beneath all oligopolistic situations.

> *Collusion* is an explicit or implicit agreement between existing firms to avoid competition with one another.

---

[2] Quotation from Professor Bishop's unpublished magnum opus 'Microeconomic Theory', on which generations of MIT economics graduates were raised.

Initially, for simplicity, we neglect the possibility of entry and focus only on the behaviour of existing firms.

The Profits from Collusion

The existing firms will maximize their *joint* profits if they behave as if they were a multi-plant monopolist. A monopolist or sole decision-maker would organize the output from the industry to maximize total profits. Hence, if the few producers in an industry collude to behave as if they were a monopolist, their *total* profit will be maximized.

Figure 10-3 shows an industry where each firm, and the entire industry, has constant average and marginal costs at the level P_c. In the last chapter we saw that a competitive industry would produce Q_c at a price P_c but a multi-plant monopolist would maximize profits by producing Q_m at a price P_m. If the oligopolists collude jointly to produce Q_m we say they are acting as a *collusive monopolist*. Having thus decided industry output, there will then be some negotiation backstage to divide up output and profits between individual firms.

However, it is hard to stop individual firms cheating on the collective agreement. In Figure 10-3 joint profit is maximized when aggregate output is restricted to Q_m and the price forced

up to P_m. Yet each firm can expand at marginal cost P_c. If one firm expands production by undercutting the agreed price P_m, its profits will rise since its marginal revenue will exceed its marginal cost. But this firm's gain is at the expense of its collusive partners. Industry output is now higher than Q_m, total profits are lower, and other firms must suffer.

Hence oligopolists are torn between the desire to collude, thus maximizing joint profits, and the desire to compete, in the hope of increasing market share and profits at the expense of rivals. Yet if all firms compete, joint profits will be low and no firm is likely to do very well. Therein lies the dilemma.

Cartels

Collusion or co-operation between firms is easiest when formal agreements are legally permitted. Such arrangements are called *cartels*. In the late nineteenth century cartels were common, and they agreed market shares and prices in many industries. Such practices are now outlawed in Europe, the United States, and many other countries. Although there are usually large penalties for being caught, informal agreements and secret deals in smoke-filled rooms are not unknown even today.

The most famous cartel is OPEC, the Organization of Petroleum Exporting Countries. Active since 1973, its members (of which the UK is not one) meet regularly to set price and output levels. Initially, OPEC was very successful in organizing quantity reductions to force up the price of oil. Real OPEC revenues rose 340 per cent between 1974 and 1980. Yet almost from the start, many economists have predicted that OPEC, like most cartels, would quickly collapse. Usually, the incentive to cheat is too strong to resist, and once somebody breaks ranks others tend to follow.

In practice, one reason OPEC was successful for so long was the willingness of Saudi Arabia, the largest oil producer, to restrict its output further when smaller members insisted on expansion. By 1986, however, Saudi Arabia was no longer prepared to play by these rules, and refused to prop up the price any longer. The oil price collapsed from just under $30 to $9 a barrel before recovering a little. Whether this signalled the end of OPEC as a major force we shall discuss shortly.

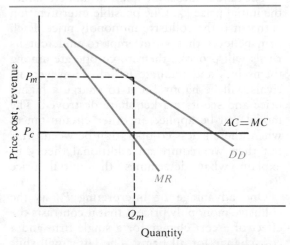

Figure 10-3 COLLUSION VERSUS COMPETITION. By colluding to restrict industry output to Q_m, joint profits are maximized and equal to those which a multi-plant monopolist would obtain. But each firm, with a marginal cost of P_c, has an incentive to cheat on the collusive agreement and expand its output.

The Kinked Oligopoly Demand Curve

Collusion is much harder if there are many firms in the industry, if the product is not standardized, and if demand and cost conditions are changing rapidly. In the absence of collusion, each firm's demand curve depends on how competitors react. Firms must guess how their rivals will behave. Before undertaking a serious analysis of how firms might make intelligent guesses, we introduce a simple model which highlights the key feature of this interdependence.

Suppose that each firm believes that its own price cut will be matched by all other firms in the industry but that an increase in its own price will induce no price response from competitors.[3] Figure 10-4 shows the demand curve DD that each firm would then face. The current price is P_0 and the firm is producing Q_0. Since competitors do not follow suit, a price increase will lead to a large loss of market share to other firms. The firm's demand curve is elastic above A at prices above the current price P_0. Conversely, a price cut is matched by other firms and market shares are unchanged. Sales increase only because the industry as a whole moves down the market demand curve as prices fall. The demand curve DD is much less elastic for price reductions from the initial price P_0.

The key feature of Figure 10-4 is that the marginal revenue curve MR is discontinuous at the output Q_0. Below Q_0 the elastic part of the demand curve is relevant, but at the output Q_0 the firm suddenly encounters the inelastic portion of its kinked demand curve and marginal revenue suddenly falls. Q_0 is the profit-maximizing output for the firm, given its belief about how competitors will respond.

The model has one important implication. Suppose the MC curve of a single firm shifts up or down by a small amount. Since the MR curve has a discontinuous vertical segment at the output Q_0, it will remain optimal to produce Q_0 and charge the price P_0. In contrast, a monopolist facing a continuously downward-sloping MR curve would adjust quantity and price when the MR curve shifted. The kinked demand curve model may explain the empirical finding that firms do not always adjust prices when costs change.

[3] This model was independently invented in 1939 by Paul Sweezy in the United States and R. L. Hall and C. J. Hitch in the UK.

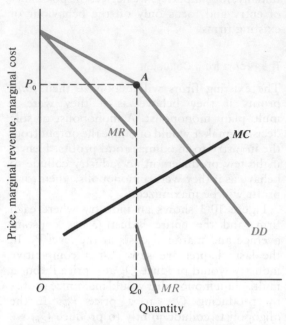

Figure 10-4   THE KINKED DEMAND CURVE. An oligopolist believes rivals will match price cuts but not price rises. The oligopolist's demand curve is kinked at A. Price rises lead to a large loss of market share, but price cuts increase quantity only by increasing industry sales. Marginal revenue is discontinuous at Q_0. The oligopolist produces Q_0, the output at which MC crosses the MR schedule.

The model does not explain what determines the initial price P_0. One possible interpretation is that it is the collusive monopoly price. Each firm believes that an attempt to undercut its rivals will provoke them to co-operate among themselves and retaliate in full. However, its rivals will be happy for it to charge a higher price and see its market share destroyed. The model can be applied in other circumstances where there is less co-operation between firms but then we require an additional theory to explain what determines the initial price P_0.

One advantage of interpreting P_0 as the collusive monopoly price is that it contrasts the effect of a cost change for a single firm and a cost change for all firms. The latter will shift the marginal cost curve up for the industry as a whole and increase the collusive monopoly price. Each firm's kinked demand curve will shift upwards since the monopoly price P_0 has increased. Thus we can reconcile the stickiness of a single firm's prices with respect to changes in its own costs alone, and the speed with which the entire industry marks up prices when all firms' costs are increased by higher taxes (as in the cigarette industry) or inflationary wage settlements in the whole industry.

10-4 Game Theory and Interdependent Decisions

A good poker player sometimes bluffs. Sometimes you can clean up with a bad hand, provided your opponents misread it for a good hand. Similarly, by having bluffed in the past and been caught, you may persuade them to keep betting even when you have a terrific hand.

Like poker players, oligopolists have to try to second-guess their rivals' moves to determine their own best action. To study how such interdependent decisions are made, we use *game theory*.

A *game* is a situation in which intelligent decisions are necessarily interdependent.

The *players* in the game try to maximize their own *payoffs*. In an oligopoly, the firms are the players and their payoffs are their profits in the long run. Each player must choose a strategy.

A *strategy* is a game plan describing how the player will act or *move* in every conceivable situation.

Being a pickpocket is a strategy. Lifting a particular wallet is a move.

In game theory, as elsewhere in economics, we are interested in equilibrium. In most games, each player's best strategy depends on the strategies chosen by other players. It is silly to be a pickpocket in an area where the police have TV cameras. Equilibrium occurs when each player chooses the best strategy, *given* the strategies being followed by other players. This description of equilibrium, invented by John Nash, is called Nash equilibrium. Nobody in the game wants to change their strategy, since other people's strategies have already been figured into the calculation of each player's best strategy.

Sometimes, but not usually, a player's best strategy is independent of those chosen by others. If so, it is called a *dominant strategy*. To introduce the use of game theory in

understanding oligopoly, we begin with an example in which each player has a dominant strategy.

Collude or Cheat?

Figure 10-5 shows a game[4] which we can imagine is between the only two members of a cartel like OPEC. Each firm can select a high-output or low-output strategy. In each box of Figure 10-5 the green number shows firm A's profits and the black number, firm B's profits for the output combination of the two firms.

When both have high output, industry output is high, the price is low, and each firm makes a small profit of 1. When each has low output, the outcome is more like the collusive monopoly of Figure 10-3. Prices are high and each firm does better, making a profit of 2. Each firm does best (a profit of 3) when it alone has high output; for then, the other firm's low output helps hold down industry output and keep up the price. In this situation we assume the low-output firm makes a profit of 0.

Now we can see how the game will unfold. Consider firm A's decision. If firm B has a high-output strategy, firm A does better also to have high output. In the two left-hand boxes

---

[4] The game is usually called the Prisoners' Dilemma, because it was first used to analyse the choices facing two people arrested and in different cells, each of whom could plead guilty or not guilty to the only crime that had been committed. Each prisoner would plead innocent if only he or she knew the other would plead guilty.

		Firm B output	
		High	Low
Firm A output	High	1 1	3 0
	Low	0 3	2 2

Figure 10-5 THE PRISONERS' DILEMMA GAME. The green and black numbers in each box indicate profits to firms A and B, respectively. Whether B pursues high or low output, A makes more profit going high; so does B, whichever A adopts. In equilibrium both go high. Yet both would make greater profits if both went low!

of Figure 10-5, firm A gets a profit of 1 by choosing high but a profit of 0 by choosing low. Now suppose firm B chooses a low-output strategy. From the two right-hand boxes. Firm A still does better by choosing high, since this yields it a profit of 3 whereas low yields it a profit of only 2. Hence firm A has a dominant strategy. Whichever strategy firm B adopts, firm A does better to choose a high-output strategy.

Firm B also has a dominant strategy to choose high output. Use Figure 10-5 to check for yourself that A does better to go high whichever strategy B selects. Since both firms choose high, the equilibrium of the game is the top left-hand box. Each firm gets a profit of 1.

Yet both firms would do better, getting a profit of 2, if they colluded to form a cartel and both produced low output – the bottom right-hand box. But neither can afford to take the risk of going low. Suppose firm A goes low. Firm B, comparing the two boxes in the bottom row, will then go high, preferring a profit of 3 to a profit of 2. And firm A will get screwed, earning a profit of 0 in that event. Firm A can figure all this out in advance, which is why its dominant strategy is to go high.

This is a particularly clear illustration of the tension between collusion and competition which we discussed earlier. In this example, it appears that the output-restricting cartel will never get formed, since each player can already foresee the overwhelming incentive for the other to cheat on such an arrangement. How then can cartels ever be sustained? One possibility is that there exist binding pre-commitments.

A *pre-commitment* is an arrangement, entered into voluntarily, which restricts one's future options.

Suppose both players in Figure 10-5 could simultaneously sign a legally enforceable contract to produce low output. They could then achieve the co-operative outcome in the bottom right-hand box, each earning profits of 2. Clearly, they then do better than in the top left-hand box, which describes the non-co-operative equilibrium of the game. Without any pre-commitment, neither player can go low because then the other player will go high. Binding pre-commitments, by removing this

temptation, enable both players to go low, and both players gain.

This idea of pre-commitment is an important one, and we shall encounter it many times. It crops up in numerous guises. Just think of all the human activities that are the subject of legal contracts, a simple kind of pre-commitment simultaneously undertaken by two parties or players.

Although this insight is powerful, its application to oligopoly requires some care. Cartels within a country are usually illegal, and we don't seriously believe that OPEC is held together by a signed agreement which could be upheld in international law! Is there some less formal way in which oligopolists can pre-commit themselves not to cheat on the collusive low-output solution to the game?

If the game is played only once, this may be difficult. In the real world, the game is repeated many times: firms choose output levels day after day. Suppose two players get together and try to collude on low output. Furthermore, each announces a *punishment strategy*. Should firm A ever cheat on the low-output agreement, firm B promises that it will subsequently react by raising its output. Firm A makes a similar promise.

Suppose the agreement has been in force for some time and both firms have stuck to their low-output deal. Firm A assumes that firm B will go low as usual. Figure 10-5 shows that firm A will make a *temporary* gain today if it cheats and goes high. Instead of staying in the bottom right-hand box with a profit of 2, it can move to the top right-hand box and make 3. However, from tomorrow onwards, firm B will also go high, and firm A can then do no better than continue to go high too, making a profit of 1 for evermore. But if A refuses to cheat today it can continue to stay in the bottom right-hand box and make 2 forever. In cheating, A is swapping a temporary gain for a permanent reduction in profits, and it may well conclude that this is a poor deal. Thus, punishment strategies can sustain an explicit cartel or implicit collusion even when no formal mechanism of precommitment exists.

One final point of great importance should be made. It is all very well to say that you will adopt a punishment strategy in the event that the other player cheats. But you can expect this to have an effect on the other player's behaviour only if your threat is not an empty one.

> A *credible threat* is one which, after the fact, you would then find it optimal to carry out.

In the preceding example, once firm A has cheated and gone high, it is then in firm B's interest to go high anyway. Hence a threat to go high if A ever cheats *is* a credible threat.

Let us see if we can use these insights to interpret the actual behaviour of OPEC in 1986, when Saudi Arabia dramatically raised its output leading to a collapse of oil prices. During the 1980s, other members of OPEC had gradually cheated on the low-output agreement, trusting that Saudi Arabia would continue to produce low, and perhaps even cut its output, to sustain a high price and the cartel's prestige. They hoped Saudi threats to adopt a punishment strategy were empty threats. And they were wrong. Figure 10-5 shows that, once the others go high, Saudi Arabia may as well go high too. Moreover, since the top left-hand box is clearly less desirable than the bottom right-hand box, the Saudi action may then have persuaded other players to return to the co-operative low-output solution. If so, the temporary period of high output and low prices was a good investment for the Saudis, and was a good reason why its punishment strategy should have been viewed as a credible threat.

10-5 Entry and Potential Competition

So far in this chapter we have discussed imperfect competition between existing firms. To complete our understanding of such markets, we must also think about the effect of potential competition from new entrants to the industry on the behaviour of existing or incumbent firms. Three cases must be distinguished: where entry is trivially easy, where it is difficult by accident, and where it is difficult by design.

Contestable Markets

In the previous chapter we saw that free entry to, and exit from, the industry was a key feature of perfect competition, a market structure in which each firm is tiny relative to the industry. Suppose, however, that we observe an industry with few incumbent firms. Before assuming that our previous analysis of oligopoly will be required, we must think hard about entry and

exit. It is possible that this industry is a contestable market.

> A *contestable market* is characterized by free entry and free exit.

By free entry, we mean that all firms, including both incumbents and potential entrants, have access to the same technology and hence have the same cost curves. By free exit, we mean that there are no *sunk* or irrecoverable costs; on leaving the industry, a firm can fully recoup its previous investment expenditure, including money spent on building up knowledge and goodwill.

A contestable market allows *hit-and-run* entry. If the incumbent firms, however few, are not behaving as if they were a perfectly competitive industry at long-run equilibrium ($p = MC = $ minimum AC), an entrant can step in, undercut them, and make a temporary profit before quitting again.

The theory of contestable markets is controversial. There are many industries in which sunk costs are hard to recover or where the initial expertise may take an entrant some time to acquire, placing it at a temporary disadvantage against incumbent firms. Nor, as we shall shortly see, is it safe to assume that incumbents will not change their behaviour when threatened by entry. But the theory does vividly illustrate that market structure and incumbent behaviour cannot be deduced simply by counting the number of firms in the industry.

That is why, in the previous chapter, we were careful to stress that a monopolist is a sole producer *who can completely discount fear of entry*. More generally, we must now refine the classification of Table 10-1 by discussing entry in more detail.

Innocent Entry Barriers

Our discussion of entry barriers distinguishes those that occur anyway and those that are deliberately erected by incumbent firms. First we discuss the former.

> An *innocent entry barrier* is one not deliberately erected by incumbent firms.

In his pioneering study in 1956, the American economist Joe Bain highlighted three types of entry barrier: product differentiation, absolute cost advantages, and scale economies. The first of these is not an innocent barrier, as we shall shortly explain. Absolute cost advantages, where incumbent firms have lower cost curves than those that entrants will face, may be innocent. For example, if it takes time to learn the business, incumbents will face lower costs, at least in the short run; if they are smart, they may already have located in the most advantageous site. In contrast, if incumbents have undertaken investment or R & D specifically with a view to deterring entrants, this is not an innocent barrier. We take up this issue shortly.

Figure 10-1 allows us to see the role of scale economies as an innocent entry barrier. There we explained that, if minimum efficient scale is large relative to the industry demand curve, an entrant cannot get into the industry without considerably depressing the market price, and it may prove simply impossible to break in at a profit.

The greater are such innocent entry barriers, the more appropriate it will be to neglect potential competition from entrants. The oligopoly game then reduces to competition between incumbent firms along the lines we discussed in the previous section. Where innocent entry barriers are low, one of two things may happen. Either incumbent firms accept this situation, in which case competition from potential entrants will prevent incumbent firms from exercising much market power – the outcome will be closer to that of perfect competition – or else incumbent firms will try to design some entry barrier of their own. It is to this important question that we now turn.

10-6 Strategic Entry Deterrence

Earlier, we defined a strategy as a game plan when decision-making is interdependent. The word 'strategic' is much used in everyday language, but it has a precise meaning in economics.

> A *strategic move* is one that influences the other person's choice, in a manner favourable to one's self, by affecting the other person's expectations of how one's self will behave.

We have already introduced pre-commitment as a strategy move, and we now extend that idea to entry deterrence.

To do so we use Figure 10-6. For simplicity,

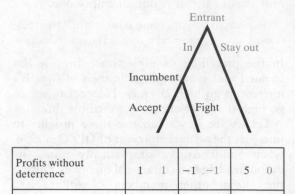

	Profits					
Profits without deterrence	1	1	−1	−1	5	0
Profits with deterrence	−2	1	−1	−1	2	0

Figure 10-6 STRATEGIC ENTRY DETERRENCE. In the absence of deterrence, should the entrant enter, the incumbent does better to accept entry than to fight. The entrant knows this and hence enters. Equilibrium is the top left-hand box, and both firms make a profit of 1. But if the incumbent pre-commits an expenditure of 3 which is recouped *only* if there is a fight, the incumbent will resist entry, the entrant will stay out, and equilibrium is the bottom right-hand box. The incumbent does better, making a profit of 2.

there is only one incumbent firm and the game is against a potential entrant. The entrant can choose to come in or stay out. If the entrant comes in, the incumbent can either opt for the easy life, accept the new rival, and agree to share the market – or it can fight. If the entrant is large, the easy life may actually involve an output reduction by the incumbent, so that the two firms' joint output will not depress the price too much. Fighting entry means producing at least as much as before, and perhaps considerably more than before, so that the industry price collapses. In this *price war*, sometimes called *predatory pricing* by the incumbent, both firms do badly and make losses. The top row of boxes in Figure 10-6 show the profits to the incumbent (in black) and the entrant (in green) in each of the three possible outcomes.

If the incumbent is unchallenged it does very well, making profits of 5. The entrant of course makes nothing. If they share the market, both make small profits of 1. In a price war, both make losses. How should the game go?

Suppose the entrant comes in. Comparing the left two boxes of the top row, the incumbent does better to cave in than to fight. The entrant can figure this out. Any threat by the incumbent to resist entry is not a credible threat – when it comes to the crunch, it will be better to cave in. Much as the incumbent would like the entrant to stay out, in which case the incumbent would make profits of 5, the equilibrium of the game is that the entrant will come in and the incumbent will not resist. Both make profits of 1, the top left-hand box.

The incumbent, however, may have got its act together before the potential entrant appears on the scene. It may be able to invent a binding pre-commitment which forces itself to resist entry and thereby scares off any future challenge. The incumbent would be ecstatic if a Martian appeared and guaranteed to shoot the incumbent's directors if they ever allowed an entry to be unchallenged. The entrants would expect a fight, would anticipate a loss of 1, and would stay out, leaving the incumbent with a permanent profit of 5.

In the absence of Martians, the incumbent may be able to achieve the same effect by economic means. For example, suppose the incumbent invests in spare capacity. This capacity is expensive, and is unused at low output. The incumbent has low output in the absence of entry or if an entrant is accommodated without a fight. Suppose in these situations the incumbent loses 3 by carrying this excess capacity. The second row of boxes in Figure 10-6 reduces the incumbent's profits by 3 in these two outcomes. In a price war, however, the incumbent's output is high and the spare capacity is no longer wasted; hence we do not need to reduce the incumbent's profit in the middle column of boxes in Figure 10-6. Now consider the game again.

If the entrant comes in, the incumbent loses 2 by caving in but only 1 by fighting. Hence entry is resisted. Foreseeing this, the entrant does not enter, since the entrant loses money in a price war. Hence the equilibrium of the game is the bottom right-hand box and no entry takes place. Strategic entry deterrence has been successful. It has also been profitable. Even allowing for the cost of 3 of carrying the spare capacity, the incumbent still makes a profit of 2, which is better than the profit of 1 that was made in the top left-hand box when no deterrence was attempted and the entrant came in.

Does deterrence always work? No. Suppose in Figure 10-6 we change the right-hand column. In the top row the incumbent gets a profit of 3 if no entry occurs. Without the pre-commitment, the equilibrium is the top left-hand box as before. But if the incumbent has to spend 3 on a spare capacity pre-commitment, it now makes a profit of 0 in the bottom right-hand box when entry is deterred. The entrant is still deterred, but the incumbent would have done better not to invest in spare capacity but to let the entrant in, and make a profit of 1.

We can extend this analysis in two ways. First, the above model suggests that price wars should never happen. If the incumbent is really going to fight, then the entrant should not have entered. This of course requires that the entrant knows accurately the profits of the incumbent in the different boxes and therefore can correctly predict its behaviour. In the real world, entrants sometimes get it wrong. Moreover, if the entrant has much better financial backing than the incumbent, a price war may be a good investment for the entrant. The incumbent will exit first, and thereafter the entrant will be able to cash up and get its losses back with interest.

Second, is spare capacity the only kind of pre-commitment available to incumbents? Pre-commitments must be irreversible, otherwise they are an empty threat; and they must increase the chances that the incumbent will fight. Generally, anything with the character of fixed and sunk costs will be of interest: fixed costs artificially increase scale economies and make the incumbent more keen on high output, and sunk costs cannot be reversed. Advertising to invest in goodwill and brand loyalty is a good example. So is product proliferation. If the incumbent has only one brand, an entrant may hope to break in with a different brand. But if the incumbent has a complete range of brands or models, an incumbent will have to compete across the whole product range, which ups the ante.

10-7 The Lessons of the New Industrial Economics

Few industries in the real world closely resemble the textbook extremes of perfect competition and pure monopoly. Most are imperfectly competitive. In this chapter, we have introduced you to some developments in how to think about imperfect competition. Game theory in general, and notions such as pre-commitment, credibility, and deterrence in particular, have allowed economists to analyse many of the practical concerns of big business.[5] These developments are known as the New Industrial Economics.

What have we learned from the New Industrial Economics of imperfect competition? First, market structure and the behaviour of incumbent firms are determined *simultaneously*. Economists used to start with a market structure, determined by the extent of scale economies relative to the industry demand curve, then deduce how the incumbent firms would behave (monopoly, oligopoly, perfect competition), then check out these predictions against performance indicators, such as the extent to which prices exceeded marginal cost. Now we realize that strategic behaviour by incumbent firms can affect entry, and hence market structure, except where entry is almost trivially easy.

Second, and related, we have learned the importance of *potential* competition, which may come from domestic firms considering entry, or from imports from abroad. The number of firms observed in the industry today conveys little information about the extent of the market power they truly exercise. If entry is very easy, even a single incumbent or apparent monopolist may find it unprofitable to depart significantly from perfectly competitive behaviour.

Finally, we have seen how many business practices of the real world – price wars, advertising, brand proliferation, excess capacity or excessive research and development – can be understood as strategic competition in which, to be effective, threats must be made credible by pre-commitments.

Summary

1 Imperfect competition exists when indi-vidual firms believe they face downward-sloping demand curves. The most important forms are monopolistic competition, oligopoly, and pure monopoly.

2 Pure monopoly status can be conferred by legislation, as when an industry is nationalized or a temporary patent is awarded. When minimum efficient scale is very large relative to the industry demand curve, this innocent entry barrier may be sufficiently high to produce a natural monopoly in which all threat of entry can be ignored.

3 At the opposite extreme, entry and exit may be costless. The market is contestable, and incumbent firms must mimic perfectly competitive behaviour, otherwise they would be undercut by a flood of entrants. With intermediate degrees of innocent entry barrier, the industry is likely to be an oligopoly.

4 Monopolistic competitors face free entry and exit to the industry, but are individually small and make similar though not identical products. Each has limited monopoly power in its special brand. In long-run equilibrium, price equals average cost but exceeds marginal revenue and marginal cost at the tangency equilibrium.

5 Oligopolists face a tension between collusion to maximize joint profits and competition for a larger share of smaller joint profits. Collusion may be formal, as in a cartel, or informal. Without credible threats of punishment by other collusive partners, each firm faces a temptation to cheat.

6 Game theory describes interdependent decision-making in which each player chooses a strategy. In the Prisoners' Dilemma game, each firm has a dominant strategy but the outcome is disadvantageous to both players. With binding pre-commitments, both could be better off by guaranteeing not to cheat on the collusive solution.

7 Innocent entry barriers are made in heaven, and arise from scale economies or absolute cost advantages of incumbent firms. Strategic entry barriers are made in boardrooms and arise from credible pre-commitments to resist entry if challenged. Only in certain circumstances is strategic entry deterrence profitable for incumbents.

[5] In his excellent review of these recent developments, John Vickers notes wryly his conversation with an eminent business-man, who, having just been told of the new economics of industry, exclaimed: 'I feel like the character in Molière who learns that all the while he has been speaking prose.' (See J. Vickers, 'Strategic Competition among the Few', *Oxford Review of Economic Policy*, vol. 1, no. 3.)

8 The New Industrial Economics is the application of modern game theory to strategic competition between large firms. In practice, many sectors of an advanced economy are characterized by such firms.

Key Terms

Imperfect competition
Natural monopoly
Oligopoly
Monopolistic competition
Collusion
Cartel
Tangency equilibrium
Product differentiation
Game theory
Strategy
Pre-commitment
Credible threat
Innocent entry barrier
Strategic entry barrier
Strategic entry deterrence
Contestable market

Problems

1   An industry faces the demand curve:

Price	1	2	3	4	5	6	7	8	9	10
Quantity	10	9	8	7	6	5	4	3	2	1

(a) Suppose it is a monopolist whose constant MC equals 3: what price and output are chosen? (b) Now suppose there are two firms, each with $MC = AC = 3$: what price and output will maximize joint profits if they collude? (c) Why do the two firms have to agree on the output each will produce? (d) Why might each firm be tempted to cheat if it can avoid retaliation by the other?

2   Suppose in the above problem the two firms, call them A and Z, begin with half the market each when charging the monopoly price. Z decides to cheat and believes A will stick to its old output level. (a) Show the demand curve Z believes it faces. (b) What price and output would Z then choose? (c) How is A likely to respond if Z does cheat in this way?

3   Go back to problem 1 with a sole supplier producing at $MC = AC = 3$. Suppose there are potential entrants who can produce at $MC = AC = 5$. (a) What price will the sole supplier charge? (b) If entry became prohibited, what would the sole supplier do?

4   Vehicle repairers have sometimes suggested that mechanics should be licensed so that repairs are done only by qualified people. Some economists argue that customers can always ask whether a mechanic was trained at a reputable institution without needing to see any licence. (a) Evaluate the arguments for and against licensing car mechanics. (b) Are the arguments the same for licensing doctors?

5   Think of five adverts on television. Do you think their function is primarily informative, or the erection of entry barriers to the industry?

6   A good-natured parent knows that children sometimes need to be punished, but also knows that, when it comes to the crunch, the child will be let off with a warning. Can the parent undertake any pre-commitment to make the threat of punishment credible?

7   Common Fallacies Show why the following statements are incorrect: (a) Competitive firms should get together to restrict output and drive up the price. If they don't do this they cannot be maximizing profits. (b) Firms wouldn't advertise unless they expected it to increase sales. (c) Monopoly power is measured by the extent to which firms can raise price above marginal costs. Average costs don't come into it. Hence market structure has nothing to do with economies of scale.

11

The Analysis of Factor Markets: Labour

In winning a golf tournament, a top professional earns more in a weekend than a professor earns in a year. Students studying economics can expect higher career earnings than those of equally smart students studying philosophy. An unskilled worker in the UK earns more than an unskilled worker in India. Few market economies manage to provide jobs for all their citizens wanting to work. How can we explain these aspects of the real world?

In each case the answer depends on the supply and demand for that particular type of labour. In this chapter and the next we discuss the supply and demand for labour. We begin our analysis of the markets for the factors of production – labour, capital and land. We discuss what determines the equilibrium prices and quantities of factors of production in different industries and in the economy as a whole. Although we begin with the factor called 'labour', we shall see in Chapter 13 that many of the same principles apply in analysing the markets for other factors of production.

We have already studied at some length the market for goods. There is nothing intrinsically different about our approach to factor markets. You should already be able to guess the general structure of this chapter: demand, supply, equilibrium, problems of disequilibrium and adjustment.

Table 11-1 gives some actual data on UK earnings in 1988 and compares these with inflation-adjusted earnings a decade earlier. By 1988 workers in the public utilities (gas, electricity and water) earned nearly £20 a week more than the national average and earned considerably more than workers in the textile industry. Table 11-1 also shows that workers in textiles had suffered a further reduction in their relative position in the earnings league table over the period 1978–88.

Another question considered in this chapter is why different methods of production are used in different countries. A snack bar in a poor country has several waiters; in a rich country it has several vending machines. The relative cost of using capital and labour in rich and poor countries affects the way in which goods and services (here, fast food) are produced. How does this work?

The economics of factor markets differ from the economics of output markets not because we depart from the usual reliance on supply and demand, but because there is something special about demand in factor markets. It is not a direct or final demand, but a *derived* demand. It is only because firms want to produce output that they demand factors of production. To know the quantities of factors a firm will demand we need to think about the demand for the firm's output that will influence how much the firm wishes to produce.

The demand for factors of production is a *derived demand* because it is derived from the demand for the output that the factors are used to produce.

Table 11-1 Weekly real earnings in the UK (£/week at 1988 prices)

INDUSTRY	1978	1988
All industries	182	218
Gas, electricity, water	191	236
Textiles	165	184

Source: Department of Employment, *Gazette.*

Each firm simultaneously decides how much output to supply and how many factors to demand. The two are inextricably interlinked. But it is the demand for the firm's output that drives the whole process.

On the supply side we must distinguish between the supply of factors to the economy as a whole and the supply of factors to an individual firm or industry. It takes a long time to train helicopter pilots. Thus the supply of helicopter pilots is almost fixed in the short run. But this total supply of pilots can choose in which industry to work. They will tend to work in the industry offering the highest wages.

Does this mean that all industries will have to pay the same wage rate for pilots of they wish to stop pilots moving to higher paying industries? Not quite. Different jobs have different non-monetary characteristics. Helicopter flights to North Sea oil rigs may be more dangerous because of bad weather, and may involve working irregular shifts that make it hard to plan leisure activities during time off. To attract pilots to this industry, it will be necessary to pay a higher than average wage rate to offset these disadvantages of the job.

> An *equalizing wage differential* is the monetary compensation for differential non-monetary characteristics of the same job in different industries so that workers with a particular skill have no incentive to move between industries.

Thus unpleasant or dangerous jobs will pay more than the national average for that skill and pleasant jobs will pay less than the national average. The total returns, monetary and non-monetary, will then be equated in different industries and workers with that skill will have no incentive to move.

In the short run, with an almost fixed supply of pilots to the economy as a whole, any increase in the total demand for pilots (e.g., the discovery of North Sea oil) will raise the equilibrium wage of pilots in all industries. To retain some of their pilots, other industries will have to match the total rewards (lucrative wages adjusted for non-monetary drawbacks) offered by the North Sea oil industry. But in the longer run the supply of pilots is not fixed. High wages will act as a signal for young workers to abandon plans to train as fixed-wing pilots or engine drivers and move instead into the lucrative helicopter business. Another theme of our analysis of factor markets will be the need to distinguish between supply possibilities in the short run and in the longer run.

Putting demand and supply together we can determine equilibrium prices and quantities in different factor markets. But are these markets always in equilibrium? When examining goods markets we showed how excess supply or excess demand would lead to changes in output price that tend to restore equilibrium. In the labour market the wage rate is the price of labour. Are wages sufficiently flexible to restore labour market equilibrium or can we envisage circumstances in which wage responses will be sluggish and the labour market can be out of equilibrium for some time? How does this relate to unemployment? These are questions we examine in more detail towards the end of the chapter.

11-1 The Firm's Demand for Factors in the Long Run: Factor Prices and the Choice of Technique

We begin by discussing the long run in which all factors of production can be fully adjusted. In Chapter 8 we showed how to construct the firm's long-run average cost curve *LAC* and long-run marginal cost curve *LMC*. In Chapters 9 and 10 we considered various descriptions of the demand curve facing the firm and showed how the firm would choose output supplied to maximize profits.

Although it is all part of the same decision, we now switch our attention from the firm's behaviour in the output market to its behaviour in the corresponding input markets. Recall that a firm's cost curves show the minimum cost way to produce each possible output level. The minimum cost method for producing any output level depends on two things: the production function, summarizing the alternative production techniques available, and the prices at which different factors of production can be employed.

Table 11-2 shows data for two possible techniques for making 100 snarks per week. Technique A is more capital intensive than technique B. In technique A the ratio of capital

Table 11-2 Making 100 snarks: factor prices and the choice of technique

TECH-NIQUE	INPUT		RENTAL RATE (£)	WAGE RATE (£)	TOTAL COST (£)
	CAPITAL	LABOUR			
A	4	4	320	300	2480
B	2	6	320	300	2440
A	4	4	320	340	2640
B	2	6	320	340	2680

to labour input quantities is 1 to 1. In technique B the ratio is 1 to 3. Technique A uses relatively more capital and relatively less labour to make 100 snarks.

To construct the total cost curve the firm chooses the minimum cost technique at each possible output level. Table 11-2 is relevant to the particular output level of 100 snarks. When each unit of capital input costs £320 per week and each unit of labour input £300 per week, the first two rows of Table 11-2 show the cheapest way to produce 100 snarks is to use technique B. The total cost is then £2440.

The second two rows show what happens when labour is more expensive. When each unit of labour now costs £340 per week, technique A is now the cheapest way to produce 100 snarks per week. But the total cost of producing 100 snarks has risen to £2640 per week.

This simple example illustrates a general principle. In producing a *given* output by the cheapest available technique, a rise in the price of a unit of labour relative to the price of a unit of capital will lead the firm to switch to a more capital-intensive technique. Conversely, if capital becomes relatively more expensive, the cost-minimizing technique to produce a given output will now be a more labour-intensive technique. The firm substitutes away from the factor of production that has become relatively more expensive.

This principle helps explain why there are substantial differences across countries in the capital–labour ratios in the same industry. In the UK and the USA, farmers face high wages relative to the cost of renting a combine harvester. Mechanized farming economizes on expensive workers. In contrast, India has cheap and abundant labour, but capital is relatively scarce and expensive. Indian farmers use much more labour-intensive techniques.

Workers with scythes and shovels perform tasks undertaken by combine harvesters and bull-dozers in the UK and USA.

Table 11-2 shows that when output is 100 snarks per week the firm will demand 4 units of labour and 4 units of capital when a unit of capital costs £320 per week and a unit of labour £340 per week. When output is 100 snarks per week, but the cost of labour is only £300 per week, the firm will demand 6 units of labour and 2 units of capital. This suggests that the demand for factors of production depends on the level of output and the relative price of the factors themselves.

However, this is not a particularly helpful way to think about the demand curve for factors of production. Why not? Because although Table 11-2 tells us how the firm selects the minimum cost technique to produce a given output, it does not tell us which output the firm will choose to maximize profits. To determine profit-maximizing output, and the corresponding quantities of factors demanded, we have to repeat the calculations of Table 11-2 for each and every output, calculate the entire total cost curve for all output levels, and then choose profit-maximizing output by equating marginal cost and marginal revenue.

An increase in the wage rate from £300 to £340 per week will cause the firm to substitute away from labour and towards capital in the production technique required to produce a given output level. But it will also raise the total cost of producing each and every output level. Even with more capital-intensive techniques firms will still use some labour for which they have now to pay more. With higher marginal costs, but unchanged demand and marginal revenue curves, firms will produce less output.

Although it is tempting to say that a decrease in output, an increase in wage rate, or a fall in the price of capital, will decrease the quantity of labour demanded, we can now see the problem. A change in the price of one factor will lead not merely to changes in factor intensity at a given output, but to changes in marginal output costs and hence the profit-maximizing level of output itself.

When we studied consumer decisions in Chapter 6 we saw that a change in the price of a good has both a substitution effect and an income effect. The substitution effect reflects the change in relative prices of different goods and the income effect reflects changes in real income as a result of the price change. We have now established that the demand for factors works exactly the same way.

Table 11-2 illustrates the pure substitution effect at a given level of output. A higher relative price of labour leads firms to substitute towards the factor that has become relatively cheaper. But there is also an income or output effect. By shifting the marginal cost of producing output, a change in a factor price leads to a different profit-maximizing output.

In the long run we can be fairly sure that an increase in the wage rate will reduce the quantity of labour demanded. The substitution effect leads to more capital-intensive techniques at each output level and the higher marginal cost of output will reduce the amount of output it is most profitable to supply. Similarly, an increase in the price of capital will reduce the quantity of capital demanded. The substitution effect and the output effect go in the same direction.

What about the effect of an increase in the wage rate on the quantity of capital demanded? There will be a substitution effect towards more capital-intensive techniques, but an output effect tending to reduce output and the quantity of all factors demanded. The easier it is to substitute capital for labour the more likely is the substitution effect to dominate. Firms will substitute a lot of capital for labour. With much

less labour than before, marginal output costs will rise only a little and the profit-maximizing output is likely to fall only a little. On balance the quantity of capital demanded is likely to rise.

We began the chapter by pointing out that the demand for factors of production is a derived demand. It depends on the demand for the firm's output. Where does the output demand curve enter the analysis? The answer is that it plays a large part in determining the output effect of a change in the price of a factor.

Figure 11-1 shows the shift upwards in the long-run marginal cost curve LMC when there is an increase in the wage rate. At the old wage rate the marginal output cost curve is LMC_0 but at the higher wage rate the marginal cost curve is LMC_1. The original profit-maximizing point is A. If the firm faces a horizontal demand curve DD, the upward shift in marginal costs leads to a new profit-maximizing output at B. Output falls from Q_0 to Q_1. With the much less elastic demand curve $D'D'$, the firm is still initially at A where LMC_0 equals MR' the marginal revenue curve corresponding to $D'D'$. Now the shift to LMC_1 leads to a much smaller reduction in profit-maximizing output. The new output level is Q_2 and the firm is at point C.

Hence, the more elastic is the demand curve for the firm's output, the more a given increase in the price of a factor of production, and a

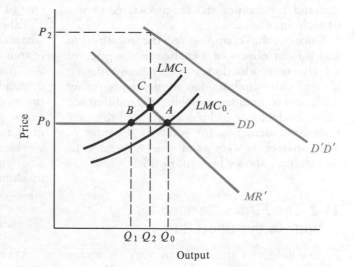

Figure 11-1 THE OUTPUT EFFECT OF A WAGE INCREASE. A wage increase will have a substitution effect leading firms to substitute relatively more capital-intensive techniques. Nevertheless, total costs and marginal costs of producing output will be greater than before. Facing the horizontal demand curve DD, a shift from LMC_0 to LMC_1 will lead the firm to move from A to B and output will fall from Q_0 to Q_1. This tends to reduce the demand for all factors of production. Facing the demand curve $D'D'$ and corresponding marginal revenue curve MR', the upward shift from LMC_0 to LMC_1 leads the firm to move from A to C at which marginal cost and marginal revenue are again equal. The output effect reduces output only from Q_0 to Q_2.

BOX 11-1

THE FIRM'S LONG-RUN FACTOR DEMANDS AND THE CHOICE OF TECHNIQUE

In the long run all factors of production can be varied. The firm's long-run total cost curve, and the average and marginal cost curves derived from it, embody the minimum cost production technique at each output level. At each output level the minimum cost technique reflects both the technical possibilities summarized in the production function and the prices of the factors employed. For a given long-run cost curve, the firm will choose to supply the output at which long-run marginal cost is equal to marginal revenue. Knowing this output, we can then determine the technique chosen and the quantity of each factor employed.

An increase in the price of one factor will have both a substitution effect and an output effect. The substitution effect leads the firm to produce a given output using a technique which economizes on the factor that has become relatively more expensive. Thus, a rise in the wage rate of labour leads to a substitution effect towards more capital-intensive production methods at each output.

But an increase in the price of a factor will also increase both total costs and marginal costs. Since the marginal revenue curve is unaltered the profit-maximizing output must fall. This is the pure output effect. It tends to reduce the quantity demanded for all factors. The output effect is larger the more elastic is the demand curve for the firm's output.

For a given output demand curve, an increase in the price of one factor will lead to a reduction in the quantity of that factor demanded. The substitution effect and output effect operate in the same direction. But the effect on the quantity of the other factor demanded is ambiguous. A rise in the wage rate leads to substitution towards more capital-intensive techniques but also leads to lower total output. The net effect on the quantity of capital demanded is more likely to be positive the easier it is to substitute capital for labour at each output level and the more inelastic is the demand curve for the firm's output.

An upward shift in the firm's output demand curve will increase the profit maximizing output. This output effect will tend to increase the quantity demanded of all factors.

---

given shift in the long-run marginal cost curve for output, will lead to a large reduction in the quantity of output produced. And the larger the output effect, the greater will be the reduction in the quantity of all factors demanded.

Box 11-1 summarizes our analysis of the influences determining the firm's long-run demand for factors and the associated choice of technique.

Since we have emphasized the substitution and output effects of a change in the price of a factor of production, you may be wondering if we can analyse factor demands using analytical techniques resembling the indifference curve–budget line techniques we used to study household demands for goods in Chapter 6. The answer is 'yes' and the Appendix to this chapter shows how to do this.

11-2 The Firm's Demand for Labour in the Short Run

In the long run the firm can vary its factor intensity by switching from one production technique to another. But in the short run the firm has some fixed factors of production, which we normally take to be machines, and may have little scope to vary the production technique in operation. We now consider the firm's short-run demand for labour when the quantity of capital it employs, and thus the cost of employing that capital, are fixed.

Table 11-3 extends the ideas we introduced in Chapter 8 in looking at the firm's short-run output decision with a fixed capital stock. Now we focus on the implications for labour demand. From columns (1) and (2) we calculate the marginal product of labour, how much each extra worker adds to total output. The marginal product increases as the first few workers are added because it is hard for the first and second worker to handle all the machinery. By the time the third worker is added, the *diminishing marginal productivity* of labour has set in. With all existing machines fully utilized, there is less and less for each new worker to contribute.

As in our discussion of output, we concentrate on the *marginal principle*. Does the cost of a

Table 11-3 Output and employment in the short run

(1) LABOUR INPUT (workers)	(2) OUTPUT pgoods)	(3) MARGINAL PRODUCT OF LABOUR (MPL) (goods/extra worker)	(4) MARGINAL VALUE PRODUCT (MPL × £500)	(5) WAGE RATE (£)	(6) EXTRA PROFITS (£)
0	0				
1	0.8	0.8	400	300	100
2	1.8	1.0	500	300	200
3	3.1	1.3	650	300	350
4	4.3	1.2	600	300	300
5	5.4	1.1	550	300	250
6	6.3	0.9	450	300	150
7	7.0	0.7	350	300	50
8	7.5	0.5	250	300	−50

new worker exceed the benefit from having an extra worker? Table 11-3 assumes we are discussing a competitive firm which can hire as many workers as it wishes at the wage rate of £300 and can sell as much output as it wishes at a price of £500. Column (4) shows the extra revenue from taking on another worker.

> The *marginal value product of labour* is the extra revenue obtained by selling the output an extra worker produces.

Since the firm is perfectly competitive, the marginal value product of another worker is simply the marginal product in physical goods multiplied by the price for which these extra goods can be sold. From this extra revenue from an additional worker, the firm must subtract the extra wage cost. The final column of Table 11-3 shows the increase in profits when an extra worker is taken on.

The firm keeps expanding employment so long as the marginal value product of another worker exceeds the wage cost. After the third worker, diminishing returns set in. Further employment expansion starts to reduce the marginal product of labour in' physical goods and hence its marginal value product. It is profitable to expand as far as 7 workers. The seventh worker has a marginal value product of £350, which just covers the wage of £300 for this extra worker. But the eighth worker's marginal value product is only £250. The optimal level of employment is 7 workers.

Note that the firm is simultaneously choosing the employment level and the output level: 7 workers make 7 units of output. In moving

from 6 workers and 6.3 units of output to 7 workers and 7 units of output, the firm's marginal revenue is £350 ($= 0.7 \times £500$). Labour is the only variable factor and the marginal cost of the extra 0.7 output unit is just the wage rate £300 of the extra worker. Seven units of output is the level to which the profit-maximizing firm would be led by thinking about marginal cost and marginal revenue. The marginal revenue of moving from 7 to 7.5 output units would not cover the marginal labour cost. It is just another way of looking at the same thing.

The firm's employment rule is thus: expand (contract) employment if the marginal value product of labour is greater than (less than) the wage of a extra worker. When labour can be smoothly adjusted, as for example when the correct measure of labour input is workers times hours worked, the firm's demand for labour must satisfy the condition:

wage = marginal value product of labour   (1)

Figure 11-2 illustrates this principle when we can assume that there is diminishing marginal productivity at all employment levels. The marginal value product of labour (*MVPL*) slopes down. A competitive firm can hire labour at the constant wage rate W_0 since it is a price-taker in the labour market. Below L^* profits can be increased by expanding employment, since *MVPL* exceeds the wage rate or marginal cost of taking on extra labour. Above L^* it is profitable to contract employment, since the wage exceeds the *MVPL*. L^* is the profit-maximizing level of employment.

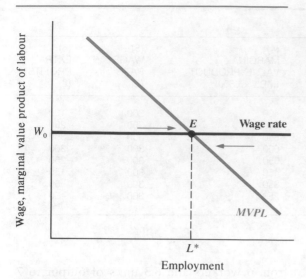

Figure 11-2   THE FIRM'S CHOICE OF
EMPLOYMENT.   The firm sells output for a given
price and hires labour at the given wage W_0.
Diminishing marginal productivity makes the $MVPL$
schedule slope down. Below L^* extra employment
adds more to revenue than labour costs. Above L^*
extra employment adds more to costs than revenue.
L^* is the profit maximizing employment level where
the wages equals the $MVPL$.

Monopoly and Monopsony Power

This theory is easily amended when the firm has
monopoly power in its output market (a
downward-sloping demand curve for its product) or *monopsony power* in its input markets
(an upward-sloping supply curve for its inputs
so that the firm must offer a higher factor price
the more of a factor it wishes to employ).

A firm with monopsony power is not a
price-taker in its input markets. Because the
firm faces an upward-sloping factor supply
curve, it must offer a higher factor price to
attract more factors. Hence the marginal cost
of an additional unit of the factor *exceeds*
the factor price. In expanding its factor use,
the firm must recognize it bids up the
price paid to all units of the factor already
employed.

For a perfectly competitive firm, the $MVPL$
schedule depicts its marginal revenue from
taking on an extra worker. We usually reserve
the term *marginal value product of labour*
($MVPL$) for competitive firms who are price-
takers in their output markets. $MVPL$ is simply

the marginal product of labour in physical
goods MPL multiplied by the output price. We
reserve the term *marginal revenue product of
labout* ($MRPL$) for firms facing a downward-
sloping demand curve for their output.

To calculate the marginal revenue product of
labour we first find the marginal physical
product of labout MPL and then calculate
the change in the firm's total revenue when
it sells these extra goods.

Figure 11-3 shows the $MVPL$ and $MRPL$
schedules for two firms with the same technology. Both schedules slope down because of
diminishing marginal productivity – a technical
property of production – but the $MRPL$
schedules slopes down more steeply because the
firm faces a downward-sloping demand curve
for its output and recognizes that additional
output reduces the price and hence the revenue
earned on previous units of output.

Similarly, although W_0 is the marginal cost
of a unit of labour for a competitive firm that
is a price-taker in its input market, a monopsonist must recognize that an expansion of
employment will bid up the wage rate. Since
all workers must be paid the same wage, the
marginal cost of an extra worker is not merely
the wage paid to that worker but the increase
in the wage bill for previously employed
workers. The monopsonist's marginal cost of
labour exceeds the wage rate and increases with
the level of employment. It is shown in Figure
11-3 as the MCL schedule.

Any firm will maximize profits when the
marginal revenue from an extra worker equals
its marginal cost. Otherwise, the firm has the
wrong employment level. Thus, a firm that is
a price-taker in both its output and input
markets will set W_0 equal to $MVPL$ to employ
L_1 workers in Figure 11-3. A firm that is a
price-taker in the labour market but not in the
output market will set $MRPL$ equal to W_0
and use L_3 workers. A firm that is a price-taker
in its output market but not in the labour
market will set $MVPL$ equal to MCL to employ
L_2 workers. And a firm that is both a
monopolist and a monopsonist will set MCL
equal to $MRPL$ to employ L_4 workers.

Thus the general principle is straightforward:
choose employment such that the marginal cost
of the last unit of labour equals the marginal
revenue earned from that last unit of labour.

Figure 11-3 MONOPOLY AND MONOPSONY POWER. As in Figure 11-2, a perfectly competitive firm sets *MVPL* equal to W_0 and employs L_1 workers. Facing a downward-sloping demand curve in its output market, the firm must recognize that its marginal revenue from extra output will be less than *MVPL*. It sets *MRPL* equal to W_0 and employs L_3 workers. A monopsonist recognizes that additional employment bids up wages for existing workers so that *MCL* depicts the marginal cost of an extra worker. Facing a given goods price, the monopsonist sets *MCL* equal to *MVPL* to employ L_2 workers, but facing a downward-sloping demand curve in the output market, the monopsonist would set *MCL* equal to *MRPL* to employ L_4 workers. Thus, monopoly and monopsony power tend to reduce the firm's demand for labour.

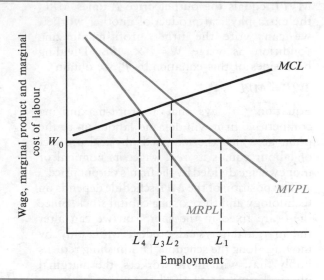

Formally, we can say the firm should set

$$\frac{\text{marginal cost}}{\text{of labour } MCL} = \frac{\text{marginal revenue}}{\text{product of labour } MRPL} \quad (2)$$

When the firm is a price-taker in the labour market, *MCL* is just the wage rate itself. When the firm is a price-taker in the output market, *MRPL* is simply the marginal value product of labour *MVPL*. For a perfectly competitive firm, equation (2) thus reduces to equation (1). For the rest of this chapter we assume that both output and labour markets are competitive. The analysis is easily amended when it is known that the firm has monopoly power in its output market or monopsony power in the labour market.

Changes in the Firm's Demand for Labour

Consider the effect of a rise in the wage W_0 faced by a competitive firm. Using Figure 11-2 or 11-3, we see that the firm will now employ fewer workers than before. The marginal cost of labour has risen, but diminishing labour productivity makes the *MVPL* schedule slope down. Hence it requires a reduction in employment to raise the marginal value product of labour in line with its higher marginal cost. The marginal revenue earned from the last workers in the original position no longer covers their marginal cost.

Next, suppose that the competitive firm faces a higher output price. Although the *MPL* remains unaltered in physical goods, this output brings in more money. The *MVPL* schedule shifts up at each level of employment. Hence in Figure 11-2 or 11-3 the horizontal line through the wage W_0 crosses the new *MVPL* schedule at a higher employment level. With the marginal cost of labour unaltered and the marginal revenue from labour increased, output and employment expand until diminishing marginal productivity drives *MVPL* back down to the wage W_0.

Finally, suppose the firm had begun with a higher capital stock. Each worker has more machinery with which to work and will be able to make more output. Although wages and prices remain unchanged, there is an increase in *MPL* in physical goods at each employment level. Hence the *MVPL* schedule shifts upwards, since *MVPL* equals *MPL* times output price. As in the case of an increase in output price, this upward shift in the *MVPL* schedule leads the firm to expand employment and output.[1]

For a competitive firm there is a neat way to combine our first two results. Noting that

---

[1] These three employment predictions carry over to firms with monopoly and monopsony power. An upward shift in the output demand curve or a larger capital stock will shift the *MRPL* curve upwards in Figure 11-3, increasing the labour demanded by a firm with monopoly power. An upward shift in the *MCL* schedule will reduce the labour demanded by a monopsonist.

$MVPL$ equals the output price P times MPL, the extra physical product of another worker, we can write the firm's profit-maximizing condition as wage $W = P \times MPL$. Dividing both sides of this equation by P, we obtain

$$W/P = MPL \qquad (3)$$

Equation (3) says that a profit-maximizing competitive firm will demand labour up to the point at which the marginal physical product of labour equals its *real* wage, its nominal or money wage divided by the firm's output price.

The position of the MPL schedule depends on technology and the existing capital stock. Since these are fixed in the short run we can alter the marginal physical product MPL only by moving along the schedule. Diminishing returns imply that, with more workers, the marginal physical product of the last worker is lower. From the particular level of the marginal physical product of labour we can deduce how many workers are being employed. Equation (3) tells us that if nominal wages and output prices both double, real wages and employment will both be unaffected. But changes in either the nominal wage or the output price, if not matched by a corresponding change in the other, will alter employment by affecting the real wage. Lower real wages lead the firm to move down its MPL schedule, taking on more workers until the marginal physical product of labour once again equals the real wage.

Having studied the firm's demand for labour in the short run, we now turn to the demand by the industry as a whole. Although each competitive firm regards itself as a price-taker in both its output and input markets, an expansion by the whole industry is likely to change output prices and wage rates. In moving from the firm's demand curve to the industry demand curve for labour, we need to take account of these effects.

11-3 The Industry Demand Curve for Labour

For a given price P_0 and wage W_0 each firm in a competitive industry chooses employment to equate the wage and the $MVPL$. In Figure 11-4 we horizontally add the marginal value product of labour curves for each firm to obtain the

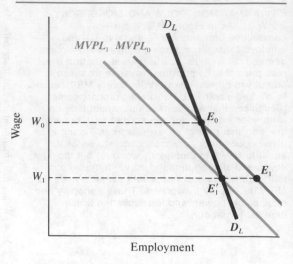

Figure 11-4 THE INDUSTRY DEMAND FOR LABOUR. $MVPL_0$ is the horizontal sum of each firm's $MVPL$ schedule at the price P_0. Each firm, and the industry as a whole sets $MVPL$ equal to W_0. Hence E_0 is a point on the industry demand curve for labour. A lower wage W_1 leads each firm and the industry as a whole to move down their $MVPL$ schedules to a point E_1. However, extra employment and output by the whole industry (a shift to the right in the industry supply curve of goods) leads to excess goods supply at the original price P_0. To clear the output market the price must fall, and this shifts to the left each firm's $MVPL$ schedule. The new industry schedule is $MVPL_1$ and the chosen point is E_1'. Joining all the points such as E_0 and E_1', we obtain the industry demand curve $D_L D_L$.

$MVPL_0$ schedule for the industry. At the wage W_0 and the price P_0, the industry will choose the point E_0. This must be a point on the industry demand curve for labour.

However, $MVPL_0$ is *not* the industry demand curve for labour. It is drawn for a particular output price, P_0. Suppose the wage is cut from W_0 to W_1. At the output price P_0 each firm will wish to move down its $MVPL$ schedule and the industry will wish to expand output and employ labour to the point E_1 in Figure 11-4. In terms of the supply and demand for output, the cut in wages has shifted the industry supply curve to the right.

At the price P_0 there will now be an excess supply of goods. The increase in supply must bid down the equilibrium price for the industry's product to some lower price P_1. The lower price shifts each firm's $MVPL$ schedule to the left. $MVPL_1$ is thus the new $MVPL$ schedule for the industry at the new price P_1. Hence the industry chooses the point E_1' at the new wage W_1.

By connecting points such as E_0 and E_1', we obtain the *industry demand for labour schedule* $D_L D_L$ in Figure 11-4. Although each firm constructs its *MVPL* schedule as if it were a price-taker, the industry demand curve has a steeper slope, since it takes account of the fact that a lower wage will shift the industry output supply curve to the right and reduce the equilibrium price.

Production technology determines how steep the *MVPL* schedules are. The faster the *MPL* diminishes as labour is increased, the steeper will be the *MVPL* schedule of the firm and of the industry. But the slope of the industry demand curve for labour depends on a second influence, the elasticity of the market demand curve for the industry's product. The more inelastic is market demand, the more a wage cut – through increasing the supply of output will reduce market price and shift *MVPL* schedules to the left when the industry supply curve for goods shifts to the right; and the steeper will be the industry demand curve $D_L D_L$ for labour.

This last observation takes us back to where we began the chapter. The demand for factors of production is a *derived* demand. Firms want factors only because they perceive a demand for their output that it is profitable to supply. It is unsurprising that the elasticity of demand for labour in a particular industry should reflect the elasticity of demand for the product the industry supplies.

11-4 The Supply of Labour

In this section we discuss the supply of labour, beginning with the decision of an individual and ending with the supply of labour to an industry and to the economy as a whole. It will then be possible to put together the labour demand curve and the labour supply curve to determine the equilibrium level of wages and employment.

The Individual's Labour Supply Decision: Hours of Work

The effective labour input to the production process is the number of workers multiplied by the number of hours they work. We approach the analysis of labour supply in two stages: how many hours people wish to work given that they are in the labour force, and whether or not people wish to be in the labour force at all.

The *labour force* is all individuals in work or seeking employment.

Suppose the individual is in the labour force. How many hours will that individual wish to work?

Note first that this will depend on the *real* wage, W/P, the nominal wage divided by the price of goods. If both W and P double, the individual will be able to buy exactly as many goods as before. It is the real wage that measures the amount of goods that can be bought with a pay packet, so it is the real wage that we should expect to influence labour supply decisions.

Figure 11-5 shows two possible labour supply curves relating hours of work supplied to the real wage. The labour supply curve SS_1 slopes upwards. Higher real wages make people want to work more. But the labour supply curve SS_2 is *backward bending*. At low real wages the supply curve slopes upwards, but beyond A, further real wage increases make people want to work fewer hours.

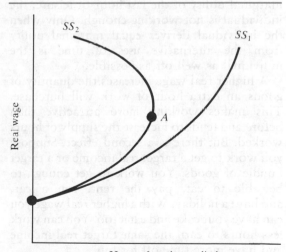

Figure 11-5 THE INDIVIDUAL'S SUPPLY OF LABOUR
The labour supply curve SS_1 slopes up and more hours of work are supplied as the real wage increases. But the labour supply curve might bend back. Along SS_2 higher real wages reduce labour supply once we reach the point A.

You may think it obvious that labour supply curves will usually correspond to SS_1, where higher real wages always increase hours of work supplied. The alternative to working another hour is staying at home and having fun. Each of us has only 24 hours a day and we have to decide how to divide these hours between work and leisure. More leisure is nice but by working longer we can get more real income with which to buy consumer goods. How should an individual trade off leisure against consumer goods in deciding how much to work?

This is a straightforward application of the model of consumer choice that we developed in Chapter 6. The choice is no longer between one good and another good, but between goods as a whole and leisure. An individual will want to work until the marginal utility derived from the goods an extra hour of work will provide is just equal to the marginal utility from the last hour of leisure. If the marginal utility of an extra hour of leisure exceeds the marginal utility of the goods financed by the last hour of work, the individual is working too much. Swapping an hour of work for an hour of leisure would make the individual better off. Conversely, if the marginal utility of the goods financed by an extra hour of work exceeds the marginal utility of the last hour of leisure, the individual is not working enough. Only when the individual derives equal marginal utility from the alternative uses of time is the individual as well off as possible.

A higher real wage increases the quantity of goods an extra hour of work will purchase. This makes working more attractive than before and tends to increase the supply of hours worked. But there is a second effect. Suppose you work to get a target real income or a target bundle of goods. You work to get enough to be able to eat, pay the rent, run a car, and have a holiday. With a higher real wage you can have your cake and eat it too. You can work less hours to earn the same target real income and have more time off for fun.

These two effects are precisely the *substitution and income effects* we introduced in the standard consumer choice model of Chapter 6. An increase in the real wage increases the relative return on working. It leads to a substitution effect or pure relative price effect that makes people want to work more. But a

higher real wage also tends to raise people's real income. This has a pure income effect. Since leisure is probably a luxury good, we expect the quantity of leisure demanded to increase sharply when real incomes increase. This income effect tends to make people work less. The overall effect of a real wage increase, and the shape of the supply curve for hours worked, thus depends on which of these effects is larger.[2]

To decide whether or not the substitution effect will dominate the income effect, we must look at actual data on what people do. Economists have tried three techniques in an attempt to discover how people actually behave. Interview studies simply ask people how they behave. Econometric studies of the kind discussed in Chapter 2 try to disentangle the separate effects from data on actual behaviour. And, especially in the USA, experiments have been conducted by giving different people different amounts of take-home pay and recording their behaviour.

The empirical evidence for the UK, the USA, and most other Western economies is as follows.[3] For adult men, the substitution effect and the income effect almost exactly cancel out. A change in the real wage has almost no effect on the quantity of hours supplied. The supply curve of hours worked is almost vertical. In terms of Figure 11-5, adult men are on the part of the supply curve to the point A where changes in the real wage have almost no effect on hours supplied.[4]

For women, the substitution effect seems to dominate the income effect. The supply curve

---

[2] You might like to try drawing a diagram with real income or goods purchased on one axis and leisure on the other axis. The maximum possible is 24 hours leisure. For each hour of leisure sacrificed you can work at the given real wage rate and earn income. Can you show the budget line on your diagram? Can you draw an indifference curve map and show which point the individual will choose? Can you represent a change in the real wage rate as a rotation of the budget line and hence illustrate the income and substitution effects? If you can, well done. If not, don't worry. It is quite tricky the first time you think about it. We will shortly use this approach to discuss the decision to be in the labour force. After that, you can come back and try this exercise again.

[3] See C. V. Brown, *Taxation and the Incentive to Work*, Oxford University Press, 1980, and 'Tax cuts, work incentives, and revenue', *Fiscal Studies*, 1988.

[4] This conclusion applies to relatively small changes in real wage rates. In most Western countries, the large rise in real wages over the last 100 years has been matched by *reductions* of ten hours or more in the working week.

for hours slopes upward, as in Figure 11-5. Higher real wages make women work longer hours.

Although at present the focus of our analysis is the labour market itself, we shall return to these issues in Chapter 16 when discussing the government and taxation. Workers care about take home pay after deductions of income tax. A reduction in income tax rates thus serves to raise after-tax real wages. For the moment we merely note that the empirical evidence on labour supply implies that lower income tax rates should not be expected to lead to a dramatic increase in the supply of hours worked. In fact, for adult men, changes in income tax rates should have almost no effect on hours of work supplied.

Individual Labour Supply: Participation Rates

If the effect of real wages on the supply of hours is smaller than is often supposed, the more important effect of real wages on labour supply may be the effect on the incentive to enter or participate in the labour force.

> The *participation rate* is the percentage of a given group of the population of working age who decide to enter the labour force.

Table 11-4 presents UK data on participation rates for different groups of the population of working age. Most men are in employment or are seeking employment. A smaller but still quite stable percentage of unmarried women are in the labour force. Table 11-4 shows that there has been a substantial increase in the number of married women in the labour force, a trend continuing steadily since 1951 when only 25 per cent of married women were in the UK labour force.[5] Similar patterns are observed

in other Western countries. Can we use our model of consumer choice to explain these trends?

We shall now develop a model of consumer choice with the following properties: individuals are more likely to participate in the labour force (a) the more they like the benefits of working (ability to buy goods or job status) relative to the benefits of leisure, (b) the lower their income from non-work sources, (c) the lower the fixed costs of working, and (d) the higher the real wage rate. To do so, we use the indifference curve-budget line techniques we employed in Chapter 6 when discussing consumer choice between alternative goods.

In Figure 11-6 we plot leisure on the horizontal axis. The maximum possible leisure per day is 24 hours. On the vertical axis we plot total real income from work and other sources. This shows the ability to buy consumer goods and services. We begin by developing the budget constraint. Suppose the individual has a non-labour income represented by the vertical distance BC. This may be income earned by a spouse, income from rent or dividends, or welfare payments received from the government.

Thus an individual who is not working at all can have 24 hours of leisure a day plus a daily income BC. The individual can consume at the point C. Now suppose the individual works. There may be fixed costs in working. Unemployment benefit from the government may be lost immediately, the right clothes or uniform must be purchased, and travel expenses must be incurred to get to the place of work. These costs are independent of the number of hours worked provided any work is done. They are a fixed cost of working.

In Figure 11-6 we show these costs as the vertical distance AC. Instead of being able to consume at C, the net non-labour income BC is reduced to BA after these fixed costs of working have been incurred. Having taken the decision to work, the individual can then move along the budget line AD sacrificing hours of leisure to gain wage income. The higher the real wage the steeper will be the budget line AD. Giving up a given number of leisure hours earns a higher real income when the real wage is higher.

Because of the fixed costs of working, the individual faces the kinked budget line CAD. Thus working a small number of hours can

---

Table 11-4 UK participation rates (%)

	1971	1975	1985
Men	92	93	89
Unmarried women	72	72	74
Married women	50	59	62

Source: General Household Survey.

---

[5] See Richard Layard *et al.*, 'Married Women's Participation and Hours', *Economica*, 1980.

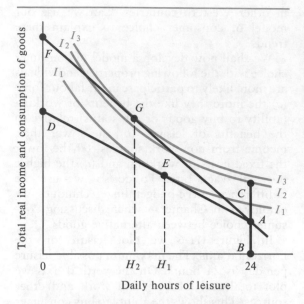

Figure 11-6 LABOUR FORCE PARTICIPATION.
With a non-labour income BC the individual can do
no work and consume at C on the indifference curve
I_2I_2. Any work incurs the fixed cost AC. At a low
hourly wage rate the total budget line is CAD and
the best point attainable by working is E. But this
lies on the indifference curve I_1I_1 and the individual
is better off at C where no work is done. At a higher
hourly wage rate the new budget line is CAF. By
working $(24 - H_2)$ hours the individual can reach G on
the indifference curve I_3I_3 which is better than being
at C. The higher the real hourly wage rate the more
likely is the individual to participate in the labour force.

actually reduce total real income. The small
wage income is insufficient to cover the fixed
costs of working. The lower the real wage rate,
the flatter will be the line AD, and the more
hours an individual will have to work merely
to recoup the fixed costs. This phenomenon is
sometimes called the *poverty trap*. Unskilled
workers may be offered such a low wage
rate that they actually lose out by working.

To complete the model of consumer choice
we must superimpose an indifference map on
the kinked budget line CAD. Individuals like
both leisure and the goods that real income can
buy. Each indifference curve has the usual slope
and curvature discussed in Chapter 6, and a
higher indifference curve means that the
individual is better off. We can now give a
general analysis of the participation decision
and establish the four effects we cited above.

The indifference curve I_2I_2 shows how well
off the individual will be by refusing to

participate and consuming at the point C. Given
the budget line CAD, the best the individual
can do by working is to work $(24 - H_1)$ hours,
consume H_1 hours of leisure, and choose the
point E to reach the highest possible indifference
curve I_1I_1 given that some work is done.
But the individual can reach a higher indifference
curve I_2I_2 by refusing to participate. This
individual will choose not to work.

Now suppose the real wage rate rises. Each
hour of leisure now earns a higher real wage
income. The budget line AD rotates to AF and
the complete budget line is now CAF. Figure
11-6 shows that by choosing the point G the
individual can now reach the indifference curve
I_3I_3 and be better off than at C. Hence higher
real wages tend to increase the number of
people wishing to participate in the labour
force. As the real hourly wage becomes
higher, the fixed costs of working become less
and less important.

A reduction in AC, the fixed cost of working,
will also tend to increase labour force participation.
The point C remains fixed but the point
A shifts up. Hence there is a parallel upward
shift in the sloping part of the budget line such
as AD or AF. This makes it more likely that
the highest indifference curve attainable by
working will lie above the indifference curve
I_2I_2 through the point C at which no work is
done.

Although we do not show it in Figure 11-6, a
decrease in non-labour income BC will also lead
to an increase in labour force participation.
Changes in non-labour income have no effect
on the relative return of an hour's work and
an hour's leisure. There is no substitution effect,
but there is an income effect. Higher non-labour
income tends to increase the quantity demanded
of all normal goods including leisure. Conversely,
a lower non-labour income tends to
make people want less leisure. They are
more likely to work.

Finally, consider the effect of a change in
tastes. Suppose people decide they think leisure
is less important and work more important.
Each indifference curve in Figure 11-6 will
become flatter. To preserve a given level of
utility along an indifference curve, people will
now be prepared to sacrifice more leisure in
exchange for the direct and indirect benefits of
extra work. Consider again the budget line
CAD. The flatter are all indifference curves the

more likely is it that the indifference curve through the point C will cross the portion of the budget line AD on which work is done. But if it crosses AD there must be another point on AD yielding even higher utility. You can check this either by drawing a diagram for yourself or by using Figure 11-6 directly. Figure 11-6 shows the indifference curve I_2I_2 crossing the budget line AF and shows that it is possible to attain a higher indifference curve by choosing the point G on AF. Exactly the same argument applies if the flatter indifference curve through C crosses the line AD.

We have thus confirmed our initial assertions. Labour force participation will be increased by (a) an increase in the real hourly wage rate, (b) a reduction in the fixed costs of working, (c) lower income from non-labour sources, and (d) changes in tastes in favour of more work and less leisure. Can we use these general propositions to explain the steady increase of participation by married women?

Three of these forces seem especially important. First, there has been an important change in social attitudes to work, especially to work by married women. Their indifference curves have become flatter. Second, the pressure for equal opportunities for women has tended to increase women's real wages toward the higher levels earned by men. It is as if the budget line for women working has rotated from AD to AF in Figure 11-6. Finally, the fixed costs of working may have been reduced for married women. Automatic ovens, labour-saving devices for housework, a second family car, and many other changes, not least in the attitude of husbands, may have made it possible for married women to contemplate working. It is as if the fixed cost of working had been substantially reduced.

Hence the data of Table 11-4 suggest that we are thinking about labour supply in the right way. For the remainder of the chapter the most important conclusion of our analysis of labour supply is that an increase in the real wage rate will increase total labour supply. And the most important effect of higher real wages on the total supply of people times hours may be the participation effect on the supply of people rather than the effect on the supply of hours by those already in the labour force.

One final point. It is best to think of this analysis of labour supply as relating to the supply of unskilled workers. Acquiring skills takes time. We shall examine the decisions about whether or not to acquire training and skills in the next chapter.

The Supply of Labour to an Industry

So far we have discussed the supply of labour to the economy as a whole. Now we discuss the supply of labour to an individual industry. Suppose that the industry is very small relative to the economy as a whole and that it wishes to employ workers with very common skills.

Essentially there are economy-wide markets for welders, drivers, and other types of worker. The small individual industry will simply have to pay the going rate. The going rate may not be the monetary wage paid elsewhere. Jobs in different industries have different non-monetary characteristics, such as risk, comfort, or anti-social hours like night shifts. The idea of the going wage rate must be adjusted industry by industry to allow for the *equilibrium wage differential* which offsets these non-monetary characteristics and makes workers indifferent about the industry in which they work.

Given this adjustment, any particular small industry will be able to hire as many workers as it wants from the economy-wide labour pool. At this wage rate the industry faces a horizontal labour supply curve.

In practice, few industries are this small relative to all the skills they wish to employ. The steel industry is a significant user of welders and the freight industry a significant user of lorry drivers. When an industry is a significant user of a particular skill, an expansion of employment in the industry will tend to bid up the wages of that particular skill whose short-run supply is relatively fixed to the economy as a whole. In the short run it will generally be correct to assume that expansion of the industry will bid up the wages of at least some of the workers it employs. The industry's labour supply curve slopes upwards.

In the long run the industry's labour supply curve may be a little flatter. When short-run expansion bids up the wages of computer programmers, more school-leavers will start to train in this skill. In the long run the economy-wide supply will increase and the wages that these workers can earn will fall back again. The individual industry will not have to offer such a high wage in the long run to increase the supply of that type of labour to the industry.

To sum up, real wages determine total labour supply to the economy. In the short run the supply of a given skill may be relatively fixed. To obtain a larger share of the total pool an individual industry will typically have to offer higher relative wages than other industries to bid workers into that industry. In depleting the labour pool available for other industries, expansion by one industry also bids up the wages that other industries will have to pay for workers who have become more scarce in the whole economy. To the extent that the supply of scarce skills is augmented in the long run, each industry may face a flatter long-run labour supply curve than in the short run.

11-5 Industry Labour Market Equilibrium

Figure 11--7 shows equilibrium in the labour market for a particular industry. Its labour demand curve $D_L D_L$ slopes down and crosses the upward-sloping labour supply curve $S_L S_L$ at the equilibrium point E where employment is L_0 and the wage rate is W_0. We do not bother to distinguish long-run and short-run supply curves though this is easily done.

Suppose wages and prices are fixed in all other industries. We can think of W as the nominal wage the industry must pay to attract workers away from other industries. Since other wages and prices are fixed, a higher nominal wages W also implies a higher real wage. We now use this model of industry equilibrium in the labour market to investigate demand and supply shocks to the industry.

We draw the industry labour demand curve $D_L D_L$ for a given output demand curve. Suppose there is a recession in the building industry which shifts the demand curve for cement to the left. The equilibrium price of cement falls. This shifts to the left the marginal value product of labour curve $MVPL$ for each cement manufacturer. Hence $D_L D_L$ shifts to $D'_L D'_L$ for the cement industry. At the new equilibrium E_1 in the labour market for the cement industry, wages and employment are reduced in the industry.

Conversely, suppose there is a spurt of

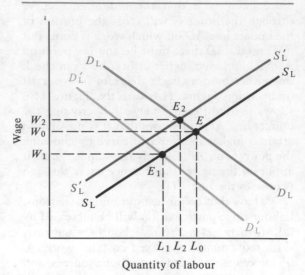

Figure 11-7 EQUILIBRIUM IN AN INDUSTRY LABOUR MARKET. The industry labour supply curve $S_L S_L$ slopes up. Higher wages are needed to attract workers into the industry. For a given output demand curve, the industry's labour demand curve $D_L D_L$ slopes down because of diminishing marginal labour productivity and because higher industry output bids down its output price. A leftward shift in the output demand curve thus shifts the derived demand for labour from $D_L D_L$ to $D'_L D'_L$ and moves labour market equilibrium from E to E_1. An increase in wages elsewhere in the economy shifts the industry's labour supply curve from $S_L S_L$ to $S'_L S'_L$ and shifts equilibrium from E to E_2.

investment in new machinery in every industry except cement. With more capital to work with, labour becomes more productive in all other industries. Setting wages equal to the $MVPL$, these industries now pay a higher wage rate. This shifts the supply curve of labour to the cement industry to the left to $S'_L S'_L$. For each wage rate in the cement industry, the industry now attracts fewer workers from the general pool than before.

The new equilibrium for cement workers occurs at E_2. Employment has contracted from L_0 to L_2. Since the remaining workers have more capital to work with they have a higher marginal product. In addition, the contraction in cement output shifts the output supply curve to the left and bids up the cement price. Together these effects move the industry up its demand curve $D_L D_L$ and allow it to pay a higher wage rate to its remaining workers.

Thus wage increases in one industry spill

over into other industries. The crucial link between industries is the assumption of *labour mobility*. It is because cement workers are lured away from the industry by wage rises elsewhere that the cement industry's labour supply curve shifts to the left in Figure 11-7. The degree of labour mobility between industries affects not only how much an industry's labour supply curve will shift when conditions change elsewhere, it also affects the slope of the industry's labour supply curve. This can be understood most easily by considering the two extreme cases.

Suppose first that workers can move effortlessly between similar jobs in different industries. If each industry is small relative to the economy, it will face a completely elastic (horizontal) labour supply curve at the going wage rate (adjusted for non-monetary advantages). When all other industries pay higher wages, the horizontal supply curve of labour to the cement industry will shift up by the full amount of the wage increase elsewhere. Unless the cement industry continues to match the going rate, it will lose all its workers.

At the opposite extreme, consider the market for concert pianists. Suppose there is no other job they are capable of doing. They have to work in the music industry. The industry faces a vertical supply curve of concert pianists at the given number of pianists currently in existence. Even if all other industries pay higher wages this will have no effect on the equilibrium in the market for concert pianists.[6] In the short run there is no question of anyone entering or leaving the occupation of concert pianists.

The general case depicted in Figure 11-7 lies between these extremes. With limited mobility between industries, the cement industry can attract more workers if it offers higher wages. But, because it is not insulated from other industries, its labour supply curve will shift to the left when wages rise in other industries.

11-6 Transfer Earnings and Economic Rents

Top pianists and top footballers are doubtless

delighted with the high salaries they can earn, but they would almost certainly choose the same career even if the pay was less good. Why then do they get paid so much? To answer this question we need to distinguish between transfer earnings and economic rent.

The *transfer earnings* of a factor of production in a particular use are the minimum payments required to induce that factor to work in that job. *Economic rent* (not to be confused with income from renting out property) is the extra payment a factor receives over and above the transfer earnings required to induce the factor to supply its services in that use.

Figure 11-8 helps make sense of these concepts. *DD* is the labour demand curve for concert pianists and *SS* the supply of pianists to the music industry. Even at a zero wage some dedicated musicians would be concert pianists.

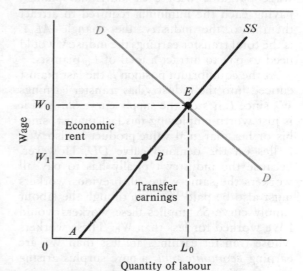

Figure 11-8 **TRANSFER EARNINGS AND ECONOMIC RENT.** *DD* is the industry demand curve for labour. A quantity *A* of labour would work in the industry even at a zero wage. Thereafter, higher wages are required to attract additional workers to the industry. *SS* is the industry labour supply curve. If each worker were paid only the transfer earnings required to attract them to the industry (to keep them on their supply curve), the industry need only pay AEL_0 in wages. If all workers must be paid the highest wage rate necessary to attract the last worker to the industry, equilibrium at *E* implies workers as a whole derive economic rent $OAEW_0$. For workers who would work in the industry for a zero wage rate, W_0 is economic rent, a pure bonus.

---

[6] Of course, if people spend their higher wages on going to more concerts there will be a small increase in the demand for concerts and the derived demand curve for concert pianists will shift up a little. If so, concert pianists will get a higher wage after all, even though their supply curve is unaltered.

Higher wages attract into the industry concert pianists who could have done other things. The supply curve slopes upwards.

Because all workers must be paid the same wage rate, equilibrium occurs at E where the wage is W_0 and the number of pianists is L_0. In the market for concert pianists or footballers W_0 may be a very large wage. Each firm in the music industry is happy to pay W_0 because their workers are very talented. They have a high marginal product. In the output market (concerts) firms can earn a large revenue. The derived demand curve DD for concert pianists is very high.

The supply curve SS shows the transfer earnings that the industry may pay to attract pianists into the industry. The first A pianists would work for nothing. A wage W_1 would be required to expand the supply of pianists to B and W_0 must be paid to increase supply to L_0. If the industry as a whole could make separate wage bargains with each individual pianist, paying each the minimum required to attract them into the industry, the triangle AL_0E is the total transfer earnings the industry would need to pay to attract a total of L_0 pianists.

At the equilibrium position E the last pianist enticed into the industry has transfer earnings W_0 since E lies on the supply curve SS. And it is just worth employing this last pianist, since his or her marginal value product is also W_0. E lies on the demand curve DD. However, because the industry typically has to pay all workers the same wage, all previous workers must also be paid W_0 even though the labour supply curve SS implies these workers would have worked for less than W_0. These workers whose transfer earnings are less than W_0 are earning *economic rent*, a pure surplus arising because W_0 is needed to attract the last pianist. Rent reflects differences in pianists' *supply* decisions not their *productivity* as musicians.

Thus in Figure 11-8 the industry as a whole makes total wage payments equal to the rectangle OW_0EL_0. It pays L_0 workers W_0 each. But these payments can be divided into the total transfer earnings AL_0E and the economic rent $OAEW_0$.

Economic rent arises whenever the supply curve of a factor is not horizontal. Try drawing a horizontal supply curve SS in Figure 11-8. No worker earns more than the going rate required to keep pianists in the industry. All earnings are transfer earnings. When the factor supply curve to the industry slopes up, any further expansion of supply can be achieved only by higher payments to entice additional factor supply into the industry. This is a pure bonus or economic rent for those who were already happily working in the industry.

Notice the distinction between the firm and the industry. Economic rent is an unnecessary payment as far as the industry is concerned. By colluding to wage-discriminate, paying each worker his or her transfer earnings alone, the industry could retain all its workers without paying them economic rent. But the entire wage W_0 is a transfer earning as far as a single competitive firm is concerned. If the firm does not match the going rate for the industry its workers will go to another firm who will employ them, since their marginal value product covers the wage at the equilibrium position E.

In the UK football industry[7] and the US baseball industry, it is currently being asserted that high player salaries are bankrupting the industry. What light does our analysis shed on this issue? First, wages are high because the derived demand is high – crowds at the ground and television rights make it profitable to supply this output – and because the supply of talented players is scarce. The supply curve of good players is steep: even by offering very high wages the industry cannot increase the number of good players by much. Thus there is no simple link between high salaries and the ruin of the game. If supplying the output were not profitable, the derived demand for players would be lower and their wages would be correspondingly reduced.

Our analysis also suggests that clubs may collude to pay equally skilled players different wages, thereby reducing the economic rent that the industry as a whole must pay the players. By paying each player his transfer earnings, the industry could reduce its wage bill from OW_0EL_0 to AEL_0 in Figure 11-8.

11-7 Do Labour Markets Clear?

Thus far we have assumed that wage flexibility

---

[7] Football clubs pay transfer fees to another club from whom they wish to take over a player. This idea of transfer fees between clubs should not be confused with the economist's concept of transfer earnings of players, the amount necessary to keep them in the industry.

ensures that labour markets for each industry and for the economy as a whole are in equilibrium. Each market clears at the equilibrium wage and employment level that equates supply and demand. In Part 4 we shall see that many questions in macroeconomics turn on whether or not it is correct to assume that wage flexibility is sufficient to maintain labour markets close to their equilibrium positions. We now examine some of the arguments that have been put forward to explain why it may not be possible to take labour market equilibrium for granted.

Minimum Wage Agreements

In some countries such as the United States there is a law specifying a national minimum wage. Particular UK industries used to be the subject of minimum wages through industry wage councils, though these were dismantled in the mid-1980s.

Figure 11-9 shows the demand curve $D_L D_L$ and the supply curve $S_L S_L$ for a particular labour skill in a particular industry. Free market equilibrium is at E. For skilled workers the

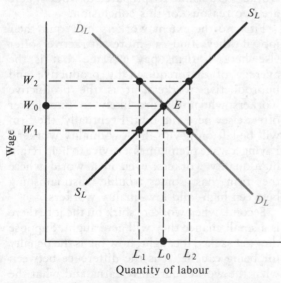

Figure 11-9 A MINIMUM WAGE. Free market equilibrium occurs at the wage W_0 and a quantity of employment L_0. A minimum wage W_1 below W_0 is irrelevant. However, a minimum wage W_2 above W_0 will restrict the actual quantity of employment to L_1, leaving a quantity $L_2 - L_1$ of workers involuntarily unemployed. They would like to work at this wage rate but cannot find jobs.

equilibrium wage W_0 is likely to exceed a minimum wage agreement at the level W_1 so the agreement is irrelevant. At W_1 there would be excess labour demand $L_2 - L_1$, which would bid wages back to their equilibrium level W_0. Putting the argument differently, at the minimum wage W_1 the labour supply L_1 would have a marginal value product equal to W_2, the height of the industry labour demand curve at L_1. Firms have an incentive to pay higher wages to attract additional workers until the differential between the wage and the $MVPL$ is eroded.

For low-skill labour the situation may be very different. Assume that the minimum wage W_2 exceeds the free market equilibrium wage W_0. At W_2 there is an excess labour supply $L_2 - L_1$. Since firms cannot be forced to employ workers they do not want, employment will be L_1 and the quantity of workers $L_2 - L_1$ will be involuntarily unemployed.

> Workers are *involuntarily unemployed* if they are prepared to work at the going wage rate but cannot find jobs.

Thus, for low-skill occupations a minimum wage in excess of the free market equilibrium wage will raise the wage for those lucky enough to find jobs but will reduce the total amount of employment relative to the free market equilibrium level of employment. Minimum wage agreements may explain involuntary unemployment among low-skilled workers.

Trade Unions

A strong trade union may act in a similar way. Figure 11-9 implies that, if unions in an industry are successful in forcing employers to pay a wage W_2 which is higher than the wage W_0 that would have prevailed under free competition, the consequence will be a lower level of employment in the industry. By forcing the wage up from W_0 to W_2, the union must accept a loss of employment from L_0 to L_1. How unions trade off higher wages for lower employment is a question we consider in the next chapter. However, the consequence of such behaviour is already clear. If the union chooses a wage W_2, the resulting unemployment is collectively voluntary for the union – it chose this action – but may be involuntary for some of the unlucky union members who lose their jobs. To say more, we need to develop models of how decisions are made within unions.

Scale Economies

Professor Martin Weitzman[8] has suggested that involuntary unemployment may arise from the interaction of scale economies and imperfect competition, which we discussed in Chapter 10. We saw how these would create entry barriers and prevent new firms from joining an industry. Weitzman argues that these entry barriers prevent the unemployed from starting new firms even if these unemployed workers were prepared to work for a wage below that earned by workers in existing firms.

Insider–Outsider Distinctions

Whereas the previous explanation emphasizes entry barriers in the formation of new firms, the insider–outsider theories emphasize barriers to entering employment in existing firms. The insiders already have a job with a firm and the outsiders are the unemployed. Entry barriers may take several forms: the cost of the firm of advertising for workers, interviewing them, and evaluating what sort of job they should be offered; costs of training new workers in activities specific to the firm; and the time taken to build up teamwork and for new employees to master their new jobs. In the terminology of Chapter 10, these may be all innocent entry barriers.

But existing workers (insiders) may also succeed in erecting strategic barriers to entry by outsiders, even without the presence of formal trade unions at plant level. For example, they may threaten various forms of industrial disruption if too many outsiders are admitted too quickly, and in many circumstances they would find it easy to obtain mass insider support for such threats if there were any proposal to admit outsiders at a *lower* wage than that currently being paid to insiders.

When such entry barriers confront outsiders, the insiders will be able to raise their own wage above that for which outsiders would be prepared to work *without* inducing a spate of hiring of outsiders. The outsiders might like to work at the wage currently enjoyed by insiders, but outsiders do not find it attractive to work for the very much lower wage that would be necessary to induce firms to hire them when the economic cost of these various entry barriers is large. Just as in the discussion of new entry by firms in Chapter 10, the market power of the incumbents or insiders will depend on the size of the entry barriers.

Efficiency Wage Explanations

Thus far, we have assumed that information is trivially easy (i.e., cheap) to come by. In the real world, employers face two kinds of problem: they find it hard to tell whether an applicant for a job will be a productive or unproductive worker (a matter of innate ability); and they find it hard to monitor whether workers are trying or shirking even once they are employed.[9]

Given the costs of evaluating or screening new workers, and the subsequent costs of monitoring their performance on the job, what is the best policy for a firm? The efficiency wage theory argues that it will be profitable for firms to respond by paying existing workers a wage which on average exceeds the wage for which workers as a whole are prepared to work. There are two reasons for this conclusion.

First, to the extent workers may quit their job if they find a more attractive offer elsewhere, if firms pay a wage that is the average of that required by productive and unproductive workers, it is the productive workers who are more likely to find better offers elsewhere and quit. Eventually, the firm will be left only with the low-quality workers. Paying a wage premium is a device to help retain high-quality workers, even in a world where the firm has some trouble distinguishing between high- and low-quality workers.

Second, when workers shirk on the job. there is a small chance they will get caught. Suppose they get sacked if caught: how big is the penalty for being caught? It is the difference between what the worker currently earns and what the worker will get in unemployment benefit or in some subsequent job. The higher the wage paid

---

[8] See Martin Weitzman, 'Increasing Returns and the Foundations of Unemployment Theory', *Economic Journal*, 1982.

[9] Technically, economists refer to these problems as adverse selection and moral hazard. We discuss them in detail in Chapter 14 when we turn to the interesting issues that arise in the economics of information.

by the existing employer, the larger the penalty of being caught shirking. Hence the efficiency wage theory concludes that, to increase the penalty and reduce the incentive to shirk, firms will pay existing workers a higher wage than on average would be necessary to get them to supply their labour. Again, the implication is that some workers may be involuntarily unemployed, in the sense that they might be happy to work for wages at or below those paid to existing workers, but have little practical chance of actually securing a job at such wages.[10]

Minimum wage agreements, trade union power, scale economies, insider–outsider distinctions, and efficiency wages are all possible explanations for insufficient wage flexibility in the short run to maintain the labour market in continuous equilibrium. Whether the labour market is always in equilibrium, and the length of time for which any disequilibrium might persist, are questions to which we return repeatedly in Part 4. In this section we have briefly examined some of the arguments that have been advanced to suggest that labour market equilibrium is not inevitable in the short run.

11-8 Wages and Employment in the UK

We began the chapter by looking at real earnings in public utilities and textiles. We end the chapter by re-examining earnings in selected industries. It allows us to draw together some of the themes of the chapter.

Table 11-5 shows changes in real earnings and employment share for three selected industries.[11] Throughout the economy, real earnings rose 46 per cent between 1977 and 1988. Technical advances, better machinery, and an improvement in workforce skills and practices tended to increase labour's marginal value product and shift the derived demand curve for labour to the

Table 11-5 UK real earnings and employment, 1977–88

INDUSTRY	% change in	
	REAL EARNINGS	INDUSTRY EMPLOYMENT
All industries	+46	−5
Public utilities	+60	−12
Textiles	+35	−39
Financial services	+81	+102

Source: Department of Employment, *Gazette.*

right. But this process was very different in different industries.

Facing severe international competition, especially from the Far East, the textile industry's output demand curve shifted to the left. This tended to shift its derived demand curve for labour to the left and reduce the equilibrium real wage in the textile industry relative to the economy as a whole. Textile wages rose much less fast than wages elsewhere. In consequence, the supply of workers to the textile industry fell and textile employment became a smaller fraction of employment in the whole economy.

In Chapter 9 we saw that the OPEC oil price shocks increased the demand for substitute fuels such as gas, coal, and electricity. With their demand curve shifting outward, these industries' derived demand curves for labour also shifted out. In the UK, the gas, electricity, and water industries were able to pay increases in real earnings well in excess of the national average. Yet employment in the public utilities fell little more than the national average. This suggests that their labour supply curve is very steep. Since these industries have strong trade unions, it is possible that the unions were able to restrict labour entry to these industries to make the labour supply curve very steep. Given a steep supply schedule, an outward shift in labour demand leads to large wage rises but little change in employment. We study the role of trade unions in more detail in the next chapter.

Financial services (such as banking and insurance) boomed during the 1980s. The demand for these products increased sharply as the industry was deregulated and as it took advantage of its stronger position in world markets. The large increases in both employment and real earnings per person suggest

---

[10] For an excellent review of these competing explanations of involuntary unemployment, see A. Lindbeck and D. Snower, 'Explanations of Unemployment', *Oxford Review of Economic Policy*, 1985.

[11] The earnings data refer to all employees and do not quite correspond to the earnings data in Table 11-1 that refers only to male employees, but the pattern of changes is very much the same.

that the supply curve of labour to this industry is less steep than in public utilities. One reason is that financial services employ an above-average percentage of women, whose labour force participation increased in the 1980s.

Summary

1   In the long run, the firm chooses the technique of production to minimize the cost of producing a particular output. From the total cost curve showing the cheapest way to produce each output level the firm then calculates long-run marginal cost and equates this to marginal revenue to determine the profit-maximizing output. An increase in the relative price of one factor of production will tend to reduce the intensity with which that factor is used. Thus a rise in the wage rate relative to the rental cost of capital will tend to lead firms to choose more capital-intensive techniques in the long run. The capital–labour ratio will rise.

2   In the long run, a rise in the price of labour (capital) will have both a substitution effect and an output effect. The substitution effect reduces the quantity of labour (capital) demanded as the capital–labour ratio rises (falls) at each output. But total costs and marginal costs of output increase. The more elastic is the firm's demand curve and marginal revenue curve, the more this upward shift in the marginal cost curve will reduce output, and this will tend to reduce the demand for both factors. For an increase in the own price of a factor the substitution and output effects work in the same direction to reduce the quantity of that factor demanded in the long run.

3   In the short run, the firm has fixed factors and probably has a fixed production technique. The firm can vary short-run output by varying its variable input, labour. But labour is subject to diminishing returns when other factors are fixed. The marginal physical product of labour falls as more labour is employed.

4   The statement that a profit-maximizing firm produces output up to the point at which marginal output cost equals marginal output revenue is identical to the statement that the firm hires labour up to the point where the marginal cost of labour equals its marginal revenue product. One implies the other. If the firm is a price-taker in its output market, the marginal revenue product of labour is its marginal value product, the output price times its marginal physical product. If the firm is a price-taker in the labour market, the marginal cost of labour is the wage rate. A perfectly competitive firm equates the real wage to the marginal physical product of labour.

5   Thus the downward-sloping marginal physical product of labour schedule is the short-run demand curve for labour (in terms of the real wage) for a competitive firm. Equivalently, the marginal value product of labour schedule is the demand curve in terms of the nominal wage. The *MVPL* schedule for a firm shifts up if the output price increases, the capital stock increases, or if technical progress makes labour more productive.

6   The industry's labour demand curve is not merely the horizontal sum of firms' *MVPL* curves. Higher industry output in response to a wage reduction will also reduce the output price in equilibrium. The industry labour demand curve is steeper (less elastic) than that of each firm and is more inelastic the more inelastic is the demand curve for the industry's output.

7   Thus labour demand curves are derived demands. A shift in the output demand curve for the industry will shift the derived factor demand curve in the same direction.

8   For an individual already in the labour force, an increase in the hourly real wage has a substitution effect tending to increase the supply of hours worked, but an income effect tending to reduce the supply of hours worked. For men, the two effects cancel out almost exactly in practice, but the empirical evidence suggests that the substitution effect dominates for women. Thus women have a rising supply curve for hours but the supply curve for men is almost vertical.

9   Individuals with non-labour income may prefer not to work. In theory, four factors increase the participation rate in the labour force: higher real wage rates, lower fixed costs of working, lower non-labour income, and changes in tastes in favour of working rather than staying at home. These forces help explain the steady trend for increasing labour force

participation by married women over the last few decades.

10   For a particular industry the supply curve of labour depends on the wage paid relative to wages in other industries using similar skills. Equilibrium wage differentials are the monetary compensation for differences in non-monetary characteristics of jobs in different industries undertaken by workers with the same skill. Taking monetary and non-monetary considerations together, there is then no incentive to move between industries.

11   When the labour supply curve to an industry is less than perfectly elastic, the industry must pay higher wages to expand employment. For the marginal worker, the wage is a pure transfer earning required to induce that worker into the industry. For workers prepared to work in the industry at a lower wage, there is an element of economic rent. Economic rent is the difference between income received and transfer earnings for that individual. Economic rent is highest when the supply curve is steep and when the derived demand curve for labour is high. Economic rent explains the extremely high salaries in sports, entertainment, and related industries.

12   In free market equilibrium, some workers will choose not to work at the equilibrium wage rate. They are voluntarily unemployed. Involuntary unemployment is the difference between desired supply and desired demand at a disequilibrium wage rate. Workers would like to work but cannot find a job.

13   There is considerable disagreement about how quickly labour markets can get back to equilibrium if they are initially thrown out of equilibrium. Possible causes of involuntary unemployment are minimum wage agreements, trade unions, scale economies, insider–outsider distinctions, and efficiency wages.

Key Terms

Derived demand
Equalizing wage differentials
Factor intensity
Substitution and output effects
Marginal value product of labour
Marginal revenue product of labour
Marginal cost of labour

Labour force
Real wage
Participation rate
Mobility of labour
Minimum wage
Involuntary unemployment
Transfer earnings
Economic rent
Insiders and outsiders
Efficiency wages

Problems

1   In what sense is it true that a firm's decision on how much output to produce is the same thing as its decision on how much labour to demand?

2   (a) Suppose in Table 11-2 that there is a third way of making 100 snarks per week. The third technique uses 4 units of capital and 5 units of labour. Would this technique ever be used? Explain. (b) Suppose that there is another technique using 1 unit of capital and 8 units of labour. Are there any levels of the wage rate at which this technique would be used assuming that the rental rate for capital stays at £320 per week?

3   (a) Explain why the marginal product of labour eventually declines. (b) Show in a diagram the effect of an increase in the firm's capital stock on its demand curve for labour.

4   Over the last 100 years the real wage has risen but the length of the working week has fallen. (a) Explain this result using income and substitution effects. (b) Explain how an increase in the real wage could cause everyone in employment to work fewer hours but still increase the total amount of work done in the economy.

5   Why should the labour supply curve to an industry slope upwards even if the aggregate labour supply to the economy is fixed?

6   A film producer says that the industry is doomed because film stars are paid an outrageous amount of money. Evaluate the argument being sure to use the concept of economic rent.

7   Answer the questions with which we began the chapter: (a) Why can a top golfer earn more in a weekend than a university professor earns in a year? (b) Why can students studying economics expect to earn more than equally smart students studying philosophy?

8   Common Fallacies Show why the following statements are incorrect: (a) There is no economic reason why a sketch that took Picasso one minute

to draw should fetch a price of £100 000. (*b*) A national minimum wage would provide the unskilled with a reasonable living standard without undermining their employment prospects. (*c*) Unemployment can result only from greedy and unrealistic wage claims by workers.

Appendix: Isoquants and the Choice of Production Technique

In the text we used Table 11-2 to describe how a firm chooses the production technique. We now show that this problem of producer choice can be examined using techniques similar to the indifference curve–budget line approach we used to study consumer choice in Chapter 6.

Figure 11-A1 plots input quantities of capital K and labour L. Points A, B, C, and D show the *minimum* input quantities required to produce 1 unit of output using each of four different techniques of production. Technique A is, of course, the most labour-intensive technique, requiring L_A units of labour and K_A units of capital to produce 1 unit of output. Technique D is the most capital intensive. Connecting points A, B, C, and D yields a schedule called an *isoquant* ('iso' meaning 'the same' and 'quant' meaning 'quantity').

> An isoquant shows the different minimum combinations of inputs to produce a given level of output. Different points on an isoquant reflect different production techniques for making the same output level.

Although Figure 11-A1 shows only four production techniques we can imagine that there are many more available techniques. Figure 11-A2 shows smooth isoquants. Isoquant *I* corresponds to a particular output level. Each point on isoquant *I* corresponds to a different production technique, ranging from the very capital intensive to the very labour intensive. The higher isoquant *I'* shows the different input combinations needed to produce a higher output level. Higher isoquants reflect higher output levels since more inputs are required. Each isoquant shows different input combinations to produce a given output level.

The successive isoquants constitute an isoquant map. Three properties of isoquants are important. First, they cannot cross. Each isoquant refers to a different output level. Second, each isoquant slopes down. Go back

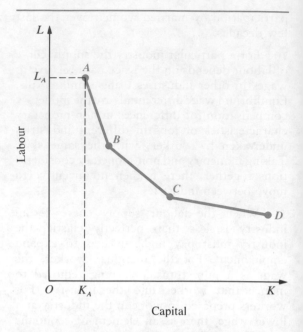

Figure 11-A1   AN ISOQUANT.   Points *A*, *B*, *C*, and *D* show different input combinations required to produce 1 unit of output. By connecting them we obtain an isoquant that shows the different input combinations which can produce a particular level of output.

to Figure 11-A1 which shows different ways to produce 1 output unit. Suppose there is a technique that uses as much labour as technique A but uses *more* capital. Such a technique would lie horizontally to the right of point A. *Nobody* would ever choose this technique. It produces the same output as A but uses more inputs. The only alternatives to technique A which make economic (as opposed to engineering) sense, are those to the north-west or south-east of A. To make a given output, a firm will consider a technique using more capital only if it uses less labour, and vice versa. Hence isoquants must slope down.

Third, Figure 11-A2 shows each isoquant getting flatter as we move along it to the right. Beginning with a very labour-intensive way to produce a given output, it gets progressively harder to produce that same output from more capital-intensive methods. Moving down a given isoquant, it takes more and more extra capital input to make equal successive reductions in the labour input required to produce a given output.

In Figure 11-A2 the line L_0K_0 is called an *isocost* line. It shows different input combina-

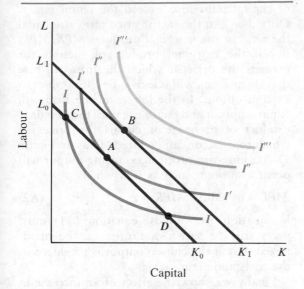

Figure 11-A2 COST MINIMIZATION. Each isoquant such as *I* shows a particular output level. Higher isoquants such as *I″* show higher output levels. Straight lines such as $L_0 K_0$ are isocost lines showing different input combinations having the same total cost. The slope of an isocost line depends only on relative factor prices. A higher isocost line such as $L_1 K_1$ implies a larger total cost. To produce a given output, such as that corresponding to the isoquant *I′*, the firm chooses the point of tangency of that isoquant to the lowest possible isocost line. Thus point *A* is the cost minimizing way to produce the output level on *I′* and point *B* the cost minimizing way to produce the output level on *I″*.

tions with the *same* total cost. With a given amount of money to spend, the firm can use more units of capital only if it uses less units of labour. Facing given prices at which different inputs may be hired, we can say two things about isocost lines. First, the slope of the isocost line reflects the relative price of the two factors of production. Beginning at K_0, where all the firm's money is spent on capital the firm can trade off 1 unit of capital for more units of labour the cheaper is the wage rate relative to the rental cost of capital. Second, facing given factor prices, if the firm spends more on inputs it can have larger quantities of both labour and capital. An isocost line parallel to but above $L_0 K_0$ thus represents a larger expenditure on hiring inputs. Thus along the isocost line $L_1 K_1$ the firm is spending a larger amount on inputs than along the isocost line $L_0 K_0$.

We now can examine the firm's decision

problem. First, how does the firm decide the cost-minimizing technique if it wishes to produce the output level corresponding to the isoquant *I′*? The complete set of parallel isocost lines, including $L_0 K_0$ and $L_1 K_1$, shows the different amounts of money the firm can spend, one amount for each isocost line. To minimize the cost of producing the output quantity corresponding to the isoquant *I′*, the firm must choose the input quantity on *I′* that allows it to reach the lowest possible isocost line. In Figure 11-A2 this is achieved at the point *A*.

> To minimize the cost of producing a given output level, the firm chooses the point of tangency of that isoquant to the lowest possible isocost line.

At the cost minimizing point the (negative) slope of the isocost line is exactly equal to the (negative) slope of the isoquant.

If w is the wage rate and r the rental cost of a unit of capital, the slope of the isocost line is $-r/w$. The higher the rental r relative to the wage rate w, the more units of labour can be gained in exchange for a reduction of capital input by 1 unit while holding constant the total cost of inputs. What about the slope of the isoquant?

By using an extra unit of capital (a change of $+1$) the firm gains MPK units of output, where MPK is the marginal physical product of capital. But along an isoquant output is constant. By shedding a unit of labour the firm gives up MPL units of output. Hence a negative change in labour input equal to $-MPK/MPL$ will maintain output constant when capital input is increased by 1 unit. Thus the slope of an isoquant is given by $-MPK/MPL$ since it tells us by how much labour must be changed to preserve a constant output level when capital is increased by 1 unit. Hence the tangency condition for cost minimization in Figure 11-A2 implies:

Slope of isocost line $= -r/w = -MPK/MPL$

           $=$ **slope of isoquant**   (A1)

The point *A* in Figure 11-A2 tells us the cost-minimizing way to produce the output level corresponding to the isoquant *I′*. We can repeat this analysis for every other isoquant corresponding to every other output level. That is how we build up the total cost curve which we

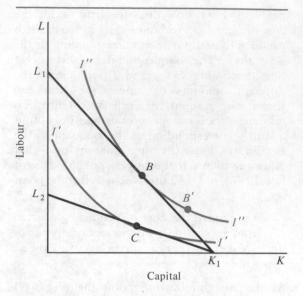

Figure 11-A3   THE EFFECT OF A WAGE INCREASE.   At the old factor prices the firm produces an output level corresponding to the isoquant I''. All isocost lines have the same slope as L_1K_1 and the firm produces its given output most cheaply by choosing the point B where the isoquant is tangent to the lowest possible isocost line L_1K_1. A wage increase makes all isocost lines flatter. The new isocost lines are parallel to L_2K_1. Each unit of capital sacrificed now allows the purchase of less additional labour. The wage increase has a pure substitution effect from B to B' where the original isoquant I'' has the same slope as the new isocost lines. Firms substitute capital for labour. But with higher marginal costs at each output level, the firm's profit-maximizing output is reduced, say to the level corresponding to the isoquant I'. On this isoquant, costs are minimized by producing at C to reach the lowest possible isocost line L_2K_1 at the new factor prices. The move from B' to C is the pure output effect induced by the shift in the firm's marginal cost curve for its output.

discussed in the text. How does the firm find the profit-maximizing output?

Suppose at point A, the marginal product of labour exceeds the wage rate w. Equation (A1) tells us that in the long run the marginal product

of capital must also exceed the rental rate r. Only then can the factor price ratio r/w equal the ratio of the marginal products MPK/MPL. But if the marginal product of each factor exceeds the price at which the firm can hire that factor, it will clearly be profitable to expand output. In the long run, the firm will expand output and factor use until the marginal product of each factor equals the price for which that factor can be hired. Thus, in Figure 11-A2, long-run profit-maximizing output will occur at a point such as B at which

$$MPL = w \quad \text{and} \quad MPK = r \qquad (A2)$$

If equation (A2) holds, equation (A1) must necessarily be satisfied. Profits can be maximized only if the chosen output is produced in the cost-minimizing way.

Finally we show the effect of an increase in the price of one factor. Figure 11-A3 shows the initial position at B where the isocost line L_1K_1 is tangent to the isoquant I''. Now suppose the wage rate rises. Each isocost line then becomes less steep. Sacrificing a unit of capital will allow less additional labour while preserving total cost. At the original output level on isoquant I'' this leads to a pure substitution effect from B to B' the point on the old isoquant tangent to an isocost line with the new flatter slope. But a higher wage rate also shifts up the total cost curve and the marginal cost curve for output and leads to a reduction in the output which maximizes profits.

The lower isoquant I' shows the new profit-maximizing output at this lower level. L_2K_1 is the lowest attainable isocost line embodying the flatter slope corresponding to the new relative input prices. The firm will thus choose the point C. The move from B' to C is the pure output effect of a higher wage-rate. The actual move from B to C can thus be decomposed into a substitution effect from B to B' and an output effect from B' to C. Both effects tend to reduce the quantity of labour demanded.

12
Human Capital, Discrimination, and Trade Unions

In most European countries men earn more than women and whites earn more than non-whites. Do these stark facts reflect discrimination in the labour market, or do they simply reflect differences in the productivity of different workers?[1]

The theme of this chapter is that labour is heterogeneous. Workers differ not merely in sex and race but in age, experience, education, training, innate ability, and in whether or not they belong to a trade union. We want to know how these differences affect pay. Table 12-1 emphasizes the difference between men and women. In manual jobs women earn only two-thirds as much per hour as men and the difference is even larger in non-manual jobs. To some extent these differences may reflect continuity of employment. For example, Christine Greenhalgh found that single women do considerably better than married or divorced women and earn almost 90 per cent as much per hour as men.[2] Whether we regard this as discrimination against women who take time off to raise a family is an issue that goes to the heart of our view about how society should be organized.

Table 12-2 considers some of the factors that influence pay differentials for men, the group on which most data are available. It shows estimates for manual and non-manual earnings

calculated in the pioneering study by Professors Richard Layard, David Metcalf and Steve Nickell. It should be remembered that earnings per person are nearly 30 per cent higher in non-manual occupations.

Table 12-2 draws attention to four sources of pay differentials. People with more schooling and higher educational attainments earn higher wages but the value of these qualifications depends on the type of job. Economics and engineering degrees are much more useful in

---

Table 12-1 Hourly earnings of men and women in the UK, 1988*

	MEN	WOMEN
Manual	£4.46	£3.11
Non-manual	£7.49	£4.68

* Adults in full-time employment.
Source: Department of Employment, *New Earnings Survey.*

Table 12-2 Pay differentials for UK men

% EXTRA PAY FOR:	MANUAL	NON-MANUAL
Extra year at school	+4	+5
University degree	+5	+38
Other post-school qualification	+30	+35
A-level school exams	+13	+22
O-level school exams	+10	+14
0–5 years' job experience	+15	+11
6–10 years' job experience	+3	+6
West Indian	−7	−14
Other non-white	0	−6
Extra 10% of work force in trade union	+5.6	−3.2

Source: R. Layard, D. Metcalf, and S. Nickell, 'The Effect of Collective Bargaining on Wages', *British Journal of Industrial Relations*, 1978.

---

[1] By 'discrimination' we mean failure to pay the going rate for the job and skill characteristics merely because a worker is female or non-white. However, other kinds of discrimination may also exist. Discrimination in education might imply that non-whites are less qualified than whites. Even if employers pay all qualified people a high wage and all unqualified people a low wage, whatever their colour, the effect of discrimination in education would be to reduce the average earnings of non-whites.

[2] See Christine Greenhalgh, 'Male–Female Wage Differentials in Great Britain: Is Marriage an Equal Opportunity?', *Economic Journal*, 1980.

non-manual jobs such as running a factory than in manual jobs such as plumbing or brick-laying. But Table 12-2 does not say it is only *relevant* or vocational degrees that contribute to higher non-manual earnings. How are we to explain the fact that history and philosophy graduates also seem to earn more, especially in non-manual jobs?

The second source of pay differentials is job experience. In most industries, workers learn skills on the job. Table 12-2 shows how earnings tend to rise with the number of years of job experience.

Third, the table confirms that non-whites, especially West Indians, earn lower wages *even after allowing for differences in education and experience*. It is prima facie evidence of discrimination in the labour market. And once we allow for the fact that non-whites typically have less education and training, their pay disadvantage is even greater than the table suggests. Finally, the table shows the effect of the proportion of the industry that is unionized. Here there is a striking difference between manual and non-manual jobs. Other things equal, Table 12-2 suggests that an industry with complete trade union membership in manual activities will pay 5.6 per cent higher wage rates than it would with no union members. In contrast, highly unionized activities in non-manual jobs earn *lower* wages.

We need to interpret Table 12-2 with some care. The highest paid non-manual workers – company executives, merchant bankers, pop stars – do not need trade unions. The demand for unions may be strongest where wages are low. Even if unions succeed in raising the wages of shop assistants *relative to what they would have been in the absence of the union*, shop workers will still earn less than company executives. Table 12-2 says that unionized non-manual workers earn less than other non-manuals. It does not say that these low paid workers would earn more if they left their unions.

Section 12-1 of this chapter examines how education, experience and skill contribute to earning by increasing workers' *human capital* – the stock of relevant expertise they have accumulated. We then examine the role of education as a filter that screens out the high-ability workers with high-career potential. History degrees may *signal* general intelligence,

even though they provide little training of direct relevance for most non-manual jobs.

Section 12-2 examines in more detail the issues of discrimination and equality of opportunity in the labour market. The final section studies the role of trade unions in the labour market.

12-1 Human Capital

Human capital is the stock of expertise accumulated by a worker. It is valued for its income-earning potential in the future.

As with physical capital such as plant and machinery, human capital is the result of past investment and its purpose is to generate future incomes. For example, in order to invest in another year of school education or a further qualification people may have to make a direct payment, as with fees for private schools, but they also forgo the opportunity to earn immediate income by working. The anticipated benefit of this initial expenditure is either a higher future monetary income or a future job yielding greater job satisfaction.

The human capital approach assumes that wage differentials reflect differences in the productivity of different workers. Skilled workers have a higher marginal value product and earn more. The problem for workers is to decide how much to invest in improving their own productivity.

Age–Earnings Profiles and Education

Table 12-2 shows that education and work experience contribute to higher earnings. Figure 12-1 shows how earnings change with age for workers with three different levels of educational qualification: university or other higher degrees, A-levels or other qualifications equivalent to the best school-leavers, and those without any formal qualifications at all.

The figure makes two points. It confirms that people with more educational qualifications typically earn more. But it also shows that the disparity grows steadily with age and experience. Healthy young people with qualifications can work hard and make quite good money. Intially they are at only a moderate pay disadvantage. But they cannot look forward to steadily rising real wages. Indeed, by the

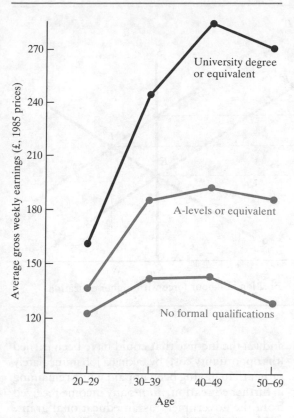

Figure 12-1 AGE-EARNINGS PROFILES BY
HIGHEST EDUCATIONAL ATTAINMENT. The figure
shows earnings in the UK for male workers in
full-time employment. Earnings increase with the
level of education and, up to a point, with age.
(*Source: General Household Survey*, HMSO.)

time they reach their early thirties their earnings
have already peaked. In contrast, the most
highly educated start at wage rates only a
modest amount above those of the completely
unqualified but they can then look forward to
steadily rising incomes over most of their
working lifetime. Figure 12-1 is compatible with
the view that the most highly educated go into
the most difficult jobs which take a long time
to master. With increasing experience and
mastery of the job, productivity and salaries rise
steadily.

At this juncture we stress that there are two
completely different interpretations of why the
most educated get the highest earnings. The
view we examine first in this section is that
education directly increases workers' productivity and allows them to command higher
earnings sooner or later. But we shall then

discuss the competing view that education
does *not* contribute the expertise that increases
worker productivity. Rather, people have different innate abilities. High-ability people have
high productivity because they can learn
difficult jobs. Also, they like studying and are
good at it. They happen to amass a lot of
educational qualifications, but they earn good
money because of the skills they were born
with. We return to this view later in the
section.

The Market for Educated Workers

Suppose higher education contributes to productivity. Figure 12-2 shows the market for
workers with higher education. On the vertical
axis we plot the difference between wages for
workers with higher education and wages for
school-leavers without higher education. It is
the *wage premium* paid for workers with higher
education. On the horizontal axis we measure
the fraction of the workforce with higher
education.

DD is the demand curve for workers with
higher education. For example, at point *B* the
wage differential is high and firms want only
a small proportion of their workers to have this
extra education. At the much lower differential
at point *C* the demand for educated workers is
much higher. The downward-sloping demand
curve *DD* thus assumes that workers with
higher education are more productive but that
firms face diminishing returns in employing
educated workers. At any instant, the supply
of such workers is fixed by past education
decisions. The short-run supply curve *SS*
is vertical. For example, in the UK about 8 per
cent of the male labour force and 3 per cent of
the female labour force have a university degree
or professional qualification of equivalent
standard.

In the long run, the supply curve *S'S'* of
workers with higher education slopes upwards.
The greater the payoff to higher education, as
measured by the wage differential, the more
school leavers will be induced to delay working
and acquire more education. We analyse this
decision in greater detail below. For the
moment all we need to note is that the long-run
supply curve of educated workers slopes
up.

Suppose the market begins in short-run and

Figure 12-2 THE MARKET FOR HIGHLY EDUCATED WORKERS. In the short run the supply of educated workers is fixed at N_0, but in the long run an increase in the wage differential for educated workers will induce more people to go to university. The long-run supply curve is $S'S'$. DD is the downward-sloping demand curve for educated workers. From the initial equilibrium at E, with a wage differential WD, an upward shift in the demand for educated workers leads initially to a sharp increase in the differential to WD'. Gradually more people get higher education, and the new long-run equilibrium is at E''.

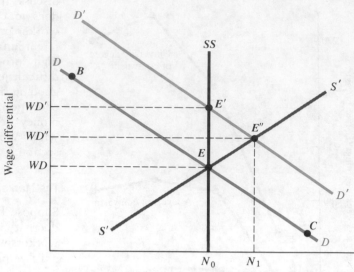

Fraction of labour force with higher education

long-run equilibrium at E. The wage differential WD just compensates workers for the effort and money they expand acquiring further qualifications and for the wages they forgo while they are being educated further.

Now suppose the demand curve for educated workers shifts up to $D'D'$. For example, there may be an expansion of high-technology firms which use educated workers intensively. In the short run, with a fixed supply SS of such workers, the differential rises to WD'. In competing for scarce educated workers firms bid up their wages. The economy is at E'.

The premium on higher education is now so high that more people decide to acquire education. Over the long run the supply of educated workers increases. As this happens the premium on scarce workers falls back. In the long run equilibrium occurs at E'' with a higher number of educated workers and a wage differential WD''.

Investing in Human Capital: Cost–Benefit Analysis

Consider the decision of a school-leaver whether to continue in education or take a job immediately. Does investment in further education make sense? There are two costs and two benefits. The immediate costs are (1) the cost of books, fees, etc., for continuing in education

and (2) the income that could have been earned (the opportunity cost) by taking a job immediately rather than having been unpaid while remaining in further education, *minus* any income received from the government as an educational grant.

The first benefit occurs in the future and is the stream of *extra* wages that workers with higher education can earn. The second occurs immediately but in a non-monetary form. It is the fun or consumption value of going to college or university. Most people, and most students themselves, think that students have a good time. They meet new people, try new sports, discover new rock bands, and do whatever students do.

Like any investment decision, the decision whether or not to continue in higher education rests on comparing current costs and benefits (usually a net cost) with the stream of future costs and benefits (usually a stream of net benefits). Figure 12-3 compares the income profile of a school-leaver entering the labour force at 18 with the income profile of a university graduate entering the labour force at 21. The cost of higher education is the grey area. It shows income forgone by not being in the labour force between 18 and 21, *plus* the direct cost of fees and books, *minus* the sum of money that the school-leavers would have paid to enjoy the pleasures of being a student. The benefits are given by the green area, the

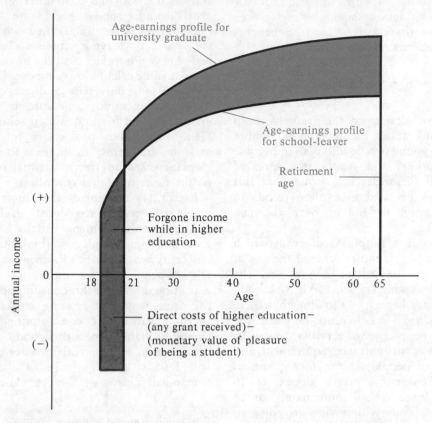

Figure 12-3 INVESTMENT IN HIGHER EDUCATION. The top half of the diagram shows the age–earnings profiles for a worker leaving school at 18 to enter the labour force and for a student who delays working until 21. The green area shows how much extra the student will eventually earn. The grey area above 0 shows the income forgone while at university. The grey area below 0 shows the money value of the other costs and benefits of being at university: the diagram assumes that these costs outweigh the benefits but this need not be the case. The decision whether or not to go to university depends on comparing the green area with the total grey area.

stream of extra income that can be earned after the age of 21.

Assuming that you will pass the final exams, it makes sense to go on to further education if the benefits outweigh the costs. But the benefits accrue in the future. Most people would rather have £100 today than a promise of £100 in five years' time. To compare like with like, it is necessary to *discount* or reduce the value of future benefits (or future costs) to place them on a par with benefits or costs incurred today. In the next chapter we discuss in detail how this should be done when we study the decisions of firms to invest in machinery that is costly today but will produce benefits (higher output) in the future.

For the moment we can skip the technical

details of how this discounting should be done. The general idea will suffice. If the present value, however calculated, of the benefits outweighs the present value of the costs incurred, the educational investment in improving human capital by going to university or college makes sense. If the present value of the benefits is less than the present value of the costs, higher education is a bad investment. It is better to start work immediately.

Cost benefit analysis is a procedure for making long run decisions such as whether to build a factory or go to university. In either case, present actions have implications far into the future. The correct way to make a decision is to compare the present value of the costs with the present value of the benefits. The action should be undertaken only if the present value of the benefits exceeds the present value of the costs.

The Demand for Higher Education in Britain

We have now developed the framework in which to think about the demand for higher education by young people who plan to become educated workers and supply that kind of labour. Chris Pissarides has shown that this approach can be used to explain trends in higher education in Britain over the last 25 years.[3]

Figure 12-3 is a simplified diagram which imagines that people must decide at the age of 18. In Britain the school-leaving age, the minimum age at which people can leave school, is 16. Pissarides begins by showing that there is a very strong relationship between the number of people who get two A-levels, the typical university entrance requirement, and the number of people who in fact go on to university. Effectively, people decide at 16 whether to leave school immediately or to embark on A-levels with a view to going to university.[4]

Pissarides shows that the fraction of 16-year-olds embarking on the A-level/university route is well explained by three factors: (1) a measure of expected future incomes in general, (2) as viewed from the age of 16, the present value of the *extra* income that university graduates enjoy after age 21 minus the present value of the income forgone (after adjusting for university grants) by not working between the ages of 16 and 21, and (3) the level of unemployment.

Factor (2) is exactly the effect examined in Figure 12-3. The more the present value of the extra income outweighs the present value of the costs of more education, the more people will go on in education. In estimating these present values, Pissarides assumed that there was no unemployment. Factor (3) says that higher unemployment tends to make people

stay on at school and go to university. This can also be understood using Figure 12-3. High unemployment hit unqualified school-leavers very hard. By leaving school at 16 a school-leaver may not in fact earn the income that the present value calculations suppose. Conversely, although some university graduates cannot find jobs, the unemployment rate is lower for graduates than for unqualified school-leavers. Hence, for given pay scales for graduates and non-graduates, an increase in unemployment increases the effective return to embarking on the route of higher education.

Factor (1) recognizes that there are non-monetary benefits to education. Earlier we pointed out that students usually have a good time. But some people also think that going to university broadens one's horizons and generally allows people to get more out of life. If education does have this consumption value, in the same way that reading books or going to the theatre have consumption value, we should probably expect this good or service to be a luxury. Higher real incomes per person will lead to a large rise in the quantity demanded. This is what factor (1) confirms.

On-the-job Training and Age–Earnings Profiles

Figure 12-1 shows that investment in education increases future earning power. But it also shows that earnings rise with experience on the job, especially in the difficult jobs which are usually done by workers of higher ability and education. Learning on the job is a central characteristic of the age–earnings profiles of the better educated but is much less important for the unqualified who frequently do relatively routine jobs which can be mastered quickly.

If on-the-job training increases worker productivity, why don't workers pay firms for the valuable learning opportunities that firms provide? In part they do. To understand how and why we must distinguish between two kinds of skills. *Firm-specific* skills help increase a worker's productivity only if he or she works for that particular firm. Firm-specific human capital could be something as simple as knowing how the filing system works or something as complicated as mastering the most efficient way to combine the various production processes of a particular factory. In

[3] C. Pissarides, 'From School to University: the Demand for Post-Compulsory Education in Britain', *Economic Journal*, September 1982.
[4] Of course, some people fail their A-level exams and some people stay on at school after 16 to do more of the lower-level GCSE exams.

either case, the skill is virtually worthless to any other firm. *General* skills are those that can be transferred to work for another firm. Examples are learning how to be a welder or understanding how the stock market works.

The firm can afford to pay for on-the-job training in firm-specific skills. Once the worker has learned them, his or her productivity will be much higher with that firm than with any other firm, where learning must begin all over again. The firm is unlikely to lose the worker. The more general or transferable the skill, the more the firm will want the worker to pay the cost of training. No firm will want to invest heavily in training its workers only to see them move to other firms. Then the firm would never reap the reward of its initial outlay.

Thus, firms offering general or transferable training will try to make the workers pay for this. How is this achieved? By offering an age–earnings profile that starts off very low, lower than the worker's marginal product, but is guaranteed to rise steeply over time. Examples are apprentice schemes, both in industry and in professional jobs such as accountancy. The worker is paying for a training by working for less than the immediate marginal product of labour even at this relatively unskilled initial level. Yet workers are prepared to pay this cost of investing in human capital because the firm is committed to an age–earnings profile that will allow the worker to recoup the initial investment with interest at a later date. Hence in Figure 12-1 age–earnings profiles rise much more steeply for people with more education, likely to be doing jobs that involve more training, than they do for unqualified workers whose training is likely to be limited.

Signalling

Why can a history graduate go on to earn big money in banking? The theory we have just developed says that education and training on the job raise worker productivity. Crudely speaking, Table 12-2 implies that staying on at school an extra year adds 5 per cent to a worker's marginal product. But there is an alternative theory of investment in education, the theory of *signalling*.[5] This theory says that

it could be rational to invest in costly education *even if education adds nothing directly to a worker's marginal product*. This theory may be more helpful in explaining why history graduates go on to earn big money in banking.

The theory assumes that people are born with different innate ability. Some people are good at most things, other people are less smart and on average less productive. But smart people do not all have blue eyes and less smart people brown eyes. The problem for firms is to tell which applicants will turn out to be the smart ones with high productivity. Looking at their eyes is not enough.

For the sake of the argument, suppose higher education contributes nothing to productivity. Before making this costly investment in human capital, how can school-leavers be assured that they will earn wages in future to offset the initial cost? Signalling theory says that, in going on in education, the smart people are sending a signal to employers that they are the high-productivity workers of the future. Higher education is *screening out* the smart high-productivity workers. Firms can pay university graduates more because they can be assured that they are the high-ability workers.

To be effective, the screening process must indeed separate the high-ability workers from the others. Why don't lower-ability workers go to university and fool firms into offering them high wages? There are two answers. First, the lower-ability workers could not be confident of passing. Here we have an interesting comparison between the two theories of investment in education. If it is studying that adds to productivity, firms should offer higher wages to people who have *attended* university, whether or not they pass the final exam. But if university works by screening out the good people, firms should be interested not in attendance but in *passing*.

Some firms hire university students before they sit their final exams. Is this evidence against the signalling theory? Not necessarily, for screening works in a second way. The lower-ability people may decide not to go to university for two reasons: first, because they do not expect to pass, and second, because they may feel that in order to scrape through they will have to work enormously and unpleasantly hard. Since most people know their own ability, firms may take it on trust

---

[5] See Michael Spence, *Market Signalling: Informational Transfer in Hiring and Related Screening Processes*, Harvard University Press, 1974.

that people who have stuck it out till their final year at university believe themselves to be at the higher end of the ability range.

It seems quite probable that education (even at the highest levels) contributes something to productivity. But there may also be an element of screening in all except purely vocational courses. Engineering, law, and business degrees presumably contribute more to productivity than philosophy, history, or politics.

There is one final issue to consider before we leave investment in education. It concerns the distinction between what is good for the individual and what is good for society as a whole. We know that university graduates earn more. It makes sense for many people to take the individual decision to invest in this human capital. If education raises productivity directly, it is also good for society. It raises the amount of output that the labour force can eventually produce. Whether individuals and society as a whole should always choose the same amount of education is an issue in welfare economics that must await Part 3 of this book.

Suppose, however, that the only function of higher education was to signal which were the higher-ability workers. It still makes sense for individuals to go to university, but does it make sense for society as a whole? There is a social gain to learning which are the smart workers. By matching smart workers to difficult jobs, society will achieve a higher output. It will not give lower-ability people jobs they are unable to do. Nor will it lead higher-ability workers to become bored in jobs that are too easy for them. But if the only function of higher education is to screen out the high-ability workers, there may be a cheaper way for society

to achieve the same result. A national IQ test, with results adjusted for disadvantages of background and previous opportunity to learn, might screen almost as well (possibly even better!) at much less cost to society as a whole.

12-2 Discrimination

In Table 12-1 we showed that women's hourly earnings in the UK are only about two-thirds the hourly earnings of men, and in Table 12-2 we showed that non-whites earn significantly less than whites. In what sense can we say that these numbers provide evidence of sex and race discrimination in the UK labour market?

For all the reasons we analysed in the last chapter, some jobs pay more than others. Differences in average earnings of different sexes or races can thus arise for two distinct reasons. The first reason is that different groups may get different shares of the high-paying jobs. They have different employment patterns. The second reason is that different groups may get paid different amounts for doing each kind of job. We begin by examining the difference between men and women of adult age in full-time employment.

Employment and Pay Differences Between Men and Women

Table 12-3 shows the weekly earnings in 1988 in different occupations and the pattern of male and female employment. Part-time working is excluded. The table shows that the patterns of male and female employment do differ. Most men are industrial manual workers or belong

Table 12-3 Pay and employment by occupation and sex in the UK, 1988

OCCUPATION	ADULT MEN		ADULT WOMEN	
	(1) WEEKLY EARNINGS (£)	(2) % OF MALE FULL-TIME EMPLOYMENT	(3) WEEKLY EARNINGS (£)	(4) % OF FEMALE FULL-TIME EMPLOYMENT
Professional, managerial, arts and sports	310	31.3	220	29.2
Clerical and selling	208	14.2	139	47.7
Personal and domestic service	159	4.3	117	8.8
Other manual	194	50.2	130	14.3

Source: Department of Employment, New Earnings Survey.

to the professional and managerial occupations. Most women do clerical or selling jobs. Yet the pattern of employment does not seem to be the major cause of the fact that women as a whole earn £90 a week less than men. For example, if women had the employment pattern shown for men in column (2) of Table 12-3 but were paid the rates shown for women in column (3), the overall average earnings of women would hardly be changed. In contrast, if women maintained the employment pattern of column (4) but earned the pay rates shown for men in column (1), women as a whole would earn almost as much as men.

Thus the source of different overall earnings does not seem to be the pattern of employment across the broad occupational categories shown in Table 12-3. Does this imply that the evidence indicates pure discrimination against women, a failure to pay them the same rate as men for doing the same job?

The numbers in Table 12-3 certainly suggest this at first sight. However, we should need a more detailed analysis to confirm this overall impression. For example, there is a big difference between a skilled manual worker and an unskilled one, or between a top manager in charge of a major company and a junior supervisor. What we can conclude from Table 12-3 is that either women get paid less than men for the identical job, however narrowly that job is defined, or else men get promoted and trained faster within these broad occupational classifications. For example, 29 per cent of women in full-time employment are in the professional or managerial occupations broadly defined, not as high a proportion as the 31 per cent of men in the same category, but the proportion of women on the boards of major companies is much smaller than the corresponding proportion of men.

Why should companies promote or train women more slowly, even if they pay men and women the same wage at each rung on the ladder? Is this overt discrimination, subtle discrimination or neither? Does our analysis of human capital and signalling in the previous section help us to make sense of this?

Suppose firms bear some of the cost of training young workers. The firm makes a hard-nosed investment decision. Assuming that men and women are of inherently equal ability and educational attainment, it will cost the firm the same to train either sex. The benefit to the firm is the stream of future profits that will accrue from the extra productivity that the trained or promoted workers will have as a result of the firm's initial outlay. Suppose that on average firms believe that women are more likely than men to interrupt or even end their careers at a young age. As a matter of biology it is women who have babies not men. Firms may conclude that the present value of the extra productivity benefits in the future is lower for women than men simply because they are likely to work fewer years in the future. Hence it is more profitable to train and promote men purely as a hard-nosed financial calculation.

Some women plan to have a full-time career, either remaining childless or returning to work almost immediately after any children are born. It would make sense for firms to invest in such people but there is a huge problem: how is a firm to tell which young women are planning to stay and which are planning to work only a few years and then have a family? Asking is no good because there is an incentive for young women not to tell the truth.[6]

Can firms and workers co-operate to devise a screening procedure that will persuade young women to reveal their true career plans? Suppose firms were to offer young workers the choice between a relatively flat age–earnings profile and a much steeper profile that begins at a lower wage but pays a suitably higher wage later in a worker's career. By making the wages in later years sufficiently high, firms could ensure that the two profiles were equally valued by someone planning a lifetime career. The early sacrifice of lower wages would be recouped with interest in later years. But someone planning to quit the labour force, say at the age of 30, would never opt for the steeper profile, for such a person would never expect to work long enough at the higher wage to recoup the early sacrifice.

By observing whether new recruits were prepared to accept the steeper age–earnings

---

[6] This is a version of the problem of *moral hazard* that we discuss in detail in Chapter 14. However, there is a presumption that single women are less likely to interrupt their career than married women. Since firms can usually discover a woman's marital status, this may explain why Christine Greenhalgh found that single women on average earn much more than married women. Firms are more likely to invest in training for single women.

profile, it might be possible for firms to persuade recruits to *reveal* their career plans. If women, or any other group with a high risk of quitting at a young age, were to accept the steeper profile the firm could then embark on training with some confidence that its investment would not be wasted.

There is, of course, an issue of credibility. Young workers would need to be assured that they really were exchanging low wages in the early years for suitably higher wages later in their career. And, initially, even career women might be reluctant to accept the steeper profile until they could see a generation of women who, having accepted such a profile and induced the firm to place its training bets, had succeeded in being promoted through the company to earn the suitably higher earnings in the later years of their career. But firms will be reluctant to place their training bets on women unless they can be persuaded to reveal their career plans.

We suspect that there are still a few firms who try to pay female workers less than male workers who are identical in every respect, including the risk of quitting. We might call this overt discrimination. In other cases, existing and traditional age–earnings profiles may give firms a purely economic reason to be cautious about large investment in the education and training of women. We have indicated how this more subtle form of discrimination might be changed. But society may discriminate against women in even more subtle ways.

For example, our analysis suggests that paternity leave for fathers, the provision of crèches for working parents, or a greater acceptance of part-time working by both sexes, would reduce the incentive for hard-nosed firms to conclude that it is more profitable to train and promote men than women. Whether or not society wishes to organize its work and home life along such principles remains a controversial issue. What it makes clear is that pay differentials · between men and women depend on much wider factors than the labour market in isolation.

Access to Education

Thus far we have discussed sex discrimination by firms assuming that they receive male and female applicants of equal calibre. However, if education contributes to human capital and potential worker productivity, it may be that firms treat workers of equal calibre equally but pay men more on average because job applicants who are male on average have more educational qualifications than job applicants who are female. If so we must seek the root cause of pay differences by sex not in the labour market, but in education itself.

Table 12-4 shows the number of males and females of a given age who are still in full-time education in the UK and how this changed in the 1970s and 1980s. We can see that more people were staying on in education in the 1980s than at the beginning of the 1970s. Also, more men than women go on to higher education in universities, polytechnics, and other training establishments. Thus it is possible that firms receive a higher proportion of educated male applicants than female applicants with equivalent qualifications. If education contributes to productivity, we should expect men to earn more on average.

Why do fewer women continue in higher education? There are three possible explanations. First, there may be genuine discrimination

Table 12-4 UK students in full-time education, by age group and sex (thousands)

AGE	1970/71		1986/87	
	MEN	WOMEN	MEN	WOMEN
18 or under	28.7	30.4	50.0	43.8
19–20	99.0	82.3	128.9	109.5
21–24	104.6	44.5	104.0	73.6
25 and over	42.0	25.3	59.9	43.2

Source: CSO, Social Trends.

in education. In schools teaching boys and girls, teachers may try harder with boys or encourage more of them to think about further education.

Second, women may have different tastes. The old stereotype of school, marriage, motherhood, and domesticity would imply that fewer women wished to embark on higher education with a view to a long career, though some women, especially those who could afford to forgo the opportunity to earn income when first reaching school-leaving age, have always stayed on, viewing higher education as a consumer good providing student fun and a certain breadth of experience and learning.

Finally, we can think about the return or payoff in higher future incomes to this initial investment in education. Equal opportunity legislation and social pressure have increased wages for women, both by reducing sex discrimination for a given job and by increasing the chances of female promotion within a firm's salary hierarchy. In contemplating whether or not to continue in education, women may now feel that there has been an increase in the future benefits through higher salary opportunities. If so, we should expect more and more women to decide to invest in education. Note, however, the crucial role of expectations or perceptions. Until it becomes evident that women really are being promoted and enjoying the benefits of higher education, the *perceived* return on higher education may continue to be lower for women than for men, and fewer women than men will decide to invest in further education.

The data of Table 12-4 are compatible with any or all of these explanations. Unequal educational opportunities, different tastes, and lower payoffs to education all tend to make it less worthwhile for women to continue into higher education. And moves towards equal educational opportunities, changes in tastes, and perceptions that wages for women are steadily rising could all explain the trend in the 1980s for the educational disparity between men and women to have shrunk.

Racial Discrimination

Exactly the same general principles may be used to analyse racial discrimination and differences in the earnings of whites and non-whites. West Indians, Indians and Pakistanis are the most important racial minority groups in the UK. Many studies have confirmed the suggestion in Table 12-2 that on average non-whites earn less than whites. The interested reader is referred to the survey of the evidence by Simon Field *et al.*, 'Ethnic Minorities in Britain' (Home Office Research Study no. 68, 1981). Interestingly, the authors conclude that the pay differential between white and non-white women is much smaller than the differential between white and non-white men.

In addition, Robert McNab and George Psacharopoulos have drawn attention to two points.[7] First, the age–earnings profiles for non-white males are much flatter than the corresponding profiles for white males. White men are much more likely to achieve steady promotion and rising earnings. From our discussion of age–earnings profiles in the previous section, we recognize that this is likely to imply that whites do more difficult jobs where training and experience are important.

Second, McNab and Psacharopoulos establish that the problem for non-white men is not so much the amount of education but the type of education they receive. The payoff to education is very low for non-whites who attend a typical state-run inner-city school.

Two interpretations are possible. Either the quality of education in inner-city schools with predominantly non-white children is poor, or attendance at such schools tends to act as a signal to firms that these children are likely to come from disadvantaged backgrounds. Firms may believe that these children have less experience in everyday skills such as reading, communicating, and concentrating and conclude that these potential workers will have lower productivity and be more expensive to train to any particular standard of performance.

Both interpretations imply that firms will be less inclined to employ such workers in jobs that are difficult and require ex .sive on-the-job training. White workers or non-whites from other educational backgrounds are much more likely to be given the skilled and demanding jobs with which the steeply rising age–earnings profiles are associated. A higher proportion of non-whites will be restricted to unskilled and low-paying jobs.

---

[7] R. McNab and G. Psacharopoulos, 'Racial Earnings Differentials in the UK', Discussion Paper 76, Centre for Labour E   omics, London School of Economics, 1980.

As in our discussion of sex discrimination, it is not easy to draw a line between discrimination in the labour market and elsewhere in society, as for example in education. And in both cases the explanation for different pay rates for different groups of workers extends far beyond the simplest notion of discrimination, which argues that firms pay women or non-whites less merely because they are not white males. The first responsibility of managers is to maximize profits for their shareholders. So long as managers perceive that different groups of workers have already acquired different characteristics, or will tend to behave differently during the course of their working lifetimes, managers will wish to pay different groups different amounts. Unless society as a whole removes the differences in characteristics, opportunities and behaviour of different groups of workers, it must be recognized that the eradication of blatant racism or sexism will go only part of the way to eliminating pay differentials between groups of workers.

12-3 Trade Unions

Trade unions are worker organizations designed to affect pay and working conditions. Do unions protect workers from exploitation by powerful employers or do they use their power to secure unjustified pay increases and oppose technical changes and productivity improvements which might threaten the employment of their members? Before examining these questions we give a brief outline of the importance of unions in the British economy.

By 1980 just over half the civilian labour force in the UK belonged to a trade union. Figure 12-4 shows the change since 1910 in the percentage of the labour force belonging to a trade union. It shows that after the steady increase in union membership until 1920 there was a massive decline and then recovery in the degree of unionization of the labour force during the inter-war years. Thereafter, there was a long period during which unionization was fairly constant until the late 1960s. The 1970s saw a sharp rise in union membership, which peaked in 1979, since when it has been falling again. Figure 12-4 is compatible with the view that unionization falls as unemployment rises.[8]

With rising female participation in the labour force, there was a much faster growth of union membership by women than men. The pattern of industrial growth may also be important. The period saw an expansion of industries, for example those in the public sector, in which unions are traditionally well organized and the degree of unionization is high. Recent attempts to reduce the relative size of the public sector in the economy may therefore tend to reduce the degree of unionization in the economy as a whole.

---

[8] See G. Bain and F. Elsheik, *Union Growth and the Business Cycle*, Basil Blackwell, 1976.

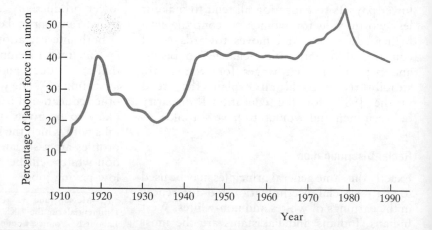

Figure 12-4 UNION MEMBERSHIP AS A PERCENTAGE OF THE CIVILIAN LABOUR FORCE.

What Unions Do

The traditional view of the role of unions is that they offset the relative power that a firm enjoys in negotiating wages and working conditions. A single firm has many workers. If each worker must make a separate deal with the firm, the firm can make a take-it-or-leave-it offer. A worker with firm-specific human capital, which will be pretty useless in any other firm, may face a large drop in productivity and wages if he or she decides to reject the firm's offer. The firm is in a strong bargaining position if it can make separate agreements with each of its workers. In contrast, by presenting a united front, the workers may be able to impose large costs on the firm if they *all* quit. The firm can replace one of its workers but not its whole labour force. Hence the existence of unions evens up the bargaining process.

Once a union is established, its aim is likely to be not merely the protection of its members but successive improvements in their pay and conditions. To be successful the union must be able to restrict the firm's labour supply. If the firm can always hire non-union labour, unions will find it hard to maintain the wage above the level at which the firm can hire non-union workers. This is one reason why unions are keen on closed-shop agreements with individual firms.[9]

A *closed shop* is an agreement that all a firm's workers will be members of a trade union.

We now analyse how unions raise wages by restricting supply. Figure 12-5 shows an industry's downward-sloping labour demand curve DD. The wage in the rest of the economy is W_0, and we assume that the industry faces a perfectly elastic labour supply curve at this wage rate. The labour supply curve to the industry is the horizontal line through W_0. In the absence of unions, equilibrium would occur at E_0 with the employment level N_0.

Now suppose everyone in the industry must belong to a trade union and that the union restricts labour in this industry to N_1. The industry faces a vertical labour supply curve at N_1. Equilibrium occurs at E_1. By sacrificing employment in the industry the union has raised the wage for each employed member from W_0 to W_1. At a higher wage and marginal cost of production, each firm will be forced to raise its price. The full effect of the trade union is not merely to raise wages and lower employment in the industry but also to raise the output price and lower equilibrium output of the industry.

This analysis raises two questions. What determines how far the union will trade off lower employment for higher wages in the industry? And what determines how much

[9] Unions frequently argue that, in the absence of a closed shop, non-union workers will benefit from improvements in pay and conditions achieved through the efforts of the union. Non-union members are getting a 'free ride' without paying their union subscriptions.

Figure 12-5   UNION EFFECT ON WAGES AND EMPLOYMENT. In the absence of a union, the industry would face a horizontal labour supply curve at the wage W_0. Given the industry demand curve DD for labour, equilibrium would occur at E_0. By restricting the industry labour supply to N_1, the union can increase the wage to W_1. It can trade-off lower employment in the industry for higher wages.

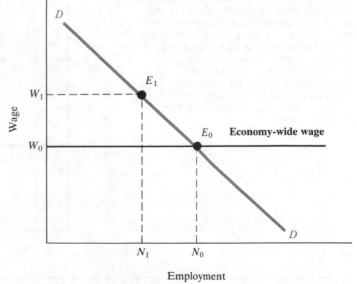

power unions have to control the supply of labour to particular industries?

We begin by assuming that the union has full control over the supply of labour to a firm or an industry. It can trade off employment for wage rises for those members employed. How far it will go in this direction depends on the preferences or tastes of the union and its members. It might try to maximize total income (wage times employment) of its members, or it might try to maximize per capita income (i.e. wages) of those in employment. A lot depends on the power and decision structure within the union.

The more the union cares about its senior members, the more it is likely to maximize the wage independently of what happens to employment. Senior workers have the most firm-specific human capital and are the least likely to be sacked if total employment in the industry must fall. Conversely, the more the union is democratic and the more it cares about its potential members as well as those actually in employment, the less likely is the union to severely restrict employment in order to ensure higher wages for those who remain employed in the industry.

Under what conditions does restricting labour supply by a given amount lead to the largest rise in wages? When the demand for labour is most inelastic. For example, in the UK in the 1970s workers in the electricity supply industry were able to secure very large wage increases. Power stations are very capital-intensive, so the wage bill is a relatively small component of total costs in the industry. Moreover, the consumer demand for electricity is relatively price-inelastic in the short run. For both these reasons, the industry was prepared to meet high wage claims which did not add much to total costs and could in any case be passed on to the consumer.

Figure 12-6 illustrates this general point. In the absence of unions industry equilibrium occurs at E_0, where the horizontal labour supply curve intersects the labour demand curve. DD shows an inelastic labour demand curve and $D'D'$ a more elastic labour demand curve. The more inelastic the labour demand curve, the larger the wage increase a union would secure by restricting labour supply from N_0 to N_1.

Suppose for example that the motor car industry is unionized. Initially the derived demand curve for car workers is quite inelastic, and by restricting employment to N_1 the unions are able to increase car workers' wages from W_0 to W_1. Then Japanese car producers start vigorously competing in the domestic market. Each firm's output demand curve becomes more price-elastic since domestic models must compete with imports. Hence, for the reasons

Figure 12-6   WAGE DIFFERENTIALS AND THE ELASTICITY OF THE DERIVED DEMAND FOR LABOUR. Suppose the union restricts labour supply from N_0 to N_1. It drives up wages in the industry and its members enjoy a wage differential compared with non-union workers elsewhere in the economy. The differential is larger, for any given reduction in industry employment, the more inelastic is the industry demand curve for labour.

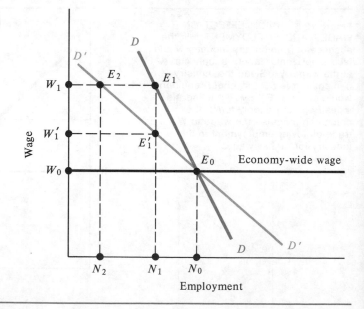

set out in the previous chapter, the derived demand curve for labour by domestic car manufacturers becomes more elastic. It rotates from DD to $D'D'$ in Figure 12-6. At the wage rate W_1 domestic producers lose market share and union employment falls from the level N_1 to the level N_2. Eventually, if the unions wish to maintain employment in the car industry at N_1 they will have to accept a wage cut to W'_1 on the new demand curve for labour $D'D'$.

Unionization and Wage Differentials

In discussing Table 12-2 we pointed out that, in order to establish the effect of union membership on wages, it is necessary not merely to control for personal characteristics such as training, education, and sex, but also to take account of the fact that different jobs and different industries exhibit very different productivity levels, for example because they have very different degrees of capital intensity.

Table 12-5 shows estimates of the union–non-union wage differential after adjusting for all these other factors. It shows how much more an individual union member typically earns than a non-union worker with similar personal characteristics in the same industry. For manufacturing industry as a whole, union members earn 7.7 per cent more than people not belonging to a union but otherwise having the same personal characteristics. Shipbuilding workers in unions do considerably better than non-union workers in the industry. In contrast, workers in the leather and fur industries tend to earn less, other things equal, if they belong to a union.

Table 12-5 Union–non-union differentials in the UK

INDUSTRY	WAGE DIFFERENTIAL
	%
Shipbuilding	18.2
Paper and printing	11.4
Clothing and footwear	10.7
Food, drink, tobacco	6.6
Textiles	6.6
Bricks, cement, glass	2.4
Electrical engineering	2.0
Leather and fur	−0.5

Source: Mark Stewart, 'Relative Earnings and Individual Union Membership in the UK', *Economica*, 1983.

Why does trade union power vary so much across industries? Let's think for a minute. Figure 12-6 identified the slope of the labour demand curve as the key determinant of trade union power to raise wages without too great a loss of employment. In the previous chapter we stressed that the demand for labour is a derived demand which depends on the demand for a firm's output.

Consider first an industry that is not very competitive, with few domestic firms and little foreign competition. Firms in this industry are making substantial supernormal profits. We would expect unions to get their hands on some of these through higher wages which eat into healthy profit margins.

At the other extreme, in a perfectly competitive industry, if a union in a single firm raises wages it will simply drive that firm out of business. Only if the union can organize across *the whole industry*, which can then pass these increases on in part to consumers, does the union stand a chance of raising wages.

In a recent study of a large number of industries, Mark Stewart of Warwick University has shown that this is exactly what happens in practice![10] In competitive industries facing significant foreign competition, unions get no wage differential at all. In industries sheltered from foreign competition but with a large number of domestic firms, union differentials exist only when the whole industry is unionized. But unions get substantial markups in industries with few domestic firms and little foreign competition.

Union Wages as Compensating Differentials

Union wage differentials may arise not only from the successful restrictions of labour supply. Union work has certain characteristics – a structured work setting, inflexibility of hours, employer-set overtime, and a faster work pace – a whole set of conditions of work that might be regarded as unpleasant. Perhaps higher wages in such industries are merely compensating wage differentials for these non-monetary aspects of the job?

[10] See M. Stewart, 'Union Wage Differentials, Product Market Influences and the Division of Rents', Warwick University, 1989.

There are two competing views. The first is that, after unions have taken over and raised relative wages, the firms respond by taking advantage of unions to raise productivity. Work patterns are standardized and the union assists in implementing these new practices. The firms claw back the wage increases by making workers operate in less pleasant but more productive ways.

The alternative view is that the change in work practices is not an employer *response* to a successful union restriction of labour supply to raise wages, but rather the rationale for the union's existence. Unions emerge in industries where large productivity gains would result from the introduction of unpleasant working conditions. The union exists not to restrict labour supply in total, but to negotiate productivity gains, ensuring that workers receive proper compensating differentials for the unpopular changes in working practices that employers find it profitable to introduce. On this view, the unions do not make separate deals for pay and working conditions; rather, their role is to secure pay increases for changes in working conditions.

To sum up, unions probably secure higher wages for their members for two distinct reasons. First, they partially restrict labour supply, deliberately trading off lower employment in the industry for higher wages. But they also play an important role in negotiating changes in working practices, securing mutually agreed changes which leave employers better off because of higher productivity but appropriate part of this gain for the workforce in the form of compensating wage differentials.

Bargaining and Strikes

How serious are strikes? Table 12-6 shows the days of work lost per employee because of industrial disputes in selected countries in the last ten years. Notice that in most countries strikes cost the whole economy less than one workday per employee per year. Even this is probably an overestimate, since employees sometimes work extra overtime after a strike to make up some of the lost production. Nor is the UK the most strike-prone country. It loses more days to strikes than France but less than Italy or Canada. Days lost through industrial disputes have been lower in most countries in the 1980s than in the late 1970s, these four-year averages obscure some considerable annual fluctuations.

Why do strikes occur? Although employers and workers are fighting for a share of the firm's total revenue, it is important to realize that they have a common interest too. If the firm does better, there may be more for employers and workers. Typically the bargaining process between a firm and a union is completed without a strike. If strikes can be avoided, there is potentially more money to divide between the shareholders and the workers.

Given this common interest, why do strikes occur at all? If both parties knew the settlement that would be reached after a strike it would be better to settle immediately on the same share out and avoid the loss of output and revenue that the strike induces. One reason is that one party may misjudge the other's position. As the strike proceeds each party becomes aware that the other had indeed meant what it initially said. Having reassessed the requirements of the other party, it then becomes possible to reach a settlement.

But not all strikes are mistakes that could have been avoided with better initial perceptions of the other side's requirements. Strikes may also occur because of issues of long-term credibility. If a firm believes that the workers will strike unless they get a fair deal, the firm

Table 12-6 Industrial disputes: workdays lost per year per 1000 employees

	FRANCE	USA	UK	CANADA	ITALY
1975–79	210	260	510	940	1510
1980–84	90	160	480	660	950
1985–87	30	150	150	430	360

Source: Department of Employment, *Employment Gazette.*

may offer a fair deal immediately. After a few years of co-operation the firm may begin to feel that the union is a pushover. The union may then strike not merely because of the current issue under dispute, but to remind the firm that it will always strike unless the firm is fair. Thus, one strike might earn the union a fair deal for many years to come because the firm *believes* that the union will strike unless the firm is fair.

Similar considerations apply the other way round.

Summary

1 Different workers get different pay. This reflects personal characteristics such as education, job experience, sex, race, and union status.

2 Skills or human capital are the most important source of wage differentials. Human capital formation includes both formal schooling and on-the-job training. Earnings profiles confirm that workers with more education and training earn higher lifetime incomes.

3 How much more employers are prepared to pay for skilled workers depends on the production technology. In the whole economy the demand for skilled workers depends on the extent to which skilled and unskilled workers can be substituted and on the output demand for industries that use skilled workers relatively intensively.

4 Skilled labour is relatively scarce because it is costly to acquire human capital. For example, education beyond minimum age has not only direct costs but the opportunity cost of earnings forgone by not working immediately. The investment decision for human capital involves comparing the present costs with the present value of the extra income or other benefits in the future.

5 These considerations are reinforced by the role of education as a screening or signalling device, which indicates to employers the workers of innate ability. Thus education has a return to high-ability workers even if it does not directly increase their productivity.

6 Women and non-white workers on average receive lower incomes than white men. Women and non-whites are concentrated in relatively

unskilled jobs with fewer opportunities for promotion. This need not reflect blatant sexism or racism by employers. It may reflect educational or other disadvantages before young workers reach the labour market. It may also reflect a low perceived rate of return by firms on the money spent in training such workers or a low perceived rate of return by such workers on the time spent in education and skill acquisition.

7 Under half the UK labour force now belongs to a trade union. Unions restrict the labour supply to firms or industries, thereby raising wages but lowering employment. Unions move firms up their demand curve for labour.

8 Unions achieve a higher wage differential for their members the more inelastic the demand for labour and the more they are willing or able to restrict the supply of labour. However, some union wage differentials should be viewed as compensating wage differentials, which unions have secured in return for changes in work practices that raise productivity but reduce the pleasantness of the job.

Key Terms

Human capital
Age–earnings profiles
Signalling and screening
Firm-specific human capital
General human capital
Discrimination
Closed shop
Compensating wage differentials

Problems

1 University-educated workers now earn a smaller wage differential than in the 1960s. (*a*) What effect would this have on the incentive to go to university? Why? (*b*) Suppose it was shown that going to university added nothing to life-time income potential. Would anyone still go to university? Why?

2 A worker can earn £20 000 a year for the next 40 years. Alternatively, the worker can take three years off to go on a training course whose fees are £7000 per year. If the government provides an interest-free loan for this training, what future income differential per year would make this a profitable investment in human capital?

3 Suppose economists form a union and establish a certificate that is essential for practising economics. How would this help to raise the relative wage of economists? How would the union restrict entry to the economics profession?

4 Apprentices are typically paid low wages. Using the concept of human capital, explain this observation.

5 Who benefits if there is economic discrimination against women? Why?

6 Show in a diagram of the labour market how a policy of restricting flight time for pilots to a specified monthly maximum number of hours affects the wage differential of unionized pilots. Why is a restriction on the number of working hours an important part of the union's attempt to raise wage differentials for pilots?

7 Common Fallacies Show why the following statements are incorrect: (*a*) Women earn less than men. Employers must be sexists. (*b*) People who study ancient history at university learn nothing about running a business. They would earn higher salaries if they joined companies at the age of eighteen. (*c*) Free schooling between sixteen and eighteen means that children from poor families can stay on in education as easily as children from wealthy families. (*d*) Since many low-paid workers belong to a trade union, this proves that unions have little effect on improving pay and conditions for their members.

13

Capital and Land: Completing the Analysis of Factor Markets

After many years of low investment, most of Europe enjoyed an investment boom in the late 1980s. Industry needed to increase its capital stock – its machinery, equipment, factory and office buildings. The car industry had to invest to compete with heavily mechanized foreign producers, the steel industry had to modernize its capital equipment, and the new growth industries such as information technology needed to invest for future production. Investment adds to the stock of capital in the economy. Thus the emphasis on investment is an emphasis on capital.

In the last two chapters our analysis of factor markets has focused on the factor of production that we call labour. In this chapter we turn our attention to the other factors of production with which labour must co-operate in the productive process. Some issues can be dealt with rather briefly. We have already studied how a firm chooses its production technique in the long run, when all factors can be freely varied, and we are already familiar with the concept of a factor's marginal product. These ideas carry over from the analysis of labour markets to the examination of the markets for other factors of production.

Apart from the irreversible decision to acquire education and skills, many aspects of labour market behaviour can be conveniently analysed within a relatively short-run time horizon. This simplification does not distort the picture too much since labour is the most variable factor of production in the short run. Since it takes much longer to adjust other factor inputs, decisions about their use must necessarily take a longer view. One theme of this chapter will be the role of time and the future in economic behaviour.

In developing this analysis, we confront explicitly the question of how decision makers today should value future benefits and costs. In the context of a firm's investment decision, we show how to discount future payments or receipts to calculate their *present value*.

As the title of the present chapter suggests, our interest in the markets for capital and land goes beyond a curiosity about the equilibrium quantity of capital or the equilibrium price of land. There are two reasons to be interested in how the complete set of factor markets work as a whole. First, firms rarely use a single factor of production in isolation. In studying the labour market we noted that the marginal product of labour schedule would shift up if the firm had a larger quantity of the other factors of production. Decisions about inputs of capital and land thus affect the demand curve for labour and the equilibrium wage rate, just as decisions about labour inputs will feed back upon the demand for other factors of production.

Second, having completed our analysis of factor markets, we shall be able to discuss what determines the *income distribution* in an economy. The price of a factor multiplied by the total quantity of the factor employed gives us the earnings or income of that factor. We need to know the prices and quantities of all productive factors if we are to understand how the economy's total income is distributed.

We conclude this chapter by pulling together our analysis in Chapters 11–13 to examine the income distribution in the UK. We shall distinguish two measures of income distribution, *functional* and *personal*.

The *functional income distribution* tells us how an economy's total income is divided between the different factors of production. For example it tells us the share going to labour through wages and salaries and the share going to landowners through property rents.

Understanding the functional income distribution might allow us to determine whether trade unions have secured a larger share of the national cake at the expense of profits or rents earned by landowners. But an individual may supply the services of several different factors of production. Individuals may supply labour services through work, capital services by renting out machinery which they own, and the services of land by renting out property.

The *personal income distribution* tells us how national income is divided between different individuals, regardless of the factor services from which they earn their income.

The personal income distribution tells us whether some people are much better off than others.

Having indicated the topics we shall cover in this chapter, we begin by defining our terms. We concentrate on the factors of production that economists call capital and land.

Physical capital is the stock of produced goods that contribute to the production of other goods and services.

The stock of physical capital includes the assembly line machinery used to make cars, railway lines that produce transport services, school buildings that produce education services, dwellings that produce housing services, and even household consumer durables such as television sets that produce entertainment services.

Physical capital is distinguished from land by the fact that the former is produced.

Land is the factor of production that nature supplies.

Clearly, this distinction between land and capital can become blurred. By applying labour to extract weeds or fertilizer to improve the soil balance, farmers can 'produce' better land. Because land and capital are sometimes hard to disentangle we discuss these two factors of production in the same chapter. Nevertheless, the distinction is often useful, as we shall see.

In Chapter 7 we introduced the idea of *depreciation*, the extent to which an asset or

durable good is used up within the time period over which we study and measure the production of goods and services. Capital and land are both assets. They do not completely depreciate during the time period, say a month or a year, during which we examine production decisions by firms.

Together, capital and land make up the *tangible wealth* of the economy. They are wealth or assets because they are durable. They are tangible because they are physical goods which we could literally touch. Financial wealth, such as a sum of money in the bank, is not tangible wealth. It cannot directly produce goods and services though it can be used to purchase factors of production which can produce goods and services. Similarly, we must distinguish between the firm's *physical* capital – its plant, machinery, and buildings, which henceforth we refer to simply as 'capital' – and its *financial* capital, the money and paper assets that it owns.

13-1 Physical Capital

Table 13-1 shows the level and composition of physical capital in the UK in 1987. 'Dwellings' are primarily owned by private individuals, but council housing provided by the state through local authorities accounts for about a quarter of the housing stock. 'Plant and machinery' is industrial equipment, for example, assembly lines and office equipment. 'Other buildings and works' include office blocks, warehouses, factories, and other outputs of the construction

Table 13-1 UK physical capital in 1987
(£ billion at 1987 prices)

	VALUE	% OF TOTAL
Road vehicles	48.7	2.9
Trains, ships, and aircraft	15.9	0.9
Plant and machinery	455.1	27.1
Other buildings and works	546.8	32.7
Dwellings	524.7	31.4
Inventories	84.3	5.0
Total	1675.5	100.0

Source: CSO, *UK National Accounts*.

industry. 'Inventories' are stocks of manufactured goods awaiting sale, partially finished goods (work in progress), and stocks of raw materials held for future production. Inventories are part of the capital stock because they are produced goods which contribute to future production.

To assess how physical capital is combined with labour in the production process, and how this is changing over time, Table 13-2 examines measures of physical capital after subtracting dwellings. The first row shows physical capital used in production (CP) in the UK in 1977 and 1987. The second row shows the ratio of CP to real national output. The capital input to the production process is approximately four times the value of annual national output. The final row shows that the quantity of capital available per employed worker rose from £40 200 to £51 800 (at 1985 prices) between 1977 and 1987.

Table 13-2 confirms that investment in physical capital is increasing the capital input to the UK's national production, not only in absolute terms but also relative to the number of workers employed. Even over a period as short as a decade, there has been a significant change in production techniques. The economy is becoming more *capital-intensive*. Each worker has more and more real capital with which to work.

In practice, it is difficult to measure the stock of capital exactly. Capital depreciates over time. It wears out, becoming less productive and less valuable. The official statistics estimate as best they can the rate at which depreciation occurs. Because capital depreciates, it takes some investment in new capital goods merely to stand still.

Gross investment is the production of new capital goods and the improvement of existing capital goods. *Net investment* is gross investment minus the depreciation of the existing capital stock.

If net investment is positive, gross investment more than compensates for depreciation and the effective capital stock is increasing. However, very small levels of gross investment may fail to keep pace with depreciation and the capital stock will then be falling over time. In the next few sections we concentrate on capital, the produced goods that are inputs to subsequent production. Later in the chapter we discuss the special features of the input that economists call 'land'.

13-2 Rentals, Interest Rates, and Asset Prices

To clarify our discussion of capital we use Table 13-3 to emphasize two crucial distinctions: between *stocks* and *flows*, and between *rental payments* and *asset prices*. We begin with the example of labour input that we studied in the last two chapters.

The labour market trades a commodity called 'hours of labour services'. The corresponding price is the hourly wage rate. Rather loosely, we sometimes call this the 'price of labour' or the 'price of one of the factors of production'. Strictly speaking, the hourly wage is the *rental payment* that firms pay to hire an hour of labour. There is no *asset* price for the durable physical asset called a 'worker' because modern societies do not allow slavery, the institution by which firms actually own workers. It is because we need not discuss slavery that we are sometimes rather careless in distinguishing between the price of labour and the rental payment to labour.[1]

Since capital can be bought and sold – there are markets for new and used vehicles and buildings – we shall have to be more careful.

A *stock* is the quantity of an asset at point in time, such as 100 machines on 1 January

---

Table 13-2 Capital input to UK production

	1977	1987
Capital input to production (CP)*	910	1131
CP/national output	3.9	3.9
CP per employed worker*	40.2	51.8

* CP and national output are measured in £ billion at 1985 prices. CP per employed worker is measured in £ thousand at 1985 prices.
Source: CSO, *UK National Accounts*; Department of Employment, *Employment Gazette*.

---

[1] In a slave society, the asset price of labour would be the market price at which slaves were bought and sold. Robert Fogel and Stanley Engerman give data on slaves prices in the United States in the nineteenth century in *Time on the Cross*, Little, Brown, 1974.

Table 13-3 Stock and flow concepts

	CAPITAL	LABOUR
Productive contribution	Flow of capital services (machine hours/week)	Flow of labour services (labour hours/week)
Payment for service flow	Rental rate (£/machine hour)	Wage rate (£/labour hour)
Asset price	Price of a unit of capital stock (£/machine)	None, except under slavery when £/slave

1990. A *flow* is the stream of services that an asset provides during a given interval, such as 40 labour hours per week per person.

The distinction between rental payments and asset prices follows immediately from this distinction between stocks and flows.

The cost of using capital services is the *rental rate* for capital.

For example, travellers pay a rental rate to hire a car for the weekend. Building contractors pay a rental rate to lease earth-moving equipment or office space for their managers. Sometimes there is no rental or leasing market for a type of capital good. It is impossible to rent a power station. When firms make a once-and-for-all purchase of a capital asset or stock they must calculate how much it is implicitly costing them day by day to *use* their capital. We return to this question in Section 13-4.

Unlike labour, capital goods can be purchased and have an asset price.

The price of an asset is the sum for which the stock can be purchased outright. By owning a capital asset the purchaser acquires title to the future stream of capital services that the stock will provide.

Buying a car for £9000 entitles a household to a stream of future transport services. Buying a factory for £100 000 entitles the owner to a stream of future rental payments on the capital services that the factory provides.

What will a purchaser be prepared to pay for a capital asset? Clearly, the answer depends on the value of the rental payments that will be paid in the future for the capital services that the asset stock provides. Can we simply add together the future rental payments over the life of the capital asset to calculate its current asset price or value? Not quite.

We have to pay more attention to the role of *time* and *interest payments*.

Interest and Present Values

Suppose a lender makes a loan to a borrower. At the outset the borrower agrees to pay the initial sum (the principal) *with interest* at some future date. If the loan is £100 for one year at 10 per cent interest per annum, the borrower must repay £110 at the end of the year. The extra £10 (10 per cent of £100) is the interest cost of borrowing £100 for a year. *Interest rates* are usually quoted as a percentage per annum. Thus, an interest rate of 20 per cent means that the borrower must pay an additional annual payment of 20 per cent of the principal at the end of the loan contract.

Suppose we lent £1 and re-lent the interest as it accrued. The first row of Table 13-4 shows what would happen if the interest rate were 10 per cent per annum. After one year we should have £1 plus an interest payment of £0.10. Re-lending the whole £1.10, we should have £1.21 by the end of the second year. The concept of *compound interest* reminds us that the absolute amount by which our money grows increases every year. The first year we increase our money by £0.10, which is 10 per cent of £1. Since we re-lend the interest, our money grows by £0.11 in the next year since we earn 10 per cent on £0.10. If we lend for yet another year, our money will grow by £0.121 to £1.331 at the end of the third year.

At 10 per cent interest per annum, £1 on year 0 is worth £1.10 in year 1 and £1.21 in year 2. Now let us ask the question the other way round. If we offered you £1.21 in two years' time, what sum today would be just as valuable? The answer is £1. If you had £1 today you could always lend it out to get exactly £1.21 in two years' time. The second row of Table 13-4

Table 13-4 Lending, interest, and present values

	YEAR 0	YEAR 1	YEAR 2	INTEREST RATE
Value of £1 lent today in:	£1	£1.10	£1.21	10%
Present value of £1 earned in:	£1	£0.91	£0.83	
Value of £1 lent today in:	£1	£1.05	£1.10	5%
Present value of £1 earned in:	£1	£0.95	£0.91	

extends this general idea. If £1.21 in year 2 is worth £1 today, then £1 in year 2 must be worth £1/1.21 = £0.83 today. £0.83 today could be lent out at 10 per cent interest to accumulate to £1 in year 2. Similarly, £1 in year 1 is worth only £1/1.10 = £0.91 today.

> The present value of £1 at some future date is the sum that, if lent out today, would accumulate to £1 by that future date.

The law of compound interest implies that lending £1 today accumulates to ever larger sums the further into the future we maintain the loan and re-lend the interest. Conversely, the present value of £1 earned at some future date becomes smaller and smaller the further into the future the date at which the £1 is earned.

The present value of a future payment also depends on the interest rate. The third row of Table 13-4 shows that a loan of £1 will accumulate less rapidly over time if the interest rate is lower. At 5 per cent interest a loan of £1 cumulates to only £1.10 after two years, compared with £1.21 after two years when the interest rate was 10 per cent in row 1. Hence the fourth row of Table 13-4 shows that the present value of £1 in year 1 or year 2 is larger when the interest rate is only 5 per cent than in the corresponding entry in row 2 where the interest rate is 10 per cent.

Figure 13-1 makes the same points in a diagram. It shows how lending £1 today would accumulate at compound interest rates of 5 and 10 per cent. After 10 years the loan fund is worth £2.59 at 10 per cent interest but only £1.62 at 5 per cent interest. Higher interest rates imply more rapid accumulation through lending. The same diagram can be used to work out present values. A payment of £2.59 in 10 years' time has a present value of £1 if the interest rate is 10 per cent. Thus the present value of £1 in 10 years' time is £1/2.59 = £0.386. However, if interest rates are only 5 per cent the value of £1 in 10 years' time is £1/1.62 = £0.617.

Using interest rate to calculate present values of future payments tells us the right way to add together payments at different points in time. For each payment at each date we calculate its present value. Then we add together the present values of the different payments.

Now we see how the price of a capital asset should be related to the stream of future payments that will be earned from the capital

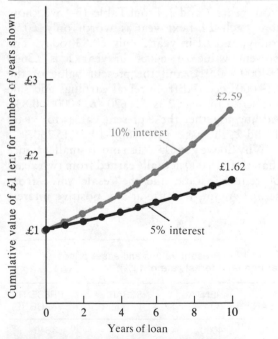

Figure 13-1 ACCUMULATION THROUGH INTEREST. At 10 per cent interest per annum, £1 accumulates to 1.59 after 10 years. At the lower interest rate of 5 per cent per annum, the accumulated interest value rises much more slowly, reaching only £1.62 after 10 years.

services it provides. We calculate the present value of the rental payment earned by the asset in each year of its working life and add these present values together. This tells us what the asset is worth today. In equilibrium it should be the asset price. If you can buy an asset for a lower price than the present value of its future stream of rental earnings, you have got a good deal. Unfortunately, others are likely to reach the same conclusion. If you all try to buy the asset you will bid up its price. Where does the process end? When the asset price equals the present value of the stream of future rental earnings and the equilibrium price is reached.

Valuing an Asset: An Example

How much would you bid for a machine that earns £4000 in rental for two years and can then be sold for scrap for £10 000? If you bid anything before asking what the interest rate is you have not understood the previous section! Suppose the interest rate is 10 per cent per annum. The first two rows of Table 13-5 show the money received in each year. The final column shows the present value of receipts from years 1 and 2. From Table 13-4 we know that each £1 next year is worth only £0.91 today, and £1 in year 2 only £0.83 today. The present value of £4000 in year 1 is £3640 (£4000 × 0.91), and the present value of the £14 000 received from rental earnings and sale for scrap in year 2 is £11 620 (£14 000 × 0.83). Adding together these present values for years 1 and 2, the asset price should be £15 260.

Why do we get £15 260, a much smaller figure than the £18 000 actually earned from two years of rental income and the resale value from scrap? Again, because at any positive interest

Table 13-5 Present values and asset prices (at annual interest rate of 10%)

YEAR	RENTAL (£)	SCRAP VALUE (£)	PRESENT VALUE (£)
1	4000		3 640
2	4000 +	10 000	11 620
Asset price			15 260

Note: From Table 13-4, the present value of each £1 in year 1 is £0.91 and in year 2 is £0.83.

rate £1 tomorrow is worth less than £1 today. £1 today would accumulate to more than £1 tomorrow. We convert future payments to current values by *discounting* the future.

A useful way to understand the role of interest rates in present-value calculations is to realize that the interest rate represents the *opportunity cost* of the money used to buy the asset. The same money could have been lent to a bank or a building society to earn interest. At an interest rate of 10 per cent per annum a payment next year of £110 has a present value of £100 today. We would not bid more than £100 today for the entitlement of £110 next year because we can get at least £110 next year by lending £100 to a bank today.

The principles we have outlined can be used to calculate the present value of any future income stream once the interest rate is known. We go into more detail in the appendix to this chapter. It turns out that the calculation is particularly simple in one special case, when the asset lasts for ever and the income stream per time period is constant. For example, governments sometimes borrow by selling a *perpetuity*, a bond (simply a piece of paper) promising to pay the owner a constant interest payment (called the 'coupon') for ever. In the UK these are called 'consols' (after a famous bond issue called Consolidated Stock). The present value of a consol, the price the stock market will offer for this piece of paper, obeys the simple formula

$$\frac{\text{Present value}}{\text{of a perpetuity}} = \frac{\text{constant coupon payment per annum}}{\text{interest rate per annum}} \quad (1)$$

If you look in the financial pages of a newspaper you will find $2\frac{1}{2}$ per cent consols. This perpetuity promises to pay £2.50 per annum for ever. (£2.50 was $2\frac{1}{2}$ per cent of the price the government happened to sell the bonds for many years ago.) Suppose the current rate of interest is 10 per cent. You should find that $2\frac{1}{2}$ per cent consols are worth around £25 (£2.5, the annual coupon, divided by 0.1, the annual interest rate expressed as a decimal fraction).

If interest rates fall to 5 per cent per annum the $2\frac{1}{2}$ per cent consols will be worth £50 (= £2.5 divided by 0.05). Although government bonds are pieces of financial paper and not physical capital, exactly the same principles of present values apply. Calculating present values and asset prices of real capital goods is more difficult than for government bonds. Whereas the latter have a known future coupon or rental payment, the rental rates on physical capital in the future will depend on the state of the economy, the level of production, and so on. Nevertheless, the level of production, and so on. Nevertheless, the formula given in equation (1) may provide a useful approximation in calculating the asset price of some long-lived physical asset such as land if the annual rental is expected to remain roughly constant over time.

Real and Nominal Interest Rates: Inflation and Present Values

Thus far we have discussed future payments valued in nominal terms. For example, the first column of Table 13-5 shows rental receipts in actual pounds without any adjustment for inflation between years. Similarly, the interest rate of 10 per cent tells us how many actual pounds we will earn by lending £1 for a year.

> The *nominal interest rate* tells us how many actual pounds will be earned in interest by lending £1 for one year.

At a nominal interest rate of 10 per cent, £100 lent today will accumulate to £110 by next year. But we may well be interested in how many goods that £110 will then buy.

> The *real interest rate* measures the return on a loan as the increase in goods that can be purchased rather than as the increase in the nominal or the money value of the loan fund.

The distinction between nominal and real interest rates is very important. Suppose the nominal interest rate is 10 per cent and inflation is 6 per cent, so that goods prices rise by 6 per cent each year. Lending £1 for a year gives us £1.10, but after a year it also costs us £1.06 to buy the goods we could have bought for £1 today. With £1.10 to spend next year, we can increase the number of goods we can purchase by only 4 per cent. We say that the real interest rate is 4 per cent because that is the number of extra goods we can buy next year as a result of lending our money for a year.[2] Thus we can use the general formula

$$\text{Real interest rate} = \text{inflation adjusted interest rate}$$
$$= \text{nominal interest rate} - \text{inflation rate} \quad (2)$$

To confirm this formula, let us try a second example. Nominal interest rates are 17 per cent and the inflation rate is 20 per cent. Lending £100 for a year, you can have £117. But it will cost you £120 to buy the goods you could have bought this year for £100. You are actually worse off by delaying purchases for a year and lending out your money at the apparently high rate of 17 per cent. In fact, real interest rates are *negative*. Equation (2) says that the real interest rate is $(17 - 20)$ per cent $= -3$ per cent. In real terms it is *costing* you to be a lender. The nominal interest you receive will not compensate for rises in the prices of goods you ultimately wish to purchase.

What Determines the Real Interest Rate?

Most lenders and borrowers are capable of working out the real interest rate involved in a loan agreement. Do we expect real interest rates to be positive or negative? There are two forces that tend to lead to positive real interest rates, though a full discussion of these will have to wait until Chapter 19.

First, people are impatient by nature. Given the choice of an equal number of goods tomorrow or today, they would rather have them today. To delay spending on goods and services, lenders usually have to be bribed with a positive real interest rate which allows them to consume *more* goods in the future if they postpone consumption and lend today. But wanting a positive real interest rate is not enough; there also has to be a way of earning positive real returns, or borrowers would never wish to borrow. Investing in physical capital is

---

[2] In fact, the real interest rate is a little less than 4 per cent. We have £0.04 extra to spend next year after allowing for the rise in goods prices. But each good is 1.06 times as expensive as this year. We can increase the number of goods purchased by only $0.04/1.06 = 0.0377$. Thus, the true real interest rate is 3.77 per cent. However the difference between 3.77 per cent and 4 per cent is tiny compared with the difference between the nominal interest rate of 10 per cent and our simple estimate of 4 per cent for the real interest rate. In practice, economists use the simpler estimate of 4 per cent for the real interest rate rather than the more sophisticated estimate of 3.77 per cent.

a way of making a real return even after paying back interest. Thus borrowers are willing to pay positive real interest rates because they can find investment opportunities in physical capital goods that provide a stream of returns more than sufficient to meet the interest cost.

Impatience to consume and the productivity of physical capital are thus the two forces that lead us to expect a positive real interest rate. Table 13-6 shows data on nominal interest rates, inflation, and real interest rates over the last two decades. The table confirms the pattern found in many countries in many decades. Real interest rates are usually small and positive though they can occasionally be negative. Since real interest rates change only a little, it follows that large changes in nominal interest rates occur specifically to offset large changes in inflation rates, thus preserving real interest rates in their normal range as determined by the forces of impatience and capital productivity. The simple proposition that a 1 per cent increase in inflation will be matched by a 1 per cent increase in nominal interest rates to leave real interest rates unchanged is a pretty useful rule of thumb.

What is the implication of this distinction between nominal and real interest rates for the calculation of present values? It is necessary only to be consistent. If we wish to calculate the present value of a future payment expressed in nominal terms, we should use the discount factor based on the current nominal interest rate. However, if the future payment is expressed in real terms, we should use a discount factor based on the real interest rate.

What we must not do is confuse the two. The following is quite a common mistake. You want to buy a farm whose rental this year is £10 000. Today's interest rate is 20 per cent. You reckon that the farm's output, and hence its rental,

should not change much over time. Hence you apply the formula of equation (1) for a perpetuity, divide £10 000 by 0.2, and get £50 000. The farmer is asking a price of £100 000 for the farm so you decide not to buy. The present value of the rental stream is only £50 000.

You have just missed a financial killing. Current interest rates are 20 per cent only because the market believes that inflation on average will be something like 17 per cent, leaving a real interest rate of 3 per cent. Doing the calculation in real terms at constant prices, we should divide £10 000 for ever by 0.03 to obtain £333 000 as the correct price for the farm. Equivalently, if we wish to calculate in nominal terms, we can use discount factors based on the 20 per cent nominal interest rate, but we must remember that the likely inflation rate of around 17 per cent will steadily increase the nominal farm rental over time. If we do this calculation, we shall again conclude that at £100 000 asking price the farm is a real bargain. Would you have got the right answer?

13-3 The Demand for Capital Services

The analysis of the demand for capital services by an industry closely parallels the analysis of labour demand in Chapter 11. The rental rate for capital takes the place of the hourly wage rate. Each represents the cost of employing or using factor services. We emphasize the *use* of *services* of capital. The example to bear in mind is a firm renting a vehicle or leasing office space.

We begin the demand for capital services by a firm. As with labour, the firm considers how much one more hour of capital services will add to the value of the firm's output.

Table 13-6 Nominal and real interest rates and inflation in the UK (% per annum)

	1961	1966	1971	1976	1981	1985	1988
Nominal interest rate	6.3	6.9	8.9	14.4	13.8	10.6	10.3
Inflation rate	3.9	3.9	9.4	16.5	11.9	6.1	5.3
Real interest rate	2.4	3.0	−0.5	−2.1	1.9	4.5	5.0

Source: CSO, *Economic Trends*; IMF, *International Financial Statistics.*

The *marginal value product of capital* is the increase in the value of the firm's output when one more unit of capital services is employed.

As in our discussion of labour in Chapter 11, we can generalize our analysis to the case where the firm has monopoly power in its output market or monopsony power in its input markets. Having discussed that extension in Chapter 11, we confine our discussion of capital services to the simpler case in which the firm is competitive.

Given the amounts of labour (and any other factor, such as land) that the firm employs, the marginal value product of capital $MVPK$ declines as the amount of capital per worker increases. Although the firm's output price is fixed since it is competitive, the marginal physical product of capital is subject to diminishing returns. Figure 13-2 shows a downward-sloping $MVPK$ curve just like the $MVPL$ curve in Chapter 11.

Suppose the firm can rent units of capital at the rental rate R_0. For example, we can think of this as the monthly payment for leasing an office. The firm will rent capital up to the point at which its marginal cost – the rental rate – equals its marginal value product. It will demand K_0 units of capital services at the rental rate R_0.

For a given price and quantity of other factors of production, $MVPK$ is the firm's demand curve for capital services. For any rental rate we can read off the profit-maximizing level of capital services from the $MVPK$ curve. As with the firm's $MVPL$ curve, showing its labour demand, the firm's $MVPK$ curve showing its capital demand curve can be shifted outwards by one of three things: (1) an increase in its output price, which makes the marginal *physical* product of capital more valuable, (2) an increase in the level of other factors (chiefly labour) with which capital works to produce output, thus increasing the marginal physical product of capital and hence its marginal value product, and (3) a technical advance, which increases the physical productivity of capital for any given quantity of other factor inputs.

The Industry Demand Curve for Capital Services

As with labour, we can move from the firm's demand for capital services to the industry demand curve for capital services by horizontally adding the marginal value product of each firm. As in Figure 11-4, which added together the $MVPL$ curves of each firm to obtain the industry demand curve for labour, again we must recognize that, in expanding output, the industry will bid down the equilibrium price of its output.

Thus the industry demand curve for capital services is steeper than the horizontal sum of each firm's $MVPK$ curves. The industry demand curve recognizes that output prices will change when industry output is changed. The more inelastic is the demand curve for the industry's output the more inelastic will be the industry's derived demand curve for capital services.

13-4 The Supply of Capital Services

Capital services are produced by capital assets. Owning or renting a machine allows a firm to use the input machine-hours. The economist's

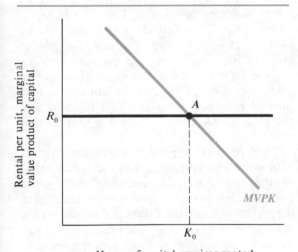

Figure 13-2   THE DEMAND FOR CAPITAL SERVICES. Diminishing marginal productivity implies a falling $MVPK$ schedule as capital input is increased holding constant the quantity of other inputs. At any given rental, the firm hires capital services up to the point which the rental per unit equals the $MVPK$. Thus the $MVPK$ curve is also the firm's demand curve for capital services. For example, at a rental rate R_0 the firm will hire K_0 capital services.

approach to capital is first to analyse the market for capital services used in production, then to consider what this implies for the market for machines themselves. In so doing, we usually assume that the flow of capital services is directly determined by the stock of capital assets such as machines.

It should be remembered that this is only a first approximation. By working overtime shifts, a firm can alter the effective flow of machine services it gets from a given machine bolted to the factory floor. Even if firms cannot quickly change the stock of machines, it may thus be possible to vary, at least in part, the flow of capital services derived from these assets, even in the short run.

Nevertheless, in normal times firms have only a limited ability to vary the flow of capital services that can be extracted from a given capital stock. We shall understand the most important features of the market for capital if we assume that the flow of capital services is essentially determined by the stock of capital available. We must now distinguish between the long run and the short run, and between the supply of capital services to the whole economy and to a particular industry.

The Short-run Supply of Capital Services

In the short run the total supply of capital assets (machines, buildings, and vehicles), and thus the services they provide, is fixed to the economy as a whole. It takes time to change the capital stock. New factories cannot be built overnight. For the whole economy, it makes sense to think of the supply of capital services as fixed in the short run. The supply curve is vertical at a quantity determined by the existing stock of capital assets.

Some types of capital are fixed even for the individual industry. The steel industry cannot change overnight its number of blast furnaces. However, some industries may be able to increase their supply of some types of capital, even in the short run. By offering a higher rental rate for delivery vans, the supermarket industry can attract a larger share of the total quantity of delivery vans that the economy currently possesses. For such types of capital services the industry faces an upward-sloping supply curve. By offering a higher rental rate the industry can increase the supply of delivery van services to that industry.

The Supply of Capital Services in the Long Run

In the long run the total quantity of capital in the economy can be varied. New machines and factories can be built to increase the capital stock. Conversely, with no new investment in capital goods the existing capital stock will depreciate and be effectively reduced. Similarly, individual industries can adjust their stocks of capital.

The Required Rental on Capital   To discuss the supply side of the market for capital, we consider the rental rates at which owners or potential owners of capital would be willing to buy or build.

> The *required rental on capital* is the rental rate that just allows the owner of capital to cover the opportunity cost of owning the capital.

Suppose you want to borrow from a bank to buy a machine to be rented out as business. The machine costs £10 000, which you have to borrow. How much must the machine earn if you are to break even as a machine services supplier? First you have to cover the interest cost. Suppose the *real*, or inflation-adjusted, interest rate is 5 per cent. You have to pay the bank £500 (£10 000 × 0.05) a year in real terms.

Then you have expenditure on maintenance. You must also recognize that the resale value of the machine is depreciating each year. Suppose that in real terms maintenance and depreciation cost you £1000 per annum. This is 10 per cent of the purchase price, and we say the depreciation rate is 10 per cent per annum. Thus your annual cost of renting out a machine in working order is

$$\begin{aligned}
\frac{\text{Annual}}{\text{cost}} &= \frac{\text{interest}}{\text{cost}} + \frac{\text{maintenance and}}{\text{depreciation}} \\
&= \frac{\text{asset}}{\text{price}} \times \left\{\frac{\text{interest}}{\text{rate}} + \frac{\text{depreciation}}{\text{rate}}\right\} \\
&= £10\,000 \times (0.05 + 0.1) \\
&= £1500
\end{aligned} \qquad (3)$$

The required rental if you are to break even must therefore be £1500 at constant prices. Frequently we show the required rental as a percentage of the purchase price of the capital good. In this example the required *real rate of return* is 15 per cent per annum.[3] It is worth borrowing from a bank to buy a machine if, after allowing for inflation, its rental is at least £1500 per annum. You will at least cover the costs, including interest and depreciation, of being in the business of renting out machines.[4]

What Determines the Required Rental? Equation (3) shows that the required rental rate or cost of capital depends on three things: the price of the capital good, the real interest rate, and the depreciation rate. Depreciation depends largely on technology; on how fast the machine wears out with use and age. The real interest rate is determined by economy-wide forces, and we have seen in Table 13-6 that it changes only slowly. Treating the depreciation rate and the real interest rate as given, we examine how the purchase price of capital goods affects the required rental on capital.

The Long-run Supply Curve for the Economy
In the long run, a given quantity of capital services is supplied to the economy only if it earns the required rental. If it earns more, people will build new capital goods. If it earns less, owners of capital will allow their goods to depreciate without building new ones.

Figure 13-3 shows the long-run supply curve of capital services to the economy. Imagine that these are industries that produce capital goods. For example, the construction industry produces buildings and the motor industry produces container lorries. Each industry has an upward-sloping supply curve. The higher the

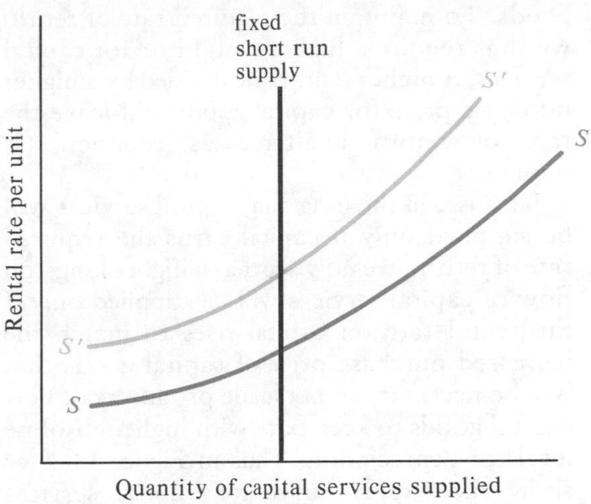

Figure 13-3 THE SUPPLY OF CAPITAL SERVICES TO THE ECONOMY. In the short run, the stock of capital goods, and the services they supply, is fixed by past investment decisions. New capital goods cannot be produced overnight. In the long run, a higher rental rate is required to call forth a higher supply of capital services and a permanently higher capital stock. The higher rental rate just offsets the higher price for capital goods required to induce higher output of new capital goods to match the higher total depreciation of a larger capital stock. Thus the required rate of return is met at all points on *SS*. If real interest rates increase, the required rate of return will also increase to match the opportunity cost of funds tied up in capital goods. Hence the long-run supply curve of capital services shifts up to *S'S'* providing a higher rental at each level of the capital stock and its corresponding purchase price. Each point on *S'S'* matches the new required rate of return.

price of the capital good, the more the capital goods producing industry will choose to supply.

In the long run there can be a larger flow of capital services only if there is a permanently higher capital stock. But capital depreciates. The higher the capital stock the larger will be the total amount of depreciation. With a 10 per cent depreciation rate, the depreciation per annum on a stock of £200 million is £20 million or twice the depreciation of £10 million per annum on a capital stock of only £100 million. Thus, a higher long-run flow of capital services requires a permanently higher capital stock, which in turn requires a higher flow of new capital goods to offset depreciation and maintain the capital stock intact.

But producers of new capital goods will require a higher price for capital goods if they

---

[3] To simplify the calculation, we assumed that both the machine and the bank loan last for ever. You may be wondering if equation (3) has any connection with our earlier discussion of the present value of a perpetuity. Equation (1) said that the price p of a perpetuity should equal the annual payment c divided by the required rate of return r that lenders could get by lending to a bank. If $p = c/r$, then $r = c/p$. Equation (3) says that when c is the annual cost and p is the initial price of a machine, you need a rate of return $r = c/p$ to decide to go into the business of renting out machines.

[4] If the firm using the capital services also owns the capital good, the required rental is the cost the firm should charge itself for using the capital when calculating economic costs. You might like to refer back to our discussion of accounting costs and economic costs in Chapter 7.

are to produce a larger quantity of new capital goods. To maintain the required rate of return we thus require a higher rental rate for capital services. A higher rental rate divided by a higher purchase price for capital goods will leave the rate of return unaltered as equation (3) implies.

Because, in the long run, capital services will be supplied only if capital earns the required rate of return, we now see that a higher long-run flow of capital services will be supplied only if the rental rate on capital rises to match the increased purchase price of capital goods that will be necessary to persuade producers of new capital goods to keep pace with higher absolute levels of depreciation. Thus in Figure 13-3 we show the supply curve for capital services sloping upwards in the long run when plotted against the rental rate on capital.

We draw the upward-sloping supply curve for capital services SS for a given real interest rate. What happens if the real interest rate increases? Equation (3) says that, for a given purchase price of capital goods, the required rental must increase. Suppliers of capital services need a higher return to offset the higher opportunity cost of the money they tie up in purchasing capital goods. Unless the rental rate rises the required rate of return cannot rise to match the increase in the opportunity cost of funds, namely the real interest rate.

Hence, in Figure 13-3 we show the effect of an increase in real interest rates as shifting upwards the long-run supply curve for capital services, from SS to $S'S'$. At each level of capital services, and the corresponding price of capital goods necessary to persuade producers of new capital goods to produce just enough to maintain the corresponding capital stock intact in spite of depreciation, the rental rate on capital services, and hence the rate of return, is now higher.

The Long-run Supply Curve for the Industry
Again, our discussion parallels the discussion of labour supply in Chapter 11. The preceding analysis determines the supply of capital services to the whole economy. In the long run a very tiny industry can obtain as much of this capital as it wishes, provided it pays the going rental rate. A larger industry may have to pay an increasing rental rate per unit of capital

services the larger the fraction of the economy-wide supply it wishes to attract. Thus an industry whose use of capital is significant relative to the whole economy will face an upward-sloping supply curve for capital services.

In the next section, we analyse only the case of a small industry facing a horizontal long-run supply curve for capital services at the going rental per unit. The analysis is easily extended to the case of an upward-sloping long-run supply curve for capital services for the industry.

13-5 Equilibrium and Adjustment in the Market for Capital Services

Figure 13-4 shows the market for capital services for an industry. Long-run equilibrium occurs at E, where the horizontal supply curve SS crosses the industry demand curve DD derived from firms' $MVPK$ curves. The industry employs K_0 capital services and pays the going rental per unit R_0.

Adjustments in the Market for Capital Services

Suppose workers in this industry now secure a wage increase. If you mastered Chapter 11 you

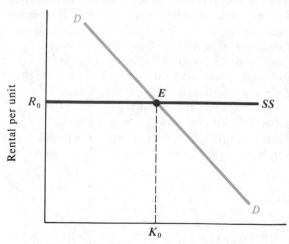

Figure 13-4 EQUILIBRIUM IN THE MARKET FOR CAPITAL SERVICES. The industry faces a long-run horizontal supply curve SS. It must pay the going rental for capital services. DD is the industry demand curve derived from individual firms' $MVPK$ curves. Equilibrium for the industry occurs at E with a quantity K_0 of capital services.

should already be able to analyse the long-run effect on the quantity of capital services demanded by the industry.

In the long run all factors of production can be freely varied. A higher wage rate will have a *substitution effect* and an *output effect*. A higher wage rate increases the cost of labour services relative to capital services. The substitution effect leads firms in the industry to switch to more capital-intensive techniques in order to economize on labour that is now more expensive. This effect tends to increase the quantity of capital services demanded at any rental rate.

But there is also an output effect. By raising the total cost and marginal cost of producing output, a wage increase causes an upward shift in the industry supply curve for output and reduces the quantity of output supplied. This tends to reduce the quantity of all factors demanded by the industry. The more elastic is the demand curve for the industry's output, the more a given upward shift in its supply curve will reduce the equilibrium quantity of output and the larger will be the output effect on the quantity of capital demanded.

This analysis is based on our discussion of the choice of technique in the text and appendix of Chapter 11. It concludes that a wage increase is more likely to reduce the demand for capital services the more elastic is the industry's output demand curve. We can reach the same conclusion by arguing directly from marginal product schedules.

We draw the marginal product of capital schedule for a given quantity of other factors including labour. A rise in the wage rate will reduce the quantity of labour demanded. This effect tends to cause a leftward shift in the marginal value product of capital by reducing the marginal physical product of capital, which now has less labour with which to work. However, a wage increase also shifts the industry supply curve upwards and raises the equilibrium price for the industry's output. This tends to increase the marginal value product of capital and shift the schedule to the right. This effect will be smaller the more elastic is the demand curve for the industry's output. Again, we reach the conclusion that the demand for capital services is more likely to shift to the left the more elastic is the demand curve for the output of the industry.

Short-run and Long-run Adjustment

The above analysis applied only in the long run when the industry can completely adjust to the wage increase. Figure 13-5 examines short-run and long-run adjustment to a wage increase for the case in which the long-run effect is to shift the demand curve for capital services inwards from DD to $D'D'$.

Originally the industry was in equilibrium at E. Overnight, capital is a fixed factor and the industry supply of capital services is vertical at the initial quantity K_0. Thus, when the demand curve first shifts from DD to $D'D'$, the firm cannot immediately respond by cutting its input of capital services. With a vertical short-run supply curve, the new short-run equilibrium occurs at E'. The rental on capital falls from R_0 to R_1.

However, this small industry faces a long-run supply curve $S'S'$ for capital services. Eventually it must pay the going rate. At E' owners of

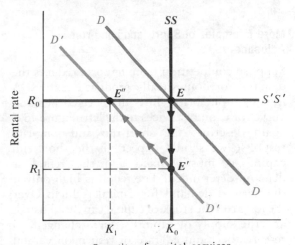

Quantity of capital services

SHORT- AND LONG-RUN
ADJUSTMENT OF CAPITAL TO A WAGE RISE.
The industry begins in equilibrium at E. Overnight its short-run supply of capital is fixed at K_0, but in the long run it faces the horizontal supply curve $S'S'$ at the going rental R_0. Suppose a wage increase shifts the demand curve for capital from DD to $D'D'$. The new short-run equilibrium is at E'. Since the rental R_1 fails to provide the required rate of return, owners of capital goods allow these goods slowly to depreciate without buying any new capital goods. The industry's capital stock and the services it provides gradually fall back. Eventually the industry reaches long-run equilibrium at E''. Since capital is again earning the required rate of return, owners of capital goods now replace goods as they depreciate.

capital are not receiving the required rental for the capital services they supply. They will allow their existing capital stock to depreciate without taking steps to maintain it, let alone replace it. Over time, the industry's capital stock and supply of capital services will gradually fall until the new equilibrium is reached at E''. The capital services used by the industry have fallen to K_1. For a given quantity of labour, lower capital means a higher marginal product of capital. In the long-run equilibrium at E'', users of capital are once more prepared to pay the required rental R_0.

The arrows in Figure 13-5 show the dynamic path that the industry will follow. When demand for capital is first reduced there is a sharp fall in the rental on capital, but owners of the fixed factor are unable to respond in the quantity of capital services they supply. As time elapses it becomes possible to adjust the quantity, in this instance by allowing capital goods to depreciate, and the rental gradually recovers.

More Examples of Short- and Long-run Adjustment

Suppose competition from imports reduces the demand for domestically produced textiles. A lower output price shifts the derived demand curve for capital services to the left. Figure 13-5 again describes the short-run and long-run response we should expect. In the short run capital is mostly fixed and the rental is demand-determined. The rental is high only if the derived demand for capital is high. Over the long run the stock of capital can be adjusted, and the supply of capital services changed, to restore the required rate of return on capital goods.

The German textile industry provides a striking example. Facing severe competition from imports, the industry experienced a sharp reduction in the rental on capital. Gradually the existing capital stock moved out of the industry. It was literally stripped down, loaded on to trains, and moved to low-wage Greece, where it was used to produce textiles for sale in Germany.

Table 13-7 shows the change in the real capital stock of selected industries in the UK in recent years. To some extent, rising real wages have led all industries to substitute

Table 13-7 UK real capital 1974–87 (£ billion at 1985 prices; excluding inventories and dwellings)

	1987	% INCREASE 1974–87
All industries	1070.0	+33
Oil and gas	35.7	+743
Textiles	12.3	−14

Source: CSO, UK National Accounts.

capital for labour over the period. However, the table makes clear that industries such as textiles, facing difficult demand conditions in their output market, have reduced their capital stock, in contrast to the national trend. In contrast, industries such as petroleum and natural gas, which faced spectacular increases in their output price after 1973, have experienced rapid increases in their capital stock, as the analysis of derived demand in this chapter would lead us to expect.

13-6 The Price of Capital Assets

Having studied the market for capital services, we now ask: what is going on in the market for capital goods themselves? Capital goods are the output of the capital goods producing industries, which have the usual upward-sloping output supply curve. They supply more capital goods if the price is higher.

Capital goods are demanded by firms who wish to supply capital services. Think of Hertz renting out cars, or property companies renting out office space. Anticipating a stream of rentals, the suppliers of capital services work out the present value of this stream of rentals at the going interest rate. This tells us how much they should be prepared to pay to obtain a capital good today. Each potential supplier of capital services will be prepared to pay a higher purchase price for a capital asset the higher the anticipated rental stream or the lower the interest rate. Both tend to increase the present value of the future rental stream.

People anticipating a higher stream of rental earnings will be prepared to pay a high purchase price for capital assets. At a lower price, people with slightly lower anticipated streams will now find it profitable to demand capital goods.

Hence we have the downward-sloping demand curve for capital goods. The lower the price, the higher the quantity demanded, since more potential suppliers of capital services are able to cover the purchase price by the present value of the rental earnings that the capital good will provide. The upward-sloping supply curve and downward-sloping demand curve together determine the equilibrium price and quantity of capital goods for the economy. The quantity determines the flow supply of capital services that this stock will provide.

What happens when an individual industry faces a leftward shift in its derived demand for capital services, as in Figure 13-5? In the short run the rental per unit of capital services falls to R_1. Moreover, everyone can work out that it will take some time before the rental rate climbs back to R_0. At the going interest rate the present value of rental earnings on new capital goods in this industry falls.

But the industry is small relative to the economy. To buy capital goods it has to pay the going price. Since the price this industry is prepared to pay has fallen below the going price, the industry buys no new capital goods. Nor does it replace existing goods that depreciate. The capital stock falls until the rental rate has climbed back to the rate prevailing throughout the economy. At this point, the present value of anticipated future rentals once more matches the price of capital goods in the whole economy. The industry is now prepared to buy capital goods to replace goods as they depreciate. The capital stock is maintained, and we have reached the new long-run equilibrium for the industry.

Thus for the industry and for the whole economy the long-run equilibrium price of a capital asset is both the price required to induce the capital-producing industries to supply capital goods and the price that, buyers of capital goods are prepared to pay, namely the present value of the anticipated rental stream for capital services discounted at the going rate of interest.

13-7 Land and Rents

The distinguishing feature of land is that it is essentially in fixed supply to the whole economy even in the long run. This is not literally true. For example, the Dutch have been able to reclaim from the sea some areas of low-lying land. Similarly, fertilizers may enhance the effective input of land for farming. Nevertheless, it makes sense to think about a factor whose total long-run supply is fixed as a guide to the most important single feature on the market for land.

Figure 13-6 shows the derived demand curve for land DD exactly analogous to the derived demand for capital services. With a fixed supply the equilibrium rental per acre is R_0. An increase in the derived demand, for example because wheat prices has risen, leads only to an increase in the rental to R_1. The quantity of land services is fixed by assumption.

Consider a tenant farmer who rents land. Wheat prices have risen but so have rents. Not only may the farmer be no better off, but the connection between the two rises may not even be recognized. The farmer may complain that high rents are making it hard to earn a decent living. As in our discussion of footballers' wages in Chapter 11, it is the high derived demand combined with the inelastic factor supply that cause the high payments for factor services.

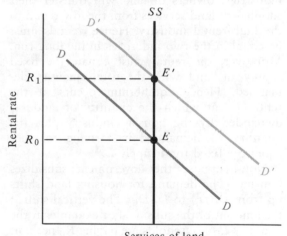

Figure 13-6 THE MARKET FOR LAND SERVICES. The total supply of land is fixed to the economy. The supply curve is vertical. The derived demand curve for land services reflects the marginal value product of land. Its derivation is exactly the same as the demand curves for labour and capital from the $MVPL$ and $MVPK$ schedules. The demand curve DD for land services determines the equilibrium land rental rate R_0. If the derived demand curve for land services shifts up to $D'D'$, the equilibrium land rental will increase to R_1.

Because land is traditionally viewed as *the* asset in fixed supply, economists have taken over the word 'rent', the payment for land services, to the concept of *economic rent*, the excess of actual payments over transfer earnings, which we introduced in Chapter 11.

13-8 Allocating a Fixed Land Supply Between Competing Uses

Land can be used for crops, for grazing, for housing or offices, and even for building roads. How do land prices and land rentals guide the allocation of the fixed total supply between the different possible uses?

Suppose there are two industries, housing and farming. Given each industry's output demand curve, we can derive its demand curve for land. Figure 13-7 shows $D_H D_H$ the demand curve for housing land and $D_F D_F$ the demand demand curve for farming land. SS shows the fixed total supply of land to be allocated between the two industries.

Although in the long run the supply in total is fixed, its allocation between the two industries is not. If rentals are different in the two industries, owners of land will transfer their supplies of land services from the low-rental to the high-rental industry. Hence, rentals must be equal in the two industries in the long run. Moreover, the rental must equate the fixed supply of land with the total quantity demanded. Hence equilibrium occurs at the rental R_0 at which the quantity of land L_H demanded by the housing industry plus the quantity L_F demanded in farming together equal the fixed total supply L.

Now suppose the government subsidizes housing. The demand for housing land shifts up from $D_H D_H$ to $D'_H D'_H$. The vertical shift is the amount of the subsidy. For example, at the quantity L_H households are paying R_0 per unit as before but the government is contributing $R_1 - R_0$ to owners of land, who thus receive R_1 in total.

At the original allocation of L_H and L_F landowners have an incentive to transfer land services from farming to housing, from which they now receive a higher rental. The new equilibrium occurs at R_2, which again equalizes rentals earned in the two sectors while ensuring that the total quantity demanded equals the

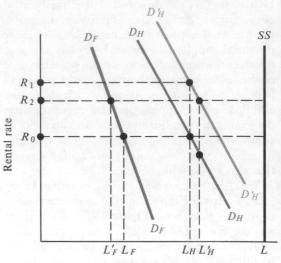

Quantity of land services

Figure 13-7 ALLOCATING LAND BETWEEN COMPETING USES. The vertical supply curve SS shows that the total supply of land is fixed. $D_F D_F$ is the demand curve for farming land and $D_H D_H$ the demand curve for housing land. In the long run, landowners will transfer land services between industries unless the rental in the two industries is the same. The equilibrium rental R_0 ensures that the total quantity of land services demanded $L_F + L_H$ just equals the total supply. With a government housing sudsidy, $D_H D_H$ still shows the demand curve for housing land net of the subsidy and $D'_H D'_H$ shows the rental the housing landowners will receive inclusive of the subsidy. Overnight, the supply of land to the two industries is fixed (at L_F and L_H) and the subsidy merely raises the rental received by owners of housing land to R_1. It is they not households who benefit. Since the rental for farmland remains R_0 in the short run there is an incentive to transfer land from farming to housing. The new long-run equilibrium occurs at rental R_2 though households pay less than this because the government subsidizes housing land. The total demand $L'_F + L'_F$ again just equals the total supply of land.

total quantity supplied. The housing subsidy increases general land rentals and leads farmers to economize on land until its marginal value product once more equals the rental per unit of land services.

What about land prices? When rentals were R_0 the land price was simply the present value of this rental stream at the going interest rate. When rentals rise to R_2 the present value of the stream increases and prices rise correspondingly.

Again, we should distinguish between short- and long-run adjustment. Overnight the land supplied to each industry is fixed. When housing is first subsidized landowners can immediately charge at rental R_1 to the housing industry at the original quantity L_H. This high rental provides the incentive for landowners to transfer land from farming to housing, bidding up farm rentals but bidding down housing rentals. In the short run housing rentals received by landowners actually *overshoot* the increase required in the long run.

13-9 The Facts Again

We began this chapter by noting that the economy is becoming more capital-intensive in its production techniques. This is a general phenomenon in Western economies. How does the analysis of this chapter help us make sense of the facts?

Table 13-8 shows UK data on capital intensity in different sectors in 1987. It shows the amount of fixed capital (productive capital minus inventories of working capital) available per production worker in each sector.

Let us assume that all industries are in long-run equilibrium so we can neglect any short-run adjustment problems. For the questions we are now asking, this seems a reasonable simplification. The ranking of industries by capital intensity in 1987 is very similar to the position ten years later.

In the long run we expect the rental on capital to be equalized in different sectors. Otherwise capital would move between sectors in search of a higher return. Similarly, long-run wage differentials should primarily reflect non-monetary job characteristics, so there is no incentive for labour to move between sectors. We should not be surprised that miners earn more than farm labourers; other things being

equal, most people would rather work in the fields than in a dark and sometimes dangerous mine shaft.

These offsetting wage differentials apart, different sectors essentially face the same relative factor rentals in the long run. Our model of the choice of technique predicts that the main determinant of different capital–labour ratios across sectors will be differences in technology. It all depends on the technical ease with which labour can be substituted for capital.

Table 13-8 confirms this prediction. A modern electricity-generating station or sewage plant can be run by only a few technical supervisors who keep an eye on the computer screens. Although a large capital-intensive plant is expensive, it can produce a large output at low average cost. It would be much more expensive to produce the same output in a labour-intensive way. Thus it makes sense to choose very capital-intensive production techniques in the gas, electricity, and water industries.

Conversely, construction is very labour-intensive and capital per employee very low. Building a factory involves a large number of different tasks which cannot easily be automated. Service industries such as restaurants, theatres, and haircutting are also necessarily labour-intensive. Human contact and personal services cannot be reproduced by machines.

Why did capital intensity increase during the 1980s, as in almost every previous decade? Two separate reasons can be given. First, the wage–rental ratio increased, leading industries to substitute capital for labour. Between 1977 and 1987 the wage–rental ratio in the UK increased by roughly 10 per cent. With more human and physical capital with which to work, labour's marginal product steadily increased and real wages rose to reflect this. In the long run the supply of labour is less elastic than the supply of capital, so real wages rise more than the real rental on capital. The consequence of this change in relative factor rentals is to lead to further substitution towards capital-intensive techniques.

Second, the steady stream of new inventions led to technical advances in production methods. To take advantage of these improvements, firms may actually have to install new capital that *embodies* the latest techniques. There is

Table 13-8 Real fixed capital per employee, 1987 (£ thousand per worker, 1985 prices)

Energy and water	382
Agriculture, forestry, fishing	95
Transport, communications	84
Financial services	58
Manufacturing	52
Distribution, hotels, catering, repairs	22
Construction	16

Source: CSO, UK National Accounts.

BOX 13-1

FACTOR MARKETS: A SUMMARY

In the last three chapters we have studied the markets for the factors of production – labour, capital, and land. In the long run when all inputs can be freely varied, the firm's choice of technique at each output level will be determined by relative factor prices or rentals. At a given output level, an increase in the relative price of one factor will lead the firm to substitute towards techniques that use that factor less intensively. The long-run total cost curve shows the cheapest way to produce each output level when the production technique is optimally chosen. From long-run total cost we can then determine long-run marginal cost and hence the profit-maximizing output at which marginal cost and marginal revenue are equal.

For each factor, the firm's demand curve is a derived demand that depends on the factor's marginal physical product in making extra output and on the marginal revenue that the firm obtains by selling that extra output. For a competitive firm, the demand curve for a factor is precisely its marginal value product schedule. We construct a marginal value product schedule for a given output price, given quantities of all other factors of production, and a given technology. Changes in any of these three things will shift the marginal value product schedule. In the short run, a competitive firm will demand that quantity of its variable factor that equates the factor's marginal value product and its factor price or rental. But in the long run, every factor can be freely varied.

Each factor will be demanded up to the point at which its factor rental equals its marginal value product *given that the quantity of all other factors has already been optimally adjusted to the same criterion.*

What then distinguishes the three factors of production we call labour, capital, and land? Primarily the speed with which the supply of that factor can adjust. At one extreme we have casual labour employed on a day-to-day basis on construction sites or on farms during the crop picking season. The supply of this factor to the firm, the industry, and possibly even to the economy as a whole, is quite free to vary even in the short run. The supply of highly skilled workers with extensive training can be changed less quickly and the supply of many capital goods, such as factories and power stations, takes even longer to adjust. And land is the factor the supply of which to the whole economy is essentially fixed, even in the long run. The slower is the speed of adjustment, and the more irreversible the process, the more current decisions must be based on future as well as present conditions. Beliefs about future conditions, and estimates of the rate of return over a long future period, could be neglected in our discussion of unskilled labour in Chapter 11, but were intrinsic to our discussion of investment in human capital in Chapter 12 and in physical capital in the present chapter.

These general principles form the basic toolkit for thinking about factor markets.

no point knowing that a breakthrough has been made in robot assembly-line technology unless the robot assembly is actually installed. Labour-saving inventions may thus provide an incentive to introduce more capital-intensive methods.

In fact, the rate of new investment in capital goods was very different in different sectors. The very capital-intensive industries – gas, electricity, water, transport and communications – had already substituted large amounts of capital for labour by 1977. Even though the wage–rental ratio continued to rise after 1977, it was technically less easy to achieve additional factor substitution in these industries such as manufacturing or financial services.

In contrast, the labour-intensive industries – financial services, and construction – achieved a

substantial substitution of capital for labour. Construction firms used more prefabricated materials which could be constructed on assembly lines. Banks and insurance companies bought computers. Since technical substitution was easier in those industries, they were more able to respond to the increase in the relative price of labour services compared with capital services.

13-10 Income Distribution in the UK

As we noted in the introduction to this chapter, the income of a factor is simply its rental rate multiplied by the quantity of the factor that is employed. In this final section we pull together

Table 13-9 UK functional distribution of income

SOURCE (factor of production)	1987 INCOME (£m)	INCOME SHARE (%) 1987	1960
Employment	226.3	64.4	69.1
Self-employed	32.5	9.3	8.7
Profits	67.7	19.3	17.1
Property rents	24.8	7.0	5.1
Total	351.3	100.0	100.0

Source: CSO, *UK National Accounts.*

our discussion of factor markets to examine the distribution of income in the UK.

The Functional Distribution of Income

The *functional income distribution* shows the division of national income between the different factors of production. Table 13-9 shows the total earnings of the different factors of production in the UK in 1987 and compares their shares of national income with the shares they received in 1960.

The most interesting feature of Table 13-9 is that there has been relatively little change in the pre-tax earnings of the different factors of production over the last three decades. As the real incomes of the nation has increased, the total real incomes of the different factors of production have broadly kept pace.

In Chapter 11 we saw that the aggregate labour supply curve to the economy is relatively inelastic. With an almost vertical labour supply curve, the total number of employed workers was little higher in 1987 than it was in 1960. Tables 13-2 and 13-8 show that the UK capital stock grew considerably faster than the UK labour force. With more capital to work with, labour's marginal product schedule shifted outwards and upwards. When confronted with an almost vertical labour supply curve, the consequence of this steady increase in the demand for labour was to increase the equilibrium real wage. And the combination of real wage growth and a slight increase in the labour force has increased real income from employment since 1960, though the share of income from employment in national income fell over this period.

Table 13-9 shows that the share of income from profits grew only a little between 1960

and 1987. From Table 13-2, we know that the quantity of capital employed has been steadily rising, but at roughly the same rate as national output. Since the ratio of capital to output has been fairly constant, the constant share of profits in national income suggests that the rate of return on capital has also been fairly constant over the period.

Since the quantity of capital has increased without a consequent fall in its rate of return, the economy cannot simply have moved down a given marginal product of capital schedule; otherwise, the rental on capital and its rate of return would have been reduced. Rather, the marginal product schedule must have shifted outwards, a move tending to increase the rate of return for any given capital stock. Together with the increase in capital employed, this explains why the rental on capital and its rate of return remained roughly the same in 1987 as in 1960.

This outward shift in the marginal product of capital schedule was chiefly caused not by an increase in the quantity of labour employed, which scarcely changed, but by technical progress. Technical progress both directly increased the productivity of capital for a given effective quantity of labour input, and increased the quantity of labour effectively employed by raising its productivity. Together, these explain the facts shown in Table 13-9.

Finally, we come to property rents earned on land. We know that the supply of land is very inelastic and that the demand for land is a derived demand. As national income increases the derived demand curve for land will shift upwards. Thus it is not surprising that property rents have risen a little faster than national income itself.

The Personal Income Distribution

The *personal income distribution* shows how national income is divided between different individuals, regardless of the factor services from which these individuals earn their income. The personal income distribution is relevant to issues such as equality and poverty.

Table 13-10 does not show people whose income is so low that the Inland Revenue do not need to record what their income actually is. Even confining our attention to people with sufficiently high pre-tax incomes that they may

Table 13-10 UK personal income distribution, 1989

INCOME RANGE (£000)	PERCENTAGE OF	
	TAXPAYERS	NATIONAL INCOME
Under 5.0	12.4	3.6
5.0–7.5	17.6	8.3
7.5–10.0	15.7	10.5
10.0–15.0	24.8	22.9
15.0–30.0	24.8	37.5
Over 30.0	4.7	17.2

Based on 21 million taxpayers.
Source: HMSO, *Social Trends.*

Table 13-11 UK wealth distribution, 1985

OWNED BY (% OF POPULATION)	% OF TOTAL WEALTH	% OF WEALTH PLUS PENSION RIGHTS
Richest 1%	20	11
5%	40	25
10%	54	36
25%	76	58
50%	93	83

Source: HMSO, *Social Trends.*

be liable for income tax, we can see that pre-tax income is quite unequally distributed in the UK. Looking at the bottom of Table 13-10, 4.7 per cent of all taxpayers earn 17.2 per cent of national income. Why should some people earn so much while others earn so little?

Chapters 11 and 12 discussed some of the reasons why people earn different wages and salaries. Unskilled workers have little training and low productivity. Workers with high levels of training and education earn much more. Some jobs, such as coal mining, pay high compensating differentials to offset unpleasant working conditions. Very pleasant, but un-skilled, jobs pay much less since many people are prepared to do them. Talented superstars in scarce supply but strong demand may earn very high economic rents.

However, Table 13-10 refers not just to income from the supply of labour services. A major reason why the distribution of personal income is so unequal is that the ownership of *wealth*, which provides income from profits and rents, is even more unequal. Table 13-11 shows details for the UK for 1985.

Table 13-11 shows that the most wealthy 1 per cent of the population owns 20 per cent of the nation's marketable wealth and the most wealthy 25 per cent of the population own 76 per cent of the nation's marketable wealth. The stream of profit and rent income to which such wealth gives rise lays a large part in determining the personal distribution of pre-tax *income*.

The final column of Table 13-11 includes pension rights in wealth. A 50-year-old worker will have accumulated substantial pension rights, and an economist would wish to treat the present value of these future payments as part of that worker's wealth. Since most workers have some kind of pension, if only from the state, inclusion of pension rights tends to make the wealth distribution more equal, as the final column of Table 13-11 shows. However, accumulated pension rights are not relevant to the distribution of income shown in Table 13-10. Pension rights lead to incomes in the future, whereas marketable wealth – shares held on the stock market, property rented out, or bank deposits – give rise to actual income in the current year and shows up directly in Table 13-10.

Summary

1   Physical (as opposed to financial) capital comprises real assets yielding useful services to producing firms or consuming households. The main categories of physical capital are plant and machinery, residential structures, other buildings, consumer durables, and inventories. Tangible wealth is physical capital plus land.

2   Present value calculations convert future receipts or payments into current values. Because lenders can earn – and borrowers must pay – interest over time, a pound tomorrow is worth less than a pound today. How much less depends on the interest rate. The higher the interest rate, the lower the present value of a given future payment.

3   Since lending or borrowing cumulates at compound interest, for any given annual interest rate the present value of a given sum is smaller the further into the future that sum is earned or paid.

4   The present value of a perpetuity is the

constant annual payment divided by the rate of interest. At a 10 per cent interest rate per annum a payment of £100 per annum for ever is worth £1000 today.

5   Nominal interest rates measure the monetary interest payments on a loan. The real, or inflation-adjusted, interest rate measures the extra goods a lender can buy by lending for a year and delaying purchases of goods. The real rate of interest is the nominal interest rate minus the inflation rate over the same period.

6   The demand for capital services is a derived demand. The firm's demand curve for capital services is its marginal value product of capital curve. Higher levels of the other factors of production and higher output prices shift the derived demand curve up. The industry demand curve is less elastic than the horizontal sum of each firm's curve because it also allows for the effect of an industry expansion in bidding down the output price.

7   In the short run the supply of capital services is fixed. In the long run it can be adjusted by producing new capital goods or allowing the existing capital stock to depreciate.

8   The required rental is the rental that allows a supplier of capital services to break even on the decision to purchase the capital asset. The required rental is higher the higher is the interest rate, the depreciation rate, or the purchase price of the capital good.

9   A rise in the industry wage has two effects on the derived demand curve for capital services. By reducing labour input it reduces the marginal physical product of capital. By reducing the industry output it increases the output price. When output demand is very inelastic the latter effect will dominate. The derived demand curve for capital services shifts up. Essentially the industry substitutes capital for labour to produce almost the same output. When output demand is very elastic the former effect dominates. The demand curve for capital services shifts down. The industry contracts its use of labour and capital and produces a much lower output.

10   The asset price is the price at which a capital good is bought and sold outright rather than rented. In long-run equilibrium it is both the price at which suppliers of capital goods are willing to produce and the price at which buyers are willing to purchase. The latter is merely the present value of anticipated future rentals earned from the capital services that the good provides in the future.

11   Land is the special capital good whose supply is fixed even in the long run. However, land and capital can move between industries in the long run. They will move until rentals on land or on capital are equalized in different industries.

12   Technology and the ease of factor substitution dictate the very different capital intensity of different industries in the long run. Although most industries are becoming more capital-intensive over time, the rate of change is different in different industries. In part this reflects the ease with which industries can substitute capital for labour as wage rates rise relative to capital rentals. In part it is a reflection of the discovery and implementation of technical advances in different industries.

13   The functional distribution of income shows how national income is divided between the factors of production. The share of each factor has remained fairly constant over time. This conceals a rise in the quantity of capital relative to labour and a corresponding fall in the ratio of capital rentals to labour wages.

14   The personal distribution of income shows how national income is divided between different individuals regardless of the factor services from which income is earned. A major cause of income inequality in the UK is a very unequal distribution of income-earning wealth.

Key Terms

Physical and financial capital
Land
Tangible wealth
Asset stocks and service flows
Present value
Marginal value product of capital
Rental on capital
Required rate of return on capital
Opportunity cost of capital
Depreciation rate
Capital–labour ratio
Wage–rental ratio
Nominal and real interest rates

Functional income distribution
Personal income distribution

Problems

1 Rich countries tend to have a relatively large share of the capital stock in the form of consumer capital. Why do you think this is?

2 (a) Consumer durables – washing machines, televisions, etc. – are part of the capital stock but do not generate any financial income for their owners. Why do we include consumer durables in the capital stock? (b) To wash your clothes you can take them to a laundromat and spend £2 per week indefinitely or buy a washing machine for £400. It costs £1 per week (including depreciation) to run a washing machine, and the interest rate is 10 per cent per annum. Does it make sense to buy the washing machine? Does this help you answer part (a).

3 A bank offers you £1.10 next year for every £0.90 you give it today. What is the implicit interest rate?

4 A firm buys a machine for £10 000, earn rentals of £3600 for each of the next two years, and then sell it for scrap for £9000. Use the data of Table 13-4 to determine if the machine is worth buying when the interest rate is 10 per cent per annum.

5 Discuss the main determinants of the firm's demand curve and the industry's demand curve for capital services. How do these determinants affect the way a tax on the industry's output will shift the industry demand for capital services?

6 The interest rate falls from 15 to 10 per cent. Discuss in detail how this affects the rental on capital services and the level of the capital stock in an industry in the short and long run.

7 Suppose a plot of land is suitable only for agriculture. Can it be true that the farming industry will experience financial distress if there is an increase in the price of land? How would your answer be affected if the land could also be used for housing?

8 Common Fallacies Show why the following statements are incorrect: (a) Inflation makes nominal interest rates go up. This must reduce the present value of future income. (b) If the economy continues to become more capital-intensive, eventually there will be no jobs left for workers to do. (Hint: what happens to labour productivity, wage income, and consumer demand?) (c) Since the economy's supply of land is fixed, it would be supplied even at a zero rental. Land rents should therefore be zero in long-run equilibrium. (Hint: is land supply fixed to each firm in the long run?)

Appendix: The Simple Algebra of Present Values and Discounting

Suppose we lend £K today at an annual interest rate i. For example, K might be 100 and i might be 0.1, which would imply an annual interest rate of 10 per cent. After one year our money has grown to £$K(1+i)$. We get our £K back plus an interest payment equal to £K times the interest rate. With $K=100$ and $i=0.1$, we get £110 back after a year. Suppose we re-lend the money for another year at the same interest rate. By the same principle we lend out £$\{K(1+i)\}$ and get back £$\{K(1+i)\}(1+i)$ at the end of the second year. For example, our £100, which had grown to £110 after one year, has grown to £121 after two years. If we lend this sum for yet another year we get back £$\{K(1+i)^2\}(1+i)$ or £$K(1+i)^3$ at the end of the third year.

The law of compound interest makes this into a general principle. Lending an initial sum £K (which we call the *principal*) for a period of N years at an annual interest rate of i, we get back £$K(1+i)^N$ after N years.[5]

Let us call £X the amount we get after N years. The law of compound interest promises us that £K today will convert into an amount £X in N years' time such that

$$£X = £K(1+i)^N \qquad (A1)$$

Beginning with £K we can get exactly £X after N years. Since one can be converted into the other, they are worth the same amount. Suppose we divide through equation (A1) by $(1+i)^N$ to obtain

$$£X\left\{\frac{1}{(1+i)^N}\right\} = £K \qquad (A2)$$

This tells us that we need £K today to be able to get £X after N years. £K is the present value of a payment £X in N years' time if the interest rate is i. We call $1/\{(1+i)^N\}$ the *discount factor*. Since i is a positive number, the discount factor must be a positive fraction. For example, with $i=1$ (an interest rate of 100 per cent per annum) and $N=3$, the discount factor is $(\frac{1}{2})^3=\frac{1}{8}$. It discounts or reduces the value of £X in three

---

[5] Since $z^0=1$ for *any* value of z, the compound interest formula even gives the correct answer when $N=0$. After zero years our money is worth £$K \times 1 = £K$.

years' time to give a present value only one-eighth as large.

Equation (A2) is the general formula we use in calculating the present value of a payment received in N periods' time. Its present value is simply the payment divided by $(1 + i)^N$ where i is the interest rate expressed as a decimal fraction. The table shows the present value of £1 N years from now using this formula when the interest rate is 10 per cent per annum and $i = 0.1$.

Present value (PV) of £1 N years from now when annual interest rate is 10 per cent

	$N = 1$	$N = 5$	$N = 10$	$N = 20$	$N = 30$	$N = 40$
PV	£0.91	£0.62	£0.39	£0.15	£0.06	£0.02

Alternatively, we can view the table as telling us the discount factors that are implied by equation (A2). Thus $0.39 = 1/(1 + i)^{10}$ when $i = 0.1$. A pound in 10 years' time discounts to only 0.39 of its face value when the interest rate is 10 per cent per annum. To calculate the present value of a whole stream of future payments, we simply multiply the face value of each payment by the relevant discount factor.

Thus the present value of £100 after 10 years and £200 after 40 years is (£100 × 0.39) + (£200 × 0.02) = £43. Notice that payments will not be received or made for many years have a very small present value.

Finally, we can relate our general formula to the formula we gave in equation (1) of the text for the value of a perpetuity. Suppose an asset earns £K per annum for ever. Letting PV_N be the present value of £1 received after N years the present value of the constant stream £K per annum is $K(PV_0 + PV_1 + PV_2 + PV_3 + PV_4 + ...)$. Fortunately we do not have to add up every term in this series. The algebra of geometric series promises us that the answer to this infinite sum is given by £$K(1 + i)/i$. If each payment is made more frequently than once a year, we must use the interest rate i (expressed as a decimal) over this shorter period. Thus, the more frequent the payments, the lower the interest rate. When the money is paid almost continuously, i will be very small per period and $(1 + i)$ is very close to 1. We then obtain the formula given in the text for the present value of a perpetuity paying £K per period:

Present value of
£K per period for ever $= £K/i$ (A3)

14

Coping with Risk in Economic Life

The only certainties are death and taxes. Nevertheless, you do not know when you are going to die or the extent of the taxes you will pay through various means. *Every* action we take today has a future outcome that is less than perfectly certain. It is risky. When we add to our bank account we do not know how much the money will buy when we want to use it because we are not certain how much the prices of goods will rise in the meantime. When we start a job we do not know how fast we will be promoted. When we start studying economics we have only a rough idea what is involved and even less idea about the purpose to which we shall put this skill once we have acquired it.

The world is a risky place. In this chapter we ask two questions: How does the presence of risk affect our actions? And how have economic institutions evolved to help us deal with the risky environment in which we are forced to live?

Although there is a degree of risk in everything we do, some activities increase the risk we face while other activities reduce it. UK citizens spend billions of pounds on insurance, which reduces the net risks they face, but they also spend over £1 billion on legal forms of betting and gambling, an activity that has the sole purpose of artificially increasing the risks people face. Can we deduce anything about people's general attitude to risk by examining their revealed behaviour in gambling and insurance activities?

We shall argue that people generally dislike risk and are therefore prepared to pay to have their risks reduced. We shall see that this idea allows us to explain the existence of many economic institutions that, at a price, allow those people who dislike risk most to pass on their risks to others who are more willing or more able to bear these risks.

14-1 Individual Attitudes to Risk

A risky activity has two characteristics: the likely outcome (for example the likely return on an investment) and the degree of variation in all the possible outcomes. Suppose we are offered a 50 per cent chance of making £100 and a 50 per cent chance of losing £100. On average you will make no money by taking such gambles. We call them fair gambles.

> A *fair gamble* is one which on average will make exactly zero monetary profit.

In contrast, a 30 per cent chance of making £100 and a 70 per cent chance of losing £100 is an unfair gamble. On average you will lose money. With the probabilities of winning and losing reversed, the gamble would on average be profitable. We say the oods on this gamble are *favourable*. Now compare a gamble offering a 50 per cent chance of making or losing £100 with a gamble with the same chances of winning or losing £200. Both are fair gambles, but we say the second is *riskier*. Depending on the outcome you will either do better or do worse, but the range of possible outcomes is greater.

Having discussed the type of gambles the market may offer, we turn now to individual tastes. Economists classify individual attitudes under three headings: risk-averse, risk-neutral, and risk-loving. The crucial question is whether or not the individual would accept a fair gamble. A *risk-neutral* person pays no attention to the degree of dispersion of possible outcomes, betting if and only if the odds on a monetary profit are favourable. Although any individual bet may turn out to be a loser, and there may even be quite a long string of unlucky losing bets, a risk-neutral person is interested only in whether the odds will yield a profit *on average*.

A *risk-averse* person will refuse a fair gamble.

This does not mean he or she will never bet. If the odds are sufficiently favourable the probable monetary profit will overcome the inherent dislike of risk. But the more risk-averse the individual, the more favourable must the odds be before that individual will take the bet. In contrast, a *risk-lover* will bet even when a strict mathematical calculation reveals that the odds are unfavourable. The more risk-loving the individual, the more unfavourable must the odds be before the individual will decline the bet.

Some people play poker for high stakes because they know that by superior card play and psychology they can turn the odds in their favour. People with perfect memories have the odds very slightly in their favour when they play blackjack in a casino. Perhaps such gamblers are risk-lovers, or perhaps they merely reckon that the odds are sufficiently favourable to offset their relatively low degree of risk aversion. But we all know the inveterate gambler who will bet on almost anything, even when the odds are clearly unfavourable. Such people are definitely risk-lovers.

Insurance is the opposite of gambling. Suppose you own a £50 000 house and there is a 10 per cent chance it will burn down by accident. Thus you have a 90 per cent chance of continuing to have £50 000 but a 10 per cent chance of having nothing. Our risky world is forcing you to take this bet. The average outcome is that you will end up with £45 000 which is 90 per cent of £50 000 plus 10 per cent of nothing.

An insurance company offers to insure the full value of your house for a premium of £10 000. Whether or not your house burns down, you pay the insurance company the £10 000 premium, but they pay you £50 000 if it does burn down. Whether or not your house burns down, you will end up with £40 000. You are worse off by the £10 000 premium, but you then have a £50 000 house or the equivalent in cash.

Would you insure? The insurance company is offering you unfavourable odds, which of course is how they make their money. If you do nothing the average outcome is £45 000 but the actual outcome could be £50 000 or zero. Insuring guarantees you £40 000 either way. A risk-neutral person would decline the insurance company's offer. The straight mathematical

Table 14-1 Behaviour towards risk

TYPE OF PERSON	BETTING	INSURANCE AT UNFAIR PREMIUM
Risk-averse	Needs favourable odds	May buy
Risk-neutral	Except at unfavourable odds	Will not buy
Risk-lover	Even if odds against	Will not buy

calculation in monetary terms says it is on average better to stand the risk of a fire. The risk-lover will also decline. Not only is the insurance company offering bad odds, there is also the added enjoyment of standing the risk. But a person who is sufficiently risk-averse will accept the offer, happy to give up £5000 on average to avoid the possibility of catastrophe. Table 14-1 summarizes this discussion of attitudes to risk.

Risk Aversion and Diminishing Marginal Utility

Decisions about gambling or insurance depend on two distinct considerations. First, there is the pleasure or pain from the risk itself. The thrill of the occasional flutter on the Grand National resembles the pleasure of seeing a good film. It has a component of pure entertainment. For other people the stress in not knowing the outcome is painful. Occasional gambling for the sheer fun of it is a legitimate form of consumption for people who enjoy it, and the standard model of consumer choice suggests that people will be prepared to pay for this modest form of entertainment. A roulette wheel does not quite offer fair odds. Yet many of us would play roulette on our birthday and regard the slightly unfavourable odds as the implicit price of our fun.

Such leisure activities form only a trivial part of the risk that we face in our everyday lives. This approach is not helpful in thinking about the risk of our house burning down or the risk a firm takes in deciding whether or not to build a new factory. It is not the spectacle that counts but the fact that different outcomes will have different implications for the financial well-being of the household or the firm.

At given prices suppose you calculate how much *utility* or happiness £1000 would yield through the goods it would let you buy. Now you calculate your utility if you had £2000 to spend. Since you have more goods, we can assume your utility has gone up. How much it goes up is the *marginal utility* of the extra £1000 which increased your wealth from £1000 to £2000.

Now you get another £1000. You have more goods and your utility rises still further. What about the marginal utility of this extra £1000? When you had only £1000 you could only just afford the essential of life. Another £1000 allowed you to buy some things you really needed but could not previously afford. Yet another £1000 allows you to buy some nice things, but they are really luxuries that you could have done without. As we gave you more and more money in blocks of £1000 a time, you find fewer and fewer things to spend it on.

Thus the marginal utility of the first £1000 is very high. You really needed it. The marginal utility of the next £1000 is high but not quite so high. As you get more and more, the marginal utility of the extra money tends to diminish.

Economists assume that individual tastes satisfy the principle of *diminishing marginal utility of wealth*. Successive increases of equal monetary value add less and less to total utility.

Of course, we can all think of exceptions to this general rule. Some people *really* want a yacht, and their utility takes a huge jump when they are finally rich enough to afford one. But most of us first spend our money on the things we most need and get less and less extra satisfaction out of successive equal increases in our spending power.

Suppose you own £15 000 and you are then offered an equal chance of winning or losing £10 000. This is a fair bet in money terms since the average profit is £0. But it is not a fair bet in utility terms. Diminishing marginal utility implies that the extra utility you enjoy if the bet wins, taking your total wealth from £15 000 to £25 000, is much smaller than the utility you sacrifice if the bet loses, taking your wealth from £15 000 to £5000. You get a few extra luxuries with the £10 000 you might win, but you have to give up a lot of essential goods if you lose and have to cut back to only £5000.

We said a person is risk-averse if he or she declines a fair bet in money terms. We can now see that the hypothesis of diminishing marginal utility implies that, except for the occasional small gamble for pure entertainment, people should generally be risk-averse. They should refuse fair money gambles because they are not fair utility gambles. As we shall see, this story seems to fit many of the facts.

Two implications of this analysis recur throughout the chapter. *First, risk-averse individuals will devote resources to finding ways to reduce risk.* As the booming insurance industry confirms, people will be prepared to pay to get out of some of the risks that our environment would otherwise force them to bear. *Second, individuals who take over or bear the risk will have to be rewarded for doing so.* Many economic activities consist of the more risk-averse bribing the less risk-averse to take over the risk.

14-2 Insurance and Risk

We begin with a simple example of home-made insurance. A farmer and an actress have risky incomes which fluctuate from month to month. But these risks are *independent*. Whether or not the farmer has a good month is completely unconnected with whether or not the actress has a good month. Table 14-2 shows what happens if the two get together to *pool* their incomes and their risks. Suppose they share out their total incomes in proportion to their average earnings over the past few years. If they have a good month (case I) or both have a bad month (case IV), the pooling arrangement makes no difference. They each get what they would have got on their own. But in cases II and III the success of one partner offsets the failure of the other. Together they have a more *stable* income than they would have as indiv-

Table 14-2 Risk-pooling

	FARMER	
	GOOD MONTH	BAD MONTH
ACTRESS		
GOOD MONTH	I	II
BAD MONTH	III	IV

iduals. If the farmer and the actress are risk-averse, they can gain by pooling their risky incomes. If it were not so hard to set up such deals (lawyers' fees, the problem of cheating, tax problems) we would see a lot more of them.

Pooling of independent risks is the key to the insurance business. Suppose we look up the mortality tables and see that on average 1 per cent of people aged 55 will die during the next year. Deaths result from heart disease, cancer, road accidents, and other causes but in fairly predictable proportions.

Now let us randomly choose any 100 people aged 55 knowing nothing about their health. Throughout the nation 1 per cent of such people will die in the next year. But in our sample of 100 people it could be 0, 1, 2, or even more. The larger we make our sample of 55-year-olds, the more likely it is that around 1 per cent will die in the next year. With 1 million 55-year-olds we could be pretty confident that around 10 000 would die, though we could not of course say which ones. By putting together more and more people we reduce the risk or dispersion of the aggregate outcome.[1]

Suppose these 100 people would like to leave their family some money in the event that they die in the next year. Each person puts up £100 to give a total of £10 000 to be shared out among the families of those who die in the next year. If this small sample of 100 55-year-olds behaves like the national average, one person will die and that family will get £10 000. But four people might die and their families would get only £2500 each. The payment to the family of someone dying in the next year is risky. It cannot be forecast for sure. But if 1 million people enter the scheme, almost exactly 10 000 will die and their families will get almost exactly £10 000 each. The risk has been enormously reduced.

Life assurance companies take in premium payments in exchange for a promise to pay a much larger amount to the family if the insured person dies. The company can make this promise with a high degree of certainty because it pools its risks over a huge number of clients. Since the company cannot guarantee that precisely 1 per cent of its large number of 55-year-olds will die in any one year, there is

a small element of residual risk for the company to bear and it will make a small charge for this in calculating its premiums. However, the company's ability to pool the risk means that it will make only a *small* charge. If life assurance companies try to charge more, new entrants will be attracted to the industry knowing that the profits more than compensate for the small residual risk to be borne.

Risk-pooling works only when the risk can be spread over a large number of individuals, each of whose risks are essentially independent of the risks faced by all other individuals. It works in our example because the risk that one person is run over by a bus makes no difference to another person's risk of getting cancer or being run over by a bus. Risk-pooling will not work when all individuals face the *same* risk.

Suppose there is a 10 per cent risk of a nuclear war in Europe alone during the next 10 years. If it happens everyone in Europe will die. In that event they would like to leave some money to their nearest surviving relative in the rest of the world. Ten million people in Western Europe offer to pay £100 each to an American insurance company. Since 10 million is a large number, they expect the premium to be a small percentage of the pay-out in the event of European catastrophe. Surely the residual risk for the insurance company is very small if it can spread the risk over this many people?

Not so. Since *everybody* in Europe dies if *anybody* dies, the insurance company either pays out to everybody's relatives or it pays out nothing. Even in the aggregate there is still exactly a 10 per cent chance of having to pay out, just as the individual faced a 10 per cent chance of disaster. When the same thing happens to everybody if it happens at all, the aggregate behaves like the individual and there is no risk reduction to be achieved by pooling.

This explains why many insurance companies will not provide insurance against what they call 'acts of god' – floods, earthquakes, epidemics. Such diasters are no more natural or unnatural than a heart attack. But earthquakes will affect large numbers of the insurance company's clients if they happen at all. Their risk cannot be reduced by pooling. Hence companies cannot quote the low premium rates that apply for heart attacks, where one person's outcome has no implication for the

---

[1] This proposition is called the 'Law of Large Numbers'. A proof can be found in most statistics textbooks.

outcome of others and the aggregate outcome is relatively certain.

Risk-pooling works by aggregating independent risks to make the aggregate more certain. But there is another way to reduce the cost of risk-bearing. This second method is known as *risk-sharing*, and the most famous example is the Lloyd's insurance market in London. Risk-sharing is necessary when it has proved impossible to reduce the risk by pooling. Lloyd's offer insurance on earthquakes in California, which would hit many of their clients, and one-off deals such as insurance of a film star's legs.

To understand risk-sharing we must return to diminishing marginal utility. We argued that the utility from an extra £10 000 was less than the utility sacrificed when £10 000 must be given up. However, this difference in marginal utility for equivalent financial gains and losses is smaller, the smaller the gain and loss. The marginal utility from an extra £1 is only fractionally less than the utility lost by sacrificing £1. When the stakes are very small people are close to being risk-neutral. You would probably toss a coin with us to win or lose £0.10, but not to win or lose £10 000. The larger the stake, the more diminishing marginal utility begins to bite.

Risk-sharing works by reducing the stake. You go to Lloyd's to insure the US space shuttle launch for £20 billion. That is a big risk. Only part of this risk can be pooled as part of a larger portfolio of risks. It is too big for anyone to take on at a reasonable premium.

The Lloyd's market in London is a big room with hundreds of 'syndicates', each a group of 20 or so individuals who have each put up £100 000. Each syndicate will take perhaps 1 per cent of the £20 billion deal and then resell some of the risk to yet other people in the insurance industry. By the time the deal has been subdivided and subdivided again, each syndicate or insurance company is holding only a tiny share of the total. And each syndicate risk is further subdivided among its 20 members. The risk has been shared out until each individual's stake has been so reduced that there is only a small difference between the marginal utility in the event of a gain and the marginal loss of utility in the event of a disaster. It now requires only a small premium to cover this risk, and the whole package can be sold to the client at a premium that is low enough to attract the business.

By pooling and sharing risks, insurance allows individuals to deal with many risks at affordable premiums. But there are two interesting and complicating factors which further inhibit the operation of insurance markets, tending to reduce the extent to which individuals can use insurance to buy their way out of risky situations.

Moral Hazard

Insurance companies employ actuaries to calculate the average or statistical chances for aggregate behaviour. They work out how many houses per million will have a fire next year. Since fires in different houses are essentially independent risks, we expect insurance firms to be able to pool the risk over a large number of clients and charge only a low premium for fire insurance.

You are sitting in a restaurant and remember you left your car unlocked. Do you abandon your nice meal and rush outside to lock it? You are less likely to if you know the car is fully insured against theft. With full health insurance you are less likely to bother about precautionary check-ups. If the act of insuring increases the likelihood of the occurrence of the thing you wish to insure against, we call this the problem of *moral hazard*.[2]

Actuarial calculations for the whole population, many of whom are uninsured and will take greater care, are no longer a reliable guide to the risks the insurance company faces and the premiums it should charge. The problem of moral hazard makes it harder to get insurance and more expensive when you do get it.

Frequently insurance companies will insure your property only up to a certain percentage of its replacement cost. They will take a large part of the risk, but you will still be worse off if the nasty thing happens. The company is providing you with an incentive to take care and hold down the chances of the nasty thing

---

[2] Similarly for safety regulations. It has been argued by Professor Sam Peltzman that the introduction of safety belts resulted in more accidents since drivers thought they could safely go faster. See 'The Effects of Automobile Safety Regulations', *Journal of Political Economy*, 1975.

happening. On average, they have to pay out less frequently and they can charge you lower premia.

Adverse Selection

Suppose some people smoke cigarettes but others do not. People who smoke are more likely to die young. Individuals know whether they themselves smoke, but suppose the insurance company cannot tell the difference and must charge all clients the same premium rate for life assurance.

Suppose the premium is based on mortality rates for the nation as a whole. People who do not smoke know they have an above-average life expectancy and will find the premium too expensive. Smokers know their life expectancy is lower than the national average and realize that the premium is a bargain. Even though the insurance company cannot tell the difference between the two groups, it can work out that if it charges the premium based on the national average it will attract only smokers and will end up paying out more than it expected.

One solution is to assume that all clients are smokers and charge the correspondingly high premium to all clients. Non-smokers effectively find it impossible to get insurance at what they believe is a reasonable price. They might be able to volunteer a medical examination in an attempt to prove they are low-risk clients who should be charged a lower price. Medical examinations are in fact compulsory for many insurance contracts now.

To check that you understand the difference between moral hazard and adverse selection, say which is which in the following examples. (1) A person with a fatal disease signs up for life insurance. (2) Reassured by the fact that he took out life assurance to protect his dependants, a person who has unexpectedly become depressed decides to commit suicide. (The first was adverse selection, the second moral hazard.)

Discrimination or Sound Insurance?

Risk-pooling and risk-sharing allow insurance companies to offer cheap insurance against some important risks. But when all clients must be charged the same premium rate for apparently similar risks, we have seen that moral hazard and adverse selection make things much harder for the insurance companies. They may refuse to insure at all, or may charge such high premiums that even risk-averse clients find there is little gain in taking out an insurance policy.

In the previous section we argued that the solution might lie in *price discrimination*. If insurance companies can distinguish between low-risk non-smokers and high-risk smokers they can quote them different premium rates. High-risk clients will pay a higher premium which properly reflects their greater risk. But price discrimination raises issues of fairness.

Women live longer than men. In 1980 the life expectancy at birth was about 70 years for a male child in many Western countries including the UK, but the life expectancy of a female child was six or seven years longer. Since insurance companies can easily tell the difference between men and women, this suggests that life insurance premiums should be lower for woman than for men. Nor does this seem particularly unfair.

But now consider pensions. Retirement pensions are typically paid for as long as the person lives after retiring from a job. Suppose a man and a woman have been earning the same amount each year in a job and have paid the same amount towards a pension. If they retire at the same age, on average the woman will live longer. If they receive the same annual pension, on average the woman will receive more pension income over the rest of her life than the man although they made the same contributions to the pension plan while in employment. Is that fair? There is no easy answer.

This example reminds us that pricing policies are not always exclusively determined by the market forces of supply and demand. Social considerations such as fairness sometimes have to be taken into account. This forms an important theme in welfare economics, which we begin to study in the next chapter.

14-3 Uncertainty and Asset Returns

There are many ways of carrying wealth from the present to the future. People can hold money, government bills or bonds, company shares, housing, gold, and so on. We now compare the rates of return that can be earned on shares and Treasury bills, two particular ways in which wealth might be held. In the next section we discuss the general problem faced by a wealth-holder trying to decide how to choose the composition of that wealth portfolio.

Treasury bills are issued by the government usually for a period of three months. The government sells a bill for say £97 and simultaneously promises to buy back the bill for £100 in three months' time. People who buy the bill and sell it back to the government earn just over 3 per cent on their money in three months. By re-investing the proceeds to buy three more bills in the course of the year, they will earn something over 12 per cent during the year. Each time an individual buys a bill, the implicit nominal interest rate over the three-month period is known for certain since the government has guaranteed the price at which the bill will be re-purchased.

The real return on Treasury bills is a little less certain. The *real return* is the nominal return minus the inflation rate over the period the bill is held. People do not know what the inflation rate will be over each three-month period during which the bill is held. On the other hand, they have a pretty good idea about what inflation is *likely* to do over the next three months. Hence even the real return on Treasury bills is not very risky.

Company shares pay out a return in two different ways. First, shareholders are entitled to dividend payments. *Dividends* are the regular payments that the firm makes out of profits after deciding how much to keep back to finance future spending on plant and machinery. Second, shareholders may make *capital gains* or suffer *capital losses*. The capital gain is the increase in the share price during the period in which the share is held. If a share can be bought at a low price and subsequently sold at a higher price, this contributes to the return earned while holding the share.

We express the rate of return as a percentage of the money initially laid out. Again we are interested in the real wage of return after allowing for inflation. Thus the general formula for the real rate of return during a given period is

$$\begin{aligned} \frac{\text{Real rate}}{\text{of return}} &= \frac{\text{nominal rate}}{\text{of return}} - \frac{\text{inflation rate}}{\text{over period}} \\ &= \frac{\text{dividend} + \text{capital gain}}{\text{purchase price}} - \frac{\text{inflation}}{\text{rate}} \quad (1) \end{aligned}$$

Figure 14-1 shows the annual real rate of return on Treasury bills and on company shares in the UK during the 30-year period 1955–85. There are two important points to note about the figure. First, the rate of return on company shares has been enormously more variable than that on Treasury bills. In fact, as we argued in the previous chapter, the real rate of return on Treasury bills is relatively constant over time. The real rate of return on shares was as high as 130 per cent during 1975 and as low as −70 per cent in 1974. Even excluding these two years, there are several years when the real return on shares exceeded 20 per cent and some years in which it was worse than −10 per cent. Shares are much riskier than Treasury bills.[3]

The second thing to note about Figure 14-1 is the average real rate of return on the two assets over the whole period. The real rate of return on Treasury bills is very close to zero on average. In fact, it is very slightly negative.

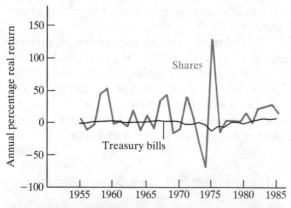

Figure 14-1   ANNUAL REAL RETURN ON SHARES AND TREASURY BILLS, 1955–85, UK. (*Source: Frank Russell International, UK Capital Market History and Asset Market Allocations 1919–1985.*)

[3] There are strong grounds for believing the large positive or negative returns on shares were unanticipated by the market. Why? Because if the market had foreseen a return of say 30 per cent in real terms it would surely have seen people trying to buy these bargain stocks. Their prices would have been bid up, and equation (1) tells us that this increase in the purchase price would have reduced the real return to a more typical level. Similarly, if large capital losses have been foreseen, share prices would already have been lower, and the return higher, as people tried to dump these shares.

In contrast, shares on average yield around 10 per cent per annum in real terms. Why such a discrepancy?

Figure 14-1 shows that shares were very much riskier than Treasury bills. The person who buys shares has to take a much bigger risk but is compensated *on average* by a higher return. Since the risk is quite a big one – many people lost huge sums of money in 1974 – it requires the carrot of a large real return on average to induce people to take this risk.

Shares are riskier for two reasons. First, nobody is quite sure what dividend the firm will announce during the year. It all depends how much profit it makes and how confident it is about the future. The more they anticipate bad times in the future, the more inclined firms may be to pay a low dividend in order to keep a contingency reserve within the firm.

Second, views about the likely capital gains may change quite radically. If people thought firms were doing well they will have anticipated rising share prices. They expect to make capital gains. Equation (1) shows that these add to the return people expect to make in shares. If the shares are offering a higher expected return, people will want to buy them and the current share prices will be bid up. Thus one reason why share prices may be high is because people have bought the shares in anticipation of capital gains.

If it suddenly becomes apparent that the company's prospects are less good, the happy scenario of steadily rising share prices can quickly vanish. Share prices may collapse. We discuss this phenomenon in more detail in Section 14-6 under the heading of 'speculative bubbles'. For the moment we merely note that current share prices and current returns are crucially dependent on current expectations of future share prices and hence capital gains. In speculative markets there can be little certainty that current views about future share prices will persist without revision. In large part it is revisions in beliefs about likely capital gains which lead to volatile share prices and share returns.

14-4 Portfolio Selection

The *portfolio* of a financial investor is the collection of financial and real assets – bank deposits, Treasury bills, government bonds, ordinary shares of industrial companies, gold, works of art – in which the financial investor's wealth is held. How does a risk-averse investor select which portfolio or wealth composition to hold?

In Chapter 6 we set out the basic model of consumer choice among goods. The budget line summarized the market opportunities, the goods that a given income would buy. Indifference curves represented individual tastes, and the consumer chose the bundle that was on the highest possible indifference curve given the budget constraint describing which bundles were affordable. We use the same basic approach to the choice of a portfolio.

Instead of the choice between two different goods, we now focus on the choice between the average or expected return on the portfolio and risk that the portfolio embodies.

The Risk–Return Choice

Tastes   The risk-averse consumer (or financial investor) prefers a higher average return on the portfolio but dislikes higher risk. To take more risk he needs to think they will receive a higher average return. By 'risk' we mean the variability of returns on the whole portfolio. From the previous section, we know that a portfolio composed exclusively of industrial shares would be much riskier than a portfolio composed exclusively of Treasury bills.

Opportunities   To highlight the problem of portfolio selection we assume there are only two possible assets in which to invest. Bank deposits are a relatively safe asset. The investor has a relatively good idea of the rate of return on bank deposits. The other asset is industrial shares, which are much riskier since their return is more variable.

The investor has a given wealth to invest. If all wealth is put into bank deposits the whole portfolio will earn the return on bank deposit and this will be relatively riskless. The higher the fraction of the portfolio held in industrial shares, the more closely the return on the whole portfolio resembles the return on shares and the riskier it becomes.

Portfolio Choice   Suppose the average return on the risky asset (shares) is lower than the average return on the safe asset (bank deposits). Putting more of the portfolio into bank deposits both increases the portfolio return *and* reduces the risk of variability of the return on the whole portfolio. The risk-averse investor will put the whole portfolio into the safe asset.

To consider buying the risky asset, the investor must believe the average return on the risky asset exceeds the average return on the safe asset. Suppose this is the case. How much of the portfolio will be put into the risky asset? It all depends how risky the risky asset is and how big the differential is between the average return on the two assets. Generally, however, the fraction of the portfolio held in the risky asset will be higher (1) the higher the average return on the risky asset compared with the safe asset, (2) the less risky is the risky asset, and (3) the less risk-averse is the investor.

Diversification

When there are several risky assets the investor may be able to reduce the risk on the whole portfolio *without* having to accept a lower average return on the portfolio. We illustrate this possibility using Table 14-3 whose structure resembles the problem of the actress and the farmer we studied in Table 14-2. There are two risky assets, say, oil shares and banking shares. Each has two possible returns: £4 if things go well and £2 if things go badly. Each industry has a 50 per cent chance of good times and a 50 per cent chance of bad times. Finally, we assume that the returns in the two industries are independent. Good times in the oil industry tell us nothing about whether the banking industry is having good or bad times.

You have £2 to invest, and oil and bank shares each cost £1. Which portfolio gives the best risk–return combination? First note that both shares have the same payoff characteristics – the same returns and the same chances. You should be indifferent between buying only oil

shares and only bank shares. But a superior strategy is to buy one of each and *diversify* the portfolio.

Diversification is the strategy of reducing risk by risk-pooling across several assets whose individual returns behave differently from one another.

Diversification means not putting all your eggs into one basket.[4] Suppose you buy only one kind of share. Buying two shares for your £2, you have a 50 per cent chance of earning £8 and a 50 per cent chance of earning £4. It all depends whether the industry in which you invest has good or bad times. The average return is £6, but the actual return will either be £4 or £8.

Table 14-3 shows the payoffs from the diversified portfolio with one of each share. If both industries do well you will make £8, but this is only a 25 per cent chance. There is a 50 per cent chance of oil doing well but, since returns in the two industries are independent, on only half of those occasions will banking also be having good times. Similarly, there is a 25 per cent chance of both industries doing badly at the same time. There is also a 25 per cent chance that one industry does well while the other one does badly. Each of the four portfolio returns shown in Table 14-3 is a 25 per cent chance.

The average return on the portfolio is still £6, just as when you put all your £2 into one kind of share, but the variability of portfolio returns has been reduced. Instead of a 50/50 chance of £4 or £8, you now have only a 25 per cent chance of each of the extreme outcomes and a 50 per cent chance of earning the average return of £6.

Diversification reduces the risk by pooling it without altering the average rate of return. It offers you a better deal. As in our earlier discussion of risk-pooling by insurance com-

---

[4] When Professor James Tobin of Yale received the Nobel Prize for economics in 1981 for, among other things, his work on portfolio choice, reporters asked him to summarize as simply as he could what his work was about. He replied that it showed that it was not wise to put all your eggs in one basket. This reply prompted several cartoons in which people were given Nobel Prizes for other discoveries such as 'A stitch in time saves nine'. Of course Tobin's work went well beyond the simple slogan. It showed precisely what trade-offs were involved in making portfolio choices and what portfolios the consumer would end up choosing.

Table 14-3 Payoff to a diversified portfolio

		BANKING	
		GOOD	BAD
OIL	GOOD	£8	£6
	BAD	£6	£4

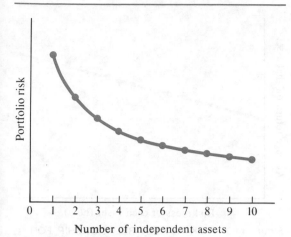

Figure 14-2 RISK REDUCTION THROUGH DIVERSIFICATION. The riskiness of a portfolio, the variability of its total return, can be reduced through diversification, but the gains to further diversification diminish quite rapidly.

panies, the greater the number of risky assets with independent returns across which the portfolio pools the risk, the lower will be the total risk of the portfolio.

Figure 14-2 shows the typical relationship between the total portfolio risk and the number of independent assets in the portfolio. The figure not only shows that portfolio risk declines as the number of independent risky assets is increased; it also shows that most of the gains of risk reduction through diversification come very quickly. Even a few assets cut the total risk a lot. (This explains why people carry one spare tyre in their cars rather than five.)

Because it is more expensive to buy in quantities of under 100 shares, small investors typically hold a dozen different shares rather than a hundred. They get many of the benefits of diversifying without having to buy too few shares at a time. People who are even more risk-averse and really want to hold a large number of shares are better advised to buy shares in a mutual fund or unit trust, a professionally run fund that buys large quantities of many different shares and then retails small shares in the total fund to small investors.

Diversification When Asset Returns Are Correlated

Risk-pooling works because asset returns are independent of each other. When asset returns

move together, we say that they are *correlated*. When returns on two assets tend to move in the same direction we say they are *positively correlated*. For example, a general expansion of the whole economy will tend to be good for bank shares and shares of motor car manufacturers. If returns tend to move in opposite directions, we say they are *negatively correlated*. For example, if people buy gold shares during financial crises, gold shares will tend to rise when other shares are falling and vice versa.

Positive and negative correlations have different implications for the effect of diversification in reducing risk. Suppose bank shares have good times *only* when oil shares have good times and vice versa. Buying one of each is just like putting all your money in one kind of share. Diversification achieves nothing. When returns are perfectly positively correlated risk-pooling does not work, just as it did not work in the 'acts of God' example we discussed for the insurance industry.

Conversely, diversification is a spectacular success when returns are negatively correlated. Suppose bank shares do well only when oil shares are doing badly and vice versa. Buying one of each, you earn either £4 from oil and £2 from banking or £2 from oil and £4 from banking. On the diversified portfolio you earn £6 for certain. You have diversified away all the risk, even though each of the individual shares is quite risky.

In practice, returns on different shares are never perfectly correlated. Some *tend* to vary together and some *tend* to vary in opposite directions, but over any particular period actual returns on two shares may not exhibit their usual correlation. Thus it is impossible to completely diversify away all portfolio risk. But smart fund managers are always on the lookout for an asset that tends to have a negative correlation with the assets in the existing portfolio. On average, extending the portfolio to include this asset will improve the risk–return characteristics of the portfolio.

Beta

Beta is a measurement of the extent to which a particular share's return moves with the return on the whole stock market. Table 14-4 gives some examples. The first row shows returns on the market as a whole in booms, normal times,

Table 14-4 Share returns and beta

ASSET	RETURNS		
	BOOM	NORMAL	SLUMP
	%	%	%
Stock market	14	6	−2
High beta	20	10	−8
Beta = 1	14	6	−2
Low beta	5	4	3
Negative beta	2	3	5

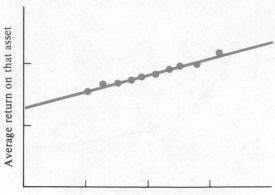

Riskiness of each asset (beta)

Figure 14-3   RISK–RETURN RELATIONSHIP FOR COMPANY SHARES, 1931–65.   Each share's risk is measured by its beta, which shows how that share's returns move with returns in the market as a whole. The higher the beta, the more the inclusion of the share in a portfolio will increase the total portfolio risk. The data show that riskier shares with higher betas must offer a higher return on average to compensate for this disadvantage.

and slumps. A share with beta = 1 moves exactly the same way as the whole market. A high beta share does even better when the market is up but even worse when the market is down. A low beta share moves in the same general direction as the market but more sluggishly than the market. Negative beta shares move against the market trend.

Most shares move pretty much with the market and have a beta close to one. There are not too many negative beta shares, but some gold shares have betas that are close to zero. This suggests that most people should have some gold shares in their portfolios.

Bankers and stockbrokers calculate betas from the past behaviour of individual shares and the whole stock market. Ideally, they are looking for negative beta shares which will greatly reduce the risk of a portfolio whose other components vary with the market as a whole. Even low beta shares are partly independent of the rest of the market and allow some risk to be pooled. High beta shares are doubly undesirable. Not only are their own returns highly variable but, because they vary in the same direction as the whole market, they cannot be used to pool risk.

A share with a low (or even negative) beta will be in high demand. Risk-averse purchasers are anxious to buy low beta shares whose inclusion in their portfolios will reduce the total portfolio risk. High demand will bid up the share price and reduce the average return, but investors are happy to trade off a lower return for the success of low beta shares in reducing the total risk of their portfolios.

Hence in stock market equilibrium low beta shares should have high prices and low rates of return on average. High beta shares add to investors' portfolio risk and will be purchased only because they have low prices and high

rates of return on average which compensate for their undesirable risk characteristics. Figure 14-3 shows the results of an early study by Professors Black, Jensen, and Scholes using stock market data from 1931 to 1965. They found clearly that average returns on individual shares rise steadily with the shares' beta as the theory predicts.

To sum up, in stock market equilibrium individual share prices depend both on expected or average returns and on risk characteristics. The risk characteristics of the firm's shares determine the expected return the share must offer if it is to compete with other shares. For a given required return, equation (1) implies that higher anticipated dividends or capital gains will mean a higher current share price. Unless shares with anticipated high dividends or capital gains have high share prices, they will have above-average expected rates of return for their risk characteristics. They will be a bargain and people will buy them, bidding up the share price until it reaches its equilibrium level.

In considering the risk characteristics of the firm's shares the crucial point is that we are not concerned with the variability of the share's return in isolation from the rest of the market. This is why beta matters. Adding a risky asset to the portfolio will reduce the risk of the portfolio provided the share's beta is less than 1. Low beta shares can be individually risky; nevertheless, taken with other shares they reduce portfolio risk and are therefore desirable since people are risk-averse. In equilibrium, low beta shares will have an above-average price and a below-average rate of return to offset this advantage.

Diversification in Other Situations

Diversification is an important facet of behaviour by risk-averse people in many other situations. Countries diversify their sources of supply of raw materials. No country likes buying all its oil, copper, or titanium from a single producer. If anything disrupts that producer's ability or willingness to sell, the country may face a disaster. Similarly, an individual farmer will be reluctant to rely on a single crop.

It may be much better for a navy to have two small aircraft carriers than one large one. If the only aircraft carrier is sunk the navy will be completely without air cover. Again, diversification is important.

14-5 Efficient Asset Markets

There are two basic images of the stock market. One is that of a casino, where there is no rational basis for speculation; it is all a matter of luck. The other view – the theory of *efficient markets* – is that the stock market is a sensitive processor of information, quickly responding to new information to adjust share prices correctly. The second view recognizes that share prices fluctuate a lot but argues that these flucutations are the appropriate response to new information as it becomes available.

Shares are claims on future dividends of companies. Individuals, and society, should value a company more highly (1) the higher the profits the company earns and hence the dividends it can pay its shareholders, and (2) the lower its beta. Companies that do well when everyone else is in a slump not merely reduces the risk of portfolios that include their shares; they also help to stabilize the economy. They are providing high output, employment, and profits when other firms are doing badly.

If companies with high average returns and low betas have high share prices, it is easier for

these companies to expand by issuing new shares. The higher the share price, the more money the company will raise by floating a new share issue and the more likely the company is to invest in plant and machinery financed by a new share issue. Share prices are guiding the right firms to invest. Companies with low average returns and high betas are valued neither by financial investors nor by society at large. Low share prices make it hard for them to raise money to finance new plant and equipment, and they will tend to contract.

Hence it matters which of the two views of the stock market is correct. If share prices correctly reflect prospective dividends and risk characteristics – the efficient market view – a free market in industrial shares is essentially guiding society's scarce resources towards the right firms. But if share prices are purely pot luck, as in a casino, the wrong firms may be guided to expand just because their share prices are high.

Testing for Efficiency

Suppose everybody has all the information available today about the likely risks and returns on different shares. Equilibrium share prices should equate the likely return on all shares with the same risk characteristics. Otherwise there would be an obvious opportunity to switch from the low return shares to higher return shares with equivalent risk characteristics. If the market has got it right, it does not matter which share you buy in any risk class. They are all expected to yield the same return. The efficient market view says there is no way of beating the market to earn an above-average return on a share of a given risk class.

If the market neglects some available information you could use this information to beat the market. For example, if the market failed to spot that hot weather increases ice cream sales it would never mark up share prices in ice cream companies when good weather occurred. By buying ice cream shares when the sun shone you would make money and beat the market. The market would be surprised by high dividends from ice cream companies and realize too late that it would have been a bargain to have bought ice cream shares for the price being quoted. But you bought them, having figured all this out by using extra information. You knew ice cream shares would pay a higher rate of return than the market thought. You spotted an inefficiency in the market.

In contrast, the efficient market view says that all the relevant available information is immediately incorporated in the share price. Given the long-range weather forecast, the market makes the best guess about profits and dividends in the ice cream industry and sets the current price to give the required rate of return for shares with the same risk characteristics as ice cream shares. If the weather forecast is correct, the return will be as predicted. If unexpectedly there is a hot spell, the market will immediately mark up ice cream shares to reflect the new ·information that ice cream profits will be higher than previously expected. How high are ice cream shares marked up? To the price that reduces the expected rate of return back to the average for that risk class.

Thus the crucial implication of the efficient market theory is that asset prices correctly reflect all existing information. It is unforeseen new information that changes share prices as the market quickly incorporates this unantici- pated development to restore expected returns to the required level. But there is no way existing information can systematically be used to get above-average returns for that risk class of asset.

The theory of efficient markets has been tested extensively to see whether there is any *currently available* information that would allow an investor systematically to earn an above-average return for that risk class. The vast majority of all empirical studies conclude that there is no readily available information that the market neglects. In particular, rules of the form 'buy shares when the price has risen two days in a row' do not work. Nor do rules that use existing information about how the economy or the industry is doing. Smart investors have taken this information on board as it became available. It is already in the price.

The empirical literature usually concludes you may as well stick a pin in the financial pages of a newspaper as employ an expensive financial adviser. Paradoxically, it is because the market has *already* used all the relevant economic information correctly that there are no bargains around. The theory of efficient markets does not say share prices and returns are unaffected by economics; it says that, because the economics has been correctly used to set the existing price, there are no easy pickings.

Financial newspapers and stock market insti- tutions run competitions for the investor of the year. If the theory of efficient markets is right, why do some portfolios do better than others? Why, indeed, are financial portfolio advisers in business at all? The world is uncertain, and there will always be new surprises that could not have been previously forecast. As this new information is incorporated in share prices some lucky investors will find they happen to have already invested in shares whose prices has unexpectedly risen. Others will have been unlucky, holding shares whose price unexpec- tedly falls.

Thus one interpretation of why some in- vestors do better than others is pure chance. This story could even explain why some investors have above-average returns for several years in a row. Even with a fair coin there is roughly one chance in a thousand of tossing ten consecutive heads. Even if there is no systematic way to beat the market, there are thousands of investors, and someone is going to have a lucky streak for ten years.

But there is also a more subtle interpretation. When a piece of new information first becomes available someone has to decide *how* share prices should be adjusted. The price does not change by magic. And there is an incentive to be quick off the mark. The first person to get the information, or correctly to calculate where the market will soon be setting the price, may be able to buy a share just before everyone else catches on and the share's price rises. The empirical evidence is compatible with the view that the non-specialist investor cannot use *past* information to make above-average profits. But it is also compatible with the view that the specialist investors, by reacting very quickly, can make capital gains or avoid capital losses within the first few hours of new information becoming available. It is their actions that help to change the price, and the small profits that they make from fast dealing are what pay the portfolio industry's salaries. It is the economic return to their time and effort in gathering and processing information. If the return is high, more people will be attracted into the industry. For example, in the UK employment in the industry increased during the period 1977–82, when stock markets were very volatile, even though employment in the whole economy fell substantially. Similarly, the enhanced opportunities for trading profits following deregulation under Big Bang led to an explosion of City salaries and employment in 1986.

Speculative Bubbles

Consider the market for gold. Unlike shares or bonds, gold pays no dividend or interest payment. Its return accrues entirely through the capital gain element in equation (1). Today's prices depend on the anticipated capital gain, which in turn depends on expectations of tomorrow's price. But tomorrow's price will depend on the capital gain then expected, which will depend on expectations of the price the day after; and so on.

In such markets there is no way for the *fundamentals*, the economic calculations about future dividends or interest payments, to influence the price. It all depends on what people today think people tomorrow will expect people the next day to expect. Such a market is vulnerable to *speculative bubbles*. If everyone believes the price will rise tomorrow, it makes sense to purchase the asset today. So long as people expect the price to keep rising, it makes sense to keep buying even though the price may already have risen a lot.[5]

A famous example of a speculative bubble is the South Sea Bubble of 1720. A company was set up to sell British goods to people in the South Seas and to bring home the wonderful and exotic goods produced there. The shares were issued long before any attempt was made actually to trade these goods. It sounded a great idea and people bought the shares. The price rose quickly, and soon people were buying not in anticipation of eventual dividends but purely to resell the shares at a profit once the price had gone even higher. The price rose even faster, till one day it became apparent that the company's proposal was a fiasco with no

chance of success and the bubble burst. Even Sir Isaac Newton lost money in the bubble.

More recently the great English economist John Maynard Keynes has argued that the stock market is like a casino because it is dominated by short-term speculators who buy not in anticipation of future dividends but purely to resell at a quick profit.[6] In terms of equation (1) again, it is capital gains not dividends that matter. Since next period's share price depends on what people then think the following period's share price will be, Keynes likened the stock market to a beauty competition in a newspaper, where the winner is the reader who guesses the beauty who will receive most votes from all readers. Thus, Keynes argued, share prices will reflect what average opinion expects average opinion to be.

Keynes made a lot of money on the stock market, so his views deserve some attention. Nor does the empirical evidence on the 'efficient market' theory necessarily reject the 'casino' theory. If share prices are set by beliefs or whims about what other investors will think, share prices will move quite randomly and empirical investigators will conclude that no available information can be used to systematically beat the market.

Undoubtedly, financial markets do sometimes exhibit temporary bubbles. Nevertheless, they *are* usually temporary. Eventually it becomes obvious that the share price has moved away from the price that could be justified by fundamentals. Bubbles are less likely the larger the share of the total return that comes in the form of dividends rather than capital gains. And we do have some evidence that, although there are no systematic opportunities to beat the market, market prices themselves are more compatible with the efficient market theory than the pure casino theory. For example, the relation between share prices and betas shown in Figure 14-3 is evidence in favour of efficient markets and against the pure 'casino' theory.

14-6 More on Risk

Risk is a central characteristic of economic life. Every topic in this book could be extended to include uncertainty. Although individual applications differ, two features recur: individuals try to find arrangements to reduce risk, and those who take over the risk-bearing have to

---

[5] For a lively account of bubbles and other exciting forms of market behaviour, see Charles Kindleberger, *Manias, Panics, and Crashes*, Basic Books, 1978.
[6] John Maynard Keynes, *The General Theory of Unemployment, Interest, and Money*, Macmillan, 1936, Chapter 12.

BOX 14-1

BLACK MONDAY: THE STOCK MARKET CRASH OF 19 OCTOBER 1987

From its level of January 1987, the UK stock market had risen 75 per cent by October. Wall Street had risen 30 per cent, and stock markets as diverse as Hong Kong and Frankfurt were also showing major gains. World stock markets were valuing the firms of the world 40 per cent more highly in October than they had been in January. And the volume of trading had reached unprecedented levels.

On Black Monday, world stock markets crashed. London and New York each fell 30 per cent. It was the same story throughout Europe. In Hong Kong the index fell 50 per cent and the exchange actually closed for several days. The increasing globalization of world financial markets made the crash spread like a forest fire. Only Tokyo escaped the crash.

Why did stock markets crash? The simplest explanation is that it was the collapse of a speculative bubble. Alan Greenspan, chairman of the US Federal Reserve System, described it as 'an accident waiting to happen'. But other explanations have been put forward.

First, there had been bad news over the weekend – spiralling US trade and budget deficits, the Iran–Contra affair, the Gulf War. But it seems unlikely the new information in itself justified such a severe revision of beliefs about expected profits and share prices. The news might have justified a belief that uncertainty had risen and share prices would be more volatile. Other things equal, if equities are riskier relative to other kinds of investment, share prices

ought to fall.

A second possibility is fear that financial markets would fail. If the firms acting as market-makers – people with inventories of shares who quote buying and selling prices – have insufficient financial backing, a fall in share prices can make them bankrupt when the value of their inventories falls. Fearing this, investors tried to get off this ship before it sank, thereby making the crisis worse. This may explain why Tokyo was different; Japanese market-makers have much greater financial backing than those in the other countries.

Third, some investors specialize in being highly informed (a costly activity), but others know they don't know much. To limit potential losses, they have automatic orders in place to sell when the market falls more than a certain amount. A modest fall can trigger massive selling and a bigger fall. Again, Tokyo was rather special. The Tokyo market automatically closes for the day when the index has fallen 15 per cent, thereby giving panicking investors a chance to regain their nerve before the following day.

Finally, unlike countries where the government believes that promotion of vigorous stock market trading is an end in itself, the Japanese believe that the stock market is too important to the rest of the economy to be allowed to inflict damage on the real economy. The Japanese Ministry of Finance organized a rescue operation to buy shares and prop up the index to prevent a major stock market crash.

Adapted from David Blake, *Financial Market Analysis* (McGraw-Hill, 1990, Chapter 17).

---

be compensated for so doing. In this section we outline two further applications of these themes.

Hedging and Forward Markets

A *forward market* deals in contracts made today for delivery of goods at a specified future date at a price agreed to day. There are forward markets for many commodities and assets including corn, coffee, sugar, copper, gold, and foreign currencies.

Suppose the current price of copper is £800 a ton and people expect the price to rise to £880 a ton after 12 months. Some people will hold

copper in their portfolios. The expected capital gain is 10 per cent of the purchase price, and it may be interesting to diversify a portfolio by including copper. However, that is not our concern at present.

Suppose you own a copper mine and know you will have 1 ton of copper to sell in 12 months' time. The *spot* price of copper is the price for immediate delivery. Today's spot price is £800 and people expect the spot price to be £880 at this time next year. One option is for you simply to sell your copper at the spot price at this time next year. You expect that to be £880 but you cannot be sure today what the price next year will actually be. It is risky.

Alternatively, you can *hedge* against this risk in the forward market for copper. Suppose today you can sell 1 ton of copper for delivery in 12 months' time at a price of £860 agreed today. You have hedged against the risky future spot price. You know for certain what you will receive when your copper is available for delivery. But you have sold your copper for only £860, even though you expect copper then to sell for £880 on the spot market. You regard this as an insurance premium to get out of the risk associated with the future spot price.

To whom do you sell your copper in the forward market? You sell it to a trader whom we can call a *speculator*. The speculator has no interest in 1 ton of copper *per se*. But the speculator, having promised you £860 for copper to be delivered in one year's time, currently expects to resell that copper immediately it is delivered. The speculator expects to get £880 for that copper in the spot market next year. He or she expects to make £20 as the compensation for bearing your risk. If spot copper prices turn out to be less than £860 next year the speculator will actually lose money. £20 is the risk premium necessary to attract enough speculators into the forward market to take up the risky positions that hedgers wish to avoid.

Whereas someone buying spot copper today at £800 for possible resale next year at £880 must compare the expected capital gain of 10 per cent with returns and interest rates on offer in other assets – copper must cover the opportunity cost of the returns that could have been earned by using this money elsewhere – the speculator in the forward market need not make this comparison. No money is currently tied up in the forward contract. Although the price has been agreed today at £860, the money is handed over only next year when the copper is delivered. Provided that the speculator then resells in next year's spot market, no money is actually tied up. All the speculator has to think about is the likely spot price in 12 months' time and how much it could vary either side of this estimate. The riskier the future spot price, the larger premium the speculator will require and the more the current forward price will lie below the expected future spot price.

In the previous example, the speculator had an open position. The speculator had taken

forward delivery of copper only in order to resell it at a likely profit. Suppose you use copper as an input to a production process. You may wish to *buy* copper for delivery in 12 months' time at a price agreed today. Again, you wish to hedge against the risky future spot price. A speculator who can make two forward contracts, one to take delivery of copper from the copper miner, the other to sell copper to a copper user, does not have an open position. The speculator's book is balanced and there is no residual risk. The risky future spot price is irrelevant, since the speculator need neither buy in the future spot market (to find copper for people the speculator has contracted to deliver to in 12 months' time) nor sell in the future spot market (to offload copper which the speculator has promised to accept in 12 months' time).

In forward markets with roughly equal numbers of people wishing to hedge by buying and hedge by selling, speculators' books will roughly balance and the residual risk is small. Hence the speculators need only a little compensation to cover this residual risk and the administration costs. The current price of forward copper should be close to the expected future spot price. This seems to fit the facts. There is little systematic discrepancy between today's forward price and the spot price that subsequently transpires. Among other things, this suggests that speculators on average guess future spot prices correctly. However, it is a risky business if buyers and sellers cannot be matched up in the forward market. In practice, the spot prices that subsequently transpire can vary by a large amount on either side of the estimate implicitly contained in the current forward price.

Why are there forward markets for copper and silver but not for cars and washing machines? Again, we return to the questions of moral hazard and adverse selection which we said could inhibit the development of insurance markets. Suppose today you make a contract for delivery of a new car model in 12 months' time. Suppose the motor car manufacturer has sold 5 million of its new model in today's forward market. At £5000 each, the company has a guaranteed revenue of £25 billion next year whatever kind of car it develops. You thought you were buying a de luxe family saloon, but the company brings out a low-

BOX 14-2

SPOT MARKETS AND FORWARD MARKETS

At first most people find it hard to keep track of all the different terms – spot price, future spot price, expected future spot price, and forward price. Here is a chance to see if you have got them straight. Suppose there is a spot market for copper open every weekday of the year. There is also a forward market for copper also open every weekday of the year. For simplicity, suppose the only type of forward contract that exists is for delivery of copper one year after the deal is struck but at a price agreed immediately. However, the money only changes hands when the copper is delivered in one year's time. Suppose today is 1 June 1990.

TERM	DEFINITION	EXAMPLE
Today's spot price	Price of copper on 1 June 1990 for delivery and payment on 1 June 1990	£800/ton
Future spot price	Price of copper being traded in the spot market at some future date, say 1 June 1991	Whatever it then is, say £900/ton or £820/ton
	As of today we cannot be certain what the spot price will be on 1 June 1991	
Expected future spot price	The best guess today (1 June 1990) about what the spot price will be on 1 June 1991	£860/ton
Forward price	Price in forward market on 1 June 1990 at which copper is being traded for delivery and payment on 1 June 1991	£840/ton
Risk premium	Difference between expected future spot price and the current forward price. The amount of money a hedger expects on average to lose by making a forward contract on 1 June 1990 to sell copper which is delivered on 1 June 1991 rather than taking a chance on the spot price that will be prevailing on 1 June 1991 when the copper is actually available for delivery and sale. The amount the hedger is prepared to pay to get out of the risk. Also, the amount the speculator expects to make by offering the forward contract and then reselling the copper in the spot market on 1 June 1991	£860 − £840 = £20/ton

quality car and says 'this is our new model'. Either you pay up or there is an expensive court wrangle. By making all these forward contracts the motor car manufacturer has affected its own quality incentives.

Forward markets do not exist for the vast majority of goods because it is impossible to write legally binding and cheaply enforceable contracts that specify the characteristics of the commodity being traded. Where forward markets do exist they are for very standardized commodities – 18-carat gold, copper of a certain grade, Japanese yen – which are easily defined. Thus, although forward markets are an important mechanism by which individuals can reduce the risks they face, there are only a limited number of risks that can be hedged in this way.

Compensating Differentials in the Return to Labour

Since people are risk-averse, we expect people with risky jobs to earn more on average than people whose jobs are safe. Broadly speaking this seems confirmed by the facts. Divers who inspect North Sea oil pipelines earn high hourly rates because the death rate in this activity is high in comparison with other jobs of equivalent skill and unpleasantness. University academics earn relatively low wages in the UK because many of them have secure jobs, unlike industrial managers who may find themselves out of a job if their company has a bad spell.

At a broad level, profits are often seen as a reward given to entrepreneurs, individuals who set up and run firms, for taking big risks. The average person who starts a business works long hours for small rewards initially. In the early stages there is the continual threat of failure, and many small firms never get off the ground. The possibility of becoming a millionaire, like Richard Branson of Virgin in the UK or Edwin Land of Polaroid in the United States, is the carrot that is required to persuade people to embark on this risky activity.

Summary

1   Uncertainty pervades economic life. Although some people gamble occasionally for fun and some addicts gamble in spite of themselves, most people seem to be risk-averse. They volunteer to take risks only if they are offered favourable odds which on average will yield a profit. Conversely, most people pay for insurance at less than fair odds in order to reduce some of the risks they would otherwise face.

2   Risk aversion may be explained by diminishing marginal utility of wealth. A fair gamble in monetary terms yields less extra utility when it succeeds than it sacrifices when it fails. Hence people usually refuse fair gambles except for very small stakes. The prevalence of risk aversion implies that individuals look for ways to reduce risk and must compensate people who take over their risk-bearing.

3   Insurance schemes work by pooling risks that are substantially independent to reduce the aggregate risk, and by spreading any residual risk across a large number of people so that each insurer has a very small stake in the risk that cannot be pooled away.

4   Insurance markets are inhibited by adverse selection and moral hazard. The former means that high-risk clients are more likely to take out insurance; the latter means that the act of insuring may increase the likelihood that the undesired outcome will in fact occur.

5   Industrial shares have a higher average return but a much more variable return than that on Treasury bills or bank deposits.

6   Portfolio choices depend on the investor's tastes – the trade-offs between risk and average return that yield equal utility – and on the opportunities that the market provides – the risk and return combinations on existing assets.

7   When risks on different asset returns are independent, the risk of the whole portfolio can be reduced by diversification across many assets.

8   The risk that an asset contributes to a portfolio is not measured by the variability of that asset's own return. Much more important is the correlation of its return with the return of other available assets. An asset that is negatively correlated with other assets will actually reduce the risk on the whole portfolio even though its own return is risky. Conversely, assets with a strong positive correlation with the rest of the portfolio will increase the overall risk. The value of beta for an asset measures its correlation with other assets.

9   In equilibrium risky assets can earn higher rates of return on average to compensate portfolio holders for bearing this extra risk. High beta assets have high returns. If an asset is offering too high an expected return for its risk class, people will buy the asset, bidding up its price until the expected return is forced back to its equilibrium level.

10   In an efficient market assets are priced to reflect the latest available information about their risk and return. There are no easy systematic investment opportunities to beat the market unless you systematically get or use new information faster than other people. Evidence from share prices is compatible with stock market efficiency, but speculative bubbles sometimes occur.

11   Forward markets set a price today for future delivery of and payment for goods. They allow people to hedge against risky spot prices in the future by making a contract today. Speculators take over the hedgers' risk and will require a premium unless they can match buyers and sellers. In practice, matching is quite close

and forward prices agreed today on average are close to today's expectation of the spot price in the future. But over the life of the forward contract there will usually be a lot of new information which leads the spot price to deviate from the level previously expected.

Key Terms

Risk-neutrality
Risk-aversion
Risk-loving
Diminishing marginal utility of wealth
Risk-pool
Risk-sharing
Moral hazard
Adverse selection
Diversification
Capital gains and losses
Correlation of returns
Beta
Efficient asset markets
Speculative bubbles
Forward markets and spot markets
Hedgers
Speculators
Compensating differentials

Problems

1   A fair coin is to be tossed. If it comes down heads the player wins £1. If it comes down tails the player loses £1. Person A doesn't mind whether or not she takes the bet. Person B will pay £0.02 to play the game. Person C demands £0.05 before being willing to play. Characterize the three people's attitude to risk. Which would be most likely to take out insurance for car theft?

2   It is sometimes said that the family is one of the main forms of insurance. Can you give several reasons why people might think this?

3   You hear a radio commercial for life insurance for anyone over 45 years old. No medical examination is required. Do you expect the premium rates to be high, low, or average? Why?

4   In which of the following are the risks being pooled: (a) life insurance; (b) insurance against the Thames flooding? (c) insurance for a pop star's voice?

5   You set up a firm to advise the unemployed on the best way to use their time to earn money. Your firm issues shares on the stock market. In equilibrium, will your shares be expected to earn a higher or lower return than the stock market average? Why?

6   Why did the US stock market fall sharply when it was announced that President Kennedy had been shot?

7   Someone gives you a tip that a firm has invented a fine new product. (a) Assuming that you are an active investor, what do you do about it: (b) Why are stock markets regulated to prevent 'inside trading' where a firm's managers use inside information about the firm to buy and sell its shares?

8   Common Fallacies   Show why the following statements are incorrect: (a) Economists cannot predict changes in the stock market. This proves that economics is useless in thinking about share prices. (b) It is silly to take out insurance. If the insurance company is making a profit on average its clients must be losing money. (c) Prudent investors should not buy shares whose returns are more volatile than those of the 'blue chip' companies such as GEC and ICI. (d) You make money by buying at the bottom and selling at the top. Hence you should buy shares whose price has fallen a lot and sell shares whose price has risen a lot.

3

Welfare Economics

15

Introduction to Welfare Economics

'We want to see an economy in which firms, large and small, have an incentive to expand by winning extra business and creating jobs. . . . Only a government which really works to promote *free enterprise* can provide the right conditions for that dream to come true.'

Conservative Election Manifesto

'The Tories say that "competition" ensures that shoppers get a fair deal. The customers know better. Stronger *legal safeguards* are essential to protect customers . . . We must rebuild . . . under a Labour Government working together with unions and managers to *plan* Britain's industrial development.'

Labour Election Manifesto
[Italics added by the authors]

In Chapter 1 we pointed out that markets are not the only device by which society can resolve the questions, what, how, and for whom to produce. Communist economies, for example, rely much more heavily on central direction or command. Are markets a good way to allocate scarce resources? What does 'good' mean? Is it fair that some people earn much more than others in a market economy? These are not positive issues about how the economy works but normative issues about how well it works. They are normative because the assessment will depend in part on the value judgements adopted by the assessor.

Welfare economics is the branch of economics dealing with normative issues. Its purpose is not to describe how the economy works but to assess how well it works.

The election manifestos of the Conservative and Labour parties fundamentally disagree about how well a market economy works. But how are we to cut through the political rhetoric to see what lies behind the disagreement? Two themes recur throughout our discussion of welfare economics in Part 3. The first is the question of *allocative efficiency*. Is the economy getting the most out of its scarce resources or are they being squandered? The second is the question of *equity*. How fair is the *distribution* of goods and services between different members of society?

15-1 Equity and Efficiency

We begin by defining what we mean by these terms.

Equity

Economists use two different concepts of equity or fairness.

Horizontal equity is the identical treatment of identical people. *Vertical equity* is the different treatment of different people in order to reduce the consequences of these innate differences.

Whether or not either concept of equity is desirable is a pure value judgement. Horizontal equity would rule out racial or sexual discrimination between people whose economic characteristics and performance were literally identical. Vertical equity is the Robin Hood principle of taking from the rich to give to the poor.

Most people would agree that horizontal equity is a good thing. In contrast, although few people believe that the poor should starve, the extent to which incomes or resources should be redistributed from the 'haves' to the 'have-nots' to increase the degree of vertical equity is an issue on which different people take very different positions.

Efficient Resource Allocation

By a *resource allocation* for an economy we mean a list or complete description of who does what and who gets what. To emphasize that markets are not the only possible allocation devices, we begin by assuming that allocations are chosen by a central dictator. Feasible or producible allocations depend on the technology and resources available to the economy. The ultimate worth of any allocation depends on consumer tastes, which determine how people value what they are given.

Figure 15-1 shows an economy with only two people, David and Susie. The initial allocation at point A gives David a quantity of goods Q_D and Susie a quantity of goods Q_S. Are society's resources being wasted? Suppose by reorganizing production it was possible to produce at point B to the north-east of A. If David and Susie assess their own utility by the quantity of goods they themselves receive, and if they would each rather have more goods than less, B is a better allocation than A since both David and Susie get more. It is inefficient to produce at A if production at B is possible. Similarly, a move from A to C makes both David and Susie worse off. If it is possible to be at A, it is definitely inefficient to be at C.

But what about a move from A to E or F? One person gains but the other person loses. Whether we judge such a change desirable depends on how *we* value David's utility relative to Susie's. If we think David's utility is terribly important we might consider a move from A to F a good thing, even though Susie's utility will be severely reduced.

Value judgements about equity, the fairness of the distribution of goods between people, have got mixed up with our attempt to make statements about waste or inefficiency. Since different people will make different value judgements, there can be no unambiguous answer to the question of whether a move from A to D, E, or F is desirable. It all depends who is making the assessment.

In an effort to separate as far as possible the discussion of equity from the discussion of efficiency, modern welfare economics uses the idea of *Pareto-efficiency* named after the economist Vilfredo Pareto whose *Manuel D'Economie Politique* was published as long ago as 1909.

> An allocation is *Pareto-efficient* for a given set of consumer tastes, resources, and technology, if it is impossible to move to another allocation which would make some people better off and nobody worse off.

In terms of Figure 15-1 a move from A to B or A to G is a *Pareto gain*. In either case Susie is better off and David no worse off. If B or G is a feasible allocation which could be produced then point A is *Pareto-inefficient*.

How about a move from A to D? David is better off but Susie is worse off. The Pareto criterion has nothing to say about such a change. Without bringing in an explicit value judgement about the relative importance of David's and Susie's utility we cannot evaluate this change. Thus the Pareto principle is of only limited use in comparing allocations on efficiency grounds. It only allows us to evaluate moves to the north-east or the south-west in Figure 15-1, but it is the most we can say about efficiency without becoming entangled in value judgements about equity.

Figure 15-2 takes the argument one stage further. Suppose by all possible reorganizations of production, the dictator decides that the economy can produce anywhere inside or on the frontier AB. From any allocation inside the

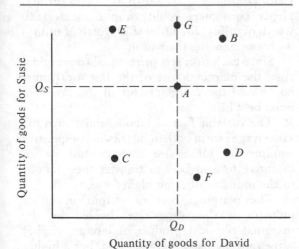

Figure 15-1 ALLOCATING GOODS TO TWO PEOPLE. Provided people assess their own utility by the quantity of goods that they themselves receive, B is a better allocation than A which in turn is a better allocation than C. But a comparison of A with points such as D, E or F, requires us to adopt a value judgement about the relative importance to us of David's and Susie's utility.

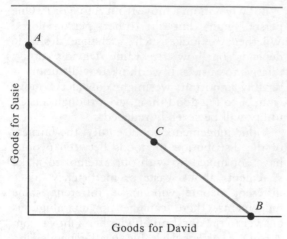

Figure 15-2 THE EFFICIENT FRONTIER. The frontier *AB* shows the maximum quantity of goods which the economy can produce for one person given the quantity of goods being produced for the other person. All points on the frontier are Pareto-efficient. David can only be made better off by making Susie worse off, and vice versa. The distribution of goods between David and Susie is much more equal at point *C* than at points *A* or *B*.

frontier it is always possible to achieve a Pareto gain by moving to the north-east onto the frontier. Hence any point inside the frontier must be Pareto-inefficient. It is possible to make one person better off without making the other person worse off. But *all* points on the frontier are Pareto-efficient. Beginning at a point such as *C*, it is possible to give one person more only by giving the other person less. Since no Pareto gain is possible, every point such as *C* lying on the frontier must be Pareto-efficient.

Thus the dictator should never choose an inefficient allocation inside the frontier. Which of the Pareto-efficient points on the frontier is most desirable will depend on the dictator's value judgement about the relative importance of David's and Susie's utility. It is purely a judgement about equity.

15-2 Perfect Competition and Pareto-Efficiency

Will a free market economy find a Pareto-efficient allocation on its own, or must it be guided there by government intervention? If we can answer this question, we shall have gone some way to understanding the different claims made in the Conservative and Labour mani-

festos. Under certain conditions, soon to be elaborated, we can prove the following striking result: *If every market in the economy is a perfectly competitive free market, the resulting equilibrium throughout the economy will be Pareto-efficient.* Formalizing Adam Smith's remarkable insight of the Invisible Hand, this result is the foundation of modern welfare economics.

Competitive Equilibrium in Free Markets

Suppose there are many producers, many consumers, but only two goods, meals and films. Each market is a free, unregulated market and is perfectly competitive. Suppose the equilibrium price of meals is £5 and the equilibrium price of films is £10. Finally, we suppose that labour is the variable factor of production and that workers like equally the non-monetary aspects of jobs in the films and meals industries.[1] We now argue through the following stages:

1 The last film produced must yield consumers £10 worth of extra utility. If it yielded less (more) extra utility than its £10 purchase price, the last consumer would buy less (more) films. Similarly, the last meal purchased must yield consumers £5 worth of extra utility. Hence consumers could swap 2 meals (£10 worth of utility) for 1 film (£10 worth of utility) without changing their utility.
2 Since each firm sets price equal to marginal cost, the marginal cost of the last meal must be £5 and the marginal cost of the last film must be £10.
3 The variable factor (labour) must earn the same wage rate in both industries in competitive equilibrium. Otherwise there would be an incentive for workers to transfer their labour to the industry offering higher wages.
4 The marginal cost of output in either industry is the wage rate divided by the marginal physical product of labour. Higher wage rates increase marginal cost, but a higher marginal physical product of labour means that less extra workers are needed to make an additional unit of output, thus reducing marginal cost.

---

[1] Otherwise the analysis is more complicated because we need to keep track of changes in job satisfaction when workers transfer between industries.

5   Since wage rates are equal in the two industries and the marginal cost of meals (£5) is half the marginal cost of films (£10), the marginal physical product of labour must be twice as high in the meals industry as in the film industry.

6   Hence reducing film output by 1 unit and transferring the labour thus freed to the meals industry would increase the output of meals by 2 units. The marginal physical product of labour is twice as high in meals as in films. Feasible resource allocation between the two industries thus allows society to exchange 2 meals for 1 film.

7   Stage (1) says that consumers can swap 2 meals for 1 film without changing their utility. Stage (6) says that, by reallocating resources, producers swap an output of 2 meals for 1 film. Hence there is no feasible reallocation of resources that can make society better off. Since no Pareto gain is possible, the initial position – competitive equilibrium in both markets – is Pareto-efficient.

Notice the crucial role that *prices* play in this remarkable result. Prices do two things. First, they ensure that the initial position of competitive equilibrium is indeed an *equilibrium*. By balancing the quantities supplied and demanded, prices ensure that the final quantity of goods being consumed can be produced. They ensure that it is a feasible allocation.

But in *competitive* equilibrium prices are performing a second role. Each consumer and each producer is a price-taker and knows that he or she cannot affect market prices. In our example, each consumer knows that the equilibrium price of meals is £5 and the equilibrium price of films is £10. Knowing nothing at all about the actions of other consumers and producers, each consumer will automatically ensure that the last film he or she purchases yields twice as much utility as the last meal purchased. Otherwise that consumer could rearrange purchases out of a given income to make himself or herself better off.[2]

_____

[2] A formal proof of this intuitive statement was given in Chapter 6 where we showed that each consumer would maximize his or her own utility by choosing the point on the budget line tangent to the highest possible indifference curve. The slope of the indifference curve – the utility trade-off between films and meals – must therefore be equal to the relative price of films and meals.

Thus by their individual actions facing given prices, each and every consumer will automatically arrange that 1 film could be swapped for 2 meals with no change in utility. Similarly, each and every producer, merely by setting their own marginal cost equal to the price of their output, will ensure that the marginal cost of films is twice the marginal cost of meals. Thus it takes society twice as many resources to make an extra film rather than an extra meal. By rearranging production, transferring labour between industries, society can swap 2 meals for 1 film, exactly the trade off that would leave consumer utility unaffected.

Thus, as if by an Invisible Hand, prices are guiding individual consumers and producers, each acting only in their own self-interest, to an allocation of the economy's resources that is Pareto-efficient. Nobody can be made better off without someone else worse off.

Figure 15-3 makes the same point in a simple diagram. *DD* is the market demand curve for one of the goods, say films. At a price P_1 a total quantity of films Q_1 will be demanded. But we know that the last film demanded must yield consumers exactly P_1 pounds worth of utility; otherwise they would buy more films or less films than the quantity Q_1. Hence we can think of *DD* as showing also the marginal utility of the last unit of films which consumers purchase. When a total quantity of Q_1 films is purchased the last film yields exactly P_1 pounds worth of extra utility to consumers.

In a competitive industry, the supply curve for films *SS* is also the marginal cost of providing films. Variable factors (labour in our simple example) are paid not only their marginal value product in the film industry, but also their marginal value product in the meals industry. Why? Because labour mobility between industries ensures that wage rates are equated in the two industries. Hence the marginal cost of producing the last film must be the value of the meals sacrificed by using the last units of labour to make films rather than meals.

Prices ensure that both industries are in equilibrium. Figure 15-3 shows that at the equilibrium point *E* the marginal utility of the last film equals its marginal cost. But the marginal cost of the last film equals the value of meals sacrificed, the price of meals multiplied by the quantity of meals forgone by using labour to make that last film. However, the meals

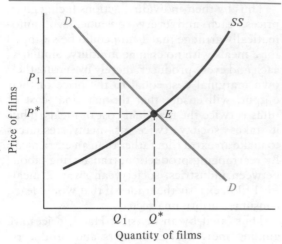

Figure 15-3 COMPETITIVE EQUILIBRIUM AND PARETO-EFFICIENCY. *DD* is the demand curve for films. At any output such as Q_1 the last film must yield consumers P_1 pounds worth of extra utility; otherwise they would demand a different quantity from Q_1. The supply curve *SS* for the competitive film industry is also the marginal cost of films. If the meals industry is in competitive equilibrium, the price of a meal is also the value of its marginal utility to consumers. Thus the marginal cost of a film is not only the market value of extra meals that could have been produced, but is also the value of the marginal utility consumers would have derived from those meals. Hence at any film output below Q^* the marginal utility of films exceeds the marginal utility of meals sacrificed to produce an extra film. Above Q^* the marginal utility of films is less than the marginal utility of meals sacrificed. The equilibrium point E for films and the corresponding equilibrium point in the market for meals thus ensure that resources are efficiently allocated between the two industries. No reallocation of resources could make all consumers better off.

industry is also in equilibrium. An equivalent diagram for the meals industry shows that the equilibrium price of meals is also the marginal utility of the last meal purchased. Hence the value of meals sacrificed to make the last film is also the marginal utility of the last meal times the number of meals sacrificed.

Thus, provided the *meals* industry is in competitive equilibrium, the marginal cost curve for the *film* industry is simply the extra pounds worth of utility sacrificed by using scarce resources to make another film instead of extra meals. It is the opportunity cost in utility terms of the resources being used in the film industry. And equilibrium in the film industry, by equating the marginal utility of

films to the marginal utility of the meals sacrificed to make the last film, guarantees that society's resources are allocated efficiently.

At any output of films below the equilibrium quantity Q^*, the marginal consumer benefit of another film would exceed the marginal consumer valuation of the meals that would have to be sacrificed to produce that extra film. At any output of films in excess of Q^*, society would be devoting too many resources to the film industry. The marginal value of the last film would be less than the marginal value of the meals that could have been produced by transferring resources to the meals industry. Competitive equilibrium ensures that there is no resource transfer between industries that would make all consumers better off.

Equity and Efficiency

In the previous section, we saw that there are an infinity of Pareto-efficient allocations, each with a different distribution of income or utility between different members of society. We have now discovered that a competitive equilibrium in all markets would generate one particular Pareto-efficient allocation. What determines which of the possible Pareto-efficient allocations it picks out?

People have different innate abilities. At any instant, people also have different amounts of human capital and financial wealth. In Chapter 13 we saw that these differences allow people to earn very different income levels in a market economy. They also affect the pattern of consumer demand.

Brazil, which has a very unequal distribution of income and wealth, has a high demand for luxuries such as servants. In Sweden, where there is a much more equal distribution of income and wealth, almost nobody can afford servants. Thus, the initial distribution of abilities, human capital and wealth, by affecting income-earning potential, determines the pattern of consumer demand in the economy. Different patterns of demand imply different demand curves for individual goods and services and determine different equilibrium prices and quantities. In principle, by varying the distribution of initial income-earning potential, we could induce the economy to pick out each and every one of the possible Pareto-efficient allocations at its competitive equilibrium.

Now we come to a very attractive idea. The government is elected by the people to express the value judgements of the majority. Ideally, we should like the government to ensure that the economy is on the Pareto-efficient frontier, shown in Figure 15-2, but take responsibility for making the value judgement about which point on this frontier the economy should attain. Since every competitive equilibrium is Pareto-efficient, and since different Pareto-efficient allocations correspond to different initial distributions of income-earning potential in a competitive economy, it appears that the government can confine itself to redistributing income and wealth through income and inheritance taxes or welfare benefits *without having to worry about interventions to ensure that resources are allocated efficiently*. Free competitive markets will automatically take care of allocative efficiency.

This seems like a pretty powerful case for the free enterprise ideal espoused in the Conservative Election Manifesto that we quoted at the beginning of the chapter. The government should let markets get on with the the job of allocating resources efficiently. Governments should not interfere by introducing a host of regulations, investigatory bodies, or state-run enterprises. Nor need the free enterprise ideal be uncompassionate. The government can make its value judgements about distribution or equality and can pursue its views about the desirable degree of vertical equity without impairing the efficient functioning of a free market economy. The Conservative case is more than a political ideal: it can be backed up by rigorous economic arguments.

But surely the Labour Party must be aware of these arguments? Before you conclude that the case of free markets has been convincingly made you should remember to read the fine print. We began this section by stating that *under certain conditions* we could show that free enterprise or free markets led to a Pareto-efficient allocation. It is time to study these conditions in more detail. In so doing, we shall begin to understand the difference between the two views of how a market economy works. The Conservative Party believes that these are *minor* qualifications that do not seriously challenge the case for a free market economy. The Labour Party believes that these qualifications are so serious that

they remove any presumption that the government can rely on a free market economy. Accordingly, they believe that a considerable amount of government intervention is necessary to *improve* the way the economy works.

15-3 Distortions and the Second Best

Competitive equilibrium is Pareto-efficient because the independent actions of producers setting marginal cost equal to price, and consumers setting marginal benefits equal to price, ensure that the marginal cost of producing a good just equals its marginal benefit to consumers.

> A *distortion* exists whenever society's marginal cost of producing a good does not equal society's marginal benefit from consuming that good.

It is simplest to begin straight away with an example of a distortion. In the previous section we suggested that a government could use taxes and welfare benefits to redistribute income-earning potential and thereby enforce its value judgements about equity while leaving the market economy to take care of allocative efficiency. We now explain why this apparently neat solution will not in fact be possible.

Taxation as a Distortion

Suppose the government wishes to subsidize the poor. To pay for these subsidies the government must tax the rich. It does not matter much whether the government taxes the incomes of rich people or taxes the goods that rich people buy. Let us extend our example from the previous section where there are only two goods, films and meals. Suppose everyone buys meals, but only the rich can afford to go to the cinema. If the government wishes to raise tax revenue in order to subsidize the poor, it should levy a tax on films.

Figure 15-4 shows that tax on films makes the gross-of-tax price of films to consumers exceed the net-of-tax price received by producers of films. The difference between the price to consumers and the price for producers is exactly the amount of the tax on each unit of films sold. Consumers equate the gross price to the

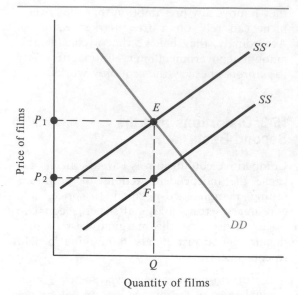

Figure 15-4   A TAX ON FILMS. *DD* shows the demand for films and the marginal benefit of the last film to consumers. *SS* shows the quantity of films supplied at each price received by producers and is also the marginal social cost of producing films. Suppose each unit of films bears a tax equal to the vertical distance *EF*. To show the tax-inclusive price required to induce producers to produce each output, we must draw the new supply curve *SS'* that is a constant vertical distance *EF* above *SS*. The equilibrium quantity of films is *Q*. Consumers pay a price P_1, producers receive a price P_2, and the tax per film is the distance *EF*. At the equilibrium quantity *Q* the marginal consumer benefit is P_1 but the marginal social cost is P_2. Society would make a net gain by producing more films. Hence the equilibrium quantity *Q* is socially inefficient.

value of the marginal benefit they receive from the last film, but producers equate the marginal cost of films to the lower net-of-tax price of films.

Hence in competitive equilibrium the price system no longer equates the social marginal cost of producing films with the social marginal benefit of consuming films. In this example, the marginal benefit of another film exceeds the marginal cost of producing another film. The tax on films is causing too few films to be produced. Producing another film would add more to social benefit than it would add to social cost.

When the other industry (meals) is untaxed and in competitive equilibrium, we showed in the last section that the marginal cost of producing films is exactly the value of the

marginal utility sacrificed by not using the same resources to produce more meals. But when films are taxed we have just seen that the marginal social benefit of another film exceeds its marginal cost. Hence the marginal value to consumers of another film exceeds the marginal value of the last meal currently being produced by the resources that would be necessary to make another film. By transferring resources from meals into films, consumers of extra films could compensate meals consumers for the meals sacrificed *and still have some extra utility left over.* Hence it would be possible to achieve a Pareto gain, making some people better off without making anyone else worse off.

A similar argument holds for any other commodity we try to tax. A tax will cause a discrepancy between the price the purchaser pays and the price the seller receives. Suppose there is an income tax. Firms equate the marginal value of labour to the gross wage rate, but suppliers of labour equate the after-tax wage rate to the marginal value of the leisure that they sacrifice in order to work another hour. The income tax ensures that the marginal value product of labour, society's benefit from another hour of work, now exceeds the marginal value of the leisure being sacrificed in order to work. Again this is inefficient. With another hour of work, society would gain more than sufficient to compensate workers fully for the value of the extra leisure forgone.

We can now pose the choice between efficiency and equity in a stark form. If the economy is perfectly competitive, and if the government is quite happy with the distribution of income-earning potential that currently exists, the government need raise no taxes. Perfectly competitive free market equilibrium will then allocate resources efficiently. There will be no possibility of reallocating resources to make some people better off without making others worse off. The economy is not wasting resources.

However, if as a pure value judgement the government considers that this distribution of income-earning potential is inequitable, the government will need to raise taxes from some people in order to provide subsidies for others. Yet the very act of raising taxes introduces a *distortion.* The price system, operating through competitive free markets, will no longer equate the marginal benefits of taxed commodities with their marginal cost. The resulting equilibrium in the economy will be allocatively inefficient. Society will be wasting resources by producing the wrong output levels of different goods.

What should the government do? The answer depends a good deal on the value judgements of the government in power. The more the government dislikes the income distribution thrown up by the free market, a distribution reflecting differences in innate ability, human capital, and financial wealth, the more the government is likely to judge that the inefficiency costs of distortionary taxes are a price worth paying in order to secure a more equitable distribution of income and utility. Conversely, the more the government feels able to tolerate the income distribution thrown up in a free market economy, the more the government can resist distortionary taxation and allow competitive free markets to allocate resources as efficiently as possible.

Thus one explanation for the differing attitudes to the market economy expressed in the election manifestos cited at the beginning of the chapter is a difference in value judgements about equity. Caricaturing the argument so far, the Conservative Party supports a free enterprise economy because it considers the most important objective is to maximize the size of the national cake by allocating resources as efficiently as possible. The Labour Party supports considerable state intervention because it considers that it is more important to divide the cake more fairly, even if this means having more allocative inefficiency and a smaller cake to share out.

But this is only part of the disagreement. The pursuit of equity through redistribution taxation is not the only distortion that can lead to allocative inefficiency. We shall consider only distortions in the next section. Before leaving our simple tax example, there is one final point that it is important to make.

The Second Best

Thus far we have shown that when there is no distortion in the market for *meals*, a tax on *films* will lead to an inefficient allocation. Because the market for meals is in competitive

equilibrium we saw that the marginal cost curve for films also told us the marginal value of the meals being sacrificed to make the last film. Hence, any tax on films, by driving a wedge between the marginal value of films and the marginal cost of films, drives a wedge between the marginal benefit of employing scarce resources in the film industry and employing these same resources in the meals industry.

Suppose, however, that there is a tax on *meals*. What should we do in the film industry? If we could abolish the tax on meals, then we could get back to free competitive equilibrium in both industries which we know is Pareto-efficient. We sometimes call this the *first-best* allocation to remind ourselves that it is fully efficient.

Suppose, however, that we cannot get rid of the tax on meals. The government needs some tax revenue to pay for national defence or its budget contribution to the European Community. Given that there is an unavoidable tax on meals, do we allocate resources more efficiently by ensuring that at least there are no distortions in the film industry?

In a seminal article Professors Richard Lipsey and Kelvin Lancaster showed that the answer is 'No!'[3] Suppose both industries are in equilibrium but there is a tax on meals. The marginal cost curve for films shows the opportunity cost to private producers of the resources they employ to make films rather than meals. But this is no longer society's opportunity cost of these resources in the film industry. Why not? Because producers are valuing the resources in terms of the price *producers* could get by transferring them to the meals industry. But the price of meals to consumers is higher than the price of meals received by producers. To check you understand this, try drawing a diagram like Figure 15-4 for the meals industry.

Since consumers of meals equate the value of the marginal utility of the last meal to the tax-inclusive price that must be paid, society's valuation of the last meal exceeds the net-of-tax price to which producers of meals are equating marginal cost. Hence the private producers' marginal cost curve for films reflects the market value to producers of using these resources to

---

[3] R. G. Lipsey and K. Lancaster, 'On the General Theory of the Second Best', *Review of Economic Studies*, 1956–57.

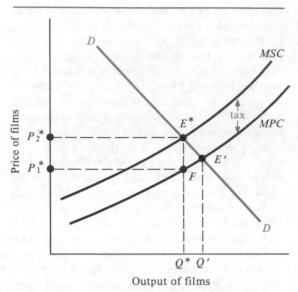

Figure 15-5 THE SECOND BEST. *DD* shows the demand curve and marginal consumer benefit of films. *MPC* is the marginal private cost of films and reflects what the resources could earn for producers if they were employed in the meals industry. With a tax on meals, the consumer price and marginal consumer benefit of meals will exceed the net-of-tax price received by producers of meals. Hence the social opportunity cost of using resources in films, the value of the marginal consumption benefits of meals forgone, exceeds the private producers' opportunity cost of using these resources in films. *MSC* shows the marginal social cost of the forgone utility by using resources in films rather than meals. With no film tax, competitive equilibrium is at E'. At the output Q' the marginal social benefit of films is less than the marginal social cost of films. Q^* is the efficient output of films at which marginal social cost and marginal social benefit of films are equal. A tax on films equal to the distance E^*F would induce a competitive film industry to produce Q^*. Consumers would pay P_2^* and producers would receive P_1^*.

make meals instead, but it no longer reflects the opportunity cost or utility valuation of forgone meals to society. It understates the social valuation of the meals forgone in order to make films. Figure 15-5 shows what happens in the market for films when there is a tax-induced distortion in the market for meals. *DD* is the demand curve for films and reflects the marginal valuation of the last film by consumers of films. *MPC* is the marginal private costs to film producers of using resources to make films. It shows what the resources could have earned in producing meals on which meal producers would receive the

net-of-tax price. *MSC* is the marginal *social* cost of using these resources to make films rather than meals. It exceeds the marginal private cost to producers because the consumer benefits of extra meals exceed the value of extra meals to producers.

With no tax on films, competitive equilibrium in the film industry would occur at E' where the demand curve crosses the private marginal cost curve which is also the competitive supply curve of the film industry. At this output Q' the marginal social cost exceeds the marginal social benefit as given by the height of the demand curve *DD*. To equate the marginal social cost of films and their marginal social benefit it is necessary to levy a tax FE^* on films. Competitive film producers would then produce an output Q^*, receiving a net-of-tax price P_1^* equal to their marginal private cost at this output. Consumers would pay the tax-inclusive price P_2^*. Marginal social cost and marginal social benefit would then be equated at the point E^*.

In contrast to the *first-best* allocation, when we achieve full efficiency by removing all distortions, we have now developed the principle of the *second best*. The principle of the second best says the following. Suppose we are interested only in allocative efficiency. However, there is an inevitable distortion somewhere else in the economy that we are unable to remove. It is inefficient to treat other markets as if that distortion did not exist. Thus in the film industry it is inefficient to aim to equate private marginal cost and private marginal benefit, the efficient outcome in the absence of a meals tax. Rather, it is efficient to deliberately introduce a new distortion to the film industry to help counterbalance the inevitable distortion in the meals industry.

In effect, the theory of the second best says that if there must be a distortion, for example if the government has to raise some taxes, it is a mistake to concentrate the distortion in one market. It is more efficient to spread its effect more thinly over a wide range of markets. In the example of Figure 15-5 a tax on meals leads to too few meals being produced. The only place the resources can go is the film industry, so too many films are being produced. A tax on films helps redress the balance.

Several applications of this general principle will be found in the ensuing chapters. The real world in which we live unfortunately provides us with several inevitable distortions. Given their existence, the argument of this section implies that the government may *increase* the overall efficiency of the whole economy by introducing *new* distortions to offset distortions that already exist. By now you will rightly be wanting to know the source of these inevitable distortions that the government should take action to offset. We now list the most important ones.

15-4 Market Failure

We began by showing that in the absence of any distortions a freely competitive equilibrium would ensure allocative efficiency. We use the term *market failure* to cover all the circumstances in which equilibrium in free unregulated markets (i.e., markets not subject to direct price or quantity regulation by the government) will fail to achieve an efficient allocation. Market failure describes the circumstances in which distortions prevent the Invisible Hand from allocating resources efficiently.

We now list the possible sources of distortions that lead to market failure.

1 Imperfect competition It is perfect competition that leads firms to set marginal cost equal to price and thus to marginal consumer benefit. Under imperfect competition, producers set marginal cost equal to marginal revenue, which is less than the price at which the last unit is sold. Since consumers equate price to marginal benefits derived from the last unit, in general marginal benefit will exceed marginal cost in imperfectly competitive industries. Such industries will tend to produce too little. Expanding output would add more to consumer benefit than it would to production costs or the opportunity cost of the resources used. This idea forms the theme of Chapter 17.

2 Social priorities such as equity We have already examined how redistributive taxation in the pursuit of equity will induce allocative distortions by driving a wedge between the price the consumer pays and the price the producer receives. We study the principles of taxation more fully in Chapter 16.

3 Externalities Externalities are things like pollution, noise, and congestion. What they have in common is that one person's actions have direct costs or benefits for other people which that individual does not take into account. Much of the remainder of this chapter is devoted to analysing this distortion. We shall see that the problem arises because there is neither a market nor a market price for things like noise. Hence we cannot expect markets and prices to ensure that the marginal benefits of making a noise are equated to the marginal cost of that noise to other people.

4 Other missing markets: future goods, risk, and information These are further examples of commodities for which markets are absent or limited. In Chapter 14 we saw how moral hazard and adverse selection tend to inhibit the setting up of insurance markets to deal with risk. As with externalities, we cannot expect markets to allocate resources efficiently if the markets do not exist in the first place. We pursue this theme at the end of this chapter. But we begin by looking more closely at the problem of externalities.

15-5 Externalities

An *externality* arises whenever an individual's production or consumption decision directly affects the production or consumption of others *other than through market prices.*

Suppose a chemical firm discharges waste into a lake, polluting the water and directly imposing an additional production cost on anglers (fewer and smaller fish, which are harder to catch) or a consumption cost on swimmers (less pleasant swimming and a dirty beach). If there is no 'market' for pollution, the firm can pollute the lake without cost. Its self-interest will lead it to pollute until the marginal benefit of polluting (a cheaper production process for chemicals) equals its own marginal cost of polluting, which is zero. It takes no account of the marginal cost its pollution imposes on anglers and swimmers.

Conversely, by painting your house you make the whole street look nicer and give consumption benefits to your neighbours. But you paint only up to the point on which your *own* marginal benefit equals the marginal cost of the paint you buy and the time you spend. Your marginal costs are also society's marginal costs, but society's marginal benefits exceed your own. Hence there is too little house-painting.

In both cases there is a divergence between the individual's comparison of marginal costs and benefits and society's comparison of marginal costs and benefits. Free markets cannot induce people to take account of these indirect effects on other people if there is no market in these indirect effects.

Divergences between Private and Social Costs and Benefits

Suppose a chemical firm discharges a pollutant into a river, the quantity of pollutant discharged being in proportion to the level of chemical production. Further down the river there are food-processing companies using river water as an input in making sauce for baked beans. There are also farmers with agricultural land.

At small levels of chemical output, pollution is negligible. The river can dilute the small amounts of pollutant discharged by the chemical producer. But as the discharge rises the costs of pollution rise sharply. Food processors must worry about the purity of their water intake and build expensive purification plants. Still higher levels of pollution start to corrode pipes and contaminate agricultural land.

Figure 15-6 shows the marginal private cost *MPC* of producing chemicals. For simplicity, we assume that marginal private costs are constant. It also shows the marginal *social* cost *MSC* of chemical production. The divergence between marginal private cost and marginal social cost reflects the marginal cost imposed on other producers by an extra unit of the *production externality* of pollution that the chemical producer disregards. The demand curve *DD* shows how much consumers are willing to pay for the output of the chemical producer. If that producer acts as a price-taker, equilibrium will occur at *E* and the chemical producer will produce an output *Q* at which the marginal private cost equals the price received by the firm for its output.

However, at this output *Q* the marginal social cost *MSC* exceeds the marginal social benefit of chemicals as given by the corresponding point on the demand curve *DD*. The market

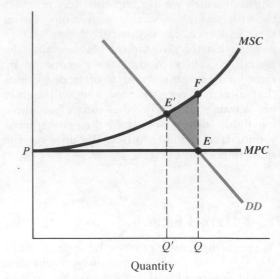

Figure 15-6 THE SOCIAL COST OF A PRODUCTION EXTERNALITY. Competitive equilibrium occurs at *E*. The market clears at a price *P* which producers equate to marginal private cost *MPC*. But pollution causes a production externality which makes the marginal social cost *MSC* exceed the marginal private cost. The socially efficient output is at *E'* where marginal social cost and marginal social benefit are equal. The demand curve *DD* measures the marginal social benefit because consumers equate the value of the marginal utility of the last unit to the price. By inducing an output *Q* in excess of the efficient output *Q'*, free market equilibrium leads to a social cost equal to the area of the triangle *E'EF*. This shows the excess of social cost over social benefit in moving from *Q'* to *Q*.

for chemicals takes no account of the production externality inflicted on other firms. Since at the output *Q* the marginal social benefit of the last output unit is less than the marginal social cost inclusive of the production externality, the output *Q* is not socially efficient. By reducing the output of chemicals society would save more in social cost than it would lose in social benefit. Reducing the output of chemicals and the corresponding amount of pollution would allow society to make some people better off without making anyone worse off.

In fact the socially efficient output is *Q'*, at which the marginal social benefit of the last output unit equals is marginal social cost. *E'* is the efficient point. How much does society lose by producing at the free market equilibrium point *E* rather than at the socially efficient point

E'? The vertical distance between the marginal social cost MSC and the marginal social benefit as given by DD shows the marginal social loss of producing the last output unit. Hence, by expanding from Q' to Q, society loses a total amount equal to the triangle $E'EF$ in Figure 15-6. This measures the social cost of the market failure caused by the production externality of pollution.[4]

Production externalities lead to a divergence between marginal private production costs and marginal social production costs. Similarly, a consumption externality leads to a divergence between marginal private benefits and marginal social benefits. Figure 15-7 illustrates a beneficial consumption externality as when painting your house or planting roses in your front garden gives pleasure also to your neighbours.

Since there are no production externalities MPC is both the marginal private cost and the marginal social cost of making your house and garden look nicer. It is the cost of the paint and plants plus the opportunity cost of your time. DD is the marginal private benefit of house improvements and, comparing your own costs and benefits, you will undertake a quantity Q of improvements.

But you do not take account of the consumption value these improvements have for your neighbours. Since these are benefits too, the marginal social benefit MSB is greater than your marginal private benefit. In comparison with the free market equilibrium at E, the socially efficient quantity of improvements is Q'. At E' the marginal social benefit and marginal social cost are equated.

Free market equilibrium leads to too few improvements. Society could gain the triangle EFE', measuring the excess of social benefits over social costs, by increasing the quantity of improvements from Q to Q'. Alternatively, this same triangle measures the social cost of the market failure that leads free market equilibrium to a social inefficient allocation.

---

[4] Conversely, some production externalities have beneficial effects on other producers. A farmer who spends money on pest control on his or her own property may reduce the cost of pest control on neighbouring farms. When production externalities are beneficial the marginal social cost of an individual producer's activity will lie *below* the marginal private cost to that individual. Suppose we re-label the MSC curve as MPC in Figure 15-6 and re-label the MPC curve as MSC. Free market equilibrium will then occur at E' but E will now be the socially efficient allocation.

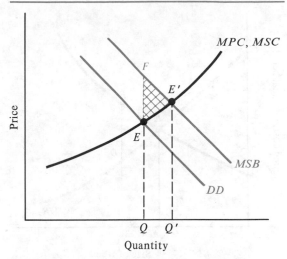

Figure 15-7 A BENEFICIAL CONSUMPTION EXTERNALITY. With no production externality, marginal private cost and marginal social cost coincide. DD measures the marginal private benefit and free market equilibrium occurs at E. The beneficial consumption externality makes marginal social benefit MSB exceed marginal private benefit. E' is the socially efficient point. The consumption externality leads to market failure. By producing output Q instead of the efficient output Q', free market equilibrium causes a social loss equal to the triangle EFE'.

Property Rights and Externalities

Suppose your neighbour's tree grows into your garden, obscuring your light and giving you a harmful consumption externality. If the law says that you must be compensated for any damage suffered, your neighbour will either have to pay up or cut back the tree. What is the smart thing for your neighbour to do, and how much compensation will you get?

Your neighbour really likes the tree and wants to know how much it would take to compensate you to leave the tree at its current size. Figure 15-8 shows the marginal benefit MB that your neighbour gets from the last inch of tree size and the marginal cost MC to you of that last inch of tree size. At the tree's current size S_1 the *total* cost to you is the area $OABS_1$. You simply take the marginal cost OA of the first inch, then add the marginal cost of the second inch, and so on till you get to the existing size S_1. The area $OABS_1$ is what you require in compensation if the tree size is S_1.

Your neighbour is about to pay up this

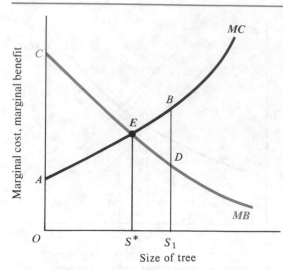

Figure 15-8 THE EFFICIENT QUANTITY OF AN EXTERNALITY. *MB* and *MC* measure the marginal benefit to your neighbour and marginal cost to you of a tree of size *S*. The efficient size is S^* where the marginal cost and benefit are equal. Beginning from a size S_1 you might bribe your neighbour the value S^*EDS_1 to cut back to S^*. Below S^* you would have to pay more than it is worth to you to have the tree cut back further. Alternatively, your neighbour might pay you the value $OAES^*$ to have a tree of size S^*. Property rights, in this case whether you are legally entitled to compensation for loss of light to your garden, determine who compensates whom but not the outcome S^* of the bargain.

amount. But he has a daughter who is studying economics. She points out that at the size S_1 the marginal benefit of the last inch is less than the marginal cost to you, which is also the amount you must be compensated for that last inch on the tree. It is not worth your neighbour having a tree this big. Nor, she points out, it is worth cutting the tree down altogether. The first inch yields a higher marginal benefit to your neighbour than the amount that you require in compensation to offset the marginal cost to you of that first inch. A tiny tree has little effect on your light and makes the garden next door look nicer.

The efficient allocation or tree size S^* occurs where the marginal benefit to your neighbour equals the marginal cost to you. Above S^* it is worth cutting back the tree since the marginal cost (and hence the compensation) exceeds the marginal benefit. Below S^* it is worth increasing the tree size and paying the marginal compensation that is less than the marginal

benefit. At the efficient size S^* your total cost is the area $OAES^*$ and this is the total amount of compensation you will be paid.

Notice that since a larger tree benefits one party but hurts the other party, *the efficient tree size and efficient quantity of the externality will not be zero*. Rather, it occurs where the marginal benefits equals the marginal cost.

Property rights, in this case the legal right for you to be compensated for infringement of your garden and light, enter in two distinct ways. First, they affect who compensates whom. They have a distributional implication. Suppose there was no law requiring compensation. Would you just sit there and allow your neighbour's tree to grow to a size S_1 that inflicts a huge cost on you? Of course not. You would bribe your neighbour to cut it back. You would compensate your neighbour for the loss of his marginal benefit. It would be worth you paying to have the tree cut back as far as S^* but no further. Beyond that size, you would be paying more in compensation for the loss of marginal benefit of another inch than you would be saving yourself in reduced cost of the externality. So you would pay your neighbour a *total* of EDS_1S^* to compensate for the loss of benefit in cutting the tree back from S_1 to S^*. Who has the property rights determines who must compensate whom, but it does not affect the quantity that the bargain will determine. It must pay to reach the point at which the marginal benefit to one of you equals the marginal cost to the other.

Property rights thus have a distributional implication – who compensates whom – but also act to achieve the socially efficient allocation. They implicitly set up the 'missing market' for the externality. The market ensures that the price equals the marginal benefit and the marginal cost, and hence equates the two.

Sometimes economists say that property rights are a way to 'internalize' the externality.[5] If people must pay for it they will take its effects into account in making private decisions and there will no longer be market failure. Why then do externalities like congestion and pollution remain a problem? Why don't private individuals establish the missing market through a system of bribes or compensation?

---

[5] This argument was first advanced by R. Coase, 'The Problem of Social Cost', *Journal of Law and Economics*, 1960.

There are two obvious reasons why it may be hard to set up this market. The first is the cost of organizing the market. If a factory chimney dumps smoke on a thousand gardens nearby it may be very expensive to collect £1 from each household to bribe the factory to cut back to the socially efficient amount. If cars joining a crowded road take no account of the extent to which they slow down *other* road users, it may be almost impossible to rush from car to car offering or collecting bribes!

Second, there is the *free-rider* problem. Suppose someone knocks on your door and says: 'I am collecting bribes from people who mind the factory smoke falling on their gardens. The money I collect will be paid to bribe the factory to cut back. Do you wish to contribute? I am going round 5000 houses in the neighbourhood.' Whether you mind or not, you say: 'I don't mind and won't contribute.' Provided everybody else pays, the factory will cut back and you cannot be prevented from getting the benefits. The smoke will not fall exclusively on your garden merely because you alone did not pay up. Regardless of what other people contribute, there is no incentive for you to contribute: you are a *free-rider*. But everyone else will reason similarly; hence no one will pay, even though you would all have been better off paying and getting the smoke cut back.

15-6 Environmental Issues

When, for either of these reasons, there is no implicit market for pollutants, there will be an overproduction of pollutants. Because private producers fail to take account of the costs they impose on others, in equilibrium the social marginal cost will exceed the social marginal benefit.

If the private sector cannot organize charges for the marginal externalities pollution creates, perhaps the government can? By charging (through taxes) for the divergence between marginal private and social cost, the government could then induce private producers to take account of the costs inflicted on others. This argument for government intervention through taxes is examined in the next chapter.

Pollution taxes, especially for water pollution, have been used in France, Italy, Germany, and the Netherlands. But most policy takes a different approach, the imposition of pollution standards that regulate the maximum amount of allowed pollution.

Air Pollution

Since the Clean Air Act of 1956 governments in the UK have taken responsibility for designating clean air zones in which certain types of pollution, notably the smoke caused by burning coal, are illegal. The number of designated clean air zones has increased steadily during the last 25 years, and Table 15-1 shows the dramatic reduction in smoke pollution in the UK.

Adding lead to petrol improves the fuel economy performance of cars. However, lead emissions from car exhausts are an atmospheric pollutant that may be harmful to people's health. Since 1972 the UK government has adopted a policy of progressive reductions in the quantity of lead permitted in petrol. Table 15-2 shows that lead emission from petrol-engined vehicles has fallen since 1973 even though total consumption of petrol has risen by 20 per cent.

Water Pollution

Since 1951 governments in the UK have imposed increasingly stringent controls on discharges into inland waters. Although we

Table 15-1 Smoke emission in the UK (million tonnes per annum)

1958	1966	1974	1980	1987
2.01	1.06	0.46	0.29	0.23

Source: Department of Environment, *Digest of Environmental Pollution and Water Statistics.*

Table 15-2 Petrol consumption and lead emission

	PETROL	LEAD EMISSION*
1971	88	87
1973	100	100
1977	102	88
1987	121	36

* 1973 level = 100
Source: as in Table 15-1.

Table 15-3 Water pollution in England and Wales
(badly polluted mileage as % of total)

	1980	1985
Freshwater rivers, canals	10	11
Estuaries	9	8

Source: as in Table 15-1.

tend to think of *industrial* effluent, sewage is a more important source of pollution. During the 1970s regional water authorities in England and Wales spent (at 1989 prices) an annual average of £2.4 billion on water purification and sewage treatment. Table 15-3 shows that this expenditure has been only moderately successful in reducing water pollution. By the late 1980s an even more important problem has been recognized: water pollution from nitrates used as fertilizers on agricultural land. The European Community has laid down tough standards for water purity which will take many years to achieve in countries like the UK.

Evaluating Pollution Policy in the UK

Direct regulation of pollution has met with mixed success over the last 25 years. In some cases, for example the smoke pollution which used to be especially acute in winter when smoke and fog mixed to produce dense and harmful 'smog', tougher standards have led to dramatic improvements in environmental quality. Many rivers are also cleaner, and fish have reappeared.

In other cases, governments have tried to regulate but often been ineffective; it is hard to enforce regulations such as those that prevent ships discharging oil at sea. In yet other cases there has been little attempt to intervene. For example, coal-fired power stations continue to emit large quantities of sulphur dioxide, which the high chimneys are only partially successful in dispersing. And ecologists continue to oppose government policies that allow new coal mines in previously green countryside, or permit the disposal of nuclear waste at sea.

Having described the consequences of anti-pollution policy in the UK, how should we assess its success? Has the government been tough enough on polluters? Recall from Figures 15-6 and 15-8 that the efficient quantity of

pollution is not zero but rather the level at which the social marginal cost of cutting back pollution equals its social marginal benefit. The fact that pollution still exists is not sufficient to establish that policy has not been tough enough.

What we can say is that where pollution control has been attempted it has usually taken a crude and simple form. Calculations of the social marginal costs and benefits of cutting back pollution tend to be conspicuous by their absence. In part this reflects the genuine difficulty in measuring marginal benefits. For example, in considering how much to reduce lead emissions from cars it is not impossible to calculate the marginal social cost of producing cars with anti-pollution exhaust systems and the marginal social cost of cars that use more fuel per mile. But even if doctors were unanimous about the effects of lead emission on health, how should society value a marginal increase in the health of current and future generations?

This is not merely a question of allocative efficiency, which we might answer by considering the resources tied up in looking after the sick or the extra output that healthier workers could produce. It is also a question of equity, both within the current generation – poor inner-city children may be most vulnerable to arrested development caused by inhaling lead-polluted air – and across generations. Devoting more resources to reducing lead pollution today may reduce the resources producing consumer goods for today's consumers, but will improve the quality of life for tomorrow's consumers.

Prices versus Quantities

Although it is difficult to reach a clear judgement about whether there is enough pollution control, we can discuss whether the current mechanism of pollution control is sensible. We began this section by noting that, if free markets tend to overpollute, society can reduce pollution either by regulating the quantity of pollution (as it does) or by using the price system to discourage such activities by taxing them. Would it be more sensible to intervene through the tax system than to regulate quantities directly?

Many economists believe the answer to this

BOX 15-1

ACID RAIN: A BITTER CONTROVERSY

Gases such as sulphur dioxide and oxides of nitrogen are discharged into the atmosphere, dissolved in water vapour, and fall as acid rain. Acid rain poisons fish, destroys forests, and corrodes buildings. The following table shows data for European emissions of sulphur ('000 tonnes a year).

	E. EUROPE	UK	FRANCE, ITALY, W. GERMANY	SOVIET UNION	SCANDINAVIA	OTHER EUROPE
Produced	6548	1271	2303	2558	107	2576
Received	3753	702	2143	3584	501	3105

Notes: (i) only European part of Soviet Union; (ii) 'E. Europe' is Poland, E. Germany, Hungary, and Czechoslovakia; (iii) 2532 tonnes of sulphur production can't be traced to any particular country.

It reveals the appalling pollution in Eastern Europe and the Soviet Union, mainly from power stations fuelled by low-grade coal. In Western Europe, the UK is a big exporter of acid rain: prevailing winds blow it east, and Scandinavia is a big loser.

Installing and operating enough flue gas desulphurization plants to cut UK power station emissions of sulphur dioxide by 50 per cent would add 6 per cent to UK electricity prices. Since much of the damage occurs in Swedish lakes and German forests, UK voters are unwilling to pay the extra cost. It needs a concerted European policy, perhaps even with transfer payments between governments, to deal with externalities across national borders.

Europe is trying to agree a 20 per cent cut in sulphur dioxide emissions and a freeze on emissions of oxides of nitrogen (mainly from car exhausts). But when different countries face a different marginal cost of pollution abatement, and inflict different amounts of marginal damage (polluting unpopulated areas is less costly than polluting densely populated areas), equal cutbacks for all is not the efficient solution. For a given overall reduction, the efficient solution equates the marginal net benefit (damage reduction minus abatement cost) across different polluters. The following table shows estimates by Professor David Newberry of Cambridge University of the efficient way to achieve a 30 per cent reduction in sulphur dioxide emissions in Europe.

% reduction by country in sulphur dioxide emissions

Belgium	69	Luxemburg	38	Austria	16	Yugoslavia	7
Holland	65	UK	31	Czech.	14	Portugal	7
W. Germany	61	Italy	27	Spain	10	Sweden	4
Switz.	44	E. Germany	21	Hungary	8	Norway	3
France	40	Denmark	18	Poland	8	Sov. Union	3

Data in this box are from D. Newbery, 'Acid rain', *Economic Policy*, 1990.

question is yes.[6] One reason is that, if each firm were charged the same price or tax for a marginal unit of pollution, then every firm would pollute up to the point at which the marginal cost of reducing pollution was equal to the price of pollution. Any allocation in which different firms have different marginal costs of reducing pollution is a socially inefficient way to reduce the total quantity of pollution. By having the firms with low marginal reduction costs contract further and firms with high marginal reduction costs contract less, the same total reduction in pollution could be achieved at less cost.

However, there are two important qualifications to this argument. First, it would be necessary to monitor the quantity of pollution of each firm in order to assess its tax liability. Second, in order to assess the tax rate or charge for pollution it would still be necessary to

---

[6] In the next chapter we spell out how such taxes would work.

calculate the overall costs and benefits of marginal changes in the amount of pollution. If the government has to make a decision on the socially efficient level of pollution anyway, it may be simpler to regulate the quantity directly.

Finally, there is the issue of the uncertainty of the effect of the legislation.[7] Suppose pollution beyond a certain critical level would have disastrous social consequences, for example irreversibly damaging the ozone layer above the earth. By regulating the quantity directly it is at least possible to ensure that the disaster is avoided. Indirect control through taxes or charges runs the risk that the government might do its sums wrong and set the tax too low. Pollution will then be higher than intended, and possibly disastrous.

Thus, regulating the total quantity of pollution and conducting a series of spot checks on individual producers to see that they are not violating agreed standards is a relatively simple policy which may avoid the worst outcomes. However, by failing to take account of differences in the marginal cost of reducing pollution across different polluters, it does not reduce pollution in the manner that is cost-minimizing to society, for that would involve the equalization across polluters of the marginal cost of reducing pollution. There is no simple answer in an uncertain world where monitoring and enforcement also use up society's scarce resources.

Lessons from the United States

The United States has gone furthest in trying to use property rights and the price mechanism to cut back pollution in a manner that is economically efficient. The US Clean Air Acts (1955, 1970, 1977) have established an environmental policy that includes an *emissions trading programme* and *bubble policy*.

The Acts lay down a minimum standard for air quality, and impose pollution emission controls to particular polluters. Any polluter emitting less than their specified amount obtains an *emission reduction credit* (ERC), which can be sold to another polluter which wants to go over its allocated pollution limit.

Thus, the total quantity of pollution is regulated, but firms that can cheaply reduce pollution have an incentive to do so, and sell off the ERC to firms for which pollution reduction is more expensive. In this way we get closer to the efficient solution in which the marginal cost of pollution reduction is equalized across firms.

When a firm has many factories, the bubble policy applies pollution controls to the firm as a whole rather than individual factories. To achieve the specified overall reduction in pollution, the firm can cut back most in the plants in which pollution reduction is cheapest. The bubble policy is efficient because it encourages equalization of the marginal cost of cutting back pollution at different plants within the firm.

Thus, the US policy manages to combine 'control over quantities' for aggregate pollution, where the risks and uncertainties are greatest, with 'control through the price system' for allocating efficiently the way these overall targets are achieved.

15-7 Other Missing Markets: Time and Risk

The previous two sections have been devoted to a single idea. When externalities exist, free market equilibrium will lead to an inefficient resource allocation because the externality itself does not have a market or a price. People take no account of the costs and benefits their actions inflict on others. Without a market for externalities the price system cannot be expected to bring marginal costs and marginal benefits of these externalities into line. In this section we discuss two other types of 'missing market', those associated with time and with risk.

The present and the future are linked. People save, or refrain from consumption, today in order to consume more tomorrow. Firms reduce current output by devoting resources to training or building in order to produce more tomorrow. How should society make plans today for the quantities of goods to be produced and consumed in the future? Ideally we should like to organize everyone's plans today so that the social marginal cost of goods in the future just equals the social marginal benefit.

[7] This argument is due to Martin Weitzman, 'Prices versus Quantities', *Review of Economic Studies*, 1974.

BOX 15-2

A LOT OF HOT AIR?

Chlorofluorocarbons (CFCs) are gases that are useful in things like aerosols. But they are thought to destroy the ozone layer, which protects the earth from the sun's rays. Without this sunscreen, more people will get skin cancers.

As with acid rain, there is a major problem in co-ordinating the policy of different countries. Each is tempted to act as a free rider: if other countries cut back on atmospheric pollution, everyone will enjoy

the benefit. But governments are beginning to get their act together. The Montreal Protocol on Substances that deplete the Ozone Layer was concluded in 1987, and 46 countries, including most of the big polluters, have now signed. The following table, based on estimates by the US Environmental Protection Agency, offers an optimistic assessment of the results of the Protocol:

DEPLETION OF THE OZONE LAYER (%)				
By year:	2000	2025	2050	2075
Without any controls	1	5	16	50
With Montreal Protocol	1	2	2	2

A second type of atmospheric pollution is potentially of much greater significance, though as yet it remains the subject of considerable scientific controversy. The greenhouse effect arises from emissions of CFCs, methane, nitrous oxide, and especially carbon dioxide. Greenhouse gases are the direct result of pollution, and the indirect result of a reduction in the atmosphere's ability to absorb them. Plants convert carbon dioxide into oxygen. Chopping down forests to clear land for cattle, as world demand for hamburgers soars, may be good business in the short run, but its long-run effect on the accumulation of greenhouse gases is significant.

The consequence is global warming. People in London and Stockholm may get better suntans, but in Africa the likelihood of drought and famine is magnified many times; and, as icecaps melt, the sea

level will rise, flooding many low-lying areas. In 1990 the Intergovernmental Panel on Climate Change forecast that by 2070 the temperature would increase by 3.5°C, implying a rise of 45 centimetres in the sea level.

As with acid rain and ozone depletion, international co-ordination of government policy is required to tackle the free rider problem. But progress is likely to be slow for two reasons. First, greater scientific uncertainty about the greenhouse effect provides an excuse for the big polluters who have the strongest interest in delaying a change of policy. Second, in many cases it is the poorer countries who will be most affected by the greenhouse effect. It is hard for them to convince the rich countries to make sacrifices on their behalf.

In Chapter 14 we introduced the concept of a *forward market*, in which buyers and sellers made contracts today for goods to be delivered in the future at a price agreed today. Suppose there was a forward market for delivery of copper in 1995. Consumers would equate the marginal benefit of copper in 1995 to the forward price, which producers would equate to the marginal cost of producing copper for 1995. A complete set of forward markets for all commodities for all future dates would lead producers and consumers *today* to make consistent plans for future production and

consumption of all goods, and the social marginal benefit of every future good would equal its social marginal cost.

In Chapter 14 we explained why only a very limited set of future markets actually exists. You can trade gold one year forward but not cars or washing machines. Since nobody knows the characteristics of next year's model of a car or a washing machine, it is impossible to write legally binding contracts which could be enforced when the goods are actually delivered. Yet without these forward markets the price system cannot be expected to ensure that the marginal cost and marginal benefits of planned future goods are equal.

Similarly, there is only a limited set of *contingent* or insurance markets for dealing with risk. In Chapter 14 we argued that people are typically risk-averse and dislike risk. Risk is costly to individuals because it reduces their utility. But does society undertake the efficient amount of risky activities?

A complete set of insurance markets would allow risk to be transferred from those who dislike risk to those who are prepared to bear risk at a price. The equilibrium price or insurance premium would equate the marginal cost and marginal benefit of risk-bearing. The equilibrium price of risky activities would include the insurance premium, and the price system would ensure that social marginal costs and benefits of risky activities were equated.

However, we saw that problems of adverse selection and moral hazard would inhibit the organization of private insurance markets. If some risky activities are uninsurable at any price, again we cannot expect the price system to guide society to an allocation at which social marginal costs and benefits are equal.

Future goods and risky goods are examples of commodities with missing markets. Like externalities, they induce market failure. Free market equilibrium will not generally be efficient. As we have seen, an important problem which inhibits the development of forward and contingent markets is the provision of *information*. For example, it is the problem of acquiring the relevant information about purchasers of insurance policies that leads insurance companies to face problems of moral hazard and adverse selection. We now study some practical examples of how informational problems affect the way in which markets work.

15-8 Quality, Health, and Safety

In the real world, information is incomplete because gathering information is costly. This may lead to socially inefficient allocations. For example, a worker who is unaware that exposure to high levels of benzene, as happens in some chemical plants, might cause cancer will be willing to work for a lower wage than she would if this information were widely available. The firm's production cost will understate the true social cost and the good will be overproduced.

In most countries, governments have accepted an increasing role in regulating health, safety, and quality standards because it has been recognized that this is a potentially important area of market failure. Although imperfect information would be sufficient to cause a divergence between private and social cost, in practice the argument for intervention is usually reinforced by externalities. With better information, the chemical worker would ask for a wage that compensated for the danger of illness but would still neglect the marginal cost that illness would impose on society through expensive health care, which uses society's resources but may be free to the individual.

Examples of government regulation in the UK are the Health and Safety at Work Acts, legislation controlling food and drugs production, the Fair Trading Act which governs consumer protection, and the various traffic and motoring regulations. The purpose of such legislation is twofold: to encourage the provision of information that will allow individuals more accurately to judge costs and benefits, and to set and enforce standards designed to reduce the risks of injury or death.

Providing Information

Figure 15-9 shows the supply curve SS for a drug that is potentially harmful. DD is the demand curve when consumers are unaware of the full extent of the danger. In equilibrium at E the quantity Q is produced and consumed. With full information about the dangers, people would buy less of the drug. The demand curve DD' shows the marginal consumer benefit with full information. By moving to the new equilibrium at E' society avoids the deadweight burden $EE'F$ from overproduction of the drug.

If information were free to collect, everyone would already know the true risks. From the social get $EE'F$ we should subtract the resources that society expends in discovering this information. In saying that the free market equilibrium would be at E, we are really saying that it would not be worth while for each individual to check up privately on each and every drug on the market. But it makes sense for society to have a single regulatory body that does the checking

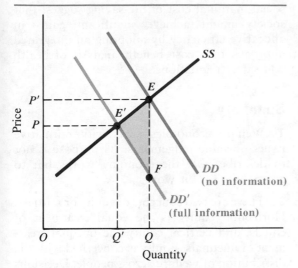

Figure 15-9 INFORMATION AND UNSAFE GOODS.   Consumers cannot individually discover the safety risks associated with a particular good. Free market equilibrium occurs at *E*. A government agency now provides information about the product. As a result, the demand curve shifts down and the new equilibrium is at *E'* where the *true* or full information valuation of an extra unit of the good equals its marginal social cost. Providing information prevents a welfare cost *E'EF* that arises when uninformed consumers use the wrong marginal valuation of the benefits of the good.

and a law whose enforcement entitles individuals to assume that drugs being sold have been checked out as safe.

Certification of safety or quality need not be carried out by the government. Sotheby's certify the quality of Rembrandts, and the private University College at Buckingham certifies educational attainments of its students. People arrested on suspicion of drunk driving in the UK are allowed to send half their blood sample to a private certification agency to corroborate the results of the police analysis.

Nevertheless, two factors tend to inhibit the use of private certification in many areas of health and safety. The first· concerns the incentive to tell the truth. If private certification firms are in business to earn profits, which they do by charging firms for a certificate attesting the quality or safety of a product, which then allows firms to sell more of the product at any given price, will not firms have an incentive to bribe the certifier to obtain the certificate? And even if they do not, will people believe that they have not done so? Firms

issuing false certificates might be subject to lawsuits, but these are expensive. Private individuals might not be able to afford to sue, and society might not wish to devote a large quantity of resources to court cases.

Second, a private certification agency would have to decide on standards. What margin of error should be built into safety regulations? How safe does a drug have to be before it receives a certificate? These are questions on which society has views. They involve externalities and may have important distributional implications. Even where society relies on private agencies to *monitor* regulations, society will probably want to set the standards itself.

Imposing Standards

The public interest may be especially important when little is known about a product and where the consequences for society of any error may be catastrophic. Few people would argue that safety standards for nuclear power stations can be adequately determined within the private sector.

In imposing standards, governments increase the private cost of production by preventing firms from adopting the cost-minimizing techniques that would otherwise have been employed. Sometimes the justification is that the government has access to better information than the private sector and judges the true social cost to be in excess of the private cost. The imposition of standards then increases private marginal cost, shifts private supply curves upwards, and reduces the overproduction of the good that occurred when the market ignored the divergence between private and social cost.

Frequently, however, the imposition of standards reflects a judgement that important externalities exist or is simply a pure value judgement based on distributional considerations. One particularly contentious area in the field of health and safety is the valuation of human life itself.

Politicians often claim that human life is beyond economic calculation and must be given absolute priority whatever the cost. An economist will raise two points in reply. First, it is quite impossible for society to implement such an objective. It is simply too expensive in resources to attempt to eliminate all risks of premature death, and in fact we do not do so. Second, in making occupational and recreational choices, for example being a racing driver or going climbing, people do take risks. Society must ask how much more risk-averse it should be than the people it is trying to protect.

Thus, beyond a certain point the marginal social benefit of further risk reduction will exceed the marginal social cost. It will take an enormous effort to make the world just a little safer, and the resources might have been used elsewhere to greater effect. Zero risk does not make economic sense. Economists have long been calling for safety regulations to be subject to cost–benefit analysis. We need to know the costs of making the world a little safer, and we need to encourage society to make a decision about how much it values the benefits.

However society decides to value the benefit of saving human life, an efficient allocation would adopt health and safety regulations up to the point at which the marginal social cost of saving life by each and every means was equal to the marginal social benefit of saving life. By shying away from the 'unpleasant' task of spelling out the costs and benefits, society is likely to produce a very inefficient allocation in which the marginal costs and marginal benefits are very different in different activities.

Suppose we assume that each regulation is enforced up to the point at which the marginal cost and marginal benefit of saving life are equal *for that activity*. If we can measure the marginal cost directly, we can infer the implicit marginal benefit from saving life through that activity. Economists frequently complain that such calculations reveal very different implicit marginal benefits across activities, which is unsurprising when those responsible for safety standards in building, motoring, medicine, and other areas make no attempt to reach a common view of the marginal social benefit from saving life. For example, estimates for the implicit marginal social benefit from saving life in the UK range from £20 million in the case of building regulations introduced after the Ronan Point disaster to £50 for a rarely used test in pregnant women that might prevent some still-births.[8] Such wide disparities in the

social marginal cost of life-saving suggest that society might achieve significant gains in allocative efficiency by adopting an integrated approach to a cost–benefit analysis of health and safety regulations.

Summary

1 Welfare economics deals with normative issues or value judgements. Its purpose is not to describe *how* the economy works but to assess *how well* it works.

2 There are two concepts of equity or fairness. Horizontal equity is the equal treatment of equals, and vertical equity the unequal treatment of unequals. Equity is concerned with the distribution of welfare across people. Decisions about the desirable degree of equity are pure value judgements.

3 A resource allocation is a complete description of what, how, and for whom goods are produced. To separate as far as possible the concepts of equity and efficiency, economists use the concept of Pareto efficiency. An allocation is Pareto-efficient if there is no reallocation of resources that would make some people better off without making some people worse off. If an allocation is inefficient it is possible to achieve a Pareto gain, making some people better off and none worse off. Many reallocations make some people better off and others worse off. We cannot say whether such changes are good or bad without making explicit value judgements about the comparison of different people's welfare.

4 For a given level of resources and a given technology, the economy has an infinite number of Pareto-efficient allocations which differ in the distribution of welfare across people. For example, every allocation that gives the maximum attainable output to a single individual is Pareto-efficient. But there are many more allocations that are inefficient.

5 Under strict conditions, competitive equilibrium is Pareto-efficient. Different initial distributions of human and physical capital across people will generate the different competitive equilibria corresponding to each of the possible Pareto-efficient allocations. When price-taking producers and consumers face the same prices, marginal costs and marginal benefits

---

[8] See C. Mooney, 'Human Life and Suffering', in D. W. Pearce (ed.), *The Valuation of Social Cost*, George Allen and Unwin, 1978.

are equated to prices (by the independent actions of individual producers and consumers) and hence to each other.

6   In practice, governments face a conflict between the objectives of equity and efficiency. Redistributive taxation drives a wedge between prices paid by consumers (to which marginal benefits are equated) and prices received by producers (to which marginal costs are equated). Free market equilibrium will not equate marginal cost and marginal benefit and there will be scope for Pareto gains. Equilibrium will be inefficient.

7   Distortions occur whenever free market equilibrium does not equate marginal social cost and marginal social benefit. Distortions lead to inefficiency or market failure. Apart from taxes, there are three other important sources of distortions: imperfect competition (failure to set price equal to marginal cost), externalities (divergence between private and social costs or benefits), and other missing markets in connection with future goods, risky goods, or other informational problems.

8   When only one market is distorted the first-best solution is to remove the distortion, thus achieving full Pareto efficiency. The first-best criterion relates only to allocative efficiency. Governments caring sufficiently about redistribution might still prefer inefficient allocations with greater vertical equity. However, when a distortion cannot be removed from one market it is not generally efficient to ensure that all other markets are distortion-free. The theory of the second-best says that it is allocatively more efficient to spread inevitable distortions thinly over many markets than to concentrate their effects in a few markets.

9   Production externalities occur when decisions by one producer affect the production costs of another producer directly, as when one firm pollutes another's water supply. Consumption externalities imply that one person's decisions affect another consumer's utility directly, as when one person's garden gives pleasure to the neighbours. External effects shift indifference curves or production functions.

10   Externalities lead to divergence between private and social costs or benefits because there is no implicit market for the externality itself. When only a few people are involved, a system of property rights may establish the missing market. The direction of compensation will depend on who has the property rights, but the consequence would be to achieve the efficient quantity of the externality at which marginal cost and marginal benefit are equated. The efficient solution is rarely to have a zero quantity of the externality. Transactions costs and the free-rider problem may prevent implicit markets being established. Equilibrium will then be inefficient.

11   When externalities lead to market failure the government could set up the missing market by pricing the externality through taxes or subsidies. If it was straightforward to assess the efficient quantity of the externality and hence the correct tax or subsidy, and straightforward to monitor the quantities produced and consumed, such taxes or subsidies would allow the market to achieve an efficient resource allocation.

12   In practice, governments often regulate externalities such as pollution or congestion by imposing standards that affect quantities directly rather than by using the tax system to affect production and consumption indirectly. Overall quantity standards may fail to equate the marginal cost of pollution reduction across different polluters, in which case the allocation will not be efficient. However, simple standards may use up less resources in monitoring and enforcement and may prevent disastrous outcomes when there is uncertainty.

13   Moral hazard, adverse selection, and other informational problems prevent the development of a complete set of forward and contingent markets. Without these markets the price system cannot equate social marginal cost and benefit for future goods or risky activities.

14   Incomplete information may lead to private choices which do not represent the best interests of individuals or society as a whole. Health, quality, and safety regulations are designed both to provide information and to express society's value judgements about intangibles such as life itself. By avoiding explicit consideration of social costs and benefits, government policy may be inconsistent in its implicit valuation of health or safety in different activities under regulation.

Key Terms

Welfare economics
Horizontal and vertical equity
Pareto efficiency of resource allocations
Distortions and market failure
First-best and second-best efficiency
Production and consumption externalities
Property rights
Free-rider problem
Government regulation
Forward and contingent markets

Problems

1   An economy has 10 units of goods to share out between two people. (x, y) denotes that the first person gets a quantity x and the second person a quantity y. For each of the following allocations say whether they are (i) efficient and (ii) equitable: (a) (10, 0) (b) (7, 2) (c) (5, 5) (d) (3, 6) (e) (0, 10). What does 'equitable' mean? If you were making the choice, would you prefer allocation (d) to allocation (e)?

2   Suppose the equilibrium price of meals is £1 and of films £5. There is perfect competition and no externality. What can we say about (a) the relative benefit to consumers of a marginal film and a marginal meal? (b) the relative marginal production cost of films and meals? (c) the relative marginal product of variable factors in the film and meal industries? Hence explain why competitive equilibrium is Pareto-efficient.

3   In deciding whether or not to drive your car during the rush hour, you think about the cost of petrol and the time of the journey. Do you slow other people down by driving in the rush hour? Is this an externality? Does this mean that too many or too few people drive cars in the rush hour? Would it make sense for city authorities to restrict commuter parking in cities during the day?

4   Explain how an economist might defend laws making it compulsory to wear seat belts in cars.

5   In 1965, 200 people died when the steam boiler exploded on a Mississippi river boat. This prompted Jeremiah Allen and three friends to form a private company offering to insure any boiler that they had inspected for safety. The idea of boiler inspections caught on and boiler explosion rates plummeted.[9] (a) Would Jeremiah Allen's company have been so successful if it had certified boilers but not insured them as well? Explain. (b) Could this idea be carried over from boiler inspections to drug inspections? If not, why not?

6   (a) Why might society wish to ban drugs that neither help nor harm the diseases they are claimed to cure? (b) It is sometimes argued that regulatory bodies will be blamed for bad things that happen in spite of the regulations (e.g. a plane crash) but not blamed so much for good things that are prevented (e.g. the quick availability of a safe and useful drug) by stringent tests and regulations. Does this mean that regulatory bodies will tend to be too conservative and will over-regulate the activities under their scrutiny?

7   Why is it inefficient for different government departments to have different rules of thumb about the marginal value of human life?

8   Common Fallacies   Show why the following statements are incorrect. (a) Irresponsible firms discharge toxic waste with no thought for the damage inflicted on others. Society should ban all such discharges. It would be much better off without them. (b) Anything governments can do the market can do better. (c) Anything the market can do the government can do better.

---

[9] For details, see Earl Ubell, 'The Privatisation of Regulation', *Newsweek*, 23 November 1982, p. 35.

16

Taxes and Public Spending:
The Government and Resource Allocation

By the 1980s many people felt that the government had too big a role in the economy. They believed that high levels of government spending were pre-empting resources that could have been used more productively in the private sector, that high taxes were stifling private enterprise, and that the abolition of the complex system of government regulations, interventions, and subsidies would unleash a new wave of private initiative and energy.

These were not quack ideas that never made it in practice. On the contrary, electorates in many countries turned to the political leaders who promised to implement these new policies – Mrs Thatcher in the UK, President Reagan in the United States, and Chancellor Kohl in West Germany.

This chapter is about the extent of government involvement in the economy. How much should the government raise in taxation? Are there good taxes and bad taxes? If taxes are needed to pay for government spending, why do we need government spending in the first place?

We begin with three tables that provide some historical perspective. Table 16-1 shows the scale of government spending in the UK over three decades. It is important to distinguish government spending on goods and services – schools, defence, the police, and so on – from government spending on *transfer payments*, such as social security and state pensions. Whereas spending on goods and services directly uses up factors of production that could otherwise have been employed in the private sector, transfer payments do not directly pre-empt society's scarce resources. Rather they transfer purchasing power from one group of consumers, those paying taxes, to another group of consumers, those in receipt of transfer payments or subsidies.

Table 16-1 shows that between 1956 and 1976 there was a moderate increase in the share of national income and national resources directly pre-empted by the government through government spending on goods and services. It also shows that the Thatcher government found it difficult to implement its objective of quickly reducing this percentage. Nevertheless, the share of national income going to government spending on goods and services is now falling.

The second row of Table 16-1 shows that government spending on transfer payments has also risen faster than national income. In part this reflects increasing expenditure on state pensions as more and more people live to a ripe old age. However, the most important source of the large rise in transfer payments was the steady rise in unemployment until the mid-1980s. The subsequent decline in unemployment has also been responsible for the fall in the share of transfer payments since 1984. The last row of Table 16-1 shows the turnaround in total spending since 1984.

One reason for trying to reduce government spending is to make room for tax cuts. Table 16-2 picks out the most controversial aspect of the tax system, *the marginal rate of income tax*.

The *marginal rate* of income tax is the percentage taken by the government of the last pound that an individual earns. In contrast, the *average* tax rate is the percentage of *total* income that the government takes in income tax.

A *progressive* tax structure is one in which the average tax rate rises with an individual's income level. The government takes proportionately more from the rich than from the poor. A *regressive* tax structure is one in which the

Table 16-1 Government spending as a percentage of UK national income*

SPENDING ON	1956	1966	1976	1984	1988
Goods and services	20.7	21.6	25.9	23.8	22.0
Transfer payments	13.2	16.5	21.0	22.7	20.0
Total spending	33.9	38.1	46.9	46.5	42.0

* Spending of central and local government as a percentage of gross domestic product at market prices.
Source: CSO, *UK National Accounts.*

Table 16-2 Marginal income tax rates in the UK (Tax rates on an extra pound of income)

TAXABLE INCOME* (1990 £)	MARGINAL TAX RATE (%)		
	1978–79	1986–97	1990–91
6 000	34	29	25
12 000	34	29	25
18 000	45	29	25
24 000	50	40	40
30 000	65	45	40
36 000	70	50	40
54 000	83	60	40

* Taxable income after deduction of allowances. In 1990–91 the single person's allowance was £3005.
Source: HMSO, *Financial Statement and Budget Report 1990–91.*

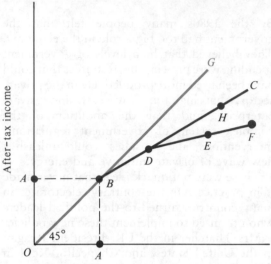

Figure 16-1 A PROGRESSIVE INCOME TAX. The line *OG* with a slope of 45 degrees shows what would happen in the absence of any income tax. A pre-tax income measured on the horizontal axis would convert into the same amount of post-tax income measured on the vertical axis. An income tax plus an allowance *OA* implies that the first *OA* pounds of pre-tax income are still retained after-tax. If income above *OA* is taxed at a constant marginal rate, the individiual is then on the schedule *BC* with a constant slope. The slope is less than 45 degrees because for each extra pound earned the individual is only allowed to keep a constant fraction of it. Higher pre-tax incomes move the individual up *BC* and imply that the government is taking a larger and larger fraction of total pre-tax income. The individual is falling further and further below the no-tax schedule *OG*. With a rising *marginal* tax rate, the schedule falls even further below *OG*.

average tax rate falls as income level rises. The government takes proportionately less from the rich.

Table 16-2 shows that, as in most countries, the UK has a progressive income tax structure. Figure 16-1 explains why. We plot pre-tax income on the horizontal axis and post-tax income on the vertical axis. The line *OG* with a slope of 45 degrees would correspond to no taxes. A pre-tax income *OA* on the horizontal axis corresponds to the same post-tax income *OA* on the vertical axis. Now suppose there is an income tax with a tax allowance *OA*. The first *OA* pounds of income are untaxed. If the marginal tax rate on taxable income is constant, individuals face a schedule such a *OBC*. The individual gets to keep only a constant fraction of each pound of pre-tax income above *OA*. The higher the marginal tax rate the flatter the portion *BC* of the schedule.

How do we calculate the average tax rate at a point such as *D*? We join up *OD*. The flatter the slope of this line the higher the average tax rate. Hence, even with a constant marginal tax rate and a constant slope of the portion *BC* of the tax

schedule, the presence of an initial tax allowance makes the tax structure progressive. If we join up *OH* we get a line with a flatter slope than *OD*, which in turn has a flatter slope than *OB*. The higher an individual's gross income, the smaller is the tax allowance as a percentage of this gross income so the larger is the percentage of total income on which the individual is paying tax.

But Table 16-2 shows that *marginal* tax rates also rise with income. The tax schedule in the UK looks more like the schedule OBDEF. As individuals move into higher tax bands they pay higher marginal tax rates and move on to even flatter portions of the tax schedule. The average tax rate now rises sharply with income. The line joining OF has a much flatter slope than the line joining OD.

Table 16-2 shows that the first Thatcher government was able to reduce marginal tax rates substantially, especially for the very rich. A millionaire paying an 83 per cent tax rate on

Table 16-3 Income tax reform 1975–90
(Marginal tax rates, %)

	INITIAL RATE		TOP RATE	
	1975	1990	1975	1990
Holland	27	35	71	60
France	5	5	60	57
Germany	22	19	56	53
Italy	10	10	72	50
Japan	10	10	75	50
Australia	20	24	65	49
Sweden	35	25	56	42
UK	35	25	83	40
USA	14	15	70	33
New Zealand	19	24	57	33

Source: J. Kay, 'Tax Policy: A Survey', *Economic Journal*, 1990.

all taxable income except the first £54 000 in 1978–79 was paying only 40 per cent per cent in 1990–91.

Table 16-3 shows a worldwide move to cut tax rates, especially for the very rich. Were the tax cuts designed to make the rich richer? Or was their purpose to revive hard work and enterprise? If so, will they work? These questions go to the heart of the current debate and form the background to much of the discussion of this chapter.

16-1 Taxation and Government Spending

Table 16-1 shows that government spending, and the taxation that finances it, are now running at over 40 per cent of national income. Table 16-4 shows the composition of government spending and revenue in 1987.

Table 16-4 shows that in 1987 £82.4 billion, almost half of total government spending, went on transfer payments such as unemployment benefit and debt interest. Of the remaining £92.1 billion spent directly on goods and services, the most important spending categories were the National Health Service, defence, and education.

Why is the government directly involved in providing defence, schools, and health services? How much of each should be provided? Would it make sense for these activities to be provided by the private sector in the same way as haircuts and cars? If refuse collection can be 'privatized',

Table 16-4 Expenditure and revenue of UK central and local government 1987

EXPENDITURE	£ billion	REVENUE	£ billion
Health	21.3	Income tax	39.8
Education	21.2	Corporation tax	14.0
Defence	18.9	Expenditure taxes	68.0
Other current spending	24.4	Social security contributions	28.5
Capital investment	6.3	Taxes on capital	3.4
All goods and services	92.1	Petroleum revenue tax	1.8
Social security	51.9	Tax revenue	155.5
Debt interest	17.7	Rent, interest and other receipts	13.1
Other transfer payments	12.8	Borrowing	5.9
All transfer payments	82.4		
TOTAL EXPENDITURE	174.5	TOTAL REVENUE	174.5

Source: CSO, *UN National Accounts.*

why not defence? To deal with these issues in democratic decision-making, we shall need a large dose of economics and a fair helping of political science.

Table 16-4 shows that most government spending is financed through taxation. The most important taxes are income tax and expenditure taxes such as value added tax (VAT). Since state provision of retirement pensions is included on the expenditure side under transfer payments, the pension contributions under the National Insurance Scheme must be included on the revenue side.

Against this background, we begin by discussing the reasons for government spending. Then we ask how spending should be financed. Are there good and bad taxes? The answer depends on the criteria of efficiency and equity that we developed in the last chapter.

16-2 The Government in the Market Economy

In this section we consider the argument that can be used to justify government spending in a market economy. We begin with public goods.

Public Goods

A *private* good is a good that, if consumed by one person, cannot be consumed by another person.

Ice cream is a private good. If you eat an ice cream it prevents anyone else from eating the same ice cream. For any given supply of ice cream, your consumption reduces the quantity available for others to consume. Most goods are private goods.

A *public* good is a good that, even if consumed by one person, can still be consumed by other people.

Clean air and defence are examples of public goods. If the air is pollution-free, your consumption of it does not interfere with our consumption of it. If the Royal Navy is patrolling Britain's coastal waters, your consumption of national defence does not affect our quantity of national defence. In fact, for a *pure public good* we must all necessarily

consume the same quantity, namely, whatever quantity is supplied in the aggregate. We may of course get different amounts of utility if our tastes differ, but we all consume the same quantity.

The key aspects of public goods are (1) that it is technically possible for one person to consume without reducing the amount available for someone else, and (2) the impossibility of excluding anyone from consumption except at a prohibitive cost. A football match could be watched by a lot of people, especially if it is televised, without reducing the quantity consumed by any individual; but *exclusion* is possible – the ground holds only so many, and the club can refuse to allow the game to be televised. The interesting issues in economics arise when, as with national defence, exclusion of certain individuals from consumption is effectively impossible.

Free-Riders   In the last chapter we introduced the *free-rider problem* when discussing why bribes and compensation for externalities might not occur. Public goods are likely to be especially vulnerable to the free-rider problem if they are supplied by the private sector. Since you get the same quantity of national defence as everyone else, *whether or not you pay for it*, it would never be in your interest to purchase national defence in a free private market. Everybody else would adopt similar reasoning, and no defence would be demanded even if we all wanted defence.

Public goods are like a very strong externality. If you buy defence everyone else gets the benefits. Since marginal private and social benefits diverge, private markets will not produce the socially efficient quantity. There is a case for government intervention to make sure marginal social cost and marginal social benefit are equated.

The Marginal Social Benefit   Suppose the public good is the purity of the public water supply. The more infected the water, the more likely it is that everyone will be hit by an epidemic of cholera or some other disease. Figure 16-2 supposes there are two people. The first person's demand curve for water purity is $D_1 D_1$. Each point on the demand curve shows what the individual would pay for the last unit of purer water. It shows the marginal benefit

Figure 16-2 A PURE PUBLIC GOOD.
D_1D_1 and D_2D_2 are the separate demand curves of two individuals and show the marginal private benefit of the last unit of the public good to each individual. What is the social marginal benefit of the last unit to the group as a whole? Since both individuals consume whatever quantity of the good is produced, we must add up *vertically* the price each is prepared to pay for the last unit. At the output Q the marginal social benefit is thus $P_1 + P_2$. The curve DD showed the marginal social benefit and is obtained by vertically adding the demand curves of the two individuals. If MC is the private and social marginal cost of producing the public good the socially efficient output is Q^* at which social marginal cost and social marginal benefit are equal.

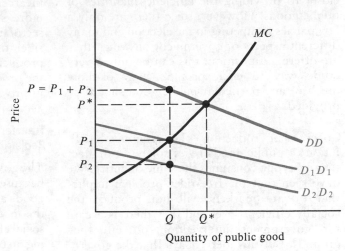

to the individual. D_2D_2 shows the marginal benefit of purer water to the second individual.

The curve DD gives the marginal social benefit of purer water. At each output level for the public good, we *vertically* sum the marginal benefit of each individual to get the social marginal benefit. Thus at the output Q the social marginal benefit is $P = P_1 + P_2$. We sum vertically *at a given quantity* because everyone consumes the same quantity of a public good by definition.

Figure 16-2 also shows the marginal cost of producing the public good. If there are no production externalities the marginal private cost and the marginal social cost of production will coincide. The socially efficient level of production of the public good is at Q^*, where the marginal social benefit equals the marginal social cost.

What would happen if the good were privately produced and marketed? Person 1 might pay a price P_1 to have a quantity Q produced by a competitive supplier pricing at marginal cost. At the output Q the price P_1 just equals the marginal private benefit which person 1 derives from the last unit of the public good. Would person 2 be prepared to pay to have the output of the public good increased beyond Q? The answer is, 'No'. Because it is a public good, person 2 cannot be excluded from consuming the output Q which person 1 has commissioned. But at the output Q, person 2's marginal private benefit is only P_2, which is less than the current price P_1.

Person 2 would certainly not pay the higher price necessary to induce a competitive supplier to expand production beyond the output Q. Person 2 is thus a free-rider enjoying person 1's purchase Q. And the total quantity privately produced and consumed in a competitive market lies below the socially efficient quantity Q^*.

Revelation of Preferences By constructing the marginal social benefit curve DD, the government can decide how much of the public good it is socially efficient to produce. But how does the government find out the individual demand curves that must be vertically added to get DD? If people's payments for the good are related to their individual demand curves everyone has an incentive to lie because of the free-rider problem. People will understate how much they value the good in order to reduce their own payments, just as in a private market.

Conversely, if payments are divorced from the question of how much people would like, people will overstate their private valuations. We are all for safer streets if we do not have to contribute to the cost. In practice, democracies try to resolve this problem through elections of governments. Different parties offer different quantities of public goods together with a statement of how the money will be raised through the tax system. By asking the question, 'How much would you like, given that everyone will be charged for the cost of providing public goods?' society can come closer to providing the efficient quantities of public goods. However, since there are only a few parties competing in the election and many different aspects of government on which they are offering a position, this can be only a very crude way to elicit people's view of how much of any particular public good should be provided.

Government Production   The economist's definition of public goods relies solely on the fact that everyone consumes the same quantity. We have seen that the free-rider problem implies that private markets will not produce the socially efficient level and that there is a case for government intervention on efficiency grounds. But this merely says that the government must determine how much is produced. It does not imply that the government must produce the goods itself. Public goods are not necessarily the goods the government happens to produce.

For example, in the UK, as in most countries, national defence is a public good and is also produced largely within the public or government sector. We have few private armies. On the other hand, street-sweeping, though a public good, can be subcontracted to private producers, even if local government determines its quantity and pays for it out of local tax revenue. Conversely, state hospitals in the National Health Service involve public sector production of private goods. One person's hip replacement operation certainly prevents the busy surgeon from doing something else at the same time.

In the next chapter we examine why the public sector may wish to produce private goods. Whether public goods need be produced by the public sector depends not on their consumption characteristics, on which our definition of public good relies, but on their production characteristics. There is nothing special about street-sweeping, and it can as easily be produced by the public or the private sector. In contrast, armies and navies rely on discipline and secrecy. Generals and admirals may believe, and society may agree, that offences against these regulations should receive unusual penalties which would not be generally sanctioned in private firms. Few people believe that insubordination is an important offence for street-sweepers and should be punished by

incarceration or even death. Hence it may make more sense for soldiers to be in the public sector than street-sweepers. Where such considerations do not arise, for example in the production of uniforms, it is more likely that the production of defence goods will take place in private firms.

Transfer Payments and Income Redistribution

The government spends money on public goods because there is a market failure when public goods are left entirely to private markets. Thus the motivation for this type of intervention is social efficiency. In contrast, government spending on transfer payments is primarily concerned with *equity* and *income redistribution*. By spending money on the unemployed, the old, and the poor (who in the UK are entitled to supplementary benefit if their total income from whatever source falls below a certain minimum level), the government seeks to ensure that the distribution of income and welfare that a totally free market economy would otherwise have produced is at least truncated: there is a minimum standard of living below which no citizen should fall. The specification of this standard is of course pure value judgement.

Where does the money come from to pay the poor and the disadvantaged? Primarily from those who can most afford to pay. Table 16-2 shows that the income tax system in the UK is *progressive*. Increasing marginal tax rates on income ensure that each individual's average tax rate, the proportion of total income paid in taxes, increases with income. Taken as a whole, the tax and transfer system takes money from the rich and gives to the poor. The poor receive not merely the direct financial transfer in the form of transfer payments such as supplementary benefit, but also the consumption of public goods that have been paid for by income taxes raised from the rich.

As we pointed out in the last chapter, not only is the amount of redistribution to be undertaken by the government a pure value judgement on which different individuals and different political parties will disagree, but there is an inevitable trade-off between the competing objectives of efficiency and equity. To undertake more redistribution the government will have to increase tax rates, thereby driving a larger wedge between the price paid by the purchaser and the price received by the seller of the good or service. Since the price system achieves Pareto efficiency by inducing each individual to equate marginal cost or marginal benefit to the price received or paid, and hence to one another, taxes that imply that buyers and sellers face different prices ensure that the marginal cost to a seller no longer equals the marginal benefit to a buyer. Taxes are generally distortionary and tend to reduce efficiency.

In Table 16-2 we saw that the Thatcher government succeeded in reducing marginal tax rates, especially for the very rich. Opponents of the government argued that the objective as well as the consequence of the legislation was to increase the after-tax incomes of the rich at the expense of the poor. The government argued that reducing distortions in the labour market by cutting income tax would lead to efficiency gains that would far outweigh the valuation that society should put on a more equal income distribution. If society's resource could be used to make more output, even the poor might be better off in the long run.

Merit Goods and Bads

Merit goods (bads) are goods that society thinks everyone ought to have (ought not to have) regardless of whether they are wanted by each individual.

Examples of merit goods are education and health. Merit bads are products such as cigarettes. Since society places a different value on these goods from the value placed on them by the individual, it follows that individual choice within a free market economy will lead to a different allocation from the allocation that society wishes to see.

There are two distinct reasons for designating merit goods. The first is a version of the externality argument we examined in the previous chapter. If more education raises the productivity not merely of an individual worker but of all other workers with whom this worker co-operates, there is a production externality that the individual does not take into account in choosing how much education to purchase. If individuals demand too little education, society should encourage the provision of education. Free schooling to ensure a minimum level of education, communication, and social

interaction might be one way to achieve this.

Conversely, if people take account of the costs to themselves but not the burden on the National Health Service in deciding whether or not to smoke and damage their health, society may regard smoking as a merit bad that should be discouraged. We shall shortly see how the tax system, in this case a tax on cigarettes, may be used to offset externalities that individuals fail to take into account.

The second aspect of merit goods is where society believes that individuals are no longer acting in their own best interests. Addiction to drugs, tobacco, or gambling are obvious examples. Economists rarely subscribe to the value judgement of whole-scale paternalism. The function of government intervention is less to tell people what they ought to like than to allow them better to achieve what they already like. However, the government will sometimes have more information or be in a better position to take a decision. Much as some people hate going to school, they will frequently be glad afterwards that they were made to do so.

Thus the government may spend money on compulsory education or compulsory vaccination because is recognizes that, left to their own decisions, individuals will act in a way they will subsequently regret.

16-3 The Principles of Taxation

This section is in three parts. First we consider the different kinds of taxes through which the government can raise revenue. Then we consider again the equity implications of taxation. Finally, we examine the efficiency implications of taxation.

Variety of Taxes

Governments can raise tax revenue only if they can identify the activities on which the tax rates apply. Before sophisticated records of income or sales were ever kept, governments raised most of their revenue through customs duties and road tolls, the two places where transactions could be easily monitored. Income tax in peacetime was not introduced in the UK until the 1840s, and VAT – a general tax on goods and services (with a few specified exemptions such as good and children's clothing) – was not introduced until the 1970s. We briefly outline the main taxes shown in Table 16-5, grouped under three headings: taxes on income, or *direct taxes*; taxes on expenditure, or *indirect taxes*; and taxes on assets, or *wealth taxes*.

Direct Taxes   Individuals pay income tax on earnings from labour, rents, dividends, and interest. In Chapter 14 we saw that the return on an asset is not just the dividend or interest payment but also the capital gain. Although many economists would argue that capital gains, as for example when ICI shares are purchased for £2 and subsequently sold for £3, are as much income as the dividend component of the return on an asset, in practice the Inland Revenue assesses and taxes capital gains separately. National insurance contributions by individuals are also a form of direct personal taxation.

Companies pay corporation tax calculated on their taxable profits after allowance for interest payments and depreciation. They also make a national insurance contribution on behalf of their employees.

Indirect Taxes   Indirect taxes are taxes levied on expenditure on goods and services. The most important source of indirect tax revenue is value added tax (VAT), which is effectively a retail sales tax. Whereas a sales tax is collected only at the point of final sale to the consumer, VAT is collected at different stages of the production process.

Suppose a firm mines iron ore and converts it into £200 worth of high-grade steel, which is then sold to a car producer. The car producer converts the steel into a car costing £3200. A simple sales tax levied at 15 per cent would raise the cost to the consumer to £3200 + £480 (15 per cent of £3200) or £3680. In contrast, VAT works as follows. The steel firm has a value added or net output of £200 on which it pays 15 per cent or £30 in tax. Passing the tax on to the car producer, the steel is sold for £230. The car producer has a value added or net output of £3000 and pays 15 per cent or £450 in tax. Since the car firm paid £230 for the steel, the final price to the consumer is £230 + £3000 + £450 = £3680. As far as the consumer is concerned this is just the same as a 15 per cent sales tax.

This example makes it seem that the consumer price is raised by the full amount of the tax. But a higher consumer price will reduce the quantity demanded. In turn this will move producers back down their marginal cost curves and alter the net-of-tax price producers require. Later in this section we show how to analyse these induced effects to determine how the burden of the tax is ultimately divided between producers and consumers.

Revenue from VAT is supplemented by other indirect taxes including special duties on tobacco and alcohol, licence fees for motor cars and televisions, and customs duties on imports.

Wealth Taxes   In the UK there used to be two taxes that tax wealth *per se* rather than the income that is derived from wealth. The first was the tax on property values, which formed the main source of revenue for local government. That is the tax that was replaced by the poll tax (a simple flat-rate tax per person) in the reform of UK local government finance during 1988–90. The second, which still exists, is capital transfer tax, which applies to transfers of wealth between individuals, whether as gifts during life or as inheritances after death.

How does the UK tax structure compare with that in other countries? Table 16-5 shows data for several advanced countries in 1983. The most notable feature of the UK tax system appears to be its low reliance on social security taxes for state pension and unemployment provisions. Table 16-5 also suggests that the UK relies quite heavily on indirect taxes rather than direct taxes.

Tax revenue is necessary to pay for government expenditure. We now assess the UK tax system against our two welfare criteria, equity and efficiency.

How To Tax Fairly

In the last chapter we introduced two notions of equity: *horizontal equity*, or the equal treatment of equals, and *vertical equity*, the redistribution from the 'haves' to the 'have-nots'.

In Table 16-2 we showed that income tax is progressive. In taking proportionately more from the rich than from the less well off, income

Table 16-5 Sources of tax revenue in 1983 (percentage of total taxes*)

COUNTRY	TAXES ON INCOME	INDIRECT TAXES	SOCIAL SECURITY TAXES	TAXES ON PROFITS AND CAPITAL
UK	28.7	41.9	18.0	11.3
Italy	30.6	28.4	34.4	5.8
Sweden	39.2	30.5	26.5	3.7
Japan	25.2	27.1	29.6	18.0
USA	38.4	29.7	23.8	8.1

* Percentages for a country may not add to 100 because of miscellaneous taxes and rounding errors.
Source: CSO, *Economic Trends, May 1986.*

tax reflects the principle of *ability to pay*. There are two reasons society might think it fair that the rich should pay more. First, society may wish to take from the rich in order to give to the poor. Second, if money has to be raised to pay for public goods, society may wish to avoid taxing those whose incomes are already low. The principle of ability to pay thus reflects a concern about vertical equity.

A second principle is sometimes applied in discussing the extent to which unequal people should be treated unequally. *The benefits principle* argues that people who receive more than their share of public spending should pay more than their share of tax revenues. Car users should pay more towards public roads than people without a car should pay. And to some extent they do. Car users pay heavy duties on petrol and must pay licence fees for running a car.

However, the benefits principle often conflicts directly with the principle of ability to pay. If people who are most vulnerable to unemployment must pay the highest contributions to the government unemployment insurance scheme, it becomes very difficult to achieve a significant redistribution of income, wealth, or welfare. If the main objective is vertical equity, the ability to pay principle must usually take precedence.

Although Table 16-2 shows that the income tax system in the UK is progressive, it is the entire structure of taxes, transfers, and public spending that we must examine before we can judge how much the government is effectively redistributing from the rich to the poor. We have already mentioned two factors that make the entire structure more progressive than an examination of income tax alone would

suggest. First, transfer payments actually give money out to the poor. The old get pensions, the unemployed get unemployment benefit, and, as a final safety net, anyone whose income from whatever source falls below a certain minimum is entitled to supplementary benefit. Second, the state provides public goods that can be consumed by the poor, even if they have not paid any taxes to finance these goods. In addition to pure public goods, such as defence, the state also makes free provision of certain goods, such as parks and swimming pools, which have part of the characteristics of a pure public good. Although the whole population cannot squeeze into Hyde Park, quite a few people can enjoy its amenities without spoiling the enjoyment of others. And since the rich tend to sit in their own gardens, public parks help redistribute enjoyment towards the poor.

As against these progressive elements of the tax, transfer, and spending structure, it should be noted that there are some important *regressive* elements that take proportionately more from the poor. Beer and tobacco taxes are huge revenue-earners for the government. Yet the poor spend a much higher proportion of their income – in some cases even a larger absolute amount – on these goods than do the rich. Such taxes reduce the effectiveness of the tax, transfer and spending structure in redistributing from the rich to the poor.

Tax Incidence

The *incidence* of a tax measures the final tax burden on different people once we have allowed for the indirect as well as the direct effects of the tax. The ultimate effect of a tax

Figure 16-3 A TAX ON WAGES. In the absence of a tax, free market equilibrium is at *E* and the wage is *W*. A wage tax makes the gross wage paid by firms higher than the net wage received by workers. Measuring gross wages on the vertical axis, the demand curve *DD* is unaltered by the imposition of the tax. Firms still choose the quantity of labour demanded to equate the gross wage to the marginal value product of labour. *SS* continues to show labour supply, but as a function of the *net* wage. To get labour supply in terms of the gross wage we must draw the new supply curve *SS'*. At each quantity of hours, *SS'* lies vertically above *SS* by a distance reflecting the tax on earnings from the last hour worked. The new equilibrium is at *E'*. The gross wage paid by firms is *W'* but the net wage received by workers is *W"*. The vertical distance *A'E'* shows the amount of the tax. Whether the government *collects* the tax revenue entirely from firms or entirely from workers, the *incidence* of the tax is the same. It falls partly on firms, who must pay a higher gross wage *W'*, and partly on workers, who receive the lower net wage *W"*. The area of pure waste *A'E'E* will shortly be discussed in the text.

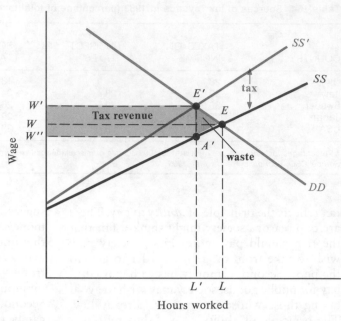

can be very different from its apparent effect. Thus to get a really good idea of the extent to which taxes (or subsidies) alter people's spending power and welfare, we need to examine the issue of tax incidence in more detail.

Figure 16-3 shows the market for labour. *DD* is the market demand curve for labour and *SS* is the supply curve for labour, which we assume slopes upwards. Thus a higher wage rate increases the supply of hours of work, but reduces the demand for hours of work. In the absence of an income tax (a tax on wages), the labour market will be in equilibrium at point *E*.

Now suppose the government imposes an income tax. If we measure the gross wage on the vertical axis, the demand curve *DD* is unaltered since it is the comparison of the gross wage with the marginal value product of labour that determines the quantity of labour demanded by firms. Workers' preferences or attitudes are also unchanged, but it is the wage net of tax that workers compare with the marginal value of their leisure in deciding how much labour to supply. Thus, although *SS* continues to show the labour supply curve in terms of the after-tax wage, we must draw in the higher schedule *SS'* to show the supply of

labour in terms of the gross or pre-tax wage. The vertical distance between *SS'* and *SS* measures the amount of tax being paid on earnings from the last hour's work.

Since *DD* and *SS'* now show the behaviour of firms and workers at any gross wage, the new equilibrium will be at the point *E'*. The new equilibrium gross wage is *W'* at which firms demand a quantity of hours *L'*. The vertical distance between *A'* and *E'* measures the tax being paid on earnings from the last hour of work. Thus the after-tax wage is *W"* at which workers are happy to supply a quantity of hours *L'*.

Relative to the original equilibrium wage *W*, the imposition of the tax on wages has *raised* the pre-tax wage to *W'*, but *lowered* the after-tax wage to *W"*. It has raised the wage that firms must pay but lowered the take-home wage for workers. The incidence of the tax has fallen on *both* firms and workers even though, as a matter of administrative convenience, the tax may be collected by the government directly from workers.

The lesson from Figure 16-3 is an important one: the incidence or burden of a tax cannot be established by looking at who actually hands

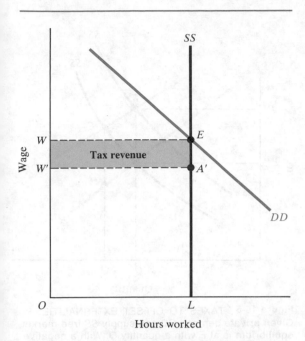

Figure 16-4 TAXING A FACTOR IN INELASTIC SUPPLY. If the supply curve *SS* is vertical, a tax *A'E* per unit leaves the quantity *L* unaffected. Since the demand curve *DD* is unaltered, the tax has no effect on the pre-tax wage rate. The full incidence of the tax falls on workers whose after-tax wage is reduced by the full amount of the tax.

over the money to the government. Taxes usually alter equilibrium prices and quantities and these induced effects must also be taken int account. However, we can draw one very general conclusion. The more inelastic the supply curve and the more elastic the demand curve, the more the final incidence will fall on the seller rather than the purchaser.

Figure 16-4 depicts the extreme case in which the supply curve is completely inelastic. In the absence of a tax, equilibrium is at *E* and the wage is *W*. Since the vertical supply curve *SS* implies that a fixed quantity of hours *L* will be supplied whatever the after-tax wage, the imposition of a tax on wages leads to a new equilibrium at *A'*. Only if the pre-tax wage is unchanged will firms demand the quantity *L* that is supplied. Hence after-tax wages fall by the full amount of the tax. The entire incidence falls on the workers.

To check you have grasped the idea of incidence, try drawing for yourself a market with a relatively elastic supply curve and a relatively inelastic demand curve. Show that the

incidence of a tax will now fall mainly on the purchaser.[1]

Taxation, Efficiency, and Waste

So far, we have been considering the equity implications of a tax. But we must also think about the efficiency implications of a tax. We can use Figure 16-3 again.

Before the tax is imposed, labour market equilibrium is at *E*. The wage *W* measures both the marginal social benefit of the last hour of work and its marginal social cost. The demand curve *DD* tells us the marginal value product of labour, the extra benefit society could have from extra goods produced. The supply curve *SS* tells us the marginal value of the leisure being sacrificed in order to work another hour, the marginal social cost of extra work. Before the tax is imposed, the labour market is in equilibrium at *E*. Since marginal social cost and benefit are equal, this initial position is socially efficient.

When the tax is imposed, the new equilibrium is at *E'*. We have already discussed the incidence of the tax on firms and workers. The tax *A'E'* increases the wage to firms to *W'* but reduces the after-tax wage for workers to *W''*. But there is an additional tax burden or deadweight loss that is pure waste. It is the triangle *A'E'E*. By reducing the quantity of hours from *L* to *L'*, the tax causes society to stop using hours on which the marginal social benefit, the height of the demand curve *DD*, exceeds the marginal social cost, the height of the supply curve *SS*. By driving a wedge between the wage firms pay and the wage workers receive, the tax induces a distortion which destroys the efficiency of free market equilibrium.

Must Taxes Be Distortionary?

Government need tax revenue to pay for public

---

[1] By now you may be wondering whether we always show the effect of a tax as a shift in the supply curve. We do, provided we wish to measure the pre-tax price of the good or service on the vertical axis. If we want to measure the after-tax price on the vertical axis, the effect of the tax will be to shift not the supply curve but the demand curve. If you look again at Figures 16-3 and 16-4, you can see that in terms of the after-tax wage, the demand curve must shift down until it passes through the point *A'*. The distance between *A'* and *E* still measures the tax and we get exactly the same conclusions as before.

goods and to make transfer payments to the poor. Must taxes create distortions and lead to the waste or inefficiency which Figure 16-3 suggests?

Figure 16-4 showed what happens when a wage tax is levied but the supply of labour is completely inelastic. Although the tax reduces the take-home pay of workers, there is no change in the gross wage or the equilibrium quantity of hours. Since the quantity is unchanged, there is no distortionary triangle or deadweight burden. The equilibrium quantity remains the socially efficient quantity.

We can make this into a general principle.[2] When either the supply or the demand curve for a good or service is very inelastic, the imposition of a tax will lead only to a small change in quantity. Hence the deadweight burden triangle must be small. Given that the government must raise some tax revenue, the smallest amount of total waste will be achieved when the goods that are most inelastic in supply or demand are taxed most heavily.

This principle finds practical expression in the UK tax system. The three most heavily taxed commodities are alcohol, tobacco, and the oil being extracted from the North Sea. For these commodities tax rates range from 50 to 90 per cent. Alcohol and tobacco are generally assumed to be products with a very inelastic demand. North Sea oil is in inelastic supply. Having spent large amounts of money on exploration and drilling, oil companies are quite keen to recoup their investment, even if the government is taking a big slice off the top.[3]

So far, we have discussed the taxes that would do least harm to the allocative efficiency of the economy. Sometimes the government has the opportunity to levy taxes which will actually improve efficiency and reduce waste. The most important example is when externalities exist.

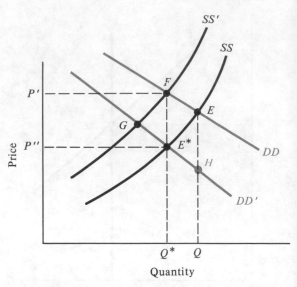

Figure 16-5   TAXES TO OFFSET EXTERNALITIES. Given private demand *DD* and supply *SS* free market equilibrium is at *E* with a quantity *Q*. With a negative consumption externality, the social marginal benefit is *DD'* lying below *DD*. *E** is the socially efficient point at which output is *Q**. At this output the marginal externality is *E*F*. By levying a tax of exactly *E*F* per unit, the government can shift the private supply curve from *SS* to *SS'* leading to a new equilibrium at *F* at which the socially efficient quantity *Q** is produced and the deadweight burden of the externality *E*HE* is eliminated.

Cigarette smokers pollute the air for other people but take no account of this in deciding how much to smoke. They give rise to a harmful consumption externality. Figure 16-5 shows the supply curve *SS* of cigarette producers. Since there are no production externalities, this marginal private cost curve is also the marginal social cost curve. *DD* is the private demand curve showing the marginal benefit of cigarettes to smokers. Because there is a harmful consumption externality, the marginal social benefit *DD'* of cigarette consumption is lower than *DD*.

In the absence of a tax, free market equilibrium is at *E*, but there is over-consumption of cigarettes. The socially efficient quantity is *Q** since marginal social cost and marginal social benefit are equated at *E**. Suppose the government levies a tax, equal to the vertical distance *E*F*, on each packet of cigarettes. With the tax-inclusive price on the vertical axis, the demand curve *DD* is unaffected, but the

[2] This insight is more than 60 years old. See Frank Ramsey, 'The Optimal Structure of Commodity Taxation', *Economic Journal*, 1927.

[3] Why are tax rates not even higher? Recall from Chapter 5 that, if a demand curve is close to a straight line, the price elasticity of demand becomes more elastic as we move up the demand curve. The tax-inclusive price of alcohol and tobacco is now reaching a point where demand becomes elastic so that the government would actually lose revenue if duties were raised much further. Similarly, although the short-run supply of North Sea oil may be quite inelastic, the long-run supply may be much more elastic. If the tax rate becomes too high oil companies will stop searching for new oil.

supply curve shifts up to SS'. Each point on SS' then allows producers to receive the corresponding net-of-tax price on SS.

After the tax is introduced, equilibrium is at the point E. The socially efficient quantity Q* is produced and consumed. Consumers pay the price P' and producers receive the price P'' after tax has been paid at the rate E*F per unit.

Only the particular tax rate E*F per unit will guide the free market to the socially efficient allocation. A lower tax rate (including a zero tax rate) leads to too much consumption and production of cigarettes. A higher tax rate than E*F will move consumers further up their demand curve and lead to under-consumption and under-production.

Why must the tax rate be exactly E*F if the efficient quantity is to be achieved? Because this is exactly the amount of the externality on the last unit when the efficient quantity Q* is produced. By levying a tax at precisely this rate, the government raises the price to the consumer above the price to the producer by the amount of the externality. Consumers are induced to behave as if they took account of the externality, though in fact they take account only of the after-tax price.

Whenever consumption or production externalities induce distortions in the free market equilibrium allocation, the government can improve efficiency and reduce waste by levying taxes. The fact that alcohol and tobacco have farmful externalities provides another reason for taxing them heavily.

16-4 Taxation and Supply-side Economics

We began the chapter by noting that many Western countries have become disenchanted with the extent of government involvement in the economy. In part, it was felt that governments were spending too much. Resources used to produce goods and services for the government cannot be used to make goods in the private sector. We shall have more to say about this in the next chapter. However, the major objection to high levels of government expenditure seems to have been associated with the need for correspondingly high levels of revenue collection. Table 16-3 reminds us that some government expenditure is financed by

borrowing. In the UK this is known as the public sector borrowing requirement (PSBR). In Part 4 we shall examine the argument that a high PSBR leads to high inflation, high interest rates, or both. For the moment we ignore government borrowing and consider the argument that high taxation to pay for high levels of public spending necessarily strangles the economy.

We have already seen that in order to pay for public goods and redistribution the government must raise tax revenues, which typically introduces allocative distortions and leads to a dead-weight burden. Suppose the government adopts a less ambitious spending programme and is therefore able to reduce income tax rates. What will be the consequences?

First, by spending less on goods and services, the government will free some resources which can now be used by the private sector. If it were true that the private sector uses resources more productively than the public sector, the transfer of resources might directly produce more output. The total supply of goods and services would rise. Whether or not the private sector does use resources more productively on average than the government remains a contentious issue.

What about the effects of lower income tax rates? Figure 16-3 suggests that income taxes introduce a distortion that leads to a level of work that is socially inefficient. With lower taxes and a smaller distortion there would be a lower dead-weight burden. Since the distortion leads to a level of work that is lower than the socially efficient amount, cutting income taxes would also increase the amount of work done in the economy.

How large could this effect be? It all depends on the elasticity of labour supply. The more inelastic the labour supply, the lower is the distortion introduced by any particular income tax rate. When labour supply is completely inelastic as in Figure 16-4, income tax does not induce any distortion at all and there will be no allocative gain in reducing income tax rates.

In Chapter 11 we showed that an increase in the after-tax wage (as for example when income tax rates are cut) will have a substitution effect, tending to make people work longer hours, but an income effect, tending to make them work fewer hours. With higher after-tax wages it takes fewer hours to earn any given target income. Hence we argued that, for people already in work, changes in after-tax rates have only a small effect on hours of work supplied. Then we showed that increasing the after-tax wage *would* encourage labour force participation by those not currently in the labour force. Hence, taking hours and participation together, the supply curve of labour input (hours times people) will not be completely vertical. Cutting income tax *will* increase the supply of labour input, chiefly by attracting new workers into the labour force. But the total effect on labour supply might not be as large as some proponents of tax cuts believe.

In contrast, the tax cut enthusiasts believe that income tax is a major distortion and labour supply is very elastic. The socially efficient quantity of labour input would then be much larger than the equilibrium level under current tax rates. One illustration of this view is the famous Laffer curve, named after Professor Arthur Laffer, one of President Reagan's most influential economic advisers.

Suppose, for example, that all government tax revenue was raised through income tax. Figure 16-6 shows that with a zero tax rate the government would raise zero revenue. At the opposite extreme, with a 100 per cent income tax rate, there would be no point working and again tax revenue would be zero. Beginning from a zero rate, a small increase in the tax rate will yield some tax revenue. Initially revenue rises with the tax rate, but beyond the tax rate t^* higher taxes have major disincentive effects on work effort and revenue starts to fall.

Professor Laffer's idea was that many 'big government–big tax' countries are now at tax rates above t^*. If so, tax cuts would be the miracle cure. Everybody likes a tax cut but the government would actually raise *more* revenue by cutting taxes. By reducing the tax distortion and increasing the amount of work *a lot*, lower taxes would be more than compensated by the extra work and incomes to which the tax rates were applied.

It is not the shape of the Laffer curve that is in dispute. Rather, what many professional economists in the UK, the United States, and other Western countries have disputed is that these economies do *in fact* have tax rates above t^*. Most economists' reading of the empirical evidence is that our economies lie to the left of t^*. Figure 16-3 implies that cutting income tax rates may eliminate some of the deadweight burden of distortionary taxation, but governments should probably expect their tax revenue to decline if such policies are put into effect. Hence, if governments do wish to reduce tax rates without adding to government borrowing it is essential that they reduce their spending.

16-5 Local Government

Thus far we have been chiefly interested in the principles of central government. In this section we examine the economics of local government. Local government expenditure may cover a variety of things, from sweeping the streets to providing local schooling. In turn this must be

Figure 16-6   THE LAFFER CURVE.   The Laffer curve shows the relationship between tax rates and tax revenue. Moderate tax rates raise some revenue. Beyond t^*, higher tax rates reduce revenue because disincentive effects greatly reduce the supply of the quantity being taxed. At 100 per cent tax rate, supply and revenue will be zero again.

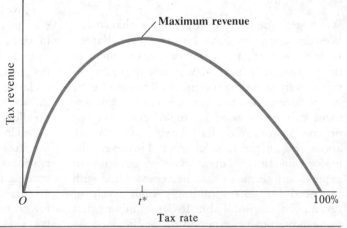

financed through taxes. Some of these taxes will be local, but some will come from central government revenue raised through the national tax system. Finally, local government is responsible for some types of regulation, for example land use or *zoning* laws.

Economic Principles

Why don't we make central government responsible for everything? Two arguments are usually used. First, diversity matters. People are different and they don't want to be treated the same. Civic pride is necessarily local. Second, people feel that central government is remote from their particular needs. Even if central government wished to pay attention to local considerations, it would find it hard to do so efficiently.

We turn now to two important models of local government. The first is the Tiebout model.[4] This model emphasizes diversity. Some people want a lot of local expenditure on public services and are prepared to pay high local taxes; others want to pay lower local taxes even though this means lower public services. If all local governments are the same, everyone will be unhappy with the compromise. The Tiebout model is sometimes called the *invisible foot*: people will cluster together in the area providing the package of spending and taxes they want. The invisible foot brings about an efficient allocation of resources through competition between local governments.

In practice, the invisible foot is sometimes a very imperfect incentive structure. First, it may be hard to move between local authorities. For example, being born in a neighbourhood may entitle you to a higher place in the queue for housing provided by that local authority. Second, if much of local authority revenue comes from central government, the levels of spending and taxes may be insensitive to the wishes of local residents. We discuss this more fully for the UK in Box 16-1.

Earlier in the chapter, we stressed the distinction between efficiency and equity. Even if the invisible foot led to efficiency, it might also lead to inequity. The rich are likely to cluster together in suburbs. Then they pass zoning laws specifying a minimum size for a

house and its garden. This makes it impossible for the poor to move to that neighbourhood. By forming an exclusive club, the rich have ensured that their tax contributions do not have to go to supporting the poor in their neighbourhood. And the poor get stuck with one another in inner-city areas whose governments face the biggest social needs but the smallest local tax base.

The Tiebout model assumes that residents mainly consume the public services provided by their own local authority. But when each unit of local government is responsible for a small geographical area, this may be a poor assumption. If an inner-city supplies free art galleries, financed out of taxes on inner-city inhabitants, the rich still come in from the suburbs to make use of these facilities. Conversely, inner-city inhabitants spend their Sundays enjoying countryside facilities supported by taxes raised out of town. In these cases, provision of public services in one area confers a beneficial externality on neighbouring areas.

Economic theory suggests the right answer to this problem. Unless the externality can be priced (charging suburban users but not city dwellers for entry to subsidized galleries and opera houses), the most efficient solution is to widen the geographical area of each local government until it includes most of the people who will use the public services it provides. Thus, for example, it may make sense to have an integrated commuter rail service and inner-city subway, and to subsidize it to prevent people driving through congested streets; but only a local government embracing both the suburbs and the inner city is likely to get close to the efficient policy.

These two theories of local government pull in opposite directions, and the right answer is likely to lie somewhere in between. The assumptions of the Tiebout model favour a lot of small local government jurisdictions to maximize choice and competition between areas. The model emphasizing externalities across areas suggests larger jurisdictions to 'internalize' externalities that would otherwise occur.

Summary

1 In industrialized economies, government revenues come mainly from direct taxes on

---

[4] Charles Tiebout, 'A Pure Theory of Local Expenditures', *Journal of Political Economy*, 1956.

BOX 16-1

POLL POSITION: UK LOCAL GOVERNMENT REFORMS

Until the late 1980s, local government in the UK was financed from three sources. First, domestic households paid *rates*, a property tax assessed on rateable values or hypothetical house prices. Second, local firms paid *business rates* on their property. The third, and much the largest source, was from central government through the *rate support grant*, which took some account of the needs of the area.

The Thatcher government believed this system has a bias towards overspending by local authorities. Many poor households were exempt from domestic rates but still had a vote in the local election; they had an incentive to vote for high spending programmes. Firms paid rates but had no vote at all in local elections. Only about 20 per cent of local government revenue was being raised from households actually required to pay rates. A subsidiary problem was a reluctance to raise rateable values, the basis of the property tax, in line with market prices.

Mrs Thatcher believed that greater local democracy would lead to a voter rebellion against high spending local authorities, forcing them to be less ambitious and more efficient. The reform of local government, which took effect in Scotland in 1989 and the rest of the UK in 1990, made three changes. First, education in state schools (the largest component of local expenditure) was moved from local to central government. Second, local business rates were replaced by a *uniform business rate*, a single tax rate nationwide. Simultaneously, the rateable values for business were moved more into line with market values, leading to enormous (and justified!) increases in the tax assessment for firms in the south-east, where property prices had risen substantially since the previous assessment of rateable values years earlier. Whereas previously each local authority had access to its own business rate revenue, now the central government collected all this revenue and redistributed it to local authorities in proportion to the local population. The consequence was to redistribute money from the rich south, where property prices were high, to the poorer north. Third, domestic rates were replaced by the community charge or 'poll tax', a flat-rate tax per head with some *partial* relief for the poorest households.

The logic of the reforms was to move local government closer to the Tiebout model, making it more transparent that 'you get what you pay for'. Greater transparency is almost certainly a good idea. In the text, we discuss the pros and cons of the Tiebout principle itself. Whatever its merits, this principle should be clearly separated from the government decision about how progressive the community charge should be. It was violation of the ability-to-pay principle that caused much of the public hostility to the poll tax.

If future policy decides to abandon the flat-rate community charge, this reopens the question of how a more progressive local tax should be designed. This year's income may be a poor indicator of a household's true economic spending power, and there is something to be said for basing the tax assessment on property values. But this creates difficult administrative problems about how often official valuations of property values are revised. Some countries do use property taxes in this way. Others, such as the United States, prefer a progressive local income tax, which may be simpler to administer.

---

personal incomes and company profits, indirect taxes on purchases of goods and services, and contributions to state-run social security schemes. Government spending comprises spending on goods and services and transfer payments.

2   Government intervention in a market economy should be assessed against the criteria of distributional equity and allocative efficiency. A progressively tax and transfer system takes most from the rich and give most to the poor. The UK tax and transfer system is mildly progressive. The less well off do receive transfer payments and the rich face the highest rates of income tax. Although some necessities, notably food, are exempt from VAT, other goods intensively consumed by the poor, notably cigarettes and alcohol, are heavily taxed.

3   Externalities and public goods are classic cases of market failure where intervention may improve allocative efficiency. By taxing or subsidizing goods that involve externalities, the government can induce the private sector to behave as if it takes account of the externality, thus eliminating the deadweight burden arising from the misallocation induced by the externality distortion.

4   A pure public good is a good for which one person's consumption does not reduce the quantity available for consumption by others. Together with the impossibility of effectively excluding people from consuming it, this implies that all individuals consume the same quantity, although they may attach different utility to this consumption if their tastes differ.

5   A free market will undersupply a public good because of the free-rider problem. Individuals need not offer to pay for a good that they can consume if others pay for it. The socially efficient quantity of a public good equates the marginal social cost of production to the *sum* of the marginal private benefits over all people at this output level. Diagrammatically, this implies that individual demand curves are vertically added to get the social demand or marginal benefit curve.

6   Except for taxes designed to offset externalities, taxes are generally distortionary. By driving a wedge between the selling price and the purchase price, they prevent the price system achieving the equality of marginal costs and marginal benefits. The amount of the deadweight burden is higher the higher is the marginal tax rate and the size of the wedge, but it also depends on supply and demand elasticities for the taxed commodity or activity. The more inelastic are supply and demand, the less the tax will change equilibrium quantity and the smaller will be the deadweight burden triangle.

7   The incidence of tax describes who ultimately pays the tax. The more inelastic is demand relative to supply, the more a tax will fall on purchasers as opposed to sellers.

8   Rising tax rates initially increase tax revenue but eventually lead to such large falls in the equilibrium quantity of the taxed commodity or activity that revenue starts to fall again. Cutting tax rates will usually reduce the deadweight tax burden but might increase revenue if taxes had initially been sufficiently high. Most Western economies do not appear to have reached this position. If governments wish to reduce the deadweight tax burden and balance spending and revenue, it is necessary to reduce government spending in order to cut taxes.

Key Terms

Marginal income tax rate
Transfer payments and governing spending on goods and services
Direct, indirect, and wealth taxes
Public goods
Merit goods
Ability to pay
Benefits principle
Progressive taxes
Tax wedge and deadweight tax burden
Value added tax (VAT)
Laffer curve
Tiebout model
Rateable value
Poll tax

Problems

1   Which of the following are public goods? (*a*) the fire brigade; (*b*) clean streets; (*c*) refuse collection; (*d*) cable television; (*e*) social toleration; (*f*) the postal service. Explain and discuss alternative ways of providing these goods or services.

2   Why does society try to ensure that every child receives an education? Discuss the different ways this could be done and give reasons for preferring one method of providing such an education.

3   How would you apply the principles of horizontal and vertical equity in deciding how much to tax two people, each capable of doing the same work, but one of whom chooses to devote more time to sun-bathing and therefore has a lower income?

4   Whereas a progressive tax takes proportionately more of a rich person's income, a regressive tax takes proportionately more of a poor person's income. Classify the following taxes as progressive or regressive. (*a*) 10 per cent tax on all luxury goods; (*b*) taxes in proportion to the value of owner-occupied houses; (*c*) taxes on beer; (*d*) taxes on champagne.

5   There is a flat-rate 30 per cent income tax on all income over £2000. Calculate the average tax rate (tax paid divided by income) at income levels of £5000, £10 000, and £50 000. Is the tax progressive? Is it more or less progressive if the exemption is raised from £2000 to £5000?

6   (*a*) Suppose labour supply is completely inelastic. Show why there is no deadweight burden if wages are taxed. Who bears the incidence of the tax? (*b*) Now suppose labour supply is quite elastic. Show the area that is the deadweight burden of the tax. How

much of the tax is ultimately borne by firms and how much by workers? (*c*) For any given supply elasticity show that firms bear more of the tax the more inelastic is the demand for labour.

7 Common Fallacies Show why the following statements are incorrect: (*a*) The only reason for taxation is to provide for shirkers by penalizing people who do an honest day's work. (*b*) It is obvious that the government is supplying too many goods and services. In a free enterprise economy it would be profitable only to supply a fraction of the amount to which the government is currently committed. (*c*) The government spends all its revenue. Taxes cannot be a burden on society as a whole.

17

Competition Policy and Industrial Policy

What do Durex, Valium, and Cornflakes have in common with electricity and coal? The answer is that the London Rubber Company, Hoffman LaRoche, Kelloggs, the Central Electricity Generating Board, and the National Coal Board have all been the subject of investigations by the Monopolies and Mergers Commission. Chapters 17 and 18 are about the very large firms that exist when economies of scale are very imporant. This chapter is about firms in the private sector; the next chapter about public sector firms.

When economies of scale are important, industries will not be perfectly competitive. There will be a few large firms in the industry. In an unregulated free market, each firm will maximize profits by setting marginal cost equal to marginal revenue, which is less than price and marginal consumer benefit. Since marginal cost is less than marginal consumer benefit, society would gain by expanding the output of such industries. Imperfectly competitive industries are a source of market failure because free market equilibrium is no longer Pareto-efficient.

Different governments adopt very different solutions to this problem. In the United States the Anti-Trust laws have been used to break up existing private monopolies and prevent the formation of new monopolies through mergers of existing companies. European governments have tended to take a more lenient view of merger activity and have sometimes actively encouraged it. Natural or inevitable monopolies such as electricity generation enjoy huge economies of scale. In some countries they are private industries subject to state regulation; in other countries they are state-run or nationalized industries. Whether nationalization improves the efficiency of resource allocation, or whether we would do better to privatize existing public corporations, is an issue we take up the next chapter. This chapter analyses

government policy towards private sector firms that are necessarily imperfectly competitive.

In some cases there are no clear and simple answers. This is an area of economic as well as political controversy. But at least we can sort out the issues involved. We begin by discussing the social cost of monopoly and other forms of imperfect competition.

17-1 The Social Cost of Monopoly Power

In Chapter 15 we saw that, in the absence of externalities and other sources of market failure, competitive equilibrium would be Pareto-efficient. Each firm's private assessment of its marginal cost would coincide with society's assessment of the social marginal cost of the resources employed. Each firm's private assessment of the marginal benefit of output, namely the output price received, would coincide with society's view of the marginal value of output to consumers. Competitive equilibrium would ensure that each industry expanded its output up to the point at which price equals marginal cost and therefore social marginal benefit equals social marginal cost. No resource reallocation would make consumers as a whole better off.

When an industry is imperfectly competitive we say that each firm in the industry enjoys a degree of *monopoly power*. Equating marginal cost and marginal revenue, each firm will produce an output at which price exceeds marginal cost. This excess of price over both marginal revenue and marginal cost is a convenient measure of the firm's monopoly power.

When firms have monopoly power, price and social marginal benefit of the last output unit exceed the private and social marginal cost of producing that last output unit. From society's viewpoint the industry is producing too little. Expanding output would add more to social benefit than to social cost. How should we measure the social cost of monopoly power and inefficient resource allocation?

Later we take up the case of natural or pure monopoly where huge economies of scale allow only a single producer to survive in an industry. We begin with a more general discussion of all forms of imperfect competition and monopoly power. As we saw in Chapter 10, intermediate forms of imperfect competition require some economies of scale to limit the number of firms an industry can support. Nevertheless, to introduce the idea of the social cost of monopoly power it is convenient to ignore economies of scale altogether. We thus ask the following question: what would happen if a competitive industry were taken over by a single firm which then operated as a multi-plant monopolist? Figure 17-1 shows how this question may be answered. Under perfect competition LMC is both the industry's long-run marginal cost curve and its supply curve. With constant returns to scale, LMC is also the long-run average cost curve of the industry. Given the demand curve DD, competitive equilibrium is at B. The competitive industry produces an output Q_C at at price P_C.

When the industry is taken over by a monopolist, the monopolist recognizes that marginal revenue MR is less than price at each output. The monopolist produces an output Q_M at a price P_M thus equating marginal cost and marginal revenue. The area $P_M P_C AC$ shows the monopolist's profits from selling Q_M at a price in excess of marginal and average cost. The area of the triangle ACB shows the deadweight burden or social cost of monopoly power. Why? Because at Q_M the social marginal benefit of another unit of output is P_M but the social marginal cost is only P_C. Society would like to expand output up to the competitive point B at which social marginal benefit and social marginal cost are equal. The triangle ACB measures the social profit or excess of benefits over costs from such an output expansion. Conversely, by reducing output from Q_C to Q_M the monopolist imposes a social cost equal to the area ACB.

For the whole economy the social cost of monopoly power is obtained by adding together

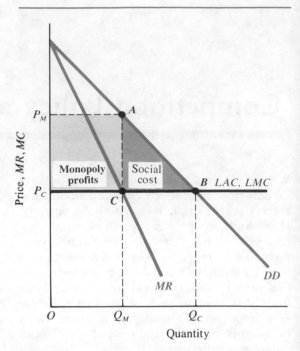

Figure 17-1 THE SOCIAL COST OF MONOPOLY. The industry has horizontal long-run average and marginal costs. A perfectly competitive industry produces at B, but a monopolist sets $MR = MC$ to produce only Q_M at a price P_M. The monopolist earns excess profits $P_M P_C CA$, but there is a social cost or deadweight burden equal to the triangle ACB. Between Q_M and Q_C social marginal benefit exceeds social marginal cost and society would gain by expanding output to Q_C. The triangle ACB shows how much society would gain by this expansion.

the deadweight burden triangles such as ACB for all industries in which marginal cost and marginal revenue are less than price and social marginal benefit. An early study by Professor Arnold Harberger suggested that the social cost of monopoly power, as measured by these deadweight burden triangles, was considerably less than 1 per cent of national income.[1] If social costs are really this small, perhaps there are more important things for the government to worry about in designing economic policy. Professor George Stigler, a recent Nobel Prize winner in economics, has argued that 'Economists might serve a more useful purpose if they fought fires or termites instead of monopoly.'[2]

However, other economists believe that the social costs of monopoly cannot be ignored.

[1] Arnold Harberger, 'Monopoly and Resource Allocation', *American Economic Review*, 1954.

Professor F. M. Scherer of Yale, whose work on industrial structure we cited in Chapters 8–10, has argued that in the United States the social cost of monopoly is large enough 'to treat every family in the land to a steak dinner at a good restaurant'.[3]

Moreover, Professors Keith Cowling and Dennis Mueller have argued that the social cost of monopoly could be as high as 7 per cent of national income.[4] Why is there such disagreement about the cost of monopoly? First, the area of the deadweight burden triangle in Figure 17-1 depends on the elasticity of the demand curve. In calculating the size of deadweight burden triangles under monopoly, different economists have used different estimates of the elasticity of demand.

Second, the welfare cost of monopoly is greater than the deadweight burden triangle itself. Since monopoly may yield high profits to the firm, it is likely that firms will expend large quantities of resources in trying to acquire and secure monopoly positions. In Chapter 10 we saw that existing oligopolists would have an incentive to advertise too much, not because advertising provides additional consumer information about the product, but because it raises the fixed cost of being in the industry, thereby making it harder for new firms to enter the industry. How much should society view this advertising expenditure as a waste of resources?

Similarly, firms may devote large quantities of resources trying to influence the government in order to obtain favourable judgements which will enhance or preserve their monopoly power. They may also deliberately maintain extra production capacity so that potential entrants can see that any attempt at entry will be matched by a sharp increase in production by existing firms, forcing price reductions which in the short run will be unprofitable for all but which may bankrupt the entrant first. From the economy's viewpoint, resources devoted to lobbying the government or maintaining deliberate over-capacity may also be largely wasted.

For these reasons, the precise extent of the social cost of monopoly remains a subject of continuing controversy. Different economists will continue to disagree about its measurement and extent. Nevertheless, few governments believe that the social cost of monopoly is sufficiently small that it can safely be ignored. We will shortly examine the policies which have been adopted to restrict the degree of monopoly power exercised by large firms.

Our discussion relates only to the efficiency losses arising from imperfect competition. Society might also have views on two other aspects on monopoly performance: the amount of *political* power that large companies are in a position to exert, and the *distributional* issue of fairness in relation to the large supernormal profits that a monopolist can earn.

The Distribution of Monopoly Profits

In Figure 17-1 the area $P_M P_C CA$ shows pure monopoly profits after all economic costs. Should society tolerate such privately collected taxes? Whether we think the high price P_M charged by a monopolist is a rip-off or the just reflection of what consumers are prepared to pay is a pure value judgement about equity. In passing, it is worth remarking that the ultimate recipients of monopoly profits are the monopolist's shareholders. Since a large fraction of the stock market is held by pension funds and insurance companies which will eventually make payments to workers, monopoly profits may indirectly pay income to some relatively poor people.

Nevertheless, in addition to any efficiency argument against monopoly, society may decide that it dislikes monopoly profits purely on the grounds of equity. Suppose the government imposes a profits tax on a monopolist: what effect would this have on the monopolist's output decision?[5]

The simple answer is that it would have no effect! Why not? Because, whatever the tax rate (assuming it is less than 100 per cent), the way to maximize after-tax profits is to maximize pre-tax profits. Provided the government does not take all the extra pre-tax profit in taxes,

---

[2,3] The quotations come from J. Siegfried and T. Tiemann, 'The Welfare Cost of Monopoly: An Interindustry Analysis', *Economic Inquiry*, Journal of the Western Economic Association, 1974.

[4] Keith Cowling and Dennis Mueller, 'The Social Costs of Monopoly Power', *Economic Journal*, 1978.

[5] For example, in the UK in 1981 the Chancellor of the Exchequer levied a one-off excess profits tax on banks whose profits had been temporarily inflated by very high interest rates.

increasing pre-tax profits must always increase post-tax profits. Hence the monopolist will produce exactly the same output as in the absence of a profits tax and, facing the same demand curve, will charge the same price as before.

Since it is always open to the government to tax away a monopolist's excess profits, it is the allocative inefficiency of monopoly on which economists have focused their criticisms.

17-2 Regulating Private Monopolies in the UK

Suppose it is recognized that economies of scale may lead to monopoly or other forms of imperfect competition that tend to misallocate resources. Government intervention may take one of two forms. Either the government can order large firms to be split up into smaller independent companies, which it is hoped will act more competitively (the so-called 'structural approach'), or the government can leave monopoly firms intact but seek to control their performance, for example by monitoring

prices and profits and ordering price reductions when firms appear to be exerting their potential monopoly power.

In the UK policy has typically followed the second route, seeking to regulate rather than remove monopolies.[6] One reason why this might be a sensible approach is that, if the original monopoly arose from technical economies of scale, breaking up large firms will not change technical know-how or remove the advantages to large scale. Under these circumstances, market forces will tend to re-establish large firms again.

Indeed, this suggests that there may be some compensating advantages of monopoly, in particular the ability to operate at larger scale and with lower average costs. Figure 17-2 shows how these advantages should be compared with the disadvantage of the deadweight burden caused by the failure to equate marginal cost and price and hence marginal cost and marginal benefit.

---

[6] An important exception is the UK privatization of electricity and water, where nationalized industries were broken up into several companies on privatization.

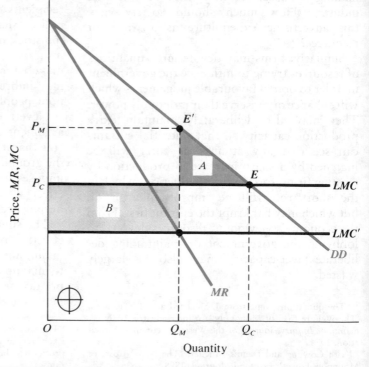

Figure 17-2 MONOPOLY WITH COST REDUCTION. Facing the marginal cost schedule LMC, a competitive industry produces at E. If a monopoly can produce at the lower cost LMC' it will equate this to MR to produce Q_M at a price P_M. The deadweight loss to consumers from lower output and higher prices is measured by the triangle A, but society gains because output is now produced using less resources. The rectangle B measures the cost savings and it could outweigh the triangle A if cost savings are sufficiently large.

Suppose a competitive industry of small firms has the supply curve and long-run marginal cost curve LMC whereas a monopolist, by taking advantage of scale economies, would face the long-run marginal cost curve LMC'. The competitive industry would produce Q_C to be in equilibrium at E, whereas the monopolist, equating MR to the lower curve LMC', would produce Q_M to be in equilibrium at E'.

Which outcome is better for society? Begin from the output Q_M produced by the monopoly. If the same output were produced by a competitive industry, society would lose the light green rectangle B shown in Figure 17-2. That is the quantity of extra resources that a competitive industry would use because it has higher average and marginal costs. But a competitive industry would produce at E, not at E'. Using the long-run marginal cost curve relevant to the competitive industry, this move from E' to E would produce a social gain equal to the area of the triangle $AE'E$. Thus, the more a monopolist can achieve economies of scale and lower production costs, the more likely it is that the area of the rectangle B will exceed the area of the triangle A. On balance the cost savings arising from monopoly would then more than offset the deadweight burden triangle, and society would actually gain from monopoly.

Thus in the UK monopoly policy is relatively pragmatic. Although the existence of monopoly power may provoke a government investigation, each investigation is a cost–benefit analysis attempting to identify the costs and benefits on a case by case basis. Some investigations conclude that on balance the existence of a large firm is actually in the public interest. This approach is fundamentally different from the approach adopted in the United States, where the law tends to assume that the very existence of monopoly power is against the public interest.

Competition Law in the UK

Legislation has been steadily extended since the Monopoly and Restrictive Practices Act of 1946. Restrictive practices, which we discuss shortly, have been separately examined since the establishment of the Restrictive Practices Court in 1956. Monopoly policy was compre-hensively reassessed in the 1973 Fair Trading Act and has been amended in the 1980 Competition Act.

The 1973 Act introduced a Director-General of Fair Trading to supervise many aspects of competition and consumer law including the regulation of quality and standards discussed in Chapter 15. The Director-General is respon-sible for a monitoring company behaviour and, subject to a ministerial veto, can refer individual cases to the Monopolies and Mergers Com-mission (MMC) for a thorough investigation.

A company can be referred if it supplies more than 25 per cent of the total market. The Commission can also be given cases where two or more distinct firms by implicit collusion operate to restrict competition. There is no presumption that monopoly is necessarily bad, and the Commission is charged to investigate whether or not the monopoly acts against the public interest, a brief that may be widely interpreted though in recent years there has been increasing emphasis on the 'maintenance and promotion of effective competition'.

The Restrictive Practices Court examines agreements between firms supplying goods and services in the UK, for example agreements on collusive pricing behaviour. All agreements must be notified to the Director-General of Fair Trading, who will refer them to the Court unless they are voluntarily abandoned or judged of trivial significance. The Court will find against these agreements unless they satisfy one of eight 'gateways' or justifications, for example that their removal would cause serious and persistent unemployment in the area. Thus for restrictive practices the burden of proof lies on the companies to show that they are acting in the public interest: in contrast, the legislation on monopolies is more open-minded, requiring the MMC to make the case that companies are acting against the public interest.

The UK is now subject to the monopoly legislation of the European Community as well. Article 85 of the Treaty of Rome is rather similar to the UK legislation on restrictive practices. Agreements have to be notified and they are likely to be outlawed. Article 86 bans the abuse of a 'dominant position' as a monopolist, but exactly what this means is rather vague. The UK legislation, allowing any firm with more than 25 per cent of the market to be referred to the MMC, is more clear-cut.

Monopolies Policy in Practice in the UK

The MMC has wide powers to make recommendations, and the Secretary of State to act on these recommendations, yet on only a few occasions have companies been formally penalized as a result of MMC investigations. More frequently, the MMC has relied on informal assurances that criticized behaviour will be discontinued. In fact, it is only a slight exaggeration to say that the main deterrent effect of monopoly policy has been not the threat of what changes might be required as a result of the MMC investigation, but the threat of having to tie up a large quantity of senior executives' time to argue the firm's case in the event that its activities attract a reference to the MMC.

The Commission has investigated a wide range of cases, from beer to breakfast cereals and from contraceptives to cross-Channel ferries. Because the MMC is charged to investigate each case with an open mind, its judgements have tended to stress different aspects of behaviour in different cases. Certainly a high market share has not been sufficient to attract an unfavourable judgement.

For example, Pilkington's Glass (making car windscreens) and Rank Xerox (making copiers) were honourably acquitted in spite of huge market shares and healthy profits. In both cases the MMC held that these companies were efficiently run and had contributed to substantial cost savings, the Schumpeterian view of monopoly to which we referred in Chapter 9 and illustrated in Figure 17-2.

On the other hand, cost reduction has not been sufficient to avoid censure by the MMC. Hoffman LaRoche was praised as 'a highly competent organization with a product range of high quality', but its enormous profits, sometimes as high as 60 or 70 per cent on capital employed, were held to be unjustified and the MMC recommended that the price of both Librium and Valium be halved.

In only one instance, the tobacco industry, has the MMC recommended companies actually be split up; it recommended that Imperial Tobacco should sell its 42.5 per cent share in Gallaghers, but the Secretary of State did not accept this recommendation. One other case deserves special mention. As we noted in Chapter 10, oligopolists have an incentive to carry out socially unproductive advertising in order to make it harder for new entrants to meet the fixed costs of breaking into the industry, thereby leaving more of the market and the profit for existing firms. In 1966 the MMC judged that Proctor & Gamble and Unilever, the two giants of the detergent industry, were guilty of this practice, and it recommended that advertising be reduced and product prices cut. In 1981 the Conservative government withdrew this restriction on advertising, partly in the belief that competition from 'own brand' soap powders sold in supermarkets would provide an effective check. Advertising spending by Proctor & Gamble took off immediately.[7]

Restrictive Practices

Since restrictive practices legislation was first introduced, almost 5000 agreements have been registered, the vast majority of which were abandoned even before they were taken to the Court. Most explicit price-fixing has gone. Although these facts look impressive, they may overstate the success of policy against restrictive practices.

First, they may simply have forced collusive agreements underground. Where oligopolistic market structures remain it seems likely that some firms will resort to informal agreements and the other collusive devices examined in Chapter 10. An important aspect of recent legislation and policy has been to tighten up on 'information agreements', which could form the basis of secret collusion.

Second, the various 'gateways' have permitted some agreements to be ratified, and the wisdom of some of these ratifications has been challenged.[8] Finally, it is possible that tighter control of restrictive practices agreements between firms is one of the factors that provide an incentive for mergers, a subject we take up in the next section. By formally merging, companies could continue their old practices within the merged company and take their chance if they got investigated by the MMC.

---

[7] In 1980 Proctor & Gamble spent £17.3 million on advertising. By 1982 this figure had jumped to £45.8 million. See Torin Douglas, 'Big Spending Brands in Fierce Battle', *The Times*, 12 July 1983.

[8] See D. Swann *et al.*, *Restrictive Practice Legislation in Theory and Practice*, George Allen and Unwin, 1974.

Assessing Competition Policy in the UK

To assess UK competition policy we need ideally to compare the evolution of the UK economy under the policy with the evolution that would have occurred under some different policy, for example a policy of *laissez-faire* or complete non-intervention. Such an assessment would be a major undertaking.

At a more modest level, we can say that legislation on restrictive practices has eliminated many cases of blatant anti-competitive behaviour and that the Director-General of Fair Trading now has powers to promote the provision of better consumer information (e.g. the Trade Descriptions Act) and to monitor general company behaviour. And the MMC has identified some practices, such as wasteful advertising, that most people would regard as undesirable.

If these seem relatively modest benefits, it is perhaps more useful to consider whether a more radical and comprehensive anti-monopoly policy would have been better for society. We began this section by noting that, unlike the United States which takes a structural approach to anti-trust policy, in which the possession of monopoly power is itself regarded as objectionable, the UK has taken a more open view of the benefits of promoting competition.

Large scale may be necessary to achieve minimum efficient plant size, and the cost of breaking up large companies may be considerable, an argument we develop in Section 17-4. Large scale may also promote better management, co-ordination, and research, a version of the Schumpeterian argument in favour of monopoly. Co-ordination via cartels or single ownership may facilitate better planning when different products are close complements in production.

As we stressed in Chapter 9, the Rover Group may produce a large share of the motor cars manufactured in the UK but this does not necessarily mean it has significant market power. When tariffs on imports are low and transport costs are moderate, domestic producers may face severe international competition. Without knowing the size of the relevant market in which firms are competing, large size cannot immediately be equated with uncompetitive behaviour.[9]

Nor is it obvious that the government should always oppose large profits. As we pointed out in Chapter 14, profits are the carrot that encourages firms to take risks in a market economy. Many firms take risks that do not come off. But if potential risk-takers are assured that success will immediately invite investigation by the MMC and an order to cut prices and eliminate excess profits, there will be less risk-taking in the economy. Society has to decide how much risk-taking it wishes to encourage and to allow a proper return to risk-taking as an economic cost against accounting profits.

These doubts about the merit of a blind pursuit of perfect competition lie behind the UK policy and the judgements of the MMC. Thus policy has considered each case on its merits. Notice, finally, that this approach suggests that monopoly policy should not be independent of other aspects of government policy. Large firms make more sense when the UK is competing within a large European market. We might wish to be tougher on large firms if the government is pursuing a policy of protection with high import tariffs.

17-3 Mergers

Two existing firms can join together in two different ways. First, one firm may make a *takeover bid* for the other by offering to buy out the shareholders of the second firm. Managers of the 'victim' firm will usually resist since they are likely to lose their jobs, but the shareholders will accept if the offer is sufficiently attractive. In contrast, a *merger* is the voluntary union of two companies where they think they will do better by amalgamating.

When one firm is sufficiently large it is difficult for another firm to raise the money to buy out all the first firm's shareholders in a contested takeover bid. Hence very large firms created by amalgamation are usually the result of mergers. In deciding to get together the two firms reveal that they think this union will be in their private interest, but we must ask whether mergers are in the public interest. Since mergers help to create monopoly power the discussion of this section is largely an extension

---

[9] More generally, in Chapter 10 we argued that *potential* competition (from new firms as well as imports) is important.

of the analysis of competition policy in the previous section.

It is important to distinguish three types of merger. The production process typically has several stages. For example, the first stage might be iron ore extraction, the second stage steel manufacture from iron ore, and the third stage production of cars from steel. By a *horizontal merger* we mean the union of two firms at the same production stage in the same industry, for example the merger of two steel producers or two motor car manufacturers. By a *vertical merger* we mean the union of two firms at different production stages in the same industry, as when a car manufacturer merges with a steel producer.

Finally, there are *conglomerate mergers*, where the production activities of the two firms are essentially unrelated. For example, a tobacco manufacturer perceiving that the cigarette market is in long-term decline might decide to join forces with a perfume company or a sugar producer.

What do firms think they stand to gain by merging? In horizontal mergers it is possible that a merger will allow exploitation of economies of scale. One large motor car factory may be better than two small ones. (Notice that this requires that each of the original companies were producing at an output below minimum efficient scale.) In vertical mergers it is often claimed that there are important gains to co-ordination and planning. It may be easier to make long-term decisions about the best size and type of steel mill if a simultaneous decision is taken on the level of car production to which steel output forms an important input. Since conglomerate mergers involve companies with completely independent products, these mergers have only small opportunities for a direct reduction in production costs.

Two other factors are frequently mentioned as potential benefits of mergers. First, if one company has an inspired management team it may be more productive to allow this team to run both businesses. Managers of course are very fond of this explanation for mergers. Economists have tended to be more sceptical. Second, by pooling their financial resources, the merging companies may enjoy better credit-worthiness and access to cheaper borrowing, enabling them to take more risks and finance larger research projects. There may also be some economies of scale in marketing effort. These managerial and financial gains could explain why mergers make sense even for companies producing completely distinct products.

If companies achieve any or all of these benefits they will increase productivity and lower the cost of making any specified output level. These private gains are also social gains, since society can use less resources to achieve the same output. If these were the only considerations, merger policy might be confined to ensuring that companies formed accurate assessments of the costs and benefits of mergers. Social and private calculations would coincide.

However, there are two important reasons for private and social assessments to diverge. First, the merger of two large firms will give them the immediate monopoly power that derives from a large market share. The merged company is likely to restrict output and increase prices, providing private profits but a dead-weight burden to society as a whole.

Second, the merged company may be able to use its *financial* power as distinct from its power derived from current market share. This danger is especially apparent in conglomerate mergers. A car producer and a food manufacturer cannot merge to gain economies of scale in production or any direct reduction in costs; but they can use their joint financial resources to start a price war in one of these industries. Because they have extra financial resources they will not be the first company to go bust. By forcing out some existing competitors, or merely holding this increased threat over potential entrants, they may be able to increase their market share in the long run, deter entry, and charge high prices for every more.

In framing merger policy, the government must therefore decide whether the potential social gains from reduced costs and more efficient production are outweighed by the social costs of monopoly power and inefficient resource allocation between firms and industries that might arise.

Concentration and Mergers in the UK

British industry is becoming increasingly concentrated in the hands of a few producers, and oligopoly seems to be the commonest market structure in manufacturing industry. By 1970 the 100 largest firms produced nearly half of the output of British industry.[10] The concentration of production in a few firms was considerably more marked in 1970 than it had been 15 years earlier, and many economists attribute around half the increase in concentration in the 1960s to the merger boom during those years.[11] From 1964 onwards many mergers were actively encouraged by a Labour government seeking to reorganize British industry into large modern units capable of taking on foreign competition.

Mergers have continued since 1970. Table 17-1 shows the average number of mergers per annum of industrial and commercial companies, and the value of the assets involved. The table shows a new UK merger boom starting in 1985. Notice that it reflects less a dramatic change in the *number* of mergers and more a spectacular increase in the size of companies involved. Nowadays not even the largest companies are safe from a takeover. One reason for this change is the greater competition among banks and the more aggressive lending policies that ensue. Several of the most recent supermergers have seen one company *borrow* large amounts in order to be able to afford to acquire another company. Little fish can now swallow bigger fish.

Table 17-2 shows the composition of mergers in the UK since 1965. The numbers refer only to mergers of large companies where assets worth over £5 are acquired through the merger. These of course are the mergers most relevant to the

Table 17-2 Proposed UK mergers: percentage by type

	1965–69	1970–77	1978–84
Horizontal	82	71	62
Vertical	6	6	6
Conglomerate	12	23	32

Source: Office of Fair Trading.

formation of even larger companies with potential monopoly power. It can be seen that vertical mergers are relatively rare. Whereas horizontal mergers, the type most likely to yield production economies of scale, were the vast majority in the 1960s, there has been a steady trend away from horizontal mergers and towards conglomerate mergers more recently.

Since 1970 industrial concentration has continued to increase and mergers have continued to play a major role in this process. Professor Keith Cowling and his research team have argued that mergers continue to explain half of the increase in industrial concentration in the UK.[12]

Merger Policy in the UK

This significant increase in industrial concentration through merger activity would not have been possible if the government had been operating a tough anti-merger policy. In Section 17-2 we saw that the United States takes a structural approach to monopoly, believing that concentration and monopoly power are undesirable *per se*. This has the natural corollary that the United States also operates rigorous controls on mergers that promote new monopolies. In contrast, the UK takes a more neutral view of monopoly, requiring the Monopolies and Mergers Commission to demonstrate that a monopoly is acting against the public interest, and the same principle carries over to the assessment of prospective mergers.

Indeed, it is only since 1965 that mergers have been subject to public scrutiny at all. There are now two grounds for referring a prospective merger to an investigation by the MMC: (1) that the merger will promote a new monopoly as defined by the 25 per cent market share used in deciding references for existing monopoly

Table 17-1 UK takeovers and mergers, 1972 88 (annual averages)

	NUMBER	VALUE (1989 £b)
1972–78	640	1.0
1979–84	490	2.0
1985–88	880	14.5

Source: British Business, August 1989.

[10] Very similar estimates are given in M. A. Utton, 'The Effect of Mergers on Concentration', *Journal of Industrial Economics*, 1971, and S. J. Prais, *The Evolution of Giant Firms in Great Britain*, Cambridge University Press, 1976.

[11] See, for example, L. Hannah and J. Kay, *Concentration in Modern Industry*, Macmillan, 1977.

[12] See K. Cowling *et al.*, *Mergers and Economic Performance*, Cambridge University Press, 1980.

positions, or (2) that the merger involves the transfer of at least £30 million worth of company assets.[13]

Since the legislation was introduced in 1965, only about 3 per cent of all merger proposals have been referred to the MMC. Thus for much of the period government policy has been to consent to, or actively encourage, mergers. The reason for this may be understood using Figure 17-2. By creating a larger firm with more monopoly power, a merger will tend to produce a deadweight burden since the new firm will use this power to restrict output and drive up the price. However, the merger may achieve a cost reduction and saving on scarce resources that more than offset this social cost.

In believing that the benefits would outweigh the costs, British merger policy reflected two underlying assumptions. The first was that the cost savings from economies of scale and more intensive use of scarce management talent could be quite large. The second was that the UK was effectively part of an increasingly competitive world market so that the monopoly power of the merged firms, and the corresponding social cost of the deadweight burden, would be small. Large as they were, the merged firms would still be small in relation to European or world markets, and would face relatively elastic demand curves which gave little scope for raising price above marginal cost.

Nevertheless, it would be wrong to suppose that all mergers were approved. Most of the mergers actually referred to the MMC were found to be against the public interest, and the effects of the legislation went beyond the cases actually referred. Investigation was a lengthy process taking many months, a delay during which company share prices could move considerably and upset the original negotiations about the terms on which the relative shares of the companies should be valued. In practice, even the threat that a merger might be referred to the MMC was often sufficient to induce the companies to drop their merger proposals.

Were Mergers Successful?

Merging companies believed they could achieve significant gains in productivity and profits,

and government policy assumed that these would offset any adverse effects from an increase in monopoly power. Yet recent investigations of the post-merger record of these firms suggests that few of these gains materialized. Even where post-merger firms did achieve productivity gains, they did little better than the productivity performance of the industry as a whole.[14] In contrast, mergers led to a significant increase in industrial concentration and monopoly power in the UK. In terms of Figure 17-2, it is highly questionable whether the cost saving rectangle B was larger than the deadweight burden triangle A.

17-4 Regulating Natural Monopoly

In the theory of market structure developed in Chapter 10 we saw that the key relation was the size of economies of scale relative to the size of the market. Most of the firms in private industry to which monopolies and mergers legislation is relevant are in fact oligopolists. They do not control the entire market and are not free from the threat of entry from new firms or foreign competitors.

We turn now to the analysis of *natural monopolies*, the industries that really do have such enormous economies of scale that only one firm can survive in them. These industries have falling long-run average cost curves, as for example in British Telecom, where the cost of transmission lines dwarfs the marginal cost of providing an extra phone call for a user already connected to the system. Nor does the industry have to worry about imports or the world market.

The Problem of Natural Monopoly

Figure 17-3 shows an industry with steadily decreasing long-run average costs reflecting the technological advantages of producing a very large output. In Chapter 10 we explained that only one private firm could survive in such an

---

[13] The asset valuation was £5 million between 1965 and 1980, and £15 million between 1980 and 1984.

[14] For detailed investigations of this interesting issue, you might like to look at Michael Firth, 'The Profitability of Takeovers and Mergers', *Economic Journal*, 1979; G. Meeks, *Disappointing Marriage: A Study in the Gains from Mergers*, Cambridge University Press, 1977; and Keith Cowling *et al.*, *Mergers and Economic Performance*, Cambridge University Press, 1980.

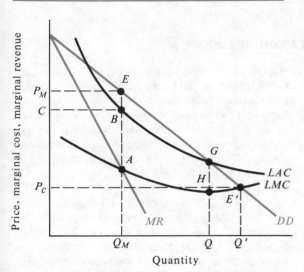

Figure 17-3 NATURAL MONOPOLY. The socially efficient point E' occurs where long-run marginal cost LMC equals marginal benefit DD. A private monopolist sets $MR = MC$, produces Q_M, and earns profits $P_M CBE$. The deadweight loss under private monopoly is therefore the area AEE'. Since LMC passes through the lowest point on LAC, a natural monopolist with steadily falling LAC must face LMC below LAC. If by law the monopolist was forced to charge a fixed price P_C, the monopolist would face a horizontal demand curve $P_C E'$ up to the output Q'. Since P_C would then also be marginal revenue, the monopolist would produce at E' where the marginal revenue and marginal cost coincide. Although Q' is the socially efficient output, society cannot force the monopolist to produce here in the long run. Since E' lies below the corresponding point on LAC at the output Q', the monopolist is making losses and would rather go out of business.

industry. With many firms, the firm that expands output will always be able to reduce costs and undercut its rivals. Facing a demand curve DD and the corresponding marginal revenue curve MR, the resulting monopolist will produce Q_M and earn profits $P_M CBE$.

At this output the social marginal benefit P_M exceeds the social marginal cost at A. The monopolist produces too little. Social marginal cost and marginal benefit are equal at the output Q' and the efficient point for society is E'. The private monopoly creates a deadweight burden AEE'.

Suppose you sat on the Monopolies and Mergers Commission and were investigating this monopolist. What are your options? If you split the firm up you will have a lot of small firms each producing at higher averge cost, a waste of society's resources. You could order the firm to produce at the socially efficient point E'. Then you will get the desired output Q'. However, the price P_C will be less than the firm's average costs at Q' so it will be making losses. You cannot force private firms to make losses. They will shut down instead.

Few countries allow unregulated natural monopolies to produce at E and impose the full deadweight burden AEE' on society. The first solution is a regulatory body such as OFTEL, which regulates British Telecom. The aim is to get as close as possible to the socially efficient allocation E' while allowing the monopolist to break even after allowing a proper deduction for all economic costs. For example, by ensuring that the monopolist produces Q at the price corresponding to average cost at this output, the social cost of the deadweight burden can be reduced from AEE' to GHE'.

An even better solution is to allow the monopolist to charge a two-part tariff.

A *two-part tariff* is a price system where users pay a fixed sum for access to the service and then pay a price per unit which reflects the marginal cost of production.

Thus the aim of a two-part tariff is to use fixed charges to pay for fixed costs and then to levy marginal charges to cover marginal costs. It acts as a lump-sum tax on users of the system.

Hence in Figure 17-3 the monopolist can be instructed to charge P_C for each unit of the good. Consumers will demand the socially efficient quantity Q'. Since the monopolist is now a price-taker at the controlled price P_C, it will be loss-minimizing for the monopolist to produce Q', at which price and marginal revenue and equal marginal cost. If the regulatory body does its sums correctly, it will then allow the monopolist to levy the minimum fixed charge necessary to ensure that the monopolist breaks even after allowing for all relevant economic costs.

The two-part tariff is not always a feasible solution. If the fixed charge has to be *very* high it may induce people to abandon consumption of the commodity altogether. Moreover, whereas it may be easy to collect fixed charges from consumers with telephone or gas installations, it is harder to enforce a fixed charge for the right to travel by rail and a fare per journey

BOX 17-1

AIRLINE DEREGULATION IN EUROPE

Although the charter market for package holidays is very competitive, scheduled flights in Europe are heavily regulated. The extent of airline regulation illustrates many of the principles we are studying in Part 3. It is also of interest because the US airline deregulation provides a live case study of the effects of completing the internal market. We discuss 1992 and the completion of the single market in Europe in Chapter 34.

Lessons from the United States   Internal US flights were deregulated in 1978. With the removal of legal barriers to entry, the industry quickly became more competitive. By 1984 the number of airlines had risen from 36 to 120, fares were down 30 per cent, and passengers use was up 50 per cent. Planes were fuller so airline costs fell. And a more frequent service meant greater passenger convenience. Free marketeers rejoiced as their predictions came true.

But the story after 1984 was rather different. Cutthroat competition led to a lot of bankruptcies and mergers. By 1989 only 27 airlines survived, and the top 12 controlled 97 per cent of the market. Fares were rising again. Powerful incumbent airlines found three ways to erect strategic entry barriers and consolidate their market power. First, they moved to a hub-and-spoke system. Each airline had a single airport (the hub), out of which long-haul flights operated. They operated a system of feeder services (the spokes) to get you to the hub. The hub-and-spoke system made it harder for small airlines to mount an effective challenge to major networks. Second, the big airlines also owned the computerized reservation systems (CRS) which travel agents use to locate empty seats. By programming the computer to ensure that their own flights appeared first on the screen, incumbent airlines put new entrants at a disadvantage. Finally, they offered 'frequent flier discounts'. Passengers clocked up bonus points by flying with a particular airline, but these could be cashed in only with the same airline. These tactics illustrate how strategic behaviour can be used to consolidate existing market power. And the US authorities operated a very lax merger policy: essentially, they approved all proposed mergers. Thus some of the benefits of deregulation had been eroded by 1990.

Regulation in Europe   European scheduled air travel has been the subject of extensive regulation by government agreement. Until the late 1980s, flights between two European capitals were restricted to one national carrier from each of the two countries (e.g. British Airways and Sabena on the London–Brussels route). And competition was often nominal. In some cases, the two airlines actually agreed to divide their joint revenue equally. Fares were strictly controlled by international agreement. Scheduled air travel was specifically exempt from EC Competition Law, Articles 85 and 86 of the Treaty of Rome.

What would you predict that the consequences of such intensive regulation would be? High fares. It is alleged that London–Brussels is the most expensive journey per mile in the world. And there is a second implication. In Chapter 12 we argued that, when firms have extensive product market power, trade unions will succeed in grabbing a big slice of these excess profits for their members. Hence the lack of competition shows up in abnormally high airline costs. The following table shows how beautifully this theory fits the facts. Apart from the UK, which has begun to deregulate the airline industry, all continental airlines pay workers substantially more than in the United States, even though countries like Spain and Portugal have much lower living standards in general.

The future of regulation in Europe   In 1987 the

Average labour cost per employee 1987 ($'000)

	Pilots	Other cockpit staff	Cabin crew
8 US major airlines	92	40	28
British Airways	65	48	19
Sabena (Belgium)	—	123	39
UTA (France)	164	119	45
Lufthansa (Germany)	—	130	40
Alitalia (Italy)	—	93	59
TAP (Portugal)	96	67	26
SAS (Scandinavia)	—	103	41
Iberia (Spain)	109	80	37

European Commission reached a deal with airlines in the European Community extending the block exemption from EC Competition Law until 1991 in exchange for some small steps towards immediate increases in competition. The EC clearly intends to keep up the pressure. For example, when the UK government approved the merger of Britain's two largest airlines, British Airways and British Caledonian, in 1988, the EC Commission exercised its power to override national policy and insisted on some tough additional requirements (e.g. BA giving up some of its routes from Gatwick) before approving the merger.

What principles should inform European airline regulation in the future? First, we should distinguish general externalities from things that directly affect market structure and the degree of competition. Externalities requiring the regulation of safety and noise can be treated separately from competition policy. The US experiment indicates that, contrary to popular belief, existing safety regulations were quite adequate: the US industry's safety record did not deteriorate after deregulation.

Second, in a completely free market, the US experiment indicates that existing airlines can exert too much market power, less through scale economies

and innocent entry barriers than through strategic barriers erected by predatory behaviour. Some regulation is still required to *promote* competition. For example, unlike the United States, mergers should be very closely scrutinized. And in Europe there is one additional consideration that is relatively unimportant in the United States. Many of Europe's major airports are heavily congested. This means that the allocation of 'slots' – the time flights can take off or land – is extremely important. At present, existing airlines have the good slots. If they are allowed automatically to keep them, this becomes a major barrier to new entry. The right solution is to auction off slots to the highest bidder.

If the reform of Europe's airline regulation is carried out intelligently, the gains will be substantial. Cheaper flights, greater efficiency, and lower airline costs as sheltered workers are forced to settle for more realistic wages. But the US experience warns us that, unless we do it right, deregulation will not automatically yield substantial benefits.

This box draws heavily on the excellent article by Francis McGowan and Paul Seabright, 'Deregulating European Airlines', *Economic Policy*, 1990.

---

reflecting marginal cost. The costs of enforcing such a system might be enormous.

The third solution to the natural monopoly problem is to order the monopolist to produce at the socially efficient point E' and the corresponding price P_C but to provide a government subsidy to cover the losses that this will inevitably imply. However, the government will wish to be closely concerned with the operation of the company to ensure that this does not provide a blanket guarantee to underwrite whatever losses the company makes through its own stupidity or inefficiency. It is still socially desirable to produce the efficient output Q' in the cost-minimizing way. Thus, where the subsidy solution is adopted there is a pressure for the government to take over the entire running of the industry so that all operations can be carefully monitored. Where this has been done in the UK these natural monopolies are called *nationalized industries*, and we discuss them more fully in the next chapter.

However, it is important immediately to dispose of one popular fallacy. We have just

demonstrated that natural monopolies cannot both survive as profit-making industries and produce the socially efficient output by pricing at marginal cost unless they have very favourable opportunities for levying two-part tariffs. If such industries are nationalized in order that they can produce closer to the socially efficient output, it is inevitable that they will make losses and require a subsidy from the government.

The fact that nationalized industries make losses is *not* sufficient to prove that they are not minimizing costs or they they are producing the wrong output from society's view-point.

Two problems recur in attempts to adopt any of the above solutions to the problem of natural monopoly. The first is that it is hard to ensure that the industry really does minimize costs. Unnecessarily high costs can be passed on under average cost pricing (solution 1), can result in a higher fixed charge to ensure break-even under a two-part tariff (solution 2), or can require a larger subsidy (solution

3).[15] In each case the regulatory body has the difficult task of trying to ensure that the management of the natural monopoly is as efficient as possible.

One practical attempt to overcome this problem of regulation is the 'RPI − x' formula, first introduced in the UK when OFTEL was established to regulate the newly privatized British Telecom (BT). The government believed that BT could reduce the real price of phone calls in subsequent years for two reasons: unusually good opportunities for cost-saving technical advances, and a previous lethargy as a public industry which it was hoped privatization would dispel.

OFTEL was instructed to ensure that, on average, the nominal price of BT phone calls rose x per cent per year less than the inflation rate of the retail price index. Initially, x was set at 3 per cent.

The second practical problem is regulatory capture.

Regulatory capture implies that the regulator gradually comes to identify with the interests of the firm is regulates, eventually becoming its champion, not its watchdog.

Clearly, the regulated devote considerable time, effort, and money to lobbying and otherwise trying to influence the regulator. A sense of public duty is the only reason for the regulator to resist. It can become an unequal contest.

More subtly, the regulated firm has all the inside information about its own activities, information which it is the whole purpose of the regulatory to try to acquire. Of necessity, regulators have to build up contacts with the regulated. At the end of long conversations, it is unsurprising that the regulator can feel quite sympathetic to the problems as perceived by the regulated.

Recap

In this chapter we have discussed aspects of competition policy, the process through which governments seek to prevent large private firms from abusing their potential monopoly power.

Some issues remain to be discussed, most notably the questions of whether some industries should be nationalized or whether existing public sector industries should be privatized. This we take up in the next chapter.

We conclude this chapter by discussing industrial policy in a wider context.

17-5 Industrial Policy

Competition policy and industrial policy are closely related. In Chapter 15 we set out the basic case for allowing free markets to allocate resources. We argued that this allocation would be efficient only if market failures did not occur. Competition policy aims to offset market failures arising from scale economies and market power. When marginal revenue is less than price, profit-maximizing firms no longer set price (and marginal consumer benefit) equal to marginal cost.

Industrial policy is designed to offset other sources of market failure which arise in the production process. In this section we highlight some of the issues that arise in industrial policy.

Inventions and the Patent System

In Chapter 14 we saw that information is a very special economic commodity which frequently causes indigestion in freely competitive markets. It is hard to trade information: the buyer needs to see the information before being willing to offer a price, and having seen the information then has no incentive to pay for it!

Inventions – the discovery of new information about the production process – are a particular example of this general theme. Suppose a company develops a product in secret, and then markets it. If other firms can quickly imitate the new invention, competition will rapidly compete away the profits on this new product. Since everyone can foresee that this will occur, few resources will be devoted to searching for inventions, even though they are socially valuable.

Inventions are an example of a public good, which we discussed in Chapter 16. The problem arises because the inventor cannot privately appropriate the benefits since imitators cannot be excluded. The solution to this market failure is a *patent system*, which confers a *temporary*

---

[15] The problem arises not from the fact that the monopoly is regulated, but from the fact that it need not fear competition from other firms. Even private monopolists may take things easy under these circumstances. See R. Cyert and J. March. *A Behavioural Theory of the Firm*, Prentice-Hall, 1963.

legal monopoly on the inventor who registers or patents the invention. The temporary monopoly provides, before the fact, the assurance that if the search for a new discovery is successful the inventor will be able to cash up after the fact. In the language of Chapter 10, it is a credible pre-commitment.

Why is it important that the legal monopoly should be only temporary? Otherwise, successful inventors would have an entrenched entry barrier which would prevent competition from other firms or new entrants for all time. The trick in designing a successful patent system is to provide a big enough incentive for invention, but not such a large and long-lived cushion that the benefits of competition are suppressed for ever.

The New Industrial Economics, which we introduced in Chapter 10, suggests that this is not a trivial problem, especially when considerations of strategic competition are introduced. For example, there are documented cases of pre-emptive patenting by incumbent firms.[16] The incumbent may discover a new process or product, patent it, but *not* actually introduce it. Potential entrants are aware that any attempt at entry will be met with the launch of this new product, which will place the entrant at a disadvantage. Thus, pre-emptive patenting can be a highly effective strategic entry barrier. This example shows that intelligent industrial policy and competition policy must work hand in hand. Evidence of pre-emptive patenting is the type of information the Monopolies and Mergers Commission seeks in evaluating whether incumbents are abusing their market power.

Research and Development (R & D)

In many countries, including the UK, one of the chief aims of industrial policy is to promote R & D. In Western Europe, the United States, and Japan, R & D accounts for between 2 and 3 per cent of national output. Table 17-3 shows UK government expenditure on R & D in recent years. Why should governments, even the Thatcher government, which is strongly committed to allowing market forces to work, spend several billion pounds of taxpayers' money promoting R & D?

Table 17-3 UK government expenditure on R & D (% of GDP)

	1981	1985	1989
Civil	0.7	0.6	0.5
Defence	0.7	0.7	0.5
Total	1.4	1.3	1.0

Source: HMSO, *Annual Review of Government Funded R & D.*

Roughly half the spending shown in Table 17-3 relates to military projects in the field of defence. But what about the other half? This seems to indicate widespread agreement that there are market failures in R & D which the patent system alone is insufficient to offset. Economics can provide several insights into what may go wrong with market forces in R & D.

First, large projects can be very risky for an individual company. Nowhere are these projects larger than in the development of a major new commercial airliner, and the chief executive of Boeing, the largest plane manufacturer in the world, has described each major new project as 'betting the company'. In other words, failure on one new project could threaten the very existence of the company. In Chapter 14 we described why private individuals may be risk-averse, and this applies even to executives of large corporations. Consequently, private firms may undertake less R & D than is socially desirable.

This implies that the social return on such projects exceeds the private return to those making the decisions. If the private decision-makers require a large risk premium, or on average a high expected return, before being willing to assume such risks, why should society demand any less? Essentially for two reasons. First, the government may be able to *pool* the risks across a large number of projects in its portfolio. Second, even if projects go wrong, the government can spread the burden very thinly across the population: $\frac{1}{2}$ per cent on everybody's income tax rate for a year should cover even the biggest disaster. Thus, the population as a whole should require only a small risk premium, much smaller than that required by executives in an individual company who may face personal disaster if the project turns sour. And these arguments have generally

---

[16] See P. Geroski and A. Jacquemin, 'Corporate Competitiveness in Europe', *Economic Policy*, 1986.

been found persuasive by governments. Hence their provision of public subsidies for R & D expenditure.

It should also be noted that no patent system can be watertight. Indeed, as we remarked above, to make it so would effectively be to suppress all future competition indefinitely. In these circumstances, a further argument for public support of R & D may be because private firms realize they will not be able to appropriate for themselves all the benefits of their efforts. Some imitation will occur, but it will be insufficiently clear-cut to guarantee that a law suit will not be protracted and expensive. Moreover, other inventors may be stimulated by what they see to make a breakthrough in an entirely different area. New breakthroughs build on past discoveries. These provide additional motives for R & D support as part of an effective industrial policy.

Strategic International Competition

In Chapter 10 we discussed how individual firms might try to erect strategic entry barriers to preserve and enhance their market power. Such considerations also apply in international competition between large firms.

For a concrete example, consider again the commercial airliner industry. Effectively, there are three large airliner firms left in the world market. Boeing is much the largest and has an entire product range, from the relatively small twin-engined 737 to the massive 747, the Jumbo. Another American firm, McDonnell-Douglas, has a smaller product range, and by the mid-1980s was wondering whether to get out of the industry entirely rather than compete in the next generation of civil airliners. The European consortium Airbus Industrie, in which British Aerospace (BAe) has a stake, is a relatively recent entrant, still building up its product range.

Airbus Industrie asked the governments of its member producers (Germany, France, the UK, and Spain) for *launch aid*, a grant or loan on favourable terms to help with R & D on a new type of aircraft. In addition to the standard arguments for R & D support, what extra issues does internatonal competition raise? What must the UK government consider in deciding whether to put in taxpayers' money?

First, will Airbus succeed even without

government support? If the answer is yes, public subsidies are simply a transfer payment to Airbus shareholders, for which there is no strong economic rationale. Second, will other European governments support Airbus even if the UK does not? If so, the UK government may be able to act as a free-rider. However, while it may be wise to attempt the free-rider strategy occasionally, governments that systematically try to do this will eventually get a bad reputation.

Suppose the UK government has decided that it cannot free-ride on other governments: either it pays its share of launch aid or the whole project collapses. What are the benefits of providing launch aid?

If Airbus pulls out, McDonnell-Douglas may still survive, or it too may pull out of the industry, leaving Boeing the sole producer without fear of competition. In that event, Boeing will surely cash up, raising the price of aircraft. British airlines and ultimately British consumers will pay high prices, and Boeing can earn monopoly profits. It may well be worth preventing this.

If the UK could be sure that McDonnell-Douglas would stay in, and provide effective competition to Boeing, it *might* be worth allowing Airbus to fold: European consumers would still get the benefit of cheaper planes. But this strategy is risky. And there are further considerations.

First, launch aid may be seen as a pre-commitment by European governments not to allow Airbus to be bullied out of the industry. With such a commitment, McDonnell-Douglas may then decide to pull out if it concludes that the industry is not big enough for three profitable producers. If so, launch aid will have directly enhanced the market share of Airbus. Second, in the presence of such a pre-commitment, Boeing may conclude that there is no point attempting a price war to try to force Airbus out. If European governments can display the credible threat to back Airbus if necessary, Boeing shareholders are only going to lose by an unsuccessful price war. Hence, the pre-commitment may *prevent* a price war which might otherwise have occurred.

This example draws on the ideas of the New Industrial Economics of Chapter 10 to show how strategic international competition can provide a rationale for strategic industrial policy. Just as industrial policy is related to competition policy, so it is closely related to international trade policy, an issue to which we return in Chapter 32.

Sunrise and Sunset Industries

The final aspect of industrial policy which we examine concerns dynamic change, the rise and fall of industries and the firms within them.

> *Sunrise* industries are the emerging new industries of the future, such as those in hi-tech.
> *Sunset* industries are those in long-term decline.

Currently, sunrise industries include information technology and genetics. Sunset industries in Western economies include the old heavy industries such as steel and shipbuilding which are now suffering from massive excess capacity as these industries have been undercut by more efficient producers in the Pacific basin.

Why not leave such changes to market forces? What are the market failures that might justify government intervention through industrial policy? We begin with the sunrise industries.

Three types of market failure have sometimes been put forward to justify the case for intervention, though it should be stressed that those who believe in the efficiency of market forces would argue that it is easy to exaggerate the importance of these factors. First, there may be imperfections in the market for lending to new companies and new industries. Banks and other lenders may be too risk-averse, or too unfamiliar with the new business, to lend the money needed through the early loss-making years. Second, the market may be slow to provide the relevant training and skills: Catch 22 (until the industry exists, people won't perceive the need for developing such skills; but without the skills, the industry cannot exist). Third, there may be important positive externalities when similar producers locate in the same place, as in the concentration of information technology firms in Silicon Glen in Scotland or Route 128 round Boston in the United States.

These arguments suggest that it may be possible to provide a rationale for an industrial policy to subsidize sunrise industries. But certain questions must be answered satisfactorily.

First, why are markets so short-sighted and uninformed? If existing lenders or trainers are getting it wrong, why don't new firms come in and do a better job? If the answer is entry barriers, this again demonstrates the close relation between industrial policy and competition policy.

Second, even if markets get it wrong, can the government do better? The strategy of trying to outguess the market by 'picking winners' is now highly discredited. It seems implausible that civil servants or politicians can do better than trained analysts in industry and finance. Rather, if such industrial policy is to be attempted, it seems preferable to diagnose the cause of the market failure and provide a generalized incentive which market decision-makers then take into account when undertaking their professional analysis.

Sunset industries present different problems. For example, the government may or may not attach importance to local unemployment when industries with a heavy geographical concentration are allowed to go under all at once. It *may* be desirable to spend what could otherwise be dole money on temporarily subsidizing lame ducks to ease the transition. Sometimes, however, a sharp shock is required to signal the extent of the adjustment eventually required and the government's commitment to seeing that adjustment is actually made.

Strategic considerations may be important here too. Suppose for example there are two remaining producers in an industry which has now contracted to the point when it can profitably support only one firm. Each firm would like to be the one to survive. They are playing an exit game of chicken. It seems plausible that one of two things may happen, neither of which is socially desirable. First, the industry survives with two firms for much longer than is socially efficient. Second, the firm with the smaller financial backing will be the first to crack, even though it may be able to produce at slightly lower cost than its richer rival. In such circumstances, an industrial policy that seeks faster and more efficient rationalization of the sunset industry may be advantageous.

Strategic international considerations may also apply. In the late 1980s, the European steel industry had an enormous over-capacity, partly because it had been undercut by Korean,

Japanese, and other producers in the Pacific, partly because of a wave of added Italian steel capacity in the 1970s. Clearly, the European governments were engaged in a game to see who would close capacity to leave a profitable market share for the survivors. In such circumstances, each country's steel industry needs effective government representation, and *laissez-faire* industrial policy may be a poor policy. In fact, in the first half of the 1980s, British Steel achieved a larger reduction in its capacity than the steel industry in any other major EC country. Far from being a free-rider, British Steel actually eased the adjustment problem for other European steel producers.

Summary

1   The social cost or deadweight burden of imperfect competition and monopoly power arises because marginal cost is set equal to marginal revenue, which is less than price and marginal consumer benefit. The social cost is measured by the cumulative difference between the value that consumers place on the lost output and its marginal production cost. The social cost is higher still if oligopolists waste society's resources lobbying for monopoly power or incurring unnecessary expenditure to deter entrants.

2   For the UK the highest estimate of this social cost is 7 per cent of company output, but most economists think the cost is much lower. Estimates refer only to the cost of allocative inefficiency. The distributional implication of high monopoly profit is less important, since it could always be taxed away.

3   In the UK any firm with more than 25 per cent of the market can be referred to the Monopolies and Mergers Commission, which must then consider whether or not the monopoly is against the public interest. The MMC takes account of a wide range of factors in making a judgement.

4   Anti-competition agreements between firms, such as collusive price-fixing, must be notified and are generally outlawed. The Restrictive Practices Court does recognize certain gateways through which such agreements may be ratified as being in the public interest.

5   Mergers may be horizontal, vertical, or conglomerate. Conglomerate mergers have the smallest scope for obvious gains through economies of scale but have become increasingly common in recent years. Mergers account for about half of the increase in industrial concentration in the UK. In spite of this, most studies agree that mergers have not on average improved the subsequent performance of the merging companies.

6   In principle, mergers can be referred to the MMC if they will create a firm with a 25 per cent market share or if they involve assets of over £30 million. In practice, a very small number of mergers satisfying these criteria are actually referred to the MMC. In part this may be justified because the UK competes in large world markets where the firms will have little monopoly power, but, given the documented lack of success of merged companies, successive governments may have encouraged too many mergers.

7   A natural monopolist with large economies of scale may continue to make profits by severely restricting output below the socially efficient level. But when the average cost curve is falling the marginal cost curve lies below average cost. Pricing at marginal cost might equate marginal cost and benefit but would entail losses. Average cost pricing or two-part tariffs may come close to the socially efficient output while allowing the monopolist to survive as a private company. Alternatively, the industry may be nationalized.

8   Regulators find it difficult to ensure that the regulated really do produce on the lowest possible cost curve. The 'RPI − x' formula is one attempt to solve this problem. Regulatory capture is also a danger.

9   Industrial policy seeks to offset market failures in production which do not arise directly from scale economies in the domestic market and the imperfect competition to which these give rise; offsetting the latter is the object of competition policy. The two are frequently related.

10   Patents provide a temporary legal monopoly for successful inventors, and hence an incentive to look for inventions. Otherwise the incentive for inventors would be low since they could foresee that profits on successful inven-

tions would quickly be competed away by imitators.

11   Many governments believe that the social return on R & D exceeds its private return. In part, this stems from society's ability to handle risk better than the private individuals on whom it falls, and who therefore require large profits in compensation. Some benefits of R & D may also spill over to other firms, creating an externality.

12   When international competition is strategic between superfirms, the industrial policies of national governments towards their own 'national champions' may be an important precommitment which affects the bargaining power of their firms in the international market.

13   Sunrise and sunset industries may involve other market failures. Before taking this as a general licence for an active industrial policy to manage change, governments must ask why the market is not doing a better job, and whether intervention can itself improve on the existing situation. Generally, picking winners has not been a success, but decentralized incentives may be effective if their rationale has been clearly identified.

Key Terms

Social cost of monopoly
Deadweight loss
Monopolies and Mergers Commission
Restrictive Practices
Takeovers and mergers
Horizontal, vertical, and conglomerate mergers
Industrial concentration
Natural monopoly
Marginal cost pricing
Two-part tariffs
Regulatory capture
Competition policy

Industrial policy
Patents
Research and development (R & D)
Sunrise and sunset industries

Problems

1 With constant AC and MC equal to £5, a competitive industry produces 1 million output units. Taken over by a monopolist, output falls to 800 000 units and the price rises to £8. AC and MC are unchanged. How would you calculate the social cost of monopoly? What is it?

2 Explain the difference between UK and US policy towards monopolies and mergers.

3 Why do sports clubs have both an initial membership fee and an annual subscription for people who are already members?

4 In 1986 there was a major debate about whether Westland Helicopters should be allowed to merge with the US helicopter giant Sikorsky, or whether it should be forced into a European partnership. What arguments can be used to support each of these viewpoints?

5 Compared with other countries, a relatively large fraction of UK R & D expenditure by the government is devoted to defence projects. Is this necessarily economically undesirable?

6 Quite apart from aid to sunrise industries, UK policy provides substantial tax breaks for those investing in small firms. Do you think the issues discussed in this chapter can be used to justify such a policy?

7 Common Fallacies Show why the following statements are fallacious. (a) Monopolies make profits and must therefore be well-run companies. (b) Monopolies create social waste. Society should prohibit any firm from having more than 20 per cent of the domestic market. (c) It does not matter what other governments do; ours should not get involved in industrial policy. (d) Mergers are obviously beneficial; otherwise companies would not bother merging.

18

Nationalization and Privatization

'In every great monarchy in Europe the sale of the Crown lands would deliver a much greater revenue than any which these lands ever afforded to the Crown. . . . When the Crown lands had become private property, they would, in the course of a few years, become well improved and well cultivated.'

Adam Smith, *The Wealth of Nations* (1776)

This chapter deals with the boundary between the public sector and the private sector. As suggested by the quotation above from Adam Smith, the father of modern economics, the controversy is more than 200 years old.

State intervention can take many forms. In previous chapters we have discussed tax incentives, competition policy, and industrial policy. The main focus of this chapter is whether these policies are sufficient, or whether it is necessary for the state to have direct control of certain industries through public ownership. Conversely, if public ownership has in the past been tried and found wanting, should the government now return these public sector corporations to private ownership?

Nationalization is the acquisition of private companies by the public sector.
Privatization is the sale of public sector companies to the private sector.

In the UK, the great wave of nationalizations – industries such as rail and steel – occurred during the Attlee government elected in 1945. By the 1960s, most countries in Europe had a significant sector of industrial production under public ownership and control. The tide has truly turned. Major privatization programmes are under way not only in the UK but also in countries as different as France, Japan, Taiwan, Mexico, Poland, and Hungary.

In this chapter we analyse the nationalized industries, explain how they have been run, and assess their performance. Then we discuss the case for privatization. Finally, we examine the UK privatization programme in practice.

18-1 Nationalized Industries

In Chapter 16 we distinguished between government production of public goods such as defence and government production of private goods such as steel. The nationalized industries are basically the part of government production that covers the provision of private goods for sale through the market place. Thus the nationalized industries include British Rail and British Coal, but not the provision of defence or the provision of social services such as education or housing, which are not sold commercially.

Nationalized industries tend to be much more capital-intensive than the rest of the economy, and it is precisely the presence of these large capital costs that generates the economies of scale that make many of these industries natural monopolies.

Nationalized industries or other forms of public ownership are not confined to the UK. Other Western countries face the same problem of natural monopoly in these industries. The precise extent and nature of public involvement differs from country to country (for example, France had a very large degree of state involvement in industry), but the basic pattern is essentially the same. Whereas European countries tended to acquire public ownership of the assets of natural monopolies, the United States preferred to handle the same problems through public regulation of industries whose assets were left in private ownership. Regulatory agencies set prices and specify quality and quantity of output.

Hence, when countries concluded that the public sector was too involved in the economy, the initial policy priorities differed in Europe and the United States. Having few nationalized industries, the US emphasis was immediately on deregulation, which began with airlines in 1978. In Europe, privatization came first, but deregulation is now also under way.

Reasons for Nationalization

We distinguish three reasons why governments may wish to nationalize industries. The first is the natural monopoly problem, which we examined in the previous chapter. Large economies of scale mean that marginal cost lies below average cost. Social efficiency requires that prices be close to marginal cost but this will imply losses for the natural monopolist. Public subsidy may therefore be desirable, but the public commitment to pick up the bills requires public monitoring to ensure that the monopolist continues to minimize costs and produce efficiently. Public management may be the simplest solution. Since private shareholders cannot be expected to subsidize the wider goals of society as a whole, public ownership may then be inevitable.

Second, externalities may be important. The social gains from an efficient road or rail network may exceed the private benefit for which direct users are prepared to pay. In Chapter 16 we argued that taxes and subsidies could sometimes be used to offset externalities and guide market equilibrium to the efficient allocation. But taxing road use may be administratively difficult and expensive, and direct regulation may be preferable.

Third, important judgements of equity or distribution may be involved. A private profit-maximizing railway would close most rural railway lines. Society might judge that this severely reduced the welfare of citizens in remote areas or that it promoted regional dissent which reduced the sense of national unity. Again, society faces two options. It can order a private supplier to provide these services, perhaps with the carrot of an explicit bribe or subsidy, or it can directly take over production to run the industry in the interests of the nation as a whole.

We now consider the principles by which nationalized industries should be run. We distinguish investment policy and pricing policy, though the two are closely connected. Decisions

on pricing will affect the rate of return on investment and the incentive to carry out new investment, but past investment, by affecting the current capital stock, will affect current marginal costs to which prices will be related.

Investment Decisions

In Chapter 13 we discussed the demand for capital and the investment decision by a private firm. We saw that we can think about this on a stock basis at a point in time or on a flow basis per period of time. Using the stock concept, at a point in time an investment project is profitable if the present value of net operating benefits – the stream of future operating profits discounted at the interest rate at which firms must borrow funds – exceeds the initial purchase price of the new capital good. Thus investment or additions to the capital stock will proceed up to the point at which the present value of the future profits equals the initial purchase price of new capital goods.

Equivalently, on a flow basis, firms compare the rate of return on a new investment with the interest rate at which they must borrow to finance the project. Investment is profitable if the rate of return exceeds the interest rate. Hence investment will proceed up to the point at which the rate of return just equals the interest rate at which firms can borrow.

Exactly the same principles carry over to social investment decisions provided we are careful to use social rather than private measures of costs, benefits, and the interest or discount rate. We discuss these in turn.

The Initial Cost of the Capital Good   In the absence of any distortions, the private cost or market price of a capital good also measures its social cost, the opportunity cost of the resources used to make the capital good, or the value of the goods these resources could otherwise have made. There are two reasons why society might consider that the social cost of a capital good is less than its private cost.

The first is unemployment. If British Rail builds a railway line in South Wales by employing construction workers who would otherwise have been unemployed, the cost includes the wages of construction workers, but these do not represent a social cost if they would not otherwise have produced any goods. Their social opportunity cost may be close to zero. Governments are sometimes suspicious of this argument because they are more accustomed to thinking as accountants about financial payments than as economists about production and distribution of goods and services that the price system is merely a mechanism to facilitate. Nevertheless, you should be able to convince even an accounting-oriented government that it will save on unemployment payments if some of the unemployed are put to work.

A second reason why private and social costs may diverge is a production or consumption externality arising from the production of the capital good. For example, the production of Concorde may generate advances in technical knowledge that would be of wider benefit to society. Whether these are reflected in the market price that a *private* supplier of capital goods would charge depends on how well the patent system allows the private producers to reap the benefits of these advances. If society gains more than the private supplier would gain, the social cost of the capital good is less than the market price that a private supplier would have to charge.

Valuing the Stream of Future Benefits and Costs

Whereas a private firm would simply use market prices to determine the stream of private operating costs and benefits, and hence the stream of future profits, to which the new investment gives rise, society will wish to value the social marginal costs and benefits of future output. It will have to take into account externalities and distributional effects. For example, the social profit in investing in rural transport almost certainly exceeds the private profit.

We shall shortly explain how prices should be set to reflect marginal *social* costs. When a nationalized industry is committed to pricing in this way, it should use these prices to calculate the stream of social profit and the social rate of return on the investment project.

Choosing the Discount Rate

Private firms should invest if the rate of return on the project exceeds the market interest rate at which they can borrow funds. That is the private opportunity cost of the funds tied up in the project. Should nationalized industries use the same interest rate as private firms?

To assess the social opportunity cost of tying up resources in a project in the nationalized industries, we need to ask what would have happened to the resources had the project not been undertaken. Suppose first that investment in the nationalized industries simply displaces private investment; resources used by British Rail are resources no longer available for investment projects in ICI or Shell.

Unless the nationalized industries use the *same* interest rate as private firms, there will be misallocation of investment resources between the private and the public sector: society can gain by reallocating resources to the sector with the higher rate of return.

This is a powerful argument. Nevertheless, there are two reasons why society may wish to use a lower discount rate in public sector investment projects, thus requiring them to earn a lower rate of return than in private industry. First, there is the question of risk. In Chapter 14 we saw that risky activities on average will need to earn a higher rate of return to compensate for the higher risks involved. But social risk can be reduced by spreading it thinly across a large number of people.

Private shareholders in Concorde would have required a high expected return to entice them into such a risky project. A private Concorde producer could have borrowed only at a very high interest rate. And as it turned out, private investors in Concorde would have lost a lot of money and minded terribly. Even a disastrous outcome in the *public* sector can be financed by a fraction of a penny on everyone's income tax, which does not have nearly such disastrous consequences. Hence, on average, risky projects in the nationalized industries do not require as high a rate of return as such projects in private industry.

The second reason arises from the fact that public projects do not displace just private sector *investment* projects. Where public projects are financed by taxation, their effect is to reduce private household *consumption* by reducing the after-tax incomes that households can spend on goods and services. When this happens, the social opportunity cost of the resources tied up in the public project is the return that households could have obtained on the same resources.

How do we measure this return? Households will so arrange their affairs that the utility return on future as opposed to present consumption is just equal to the real interest rate at which households can lend out money. Why? Because if the marginal utility of future consumption relative to present consumption differs from the rate at which households can convert current spending power into future spending power by saving and lending this money out at interest, households could improve their long-run utility by saving and lending a different amount. This argument is spelled out in detail in Chapter 19.

Hence the rate of return on household savings is the relevant measure of the social opportunity cost of public sector resources that could have been used in private consumption. But whereas firms borrow at the gross of tax interest rate to finance investment projects, households must pay income tax on interest earnings as a result of saving and lending. It is the lower after-tax interest rate that measures the social opportunity cost of resources that could have been devoted to private consumption.

These two reasons – the public sector's ability to spread risk more thinly and the lower after-tax interest rate relevant to resources displaced from private consumption – justify the use of a public sector discount rate that is a little lower than the interest rate inclusive of tax and risk at which private firms must borrow. The public sector should undertake some investment projects whose rate of return would be too low to justify the project in a private industry.[1]

Pricing Decisions

If there are no distortions elsewhere in the economy, nationalized industries should set prices at social marginal cost. Private marginal cost should be adjusted for any production or consumption externalities that arise, thus ensuring that society equally values the marginal cost and marginal benefit from the last unit of output. Social marginal cost also takes account of any distributional value judgements the government wishes to impose.

Thus, for example, the price of a rural railway line should be less than the private marginal cost if society judges it a good thing to protect the living standards of people in

remote areas or to foster a sense of national cohesion. Conversely, bus fares should take account (among other things) of the social cost of the damage inflicted as a result of pollution from lead emissions from their exhaust systems.

We now consider some aspects of nationalized industry pricing that deserve special attention.

Short-run or Long-run Marginal Cost Pricing? We have said that nationalized industries should price at social marginal cost, but should this be short-run marginal cost (SMC) or long-run marginal cost (LMC)? In the short run capital or plant capacity is fixed but in the long run it is variable. Thus LMC must also include the cost of providing plant capacity.

The once-and-for-all cost of building a plant is a *stock* concept. The cost is incurred at the point in time when the plant is built. But LMC is a *flow* concept, relating to the cost *per period* of producing output. In Chapter 13 we explained how stocks and flows are related. At the discount rate r the present value PV (a stock concept) of a permanent flow of c_k per period is given by the perpetuity formula $PV = c_k/r$. Conversely, the per period cost c_k of an initial outlay PV can be expressed as $c_k = r \times PV$. The flow cost is the opportunity cost of the money or social resources tied up in the plant and is measured by the initial capital cost multiplied by the discount rate r. In the absence of any divergence between private and social costs, it would simply be the interest payments on the money originally borrowed to build the plant. Society will wish to evaluate this cost as the social cost of building the plant multiplied by the social rate of discount which we discussed above.

Figure 18-1 shows the short-run marginal cost SMC_0 of producing output. For simplicity, we assume that existing plant has a maximum capacity of Q_0 units of output and the SMC_0 is constant at the level c up to full capacity and then becomes vertical. No matter how much is spent, output cannot be increased beyond Q_0 given the existing level of plant or capital capacity.

Since SMC_0 measures the marginal social opportunity cost in the short run of the resources used to produce this good, price should be set at SMC_0 to equate marginal social cost and marginal social benefit. Thus if

---

[1] For a fuller discussion of these issues see R. Layard, *Cost Benefit Analysis*, Penguin, 1972.

Figure 18-1   MARGINAL COST PRICING. For simplicity we assume that short-run marginal cost is constant at c until full capacity is reached, after which short-run marginal cost curves become vertical. Thus SMC_0 corresponds to plant with a maximum capacity Q_0 and SMC_2 to plant with a maximum capacity Q_2. Suppose SMC_0 is relevant and demand is D_1D_1. In the short run the efficient output is Q_1 and price should be set at c. If demand is D_2D_2, pricing at short-run marginal cost leads to a price P_2 on the vertical part of SMC_0. LMC also includes the capital charge c_k. Beginning from the plant size with maximum capacity Q_0, in the long run society can gain the triangle ABE by expanding plant capacity until LMC equals social marginal benefit at E. At this plant size Q_2 the price is P_1 and still lies on the short-run marginal cost curve which is now SMC_2. Short-run marginal cost pricing equates immediate marginal costs and marginal benefits. In the long run it is by making efficient investment decisions that capacity is adjusted to ensure that this price also reflects long-run marginal cost.

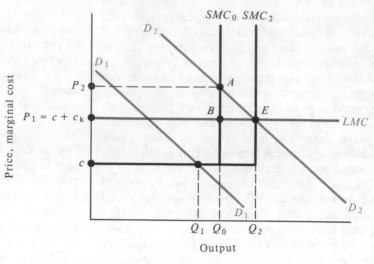

demand is low the industry should produce Q_1 and will operate at less than full capacity. Given the higher demand curve D_2D_2, short-run marginal cost pricing will lead to a price P_2 and the industry will produce at full capacity. Since output cannot be increased above Q_0, a price P_2 higher than c is required to ensure that the quantity demanded is no larger than the maximum available quantity that can be supplied.

Suppose in the long run the industry can build more identical factories. For example, with a slightly higher capital stock the industry will then face the short-run marginal cost curve SMC_2 with constant marginal cost c up to the new level of full capacity Q_2, after which marginal costs become vertical.

But LMC also includes the per-period opportunity cost of the resources tied up in the capital stock, what we might call the capital charge c_k, whose calculation we described above. Figure 18-1 assumes that this capital charge c_k is given by the vertical distance $P_1 - c$. Thus we draw the LMC curve as a horizontal line at the height $P_1 = c + c_k$. The long-run marginal cost of another output unit is both the marginal operating cost and the capital charge c_k per unit of output.

Suppose the demand curve, reflecting social marginal benefit, is given by D_2D_2 and that the industry begins with the capital stock for which Q_0 is the maximum output and SMC_0 the relevant short-run marginal cost curve. Pricing at short-run marginal cost, the industry will charge a price P_2. Although this is the socially efficient output in the short run it is not efficient in the long run. Once capacity can be varied society will wish to produce at point E, where marginal social benefit equals long-run social marginal cost LMC. By increasing the capital stock until its maximum output is Q_2 society can gain the area of the triangle ABE, which reflects the excess of marginal benefit over marginal cost when output is increased from Q_0 to Q_2.

We can now see how pricing and investment decisions are interconnected. In the short run output should be priced at SMC, which is the social opportunity cost of the resources employed. However, in the long run society should invest if the present value of future benefits exceeds the cost of adding to the capital stock. Instead of this stock evaluation of investment decisions we can use the equivalent flow evaluation. The capital stock should be increased if the marginal social benefit exceeds the long-run marginal cost inclusive of the capital charge. Thus, although prices are set according to *SMC*, in the long run investment will change full capacity and shift the *SMC* curve.

If price exceeds *LMC* it will be socially profitable to increase capital capacity, and this process will continue until price and marginal benefit equal *LMC*. Hence, although prices are set according to *SMC*, in the long run investment will adjust the capital stock and full capacity output until price also equals *LMC*. In the long run the efficient allocation is at point E in Figure 18-1, where marginal benefit, *SMC*, and *LMC* coincide.

Peak Load Pricing   In Chapter 9 we argued that a private monopolist would make higher profits if it were possible to price-discriminate, charging different prices to customers whose demand curves were effectively distinct. The problem with price discrimination in *goods* is that a secondary market is likely to be established in which low-price customers resell to higher-price customers, thus tending to equalize the prices customers actually pay. Resale is not a problem when the commodity is a service (train journeys, electricity supply), which must be consumed as it is purchased.

Consider the problem faced by a producer of electricity. It faces a high demand for electricity at breakfast time and dinner time, moderate demand throughout the rest of the day, and very little demand at night. To cater for demand at peak times it has to build extra power stations, which are then idle during times of day when demand is lower. Thus in the long run, taking account of the capacity cost of building the extra power stations, the marginal cost of supplying peak users is very high.

It does not make sense to charge all users the same rate, for users at different times impose very different marginal costs on society. It makes sense to charge peak users higher prices to reflect the higher marginal costs they impose.

Peak load pricing is a system of price discrimination whereby peak time users pay higher prices to reflect the higher marginal cost of supplying them.

Peak load pricing has two attractive consequences. Not only are peak users paying for the high marginal costs they impose, but also those users who would not mind consuming at a different time (e.g. households with night storage heaters, who can use electricity at a time when marginal costs are low) are induced by cheaper prices to switch to consuming at off-peak times. By spreading total daily consumption more evenly, society reduces peak demand and has to devote less resources to building power stations whose number is determined by peak usage.

In terms of Figure 18-1, the efficient pricing policy makes prices vary with short-run marginal cost. Off-peak users, with the lower demand curve D_1D_1, do not exhaust full capacity and pay the marginal operating cost c exclusive of capacity charges for the marginal plant. Peak users with the higher demand curve D_2D_2, pay a higher price P_2 on the vertical part of the *SMC* curve through which their demand curve passes.

Given this efficient pricing structure, what is the efficient quantity of investment? Investment should increase capacity up to the point at which the once-and-for-all cost of a new plant equals the present value of operating profits when the efficient pricing structure is in operation. Equivalently, on a flow basis, the average daily price (in Figure 18-1, the average of the prices P_2 and c, weighted by the fraction of the day for which the demand curves D_1D_1 and D_2D_2 are relevant) should cover long-run marginal cost inclusive of capacity costs. Thus in Figure 18-1 the efficient level of capacity might be Q_0 if the weighted average of P_2 and c is equal to $P_1 = c + c_k$.

To sum up, prices should be set at short-run marginal cost. This reflects the actual opportunity cost of the resources to society as a whole. When there is a daily or seasonal pattern in demand, peak load pricing reflects the different short-run marginal costs of supplying different customers at different times of day or times of year. When these principles are implemented, the amount of total demand met on the vertical part of short-run marginal cost curves will depend on the level of total capacity. At low capacity, prices will frequently be high since they are set on the vertical part of the short-run marginal cost curves. In the long run, investment and the efficient level of capacity should be determined to ensure that, when pricing at short-run marginal cost, average daily or yearly prices equal long-run marginal cost.

Electricity Pricing in the UK   The following example combines the principle of peak load pricing with the idea of a two-part tariff that we introduced in Section 17-4. (In the UK electricity generation used to be a nationalized industry known as the Central Electricity Generating Board (CEGB). We expect the underlying pricing structure to remain rather similar when the electricity industry is privatized, but closely regulated, in the early 1990s.)

Marginal costs are highest during peak hours, both because LMC is high, reflecting the fact that peak demand requires additional capacity which is costly, and because SMC is high. Figure 18-1 explains one reason why SMC is high during peak use. At full capacity SMC is vertical and high prices are required to choke off demand. However, Figure 18-1 is simplified by assuming constant average and marginal short-run operating costs up to full capacity. In practice, the CEGB had a range of different power stations and used the less efficient higher-cost stations only when demand was at its peak. When these stations are in use SMC is higher than during off-peak hours.

The CEGB operated peak load pricing in two distinct ways. It used capacity charges to directly recoup costs of building plant, and then it sold electricity by the kilowatt hour. In 1986–87 the CEGB charged area boards £10 for every kilowatt of basic demand plus £23 charge per kilowatt demanded during peak hours. These capacity charges were intended to cover the annual cost of the interest payments (at the social rate of discount) on the money used to build the plant. Peak users paid more because they force extra plant to be built.

In addition, there were energy charges intended to cover short-run marginal costs of operating the plant. These too followed peak load principles. In 1986–87 the CEGB had a complex structure of energy charges, ranging from 1.4 pence per kilowatt hour (p/kWh) for use at night during weekends to 3.8 p/kWh for use at breakfast time on a weekday. In addition, there was a further surcharge of 2.5 p/kWh during the hour and a half of heaviest demand during the day, at whatever time that occurred.

Thus, the CEGB had explicitly tried to implement the pricing principles we have been discussing.

18-2 Nationalized Industries and Government Policy

When industries were first nationalized, many of them immediately after the Second World War, the government had two concerns. First, that nationalized industries should broadly break even, and second, that they should be run not directly by ministers but through boards with a considerable measure of managerial independence.

In 1967 the government accepted many of the economic principles we have set out in the last two chapters. Nationalized industries were directed to adopt marginal cost pricing. The government fixed the social rate of interest or *test discount rate* at 8 per cent and urged nationalized industries to undertake explicit present value calculations for investment decisions using this discount rate. This rate was considerably closer to the discount rate being used in private investment decisions than to the after-tax interest rate faced by households. The government believed it more important to balance public investment against private investment by keeping their discount rates in line than to balance overall investment against consumption by using a test discount rate closer to the rate at which consumers would swap current for future consumption.

Finally, the government accepted the distinction between private and social costs. Where, for example, British Rail wishes to maintain a loss-making rural railway for social reasons, the government attempted to value the divergence between private and social cost and made an explicit subsidy payment to British Rail. Thus commercial considerations in running the railway could be kept distinct from the value judgements the government wished to adopt.

The 1967 policy was organized along classic first-best principles of Pareto efficiency. Gradually, however, governments came to feel that second-best considerations could not be ignored. In particular, they became increasingly worried about two things. First, to the extent that nationalized natural monopolies made losses because marginal costs lay below average costs, the government became increasingly concerned about the social cost of the distortions introduced elsewhere by the taxes required to finance these losses. Second, governments became increasingly convinced that the commitment to meet any residual losses was leading to sloppiness and a failure to minimize costs.

These concerns partly explain the switch in policy in 1978 where first-best requirements for marginal cost pricing were partially replaced by a return to an emphasis on average costs. The 1978 changes were (1) the introduction of a required real rate of return of 5 per cent, not on *new* investment projects, as the test discount rate implied, but on existing capital assets, and (2) the introduction of *cash limits* for each industry, a target profit or loss specified by the government in the light of the industry's circumstances.

In general these cash limits were tighter than the losses industries had previously been making. The cash limits were intended to reduce the social cost of distortionary taxes elsewhere, to impose 'financial discipline' in the hope of attaining a performance that was closer to that which was cost-minimizing for any output, and to increase the bargaining power of management in wage negotiations. Workers could no longer rely on wage increases that would simply increase the industry's losses and the government subsidy required.

The switch in policy in 1978 was reinforced by the 1980 Competition Act wherein the Monopolies and Mergers Commission was given powers to investigate nationalized industries as well as private companies. These investigations were intended as 'efficiency audits' to check up on management performance. These investigations such as the 1981 report on the CEGB have been quite critical of the way nationalized industries have been run.

Assessing Nationalized Industry Performance

Many people have strong views on whether or not the nationalized industries have been a success story. Sometimes these views are based on reasoning that an economist would judge fallacious. For example, unregulated private monopolists should have no difficulty earning profits. Conversely, natural monopolies in the public sector which at times have been instructed to use marginal cost pricing will almost inevitably make losses. Simple profitability is not the right yardstick by which to assess performance.

Similarly, at various times nationalized industries have been instructed to pursue social objectives or to help implement incomes policy by holding their price increases to less than the general inflation rate.

Assuming that the government has plenty of other policy measures at its disposal – tax incentives, subsidies to private activities, competition policy, industrial policy, and so on – the key question in reaching an assessment is surely a simple one: are enterprises more efficient in the public or the private sector?

Remember that economists mean two things by efficiency: first, that firms are on the lowest possible cost curve (absence of slack and waste); and, second, that the balance of activities in the economy is Pareto-efficient: resource reallocation would not increase social welfare. If, and some would say it is quite a big if, other policies can be used to get the right balance of activities in the economy, we can confine our attention to the narrower questions: are firms more likely to attain the lowest possible cost curve in the public or the private sector?

Many economists have tried to investigate this question. Before reading further, think about the last few chapters and decide what you expect their empirical studies have found.

Evaluating the results of 30 studies conducted in different industries in different countries, George Yarrow of Oxford University reached the following conclusion. Private sector firms tend to be more efficient than public sector firms, *provided* both operate in markets facing strong competition. When effective competition is absent, or when other market failures are very important, the evidence is much less clear-cut, and sometimes favours public sector firms.[2] Was that what you expected?

We now develop this theme in more detail.

18-3 Private or Public: The Issues

Firms do not become efficient by accident. It requires sustained effort and leadership by management. We need to think about the differing incentives for managers in the public and private sectors.

[2] See G. Yarrow, 'Privatisation in Theory and Practice', *Economic Policy*, 1985.

Incentives for Private Managers

In theory, private managers' performance is monitored by actual and potential shareholders. If managers do badly, the company's directors may be voted out of office at the annual general meeting of shareholders. Moreover, if bad management is perceived by the stock market, share prices will be lower than they might have been and a takeover raider may see an opportunity to buy up the company, install a better management, improve profits, and hence make capital gains when share prices subsequently rise. Together, these threats are supposed to discipline managers and keep them on their toes.

In practice, these threats are weak and not very credible. In the first place, individual shareholders face a free-rider problem: provided other shareholders monitor the management, everything will be fine. So everyone tends not to bother. Second, takeover raids typically bid up the share price significantly, so again the incumbent management has considerable leeway before it is likely to get into trouble and be out of a job. Finally, incumbent managers have a lot of insider information about the true state of the firm, information that is not available to either existing shareholders or potential raiders.

Because shareholders know all this, they try to give managers a direct incentive to care about profits and cost reduction. Senior executives get large profit-related bonuses. These are a carrot, for those who like carrots; but shareholders have no accompanying stick, which effective two-handed discipline would require.

In these circumstances, we cannot guarantee that private management will be efficient unless it is subject to effective competition and challenge, either from other competitors in the market-place or from a tough and watchful regulatory body. When the private firm is very large, and therefore subject to little domestic competition, and also produces in a sector sheltered from imports and foreign competition, it is quite likely to be a relatively sleepy monopolist unless it has regulators to whom it must account. And these regulators must be capable of resisting the regulatory capture we discussed in Chapter 17.

Incentives for Public Managers

Whereas private managers sometimes face a weak market mechanism for discipline and control, public sector managers face no market mechanism at all. Now everything depends on the effectiveness of the government as a watchdog.

In principle, the government might do this at least as effectively as private markets. It too can offer performance-related bonuses, and it does not face the free-rider problem which confronts individual shareholders. On the other hand, its civil servants probably have less training in business evaluation than do private sector analysts, and, of greatest importance, there is the overwhelming political temptation for the government of the day to hijack the nationalized industries and make them an instrument of whatever is the pressing problem of the day.

Until the 1980s, nationalized industries were often instructed to cut prices to help control inflation, increase prices to help raise revenue for the Chancellor, take on workers to alleviate unemployment, and sack workers to curtail government expenditure. Whatever else, privatization does act as a pre-commitment that there will be less political tampering with these industries. On average, this seems likely to make it easier to run them more efficiently.

Thus we are sympathetic to Yarrow's conclusion. *Provided* either competition or effective regulation provides adequate discipline on private managers, on balance, companies will tend to achieve lower cost curves in the private sector than in the public sector. If, also, market failures are relatively unimportant, or can adequately be offset by other policies, then on balance, privatization is likely to be desirable. But both caveats are important. Privatization is not everywhere and always the best policy.

The Importance of Ownership

It follows from the arguments above that the transfer of *ownership* from the public to the private sector is not in itself the most important issue. Neither public nor private owners happen to be great at monitoring managements. If ownership transfer to the private sector has any direct benefit, it is only the one we cited above; namely, that it makes it less easy for governments to use industries to meet the requirements of other political dictates.

On the other hand, it should not be imagined that private industries are immune from such considerations. If you doubt this, talk to any private oil company that has been involved in the North Sea. Such companies have at times faced a petroleum revenue tax rate of over 90 per cent, considerably in excess of anything they were led to expect when they first went into the North Sea.

Thus, most economists agree that the key issue is not ownership itself but rather the severity of the market competition, or its substitute government competition policy, which the industry faces.[3] Sheltered monopolies will be sleepy and slack no matter who owns them. Conversely, the major benefits of privatization are likely to stem not from literally returning ownership to the private sector, but rather from associated measures which make it clear to managers that they are expected to compete effectively and efficiently. The litmus test of this assertion is the fact that so many UK nationalized industries managed to improve their performance in the run-up to privatization, *while they were still in public ownership*. And industries such as British Steel dramatically improved their performance in the early 1980s, while they were nationalized industries for whom privatization at that stage was still a distant prospect.

Selling the Family Silver?

Some people worry that selling off state assets mortgages the country's future. Others think privatization makes the state better off. Is there any simple way through the confusion in the public debate?

You already know enough to work out the answer for yourself. The market price of an asset is simply the present value of the income stream to which it entitles the owner. Suppose a fair price is £100. If we sell you the asset, we get £100 in cash but you get an asset worth £100. Neither of us is better or worse off than before. Of course, if we put too low a price on the asset we are selling, perhaps

because we want large queues of buyers for this asset so we can claim how popular it is, we make a loss on the sale and you make a profit. That is one way the government could be worse off by privatization.[4]

How could the government be better off by privatization? Essentially for the reason first advanced by Adam Smith in the quotation at the start of this chapter. If nationalized industries previously had bad performances, they would have been worth little had they been sold at that stage. If management policy is changed *prior* to privatization, the present value of future profits rises at this point, and it is this that is the source of improvement to the public finances, not the subsequent change of ownership. Only if one believes that the prospect of privatization is the *only* way to improve management performance in nationalized industries can one attribute the benefit to privatization itself. The British Steel example suggests that this belief is at best doubtful.

Finally, notice that the question of mortgaging the future hinges crucially on what is done with the privatization revenue. If it is invested in physical capital for the public sector or used to retire outstanding government debt, it is not at all imprudent. Only if it is 'blown', for example on a tax-cut-financed consumer boom, can the government be said to be piling up financial trouble for future governments.

18-4 Privatization in Practice

In the UK, privatization began not with sales of companies but with the sale of public sector council housing to incumbent tenants. Between 1979 and 1983, local government sold almost 600 000 houses or flats, and at the peak were raising £2 billion a year in revenue from this source.

Table 18-1 shows the principal privatization of public sector companies in the UK. Note that revenue from sales was relatively small until the British Telecom flotation in 1984. From 1986 onwards, the Thatcher government raised £4–£6 billion a year by selling off some of the major public corporations – British Gas, British

---

[3] In addition to Yarrow (cited earlier), see also J. Kay and D. Thompson, 'Privatisation: A Policy in Search of a Rationale', *Economic Journal*, 1986; the special issue of *Fiscal Studies*, November 1985; and J. Vickers and G. Yarrow, *Privatisation and Natural Monopolies*, Public Policy Centre, London, 1985.

[4] Most UK privatizations do seem to have been underpriced. The government believed there was an important externality in encouraging wider share ownership, and was prepared to subsidize this activity.

Table 18-1 The UK privatization programme

YEAR	REVENUE (1988 £b)	MAJOR COMPANIES
1979	0.7	BP (Stage 1)
1980	0.6	Ferranti
1981	0.7	British Aerospace (Stage 1)
		BP (Stage 2)
		Cable & Wireless (Stage 1)
1982	0.6	Britoil (Stage 1)
		National Freight
1983	1.4	BP (Stage 3)
		Cable & Wireless (Stage 2)
1984	2.5	British Telecom
		Jaguar
		Enterprise Oil
1985	2.9	British Aerospace (Stage 2)
		Britoil (Stage 2)
		Cable & Wireless (Stage 3)
1986	4.7	British Gas
		National Bus
1987	5.1	British Airports
		British Airways
		BP (Stage 4)
		Rolls-Royce
1988	6.5	British Steel
		Rover Group
1989	4.7	Water supply

Source: Central Statistical Office.

Airways, and British Steel. And following the successful privatization of water supply, the early 1990s will see the privatization of electricity supply; the CEGB will be broken up into two companies (National Power and Powergen), from which the sale proceeds will dwarf the proceeds of previous privatizations.

Table 18-2 shows the price at which some of the early privatizations were offered for sale and compares this with the free market price established on the first day of trading on the stock market. While it is of course very difficult to fix an offer price several weeks or even

months in advance – who knows how share prices in general will change in the meantime? – the table does seem to confirm our earlier claim that, on average, the offer price was set below the free market price.

Earlier, we stressed the importance of the extent of competition that newly privatized companies would face. We discuss this under three headings.

Significant Competition and Little Market Failure

Examples in this category include Cable and Wireless, National Freight, Sealink, and Jaguar. Generally, these companies have been highly successful since privatization, even after account has been taken of nationwide trends affecting all companies.

Special mention should be made of the National Freight Corporation, which was exceptionally successful after privatization. This company was very special in the extent of both worker participation in management, and employee ownership. It was not a typical privatization, since *all* shares were sold to employees – what we call an *employee buyout*.

Partly Competitive/Partly Regulated Industries

Examples of this kind of industry are oil, aerospace, and air transport. Within this category, Britoil, Enterprise Oil, and British Aerospace had already been privatized by 1986, with British Airways and the British Airports Authority soon to follow.

It is too soon to reach any definitive judgement, given the relatively few companies privatized and the extreme movements of oil

Table 18-2 Offer prices and prices on first day of trading

COMPANY	OFFER PRICE (pence)	OPENING PRICE (pence)	UNDER-VALUATION (£m)
BT	50	95	1340
Cable and Wireless	142	190	47
British Aerospace	150	171	21
Jaguar	165	179	25
Enterprise Oil	100	100	0
Britoil	100	81	−50

Source: G. Yarrow, 'Privitisation in Theory and Practice', *Economic Policy*, 1985.

prices which make it hard to compare that industry with others. However, we can say that to date privatized companies in these categories, when measured against all other companies, have not displayed any dramatic improvement since privatization.

Market Power and Regulation

Having privatized most of the smaller companies first, by 1984 the government turned to sales of the giant corporations which are close to natural monopolies. Whereas water and electricity were broken up into different private companies between which there might be a degree of competition, British Telecom (BT) and British Gas were essentially privatized intact.

We have considered at length why natural monopoly leads to socially inefficient outcomes: too little output and too high a price in that industry. Moreover, in Chapter 10 we discussed how large firms enjoying a significant but not prohibitive entry barrier could erect strategic entry barriers to consolidate their market power. In short, the privatizing of giant firms not subject to severe international competition is unlikely to be attractive unless it is accompanied by regulation.

Before discussing regulation in detail, we must make one obvious point. Competition policy is the device already in place to combat market power. At a time of large-scale privatization, one should be seeking to strengthen competition policy. Privatization should not be seen as the signal for the government to withdrawn from the economy entirely.

The regulation of British Gas followed the general principles laid down for BT two years earlier, so it will suffice to concentrate on the latter. As we discussed in Chapter 17, the first element in the regulation of BT was the 'RPI − x' formula, to apply over an initial five-year period and then be reviewed, and with x equal to 3 per cent. Second, BT was required to guarantee certain public services such as public telephone boxes and the 999 emergency service. Third, one small competitor – Mercury, a subsidiary of Cable and Wireless – was licensed to compete over part of BT's activities. OFTEL was established as a regulatory body to supervise these arrangements.

Critics of this framework have argued that it is quite inadequate to cope with a firm with the market power of BT. Because BT was not restructured or broken down into more manageable units which might compete with one another (the US solution to their phone giant AT & T), competition between giant BT and tiny Mercury is unlikely to constrain BT much. All the responsibility has been thrown on to the regulatory body OFTEL, when it might have been possible to help the market work better.

Summary

1   Nationalization is the acquisition of private companies by the public sector. Privatization is the sale of public sector companies to the private sector.

2   Ideally, nationalized industries should set price at marginal social cost and invest up to the point at which the present value of output meets the initial social cost of the capital equipment. When this occurs, price just covers long-run social marginal cost, including the annual interest cost of the initial capital expenditure.

3   Given the second-best world in which we live, it may be desirable to set prices above marginal social cost, thereby reducing the distortionary taxes required to finance a deficit which would occur when marginal cost lies below average cost.

4   Peak load pricing charges the user the true social marginal cost. In consequence, by charging peak users more, it spreads demand more evenly and allows society to devote fewer resources to the provision of capacity to meet peak demand.

5   In 1967 the UK government broadly adopted first-best principles for pricing and investment in nationalized industries. Since 1978 policy has emphasized second-best principles and stricter financial control. Since 1980 the Monopolies and Mergers Commission has been empowered to make efficiency audits of nationalized industries.

6   Economic efficiency requires both that individual firms attain the lowest possible cost curve and that the correct balance of outputs is attained across firms and industries. One

aspect of the debate about whether public or private firms are more efficient rests on the incentives for managers to keep costs down. In the private sector, competition is likely to be the most effective management discipline. In the public sector, it all depends on how effectively the government monitors managers in nationalized industries.

7   Transfer of ownership is probably not the most important aspect of privatization. If that policy is to succeed, it must be accompanied either by greater competition within the market, or by increased incentives and monitoring provided by regulatory agencies.

8   Selling assets at a fair market price leaves government wealth unaltered. If public corporations become more efficient prior to privatization, this increases their value and government wealth. However, if the government hands out privatization revenues as tax cuts rather than reinvesting the proceeds, government wealth may subsequently be reduced.

9   The UK government has embarked on a large programme of privatization. It is still too early to assess its effects, but first indications suggest that the outcome may be most favourable in industries where competition is greatest. This is what our theoretical discussion suggested was likely.

Key Terms

Nationalization
Privatization
Peak load pricing
Capacity charges
Test discount rate
Required real rate of return on capital

Cash limits
Regulation
Nationalized industries
Public ownership
Offer price

Problems

1   'Season tickets make sense because they prevent commuters congesting the roads.' 'Commuters should pay more because they use trains which are idle the rest of the day.' How should British Rail treat commuters? Does the answer depend on government policy on parking charges for cars?

2   British Gas extracts gas very cheaply from shallow parts of the North Sea. When British Gas was a nationalized industry, it was required to make a large *profit*. Why?

3   Suppose you are responsible for running British Airways (BA) as a private company for the benefit of your shareholders. How would your policies differ from those of the chairman of BA when it was a nationalized industry?

4   Now you are the government. Do you want to regulate the privatized BA?

5   'The stock market is the best watchdog of British managers.' What are the arguments for and against this assertion?

6   In what circumstances will privatization benefit the government's finances *in the long run*?

7   Common Fallacies Show why the following statements are fallacious. (*a*) Some countries run their railways at a profit. If British Rail makes losses, the management should be sacked. (*b*) Transport is a public service. We should design the best train service we can and disregard any losses that service might entail. (*c*) Getting companies back into private ownership will always improve efficiency.

19

General Equilibrium and Welfare Economics

The economy is like a waterbed. Sit on any part of it and a whole series of adjustments take place elsewhere. In this chapter we analyse the interactions of markets for goods and factors, showing how the price *system* connects *all* markets. This is the analysis of the *general equilibrium* of the economy.

In Chapter 15 we introduced the main ideas of welfare economics. In particular, we gave a simple proof that, under special circumstances, free market equilibrium would lead to a Pareto-efficient allocation of resources from which it would be impossible to make one person better off without making at least one other person worse off. As Adam Smith surmised, people acting in their own self-interest might be led 'as if by an Invisible Hand' to an outcome that is socially efficient.

We have seen too that there are many potential sources of market failure that will cause the economy's general equilibrium to be inefficient. In the last four chapters we have examined how externalities, other missing markets, public goods, and imperfect competition lead to market failure which provides a rationale for government intervention. We also saw that governments might wish to intervene to change the distribution of income and welfare but would have to take account of tax-induced allocative distortions. They would face a trade-off between efficiency and equity. Different governments would make different value judgements about the level of intervention that was desirable.

We now provide a more rigorous analysis of these issues to extend and complement our earlier discussion.[1] In this chapter the emphasis is on the economy *as a whole*. Once you get the idea of how markets are interconnected you will have grasped one of the essentials of economic analysis.

The order of the material in this chapter is important. We start by asking about the *best* the economy can do. How can resources be allocated most efficiently? Initially, we do not restrict our attention to economies that use prices and markets to allocate resources. Once we have discovered how to allocate resources efficiently, we then ask whether markets work in this way. We summarize the arguments for and against a free market economy.

In the last part of the chapter we extend our discussion to the choice between present and the future. Even squirrels put nuts aside for consumption tomorrow. How much of today's resources should society set aside for the provision of goods and services in the future? We introduce the concepts of saving and investment and we show how, in a market economy, the rate of interest acts as the key price over time, or *intertemporal* price, to allocate society's current resources between provision for immediate consumption and provision for consumption in the future.

19-1 The Economy's Production Possibility Frontier

An *allocation* of resources is a complete description of the factors being used, the goods being produced, and the way these goods are distributed to consumers. It answers all three

---

[1] Some of the material in this chapter is at a more advanced level than the rest of the book. It summarizes and extends earlier material and, if mastered, will increase your economic intuition.

of the questions what, how, and for whom the economy is producing goods and services. To assess whether a particular allocation is efficient, we must ask two distinct questions.

First, could the economy produce more of some goods while producing no less of other goods? If the answer is yes, then society is wasting resources in production. People could be made better off if these resources were not wasted and more goods were produced. Hence a necessary condition for overall efficiency is *production efficiency*.

> The economy is producing efficiently if, for a given output of all other goods, the economy is producing the maximum possible quantity of the last good, given the resources and technology available to the economy as a whole.

If the only two goods are meals and films, then for any film output the economy must be producing as many meals as it possibly could.

However, production efficiency is not enough. Suppose that when no films are produced the economy is making 100 meals, the maximum it can technically produce. Nevertheless, if consumers really like films and could make do with fewer meals, the economy is not doing a good job of making consumers as well off as possible. To be fully efficient, a resource allocation must not only be productively efficient but also must make the combination of goods that consumers most want.

We return to the combination of goods in a later section. First we must determine whether the economy is producing efficiently. When production is efficient, we say that the economy is producing on the *production possibility frontier* (PPF). In the next section we show how to construct an economy's PPF. First we begin with a simple example.

Figure 19-1 shows the PPF for an economy with a given level of resources that can be used to produce either meals or films. The PPF shows the maximum quantity of one good that can be produced given the quantity of the other good that is being produced.

Notice three things. First, points such as *H* lying above the frontier are unattainable. They could be produced only with more inputs than the economy has available. Second, points such as *G* lying inside the frontier are productively inefficient since they do not use up all the

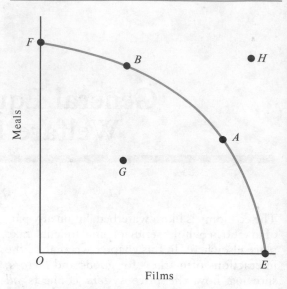

Figure 19-1 THE PRODUCTION POSSIBILITY FRONTIER (PPF). The PPF shows the maximum quantity of one good that can be produced given the output of the other good, defining output combinations that are production-efficient. Points such as *G* inside the frontier are inefficient because they do not use all available resources. Points such as *H* outside the frontier would need more resources than are available. By transferring variable factors of production between industries, the economy can move along the frontier. Thus, more of the economy's resources are devoted to film production and less to production of meals at *A* than at *B*.

available resources. By using all the available resources the economy could move to the north-east, having more of at least one good without having less of the other good. Finally, notice the shape of the PPF. As we increase production of one good we must give up increasing amounts of the other good. We now explain why the PPF has the shape shown in Figure 19-1.

19-2 Deriving the PPF

For simplicity we assume that there are only two industries, films and meals. Each industry has fixed supplies of capital and land. Relaxing this assumption would complicate the ensuing diagrams but would not change any of the basic results. Each industry has a production function showing how much output can be produced when different amounts of variable labour input are added to the stock of fixed factors in

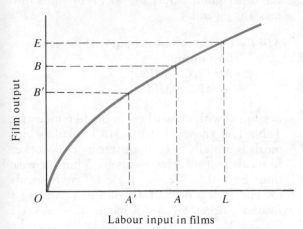

E
B
B'

Film output

O   *A'*   *A*   *L*

Labour input in films

(a) **Production function in films**

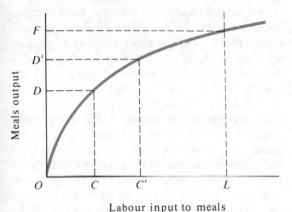

F
D'
D

Meals output

O   *C*   *C'*   *L*

Labour input to meals

(b) **Production function in meals**

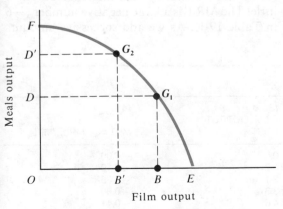

F
D'
D

Meals output

O   *B'*   *B*   *E*

Film output

(c) **The production possibility frontier**

G₂ — shown as G_2, *G₁* — shown as G_1

Figure 19-2 DERIVING THE PPF. The PPF in (c) is derived from the production functions in (a) and (b) when the total labour supply *L* is allocated between the two industries. In (c) the points *E* and *F* correspond to the same points in (a) and (b) and show the maximum output of each good when all available labour is allocated to one industry alone. Point G_1 in (c) shows that a labour input *OA* in films produces *OB* films in (a) and the remaining labour *AL = OC* produces *OD* meals in (b). Varying the proportion of total labour *L* allocated to the two industries traces out the entire PPF.

the industry. Figure 19-2 shows how we then derive the economy's PPF.

Figure 19-2(a) shows the production function for films. Increases in film labour increase output of films but, with fixed factors in the film industry, film labour has a diminishing marginal product. As more workers are added the increase in film output becomes steadily smaller. Figure 19-2(b) shows a similar production function for the output of meals from workers employed in that industry.

Suppose the total labour force in the economy is *L* and that it is all used in film production. In Figure 19-2(a) this labour input produces an output *OE* of films. With no labour left for meals output of meals is zero. Hence in Figure 19-2(c) we show that it is feasible for the economy to produce this combination of *OE* films and no meals. Conversely, with all the economy's labour force in meal production, the economy can produce *OF* meals and no films, so we can mark in the point *F* in Figure 19-2(c) showing this output combination.

Beginning with all labour in films and none in meals, suppose we move one worker from film to meal production. One worker is the distance *AL* in Figure 19-2(a) and the distance *OC* in Figure 19-2(b). In the film industry employment is now the amount *OA* and the production function for films tell us that an output *OB* will be produced. In the meals industry employment *OC* produces *OD* meals. This output combination of *OB* films and *OD* meals is shown at the point G_1 in Figure 19-2(c). Like the points *E* and *F*, G_1 must be a point on the economy's PPF.

The entire PPF is traced out by moving labour, unit by unit, from the film to the meals industry. For example, the point G_2 in Figure 19-2(c) corresponds to two workers in meals production, where an employment level OC' produces an output OD', and an employment level OA' in films produces an output OB'. Starting at point E with all workers in the film industry, successive transfers of one worker to the meals industry will trace out the entire PPF until we reach point F with all workers in the meals industry and no one in film production.

The Marginal Rate of Transformation

Table 19-1 provides a concrete example of the construction of the PPF. The economy begins at E in Figure 19-2(c) with all workers in film production. The table shows how many extra meals (the marginal product of labour in meals) we gain and how many extra films (the marginal product of labour in films) we lose each time a worker is transferred from films to meals. Adding the first worker to meals production increases meal output by 3 units, the marginal product of labour MPL_M in meal production at this employment level. Simultaneously, we lose 0.5 films, the marginal product of labour MPL_F in the film industry. Transferring another worker yields an extra 2.5 meals in exchange for 1.2 films lost; and so on. The second column shows diminishing marginal labour productivity in the meals industry and the third column, diminishing marginal productivity in the film industry. As the number of film workers shrinks, their marginal product increases.

In the last column we calculate the trade-off between the extra meals produced and the films lost as labour is moved between industries. We call this trade-off the *marginal rate of transformation* of films into meals. The marginal rate of transformation (MRT) is negative because we have to give up one good to gain more of

the other good. Thus the MRT of films into meals is given by

$MRT =$ change in meal output/change in
        film output
$= MPL_M/(-MPL_F)$
$= -MPL_M/MPL_F$ \hfill (1)

Beginning with all workers in the film industry, Table 19-1 shows that the MRT of films into meals is initially -6. Transferring one worker to meals will increase meals by 3 but increase films by -0.5. We can trade off more meals for fewer films in the ratio of 6 to 1. Adding a second worker gains 2.5 meals but loses 1.2 films so the MRT is -2.1, again showing the ratio in which we can increase meals at the expense of films.

Table 19-1 shows that successive transfers of labour from films to food reduce the ratio in which we can swap films for food, both because meal workers' MPL_M diminishes as we add more labour to meals production and because, with diminishing employment in films. MPL_F rises and we lose more film output every time another worker is transferred.

The MRT shows us the trade-off between films and meals. Hence, *the MRT must be the slope of the PPF*. It tells us how much of one good the economy can produce when it sacrifices production of the other good. Because MRT is always negative the PPF slopes down, reminding us that when production is efficient output of one good can be increased only if the output of the other good is reduced.

The MRT also tells us why the PPF is curved outwards as in Figure 19-2(c). Beginning at E with all labour in films, initially we can get a lot of extra meals by reducing film output a little. The MRT is a large negative number (-6 in Table 19-1). As we add successive amounts

Table 19-1 Reallocating labour from films to meals

(1) EXTRA WORKER IN MEALS	(2) EXTRA MEALS OUTPUT	(3) FILM OUTPUT LOST	(4) MRT $= -MPL_M/MPL_F$
1	3.0	0.5	-6.00
2	2.5	1.2	-2.10
3	2.2	2.1	-1.05
4	2.0	3.3	-0.60
5	1.9	4.6	-0.41

to the meal industry the MRT becomes a smaller negative number because of diminishing marginal productivity in both industries. Hence the slope of the PPF becomes flatter as we move to the left, as we show in Figure 19-2(c).

The MRT or slope of the PPF makes precise the idea of opportunity cost. It tells us how much of one good we have to give up to increase output of the other good when the economy is producing efficiently on the production possibility frontier.

19-3 Consumption and Efficient Resource Allocation

The PPF shows the different combinations of output that can be efficiently produced, but it is consumption that yields utility to members of the economy. To determine the efficient allocation, and thereby to explain which point on the PPF will be socially efficient, we must now bring consumption and tastes into the analysis.

Suppose there is only one consumer. This will allow us to give a simple but rigorous analysis of the problem, because anything that makes the consumer better off is a Pareto gain. This consumer is better off and there are no other consumers to be worse off. Again, this is purely an expositional device. All the results go through with many consumers, provided we retain the Pareto definition that an improvement in efficiency occurs when some consumers are better off and none is made worse off.

Figure 19-3 shows the PPF which we label EF. We also show the indifference map for the single consumer. Remember that indifference curves slope down, with each curve representing output combinations with a constant level of utility and higher curves showing greater utility. Each curve gets flatter as we move along it to the right because of a diminishing *marginal rate of substitution* (MRS) in consumption. Consumers like relatively balanced combinations of the two goods and require ever more of one good to compensate for sacrificing successive quantities of another good of which they already consume only a little.[2]

---

[2] If you want to refresh your memory about the properties of indifference curves, refer back to Chapter 6.

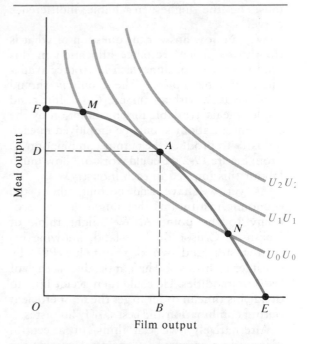

Figure 19-3 THE EFFICIENT ALLOCATION. *EF* is the economy's PPF. Points on the indifference curve U_2U_2 are unattainable. Points on U_0U_0 between *M* and *N* are attainable (inside or on the PPF) but inefficient because it is possible to move to the higher indifference curve U_1U_1 at point *A*. Point *A* is Pareto-efficient. Consumer tastes thus determine which of the production-efficient points on the PPF is the socially efficient allocation. It is the point on the PPF that is tangent to the highest attainable indifference curve.

Figure 19-3 shows three indifference curves. The curve U_2U_2 is unattainable. The economy does not have enough resources to produce any output combination on U_2U_2 which lies entirely outside the PPF. There are certainly enough resources to provide the consumer with the level of utility corresponding to U_0U_0, which crosses the PPF. Any of the output combinations on the part of U_0U_0 between *M* and *N* can be produced. However, given the economy's resources – reflected in the position of the PPF – and the consumer's tastes – reflected in the indifference map – it is possible to provide the consumer with more utility than that on the indifference curve U_0U_0. In fact, the highest indifference curve the consumer can reach is U_1U_1, when the economy produces and the consumer consumes at the point *A*. At this point the indifference curve is tangent to the PPF. It must be the highest reachable indifference curve.[3]

We can now answer the question of what is the most efficient resource allocation in this economy given consumer tastes, resource availability, and technology. The economy should produce at A, with an amount OB of films and OD of meals available for consumption by the consumer. Labour should be employed in each industry to produce the output combination A. From Figure 19-2 we could work out how much labour this implied in each industry.

As yet we have said nothing about the economic institutions that might get the economy to the point A. We might think of Robinson Crusoe on his island, knowing his own tastes and working out his PPF by considering how good he is at producing each of two commodities. He could then decide how to divide his time in order to get the most efficient output combination and best satisfy his tastes.

Alternatively, we can think of a central planner in a command economy. Knowing the economy's resources and technology, the PPF can be calculated. Knowing the tastes of all citizens, it is then possible to select the point on the PPF that gives citizens the maximum possible utility or welfare, reaching point A. As we pointed out in Chapter 1, this would require a great deal of knowledge and information. But if the central planner had all the necessary information it would be possible then to direct labour into different industries in the required amounts, so as to produce the output combination at A, and distribute this to the citizens to achieve a Pareto-efficient allocation.

Now we come to the Invisible Hand. In Chapter 15 we argued that, in the absence of any sources of market failure, free competitive equilibrium in all markets would succeed in locating the point (A) that is socially efficient. Although we have subsequently argued that market failures are too important to be neglected, in the last four chapters we have seen

that government intervention may often be interpreted as *corrective* action to offset specific distortions that induce market failure.

Thus, although most Western economies are now mixed economies with some degree of government intervention, the doctrine of the Invisible Hand suggests that government intervention need not be as extensive as in a command economy. If government intervention can offset specific sources of market failure, free market general equilibrium will take the economy to a Pareto-efficient resource allocation. So an important reason why many economists believe that the market mechanism is an important device is that it economizes on the amount of information about tastes and production technology that the government needs to collect relative to the information required by a central planner in a command economy.

Because of the significance of the claim that, in the absence of distortions, a free competitive equilibrium throughout the economy will be Pareto-efficient, it is important to restate the argument that we presented in a simplified form in Chapter 15. We do this in the context of a very simplified economy, although the proof can be extended to a much more complex economy.[4]

19-4 Getting to the PPF

This and the next section show how the price system moves a free market competitive economy to the point that is Pareto-efficient, even though firms try only to maximize profits and consumers try only to maximize utility subject to their budget lines. What is remarkable is that, even though each individual acts in a

---

[3] In Chapter 6 we explained how consumer tastes determine the shape of indifference curves. Remember the difference between the indifference curves of the glutton and the weight-watching film buff? The glutton has very flat indifference curves because it takes a lot of extra films to compensate for losing another meal. Try redrawing Figure 19-3 with flatter indifference curves. The efficient allocation will lie on the PPF but to the left of point A. This shows how consumer tastes affect how much of the two goods that society should produce.

[4] We persist with the two convenient simplifications that the only variable factor is labour and that there is only one consumer. With more mathematics, the argument is straightforwardly extended to many variable factors, though this case cannot be conveniently presented in diagram form. The assumption of a single consumer is more restrictive. It is useful because it equates a Pareto gain with an improvement in the single consumer's utility, but it neglects the distributional 'for whom' question which arises when there are many consumers. In terms of the distinction we introduced in Chapter 15, all we can prove is that the free market equilibrium is Pareto-efficient as a resource allocation. Nothing in what follows says that, as a value judgement, we should subscribe to the distribution of goods, incomes, and utility that free market equilibrium produces. We might still choose to sacrifice allocative efficiency in order to have redistributive taxes.

self-interested manner, prices provide the correct signals to achieve two things: (1) a set of mutually consistent consumption, production, and employment decisions; and (2) a Pareto-efficient allocation.

As in previous sections, we first show how the economy gets to the PPF describing production efficiency. In Figure 19-2 we showed how a central planner (or Robinson Crusoe) might *mechanically* calculate the PPF given the labour force L and the production function for each industry. Being on the frontier necessarily implied using all available labour between the two industries. How does competitive equilibrium determine not merely that all factors are fully employed but how they are allocated between industries?

From Chapter 11 we know that each firm in a competitive industry employs labour until the wage equals labour's marginal value product $MVPL$. For example, the $MVPL$ in films is the price of films P_F times the marginal physical product of labour MPL_F in the film industry. Moreover, in competitive equilibrium throughout the economy, labour will move between industries until it earns the same wage rate in all industries.[5] Hence in general competitive equilibrium

$MVPL$ in meals = wage = $MVPL$ in films

or

$$P_M \times MPL_M = \text{wage} = P_F \times MPL_F \qquad (2)$$

We now emphasize two implications of equation (2). The first is how wage flexibility ensures full employment of the economy's workforce. Suppose we begin with a particular nominal wage w_0. Given its output price, each firm demands employment until the $MVPL$ equals w_0. Suppose we add up the quantity of labour demanded by each firm in each industry. If this just equals the total labour force we can call w_0 the equilibrium full employment wage rate.

What happens if the total quantity of labour demanded is less than the labour supply? Some workers are unemployed. There is excess supply

of labour. But this will tend to bid down the wage rate as unemployed workers compete for jobs and offer to work for less than the existing wage rate. The wage rate will fall. Each firm will now move down its demand curve for labour and more workers will be employed. This process of falling wages and rising employment will continue until the equilibrium full employment wage rate is reached.[6]

Conversely, if we begin from a wage w_0 that is below the equilibrium full employment wage, each firm will demand a large quantity of labour. In terms of equation (2), it takes high employment to reduce the marginal physical product of labour and hence the $MVPL$ to the level of the low wage rate. Adding all firms' demands, there will be excess demand for labour at this wage rate, and firms, in competing for scarce labour, will bid up the wage until its equilibrium full employment level is reached.

Hence flexibility of wages and prices leads to a general equilibrium in which goods and labour markets clear. Since all labour is employed the economy is on the PPF, but at which point? We now show that this depends on the relative price of film output and meal output. You might guess that the higher the price of meals relative to films, the more the economy will want to produce meals rather than films. You would be correct, as we now show.

Equation (2) tells us that in general competitive equilibrium, each firm equates its $MVPL$ to the same wage. Hence each firm has the *same* $MVPL$.[7] Since $(P_M \times MPL_M) = (P_F \times MPL_F)$, it follows that

$$\begin{aligned} MPL_M/MPL_F &= P_F/P_M \\ &= \text{relative price of} \\ &\quad \text{films to meals} \end{aligned} \qquad (3)$$

---

[5] As in Chapter 15, we simplify by assuming that there are no equilibrium wage differentials to reflect differences in the non-monentary attractions of jobs in different industries. It is possible, though more difficult, to show the efficiency of competitive general equilibrium even when there are equilibrium wage differentials.

[6] In Chapter 11 we saw that wage inflexibility may be a cause of unemployment. For the moment we assume that free competitive markets will quickly converge upon their equilibrium position. In Part 4 we discuss this issue in greater detail.
[7] Otherwise it could not be an equilibrium. If firms with different $MVPL$ face the same wage, firms with a high $MVPL$ would still be expanding employment and firms with a low $MVPL$ would still be shedding employment. Conversely, if high $MVPL$ firms alsy pay high wages and have no incentive to change the quantity of labour demanded, labour supply would still be shifting from low-wage to high-wage firms or industries. Hence equation (2) must hold in general competitive equilibrium.

Equation (3) tells us that as the price of films rises relative to meals, more labour is moved from meal production into film production. Why? Because the initial effect of an increase in the relative price of films is to increase the marginal value product of labour in films relative to meals. Film producers bid labour away from producers of meals. As labour transfers, diminishing returns reduce MPL_F as film employment expands but increase MPL_M as employment in meals contracts. When the new equilibrium is reached, the marginal value product of labour is again equal in the two industries. The increase in the relative price of films has been offset by a corresponding reduction in MPL_F/MPL_M. But this means that MPL_M/MPL_F rises by the corresponding amount, as equation (3) points out.

Recall that the slope of the PPF equals the marginal rate of transformation MRT between films and meals. But equation (1) states that MRT equals the ratio $(-MPL_M/MPL_F)$. We thus arrive at the following conclusion. When competitive firms maximize profits and both the goods markets and the labour market are in equilibrium, not only is the economy on the PPF because labour is fully employed, but the slope of the PPF is given by the MRT and depends only on the relative price of the two goods:

$$MRT = -MPL_M/MPL_F = -P_F/P_M \qquad (4)$$

Once we are told that the economy is in competitive equilibrium with each firm maximizing its own profits, we need to know only the relative output price of the two goods to know which point on the PPF will be attained. The economy will be at the point where the MRT equals the price ratio multiplied by -1. Relative goods prices determine the production of the economy.

Another Interpretation of MRT and Price Ratio

Equation (4) may be derived and understood in a different way, namely, in the way we sketched out in Chapter 15. If labour is the only variable factor of production, the marginal cost of producing one more output unit is the wage rate times the amount of extra labour needed to produce that extra output. Suppose the marginal physical product of labour is 0.5. An extra worker produces half an extra good.

Hence it takes $(1/MPL) = (1/0.5) = 2$ extra workers to make another output unit. Hence, in general,

Marginal cost MC = wage × extra workers
of extra good = to produce an extra good

$$= \frac{\text{wage}}{MPL} \qquad (5)$$

If the film and meal industries each equate price to marginal cost,

$$\frac{P_F}{P_M} = \frac{\text{wage}/MPL_F}{\text{wage}/MPL_M} = \frac{MPL_M}{MPL_F} \qquad (6)$$

But since MRT is defined as $(-MPL_M/MPL_F)$, this equation is exactly the same as equation (4). Competitive producers, each equating price and marginal cost, will lead the economy to produce at the point on the PPF at which the MRT is the relative price of food and films multiplied by -1.

19-5 The Consumer and General Equilibrium

Figure 19-4 shows the PPF labelled EF. Forget about it for a moment. Suppose the consumer faces the budget line PP. The theory of consumer choice developed in Chapter 6 says that the consumer will choose the point on the budget line that is tangent to the highest reachable indifference curve. In Chapter 6 we saw that the slope of the budget line PP reflects only the relative price of films and meals. Its slope is equal to $(-P_F/P_M)$. The more expensive are films relative to meals, the steeper will be the negative slope of the budget line PP. To just spend the total budget income, a consumer can gain more extra meals for each film sacrificed when the relative price of films is higher.

The marginal rate of substitution (MRS) measures the slope of the indifference curve. It shows how much of one good the consumer would need to gain to compensate for losing one unit of the other good while holding utility constant. Since the theory of consumer choice says the consumer chooses the point on the budget line that is tangent to the highest possible indifference curve, it follows that the slopes of the budget line and indifference curve

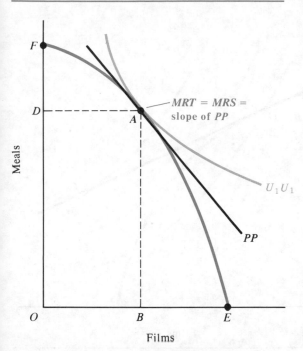

Figure 19-4   *MRT = MRS* IN EQUILIBRIUM.
Given the equilibrium price line *PP*, competitive
producers produce at *A* where *MRT* equals the slope
of *PP* (equation (4)) and price-taking consumers
consume at *A*, where *MRS* equals the slope of *PP*
(equation (7)). Not only does *A* reflect competitive
behaviour, but it is also an equilibrium since supply
and demand of each good is equated. This
competitive general equilibrium is Pareto-efficient,
since *MRS = MRT* as in Figure 19-3.

must be equal at this point. Thus,

$$MRS = -P_F/P_M \qquad (7)$$

The minus sign again reminds us that the
budget line and indifference curve both slope
down. The consumer must give up one good
to get more of another.

General Competitive Equilibrium

Now we interpret Figure 19-4 as the complete or
general equilibrium of a competitive economy.
The relative price $(-P_F/P_M)$ is the slope of the
line *PP*. Competitive production leads firms to
produce at point *A* on the PPF. This is the only
point on the PPF whose slope or *MRT* equals
the slope of the price line *PP*. This follows
directly from equation (4). Similarly, confronted
with the equilibrium price line *PP*, the consumer

will choose point *A* to maximize utility and
reach the highest possible indifference curve
U_1U_1 given this budget line.

Thus, given the slope of *PP*, point *A* is
compatible both with profit maximization by
competitive firms and with the utility-maximizing theory of consumer choice. Finally, the
point *A* is indeed an equilibrium. Since it lies
on the PPF it implies full employment in the
labour market. But in addition, the quantities
of the two goods that firms wish to produce are
precisely the quantities that the consumer
wishes to consume and will demand at these
prices.

The point *A* reflects competitive behaviour in
production and consumption. Everyone is a
price-taker. It is also an equilibrium in all
markets, and hence a general equilibrium. And,
crucially, even though each individual is
motivated only by self-interest, the general
equilibrium at *A* is Pareto-efficient. It is exactly
the same point *A* as in Figure 19-3. There is no
feasible way to reallocate production to improve
consumer welfare or utility.

Because there is only one consumer in this
example, there is a single Pareto-efficient
allocation.[8] There is also a unique general
equilibrium, and the two coincide. Figure 19-5
shows what would happen at any price ratio
other than that implied by the price line that
passes through point *A*, at which the PPF is
tangent to the highest possible indifference
curve. At the price line *PP'* competitive profit-
maximizing producers will produce at point *G*,
where the PPF has the same slope as the price
line. Competitive consumers will wish to
consume at the point *G'*, where the price line
is tangent to the highest possible indifference
curve.

The points *G* and *G'* reflect competitive
behaviour but they are not equilibrium points.
The quantity of meals supplied exceeds the
quantity of meals demanded and the converse
holds for films. At the relative price embodied

---

[8] With more than one consumer we have to ask whose tastes
the indifference curves describe in Figures 19-3 and 19-4. In
general, this depends on the distribution of goods, incomes,
and utility across consumers. By redistribution we effectively
change the indifference map for society as a whole. Hence we
determine a different point at which the PPF is tangent to the
highest indifference curve. As we stated in Chapter 15, there
is a different Pareto-efficient allocation for each possible
welfare *distribution*. That is why with a single consumer we
locate a unique Pareto-efficient allocation in this example.

Figure 19-5   DISEQUILIBRIUM PRICE RATIO. When relative prices are given by the slope of PP', firms produce at G but households want to consume at G'. There is an excess supply of meals and an excess demand for films. But this will bid up the relative price of films, making the price line steeper. When the price line is as steep as MRT and MRS at A, both markets will be in equilibrium and the relative price will remain constant thereafter.

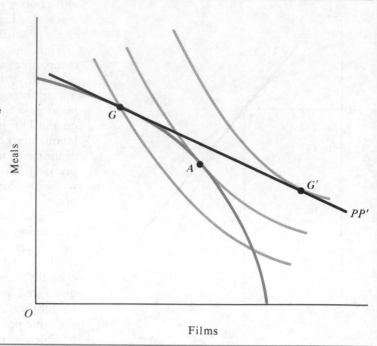

in the price line PP' there is excess demand for films and excess supply of meals. Given flexible output prices, we should expect this to bid up the price of films and bid down the price of meals. Both these effects make the relative price of films increase, making the price line steeper. A steeper price line will move both G and G' towards point A, increasing the relative supply of films and reducing the relative demand for films. Where will this process end? When the price line has become exactly as steep as the MRT and MRS at the point A. In other words, prices will stop changing when general equilibrium has been restored at point A, which is also Pareto-efficient.

Since the argument is quite involved, it is helpful to summarize it now. Box 19-1 presents a more formal summary.

1   Wage flexibility ensures labour market equilibrium at full employment and places the economy on the PPF.

2   Profit-maximizing price-taking producers, by equating the MVPL to the wage, are led to produce at the point on the PPF where its slope (the MRT) equals the relative output price of the two goods multiplied by -1.

3   Since price-taking consumers choose the point on their budget line that is tangent to the highest possible indifference curve, the slope of the indifference curve (the MRS) must equal the relative output price of the two goods multiplied by -1.

4   Hence, in competitive equilibrium the MRT must equal the MRS. This follows only from maximizing behaviour by price-taking producers and consumers.

5   Finally, since it is an equilibrium, every quantity demanded must equal the corresponding quantity supplied. Thus general equilibrium occurs at the point on the PPF where MRT = (minus the relative prices) = MRS. But the point on the PPF where MRT = MRS is the Pareto-efficient allocation.

Hence in free competitive markets where individual economic agents act only for self-interest, the price system (including wages and other factor rentals) guides the economy both to an equilibrium and to one that is Pareto-efficient. As we said at the outset, this does not prove that free markets are unambiguously wonderful. We can identify several sources of market failure, and we may dislike the

---

BOX 19-1

GENERAL EQUILIBRIUM: A REVIEW

LABOUR MARKET EQUILIBRIUM

$$P_F MPL_F = \text{wage} = P_M MPL_M \qquad (B1)$$

Firms hire labour until *MVPL* equals the wage. If jobs in different sectors have similar non-monetary characteristics, labour mobility equates wages between sectors. Wage flexibility clears the economy-wide labour market at full employment and ensures that the economy is on the PPF. Since the slope of the PPF shows the output trade-off when one worker is moved between sectors, the labour market equilibrium condition implies:

$$MRT = - MPL_M/MPL_F = - P_F/P_M \qquad (B2)$$

PRODUCTION EQUILIBRIUM

Equivalently, we can think of firms equating price to marginal cost of output. Marginal cost is increased by higher wages but reduced by higher productivity. Hence

$$P_M = \text{wage}/MPL_M \quad \text{and} \quad P_F = \text{wage}/MPL_F \qquad (B3)$$

which can also be rearranged to give equation (B2).

CONSUMERS' EQUILIBRIUM

$$MRS = - P_F/P_M \qquad (B4)$$

This follows from the tangency of the budget line to the indifference curve when utility is maximized. *MRS* is the slope of the indifference curve and $- P_F/P_M$ the slope of the budget line.

GENERAL EQUILIBRIUM

Consumers and producers face the same prices and are price-takers. Suppliers equate relative prices to relative marginal production costs. Consumers equate relative prices to the relative marginal valuation of the two goods in utility terms. Hence

$$\text{Relative marginal production costs} = - MRT = \frac{P_F}{P_M} = - MRS$$

$$= \text{Relative marginal utility valuation} \qquad (B5)$$

In the absence of market failure, resources are efficiently allocated by the price system. Point *A* is reached.

---

welfare distribution that free market equilibrium throws up. For example, ill people have a low marginal product and would earn low incomes in competitive equilibrium.

Nevertheless, the result we have established is rather suggestive. It suggests that, if the government expresses its value judgements on distribution by intervening through the tax system, and if the government intervenes to offset or regulate conditions that create market failure through externalities, imperfect competition, and other distortions, then markets and prices are capable of doing the rest.[9] If so, the

---

[9] Economists who have less faith in the market mechanism and would argue for more rather than less government intervention would stress (a) the number and size of the distortions that might lead to market failure, and (b) the theory of the second-best (see Chapter 15), which argues that if some distortions are not offset there is no presumption that the rest of the economy should be organized on first-best lines. Free marketeers believe that distortions are small and second-best effects even smaller.

task of the government in running the economy is considerably simplified in comparison with a command economy, where an efficient allocation of resources requires complete knowledge of the production conditions of all firms, the tastes of all consumers, and the extent of all resources available for production. As we saw in Chapter 3, even a shock as large as the OPEC oil price rise (backed up of course by restrictions in the quantity of oil actually supplied) was handled relatively smoothly by the price mechanism working through markets. Prices rose to restore the balance of supply and demand, to guide consumers away from oil-intensive products, and to guide firms towards producing substitutes for oil or oil-intensive commodities. Imagine having to work all that out as a central planner!

19-6 The Qualifications Restated

To be quite sure there is no misunderstanding,

we set out for the last time what we have shown and what we have not shown. What we have shown is that, in an economy with no distortions or market faioure, a competitive equilibrium will be Pareto-efficient. It will be impossible to make one person better off without making someone else worse off. Given the level of welfare of every individual except one in the economy, competitive equilibrium makes the last person as well off as is possible given the economy's resources and technology and given its citizen's tastes. Although this is a powerful result, the following qualifications must be borne in mind.

Income Distribution   Whether or not allocation occurs through a market system, for each different level of everybody else's welfare there will be a different Pareto-efficient allocation to maximize the welfare of the last person. Similarly, in a market economy the initial distribution of human and non-human capital, by affecting consumers' buying power and market demands, will affect the general equilibrium allocation. In a market economy the particular endowment of capital determines the particular Pareto-efficient allocation that general equilibrium would generate.

Governments can redistribute through taxes. However, taxes imply that different people (e.g., consumers and producers) face different prices. Individual price-taking behaviour will no longer ensure the equality of MRT and MRS which Pareto efficiency requires. Governments that wish to redistribute have to trade off gains in equity against losses in allocative efficiency because redistributive taxes introduce distortions.

Imperfect Competition   In Chapter 10 we saw that economies of scale will lead to market structures that are imperfectly competitive. If producers do not equate marginal cost to price, the price ratio will no longer reflect the MRT. Free market equilibrium will not achieve the equality of MRS and MRT. It will be Pareto-inefficient. The government may be able to regulate or nationalize such producers to reduce this distortion. However, if marginal cost pricing leads to losses for state-run industries, further distortions will be introduced by the taxes levied to meet the deficits.

Externalities and Public Goods   The price system can guide people to the socially efficient allocation only if there are no divergences between social and private assessments of marginal costs or marginal benefits. Externalities and public goods are examples where divergences will induce distortions. Government taxes might induce price-taking agents to act as if taking account of the full social cost.

Other Missing Markets   Markets for future goods, risky goods, and for information itself are inhibited by factors such as moral hazard and adverse selection. If there is neither a market nor a price, we can hardly expect the price system to equate the MRS and MRT for such goods.

The Second-best   The theory of the second-best (see Chapter 15) shows that, when there is an inevitable distortion in one market, for any or all of the above reasons, it is more efficient deliberately to distort all other markets a little in order to spread the effects of the distortion. Thus, unless we can eliminate all the above sources of distortion, we cannot prove that free markets work best. Nevertheless, in many practical instances the required distortion for second-best reasons might be quite small. It seems likely that some form of mixed economy, combining a degree of government intervention to offset some of the effects listed above but relying on markets and prices in many other instances, will be the best way to run the economy. But the precise blend of free markets and government intervention remains the subject of continuing controversy.

19-7 Saving, Investment, and the Interest Rate

In Chapter 13 we saw the key role of the real interest rate in decisions involving time and the future. The real interest rate allows us to calculate discount factors and hence the present values of future costs and benefits.

In this chapter we apply the general equilibrium framework to show how real interest rates are determined. For expositional convenience we shall consider a world without inflation so that nominal and real interest rates coincide. The following analysis can be extended to the determination of real interest rates when the economy is experiencing inflation.

Investment and the PPF

Instead of films and meals, we now consider the choice between present and future consumption of goods in general. Figure 19-6 shows the economy's PPF $A'A$, which tells us how the economy can produce different combinations of current and future consumption. For example, at A the economy is maximizing present consumption but providing nothing for future consumption; at A' society is giving up all consumption today to maximize future consumption.

The trade-offs shown by the PPF in the figure reflect different amounts of current resources being devoted to *investment* to increase the capital stock. At A the economy is combining its inherited capital stock with available labour to produce only goods for immediate consumption. The capital stock is not being maintained but is allowed to depreciate. Perhaps it is even being sold off to foreigners to pay for imports of yet more consumer goods. In consequence, the economy will have no capital in the future and be unable to produce any goods for consumption.

At the opposite extreme, all current resources are being devoted to investment, making new capital goods which will allow the economy to produce more consumer goods in the future. But people are starving today since consumption today is zero.

As we move along the PPF from A to A', more and more resources today are being transferred from producing for current consumption to producing capital goods to increase future consumption. The shape of the PPF again reflects diminishing returns. At A all resources today are making consumption goods, and productive opportunities for making consumption goods may have been almost exhausted. Making no capital goods, there must surely be some productive opportunities for adding to the capital stock. Hence, transferring a small quantity of resources from consumer goods to capital goods production exchanges a lot of extra capital goods for a small loss of consumer goods. But successive additional transfers of resources towards capital goods production run into diminishing returns and gradually raise the opportunity cost of forgone consumption goods.

The trade-off gets steadily smaller as we move more and more resources into production of new capital goods.

Since the PPF has a negative slope, $(-MRT)$ is the extra consumption in the future by diverting a unit of current output from consumption to investment. Hence the profit or *rate of return* per unit of investment is the benefit $(-MRT)$ minus the cost of giving up 1 unit of current consumption

$$\text{rate of return} = -MRT - 1 \qquad (8)$$

Only when the production possibility frontier has a negative slope in excess of $45°$ is the rate on investment greater than zero (yielding more future consumption than the sacrifice in current consumption necessary to bring this about).

Figure 19-7 shows how the rate of return on investment changes as we move from A to A' along the PPF. The rate of return starts out high but steadily declines. At point G in Figure 19-6 the rate of return becomes zero and it is negative for even higher levels of investment. How can the rate of return on investment be negative? This happens when we have to give up more than one unit of today's consumption in order to gain one extra unit of future consumption. And this happens at all points to the left of G in Figure 19-6.

Indifference Curves and Saving

To determine at which point on the PPF the economy will produce, we must bring in consumer tastes, which are shown in Figure 19-8 as indifference curves between current and future consumption.

Both current and future consumption are desirable, so indifference curves must slope down, exchanging more current consumption for less future consumption to maintain constant utility along any particular indifference curve. Since consumers like relatively balanced combinations of current and future consumption, each indifference curve reflects a diminishing marginal rate substitution and becomes flatter as we move along it to the right. Combining the PPF showing production possibilities and the indifference map showing consumer tastes, Figure 19-8 shows that the efficient allocation is at point E, which attains the highest possible indifference curve. Point E tells us the efficient way for today's resources to be allocated

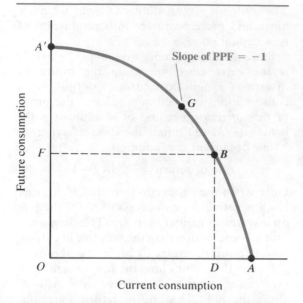

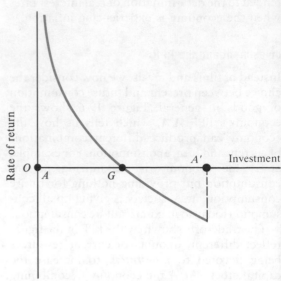

Figure 19-6   THE PPF BETWEEN CURRENT AND FUTURE CONSUMPTION.   The PPF shows the combinations of current and future consumption that a society can produce depending on how many current resources are used for investment. At A no provision is being made for the future. At A' all current resources are being used to add to the capital stock for the future. At B society is consuming OD today but sacrificing the quantity DA of current consumption in order to be able to consume OF in the future. Later, in connection with Figure 19-7, we discuss point G, at which the slope of the PPF is -1.

Figure 19-7   INVESTMENT AND THE RATE OF RETURN.   At A, where investment is zero, the rate of return on investment is initially very high. It falls steadily as resources are transferred from production of consumer goods to production of investment goods. Beyond point G in Figure 19-7, where the slope of the PPF is -1, the rate of return on investment becomes negative.

Figure 19-8   THE EFFICIENT RATES OF CURRENT AND FUTURE CONSUMPTION.   The efficient allocation is at E to reach the highest attainable indifference curve given the PPF. The price line with slope equal to $-(1 + r)$ will be referred to in the text.

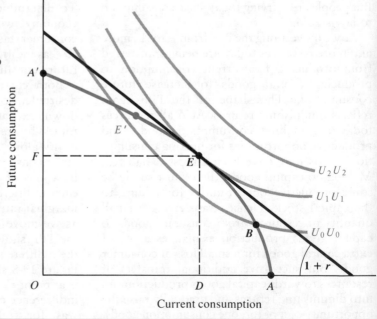

between production of consumer goods and production of capital goods that enhances future consumption possibilities.

The Equilibrium Interest Rate

We will now show how the interest rate brings a market economy to general equilibrium at the socially efficient point E. To do so, we focus on saving and investment.

> *Saving* is the difference between income and current consumption.

Savings decisions are made by households. Investment represents the amount firms want to add to the capital stock to provide for future consumption. It is the amount of current production set aside for additions to the capital stock rather than immediate consumption.

The income received in the economy equals the total costs (factor payments) of firms plus any profits that firms might earn. But profits are simply income for the owners of the firm. Hence the value of production is equal to the value of household incomes.

Hence in equilibrium savings must equal investment. Why? Saving is the amount of current income households want to set aside for future consumption. Investment is the amount of output firms want to add to the capital stock to provide for future consumption. It is the amount of current production not available for current consumption. Since the value of incomes is equal to the value of production, savings must equal investment. More formally,

Savings = income − current consumption   (9)

$$\text{Investment} = \text{total production} - \text{sales}$$
$$\text{for current consumption}$$
$$= \text{total income} - \text{consumption}$$
$$= \text{savings} \qquad (10)$$

What market forces bring saving and investment into line? The answer is the interest rates at which firms can borrow and consumers can lend. Let us begin with investment decisions by firms. Equation (8) says that, expressing the rate of return i as a decimal fraction, $i = -MRT - 1$. Hence at all points on the PPF

$$MRT = -(1 + i) \qquad (11)$$

Suppose firms wishing to invest have to borrow

at the interest rate r. If the rate of return i exceeds the interest rate r, firms will be able to invest and make a profit. Selling consumption goods in the future will more than cover the cost of borrowing. Conversely, if i is less than r, future sales will not cover the interest costs of current borrowing. Hence firms will borrow and invest up to the point at which the rate of return i is equal to the rate of interest r. Hence from equation (10) firms will invest until

$$MRT = -(1 + r) \qquad (12)$$

What about households? They can spend £1 on consumption today or they can save and have £$(1 + r)$ to spend on consumption in the future. It is as if goods today were $(1 + r)$ times as expensive as goods in the future. Households can buy more goods if they wait. Effectively, households face a budget line with slope $-(1 + r)$ telling them that they can exchange 1 good today for $(1 + r)$ times as many goods in the future. And since households equate the slope of their indifference curves to the slope of the budget line, it must follow that

$$MRS = -(1 + r) \qquad (13)$$

Figure 19-8 shows general equilibrium at E, the efficient allocation at which MRS equals MRT. The price line (shown in black) now has the slope of $-(1 + r)$. Equation (11) implies that competitive firms will equate this slope to the MRT to produce at E, and equation (13) says that households will equate $-(1 + r)$ to the slope of the highest attainable indifference curve to consume at E. OD goods will be supplied and demanded for current consumption and DA new capital goods will be produced. These allow OF to be consumed in the future. The equilibrium interest rate r is determined at the level that ensures that the price line with slope $-(1 + r)$ has the same slope as both MRS and MRT at point E.

Suppose households were more thrifty, preferring future consumption more strongly to current consumption. Each indifference curve would be flatter, showing that for a given level of utility households would trade off more current consumption to gain extra future consumption. A map of flatter indifference curves would shift point E to the left along the PPF. A more thrifty society would choose a lower level of current consumption and a higher level of future consumption.

Suppose the new equilibrium point was at E'. How would the price system guide firms to produce more capital goods and fewer goods for immediate consumption? At E' the MRT is less negative (the PPF has a flatter downward slope). Equation (11) implies that a fall in the interest rate would persuade firms to produce at E'. With lower interest rates, investment opportunities that were previously unprofitable would now become profitable. A more thrifty society will save more. The increased supply of loans will bid down interest rates and encourage the investment to ensure that savings and investment are equal in equilibrium.

In this section we have shown two things. First, the analysis of general equilibrium can be extended to the choice of present versus future consumption. In the absence of market failure, competitive general equilibrium will achieve the Pareto-efficient allocation between consumption and investment.[10] Since in equilibrium savings equal investment, the allocation between consumption and savings will also be efficient. The rate of interest is the key price that guides the market to the efficient allocation.

Second, the equilibrium level of the interest rate reflects the competing forces of productivity and thrift. Productivity determines the slope of the PPF and thrift determines the slope of indifference curves. The equilibrium and efficient point on the PPF is where the MRT equals the MRS. In market equilibrium both are equal to $-(1 + r)$. Hence productivity and thrift together determine the real interest rate.

Summary

1   A resource allocation is Pareto-efficient when it is impossible to reallocate resources to make some people better off without simultaneously making others worse off. A necessary condition for Pareto efficiency is production efficiency or being on the PPF. This means that the economy is producing the maximum possible quantity of one good given the quantities of other goods being produced. But we also need to be at the right point on the PPF if we are to attain full Pareto efficiency.

2   The efficient resource allocation occurs when the marginal rate of transformation (MRT) or slope of the production possibility frontier (PPF) equals the marginal rate of substitution (MRS) at a point on the PPF. The MRT describes the rate at which society can trade off between goods in production. The MRS is the rate at which consumers are willing to trade off one good for another while holding utility constant.

3   In the absence of market failure, competitive equilibrium will be efficient. This is the fundamental justification for allowing markets and prices to handle resource allocation. Details of these arguments are summarized in Box 19-1.

4   Nevertheless, to avoid intervention entirely the government would have to believe all the following: there are no externalities, public goods, or missing markets; there is no imperfect competition (and hence no economies of scale); the income distribution thrown up by free market equilibrium is fair and right.

5   The interest rate is the key intertemporal price in economics. It affects consumption–savings decisions of households and investment decisions of firms. The interest rate establishes equilibrium between borrowing and lending, or investment and saving, or the demand and supply of current consumption. In general equilibrium they are all the same thing.

6   The equilibrium interest rate is determined by productivity (the slope of the PPF describing possibilities of transforming current consumption into future consumption) and thrift (the rate at which consumers will exchange current for future consumption along a given indifference curve). In equilibrium, both the MRT and the MRS are equal to $-(1 + r)$.

---

[10] In fact, there may be an important externality in saving. By refraining from consumption you allow an improvement in the capital stock that will benefit not only your own children but the children of everyone else. Since you fail to take this into account, the social marginal benefit of saving will exceed the private marginal benefit. There will be too little saving. This may explain why governments are always exhorting the population to save more.

Key Terms

General equilibrium
Invisible Hand
Efficient resource allocation
Production possibility frontier

Production efficiency
Opportunity cost
Marginal rate of transformation
Marginal rate of substitution
Investment and saving
Rate of return on investment
Distortions
Income distribution

Problems

1   (*a*) Why is it inefficient to end up producing inside the PPF? (*b*) Suppose the wage is stuck at a level above the equilibrium wage: will the economy produce on the PPF? Explain.

2   (*a*) Define the *MRT* and explain what it has to do with opportunity cost. (*b*) Will all profit-maximizing firms produce on the PPF with the *MRT* equal to −1 times the price ratio?

3   Why is it only relative prices that matter for determining *MRS*, *MRT* and the equilibrium allocation? What would happen if the price of every good and the rental of every factor of production doubled?

4   Look at equation (B5) in Box 19-1. Explain where each of these equalities comes from and why together they establish that resources are efficiently allocated.

5   A union raises the wage in the film industry 20 per cent above the wage in the meals industry. (*a*) What effect does this have on the equality of *MVPL* in the two sectors? (*b*) Will the economy stay on the PPF? (*c*) Are resources in the economy allocated efficiently? (*d*) Do workers in meals production benefit from the higher wages of their fellow workers?

6   Suppose there is a technical change which raises the return on investment. What happens to the PPF in Figure 19-8? What happens to the equilibrium levels of investment and savings? Draw a diagram to show the new equilibrium.

7   Common Fallacies   Show why the following statements are incorrect: (*a*) Just because the government needs some tax revenue, it should not use this as an excuse to tax as many commodities as possible. The government should leave as many goods untaxed as possible. (*b*) The free market has many deficiencies and no advantages. The state may as well run everything. (*c*) No wonder British industry does not invest. The real rate of return is very low.

4

Macroeconomics

20

Introduction to Macroeconomics and National Income Accounting

Macroeconomics is the study of the economy as a whole.

Macroeconomics is concerned not with the details – the price of cigarettes relative to the price of bread, or the output of cars relative to the output of steel – but with the overall picture. In Part 4 we shall study issues such as the determination of the total output of the economy, the aggregate level of unemployment, and the rate of inflation or growth of prices of goods and services as a whole.

The distinction between microeconomics and macroeconomics is more than the difference between economics in the small and economics in the large, which the Greek prefixes *micro* and *macro* suggest. The purpose of the analysis is also different.

A model is a deliberate simplification to enable us to pick out the key elements of a problem and think about them clearly. Although we could study the whole economy by piecing together our microeconomic analysis of each and every market, the resulting model would be so cumbersome that it would be hard to keep track of all the economic forces at work.

Microeconomics and macroeconomics take different approaches to keep the analysis manageable.

Microeconomics places the emphasis on a detailed understanding of particular markets. To achieve this amount of detail or magnification, many of the interactions with other markets are suppressed. In saying that a tax on cars reduces the equilibrium quantity of cars we ignore the question of what the government does with the tax revenue. If the government has to borrow less money, it is possible that interest rates and the exchange rate will fall and that improved international competitiveness of UK car producers will actually increase the equilibrium output of cars in the UK.

Microeconomics is a bit like looking at a horse race through a pair of binoculars. It is great for details, but sometimes we get a clearer picture of the whole race by using the naked eye. Because macroeconomics is concerned primarily with the interaction of different parts of the economy, it relies on a different simplification to keep the analysis manageable. Macroeconomics simplifies the building blocks in order to focus on how they fit together and influence one another.

Macroeconomics is concerned with broad aggregates such as the total demand for goods by households or the total spending on machinery and building by firms. As in watching the horse race through the naked eye, our notion of the individual details is more blurred but we can give our full attention to the whole picture. We are more likely to notice the horse sneaking up on the rails.

20-1 The Issues

We now introduce some of the main issues in macroeconomics. We pose a series of questions which form the theme on the analysis in Part 4.

Inflation   The annual *inflation rate* is the percentage increase per annum in the average price of goods and services. In Chapter 2 we introduced the retail price index (RPI), a weighted average of the prices households pay for goods and services. The percentage annual growth in the RPI is the most commonly used measure of inflation in the UK.

What causes inflation? The money supply? Trade Unions? Why do people mind so much about inflation? Does inflation cause unemployment? These are among the questions we shall seek to answer.

Unemployment   Unemployment is a measure of the number of people registered as looking for work but without a job. The *unemployment rate* is the percentage of the labour force that is unemployed. The *labour force* is the number of people working or looking for work. It excludes all those, from rich landowners to heroin addicts, who are neither working nor looking for work.

Unemployment is still high. Why did it increase so much in the early 1980s? Are workers pricing themselves out of jobs by greedy wage claims? Is high unemployment necessary to keep inflation under control, or could the government create more jobs?

Output and Growth   Real gross national product (real GNP) measures the total income of the economy. It tells us the quantity of goods and services the economy as a whole can afford to purchase. It is closely related to the total output of the economy. Increases in real GNP are called *economic growth*.

What determines the level of real GNP? Does unemployment mean that real GNP is lower than it might be? Why do some countries grow faster than others?

Macroeconomic Policy   Almost every day the newspapers and television refer to the problems of inflation, unemployment, and slow growth. These issues are widely discussed; they help determine the outcome of elections, and make some people interested in learning more about macroeconomics.

The government has a variety of policy measures through which it can try to affect the performance of the economy as a whole. It levies taxes, commissions spending, and influences the money supply, interest rates, and the exchange rate.

What the government can and should do is the subject of lively debate both within the field of economics and in the country at large. As usual, it is important to distinguish between positive issues relating to how the economy works and normative issues relating to priorities or value judgements. In the ensuing chapters we try to make clear which aspects of the policy debate refer to differing beliefs about how the economy works and which aspects refer to differences in priorities or value judgements.

20-2 The Facts

To set the scene, we begin by giving some of the key facts on recent inflation, economic growth, and unemployment.

Prices and Inflation

In Chapter 2 we explained how to calculate index numbers and showed the weights used to construct the RPI in the UK. Table 20-1 shows recent inflation rates in several countries. It gives a fair picture of what has been happening in prices in general.

Table 20-1 shows the inflation picture in the late 1980s. How did this inflation compare with other countries and other decades? The first column of Table 20-2 shows that the average annual inflation rate has varied greatly from country to country. Although the UK has experienced much higher inflation than Switzerland, West Germany, or the United States, its inflation rate has still been much lower than that of many other countries. Figure 20-1 shows the annual inflation rate in the UK over a much longer period.

Economic Growth

Table 20-2 also shows the average annual rate of growth of real GNP per head in selected countries. Again, the performance of different countries has varied greatly. Brazil, Korea, and Japan have grown significantly faster than the European countries such as the UK, Switzerland and even West Germany.

Table 20-1 Inflation rates (%)

	1987	1988	1989
USA	3.7	4.1	5.0
Japan	−0.2	0.5	2.0
W. Germany	0.2	1.2	3.0
France	3.1	2.7	3.5
Italy	4.7	5.0	5.8
UK	4.2	4.9	7.5
Sweden	4.2	5.8	7.5

Source: OECD *Economic Outlook.*

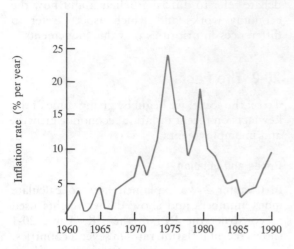

Figure 20-1 THE INFLATION RATE IN THE UK. (*Source*: CSO, *Economic Trends*.)

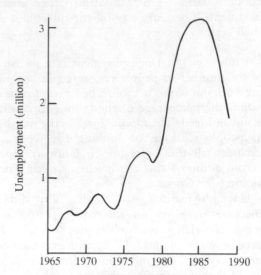

Figure 20-2 UK EMPLOYMENT (excluding school-leavers). (*Source*: CSO, *Economic Trends*.)

Table 20-2 Inflation and per capita real output growth, 1965–87 (Average % per annum)

COUNTRY	INFLATION	GROWTH
Argentina	150	0.1
Brazil	76	4.1
Israel	70	2.5
Korea	14	6.4
Italy	11	2.7
UK	9	1.7
Sweden	8	1.8
France	8	2.7
USA	6	1.5
Japan	5	4.2
W. Germany	4	2.5
Switzerland	4	1.4

Source: World Bank, *World Development Report*.

Table 20-3 Unemployment rates

COUNTRY	1985	1988
Belgium	15.8	14.5
UK	13.2	8.1
France	10.0	10.1
W. Germany	9.2	8.8
USA	6.9	5.5
Japan	2.8	2.5
Switzerland	0.9	0.7

* Unemployed, including school-leavers, as percentage of registered labour force.
Source: Department of Employment, *Employment Gazette*.

The table gives strong evidence against the popular myth that countries with high inflation rates always grow slowly. Switzerland, with the lowest inflation rate, has almost the *lowest* growth rate of real GNP per head. Brazil, with an inflation rate eight times as large as that in the UK, grew almost *three* times as quickly.

Unemployment

Figure 20-2 shows the number of people in postwar Britain wanting to work but unable to find a job. The increase in unemployment since the mid-1970s is quite dramatic. By 1985 over 3 million people in the UK were registered as unemployed but there was a substantial fall in UK unemployment in the late 1980s. Table 20-3 shows that many other countries were facing similar problems. Only Japan and Switzerland have managed to maintain the low unemployment rates that the UK experienced in the period 1955–70.

Recent Years in Perspective

The 1970s was a period of poor macroeconomic performance throughout the world. In almost every country there was a decline in the growth of both real GNP and real GNP per person, a rise in unemployment rates, and an increase in inflation. Table 20-4 contrasts the good years

Table 20-4 Inflation, unemployment, and real GNP growth, 1960–88
(Average percentage rates per annum)

	UK	USA	W. GERMANY	JAPAN
Inflation				
1960–73	5.1	3.2	3.3	6.1
1973–81	15.4	9.4	4.9	9.0
1981–88	5.5	4.6	3.0	1.3
Unemployment				
1960–73	2.9	5.0	0.8	1.3
1973–81	6.3	6.9	3.2	1.2
1981–88	10.3	8.0	6.9	2.6
Real GNP growth				
1960–73	3.2	4.2	4.8	10.5
1973–81	0.5	2.4	2.0	4.0
1981–88	3.2	2.7	1.5	4.0

Source: Economic Report of the President of the United States; United Nations, *World Economic Survey.*

1960–73 with the difficult years 1973–81 for four of the major industrial economies.

As we saw in Chapter 16, by the start of the 1980s many countries were feeling disenchanted with the economic policies of their governments. We described moves away from government intervention in the economy, moves to cut taxes and public spending and 'get the government off the backs of the people'. Table 20-4 helps provide the background to this wave of popular feeling. As Western economies started to slow down and both inflation and unemployment rose, people began to feel that the old policies were no longer working. By the end of Part 4 we shall be in a position to answer the following questions: Does the current insistence by many governments that the role of the government should be curtailed stem from a coherent analysis of why previous policies ceased to work? Or is it merely an attempt by governments to dissociate themselves from the poor performance of their economies in recent years?

20-3 The Framework: An Overview

The complete economy comprises many millions of individual economic units: households, firms, and the departments of central and local government. Together, their individual decisions determine the economy's total spending, its total income, and its total level of production of goods and services.

The Circular Flow

We begin by ignoring the government sector and the possibility of making transactions with foreigners in other countries. Table 20-5 presents a simple classification of the different transactions between households and firms within an isolated economy which also has no government. Households own the factors of production or inputs to the production process. They own their own labour, which they can rent out to firms in exchange for wages. In Chapter 7 we saw that households are also the ultimate owners of firms. It is households who put up the money as sole-traders, partners, or shareholders in exchange for the final entitlement to the firms' profits. Hence, although other factors of production such as capital and land appear to be held by firms, they are ultimately owned by households.

Table 20-5 Transactions by Households and firms

HOUSEHOLDS	FIRMS
Own factors of production which they supply to firms	Use factors of production supplied by households to produce goods and services
Receive incomes from firms in exchange for supplying factors of production	Pay households for use of factors of production
Spend on goods and services produced by firms	Sell goods and services to households

Figure 20-3 THE CIRCULAR FLOW BETWEEN FIRMS AND HOUSEHOLDS. The inner loop shows the flow of real resources. Households supply the services of factors of production to firms who use these factors to produce goods and services for households. The outer loop shows the corresponding flow of payments. Firms pay factor incomes to households but receive revenue from households' spending on goods and services that the firms produce.

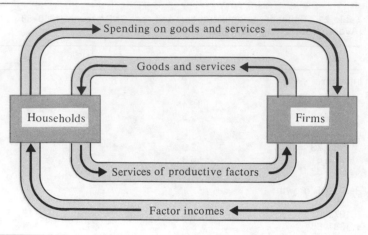

The first row of Table 20-5 shows that households supply factor services to firms which use these factors to produce goods and services. The second row shows the corresponding payments. Households earn factor incomes (wages, rents, profits) which are payments made by firms for the supply of these factor services. The third row shows that households use their incomes to buy goods and services from firms, thereby giving firms the money with which to pay for the factor services used in production.

Figure 20-3 shows this *circular flow* between households and firms. The inner loop shows the transfers of real resources between the two sectors and the outer loop shows the corresponding flows of money. As in our discussion of the role of markets and prices in microeconomics, we should think of these monetary payments as being only one of many ways in which an economy could organize the allocation of inputs and outputs. A centrally planned economy could arrange for the resource transfers on the inner loop without the use of markets, prices, or payments.

Figure 20-3 suggests that there are three ways of measuring the amount of economic activity in an economy. We could measure (*a*) the value of goods and services produced, (*b*) the level of factor earnings, which represent the value of factor services supplied, or (*c*) the value of spending on goods and services. Since all payments are the counterparts of transfers of real resources, and since for the moment we assume that all payments must be spent on purchasing real resources, we must get the same

estimate of total economic activity whether we measure the value of production output, the level of factor incomes, or spending on goods and services.

It is worth restating this important point. Factor incomes must equal household spending since we assume that all income is spent. The value of production or output must equal total spending on goods and services since we assume that all goods are sold. The value of output must equal the value of household incomes because we can always regard the management or ownership of a business as a factor of production. Since profits are residually defined as the value of output sales minus the direct payments to hire land, labour, and capital, and since these profits ultimately accrue to the households which own the business, it follows that household incomes – derived either from supplying land, labour, and capital or from entitlements to the firms' profits – must exactly equal the value of production.

Stating the arguments in this way, we can see that our model is still very simple. What happens if firms do not sell all their output? What happens if firms sell output not to households but to other firms? What happens if households do not spend all their incomes? In the next section we show that we can take account of all these possibilities. Having done so, we shall discover that our conclusion is unchanged: the level of economic activity can be measured by valuing total spending, total output, or total earnings, and all three methods give the same answer.

Once we have learned to measure the level of

economic activity through this system of *national income accounting*, we shall be in a position to begin the analysis of the basic macroeconomic issues such as inflation, unemployment, and economic growth. We will have a coherent framework in which to relate the flows of payments to the flows of factor inputs and outputs of goods and services.

This framework will allow us to explore the behaviour of the economy as a whole. We shall see how increased factor supplies or advances in technology allow the economy to achieve economic growth by producing more output, and how this leads to higher household incomes and spending, giving people a higher standard of living.

We shall see how a reduction in sales of goods and services will lead firms to contract their production levels, cut back on their use of factors of production, and create unemployment not only of labour but also of other factors such as machinery. Even our simple model shown in Figure 20-3 suggests that the consequent reduction in household incomes may lead to a reduction in spending, which forces further reductions in output and factor use. We shall wish to analyse whether this process can spiral indefinitely or whether the economy as a whole has a self-correcting mechanism which gradually restores full employment.

Finally, we shall wish to see what happens when households try to spend more than the value of the goods that are being produced. If all factors of production are already fully employed, the quantity of output cannot be increased. Does this mean that prices of output must be increased until the value of output equals the amount consumers would like to spend? And does this mean that inflation should not occur when the economy has unemployed resources that could be used to increase the quantity of output?

The circular flow diagram in Figure 20-3 allows us to keep track of the interactions that are so important in studying the economy as a whole. But the diagram is too simple. It leaves out too many of the important features of the real world: saving and investment, government spending and taxes, transactions between firms and with the rest of the world. Our first priority must be to develop a comprehensive system of national accounting which addresses all these complications.

20-4 National Income Accounting

Measuring GDP

Gross domestic product (GDP) measures the output produced by factors of production located in the domestic economy regardless of who owns these factors.

GDP measures the value of output produced within the economy. Most of this output will be produced by domestic factors of production but there are some exceptions. Suppose Nissan or Peugeot builds a car factory in the UK. They employ UK workers and use machines made in the UK. Their output is part of GDP for the UK. However, the company's profits are owned by shareholders in Japan or France. Hence the value of the factory's output cannot be expected to be the same as the value of incomes earned by UK households. Initially we shall simply suppose that we are discussing a country with no links with the rest of the world. Shortly, we shall introduce the rest of the world and show that it is precisely the issue of how to treat payment of profits and other income to foreigners that explains why we have to distinguish GDP from the concept of GNP, which we introduced earlier. When an economy has no transactions with the rest of the world we say that it is a *closed economy*.

We begin by considering how our simple circular flow diagram should be extended to recognize that transactions do not take place exclusively between a single firm and a single household. Firms hire labour services from households, but they buy raw materials and machinery from other firms. If we include the value of the output of cars in GDP we do not want also to include the value of the steel sold to the car producer which is already in the value of the car.

To avoid double counting, we use the concept of value added.

Value added is the increase in the value of goods as a result of the production process.

Value added is calculated by deducting from the value of the firm's output the cost of the input goods that were used up in the act of producing that output.

Closely related to the concept of value added is the distinction between final goods and intermediate goods.

Final goods are goods purchased by the ultimate user. They are either consumer goods purchased by households or capital goods such as machinery which are purchased by firms. *Intermediate goods* are partly finished goods which form inputs to another firm's production process and are used up in that process.

Thus, ice cream is a final good but steel is an intermediate good which some other firm uses as an input to its production process. In classifying capital goods as final goods we suppose they are not used up in subsequent production. In the language of Chapter 7, we suppose that they do not depreciate or wear out. Shortly, we shall see how depreciation may be handled within this framework.

The following example should help you sort out these concepts and it is important that you should study it until you have mastered these ideas. We assume that there are four firms in the economy: a steel producer, a producer of capital goods (machines) used in the car industry, a tyre producer, and a car producer who sells cars to the final consumers, the households. Table 20-6 shows how we may calculate GDP for this simple economy.

The steel producer makes £4000 worth of steel, one-quarter of which is sold as an intermediate good to the firm that makes machines and three-quarters of which is sold to the car producer to make cars. If the steel producer also mines the iron ore from which the steel is produced, then the entire £4000 is value added or net output by the steel firm. This revenue is directly paid out in wages and rents or is residual profits which also accrue to households as income. Hence the first two rows

of the last column also add up to £4000. Although firms have spent £4000 buying this steel output, this does not show up as expenditure on final goods since steel is entirely an intermediate good which will be used up in later stages of the production process.

The machine manufacturer spends £1000 buying steel input which is then converted into a machine to be sold to the car producer for £2000. The value added to the machine manufacturer is £2000 less the £1000 spent on steel inputs. And this net revenue of £1000 accrues directly or indirectly to households as income or profit. Since the car firm intends to keep the machine, its full value of £2000 is shown under 'Final expenditure'.

Like the steel producer, the tyre manufacturer produces an intermediate output which does not show up under final expenditure. If the tyre manufacturer also owns the rubber trees from which the tyres were made, the entire output of £500 is value added and will contribute directly or indirectly to household incomes. If the tyre company bought rubber from a domestic rubber producer we should have to subtract the input value of rubber from the tyre manufacturer's output to obtain value added or net output, but we should have to add another row showing the value added of the company producing the rubber for sale to the tyre company.

The car producer spends £3000 on steel and £500 on tyres. Since both are used up during the period in which cars are made, we subtract £3500 from the car output of £5000 to obtain the value added of the car producer. This net revenue pays households for factor services supplied, or is paid to them as profits.

Table 20-6 Calculating GDP

(1) GOOD	(2) SELLER	(3) BUYER	(4) TRANSACTION VALUE	(5) VALUE ADDED	(6) EXPENDITURE ON FINAL GOODS	(7) FACTOR EARNINGS
Steel	Steel producer	Machine producer	£1000	£1000	—	£1000
Steel	Steel producer	Car producer	£3000	£3000	—	£3000
Machine	Machine producer	Car producer	£2000	£1000	£2000	£1000
Tyres	Tyre producer	Car producer	£500	£500	—	£500
Cars	Car producer	Consumers	£5000	£1500	£5000	£1500
Total value of transactions			£11 500			
Gross domestic product (GDP)				£7000	£7000	£7000

Finally, the car producer sells the car for £5000 to the final consumer-households. Only now does the car become a final good and its full price of £5000 is entered as final expenditure.

Table 20-6 shows that the gross value of all the transactions that occurred is £11 500, but this overstates the value of the goods the economy has actually produced. For example, the £3000 that the steel producer earned by selling steel to the car producer is already included in the final value of car output. It is simply double-counting to count this £3000 twice.

Column (5) shows the value added at each stage in the production process. In total this comes to £7000, and this is the correct measure of the net output of the economy. Since each producer pays out the corresponding net revenue to households either as direct factor payments or indirectly as profits, household earnings also equal £7000 in the last column of the table. If we simply counted up the payments made to households as income and profits we would get the same measure of the economy's output or GDP.

Table 20-6 confirms that we also get the same answer if we measure spending on *final* goods and services. In this case the final users are the households buying the cars and the car producer buying the (everlasting) machinery used to make cars.

Investment and Saving

The example shown in Table 20-6 not only allows us to explain the concept of value added and the distinction between intermediate and final goods, but also allows us to deal immediately with a second complication. Total output and household incomes are each equal to £7000, but households are spending only £5000 on cars. What are they doing with the rest of their incomes? And who is doing the rest of the spending? To resolve these issues we need to introduce investment and saving.

> *Investment* is the purchase of new capital goods by firms. *Saving* is that part of income which is not spent buying goods and services.

Thus, in our example households are consuming £5000. This is the value of their expenditure on consumer goods (cars). Since their income is £7000 they are saving £2000. The car manufacturer is spending £2000 on investment (the purchase of new machinery). Figure 20-4 shows how we must amend the circular flow diagram of Figure 20-3. The bottom half of the figure tells us that incomes and the value of factor services are each £7000. But £2000 leaks out from the circular flow when households save. Only £5000 finds its way back to firms as households spending on consumer goods (cars).

The top half of the figure shows that £5000 is the value of output of consumer goods and the value of household spending on these goods. Since GDP is £7000, where does the other £2000 come from? Since it does not come from household spending it must come from spending by firms themselves. It is the £2000 of investment expenditure made by the car producer in purchasing machinery for use in car manufacturing.

The numbers in Table 20-6 relate to flows of output, expenditure, and income in a particular time period such as a year. During the same time period the economy goes once round the inner and outer loops shown in Figure 20-4. On the inner loop firms produce an output of £5000 for consumption by households but also produce an output of £2000 of capital goods for investment by other firms. On the outer loop, which relates to money payments, we show savings as a *leakage* of £2000 from the circular flow, with an arrow pointing outwards to remind us that this money does not directly find its way back to firms through household purchases of firms' output. We show investment spending by firms on new machinery as an *injection* of £2000 to the circular flow, with an arrow pointing inwards to remind us that spending decisions by firms are supplementing the payments received by firms from household spending.

Two questions immediately arise. First, is it coincidental that household savings of £2000 exactly equal investment expenditure of £2000 by firms? Second, if it is not a coincidence, how is the money saved by households transferred to firms to allow them to pay for investment spending?

Suppose we use Y to denote the value of GDP which we know is also the value of household incomes. If C denotes household spending on consumption and S denotes savings, then from

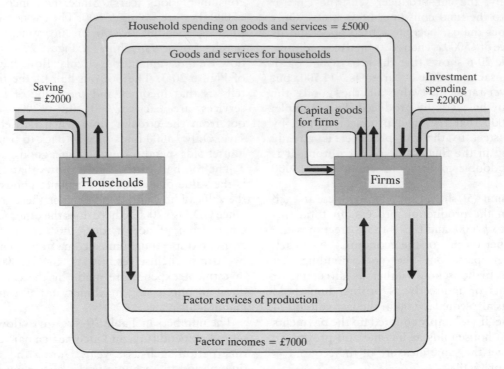

Figure 20-4 INVESTMENT, SAVINGS, AND THE CIRCULAR FLOW.   The inner loop continues to show flows of real resources between firms and households. Firms use factor services supplied by households to make consumer goods and services for households and new capital goods for other firms. The outer loop continues to show payment flows. Factor incomes are either saved by households or spent on purchasing consumer goods. Firms also earn revenue from the investment expenditure on new capital goods by other firms. Thus, saving is a leakage from the circular flow of payments.

the definition that savings are the part of income not spent,

$$S \equiv Y - C \quad \text{and} \quad Y \equiv C + S \qquad (1)$$

The symbol $\equiv$ means 'is identically equal to, as a matter of definition'. Similarly since GDP Y can be measured as the sum of final expenditure on consumption goods C and final expenditure on investment goods I,

$$Y \equiv C + I \qquad (2)$$

it follows purely from the national accounting definitions we have adopted that

$$Y \equiv C + S \equiv C + I$$

Hence it must be that

$$S \equiv I \qquad (3)$$

It is no accident that savings and investment are each £2000 in our example. Equation (3) tells

us that savings will equal investment in any example we construct. Look again at the outer loop of Figure 20-4. All consumption expenditure in the top half of the figure finds its way back to households as income in the bottom half of the figure. Hence any investment spending by firms is matched by an income flow to households in excess of their consumption expenditure. Since savings is defined as the excess of income over consumption, investment and savings must always be equal.

We cannot stress too strongly that these are purely accounting identities which follow from our definitions of investment, savings, and income. What we have shown is that *actual* savings are necessarily equal to *actual* investment. As yet we have said nothing about *desired* savings or *desired* investment; nor have we claimed that there will always be an equilibrium between the two. To investigate these issues we need to develop models or theories of desired savings and investment, a task we begin in the next chapter.[1]

What connects the leakage of savings and the injection of investment expenditure? Since firms as a whole are making income payments to households of £7000 but receiving only £5000 from households through spending on consumption, they must be borrowing £2000 to pay for the new capital goods they are purchasing. Since households are saving £2000 they must be lending it to firms who wish to make investment expenditures.

In a market economy, the financial institutions and financial markets – the banks that take in household savings as deposits and grant overdraft facilities to firms, and the stock market on which firms raise money by selling new shares to households – play a key role in channelling household savings towards the firms that wish to borrow in order to invest in new capital goods.

The introduction of investment allows us to deal with another problem glossed over in our simpler circular flow diagram. What happens if firms cannot sell all the output that they produce? Surely this leads to a difference between the output measure and the expenditure measure of GDP?

Final goods are goods not completely used up in the production process during the period. In Table 20-6 steel was an intermediate good used up in making cars and machines, but machines were a final good because the car producer could use them again in the next period.[2] Suppose in Table 20-6 that the car producer's sales were not £5000 but only £4000. The producer is left with £1000 worth of cars which must be stockpiled.

Inventories or *stocks* are goods currently held by a firm for future production or sale.

Thus the car producer may hold stocks of steel,

which will form an input to production of cars in the next period, or stocks of finished cars awaiting sale to consumers in the next period.

In Chapter 7 we described stocks as *working capital*. Because they have not been used up in production and sale during the current period, stocks are classified as capital goods. Adding to stocks is investment in working capital. When stocks are run down, we treat this as negative investment or disinvestment.

Now we see how to keep the national accounts straight. When the car producer is able to sell only £4000 of the £5000 worth of cars produced in the period, we treat the inventory investment of £1000 by the car producer as final expenditure. As in Table 20-6, the output and expenditure measures of GDP are each £7000 including the output and expenditure on the machinery for making cars. But spending on final goods now comprises: car producer (£2000 on machines, £1000 on stocks), household-consumer (£4000 on cars).

Many people find this confusing. The trick is to distinguish between classification by commodity and classification by economic use. Steel is clearly an intermediate commodity but that is not important. When a steel producer makes *and sells* steel we show this as production of an intermediate good. Since it has been passed on to someone else, our expenditure measure will pick it up further up the chain of production and sales. But when a firm adds to its stocks we must count that as final expenditure because it will not show up anywhere else in the national accounts. The firm is temporarily adding to its capital, and when it subsequently uses up these stocks we treat this as negative investment to keep the record straight.

Having dealt with transactions between firms, investment and savings, and changes in stocks because of discrepancies between output and sales, we now introduce the government sector.

The Government

Governments raise revenue both through direct taxes T_d levied on incomes (wages, rents, interest, and profits) and through indirect taxes or expenditures taxes T_e (VAT, petrol duties, cigarette taxes). Taxes are raised to meet two kinds of expenditure. Government spending on goods and services G comprises purchases by the government of physical goods and services.

---

[1] It may be helpful to think of the analogous concepts we have already developed in microeconomics. In a particular market the demand curve shows desired purchases at any price and the supply curve shows desired sales at any price. Equilibrium occurs at the price at which desired purchases equal desired sales. When the price is too high there is excess supply and some desired sales will be frustrated. But since there is a buyer and a seller in every transaction that takes place, actual purchases will equal actual sales whether or not the market is in equilibrium.

[2] Of course, the machine gradually wears out with use. We deal with depreciation shortly.

It includes spending on the wages of civil servants and soldiers, the purchase of typewriters, tanks, and military aircraft, and investment programmes in roads and hospitals.

But governments also spend money financing *transfer payments* or benefits, *B*. These include pensions, unemployment benefit, and subsidies to private firms (investment grants) and to state-owned firms (paying for loss-making rural railways). Transfer payments are payments that do not require the provision of any goods or services in return.

Transfer payments add to neither national income nor national output. They should not be included in GDP. There is no corresponding value added or net output produced. Taxes and transfer payments merely redistribute existing income and spending power away from people being taxed and towards people being subsidized. In contrast, spending *G* on goods and services produces net output, gives rise to corresponding factor earnings in the firms supplying this output, and hence gives rise to additional spending power of the households receiving this income. Hence government spending *G* on goods and services should be included in GDP.

The purpose of national income accounting is to provide a logically coherent set of definitions and measures of national output. However, in our discussion of microeconomics we have seen that taxes drive a wedge between the price the purchaser pays and the price the seller receives. Thus we can choose to value national output either at market prices inclusive of indirect taxes on goods and services, or at the prices received by producers after indirect taxes have been paid.

GDP at *market prices* measures domestic output inclusive of indirect taxes on goods and services. GDP at *factor cost* measures domestic output exclusive of indirect taxes on goods and services. Thus GDP at market prices exceeds GDP at factor cost by the amount of revenue raised in indirect taxes (net of any sudsidies on goods and services).

Our national accounts may now be constructed as follows. Measuring consumption *C*, investment *I*, and government spending *G* on goods and services, at market prices inclusive of indirect taxes, the value added or net output of the economy is given by $(C + I + G)$. Hence

GDP at market prices $\equiv C + I + G$ (4)

Higher indirect tax rates will increase the price of goods and services. Although the value of output increases at market prices, the physical quantity of output is unchanged. Hence it makes more sense to use the measure of GDP at factor cost. Thus, subtracting indirect taxes (net or subsidies) T_e,

$Y \equiv$ GDP at factor cost $\equiv C + I + G - T_e$ (5)

This measure of the value of national output is independent of indirect taxes. Higher tax rates increase the value of $(C + I + G)$ but leads to an equivalent rise in T_e, leaving GDP at factor cost unchanged.

We now use the symbol *Y* to denote GDP at factor cost. The right-hand side of equation (5) is now the final expenditure measure of GDP and the net output measure of GDP, each at factor cost. The left-hand side of equation (5) is the income measure of GDP at factor cost. Through factor payments and profits, firms pay households the exact value of net output measured at the prices, net of indirect taxes, that firms actually receive. Hence the output, expenditure, and income measures of GDP at factor cost are all equal.

Equation (5) tells us why we must not include direct taxes T_d or transfer benefits *B* in the income measure of GDP. They do not correspond to actual production. For a given total output and expenditure, direct taxes and transfer benefits merely alter the way in which the given total income is shared out between different households. They do not affect total income itself.

Figure 20-5 shows that direct taxes and transfer benefits do affect the circular flow of payments, which we now extend to take account of the government sector. Household incomes at factor cost *Y* are supplemented by benefits *B* less direct taxes T_d. This gives us personal disposable income.

Personal disposable income is household income after direct taxes and transfer payments. It shows how much households have available for spending and saving.

Thus personal disposable income equals $(Y + B - T_d)$.

We must now amend our definition of savings *S* when there is a government sector. Saving is the amount of disposable income that

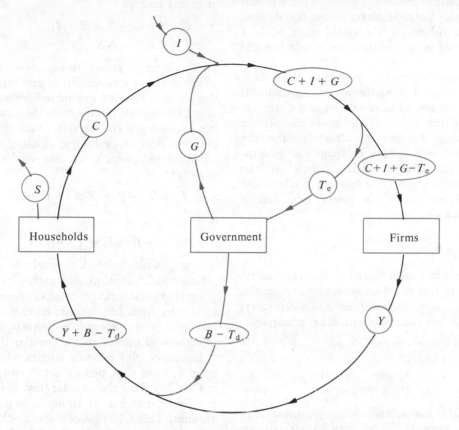

Figure 20-5   THE GOVERNMENT AND THE CIRCULAR FLOW.   The figure extends the circular flow between households and firms to include the government sector. Firms make factor payments Y to households. Disposable income $Y + B + T_d$ also includes transfer payments B less direct taxes T_d. Disposable income goes on savings S or consumption C. This spending is augmented by injections of government spending G on goods and services and by investment spending I. From $C + I + G$ or GDP at market prices, we must subtract the leakage of indirect taxes T_e to get GDP at factor cost Y which firms pay out to households.

is not spent on consumption. Thus

$$S \equiv (Y + B - T_d) - C \qquad (6)$$

Proceeding round the top loop of Figure 20-5 we see that consumption C at market prices is now supplemented by injections of investment spending I and government spending G. From $(C + I + G)$ or GDP at market prices we must finally subtract indirect taxes T_e to get back to Y or GDP at factor cost.

Equation (6) implies that GDP at factor cost is given by

$$Y \equiv C + S - B + T_d$$

Comparing this with our definition of Y in equation (5), we see that

$$C + S - B + T_d \equiv Y \equiv C + I + G - T_e$$

Since these expressions are identically equal, we can say that

$$S + T_d + T_e \equiv I + G + B \qquad (7a)$$

and

$$S - I \equiv G + B - T_d - T_e \qquad (7b)$$

Equations (7a) and (7b) allow us to confirm that our system of national income accounting makes sense. The left-hand side of equation (7a) tells us the total leakages or withdrawals from the circular flow of payments. Money leaks out through household savings and taxes to the government. The right-hand side of equation (7a) tells us the injections to the circular flow. Investment spending by firms and government spending on goods and services and on transfer benefits put money back into the system. Total leakages must equal total injections; otherwise we would have made a bookkeeping error and the sums would not add up.[3]

Equation (7b) makes the same point in a different way. Taking firms and households together, the net withdrawals from the circular flow $S - I$ (the financial surplus of the private sector) must be exactly offset by the net injections $G + B - T_d - T_e$ from the government sector (the financial deficit of the government). The private sector as a whole can run a surplus only if the government runs a deficit, and vice versa.

The Foreign Sector

Thus far we have considered a closed economy, which does not transact with the rest of the world. We now consider an *open economy*, which does have dealings with other countries.

> *Exports* (X) are goods that are domestically produced but sold abroad. *Imports* (Z) are goods that are produced abroad but purchased for use in the domestic economy.

Households, firms, and the government may purchase imports Z of raw materials or consumer goods that are not part of domestic output and do not give rise to domestic factor incomes. These goods will not show up in the output measure of GDP, which relates only to the *value added* by domestic producers. However, imports do show up in final expenditure. There are two solutions to this problem. We could subtract the import component separately from C, I, G, and X and measure only final expenditure on the domestically produced component of consumption, investment, government spending, and exports. But it is much easier to continue to measure total final expenditure on C, I, G, and X and then subtract total expenditure on imports from $(C + I + G + X)$. It comes to exactly the same thing. It is also the same as adding net exports NX – that is, exports X minus imports Z – to $C + I + G$.

Hence in an open economy we can recognize the presence of foreign trade by redefining GDP at factor cost as

$$Y \equiv C + I + G + X - Z - T_e$$
$$\equiv C + I + G + NX - T_e \qquad (8)$$

which directly extends to equation (5).

What about leakages from and injections to the circular flow of payments? Imports represent a leakage of money from the circular flow but exports are an injection of money into the circular flow. Combining equation (8) with equation (6), which remains unchanged, we now get

$$S + (T_d + T_e - B) + Z \equiv I + G + X \qquad (9a)$$

and

$$S - I \equiv (G + B - T_e - T_d) + NX \qquad (9b)$$

You might like to work through the algebra as an exercise. Equation (9a) makes the familiar point that total leakages must continue to equal total injections. Imports are an extra source of leakages and exports an extra source of injections of money to the circular flow.

Equation (9b) extends equation (7b) to an open economy. A private sector surplus $S - I$ is a leakage from the circular flow of payments. It must be matched by an injection of the same amount. This injection can come either from a government deficit $(G + B - T_e - T_d)$ or from net exports NX, the excess of export earnings over import spending. Since our trade surplus is the rest of the world trade deficit, we can summarize equation (9b) by saying that the surplus of the private sector must be matched by the budget deficit of the government plus the trade deficit of foreigners.

From GDP to GNP

To complete our description of the national accounts we must deal with two final problems. Thus far we have assumed that all factors of production are domestically owned: all net domestic output accrues to domestic households as factor incomes. But this need not be the case. When Nissan or Peugeot owns a car factory in the UK, some of the profits will be sent back to Japan or France to be spent or saved by Japanese or French households. Similarly, when immigrant workers send some of their wage packets back home to support relatives, or foreign owners of UK property or shares in UK companies send home some of

---

[3] Notice that when $T_d = T_e = G = B = 0$ there is no government sector and equation (7a) implies $S = I$, as we discovered in equation (3).

their income from property rents or company dividends, there is a discrepancy between the factor incomes earned in the UK and the factor incomes accruing to UK households.

Conversely, UK households earn income from factor services that they supply in foreign countries. Since most of these income flows between countries are not labour income but income from interest, dividends, profits, and rents, they are shown in the national accounts as the flow of *property income* between countries. The net flow of property income into the UK is the excess of inflows of property income from factor services supplied abroad over the outflows of property income arising from the supply of factor services by foreigners in the UK.

When there is a net flow of property income between the UK and the rest of the world, the output and expenditure measure of GDP will no longer equal the total factor incomes earned by UK citizens. We use the term *gross national product* (GNP) to measure GDP adjusted for net property income from abroad.

> *GNP* measures total income earned by domestic citizens regardless of the country in which their factor services were supplied. GNP equals GDP plus net property income from abroad.

Thus, if the UK has an inflow of £2 billion of property income from abroad but an outflow of £1 billion of property income accruing to foreigners, UK GNP, measuring income earned by UK citizens, will exceed UK GDP, measuring the value of goods produced in the UK, by £1 billion.

From GNP to National Income

The final complication of which we must take account is depreciation.

> *Depreciation* or capital consumption measures the rate at which the value of the existing capital stock declines per period as a result of wear and tear or of obsolescence.

Depreciation is a flow concept telling us how much our effective capital stock is being used up in each time period. Depreciation is an economic cost because it measures resources being used up in the production process.

In our simple example of Table 20-6 we ignored depreciation completely. We assumed that the machine purchased by the car producer would last for ever. We now recognize that machinery wears out. In consequence, the *net* output of the economy is reduced. Some of the economy's gross output has to be used merely to replace existing capital, and this part of gross output is not available for consumption, investment in net additions to the capital stock, government spending, or exports. Similarly, we need to reduce our measure of the incomes available for spending on these goods.

Accordingly, we subtract depreciation from GNP to arrive at net national product (NNP) or national income.

> *National income* is the economy's *net national product*. It is calculated by subtracting depreciation from GNP at factor cost.

National income measures the amount of money the economy has available for spending on goods and services after setting aside enough money to maintain its capital stock intact by offsetting depreciation.

Summary

We have now developed a complete set of national accounts. You are probably wondering how you are going to remember all these new concepts. Figure 20-6 may help to keep you straight. Table 20-7 fills in the actual numbers for the UK in 1987.

20-5 What Does GNP Actually Measure?

A company's accounts provide a picture of how the company is doing. Our system of national income accounting allows us to assess the performance of the economy as a whole. But, just as a company's accounts may conceal as much as they reveal, we must interpret the national income accounts with some care.

We concentrate on GNP as a measure of national economic performance. National income, or net national product at factor cost, differs from GNP at factor cost only because the former subtracts an estimate of the economic depreciation of the capital stock. Since depreciation is rather difficult to measure, and consequently may be treated differently in

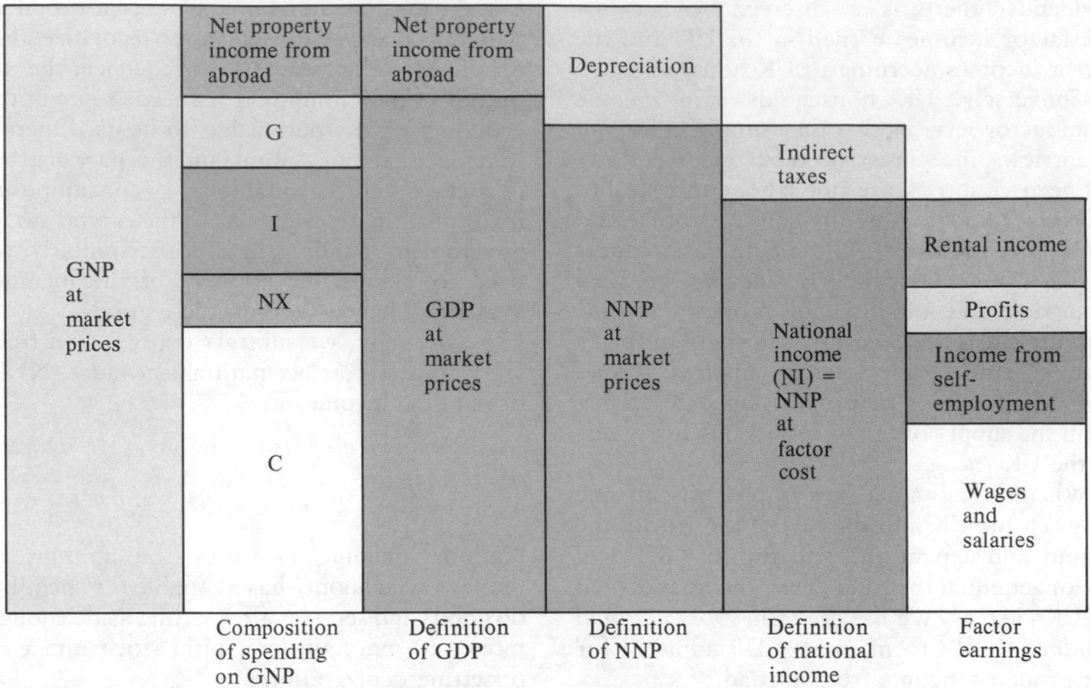

Figure 20-6   NATIONAL INCOME ACCOUNTING: A SUMMARY

Table 20-7 UK national income in 1987*
(£ billion at current prices)

OUTPUT–EXPENDITURE MEASURE		INCOME MEASURE	
At market prices		Income sources	
Consumption *C*	258.4	Employment	226.3
Investment *I*	71.3	Self-employment	33.0
Government spending *G*		Profits	65.6
on goods and services	85.8	Rent	24.8
Net exports *NX*	−4.5	Other	6.5
GDP at market prices	411.0	GDP at factor cost	356.2
Net property income from abroad	5.5	Net property income from abroad	5.5
GNP at market prices	416.5		
Factor cost adjustment			
less indirect taxes	−62.2		
GNP at factor cost	354.3	GNP at factor cost	361.7
less depreciation	−48.2	*less* depreciation	−48.2
National income	306.1	National income	313.5

* Because of problems in data measurement and collection, the output–expenditure and income measures gives slightly different estimates of UK national income.
Source: CSO, *UK National Accounts.*

different countries or during different time periods, in practice most economists make comparisons using GNP, which avoids the need to argue about the relevant measure of depreciation.

In this section we make three points. First, we recall the distinction between nominal and real variables. Real GNP adjusts nominal GNP for changes in the general price level over time, thus providing a more accurate picture of the quantity of goods and services produced by the economy as a whole. Second, we show how per capita GNP may be used to take account of population growth and provide a more accurate picture of the standard of living of a representative person in the economy. Finally, we discuss the incompleteness of GNP as a measure of the activities that provide economic welfare or satisfaction to members of society.

Nominal and Real GNP

Nominal GNP measures GNP at the prices currently prevailing when these goods and services are produced. If in successive years the economy produces the same physical quantity of output but all prices are 10 per cent higher in the second year, nominal GNP in the second year will be 10 per cent higher than in the first year. Since it is physical quantities of output that yield people utility or happiness, it can be very misleading to judge the economy's performance by looking at nominal GNP.

Real GNP, or GNP at constant prices, adjusts for inflation by measuring GNP in different years at the prices prevailing at some particular calendar date known as the *base year*. To introduce these ideas, Table 20-8 presents a simple hypothetical example of a whole economy. Nominal GNP is the value of production measured in the prices of that year. In our example it increases from £600 to £1440 between 1975 and 1990. If we take 1975 as the base year we can measure real GNP in 1990 by valuing output quantities in that year at 1975 prices. Thus, real GNP increases only from £600 to £860. This increase of 43 per cent in real GNP provides a much more accurate picture

of the change in the total quantity of goods produced by the economy as a whole.

The GNP Deflator   In Chapter 2 we introduced the retail price index (RPI), an index of the average price of goods purchased by consumers. The most common measure of the inflation rate in the UK is the percentage increase in the RPI over its corresponding value in the same month one year earlier. This measure is of interest because it shows what is happening to the prices of goods bought by consumer-households.

However, we now know that consumption expenditure is only one component of GNP. GNP also includes investment, government spending, and net exports. To convert nominal GNP to real GNP we need to use an index that reflects what is happening to the price of all goods. This index is called the GNP deflator.

The *GNP deflator* is the ratio of nominal GNP to real GNP expressed as an index.

Expressing the deflator as an index means that the ratio of nominal to real GNP is multiplied by 100.

In the hypothetical example of Table 20-8, nominal and real GNP coincide in the base year 1975. Their ratio 1 and the value of the index is 100. For 1990 the ratio of nominal to real GNP is 1.674 ($=1440/860$) and the value of the index is 167.4. According to the GNP deflator, prices for the economy as a whole increased from 100 to 167.4, a 67.4 per cent increase between 1975 and 1990. From Table 20-8 we can see that the price of apples rose by 100 per cent over the period while the price of chickens rose by 50 per cent. Thus the increase of 67.4 per cent in the GNP deflator is giving us a reasonable picture of what is happening to all the different prices in the economy.

Table 20-8 Nominal and real GNP

GOOD	QUANTITY PRODUCED		PRICE (£/unit)		VALUE OF OUTPUT (current £)		VALUE OF OUTPUT (1975 £)	
	1975	1990	1975	1990	1975	1990	1975	1990
Apples	100	150	2	4	200	600	200	300
Chickens	100	140	4	6	400	840	400	560
					600	1440	600	860
					Nominal GNP		Real GNP	

Table 20-9 presents some actual numbers for the UK economy over the last two decades. Nominal GNP in the UK rose from under £23 billion in 1960 to over £354 billion in 1987. Yet without knowing what happened to the price of goods in general it is impossible to judge what happened to the quantity of output produced by the economy as a whole over this period. The second row of Table 20-9 answers this question. On average, the price of output was nearly nine times higher in 1987 than in 1960. In consequence, the change in real GNP was much less dramatic than the change in nominal GNP over the same period. Nominal GNP doubled between 1975 and 1980, but the table shows that more than 90 per cent of this increase was due to rising prices and less than 7 per cent was due to rising physical quantities of output. At 1980 prices, real GNP increased only from £186 billion in 1975 to £199 billion in 1980. Hence we see the vital importance of distinguishing between nominal and real GNP.[4]

Per Capita Real GNP

Real GNP gives us a simple measure of the physical output of an economy, and the annual percentage increase in real GNP gives us an idea of how fast an economy is growing. Table 20-10 shows the average annual growth rate of real GNP during the 1970s in three countries, Mexico, the United States, and West Germany. The first column shows that the annual growth

[4] Even after many years of inflation this point is not universally understood. How many times have you heard statements such as 'Today the stock market hit an all-time high'? Frequently such statements refer to the *nominal* value of a variable. In times of inflation it is scarcely surprising that nominal variables increases. For many purposes it is *real* values that are of interest in assessing economic performance.

rate of real GNP in the 1970s was highest in Mexico and lowest in West Germany. Although this tells us about the growth of the economy as a whole in each of these countries, we may be interested in a different question: what was happening to the standard of living of a representative person in each of these countries? To answer this question we need to examine per capital real GNP.

Per capita real GNP is real GNP divided by the total population. It is real GNP per head.

For a given level of real GNP, the larger the population, the smaller will be the quantity of goods and services available for each individual. The second column of Table 20-10 shows that population was growing much faster in Mexico than in the United States or West Germany in the 1970s. Column (3) shows what was happening to per capita real GNP over the period. Notice that the ranking is completely reversed: GNP per person was rising fastest in West Germany and slowest in Mexico. Thus, if we wish to get a simple measure of the standard of living enjoyed by a person in a particular country, it is better to look at per capita real GNP, which adjusts for population growth, than to look at total real GNP.

Even per capita real GNP is only a crude indicator. Table 20-10 does *not* say that every person in Mexico obtained 1.8 per cent more goods and services each year throughout the 1970s. It only indicates what was happening on average. Some people's real incomes increased by a lot more than 1.8 per cent per annum and some people became absolutely poorer. The more the income distribution is changing over time, the less reliable is the change in per capita real GNP as an indicator of what is happening to any particular person.

Table 20-9 Nominal and real GNP in the UK

	1960	1965	1970	1975	1980	1984	1987
GNP at factor cost (£ billion, current prices)	22.9	31.9	44.6	96.5	199.0	277.9	354.3
GNP deflator (1980 = 100)	17.9	21.3	27.1	50.2	100.0	131.4	151.5
Real GNP at factor cost (£ billion, 1980 prices)	127.8	149.4	169.2	186.1	199.0	211.9	233.9

Source: CSO, UK National Accounts.

Table 20-10 Growth rates of real GNP and population 1970–1979
(Per cent per year)

	(1) REAL GNP GROWTH	(2) POPULATION GROWTH	(3) PER CAPITA REAL GNP GROWTH
Mexico	5.4	3.5	1.8
United States	3.5	0.9	2.6
West Germany	2.9	0.1	2.8

Source: IMF, *International Financial Statistics.*

A More Comprehensive Measure of GNP

Because we use GNP to measure the production of goods and services in the economy, it is desirable that the coverage of the GNP accounts should be as comprehensive as possible. In practice, we encounter two problems in including all production in GNP. First, some outputs, such as noise, pollution, and congestion, are nuisances. We should make an adjustment for these 'bads' by subtracting from the traditional GNP measure an allowance for all the nuisance goods created during the production process. This is a perfectly sensible suggestion but it is almost impossible to implement. These nuisance goods are not traded through markets, so it is hard to quantify the level of their output or the costs they impose on society.

There are also many valuable goods and services excluded from GNP, again because they are not marketed and therefore hard to measure accurately. These activities include household chores, do-it-yourself activities, and unreported jobs. Estimates of the value of these activities have been made, although they are necessarily highly speculative. Estimates of the size of the unreported economy range all the way from 3 per cent to 25 per cent of GNP.[5]

Net Economic Welfare   Deducting the value of nuisance outputs and adding the value of unreported and non-marketed incomes would make GNP a more accurate measure of economy's production of goods and services.

But there is another important adjustment that must be made if we are to use GNP as the basis for calculations of national economic welfare. People get enjoyment not merely from goods and services, but also from leisure time.

Suppose people in Leisuria value leisure more highly than people in Industria. Other things equal, people in Industria will work more hours and produce more goods and services. Industria will have a higher measured GNP. It would be silly to say this proves that people in Leisuria have a lower level of enjoyment. By choosing to work less hard they are revealing that the extra leisure is worth at least as much as the extra goods that could have been produced by working longer hours.

In 1972 Professors William Nordhaus and James Tobin of Yale University estimated a measured called *net economic welfare* (NEW), which adjusted GNP by deducting 'bads', adding the value of non-market activities, and including the value of leisure.[6] The value of NEW is larger than that of GNP, but on balance it is growing more slowly. Production of 'bads' (pollution) has been growing quickly, and leisure has not been increasing as rapidly as the output of goods and services. NEW estimates are of course still crude, but they remind us that GNP is far from being a perfect measure of economic welfare.

Because it is difficult and expensive to collect regular measurements on non-marketed and unreported goods and bads and to make regular assessments of the implicit value of leisure, real GNP inevitably remains the most commonly used measure of economic activity. Although

---

[5] The size of the unreported economy depends among other things on national attitudes to tax evasion. One attempt to estimate the size of the unreported economy is *The Hidden Economy in the Context of National Accounts*, published in 1981 by the Organisation for Economic Cooperation and Development (OECD) in Paris.

[6] William Nordhaus and James Tobin, 'Is Growth Obsolete?' *NBER Fiftieth Anniversary Colloquium*, Columbia University Press, 1972. Originally called the 'Measure of Economic Welfare' (MEW), 'NEW' was suggested by Professor Paul Samuelson.

far from ideal, it is the best measure we have that is available on a regular basis.

Summary

1   Macroeconomics is the study of the working of the economy as a whole. Inflation, unemployment, and growth are three of the most important macroeconomic issues.

2   To keep the analysis manageable, macroeconomics sacrifices aspects of individual detail to concentrate on the interaction of broad sectors of the economy. Households supply the services of factors of production to firms that use them to produce goods and services. Firms pay factor incomes to households, who in turn use this money to purchase the goods and services produced by firms. This process is called the circular flow of payments.

3   Gross domestic product (GDP) is the value of output of the factors of production located in the domestic economy. It can be measured in three equivalent ways: as the sum of value added in production, the sum of factor incomes including profits accruing to entrepreneurs, or the sum of final expenditure.

4   Leakages from the circular flow are those parts of payment by firms to households that do not automatically return to firms as spending by households on the output of firms. Savings and taxes net of subsidies are leakages from the circular flow. Injections are sources of revenue to firms that do not arise from household spending. Investment expenditure by firms, spending on goods and services by the government, and net exports are all injections to the circular flow. As a matter of definition or national income accounting, total leakages must equal total injections.

5   GDP at market prices values domestic output at prices inclusive of indirect taxes. GDP at factor cost measures domestic output at prices exclusive of indirect taxes. Gross national product (GNP) adjusts GDP for net property income from abroad.

6   National income is net national product (NNP) at factor cost. NNP is GNP minus the depreciation of the capital stock during the period. In practice, many assessments of economic performance are based on GNP since it is not always easy to measure depreciation accurately and the treatment of this item varies across time periods and across countries.

7   Nominal GNP measures output at current prices. Real GNP measures output at constant prices. Thus, real GNP adjusts nominal GNP for changes in the general price level as a result of inflation. The index of general prices used to make this adjustment is called the GNP deflator.

8   Per capita real GNP divides real GNP by the population. It provides a more reliable indicator of the goods and services available per person in an economy. However, this is only an average measure of what people get. The goods and services available to particular individuals also depends on the income distribution within the economy.

9   Real GNP and per capita real GNP are still very crude measures of national and individual welfare. GNP takes no account of non-market activities, bads such as pollution, and valuable activities such as work in the home. No allowance is made for production unreported by tax evaders. Nor does GNP measure the value of leisure.

10   Net economic welfare (NEW) attempts to make these adjustments to GNP to produce a more satisfactory indicator of national economic welfare. Since it is expensive, and sometimes impossible, to make regular and accurate measurements of all these activities, in practice GNP is the most widely used measure of national performance.

Key Terms

Macroeconomics
Inflation, unemployment, and economic growth
Circular flow of payments
National income accounting
GDP at market prices and at factor cost
Value added
Final and intermediate goods
Closed and open economy
Exports, imports, and net exports
Direct and indirect taxes
Government spending on goods and services
Transfer payments

Leakages and injections
GNP and national income
Depreciation
Net property income from abroad
Nominal and real GNP
GNP deflator
Per capita real GNP
Net economic welfare

Problems

1 Explain what is meant by each of the terms 'inflation', 'unemployment', and 'economic growth'. Table 20-4 shows that many countries have had higher inflation, higher unemployment, and lower growth since 1973 than in the years before 1973. Give four reasons why you think economic performance may have deteriorated since 1973. When you have finished Part 4 you can see if you still agree with the reasons you have given.

2 This question deals with the value added accounting. The table below shows final sales and purchases of intermediate goods by firms connected with car production:

	FINAL SALES	INTERMEDIATE GOODS PURCHASES
Car producer	1000	270
Windscreen producer	100	12
Tyre producer	93	30
Car radio producer	30	5
Steel producer	47	0

What is the contribution of the car industry to GNP?

3 GNP at market prices is £300 billion. Depreciation is £30 billion and indirect taxes are £20 billion. There are no subsidies. (a) What is the value of national income? (b) Explain in words why and how depreciation leads to a discrepancy between GNP and national income. (c) Explain in words why indirect taxes enter the calculation.

4 This question explores the argument that government spending on the police does not really contribute to GNP. (a) Suppose the crime rate falls

and the police force can be halved. Former police officers get jobs in private industry at (say) the same wage rate as police officers. Explain why there is no change in GNP. (b) Is society better or worse off? (c) What does this suggest about including police expenditure as part of GNP?

5 Suppose $GNP = 2000$, $C = 1700$, $G = 50$, and $NX = 40$. (a) What is investment I, (b) Suppose exports are 350. What are imports? (c) Suppose depreciation is 130. What is national income? (d) In this example net exports are positive. Could they be negative? Explain.

6 Consider an economy with the following data:

	NOMINAL GNP	GNP DEFLATOR
1990	2000	100
1991	2400	113

(a) What is 1991 GNP in constant (1990) prices? (b) What is the growth rate of real GNP from 1990 to 1991? (c) What is the inflation rate? (d) Suppose 1991 nominal GNP was 2240 with all other data above unchanged. What would 1991 real GNP be? What would the growth rate of real GNP be? Explain in words what is going on.

7 Explain why the following non-market activities should or should not appear in a comprehensive measure of GNP: (a) time spent by students in lectures; (b) the income of muggers; (c) the time spent by boxing match spectators; (d) the wage paid to traffic wardens who issue parking tickets; (e) dropping litter.

8 Common Fallacies Explain why the following statements are incorrect: (a) If a country concentrates its production on goods with a high selling price, it will automatically increase its national income. (b) Unemployment benefit helps prop up national income in years when employment is low. (c) A higher level of per capita real GNP is always a good thing. (d) In 1990 Crummy Movie earned £1 million more at the box office than Gone With The Wind has earned over the last 30 years. Crummy Movie is already a bigger box office success.

21

The Determination of National Income

Since 1960 real GNP in the UK has grown on average at about 2.3 per cent per annum. But there have been marked cycles around this rising trend in real GNP. Real GNP actually fell by 1 per cent between 1973 and 1975, then increased by 10 per cent between 1975 and 1979, then fell by 3 per cent between 1979 and 1981, then increased by 26 per cent between 1981 and 1989. And these are large fluctuations.

Technical words used by economists to describe the fluctuations – 'recession' and 'recovery', 'boom' and 'slump' – have passed into everyday language. One of the aims of macroeconomics is to explain why real GNP fluctuates as it does. In this chapter we start to analyse the forces determining the level of real GNP.

To construct a simple model, we ignore the discrepancies between national income, real GNP, and real GDP that are caused by depreciation and the net flow of property income from abroad. Henceforth, we use national income, total output, and GNP interchangeably. We begin by distinguishing *actual* output and income from *potential* output and income.

Potential output is the level of output the economy would produce if *all* factors of production were fully employed.

Potential output tends to grow smoothly over time as the economy's stock of factors of production increases. Population growth adds to the labour force. Investment in education, training, and new machinery gradually increases the stock of human and physical capital. Technical advances allow any given stock of factors to produce more output. Together, these trends explain why the UK has been able to

sustain an average growth rate of 2.3 per cent per annum since 1960.

We examine the theory of long-run economic growth in potential output in Chapter 30. For the moment we are more interested in why the economy's actual output can deviate from potential output in the short run. Since potential output changes only slowly, we begin with a short-run analysis of an economy with a given level of potential output.

Potential output is not the maximum output the economy could conceivably produce – if compelled to work 18 hours a day, doubtless we could all produce more. Rather, it is the output that could be sustained if every market in the economy were in long-run equilibrium. Every worker who wanted to work at the equilibrium wage rate could find a job, and every machine that could profitably be employed at the equilibrium rental for machinery was indeed being used. Thus, potential output includes an allowance for 'normal unemployment'. Some people don't want to work at the equilibrium wage rate, and, in a constantly changing economy, other workers are temporarily in between jobs. Potential output in the UK probably now corresponds to an unemployment rate of between 5 and 10 per cent.

Suppose actual output falls below potential output. Workers become unemployed and firms have idle machines or spare capacity. One of the key issues in macroeconomics is how quickly market forces will return output to its potential or full employment level. In microeconomics, when we studied a single market in isolation we assumed that excess supply would quickly put downward pressure on the price of that product, thus eliminating the excess supply and restoring market equilibrium. In macroeconomics, this argument cannot be taken for granted. Macroeconomics emphasizes how disturbances in one part of the economy induce changes in other parts of the economy which may feed back upon the first part again, exacerbating the original disturbance.

We cannot examine this important issue by *assuming* that the economy is always at its full employment potential output, for that would be to assume that the problem could never arise. Instead, we must construct a model in which departures from potential output are a logical possibility, examine the market forces that would then be set in motion, and thus form a judgement about the success or otherwise of market forces in restoring output to its full employment potential. That is the strategy we adopt in the ensuing chapters.

Thus we begin by studying a model with two crucial properties. First, all prices and wages are fixed at a given level. Second, at these prices and wage levels, there are workers without a job who would like to work and firms with spare capacity they would find profitable to use. Thus the economy has spare resources. Under these circumstances, we do not need to analyse the supply side of the economy in detail. Any increase in output and employment will happily be supplied by firms and workers until full employment is reached and both firms and workers are once more supplying as much as they would like.

Since, below potential output, firms will happily supply as much output as is demanded, the actual quantity of total output is *demand-determined*. It depends only on the level of *aggregate demand*, the total amount that people want to spend on goods and services in the economy as a whole. This is the essence of the model of income and output determination that we present in the next few chapters.

Of course, as soon as possible we shall want to relax the assumption that prices and wages are fixed. Not only do we want to study the important problem of inflation, but we also want to examine how quickly market forces, acting through changes in prices and wages, can eliminate the problems of unemployment and spare capacity. But first we must learn to walk. We postpone the analysis of price and wage adjustment until Chapter 26.

Until then, we focus on the demand-determined model of output and employment

first developed by John Maynard Keynes in *The General Theory of Employment, Interest, and Money*, published in 1936. Keynes used the model to explain the high levels of unemployment and low levels of output that persisted in most industrial countries throughout the 1930s in what we now call the years of the Great Depression. The unemployment rate was persistently above 10 per cent, and in both the UK and the USA it reached over 20 per cent in the early 1930s.

After the publicaton of *The General Theory* in 1936, most of the younger economists quickly became *Keynesians*, or followers of Keynes's approach. In the 1950s and 1960s this approach was challenged by a group of economists called *monetarists*, whose intellectual leader was Professor Milton Friedman. Monetarists argued, correctly, that, even if Keynesian analysis was helpful in understanding depressions, it did not provide a good explanation of inflation. As the name suggests, monetarists seek the explanation for inflation in the quantity of money in circulation. Today, most macroeconomics have absorbed the best of both approaches, though there remain extremists on both sides. With this hint of controversies to come, we now begin the task we have set ourselves in this chapter, to explain what determines the level of output in the short run and why it could deviate from its full employment potential.

21-1 The Circular Flow

In the last chapter we introduced the circular flow of income and payments between households and firms. Households spend money purchasing the output of firms. Firms pay factor incomes to households. In this chapter we build a simplified model of the interaction of households and firms. In the next chapter we extend the model by introducing the government and the foreign sector.

Since we assume output is demand-determined, the aggregate demand or spending plans of households and firms determine the level of output produced, which in turn generates the income from which households spend. Suppose households decide to save more of their income and spend less. Firms can now sell fewer goods and cut back on output and employment. But this reduces household incomes. With lower incomes, households will further reduce their spending. Output and employment will fall yet again.

Is there an end to this downward spiral? The Great Depression is evidence that the economy can spiral down far below its potential output. Fortunately, we can show the spiral cannot go on for ever. We now explain why.

21-2 Components of Aggregate Demand or Planned Spending

In the absence of the government and the foreign sector, there are two sources of demand for goods: consumption demand by households, and investment demand for new machines and buildings by firms. Using *AD* to denote aggregate demand, *C* to denote consumption demand, and *I* to denote investment demand,

$$AD = C + I \qquad (1)$$

We distinguish between consumption demand and investment demand because they are determined by different economic groups and depend on different things.

Consumption Demand

Households buy goods and services ranging from cars and food to cricket bats, theatre performances, and electricity. In practice, these consumption purchases account for about 90 per cent of personal disposable income.

> *Personal disposable income* is the income households receive from firms, plus transfer payments received from the government, minus direct taxes paid to the government. It is the income that households have available for spending or saving.

Given its disposable income, each household must decide how to divide this income between spending and saving. A decision about one is necessarily a decision about the other. One family may be saving to buy a bigger house; another may be spending more than its income, or 'dis-saving', by taking the round-the-world trip it has always wanted.

Many factors affect the consumption and savings decisions of each household and thus the aggregate level of planned consumption and planned savings. We examine these in detail in

Chapter 25. But to get started, a single simplification will take us a long way. We assume that, in the aggregate, households' consumption demand is larger the larger is aggregate personal disposable income.

Figure 21-1 shows the relationship between real consumption and real personal disposable income in the UK. Because the scatter of points lies close to the line summarizing this relationship, we can say that our simplification is a helpful one. Nevertheless, the points do not lie *exactly* along the line. Our simplification is missing some of the other influences on consumption demand which we take up in Chapter 25.

The Consumption Function   Figure 21-2 shows the relationship between desired aggregate consumption and total income that we assume in the rest of this chapter. It resembles the line fitted to the actual data in Figure 21-1 and is called the *consumption function*.

> The *consumption function* shows the level of aggregate consumption desired at each level of personal disposable income.

Recall from Chapter 2 that a function is simply a rule for going from a value of one variable to the corresponding value of another variable. The consumption function tells us how to go from personal disposable income to desired consumption.

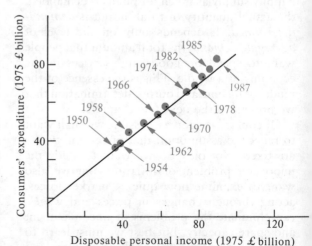

Figure 21-1   THE RELATIONSHIP BETWEEN CONSUMPTION AND INCOME. (*Source:* HMSO, *Economic Trends.*)

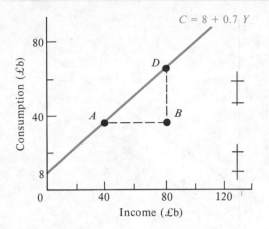

Figure 21-2   THE CONSUMPTION FUNCTION.
The consumption function shows the desired level of
aggregate consumption at each level of aggregate
income. With zero income, desired consumption is
£8 billion. This is autonomous consumption
unrelated to the level of income. The marginal
propensity to consume is 0.7. Of each extra pound of
income, 70 pence is consumed and the other 30
pence saved. At A, income is £40 billion and desired
consumption £36 billion. At D, income is £80 billion
and desired consumption £64 billion. When income
rises by £40 billion (from A to B) consumption rises
by 0.7 × £40 billion = £28 billion (from B to D).

Our simplified model has no government, no
transfer payments, and no taxes. Hence personal disposable income equals national income.
Figure 21-2 assumes this by showing desired
consumption at each level of *national* income.
The consumption function is a straight line,
and any straight line is completely described by
its intercept – the height at which it crosses the
vertical axis – and its slope – the amount it
rises for each unit we move horizontally to the
right. In Figure 21-2 the intercept is £8 billion.
We call this the amount of *autonomous*
consumption demand. By autonomous we
mean unrelated to the level of income. Households wish to consume £8 billion even when
income is zero.[1] The slope of the consumption

<hr>

[1] For example, we can think of this as the minimum
consumption needed for survival. How do households finance
this spending when their incomes are zero? In the short run
they dissave and run down their existing assets. But they
cannot do so for ever. This suggests that the consumption
function may be different in the short run from in the long
run, an idea we discuss more fully in Chapter 25.

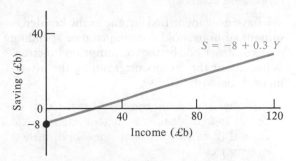

Figure 21-3   THE SAVINGS FUNCTION. The
savings function shows the amount of desired
savings at each income level. Since all income is
saved or spent on consumption, the savings function
can be divided from the consumption function or vice
versa.

function is called the marginal propensity to
consume.

> The *marginal propensity to consume* is the
> fraction of each extra pound of disposable
> income that households wish to use to
> increase consumption.

In Figure 21-2 the marginal propensity to
consume (*MPC*) is 0.7. If income rises by £1,
desired consumption rises by 70p.

Savings are the amount of income that is not
consumed. Figure 21-2 implies what when
income is zero, saving is −£8 billion. Households are dissaving, or running down their
assets.

Moreover, since 70p of every pound of extra
income is consumed, 30p of every extra pound
of income must be saved. The *marginal
property to save* (*MPS*) is thus 0.3. Since every
extra pound of income leads either to extra
desired consumption or to extra desired saving,
MPC + *MPS* must always equal unity. Figure
21-3 shows the *savings function* corresponding
to the consumption function in Figure 21-2.

In Figures 21-2 and 21-3 we write the
equations describing the consumption and
savings functions. The consumption function is
$C = 8 + 0.7Y$. When income Y is zero, consumption C is £8 billion. Each time Y rises £1,
C rises by £0.7. The marginal propensity to
consume is 0.7. The corresponding savings
function is $S = −8 + 0.3Y$. When income is
zero, savings S is −£8 billion. Each additional
£1 of income adds £0.3 to desired saving. The
marginal propensity to save is 0.3.

Investment Spending

We have now identified income as the key determinant of household consumption or spending plans as described by the consumption function. What about the factors determining the investment decision by firms?

> *Investment demand* consists of firms' desired or planned additions both to their physical capital (factories and machines) and to their inventories.

Inventories are goods being held for future production or sale.

Hence firms' demand for investment or additions to their capital depends chiefly on firms' current guesses about how fast the demand for their output will increase. There is no close connection between the current *level* of output and current guesses about how demand and output will *change*. Sometimes output is high and rising, sometimes it is high and falling. Since there is no close connection between the current level of income and firms' guesses about how the demand for their output is going to change, we begin our analysis of aggregate demand by making a simple assumption about investment demand, namely that it is autonomous.

Thus, at any particular time we assume that desired investment I is a constant amount, independent of the level of current output and income. In Chapter 25 we discuss investment demand in more detail.

21-3 Aggregate Demand

> *Aggregate demand* is the amount that firms and households *plan* to spend on goods and services at each level of income.

In our simplified model, aggregate demand is simply households' consumption demand C plus firms' investment demand I.

The Aggregate Demand Schedule

Figure 21-4 shows the *aggregate demand schedule*. In this example, the given amount I that firms wish to spend on investment is £22 billion. (Hereafter we omit the 'billions' and the pound sign.) Given the consumption function $C = 8 + 0.7Y$, the aggregate demand

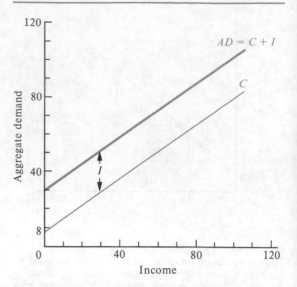

Figure 21-4   AGGREGATE DEMAND.   Aggregate demand is the sum of the amounts households plan to spend on consumption and firms plan to spend on investments. Since we assume that investment demand is constant, consumption is the only part of aggregate demand that increases with income. Vertically adding the constant investment demand to the consumption function C gives the aggregate demand schedule AD.

schedule AD is a vertical distance 22 higher than the consumption function at each income level. Since each extra unit of income adds 0.7 to consumption demand and nothing to investment demand, aggregate demand increases by 0.7. The AD schedule is parallel to the consumption function and the slope of both is given by the marginal propensity to consume.

We now show how aggregate demand determines the level of output and income.

21-4 Equilibrium Output

In our simplified model there is no government, no foreign sector, and no depreciation. National income, GNP, GDP, and personal disposable income are all equal. Firms produce output and pay out the proceeds to households as factor incomes.

Wages and prices are *fixed* and output is demand-determined. Whenever aggregate demand falls below its full employment level, firms are unable to produce as much as they would like. We say there is *involuntary* excess

BOX 21-1

MOVEMENTS ALONG THE AGGREGATE DEMAND SCHEDULE AND SHIFTS IN THE SCHEDULE

The aggregate demand schedule is a straight line whose position depends on its intercept and its slope. The intercept is the total amount of autonomous spending: autonomous consumption demand plus investment demand. The slope is the *MPC*. For a given level of autonomous demand, changes in income lead to *movements along* a given *AD* schedule.

The level of autonomous demand is influenced by many things which we examine in Chapter 25. It is not fixed for all time. But it *is* independent of income.

The purpose of the *AD* schedule is to separate out the change in demand directly induced by changes in income. All other sources of changes in aggregate demand must be shown as *shifts* in the *AD* schedule. For example, if firms get more optimistic about future demand and decided to invest more, autonomous demand increases and the new *AD* schedule is parallel to, but higher than, the old *AD* schedule. It crosses the vertical axis at a higher point, reflecting the increase in autonomous demand.

---

capacity. And workers are unable to work as much as they would like. There is *involuntary* unemployment.

We now require a definition of short-run equilibrium. We cannot use the definition that we used in microeconomics, namely the output at which both suppliers and demanders were happy with the quantity being purchased and sold. We now wish to contemplate a situation in which firms and workers would be delighted to produce more goods and supply more labour. Suppliers are frustrated. But we can at least require that demanders are happy.

> When prices and wages are fixed, the output market is in *short-run equilibrium* when aggregate demand or planned aggregate spending just equals the output that is actually produced.

Thus, spending plans are not being frustrated by a shortage of goods. Nor are firms producing more output than they can sell. In short-run equilibrium the output produced exactly equals the output demanded by households as consumption and by firms as investment.

Figure 21-5 shows income on the horizontal axis and planned spending on the vertical axis. It also includes the 45° line, which reflects any point on the horizontal axis on to the same point on the vertical axis. Beginning, for example, at the income level of 40 on the horizontal axis, we go vertically up to point B on the 45° line, then horizontally along to reach exactly the same value of 40 on the spending axis.

Now we draw in the *AD* schedule from

Figure 21.4. This crosses the 45° line at the point E. Since E in on the 45° line, we know that at E the value of income on the horizontal axis equals the value of spending on the vertical axis. Since E is the *only* point on the *AD* schedule that is also on the 45° line, it is the only point on the *AD* schedule at which income and desired spending are equal.

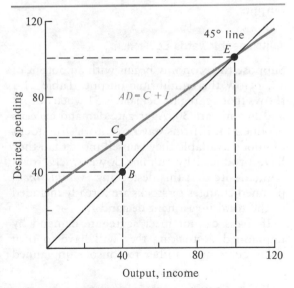

Figure 21-5 THE 45° DIAGRAM AND EQUILIBRIUM OUTPUT. The 45° line reflects any value on the horizontal axis on to the same value on the vertical axis. From an income of 40 we go vertically up to point B and horizontally along to a spending of 40. The point E, at which the *AD* schedule crosses the 45° line, is the only point at which aggregate demand *AD* is equal to income. Hence E is the equilibrium point at which planned spending equals actual output and actual income.

Hence Figure 21-5 shows that equilibrium output will be at the point E. Firms are producing 100. That output in turn is equal to income. At an income level of 100 we can read from the AD schedule that the demand for goods is equal to 100. At E the planned spending on goods or the demand for goods is exactly equal to the quantity being produced.

At any output level other than 100 in Figure 21-5 output is not equal to aggregate demand. Suppose output is only 40. Since output and income are always equal, income is also 40. Since the consumption function is $C = 8 \times 0.7Y$, consumption demand is $8 + (0.7 \times 40) = 8 + 28 = 36$. But investment demand is always 22; aggregate demand is 58; and output now is only 40. There is excess demand, and spending plans cannot be realized at this output level.

Indeed, Figure 21-5 shows that, for all output levels below the equilibrium level of 100, planned spending or aggregate demand will exceed income and output. The AD schedule lies *above* the 45° line along which spending and output would be equal. Conversely, at all outputs above the equilibrium level of 100, aggregate demand will be less than income and output.

Adjustment towards Equilibrium

Suppose the economy begins with an output of 30, below the equilibrium output. Table 21-1 shows that aggregate demand is 51 when output and income are 30. Aggregate demand exceeds production. If firms have inventories or stocks of goods available they can sell more than they have produced by running down stocks for a while. Note that this destocking is *unplanned*; planned changes of stocks are already included in the total investment demand I.

If firms cannot meet aggregate demand by unplanned destocking they will have to turn away customers. Either response – unplanned

destocking or turning away customers – is likely to act as a signal to firms that they should increase their output levels. Thus the first row of Table 21-1 shows how firms react when output is 30 but aggregate demand is 51.

Any *any* output level below 100, aggregate demand exceeds output. Firms are making unplanned reductions in stocks, turning away customers, and acting on these signals by making plans to raise output levels in future periods. Whenever output is below its equilibrium level firms get signals to start raising their output.

The fourth row of Table 21-1 illustrates what happens when output is initially above its equilibrium level. Output now exceeds aggregate demand. Firms cannot sell all they have produced and have to make *unplanned* additions to inventories. Firms respond by making plans to start cutting their output levels.

Hence, when output is below its equilibrium level, firms have an incentive to start raising output. When output is above its equilibrium level, firms have an incentive to start reducing output. As the third row of Table 21-1 shows, when output is at its equilibrium level of 100, firms are selling all their output and making no unplanned changes to their stocks. There is no incentive to change output levels.

Equilibrium Output and Employment

In this example the equilibrium level of income and output is 100. Firms are selling all the goods they produce and households and firms are able to buy all the goods they want. But there is nothing in our analysis that guarantees that 100 is the level of full employment or potential output.

The whole point of our analysis is that the economy can end up with an output level below potential without any forces being present to move output towards the potential level. Firms have no incentive to hire unemployed workers

Table 21-1 Aggregate demand and output adjustment

Y	I	$C = 8 + 0.7Y$	$AD = C + I$	$Y - AD$	UNPLANNED STOCKS	OUTPUT
30	22	29	51	−21	Falling	Rising
80	22	64	86	− 6	Falling	Rising
100	22	78	100	0	Zero	Constant
120	22	92	114	+14	Rising	Falling

since there is no prospect of increasing the level of output beyond its existing level of 100. At the given level of prices and wages, the lack of aggregate demand stands in the way of an expansion of output to the full-employment level.

21-5 Another Approach: Planned Savings Equals Planned Investment

Figure 21-5 and Table 21-1 shows that equilibrium income equals planned investment plus planned consumption. Equivalently, planned investment equals equilibrium income minus planned consumption.

$$I = Y - C \qquad (2)$$

However, planned savings S are the part of income Y not devoted to planned consumption C. Thus $S = Y - C$. Using equation (2) we see that equilibrium occurs at the point where planned investment equals planned savings:

$$I = S \qquad (3)$$

In modern economics, it is firms that make investment decisions, and the managers of these firms are not the same decision-units as the complete group of households making savings and consumption plans. But household plans depend on the level of income. Equation (3) says that the equilibrium level of income and output will be that level that just makes households plan to save as much as firms are planning to invest.

Figure 21-6 shows how this works out. Using the same data as in Figure 21-5, we know that, since the consumption function is $C = 8 + 0.7Y$, the savings function must be $S = -8 + 0.3Y$. Since planned investment I is 22 whatever the level of income, the equilibrium level of income that makes planned savings equal to planned investment is $Y = 100$, exactly as in Figure 21-5.

If income exceeds its equilibrium level of 100, households want to save more than firms want to invest. But saving is the part of income that is not consumed. Thus, households are not planning enough consumption, together with firms' investment plans, to purchase the total amount of output being produced. Unplanned inventories will pile up and firms will start to reduce output. Conversely, when output is below its equilibrium level, planned investment exceeds planned savings. Together, planned consumption and planned investment exceed actual output. Firms are making unplanned inventory reductions and starting to increase output. Either way, output tends to adjust towards its equilibrium level of 100.

Rather than think about savings and investment in the abstract, it makes sense to think of households saving by making loans to firms, and firms having to borrow from households to pay for the investment goods they buy. We can think of savings as the amount of loans that households want to make to firms and investment as the amount that firms want to borrow from households. At the equilibrium level, the amount firms want to borrow is equal to the amount households want to lend.

Figure 21-6 EQUILIBRIUM OUTPUT AT THE LEVEL AT WHICH PLANNED INVESTMENT EQUALS PLANNED SAVINGS. The equilibrium output level is 100, at which planned investment equals planned savings. The figure presents another way of viewing the determination of the equilibrium output in Figure 21-5. Planned investment is 22, as in Figure 21-5. The savings function $S = -8 + 0.3Y$ is implied by the consumption function in that figure. To the right of E, households plan to save more than firms plan to invest. Excess savings and deficient consumption demand cause unplanned stockbuilding, and firms cut production. To the left of E, households save less than firms want to invest. Stocks are being run down and firms increase output.

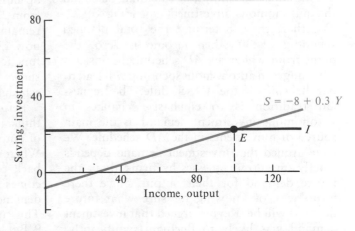

A Pitfall: Remembering the Distinction between Planned and Actual

We have shown that the equilibrium level of output and income will satisfy one of two equivalent conditions. Aggregate demand must equal income and output. In other words, planned consumption plus planned investment must equal actual income, output, and spending. Equivalently, planned investment must equal planned savings.

In the last chapter we showed that *actual* investment is *always* equal to *actual* savings, purely as a consequence of our national income accounting definitions. When the economy is not in equilibrium, unplanned investment or disinvestment in stocks or unplanned savings (frustrated consumers) always ensures that actual investment, planned plus unplanned, equals actual savings, planned plus unplanned.

21-6 A Fall in Aggregate Demand

Figure 21-5 shows how to determine the equilibrium level of output for a particular aggregate demand schedule AD. What might lead to a shift in the AD schedule, and what would happen to the equilibrium level of output?

The slope of the AD schedule depends only on the marginal propensity to consume (MPC). For a given MPC it is the level of *autonomous* spending that determines the position of the AD schedule. Autonomous spending is spending unrelated to income. In Figure 21-5 there are two items of autonomous spending, the autonomous consumption spending of 8 and the autonomous investment spending of 22. Together, these determine the total planned spending of 30 when income is zero, the point from which the AD schedule begins.

Changes in autonomous spending will lead to parallel shifts in the AD schedule. The Keynesian tradition is to emphasize changes in autonomous investment demand as the main source of movements in the AD schedule. We have argued that investment demand depends chiefly on current guesses by firms about the future demand for their output. Since there is no way of knowing for sure what future demand will be, Keynes argued that investment demand was likely to fluctuate significantly,

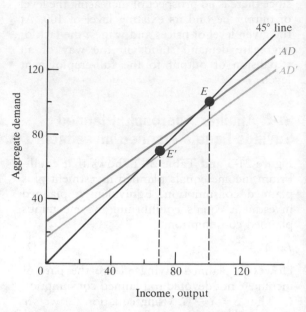

Figure 21-7   A FALL IN INVESTMENT DEMAND REDUCES EQUILIBRIUM OUTPUT. When investment demand falls from 22 to 13, the aggregate demand schedule shifts down from AD to AD' and is 9 lower at each output level. The equilibrium point moves from E to E'. Equilibrium output falls from 100 to 70. The fall of 9 in investment demand is multiplied into a fall of 30 in equilibrium output.

being strongly influenced by current pessimism or optimism about the future – what he called the *animal spirits* of investors.

Suppose firms became pessimistic about the future demand for their output. In consequence they reduce their current investment demand. Specifically, suppose planned investment falls from 22 to 13. Since autonomous consumption remains 8, the aggregate demand schedule is now 13 rather than 22 above the consumption function at each income level. Figure 21-7 shows this shift in the aggregate demand schedule from AD to AD'.

Before we go into the details, we want to think about what is likely to happen to the level of output. It will certainly fall, but how much? When investment demand falls by 9, firms cut back production. Households have lower incomes and in turn cut back their consumption demand. Firms cut back production again. Thus output will probably fall by more than 9. But how far will it fall, and what, if anything,

Table 21-2 Adjustment to a shift in investment demand

	Y	I	C = 8 + 0.7Y	AD = C + I	Y − AD	UNPLANNED STOCKS	OUTPUT
Step 1	100	22	78	100	0	Zero	Constant
Step 2	100	13	78	91	9	Rising	Falling
Step 3	91	13	71.7	84.7	6.3	Rising	Falling
Step 4	84.7	13	67.3	80.3	4.4	Rising	Falling
New equilibrium	70	13	57	70	0	Zero	Constant

brings the process of falling output and income to an end?

Figure 21-7 shows that a downward shift of the aggregate demand schedule by 9 reduces the equilibrium output level from 100 to 70. Equilibrium moves from E to E'. Although equilibrium output falls by considerably more than the reduction of 9 in investment, it does not fall all the way to zero. There is a new equilibrium level of output at 70.

Table 21-2 explains. Step 1 shows the original equilibrium from Table 21-1 with investment demand still at 22 and output at the equilibrium level of 100. In step 2 there is a drop in investment demand to 13. We assume that firms did not expect demand to change and therefore still produce 100. Output exceeds aggregate demand by 9. Firms add these goods to their inventories and respond by cutting back production.

Step 3 shows the firms producing only 91, the level that would just have met demand in step 2. But when firms reduce output, income falls. Hence step 3 shows consumption demand reduced to 71.7. This fall in consumption demand is caused entirely by firms cutting back output by 9. Since the MPC is 0.7, a reduction in income by 9 causes a reduction in consumption demand by 6.3, from 78 to 71.7. But this induced fall in consumption demand means that output at 91 still exceeds aggregate demand, which is now 84.7. Again inventories pile up, and again firms respond by cutting output.

At step 4 we assume that firms are producing enough to meet demand at step 3. Output is 84.7, but again this leads to a further reduction in consumption demand so output still exceeds aggregate demand. However, comparing steps 2, 3, and 4, we can see that the excess of output over aggregate demand is gradually getting smaller. The process will keep going until it reaches the new equilibrium, an output level of 70. Only at that level does aggregate demand equal output. There is no unplanned stock-building and output is therefore being kept constant.

How long does it take for the economy to reach the new equilibrium? That depends on how well firms can figure out what is going on during the process. If they mechanically produce during each period to meet the level of demand they saw in the previous period, it can take a long time to adjust. But smart firms will recognize that, period after period, they are producing too much and adding to unwanted inventories. They will start to anticipate that demand is still falling and cut back output much more quickly than Table 21-2 suggests.

Why does equilibrium output fall by a larger amount than 9, the reduction in investment demand? Because this fall in investment demand induces a reduction in income which then induces an additional reduction in consumption demand. Total demand falls by more than the original fall in investment demand.

The reduction in equilibrium output is exactly 30. Output does not fall for ever. To understand why not, we introduce the concept of the multiplier.

The *multiplier* is the ratio of the change in equilibrium output to the change in autonomous spending that causes the change in output.

In our example, the initial change in autonomous investment demand is 9 and the final change in equilibrium output is 30. The multiplier is thus (30/9) = 3.33. We now examine the multiplier in more detail.

21-7 The Multiplier

The multiplier tells us how much output changes when there is a shift in aggregate demand. The multiplier is larger than 1 because any given change in investment demand sets off further changes in consumption demand. This gives us a clue about the size of the multiplier. It must depend on the marginal propensity to consume. The initial effect of a 1-unit increase in investment demand is to increase output and income by 1 unit. If the *MPC* is large, this increase in income will lead to a large increase in consumption and the multiplier will be large. If the *MPC* is small, a given change in investment demand and output will induce only small changes in consumption demand and the multiplier will be small.

To obtain the exact formula for the multiplier, we go through a series of steps like those in Table 21-3, which begins with a 1-unit *increase* in investment demand. In step 2, firms react to the increase in demand in step 1 by increasing output by 1 unit. Consumption rises by 0.7, the marginal propensity to consume times the 1-unit change in income and output. At step 3, firms increase output by 0.7 to meet the increased consumption demand in step 2. In turn, consumption demand is increased by 0.49 (the *MPC* 0.7 times the 0.7 increase in income) leading to step 4 to an increase in output of $(0.7)^2$ or 0.49. Consumption increases again and the process continues.

To find the value of the multiplier, we add together all the increases in output from each step in the table and then we keep going:

$$\text{Multiplier} = 1 + 0.7 + (0.7)^2 + (0.7)^3 + (0.7)^4 + (0.7)^5 + \ldots \quad (4)$$

The dots at the end mean that we keep adding terms such as $(0.7)^6$ and so on. The right-hand side of equation (4) is called a geometric series. Each term is (0.7) times the previous term. Fortunately, we do not have to keep adding

these up indefinitely. Mathematicians have shown that there is a general formula for the sum of all the terms in such a series. It is given by

$$\text{Multiplier} = \frac{1}{1 - 0.7} \quad (5)$$

Since the formula applies whatever the (constant) value of *MPC*, it is useful to remember that the multiplier will always be given by

$$\text{Multiplier} = \frac{1}{1 - MPC} \quad (6)$$

For the particular value of 0.7 for the *MPC*, equation (5) tells us that the multiplier equals $1/(0.3) = 3.33$. Hence an initial reduction in investment demand by 9 will lead to a final reduction in equilibrium output by $(9 \times 3.33) = 30$, as Figure 21-7 confirms.

The marginal propensity to consume tells how much of each additional unit of income is spent on consumption. Thus the marginal propensity to consume will usually be a number between zero and unity. The higher the *MPC*, the lower will be $(1 - MPC)$. Dividing 1 by a smaller number leads to a larger answer; dividing 1 by 0.3 yields 3.33, whereas dividing 1 by 0.5 yields only 2. Hence the general formula for the multiplier shown in equation (6) confirms that the larger the *MPC*, the larger will be the value of the multiplier.

The Multiplier and the *MPS* Any part of an extra unit of income not spent on extra consumption must be spent on extra savings. Hence $(1 - MPC)$ equals *MPS*, the marginal propensity to save. Equation (6) says that we can think of the multiplier as $1/MPS$. The higher the marginal propensity to save, the more of each extra unit of income leaks out of the circular flow into savings and the less goes back round the circular flow to generate further increases in aggregate demand, output, and income.

Table 21-3 Calculating the multiplier

CHANGE IN	Step 1	Step 2	Step 3	Step 4	Step 5	.	.	.
I	1	0	0	0	0	.	.	.
Y	0	1	0.7	$(0.7)^2$	$(0.7)^3$	.	.	.
C	0	0.7	$(0.7)^2$	$(0.7)^3$	$(0.7)^4$	.	.	.

21-8 The Paradox of Thrift

In the previous section we used our model of income determination to investigate the effect of a parallel shift in the aggregate demand schedule caused by a change in autonomous investment demand. We now investigate the effect of a parallel shift in the aggregate demand schedule caused by a change in the autonomous component of planned consumption and savings.

Previously, we have assumed that at zero income households would plan to consume 8, which they would finance by a corresponding dissaving of 8. Hence we showed the consumption function beginning at a height of $+8$ and the savings function beginning at a height of -8. Suppose households decide they now wish to save 12 *less* at each level of income. Equivalently, they wish to consume 12 more at each income level. Figure 21-8 shows the savings function shifting down from SA to SA' and the consumption function shifting from CC to CC'.

What happens to the *actual* level of savings when households want to save less? Figure 21-9 shows that the aggregate demand schedule shifts up by 12 from AD to AD' because of the corresponding upward shift in the consumption function in Figure 21-8. The equilibrium shifts from E to E'. Equilibrium income and output increase from 100 to 140. The increase in autonomous consumption acts very much like an increase in autonomous investment. Since the marginal propensity to consume remains 0.7 we can use our previous analysis of the multiplier to say immediately that the change in equilibrium output will be 12, the change in autonomous consumption, times $1/(1-0.7)$ or 3.33, the multiplier. Thus equilibrium income and output increase by $12 \times 3.33 = 40$.

The new consumption function is $C = 20 + 0.7Y$. At the equilibrium income level of 140, consumption demand is 118. Hence savings is $140 - 118 = 22$. This should come as no surprise. We already know that in equilibrium planned investment equals planned savings. Since the level of investment demand remains at 22, the equilibrium level of planned savings must also remain at 22.

A change in the amount households wish to save at each income level leads to a change in the equilibrium level of income. There is

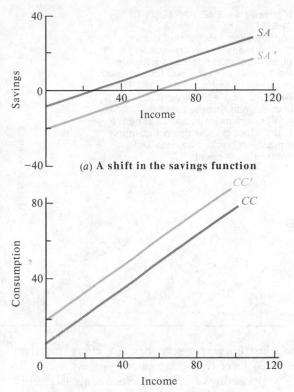

(a) **A shift in the savings function**

(b) **The equivalent shift in the consumption function**

Figure 21-8 A SHIFT IN THE CONSUMPTION FUNCTON AND IN THE SAVINGS FUNCTION. Households decide they want to save 12 units less, and consume 12 units more, at each income level. The savings function shifts down by 12 from SA to SA' and the consumption function shifts up by 12 from CC to CC'.

no change in the equilibrium level of savings, which must still equal planned investment. This is the *paradox of thrift*.

The paradox of thrift helps us to understand an old debate about the virtues of saving and spending. Does society benefit from thriftiness and a high level of desired savings at each income level? The answer depends on whether or not the economy is at full employment.

When aggregate demand is low and the economy has spare resources, the paradox of thrift shows that a *reduction* in the desire to save will increase spending and increase the equilibrium income level. Society will benefit from higher output and employment. And since investment demand is autonomous, a change

Figure 21-9 THE PARADOX OF THRIFT. The shift in the consumption function in Figure 21-8(b) leads to a corresponding shift in the aggregate demand schedule from *AD* to *AD'*. The equilibrium level of output rises from 100 to 140. Although households want to save less at each income level, equilibrium savings are 22 at both *E* and *E'*. Income rises to maintain the equality of desired savings and desired investment.

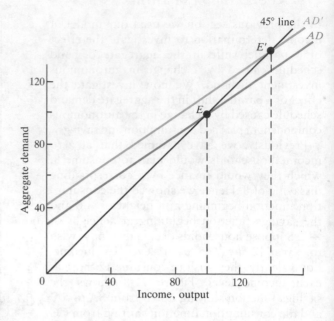

in the desire to save has no effect on the desired level of investment.

Suppose however that the economy is at full employment. In Chapter 26 we discuss how this might come about in the longer run once prices and wages have time to adjust. If the economy is in long-run equilibrium at full employment, an *increase* in the desire to save at each income level must lead to an increase in the level of savings at full-employment income. Consumption demand must fall and investment demand may increase to restore aggregate demand to its full-employment level. In the next few chapters we discuss the forces that could induce this change in autonomous investment demand in the long run. Hence, in the long run society may benefit from an *increase* in the desire to save. Investment will increase and the economy's capital stock and full-employment output level will grow more quickly.

In this chapter we have focused on the short run before prices and wages have time to adjust. Savings and investment decisions are made by different groups of people, and there is no automatic mechanism to translate a wish for higher savings into a corresponding rise in investment demand. Since planned savings depend on the level of income, it is income that adjusts to equate planned savings and planned investment.

Summary

1   Aggregate demand is the amount of planned spending on goods (and services). The aggregate demand schedule shows the level of aggregate demand at each income level.

2   In this chapter we neglect planned spending by foreigners and by the government. We focus on consumption demand by households and investment demand by firms. We treat investment demand as constant. Investment demand is firms' *desired* additions to physical capital and to inventories.

3   Consumption demand is closely though not perfectly related to personal disposable income. In the absence of taxes and transfers, personal disposable income and total income coincide.

4   Autonomous consumption is the desired consumption at a zero income level. The marginal propensity to consume (*MPC*) is the fraction by which consumption rises when income rises by a pound. The marginal propensity to save (*MPS*) is the fraction of an extra pound of income that is saved. Since income is either consumed or saved, *MPC* and *MPS* sum to 1.

5   For a given level of prices and wage rates, the goods market is in equilibrium when output

produced equals planned spending or aggregate demand. Equivalently, at the equilibrium level of income, planned savings equals planned investment. Goods market equilibrium does *not* mean that income is at its full-employment level. Rather, it means that planned spending is equal to actual spending and actual output.

6   The equilibrium level of output is demand-determined because we assume that prices and wages are fixed at a level that implies that there is excess supply of goods and labour. Firms and workers are happy to supply whatever output and employment is demanded.

7   When aggregate demand exceeds actual output there is either unplanned disinvestment (inventory reductions) or unplanned saving (frustrated customers). Actual investment always equals actual savings as a matter of national income accounting. Unplanned inventory reductions or frustrated customers act as a signal to firms to increase output when aggregate demand exceeds actual output. Similarly, unplanned additions to stocks occur when aggregate demand is less than actual output.

8   An increase in planned investment increases the equilibrium level of output by a larger amount. The initial increase in income to meet investment demand leads to further increases in consumption demand.

9   The multiplier is the ratio of the change in output to the change in autonomous demand which caused output to change. In the simple model of this chapter, the multiplier is $1/(1 - MPC)$ or $1/MPS$. The multiplier exceeds 1 because MPC and MPS are positive fractions.

10   The paradox of thrift shows that a reduced desire to save leads to an increase in output but no change in the equilibrium level of planned savings, which must still equal planned investment. Higher output is needed to offset the reduced desire to save at each output level.

Key Terms

Potential output
Consumption function
Autonomous consumption
Marginal propensity to consume (MPC)
Autonomous investment demand

Aggregate demand
Aggregate demand schedule
Savings function
Marginal propensity to save (MPS)
Multiplier
Animal spirits
Paradox of thrift
Equilibrium aggregate output

Problems

1   Suppose the consumption function is $C = 0.7Y$ and planned investment is 45. (*a*) Draw a diagram showing the aggregate demand schedule. (*b*) If actual output is 100, what unplanned actions will occur? (*c*) What is equilibrium output?

2   Suppose the *MPC* is 0.6. Beginning from equilibrium, investment demand then rises by 30. (*a*) How much does equilibrium output increase? (*b*) How much of that increase is extra consumption demand? (*c*) Construct a table like Table 21-2 to show how adjustments take place over time.

3   Planned investment is 150. People decide to save a higher proportion of their income. Specifically, the consumption function changes from $C = 0.7Y$ to $C = 0.5Y$. (*a*) What happens to the equilibrium income level? (*b*) What happens to the equilibrium proportion of income saved? Explain. (*c*) Using a savings-investment diagram, show the change in equilibrium output.

4   Which part of actual investment is not included in aggregate demand? Why not?

5   (*a*) Find the equilibrium level of income when investment demand is 400 and the consumption function is $C = 0.8Y$. (*b*) Would output be higher or lower if the consumption function were $C = 100 + 0.7Y$?

6   This question looks ahead to the next chapter. Suppose equilibrium output is below the full-employment level. We now recognize the government as a potential source of demand for goods. Can the government do anything to increase the equilibrium level of output?

7   **Common Fallacies** Show why the following statements are incorrect: (*a*) If only people were prepared to save more, investment would increase and we could get the economy moving again. (*b*) Lower output leads to lower spending and yet lower output. The economy could spiral downwards for ever. (*c*) A market economy cannot guarantee that savings and investment are equal. That is why we need central planning.

22

Aggregate Demand, Fiscal Policy, and Foreign Trade

Central and local government together buy about one-quarter of the total output of goods and services in the UK. Total taxes amount to more than one-third of GNP. Because government spending is a large component of aggregate demand, and because taxes affect the amount that households and companies have available for spending, government spending and taxation decisions have major effects on aggregate demand and output.

In this chapter we begin to analyse the macroeconomic impact of government fiscal policy.

Fiscal policy is the government's decisions about spending and taxes.

Having shown how to extend our basic model of income determination to include the effects of fiscal policy, we then take up three issues in fiscal policy.

Stabilization policy consists of government actions to control the level of output in order to keep GNP close to its full-employment level.

We analyse both the possibilities and the difficulties of using fiscal policy for stabilization.

The second issue is the significance of the government's budget deficit.

The *budget deficit* is the excess of government outlays over government receipts.

When the government is running a deficit, it is spending more than it is taking in. In the last forty years, 1969–70 and 1988–90 are the only periods when the UK government has not been in deficit. Deficits worry people. They wonder how and whether the government can keep spending more than it receives year after year without something terrible happening. We shall examine the size of the deficit and ask how much we should worry about it.

The government finances its deficit mainly by borrowing from the public through selling bonds, which are promises to pay specified amounts of interest payments at future dates. As a result of this borrowing, the government builds up its debts to the public.[1]

The national debt is the stock of outstanding government debt.

As deficits have continued year after year, the national debt has continued rising to apparently astronomical levels. By 1990 the UK national debt was well above £100 billion, or about £2000 per person. The third fiscal policy issue we examine therefore is the effects of the national debt.

Most of this chapter is about the government and aggregate demand. However, we know from Chapter 20 that GDP is not equal to $C + I + G$ but rather to $C + I + G + X - Z$. To complete our model of income determination we must add not merely the government sector but also the effect of foreign trade. Exports X and imports Z are each about one-quarter of UK GDP. The UK is a very open economy, and the effects of foreign trade are too important to be ignored even in a simple model.[2] Accordingly, we conclude this chapter by

---

[1] In the UK the government is responsible not merely for its own deficits but also for losses made by the nationalized industries. The public sector borrowing requirements (PSBR) is the government deficit plus the net losses of the nationalized industries. The public sector debt repayment (PSDR) shows the public sector surplus when the PSBR is negative.

[2] In contrast, net property income accounts for less than 1 per cent of GNP. We continue to ignore the net property income inflow from abroad and treat GNP and GDP as equivalent.

discussing how our model of income determination must be extended to include foreign trade.

22-1 The Government in the Circular Flow

Figure 22-1 shows how the government gets into the circular flow of payments which we discussed in Chapter 20. Government spending G on goods and services contributes directly to aggregate demand on the right-hand side of the figure. The government also withdraws money from the circular flow through indirect taxes T_e on expenditure and through direct taxes T_d on factor incomes (less any transfer benefits B through which the government augments factor incomes).

Although Chapter 16 presents more detailed numbers about actual spending and taxes in the UK, Table 22-1 provides a useful summary of government activity in 1989. The major components of direct spending on goods and services are the National Health Service and defence. Social security payments – state pensions, unemployment benefit, and supplementary benefit – and interest payments on government debt are the major components of transfer payments. Direct government spending G and transfer payments B were each nearly one-quarter the size of GNP.

The main sources of direct tax T_d are income tax and national insurance contributions to state schemes for pensions and unemployment benefit. Indirect taxes T_e include value added

tax (VAT), specific duties on tobacco, alcohol, and petrol, and the property taxes levied by local government in 1989 before the introduction of the poll tax.

22-2 The Government and Aggregate Demand

We now extend our model of income determination from the last chapter to include the government sector. Since it is somewhat cumbersome to keep distinguishing between GDP at market prices and GDP at factor cost, we shall assume that all taxes take the form of direct taxes. In the absence of indirect taxes, measurements at market prices and at factor cost coincide, as we explained in Chapter 20. Until the final section of this chapter, we continue to assume that we are analysing a closed economy and ignore foreign trade.

In this simplified model, aggregate demand AD equals consumption demand C, plus investment demand I plus government demand G for goods and services.[3]

$$AD = C + I + G \tag{1}$$

There is no automatic reason why government spending G should vary with the level of output and income. We assume that G is simply fixed at the level chosen by the government. This

[3] If you have forgotten why transfer benefits B should not be included in aggregate demand for goods and services, go back and read the part of Section 20-4 dealing with government spending.

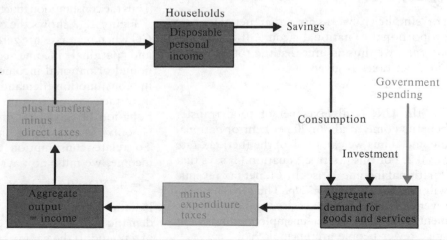

Figure 22-1 THE GOVERNMENT IN THE CIRCULAR FLOW. The government injects spending on goods and services into the circular flow but withdraws revenue from expenditure taxes and direct taxes on factor incomes. Household incomes are also augmented by transfer payments from the government.

Table 22-1 UK public sector revenue and expenditure 1989

REVENUE	£	EXPENDITURE	£b
Income tax	48.7	Social security	47.0
Tax on profits and oil revenues	22.5	Defence	20.6
Social security contributions	33.1	Health	20.0
Direct taxes T_d	104.3	Debt interest	17.7
		Other	92.4
Expenditure taxes	55.3		
Property taxes	20.1	GOVERNMENT EXPENDITURE	197.7
Indirect taxes	75.4	GOVERNMENT SURPLUS	5.7
Other taxes and government receipts	23.7	SURPLUS OF PUBLIC EXPENDITURE	1.4
GOVERNMENT REVENUE	203.4	PUBLIC SECTOR DEBT REPAYMENT	7.1

Source: HM Treasury, *Financial Statements and Budget Report 1990–91.*

level reflects how many hospitals the government wishes to build, how large it wants defence spending to be, and so on. Thus we now have three autonomous components of aggregate demand which do not directly vary with current income and output: the autonomous component of consumption demand, investment demand *I*, and government demand *G*.

The government also levies taxes and pays out transfer benefits. *Net taxes* are taxes minus transfers. Since we are assuming that there are no indirect taxes, net taxes *NT* are simply direct taxes T_d minus transfer benefits *B*. Net taxes reduce personal disposable income – the amount available for spending or savings by households – relative to national income and output. Letting *YD* denote disposable income, *Y* denote national income and output, and *NT* denote net taxes,

$$YD = Y - NT \qquad (2)$$

For simplicity, we assume that net taxes are proportional to national income. If *t* is the *net tax rate*, we thus assume that the total revenue from net taxes is given by

$$NT = tY \qquad (3)$$

For the UK, total taxes net of total transfer benefits come to about 20 per cent of national income. Thus we can think of the (net) tax rate *t* as 0.2. For this tax rate, equation (3) says that if national income *Y* rises by £1, net tax revenue will rise by 0.2 × £1 or 20p. The government's revenue from direct taxes rises and the government pays out less in unemployment benefit since fewer people are unemployed.

Disposable income *YD* is national income *Y* minus net taxes *NT*. Hence when the net tax rate is *t*, disposable income is related to national income by the formula

$$YD = Y - NT = Y - tY = Y(1 - t) \qquad (4)$$

Equation (4) tells us that households are allowed to keep only the fraction $(1 - t)$ of each pound of pre-tax income. When the net tax rate *t* is 0.2, or 20 per cent, households' after-tax or disposable income is only 0.8, or 80 per cent, of their pre-tax income *Y*. The other 20 per cent goes to the government.

We continue to assume that households' desired consumption is proportional to their personal disposable income. For simplicity, suppose that autonomous consumption is zero but that, as in the previous chapter, the marginal propensity to consume out of disposable income is 0.7. Households wish to consume 70p of each extra pound of disposable income. Thus the consumption function is now $C = 0.7YD$.

Figure 22-2 shows the consumption function *CC* when net taxes are zero. Disposable income and national income coincide. Each extra pound of national income leads to an increase in consumption demand by 70p. Now we introduce a proportional net tax rate *t*. Equation (4) says that disposable income *YD* is only $(1 - t)$ times national income *Y*. To relate consumption demand to *national* income, we must now write

$$C = 0.7YD = 0.7(1 - t)Y \qquad (5)$$

If national income riskes by £1, consumption demand will now rise by only 0.7 times $(1 - t)$ of a pound. If the net tax rate *t* is 0.2 and $(1 - t)$

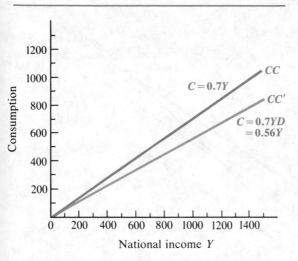

Figure 22-2 NET TAXES AND THE CONSUMPTION FUNCTION. In the absence of taxation, national income Y and disposable income YD are the same. The consumption function CC shows how much households wish to consume at each level of national income. With a proportional net tax rate of 0.2, households still consume 70p of each extra pound of disposable income. Since YD is now only 0.8Y, households consume only 0.7 × 0.8 = 0.56 of each extra unit of national income. Relating consumption to national income, the effect of net taxes is to rotate the consumption function downwards from CC to CC'.

is 0.8, consumption demand rises by only $0.7 \times 0.8 = 0.56$ pounds. Each extra pound of national income increases disposable income by only 80p, out of which households wish to consume only an additional 56p. Figure 22-2 shows this as the consumption function CC' relating the level of consumption demand to the level of national income.

In general, let MPC be the marginal propensity to consume out of disposable income and MPC' the marginal propensity to consume out of national income. With a proportional net tax rate t, disposable income will always be $(1 - t)$ times national income and MPC' will always be related to MPC by the formula

$$MPC' = MPC \times (1 - t) \tag{6}$$

Proceeding one step at a time, we now show how the introduction of the government affects the equilibrium level of national income and output. We start with an example in which autonomous investment demand $I = 300$ and the consumption function in terms of disposable income is $C = 0.7YD$.

The Effect of Government Spending on Output

First we assume that government spending G on goods and services is 200 but there are no taxes. National income and disposable income coincide. Figure 22-3 shows that an increase in government spending from zero to 200 has precisely the same effects as an increase in investment spending from 300 to 500. With the multiplier equal to $1/(1 - MPC) = 3.33$, an increase in government spending G from zero to 200 increases income and output by 666, or from 1000 to 1666. In Figure 22-3 that is shown as a move from equilibrium at E to equilibrium at E' when the aggregate demand schedule shifts from AD to AD'.

Thus, an increase in G leads to an increase in equilibrium output equal to the multiplier times the increase in G. This suggests that in a recession, when the equilibrium level of output is low, increased government spending on goods and services will increase aggregate demand and the equilibrium level of output.

The Effect of Net Taxes on Output

Now we ignore government spending and focus on net taxes. The *net* tax rate t is increased when the government raises direct tax rates such as the rate of income tax, or reduces the rate of subsidies such as unemployment benefit. Either way, the government's net tax revenue increases at each level of national income and unemployment.

Figure 22-2 shows that an increase in the net tax rate from zero to 0.2 causes the consumption function to pivot downward from CC to CC'. Its slope, the marginal propensity to consume out of national income, falls from MPC to MPC'. For any consumption function, the aggregate demand schedule is a higher parallel line because we add the constant investment demand to consumption demand at each income level. Hence Figure 22-4 shows that the rise in the net tax rate from zero to 0.2 leads the aggregate demand schedule to rotate from AD to AD'. The equilibrium point at which it crosses the 45° line – the point at which planned spending equals actual income and output – moves from E to E'. Equilibrium income and output fall from 1000 to 682.

Raising the net tax rate reduces equilibrium output and decreasing the net tax rate leads to a

Figure 22-3 GOVERNMENT
SPENDING AND EQUILIBRIUM
OUTPUT. Beginning from
equilibrium at E, government
spending G is increased from
zero to 200. AD shifts up to AD'.
The new equilibrium point is E'
and equilibrium output has
increased from 1000 to 1666. If,
instead of an increase in G, there
had been an equivalent increase
in investment demand I, the effect
on equilibrium output would have
been exactly the same.

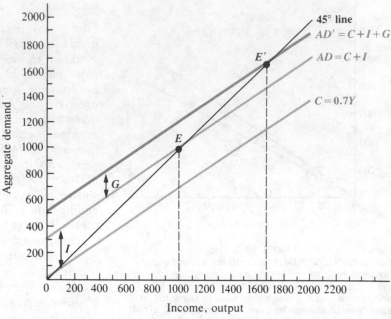

larger equilibrium output level. This suggests
that, when aggregate demand and equilibrium
output are below the full-employment level,
lower tax rates or higher rates of transfer
benefits will increase aggregate demand and
move equilibrium output closer to its full-
employment level.

The Combined Effects of Government Spending and Taxation

Next we put the two changes together.
Government spending increases from zero to
200 and the tax rate increases from zero to 0.2.
Investment remains at 300 and the MPC out of
disposable income is still 0.7. Of course, the
presence of taxation means that the marginal
propensity to consume out of national income
drops to 0.56.

Figure 22-5 shows that the introduction of
this tax and spending package increases the
equilibrium level of national income from 1000
to 1136.

The Balanced Budget Multiplier

The economy began at an equilibrium output of
1000. With a proportional tax rate of 20 per

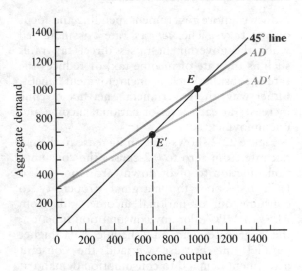

Figure 22-4 INCREASING THE NET TAX RATE.
An increase in the income tax rate or a reduction in
rate of unemployment benefit will increase the net
tax rate t. When the net tax rate increases from zero
to 0.2, the consumption function rotates from CC to
CC' in Figure 22-2. With constant investment demand,
the aggregate demand schedule is parallel to the
consumption function. Hence the aggregate demand
schedule rotates from AD to AD' in the figure. The
equilibrium level of output falls from 1000 to 682 and
the equilibrium point, where the aggregate demand
schedule crosses the 45° line, moves from E to E'.

Figure 22-5 THE COMBINED
EFFECTS OF HIGHER SPENDING AND
TAXES. Beginning from equilibrium at E,
government spending rises from zero to
200, shifting the AD schedule upwards, and
the tax rises from zero to 0.2, making the
new schedule AD' flatter. Whereas the AD
schedule has a slope of 0.7, reflecting the
original MPC, the AD' schedule has a slope
of only $0.8 \times 0.7 = 0.56$ because the
consumption function CC' in Figure 22-2
now has this slope, reflecting MPC'.
Equilibrium moves from E to E' where AD'
intersects the 45° line. Equilibrium output
increases from 1000 to 1136.

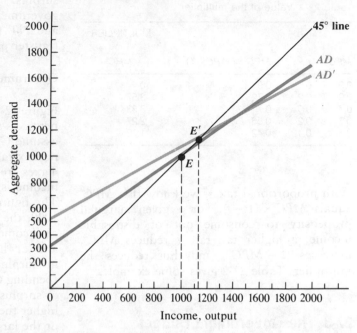

cent, the initial tax revenue was 200, precisely the amount of the government spending on goods and services.

A natural assumption would be that an equivalent increase in government spending and taxes would leave aggregate demand and equilibrium output unchanged. But Figure 22-5 shows that equilibrium output increases. The increase of 200 in government spending raises aggregate demand by 200. The tax increase reduces disposable income by 200. But since the MPC out of disposable income is only 0.7, this reduction in disposable income by 200 reduces consumption demand by only $140(0.7 \times 200)$.

Thus the initial effect of the tax and spending package is to increase aggregate demand by 200 because of government spending but to reduce aggregate demand by only 140 because higher taxes reduce consumption demand. On balance, aggregate demand is increased by 60. Output increases, and this induces further increases in consumption demand. When the new equilibrium is reached, output has risen a total of 136.

This example illustrates the famous balanced budget multiplier.

The *balanced budget multiplier* states that an increase in government spending accom-

panied by an equal increase in taxes results in an increase in output.

Higher government spending by 200 adds the full amount 200 to aggregate demand. An increase in the net tax rate which initially reduces disposable income by 200 does *not* reduce aggregate demand by the full 200. Changes in disposable income lead to changes in savings as well as consumption demand. Households reduce consumption demand by 140 and savings by 60. On balance, the government package adds to aggregate demand, causing output to rise. In turn, this leads to an increase in consumption demand and net tax revenue.

The Multiplier with Proportional Taxes

The multiplier relates changes in autonomous demand to changes in the equilibrium level of *national* income and output. The formula we worked out in Chapter 20 still applies, except we must now use MPC', the marginal propensity to consume out of national rather than disposable income. The multiplier is now given by

$$\text{Multiplier} = \frac{1}{1 - MPC'} \qquad (7)$$

Table 22-2 Value of the multiplier

MPC	t	$MPC' = MPC - (1 - t)$	MULTIPLIER $\dfrac{1}{1 - MPC'}$
0.9	0	0.9	10
0.9	0.2	0.72	3.57
0.7	0	0.7	3.33
0.7	0.2	0.56	2.27
0.7	0.4	0.42	1.72

With proportional taxes, we know that MPC' equals $MPC \times (1 - t)$. For a given marginal propensity to consume out of disposable income, a higher tax rate t reduces MPC', increases $(1 - MPC')$, and thus reduces the multiplier. Table 22-2 gives some examples.

22-3 The Government Budget

> A budget is a description of the spending and financing plans of an individual, a company, or a government.

The government budget describes what goods and services the government will buy during the coming year, what transfer payments it will make, and how it will pay for them. Usually the government plans to pay for most of its spending by making people pay taxes. When spending exceeds taxes, there is a budget deficit. When taxes exceed spending there is a budget surplus. Continuing to use G to denote government spending on goods and services, and NT to denote net taxes or taxes minus transfer payments,

$$\text{Government budget deficit} = G - NT \qquad (8)$$

Figure 22-6 shows government purchases G and net taxes tY in relation to national income. We assume G is fixed at 200. With a proportional net tax rate of 0.2, net taxes are equal to $0.2Y$. Taxes are zero when income is zero, 100 when income is 500, and 200 when income is 1000. The figure shows that at income levels below 1000, the government budget is in deficit. At an income level of 1000 the budget is balanced, and at higher income levels the budget is in surplus. Given the level of government spending G and the tax rate t, the budget deficit or surplus depends on the level of income. The higher the income level, the smaller the deficit or the larger the surplus.

The state of the budget surplus or deficit is thus determined by three things: the tax rate t, the level of government spending G, and the level of income. With a given tax rate, an increase in G will increase the equilibrium level of income. But in turn this will increase tax revenue. Is it conceivable that, by spending more, the government could increase the equilibrium level of income and tax revenue to such an extent that the budget deficit was actually *reduced* by higher spending? We now show that this is not possible.

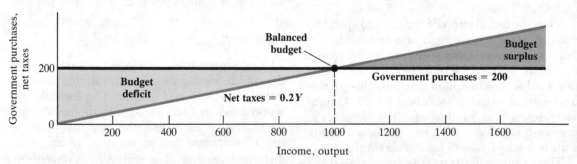

Figure 22-6   THE GOVERNMENT BUDGET.   The budget deficit equals total government spending minus total tax revenue, or government purchases of goods and services minus net taxes. Government purchases are shown as constant, independent of income, while net taxes are proportionate to income. Thus at low levels of income the budget is in deficit; at high income levels, the budget is in surplus.

Investment, Savings, and the Budget

In Chapter 20 we showed that, as a matter of definition, actual leakages from the circular flow of payments must always equal actual injections to the circular flow of payments. Payments cannot vanish into thin air. In the model we are now studying there are two leakages from the circular flow – savings by households and net taxes paid to the government – and there are two corresponding injections to the circular flow – investment spending by firms and government spending on goods and services. Thus *actual* savings plus *actual* net taxes must always equal *actual* government spending plus *actual* investment spending.

In the last chapter we saw that, when the economy is not at its equilibrium level of income, actual savings and investment will differ from *desired* or *planned* savings and investment. We saw how firms would make unplanned changes in inventories, and how households might be forced to make unplanned savings if demand exceeds the output actually available.

We defined the economy as being in equilibrium when all quantities demanded or *desired* are equal to *actual* quantities. Hence we can now say that, in equilibrium, planned savings S plus planned net taxes NT must equal planned government purchases G plus planned investment I. Planned leakages must equal planned injections.

$$S + NT = G + I \tag{9}$$

Notice that, in the absence of the government, this reduces to the equilibrium condition that planned savings equals planned investment which we used in the last chapter. Equation (9) implies that in equilibrium it is also true that desired savings minus desired investment equals the government's desired budget deficit.

$$S - I = G - NT \tag{10}$$

Equation (10) tells us immediately that an increase in planned government spending G must *increase* the budget deficit. Why? For a given tax rate, an increase in G leads to a parallel upward shift in the aggregate demand schedule. This certainly leads to an increase in the equilibrium income level. Provided the tax rate is less than 100 per cent, this must increase the equilibrium level of disposable income. Since households increase both desired consumption and desired savings when disposable income rises, some of this extra disposable income will go on extra desired savings.

Since desired investment I is independent of income, this increase in desired savings must increase the left-hand side of equation (10). Hence on the right-hand side of equation (10), net taxes NT cannot have increased by as much as the original increase in G. Equation (10) promises us that in equilibrium the budget deficit equals planned savings minus planned investment. Since higher government spending raises equilibrium output and planned savings, the induced increase in net tax revenues at the higher output level cannot fully offset the rise in government spending. The budget deficit must increase.

An increase in government spending on goods and services increases the equilibrium level of output. With a given tax rate, tax revenue rises. Nevertheless, the budget deficit increases (or the budget surplus falls).

We can analyse the effect of an increase in the tax rate in a similar way. We know from Figure 22-4 that a rise in the tax rate will cause the aggregate demand schedule to pivot downwards. The equilibrium level of income must fall. Disposable income falls both because the equilibrium level of national income has fallen and because the tax rate is higher. With a lower equilibrium level of disposable income, desired savings must fall.

Hence the left-hand side of equation (10) must fall. Equation (10) then promises us that net taxes NT increase, reducing the size of the budget deficit. Thus the higher tax rate more than compensates for the reduction in the equilibrium level of national income.

For a given level of government spending G, *an increase in the tax rate* reduces both the equilibrium level of national income and the size of the budget deficit.

22-4 The Deficit and the Fiscal Stance

In 1970 there were 600,000 people unemployed in the UK. Although this now seems a small number, it was higher than any unemployment level in the previous two decades and more than twice the level only five years earlier. The Heath government concluded that the UK was in a recession and that output was well below its full-employment level. To increase aggregate demand, taxes were cut. Between 1970 and 1973 taxes as a percentage of GNP fell from 37 to 32.3 per cent. In consequence the government budget, which has just been in surplus in 1970, was in deficit by £3.7 billion or 5 per cent of GNP by 1973, even though real output increased by over 13 per cent during this period.

This example shows the active use of fiscal policy to try to get the economy to operate close to its full-employment potential. When autonomous components of aggregate demand fall and the aggregate demand schedule shifts down, a fiscal stimulus can be used to raise aggregate demand again. We examine the use of fiscal policy to stabilize income and output levels in the next section.

First, we consider whether the size of the budget deficit is a good measure of the government's *fiscal stance*. Can we tell from the size of the deficit whether fiscal policy is *expansionary* and aiming to increase national income, or *contractionary* and trying to reduce national income?

The answer is that, in itself, the deficit is *not* a good measure of the government's fiscal stance. The deficit can change for reasons that have nothing to do with fiscal policy. Even though government spending and tax rates remain unaltered, if investment demands drops income will fall. In turn this will reduce the government's net tax revenue and increase the budget deficit. The government will take in less revenue from taxes and have to pay out more transfer payments such as unemployment benefit.

In particular, for given levels of government spending and tax rates, we expect the budget to show larger deficits in recessions, when income is low, than in booms, when income is high. Suppose aggregate demand suddenly falls. The budget will go into deficit. Someone looking at the deficit might conclude that fiscal policy was expansionary and that there was no case for further tax cuts or further increases in government spending on goods and services. But that would be wrong. The deficit exists because of the recession. It is not an argument against tax cuts or spending increases designed to restore aggregate demand to its former level.

One way in which we can use the budget deficit as an indicator of the fiscal stance is to calculate the *full-employment budget*. Suppose government spending is 200 and the tax rate is 0.2. As in Figure 22-6, the budget will be in deficit at any income level below 1000 and in surplus at any income level above 1000. If, given the other components of aggregate demand, the equilibrium level of income is 800, the actual budget will be in deficit. Net tax revenue will be 0.2×800 or 160. With government spending at 200, there is a budget deficit of 40.

However, in the last chapter we saw that the equilibrium output level is the level at which desired spending equals actual income and spending. Suppose the equilibrium output of 800 lies well below the full-employment output of the economy, say 1200. Would the government still be running a deficit if the other components of aggregate demand were higher and the economy was at full-employment output?

With output and income at 1200 and a tax rate of 0.2, net tax revenue would be 240. There would be a budget *surplus* at full-employment output. Looking at the deficit of 40 when the actual income level is 800, we might be tempted to conclude that fiscal policy is too expansionary and that the government should be raising taxes or cutting its spending levels. Once we realize that the main cause of the deficit is the low level of income, we are less likely to reach this conclusion. We might even argue that taxes should be reduced or spending increased despite the deficit in the actual budget, believing that when the economy returns to full employment, the deficit will disappear.[4]

Inflation-adjusting the Government Deficit

A second reason why the actual government deficit is a poor measure of fiscal stance concerns the distinction between real and nominal interest rates. In practice, published measures of the deficit treat the whole of the nominal interest paid by the government on the

----

[4] We should emphasize that in this chapter we are concerned only with the impact of fiscal policy on aggregate demand. There may be other reasons to worry about the consequences of a deficit. We examine these in more detail in Chapter 28.

national debt as an item of government expenditure. In fact, in a world with significant inflation, in which nominal and real interest rates may diverge considerably, it would make more sense to count only the *real* interest rate times the outstanding government debt as an item of expenditure which contributes to the deficit. Why?

Suppose inflation is 10 per cent, nominal interest rates are 12 per cent, and real interest rates are 2 per cent. From the government's viewpoint, the interest burden is only really 2 per cent on each £1 of debt outstanding. Putting the matter differently, although nominal interest rates are 12 per cent, even at constant tax rates inflation will inflate future nominal tax revenue at 10 per cent a year, providing most of the revenue required to meet the high nominal interest rates. Similarly, from the private sector's viewpoint, although bondholders are getting a nominal income of 12 per cent from the government, this represents a real return of only 2 per cent, and it is the latter that will determine the real value of the fiscal stimulus the government is providing via transfer payments in the form of debt interest to the private sector.

Thus, to interpret fiscal stance, it may be dangerous to look at the actual or simple government deficit. Table 22-3 gives data for the UK. The first column shows the UK public sector deficit as a percentage of GDP. It appears that the mid-1970s saw very high deficits which have gradually been reduced in the 1980s. This suggests that fiscal policy has been pretty expansionary. The second column shows the inflation-adjusted deficit

relative to GDP. The message is now radically altered. When we count the burden of real rather than nominal interest in the interest component of government expenditure, it turns out that the UK public sector has effectively been running a surplus during the 1970s.

The final column shows the consequences of adjusting the deficit both for inflation and for deviations from full employment over the cycle. It is the real full-employment deficit. This measure suggests that the fiscal policy was tight at the start of the 1970s and during 1980–83. It is not the conclusion we would have reached by looking at the simple deficit in the first column.

22-5 Automatic Stabilizers and Active Fiscal Policy

In Table 22-2 we showed that, for a given marginal propensity to consume MPC out of disposable income, the higher the net tax rate t the lower would be the marginal propensity to consume MPC' out of national income and the lower would be the multiplier. For example, when MPC is 0.7, the multiplier is 3.33 when the tax rate is zero but is only 2.27 when the tax rate is 0.2.

Suppose the economy is hit by a fall of 100 in investment demand. With a zero tax rate, equilibrium output will fall by 333. However, with a tax rate of 0.2, equilibrium output will fall by only 227. Similarly, if investment increased, the higher the tax rate the more damped would be the multiplier effect on equilibrium output.

Table 22-3 UK fiscal stance, 1970–84 (Public sector deficit as % of GDP, annual averages)

	ACTUAL DEFICIT	INFLATION-ADJUSTED DEFICIT	INFLATION AND CYCLICALLY ADJUSTED DEFICIT
1970–71	−0.4	−4.1	−4.2
1972–73	3.1	−0.4	−0.1
1974–75	6.5	−0.6	−1.2
1976–77	5.5	0.8	0.4
1978–79	4.6	0.2	0.0
1980–81	4.3	−0.2	−3.7
1982–83	3.2	0.2	−4.6
1984	4.0	1.6	−3.2

Source: D. Begg, 'UK Fiscal Policy since 1970', in R. Dornbusch and P. R. G. Layard (eds), *The Performance of the UK Economy*, Oxford University Press, 1987.

The proportional tax rate is an example of an automatic stabilizer.

Automatic stabilizers are mechanisms in the economy that reduce the response of GNP to shocks.

By 'shocks' we mean events such as the oil price increase in 1973, or a war. Shocks are likely to change the autonomous components of aggregate demand and shift the aggregate demand schedule.

Income tax, VAT, and unemployment benefit are important automatic stabilizers. Whenever income and output fall, government payments of unemployment benefits rise and government receipts of income tax and VAT fall. These factors help to ensure that the net tax rate is sufficiently high to reduce the size of the multiplier by a considerable amount. And this means that a given shift of the aggregate demand schedule will have a smaller effect on the equilibrium level of income and output.

Automatic stabilizers have one great advantage. They work automatically, without anybody having to decide they should go into effect. Nobody has to decide whether there has been a shock to which the government should now respond. And by reducing the responsiveness of the economy to shocks, automatic stabilizers help ensure that output does not fall to catastrophic levels. Problem 6 at the end of this chapter shows that, in an open economy, imports are another automatic stabilizer.

Active or Discretionary Fiscal Policy

Although automatic stabilizers are always at work, governments can and do embark on *active* or *discretionary* fiscal policies which alter spending levels or tax rates in order to stabilize the level of aggregate demand close to the full-employment output level. When other components of aggregate demand are thought to be abnormally low, the government stimulates demand by cutting taxes, increasing spending, or both. Conversely, when other components of aggregate demand are thought to be abnormally high, the government raises taxes or reduces spending.

In the UK, as in many other countries, the golden age of active fiscal policy to 'fine-tune' the level of aggregate demand was the 1950s

and 1960s. Output and employment were held close to their full-employment levels.

By now you ought to be – and probably are – asking yourself two questions. First, why can't fiscal policy be used to stabilize aggregate demand completely? Surely, by maintaining aggregate demand at its full-employment level, the government could eliminate booms and slumps altogether? Second, why since the mid-1970s have governments in the UK been reluctant to adopt an expansionary fiscal policy which might have offset the reductions in other sources of aggregate demand and prevented the rise in unemployment to over 3 million people? Box 22-1 provides some of the answers to these two questions.

22-6 The National Debt and the Deficit

The government's total outstanding debts are called the *national debt*. Where, as in the UK, the government is also responsible for the debts of nationalized industries, it is more interesting to consolidate debts of the government and debts of the nationalized industries and discuss the *public sector debt*. The public sector debt rises whenever the public sector runs a deficit, for then it must add to its borrowing to meet the excess of expenditure over receipts.

In Table 22-3 we showed that the UK ran large actual deficits in the 1970s. Hence we expect the nominal value of public sector debt to have increased sharply during the 1970s, and it did, from £33.4 billion in 1971 to £113 billion in 1981.

Yet Table 22-3 stressed that the public sector has effectively been running a real surplus for most of the last two decades, once the appropriate inflation-accounting is employed. This suggests that the *real* debt must have been falling, not rising. And this in fact is the case. Even if it were not, we should remember that, when the economy is growing in *real* terms, real tax revenue will be rising, and the public sector can service a growing real debt without having to increase *tax rates*.

These two arguments – inflation adjustment of the deficit and the growth of real incomes and the real tax revenue that will be raised at given tax rates – suggest that the UK debt may

BOX 22-1

THE LIMITATIONS ON ACTIVE FISCAL POLICY

WHY CAN'T SHOCKS TO AGGREGATE DEMAND IMMEDIATELY BE OFFSET BY CHANGES IN FISCAL POLICY

1 *Time lags* It takes time to recognize that aggregate demand has changed. It may take six months to collect reliable statistics on national output. Even then, it takes time to change fiscal policy. Long-term spending plans on hospital construction or on defence cannot be changed overnight. And once the policy change has been implemented it takes time to work through all the steps of the multiplier process shown in Table 21-2 before the full effect of the new fiscal policy is felt.

2 *Uncertainty* The government faces two major sources of uncertainty in deciding how much fiscal policy should be changed. First, it does not know for certain the values of key magnitudes such as the multiplier. It only has estimates obtained from past data. Mistakes in estimating the multiplier will induce incorrect decisions about the extent of the fiscal change required to change equilibrium output by a given amount. Second, since fiscal policy takes time to work, the government has to *forecast* the level that aggregate demand will have reached by the time fiscal policy has had its full effects. If investment is currently low but about to increase dramatically, it may be unnecessary to begin fiscal expansion today. Mistakes in forecasting non-government sources of autonomous demand, such as investment, may lead to incorrect decisions about the fiscal changes currently required. ·

3 *Induced effects on autonomous demand* Our simple model treats investment demand and the autonomous component of consumption demand as given. But this is only a simplification. Changes in fiscal policy *may* lead to offsetting changes in other components of autonomous demand. And if the government fails to estimate these induced effects correctly, fiscal changes will not have the expected effects. To discuss this important issue, we extend our simple model of aggregate demand in Chapter 25.

WHY DOESN'T THE GOVERNMENT CREATE A FISCAL EXPANSION WHEN UNEMPLOYMENT IS PERSISTENTLY HIGH?

1 *The budget deficit* When output is low and unemployment is high, the budget deficit is likely to be large. Fiscal expansion will make the deficit even larger. The government may refuse to undertake a fiscal expansion either because of worries about the size of the deficit itself, an issue we discuss in Section 22-6, or because of worries that a large deficit will lead to inflation, an issue we explore in Chapter 28.

2 *Maybe we're at full employment!* Our simple model assumes that there are resources that are involuntarily unemployed and would like to work. Output is demand-determined. Fiscal expansion will raise aggregate demand and output. Suppose however that we are in full long-run equilibrium at potential output. People are unemployed, and machines idle, only because they do not wish to supply their factor services at the going wages or rentals. Now there are no spare resources to be mopped up by a fiscally induced expansion of aggregate demand. If the government believes that high unemployment and low output are *not* the result of a fall in aggregate demand, but rather the result of a decline in the willingness to work or to supply output, it is likely to conclude that a fiscal expansion is pointless. Chapters 26 and 27 discuss the supply side of the economy and explore this argument in greater detail.

---

not be out of control. Although nominal deficits have dramatically raised the nominal debt, the ratio of nominal debt to nominal GDP may well have *fallen*. Table 22-4 confirms that this reasoning is correct. In fact, the debt/GDP ratio in 1984 was less than 60 per cent of its level 15 years earlier. Public fears of a UK debt explosion were completely misplaced. And of course since 1987, when the public sector has been running a surplus, debt repayments have been substantial.

Not only are public perceptions of the facts incorrect, but there are two theoretical reasons why concerns about the national debt may be overstated. First, the vast majority of UK debt is owed to UK citizens who hold government bonds. It is a debt we owe ourselves as a nation. Second, some of the money which the public

Table 22-4 UK national debt, 1969–89
(Net public sector debt as % of GDP)

1969	1973	1979	1984	1989
68.2	48.9	41.5	41.0	31.1

Source: as for Tables 22-1 and 22-3.

Table 22-5 Net public sector debt (% of GDP)

	1981	1990
Belgium	84	122
Italy	58	98
Netherlands	27	58
USA	19	29
UK	42	25
France	14	24
W. Germany	17	21
Japan	21	13
Sweden	−5	−1

Source: OECD, Economic Outlook.

sector has borrowed in the past has been used to finance physical investment or investment in human capital, which will raise *future* tax revenue and help pay off the debt. Prudent businesses sometimes borrow to finance profitable investment, and there is no reason why a prudent public sector should not do likewise.

Why, then, should a sensible economist worry about the scale of the public debt at all? Two reasons. First, *if* the debt becomes large relative to GNP, high tax rates may be required to meet the debt interest burden. High tax rates may have disincentive or distortionary effects.

Second, if the government is unwilling to raise tax rates beyond a certain point (perhaps because of the adverse effects mentioned above) or is unable to raise tax rates beyond a certain point (perhaps because businesses and rich individuals would then emigrate), a sufficiently large debt may lead to large deficits which the government can finance only by borrowing or printing money. Since borrowing merely compounds the problem, eventually the temptation to print money on a massive scale may become irresistible. That is how hyperinflations start. We shall discuss hyperinflations in Chapter 28.

While this theoretical possibility may lie behind public fears of large deficits and growing public sector debt, Table 22-4 makes clear that this has little practical relevance for the UK, where the debt burden has been falling steadily in recent decades. In this regard, the UK has been an exception. Apart from Japan, most other countries have run such large budget deficits that their debt has been growing faster than their nominal GDP. Table 22-5 shows that the public sector debt has now reached massive proportions in countries like Belgium and Italy. Such high debt levels are especially worrying at a time when real interest rates are higher than they have been for decades.

This completes our introduction to fiscal policy, aggregate demand, and the economy. We conclude the chapter by extending our model of aggregate demand and income determination to include the one sector we have so far neglected – foreign trade with the rest of the world.

22-7 Foreign Trade and Income Determination

In this section we take account of the economy's exports X, goods domestically produced to be sold to the rest of the world, and its imports Z, goods produced by the rest of the world but purchased by domestic residents. Table 22-6 shows UK exports, imports, and net exports $X - Z$. Two points should be noted.

First, net exports are very small relative to GDP. Roughly speaking, exports and imports are equal in magnitude. The UK has tended to have a roughly balanced trade with the rest of the world, although there was a sharp increase in the trade deficit in the late 1980s.

The *trade balance* is the value of net exports. When exports exceed imports the economy

Table 22-6 UK foreign trade, 1950–89
(Percentage of GDP)

	EXPORTS	IMPORTS	NET EXPORTS
1950	22.9	23.6	−0.7
1960	20.0	21.5	−1.5
1970	22.4	21.7	0.7
1980	27.4	25.1	2.3
1989	28.7	33.5	−4.8

Source: HMSO, Economic Trends.

has a *trade surplus*. When imports exceed exports, the economy has a *trade deficit*.

When a household spends more than its income, it dissaves, or is in deficit, and must run down its assets (in bank account or holdings of industrial shares) to meet this deficit. Similarly, when a country runs a trade deficit with the rest of the world, the country as a whole must sell off some assets to foreigners to pay for this deficit. In Chapter 29 we explain the mechanism through which this occurs.

Second, Table 22-6 shows that the UK is a very open economy, and increasingly so. Exports and imports have each grown from about 20 per cent of GDP in 1950 to about 30 per cent of GDP in the early 1990s. Over the same period in the United States, exports and imports have grown from about 6 per cent of GDP to about 12 per cent of GDP. Foreign trade is much more important for a country like the UK than for a country like the United States.

In Chapter 20 we explained that net exports $X - Z$ add to our income and expenditure measures of GDP. Accordingly, the equilibrium condition for the goods market must now be expanded to[5]

$$Y = C + I + G + X - Z \qquad (11)$$

What determines the desired levels of exports

and imports? We assume that the demand for our exports depends chiefly on what is happening in foreign economies. For a small country like the UK, the level of foreign income and foreign demand for our exports is largely unrelated to the level of income in our domestic economy. Hence we treat the demand for our exports as autonomous. At any particular instant it is at a given level but this level will change when demand conditions alter in the rest of the world.

Imports from the rest of the world may be raw materials for domestic production or items to be consumed directly by households, such as a Japanese television set or a bottle of French wine. Either way, demand for imports is likely to rise when domestic income and output rise. Figure 22-7 shows the behaviour of export, import, and net export demand as domestic income changes.

The export demand schedule is horizontal since export demand is independent of the level of domestic income. The level of desired imports is zero when income is zero but rises steadily as incomes rises. The slope of the

---

[5] Another way to write this equilibrium condition is $Y + Z = C + I + G + X$, which says that domestic output Y plus output Z from abroad equals final demand or final expenditure $C + I + G + X$.

Figure 22-7   EXPORTS, IMPORTS, AND THE TRADE BALANCE.   Part (a) shows the given level of exports at 50. Imports increase with the level of income. The diagram assumes a marginal propensity to import, shown by the slope of the import schedule of 0.2. The trade balance, the difference between planned exports and planned imports, is zero at an income level of 250. Imports and exports both equal 50. At higher levels of income, imports exceed 50 and there is a trade deficit. The net export schedule $X - Z$ in part (b) shows in a different way the difference between export and import demand.

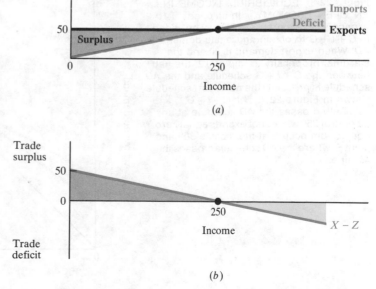

important demand schedule is called the marginal propensity to import.

> The *marginal propensity to import* (MPZ) is the fraction of each additional pound of national income that domestic residents wish to spend on extra imports.

The important demand schedule shown in Figure 22-7 assumes a value of 0.2 for the marginal propensity to import. Each additional pound of national income adds 20p to the desired level of imports. Many economists think that one of the problems facing the UK economy is that the marginal propensity to import MPZ is much higher than 0.2, so that any increase in national income leads to a large increase in the demand for imports. We shall return to this problem when we discuss in more detail the difficulties of government policy in an open economy.

At each income level, the difference between export demand and import demand is the demand for net exports. At low levels of income, net exports will be positive. There will be a trade *surplus* with the rest of the world. At high levels of income, there will be a trade *deficit* and net exports will be negative. By raising import demand while leaving export demand unchanged, an increase in income will reduce the trade surplus or increase the trade deficit.

Net Exports and Equilibrium Income

Figure 22-8 shows how equilibrium income is determined when foreign trade is introduced into the model. We start from the schedule $C + I + G$, which we described earlier in the chapter. Figure 22-7 shows that, at low income levels, net export demand is positive. Aggregate demand $C + I + G + X - Z$ will then exceed $C + I + G$. As income rises, import demand rises and the desired level of *net* exports falls. At the income level of 250, Figure 22-7 tells us that net export demand is zero. Thus in Figure 22-8 we show the new aggregate demand schedule AD crossing $C + I + G$ at an income level of 250. Beyond this income level, net export demand is negative and the aggregate demand schedule falls below $C + I + G$.

At a zero income level, Figure 22-8 shows aggregate demand equal to 150, made up of $I + G = 100$ and 50 units of export demand. We assume that the marginal propensity to consume out of national income MPC' is 0.7. Although we show that $C + I + G$ schedule with a slope of 0.7, we show the aggregate demand schedule AD with a slope of only 0.5. Why? Because although each extra pound of national income adds 70p to desired consumption, it also adds 20p to desired imports, since $MPZ = 0.2$. Since government spending and investment demand are both

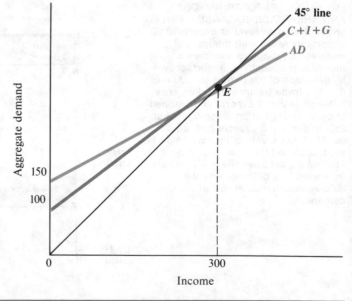

Figure 22-8 EQUILIBRIUM INCOME IN AN OPEN ECONOMY. In an open economy net exports $(X - Z)$ must be added to $C + I + G$ to obtain aggregate demand AD. When export demand is 50 and the marginal propensity to import 0.2, the gap between the $C + I + G$ schedule and the AD schedule is precisely the net export schedule shown in Figure 22-7. The $C + I + G$ schedule crosses the AD schedule at an income of 250 where net exports equal zero. Equilibrium occurs at the income 300 and point E, where the AD schedule crosses the 45° line.

constant, the extra 20p of desired imports must be going to meet consumption demand. Only 50p goes on extra demand for domestically produced consumption goods. Thus each extra pound of national income adds only 50p to aggregate demand and the *AD* schedule has a slope of 0.5.

In Figure 22-8 equilibrium occurs at *E*, where aggregate demand equals domestic income and output. Only at that point do planned spending and actual incomes and output coincide. The equilibrium level of domestic income is 300. Investment and government spending account for 100, exports are 50. Consumption is 210 (0.7 × 300), of which 150 is spent purchasing domestically produced goods. The remaining 60 (0.2 × 300) is important spending, which exceeds exports of 50. At the equilibrum output level, there is a trade deficit of 10.

The Multiplier in an Open Economy

The example of Figure 22-8 shows that each additional pound of national income raises consumption demand *for domestically produced goods* not by *MPC'*, the marginal propensity to consume goods from whatever source, but only by (*MPC' − MPZ*). Hence in an open economy, the formula for the multiplier must be amended to

$$\text{Multiplier} = \frac{1}{1 - (MPC' - MPZ)}$$

$$= \frac{1}{1 - MPC' + MPZ} \tag{12}$$

With a value of 0.7 for *MPC'*, the value of the multiplier in the absence of foreign trade would be 3.33. When the value of the marginal propensity to import is 0.2, the multiplier is reduced to 1/0.5 = 2. Higher values of the *MPZ* would reduce the value of the multiplier still further.

An Increase in Exports

An increase in export demand will lead to a parallel upward shift in the aggregate demand schedule *AD* shown in Figure 22-8. Hence the equilibrium level of income must increase. A higher aggregate demand schedule must cross the 45° line at a higher level of income. With a higher level of income, desired imports must

rise. The analysis of what happens to net exports is very similar to the analysis we used to show the effect of an increase in government spending on the budget deficit.

As a matter of national income accounting, total leakages from the circular flow must always equal total injections to the circular flow. And in equilibrium desired spending must coincide with actual income and spending on domestic goods. Hence the amended equilibrium condition for an open economy is

$$S + NT + Z = I + G + X \tag{13}$$

Desired savings plus net taxes plus desired imports must equal desired investment plus desired government spending plus desired exports. An increase in export demand *X* will increase the equilibrium level of domestic income and output. In turn, this will raise desired savings, and net tax revenue at constant tax rates, and desired imports.[6] Since *S*, *NT*, and *Z* all increase, we conclude that the increase in desired imports must be smaller than the increase in desired exports *X*. Hence an increase in export demand raises the equilibrium level of desired imports but still increases the desired level of net exports. The domestic country's trade balance with the rest of the world improves.

Import Spending and Employment

A common view is that imports steal jobs from the domestic economy. Final expenditure demand *C + I + G + X* is met partly through goods produced abroad rather than through goods produced at home. Thus, by reducing imports, we can create extra output and employment at home. This view is correct, but it may also be dangerous. It is correct because higher consumer spending on domestic rather than foreign goods *will* increase aggregate demand for domestic goods and therefore increase domestic output and employment. In terms of Figure 22-8, a reduction in the marginal propensity to import makes the *AD* schedule steeper and raises equilibrium income and output.

---

[6] Since tax rates remain constant, we can be sure that an increase in domestic income is accompanied by an increase in disposable income, and hence an increase in desired consumption and savings.

There are many different ways to restrict import spending at each level of output. In Chapter 29 we will begin the analysis of how the exchange rate affects the demand for imports (and exports). However, imports can also be restricted directly. For example, in the early 1980s we saw the United States imposing *import quotas*, or maximum quantities, on the amount of steel that can be imported from European or Japanese producers.

The view that import restrictions are always good for domestic output and employment ignores the possibility of retaliation by other countries. By reducing our imports, we cut the exports of others. If they retaliate by doing the same thing, the demand for our exports will fall. In the end, nobody gains employment but world trade disappears.[7] When the whole world is in a recession, what is needed is a worldwide expansion of fiscal policies, not a collective, and ultimately futile, attempt to steal employment from other countries.

Summary

1   The government enters the circular flow by purchasing goods and services, and by levying taxes (net of transfer benefits) which reduce disposable income below national income and output.

2   In effect, proportional taxes lower the marginal propensity to consume out of national income. Households get only a fraction of each extra pound of national income to use as a disposable income.

3   An increase in government purchases of goods and services increases aggregate demand and equilibrium output. An increase in the tax rate reduces aggregate demand and equilibrium output.

4   An equal initial increase in government spending and taxes raises aggregate demand and output. This is the balanced multiplier.

5   The government budget is in deficit (surplus) when spending is larger (smaller) than tax revenue. Higher government spending increases

---

[7] Some forms of import control may be less vulnerable to retaliation. We discuss more sophisticated proposals to limit imports in Part 5.

the budget deficit. An increase in the tax rate reduces the budget deficit.

6   In equilibrium in a closed economy, desired savings and taxes equal desired investment and government spending. Equivalently, any excess of desired savings over desired investment must be offset by an excess of government spending on goods and services over the net tax revenue.

7   The budget deficit is not a good indicator of the government's fiscal stance. Recessions automatically make the budget go into deficit. This does not mean that fiscal policy is being actively used to stabilize the economy. The full-employment budget calculates whether the budget would be in surplus or deficit if income were at its full-employment level. It is a better measure of the fiscal stance than the actual surplus or deficit. It is also important to inflation-adjust the deficit.

8   Automatic stabilizers reduce fluctuations in GNP by reducing the multiplier. Income tax, VAT, and unemployment benefit act as automatic stabilizers in a closed economy. Imports are another example in an open economy.

9   In addition, the government may also use active or discretionary fiscal policy to try to stabilize output. In practice, we should not expect active fiscal policy to be capable of perfect stabilization of output.

10   The national debt grows as a result of budget deficits. Since the debt is mainly owed to the citizens of the country, it may pose fewer problems for the economy than is often supposed. However, the national debt may be a burden if it makes it hard for firms to raise loans at reasonable interest rates or if the government is unable or unwilling to raise taxes to meet high interest payments on a large national debt.

11   Deficits are not necessarily bad. Particularly in a recession, any move to reduce the deficit might lead the economy further away from its full-employment output. But extremely large deficits create the possibility of a vicious circle of extra borrowing, extra interest payments, and yet more borrowing.

12   In an open economy, exports are a source of demand for domestic goods but imports are a leakage from the circular flow since they represent a demand for goods produced abroad.

13   Exports are determined mainly by conditions abroad and can be treated as autonomous spending unrelated to domestic income. Imports are assumed to increase in line with domestic income. The marginal propensity to import MPZ tells us how much of each extra pound of national income goes on additional demand for imports.

14   The marginal propensity to import reduces the value of the multiplier from $1/(1 - MPC')$ to $1/(1 - MPC' + MPZ)$.

15   An increase in exports increases domestic output and income. An increase in the marginal propensity to import reduces domestic output and income.

16   The trade surplus is the excess of exports over imports. The trade surplus is larger the smaller is the level of income. An increase in exports increases the trade surplus, and an increase in the marginal propensity to import reduces it.

17   In equilibrium, desired leakages $S + NT + Z$ must equal desired injections $G + I + X$. This means that any surplus $S - I$ desired by the private sector must be offset by the sum of the government deficit $G - NT$ and the desired trade surplus $(X - Z)$.

Key Terms

Fiscal policy
Stabilization policy
Budget deficit and surplus
National debt
Government spending and net taxes
Balanced budget multiplier
Full-employment budget
Inflation-adjusted budget
Automatic stabilizers
Trade balance
Net exports
Marginal propensity to import
Import restrictions

Problems

1   Suppose equilibrium output in a closed economy is 1000, consumption is 800 and investment is 80. (a) What is the level of government spending on goods and services? (b) Suppose investment rises by 50 and the marginal propensity to consume out of national income is 0.8. What is the new equilibrium level of C, I, G, and Y? (c) Suppose instead that G had risen by 50. What would be the new equilibrium of C, I, G, and Y? (d) Suppose full-employment output is 1200. By how much would G now have to be raised to get the economy to full-employment output?

2   (a) Explain why the multiplier is lower when there is a proportional tax rate. (b) Relate your answer to automatic stabilizers.

3   The government makes a transfer payment of £5 billion to the elderly. The income tax rate is 0.2 and the MPC is 0.8. (a) What is the effect of the transfer payment on equilibrium income and output? (b) Does the budget deficit rise or fall as a result of the transfer? Explain.

4   In equilibrium, desired savings equal desired investment. True or false? Explain.

5   Why does the government bother to raise taxes when it could borrow to cover its spending?

6   The MPC' is 0.8. MPZ, the marginal propensity to spend on imports, is 0.4. Suppose investment demand rises by 100. (a) What happens to the equilibrium level of income and the equilibrium level of net exports? (b) Suppose exports, rather than investment, increase by 100. How does the trade balance change?

7   The UK's trade partners have a recession. (a) What happens to the UK's trade balance? (b) What happens to the equilibrium level of UK income? Explain.

8   Common Fallacies   Show why the following statements are incorrect: (a) The Chancellor raised taxes and spending by equal amounts. It will be a neutral budget for employment and output. (b) Government policy should aim to balance exports and imports but ensure that the government follows the prudent example of the private sector in spending less than it earns. (c) To reduce the budget deficit by £1 billion it is necessary to cut government spending by £1 billion.

23

Money and Modern Banking

In songs and popular language, 'money' stands for many things. It is a symbol of success, it is a source of crime, and it makes the world go around. Economists use the word more precisely.

Money is any generally accepted means of payment for delivery of goods or the settlement of debt. It is the *medium of exchange*.

Dog's teeth in the Admiralty Islands, sea shells in parts of Africa, gold during the nineteenth century: all are examples of money. What matters is not the physical commodity used but the social convention that it will be accepted without question as a means of payment.

We now begin our study of the role of money in the economy. We explain why society uses money and how money helps us to economize on scarce resources used in the transacting process. By the end of Chapter 24 we will understand how modern banks play a key role in determining the total quantity of money in the economy and how the government, operating through profit incentives or direct controls on the banking system, seeks to control the quantity of money in the economy.

Before embarking on this detailed look at financial markets, it may be useful to indicate where this path will eventually lead us. As macroeconomists, we are interested in how the financial markets interact with the 'real economy', the markets for output of goods and inputs of factors such as labour. We begin by showing the relation between money and interest rates. Then in Chapter 25 we show how interest rates can affect aggregate demand and hence the equilibrium level of output and employment. In Chapters 26–28 we examine the relation between money, prices, and output. By then we shall be in a position to discuss the major issues of unemployment and inflation. And in Chapter 29 we discuss the relation

between money, interest rates, prices, and the exchange rate, showing how international competitiveness can affect the demand for exports and imports, and hence aggregate demand.

First, we must study the financial markets in some detail. We begin by asking why society uses money at all.

23-1 Money and its Functions

Although the crucial feature of money is its acceptance as the means of payment or medium of exchange, money has three other functions. It serves as a unit of account, as a store of value, and as a standard of deferred payment. We discuss each of the four functions of money in turn.

The Medium of Exchange

Money, the medium of exchange, is used in one-half of almost all exchange. Workers exchange labour services for money. People buy or sell goods in exchange for money. We accept money not to consume it directly but because it can subsequently be used to buy things we do wish to consume. Money is the medium through which people exchange goods and services.[1]

To see that society benefits from a medium of exchange, imagine a barter economy.

A *barter economy* has no medium of exchange. Goods are traded directly or swapped for other goods.

---

[1] For an interesting account of how cigarettes became used as money in prisoner-of-war camps, see R. A. Radford, 'The Economic Organisation of a POW camp', *Economica*, 1945.

In a barter economy, the seller and the buyer *each* must want something the other has to offer. Each person is simultaneously a seller and a buyer. In order to see a film, you must hand over in exchange a good or service that the cinema manager wants. There has to be a *double coincidence of wants*. You have to find a cinema where the manager wants what you have to offer in exchange.

Trading is very expensive in a barter economy. People must spend a lot of time and effort finding others with whom they can make mutually satisfactory swaps. Since time and effort are scarce resources, a barter economy is wasteful. The use of money – any commodity *generally* accepted in payment for goods, services, and debts – makes the trading process simpler and more efficient. Instead of having to find a restaurant that will give you a meal in exchange for your doing the washing up, you can get a job anywhere and subsequently use the money to pay for a meal; and the restaurant can sell meals in exchange for money without having to worry about what goods or services you could supply in return. By economizing on time and effort spent in trading, society can use these resources to produce extra goods or leisure, making everyone better off.

Other Functions of Money

The *unit of account* is the unit in which prices are quoted and accounts are kept.

In Britain prices are quoted in pounds sterling; in France, in French francs. It is usually convenient to use the units in which the medium of exchange is measured as the unit of account as well. However there are exceptions. During the rapid German inflation of 1922–23 when prices in marks were changing very quickly, German shopkeepers found it more convenient to use dollars as the unit of account. Prices were quoted in dollars even though payment was made in marks, the German medium of exchange.

Money is a *store of value* because it can be used to make purchases in the future.

To be accepted in exchange, money *has* to be a store of value. Nobody would accept money as payment for goods supplied today if the money was going to be worthless when they tried to buy goods with it tomorrow. But money is neither the only nor necessarily the best store of value. Houses, stamp collections, and interest-bearing bank accounts all serve as stores of value. Since money pays no interest and its real purchasing power is eroded by inflation, there are almost certainly better ways to store value.

Finally, money serves as a *standard of deferred payment* or a unit of account over time. When you borrow, the amount to be repaid next year is measured in pounds sterling. Although convenient, this is not an essential function of money. UK citizens can get bank loans specifying in dollars the amount that must be repaid next year. Thus the key feature of money is its use as a medium of exchange. For this, it must act as a store of value as well. And it is usually, though not invariably, convenient to make money the unit of account and standard of deferred payment as well.

Different Kinds of Money

In prisoner-of-war camps, cigarettes served as money. In the nineteenth century money was mainly gold and silver coins. These are examples of *commodity money*, ordinary goods with industrial uses (gold) and consumption uses (cigarettes) which also serve as a medium of exchange. To use a commodity money, society must either cut back on other uses of that commodity or devote scarce resources to producing additional quantities of the commodity. But there are less expensive ways for society to produce money.

A *token money* is a means of payment whose value or purchasing power as money greatly exceeds its cost of production or value in uses other than as money.

A £10 note is worth far more as money than as a 3 × 6 inch piece of high-quality paper. Similarly, the monetary value of most coins exceeds the amount you would get by melting them down and selling off the metals they contain. By collectively agreeing to use token money, society economizes on the scarce resources required to produce money as a medium of exchange. Since the manufacturing cost are tiny, why doesn't everyone make £10 notes?

The essential condition for the survival of

token money is the restriction of the right to supply it. Private production is illegal.[2]

Society enforces the use of token money by making it *legal tender*. The law says it must be accepted as a means of payment. However, laws cannot always be enforced. When prices are rising very quickly, domestic token money may be a very poor store of value and people will be reluctant to accept it as a medium of exchange. Shops and firms will give discounts to people paying in gold or in foreign currency, as in the later stages of the great German inflation in 1923. But such examples are the exceptions that proves the rule.

In modern economies, token money is supplemented by IOU money.

An *IOU money* is a medium of exchange based on the debt of a private firm or individual.

A bank deposit is IOU money because it is a debt of the bank. When you have a bank deposit the bank owes you money. You can write a cheque to yourself or a third party and the bank is obliged to pay whenever the cheque is presented. Bank deposits are a medium of exchange because they are generally accepted as payment. To examine how IOUs of private firms came to serve as money, we now turn to the development of the banking system.

23-2 Goldsmiths and Early Banking

The following story has some basis in fact and explains the role of banks. Once upon a time people used gold bullion as money. Wanting a safe place to store this bullion, people deposited it with goldsmiths – people who worked with gold and had guarded vaults for storing it safely – and picked it up when it was needed for making payments.

Banking

Two developments turned goldsmiths from safekeepers into bankers. First, people found

that, instead of physically handing over gold as a means of payment, they could give the seller of goods a letter transferring the ownership of the gold held by the goldsmith. This letter was what today we would call a cheque.

Once cheques became acceptable in payment of purchases, people felt that the gold at the goldsmith's was as good as gold in their pocket. To figure out how much money they had, people would count both gold in their pockets and gold held by the goldsmith.

The amount at the goldsmith's for safe-keeping was called a *deposit*.

People said their money holdings were the gold in their pockets plus their deposits. Since letters of gold ownership were more convenient to carry around than heavy gold, the invention of deposits made the payments system more efficient.

Second, and of greater significance, the goldsmiths noticed that they had a lot of gold lying idle in their values. People swapped titles of ownership much more frequently than they came to withdraw gold from the vaults.

The First Bank Loan

Suppose a firm asks a goldsmith for a loan. The goldsmith realizes some of the gold in the vault can be lent to the firm, which will eventually repay it with interest. Although the goldsmith is temporarily short of gold, it is unlikely that all the people who have previously deposited gold will suddenly ask for it back at the same time.

Table 23-1 shows what happens. Originally, the goldsmith simply had assets of £100 of gold in the vault and a corresponding liability of £100 owed to people who had deposited the gold. The second row of the table shows what happens when the goldsmith lends £10 in gold to a firm. The goldsmith's assets are still £100 but only £90 of this is now gold in the vault, while the other £10 is the value of the outstanding loan. Deposits still equal £100. The goldsmith expects to get the gold loan back with interest and is happy about the deal.

Lending a bank deposit   Since gold is difficult to carry around, the firm might be happier if, instead of borrowing physical gold, it can

---

[2] Society's success in raising the value of token money above its direct production cost is what provides the incentive for forgery of money. The existence of forgers is evidence that society is economizing on scarce resources by producing money whose value as a medium of exchange exceeds its direct production cost.

BOX 23-1

TRAVELLERS' TALES

The following contrast between a monetary and barter economy is reproduced from the World Bank, *World Development Report*, 1989.

LIFE WITHOUT MONEY

'Some years since, Mademoiselle Zelie, a singer, gave a concert in the Society Islands in exchange for a third part of the receipts. When counted, her share was found to consist of 3 pigs, 23 turkeys, 44 chickens, 5000 cocoa nuts, besides considerable quantities of bananas, lemons and oranges ... as Mademoiselle could not consume any considerable portion of the receipts herself it became necessary in the meantime to feed the pigs and poultry with the fruit.' W. S. Jevons (1898)

MARCO POLO DISCOVERS PAPER MONEY

'In this city of Kanbula [Beijing] is the mint of the Great Khan, who may truly be said to possess the secret of the alchemists, as he has the art of producing money ... He causes the bark to be stripped from mulberry trees ... made into paper ... cut into pieces of money of different sizes. The act of counterfeiting is punished as a capital offence. This paper currency is circulated in every part of the Great Khan's domain. All his subjects receive it without hesitation because, wherever their business may call them, they can dispose of it again in the purchase of merchandise they may require.' *The Travels of Marco Polo*, Book II

---

borrow from the goldsmith by being given a deposit. Today we should call this an overdraft. The third row of the table shows that happens initially when the goldsmith keeps all the gold but grants the firm a deposit of £10. Assets and liabilities are always equal but now both are £110.

Perhaps the borrower wants the loan to buy a carriage. The new deposit of £10 is used to pay for the carriage by writing a cheque. The last row of the table shows the goldsmith's balance sheet when the seller of the carriage brings in the cheque and asks for £10 in gold. Assets fall £10 as the gold is paid out, but liabilities also fall £10 because the borrower has used up the deposit. Notice that rows (2) and (4) of the table are identical. It makes no difference to the goldsmith whether the loan is initially in gold or in the form of a deposit or overdraft.

Reserves

People originally deposited £100 of gold, but, having made the loan, the goldsmith has only £90 of gold in the vault. If all depositors were suddenly to want their gold again, the goldsmith is unlikely to be able to get back at short notice the missing £10 of gold that has been lent out. As a banker, the goldsmith is relying on the fact that depositors will not all reclaim their gold simultaneously.

The *reserves* are the amount of gold immediately available to meet depositors' demands. The *reserve ratio* is the ratio of reserves to deposits.

The old-fashioned goldsmith in Table 23-1 has a 100 per cent reserve ratio. Depositors could be paid in full, making no loans, the goldsmith is making no profits from the lending business. The goldsmith–banker in the row (2) of the

---

Table 23-1 Goldsmiths as bankers

	ASSETS	LIABILITIES
(1) Old-fashioned goldsmith	Gold £100	Deposits £100
(2) Gold lender	Gold £90 + loan £10	Deposits £100
(3) Deposit lender: Step 1	Gold £100 + loan £10	Deposits £110
(4) Step 2	Gold £90 + loan £10	Deposits £100

table has a reserve ratio of 90 per cent. There is a small profit from lending out gold but only a small risk of being unable to pay depositors if some of them want their gold back. The lower the reserve ratio, the more the goldsmith is lending. Interest payments will be higher but, with less gold in the vaults, there will be a greater risk of being unable to meet depositors' claims for their gold back.

How much of the gold dare the goldsmith lend out? The more unpredictable the withdrawals by depositors, and the less able are borrowers to repay loans at short notice, the more cautious must the goldsmith be and the higher must be the reserve ratio. Conversely, the larger the interest rate, the more likely the goldsmith is to take a bit of a chance and the lower will be the desired reserve ratio.

Financial Panics

Everybody knows what the goldsmith–banker is up to. Most of the time people don't mind. Cheques are easier to use as a medium of exchange than gold. But if people believe that the goldsmith has lent too much, and will be unable to meet depositors' claims, there will be a *run* on the bank. If the goldsmith is not going to be able to repay all depositors, it makes sense to get your gold out first while the goldsmith can still pay. Since everyone is doing the same thing, they ensure that the goldsmith will be unable to pay. Whenever the goldsmith has lent at all, and the reserve ratio is less than 100 per cent, it is impossible to meet the claims of all depositors at once.

A *financial panic* is a self-fulfilling prophecy. People believe that the bank will be unable to pay. In the stampede to get their money out, they ensure that the bank cannot pay. It will go bankrupt.

Today, financial panics are rare.[3] One important reason for this, which we discuss in the next chapter, is that the Bank of England stands ready to lend to banks who get into temporary difficulties. And the mere knowledge that this is the case helps prevent the self-fulfilling stampede to withdraw deposits before bankruptcy is declared.

[3] For a highly readable account of the more spectacular panics, see Charles Kindleberger, *Manias, Panics, and Crashes*, Basic Books, 1979.

Goldsmith Banking and the Money Supply

The *money supply* is the value of the total stock of money, the medium of exchange, in circulation.

In our simple example, the money supply is gold coins in people's pockets plus the amount of deposits at the goldsmiths. Deposits are money because cheques against these deposits are accepted as a means of payment. Thus

$$\text{Money supply} = \text{gold in circulation} + \text{deposits at goldsmith} \quad (1)$$

Table 23-1 shows that goldsmiths' liabilities are always equal to their assets. Deposits are liabilities. Assets are gold in the vaults plus the value of loans. Thus we can write equation (1) another way:

$$\text{Money supply} = \text{gold in circulation} + \text{gold at goldsmiths} + \text{goldsmith's loans} \quad (2)$$

The total gold stock is gold in circulation plus gold in goldsmiths' vaults. Thus

$$\text{Money supply} = \text{gold stock} + \text{goldsmiths' loans} \quad (3)$$

The importance of this result cannot be overstated. *Loans by goldsmith–bankers increase the stock of money in the economy.* Go back to Table 23-1. When the goldsmith first lends out £10, the borrower received extra money. But nobody else had any less money than before. Existing depositors could still write cheques against the gold originally deposited. Essentially, the goldsmith took £10 out of the vaults and put it back into circulation. By making loans and putting gold back into circulation, the goldsmith increased the money supply.

Before leaving this example, we note two things. First, since the money supply is the gold stock plus goldsmiths' loans, the money supply is larger than the gold stock. Second, the money supply is larger the more goldsmiths lend. The lower their reserve ratio, the higher the money stock.

23-3 Modern Banking

The goldsmith bankers were an early example of a financial intermediary.

A *financial intermediary* is an institution that specializes in bringing lenders and borrowers together.

A *commercial bank* borrows money from the public, crediting them with a deposit. The deposit is a liability of the bank. It is money owed to depositors. In turn the bank lends money to firms, households, or governments wishing to borrow.

Banks are not the only financial intermediaries. Insurance companies, pension funds, and building societies also take in money in order to relend it. The crucial feature of banks is that some of their liabilities are used as a means of payment, and are therefore part of the money stock.[4]

Commercial banks are financial intermediaries with a government licence to make loans and issue deposits, including deposits against which cheques can be written.

We begin by looking at the present-day UK banking system. Although the details vary from country to country, the general principle is much the same everywhere. As we shall see, it is basically the principle discovered by the goldsmith–bankers in our example of the previous section.

In the UK, the commercial banking system comprises about 600 registered banks, the National Girobank operating through post offices, and about a dozen trustee savings banks. Much the most important single group is the London clearing banks.[5] The clearing banks are so named because they have a central clearing house for handling payments by cheque.

A *clearing system* is a set of arrangements in which debts between banks are settled by adding up all the transactions in a given period and paying only the net amounts needed to balance inter-bank accounts.

Suppose you bank with Barclays but visit a supermarket that banks with Lloyds. To pay for your shopping you write a cheque against your deposit at Barclays. The supermarket pays this cheque into its accounts at Lloyds. In turn, Lloyds presents the cheque to Barclays which will credit Lloyds' account at Barclays and debit your account at Barclays by an equivalent amount. Because you purchased goods from a supermarket using a different bank, a transfer of funds between the two banks is required. Crediting or debiting one bank's account at another bank is the simplest way to achieve this.

However on the same day someone else, call her Joan Groover, is probably writing a cheque on a Lloyd's deposit account to pay for some stereo equipment from a shop banking with Barclays. The stereo shop pays the cheque into its Barclays' account, increasing its deposit. Barclays then pay the cheque into its account at Lloyds where Ms Groover's account is simultaneously debited. Now the transfer flows from Lloyds to Barclays.

Although in both cases the cheque writer's account is debited and the cheque recipient's account is credited, it does not make sense for the two banks to make two separate inter-bank transactions between themselves. The clearing system calculates the *net* flows between the member clearing banks and these are the settlements that they make between themselves. Thus the system of clearing cheques represents another way society reduces the costs of making transactions.[6]

The Balance Sheet of the London Clearing Banks

Table 23-2 shows the balance sheet of the London clearing banks. Although more complex, it is not fundamentally different from the balance sheet of the goldsmith–banker shown in Table 23-1. We begin by discussing the asset aisde of the balance sheet.

Cash assets are notes and coin in the banks' vaults just as the goldsmiths held gold in their vaults. However, modern banks' cash assets also include their cash reserves deposited with the Bank of England. The Bank of England

---

[4] In fact, building societies now issue cheque books to their depositors. Although official UK statistics do not classify building societies as banks, this example illustrates the practical difficulty in deciding which intermediaries are banks and which of their deposits in practice are accepted as a medium of exchange.

[5] The big four – Barclays, Lloyds, National Westminster, and Midland – control about 90 per cent of clearing bank deposits in the UK.

[6] Society continues to find new ways to save scarce resources in producing and using a medium of exchange. Already many people use credit cards. Some supermarket tills directly debit customers' bank accounts. And shopping by TV and telephone is now possible.

Table 23-2 Balance sheet of London clearing banks, June 1989

ASSETS	£b	LIABILITIES	£b
Sterling: Cash	3.1	Sterling: Sight deposits	87.2
Bills and market loans	42.0	Time deposits	80.9
Advances	138.1	CDs (Certificates of deposit)	11.8
Securities	9.6		
Lending in other currencies	58.5	Deposits in other currencies	46.4
Miscellaneous assets	19.9	Miscellaneous liabilities	44.9
TOTAL ASSETS	271.2	TOTAL LIABILITIES	271.2

Source: Bank of England Quarterly Bulletin.

(usually known as the Bank) is the *central bank* or banker to the commercial banks. We discuss the role of the central bank in the next chapter.

Apart from cash, the other entries on the asset side of the balance sheet show money that has been lent out or used to purchase interest-earning assets. The second item, bills and market loans, shows short-term lending in liquid assets.

Liquidity refers to the speed and the certainty with which an asset can be converted back into money, whenever the asset-holders desire. Money itself is thus the most liquid asset of all.

We discuss liquidity further in Box 23-2.

The third item, advances, shows lending to households and firms. A firm that has borrowed to see it through a sticky period may not be able to repay whenever the bank demands. Thus, although advances represent the major share of clearing bank lending, they are not very liquid forms of bank lending. The fourth item, securities, shows bank purchases of interest-bearing long-term financial assets. These can be government bonds or industrial shares. Although these assets are traded daily on the stock exchange, so in principle these securities can be cashed in any time the bank wishes, their price fluctuates from day to day. Banks cannot be certain how much they will get when they sell out. Hence financial investment in securities is also illiquid.

The final two items on the asset side of Table 23-2 show lending in foreign currencies and miscellaneous bank assets whose details need not concern us. Total assets of the London clearing banks in June 1989 were £271.2 billion.

We now examine how the equivalent liabilities were made up.

Deposits are chiefly of two kinds: sight deposits and time deposits. Whereas sight deposits can be withdrawn on sight whenever the depositor wishes, a minimum period of notification must be given before time deposits can be withdrawn. Sight deposits are the bank accounts against which we write cheques, thereby running down our deposits without giving the bank any prior warning.[7] Whereas most banks do not pay interest on sight deposits or chequing accounts, they can afford to pay interest on time deposits. Since they have notification of any withdrawals, they have plenty of time to sell off some of their high-interest investments or call in some of their high-interest loans in order to have the money to pay out depositors.

Certificates of deposit (CDs) are an extreme form of time deposit where the bank borrows from the public for a specified time period and knows exactly when the loan must be repaid. The final liability items in Table 23-2 show deposits in foreign currencies and miscellaneous liabilities such as cheques in the process of clearance.

Banks as Financial Intermediaries

In what sense are banks financial intermediaries standing between lenders and borrowers? A bank is a business and its owners or managers aim to maximize profits. A bank makes profits by lending and borrowing. To get money in, the bank offers favourable terms to potential

---

[7] In the UK sight deposits are frequently called chequing accounts and time deposits are called deposit accounts.

BOX 23-2

A BEGINNER'S GUIDE TO THE FINANCIAL MARKETS

Financial asset: A piece of paper entitling the owner to a specified stream of interest payments for a specified period. Firms and governments raise money by selling financial assets. Buyers work out how much to bid for these assets by calculating the present value of the promised stream of payments. Assets are frequently retraded between individuals before the date at which the original issuer is committed to repurchase the piece of paper for a specified price.

Cash: Notes and coin, paying zero interest. The most liquid asset.

Bills: Financial assets with less than one year until the known date at which they will be repurchased by the original borrower. Suppose the government sells three-month Treasury bills. In April the government sells a piece of paper simultaneously promising to repurchase it for £100 in July. Bills do not pay interest, but if people bid £97 in April they will effectively make 3 per cent by holding the bill till July, quite a decent annual return. As July gets nearer the price at which the bill is retraded will climb towards £100. Buying it from someone else in June for £99 and reselling to the government in July for £100 still yields 1 per cent in a month, or over 12 per cent a year at compound interest. Because Treasury bills can easily be bought and sold, and because their price can only fluctuate over a small range (say, between £97.5 and £98 in May when they expire in July), they are highly liquid. People can get their money back quickly and have a good idea how much they would get if they had to sell.

Bonds: Longer-term financial assets. If you look under government bonds in the *Financial Times* you will find a bond listed as Treasury 13% 2000. In the year 2000 the government guarantees to repurchase this bond for £100 (the usual repurchase price). Until then the person owning the paper will get interest payments of £13 a year. Bond dealers claim to have a sense of humour. This particular bond is popularly called a 'Grecian' (Grecian 2000: get it?). Other bonds have similar nicknames. Bonds are less liquid than bills,

not because they are hard to sell, but because the price for which they could be sold, and the amount of cash this would generate, is more uncertain. We now explain why by looking at the most extreme kind of bond.

Perpetuities: Bonds that are never repurchased by the original issuer, who pays interest for ever. Usually called Consols (consolidated stock) in the UK. Consols $2\frac{1}{2}$% pay £2.5 a year for ever. Most consols were issued when interest rates were very low. People originally would have bid around £100 for this consol. Subsequently interest rates on other assets have risen to, say, 10 per cent. Today consols are traded between people at around £25 each so that new purchasers of these old bonds can still get about 10 per cent on their financial investment. Notice two things. The person *holding* a bond makes a capital loss when other interest rates rise and the price of the bonds falls. Second, since the price of Consols was once £100 and is now only £25, there is much more volatility in Consol prices than in the price of Treasury bills. In fact, the longer the period until the original issuer is committed to buying the bond back for £100, the more its current price can move around as existing bond-holders attempt to sell out to new buyers and offer them a rate of return in line with other assets today. Hence although bonds can easily be bought and sold, they are not very liquid. If you buy one today, you do not have a very good idea exactly how much you would get if you had to sell out in six months' time.

Gilt-edged securities: Government bonds in the UK. Gilt-edged because there is no danger of the government going bust and refusing to meet the interest payments.

Industrial shares (equities): Entitlements to receive corporate dividends, the part of firms' profits paid out to shareholders rather than retained to finance new investment in machinery and buildings. In good years, dividends will be high, but in bad years dividends may be zero. Hence a risky asset which is not very liquid. Firms could even go bust, making the shares completely worthless.

---

depositors. As of 1989, British clearing banks offer interest on sight deposits only to important customers, but they usually offer free chequing facilities to people whose sight deposits or current accounts do not fall below a certain level. They do not charge directly for the expenses of clearing and processing cheques. And they offer interest on time deposits.

Next, the banks have to find profitable ways to lend what has been borrowed. Table 23-2 shows how the London clearing banks lend out their money. Most is lent out as advances of overdrafts to households and firms, usually at interest rates well in excess of the rate simultaneously being paid to the bank customers with time deposits. Some is used to purchase securities such as long-term government bonds. Some is more prudently invested in liquid assets. Although these do not pay such a high rate of interest, the bank knows it can get its money back quickly if people start withdrawing a lot of money from their sight deposits. And some money is held as cash, the most liquid asset of all.

What economic services does the bank provide? It is transforming household loans to the bank into bank loans to a wide range of people – governments wishing to finance a budget deficit, firms borrowing to build a new factory, and individuals borrowing to start a new business or buy a new home. The bank is using its specialist expertise to acquire a diversified portfolio of investments though depositors merely observe that they get an interest rate on their time deposits or free chequing facilities. Without the existence of the intermediary, depositors would have neither the time nor the expertise to decide which of these loans or investments to make. That is the economic service that the bank as an intermediary provides.

Fractional Reserve Banking

Table 23-2 shows that, although the London clearing banks had over £87 billion in sterling sight deposits which could be withdrawn at any time, they only held just over £3 billion of cash in sterling. Surely this is imprudent? If only 4 per cent of people holding sight deposits denominated in pounds were to withdraw their money, the banks would not have enough cash to meet these withdrawals.

This shows the importance of the other liquid assets in which banks have invested. At very short notice, they could cash in much of the money shown under 'Banks and market loans'. That is precisely why banks hold some of their money in liquid assets when they could get a higher interest rate by making less liquid advances to firms and households or by

purchasing less liquid securities. The skill in running a bank entails being able to judge how much of total assets must be held in liquid assets including cash, and how much can be lent out in less liquid forms that earn higher interest rates.

23-4 Commercial Banks and the Money Supply

In the UK today, we define money as those generally accepted means of payments that are usable for *unrestricted* payments. We can use them at any time to pay any amount to anyone. This is the most straightforward definition of money, and this measure of the money supply is called 'M1'. For the UK it is measured as sterling notes and coin in circulation with the general public plus private sector sterling sight deposits with the banking system. Thus M1 measures the domestic currency in circulation plus the bank deposits or current accounts of private households and firms against which cheques may be written.

Money supply M1 = notes and coin
outside banks
+ private sector
chequing accounts
(sight deposits)   (4)

Banks as Creators of Money

As in the simple goldsmith example, modern banks create money by granting overdraft facilities, issuing sight deposits in excess of the cash reserves in the bank vaults. Without depositing any cash, some people are told they now have money in their bank accounts. These bank accounts are money because people can write cheques against them and use them as a means of payment. Equation (4) shows that this creation of new sight deposits adds to M1.

To show how modern fractional reserve banking is an intrinsic part of the process of money creation, we work through a simple example. We assume that there are ten banks, each of which is prepared to expand lending up to the point at which cash reserves in the vaults or with the central bank equal 10 per cent of all deposits.[8] Suppose one of the ten banks now has a client who pays an additional £100 in cash into his or her chequing account. That bank's cash assets have risen by £100 and its sight deposit liabilities have also risen by £100.

Is this an equilibrium position for a profit-maximizing bank? No. The bank will want to increase the lending on which it earns interest. In assuming that banks have a cash reserve ratio of 10 per cent, we assume that the bank's initial reaction is to increase lending by £90 or 90 per cent of the extra cash reserves it has just received.

To show how the banks interact, suppose first that only *one* bank increases its lending. Table 23-3 shows what happens. Bank A took in £100 in cash in exchange for a deposit of £100. In step 1, the bank lends out £90 or 90 per cent of its extra cash reserves. Suppose it gives you a deposit overdraft of £90 against which you can write cheques. Assets are £100 in cash plus the loan for £90. Deposits are also £190, comprising the sight deposit of £100 of the original cash depositor plus the additional £90 sight deposit you have been allowed to write cheques on.

In step 2 you have blown your loan of £90, running down your deposit account to zero. The shops to which you wrote the cheques have collected their £90 in cash from your bank. Although the bank has reached its desired position of holding cash equal to 10 per cent of its total deposits, that is not the end of the story. The shops now have an extra £90 in cash. If in total they use the ten banks equally, your bank will get a new deposit of £9 in cash as the shopkeepers put their money in their bank accounts. This is shown in step 3.

Step 4 shows that your bank will now lend out 90 per cent of this new deposit of £9. Its cash reserves are now £19 and its loans £98.10, the original loan to you of £90 plus a new loan of £8.10, or 90 per cent of the new cash deposit of £9. Since you have completely used up your deposit overdraft, total deposits of £117.10 are made up of the £100 deposits of the original cash deposit, £9 of new deposits when the shops paid in £9 in cash, and the new overdraft deposit of £8.10.

When this overdraft is spent, the bank will lose £8.10 in cash as people present their cheques for payment. However, it can hope to get back 10 per cent of this as a new cash deposit if it gets its share of new cash deposits across the whole banking system. And against this new cash of £0.81 it will be able to lend a little more. You might like to fill in the next few steps in the table yourself.

Table 23-3 shows that even a single bank can create money. A single client began the process by depositing £100 in cash. By step 4 there is £81 of this cash outside the bank and there are deposits of £117.10. The money supply M1 has increased from £100 to £198.10.[9] It may seem as if a single bank, acting in isolation, has been able to create a lot of money. However, this is nothing compared with the money that the banking system can create when they act together.

When a single bank expands deposits, it loses most of its cash as people write cheques against their new deposits. Although this cash will be redeposited with the banking system as a whole, a single bank will get only a small share of this redepositing. In our example of Table 23-3, in step 3 our bank got new cash of only £9 or 10 per cent of the cash withdrawals it suffered in step 2. Suppose however that all the other banks were also increasing deposits and lending whenever they got additional cash.

What happens to the £81 withdrawn from our bank in step 2 and not redeposited in step 3? It gets deposited in other banks, which then increase their lending. As people cash in cheques written against these deposits, our

Table 23-3 Direct expansion by a single bank

STEP	ASSETS	LIABILITIES
1	Cash £100, loans £90	Deposits £190
2	Cash £10, loans £90	Deposits £100
3	Cash £19, loans £90	Deposits £109
4	Cash £19, loans £98.10	Deposits £117.10

[8] Although Table 23-2 shows that modern banks can get by with cash reserves well below 10 per cent of total deposits, because of sophisticated financial markets for very liquid loans which can be quickly cashed in if required, the basic principle is the same whatever figure we assume for the cash reserve ratio desired by the banks. We use 10 per cent to keep the arithmetic simple.

[9] Even if the outstanding cash of £81 has been deposited in other banks, there will be corresponding deposit accounts. Either way we add this £81 to £117.10 to obtain £198.10.

Table 23-4 Deposit expansion by the banking system as a whole

STEP	ASSETS	LIABILITIES
1	Cash £100, loans £90	Deposits £190
2	Cash £100, loans £180	Deposits £280
⋮	Cash £100, loans £900	Deposits £1000

bank will get its share of the redeposits of this cash. Provided all withdrawn cash is redeposited in banks, *the banking system as a whole does not lose cash as it expands deposits*. Table 23-4 shows how the banking system as a whole expands deposits when it receives £100 of extra cash.

Suppose initially that each bank expects that, in making loans and creating new deposits, it will subsequently suffer cash withdrawals as people cash in these cheques. Each bank will then lend out 90 per cent of the value of its new cash. Step 1 shows that the banking system lends out £90 and creates £90 of new deposits when it begins with £100 in cash and equivalent deposits.

However, the system as a whole does not lose cash. In step 2, banks find that their cash assets are undiminished. They try lending out some more and creating even more deposits. Still they will find their cash reserve undiminished. They will try lending even more. In fact, lending will expand until £900 has been lent out and total deposits are the £900 corresponding to these loans plus the original £100 of deposits corresponding to the initial cash of £100 paid in. By the last row of Table 23-4 each bank, and the banking system as a whole, has succeeded in attaining its desired 10 per cent ratio of cash reserves to total deposits.

Originally, the money supply was the £100 of cash in people's pockets. This money is now in the banks and must be excluded from the M1 measure of the money supply since that cash is no longer in circulation. But bank deposits are now £1000, and this is the value of M1. The banking system has converted £100 of cash in circulation into £1000 of bank deposits against which people can write cheques as a means of payment. Thus banks play a crucial role in determining the level of the money supply M1.

23-5 The Monetary Base and the Money Multiplier

Because the cash reserves of commercial banks are only a small fraction of total bank deposits, bank-created deposit money forms by far the most important component of the money supply in modern economies. Although we have now mastered the basics, it is important to tie up the loose ends, which we do in this section. Banks' deposits depend on the cash reserves in the banking system. To complete our analysis of how the money supply is determined we need to examine what determines the amount of cash that will be deposited with the banking system.

Through the *central bank*, the Bank of England in the UK, the government controls the issue of token money in a modern economy. We have already seen that private creation of token money must be outlawed when its value as a medium of exchange exceeds the direct cost of its production. We shall shortly examine the role of the central bank in more detail. For the moment we simply assume that the government has instructed the central bank to issue a particular quantity of notes and coin.

> The *monetary base* or *stock of high-powered money* is the quantity of notes and coin in private circulation plus the quantity held by the banking system.

How much of the monetary base will be held by commercial banks as cash reserves? In the simplified example of the previous section, we assumed that the general public deposited all its cash with the banks. But this is only a simplification. Even people with deposit accounts and cheque-books carry some money around in their pockets. Few of us would think of trying to write out a cheque for a bus fare. And how many times have you stood behind someone writing a cheque for a rail ticket and wished that they had been paying in cash, which can be dealt with more quickly?

But there are other reasons why people hold cash. Many people do not trust banks. They keep their savings under the bed. Remarkably enough, in 1986 only 61 per cent of British households had chequing accounts.[10] Other people hold cash because they wish to make illegal or unreported transactions in the 'black economy'.

---

[10] HMSO, *Social Trends*, 1989.

How then is the money supply M1 related to the monetary base, the amount of notes and coin issued by the central bank? To answer this question we introduce the money multiplier.

> The *money multiplier* gives the change in the money stock for a £1 change in the quantity of the monetary base.

Thus we can write

Money stock = money multiplier
                  × monetary base   (5)

The value of the money multiplier depends on two key ratios, the banks' desired ratio of cash reserves to total deposits, and the private sector's desired ratio of cash in circulation to total bank deposits.

From the previous section, we know that the banks' desired ratio of cash reserves to total deposits determines how much they will multiply up any given cash reserves into deposit money. The *lower* the desired cash reserves ratio, the larger the quantity of deposits the banks will create against given cash reserves and the *larger* will be the money supply M1.

Similarly, the *lower* the private sector's desired ratio of cash in circulation to private sector bank accounts, the *larger* will be the money supply M1 for any given quantity of high-powered money issued by the central bank. Since a higher fraction of the monetary base is deposited in the banking system, the banks are able to create more bank deposits.

We give an exact formula for the money multiplier in the Appendix to this chapter. To give an idea of its possible magnitude, suppose that banks wish to hold cash reserves equal to 4 per cent of their total sight deposits and that the private sector wishes to hold cash in circulation equal to 20 per cent of the value of private sector sight deposits. The formula given in the Appendix then implies that the money multiplier would be 7. Each £100 increase in the monetary base would lead to an increase of £700 in the money supply M1.

At present, it is more important to remember that an increase in either the banks' desired cash reserves ratio or the private sector's desired ratio of cash to chequing account balances will reduce the value of the money multiplier. For a given monetary base, the money supply M1 will fall.

We have seen what determines the cash reserves ratio desired by commercial banks. The higher the interest rate banks can earn by lending relative to the interest rate (if any) that banks must pay depositors, the more banks will wish to lend and the more they will take chances with a low ratio of cash reserves to outstanding sight deposits. Conversely, the more unpredictable are withdrawals from sight deposits and the fewer lending opportunities the banks have in very liquid loans, the higher cash reserves they will have to maintain for any level of deposit lending.

What about the public's desired ratio of cash in circulation to sight deposits? In part this depends on institutional factors, for example whether firms pay wages by cheque or cash. In part it depends on tax rates and the incentive to hold cash to make untraceable payments in the process of tax evasion. And we might expect the growing use of credit cards to reduce the amount of cash used. Credit cards are a temporary means of payment, a *money-substitute* rather than money itself. When you sign a credit card slip, the slip itself cannot be used to make further purchases. Within a short period you have to settle your account by using cash or a cheque, the ultimate means of payment. Nevertheless, since credit cards allow people with chequing accounts to carry less cash in their pocket, their increasing use will probably reduce the desired ratio of cash to sight deposits with banks.

Figure 23-1 summarizes our discussion of the relation between the monetary base and the level of the money supply M1. The monetary base or stock of high-powered money is held either as cash reserves by the banks or as money in circulation. Since bank deposits are a multiple of banks' cash reserves, the money multiplier exceeds unity. The money multiplier will be larger (*a*) the lower the private sector's desired ratio of cash to bank deposits, thus giving the banks more cash with which to create a multiplied deposit expansion, and (*b*) the lower is the banks' desired ratio of cash to deposits, thus leading them to create more deposits for any given cash reserves.

23-6 Other Definitions of Money

The M1 definition of money includes a narrow range of assets that can immediately and

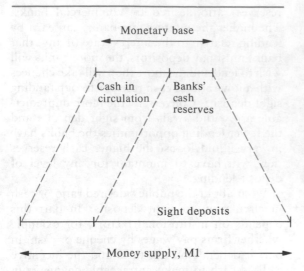

Figure 23-1 MONEY SUPPLY DETERMINATION.
The money supply M1 comprises currency in
circulation and sight deposits at banks. The
monetary base, issued by the central bank, is held
either as currency in circulation or as banks' cash
reserves. Since sight deposits are a multiple of
banks' cash reserves, the money multiplier exceeds
1. The monetary base is 'high-powered' because
part of it is multiplied up as the banking system
creates additional sight deposits, the major
component of the money supply.

without restriction be used to make payments.
But there is a host of other assets that are
'almost' as good as money. We call them *near
money*. They are stores of value that can readily
be converted into money but are not themselves
a means of payment.

The most important near money is *time
deposits*. Time deposits are interest-bearing
deposit accounts on which cheques may not be
drawn directly. Suppose you have £50 in your
chequing account and £500 earning 10 per cent
interest in a time deposit with the same bank.
If you want to write a cheque for £60 you can
always transfer £10 from your time deposit to
your sight deposit. Indeed, for important
customers banks may undertake to make such
transfers almost automatically. Having money
in a time deposit is nearly as good as a means
of payment and has the added advantage of
earning interest.

Why don't we keep the minimum in our sight
deposits and as much as possible in time
deposits? One reason is the time and effort, and
sometimes bank charges, involved in continually

transferring money between the two kinds of
deposit account. It may be simpler to keep a
'safe' working balance in your sight deposit
even though it means giving up a pound or two
in interest over the course of a year.

Table 23-5 shows the relation between the
narrowest M0 measure of money and the wider
measures used in the UK. M3, known as sterling
M3 before 1987, is M1 plus sterling time
deposits and certificates of deposit of the
private sector. The wider measure M3c, formerly
called M3, also includes UK residents' deposits
denominated in foreign currencies such as
dollars or Swiss francs. And the widest measure
M4 also includes other near money such as
deposits in building societies.

In 1989 the Abbey National, one of the
largest building societies, changed its legal
status to a private profit-making company
quoted on the stock exchange, and was
reclassified as a bank rather than a building
society. Thus, in official statistics, its deposits
were still part of M4 (which includes both
banks and building societies), but now, as a
bank, its deposits would also have been
included in M3 and M3c for the first time.
Recognizing that it was becoming increasingly
difficult to make a convincing economic case
for distinguishing bank and building society

Table 23-5 Money and near money in the UK,
June 1989 (£ billion)

Cash in circulation	14.9
Banks' till money and deposits with Bank of England	2.1
Wide monetary base, M0	17.0
Cash in circulation	14.9
Sight deposits (non-interest-bearing)	31.8
Sight deposits (interest-bearing)	67.7
Money supply, M1	114.4
+ UK private sector sterling time deposits	131.9
Money supply, M3	246.3
+ UK private sector deposits in other currencies	41.8
Money supply, M3c	288.1
M3	246.3
+ private sector holdings of building society shares and deposits (minus building society holdings M3)	143.2
M4	389.5

Source: Bank of England, *Quarterly Bulletin.*

deposits, the Bank of England responded by ending the publication of M3 and M3c data. Nowadays, M0 and M4 are the main money supply data. This example illustrates the problem other European countries will face as they proceed down the road of financial liberalization.

Thus there is a spectrum of money, ranging from cash and bankers' balances (M0) to wide definitions such as M4. In many ways, it is unhelpful to draw an artificial line and say that everything on one side of the line shall be called 'money' or 'the money supply'. In modern financial systems, one form of deposits can quickly and cheaply be converted into another. One consequence of this, which we discuss in the next chapter, is that attempts by the government to regulate one particular measure of the money supply quickly lead to people switching to forms of deposit that remain unregulated.

Summary

1 Money has four functions: a medium of exchange or means of payment, a store of value, a unit of account, and a standard of deferred payment. It is its use as a medium of exchange that distinguishes money from other assets.

2 In a barter economy, trading is costly because there must be a double coincidence of wants. Using a medium of exchange reduces the costs of matching buyers and sellers and allows society to devote scarce resources to other things. A token money has a higher value as a medium of exchange than in any other use. Because its value greatly exceeds its production cost, token money economizes still further on the resources required to facilitate trading.

3 Token money is accepted either because people believe it can subsequently be used to make payments or because the government declares it legal tender. The government controls the supply of token money.

4 The story of the goldsmith–banker illustrates the role of modern banks. Goldsmiths create money by making loans, either by releasing into circulation gold previously held in vaults or by increasing the value of deposits. The choice of how much reserves to hold involves a trade-off between interest earnings and the danger of insolvency.

5 Modern commercial banks attract deposit funds by acting as financial intermediaries. A national system of clearing cheques, which are a convenient form of payment, attracts funds into sight deposits. Interest-bearing time deposits attract further funds. In turn, banks lend out money as short-term liquid loans, as longer-term less liquid advances, or by purchasing securities.

6 Sophisticated financial markets for short-term liquid lending allow modern banks to operate with very low cash reserves relative to deposits. Since the M1 measure of the money supply is currency in circulation plus private sector sight deposits, the high ratio of deposits to cash reserves implies that the banks are responsible for creating the largest component of M1, namely sight deposits.

7 The monetary base M0 is currency in circulation plus banks' cash reserves. The money multiplier is the ratio of M1 to the monetary base, and exceeds unity. The money multiplier is larger (*a*) the smaller is the desired cash ratio of the banks and (*b*) the smaller is the private sector's desired ratio of cash in circulation to sight deposits.

8 Wider definitions of money include near money, those assets which though not means of payments, can readily be converted into means of payment. M3 is M1 plus private sector time deposits, both denominated in sterling. M3c is M3 plus residents' deposits in other currencies. Even wider measures of money include private sector building society deposits.

Key Terms

Money
Medium of exchange
Unit of account
Store of value
Token money
Legal tender
IOU money
Liquidity
Financial intermediary
Fractional reserve banking
M1 and M0
Monetary base
Money multiplier
Banks' cash–deposits ratio
Private sector cash–deposits ratio
M3, M3c, and M4

Problems

1   (a) A person trades in a car when buying another. Is the used car a medium of exchange? Is this a barter transaction? (b) Could you tell by watching someone buying mints (white discs) with coins (silver discs) which one is money?

2   A goldsmith holds 100 per cent reserves against deposits. What happens to the money supply when a customer withdraws gold from the vault?

3   Initially gold coins were used as money but people could melt them down and use the gold for industrial purposes. (a) What must have been the relative value of gold in these two uses? (b) Explain the circumstances in which gold could (i) become a token money, and (ii) disappear from monetary circulation completely.

4   In what sense do commercial banks create money? (a) Use a balance sheet to show how cheque clearance works. (b) What difference does this make to the resources that society uses in trading?

5   (a) Would it make sense to include travellers' cheques in measures of the money supply? (b) season tickets for British Rail? (c) credit cards?

6   Sight deposits = £30; time deposits = £60; banks' cash reserves = £2; currency in circulation = £12; residents' deposits in US dollars = £12. Calculate (a) the monetary base; (b) M1; (c) the banks' reserve ratio; (d) the private sector's ratio of cash to sight deposits; (e) M3; (f) M3c.

7   Common Fallacies Show why the following statements are incorrect: (a) Since their liabilities equal their assets, banks cannot *create* anything. (b) The money supply has gone up because of the expansion of the black economy. Since cash transactions are untraceable, people are putting less in the banks. (c) Since the government is responsible for printing money, it always knows the exact quantity of the money supply in the UK.

Appendix: The Money Multiplier

Suppose banks wish to hold cash reserves R equal to some fraction c_b of deposits D, and that the private sector wishes to hold cash in circulation C equal to some fraction c_p of their bank deposits D. Thus

$$R = c_b D \text{ and } C = c_p D \tag{A1}$$

Since the monetary base or stock of high-powered money H equals currency in circulation plus cash with the banks, we have

$$H = C + R = (c_b + c_p)D \tag{A2}$$

The money supply equals currency in circulation C plus banks' sight deposits D. Hence

$$M1 = C + D = (c_p + 1)D \tag{A3}$$

Comparing equations (A3) and (A2), we see that

$$M1 = \frac{c_p + 1}{c_p + c_b} H \tag{A4}$$

Thus the value of the money multiplier is $(c_p + 1)/(c_p + c_b)$. Since c_b and c_p are positive fractions, the money multiplier exceeds unity. Also, an increase in c_b, the banks' desired cash reserve ratio, or in c_p, the private sector's desired ratio of cash to sight deposits, will reduce the value of the money multiplier. Using the data of Table 23-5, and assuming that banks and the private sector were at their desired positions, for the UK in June 1989 c_p was about 0.15 and c_b about 0.02. From equation (A4) the value of the money multiplier is thus 1.15/0.17 = 7, as quoted in Section 23-5 of the text.

24

Central Banking and the Monetary System

Today every country of any size has a *central bank*. There are two basic tasks that such a bank performs. It acts as banker to the commercial banks, ensuring that the banking system runs smoothly; and it acts as banker to the government, taking responsibility for the control of the money supply and the funding of the government's budget deficit.

Originally private institutions in business for profit, central banks have come under increasing public control as their activities as bankers to their respective governments have grown in importance, and as governments have placed increasing emphasis on manipulating the quantity of money in circulation. Founded in 1694, the Bank of England was not nationalized until 1947, and the Federal Reserve System, the central bank in the United States, was not set up until 1913.

In this chapter we look in detail at the role of the central bank. Having examined its functions, we then show how it influences equilibrium in the markets for financial assets in general and money in particular. Since the central bank influences the supply of money, it is necessary to consider what determines the demand for money before a complete analysis of monetary equilibrium can be undertaken.

We conclude the chapter by discussing the techniques of monetary control available to the central bank and showing the problems that arise in practice when the Bank of England attempts to implement the money supply targets set by the government.

24-1 The Bank of England

The Bank of England, usually known simply as the Bank, is the central bank of the UK. For historical reasons, it is divided into an Issue Department and a Banking Department, each with separate balance sheets which are shown in Table 24-1.

The Issue Department is responsible for issuing banknotes, and these are shown as liabilities in Table 24-1. To introduce notes into circulation, the Issue Department purchases financial securities: bills and bonds issued by the government, commercial firms, or local authorities. These are shown as assets of the Issue Department in Table 24-1. The exchange of high powered money for financial securities is called an *open market operation*. We return to this shortly.

The Banking Department acts as banker to the commercial banks and to the government. Public deposits and bankers' deposits are deposits by the government and the commercial banking system. Reserves and other accounts are deposits by central banks of other countries, by domestic local authorities, and by nationalized industries.

Assets are government securities (loans to the government) and advances. Advances are loans to the banks, and in the UK are issued through financial intermediaries called Discount Houses. Other assets include physical capital, buildings and equipment, and securities issued by private firms or local authorities.

In practice, the activities of the Issue Department and the Banking Department are carefully coordinated. Although much of Table 24-1 resembles the balance sheet of a commercial bank, there is one crucial difference. *There is no possibility that the Bank can go bankrupt.* A £50 note is a liability of the Issue Department. Suppose you take it along to the Bank and say you want to cash it in for £50. At best, the Bank would simply give you 50 new £1

Table 24-1 Balance sheets of the Bank of England, June 1989

DEPARTMENT	ASSETS	£ b	LIABILITIES	£ b
ISSUE	Government securities	14.0	Notes in circulation	14.7
	Other securities	0.7		
	Issue Department assets	14.7	Issue Department liabilities	14.7
BANKING	Government securities	0.9	Public deposits	0.1
	Advances	0.8	Bankers' deposits	1.3
	Other assets	1.7	Reserves and other accounts	2.0
	Banking Department assets	3.4	Banking Department liabilities	3.4

Source: Bank of England Quarterly Bulletin.

coins. The unique feature of the central bank's liabilities is that it can create them in unlimited quantities without fear of bankruptcy.

This was not always so. In the days of the gold standard, notes could be cashed in for gold and the central bank might not have had sufficient gold to pay. Nowadays there is no such obligation. The Bank can always meet withdrawals by its depositors by printing new banknotes a little more quickly.

24-2 The Bank and the Money Supply

In this section we study the ways in which a central bank can affect the supply of money in the economy. The narrowest measure M1 of the money supply is currency in circulation outside the banking system plus the sight deposits of commercial banks against which the private sector can write cheques. Thus the money supply is partly a liability of the Bank (currency in private circulation) and partly a liability of commercial banks (chequing accounts of the general public).

In the last chapter we introduced the *monetary base*, the currency supplied by the Bank both to the commercial banks and to private circulation, and the *money multiplier*, the extent to which the money supply is a multiple of the monetary base. We saw that the money multiplier was larger the smaller the cash reserve ratio of the commercial banks and the smaller the private sector's desired ratio of cash to bank deposits.

We now describe the three most important instruments through which the Bank *might* seek to affect the money supply: reserve requirements, the discount rate, and open market operations.

Reserve Requirements

A *required reserve ratio* is a minimum ratio of cash reserves to deposits that the central bank requires commercial banks to hold.

If a reserve requirement is in force, commercial banks can hold more than the required cash reserves but they cannot hold less. If their cash falls below the required amount, they must immediately borrow cash, usually from the central bank, to restore their required reserve ratio.

Suppose the commercial banking system has £1 million in cash and for strictly commercial purposes would normally maintain cash reserves equal to 5 per cent of sight deposits. Since sight deposits will be 20 times cash reserves, the banking system will create £20 million of sight deposits against its £1 million cash reserves. Suppose the Bank now imposes a reserve requirement that banks must hold cash reserves of at least 10 per cent of sight deposits. Now banks can create only £10 million sight deposits against their cash reserves of £1 million.

Thus, when the central bank imposes a reserve requirement in excess of the reserve ratio that prudent banks would anyway have maintained, the effect is to reduce the creation of bank deposits, reduce the value of the money multiplier, and reduce the money supply for any given monetary base. Similarly, when a particular reserve requirement is already in force, any increase in the reserve requirement will reduce the money supply.

When the central bank imposes a reserve requirement in excess of the reserves that banks would otherwise have wished to hold, the banks are creating fewer deposits and undertaking less lending than they would really like. Thus a reserve requirement acts like a tax on banks by forcing them to hold a higher fraction of their total assets as bank reserves and a lower fraction as loans earning high interest rates. Can the banks do anything about it?

Although there are profitable lending opportunities, the banks can take advantage of them only if they can increase their cash reserves. In principle, they could try to borrow cash from the central bank. If the point of a reserve requirement is to reduce the money supply, the central bank will be reluctant to lend banks the cash they want to make additional loans, increase deposits, and expand the money supply. With lucrative lending opportunities around, the banks may be able to induce the private sector to exchange cash in circulation for bank deposits. Banks can offer more generous interest rates on time deposits or stay open later to encourage people to make greater use of chequing facilities. By attracting more cash from the general public, banks may then be able to restore former levels of deposit lending, though there is then the danger that the central bank will raise the reserve requirement still higher.

One form of reserve requirement that has been especially popular in the UK is the use of *special deposits*. Commercial banks were required to deposit some of their cash reserves in a special deposit at the Bank, and this money could *not* be counted as part of the banks' cash reserves in meeting their reserve requirements. Varying the amount required as special deposits gave the Bank another lever for controlling deposit creation by the banking system and the size of the money multiplier.

The Discount Rate

The second instrument of monetary control available to the central bank is the discount rate.

The *discount rate* is the interest rate that the Bank charges when the commercial banks want to borrow money.

When the discount rate was an important part of monetary control in the UK it used to be known as the Bank Rate, or Minimum Lending Rate (MLR).

Suppose banks think the *minimum* safe ratio of cash to deposits is 10 per cent. For the purposes of this argument it does not matter whether this figure is a commercial judgement or a required ratio imposed by the Bank. On any particular day, banks are likely to have a bit of cash in hand. Say their cash reserves are 12 per cent of deposits. How far dare they let their cash reserves fall towards the minimum level of 10 per cent?

Banks have to balance the interest rate they will get on extra lending with the dangers and costs involved if there is a sudden flood of withdrawals which push their cash reserves below the critical 10 per cent figure. This is where the discount rate comes in. Suppose market interest rates are 8 per cent and the central bank makes it known it is prepared to lend to commercial banks at 8 per cent. Commercial banks may as well lend up to the hilt and drive their cash reserves down to the minimum 10 per cent of deposits. The banks are lending at 8 per cent and, if the worst comes to the worst and they are short of cash, they can always borrow from the Bank at 8 per cent. Banks cannot lose by lending as much as possible.

Suppose however that the Bank announces that, although market interest rates are 8 per cent, it will lend to commercial banks only at the penalty rate of 10 per cent. Now a bank with cash reserves of 12 per cent may conclude that it is not worth making the extra loans at 8 per cent interest that would drive its cash reserves down to the minimum of 10 per cent of deposits. There is too high a risk that sudden withdrawals will then force the bank to borrow from the Bank at 10 per cent interest. It will have lost money by making these extra loans. It makes more sense to hold some excess cash reserves against the possibility of a sudden withdrawal.

Thus, by setting the discount rate at a penalty level in excess of the general level of interest rates, the Bank can induce commercial banks voluntarily to hold additional cash reserves.

Since bank deposits now become a lower multiple of banks' cash reserves, the money multiplier is reduced and the money supply is lower for any given level of the monetary base.

Open Market Operations

An *open market operation* occurs when the central bank alters the monetary base by buying or selling financial securities in the open market.

Whereas the previous two methods of monetary control operate by altering the value of the money multiplier, open market operations alter the monetary base. Since the money supply is the monetary base multiplied by the money multiplier, they alter the money supply.

Suppose the Issue Department of the Bank prints £1 million of new banknotes and uses them to purchase government securities on the open market. There are now £1 million fewer securities in the hands of the banks or the private sector, but the monetary base has increased by £1 million. There has been an injection of £1 million of cash into the economy. Some will be held in private circulation but most of it will be deposited with the banking system, which can now expand deposit lending against its higher cash reserves. Conversely, if the Issue Department of the Bank sells £1 million of government securities from its existing stock, exactly £1 million of cash must be withdrawn from private circulation or the banks' cash reserves. The monetary base falls by £1 million. Since banks lose cash reserves, they have to reduce deposit lending and the money supply falls.

Notice that it makes little difference whether the Bank transacts with banks directly or with members of the non-bank public. If the Bank sells securities directly to the banking system, banks' cash reserves are immediately reduced. If the Bank sells securities to the general public, individuals will write cheques on their bank accounts and banks' cash reserves are again reduced. Either way, by open market operations in financial securities, the Bank alters the monetary base, banks' cash reserves, deposit lending, and the money supply.

24-3 Other Functions of the Central Bank

Later in the chapter we return to the role of the Bank in controlling the money supply and implementing the government's monetary policy. In this section we briefly describe the other responsibility of the Bank in its role as banker to the banking system and as banker to the government.

Lender of Last Resort

Modern fractional reserve banking allows society to produce the medium of exchange with relatively small inputs of scarce resources: land, labour, and capital. However, there is a price to be paid for this efficient production of the medium of exchange. In the last chapter we saw that any system of fractional reserve banking will be vulnerable to financial panics. Since banks have insufficient reserves to meet a simultaneous withdrawal of all their deposits, any hint of large withdrawals is likely to become a self-fulfilling prophecy as people scramble to get their money out before the banks go bust.

To avoid financial panics, it is necessary to ensure that people believe that banks can never get into trouble in the first place. There must be a guarantee that banks can get cash if they really need it. And there is only one institution that can manufacture cash in indefinite quantities: the central bank. The threat of financial panics can be avoided, or at least greatly diminished, if it is known that the Bank of England stands ready to act as a lender of last resort.

The *lender of last resort* stands ready to lend to banks and other financial institutions when financial panic threatens the financial system.

The Bank's role as lender of last resort does not merely preserve a sophisticated and interconnected system of modern finance in which the failure of one bank would bring many others crashing down. It also reduces one major uncertainty in the day-to-day process of monetary control. If depositors were subject to fluctuating moods of optimism and pessimism about the solvency of banks, there would be wild swings in the private sector's desired ratio of cash in circulation to bank deposits and corresponding fluctuations in the value of the money multiplier. For a given monetary base, the fraction being held as banks' cash reserves would constantly be varying, and it would be difficult for the Bank to predict the money supply with any accuracy. By acting as a lender of last resort, the Bank can maintain confidence in the banking system and relatively stable values of the private sector's desired ratio of cash to deposits and hence of the money multiplier.

Although the mere knowledge that the Bank stands ready to act as a lender of last resort prevents most panics from arising, occasionally the Bank is required to act, for example, in the secondary banking crisis of 1973–74. In a period of rapidly rising property prices, many fringe banks overstretched their lending as they chased lucrative rates of return on property lending. When property prices started to fall, many of the loans could not be repaid by property speculators. The lending by the Bank to banks in trouble was so extensive it became known as the 'lifeboat operation'. Subsequently, the Bank has imposed a system of 'prudential control' on financial intermediaries to restrict the extent of their speculative lending.

Debt Management and Deficit Finance

The *public sector borrowing requirement (PSBR)* is the budget deficit of central and local government plus the deficit of the nationalized industries.

As banker to the government, the Bank must ensure that the government is able to meet its payments when it is running a deficit.

Neglecting for the moment the possibility that the government can borrow money from abroad, there are two ways in which the PSBR can be financed. First, the government can borrow from domestic residents. To do so, it sells financial securities, government bills and bonds, to domestic residents. How does this happen?

The government sells securities to the Bank in exchange for the cash it needs to meet its deficit. In turn, the Bank undertakes an open market operation, selling these securities on the open market in exchange for cash. At the end of the process, domestic residents are holding interest-bearing government securities but the money supply is unchanged. Through its deficit spending, the government has put back into the

economy exactly the cash it withdrew from the economy in selling securities in exchange for cash. And the Bank, through its sale of securities, has replenished the cash it initially lent the government.

Second, the government can finance the deficit by printing money. Actually, it sells securities to the Bank in exchange for cash, which is then used to meet the excess of spending over tax revenue. The stock of government securities held by commercial banks or private citizens is unaltered but the monetary base has increased. The money supply will increase by a larger amount because of the money multiplier.

The role of the Bank extends beyond ensuring that the current deficit is financed by selling securities or printing money. Because the government has run deficits in the past, there is a stock of outstanding securities in the hands of banks or private citizens. In Box 23-1 we listed the various kinds of government securities. Most have a finite *term to maturity*. When they are first issued, the government commits itself to buy back or redeem the securities for £100 each at a specified date.

Thus, at any time, some outstanding securities are being redeemed. The Bank is responsible for selling new securities to raise the money with which to buy back old securities which must now be redeemed. *Debt management* is the set of judgements by which the Bank decides the details of the new securities to be issued – the future date at which the government should be committed to redeem them, and the interest rate that must be offered on them to make them attractive to purchasers of securities.

Having described the functions of the central bank, we now begin the analysis of how the Bank influences the equilibrium prices and quantities of financial assets in general and money in particular. Thus far we have focused on the Bank's role in supplying money and other financial assets. But equilibrium also depends on demand. We must now consider how the demand for financial assets is determined.

24-4 The Demand for Money

In 1965 the amount of money (M1) in the UK was £7.6 billion. By 1989 it was £101 billion. Why were UK residents prepared to hold 13

BOX 24-1

THE FINANCIAL REVOLUTION: CENTRAL BANKING IN THE 1990s

In the old days, strict regulations kept different financial institutions separate. Banks couldn't be dealers on the floor of the stock exchange, and building societies couldn't be banks. Strict regulations controlled entry into each of these activities, limiting competition from new entrants. Codes of conduct were often implicit, and the central bank usually acted as informal policeman for the financial sector.

Beginning in the mid-1980s, financial markets throughout the world were subject to a wave of reform: enhanced competition, deregulation, and then regulation in a new form which amounted to a financial revolution. We discuss the effect on stock markets in particular in Box 34-1. Here we are concerned primarily with how it affected the central bank's role in financial supervision. We also explain its implication for the money supply and the demand for money.

London was the first European financial centre to experience the wind of change. Big Bang in October 1986 allowed banks (who have lots of financial backing) to become market-makers on the stock exchange floor. Other reforms made it easier for building societies to compete with banks. Similar reforms elsewhere were leading to a *globalization* of world financial markets. Entry barriers to particular financial sectors came tumbling down, and competition increased. Because *entry* had been deregulated, a new set of regulations for *conduct* became imperative. Relying on the old gentlemen's club – my word is my bond – was no longer enough.

It was not merely the number of institutions that was growing; the volume and type of business transacted was becoming ever fancier. Much of the new business was 'off balance sheet'. Instead of taking in money and relending it, the traditional role of a bank, banks were expanding business by acting as agents to repackaging existing loans. *Swaps* involve exchanging the income stream from two different assets (e.g. a sterling bond and a dollar bond). *Securitization* means bundling together separate illiquid investments and passing them on as a more attractive package which can be actively traded on a second-hand market.

Financial supervision had become a task that was too big for central banks alone. For example, in London the Securities and Investments Board (SIB) was established to oversee supervision of the financial sector. Each subsector, such as life assurance companies, had its own self-regulatory organization (SRO) to establish and enforce 'fit and proper' rules of conduct to protect investors. But central banks retain an important role in supervising banks themselves.

Globalization of business led to calls for all banks to be regulated in broadly the same way, to establish 'level playing fields' or equal treatment so that effective competition could take place. In 1988 the Group of 10, the world's largest economies, signed the Basle Accord, making international banking the first industry to be truly regulated at international level. The Accord was concerned with (i) *capital adequacy provisions*, specifying minimum financial backing for each type of credit risk; (ii) *risk assessment*, specifying the relative importance of different risks; and (iii) *fit and proper* rules for management conduct. Within the European Community, the 1992 programme to complete the single internal market has followed broadly similar lines in the Banking Directives, which establish regulatory rules for banking within the EC. Increasingly, therefore, the microeconomic role of a European central bank will be to implement the broad guidelines laid down at international or European Community level.

And the macroeconomic role of the central bank is also changing in the 1990s. If the European Community succeeds in moving to European Monetary Union (EMU), there will eventually be a European System of Central Banks providing unified decision-making on the common monetary policy of the Community.

The financial revolution has had two other consequences which should be borne in mind in reading the rest of this chapter. First, the definition of a bank is becoming increasingly blurred. For example UK building societies, traditionally offering interest-bearing savings accounts and relending for house purchase, are now offering chequing facilities. So the appropriate definition of money itself (whose deposits should count in the money supply?) is becoming ambiguous. Second, greater competition is raising the interest rates paid on current accounts. The consequence for the opportunity cost of holding money is discussed in the text.

times as much money in 1989 as in 1965? Answering that question will introduce us to the factors that determine money demand, which in turn sets the stage for understanding how monetary policy affects the economy.

We single out three key variables that determine money demand: interest rates, the price level or average price of goods and services, and real income. Before examining whether movements in these variables can explain the 13-fold increase in money holdings between 1965 and 1989, we reconsider why people hold money at all.

The Motives for Holding Money

Money is a stock. It is the quantity of circulating currency and bank deposits *held* at any given time. Holding money is not the same as *spending* money when we buy a meal or go to the cinema. We hold money now in order to spend it later.

The distinguishing feature of money is its use as a medium of exchange, for which it must also serve as a store of value. It is in these two functions of money that we must seek the reasons why people wish to hold it.

People can hold their wealth in various forms – money, bills, bonds, equities, and property. For simplicity we assume that there are only two assets: money, the medium of exchange that pays no interest, and bonds, which we use to stand for all other interest-bearing assets that are not directly a means of payment. As people earn income, they add to their wealth. As they spend, they deplete their wealth. How should people divide their wealth at any instant between money and bonds?

There is an obvious cost in holding any money at all.

The opportunity cost of holding money is the interest given up by holding money rather than bonds.

People will hold money only if there is a benefit to offset this cost. We now consider what that benefit might be.

The Transactions Motive In a monetary economy we use money to purchase goods and services and receive money in exchange for the goods and services we sell. Without money,

making transactions by direct barter would be costly in time and effort. Holding money economizes on the time and effort involved in undertaking transactions.

If all transactions were perfectly synchronized, we would earn revenue from sales of goods and income from sales of factor services at the same instant we made purchases of the goods and services we wish to consume. Except at that instant, we need hold no money at all.

The *transactions motive* for holding money reflects the fact that payments and receipts are not perfectly synchronized.

We need to hold money between receiving payments and making subsequent purchases. Or do we?

We could use all receipts immediately to purchase interest-earnings assets to be resold only at the instant we need money to make expenditures. Corporate treasurers of large companies do try to implement this policy, but for most of us it does not make sense. Every time we buy and sell assets there are brokerage and banking charges, which tend to be proportionately larger the smaller the level of transaction. And it takes an eagle eye to keep track of incomings and outgoings to judge the precise moment at which money is needed and assets must be sold. When relatively small sums are involved, the extra interest we could earn does not compensate for the brokerage charges and the extra time and effort required to implement such a policy. It is simpler and cheaper to hold at least some money.

How much money we need to hold depends on two things, the value of the transactions we wish to make and the degree of synchronization of our payments and receipts. Money is a nominal variable not a real variable. We do not know how much £100 will buy until we know the price of goods. If all prices double, both our receipts and our payments will double in nominal terms. To make the same transactions as before we will need to hold twice as much money. Putting this differently:

The demand for money is a demand for *real* money balances.

We need a given amount of real money, nominal money deflated by the price level, to undertake a given quantity of total transactions. Hence when the price level doubles, other things equal we expect the demand for nominal money balances to double, leaving the demand for real money balances unaltered. People want money because of its purchasing power in terms of the goods it will buy.

People hold real money balances because they want to make transactions. In practice, real national income, which measures the net output of goods and services in the economy, is a good proxy for the total real value of the transactions people undertake. Thus we assume that the transactions motive for holding real money balances will increase when real national income increases.

Although real national income is a useful measure of total transactions, it is important to recognize that we are making a simplification when we use this proxy. As we saw in our study of national accounts in Chapter 20, the value of total transactions exceeds the value of national income or net output. Total transactions include transactions in intermediate goods which do not show up in measures of *net* output or factor income. In using national income to measure total transactions, we are thus assuming that there is a stable relation between intermediate transactions and net output. We are assuming that a 1 per cent increase in national income will usually be associated with a 1 per cent increase in *total* transactions.

The second factor affecting the transactions motive for holding money is the degree of synchronization of payments and receipts. Suppose that, instead of spreading their shopping evenly throughout the week, households do all their shopping on the day they get a salary cheque from their employers. Over the week, national income and total transactions are unaltered, but people now *hold* less money over the week.

A nation's habits for making payments change only slowly. In our simplified model we assume that the degree of synchronization remains constant over time. Thus we focus on real national income as *the* measure of the transactions motive for holding *real* money balances.

The Precautionary Motive   Thus far we have assumed that people know exactly when they will obtain receipts and make payments. But of course we live in an uncertain world. This uncertainty about the precise timing of receipts

and payments gives rise to a precautionary motive for holding money.

Suppose you decide to buy a lot of interest-earning bonds and try to get by with only a small amount of money holdings. You are walking down the street and spot a great bargain in a shop window. But you do not have enough money to take advantage immediately of this opportunity. By the time you have arranged for some of your interest-earning bonds to be sold off in exchange for money, the sale may be over. Someone else may have snapped up the video recorder on sale at half price. This is the precautionary motive for holding money.

> In an uncertain world, there is a *precautionary motive* to hold money. In advance, we decide to hold money to meet contingencies the exact nature of which we cannot yet foresee.

If we had foreseen the contingency we would have had plenty of time to cash in interest-earning bonds to have money available. If we did not have to take advantage of the transactions opportunity immediately, it would not matter that it was unforeseen: we could still cash in our bonds at our leisure and buy the half-price video recorder. We forgo interest and carry money for precautionary reasons, because having ready money allows us to snap up unforeseen bargains, or stave off unforeseen crises by making immediate payments.

How can we measure the benefits from holding money for precautionary reasons? The payoff to having ready money available is likely to be larger the larger the volume of transactions we undertake and the greater the degree of uncertainty. If the degree of uncertainty remains roughly constant over time, it is the volume of transactions that will determine the benefits from holding real money balances for precautionary reasons. As with the transactions motive, we use the level of real national income to measure the volume of transactions. Thus, other things equal, the higher is real national income the stronger will be the precautionary motive for holding money.

Together, the transactions and precautionary motives provide the main reasons for holding the medium of exchange. They are the motives most relevant to the benefits from holding the narrow definition of money M1. In the last chapter we introduced wider definitions of money, such as M3, which includes interest-earning time deposits that are not directly a medium of exchange. The wider the definition of money, the less important will be the transactions and precautionary motives that relate to money as a medium of exchange, and the more we must take account of money as a store of value in its own right.

The Asset Motive   Suppose we forget all about the need to transact. We think of a wealthy individual or a firm deciding in which assets to hold wealth. At some distant date there may be a prospect of finally spending some of that wealth, but in the short run the objective is to earn a good rate of return.

Some assets, such as industrial shares, on average pay a high rate of return but are also quite risky. Some years their return is *very* high but in other years it is negative. When share prices fall, shareholders can make a capital loss which swamps any dividend payment to which they are entitled. Other assets are much less risky, but their rate of return tends to be much lower than the average return on risky assets.

How should people divide their portfolios of financial investments between safe and risky assets? We discussed this question in detail in Chapter 14 and you might like to reread Sections 14-4 and 14-5. We concluded that, since people dislike risk they will not put all their eggs in one basket. As well as holding some risky assets, they will keep some of their wealth in safe assets. Although on average this portfolio will earn a lower rate of return, it will help avoid absolute disaster in bad years.

> The *asset motive* for holding money arises because people dislike risk. People are prepared to sacrifice a high average rate of return to obtain a portfolio with a lower but more predictable rate of return.

The asset motive for holding money is important when we consider why people hold broad measures of money such as M4. It is much less relevant when we consider why people hold the medium of exchange as measured by M1. Why? Because if we are going to lend or invest money for any length of time, we can put it in a time deposit, which is safe but earns interest, rather than in a sight deposit or in cash which, though equally safe, earn no interests. Since time deposits are included in M4 but not in

M1, the asset motive is of interest chiefly for wider measures of money. However, as more sight deposits start to bear interest, this distinction is breaking down.

The Demand for Money: Prices, Real Income, and Interest Rates

We now draw together our analysis of why people hold money and discuss the demand for money. The transactions, precautionary, and asset motives suggest that there are benefits to holding money. But there is also a cost, namely the interest forgone by not holding interest-earning assets instead. People will hold money up to the point at which the marginal benefit of holding another pound just equals its marginal cost. Figure 24-1 illustrates how much money people will choose to hold.

We have already explained the role of prices. People want money only because of its purchasing power over goods. Hence, on the horizontal axis we plot quantities of real money balances, nominal money in current pounds divided by the average price level of goods and services. The horizontal line MC shows the marginal cost of holding money, the interest forgone by not holding bonds. The height of the MC line depends on the level of interest rates.

The MB schedule shows the marginal benefit of holding money. For the narrow M1 definition, we must think chiefly of the transactions and precautionary motives. We draw the MB schedule for a given level of real national income measuring the level of transactions undertaken. For this given level of transactions, it is possible to get by with a low level of real money holdings, but we have to work hard. We have to keep watching our purchases and receipts, being quick to invest money as it comes in and being every ready to sell off bonds just before we make a purchase. And we do not have much money holdings for precautionary purposes. We may be frustrated or inconvenienced if, unexpectedly, we wish to or need to make a purchase or settle a debt.

With a low level of real money holdings, the marginal benefit of another pound is high. We don't need to put so much effort into timing our transfers between money and bonds and we have larger precautionary balances to deal with unforeseen contingencies. For a given level

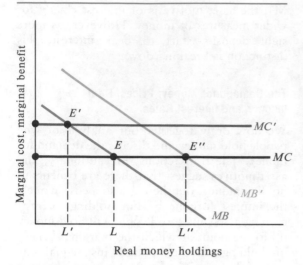

Figure 24-1 DESIRED MONEY HOLDINGS.
People hold money to make subsequent purchases of goods. The horizontal axis shows real money holdings or the purchasing power of money in terms of goods. The *MC* schedule shows the interest sacrificed by putting the last pound into money rather than bonds. The *MB* schedule is drawn for a given real income and shows the marginal benefit of the last pound of money. When real money holdings are small, the marginal benefit of the extra money holdings is high. It saves a lot of effort in managing transfers between money and bonds and provides a valuable precautionary reserve. The marginal benefit falls as money holdings increase. The desired point is *E*, at which marginal cost and marginal benefit are equal. An increase in interest rates, shown by an upward shift in the opportunity cost schedule from *MC* to *MC'*, reduces desired money holdings from *L* to *L'* as the desired point shifts from *E* to *E'*. An increase in real income reduces the adequacy of any holding of real balances for transactions and precautionary purposes, and increases the marginal benefit of adding to real balances. The *MB* schedule shifts up to *MB'*. At any given level of interest rates the desired quantity of real money increases. Facing the schedule *MC*, a shift from *MB* to *MB'* increases real money holdings to *L"* as the desired point shifts from *E* to *E"*.

of real income and real value of transactions, the marginal benefit of the last pound of money holdings declines as we hold more real money. With very high real money balances, we have plenty of money both for precautionary purposes and for transactions purposes to meet our planned purchases. We have given up leaping in and out of bonds, and life is much easier. The marginal benefit of yet more money holdings is very low.

Given the level of our real income and transactions, desired money holdings occur at point *E*. For any level of real money below the level *L*, the marginal benefit of another pound exceeds its marginal cost in interest forgone. We should hold more money. Above *L*, the marginal cost exceeds the marginal benefit and it is not worth holding as much money as this. The optimal level of money holding is *L*.

To emphasize the effect of prices, real income, and interest rates on the quantity of money demanded, we now consider changing each of these variables in turn. If all prices of goods and services double but interest rates and real income remain unaltered, neither the *MC* schedule nor the *MB* schedule shift. The desired point remains *E* and the desired level of *real* money remains *L*. Since prices have doubled, individuals will hold twice as much nominal money to preserve the level of their real money balances at *L*.

If interest rates on bonds increase, the opportunity cost of holding money rises. Figure 24-1 shows this as an upward shift from *MC* to *MC'*. The desired point is now *E'* and the desired quantity of real money holdings has fallen from *L* to *L'*. Higher interest rates reduce the quantity of real money balances demanded.[1]

Finally, we consider the effect of an increase in real income. At each level of real money holdings, the marginal benefit of the last pound is higher than before. With more transactions to undertake and a greater need for precautionary balances, a given quantity of real money does not make life as easy as it did when transactions and real income were lower. The

---

[1] In Chapter 13 we stressed the distinction between nominal interest rates and real interest rates which are measured by subtracting the inflation rate from the nominal interest rate over the same period. Although real interest rates measure the real return on lending, the increase in purchasing power over physical goods as a result of postponing spending, it is *nominal* interest rates that affect the demand for money. Why? Because the opportunity cost of holding money is the extra or differential return between bonds and money. If π is the inflation rate and r the nominal interest rate on bonds, the real return on bonds is $r - \pi$. But in purely financial terms the real return on money is $-\pi$. That is the rate at which the purchasing power of money is being eroded by inflation. Hence the differential real return between bonds and money is $(r - \pi) - (-\pi) = r$. Since we must inflation-adjust the financial return on both money and bonds by the same inflation rate, the measurement of the differential is unaffected by inflation. The nominal interest rate is the opportunity cost with which the transactions and precautionary benefits of money must be compared.

Table 24-2 The demand for money

	EFFECT OF INCREASE IN:		
	PRICE LEVEL	REAL INCOME	INTEREST RATES
Quantity of nominal money demanded	Increases proportionately	Increases	Falls
Quantity of real money demanded	Unaffected	Increases	Falls

benefit of a bit more money is now greater. Hence in Figure 24-1 we show the *MB* schedule shifting up to *MB'* when real income increases.

At the original level of interest rates and the original *MC* schedule, the desired point is now *E"* and the desired level of money balances *L"*. Thus an increase in real income increases the quantity of real money balances demanded. Table 24-2 summarizes our discussion of the demand for money as a medium of exchange.

Thus far we have focused on the demand for M1, which measured money as a medium of exchange. Wider definitions of money must also recognize the asset motive for holding money. For example, M3 is M1 plus private sector time deposits. To explain the demand for M3 we must also consider the demand for time deposits. Figure 24-1 may be used again.

Now we interpret *MC* as the *extra* return that could be obtained on average by putting the last pound into risky assets rather than time deposits, which are safe but yield a lower return. For a given wealth, *MB* shows the marginal benefit of time deposits in reducing the riskiness of the portfolio. When no wealth is invested in time deposits the portfolio is very risky. A bad year could be a real disaster. There is a high benefit in taking out insurance by having at least some time deposits. As the quantity of time deposits increases, the danger of a disaster recedes and the marginal benefit of more time deposits falls.

Point *E* shows the desired quantity of time deposits. An increase in the average *interest differential* between risky assets and time deposits shifts the opportunity cost schedule from *MC* to *MC'* and reduces the quantity of time deposits demanded. An increase in wealth shifts the marginal benefits schedule from *MB* to *MB'* and increases the quantity of time deposits demanded.

Explaining the Rise in Money Holdings from 1965 to 1989

We now return to the question with which we began this section. Why did nominal money holdings increase from £7.6 billion in 1965 to £114 billion in 1989? Our discussion has identified three factors: prices, real income, and nominal interest rates. Table 24-3 shows how these variables changed over the period.

Although nominal money holdings grew 15-fold, the average price level also grew between 1965 and 1989. Once we divide nominal money holdings by the price index to obtain an index of real money balances, the second line of Table 24-3 shows that real money balances grew only 80 per cent over the period. Yet national output as measured by real GDP rose 75 per cent over the same period. Other things equal, rising real income and real output increase the quantity of real money demanded. But other things were not equal. Nominal interest rates almost tripled. With a

Table 24-3 Holdings of M1, 1965–89

	1965	1985	1989
Nominal money, M1 (1965 = 100)	100	860	1500
Real money, M1 (1965 = 100)	100	129	180
Real GDP (1965 = 100)	100	150	175
Nominal interest rate (Treasury bills)	5.6%	10%	14%

Source: CSO, Economic Trends.

higher opportunity cost of holding money, people managed to economize on their holdings of real balances.

Between 1965 and 1985, the increase in interest rates meant that the increase in real money demand was substantially smaller than the increase in real GDP. Why then has real money demand increased much more than real GDP during 1985–89 even though interest rates kept on increasing? Table 24-3 provides the clue to the answer. The cost of holding money is the extra return sacrificed by not putting your funds into interest-bearing Treasury bills instead. It is the interest differential between what you get on Treasury bills and what you get on money (most of which is sight deposits).

The financial revolution of the late 1980s, and the intense increase in competition, forced banks to pay ever more generous interest rates on deposits, thereby *reducing* the cost of holding money even at a time when Treasury bill interest rates were rising. Table 24-3 shows that two-thirds of sight deposits are now interest-bearing. That explains the surge in real money demand in the UK in the late 1980s. Bank deposits were a good financial investment.

24-5 Equilibrium in the Financial Markets

We have explained the forces determining the supply of money and the demand for money. We now combine supply and demand to show how equilibrium is determined.

The monetary base is the outstanding stock of currency plus commercial banks' deposits at the Bank. Through open market operations the central bank can determine the level of the monetary base. The money supply, currency in private circulation plus private sector sight deposits with the commercial banking system equals the monetary base multiplier by the money multiplier. The size of the money multiplier depends on the cash reserves ratio of the commercial banks and the cash–deposits ratio of the private sector.

The central bank can affect the banks' cash reserves ratio, and hence the money multiplier, in two ways: by imposing required reserves ratios on the commercial banking system, or by setting the discount rate – the interest rate at which the central bank will lend to commercial banks – at a penalty level which induces banks to play safe and hold extra cash reserves to minimize the risk of having to borrow from the central bank. Apart from small fluctuations in the cash–deposits ratio desired by the private sector, the central bank can in principle control the level of the money supply.

The real money supply L is the nominal money supply M divided by the price level P. We now issue a warning that should never be forgotten.

The central bank controls the *nominal* money supply. When we simplify by assuming that the price of goods is fixed, the central bank also controls the *real* money supply. But in later chapters, when we allow the price level to change, we shall see that changes in nominal money tend to lead to changes in the price level. It is then much harder for the central bank to control the real money supply.

For the moment we ignore this difficulty. With given prices, the central bank can determine both the nominal money supply and the real money supply.

In the last section we emphasized that the demand for money is a demand for real money balances. The quantity of real money demanded increases with the level of real income but decreases with the level of nominal interest rates. For the moment, we focus exclusively on the financial markets for money and bonds. We examine market equilibrium for a *given* level of real income and real output of goods and services. Having mastered this analysis, in the next chapter we can study how the financial markets interact with the markets for goods and labour to determine the equilibrium level of real income itself.

Money Market Equilibrium

The money market is in *equilibrium* when the quantity of real balances demanded equals the quantity supplied.

Figure 24-2 shows the demand curve LL for real money balances for a given level of real income. The higher the interest rate and the opportunity cost of holding money, the lower the quantity of real money balances demanded. With a given

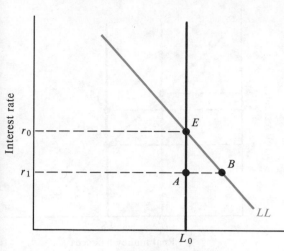

Real money balances

Figure 24-2   MONEY MARKET EQUILIBRIUM.
The demand schedule for real balances LL is drawn
for a given level of real income. The higher the
opportunity cost of holding money, the lower the real
balances demanded. The real money supply
schedule is vertical at the level L_0. The equilibrium
point is E and the equilibrium interest rate, r_0. At a
lower interest rate r_1 there is excess demand for
money AB. There must be a corresponding excess
supply of bonds. This reduces bond prices and
increases the return on bonds, driving the interest
rate up to its equilibrum level at which both markets
clear.

price level, the central bank controls the
quantity of nominal money and real money.
The supply curve is vertical at this quantity of
real money L_0. Equilibrium is at the point E.
At the interest rate r_0 the quantity of real
money that people wish to hold just equals the
outstanding stock L_0.

Suppose the interest rate is r_1, lower than the
equilibrium level r_0. There is an excess demand
for money given by the distance AB in Figure
24-2. How does this excess demand for money
bid the interest rate up from r_1 to r_0 to restore
equilibrium? The answer to this question is
rather subtle.

Strictly speaking, there is no such thing as a
market for money. Money is the medium of
exchange. It is what we use for payments or
receipts when making transactions in *other*
markets. A market for money would involve
buying and selling pounds with other pounds,
which makes no sense.

The other market of relevance to Figure 24-2

is the market for bonds. In saying that the
interest rate is the opportunity cost of holding
money, we are saying that people who don't
hold money will hold bonds instead. And it is
what is happening explicitly in the market for
bonds that determines what is happening in the
implicit market for money shown in Figure
24-2.

The stock of real wealth W is equal to the
total outstanding stock or supply of real money
L_0 and real bonds B_0. People have to decide
how they wish to divide up their total wealth
W between desired real bond holdings B^D and
desired real money holdings L^D. *Whatever
factors determine this division, it must be true
that*

$$L_0 + B_0 = W = L^D + B^D \qquad (1)$$

The total supply of real assets determines the
wealth to be divided between real money and
real bonds. And people cannot plan to divide
up wealth they do not have. Since the left-hand
side of equation (1) must equal the right-hand
side, it follows that

$$B_0 - B^D = L^D - L_0 \qquad (2)$$

An excess demand for money must be exactly
matched by an excess supply of bonds.
Otherwise people would be planning to hold
more wealth than they actually possess.

This insight allows us to explain how an excess
demand for money at the interest rate r_1 in
Figure 24-2 sets in motion forces that will bid
up the interest rate to its equilibrium level r_0.
With excess demand for money, there is an
excess supply of bonds. To induce people to
hold more bonds, suppliers of bonds must offer
a higher interest rate.[2] As the interest rate rises,
people switch out of money and into bonds.
The higher interest rate reduces both the excess
supply of bonds and the excess demand
for money. At the interest rate r_0 the supply and
demand for money are equal. Since the excess

---

[2] A bond is a commitment by the original issuer to pay a given
stream of interest payments over a given time period. In
Chapter 13 we explained that the price of a bond should be
the present value of this stream of payments. The higher the
interest rate at which this stream is being discounted, the lower
the price of a bond. Equivalently, the lower the price of a
bond, the higher the rate of return that the promised stream
of payments will yield. With excess supply in the bond market,
bond prices fall and the interest rate or rate of return on bonds
rises.

demand for money is zero, the excess supply of bonds is also zero. The money market is in equilibrium only when the bond market is also in equilibrium. People wish to divide their wealth in precisely the ratio of the relative supplies of money and bonds.

For the rest of this chapter, we focus on the implicit market for money. However equations (1) and (2) imply that, once we know total wealth, any statement about what is happening in the money market is simultaneously a statement about what is happening in the bond market. That is why we called this section 'Equilibrium in the financial markets' rather than simply 'Money market equilibrium'.

Changes in Equilibrium

A shift in either the supply curve for money or the demand curve for money will alter the equilibrium position in the money market (and the bond market). These shifts are examined in Figure 24-3.

A Fall in the Money Supply   Suppose the central bank reduces the money supply, either by undertaking an open market sale of securities to reduce the monetary base or by taking steps to make banks increase their cash reserve ratios and reduce the value of the money multiplier. Given our assumption that the price level is given, this contraction in the nominal money supply will also reduce the real money supply. Figure 24-3 shows this as a leftward shift in the supply curve. The real money stock falls from L_0 to L'. The equilibrium interest rate rises from r_0 to r'. It takes a higher interest rate to reduce the demand for real balances in line with the lower quantity supplied. Hence a reduction in the real money supply leads to an increase in the equilibrium interest rate. Conversely, an increase in the real money supply reduces the equilibrium interest rate. It takes a lower interest rate to induce people to hold larger real money balances.

An Increase in Real Income   In Figure 24-3 we draw the demand curve for real balances LL for a given level of real income. As we explained in Figure 24-1, an increase in real income increases the marginal benefit of holding money at each interest rate, and increases the quantity of real balances demanded. Hence in Figure

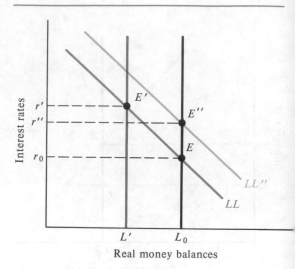

Figure 24-3 EQUILIBRIUM INTEREST RATES. With a given real income, LL is the demand schedule for real money balances. A reduction in the real money supply from L_0 to L' moves the equilibrium point from E to E'. Equilibrium interest rates increase from r_0 to r' to reduce the quantity of money demanded in line with the fall in the quantity supplied. With a given supply of real money L_0, an increase in real income shifts the demand schedule from LL to LL''. The equilibrium point moves from E to E'' and equilibrium interest rates must increase from r_0 to r''. Higher real income tends to increase the quantity of real money demanded and higher interest rates are required to offset this, maintaining the quantity of real money demanded in line with the unchanged real supply.

24-3 we show the money demand schedule LL shifting to the right, to LL'', when real income increases. Since people wish to hold more real balances at each interest rate, the equilibrium interest rate must rise from r_0 to r'' to keep the quantity of real balances demanded equal to the unchanged real supply L_0. Conversely, a reduction in real income will shift the LL schedule to the left and reduce the equilibrium interest rate.

An Increase in Banking Competition   In Figure 24-3 we also draw the demand curve LL for a given level of interest rates paid on bank deposits. Holding this rate constant, an increase in market interest rates r reduces the quantity of money demanded. A once-and-for-all increase in banking competition, reflected by a permanent increase in interest rates paid on bank deposits, will increase the demand for bank deposits at any level of market interest rates r. Again, the demand curve shifts from LL to LL''. For a given money supply, this bids up equilibrium market interest rates.

To sum up, an increase in the real money supply reduces the equilibrium interest rate. A lower interest rate reduces the attractiveness of bonds and induces people to switch from bonds to money. It is necessary to induce people to hold the higher real money stock. An increase in real income increases the equilibrium interest rate. A higher interest rate offsets the tendency of higher real income to increase the quantity of real money balances demanded, and thus maintains the demand for real balances in line with the unchanged supply. An increase in banking competition has similar effects.

24-6 Monetary Control in the UK

Our theoretical analysis tells us how the central bank can control the money supply and thus, for a given money demand schedule, determine the equilibrium level of interest rates. To see how our analysis helps us understand the real world, we now examine the Bank of England in action. We begin with a review of recent policy. In the following section we discuss the practical problems that have lain behind the search for more effective methods of monetary control.

Controls before 1971

Prior to 1971, four instruments of control were used. First, every Thursday the Bank announced the discount rate at which it would act as lender of last resort to the banking system. Known first as Bank Rate and, since 1972, as Minimum Lending Rate (MLR), this interest rate was sometimes though not invariably set at a penalty level in excess of current interest rates. Second, clearing banks were subject to reserve requirements: a cash ratio of at least 8 per cent of their deposits and a liquid asset ratio of at least 28 per cent of their deposits. Liquid assets were cash reserves plus liquid lending such as purchases of Treasury bills which could easily be resold. In addition, clearing banks were sometimes subject to Special Deposits, a requirement to hold deposits

at the Bank that could *not* be counted towards the fulfilment of required asset ratios. Third, clearing banks were subject to *ceilings* both on interest rates and on the quantity of bank lending. Finally, the Bank undertook open market operations to alter the monetary base, the money supply, and the equilibrium level of interest rates.

In practice, this system discriminated against the clearing banks. Reserve requirements and special deposits restricted their ability to make advances and other long-term loans. Other banks—the merchant banks dealing with large companies, and foreign banks—were unregulated and expanded their lending business rapidly. Moreover, they offered their depositors interest-bearing chequing accounts which formed part of the money supply. Confining monetary control to the clearing banks became increasingly ineffective.

Competition and Credit Control

In 1971 the change in Bank policy was set out in the document *Competition and Credit Control*. Interest rate ceilings for clearing bank time deposits and advances were scrapped. Banks were able to compete for deposits and advances. Reserve requirements were extended to all banks though in a modified form. Banks had to hold liquid assets equal to at least $12\frac{1}{2}$ per cent of their *eligible liabilities*, essentially their sterling deposits issued to the non-bank public. As part of this reserve requirement, clearing banks were required to hold cash balances at the Bank equal to $1\frac{1}{2}$ per cent of their eligible liabilities. MLR was retained.

In practice, 1971–73 saw a dramatic rise in the money supply, especially when broadly measured. Sterling M3 grew by more than 60 per cent in two years. To stem the flood, the Bank introduced the Supplementary Special Deposit scheme, which became popularly known as the 'Corset'. Box 24-2 gives details and illustrates the hazards of trying to regulate financial markets.

Policy since 1980

In 1981 the reserve requirements were scrapped. The Bank now relies on the desired ratios of cash and liquid assets to total deposits that commercial banks adopt in their own self-

BOX 24-2

THE CORSET: NO HELP FOR THE WEIGHT-WATCHER?

After 1971 banks faced a minimum liquid assets ratio of $12\frac{1}{2}$ per cent of eligible sterling deposits. The Bank controlled the total supply of liquid assets but not its division between banks and the non-bank public. In 1971–73 the demand for bank loans was strong. To acquire liquid assets to allow an expansion of profitable lending, banks offered such high interest rates on time deposits that the non-bank public sold their liquid assets to the banks and held their wealth in interest-bearing bank deposits instead. Banks had more liquid assets and expanded lending, which grew by 38 per cent in 1973 alone. With the rapid expansion of interest-bearing deposits, sterling M3 grew by 28 per cent in 1973, considerably faster than the growth in M1.

To combat this explosion, the Bank introduced the 'Corset', a tax on deposit-financed bank lending. The more funds commercial banks attracted through this route, the more they had to deposit in a *non-interest-bearing* account at the Bank. The Corset was not finally abandoned until 1980. It was not really a success.

The banks found two ways round its restrictions. First, they colluded with firms to ensure that firms could borrow *without* its showing up in banks'

balance sheets. Firms issued bills promising to pay interest for a certain period. The banks 'accepted' these bills. For a small fee, they guaranteed the bills against default by the issuing firm. But they did not actually buy the bills. With a bank guarantee, the non-bank public bought these new liquid assets and effectively lent to firms. Firms got their loans without it showing up in figures for bank lending, the money supply, or the deposits which triggered Corset penalties. Second, banks and firms arranged to do business abroad where Corset regulations did not apply.

This is an example of Goodhart's law, named after Professor Charles Goodhart. Unlike producers of motor cars, modern financial intermediaries can easily substitute one way of producing their services for another, and are quick to invent new, and only fractionally more expensive, means of carrying on the old business. Just as an old-fashioned corset doesn't make you lose weight but merely shifts the flab to a different place, Goodhart's law says that attempts by the Bank to regulate or tax one channel of banking business quickly lead to the same business being conducted through a different channel which is untaxed or unregulated.

---

interest. As Table 23-1 showed, with well developed markets for liquid assets, modern banks can get by with cash reserves of only 1 or 2 per cent of deposits. Although the Bank is still committed to act as lender of last resort, announced MLR has also been scrapped. Nowadays, commercial banks have to guess how much of a penalty will be imposed if they have to borrow from the Bank. To further concentrate the mind, official target paths for the money supply and the PSBR were announced in 1980 in the government's Medium Term Financial Strategy, which we discuss in detail in Chapter 28. By 1986 these targets had been considerably 'de-emphasized'.

Can we use the analysis of the last two chapters to make sense of these developments?

24-7 Practical Problems of Monetary Control

We begin by examining the practical problems entailed when the Bank tries to implement the

textbook theory of monetary control, namely the use of open market operations to determine the monetary base and the use of reserve requirements and the discount rate to influence the size of the money multiplier.

Monetary Base Control

Suppose first that the Bank imposes a cash reserve requirement on the banks, as in the 8 per cent ratio requirement before 1971. The first problem is Goodhart's law, which we set out in Box 24-2. These controls act as a tax on banks, preventing them from undertaking business that they would otherwise have found profitable. Modern banks, with access to sophisticated telecommunications, will try to find ways round these controls. They may well conduct lending business with domestic firms through foreign markets in Frankfurt, Zurich, or New York.

To avoid this problem, the Bank can dispense with a *required* cash ratio and rely on open market operations and changes in the monetary base to work through a money multiplier whose size is determined by the cash ratio that banks wish to hold for purely commercial purposes. This is one reason why formal reserve requirements were scrapped in the early 1980s.

Nevertheless, the Bank argues that there is one key problem in trying to work through the monetary base: the Bank's role as lender of last resort. When the banks wish to increase lending and deposits they can *always* get extra cash from the Bank. That is why, both before and after 1971, the Bank imposed *liquid assets* ratio requirements. The idea was that the Bank would control the total supply of liquid assets, basically cash plus short-term government bills, and the banks could always sell bills to the Bank when they were short of cash. Since the exchange of cash for bills would not alter the outstanding stock of liquid assets, the Bank could control the money supply through a liquid assets multiplier instead of a money multiplier.

In such a system, we can think of the money supply as the liquid assets multiplier multiplied by the liquid assets base or stock of liquid assets outstanding. The liquid assets multiplier is larger (*a*) the lower the banks' ratio of liquid assets to deposits and (*b*) the lower the fraction of outstanding liquid assets held by the non-bank public and the higher the fraction held by the banks. How would the Bank control the liquid assets base? Not by buying and selling bills, which simply exchanges one liquid asset for another, but by buying and selling long-term bonds, which are not liquid assets. Sales of long-term bonds take cash out of the system and reduce the liquid assets base.

But, as Box 24-2 makes clear, this system also has difficulties. Although the non-bank private sector holds cash in a very stable ratio to deposits, its demand for other liquid assets is much more sensitive to interest rates. By offering generous interest rates, banks can acquire liquid assets from the private sector and give them time deposits instead. By getting a larger share of the outstanding liquid assets, banks can increase the size of the liquid assets multiplier.

How can banks afford to pay such generous rates on time deposits? Because the demand for bank loans is not very sensitive to interest rates. If a company is in trouble it will be happy to borrow at almost any interest rate the banks charge. When the demand for loans is strong, banks increase their overdraft charges. With correspondingly high rates on time deposits, banks can induce the private sector to swap holdings of liquid assets for holdings of time deposits without any cash drain on the banking system. Thus banks acquire the extra liquid assets they need to expand lending and create new overdraft sight deposits.

Can't the central bank do anything to prevent banks expanding lending and deposits whenever they wish? One possibility is a more vigorous use of the discount rate for last-resort loans. Suppose that, when the banks want cash, the Bank forces them to apply for a loan of last resort at an interest rate not previously announced. By sometimes charging a very high penalty rate, the Bank can make the commercial banks rather wary of being caught short in this manner. This is one reason why the Bank has abandoned the policy of pre-announcing MLR. It hopes that the uncertainty will make banks more cautious and, on average, make them carry larger reserves.

Nevertheless, we can see that there are some tricky problems in trying to implement the textbook account of monetary control in the real world. In practice, the Bank has judged these difficulties to be quite important and has leant towards an alternative method of monetary control which we now examine.

Control Through Interest Rates

Figure 24-4 shows again the market for money. We draw the money demand schedule LL for a given level of real income. If the central bank were able to control the money supply, then for a given level of goods prices the central bank could fix the real money supply, say at L_0. The equilibrium level of interest rates would be r_0.

Alternatively, the central bank can fix the interest rate at r_0 and provide whatever money is required to clear the market at this interest rate. The central bank simply announces that it is ready to deal in interest-bearing assets in unlimited quantities at r_0. In equilibrium, the central bank will end up supplying exactly the quantity of money that is demanded at the interest rate r_0. The money supply will be L_0.

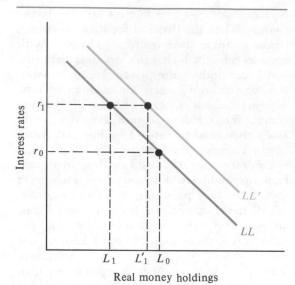

Figure 24-4 INTEREST RATES AND MONETARY
CONTROL. The money demand schedule *LL* is
drawn for a given level of real income. If the Bank
can fix the real money supply at L_0 the equilibrium
interest rate will be r_0. Alternatively, if the Bank sets
the interest rate r_0 and provides whatever money is
demanded, the money supply will again be L_0. To
control the money supply by using interest rates, the
Bank must know the position of the demand
schedule. Fixing an interest rate r_1, the resulting
money supply will be L_1 if the demand schedule is
LL but will be L'_1 if the demand schedule is *LL'*.

The central bank can fix the money supply
and accept the equilibrium interest rate
implied by the money demand equation, or
it can fix the interest rate and accept the
equilibrium money supply implied by the
money demand equation.

Faced with all the problems in trying to control
the money supply directly, the Bank has
preferred to set interest rates, directly or
indirectly, and then provide the money the
market demanded. This is one reason why, in
practice, the Bank has frequently been prepared
to act as lender of last resort without charging
a penalty rate.

How easy is monetary control through
interest rates? It too has its difficulties. To
achieve a particular monetary target, the Bank
must be able to estimate accurately the demand
schedule for money. Not only must the Bank
know the slope of the *LL* schedule; it must
know how it shifts as real income changes.

In his evidence to a House of Commons

investigation of monetary policy in 1980,
Professor Milton Friedman criticized the attempt to control the money supply indirectly
via income, interest rates, and hence money
demand, rather than directly through a system
of monetary base control.

A precise analogy is like trying to control the output of
motor cars by altering the incomes of potential purchasers
and manipulating rail and air fares. In principle, possible
but in practice, highly inefficient. Far easier to control
the output of motor cars by controlling the availability of
a basic raw material, say steel, to manufacturers – a precise
analogy to controlling the availability of base money to
banks and others.[3]

Financial Innovation: The Policy Problem

To control the money supply in the manner
suggested by Figure 24-4, it is essential that
policy-makers are able to assess accurately the
position of the money demand schedule *LL*:
only then can they infer what interest rates to
set to achieve a given monetary target.

We have already discussed the increasing
trend in the 1980s for banks to offer competitive
interest rates on sight deposits. Ten years ago
this was rare, but by 1989 two-thirds of all right
deposits bore interest, and before long this will
probably be extended even to households with
small deposits. Many other financial innovations
are also in progress, such as the use of cheques
against interest-bearing building society accounts.

Such developments reduce the opportunity
cost of holding money by reducing the interest
differential between that earned on other
lending and that earned on money itself. In
consequence, the demand for real money
increases. Since these innovations are currently
proceeding at a rapid but uncertain rate,
the monetary authorities were finding it very
difficult by the mid-1980s to be confident that
they knew the position of the *LL* schedule in
Figure 24-4. In his important Loughborough
speech in October 1986, the Governor of the
Bank of England effectively admitted that
accurate monetary control through interest
rates was impossible, at least while financial
innovation proceeded at such a pace.

In the late 1980s, the government tried to get
round this problem in two ways. The first was

[3] Milton Friedman, 'Memorandum on Monetary Policy',
Treasury and Civil Service Committee, *Memoranda on
Monetary Policy*, HMSO, 1980.

to try, on occasion, to regulate the economy through the effect of interest rates on the exchange rate rather than directly on the domestic economy. We discuss this in more detail in Chapter 29. The second method was to focus increasingly on controlling very narrow money M0 rather than wider measures of money such as M1 or M4.

Because M0 is essentially non-interest-bearing cash, it is much easier to predict the position of the demand for M0, which is much less vulnerable to the rapid but uncertain financial revolution that is still under way.

Summary

1   The Bank of England is the UK central bank acting as banker to the banks and to the government. Because it can print money it can never go bust. It acts as lender of last resort to the banks.

2   The Bank is responsible for implementing the government's monetary policy. It controls the monetary base through open market operations, purchases and sales of government securities. In addition, the Bank can affect the size of the money multiplier by imposing reserve requirements on the banks, calling for Special Deposits, or setting the discount rate for last resort loans at a penalty level which encourages banks to hold excess reserves.

3   The Bank is also responsible for managing the outstanding stock of government debt, issuing new bonds to replace old bonds which have become due for redemption or repurchase.

4   The demand for money is a demand for real balances. Money is valued for its subsequent purchasing power over goods. The demand for the medium of exchange M1 depends on comparing the transactions and precautionary benefits of holding another pound with the interest sacrificed by not holding interest-bearing assets instead. The quantity of real balances demanded falls as the interest rate rises. Increases in real income, a proxy for total transactions, increase the quantity of real balances demanded at each interest rate.

5   For wider definitions of money such as M3, the asset motive for holding money is also relevant. When other interest-bearing assets are risky, people will diversify their portfolios by holding some of the safe asset, money. When there is no immediate need to make transactions, this leads to a demand for holding interest-bearing time deposits rather than non-interest-bearing sight deposits. The demand for time deposits will be larger the larger the total wealth to be invested and the lower the interest differential between time deposits and risky assets.

6   There is no explicit market in money. Because people can only plan to hold the total supply of assets that they own, any excess supply of bonds must be exactly matched by an excess demand for money. Interest rates adjust to clear the market for bonds. In so doing, they ensure that the money market is in equilibrium.

7   An increase in the real money supply reduces the equilibrium interest rate. An increase in real income increases the equilibrium interest rate.

8   In practice, the Bank finds it difficult to control the money supply exactly. Imposing artificial regulations drives banking business into unregulated channels. Monetary base control is difficult since the bank is committed to act as a lender of last resort and supply cash when needed. Although it is easier for the Bank to control the liquid assets base, it is difficult to prevent the banks acquiring a larger share of this base when they need to attract funds to expand lending.

9   In practice, the Bank has preferred to control the money supply by operating directly on interest rates and allowing the demand for money to determine the quantity of money that must then be supplied. This indirect system of monetary control has been subject to some criticism. It has also been rendered much less predictable by rapid financial innovation, which has shifted the money demand schedule in a way that is not easy to assess accurately.

Key Terms

Central bank
Lender of last resort
Debt management
Required reserve ratio
Discount rate

Open market operations
Money multiplier
Nominal and real money balances
Transactions, precautionary, and asset motives
Opportunity cost of holding money
Money market equilibrium
Liquid assets ratio
Special deposits
The Corset
Goodhart's law

Problems

1 Suppose the Bank conducts a £1 million open market sale of securities to Mr Jones who banks with Barclays. (*a*) If Mr Jones pays by cheque, show the effect of the deal on the balance sheets of the Bank of England and Barclays Bank. (*b*) What happens to the money supply? (*c*) Would the answer be the same if Mr Jones had paid in cash?

2 Suppose the Bank required commercial banks to hold 100 per cent cash reserves against deposits. Repeat your answers to question 1. What is the value of the money multiplier?

3 What effect do you expect the widespread adoption of credit cards to have on the precautionary demand for money by households? Explain. Be sure to take account of the demand for sight deposits as well as the demand for cash.

4 Suppose banks raise interest rates on time deposits whenever interest rates on bank loans and other assets rise. (*a*) Will a rise in the general level of interest rates have a large or a small effect on the demand for time deposits? (*b*) If the government is worried about the effect of high interest rates on electors who have large loans to finance house purchases, does this imply that it will be easy or difficult for the government to reduce M3 by a large amount?

5 Explain how the Corset worked. How is Goodhart's law relevant?

6 Why has the Bank of England felt that a required cash ratio for the banks must be supplemented by a required liquid assets ratio? Why have both now been scrapped?

7 Common Fallacies Explain why the following statements are incorrect: (*a*) The abolition of reserve requirements implied that the Bank had given up any attempt to control the money supply. (*b*) When inflation exceeds nominal interest rates, real interest rates are negative. People are actually being paid to hold money. (*c*) Interest rates are high. This proves that the money supply has been tightly controlled.

25

Monetary and Fiscal Policy in a Closed Economy

In this chapter we extend the simple model of income determination developed in Chapters 20 and 21. For the moment we assume a closed economy. Exports, imports, and the foreign sector will be reintroduced in Chapter 29 once we have mastered the analysis of a closed economy. First, we relax the simple assumptions with which we began our study of aggregate demand and income determination. We give a more complete account of the determinants of consumption and investment demand and explain why lower interest rates would boost aggregate demand and national income.

Then we start to use the analysis of money and interest rates developed in the last two chapters. For a given money supply, we saw that higher income would increase equilibrium interest rates to maintain the demand for money in line with its fixed supply. Thus we now discuss a model in which the level of income affects interest rates but the level of interest rates also affects aggregate demand and equilibrium income. We explain how the money market and the output market interact to determine simultaneously the equilibrium level of income *and* interest rates.

Within this model we then examine how the government can affect the equilibrium level of income by altering the money supply, and hence interest rates and aggregate demand. We also reassess the role of fiscal policy in this extended model. Finally, we discuss how the government can use a mix of monetary and fiscal policy to manage or control the level and composition of aggregate demand.

In this chapter, we persist with the assumption that prices remain fixed. The interest rate is the key variable connecting the markets for money and output. In the following chapter, we allow prices to change and show that the price level is a second variable relating the markets for money and output. Chapter 29 shows that, in an open economy such as the UK, the foreign sector provides a third linkage between the financial markets and the 'real economy' in which output and employment are determined.

25-1 The Consumption Function Again

We begin our re-examination of aggregate demand, or total planned spending on goods and services, by looking again at the consumption function. In Chapter 21 we used a very simple model of aggregate consumption demand. The consumption function was an upward-sloping straight line relating aggregate consumption to the total personal disposable income of households. The slope of this line, the marginal propensity to consume, showed the fraction of each extra pound of disposable income that households would spend rather than save. The height of the consumption function depended on autonomous consumption demand. It captured all determinants of consumption spending except personal disposable income. Changes in disposable income moved households along the consumption function. Changes in autonomous demand shifted the consumption function.

Now we consider autonomous consumption demand in more detail. What factors shift the consumption function?

Determinants of Autonomous Consumption Spending

Household Wealth   Suppose there is an increase in the real value of household wealth, for example a boom on the stock market which increases the value of company shares held by households. If households never spend this extra wealth, they will have to leave it all to their children. In practice, households are likely to use some of their extra wealth to pay for a new car or an extra holiday. For a given level of disposable income, consumption spending will increase. Since this happens whatever the level of disposable income, the entire consumption function shifts up when household wealth increases. We say there is a wealth effect.

> The *wealth effect* is the upward (downward) shift in the consumption function when household wealth increases (decreases) and people spend more (less) at each level of personal disposable income.

Can money and interest rates affect household wealth and hence consumption and aggregate demand? Yes, in two different ways. First, since money is one of the assets in which households hold their wealth, an increase in the real money supply adds directly to household wealth. Second, to the extent that an increase in the money supply reduces equilibrium interest rates, this will increase household wealth indirectly. Using the concept of present values explained in Chapter 13, the market price of corporate shares and long-term government bonds is the present value of the expected stream of divided earnings or promised interest payments. When interest rates fall, future earnings must now be discounted at a lower interest rate and are worth more today. Thus, reductions in interest rates make the price of bonds and corporate shares rise and make households wealthier.[1]

Durables and Consumer Credit When rich people spend more than their current disposable income they simply run down their wealth, selling off some company shares or using up money in their bank account. Poorer people don't have many spare assets that can be sold

to finance an excess of spending over disposable income. They have to borrow.

Although some people borrow money to spend on things like holidays, most consumer borrowing is used to finance purchases of *consumer durables*; household capital goods such as televisions, furniture, and cars. Splashing out on a new car can cost a whole year's income.

Two aspects of consumer credit or borrowing possibilities affect consumption spending. First, there is the quantity of credit on offer. If banks decide to give more generous overdrafts or retailers extend more generous loans to customers through hire purchase instalment plans, more people are likely to overspend their current disposable income and buy the car, stereo, or dream kitchen they have always wanted. An increase in the supply of consumer credit shifts the consumption function upwards. People spend more at any level of disposable income. Second, the cost of consumer credit matters. The higher the interest rate, the lower the quantity that households can borrow while still being able to meet the interest payments and loan repayment out of their future disposable incomes.

Money and interest rates thus affect consumer spending by affecting both the quantity of consumer credit and the interest rates charged on it. An increase in the monetary base increases the cash reserves of the banking system and allows it to extend more consumer credit in the form of overdrafts. And by reducing the cost of consumer credit, lower interest rates allow households to take out bigger loans while still being able to meet the interest and repayments. Both these effects tend to increase consumer spending relative to disposable income and shift the consumption function upwards.

Those two forces – wealth effects and changes in consumer credit – account for most of the shifts in the consumption function. They are part of the *transmission mechanism* through which changes in the financial sector affect output and employment in the real economy. Operating through wealth effects or the supply and cost of consumer credit, changes in the money supply and in interest rates can shift the consumption function and the aggregate demand schedule, thus affecting the equilibrium level of income and output. We now think about these same effects from a slightly different viewpoint.

---

[1] We can reach the same conclusion using the less technical reasoning of Box 23-1. When interest rates are 10 per cent, a bond promising to pay £2.50 for ever will trade today for about £25 so that new buyers get about 10 per cent a year on their investment. If interest rates fall to 5 per cent, bond prices must rise to £50 if new buyers are to get an annual return in line with interest rates on other assets. A similar argument applies to company shares, even though share prices are based upon guesses about future dividend payments.

Modern Theories of the Consumption Function

Two closely related theories of the consumption function re-interpret these phenomena and make some of their subtleties more explicit.

The Permanent Income Hypothesis   Developed by Professor Milton Friedman, this hypothesis starts from two propositions: first, people's incomes fluctuate; second, people dislike fluctuating consumption. A few extra bottles of champagne in the years when consumption is high is little compensation for going hungry in the years when consumption is low. Rather than allowing fluctuations in income to be reflected in fluctuations in consumption, people have an incentive to even out fluctuations in consumption. People will go without champagne to avoid ever being hungry.

What determines the consumption that people can afford on average? Friedman coined the term *permanent income* to describe people's average income in the long run. And he argued that consumption depends not on current disposable income but on permanent income. When people believe that current income is unusually high they will recognize that this temporarily high income makes little difference to their permanent income or the amount of consumption they can afford in the long run. Since their permanent income has hardly risen, they will hardly increase their current consumption. Rather, they will save most of their temporary extra income and put money aside to see them through the years when income is unusually low. Only if people believe that a rise in today's income is likely to be sustained as higher future incomes will they believe that their permanent income has significantly increased. And only then will a large rise in current income be matched by a large rise in current consumption.

The Life-cycle Hypothesis   Developed by Professors Franco Modigliani and Albert Ando, this theory is very similar to the permanent income hypothesis. People form their best guess about the income they will earn over their lifetimes and form a lifetime consumption plan (including any bequests to their children) which can just be financed out of lifetime income (plus any initial wealth or inheritances).

At the level of the individual household, this theory does not require that each household plans a constant consumption level over its lifetime. There may be years of heavy expenditure (splashing out on a round-the world cruise or sending the kids to private school) and other years when spending is a bit less. However, such individual discrepancies tend to cancel out in the aggregate. As with the permanent income hypothesis, the life-cycle hypothesis suggests that it is average long-run income that is likely to determine the total demand for consumer spending.

Figure 25-1 shows a household's actual income over its lifetime. Income rises with career seniority until retirement, then drops to the lower level provided by a pension. The household's permanent income is *OD*. Technically, this is the constant annual income with the same present value as the present value of the actual stream of income. If the household consumed exactly its permanent income, it would consume *OD* each year and die penniless. The two shaded areas labelled *A* show when the household would be spending more than its

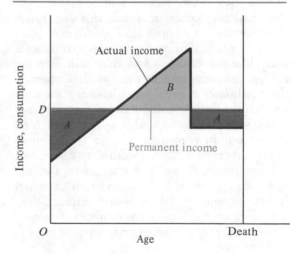

Figure 25-1 CONSUMPTION AND THE LIFE-CYCLE. Actual disposable income rises over a household's lifetime until retirement, then falls to the pension level. Permanent income is the constant income level *OD* with the same present value as actual income. Suppose consumption equals permanent income. The areas *A* show total dissaving and the area *B*, total saving. In the absence of inherited wealth and bequests, *B* must be large enough to repay borrowing with interest and also build up enough wealth to supplement actual income during retirement.

current income and the area *B* shows when the household would be saving.

Although the household spends its income over its lifetime, the area *B* is not the sum of the two areas *A*. We must also take account of interest. In the early years of low income, the household borrows. The area *B* shows how much the household has to save to pay back the initial borrowing *with interest* and accumulate sufficient wealth to see it through the final years when it is again dissaving.

Now let's think about wealth effects and consumer credit again. With more initial wealth, a household can spend more in every year of its lifetime without ever going broke. We can shift the permanent income line in Figure 25-1 upwards and consumption will rise. Although the area *B* is now smaller and the areas *A* are now larger, the household can use its extra wealth to meet this shortfall between the years of saving (the area *B*) and the years of dissaving (the two areas *A)*.

Although we again conclude that higher wealth leads to more consumption at any level of current disposable income, we pick up something we missed earlier. If households believe their *future* income will be higher than they had previously imagined, this also raises their permanent income. Households can spend more in every year and still expect to balance their lifetime budget. And they will increase *current* consumption as soon as they upgrade their estimates of their future incomes. We now see that the present value of future income plays a role very similar to wealth. It is money to be shared out in consumption over the lifetime. Friedman called it 'human wealth', to distinguish it from financial and physical assets. But the important point is that increases in expected future incomes will have wealth effects; they will shift up the simple consumption function relating *current* consumption to *current* disposable income.

How about consumer credit? An increase in interest rates reduces the present value of future incomes and makes households worse off today. In terms of Figure 25-1, households must enlarge area *B* to meet the extra interest costs of paying back money borrowed in area *A* during the early years of the lifetime. We must shift the permanent income line downwards. Thus, an increase in interest rates reduces current consumption not merely by reducing

the market value of financial assets such as company shares, but also by reducing the present value of future labour income. By reducing human wealth, it shifts the simple consumption function downwards.

Finally, how about an increase in the quantity of consumer credit on offer? Figure 25-1 assumes that people can spend more than their incomes in the early years of their lifetime. Students run up overdrafts knowing that, as rich economists, they can pay them back later. But what if nobody will lend? Then people without wealth are restricted by their actual incomes, although people with wealth can lend to themselves by running down their wealth. Hence an increase in the availability of consumer credit allows people who would like to dissave in the early years to follow this policy without being forced to keep consumption in line with their low current incomes. Total consumption will increase. More students will run up overdrafts and buy cars.

The purpose of this section has been to show how wealth effects and changes in consumer credit shift the consumption function which relates consumption to current disposable income. The modern theories of consumption allow a slightly different perspective on these same phenomena; and when we reassess fiscal policy later in the chapter, they warn us to pay attention to one final point.

A tax cut that is expected to be permanent will increase people's current and future disposable incomes. Hence it will shift their average or permanent income by quite a lot. However, a tax cut that is known to be temporary will affect only current disposable income. Since it has no effect on expected future disposable incomes, it will have little effect on permanent income. Hence *temporary* tax cuts will have little effect on current consumption; permanent tax cuts will have a much larger effect. And it is whether or not people *believe* that the tax cut is permanent that counts.

25-2 Investment Demand

In earlier chapters we treated investment demand as autonomous, or independent of the current level of income and output. In this section we begin to analyse the forces that determine the level of investment demand. Here we focus on the role of interest rates. Other determinants of investment demand are considered in greater detail in Chapter 30.

Total investment spending comprises investment in fixed capital and investment in working capital. Fixed capital includes factories, houses, plant, and machinery. Working capital consists of stocks or inventories. We begin by looking at the facts. Figure 25-2 shows recent UK data measured in billions of pounds at 1985 prices.

Total investment has fluctuated between £45 billion and £83 billion. Since real GDP is nearly £400 billion, these numbers imply that the share of investment in GDP fluctuates between 10 and 20 per cent.[2] The figure distinguishes investment in fixed capital by the private sector and the public sector (the government plus the nationalized industries). Public investment has been falling as the government has increasingly

tried to keep its spending in check. Private investment in fixed capital has fluctuated a bit but grew strongly in the late 1980s. In recent years, fluctuations in inventories have been quite dramatic. Although the total volume of stockbuilding or destocking is quite small, this component of total investment is much the most volatile and contributes significantly to changes in the total level of investment.

How are we to organize our thoughts about investment? Our model of aggregate demand in a closed economy distinguishes consumption C, investment I, and government spending G on goods and services. Public investment is part of G, and we continue to treat government demand as part of the government's general fiscal policy. Thus we assume that G is fixed at a level determined by the government. In this section it is the determination of private investment demand I on which we focus.

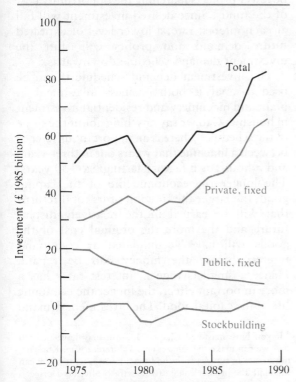

Figure 25-2   UK INVESTMENT (1985 prices). (*Source*: CSO, *Economic Trends*.)

Investment in Fixed Capital

Firms add to their plant and equipment because they foresee profitable opportunities to expand their output, or because they can reduce costs by moving to more capital-intensive production methods. British Telecom needs new equipment because it is developing new products such as car phones. The Rover Group needs new assembly lines because it is substituting robots for workers in car production.

In each case, the firm has to weigh the benefits from new plant or equipment – the increase in profits – against the cost of investment. But the benefit occurs only in the future, whereas the costs are incurred immediately as the plant is built or the machine purchased. The firm must compare the value of extra future profits with the current cost of the investment.

Here is where the interest rate comes in. The firm has to ask whether the investment will return enough extra profits to pay back *with interest* the loan used to finance the original investment. Equivalently, if the project is funded out of existing profits, the firm has to ask whether the new investment will yield a return at least as great as the return that could otherwise have been earned by lending the money out at interest. The higher the interest rate, the larger must be the return on a new

---

[2] These numbers refer to *gross* investment or the production of *new* capital goods. Since the capital stock is depreciating, or wearing out, it takes something like £20 billion of gross investment per annum merely to maintain the existing capital stock intact.

investment before it will match the opportunity cost of the funds tied up in it.

At any instant there is a host of investment projects that the firm *could* undertake. Suppose the firm ranks these projects, from the most profitable to the least profitable. At a high interest rate, only a few projects will earn enough to cover the opportunity cost of the funds employed. As the interest rate falls, more and more projects will be able to earn a return that is at least as great as the opportunity cost of the funds used to undertake the investment. Hence the firm will undertake a larger volume of investment.

Figure 25-3 plots the investment demand schedule II describing this relationship between the interest rates and the level of investment demand.

The *investment demand schedule* shows how much investment firms wish to make at each interest rate.

If the interest rate rises from r_0 to r_1, fewer investment projects will cover the opportunity cost of the funds tied up in them, and desired investment will fall from I_0 to I_1.

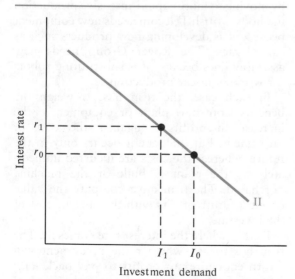

Figure 25-3   THE INVESTMENT DEMAND SCHEDULE.   For a given price of new capital goods and given expectations about the profit stream to which new investments will give rise, a higher interest rate reduces the number of projects that can provide a return matching the opportunity cost of the funds employed. As interest rates rise from r_0 to r_1, desired investment falls from I_0 to I_1.

What determines the height of the schedule II? Two things: the cost of the new machines, and the stream of profits to which new machines give rise. For a given stream of expected future profits, an increase in the purchase price of new capital goods will reduce the rate of return earned on the money tied up in investment. Hence fewer projects will be able to match the opportunity cost of any particular interest rate. Since the level of desired investment will be lower at each interest rate, an increase in the cost of new capital goods will shift the investment demand schedule II downwards.

Similarly, if the firm becomes less optimistic about the future demand for its output, it will revise downwards its estimates of the stream of profits that will be earned on each of the possible investment projects. For a given cost of new capital goods, the return on each project will fall. At each interest rate there will now be fewer projects matching the opportunity cost of the funds. Since desired investment will fall at each interest rate, a lower level of expected future demand and profits will shift the investment demand schedule downwards.[3]

The investment demand schedule II can be used to analyse both business investment in plant and machinery and residential investment in housing. Can we say anything about the slope of the schedule? There is an important difference between a machine that wears out in three years and a house or a factory lasting, say, 50 years. The longer the economic life of the capital good, the larger the fraction of its total returns that will be earned in the relatively distant future and the more the original cost of the goods will have accumulated at compound interest before the money can be repaid. Hence a small change in interest rates has a more important effect, the longer the economic life of the capital good. The investment demand

[3] If you have mastered Chapter 13, you may have realized that we can make the same points a different way. Knowing the stream of future profits and the interest rate, the firm can calculate the present value of the extra profits on a project. It will undertake all the projects for which the present value exceeds the initial price of the capital goods required. A higher interest rate reduces the present value of the profits, and some projects no longer cover the purchase price of the capital goods. Hence, higher interest rates reduce desired investment. Similarly, downgrading the stream of expected future profits, or increasing the purchase price of capital goods, reduces the present value of the extra profits relative to the purchase price, and some projects are again no longer profitable enough to undertake.

schedule will be flatter for long-lived houses and factories than for very short-term machinery.[4] A rise in interest rates is more likely to choke off long-term projects than short-term projects.

Inventory Investment

There are two reasons why firms plan to hold inventories or stocks of raw materials, partly finished goods, and finished goods awaiting sale. First, the firm may be speculating, or betting on price increases. When oil prices were rising sharply, many firms bought large stocks of oil, believing it would be cheaper to buy it now rather than later. Similarly, firms may hold finished goods off the market hoping to get a better price for them in the near future.

Second, firms may plan to hold stocks for the same reasons households plan to hold money. Corresponding to the transactions motive for holding money is the fact that many production processes take time. A ship cannot be built in a month, or even a year in many cases. Some stocks are simply the throughput of inputs on their way to becoming outputs. But there is also a motive corresponding to the precautionary motive for holding money. Suppose demand for the firm's output suddenly increases. Since plant capacity cannot be changed overnight, the firm may have to pay large overtime payments if it is to meet the upsurge in its order book; so it may be cheaper to carry some stocks in reserve with which to meet any sudden upswing in demand. Similarly, in a temporary downturn, it may be cheaper to continue production and pile up stocks of unsold goods than to incur expensive redundancy payments in order to reduce the workforce and cut back production.

These are the benefits of holding inventories. What about the costs? By holding on to goods that could have been sold, or purchasing goods whose purchase could have been delayed, the firm is tying up money that could have been used elsewhere to earn interest. Hence the cost

of holding inventories is the interest paid on the money that could have been earned by selling them or that was laid out to purchase them.

Thus we can also regard the investment demand schedule II in Figure 25-3 as being relevant to investment in increasing inventories. For any given assessment of the speculative profits to be earned from holding inventories, or of the cost savings and additional profits accruing from using inventories to smooth out production when demand is varying, an increase in the interest rate increases the marginal cost of holding inventories relative to this given marginal benefit. Hence an increase in interest rates makes firms reduce desired investment in inventories and move up the investment demand schedule. But a rise in potential speculative profits or cost reductions shifts the schedule upwards and increases inventory investment at each interest rate.

We conclude by noting two special features of inventory investment. First, unlike other components of investment, inventory investments can be negative. Firms can reduce stocks, as Figure 25-2 makes clear. Second, we must remember that the investment demand schedule shows desired or planned investment and that it will become a component in our analysis of aggregate demand or planned spending on goods and services. For investment in fixed capital, there is probably little difference between desired investment and actual investment. Firms rarely build factories they do not want at the time.

However, firms do get forced into unplanned inventory changes. In Chapter 21 we saw that, when aggregate demand is not equal to actual output, or planned investment not equal to planned savings, unplanned inventory changes take much of the strain until output and aggregate demand are brought into equilibrium. It is partly these unanticipated developments that lead to the volatility of actual inventory investment, brought out so clearly in Figure 25-2. Although it would be wrong to infer that fluctuations in interest rates lead to fluctuations in inventory investment demand of the order shown in Figure 25-2, inventory *plans* do respond to the opportunity cost of the funds tied up.

In this section we have established two points. First, an increase in interest rates will affect all types of investment decisions. From

---

[4] Equivalently, using present values, a 1 per cent rise in the interest rate has only a small effect on the present value of earnings over a three-year period but a much larger effect on the present value of earnings over the next 50 years. Note that this is exactly the same argument as we used in Chapter 23, in saying that a change in interest rates would have little effect on the price (the present value of promised payments) of a short-term bond but a much larger effect on the price of a long-term bond.

BOX 25-1

INVESTMENT, THE STOCK MARKET, AND INTEREST RATES

Firms will invest in projects whose rate of return exceeds the opportunity cost of the funds used. But which is the correct interest rate for firms to use in calculating this opportunity cost? In the UK, some investment is financed by bank borrowing through overdrafts. Since firms can deduct interest payments from profits before paying corporation tax, a tax on profits at the rate t (currently about 0.4), the opportunity cost of each pound is $£(1 - t)r$ where r is the interest rate charged by the bank: although the firm has to pay the bank $£r$ per year for each £1 borrowed, it gets out of an amount $£rt$ in profits tax, so the net cost per pound is only $£(1 - t)r$.

What if the firm has no profits on which to offset the interest? Then it does a deal with a bank. The bank buys the capital good and leases it to the firm. The bank gets the tax break instead of the firm (and banks are careful always to make profits!) Since competition between the banks for leasing business ensures that they have to pass on most of the tax break to the firms, effectively the opportunity cost to the firm remains close to $£(1 - t)r$. Leasing business boomed in Britain in the late 1970s. Since many firms

had not been making profits, they were doing deals with the banks to get the taxman to pay for as much of the investment as the accountants could wangle.

But some really large projects are financed not by normal borrowing or leasing, but by selling new company shares on the stock market. If Shell wants a lot more investment money it will sell new shares. The higher the Shell share price, the more money it can raise from a new share issue. But the share price is the present value of expected Shell dividends discounted at the interest rate. Hence an increase in interest rates reduces share prices and reduces the amount of investment Shell will wish to undertake. Thus, even when investment is financed through the stock market, our investment demand schedule II in Figure 25-4 remains relevant. Higher interest rates reduce desired investment. And higher expected future profits and dividends, by raising share prices, lead to more investment at any interest rate and shift up schedule II just as when the investment is financed by bank borrowing. Neither leasing nor the use of the stock market alters the usefulness of the investment demand schedule in analysing investment decisions.

---

now on we suppose there is an aggregate investment demand schedule relating planned investment to the level of the interest rate. Precisely which interest rate is a question we discuss in Box 25-1. Second, an increase in the cost of capital goods or a reduction in expected future profit opportunities will lead to a downward shift in the investment demand schedule. A decrease in the cost of capital goods or greater optimism about future profits will shift the schedule upwards. Since ideas about future profits can sometimes be revised quite drastically, it is possible that the investment demand schedule could shift around quite a lot.

25-3 Money, Interest Rates, and Aggregate Demand

We have now reached the following position. A fall in interest rates increases the level of investment demand by moving firms down their

investment demand schedule. And from Section 25-1 we know that a fall in interest rates will also increase consumption demand by increasing household wealth and shifting the consumption function upwards. But in the previous chapter we saw that an increase in the money supply will reduce the equilibrium interest rate to increase the quantity of money demanded and maintain money market equilibrium. Thus we have now made explicit the *transmission mechanism* through which an increase in the money supply shifts the aggregate demand schedule upwards and increases the equilibrium level of output and income.

This is shown in Figure 25-4. For simplicity we assume that government spending G is zero. Initially, the consumption function is CC_0, investment demand is I_0 and the aggregate demand schedule AD_0. The equilibrium point is E_0 where the AD_0 schedule crosses the 45° line. It is the equilibrium because aggregate demand or planned spending equals actual

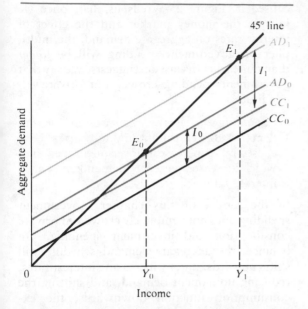

Figure 25-4 INTEREST RATES AND AGGREGATE DEMAND. Initially the consumption function is CC_0, investment demand is I_0 and equilibrium is at E_0 where the aggregate demand schedule AD_0 crosses the 45° line. A fall in interest rates shifts the consumption function to CC_1 and increases investment demand to I_1, shifting the aggregate demand schedule up from AD_0 to AD_1. Hence an increase in the money supply lowers interest rates, shifts the aggregate demand schedule upwards, and increases income and output.

income and output. Suppose now the money supply increases. A reduction in interest rate is required to increase money demand in line with the higher money supply. Lower interest rates increase investment demand to I_1 and shift the consumption function from CC_0 to CC_1. The aggregate demand schedule shifts from AD_0 to AD_1.

You may be thinking that the new equilibrium point is E_1. However this is not quite right. *Before* reading further, see if you can work out for yourself why not.

Damping Effects In the last chapter we pointed out that the quantity of money demanded depends both on interest rates and on the level of income. Since interest rates can adjust from hour to hour, the immediate effect of an increase in the money supply is to reduce interest rates to maintain equilibrium in the money market. Figure 25-4 shows that the consequence of lower interest rates is to shift

aggregate demand upwards. As firms gradually revise their investment plans upwards and households decide to consume more, income increases. But as income increases, so does the demand for money.

Unless the money supply is increased again there will now be excess demand for money, and interest rates have to rise a bit to choke this off and maintain money market equilibrium. And since interest rates have risen a bit, the aggregate demand schedule must fall back a bit. Hence the final position of the aggregate demand schedule is higher than its original position AD_0 but lower than AD_1, in Figure 25-4. Thus the new equilibrium will be between E_0 and E_1. We discuss these damping effects more fully in Section 25-5.

25-4 Fiscal Policy and Crowding Out

In Chapter 22 we showed that an expansionary fiscal policy, through tax cuts or additional government spending, leads to higher aggregate demand an an increase in equilibrium income and output. We must now modify our analysis. An increase in government spending will shift the aggregate demand schedule upwards and will tend to increase income and output. But with an unchanged real money supply, higher income will increase the demand for money and raise interest rates. This reduces investment demand and shifts the consumption function downwards. These effects tend to offset the original upward shift in aggregate demand caused by the increase in government spending, though they cannot offset it completely.[5] Figure 25-5 illustrates.

Beginning from the aggregate demand schedule AD, the immediate effect of higher government spending is to shift the aggregate demand schedule to AD', as in Chapter 22. In that chapter we said that the equilibrium point

---

[5] If falls in consumption and investment demand completely offset higher government demand, aggregate demand would then be unchanged. With unchanged income, there would be no upward pressure on the demand for money and interest rates. Without higher interest rates, investment and consumption demand would not have been reduced. Hence, increased government spending must lead to some upward shift in the aggregate demand schedule, some increase in interest rates, and to only partially offsetting falls in consumption and investment demand.

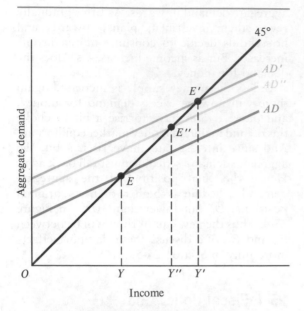

Figure 25-5   CROWDING OUT. Increased government spending initially shifts the aggregate demand schedule from *AD* to *AD'*. But higher income raises money demand and interest rates rise, thus reducing investment demand and shifting the consumption function downwards. The final aggregate demand schedule is thus *AD''* and the new equilibrium point is *E''*. Fiscal policy with a constant money supply is less expansionary than it would be if the money supply were increased to keep interest rates constant as income expanded.

moved from E to E' and that equilibrium income increased from Y to Y'. Now we must recognize that higher income will increase the demand for money and interest rates, thus shifting the aggregate demand schedule down, say to AD''. The final equilibrium point will be E'' and equilibrium income will increase only from Y to Y''.

In Chapter 21 we introduced the concept of the multiplier, and in Chapter 22 we calculated the multiplier for government spending as the ratio of the increase in equilibrium income to the increase in government spending that

caused it. Figure 25-5 tells us that, once we include the money market and the effect of interest rates on aggregate demand, the multiplier on government spending will be *lower* than our earlier discussion suggests. We say that government spending crowds out private expenditure.

> *Crowding out* is the reduction in private demand for consumption and investment caused by an increase in government spending, which increases aggregate demand and hence interest rates.

In the model of this chapter, government spending does not completely crowd out private consumption and investment spending. On balance, the aggregate demand schedule still shifts upwards. But, by increasing interest rates, reducing investment demand, and shifting the consumption function downwards, the expansionary effect of higher government spending is partially damped. Similarly, although a tax cut initially causes an upward rotation of the consumption function plotted against national income, the induced rise in income bids up interest rates, again damping the final effect of the fiscal stimulus.

Table 25-1 summarizes the steps in the crowding-out argument for the case of higher government spending. Try constructing your own table for the case of an income tax cut.

25-5 The *IS–LM* Model

In the previous two sections we have analysed the interaction of income and interest rates using the familiar aggregate demand schedule and the 45° line. Equilibrium income is the level at which the aggregate demand schedule crosses the 45° line. Changes in interest rates shift the aggregate demand schedule by altering investment demand and shifting the consumption function through wealth effects and changes in

Table 25-1   Government spending and crowding out

(1)	(2)	(3)	(4)
Higher government spending raises output and income.	Higher income raises desired real money balances.	Higher real money demand and unchanged supply bid up interest rates.	Higher interest rates crowd out consumption and investment, damping the expansion.

desired consumer borrowing. Although it is possible to use this framework to analyse the effects of the government's fiscal and monetary policy, the framework is a bit cumbersome. Any initial shift in the aggregate demand schedule induces interest rate changes and hence further shifts in the aggregate demand schedule.

In this section we introduce a different way to study the same issues. The advantage of this method is that we can see immediately how the equilibrium levels of income and interest rates are simultaneously determined. The trick is to consider the *combinations* of income and interest rates that would lead to equilibrium in each of the two markets, goods and money, and thus determine the unique combination of income and interest rates that leads to equilibrium in both markets at the same time.

The *IS* Schedule

The goods market is in equilibrium when the aggregate demand schedule crosses the 45° line so that aggregate demand and actual income are equal. In Chapter 21 we saw that this would occur at the point at which planned investment I equals planned savings S. For this reason, the set of different combinations of interest rates and income compatible with equilibrium in the goods market is called the *IS* schedule.

> The *IS schedule* shows the different combinations of income and interest rates at which the goods market is in equilibrium.

Figure 25-6 shows how we construct the *IS* schedule. We begin with a particular interest rate, call it r_0. For this interest rate, we know the level of investment demand and the level of autonomous consumption demand. Thus we know the height of the aggregate demand schedule, which we plot as AD_0 in the top half of the diagram. The equilibrium point in the output market occurs at E_0 in the top diagram and the equilibrium income level is Y_0. Hence in the bottom half of the diagram we plot the corresponding point E_0. The goods market is in equilibrium if the interest rate is r_0 and the income level is Y_0.

Now imagine a lower interest rate r_1. Since investment demand will now be higher and the consumption function will have shifted upwards, we plot the higher aggregate demand schedule AD_1. AD_1 is higher than AD_0 only because of

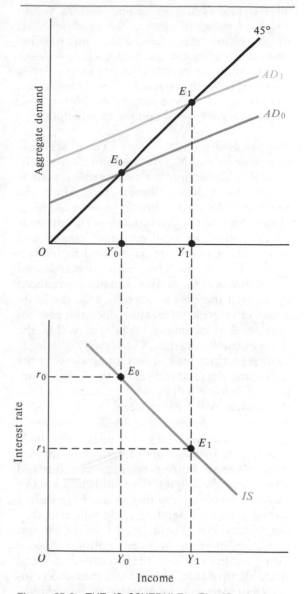

Figure 25-6 THE *IS* SCHEDULE. The *IS* schedule shows different combinations of income and interest rates at which the goods market is in equilibrium. At the interest rate r_0 the aggregate demand schedule is AD_0, say. The top figure tells us that equilibrium income is then Y_0. This combination is shown as E_0 in the bottom figure. At the lower interest rate r_1, the aggregate demand schedule is higher, say AD_1. Equilibrium income is now Y_1 and the point E_1 plots this combination in the bottom figure. Repeating this exercise for all possible interest rates, we can join up all the points such as E_0 and E_1 in the bottom figure to obtain the *IS* schedule.

the effect of lower interest rates. The new equilibrium point is E_1 and the bottom half of the diagram shows that the combination of an interest rate r_1 and an income level Y_1 would also lead to equilibrium in the goods market. By repeating this exercise for all possible interest rates, we can trace out a whole series of combinations of interest rates and income levels compatible with goods market equilibrium. Joining up all these points in the bottom half of the diagram we obtain the IS schedule.

The Slope of the IS Schedule   The IS schedule slopes downwards. For goods market equilibrium, a higher interest rate must be accompanied by a lower income level since the aggregate demand schedule must be lower. How steep will the IS schedule be? This depends on the sensitivity of investment demand and autonomous consumption demand to interest rates. The more investment demand and autonomous consumption demand are reduced by a given increase in interest rates, the more a rise in interest rates will reduce the equilibrium level of income and the flatter will be the slope of the IS schedule. Conversely, if changes in interest rates lead to only small shifts in the aggregate demand schedule, the equilibrium level of income will hardly be affected and the IS schedule will be very steep.

Shifts in the IS Schedule   The purpose of the IS schedule is to illustrate the effect of interest rates *alone* in shifting the aggregate demand schedule and changing the equilibrium level of income. Anything else that would have shifted the aggregate demand schedule will also shift the IS schedule. For a *given* level of interest rates, an increase in firms' optimism about future profits will shift the investment demand schedule upwards, increasing autonomous investment demand; an increase in households' estimate of future incomes will shift the consumption function upwards, increasing autonomous consumption demand; or an increase in government spending could increase the government component of autonomous demand directly. Any of these would shift the aggregate demand schedule upwards at a given interest rate. Hence equilibrium income would increase at any interest rate. We would show this as an *upward shift in* the IS schedule, telling us that equilibrium income is now higher at any particular interest rate.

To sum up, movements along the IS schedule tell us about shifts in the equilibrium income caused by shifts in the aggregate demand schedule as a result only of changes in interest rates. Any other cause of a shift in the aggregate demand schedule must be represented as a shift in the IS schedule. Since higher aggregate demand leads to higher equilibrium income, an upward shift in the IS schedule must always correspond to an upward shift in the aggregate demand schedule. A downward shift in the IS schedule must always correspond to a downward shift in the aggregate demand schedule. Moreover, a move down a given IS schedule must correspond to an upward shift in aggregate demand caused purely by lower interest rates.

The *LM* Schedule

We now consider money market equilibrium.

The LM *schedule* shows the different combinations of interest rates and income compatible with equilibrium in the money market.

It is the schedule along which the demand for real money balances, which Keynes originally called the liquidity preference schedule, is equal to the supply of real money balances, which we can denote by L.

Figure 25-7 shows how we construct the LM schedule. In Figure 25-7(a) we show a fixed supply of real money balances L_0. For a given income level Y_0, we plot the money demand schedule LL_0. Higher interest rates reduce the quantity of real money balances demanded. The equilibrium point is E_0 and the equilibrium interest rate, r_0. Hence in Figure 25-7(b) we show the corresponding point E_0 at which the money market is in equilibrium with the combination of an income level Y_0 and an interest rate r_0.

At the higher income level Y_1, the demand for money will be greater at each interest rate. Plotting the new money demand schedule LL_1, we see that the equilibrium interest rate is now r_1 and we plot the point E_1 in Figure 25-7(b), showing that the combination r_1 and Y_1 also leads to money market equilibrium. With a higher income, tending to increase the quantity of money demanded, and a higher interest rate, tending reduce the quantity of money demanded, the quantity of money demanded remains in line with the unchanged quantity supplied. Considering each income level in turn, plotting

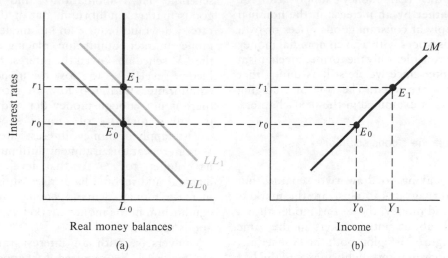

Figure 25-7 THE *LM* SCHEDULE. The real money supply is assumed fixed at L_0. For a given income Y_0 the money demand schedule is LL_0 and the equilibrium interest rate r_0. Point E_0 in figure (b) shows that r_0 and Y_0 lead to money market equilibrium. If income is Y_1, the money demand schedule in (a) shifts up to LL_1 and the equilibrium interest rate is r_1. This combination of income and interest rates is shown as point E_1 in (b). Repeating the analysis for all income levels and joining up the points such as E_0 and E_1 in (b), we get the *LM* schedule showing the different combinations of interest rates and income compatible with money market equilibrium.

the corresponding money demand schedule in Figure 25-7(a), and plotting the corresponding equilibrium points in Figure 25-7(b), we can trace out the entire *LM* Schedule.

The Slope of the *LM* Schedule   The *LM* schedule slopes upwards. With a higher income level it requires a higher interest rate to choke off money demand and maintain money market equilibrium with an unchanged money supply. The more a given increase in income tends to increase the quantity of money demanded, the larger will be the increase in the interest rate required to maintain money market equilibrium and the steeper will be the *LM* schedule. Similarly, the less responsive the quantity of money demanded to a given rise in interest rates, the larger will be the increase in interest rates required to choke off money demand for a given increase in income, and the steeper will be the *LM* schedule. Conversely, the more the quantity of money demanded responds to interest rates and the less it responds to income, the flatter will be the *LM* schedule.

Shifts in the *LM* Schedule   We construct a given *LM* schedule for a given supply of *real* money balances. Suppose we now increase the

supply of real money balances. For a given income level and a given height of the money demand schedule in Figure 25-7(a), the equilibrium interest rate will now be lower since the vertical supply curve has shifted to the right. At each income level, a lower interest rate is required to induce people to hold the additional supply of real balances. Hence in Figure 25-7(b) we must represent an increase in the supply of real money balances as a shift to the right in the *LM* schedule, showing that the equilibrium interest rate is lower at each income level, or, equivalently, that at each interest rate it requires a higher income level to induce people to hold the additional supply of real balances. Conversely, a reduction in the real money supply shifts the *LM* schedule to the left. To reduce the quantity of real balances demanded and maintain money market equilibrium with a lower real money supply, it now takes a higher interest rate at each income level.

To sum up, we draw an *LM* schedule for a given real money supply. Moving along the schedule, higher interest rates must be accompanied by higher income to maintain the quantity of real balances demanded in line with the fixed supply. Increases in the real money supply shift the *LM* schedule to the right.

Although the real money supply can be increased either by an increase in the nominal money supply at constant goods prices or by a fall in goods prices with a given nominal money supply, we consider only the former mechanism in this chapter since we are still assuming that goods prices are fixed. The role of changing goods prices is examined in the next chapter.

Equilibrium in the Goods and Money Markets

Instead of having to draw two separate but interrelated diagrams to illustrate the markets for goods and money, the *IS–LM* model allows us to think about both markets in the same diagram. Figure 25-8 plots both the *IS* schedule, showing goods market equilibrium, and the *LM* schedule, showing money market equilibrium. Only at the point *E* are both markets in equilibrium. Hence the goods and money markets interact to determine the level of equilibrium interest rate r^* and the equilibrium income level Y^*.

Suppose the interest rate is r_1. At the income level Y_1 we would be at the point *A* on the *IS*

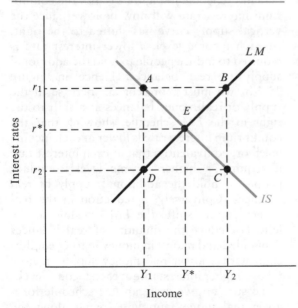

Figure 25-8 EQUILIBRIUM IN THE GOODS AND MONEY MARKETS. The goods market is in equilibrium at all points on the *IS* schedule. The money market is in equilibrium at all points on the *LM* schedule. Hence only at point *E* are both markets in equilibrium.

schedule. The combination r_1 and Y_1 lead to goods market equilibrium. But at the interest rate r_1 it would require an income level Y_2 for money market equilibrium, placing us at *B* on the *LM* schedule. Given the interest rate r_1, the income level Y_1 is too low for money market equilibrium. With too low an income level, there is not enough money demand to match the given quantity of money supply. With excess supply of money, interest rates will fall. We can repeat this argument until interest rates have fallen to r^*. At that level, aggregate demand and income have risen sufficiently to increase money demand enough to lead to equilibrium in the money market as well as the goods market.

Conversely, with an interest rate r_2, the income level Y_2 required for goods market equilibrium at the point *C* is greater than the income level Y_1 required for equilibrium in the money market at point *D*. With income too high for money market equilibrium, there is excess demand for money, bidding up interest rates. Again, the process continues until interest rates are r^*, income is Y^*, and both markets are in equilibrium.

Now we rework the analysis of monetary and fiscal policy that we undertook earlier in the chapter using the more cumbersome framework of the aggregate demand schedule and the 45° line. Previously we had to concentrate on the goods market in our diagram, but, by keeping the money market at the back of our minds, we had to remember that changes in income would alter equilibrium interest rates and induce further shifts in the aggregate demand schedule. The *IS* schedule now captures interest-rate-induced shifts in the aggregate demand schedule; and, by plotting the *LM* schedule on the same diagram, we can now explicitly keep track of both markets at once.

Fiscal Policy: Shifting the *IS* Schedule

Any change, other than a fall in interest rates, that shifts the aggregate demand schedule upwards will also shift the *IS* schedule upwards. We use Figure 25-9 to analyse the consequences of an increase in government spending, though the same diagram can be used also to discuss the effect of an increase in firms' optimism about future profits or an increase in households' estimates of their future disposable incomes.

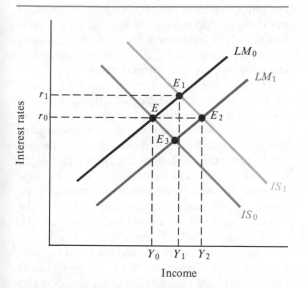

Figure 25-9 FISCAL EXPANSION SHIFTS THE *IS* SCHEDULE. A bond-financed increase in government spending shifts the *IS* curve from IS_0 to IS_1 but leaves the money supply unaltered. Hence the *IM* schedule remains LM_0. Thus, fiscal expansion moves the equilibrium from *E* to E_1. Income increases to Y_1 even though the increase in interest rates partly crowds out private investment and autonomous consumption demand. However, by simultaneously increasing the money supply, the government could shift the *LM* curve from LM_0 to LM_1, thus preventing a rise in interest rates. The equilibrium income level would then increase to Y_2, since private investment and consumption would no longer be crowded out.

The economy begins with the *IS* schedule IS_0 and the *LM* schedule LM_0. Initial equilibrium is at *E*. Suppose first that the government increases government spending *G* and finances the extra government deficit by selling bonds. Thus the money supply remains unchanged. Hence the *LM* schedule does not shift and remains LM_0. However, the additional government spending shifts the *IS* schedule upwards, say from IS_0 to IS_1. At each interest rate the equilibrium level of income is increased, since higher government spending tends to shift the aggregate demand schedule upwards.

Given the schedules IS_1, and LM_0 the new equilibrium point is E_1. Thus the effect of bond-financed government spending increases is to increase the equilibrium level of income from Y_0 to Y_1. With a fixed supply of real money balances, interest rates must rise from r_0 to r_1 to prevent the higher income level from increasing the quantity of real balances de-

manded. Although higher interest rates crowd out private consumption and investments spending, higher government spending is not completely offset by crowding out and equilibrium income increases.

Figure 25-9 allows us to make two interesting points. First, crowding out would be complete only if the *LM* schedule were vertical. Then, an upward shift in the *IS* schedule would lead to higher interest rates but not to higher income. A vertical *LM* curve implies that interest rates have *no effect* on the quantity of money demanded, which depends on income alone. Under this extreme assumption, any increase in income would lead to excess demand in the money market that could no longer be eliminated by higher interest rates. Hence, no increase in equilibrium income would be possible. Interest rates would simply increase until private consumption and investment had fallen by the amount of the original increase in government spending. Crowding out would be complete.

In practice, this is most unlikely. The demand for money is not completely insensitive to interest rates, and the *LM* schedule is not completely vertical. What we can say, however, is that the less sensitive is money demand to interest rates, the steeper will be the *LM* schedule, and the more a bond-financed increase in government spending will lead to higher interest rates rather than higher income.

Second, in Figure 25-9 we show what would happen if the increase in government spending were accompanied by an increase in the money supply. Suppose, in addition to raising spending and shifting the *IS* schedule upwards, that the government increased the money supply just enough to keep interest rates at their original level while income expanded. Increases in the money supply shift the *LM* schedule to the right. By providing enough extra money to shift the *LM* schedule as far as LM_1, the government could ensure that its fiscal expansion led to a new equilibrium at point E_2, with interest rates unchanged at r_0.

By increasing the money supply in line with the income-induced increase in money demand, the government prevents interest rates from rising and crowding out private investment and consumption. In fact, the ratio of the increase in income from Y_0 to Y_2 to the increase in government spending that had shifted the *IS* curve would then be exactly the value of the multiplier that we calculated in Chapter 22 for an increase in government spending. There, we *ignored* the possibility that interest rates could affect aggregate demand. Here, we are considering precisely the change in the money supply that would *prevent* interest rates from affecting aggregate demand.

Thus we conclude that an increase in government spending increases the equilibrium level of income even when we take account of the money market and the effect of interest rates on aggregate demand. However, the exact value of the government spending multiplier depends on the monetary policy in force when the fiscal expansion is undertaken. If the money supply is held constant, interest rates will rise, crowd out private expenditure, and partially offset the fiscal stimulus. If the money supply is increased to hold interest rates constant as output increases, the multiplier will be larger: equilibrium income will increase by a larger amount for any given increase in government spending. Thus government spending financed by printing money tends to be more expansionary than government spending financed by issuing bonds.

Monetary Policy: Shifting the *LM* Schedule

Figure 25-9 can also be used to discuss monetary policy. Suppose fiscal policy is held constant and the *IS* schedule is fixed at IS_0. Given the initial level of the real money supply, the *LM* schedule is LM_0 and equilibrium occurs at the point E. An increase in the money supply, with given goods prices, will shift the *LM* schedule to the right, say to the position LM_1. Figure 25-9 shows that the new equilibrium occurs at the point E_3.

The increase in the real money supply requires a reduction in interest rates to induce people to hold the extra real money balances. Overnight, before income has time to change, there will be a large drop in interest rates. If the money market is continuously in equilibrium, in Figure 25-9 the economy will move from point E to the point on the new schedule LM_1 vertically below E. But this point is not on the fixed schedule IS_0. Lower interest rates will increase consumption and investment

spending, increase income, and hence increase the demand for money. When the new equilibrium in both markets is reached, the economy will be at the point E_3 with the corresponding levels of income and interest rates.

Thus, Figure 25-9 summarizes our discussion of the transmission mechanism through which an increase in the money supply reduces interest rates, increases consumption and investment demand, and hence increases the equilibrium level of income. Although the final effect of an increase in the real money supply is to increase income, interest rates must nevertheless be lower in the new equilibrium than in the original one. Without a reduction in the equilibrium interest rate, there would be nothing to make aggregate demand and equilibrium income increase. With neither lower interest rates nor higher income, the demand for money would not have increased in line with the increase in its supply. Figure 25-9 summarizes this argument by noting that the new equilibrium point E_3 lies to the south-east of the original equilibrium at E. It promises us that an increase in the real money supply increases the equilibrium level of income and reduces the equilibrium interest rate.

25-6 Demand Management and the Policy Mix

Fiscal policy is the set of decisions the government makes about taxation and spending. Through such decisions, the government can shift the *IS* schedule. Monetary policy is the corresponding set of decisions about the level of the money supply. Monetary policy can shift the *LM* curve. Although fiscal decisions will determine the level of the government's budget deficit, it is not essential to finance the deficit by printing money. The government can also sell bonds and borrow from the private sector. Hence, if it chooses, the government can pursue independent monetary and fiscal policies.

Demand management is the use of monetary and fiscal policy to stabilize the level of income around a high average level.

Thus, if pessimism about the future leads the private sector (firms and households) to spend less, the government can use an expansionary fiscal policy to shift the *IS* schedule upwards, an expansionary monetary policy to shift the *LM* curve to the right, or some combination of these two policies. Nevertheless, monetary and fiscal policy are not interchangeable. They affect aggregate demand through different routes and have different implications for the *composition* of aggregate demand.

Figure 25-10 can be used to analyse the mix of monetary and fiscal policy. Suppose the government aims to stabilize income at the level Y^*. The figure shows two different ways in which this can be done. One option is to have an expansionary or *easy* fiscal policy with high levels of government spending, low tax rates, or both. This will tend to lead to a high position of the *IS* schedule, which we show as IS_1. To keep income in check with such an expansionary fiscal policy, it is necessary to have a *tight* monetary policy. With a relatively low money supply the *LM* schedule lies relatively far to the left, which we show as LM_1.

Equilibrium at E_1 meets the objective of attaining an income level Y^*. Since government

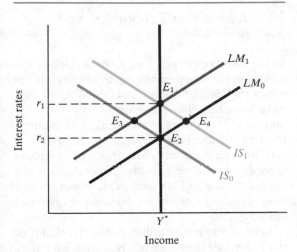

LM_1
E_1
LM_0
r_1
E_3
E_4
r_2
E_2
IS_1
IS_0
Interest rates
Y^*
Income

Figure 25-10 THE POLICY MIX AND THE COMPOSITION OF AGGREGATE DEMAND. The target income Y^* can be attained by easy fiscal policy and tight monetary policy. Equilibrium at E_1, the intersection of LM_1 and IS_1, implies relatively high interest rates r_1 and a relatively low share of private sector investment and consumption in GNP. Alternatively, with easy monetary policy and tight fiscal policy, equilibrium at E_2, the intersection of LM_0 and IS_0, still attains the target income but at lower interest rates r_2. The share of private sector investment and consumption in GNP will be higher than at E_1.

spending is a large component of aggregate demand, it requires a high equilibrium interest rate to keep investment and consumption demand in check so that total income is no larger than Y^*. Thus the combination of easy fiscal policy and tight monetary policy means that government spending G will be a relatively large share of national income Y^* and private spending $(C + I)$ will have a relatively low share.

Alternatively, the government can adopt a relatively tight fiscal policy (a lower *IS* schedule, IS_0) and a relatively easy monetary policy (a schedule LM_0, further to the right). The target income Y^* is still attained but at the lower interest rate r_2 corresponding to the new equilibrium point E_2. With easy monetary policy and tight fiscal policy, the share of private expenditure $(C + I)$ will be higher and the share of government expenditure lower than at the point E_1. With lower interest rates, there is less crowding out of private expenditure.

Of course, easy monetary policy and easy fiscal policy together are highly expansionary. With the schedules IS_1 and LM_0 the equilibrium point in Figure 25-9 is E_4, where income is much higher than Y^*. Conversely, with tight monetary policy and tight fiscal policy, the schedules LM_1 and IS_0, the equilibrium point is E_3, where income lies well below Y^*.

In the UK the Heath government in the early 1970s adopted a mix of easy monetary policy and easy fiscal policy in a famous attempt at 'a dash for growth'. And real national income rose by over 8 per cent in 1972 alone. Conversely, both fiscal and monetary policy were tight during the early years of the first Thatcher government, and real national income fell between 1979 and 1981. The subsequent sustained period of output growth was achieved against a background of gradual easing of both fiscal and monetary policy.

When the government thinks aggregate demand is too low, easy monetary and fiscal policies can help to raise it. When the government thinks aggregate demand is too high, tight monetary and fiscal policies can help reduce it. But when the government thinks the level of aggregate demand is about right, what should determine the mix of fiscal and monetary policy?

In the short run, the government may care about the total level of aggregate demand, income, and employment, but in the longer run it may also care about economic growth. High levels of investment are good for growth because they increase the capital stock more quickly, giving workers more equipment with which to work and raising their productivity. Figure 25-10 suggests that it is better to choose a tight fiscal policy and an easy monetary policy than the other way round. With lower interest rates, firms will invest more, and in the long run the economy's productive potential will grow more quickly.

However, this argument is less clear-cut than it first appears. Government spending G includes not only current expenditure (wages of civil servants) but capital investment in roads, hospitals, and many other things. Thus, tight fiscal policy typically involves cutting back on public investment, and this must be set against any benefits from higher private investment that a correspondingly easier monetary policy and lower interest rate allows; and Figure 25-2 shows that recent cuts in real government spending in the UK have fallen heavily on investment by the public sector.

Three other issues play a large role in the practical judgements of governments about the desirable mix of fiscal and monetary policies. First, there is the question of the predictability of effects, which we discussed in Box 22-1 when examining fiscal policy. In practice, neither monetary nor fiscal policy ever has exactly the effects the government anticipated. Our model is only a simplification of the complex world in which we live. Fiscal actions such as higher government expenditure do have one major advantage over monetary actions. Higher government spending adds directly to aggregate demand. In contrast, policy must work indirectly through the transmission mechanism which we have set out in this chapter. Sometimes governments feel that the effects of monetary policy are likely to be less certain because there are more stages in the transmission mechanism at which something could go wrong.

The other two issues take us beyond the scope of our simple model. First, there may be a reluctance to embark on an easy monetary policy because it is feared that an increase in the money supply will lead to inflation. Moreover, if it does, the induced rise in prices may offset the initial increase in the nominal money supply, leaving the real money supply

unaltered. If so, the *LM* schedule reverts to its original position. Easy monetary policy has brought on inflation but no stimulus to aggregate demand, income, and employment. To examine this important issue, we begin in the next chapter the analysis of how the price level is determined.

Second, in deciding the appropriate fiscal policy, the government may be concerned not merely with the effects of spending and taxes on aggregate demand but also with the *microeconomic* effects of fiscal policy. For example, it is commonly held that high tax rates discourage the incentive to work and reduce the economy's productive potential. Supply-side economics argues that the effects of fiscal policy on aggregate supply may be as important as the effects of fiscal policy on aggregate demand.

These two issues introduce us to the material we shall be studying in the next few chapters. We now take stock of what we have learned so far in macroeconomics and indicate the ground we have still to cover.

25-7 Keynesian Economics and Activism

In the last five chapters we have developed the Keynesian theme that aggregate demand determines the level of output and employment. We have seen how the government can use fiscal and monetary policy to manipulate or manage the level of aggregate demand and can aim to stabilize the economy close to its full-employment level. During periods of recession, when aggregate demand is insufficient, monetary and fiscal expansion can boost demand, output, and employment.

Britain was partly pulled out of the slump of the 1930s by the inadvertently Keynesian policy of heavy government spending on rearmament as the threat of war loomed. However, in the three decades after 1945 governments of both political parties in Britain (and other countries) attempted to implement the Keynesian policy prescription and to manage the level of aggregate demand. The government accepted responsibility for preserving a high and stable level of demand and employment, intervening actively to offset shocks to private demand.

But the policy did not work perfectly. In the

decade after 1965, both inflation and unemployment grew fairly steadily. That build-up of inflation proved to be a costly after-effect of Keynesian policies. Today we are more doubtful about the success of the activist period of the 1950s and 1960s.

We have already mentioned the two main worries that have developed about the pursuit of Keynesian activism. First, simple Keynesian economics proceeds on the assumption that the price level is given. Monetary and fiscal policy that induce increased aggregate spending therefore increase the demand for goods, output, and employment. But what happens when the price level can change, for example when the economy is near full employment and there is no longer spare capacity to make firms think twice about raising prices or paying higher wages? Then a monetary expansion may lead not to higher employment but only to higher prices, leaving the real money supply unaltered. The analysis of prices and inflation is central to a fuller understanding of macroeconomics, and we begin this task in the next chapter.

Second, Keynesian economics discussses an economy with spare capacity and workers who would like to work but cannot find a job. But it says little about what determines full-employment output or the economy's productive potential. On the one hand, the high tax rates that accompany a government sector of ever-increasing size and importance as it strives to run the economy more efficiently may provide a disincentive to work. On the other hand, the very promise of a Keynesian government to take care of the unemployment problem through demand management may make people slack and complacent. Both these effects *could* so reduce the level of productive potential that it is no longer legitimate to look at low actual output levels and conclude that we must be way below full-employment output. And if we are really close to full-employment output, we had better start to pay attention to the supply bottlenecks that can make productive potential so low, rather than focusing exclusively on aggregate demand on the happy assumption that the economy has plenty of scarce resources which can easily be put to work if only demand is increased. We tackle this issue directly in the next chapter.

Although these are important topics yet to be covered, by now we have completed the first major stage of macroeconomics. We have learned how to analyse the demand side of the economy. Even when we have mastered the analysis of supply, adjustment, and price behaviour, we shall see that the demand analysis we have mastered plays an important part in the story, especially in the short run.

Summary

1   An increase in interest rates reduces household wealth and also makes borrowing more expensive. Together, these effects reduce autonomous consumption demand and shift the consumption function downwards.

2   Modern theories of the consumption function emphasize long-run disposable income and the incentive to smooth out short-run fluctuations in consumption. They suggest that higher interest rates also reduce consumption demand by reducing the present value of expected future labour income. They also suggest that temporary tax changes are likely to have less effect on consumption demand than tax changes that are expected to be permanent.

3   For a given cost of new capital goods and expected stream of future profits, an increase in interest rates reduces the number of investment projects that earn a rate of return at least as great as the opportunity cost of the funds employed. The investment demand schedule shows this negative relationship between the interest rate and the demand for investment. Higher expected future profits or a lower cost of new capital goods will shift the investment demand schedule upwards.

4   Together, these effects of interest rates on consumption and investment spending show the transmission mechanism through which an increase in the money supply and a reduction in interest rates affect aggregate demand.

5   With a given real money supply, a fiscal expansion increases output, money demand, and interest rates, thus crowding out or partially displacing private consumption and investment demand. Thus the government spending multiplier is smaller than its value in the case where the money supply is simultaneously increased to prevent interest rates from rising as output increases.

6   The *IS* schedule shows the combinations of interest rates and income compatible with goods market equilibrium. As interest rates increase, equilibrium income falls. At given interest rates, an increase in expected future consumer incomes, higher expected profits on investment, or higher government spending would shift the aggregate demand schedule upwards. Hence they shift the *IS* schedule upwards showing higher equilibrium income at each interest rate.

7   The *LM* schedule shows combinations of interest rates and income compatible with money market equilibrium. With a given money supply, higher income must be accompanied by higher interest rates to keep money demand unchanged. An increase in the supply of real money shifts the *LM* schedule to the right. Equilibrium in both markets occurs at the point at which the *IS* and *LM* schedules intersect.

8   A given income level can be attained by easy monetary policy and tight fiscal policy or by the converse. In the latter case the equilibrium interest rate is higher and private spending will be a lower share of the given level of income and spending.

Key Terms

Transmission mechanism
Wealth effects
Consumer borrowing
Permanent income hypothesis
Life-cycle hypothesis
Human wealth
Investment demand schedule
Crowding out
IS and *LM* schedules
Mix of fiscal and monetary policy
Demand management
Easy and tight monetary or fiscal policy

Problems

1   Before the 1976 election in the United States President Ford tried to get unemployment down by giving everyone a once-off tax rebate. Most people saved their government rebate and spending hardly increased. Can modern theories of the consumption function explain why?

2   Suppose people not previously allowed bank overdrafts get credit cards on which they can borrow up to £500 each. What happens to the consumption function? Why?

3   Why do higher interest rates reduce investment demand? Be sure to discuss all the different ways in which firms might finance their investment projects.

4   'Higher money supply increases consumption and investment, and hence income. Higher income increases interest rates. Hence higher money supply increases interest rates.' Evaluate this proposition using diagrams to check your answer.

5   Fiscal policy takes the form of government subsidies to firms undertaking investment. Monetary policy involves an open-market sale of government bonds. Explain what this policy mix does to the level of GNP and to its composition as between consumption, investment, and government expenditure on goods and services.

6   Suppose firms expect a huge boom in a couple of years. What happens today to investment, income, and interest rates?

7   What is active Keynesian demand management? Give two reasons why some people believe it might fail to work.

8   Common Fallacies   Show why the following statements are incorrect: (*a*) Consumers must have gone crazy. Their take-home pay is down yet their spending is up. (*b*) Interest rates affect investment only if firms have to borrow. In practice, many firms finance investment out of existing profits. Hence we should not expect interest rates to have much effect on investment. (*c*) Keynesians believe only in fiscal policy. They ignore monetary policy.

26

Aggregate Supply, the Price Level, and the Speed of Adjustment

By assuming that prices are fixed and that the economy has spare resources, Keynesian models suggest that boosting aggregate demand will always lead to higher output. But prices are not fixed for ever. Inflation is one of the key macroeconomic issues. And, with only finite resources, the economy cannot expand output indefinitely. By introducing aggregate supply, or firms' willingness and ability to produce, we now show how demand and supply together determine both the price level and the level of output.

We shall see that printing money, or steadily increasing the money supply, must eventually create inflation since output and employment cannot expand for ever. Similarly, fiscal expansion must eventually increase prices and interest rates rather than continue to increase output. To introduce these ideas we move from the Keynesian extreme, in which wages and prices are fixed, to the opposite extreme, in which wages and prices are fully flexible.

> The *classical model* of macroeconomics analyses the economy when wages and prices are fully flexible.

In the classical model we shall show that the economy is *always* at its full-employment output. Monetary and fiscal policy then affects prices but not the aggregate level of output and employment.

In the very short run, before prices and wages have time to adjust fully to the pressures of demand and supply, the Keynesian model remains relevant. In the long run, after all prices and wages have adjusted, the classical model is relevant. The key issue in the modern macroeconomic debate is how quickly prices and wages *actually* adjust in the real world. Taken by themselves, neither the Keynesian nor the classical model is a complete description of how the economy works.

In seeking to understand macroeconomics, the challenge is to master the analysis of how the economy makes the transition from the Keynesian short run to the classical long run. Many of the policy issues most keenly debated today turn on differing assessments of how quickly the economy makes this transition. Hence in the second part of the chapter we examine in detail the process through which the economy responds to shocks to aggregate demand or aggregate supply.[1]

In this chapter we shall study the interaction of three markets: the markets for goods, money, and labour. This sounds more complicated than it is. The analysis breaks down into two parts. Aggregate demand depends on the interaction of the markets for goods and money. That is the part we have already learned. The new element is the introduction of aggregate supply, which involves the interaction of the markets for goods and labour.

26-1 The Price Level and Aggregate Demand

In this section we show that the real money supply is the key variable linking the aggregate demand for goods and the price level.

> The *price level* is the average price of all the goods produced in the economy.

---

[1] In this chapter, for simplicity we assume that the long-run equilibrium or full-employment position is constant over time. We discuss how the economy gradually works its way back to this long-run equilibrium. In practice, of course, the world does not stand still and the full-employment equilibrium is itself changing slowly over time. The economy is gradually adjusting back towards a moving target. Changes in long-run equilibrium are discussed more fully in Chapters 27 and 30.

The real money supply is defined as the nominal money supply divided by the price level. It shows the quantity of goods that a given quantity of nominal money will purchase. When the price level is fixed, the real money supply increases (decreases) only if the nominal money supply increases (decreases). But when the price level can change, the real money supply will rise (fall) if the price level falls (rises) while the nominal money supply remains unchanged.

In Figure 26-1(a) we plot real income against interest rates, and in Figure 26-1(b) we plot the price level against real income. Since we wish to isolate the effect of prices alone on aggregate demand, we hold constant all other determinants of aggregate demand such as the nominal money supply, the level of government spending and tax rates, and private sector expectations of future profits and future incomes.

Suppose the economy begins with a price level P_0. Given the fixed nominal money supply, P_0 determines the real money supply and hence the position of the LM schedule, say LM_0. Given the level of government spending and all other variables relevant to aggregate demand, we can draw the IS schedule, say IS_0, showing the different combinations of interest rates and income at which planned spending on goods equals actual output of goods. Notice crucially that for the moment we continue to assume that output is demand-determined and that firms will happily produce whatever output is demanded. Exploring whether this is true is precisely where we are going to use the aggregate supply schedule later in the chapter.

As we saw in the previous chapter, planned spending on goods equals actual output of goods at all points on the IS schedule. And the money market is in equilibrium at all points on the LM schedule. Hence only at the intersection of the IS schedule (assumed for the moment to be IS_0) and the LM schedule (assumed for the moment to be LM_0) is the money market in equilibrium and the planned spending on goods equal to the actual output of goods. In Figure 26-1(a) this point is shown as the point E_0. Hence in Figure 26-1(b) we draw the point E_0 showing that the money market clears and that planned and actual output are equal when the price level is P_0 and the level of aggregate demand is Y_0.

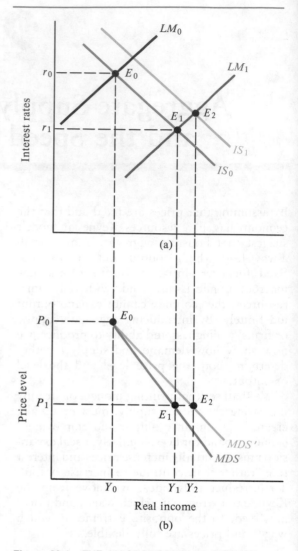

(a)

(b)

Figure 26-1   THE MACROECONOMIC DEMAND SCHEDULE.   For a given nominal money supply, a lower price level increases the real money supply, shifts the LM schedule to the right, and increases equilibrium income. Given the IS schedule IS_0, a fall from P_0 to P_1 induces the shift from LM_0 to LM_1 and an increase from Y_0 to Y_1. The macroeconomic demand schedule MDS shows the different combinations of prices and income at which the money market is in equilibrium and actual output satisfies the aggregate demand for goods. The relevance of IS_1 and MDS' is discussed in the text.

Now consider a lower price level P_1. Given the fixed nominal money supply, the lower price level means a higher real money supply and shifts the LM schedule to the right from LM_0 to LM_1. At each interest rate it takes a higher income level to induce people to hold the larger real money stock. Since the *IS* schedule remains IS_0, the point E_1 in Figure 26-1(a) now shows the combination of interest rates and income at which the money market is in equilibrium, and planned spending equals actual income *and* output. In Figure 26-1(b) we draw point E_1 showing that, when the price level is P_1, the level of income at which planned spending and actual spending are equal is Y_1. This point already recognizes the adjustment in interest rates that will be required to maintain equilibrium in the money market at this income level.

By considering each possible price level in turn, and hence the corresponding real money supply and position of the *LM* schedule, we can trace out a whole set of points such as E_0 and E_1 in Figure 26-1(b). Joining up these points, we obtain the macroeconomic demand schedule *MDS*.

The *macroeconomic demand schedule MDS* shows the different combinations of the price level and real income at which planned spending equals actual output once interest rates are set at the level required to keep the money market in equilibrium.

The macroeconomic demand schedule slopes downwards because a lower price level increases the real money supply, reduces equilibrium interest rates, and increases aggregate demand. It is drawn for a given level of the nominal money supply, government spending, and all other variables relevant to the level of aggregate demand. Real changes, such as an increase in government spending, which would shift the *IS* schedule upwards also shift upwards the *MDS*. At each price level – and hence each level of the real money supply and position of the *LM* schedule – a higher level of government spending will increase aggregate demand and increase income in the short run. Hence the macroeconomic demand schedule must shift upwards, showing a higher income at each price level. Similarly, for each price level, a higher nominal money supply will imply an *LM* schedule lying further to the right and a higher level of aggregate demand and actual income. Again, the macroeconomic demand schedule will shift upwards.

The purpose of the macroeconomic demand

schedule is to show how lower prices increase aggregate demand by increasing the real money supply and reducing the equilibrium interest rate. Because it is so important, we restate why we can think of it as a *demand* schedule. The schedule simultaneously incorporates two conditions. The first is that planned spending equals actual output, and the second is that interest rates have adjusted to keep the money market in equilibrium at this level of income and output. But we have not yet asked whether firms, whose aim is to choose the output level that maximizes their profits, *wish* to supply this output. For the moment we have simply assumed that firms will supply whatever output is demanded. The macroeconomic demand schedule assumes that there is no internal inconsistency on the demand side. Planned spending on goods equals actual output of goods, and demanders of goods are getting the quantities they desire. But we have still to investigate whether firms are happy to produce this output. Thus we can think of the macroeconomic demand schedule as the actual output that would satisfy aggregate demand for goods even when we take account of the induced changes in interest rates necessary to keep the money market in equilibrium at the same time.

In Figure 26-1 the macroeconomic demand schedule *MDS* slopes down because a lower price level shifts the *LM* schedule as a higher real money supply reduces interest rates. This moves us down a given *IS* schedule. Although this mechanism is sufficient to allow the construction of a downward-sloping macroeconomic demand schedule, we briefly examine a second mechanism which also has this effect.

The Real Balance Effect

In the last chapter we constructed the *IS* schedule to isolate the effect of interest rates on aggregate demand. Lower interest rates increase aggregate demand both by increasing investment demand and by shifting the consumption function upwards, through increasing the value of household wealth and also by making consumer borrowing cheaper. Here we note that consumer wealth may increase for a reason not directly connected with the fall in interest rates, and that in consequence the consumption function *and* the *IS* schedule will shift upwards.

The source of this additional wealth effect is the real value of that part of household wealth held in money. A lower price level increases the value of households' real money balances, adding directly to their wealth. To distinguish this wealth effect from the wealth effect operating through the effect of interest rates on the value of bonds and company shares, we call it the real balance effect.

The *real balance effect* is the increase in autonomous consumption demand when the value of consumers' real money balances increases.

Because the *IS* schedule isolates the increase in aggregate demand that is due to interest rates *alone*, we must show the real balance effect as an upward shift in the *IS* schedule. At each interest rate, aggregate demand and output increase when real balances are higher. Figure 26-1 shows the consequence of extending our analysis to include the real balance effect. Suppose we begin as before, with the price level P_0 and the schedules LM_0 and IS_0. E_0 remains the point of equilibrium in the goods and money markets. However, at the lower price level P_1, not only does the real money supply increase and the *LM* schedule shift from LM_0 to LM_1, but the real balance effects shifts the *IS* schedule from IS_0 to IS_1. Hence the new equilibrium point is E_2, which we also plot in Figure 26-1(b).

Repeating the analysis for all price levels, we now get the macroeconomic demand schedule MDS'. It is flatter than MDS because a fall in prices increases aggregate demand not only through lower interest rates, but also through the real balance effect. Even so, the main conclusion of this section is unaffected. The macroeconomic demand schedule – the set of points at which the money market clears *and* planned spending on goods equals actual income and output – is a downward-sloping schedule relating the price level and the level of real income.

To determine which of these combinations of prices and real income will be relevant, we must now turn to the linkage between the goods and labour market which is summarized in the aggregate supply schedule.

26-2 The Labour Market and Aggregate Supply

The *aggregate supply schedule* shows the quantity of output that firms wish to supply at each price level.

Since the quantity of output will depend on the quantities of inputs employed, we begin our analysis of aggregate supply by examining the labour market.

Labour Demand

Firms have a given amount of machines, buildings, and land – we shall call these resources capital – which can be combined with labour to produce output for sale in the goods market. Figure 26-2 plots the labour demand schedule *LD* showing how much labour firms demand at each real wage.

The *real wage* is the nominal or money wage divided by the price level. It shows the quantity of goods that the nominal wage will buy.

We briefly review the analysis of Chapter 11 explaining why a fall in the real wage increases the quantity of labour demanded.

The *marginal product of labour* is the increase in output produced from a given capital stock when an additional worker is employed.

If the marginal product of labour exceeds the real wage, firms will increase profits by expanding employment, since the marginal benefit of another worker (the extra output) exceeds the marginal cost (the real wage). If the marginal product of labour is less than the real wage, firms will reduce employment, thereby avoiding the losses made by hiring the last worker whose marginal cost exceeded the marginal benefit. Hence firms maximize profits by increasing employment up to the point at which the marginal product of labour just equals the real wage.

With a fixed capital stock, the marginal product of labour falls as extra workers are hired. More and more workers have to share the same capital, and an extra worker can add less and less to total output. Hence firms will demand a higher quantity of labour only if the real wage falls to compensate for the reduction in the marginal product of the last worker when more workers were employed. Thus Figure 26-2 shows a down-sloping *LD* schedule for a given capital stock. An increase in the capital stock would shift the *LD* schedule upwards. At any real wage, firms could take on more workers until marginal product of labour was reduced to equal that real wage. Hence firms would demand more labour at each real wage.

Labour Supply

We must distinguish between the people wishing to register as being in the labour force and the people who actually have accepted a job.

The *registered labour force* is the number of people registered as wishing to work. It is the number of people in employment *plus* the *registered unemployed*, those without a job who are registered as seeking a job.

In Figure 26-2 the upward-sloping schedule *LF* shows that more people join the labour force as the real wage increases. Being in the labour force has certain costs. People have to commute to work or spend time job hunting. Either way, they must give up leisure, and possibly hire babysitters or buy special clothing. As the real wage rises, more people will find it worthwhile to enter the labour force in search of a job. We discussed the decision to join the labour force in detail in Chapter 11.

The schedule *AJ* shows that as the real wage rises more people will accept jobs. In part this is because there are more people in the labour force looking for jobs, but we show the *AJ* schedule getting closer to the *LF* schedule as the real wage increases. For a given level of unemployment benefit, a higher percentage of the labour force are likely to accept jobs the higher is the real wage relative to the level of unemployment benefit.

The horizontal distance between the job acceptances schedule *AJ* and the labour force schedule *LF* shows how many people are unemployed because they are refusing to accept jobs at that real wage even though they are in the labour force and registered as seeking employment. Some people will inevitably be in between jobs. They will be temporarily unemployed in a world where the pattern of

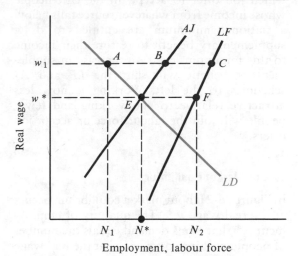

Figure 26-2 THE LABOUR MARKET. The labour demand schedule *LD* shows that firms will offer more jobs the lower is the real wage. The schedule *LF* shows that more people wish to be in the labour force the higher is the real wage. The schedule *AJ* shows how many workers have actually chosen to accept a job at each real wage. At any wage, some workers are in the labour force but have not accepted a job, either because they are holding out for a better offer or because they are temporarily between jobs. Labour market equilibrium occurs at *E*, where the quantity of employment demanded by firms equals the number of jobs that people wish to accept. The horizontal distance between the *AJ* and *LF* schedules shows the level of voluntary unemployment at each wage rate. At the equilibrium wage rate the level of voluntary unemployment *EF* as a percentage of the labour force N_2 is called the natural rate of unemployment. When the real wage exceeds w^*, some people are involuntarily unemployed. They would like to take a job but can't find one. At the real wage w_1, involuntary unemployment is *AB* and voluntary unemployment is *BC*.

employment is continually changing. Others may have been tempted into the labour force at a particular wage rate in the hope of finding an unusually good employment offer which pays more than the average wage. They are still searching for better offers.

Other things equal, we expect an increase in the population of working age to shift both the *LF* and the *AJ* schedules to the right. At any real wage, more people will enter the labour force and more will accept jobs. An increase in the real level of unemployment benefit will shift the *AJ* schedule to the left since people in the labour force can now be more choosy about which job offer to accept. In the UK, people whose income from whatever source falls below a national minimum are entitled to draw supplementary benefit to restore their income to this minimum level. An increase in supplementary benefit will shift the *LF* and *AJ* schedules to the left. Working is now less attractive relative to not working and fewer people will join the labour force or accept job offers.

Labour Market Equilibrium

In Figure 26-2 labour market equilibrium occurs at the real wage w^*. The quantity of employment N^* that firms demand equals the number of people wishing to take jobs at the real wage w^*. Everyone who wants a job at this real wage has found a job. Although we call this position the *full-employment equilibrium*, registered unemployment is not zero. Figure 26-2 shows that *EF* people are registered as unemployed. They want to be in the labour force but do not want a job at this real wage.

> The *natural rate of unemployment* is the percentage of the labour force that is unemployed when the labour market is in equilibrium. They are *voluntarily unemployed* because they choose not to work at that wage rate.

At any real wage above w^* some people are *involuntarily unemployed*.

> People are *involuntarily unemployed* when they would like to work at the going real wage but cannot find a job.

At the real wage w_1 there are thus two kinds of unemployment. A number of workers *AB* are involuntarily unemployed. They would like to accept jobs but firms are only offering N_1 jobs at this real wage. In addition a number of workers *BC* are voluntarily unemployed. The real wage w_1 has tempted them into the labour force, perhaps in the hope of securing an unusually good offer in excess of w_1, but they are not actually prepared to take a job at the wage rate w_1.

When the labour market clears at the real wage w^*, employment can be increased only if firms are prepared to take on more workers at each wage rate (a rightward shift in the labour demand schedule) or if workers are prepared

to work for lower wages (a rightward shift in the job acceptance schedule). Moreover, since the *AJ* schedule is probably quite steep in practice, the main consequence of a rightward shift in labour demand will probably be to bid up the equilibrium real wage rather than to increase equilibrium employment by very much. In contrast, when the real wage exceeds w^* and there are involuntarily unemployed workers, an increase in labour demand will lead to an increase in employment without increasing the real wage. In Figure 26-2 the number of workers *AB* would be happy to work at the real wage w_1 if only firms were offering more jobs.

Money Wages, Prices, and Real Wages Figure 26-2 says that it is *real* and not *money* wages that matter in the labour market. Real wages tell firms the cost of a worker relative to the extra output that he or she can produce, and real wages tell households how many goods they can buy if they supply their labour. If all prices and all money wages double, nothing real changes. Workers can still buy as many goods with their wage income and firms' money wage costs have risen exactly in line with their output prices. Firms and workers who recognize that it is real wages that matter are said not to suffer from money illusion.

> *Money illusion* exists when people confuse nominal and real variables.

Suppose all wages and prices double. If firms reduce employment because *money wages* have risen, they are suffering from money illusion. In fact, real wages are no higher than before. Any time people respond to changes in nominal values rather than real wages there is money illusion.

If prices and money wages are fully flexible, real wages are also fully flexible. In the classical model this means that the labour market is *always* in equilibrium. Any excess supply of labour or demand for labour will (instantaneously) bid real wages back to their equilibrium level. Combining the assumption of full flexibility with the assumption of an absence of money illusion has two strong implications. First, only real changes (a higher capital stock, higher population, etc.) shift labour demand and supply schedules and alter the equilibrium real wage. Hence any price increase *not* caused by a shift in these schedules must be matched by an equivalent change in money wages to leave real wages at their unchanged equilibrium level. Second, because real wages are unchanged, equilibrium employment must also be unchanged. We now develop these two points which are central to the classical model of output determination.

Suppose that output prices double but neither the labour supply nor labour demand schedules shift. At the original money wages the real wage has now been halved. Hence there is excess demand for labour which bids up the money wage as firms compete for scarce workers. Only when the money wage doubles will real wages be restored to the equilibrium level and excess labour demand be eliminated. But at that point, employment also will have returned to its equilibrium level. Thus, if neither the labour supply nor the labour demand schedules shift, and if wages are instantly and fully flexible, a change in prices will be instantly matched by a change in money wages precisely because both firms and workers care about real wages rather than money wages. And prices will have no effect on either the real wage or the level of employment. This is the strong result obtained in the classical model.

Employment, Output, and Prices

The last step on the supply side is to link employment, output, and prices. In the classical model, where both prices and money wages are flexible, real wages adjust to keep the labour market in equilibrium continuously. Employment is always at its full-employment level, where nobody is involuntarily unemployed. And this employment level is unaffected by changes in prices in the absence of any real shocks to the labour market.

Together with the existing capital stock, this full-employment level determines the quantity of output firms are willing and able to produce. *Potential output* is the output produced when labour is fully employed. Since the level of full employment is unaffected by changes in prices alone, we conclude that the level of output supplied by firms must also be independent of prices alone. Firms always supply full employment output or potential output in the classical model. In Figure 26-3 we show this result

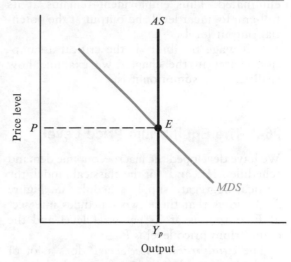

Figure 26-3   FULL EQUILIBRIUM IN THE CLASSICAL MODEL. With flexible wages and prices, the real wage always adjusts to maintain full employment in the labour market. Given this labour input, firms produce potential output Y_p. The classical aggregate supply schedule AS is vertical at Y_p. Any change in prices is immediately reflected in a change in wages to maintain equilibrium real wages, full employment, and potential output. The macroeconomic demand schedule MDS shows points at which money demand equals money supply and planned spending on goods equals actual output. Hence, at E the markets for labour, goods, and money are all in equilibrium. The equilibrium price level is P, determined jointly by aggregate supply and macroeconomic demand.

as a vertical aggregate supply schedule at the level of potential output Y_p.

> The *aggregate supply schedule AS* shows the quantity of output firms wish to supply at each price. In the *classical model* there is no money illusion and money wages are flexible. The quantity of output supplied is then independent of prices, and the aggregate supply schedule is vertical at the level of potential output.

Before reading the next sentence, explain to yourself why in the classical model a fall in prices does *not* result in a reduction in the output that firms wish to supply. The answer? Beginning from labour market equilibrium, a fall in prices with a given money wage would increase the real wage, causing excess labour supply. Flexible money wages are immediately bid down until the real wage is restored to its equilibrium level and the excess supply is eliminated. Thus employment remains at its full-employment level and output at the potential output level.

Full wage flexibility is the critical assumption. Later in the chapter we examine how realistic an assumption it is.

26-3 The Equilibrium Price Level

We have developed the macroeconomic demand schedule MDS and, for the classical model, the vertical aggregate supply schedule AS. Figure 26-3 shows that these two schedules intersect at E: output is at its potential level and the equilibrium price level is P.

The *equilibrium price level P* does a lot of work. It clears the markets for goods, labour, and money. The labour market is in equilibrium anywhere on the classical aggregate supply schedule. But at E we are also on the macroeconomic demand schedule along which the money market clears and aggregate demand for goods equals the actual output of goods.

Suppose prices were higher than P. The real money stock would be lower and interest rates higher. Hence aggregate demand would be lower. At any price above P, firms could not sell the output Y_p they wish to produce. In the classical model, firms immediately cut prices to eliminate excess demand. In so doing, they increase the real money supply, lower interest rates, and boost aggregate demand until they get back to equilibrium at E again. Conversely, if prices were below P, real money supply would be higher, interest rates lower, and aggregate demand would exceed potential output. Excess demand would bid up prices and return the economy to equilibrium at the point E, at the equilibrium price level P. Given this price level, we can calculate the money wage level that secures the real wage required for equilibrium in the labour market.

What Determines Prices?

The equilibrium price level P depends on a number of factors reflected in the positions of the macroeconomic demand schedule and the aggregate supply schedule. On the supply side, the level of potential output Y_p depends chiefly on the labour supply and demand schedules that determine the equilibrium level of employ-

ment. If more workers want to work at each real wage, the labour supply schedule shifts to the right and the equilibrium level of full employment and potential output increases. Similarly, if firms have a larger capital stock, the marginal product of labour will rise at each level of employment, shifting the labour demand schedule to the right and increasing the level of equilibrium employment and potential output. Thus an increase in the willingness to work, or an increase in the stock of capital available, will increase potential output, shift the aggregate supply schedule to the right in Figure 26-3, and reduce the equilibrium price level. Lower prices boost aggregate demand in line with the increase in the potential output that firms wish to supply.

Although we have seen that many factors can affect the macroeconomic demand schedule, we concentrate on those directly under government control. Other changes may be analysed in a similar manner. Under Keynesian assumptions, with prices given and output determined *only* by demand, we showed in the previous chapter that an increase in the nominal money supply, or in the level of government spending, boosts aggregate demand and increases output. We now show that the situation is very different under the assumptions of the classical model.

26-4 Monetary and Fiscal Policy

Movements along the macroeconomic demand schedule show how changes in prices alter the real money supply, thus changing aggregate demand both by altering the interest rate and through the real balance effect on consumption demand. But changes in the nominal money supply, or in fiscal policy, *shift* the macroeconomic demand schedule by altering the level of aggregate demand at each price level.

Monetary Policy

Suppose the economy begins in equilibrium at point E in Figure 26-4 and that the nominal money supply is now doubled because the central bank purchases government securities through an open-market operation. At each price level, the real money stock is now higher than before and the macroeconomic demand schedule shifts upwards from MDS to MDS'.

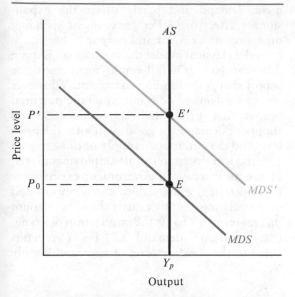

Figure 26-4   MONETARY AND FISCAL EXPANSION.   The macroeconomic demand schedule is drawn for a given nominal money supply and a given fiscal policy. A doubling of the nominal money supply increases aggregate demand at each price level, shifting the macroeconomic demand schedule from *MDS* to *MDS'*. Since the equilibrium point moves from *E* to *E'*, in the classical model an increase in the money supply leads to higher prices but not higher output, which remains Y_p. In fact, if nominal money doubles, equilibrium prices must also double. Only then is the real money supply unaltered. Since interest rates are unaltered, aggregate demand will remain exactly Y_p as required. Fiscal expansion also shifts the macroeconomic demand schedule upwards. Since output supply remains Y_p, in the classical model prices must rise just enough to reduce the real money supply and increase interest rates enough to completely crowd out private expenditure, leaving aggregate demand unaltered at Y_p.

At each price level, interest rates are lower and there is also a real balance effect on consumption.

The new equilibrium point is E'. When all wages and prices have adjusted, the only effect of an increase in the nominal money supply is to increase the price level. There is no effect on output, which remains Y_p since the classical aggregate supply schedule is vertical. We can be even more specific. When the nominal money supply doubles, the macroeconomic demand schedule in Figure 26-4 must shift up from *MDS* to a position *MDS'* such that the equilibrium price level exactly doubles in moving from P_0 to P'. Why?

With a vertical supply schedule, real aggregate demand must remain unchanged at Y_p in the new equilibrium. This can happen only if the *real* money supply also remains unchanged. Otherwise interest rates would change, thus affecting aggregate demand. There would also be a real balance effect on consumption if the real money balances of households changed.

> In the classical model, a change in the nominal money supply leads to an equivalent percentage change in nominal wages and the price level. The real money supply, interest rates, output, employment, and real wages are unaffected.

This proposition, that changes in the nominal money supply lead to changes in prices and wages, rather than to changes in output and employment, is one of the central tenets of the group of economists called *monetarists*. Figure 26-4 shows that the proposition is correct in the classical model in which there is full wage and price flexibility and an absence of money illusion.

It is helpful to spell out the process through which the economy adjusts (instantaneously in the classical model) from point E to point E' when the nominal money supply is increased. Beginning from E, where the price level is P_0, an increase in the nominal money supply increases the real money supply, lowers interest rates, and increases aggregate demand. Aggregate demand exceeds potential output but firms wish to supply Y_p whatever the price level. Excess demand for goods instantaneously bids up the price level until equilibrium is restored. Higher prices have offset the initial increase in the nominal money supply. The real money supply and interest rates have returned to their original level. And in the labour market, higher money wages have matched the increase in the price level, maintaining real wages at their original level. The economy has returned to full employment and potential output. In the classical model all these adjustments happen instantaneously.

Fiscal Policy

Figure 26-4 may also be used to examine the effect of a fiscal expansion. At each price level, and the corresponding value of the real money supply, an increase in government spending (or a cut in taxes) will increase aggregate demand, shifting the macroeconomic demand schedule from MDS to MDS'. Again, since the classical aggregate supply schedule is vertical, the consequence of fiscal expansion must be a rise in prices from P_0 to P' but not an increase in output, which remains at its full-employment level Y_p.

The impact of the fiscal expansion is to increase aggregate demand if prices remain unchanged. But since firms wish to supply potential output, there is excess demand. Prices are bid up (instantaneously) until excess demand for goods is eliminated. Since firms wish to supply Y_p whatever the price level, higher prices must eliminate excess demand entirely by reducing the demand for goods. With a given nominal money supply, higher prices reduce the real money supply, drive up interest rates, and reduce private expenditure on consumption and investment. When aggregate demand has fallen to its full-employment level again, full equilibrium is restored. The economy has higher prices and nominal wages, a lower real money stock, and higher interest rates. Government spending is higher but private consumption and investment are sufficiently lower that aggregate demand remains at its full-employment level. The increase in government spending is exactly offset by a reduction in private expenditure on consumption and investment.

An increase in government spending *crowds out* an equal amount of private expenditure in the classical model, leaving aggregate demand unaltered at the level of potential output.

There is a subtle difference between partial crowding out in the Keynesian model and this complete crowding out in the classical model. In the Keynesian model discussed in the previous chapter, prices and wages were fixed and output was demand-determined in the short run. Although the nominal and real money supplies were both fixed, an increase in government expenditure bid up the equilibrium level of interest rates through its effect on aggregate demand and actual output. Higher output increased the demand for money and required a higher interest rate to maintain money market equilibrium. In turn, the higher interest rate reduced consumption and invest-

ment demand and partly offset the expansionary effect of higher government spending on aggregate demand and output.

In the classical model the mechanism is quite different. Now it is full-employment aggregate supply that is the binding constraint. Whenever aggregate demand does not equal the potential output that firms wish to produce, excess supply or demand for goods will alter the price level and the real money supply until aggregate demand is restored to its full-employment level. Hence an increase in government expenditure (in real terms) must reduce consumption and investment together by exactly the same amount (in real terms). That is the implication of saying that aggregate demand $C + I + G$ remains equal to the constant level of aggregate supply Y_p.

A Moment for Perspective

Before proceeding, it is worth stopping for a moment to take stock. Figure 26-5 is useful. Suppose the economy begins with the macroeconomic demand schedule MDS and is in full equilibrium at the point E. There is now a downward shock to aggregate demand, say because firms get pessimistic about future profits and reduce investment demand, or because consumers get pessimistic about future incomes and reduce consumption demand. Hence the macroeconomic demand schedule shifts down from MDS to MDS'.

In the classical model, prices fall from P to P'. There is a corresponding fall in money wages to maintain real wages at the full-employment level. Lower prices increase the real money supply. The real balance effect on consumption, together with the lower interest rates required to induce people to hold the larger real money supply, increase aggregate demand again. They completely offset the initial downward shock to aggregate demand, restoring it to Y_p. The new equilibrium is at E'.

In contrast, the Keynesian model assumes that wages and prices are fixed. Beginning from equilibrium at E, the downward shift in the macroeconomic demand schedule leads to a new equilibrium at A, with the price level still at P. This is an equilibrium in the sense that the money market clears and that planned spending on goods equals actual output of goods. But it is not a *full* equilibrium. Suppliers would really like to be producing Y_p but are only producing Y. Output is demand-determined.

What happens next in this story? One of two things. First, a Keynesian government may adopt an expansionary fiscal or monetary policy to shift the macroeconomic demand schedule up from MDS' to MDS, in which case suppliers will happily produce the extra output, taking them back on to their desired supply curve. Income will increase from Y to Y_p. Fiscal or monetary policy will be capable of increasing output precisely because the economy had spare resources at point A. Suppliers were producing less than they wished. In consequence, they were demanding less labour than households wished to supply. At point A there was involuntary unemployment in the labour market, since the quantity of employment had been reduced but the real wage had remained unchanged.

Alternatively, in the absence of a government boost to aggregate demand, it is possible that firms will begin to cut prices to try to raise output towards the level they would like to produce, and that workers will accept nominal wage cuts as involuntary unemployment puts downward pressure on wage rates. Thus it is possible that the economy will gradually drag its way down the schedule MDS' from point A to point E', where full employment and equilibrium in all markets are restored.

Thus, on the one hand the classical model asserts that these price and wage adjustments happen immediately, or at least sufficiently quickly that, for the purpose of practical analysis, we can ignore the short time interval during which this adjustment occurs. On the other hand, the extreme Keynesian model assumes that, in spite of the fact that at point A firms are not selling as much output as they wish and workers are not finding as many jobs as they wish, there is nevertheless no downward movement of prices and wages.

Viewed in this way, we can regard the Keynesian story as describing the behaviour of the economy in the short run, before prices and wages have time fully to adjust, and the classical story as describing the behaviour in the long run, after all wages and prices have had time to adjust. The crucial issue is how quickly this adjustment takes place in practice. The analysis of this issue is the focus of the rest of

the chapter. How quickly does the classical long run become relevant?

Before leaving Figure 26-5 we should note two final points. First, there is no disagreement between the Keynesian model and the classical model about the fact that monetary and fiscal policy can shift the macroeconomic demand schedule. Expansionary policies shift the schedule upwards. In the Keynesian model the economy has spare resources which the expansion can mop up; below full employment, output is demand-determined. In contrast, in the classical model we are always at full employment;

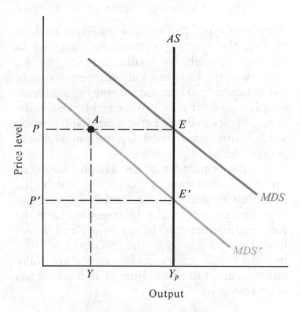

Figure 26-5 KEYNESIAN AND CLASSICAL MODELS COMPARED. The economy begins in equilibrium at E. Given a downward shock, the macroeconomic demand schedule shifts from MDS to MDS'. In the classical model prices fall from P to P' to keep aggregate demand equal to potential output. Money wages fall to maintain equilibrium real wages in the labour market. In the Keynesian model, the failure of prices and wages to adjust leads to equilibrium at A. The money market clears and planned spending on goods equals actual output. But this is less than the output that firms wish to supply. And with lower output and employment, but unchanged real wages, there is involuntary unemployment. Output and employment are demand-determined. Fiscal and monetary policy can shift the demand schedule upwards from MDS' to MDS. In the classical model this leads only to higher prices and higher money wages, a move from E' to E. In the Keynesian model it leads to an expansion of output and employment, a move from A to E.

the aggregate supply schedule is vertical at this output, and the only consequence of expansionary policy is to bid up prices to knock out the effect of the expansion on aggregate demand and maintain demand at the level of potential output Y_p.

Finally, in the classical model in which output is always Y_p, the way for the government to increase output and employment is not to adopt demand management policies to boost demand, but to adopt supply-side policies to boost full employment output.

> *Supply-side economics* is the pursuit of policies aimed not at increasing aggregate demand but at increasing aggregate supply.

Supply-side policies include measures such as cutting the rate of income tax (designed to increase households' willingness to work), increasing the level of equilibrium employment in the labour market, and shifting the aggregate supply curve for goods to the right. We discuss such policies in detail in the next chapter, when we examine employment and unemployment in greater detail.

For the remainder of this chapter we focus on the adjustment process by which the economy responds to an initial shock. How does the economy make the transition from the Keynesian short run, before prices and wages have time to adjust, to the classical long run, in which all prices and wages have fully adjusted and full equilibrium in all markets has been restored?

26-5 The Labour Market and Wage Behaviour

In modern industrial economies such as those of the UK, Western Europe, and the United States, downward shocks to aggregate demand are followed by periods of unemployment that can be severe and persistent. Recessions are usually measured in years rather than weeks or months. Although the classical model is a useful guide to the long-run equilibrium to which the economy is adjusting, that adjustment can be slow and painful.

Adjustment is not immediate because prices and wages do not leap immediately to their new long-run equilibrium positions as the extreme classical model suggests. But why don't they?

We must now come to grips with how wages and prices are actually set in the short run. Since firms must cover their costs of production, and since wages are usually the most important component in these costs, it is sluggish wage adjustment that is the most likely cause of a slow adjustment of prices to changes in aggregate demand. Thus we begin by examining how wages are actually set in the labour market.

To examine wage-setting behaviour we must think about the general relationship between firms and their workforces.

Long-term Job Commitments

From the viewpoint of both firms and workers, a job is typically a long-term commitment. For the firm, it is expensive to hire and fire workers. Firing an existing worker usually means a severance or redundancy payment. It also means the loss to the firm of whatever special expertise the worker has built up on the job. Hiring a worker means advertising, interviewing, and training the new worker in the special features of work within that firm. Thus, firms are reluctant to hire and fire workers merely because of short-term fluctuations in demand and output.

From the worker's viewpoint, looking for new jobs is costly in time and effort. It can also mean beginning from scratch, throwing away experience, seniority, and perhaps the high wages that go with the high productivity that comes from having mastered a particular job in a particular firm. Like firms, workers are concerned with long-term arrangements. Since both firms and workers view job arrangements as long term, both want to reach some explicit or implicit understanding about the terms of work. This includes agreements about wages and how to handle fluctuations in the output produced by the firm.

Adjustments in Labour Input

A firm and its workers have *explicit* or *implicit labour contracts* specifying working conditions. These include normal hours, overtime requirements, regular wages, and pay schedules for overtime work. It is then up to the firm to set the number of hours, within the limits of these conditions, depending on how much output it wishes to produce in that week.

> The firm's *labour input* is the total number of labour hours it employs in a given period.

Labour input may be changed by changing the number of hours worked by a given number of people, by changing the number of workers employed to work a given number of hours, or by some combination of the two. When the firm wishes to change its output, and hence its labour input, how does it choose whether to change the hours worked or the number of workers it employs?

Suppose the demand for a firm's output falls. Given the costs of hiring and firing labour, in the short run the firm's first reaction will be to abolish overtime and try to get by with the same labour force but a shorter working week. Factories may even close before the end of a normal working day. If demand does not recover, or declines still more, firms may then lay off some of their workers.

> A *lay-off* is a temporary separation of workers from the firm.

Workers are made unemployed but they are not fired. Given their skills are specialized to that firm, there is a mutual understanding that the workers will be rehired when demand improves. The lay-off makes sense for the firm, which does not lose its skilled workers for ever, and makes sense for the workers, who need not look for jobs in which they will have to start learning skills from scratch. But when the firm finally concludes that demand prospects are poor, it may make workers redundant, or fire them permanently.

Conversely, during a boom a firm's reaction will be to get its existing workforce to work overtime. Then it may seek temporary workers to supplement the existing labour force. Only when the firm is confident that higher sales can be sustained is it likely to embark on a major recruiting programme. We now discuss the implications of this pattern of hours and employment adjustment for wage settlements.

Wage Adjustment

In modern industrial economies, wages are not set in a daily auction in which the equilibrium wage clears the market for labour. We have explained that firms and workers both stand to gain by reaching long-term understandings. To some extent this mutual commitment insulates a firm and its workforce from conditions in the labour market as a whole.

Nor can a firm and its workforce spend every day haggling about terms and conditions of employment. Bargaining is a costly process, using up valuable time which workers and managers could have been using to produce and sell output. Although there may be regular meetings to deal with minor grievances, in practice the costs of bargaining about the firm's general wage structure mean that such negotiations can be undertaken only infrequently. In the UK this usually means once a year. In the United States many bargains are for a three-year period.

The existence of bargaining costs (which may include the use of strikes initiated by the workforce or lock-outs initiated by the managers) provides a microeconomic rationale for wage changes only at discrete intervals. The macroeconomic consequence is that immediate wage adjustment to demand shocks is ruled out. At best, many firms will have to wait until the next scheduled date for a revision in the wage structure. In practice, complete wage adjustment is unlikely to take place even then. We now examine some of the reasons why adjustment is even more sluggish.

Suppose there is a fall in aggregate demand and some firms have made workers unemployed. Other firms may still be doing all right. Merely because there is a pool of involuntarily unemployed workers prepared to work at, or perhaps even below, the going wage it does not mean that all firms will use this excuse to reduce wages. First, a new worker is a poor substitute for an existing worker familiar with the job and the firm. Second, and of greater importance, long-term co-operation between a firm and its workforce is more important than short-term gains from forcing wages down a little. The reputation of a firm as an employer is an important determinant of the firm's ability to attract and retain its skilled workers in the long run.

If its existing labour force dislikes fluctuations in the wage rate, the firm will have an incentive to smooth out wages in the long run to keep its labour force happy. The firm will lose out in the times when it would like to be cutting wages, but it will correspondingly gain in the times when demand is high and labour market pressures are tending to raise wages. Thus, firms and workers may reach an implicit understanding that wages will neither be drastically cut during slumps nor drastically raised during booms.

In Section 11-7 we discussed other reasons why involuntary unemployment might not be immediately eliminated by instantaneous wage adjustment. We grouped these arguments under the headings of trade union effects, the effect of scale economies, insider–outsider effects, and arguments based on efficiency wages when information on worker quality and effort is expensive for the firm to collect. If you do not recall these arguments in detail, we strongly suggest that you go back to Section 11-7 before continuing with this chapter.

Recap

Table 26-1 summarizes our discussion and provides a road map for the rest of the chapter. The table lays out the labour market adjustment in the short run, the medium run, and the long run. Based on our own reading of the empirical evidence, we also give our view about how long each of these 'runs' might be. We suggest three months for the short run, one year for the medium run, and four to six years for the long run. We should emphasize that it is precisely on this assessment that many macroeconomists disagree. Many modern monetarists think that adjustment will be faster than we have suggested and some modern Keynesians think it will be considerably slower than we have suggested. But the assessment of Table 26-1 corresponds to the view of a large number of mainstream economists.

The table shows, in the short run, variations in labour input largely take the form of changes in the work week, perhaps supplemented by lay-offs or recalls from lay-offs. In the medium run, as changes in labour demand persist, the firm begins to alter its permanent workforce. The alternative, continuing to run a factory with large overtime or short-time working, is simply too expensive. And in the long run, adjustment becomes complete. By then, firms have fully adjusted to the new long-run equilibrium and the classical model becomes relevant.

In the short run the wage structure within a firm is largely given. The firm has a bit of flexibility over earnings as distinct from negotiated wage rates, because fluctuations in overtime and short time affect average hourly earnings. But this flexibility is limited. In the medium run the firm begins the process of adjusting the wage structure, and in the long run this process has been completed and the economy as a whole is back on the vertical classical aggregate supply schedule at full-employment output.

Although the table suggests that firms will be slow to fire workers, the fact that firms make long-run decisions means that they will also be slow to take on new workers when demand picks up or wages are reduced. While this means that involuntary or Keynesian unemployment may be slow to build up, it also means that it is not quickly eliminated once it has built up.

Having examined behaviour in the labour market, we turn now to the link between the labour market and the goods market.

26-6 Wages, Prices, and Aggregate Supply

Figure 26-6 shows the implications of our discussion of short-term wage adjustment. Suppose the economy begins at full employment

Table 26-1 Adjustment in the labour market

	SHORT-RUN (3 months)	MEDIUM-RUN (1 year)	LONG-RUN (4–6 years)
Wages	Largely given	Beginning to adjust	Clearing the labour market
Hours	Demand-determined	Hours/employment	Normal work week
Employment	Largely given	mix adjusting	Full employment

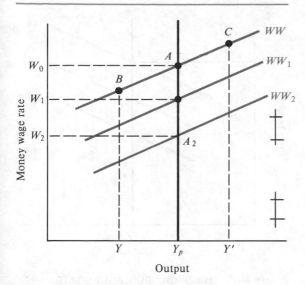

Figure 26-6 WAGE ADJUSTMENT. Beginning at the full employment point A, there is a short-run money wage schedule WW along which output changes are met primarily by changing hours of work and overtime bonuses. A permanent fall in aggregate demand will be met by a move from A to B. Output is cut and short-time working introduced. As time elapses, workers are fired and wage adjustment begins. The new wage schedule is WW_1. Since wages have not fallen enough to restore full employment, the economy is at a point on WW_1 to the left of Y_p. Only in the long run do money wages and prices fall enough to restore aggregate demand and attain full employment and potential output, at the point A_2. Temporary fluctuations in demand around full employment will then be met by movements along WW_2 and will be reflected chiefly in temporary fluctuations in hours worked.

at the point A. In the short run there is a very flat wage schedule WW. If firms wish to produce more output, their first reaction will be to use overtime payments to get more labour input out of their existing labour force, producing at a point such as C. Conversely, if demand for their output falls, firms will initially meet this reduction in demand and output by reducing the working week, ending overtime, and slightly reducing hourly earnings in consequence. Faced with this reduction in demand, the short-term response will be to produce at a point such as B.

If demand does not pick up, in the medium run firms will begin making workers unemployed and cutting wages. However, wage rates are unlikely to be reduced all the way to W_2, the level we assume would restore full employment in the classical long run. Rather, in the medium run there will be partial adjustment, say to the wage schedule WW_1. As we shall shortly explain, lower wages will allow lower prices, and this will partly restore the level of aggregate demand by increasing the real money supply and reducing interest rates. But sluggish wage adjustment implies that this adjustment will not be accomplished fully in the medium run. Hence firms will still be producing an output below potential output Y_p.

Only in the long run is the wage schedule finally reduced to WW_2. Now, wages and prices have fallen sufficiently to increase the real money supply and lower interest rates to the extent required to restore aggregate demand to its full-employment level. In the absence of any further shock to aggregate demand, firms will now be at the new long-run equilibrium point A_2 and the wage rate will be W_2. Any temporary fluctuations in demand around this new full-employment position will be met by temporary movements along the new wage schedule WW_2.

Now we make explicit the link between wages in the labour market and prices in the goods market.

The Short-run Aggregate Supply Schedule

Only in some markets, notably agricultural markets such as wheat and soya beans, where there is a standardized product, are prices set in a competitive auction. In most cases prices are set by sellers. Ford sets the price of its cars and Sony the price of its televisions. How are prices set in practice?

In Part 2 we examined a number of microeconomic theories of pricing and saw that market structure would play an important role. In some market structures, such as perfect competition or pure monopoly, prices were related to the marginal cost of producing the last unit of output, with the mark-up of price over marginal cost being determined by the extent of the firm's monopoly power, if any. In other theories, such as the limit pricing model of competition between a few firms in an industry, prices were set as a mark-up on average costs, with the size of the mark-up depending on the threat of entry of new firms to the industry if profits became too large.

Whether we base our analysis of pricing on

rigorous microeconomic analysis or on the view of pragmatic managers that prices should cover prime costs (average variable costs) and over-heads and leave a reasonable profit margin, we reach the same conclusion: when firms' costs rise, they will have to raise the prices they charge.

In modern industrial economies, labour costs are the major part of the costs of production. Of course raw materials, land, and capital are also important. But for the moment we concentrate on wages as the chief determinant of costs. Once our analysis is developed, it will be easy to introduce other cost items.

Thus, we simplify by assuming that firms base output prices on the wages they have to pay. Although we could adopt a much more complex analysis, recognizing the role of other costs, of changes in labour productivity, and of changes in firms' profit margins, in practice none of these complications would change significantly the analysis we now present. Ignoring these complications greatly simplifies the exposition and justifies the sacrifice of realism.

With this simplification we can move directly from a wage schedule WW in Figure 26-6 to an equivalent short-run aggregate supply schedule SAS in Figure 26-7. All we have done is change the label on the vertical axis from 'wages' to 'prices'.

> The *short run aggregate supply schedule* shows the prices charged by firms at each output level, given the wages they have to pay.

Figure 26-7 shows the short-run aggregate supply schedule SAS corresponding to the wage schedule WW. Suppose we begin at the point A in both diagrams. The economy is at full employment and all markets clear. Prices are at level P_0 in Figure 26-7 because negotiated money wages are at level W_0 in Figure 26-6. Beginning from this inherited level of money wage settlements, firms will move along the supply schedule SAS in the short run. Firms can supply a lot of extra output in the short run at only a slightly higher price. A slightly higher price allows firms to cover the overtime payments needed to produce extra output. But, facing a lower price, firms will want to cut back output a lot. At the inherited wage rates, firms have only limited scope for cutting costs, and

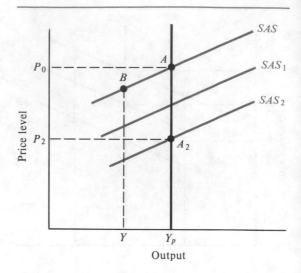

Figure 26-7   THE SHORT-RUN AGGREGATE SUPPLY SCHEDULE.   Firms base prices on wage costs. The short-run aggregate supply schedules correspond to the wage schedules in Figure 26-6. For a given negotiated money wage rate and height of the wage schedule, firms can vary labour costs only by affecting overtime payments and other bonuses. Hence, in the short run they require only a small increase in price to produce more output but can afford to charge only a slightly lower price when producing less output. In the longer term, as firms negotiate lower wages and move on to lower wage schedules, they can also cut their prices. The short-run supply schedule shifts down. At A_2 prices have fallen enough to restore the full-employment level of aggregate demand, and full equilibrium is restored.

will have to reduce output a lot if prices fall. In the medium run, however, negotiated wage rates gradually adjust. If demand and output remain low, wage rates will gradually fall, allowing firms to move on to a lower wage schedule in Figure 26-6 and a lower short-run aggregate supply schedule such as SAS_1 in Figure 26-7. And if full employment and potential output are still not restored, in the longer run negotiated wage rates will fall yet again, leading to a short-run aggregate supply schedule such as SAS_2.

Thus, if demand falls, firms cannot cut their prices much in the short run. They can only move back along the relatively flat short-run aggregate supply schedule SAS. In the medium run, firms will be able to negotiate lower wage settlements if demand remains low and they have to start sacking workers. When the wage schedule shifts down to WW_1 in Figure 26-6, firms will be able to cut prices much more. Corresponding to this wage schedule, the short-run aggregate supply schedule in Figure 26-7 will now be SAS_1. And in the long run, with the wage schedule down to WW_2, the short-run aggregate supply schedule will be SAS_2. Firms will have reached the point A_2, at which they are back on their vertical long-run aggregate supply schedule. There is full employment, and firms are producing potential output. Prices have fallen enough to increase the real money supply and reduce interest rates to the extent required to restore aggregate demand to its full-employment level.

We now use the short-run aggregate supply schedule to develop a realistic picture of the adjustment of the economy to disturbances. Anticipating our main results, we shall show the following. Because the short-run aggregate supply schedule is very flat, a shift in aggregate demand will lead mainly to changes in output rather than changes in prices in the short run. This is the Keynesian feature. But because deviations from full employment gradually change wages and prices over time, the economy gradually works its way back to full employment. That is the classical feature.

26-7 The Adjustment Process

We now combine the macroeconomic demand schedule with the short-run aggregate supply schedule to show how demand or supply disturbances work themselves out in the adjustment process. In combining the macroeconomic demand schedule and the short-run aggregate supply schedule, we are assuming that even in the short run the goods market clears. Demand for goods and supply of goods are equal. But short-run aggregate supply gradually changes over time as firms are able to secure wage adjustment towards the level of wages that will restore full employment and potential output, placing firms eventually on their long-run aggregate supply schedule.

In this more sophisticated analysis, we have finally abandoned the simplifying assumption that output is demand-determined when aggregate demand lies below the level of potential output. In the short run, firms are also on their short-run supply schedules producing as much as they wish, *given the inherited level of money wage bargains*.

Which market is not clearing in the short run? The labour market. Sluggish wage adjustment is preventing immediate adjustment back to full-employment equilibrium. As we shall see, when aggregate demand for goods is reduced, firms cut back on the output they wish to produce and the jobs they wish to offer. Since wages do not fall immediately, there is involuntary unemployment. Until wages fall in the long run to restore full employment, there will be more people wishing to take a job than there are jobs on offer. Some people will want to take a job at the going wage but be unable to find a job. Since there is excess supply of labour at the wage rate ruling in the short run, *employment* is demand-determined in the short run. Only when wages have eventually fallen to eliminate involuntary unemployment will full employment be restored.

We can use Figure 26-8 to analyse the effect of a downward shift in the macroeconomic demand schedule. To be specific, suppose there is a once-and-for-all reduction in the nominal money supply. Initially the economy is at point E in full equilibrium, producing potential output Y_p at an equilibrium price level P. Money wages W are at the level that clears the labour market at the equilibrium real wage $w = W/P$. The point E lies on the macroeconomic demand schedule MDS along which the money market clears and actual output equals planned spending. It also lies on the long-run aggregate supply schedule which is vertical at potential output Y_p.

When the nominal money supply is reduced, there is a lower level of aggregate demand at each price level. The macroeconomic demand schedule shifts down from MDS to MDS'. In the classical model there is immediate price and wage adjustment to maintain the economy at full employment and potential output. The equilibrium price level falls immediately to P_3 and the level of money wages falls to W_3 such that the real wage W_3/P_3 remains at its unchanged full-employment level. The new equilibrium point is E_3.

The reduction in the price level from P to P_3 has just matched the reduction in the nominal money supply. The real money supply is unaltered. Interest rates are unaltered. Aggre-

Figure 26-8   A REDUCTION IN THE NOMINAL MONEY SUPPLY.   Beginning from long-run equilibrium at E, a reduction in the nominal money supply shifts the macroeconomic demand schedule from MDS to MDS'. Given the inherited money wage level, and the short-run supply schedule SAS, the goods market clears at E'. There is a large output fall, from Y_p to Y'. Since prices have fallen from P to P' but money wages are unaltered, real wages have risen. There is involuntary unemployment in the labour market. Gradually this leads to reductions in money wages. Hence the short-run supply schedule for goods shifts from SAS to SAS' and the goods market now clears at P''. As money wages keep falling, the short-run aggregate supply schedule shifts down until it reaches SAS_3. Money wages have now fallen in the same proportion as the original reduction of the nominal money supply. Prices have also fallen by this proportion. Full equilibrium is re-established at E_3.

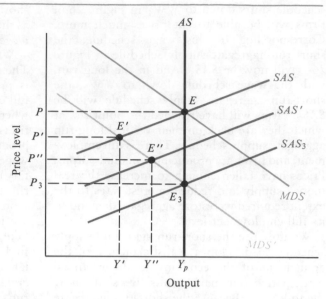

gate demand remains at its full-employment level. No real variables have changed. That is why the economy is able to remain at its full-employment position.

Now we recognize that the classical results will be valid only in the long run. Eventually the economy will move from E to E_3 in Figure 26-8, but we wish to study the adjustment process while wages, and hence prices, are slow to adjust. When the money supply is first reduced, the economy faces the short-run aggregate supply schedule SAS, reflecting the money wage settlements already in force.

In the short run, the downward shift in the macroeconomic demand schedule is met by a move from E to E'. Since firms have few opportunities for reducing costs per unit output, they will want to cut back output a lot. At E' the goods market is clearing. We are on both the demand schedule MDS' and the short-run supply schedule SAS but prices have not fallen much. Output has fallen a lot. Since money wages have not yet adjusted, *real* wages have actually risen. The money wage is unaltered and the price level is lower. Once firms start adjusting employment, they will be offering fewer jobs but more workers will want to take a job. That is why there will be involuntary unemployment.

In the medium run this starts to put downward pressure on money wages. With a

lower wage settlement, firms move on to a lower short-run aggregate supply schedule, say SAS'. The goods market now clears at the point E''. Lower goods prices mean that the original money wage cut turns out not to have reduced real wages so much. Some involuntary unemployment persists. But since prices are lower at E'' than E', aggregate demand for goods has increased. The real money supply has begun to increase, interest rates have fallen, and the economy has moved down the demand schedule MDS', showing that output has begun to move back towards its full-employment level.

Only in the long run is full adjustment completed. Money wages have fallen in proportion to the original reduction in the nominal money supply. And so have prices. The short-run aggregate supply schedule has shifted down to SAS_3 in Figure 26-8 and the economy is in full equilibrium at the point E_3, lying both on the short-run and the long-run aggregate supply schedules. Prices have fallen sufficiently to restore the real money supply to its original level. Interest rates and aggregate demand have been restored to their original full-employment position. And in the labour market, the real wage has returned to its full-employment level. Involuntary unemployment has been eliminated.

Figure 26-9 shows how the decrease in the nominal money supply has affected output and

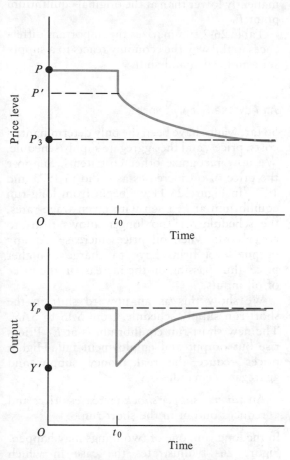

Figure 26-9 ADJUSTMENT PATHS FOR PRICES AND OUTPUT. The economy begins at potential output Y_p with an equilibrium price level P. At time t_0 there is a once-and-for-all reduction in the nominal money supply. In Figure 26-8 the economy moves from E to E'. Here this is shown as a fall in the price level to P' and a fall in output to Y'. Thereafter, as wages slowly fall, the price level gradually falls to its new long-run equilibrium level P_3. As the real money supply gradually increases again, output rises slowly back to its full-employment level Y_p. Employment follows a path similar to that shown for output.

prices. The economy began in full employment at E. At time t_0 there was a once-and-for-all reduction in the nominal money supply. Initially output fell sharply to Y' but then it began to move back towards its full-employment level as wage and price reductions increased the real money supply, reduced interest rates and boosted aggregate demand. Once wages and prices had fallen in proportion to the original fall in the nominal money supply, all real

variables were back to their original position and full equilibrium had been restored.

Figure 26-9 provides a good way of seeing how the real world lies between the extreme simplifications adopted by the simple Keynesian model and the simple classical model. In practice, prices and wages are neither fully flexible nor fully fixed. A monetary contraction has real effects in the short run since output and employment are reduced. But after wages and prices have fully adjusted, the only consequence of a monetary contraction is a reduction in nominal wages and prices. No real variables have changed, and the economy has returned to full employment and potential output.

Similar conclusions apply in other contexts. We strongly suggest that you use a figure like Figure 26-8 to analyse for yourself the short-run and long-run effects of a once-and-for-all increase in the nominal money supply. Similarly, in problem 7 at the end of this chapter we ask you to analyse the effect of a change in fiscal policy.

This analysis also demonstrates the possibility of a *business cycle*. An initial expansion (a boom) or an initial contraction (a slump) will set in motion forces that gradually reverse the initial movement and bring the economy back to full employment and potential output. But it takes time. We examine business cycles in detail in Chapter 30.

26-8 A Shift in Aggregate Supply

When aggregate demand increases and the MDS schedule shifts upwards, output and employment temporarily increase until a temporary period of inflation has reduced the real money supply sufficiently to restore aggregate demand to the level of potential output. The effect of a shift in aggregate supply is very different. Suppose a change in social attitudes towards women working leads to more people wishing to work at each real wage rate. The labour supply schedule shifts to the right, increasing the level of equilibrium employment in the long run. Figure 26-10 shows this as an increase in potential output from Y_p to Y_p'.

Until this pool of extra labour starts to reduce wage settlements, there will be no effect on the short-run aggregate supply schedule. Beginning

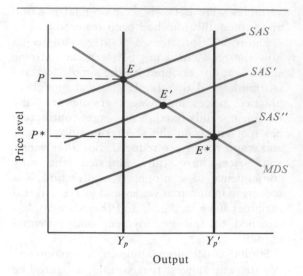

Figure 26-10 AN INCREASE IN POTENTIAL OUTPUT. An increase in the willingness to work increases the level of full employment and increases potential output from Y_p to Y_p'. Beginning from E, initially there is no effect on output or prices, so unemployment increases. Gradually this leads to lower wages. The short-run aggregate supply schedule shifts from SAS to SAS' and the new equilibrium is at E'. Eventually wages fall sufficiently to shift SAS' to SAS'', and full employment is attained at E^*. Prices are permanently lower and output permanently higher in the long run.

from the point E, the schedule remains SAS in the short run. Prices, output, and employment are unaffected. Since more people wish to work, recorded unemployment will rise.

Over time, this will put downward pressure on wages, and the short-run aggregate supply schedule will shift from SAS to SAS'. With lower wages and prices, the real money supply and aggregate demand will increase and the new equilibrium point will be E'. Unemployment has been reduced but not eliminated. Only in the long run do wages and prices fall sufficiently to establish equilibrium at point E^*. At this point, output and employment are per-

manently lower than at the original equilibrium point E.

Table 26-2 summarizes the important differences in the way the economy reacts to a supply shift and a demand shift.

An Adverse Supply Shock

So far, wages have been the only determinant of costs, prices, and the aggregate supply schedule. We now recognize other cost items. Suppose the price of oil increases as it did in 1973 and 1979. In Figure 26-11 we begin from long-run equilibrium at E. Even with given wage rates, the schedule SAS no longer allows firms to cover costs when oil prices increase. At any output level firms have to charge a higher price, thus passing on the increase in the price of oil inputs.

We show this as an upward shift in the short-run supply schedule, from SAS to SAS'. The new short-run equilibrium is at E'. Prices rise but output and employment fall. Higher prices reduce the real money supply and aggregate demand.

> An *adverse supply shock* increases prices and reduces output in the short run.

In the long run, one of two things may happen. Figure 26-11 illustrates the case in which unemployment gradually bids down wages, the short-run supply schedule gradually shifts downwards, and the economy gradually moves down the MDS schedule back to the original equilibrium at E.

Although oil prices are permanently higher, wages and other prices have fallen sufficiently that the aggregate price level has returned to P, thus restoring aggregate demand to the level of potential output Y_p.

In practice, a second outcome is more probable. Since the price of oil has risen relative to other commodities, firms will try to get by

Table 26-2 Reactions of the economy to shifts in demand and supply

RIGHTWARD SHIFT OF:	EFFECT ON OUTPUT		EFFECT ON PRICE LEVEL	
	SHORT RUN	LONG RUN	SHORT RUN	LONG RUN
Aggregate demand	Rise	Zero	Rise	Higher
Aggregate supply	Zero	Higher	Zero	Lower

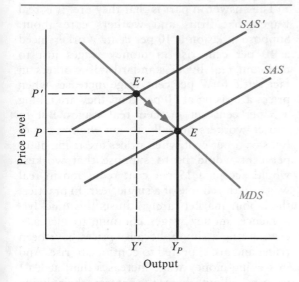

Figure 26-11 AN ADVERSE SUPPLY
SHOCK.   Higher oil prices force firms to charge
more for their output. In the short run, the supply
schedule shifts from SAS to SAS' and equilibrium
from E to E'. Higher prices reduce aggregate
demand and output falls to Y'. Unemployment
gradually reduces wages and allows SAS' to shift
down gradually towards SAS again.

with less oil. Since oil is one of the inputs with
which labour works to produce output, labour
will now have fewer materials with which to
work in producing output. Thus, at each
employment level the marginal product of
labour is likely to be reduced. The labour
demand schedule will shift downwards. Because
it will now cross the labour supply schedule at
a lower level of employment, full employment
and potential output will be reduced. Hence a
more complete analysis of an oil shock would
have to take account not merely of the
short-term effect of higher prices in reducing
aggregate demand, as shown in Figure 26-11,
but also of the possibility that the level of
potential output Y_p may be permanently
reduced. If so, the new long-run equilibrium
will occur at a point higher up the MDS
schedule than point E in Figure 26-10. Output
will be lower and the price level higher in the
long run.

A Wage Increase   Figure 26-11 can also be used
to show the effect of an increase in trade union
power or militancy. Beginning from E, an
'unjustified' wage increase will force firms to

raise prices and will move the supply schedule
from SAS to SAS'. Output will fall and
unemployment increase. Gradually, this is
likely to put downward pressure on wages and
to allow the supply schedule to shift back to
SAS again. Workers who keep their jobs during
the transitional period will temporarily have
higher real wages, but other workers will be
temporarily priced out of a job while aggregate
demand is reduced by higher prices and a lower
real money supply. Nevertheless, those who
expected (correctly or mistakenly) to keep
their jobs during the transitional period may
succeed in outvoting the other workers and
forcing the union to press for the wage increase.

26-9 The Business Cycle

Shifts in aggregate supply and demand generate
changes in the level of output and prices and
affect the inflation rate during transitional
periods of adjustment. Shifts in aggregate
supply and demand are thus the underlying
source of the business cycle.

> The *business cycle* is the tendency for output
> and employment to fluctuate around their
> long-term trends.

Although the economy is continuously buffeted
by small shocks, major shocks are infrequent.
The UK got through the 1960s without a major
supply-side shock, but in both 1973 and 1979
there were major supply-side shocks in the form
of the oil price increases. In the UK the latter
was exacerbated by an increase in VAT from
8 to 15 per cent, which also dramatically
increased the prices that suppliers had to charge
their customers.

Figure 26-12 shows that these two supply-
side shocks, displayed as temporary increases
in the annual inflation rate, were quickly
followed by sharp rises in the unemployment
rate, as Figure 26-11 predicts. But we can also
identify periods in which demand-side shocks
were occurring. In previous chapters we have
discussed the Heath government's 'dash for
growth', when monetary and fiscal expansions
were undertaken during 1971–73. Figure 26-12
shows that unemployment was falling immediately prior to the first oil price shock but
that prices had already started to rise quite
sharply, as Table 26-2 predicts. Similarly,

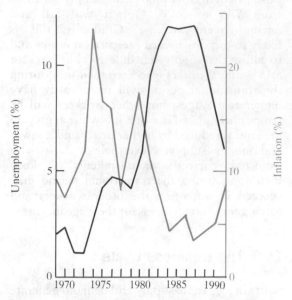

Figure 26-12 INFLATION AND UNEMPLOYMENT IN THE UK. (*Source*: CSO, *Economic Trends*.)

during 1980–82, tight fiscal and monetary policy succeeded in reducing the inflation rate slowly, but in the short run they also contributed to rising unemployment. In the late 1980s unemployment fell sharply, but inflation began to increase again.

Thus recent economic history illustrates the usefulness of the supply and demand apparatus we have developed in this chapter to analyse short-run adjustment. Of course, we could have made the theory more sophisticated, allowing for example a better understanding of the exact timing of the adjustment responses. But the big picture comes through clearly. The rate of inflation and the level of output are being moved around by shifts in aggregate supply and aggregate demand to which the economy responds only sluggishly.

Persistent Inflation   A close look at Figure 26-12 leaves us with one remaining puzzle. Although swings in unemployment reflect shifts in aggregate supply or demand, there is *always* inflation. Inflation slows down when unemployment is high but prices never actually fall. Since prices rise essentially because wages rise, this means that money wages are rising even when unemployment is 10 per cent of the labour force. Why aren't workers taking wage cuts?

The answer in part is that they are. It is real wages that firms and workers care about. Suppose inflation is 10 per cent. Workers need a 10 per cent rise in money wages just to maintain real living standards. If workers in fact settle for 7 per cent wage increases when prices are rising at 10 per cent, they are taking a 3 per cent cut in their real wages. But to expect workers actually to cut *money* wages by, say, 5 per cent when prices are rising at 10 per cent would be to suppose that workers would accept a 15 per cent reduction in real wages in the course of a single year. In practice, the labour market rarely adjusts this quickly.

Hence, money wages continue to increase, even during a slump, because prices have been rising and are expected to continue to rise. And in seeking money wage increases that, at least in part, allow them to protect their living standards, workers reach deals with firms that ensure that wage costs will keep rising and that prices will have to be raised again. We examine the interaction of rising wages and rising prices at length in Chapter 28, where we deal explicitly with the question of inflation.

Summary

1   The classical model of macroeconomics assumes full flexibility of wages and prices, and the absence of money illusion.

2   The macroeconomic demand schedule shows at each price level the level of income at which planned spending on goods equals actual output when the money market is also in equilibrium. The schedule slopes downward. Lower prices increase the real money supply, thus increasing aggregate demand both through lower interest rates and through the real balance effect on consumption.

3   An increase in the real wage increases the quantity of labour supplied but reduces the quantity of labour demanded. Since the marginal product of labour declines as employment increases, firms need a lower real wage to match the declining marginal product of labour when more workers are employed.

4   In the classical model, there is always full employment and the aggregate supply schedule is vertical at the corresponding level of potential output. The equilibrium price level is deter-

mined by the intersection of the aggregate supply schedule and the macroeconomic demand schedule. The markets for goods, money, and labour are all in equilibrium.

5   In this model, fiscal or monetary expansion cannot increase output. Rather, they increase prices until the real money supply has fallen sufficiently to restore aggregate demand to the level of potential output that firms wish to supply.

6   Supply-side economics considers how potential output can be increased by providing incentives to increase the supplies of factor inputs.

7   In practice, wages change only slowly in response to shocks since job arrangements are long term. Firms incur costs in hiring and firing, and workers lose seniority when they switch jobs and have to learn particular skills afresh. Firms and workers reach implicit understandings about terms and conditions of work.

8   In the short run, variations in labour input are met chiefly by changing hours. Only in the longer run is the quantity of workers adjusted.

9   Wage adjustment is sluggish not merely because wage bargaining is infrequent, but because workers prefer their long-term employers to smooth wages. Trade unions, scale economies, insider–outsider distinctions, and efficiency wages may all act to reduce short-run wage flexibility.

10   Prices are based chiefly on labour costs. The short-run aggregate supply schedule shows how much firms wish to produce given the wage settlement in force. Output is responsive to small price changes since small variations in overtime and other bonuses allow firms to produce the extra output at only slightly different labour costs. As wage adjustment takes place, the short-run supply schedule shifts and prices change much more.

11   Thus, in the short run prices and wages are capable only of small changes. In the long run, a period of several years, they are fully flexible. Hence the Keynesian model is a good guide to short-term behaviour but the classical model describes behaviour in the long run.

12   A shift in the macroeconomic demand schedule, whether caused by changes in private expenditure or by changes in fiscal and monetary policy, will thus affect output more than prices in the short run. But in the long run the economy returns to potential output as induced prices changes alter the real money supply and the level of aggregate demand.

13   A shift to the right in the aggregate supply schedule may have little short-run effect, but in the long run output is permanently higher at the new level of potential output and prices are permanently lower, thus ensuring a corresponding increase in aggregate demand.

14   Sluggish adjustment implies that shocks to aggregate demand or aggregate supply set off a business cycle. Because shocks are irregular, but business cycle is also irregular.

Key Terms

Classical model
Wage and price flexibility
Macroeconomic demand schedule
Money illusion
Crowding out
Real balance effect
Voluntary and involuntary unemployment
Labour force schedule
Job acceptance schedule
Supply-side economics
Aggregate supply schedule
Lay-offs
Overtime and short time
Short-run aggregate supply schedule
Adverse supply shock
Business cycle

Problems

1   (a) Define the macroeconomic demand schedule. (b) What happens to the schedule if (i) consumers' propensity to save increases? (ii) prices fall? (iii) investment demand increases?

2   Explain how and whether an increase in the money supply affects prices and output in the classical model.

3   How does a larger capital stock affect the long-run aggregate supply schedule?

4   How do the following affect the short-run supply

schedule and hence output and prices in the short run: (a) a higher income tax rate? (b) an increase in labour productivity? (c) an increase in the money supply?

5 'Higher unemployment means lower inflation.' Is this true for (a) a supply schedule shift? (b) a demand schedule shift?

6 Using aggregate supply and demand schedules, explain why a cut in the money supply aimed at reducing the price level could be costly to society in the short run.

7 In 1979 the UK rate of VAT was raised from 8 to 15 per cent. Draw a diagram showing how you expect the economy to react.

8 Common Fallacies Show why the following statements are incorrect: (a) The money supply affects only the price level. (b) Fiscal expansion would increase output for ever. (c) The government can do nothing about the level of unemployment. (d) Higher unemployment always means lower inflation.

27

Unemployment

In the early 1930s, more than one quarter of the UK labour force was unemployed. In particular regions and occupations the unemployment rate was very much higher. High unemployment means that the economy is throwing away output by failing to put its people to work. It also means misery, social unrest, and hopelessness for the unemployed. Over the following 40 years, macroeconomic policy was geared to avoiding a rerun of the 1930s. Figure 27.1 shows that it succeeded.

In the 1970s views about unemployment began to change. People began to reject the Keynesian pessimism about the capacity of the economy to respond to shocks by quickly restoring full employment. The classical model began to be more widely accepted as a description of the way the economy works even in the fairly short run. Since in the classical model unemployment is voluntary, there is less presumption that unemployment means extreme human suffering.

By the 1970s governments in many countries began to perceive an even greater danger to economic and social stability, the danger of high and rising inflation. Thus by the end of the 1970s many governments had embarked on tight monetary and fiscal policies to try to keep inflation under control. The combination of restrictive demand policies and adverse supply shocks led to a dramatic increase in unemployment in most of the industrial countries in the 1980s. Figure 27-1 shows data for the UK. Data for other countries are shown later in the chapter.

High unemployment was one of the major problems in the 1980s. Will it continue? Is it a drain on society or a signal that at last people are getting out of dead-end jobs into something better? What can and should the government be doing? These are the questions we set out to answer in this chapter. We begin by looking at the facts.

27-1 The Facts

Not everyone wants a job. Those people who do are called the labour force.

> The UK *labour force* comprises all those people holding a job or registered with the local office of the Department of Employment as being willing and available for work.

The *participation rate* is the percentage of the population of working age who declare themselves to be in the labour force. In Chapter 11 we pointed out the postwar growth of the UK labour force has been caused less by an increase in the population of working age than by an increase in participation rates, most notably by married women.

> The *unemployment rate* is the percentage of the labour force who are without a job but are registered as being willing and available for work.

Of course, some people without a job are really looking for work but have not bothered to register as unemployed. These people will not be included in the official statistics for the registered labour force, nor will they appear as registered unemployed. Yet from an economic viewpoint, such people *are* in the labour force and *are* unemployed. This is an important phenomenon to which we return shortly. For the moment, when we present evidence on the size of the labour force or the number of people unemployed, it should be understood that data refer to the registered labour force and the registered unemployed.

Figure 27-1 makes two main points about the unemployment rate in the UK. First, unemployment was high during the interwar years, especially during the Great Depression of the 1930s. It was the persistence of high unemployment that led Keynes to develop his *General Theory*. Second, by comparison, the postwar

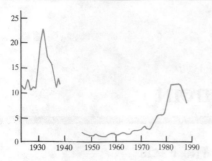

Figure 27-1   UK UNEMPLOYMENT (%).
(*Sources*: B. R. Mitchell, *Abstract of British Historical Statistics* and B. R. Mitchell and H. G. Jones, *Second Abstract of British Historical Statistics*, Cambridge University Press; CSO, *Economic Trends*.)

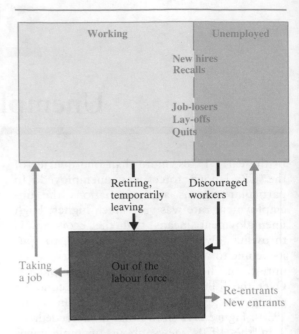

Figure 27-2   LABOUR MARKET FLOWS. A person may be working, unemployed, or out of the labour force. The arrows show the routes along which people move. Each route carries a surprisingly heavy flow.

unemployment rate was tiny until the late 1970s. By the early 1980s it was starting to get back to prewar levels. This basic pattern applies in many other industrialized countries. However, the UK has been more successful than other countries, especially in Western Europe, in bringing unemployment down in the late 1980s.

Alternative Definitions of the Unemployment Rate

The basis for compiling UK unemployment statistics changed several times in the 1980s.

Previously, the unemployment rate referred to the percentage of the labour force who were registered as unemployed. Since 1986, however, the unemployment rate in the UK refers to the percentage of the working population who are unemployed. The working population is the labour force plus those in the armed services plus the self-employed. Since the working population exceeds the labour force, figures on the new basis show a lower unemployment rate, even if the actual number of people unemployed has not changed. Figure 27-1 plots postwar data on this new basis. Later in the chapter we discuss unemployment elsewhere in Europe.

Stocks and Flows

Unemployment is a stock concept measured at a point in time. Like a pool of water, its level rises when inflows (the newly unemployed) exceed outflows (people getting new jobs or quitting

the labour force altogether). Figure 27-2 illustrates this important idea.

Beginning with people working, there are three ways to become unemployed. Some people are sacked or made redundant (job-losers); some are temporarily laid off but expect eventually to be rehired by the same company; and some people voluntarily quit their existing jobs. But the inflow to unemployment can also come from people not previously in the labour force: school-leavers (new entrants), and people who once had a job, then ceased even to register as unemployed, and are now coming back into the labour force in search of a job (re-entrants).

People leave the unemployment pool in the opposite directions. Some get jobs. Others give up looking for jobs and leave the labour force completely. Although some of this latter group may simply have reached the retirement age at which they can draw a pension, many of them are *discouraged workers*, people who have become depressed about the prospects of ever finding a job and decide to stop even trying.

Table 27-1 shows that the pool of unemployment is not stagnant. Even with 3 million

Table 27-1 Flows into and out of unemployment
(Millions of people)

	1988
Excluding school-leavers:	
Inflow to unemployment	3.75
Outflow from unemployment	4.40
Excess of inflow over outflow	−0.65

Source: Department of Employment Gazette.

unemployed, this number is less than the number of people entering and leaving the pool *every* year.

The Duration of Unemployment   When unemployment is high, people have to spend longer in the pool before they find a way out. Table 27-2 gives data on the duration of unemployment. As the level of unemployment has risen, the problem of the *long-term unemployed* has returned. Whereas in 1974 only 20 per cent of the people unemployed had been out of work for longer than one year, by April 1988 this proportion had risen to 40 per cent. And over the same period, the fraction of the unemployed who had been unemployed for less than eight weeks fell from 44 to 17 per cent. Unemployment can no longer be regarded as a temporary stopover on the way to better things.

The Composition of Unemployment

Table 27-3 gives a recent breakdown of unemployment by sex and by age. A recession hits young workers badly. Unlike established workers with accumulated skills and job experience, young workers have to be trained from scratch, and firms frequently cut back on training when times are tough. To combat this, in 1983 the Thatcher government introduced the Youth Training Scheme (YTS), which offers young workers a temporary chance of a job. Table 27-3 shows that youth unemployment fell after the introduction of the scheme.

Table 27-3 also shows that the unemployment rate is lower for women than for men. In part this may reflect the fact that employment in the declining heavy engineering industries had traditionally been predominantly male, so men are worst hit by redundancies in steelworks and shipyards. However, although established women have managed to hang on to their jobs, young women are finding it nearly as tough as young men to get started.

Labour economists believe that the discrepancy between male and female workers is smaller than the table suggests, because unemployed women are less likely than unemployed men to register as unemployed. Hence the true unemployment rates for women are probably higher than the table suggests.

Table 27-3 UK unemployment rates
(Percentage of relevant group)

	MEN		WOMEN	
AGE	1982	1986	1982	1986
Under 25	24.2	21.9	20.5	16.5
25–54	11.3	12.8	6.3	7.3

Source: Department of Employment *Gazette.*

Table 27-2 The duration of unemployment in the UK

| THOUSANDS | WEEKS SINCE ENTERED UNEMPLOYMENT | | | | |
UNEMPLOYED AT	UNDER 2	2–8	8–26	26–52	OVER 52
April 1974	136	153	161	72	132
April 1979	85	230	396	507	367
April 1981	158	486	845	620	516
April 1983	185	362	760	719	1143
April 1988	136	303	767	484	1029

Source: Department of Employment *Gazette.*

27-2 The Framework

Having introduced some of the most important facts about unemployment in the UK, we now develop a theoretical framework in which to discuss the subject. We begin with the old-style classification of types of unemployment, which emphasizes the source of the problem. Then we discuss the modern approach to unemployment which emphasizes the way people in the labour market are behaving.

Types of Unemployment

Economists used to classify unemployment as frictional, structural, demand-deficient, or classical. We discuss each in turn.

Frictional Unemployment   This is the irreducible minimum level of unemployment in a dynamic society. It includes people whose physical or mental handicaps make them almost unemployable, but it also includes the people spending short spells in unemployment as they hop between jobs in an economy where both the labour force and the jobs on offer are continually changing.

Structural Unemployment   In the longer run, the pattern of demand and production is always changing. In Chapter 32 we discuss the reasons why particular countries in the world economy come to specialize in the production of particular commodities at particular times. In recent decades industries such as textiles and heavy engineering have been declining in the UK. Structural unemployment refers to unemployment arising because there is a mismatch of skills and job opportunities when the pattern of demand and production changes. For example, a skilled welder may have worked for 25 years in shipbuilding but is made redundant at 50 when the industry contracts in the face of foreign competition. That worker may have to retrain in a new skill which is more in demand in today's economy. But firms may be reluctant to take on and train older workers. Such workers become the victims of structural unemployment.

Demand-deficient Unemployment   This refers to Keynesian unemployment, when aggregate demand falls and wages and prices have not yet adjusted to restore full employment. Aggregate demand is deficient because it is lower than full-employment aggregate demand.

In Chapter 26 we saw that, until wages and prices have adjusted to their new long-run equilibrium level, a fall in aggregate demand will lead to lower output and employment. Some workers will want to work at the going real wage rate but will be unable to find jobs. Only in the longer run will wages and prices fall enough to boost the real money supply and lower interest rates to the extent required to restore aggregate demand to its full-employment level, and only then will demand-deficient unemployment be eliminated.

Classical Unemployment   Since the classical model assumes that flexible wages and prices maintain the economy at full employment, classical economists had some difficulty explaining the high unemployment levels of the 1930s. Their diagnosis of the problem was partly that union power was maintaining the wage rate above its equilibrium level and preventing the required adjustment from occurring. Classical unemployment describes the unemployment created when the wage is deliberately maintained above the level at which the labour supply and labour demand schedules intersect. It can be caused either by the exercise of trade union power or by minimum wage legislation which enforces a wage in excess of the equilibrium wage rate.

The modern analysis of unemployment takes the same types of unemployment but classifies them rather differently in order to highlight their behavioural implications and consequences for government policy. Modern analysis stresses the difference between *voluntary* and *involuntary* unemployment.

The Natural Rate of Unemployment

Figure 27-3 shows the market for labour. The labour demand schedule *LD* slopes downwards, showing that firms will take on more workers at a lower real wage. The schedule *LF* shows how many people want to be in the labour force at each real wage. We assume that an increase in the real wage increases the number of people wishing to work. The schedule *AJ* shows how many people accept job offers at each real wage. The schedule lies to the left of the *LF*

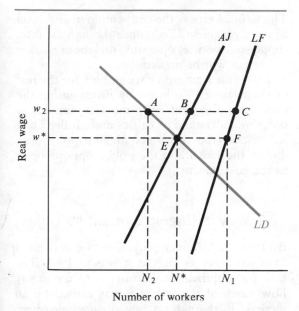

Figure 27-3 THE NATURAL RATE OF
UNEMPLOYMENT.   The schedules *LD*, *LF*, and *AJ*
show, respectively, labour demand, the size of the
labour force, and the number of workers willing to
take job offers at any real wage. *AJ* lies to the left of
LF both because some labour force members are
between jobs and because some optimists are
hanging on for an even better job offer. When the
labour market clears at *E*, *EF* is the natural rate of
unemployment, the number of people in the labour
force not prepared to take job offers at the
equilibrium wage *w**. If union power succeeds in
maintaining the wage *w₂* in the long run, the labour
market will be at *A*, and the natural rate of
unemployment *AC* now shows the amount of
unemployment chosen by the labour force
collectively by enforcing the wage *w₂*.

schedule, both because some people are inevitably between jobs at any instant, and because
a particular real wage may tempt some people
into the labour force even though they will
accept a job offer only if they find an offer with
a rather higher real wage than average. Labour
market equilibrium occurs at the point *E*. The
employment level N^* is the equilibrium or
full-employment level. The distance *EF* is called
the natural rate of unemployment.

> The *natural rate of unemployment* is the rate
> of unemployment when the labour market is
> in equilibrium.

This unemployment is entirely *voluntary*. At
the equilibrium real wage w^*, N_1 people want
to be in the labour force but only N^* want to

accept job offers; the remainder don't want to
work at the equilibrium real wage.

Which of our earlier types of unemployment
must we include in the natural rate of
unemployment? Certainly all frictional unemployment. But we should also include
structural unemployment. Suppose a skilled
welder earned £150 a week before being made
redundant. The issue is not why the worker
became redundant (the decline of the steel
industry), but why the worker refuses to take
a lower wage as a dishwasher in order to get
a job, or why steelworkers as a whole did not
take a sufficient wage cut to allow the steel
industry to remain profitable and competitive
at its former levels of output and employment.
If the answer is that steelworkers refuse to
accept that the equilibrium wage for their skill
has fallen, and refuse to work at wages lower
than those to which they have been accustomed,
then we must count this unemployment as
voluntary and include it in the natural rate.
They are not prepared to work at the going
wage rate but still want to be considered part
of the labour force.

What about classical unemployment, for
example where unions maintain wages above
their equilibrium level? This is shown in Figure
27-3 as a wage rate w_2 above w^*. Total
unemployment is now given by the distance
AC. As individuals, a number of workers *AB*
would like to take jobs at the wage rate
w_2 but will be unable to find them since firms
will wish to be at the point *A*. As individuals,
these workers are involuntarily unemployed.

> A worker is *involuntarily unemployed* if he
> or she would accept a job offer at the going
> wage rate.

However, through their unions, workers collectively decide to opt for the wage rate w_2 in
excess of the equilibrium wage, thereby reducing
the level of employment. Hence for workers as
a whole we must regard the extra unemployment as voluntary. Thus we also include
classical unemployment in the natural rate of
unemployment. If in the long run unions
maintain the wage w_2, the economy will
remain at *A* and *AC* is the natural rate of
unemployment.

This leaves only Keynesian or demand-
deficient unemployment. Such unemployment
is involuntary, being caused by sluggish labour

market adjustment beyond the control of individual workers or unions. Thus we can divide total unemployment into the equilibrium or natural rate – the equilibrium level determined by normal labour market turnover, structural mismatch, union power, and incentives in the labour market – and Keynesian unemployment, sometimes called demand-deficient or cyclical unemployment – the disequilibrium level of involuntary unemployment caused by the combination of low aggregate demand and wage adjustment which is sluggish for the reasons we examined in the previous chapter.

This division helps us think clearly about the government policies required to tackle the unemployment problem. Since we have argued that in the long run the economy will gradually manage to get back to full employment through a slow process of wage and price adjustment, Keynesian unemployment will eventually get rid of itself. But in the short run, Keynesian unemployment is the part of total unemployment that the government could help mop up by using fiscal and monetary policy to boost aggregate *demand*, rather than waiting for wage and price reductions to increase the real money supply and lower interest rates.

In contrast, the natural rate of unemployment tells us the part of unemployment that will not be eliminated merely by restoring aggregate demand to its full-employment level.

The natural rate is the 'full-employment' level of unemployment. To reduce the natural rate, *supply-side* policies operating on labour market incentives will be needed.

This is the framework we employ for the rest of the chapter. We begin by investigating the high unemployment over the last decade, in order to understand its causes more fully. Then we discuss the prospects for unemployment during the 1990s and the policy options open to the government.

27-3 Why is Unemployment so High?

By 1986 the UK unemployment rate was more than ten times as high as it was in 1965. The task for empirical economists is to try to say how much of this increase was caused by an increase in the natural rate of unemployment and how much was caused by deficient demand and sluggish wage adjustment. In Table 27-4 we give some estimates of the forces at work, based on work by Professor Steve Nickell of Oxford and Professor Richard Layard of the London School of Economics. Their estimates were derived from data on male unemployment, which is more comprehensively and reliably documented than the unemployment of women.

The top part of Table 27-4 shows the contribution of various forces to changes in the average rate of male unemployment between

Table 27-4 The causes of male unemployment in the UK
(Percentage points of unemployment)

CHANGES IN	EFFECT ON UNEMPLOYMENT RATE		
	1956–66 to 1967–74	1967–74 to 1975–79	1975–79 to 1980–83
Employers' labour taxes	0.25	0.38	0.44
Unemployment benefit	0.54	−0.09	−0.10
Trade union power	1.18	1.17	0.80
Real import prices	−0.58	1.47	−0.93
Mismatch of skills	0.16	0.20	0.49
Incomes policy	—	−0.36	0.49
Demand factors	0.12	0.54	6.56

	1956–66	1967–74	1975–79	1980–83
Estimated 'natural' rate of unemployment	2.0	4.2	7.6	9.1
Actual rate of unemployment	2.0	3.8	6.8	13.8

Source: P. R. G. Layard and S. J. Nickell, 'Unemployment in Britain', *Economica*, 1986.

four periods: 1956–66, 1967–74, 1975–79, and 1980–83. Figure 27-3 is useful to interpret some of these effects. A rise in taxes on labour drives a wedge between the gross wage paid by the firm and the net wage received by the worker. It is as if the firm is at point A in Figure 27-3, but with unemployment only N_2, the net wage is the point on the AJ schedule vertically below A. The gap is the tax rate. We discuss this more fully in the next section. Table 27-4 says higher tax rates on labour made some contribution to a rising natural rate of unemployment.

When unemployment benefit rises relative to wages from working, we say the *replacement ratio* has risen. This should shift the AJ schedule to the left in Figure 27-3: workers get more choosy in looking for jobs. Table 27-4 says that in practice this is *not* an important explanation for higher UK unemployment, and the reason is simple: unemployment benefit has *not* risen significantly relative to wages from working!

Table 27-4 says that increases in trade union power have been a major source of higher UK unemployment. Over the whole period, they account for 3.15 of the 11.8 percentage points by which unemployment increased.

In contrast, changes in real import prices, skill mismatch, or incomes policy have not been important causes of the long-term growth in UK male unemployment.

The last line of the top part of the table shows that deviations of aggregate demand from the full-employment level were not important before the end of the 1970s. This is hardly surprising, since until that date governments were committed to demand management policies whose specific purpose was to stabilize aggregate demand. However, Table 27-4 makes very clear the magnitude of the Keynesian recession in the early 1980s. It accounts for nearly 7 percentage points of the rise in UK unemployment in the late 1970s.

The bottom part of Table 27-4 makes the same points in a different way. Until the end of the 1970s, there was little discrepancy between actual unemployment and the natural rate of unemployment. The slow but remorseless increase in UK unemployment up to that date was almost entirely explained by forces that had increased the natural rate. However, in the first half of the 1980s the story was very different. Although the natural rate continued to increase, a substantial bout of

Keynesian recession or deficient demand was overlaid. That is why unemployment rose so sharply.

Conversely, UK unemployment fell rapidly in the late 1980s partly because the natural rate of unemployment fell, for reasons we discuss shortly, and partly because of a strong expansion of aggregate demand. The latter was caused not merely by the fiscal stimulus of tax cuts but also because the financial revolution made available consumer credit to an extent never previously encountered.

27-4 Supply-side Economics

Keynesians believe that the economy can deviate from full employment for quite a long time, certainly for a period of several years. Monetarists believe that the classical full-employment model is relevant much more quickly. But everyone agrees that in the long run the performance of the economy can be changed only by affecting the level of full employment and the corresponding level of potential output.

> *Supply-side economics* is the use of microeconomic incentives to alter the level of full employment, the level of potential output, and the natural rate of unemployment.

Although in this section we are interested chiefly in how to change the natural rate of unemployment, it is convenient to discuss some of the wider implications of supply-side economics at the same time. We return to the determination of potential output in Chapter 30.

Income Tax Cuts

One of the key themes of supply-side economists is the benefits that stem from reducing the marginal rate of income tax.

> The *marginal rate of income tax* is the fraction of each extra pound of income that the government takes in income tax.

We discussed tax rates and work incentives in detail in Chapter 11. We pointed out that a cut in marginal tax rates, and a consequent increase in the take-home pay derived from the last hour's work, tend to make people substitute work for leisure. But against this *substitution effect* must be set an *income effect*. To the extent that people now pay less in taxes, they will have to do less work to obtain any given target living standard. Thus, theoretical economics cannot prove that income tax cuts increase the desired labour supply, and in fact most empirical studies confirm that, at best, tax cuts lead to only a small increase in the supply of labour. We gave some details in Chapter 11 and give some more in Box 27-1.

Figure 27-4 may be used to analyse the effect of a cut in marginal tax rates. The labour demand schedule *LD* shows that firms demand more workers at a lower real wage. We draw a steep schedule *LF* showing that higher after-tax real wage rates, at best, lead to only a small increase in the number of people

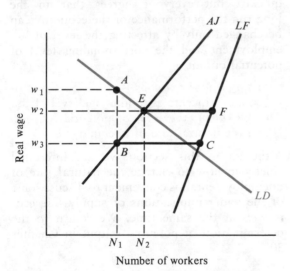

Figure 27-4   A CUT IN MARGINAL INCOME TAX RATES. An income tax makes the net-of-tax wage received by households lower than the gross wage paid by firms. When the vertical distance *AB* measures the amount each worker pays in income tax, equilibrium employment is N_1, the quantity that households wish to supply at the after-tax wage w_3 and that firms demand at the gross wage w_1. At the after-tax wage w_3 the natural rate of unemployment is the horizontal distance *BC*. If income tax were abolished, equilibrium would be at *E*. Employment would rise from N_1 to N_2 and the natural rate of unemployment would fall from *BC* to *EF*. Relative to the fixed level of unemployment benefit, the rise in take-home pay from w_3 to w_2 reduces the level of voluntary unemployment.

wishing to be in the labour force. The schedule *AJ* shows how many people wish to accept job offers at each real wage. It is drawn for a given (real) level of unemployment benefit. Hence the horizontal distance between the *AJ* and *LF* schedules – the number of people in the workforce refusing to work at each real wage, or the amount of voluntary unemployment – decreases as the real wage rises relative to the given level of unemployment benefit. Thus the figure incorporates the fact that a reduction in the replacement ratio, the ratio of unemployment benefit to wage rates, reduces voluntary unemployment.

Suppose initially that there is a marginal income tax rate equal to the vertical distance *AB*. The equilibrium level of employment will then be N_1. Why? Because income tax drives a wedge between the gross-of-tax wages paid by firms and the net-of-tax wages received by workers. At the employment level N_1 firms are happy to hire this quantity of labour at the gross wage w_1. Subtracting the income tax rate *AB*, N_1 workers want to take job offers at the after-tax wage w_3. Thus N_1 is the equilibrium level of employment. The horizontal distance *BC* shows the natural rate of unemployment, the number of workers in the labour force not wishing to work at the going rate of take-home pay.

To show the effect of a cut in marginal tax rates, suppose that income taxes were abolished. The gross wage and the take-home pay now coincide, and the new labour market equilibrium is at *E*. Note that two things have happened. First the equilibrium level of employment has risen. Second, although more people wish to be in the labour force because take-home pay has increased from w_3 to w_2, the natural rate of unemployment has fallen from the distance *BC* to the smaller distance *EF*. A rise in take-home pay relative to unemployment benefit reduces the level of voluntary unemployment.

Similar effects would be obtained if, instead of cutting income tax, the level of unemployment benefit were cut. For a given labour force schedule *LF*, fewer people would now wish to be unemployed at any real wage. Hence the schedule *AJ*, showing acceptances of job offers, would shift to the right. Again, the effect would be both to increase the equilibrium level of employment (and hence of potential output)

BOX 27-1

DOES THE TAX CARROT WORK?

THE EVIDENCE FROM THE PAST

A lower *marginal* tax rate makes people *substitute* work for leisure. But tax cuts also make workers better off. This *income effect* makes them want to consume more leisure, and hence work less. The combined effect on hours of work is small for those already in work. Of more importance is the decision about whether to work at all. In Chapter 11 we showed that higher take-home pay, for example because of tax cuts, *will* encourage more people to join the labour force by reducing the significance of the fixed costs of working (commuting, babysitters, giving up social security).

The UK evidence, surveyed in C. V. Brown, *Taxation and the Incentive to Work*, Oxford University Press, 1980, shows that tax cuts have a negligible effect on the labour supply decision of men and single women. But for married women, higher take-home pay does encourage labour force participation, if only a little.

THE THATCHER PROGRAMME

During the 1980s the Thatcher government embarked on a major programme of tax cuts and tax reforms. The real value of personal allowances – how much you can earn before paying income tax – was increased by 25 per cent. The basic rate of income tax fell from 33 to 25 per cent and for top income-earners from 83 to 40 per cent. Many politicians anticipated a considerable increase in the labour supply, yet most economists were pessimistic because of the evidence from the past.

THE NEW EVIDENCE

The effect of the Thatcher programme is assessed by C. V. Brown, 'The 1988 Tax Cuts, Work Incentives and Revenue', *Fiscal Studies*, 1988. Brown finds that the substantial increase in tax allowances led to less than 0.5 per cent extra hours of labour supply. The cut in the basic rate of income tax had no detectable effect at all. The massive cut in the marginal tax rate of top earners had a small effect in stimulating extra hours of work by the rich. The evidence from the past stood up well to this major change of tax policy.

---

and to reduce the natural rate of unemployment by reducing the replacement ratio.

What about the effect of changes in the national insurance contributions paid both by firms and by workers? These are mandatory contributions to state schemes which provide unemployment and health insurance. They act like an income tax in driving a wedge AB between the total cost to a firm of hiring another worker and the net take-home pay of a worker. Figure 27-4 shows that a reduction in these contributions will increase the equilibrium level of employment, increase the equilibrium level of take-home pay, reduce the replacement ratio, and reduce the natural rate of unemployment.

Other Policies Aimed at Labour Supply

In Figure 27-3 we showed that, by restricting labour supply, unions could force firms up their labour demand schedule. In consequence, the equilibrium real wage would be higher but the equilibrium level of employment lower. Since a higher real wage reduces employment but (slightly) increases the number of people wishing to be in the labour force, we said that in raising real wages unions had increased the natural rate of unemployment. Collectively, labour had opted for higher wages and more unemployment.

Conversely, the natural rate of unemployment will be reduced if the power of organized labour is weakened. Unions will then be less successful in restricting labour supply and forcing up wages. Hence any government intervention in the labour market to weaken the monopoly power of trade unions should be classified as a supply-side policy aimed at reducing the natural rate of unemployment and increasing equilibrium employment and potential output. Such policies would include changes in the law governing trade union activities, or *incomes policies* – direct regulation of wages – if the aim of the latter is to reduce *real* wages. This need not be the sole aim of incomes policies, as we explain in the next chapter.

Earlier, we pointed out that frictional and structural unemployment are important components of the natural rate of unemployment. Policies aimed at reducing frictional and structural unemployment should also be included in supply-side economics. Their objective is to shift the *AJ* schedule to the right relative to any given position of the labour force schedule *LF*.

Among such policies we include grants that allow redundant workers to retrain in relevant skills, various government measures introduced to help school-leavers develop skills and job experience for the first time, and special measures to encourage the long-term unemployed back into the labour force. By making the labour force more suited to employers' needs, such policies aim to allow firms to make wage offers that unemployed workers will find acceptable. Hence such measures reduce voluntary unemployment.

Policies Aimed at the Demand for Labour

Thus far, we have emphasized policies aimed at the supply of workers for employment. We now turn to the demand for workers by firms. In the previous chapter we saw that an adverse supply shock could reduce the demand for labour, shifting the *LD* schedule downwards.

It seems plausible that the two dramatic rises in real oil prices in the 1970s had this effect. Overnight, many energy-intensive factories were made economically obsolete by the rise in oil prices. They could no longer compete with more modern energy-saving plant. It was as if many existing firms had suffered a reduction in their useful capital stock. Since labour now had to work with a smaller quantity of relevant capital equipment, the marginal product of labour was reduced at each employment level. This can be represented in Figure 27-4 by a downward shift in the labour demand schedule *LD*.

Try constructing your own diagram to show the effect of this. (Forget about income taxes and start from the point *E* in Figure 27-4.) If you draw the diagram correctly you will discover two things. First, the downward shift in the *LD* schedule reduces equilibrium employment. Second, because equilibrium real wages fall, the replacement ratio must rise and

the natural rate of unemployment must increase. Some redundant steelworkers decide to go on the dole rather than work for lower wages.

Supply-side economics aims to reverse this effect. If firms can be encouraged to install modern capital equipment, the labour demand schedule will shift upwards. Hence the equilibrium wage rate will rise and the natural rate of unemployment will fall. What kind of policies could induce this favourable outcome?

We saw that firms' investment demand depends on three things: future output and profit prospects, the cost of new capital goods, and the rate of interest. The government can affect the price of new capital goods by grants (investment subsidies) or tax breaks. For example, firms can be allowed to set the cost of buying new capital goods against their pre-tax profits, thus reducing their liability to corporation tax on profits.

Second, the government can try to get interest rates down. Surely interest rates come under the heading of demand management rather than supply-side policies?

Not in the long run. If the economy is at full employment, the purpose of lower interest rates is not to increase aggregate demand. Rather, it is to alter the *composition* of full-employment aggregate demand, allowing the share of investment to increase. Of course this means that some other components of aggregate demand must fall; otherwise excess demand for goods will simply bid up prices, reduce the real money supply, and bid up interest rates again. An important element in the Thatcher government's supply-side strategy has been to try to reduce government spending, thus leaving more room for private investment as a component of full-employment aggregate demand.

In this section we have discussed how supply-side policies could be used to reduce the natural rate of unemployment. Supply-side policies may offer some hope in the long run, but many of them, for example measures to increase the capital stock, cannot be expected to have a dramatic effect in the short run. Slashing the level of unemployment benefit is one supply-side policy that would have an immediate effect. However, it would make life pretty miserable for those who still could not find a job. Whether the government is prepared to entertain this policy option remains to be seen.

27-5 Eliminating Keynesian Unemployment

We have argued that about one-third of UK unemployment in the early 1980s was Keynesian unemployment arising from deficient demand. In the previous chapter we showed that, eventually, wage and price adjustment will eliminate Keynesian unemployment by boosting the real money supply and reducing interest rates. But this process can take half a decade or more.

Suppose the government boosts aggregate demand: what effect will this have on employment and unemployment if the economy begins with spare capacity and Keynesian unemployment? The answer depends in part on which components of aggregate demand are increased. Government expenditure on extra police officers will add more to employment than an equivalent increase in the value of spending on electricity, whose production is very capital-intensive.

It is also extremely important to understand the cyclical relationship between demand and output, employment, and unemployment. On average, boosting aggregate demand by 1 per cent will not increase employment by 1 per cent or reduce unemployment by 1 percentage point. Table 27-5 helps us to see why. It shows a period of rapid demand growth, 1972 quarter I to 1974 quarter IV, and a period of rapid demand contraction, 1979 (II) to 1981 (II). In practice, booms lead initially to a sharp increase in shift lengths and hours worked; slumps lead to the abolition of overtime, the introduction of short time, and a marked decline in hours worked.

Hence the table confirms that changes in demand and output lead to smaller changes in the level of employment. For example, when

output grew 17 per cent between 1972 (I) and 1974 (IV), employment increased by only 3.1 per cent. Moreover, changes in employment do not lead to corresponding changes in unemployment. The last two rows of the table show that rapid expansion or contraction of employment leads to significantly smaller changes in the level of unemployment.

One important reason for this result is the 'discouraged worker effect', which we discussed earlier in the chapter. When unemployment is high and rising, some people who would really like to work get so pessimistic that they give up looking for a job. Since they are no longer registered as looking for work, they are not recorded in the labour force or considered to be among the unemployed. Conversely, in a boom many people who had previously given up looking for work come back into the labour force since there is now a good chance of finding a suitable job. Hence in booms and slumps recorded employment data usually change by more than recorded unemployment data.

The period of rapid output growth during 1986(II)–88(II) deserves special mention. As in the other examples, the change in output greatly exceeded the change in employment. But the change in unemployment was even larger. In part this reflects the success of government programmes such as the Youth Training Scheme, which reduces unemployment without adding to employment, and in part it reflects a crackdown on those registering for unemployment benefit. Those not genuinely looking for work were forced off the register.

27-6 The Private and Social Cost of Unemployment

In this section we discuss the private and social

Table 27-5 Output, employment, and unemployment

	1972(I)–74(IV)	1979(II)–81(II)	1986(II)–88(II)
Change in real GDP (percentage)[*]	+17%	−7.8%	+9.1
Change in employment (percentage)	+3.1%	−6.3%	+2.5
Change in employment (thousands)	+240	−1688	+544
Change in unemployment (thousands)	−187	+1336	−913

[*] For 1979(II)–81(II) data refer to GDP excluding North Sea oil.
Source: CSO, *Economic Trends.*

BOX 27-2

HYSTERESIS AND HIGH UNEMPLOYMENT IN EUROPE

Supply and demand curves are supposed to be independent of one another. The labour supply curve or job acceptances schedule *JA* shows the number of people willing to work at each real wage whatever the position of the labour demand curve *LD*, and vice versa. But this assumption may be wrong.

In the diagram, the initial equilibrium is at *E*. Something then makes the labour demand curve shift left to *LD'*. Suppose this in turn *causes* a permanent reduction in labour supply: *JA* shifts to *JA'*. When labour demand reverts to its original level *LD*, the new equilibrium is at *F*, not *E*. The short-run history of the economy has affected its long-run equilibrium.

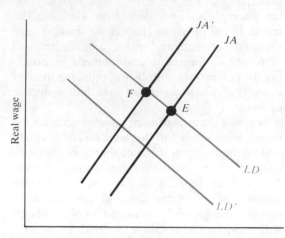

> An economy experiences *hysteresis* when its long-run equilibrium depends on the path it has followed in the short run.

In the late 1980s, economists became excited about hysteresis as a possible explanation of high and persistent unemployment in Europe. We now examine four channels through which it might work.

The insider–outsider distinction Outsiders are the unemployed without jobs. Only insiders with jobs participate in wage bargaining. At the original equilibrium *E*, there are lots of insiders in work and they ensure that real wages are low enough to preserve their own jobs. When a recession occurs, *LD* shifts to *LD'*. Some insiders get fired and become outsiders. Eventually, as we explained in Chapter 26, market forces will restore labour demand to *LD* again. But now there are fewer insiders than originally. They exploit their scarcity by pressing for higher wages for themselves, rather than encouraging their firms to rehire. The economy gets trapped in the high-wage, low-employment equilibrium at *F* instead of the low-wage, high-employment equilibrium at *E*. Thereafter, only long-run supply-side measures aimed at breaking down insider power (e.g. less job protection) can gradually break the economy out of this low-employment equilibrium. This explanation has been emphasized by Professors Dennis Snower and Assar Lindbeck in Europe, and Professors Olivier Blanchard and Larry Summers in the United States.

Discouraged workers Again, the economy begins at *E*. It has a skilled and energetic labour force. A temporary recession leads to unemployment. If the recession is protracted, we see the emergence of the long-term unemployed and a culture in which people stop looking for jobs. Again, when demand picks up, labour supply has been permanently reduced and equilibrium reverts to *F*, not *E*. Only long-term supply-side measures to restore the work culture will succeed. This effect has been emphasized by Professor Richard Layard.

Search and mismatch When unemployment is low at *E*, firms are busily trying to find scarce workers and potential workers are searching hard for a good job. A recession makes firms advertise fewer vacancies, and workers realize it is a waste of time searching for jobs. When demand picks up again, both firms and workers have became accustomed to low levels of search; so new jobs don't get created. This explanation has been emphasized by Professor Chris Pissarides.

The capital stock At *E* the economy has a lot of capital, so labour productivity is high and firms want lots of workers. During a temporary recession, firms save money by abandoning investment. When the demand for goods picks up again, firms have permanently lower capital. Hence the demand for labour, which depends on the marginal product of labour, never rises to its original level. Again, the economy returns to an equilibrium with lower employment than at *E*. This channel has been studied by Professor Charlie Bean.

Policy implications of hysteresis All these explanations imply that a temporary fall in demand leads to a permanently lower level of employment and output, and a rise in the natural rate of unemployment. There are two policy implications. First, once the problem has emerged, it is dangerous to try to break out of it simply by expanding aggregate demand. Before long-run supply can respond, you are likely to get a major bout of inflation. Supply-side policies are needed to restore aggregate supply, and this will take a long time.

Second, precisely because the problem is so hard to cure once it occurs, it is even more important not to let demand fall in the first place. The payoff to demand management is higher than in an economy with a *unique* long-run equilibrium, where all that is at stake is how quickly the economy gets back to its original point.

---

cost of unemployment. We begin with the private cost.

The Private Cost of Unemployment

It is important to distinguish between voluntary and involuntary unemployment. When individuals are voluntarily unemployed, they reveal that they do better by being unemployed than by accepting the job offers that they face at the going wage rate. Under these circumstances the private cost of unemployment (the wage forgone by not working) is less than the private benefits for being unemployed. What are these benefits?

First, the individual is entitled to transfer payments from the government. These are of two kinds. Workers who have previously contributed to the national insurance scheme are entitled to unemployment benefit for the first 12 months after they become unemployed. Thereafter they become entitled to supplementary benefit, the ultimate backstop in the British welfare state.

Whereas most workers are entitled to unemployment benefit as of right, supplementary benefit is *means-tested*. Individuals have to make a full disclosure of their financial position before the benefit level is assessed, a procedure many people find invidious. For this reason, some people do not apply for supplementary benefit even though they would be entitled to it. Moreover, although the popular myth of 'scroungers' living well off the welfare state is not completely without foundation, in practice many people on supplementary benefit are among the poorest people in the country.

Are there any other benefits to be had from being unemployed? First, there is the value of leisure. By refusing a job, some people are revealing that the extra leisure is worth more to them than the extra disposable income if they took a job. Second, some people expect to get a better job after a temporary spell of unemployment. These future benefits must be set against the current cost of lower disposable income.

When people are involuntarily unemployed, the picture changes. Involuntary unemployment means that people would like to work at the going wage but cannot find a job because there is excess labour supply at the existing wage rate. These people are worse off as a result of being unemployed.

The distinction between voluntary and involuntary unemployment is important because it may affect our value judgement about how much attention should be paid to the unemployment problem. When unemployment is involuntary, more people are suffering and the case for helping them is stronger.

The Social Cost of Unemployment

Again we distinguish between voluntary and involuntary unemployment. When unemployment is voluntary, individuals reveal that they prefer to be unemployed. Does this mean that unemployment is also good for society as a whole?

There is one very obvious discrepancy between individual benefit and social benefit. For an individual, unemployment and supplementary benefit are part of the benefits of being unemployed. But these transfer payments give no corresponding benefit to society as a whole. They may ease the collective conscience about poverty and income inequality, but they are not payments in exchange for the supply of any goods or services that other members of society may consume. To this extent, the value judgement that we ought to support the unemployed inevitably entails a cost in allocative inefficiency. It encourages too many people to be voluntarily unemployed.

However, this does not mean that society should go to the opposite extreme and try to eliminate voluntary unemployment completely. First, society is perfectly entitled to adopt the value judgement that it will maintain a reasonable living standard for the unemployed, whatever the cost in resource misallocation. Second, even in terms of allocative efficiency, the efficient level of voluntary unemployment is certainly above zero.

In a changing economy, it is important to match up the right people to the right jobs. Getting this match right allows society as a whole to produce more output. Freezing the existing pattern of employment in a changing economy will eventually lead to a mismatch of people and jobs. The flow through the pool of unemployment is one of the mechanisms through which society reallocates people to more suitable jobs and increases total output in the long run. If unemployment benefits make this transition smoother, society as a whole may gain.

Our earlier discussion of the duration of unemployment showed that, during the postwar years of low unemployment, a high percentage of the unemployed were quickly re-employed. In the 1980s many more of the unemployed were unemployed in the long term. It can no longer be maintained that most of our unemployment is the inevitable consequence of reallocation of the workforce to more appropriate jobs.

Involuntary or Keynesian unemployment has an even higher social cost. Since the economy is producing below capacity, it is literally throwing away output that could have been made by putting these people to work. Moreover, since Keynesian unemployment is involuntary, there may be a presumption that it entails more human and psychological suffering than voluntary unemployment. Although this is hard to quantify, it should also be counted as part of the social cost of unemployment.

Since we have focused largely on unemployment in the UK, we conclude the chapter with a brief review of what has been happening to unemployment in other countries.

27-7 International Comparisons

Table 27-6 shows recent unemployment rates in selected countries. Apart from Japan and Sweden, unemployment rates in other countries were high and rising in the 1980s. Two of the explanations of high UK unemployment – the adverse supply shock caused by the doubling of real oil prices in 1979–80 and the determination to adopt restrictive monetary and fiscal policies to get inflation under control – apply in most of the countries shown in Table 27-6.

Obviously, there are different forces at work in different countries. For example, in Japan workers are rarely fired and seldom quit, there is an implicit agreement between firms and workers that the workers have lifetime jobs, provided that they are male. (Women who lose jobs tend not to become unemployed but rather to move out of the labour force.) In Sweden it is extremely expensive to sack a worker; firms have to pay large redundancy payments and go to some lengths to avoid having to fire workers. And the government has deliberately created public sector jobs to hold down unemployment.

Table 27-6 Unemployment rates (%)

	1969–73	1974–79	1980–85	1986–88
USA	4.8	6.9	6.8	6.1
Japan	1.2	2.2	2.4	2.7
Sweden	2.2	1.9	2.9	3.1
Australia	2.0	5.0	7.6	7.7
UK	3.5	5.0	10.5	9.9
Italy	5.8	6.6	8.6	11.0
France	2.6	5.2	8.3	10.3
Germany	0.9	3.2	6.0	6.3
EC average	2.9	4.8	9.3	10.1

Source: OECD Economic Outlook.

Summary

1   People are either employed, unemployed, or out of the labour force. The level of unemployment rises when inflows to the pool of the unemployed exceed outflows. Inflows and outflows are large relative to the level of unemployment.

2   As the level of unemployment has risen, the

average duration of unemployment has increased. More than half the unemployed in the UK in the 1980s had been unemployed for more than six months.

3 Women face lower unemployment rates than men. The unemployment rates for old workers, and especially for young workers, are well above the national average.

4 Unemployment can be classified as frictional, structural, classical, and demand-deficient. In modern terminology, the first three types are voluntary unemployment and the last is involuntary, or Keynesian, unemployment. The natural rate of unemployment is the equilibrium level of voluntary unemployment.

5 Roughly one-third of UK unemployment in the early 1980s was explained by a Keynesian recession. The rest, and almost all the increase prior to 1980, is explained by a rise in the natural rate of unemployment. Since 1986 UK unemployment has fallen sharply.

6 Supply-side economics aims to increase equilibrium employment and potential output, and to reduce the natural rate of unemployment, by operating on incentives at a micro-economic level. Supply-side policies include income tax cuts, reductions in unemployment benefit, retraining and relocation grants, investment subsidies, and policies such as lower interest rates coupled with lower government spending, aimed at 'crowding in' investment's share of full-employment aggregate demand.

7 A 1 per cent increase in output is likely to lead to a much smaller reduction in Keynesian unemployment. Some of the extra output will be met by longer hours. And as unemployment falls some people, effectively in the labour force but not registered, will start looking for work again.

8 Hysteresis means that short-run changes can move the economy to a different long-run equilibrium. It may explain why the European recession of the early 1980s seems to have raised the natural rate of unemployment substantially.

9 Although people who are voluntarily unemployed reveal that the private benefits from unemployment exceed the private cost in wages forgone, society derives no direct return from the payment of unemployment benefit which individuals regard as a private benefit from being unemployed. Nevertheless, society would not benefit by driving the natural rate of unemployment to zero. Some social gains in higher productivity are derived from the improved matching of people and jobs that temporary spells of unemployment allow.

10 Keynesian unemployment is involuntary and therefore a disadvantage to private individuals who would prefer to be employed. Socially it represents wasted output. Society may also care about the human misery inflicted by involuntary unemployment.

11 In most European countries unemployment was high and rising in the 1980s. However, Japan and Sweden have managed to retain very low rates of unemployment.

Key Terms

Labour force
Registered unemployed
Long-term unemployed
Discouraged workers
Frictional and structural unemployment
Classical and Keynesian unemployment
Voluntary and involuntary unemployment
Natural rate of unemployment
Replacement ratio
Unemployment and supplementary benefit
Supply-side economics
Income and substitution effects
Incomes policy
Private and social cost of unemployment
Hysteresis

Problems

1 What is the discouraged-worker effect? Suggest two reasons why it occurs.

2 'The average duration of an individual's unemployment rises in a slump. This suggests that the problem is a lower outflow from the pool of unemployment, not a higher inflow.' Do you agree?

3 Why is teenage unemployment so high?

4 'The microchip will inevitably cause a permanent increase in the level of unemployment.' Carefully examine this assertion.

5 How would the high unemployment in the 1980s be explained by (a) a Keynesian, (b) a classical or monetary economist?

6 Shouldn't we pay the unemployed an amount equal to the after-tax wage they earned in their last job, thereby eliminating the disadvantage they suffer on becoming unemployed?

7 Common Fallacies Show why each of the following statements is incorrect. (*a*) Unemployment is always a bad thing. (*b*) So long as there is unemployment, there should be pressure on wages to fall. (*c*) Unemployment arises only because greedy workers are pricing themselves out of a job.

28

Inflation

In the 1980s President Reagan, Mrs Thatcher, Chancellor Kohl, and many other national leaders named inflation as public enemy number one. Getting inflation down became their top priority.

Inflation is a rise in the average price of goods over time. *Pure inflation* is the special case in which all prices of goods and factors of production are rising at the same percentage rate.

Persistent inflation over many years is in fact quite a recent phenomenon. Before 1950, prices tended to rise in some years but fall in other years. In the UK the *price level* – the average price of goods as a whole – was no higher in 1950 than it had been in 1920. Figure 28-1 shows that the UK price level fell quite sharply during some of the interwar years when inflation was negative. Yet since 1945 there has not been a single year in which the price level fell. Since 1950 the price level has increased by a factor of ten, more than its increase over the previous three centuries. This broad picture applies not only in the UK but also in most of the advanced economies.

In this chapter we shall try to explain why inflation is thought to be so bad as to justify its title of public enemy number one. Inflation does have bad effects, but we shall see that some of the popular criticisms of inflation are based on spurious reasoning. It requires some care to distinguish between the good and bad arguments about why inflation is costly for the economy as a whole.

To understand the costs of inflation we need to understand the effects of inflation. But these effects may depend on what is causing the inflation in the first place. Hence the chapter is divided into three parts. First we examine the causes of inflation. Monetarists such as Milton Friedman say that inflation is caused

by too much money chasing too few goods. And they attribute this excess demand for goods to an increase in the nominal money supply. Friedman has asserted that 'inflation is always and everywhere a monetary phenomenon'.[1] Thus we begin by examining the link between the money supply and the price level. And we take this argument a stage further by asking whether it is large budget deficits that lead the government to print large quantities of money in order to finance these deficits.

We then turn to the consequences of inflation. How does it affect the markets for goods and labour? Is high inflation bad for output and employment? And does it matter whether the inflation was previously expected or whether it takes people by surprise?

Finally, we return to the theme of this chapter. To what extent is inflation a bad thing? We distinguish the costs that inflation might impose on individuals and the costs it might impose on society as a whole. We conclude by considering what the government can do about inflation.

28-1 Money and Inflation

In this section we develop the basic link between the nominal money supply and the price level. In turn, this provides a link between the rate of growth of the nominal money supply and inflation, or the rate of growth of the price level.

The analysis focuses on the market for money which we discussed in Chapters 24 and 25.

The *real money supply* M/P is the nominal money supply M divided by the price level P.

People demand money because of its purchasing power in terms of goods. In Chapter 24 we

[1] Milton Friedman, *Dollars and Deficits*, Prentice-Hall, 1968.

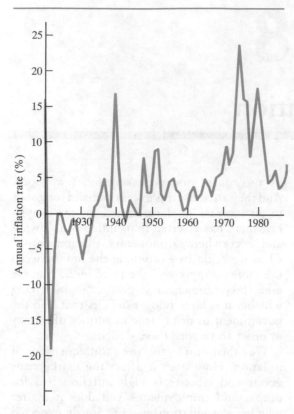

Figure 28-1 THE ANNUAL UK INFLATION RATE 1920–88. (*Source*: B. R. Mitchell, *European Historical Statistics 1750–1970*, Macmillan, 1975, and CSO, *Economic Trends*.)

explained that the demand for money will be a demand for *real* money balances. Because Keynes happened to use the term *liquidity preference* to mean the demand for money, economists often use the symbol L to denote the demand for real money balances. We use the symbol $L(Y, r)$ to denote the quantity of real balances demanded when real income is Y and the interest rate is r. An increase in real income increases the quantity of real balances demanded since people are undertaking more transactions. By increasing the opportunity cost of holding money rather than bonds or other interest-bearing assets, an increase in the interest rate r will reduce the quantity of real balances demanded.

If the money market is in equilibrium, the supply of real balances M/P must equal the quantity of real balances demanded. Equation (1) summarizes this equilibrium condition.

$$M/P = L(Y, r) \qquad (1)$$

Throughout this chapter we shall assume that interest rates are very flexible. Whenever there is excess demand for money, interest rates are bid up until the quantity of real money demanded is sufficiently reduced that it is brought into line with the supply of real balances. Conversely, an excess supply of money reduces interest rates and immediately increases the quantity of real balances demanded. Thus we assume that flexible interest rates keep the money market continuously in equilibrium. Equation (1) holds at all points in time.

Suppose, as we have previously assumed, that nominal wages and prices are slow to adjust in the short run. An increase in the nominal money supply M leads initially to an increase in the real money supply M/P since prices P have not yet had time to adjust fully. There is now an excess supply of real money balances which bids interest rates down until the demand for real balances has increased enough to restore money market equilibrium. Lower interest rates boost aggregate demand for goods. Gradually this excess demand for goods bids up goods prices, and in the labour market the increased demand for employment starts to bid up money wages. In Chapter 26 we saw that, when wages and prices have fully adjusted, a once-and-for-all increase in the nominal money supply leads to an equivalent once-and-for-all increase in wages and prices. Output, employment, interest rates, and the real money supply are restored to their original levels.

Equation (1) allows us to state this argument succinctly. When adjustment is complete and long-run equilibrium has been restored, real income, interest rates, and hence the demand for real balances are all unchanged. Hence the price level must have changed in proportion to the original increase in the nominal money supply. Only then will the real money supply be unchanged and the money market have returned to its long-run equilibrium position. This result is the essence of the quantity theory of money.

The *quantity theory of money* says that changes in the nominal money supply lead to equivalent changes in the price level (and money wages) but do not have effects on output and employment.

The theory is at least 500 years old and is

sometimes claimed to date from Confucius. Today the quantity theory is defended by monetarists, who argue that *most* changes in prices are due to changes in the nominal money supply.

However, the theory must be interpreted with some care. Effectively, the quantity theory says that, since the demand for real balances must always be constant, the supply of real balances must also be constant. Hence changes in nominal money must be matched by equivalent changes in prices to keep the real money supply constant. There are two issues we must now investigate. First, even if the demand for real balances does remain constant, is it changes in nominal money that cause changes in prices, or is it changes in prices that cause changes in nominal money? Second, it is in fact true that the demand for real money balances remains constant? We discuss each issue in turn.

Money, Prices, and Causation

Suppose the demand for real balances remains constant over time. We have just seen that an increase in the nominal money supply must eventually lead to an equivalent increase in the price level. We can say that a change in the money supply causes a change in prices. Now let us ask the question the other way round. Suppose workers manage to secure higher money wages from firms. In consequence firms have to put their prices up to cover their costs. What happens next?

Equation (1) says that one of two things can happen. If the government does *not* increase the nominal money supply in response to the supply shock that has increased costs and goods prices, the real money supply will be reduced. Interest rates will have to increase to maintain money market equilibrium. In the short run this will reduce the quantity of real balances demanded. But higher interest rates will reduce the aggregate demand for goods and create excess goods supply, putting downward pressure on goods prices and the quantity of employment demanded. Eventually, prices and wages will fall back to their original level. Full-employment equilibrium is then restored. Prices, wages, the real money supply, and interest rates are back to their original level. The attempt to

raise wages and prices will be defeated once full adjustment has taken place.

Alternatively, the government may react to the initial rise in wages and prices by *accommodating* this shock.

> Monetary policy *accommodates* a shock when a change in prices induces the government to provide a matching change in the nominal money supply precisely to avoid any change in the real money supply in the short run.

When a rise in prices is accommodated by an increase in the money supply, the real money stock remains constant and there is no change in equilibrium interest rates. The economy remains at full employment but with a higher level of the nominal money supply, prices, and nominal wages.

We can now understand Friedman's claim that inflation is a monetary phenomenon. Once wages and prices have had time to adjust, the economy will always be at full-employment output. If the demand for real balances is always the same at full employment, only two things allow a rise in the price level. First, a rise in the money supply will cause a rise in prices to restore the real money supply to its full-employment level, which is equal to the full-employment demand for real money balances. Second, if something else makes the price level increase, and the government accommodates this price increase by printing money, again money and prices will be higher. Thus, directly or indirectly the government is responsible for the higher price level by printing extra money. If the government refuses to print extra money, increases in the price level, however caused, will reduce the real money supply and set up deflationary pressures which will reduce the price level again.

The Demand for Real Money Balances

This exact relationship between money and prices depends crucially on the assumption that the demand for real balances remains constant. It is this that means that the supply of real money must also remain constant. But is this assumption likely to be true?

Table 28-1 shows the behaviour of nominal money (M1), prices, real money, and real income over a 30-year period. The simple

Table 28-1 Nominal money and prices, 1988
(1960 = 100)

	JAPAN	FRANCE	UK
Nominal money	2620	1265	1340
Prices	470	608	810
Real money	560	273	166
Real income	610	278	190

Source: IMF, *International Financial Statistics.*

quantity theory is not a good approximation to reality. Nominal money rose six times as much as prices in Japan but more nearly matched prices in the UK. The last line of the table shows that changes in real income were very different in the three countries. Equation (1) suggests that real income growth increases real money demand and requires a matching increase in the real money supply. Nominal money must grow more quickly than prices.

Two other forces help to explain the data of Table 28-1. First, banking innovations, such as provisions for automatic transfers between time deposits and chequing accounts, have made near-money almost as good as M1 for transactions purposes. With a wider definition of money than M1, we would have found a larger increase in real money in the UK over the period. The real value of M3 almost tripled between 1960 and 1989.

Second, we must still take account of the effect of interest rates on real money demand. Higher interest rates have tended to reduce real money demand. We investigate the role of interest rates in the next section. Already, we can reach one conclusion: even in the long run, changes in real income and interest rates significantly alter real money demand. Hence we cannot expect real money supply to remain constant in the long run. In many practical contexts, it is dangerous to assume that an increase in the nominal money supply will lead to an equivalent change in money wages and prices, even though one cannot dispute the theoretical proposition that, *if* real income and interest rates were unaltered, changes in nominal money would eventually lead to equivalent change in money wages and prices.

Inflation

So far we have talked about levels. Now we talk

about rates of change per annum. Equation (1) implies that the growth in real money demand must equal the growth in the real money supply, namely the excess of nominal money growth over the growth in prices. But inflation is the growth in prices. Thus,

$$\begin{aligned}\text{Inflation}\\ \text{rate}\end{aligned} = \begin{aligned}&\text{growth of nominal}\\ &\text{money supply}\\ &- \text{growth of real}\\ &\text{money demand}\end{aligned} \qquad (2)$$

The simple quantity theory says that, when the growth of real money demand is zero, the inflation rate equals the rate of nominal money growth. Table 28-1 showed how this prediction gets screwed up by the fact that real money demand does change. Can we think of circumstances in which changes in real money demand will be small relative to changes in nominal money and prices? Yes. Since real income and interest rates *usually* change only a few percentage points a year, real money demand usually changes only slowly.[2] When nominal money is growing rapidly it will essentially have to be matched by rapidly growing prices to make sure that the real money supply changes only slowly in line with changes in money demand.

Figure 28-2 shows some countries with high inflation and high nominal money growth. Inflation and money growth are very similar, as equation (2) predicts. The points in Figure 28-2 lie close to the line along which inflation and nominal money growth are equal.

The essential insight of the quantity theory of money is that real variables usually change slowly. Hence very large changes in one nominal variable (nominal money supply) must be accompanied by very large changes in other nominal variables (prices and money wages) in order to maintain real money supply (and real wages) at their equilibrium values. This is a useful first look at inflation, but we have simplified a little too much. We shall now put this right.

28-2 Inflation and Interest Rates

Table 28-2 shows interest and inflation rates for selected countries for 1989. Countries with high

---

[2] For an exception, see the hyperinflation example of the next section.

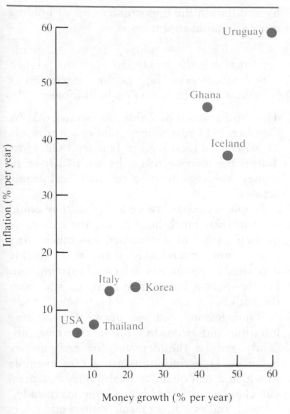

Figure 28-2   MONEY GROWTH AND
INFLATION 1970–88 (average annual growth rates).
(*Source*: IMF, *International Financial Studies*.)

Table 28-2 Inflation and interest rates, 1987
(Per cent per annum)

	INFLATION RATE	INTEREST RATE
Brazil	230	390
Mexico	130	95
Greece	16	20
Spain	5	8
UK	4	9
Switzerland	1	3
Germany	0	2
Japan	0	2

Source: IMF, *International Financial Statistics.*

inflation have high interest rates. In fact, the data suggest that a 1 per cent higher inflation rate is pretty much accompanied by a 1 per cent higher interest rate, a proposition first suggested by Irving Fisher.[3]

The *Fisher hypothesis* says that a 1 per cent increase in inflation will be accompanied by a 1 per cent increase in interest rates.

Suppose the inflation rate is 10 per cent per annum. With £100 you can buy ten books at £10 each today, but you will need £110 to buy the same number of books next year. If the actual or nominal interest rate is 12 per cent per annum, by postponing buying books you could lend £100 today and have £112 next year, spending £110 to buy the same ten books but having £2 left over to compensate you for

waiting a year to buy the books. We say that 2 per cent is the *real interest rate*, or increase in your purchasing power as a result of lending. In general,

Real interest rate = nominal interest rate

$$- \text{inflation rate} \qquad (3)$$

The Fisher hypothesis says that the *real* interest rate does not change much. Otherwise there would be large excess supply or demand for loans. Hence higher inflation must largely be offset by equivalently higher nominal interest rates to maintain the equilibrium real interest rate. Table 28-2 shows that, although not exactly correct, the hypothesis is not a bad approximation.

Hence an increase in the rate of money growth will lead not merely to an increase in the inflation rate but also to an increase in nominal interest rates. This will alter the demand for real money balances and hence will require money and prices to grow at *different* rates until the real money supply has adjusted to the change in real money demand. To show how this works, we consider a particularly spectacular example, the German hyperinflation.

Hyperinflation

Hyperinflations are periods when inflation rates are very large.

Chile had a hyperinflation during the last stages of the Allende government in the late 1970s, and Bolivian inflation reached 11 000 per cent in 1985. The most famous example is the German experience of 1922–23.

---

[3] Fisher was a professor at Yale. He wrote books about health as well as economics and believed in sleeping in the fresh air and eating wheatgerm.

Germany lost the First World War. To the problems of a ravaged economy with low output and low tax revenues were added the reparations payments imposed by victorious countries such as France and the UK. The German government had a big deficit, which it financed largely by printing money. Table 28-3 shows what happened. The sixteenfold increase in the nominal money supply in 1922 was tiny compared with the increase in 1923. The government had to buy faster printing presses. In the later stages of the hyperinflation they took in old notes, stamped on some more zeros, and reissued them as larger-denomination notes in the morning.

The second column in the table shows that prices increased by a factor of 75 in 1922 but by considerably more in 1923. By October 1923 it took 192 million reichmarks to buy a drink that had cost 1 reichmark in January 1922. People carried money around in wheelbarrows when they went shopping. According to the old joke, thieves used to steal the barrows but leave the almost worthless money behind.

The Flight from Money   When the inflation rate is π and the nominal interest rate r, the real interest rate is $(r - \pi)$ but the real return on non-interest-bearing money is simply $-\pi$, which shows how quickly the real value of money is being eroded by inflation. Hence the differential real return on holding interest-bearing assets rather than money is $(r - \pi) - (-\pi) = r$. Even though people care about real rates of return, it is the *nominal* interest rate that measures the opportunity cost of holding money.

We have seen that nominal interest rates rise with inflation. Hence during the German hyperinflation the opportunity cost of holding money became enormous.

The *flight from money* is the dramatic reduction in the demand for real money when high inflation and high nominal interest rates make it very expensive to hold money.

The third column of Table 28-3 shows that by October 1923 real money holdings were only 11 per cent of their level in January 1922. How did people manage to get by with such small money holdings relative to their real transactions?

People were paid twice a day so they could shop in their lunch hour before the real value of their cash had depreciated too much. Any money not immediately spent was quickly deposited in a bank where it could earn interest. People spent a lot of time going to and from the bank.

What lessons can we draw? First, *rising* inflation and *rising* interest rates can significantly reduce the demand for *real* money balances. Hyperinflations are a rare example in which a real quantity (real money balances) can change quickly and by a large magnitude.[4] Second, and as a direct result, money and prices can get quite out of line during the period when inflation and nominal interest rates are rising. Table 28-3 shows that prices rose by six times as much as nominal money between January 1922 and July 1923, thus reducing the real money supply by 82 per cent, in line with the fall in real money demand.

---

[4] Even if nominal interest rates keep up with inflation and the real interest rate on bonds remains unchanged, the real return on cash is simply the negative of the inflation rate. It is because changes in inflation affect this *real* return that large changes in inflation lead to large changes in *real* money demand.

Table 28-3 The German hyperinflation, 1922–23
(January 1922 = 1)

	CURRENCY	PRICES	REAL MONEY	INFLATION (% per month)
January 1922	1	1	1.00	5
January 1923	16	75	0.21	189
July 1923	354	2 021	0.18	386
September 1923	227 777	645 946	0.35	2 532
October 1923	20 201 256	191 891 890	0.11	29 720

Source: Data adapted from C. L. Holtfrerich, *Die Deutsche Inflation 1914–23*, Walter de Gruyter, 1980.

THE QUANTITY THEORY OF MONEY

Economists used to express the quantity theory of money as the equation

$$MV = PY$$

The velocity of circulation V is the ratio of nominal income PY (prices P times real income Y) to nominal money M. When prices adjust to maintain real income at its full employment level, assumed constant, then a change in nominal money supply M leads to an equivalent change in prices P, *provided velocity V stays constant*. What is velocity? It is the speed at which the outstanding stock of money is passed round the economy as people make transactions. If everyone holds money for a shorter period and passes it on more quickly, the economy can get by with a lower money stock relative to nominal income. But how do we assess whether velocity is likely to remain constant, as the simple quantity theory requires?

The quantity theory equation can be rearranged as

$$M/P = Y/V$$

The left-hand side is the real money supply. We can think of the right-hand side as real money demand. It rises if real income rises and falls if velocity rises.

But we have argued that real money demand is determined by real income and nominal interest rates, which measure the opportunity cost of holding money. Hence velocity just measures the effect of interest rates on the demand for real money balances. Higher nominal interest rates reduce real money demand. People *hold* less money relative to income. Velocity rises. Hence, while inflation and nominal interest rates are increasing, velocity is rising. But if inflation and nominal interest rates settle down at some particular level, velocity will become constant. For a given income level, changes in money will then be accompanied by equivalent changes in prices and the simple quantity theory once more applies.

This discussion assumes that prices (and wages) are fully flexible. In the short run, if prices are sluggish, changes in nominal money must change the real money supply. Changes in interest rates or real income will be required to change the quantity of real balances demanded and maintain money market equilibrium. When prices are slow to adjust, changes in nominal money will not be immediately matched by changes in prices, and the quantity theory of money will not hold in the short run.

Third, the table emphasizes the effect of *rising* inflation. Suppose inflation had risen to 1000 per cent per annum but then remained constant at this rate. Nominal interest rates would then settle down at about 1000 per cent per annum. Provided real income remained constant, real money demand would then become constant (at a low level). Therefore, nominal money and prices would each grow at 1000 per cent per annum to maintain the real money supply at the constant level of real money demand. Once again the simple quantity theory would be re-established. Box 28-1 summarizes our discussion to date.

28-3 Inflation, Money, and Deficits

We have argued that persistent inflation must be accompanied by continuing money growth. The example of the German hyperinflation suggests that printing money to finance a large deficit may be the source of inflation. Do large budget deficits necessarily lead to inflation by forcing the government to print large quantities of extra money to finance these deficits? If so, tight *fiscal* policy will be required to fight inflation by keeping the deficit small and the rate of money growth low.

In 1980 the Thatcher government introduced a Medium-Term Financial Strategy (MTFS) for the UK. The MTFS assumed that fast money growth causes high inflation and that high budget deficits lead to fast money growth. Hence the MTFS emphasized the need to reduce the budget deficit in order to reduce the rate of money growth and get inflation down. Since in the UK the government is responsible for funding not only its own deficit but also any losses incurred by the nationalized industries, the relevant measure of the deficit is the public sector borrowing requirement (PSBR), the combined deficit of the government and the nationalized industries. Table 28-4 shows the original targets when the MTFS was introduced in 1980.

Table 28-4 The medium-term financial strategy (Original targets)

	1980–81	1981–82	1982–83	1983–84
Target annual percentage growth of M3	7–11	6–10	5–9	4–8
Target PSBR as percentage of GDP	3.75	3.0	2.25	1.5

Source: HMSO, *Financial Statement and Budget Report, 1980–81.*

Three points should be noted about the MTFS. First, it was originally assumed that the wide measure of money, M3, was the measure most relevant for inflation. We shall see shortly that in recent years the growth of M3 has been less closely related to inflation than in the past. In consequence, by the mid-1980s the MTFS began to specify targets for the growth of the narrower M0 measure of money and paid less attention to M3. Second, from the outset the government recognized the practical difficulties in trying to control the money supply which we discussed in Chapter 24. Hence monetary targets referred to a *range* of money growth, such as 7–11 per cent in 1980–81, rather than to more precise targets. Finally, since the PSBR is determined primarily by the government's *fiscal* policy, the MTFS insisted that fiscal and monetary policy could not be conducted independently. Tight fiscal policy, and hence a small deficit, was seen as essential for the pursuit of tight monetary policy. By the late 1980s the Thatcher government had achieved a substantial budget surplus.

In this section we look first at the direct link between the government deficit and inflation. Then we look more carefully at the reasoning behind the MTFS, and study the empirical evidence.

Figure 28-3 shows that there is no direct and immediately obvious link between the size of the budget deficit and the inflation rate. If we are to establish a relation between the deficit and the inflation rate, we shall have to analyse the linkage or transmission mechanism more carefully.

Deficits and Money Growth

A deficit by the government or the public sector can be financed in two ways. First, the government can borrow from the private sector by selling bonds. The money received can then

be used to meet the excess of expenditure over revenue. Second, the government can print money and spend it directly. In Chapter 24 we explained how the Bank of England helps the government to finance a deficit through one or both of these channels.

In a hyperinflation it is quite clear what is happening: deficits are being financed by printing large quantities of money. But this need not be the case. It is logically possible for the government to finance a deficit entirely by selling bonds. Although the government *might*

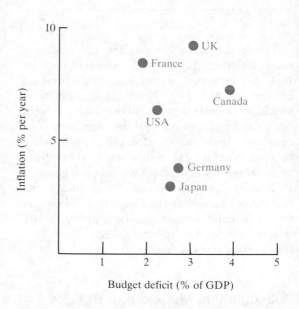

Figure 28-3 BUDGET DEFICITS AND INFLATION 1978–89. The figure shows there is little obvious relationship between the average inflation rate and the average government deficit. (*Source:* IMF, *World Economic Outlook*.)

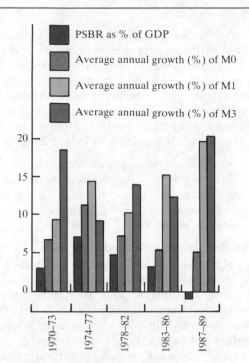

Figure 28-4 DEFICITS AND MONEY GROWTH IN THE UK. (*Source:* CSO, *Economic Trends.*)

debt, and hence the size of the public sector deficit, become so large that they cannot be met by new bond issues alone. If so, then unless the government takes fiscal action to reduce the deficit, it will have no option but to resort to financing the deficit by printing money. That is how hyperinflation starts.

Money Growth and Inflation in the UK

We conclude this section by looking at the short-run relationship between money growth and inflation, each expressed in percentage per annum, between 1970 and 1989. Figure 28-5 shows data comparing inflation in the UK with the annual growth rate of M0 and M3.

The figure shows that UK inflation peaked at 25 per cent in 1975. The figure shows why in the late 1970s many people believed that UK inflation was determined by the rate of growth of M3 two years earlier. This view depended heavily on the behaviour of M3 and inflation in the mid-1970s. With hindsight, we can see that the relationship has been much less close since then. Moreover, the M0 measure of the UK nominal money supply never grew by more than 14 per cent in any year. Hence there is no close relation between M0 and inflation, which reached 25 per cent in the mid-1970s.

Looking at the whole period shown in Figure 28-5, we can draw two conclusions. First, there is no simple relation between nominal money growth and inflation: changes in interest rates

decide to finance a constant fraction of its deficit by printing money, it need not do so. Figure 28-4 shows data for the UK. It shows that PSBR as a percentage of GDP, and the corresponding annual rates of growth in nominal money, measured both by the narrow M0 definition and the broader M1 and M3 definitions. Particularly on the wider definitions, there seems little short-run relation between money and the PSBR even when we average annual data over four-year periods.

In the longer run, the relationship between the size of the public sector deficit and the growth of the money supply is more likely to be significant. Suppose the government tries to run a persistently high deficit and finance it by bond issues alone. As the stock of bonds increases, interest payments on existing government debts rise. This tends to increase the government deficit, requiring yet more bond issues. And the government may have to offer higher interest rates to induce people to hold ever larger stocks of government debt. Thus it is possible that interest payments on existing

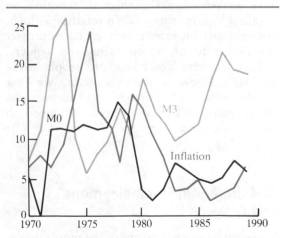

Figure 28-5 INFLATION AND MONEY GROWTH (%). (*Source:* CSO, *Economic Trends.*)

and in real income lead to changes in real money demand that destroy any simple relationship.

Second, since changes in nominal money are not immediately reflected in changes in prices, the evidence of Figure 28-5 is compatible with the account of sluggish adjustment we developed in Chapter 26. In the short run, changes in nominal money lead to changes in the real money supply, inducing changes in interest rates and income. Only in the longer run is there a tendency for prices and wages to adjust fully to restore full employment in the labour market and potential output in the goods market.

Recap

Although the demand for real money balances changes with changes in real income and in interest rates, in the long run changes in real money demand are usually quite small. Hence the equilibrium real money supply usually changes slowly. Thus persistent inflation is possible only if the government is printing money. High budget deficits may increase the temptation to print money in the long run, but there need not be a close short-run relation between the size of the budget deficit and the rate of money growth. Moreover, since real income and interest rates can change in the short run, there need not be a close relation between money growth and inflation in the short run.

Having examined the causes of inflation, we now turn our attention to its consequences. We have already seen the effect of inflation on nominal interest rates. When inflation is high, nominal interest rates must increase to protect the real rate of return earned by lenders. Otherwise there won't be many people in the lending business. In the next section we look at the effect of inflation on output and employment. We shall then be equipped to discuss the costs of inflation.

28-4 Inflation, Unemployment, and Output

We begin by discussing one of the most famous and infamous relationships in postwar macroeconomics. It is known as the Phillips curve.

The Phillips Curve

In 1958 Professor A. W. Phillips of the London School of Economics demonstrated that there was a strong statistical relationship between the annual inflation rate and the annual unemployment rate in the UK. Similar relationships were found to hold in other countries and this relationship quickly became known as the Phillips curve. It is shown in Figure 28-6.

> The *Phillips curve* shows that a higher inflation rate is accompanied by a lower unemployment rate, and vice versa. It suggests we can *trade off* more inflation for less unemployment, or vice versa.

The Phillips curve seemed the answer to the problem of choosing macroeconomic policy in the 1960s, when Keynesian economics was at its most fashionable and economists were pessimistic about the speed with which the economy was capable of returning to full employment automatically through wage and price adjustments. Keynesian governments saw the policy choice as follows. By selecting fiscal and monetary policy, the government could determine the level of aggregate demand and the extent of involuntary unemployment. The Phillips curve showed the level of inflation that would then ensue: higher aggregate demand put upward pressure on wages and prices and led

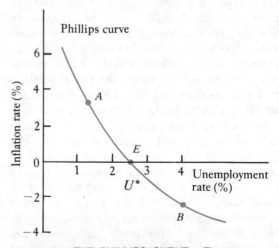

Figure 28-6 THE PHILLIPS CURVE. The Phillips curve shows the trade-off between higher inflation and lower unemployment. In the 1960s people believed that an unemployment rate of 2.5 per cent would be accompanied by zero inflation.

to higher inflation but lower unemployment. It showed the menu of choices available. Governments simply had to decide how much extra inflation they were prepared to tolerate in exchange for lower unemployment. They picked a point on the Phillips curve and set fiscal and monetary policies to achieve the corresponding level of aggregate demand and hence unemployment.

The Phillips curve shown in Figure 28-6 shows the trade-off that people believed they faced in the 1960s. In those days UK unemployment was scarcely ever over 2 per cent of the labour force. But people sincerely believed that if they did the unthinkable, and cut back aggregate demand until unemployment rose to 2.5 per cent, the inflation rate would fall to zero.

Today, of course, we know that there have been many years since 1970 when *both* inflation and unemployment were over 5 per cent in the same year. Something happened to the Phillips curve. The rest of this section explains how macroeconomists gradually managed to solve the puzzle of why the simple Phillips curve of Figure 28-6 ceased to fit the facts.

As we shall shortly see, many of the important clues were discovered by Milton Friedman. However let's try to work it out for ourselves using the analysis of aggregate demand and aggregate supply that we developed in Chapter 26. Consider a model of the economy in which the level of full employment and potential output are fixed in the long run, but where there is sluggish wage and price adjustment. In response to an initial shock, wages and prices change only slowly and the economy gradually works its way back to full employment as changes in prices alter the real money supply.

We begin by assuming that *in the long run* the nominal money supply is fixed. When the economy gets back to full employment, inflation will eventually be zero, maintaining the real money supply in line with the quantity of real money demanded when income equals potential output and nominal interest rates are at their long-run equilibrium level.

From an initial position of equilibrium in all markets, suppose aggregate demand increases. For example, suppose there is a once-and-for-all increase in the nominal money supply. Since prices and wages do not immediately increase very much, the real money supply increases and

it takes lower interest rates to induce people to hold a larger quantity of real money balances. In the short run, higher aggregate demand for goods leads to higher output. Employment rises and unemployment falls.

In terms of Figure 28-6, we begin in equilibrium at point E with zero inflation and unemployment equal to its natural rate U^*, the level of recorded unemployment when the labour market is in long-run equilibrium. The immediate effect of the increase in aggregate demand is to move the economy to a point such as A on the Phillips curve. Since prices have risen a bit, inflation is greater than zero, but higher aggregate demand and output have increased employment and reduced unemployment below the natural rate U^*.

However, this is only the first step. The economy does not stay at A for ever. Gradually wages rise in response to higher demand for workers, and prices rise as firms pass on these wage increases. In Chapter 26 we described this response as a slow shift upwards in the short-run aggregate supply schedule. What happens as this process continues? First, higher prices reduce real money supply and push up interest rates to choke off the demand for real money balances. Aggregate demand starts to fall and unemployment starts to rise again. Second, although wages and prices are still rising, they are rising at an ever slower rate. Since a higher price *level* is reducing the real money supply and aggregate demand relative to the level of potential output that firms wish to supply in the long run, there is less and less additional upward pressure on money wages and prices the longer the adjustment process continues.

In terms of Figure 28-6, the economy is simply moving down the Phillips curve from A back to its long-run equilibrium position at E, which it will eventually reach. When prices and money wages have risen sufficiently to reduce the real money supply and raise interest rates to the levels that equate aggregate demand and potential output, the economy is back to long-run equilibrium. Since the nominal money supply is constant by assumption, inflation is then zero. There is no further pressure for wages or prices to change.

The same story may be told in reverse. If the initial shock is a downwards shift in aggregate demand, two things will happen in the short run. A partial fall in wages and prices will make inflation negative in the short run. But because wage and price adjustment is only partial, lower aggregate demand will increase unemployment. The economy will move to a point such as B on the Phillips curve in Figure 28-6. Thereafter involuntary unemployment will gradually bid down wages and prices, thereby increasing the real money supply, lowering interest rates, and increasing aggregate demand. The economy will gradually move back up the Phillips curve from B to E, where full employment is restored and inflation is zero again.

We draw two conclusions from this analysis. First, it was wrong to interpret the Phillips curve as a *permanent* trade-off between inflation and unemployment. Rather, it shows the temporary trade-off while the economy is adjusting to a shock to *aggregate demand*. An increase in aggregate demand requires a *temporary* period of inflation to reduce real money balances and get aggregate demand back to its full-employment level.

Second, the speed with which the economy moves back along the Phillips curve depends on the degree of flexibility of money wages, and hence of prices. Extreme monetarists believe that this flexibility is almost instantaneous. In this extreme version, it is only the fact that workers make annual wage settlements that prevents the economy from being continuously at its long-run equilibrium position. Changes in aggregate demand that were not foreseen when money wages were set mean that money wages and prices are temporarily at the wrong level to secure the real money supply which will equate aggregate demand and potential output. But such mistakes are rectified as soon as wages are renegotiated. In contrast, the model of more sluggish wage adjustment that we developed in Chapter 26 means that the economy takes much longer to adjust fully to any shock to aggregate demand. Movements along the Phillips curve back to long-run equilibrium take much longer.

This examination of short-run adjustment is a useful beginning to our analysis. But it is only a beginning. First, we have assumed that the long-run equilibrium involves a constant nominal money supply and zero inflation. Second, we have assumed that all shocks are to aggregate demand rather than to aggregate supply. And finally, we have assumed that the natural rate of unemployment remains constant over time. Once we recognize these three complications we shall be able to understand the complete picture.

The Vertical Long-run Phillips Curve

Suppose we now recognize that the nominal money supply need not be constant in the long run. Suppose in long-run equilibrium the nominal money supply is growing at 20 per cent per annum. Inflation is 20 per cent per annum and nominal interest rates are, say, 22 per cent, so that the real interest rate is 2 per cent. Money wages are also growing at 20 per cent every year, so that real wages remain constant at their full-employment level. The real money supply is constant, since prices and nominal money are growing at the same rate, and equals the level of real balances demanded given the nominal interest rate of 22 per cent and the level of real income corresponding to full-employment output.

Is there any reason why the levels of output, employment, and unemployment in this long-run equilibrium should differ from the levels that these variables would attain if there were no inflation? In 1968 Milton Friedman asked this question and provided the answer: essentially, there should be little difference.[5] In the absence of money illusion, people care about real variables not nominal variables. In long-run equilibrium with 20 per cent inflation, or any other rate of inflation, nominal money and money wages are growing at the *same* rate as prices. Neither the real money supply nor real wages are being eroded by inflation. Since the Fisher hypothesis says that nominal interest rates will rise in line with inflation to maintain the real interest rate, neither lenders nor borrowers are doing better or worse as a result of inflation.

In thinking about the Phillips curve, Friedman suggested that we recognize that the long-run equilibrium values of full employment, potential output, real wages, and unemployment will be unaffected by the inflation rate. Since all nominal variables can adjust to keep up with inflation and maintain the values of the corresponding real variables, and since

---

[5] Milton Friedman, 'The Role of Monetary Policy', *American Economic Review*, 1968.

people care only about real variables, the
equilibrium values of these real variables will
be unaffected by inflation in the long run when
everyone has had the chance to adjust fully to
the equilibrium inflation rate.

In Figure 28-7 we show this as a vertical
long-run Phillips curve. Whatever the long-run
rate of money growth and inflation, eventually
everyone can adjust to it and the economy will
get back to the natural rate of unemployment
U^*, which is unaffected by inflation. Thus, if
the money supply increases at 10 per cent a
year for ever, eventually the economy will
reach long-run equilibrium at the point E.
Inflation will be 10 per cent, money wages will
grow at 10 per cent, and unemployment will
be at the natural rate U^*.

Suppose we begin from long-run equilibrium

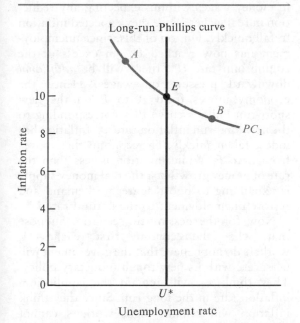

Figure 28-7 THE LONG-RUN PHILLIPS
CURVE. Since people care about real variables not
nominal variables, when full adjustment has been
completed people will arrange for all nominal
variables to keep up with inflation. The vertical
long-run Phillips curve shows that eventually the
economy gets back to the natural rate of
unemployment U^*, whatever the long-run inflation
rate. There is no long-run trade-off between inflation
and unemployment. The short-run Phillips curve PC_1
shows short-run adjustment as before. The height of
the short-run Phillips curve depends on the rate of
inflation and nominal money growth in long-run
equilibrium, as shown by the position of the point E
on the long-run Phillips curve.

at E. We can repeat the analysis of short-run
adjustment we discussed using Figure 28-6. Any
stimulus to aggregate demand will temporarily
boost output and reduce unemployment. But
this will put upward pressure on wages and
prices until a temporary period of extra
inflation, during which prices grow faster than
nominal money, reduces the real money supply
and restores aggregate demand to its full-
employment level.

Hence we draw the short-run Phillips curve.
PC_1. The long-run equilibrium point E is a
point on this Phillips curve. But in the short
run, a boost to aggregate demand will take the
economy to the point A. Thereafter, pressure
on wages and prices will reduce the real money
supply and aggregate demand and take the
economy back along PC_1 until it gets back to
E again. Conversely, any drop in aggregate
demand will initially take the economy to a
point such as B. Higher unemployment will
then moderate the rate of growth of money
wages and prices, boost the real money supply
and aggregate demand, and move the economy
along PC_1 back to E.

As in Figure 28-6, the short-run Phillips curve
describes the temporary trade-off between
inflation and unemployment *while the economy
is adjusting to a change in aggregate demand*.
But the height of the short-run Phillips curve is
determined by the height of the point at which
it crosses the vertical long-run Phillips curve,
namely the rate of money growth and inflation
in long-run equilibrium.

Friedman's insight allows us to explain why
the UK and most other economies had higher
inflation at each unemployment rate in the
1970s than in the 1960s: the short-run Phillips
curve had shifted upwards. Why? Because in
the 1970s governments were printing money at
a faster rate than in the 1960s. Hence the
long-run equilibrium inflation rate had risen.
The point E lay further up the long-run
Phillips curve in Figure 28-7. The short-run
Phillips curve passing through this point had
shifted upwards.

Expectations and Credibility

Figure 28-8 allows us to put this apparatus to
work to discuss what happens when a new
government is elected with a commitment to
get inflation down. It is relevant to the election

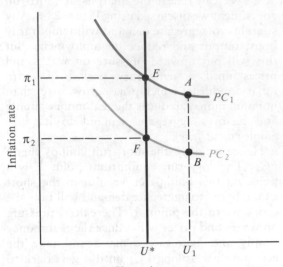

Figure 28-8 EXPECTATIONS AND CREDIBILITY. Beginning from long-run equilibrium at E, the government reduces the rate of money growth from π_1 to π_2. Initially this reduces the real money supply and moves the economy from E to A. Unemployment increases to U_1. If people believe that money growth will remain π_2, they realize that the new long-run equilibrium will be at F. The short-run Phillips curve shifts from PC_1 to PC_2 and the economy moves from A to B. There is a sharp fall in money wage growth because people realize that inflation will be lower and cost of living wage claims can be moderated. Thereafter the economy moves up PC_2 from B to F. However, if people believe that the rate of money growth will soon return to its original level π_1, they cannot moderate wage increases in anticipation of falling inflation. The short-run curve *remains* PC_1. In the short run, nominal money is growing at π_2, but inflation is higher. Hence the Keynesian slump intensifies since the real money supply is still being reduced.

of the Thatcher government in the UK in 1979, or the Reagan administration in the United States in 1980.

Suppose the economy begins in long-run equilibrium at E facing the short-run Phillips curve PC_1. Nominal money, prices, and money wages are all rising at the rate π_1. The government believes that inflation is unacceptably high and in the long run wants to get inflation down to the lower rate π_2. It wants to get to the new long-run equilibrium position F. The day the government is elected it announces that the rate of nominal money growth is to be permanently reduced from π_1 to π_2.

In the short run, firms are locked into their previous agreements to increase money wages at the old inflation rate π_1. They have little scope for reducing the rate at which prices are rising in the short run. Hence a reduction in the rate of nominal money growth leads to a reduction in the real money supply. Prices are rising faster than nominal money. Aggregate demand falls and there is involuntary unemployment. The economy moves along the short-run Phillips curve PC_1 to the point A. Unemployment is higher and inflation is only slighly reduced. The key question is, what happens next?

On the optimistic scenario, workers believe that the government will stick to its tighter monetary policy and inflation will quickly fall. In the next round of wage bargaining, they can afford to ask for a much lower rate of increase in money wages without expecting any reduction in real wages, since they expected inflation to fall quickly. On top of this, since unemployment has now reached U_1, in excess of the equilibrium rate U^*, there will be *additional* downward pressure on wages. Hence the economy moves from A to B on the new short-run Phillips curve PC_2 corresponding to the new long-run inflation rate π_2. Inflation has indeed fallen quickly. The economy then moves from B to F. While inflation is less than the rate of money growth π_2, the real money supply is expanding to boost aggregate demand and restore unemployment to the natural rate U^*.

Now for the pessimistic scenario. Suppose that, when the economy first reaches A, workers do not believe that the government will persevere with its new tough monetary policy. They think π_1 will remain the equilibrium inflation rate in the long run. Since they think inflation will remain high, workers cannot afford to take nominal wage cuts in anticipation of lower inflation. They believe that it is the short-run Phillips curve PC_1 not PC_2 that is relevant. But if the economy stays at A while the government in fact is only increasing the money supply at the lower rate π_2, in the short run prices are rising more quickly than nominal money. The real money supply is falling yet again, aggregate demand is further reduced, and unemployment increases as the economy moves further down PC_1. Moreover, the worse this slump becomes, the more likely it is that the government's nerve will crack and it will conclude that unemployment has reached such unacceptable proportions that the money supply must be increased to boost aggregate demand again. A belief that the government's nerve will crack can become a self-fulfilling prophecy. The economy will stay on PC_1, and the attempt to reduce inflation substantially will have failed. Gradually the economy will move back along PC_1 to equilibrium at E.

This insight explains why the Thatcher government went to such lengths to proclaim that there would be no U-turn from the tight monetary policy. The sooner people accepted that the long-run inflation rate really would be lower, the sooner wage claims would moderate. To help convince people that the government would stick to its tight monetary targets, the Thatcher government introduced the Medium-Term Financial Strategy, a public, announced commitment to low money growth targets for several years into the future.

Changes in The Natural Rate of Unemployment

In the long-run, the Phillips curve is vertical at the natural rate of unemployment U^*, the level of voluntary unemployment when the labour market is in equilibrium. In the previous chapter we discussed the forces that could change the natural rate of unemployment. We also argued that the natural rate had steadily increased in the UK since the mid-1960s. Structural unemployment had increased, and organized workers had secured real wage increases in excess of their productivity increases. The natural rate has also increased in most other countries during this period.

In terms of Figure 28-8, an increase in the natural rate of unemployment shifts the vertical long-run Phillips curve to the right. It continues to pass through the natural rate of unemployment, which has increased.

Inflation and Unemployment since 1960

The original Phillips curve seemed to offer a permanent trade-off between inflation and unemployment. Moreover, it suggested that both inflation *and* unemployment could be extraordinarily low by post-1970 standards.

In the 1960s and the early 1970s, many governments were committed to maintaining full employment even in the short run. Any shock that tended to increase inflation – whether a wage claim by a trade union or a rise in the cost of a raw material – was accommodated by an increase in the money supply to prevent a reduction of the real money supply in the short run. Since governments were often raising the rate of money growth but rarely reducing it, money growth and inflation gradually increased. That explains why inflation rose above its level of the 1960s. Since the mid-1970s, government policy has changed in many countries. The emphasis is now on getting inflation down even if this means a short-term rise in unemployment. That is why inflation has fallen since the early 1980s.

What about unemployment? We now understand that the Phillips curve is vertical in the long run at the natural rate of unemployment. An increase in the natural rate of unemployment in many countries is an important component of the rise in actual unemployment in those countries. But it is not the whole story. We understand now that the long-run Phillips curve shows the *temporary* trade-off between inflation and unemployment while the economy is adjusting to an aggregate demand shock and gradually working its way back to potential output and the natural rate of unemployment. The height of the short-run Phillips curve depends on current expectations about future inflation and money growth.

At the beginning of the 1980s, inflation was high because it had been high in the past. Anti-inflation policies were only just beginning to bite. When tight money was first introduced, the real money supply was cut since inflation did not fall immediately. Aggregate demand fell and the economy moved to the right along the short-run Phillips curve. In addition to a high natural rate of unemployment, many countries were experiencing a short-run Keynesian slump. Involuntary unemployment was also high.

This combination of high inflation and high unemployment was made worse by a major aggregate supply shock, the doubling of oil prices during 1979–80.

An Aggregate Supply Shock

What is the effect of an aggregate supply shock such as the doubling of oil prices? Overnight, inflation increases as firms pass on increased costs in higher prices. Suppose there has not yet been time for employment to change. What happens next depends on what the government does, and on what people expect the government to do.

Suppose the government does *not* accommodate the shock. Money growth remains unchanged. With higher inflation, the real money supply is reduced, interest rates rise, and aggregate demand falls. There is a Keynesian slump and stagflation.

> *Stagflation* is a period of both high inflation *and* high unemployment. It is often caused by an adverse supply shock.

Gradually, involuntary unemployment bids down wages or moderates wage increases. The inflation rate falls below the fixed rate of money growth, and the real money supply starts to expand again. Eventually the economy gets back to the natural rate of unemployment. Since money growth has remained unchanged, in the long run the inflation rate has not been altered by the adverse supply shock.

Suppose instead that the government *had* accommodated the aggregate supply shock. When inflation first increased, the government simply raised permanently the rate of money growth to match this higher inflation rate. There would be no reduction in the real money supply, even in the short run. Aggregate demand would not be reduced in the short run and there would be no increase in unemployment. But the economy would be left with a permanently higher rate of money growth and a permanently higher inflation rate.

This example highlights the policy dilemma. If the government refuses to accommodate the shock, it will take a painful period of unemployment before wage and price adjustment restores the economy to its original equilibrium position in the long run. But long-run inflation will not have increased. However, by accommodating the original supply shock to prices, the government can avoid the Keynesian slump by maintaining aggregate demand; but only at the price of permanently higher inflation.

In the UK the government accommodated much more of the 1973 OPEC shock than of the 1979–80 OPEC shock. Hence the 1973 shock caused only a little extra Keynesian unemployment but a lot of extra inflation, whereas the 1979–80 shock caused much more extra Keynesian unemployment but less extra inflation.

Again, the credibility of policy is crucial. Before the Thatcher government took office in the UK, workers recognized that governments were so frightened of high unemployment that they would accommodate almost any shock. Extravagant wage claims would buy temporarily higher real wages until prices adjusted fully. And in the long run the government would increase the money supply to maintain aggregate demand at full employment, so there was little danger of additional Keynesian unemployment. By refusing to accommodate high money wage claims, the Thatcher government gradually convinced workers that such claims reduce the real money supply, reduce aggregate demand, and push up unemployment. In the 1980s many union leaders found little support from their union members when they proposed large wage increases.

Once the Thatcher government had established the credibility of its determination to fight inflation, it was then able to relax policy a bit in the mid-1980s and achieve a sustained boom. For five or six years inflation remained low. Wage-setters believed that, in spite of a monetary and fiscal expansion, any outbreak of inflation would quickly be met by a return to restrictive policies. But the longer policy remained looser, the more wage-setters began to wonder whether the government really would tighten policy if required. When inflation began to climb again in 1989, the government was forced to raise interest rates substantially to try to restore its credibility.

Recap of the Relation between Inflation and Unemployment

We have reached the following conclusions. There is essentially *no* long-run trade-off between inflation and unemployment. The long-run Phillips curve is vertical at the natural rate of unemployment. The short-run Phillips curve is a temporary trade-off between inflation and unemployment when the economy is adjusting to shocks to aggregate demand. The height of this short-run trade-off depends on beliefs about money growth and inflation in the long run. But there is no trade-off *between* inflation and unemployment in the short run when shocks come from the supply side. Initially, higher inflation is likely to be accompanied by higher unemployment. What happens next depends crucially on the extent to which the government accommodates the supply-side shock.

28-5 The Costs of Inflation

People dislike inflation. And governments think it worth while to adopt tight fiscal and monetary policies aimed at reducing inflation, even though in the short run these policies may mean higher unemployment and lower output. Why exactly is inflation such a bad thing? Now that we understand what causes inflation and what some of its effects are, we are in a much better position to answer this question.

Inflation Illusion?

Some of the arguments most commonly used to show why inflation is a bad thing are in fact quite spurious, and suggest that people may suffer from inflation illusion.

> People have *inflation illusion* when they confuse nominal and real changes. People's welfare depends on real variables, not nominal variables.

It is incorrect to say that inflation is bad because it makes goods more expensive. If *all* nominal variables are increasing at the same rate, people have larger nominal incomes and can buy the same physical quantity of goods as before. If people think about their nominal expenditure without recognizing that their nominal incomes are also increasing, they have inflation illusion. It is real incomes that tell us how many goods people can afford to buy.

A second kind of illusion is more subtle. Suppose there is a sharp increase in the real or relative price of oil. In countries that import large quantities of oil, people will now be worse off. The country as a whole has to divert goods from domestic consumption to exports in order to earn the extra foreign currency with which to purchase the more expensive oil imports. Hence domestic consumption per person has to fall. However, it can fall in one of two ways.

The first way is if workers do not ask for 'cost-of-living' wage increases to cover the higher cost of oil-related products. Real wages

fall since the old level of money wages now buys a smaller quantity of goods as a whole. Suppose also that domestic firms absorb the increase in their oil-related fuel costs and do not pass on these costs in higher prices. There is no increase in either domestic prices or domestic money wages. The domestic economy has adjusted to the adverse supply shock without any inflation. And people are inevitably worse off.

Suppose instead that people try to maintain their old standard of living. Workers put in for cost-of-living increases to restore their real wages, and firms protect their profit margins by increasing prices in line with higher wage and fuel costs. There is a lot of domestic inflation, which the government accommodates by printing extra money. Eventually the economy settles down in its new long-run equilibrium position, but what does this new equilibrium look like?

People must still be worse off. The rise in the real oil price has not disappeared by magic. It still takes more domestic exports, made possible by lower domestic consumption, to pay for the more expensive oil imports. Hence in the new long-run equilibrium workers will find that their real wages have been reduced and firms may find that their profit margins have been squeezed. This is the market mechanism that brings about the required fall in domestic expenditure and allows resources to be transferred to the export industries.

What people notice is that there has been a period of rising wages and rising prices, but that somehow wages did not manage to keep up with price rises. Real wages fell. But people draw the wrong conclusion. It was not the inflation that made them worse off, but the rise in oil prices. Real wages would have fallen whether or not there had been a domestic inflation. When inflation is caused by an adverse supply shock, and is allowed to persist because the government adopts an accommodating monetary expansion, it is neither the inflation nor the monetary expansion that makes people worse off: it is the adverse supply shock. The inflation is merely a symptom of the initial refusal to accept the new reality.

So far, we have examined some spurious arguments about why inflation is a bad thing. We now turn to more serious arguments. The subsequent discussion has two central themes.

First, was the inflation fully expected in advance? Or are people still in the process of adjusting to inflation which took them by surprise? Second, do our institutions, including government regulations and the tax system, enable people to adjust fully to inflation once they have come to expect it? The costs of inflation depend on the answer to these two questions.

Complete Adaptation and Full Anticipation

Imagine an economy in which inflation is 10 per cent a year for ever. Everybody knows it, anticipates its continuation, and can take it into account when making wage bargains or lending money. All prices, money wages, and the nominal money supply are growing at 10 per cent a year. Inflation is eroding neither real incomes nor the real money supply. The economy is at full employment. Government policy is also fully adjusted. Nominal taxes are being changed every year so that the real tax revenue remains constant. Nominal government spending is increasing at 10 per cent a year so that real government spending is constant.[6]

Nominal interest rates have risen to the constant level necessary to maintain the equilibrium real interest rate when inflation is 10 per cent a year. Share prices are rising with inflation to maintain the real value of company shares on the stock exchange. The tax treatment of interest earnings and capital gains has been adjusted to take account of inflation. In real terms, taxation of interest earnings and capital gains remains unaffected by inflation.[7] Pensions and other transfer payments are being raised every year, in line with expected inflation.

This economy does not suffer from inflation illusion. Individuals and the government fully expect a 10 per cent inflation and have adjusted as fully as they can to minimize its effect on real variables. This was the insight that lay behind the long-run vertical Phillips curve in the previous section. But even in this ideal world, is complete adjustment possible?

Shoe-leather Costs   Earlier in this chapter, we explained that nominal interest rates usually rise in line with inflation in order to preserve the real rate of interest. But we have also seen that it is the nominal interest rate that is the opportunity cost of holding money. Hence when inflation is higher, people hold less money balances. In Section 28-2 we examined the flight from money during the German hyperinflation as an extreme example of this relation between inflation and the demand for real balances.

We began our study of money in Chapter 23 by showing that society uses money to economize on the time and effort involved in undertaking transactions. When high nominal interest rates induce people to economize on holding real money balances, society must use a greater quantity of resources in undertaking transactions and therefore has less resources available for production and consumption of goods and services. We call this the *shoe-leather cost* of higher inflation.

With higher inflation and nominal interest rates, people will hold less of their wealth in cash and more of it in interest-bearing assets such as bank accounts. Instead of withdrawing £50 at a time from an interest-bearing bank account and visiting the bank only once a month, people will withdraw £10 a time but visit the bank five times a month. For a given level of transactions, this enables people to hold less of their wealth in non-interest-bearing cash, but it makes people wear out their shoe-leather in walking to the bank more frequently. Shoe-leather costs stand for all the extra time and effort people put into transacting when they try to get by with lower real balances.

Menu Costs   When prices are rising, price labels have to be changed. For example, menus have to be reprinted to show the higher price of meals. The *menu costs* of inflation refer to the physical resources required to reprint price tags when prices are rising (or falling). The faster the rate of price change, the more

---

[6] For simplicity we assume there is no productivity growth, no changes in supply or demand conditions, and hence a given level of full employment and potential output. Pure inflation could also happen, of course, in an economy with underlying real growth of output and employment.

[7] During times of inflation many people worry about a country's international competitiveness. We discuss international transactions in the next chapter. We shall see that it is also possible to adjust the exchange rate over time so that a country's real competitiveness remains unaffected by inflation.

frequently menus have to be reprinted if real prices are to remain constant.

Among the menu costs of inflation we should probably include the effort of doing mental arithmetic. When the inflation rate is zero it is easy to walk into a shop and see that a pound of steak costs the same as it did three months ago. But when inflation is 25 per cent a year, it takes a bit more effort to compare the price of steak today with that of three months ago so as to see what has happened to the real or relative price of steak. Although people without inflation illusion try to think in real terms, the mental arithmetic required involves real time and effort.

How significant are menu costs? In supermarkets it may be relatively easy to change price tags. But the cost of changing parking meters, pay telephones, and slot machines are more substantial. In fact, in countries where inflation rates are high, pay telephones usually take tokens whose price can be easily changed without having to physically alter the machines.

Even when inflation is perfectly anticipated and the economy has fully adjusted to inflation, it is impossible to avoid shoe-leather costs and menu costs. Although these costs become very significant when the inflation rate reaches hyperinflation levels, they suggest that the social cost of living with 20 per cent inflation for ever might not be too large. However, this applies to the case in which society is best able to adjust to inflation. As we now see, the costs of inflation will be larger in other situations.

Fully Anticipated Inflation When Institutions Fail to Adapt Fully

In this section we assume that the inflation is fully anticipated but that institutional factors prevent people from implementing some of the changes that would be required if nominal variables are to adjust in line with expected inflation. Because nominal variables are prevented from fully adjusting, inflation then affects more real variables than the shoe-leather and menu effects identified above.

Interest Rate Controls   To preserve real interest rates, nominal interest rates must be allowed to rise in line with inflation. If chequing accounts paid interest, shoe-leather costs would apply only to cash itself since, as yet, we have found no way to pay interest on cash.

In many countries chequing accounts either pay no interest or pay a small interest rate which typically does not rise with inflation. Since the introduction of Competition and Credit Control in the UK in 1971 (see Chapter 24), time deposits do pay competitive interest rates; these vary in line with market interest rates and inflation. Prior to 1971, banks rarely adjusted interest rates on time deposits. This institutional sluggishness meant that a rise in inflation reduced the real interest rate on all assets whose nominal interest rate was essentially fixed. It extended the shoe-leather costs. With lower real returns, people had to economize not merely on real cash holdings but also on real holdings of chequing accounts and deposit accounts. People spent more time and effort keeping a close eye on their holdings of quite a wide range of liquid assets.

Whether these are permanent costs of inflation remains to be seen. One effect of persistently high inflation is that people start pressing for institutional changes to allow nominal variables to keep up with inflation. The longer high inflation continues, the more likely it is that banks and other institutions will be forced to pay competitive nominal interest rates on various kinds of bank deposits. But since institutional change is usually quite slow, in the short run the effect of a move from low inflation to high inflation may be to reduce real interest rates on many kinds of borrowing and lending, thereby benefiting borrowers and penalizing lenders.

Taxes   The second major effect of fully anticipated inflation when institutional adjustment is incomplete is that tax rates may not be fully inflation-adjusted. The first problem is fiscal drag.

Fiscal drag is the increase in real tax revenue when inflation raises nominal incomes and pushes people into higher tax brackets in a progressive income tax system.

Here is a simple example. Suppose income below £2000 is untaxed but people pay income tax at 30 pence in the pound on all income over £2000. Initially, a person with an income of £3000 pays tax at 30 per cent on the income over £2000. Thus income tax paid is £300.

Suppose that after ten years of inflation all wages and prices have doubled but the tax brackets and tax rates remain as before. The person's income is now £6000. Nominal tax paid is 30 per cent on the £4000 by which nominal income exceeds £2000. Hence nominal tax paid is £1200. Thus, although wages and prices have only doubled, nominal taxes paid have increased fourfold. Fiscal drag has increased the real tax burden. The government is benefiting from the inflation at the expense of private individuals.

To make the tax system inflation-neutral, nominal tax brackets must be increased in line with inflation. In the above example, if the real tax exemption limit had been preserved by raising the nominal limit from £2000 to £4000 when other nominal variables doubled, everything would be inflation-adjusted. The person now earning £6000 would have to pay 30 per cent on only the last £2000 of income, a nominal tax payment of £600, having exactly the same real value as the original payment of £300 when all nominal variables were only half their current value.

When governments adjusted the nominal tax bands upwards to offset inflation this used to be portrayed as a cut in income tax or increased government generosity. We now see that this is pure inflation illusion. The adjustments are required merely to maintain the real burden of income tax unchanged. In countries such as the UK and the United States, this logic has now been accepted. Tax bands are now automatically increased in line with inflation unless a deliberate government policy to the contrary is adopted. And the press no longer hails as income tax cuts the increases in tax bands that are necessary purely to keep up with inflation.[8]

Taxing Capital   Income tax levied on interest income is also affected by inflation. Suppose there is no inflation and the nominal and real interest rates are both 4 per cent. With a 30 per cent tax rate, the after-tax real return on lending

is 2.8 per cent a year. Now suppose inflation is 10 per cent a year and nominal interest rates rise to 14 per cent to maintain the pre-tax real interest rate of 4 per cent. But in the current tax system in most countries, lenders must pay income tax at 30 per cent on nominal income. Hence the after-tax nominal interest rate is 9.8 per cent (0.7 × 14). Subtracting the 10 per cent inflation rate, the after-tax *real* interest rate is actually *negative*. This compares with the 2.8 per cent after-tax real interest rate when inflation was zero.

What goes wrong? When inflation is 10 per cent, nominal interest rates are 14 per cent. But 10 per cent of this is not real income, merely a payment for keeping up with inflation. Only 4 per cent is the real interest rate providing real income. But income tax applies to the whole 14 per cent. Hence higher inflation reduces the real return on lending because the tax system is not properly inflation-adjusted.

Higher inflation rates must have real effects in such a system. If, as we have assumed, the pre-tax nominal interest rate rises fully in line with inflation to preserve the pre-tax interest rate to borrowers, then higher inflation makes lenders lose out. Conversely, higher inflation *could* lead to even higher nominal interest rates to preserve the real after-tax interest rate to lenders. But then the real pre-tax interest rate to borrowers would rise with inflation. Either way, the government is benefiting by higher real tax revenue. Individual borrowers or lenders are losing out.

Capital gains taxation provides another example. Suppose people have to pay the government 30 per cent of any capital gains they make when buying and selling shares. When inflation is zero only real gains are taxed. But when inflation is 10 per cent, nominal share prices must rise merely to preserve their real value. People have to pay capital gains tax even though they are not making real capital gains.

Taxing Profits   Inflation may also increase the real burden of taxation on company profits. Here is a simple example. Suppose a company holds some stocks of finished goods awaiting sale. In an inflationary world, the nominal value of these stocks will increase over time. If these capital gains are treated as taxable company profits, firms will have to pay more taxes even

---

[8] How about indirect taxes? Percentage taxes on value, such as VAT, automatically increase nominal tax revenue in proportion to inflationary rises in the price level. However *specific* duties, such as £5 a bottle on whisky, need to be raised as the price level rises. In the UK where is no *automatic* formula for raising such duties. Each year the government makes a decision about how much to raise them.

though the real value of their stocks remains unchanged. Such inconsistencies in the tax system would disappear if firms and the government moved over to inflation accounting.

> *Inflation accounting* is the adoption of definitions of costs, revenue, profit and loss that are fully inflation-adjusted.

Thus institutional imperfections help explain why inflation can have real effects even when individuals have fully anticipated that inflation. Until institutions are fully adjusted to inflation, these effects can be quite significant. It is worth noting that in many instances it is the government that stands to gain most by inflation.

Earlier in the chapter we argued that a period of high unemployment and lower output may be required if inflation is to be reduced. Before assuming that the economy should pay this price for reducing the costs of inflation, it is important to ask whether it might not be cheaper to adjust the institutions so that inflation no longer imposed these costs. We discuss 'living with inflation' later in the chapter. For the moment we merely note that institutional adjustment would imply both the once-and-for-all cost of thinking how to design inflation-adjusted institutional rules, and the menu costs of calculating and implementing adjustments as they were required to offset steadily rising prices.

Unexpected Inflation

Previously, we assumed that inflation was fully anticipated. Now we discuss the special problems that arise when inflation takes people by surprise.

Redistribution   When prices rise unexpectedly, the losers are people who own nominal assets and the gainers are people with liabilities denominated in nominal terms. The terms of the original nominal contract to buy or sell, lend or borrow, may have been written to take full account of expected inflation, but they cannot have incorporated inflation that subsequently takes people by surprise.

Suppose you expect inflation to be 10 per cent and agree to lend £100 for a year at 12 per cent, expecting a real interest rate of 2 per cent.

Unexpectedly, inflation jumps to 20 per cent. Whereas you thought you would have £112 next year with which to buy goods whose price had risen from £100 to only £110, in fact goods cost £120 next year and you have lost out by lending. The real interest rate is −8 per cent. Conversely, the borrower has gained. Having borrowed £100 today and promised to repay £112 next year, the borrower suddenly finds that all nominal variables, including the borrower's nominal income, have risen by 20 per cent. The real interest rate of −8 per cent tells us that, if the borrower had put the £100 into durable goods today, these could be sold for £120 the next year, allowing the borrower to repay £112 as promised, and leaving a clear profit of £8.

In one sense, since to every borrower there corresponds a lender, one person's gain is another person's loss. In the aggregate the two cancel out. But unexpected inflation results in a redistribution of income and wealth, in this case from lenders to borrowers. This has two consequences. First, it may lead to a certain amount of economic dislocation. For example, some people may have to declare bankruptcy, which in turn may affect other people. Second, we have to adopt a value judgement about whether we like or approve of the redistribution that is taking place. For example, if rich lenders are losing out to poor borrowers, political parties that believe in a more equal income distribution may not mind this effect, whereas political parties supported by the rich may think that this is a very bad thing.

One of the most important redistributions is between the government and the private sector. Unexpected inflation reduces the real value of all outstanding nominal government debt. Not only is the real money supply reduced, but the real price at which the government has to buy back its bonds is reduced. Equivalently, the government has a higher nominal tax revenue with which to buy back bonds at the already agreed nominal price.[9]

---

[9] Why do we emphasize *unexpected* inflation? Because expected inflation was already built into the terms on which bonds were originally issued. Since expected inflation is incorporated into nominal interest rates, either the government had to offer a high nominal payment per annum or it had to issue the bonds at a lower price than it promised to repurchase them at, so that people could make capital gains to offset expected inflation.

Does this redistribution matter? This is a tricky question. If the government is better off it may be able to cut taxes and undo the effect of such a redistribution. But typically, the people who have lent to the government and lost out through unexpected inflation tend not to be the same people who will benefit from any tax cuts the government is then able to offer.

The Old and the Young   In practice, many of the people who lend by buying nominal assets are the old. Having paid off their mortgages and built up savings during their working life, they may well have put their wealth into nominal bonds to provide income during retirement. These people lose out when there is unexpected inflation and the real value of the bonds falls. They also lose out if they are keeping their wealth in non-interest-bearing money, either in a current account or under the bed.

The nominal debtors are the young, and especially those just entering middle age, who have frequently taken out a large mortgage to move into a large house to see them through the process of bringing up a family. Having borrowed a fixed sum to buy a house, they gain when unexpected inflation increases house prices and nominal incomes without any matching increase in the nominal sum they owe the bank or building society.

Unexpected inflation redistributes from the old to the young. If we believe at all in equality, this redistribution is likely to be viewed as undesirable. With technical progress and productivity increases, each generation is already likely to have a higher lifetime standard of living than its predecessor. Further redistribution from the old to the young merely accentuates this inequality between generations.

Uncertainty about Inflation

Uncertainty about future inflation rates imposes two kinds of costs. First, it increases the complexity of making long-term plans since a much wider range of possible (nominal) outcomes must be carefully investigated. As with shoe-leather costs, this increases the real resources that society must expend in making plans, undertaking transactions, and doing business. Second, people dislike risk. In Chapter

14 we explained why in detail. Briefly, the extra benefits of the champagne years are poor compensation for the years of starvation. People would rather average out these extremes and live comfortably all the time. The psychic costs of worrying about how to cope with the bad years may also be important.

When people must enter into nominal contracts, an increase in uncertainty about the inflation rate increases the uncertainty about the eventual real value of the nominal bargains that people are currently making. This is a genuine cost of inflation. However, the next stage in the argument is more tricky. It is frequently argued that reducing the average level of inflation also reduces the uncertainty about inflation. In fact, it is hard to show in any theoretical model why, if people expect 2 per cent inflation but think it could be as high as 4 per cent or as low as zero, then when people expect 20 per cent inflation the same range of outcomes (namely as high as 22 per cent or as low as 18 per cent) should not apply. Nevertheless, there is some empirical evidence that inflation rates change by more when inflation is already high. Hence higher average inflation rates may be accompanied by more uncertainty about inflation. If so, this imposes a real cost. It may be a very important cost.

28-6 What Can Be Done About Inflation

There are three ways of dealing with inflation. First, we can adopt tough policies designed to keep inflation under control. Second, we can change laws and institutions to make it hard for inflation to emerge. Third, we can learn to live with inflation.

Getting Rid of Inflation

We have already explained that in the long run the inflation rate will be low if the rate of money growth is low. For this it may be necessary to keep fiscal policy fairly tight so that deficits are also low. However, to get to this position from an initial position of high inflation, it may be necessary to get through an intermediate period of high unemployment. Until prices and wages adjust to the new tight monetary and fiscal policies, real aggregate demand will fall. We have argued that this recession could last for a period of years rather than months. To incur the permanent benefits of lower inflation, the economy must first undergo a period of low output and employment.

Could this transition be made more quickly and less painfully? We have already explained that, the more credible the new policy, the faster is likely to be the speed of adjustment of wages and prices. We now examine other policies designed to speed up the process.

Incomes Policies

Incomes policy is the attempt to influence wages and other incomes directly.

Suppose the government wishes to get inflation down from 10 per cent to 5 per cent. If, by explicit legislation or implicit pressure, it can persuade everyone to seek wage increases of only 5 per cent, price inflation will quickly fall to 5 per cent. If this transition happens quickly enough, *real* wages need not suffer.

It is commonly said, and essentially correct, that all previous attempts at incomes policy have been a failure, at best lasting for a short time before a new explosion of wages and prices took place. However, this need not be inevitable. We discuss several reasons why past incomes policies have been unsuccessful.

First, while governments have been in the business of direct intervention in the labour market, they have often been unable to resist pursuing other aims at the same time. For example, in the UK in the 1970s the Labour government tried to reduce the differential between high-wage jobs and low-wage jobs by adopting an incomes policy that allowed an absolute rather than a percentage increase: £6 a week means much more to a worker getting £40 a week than to a worker getting £100 a week. By changing relative wages and real wages, such policies alter real wages from their equilibrium levels, lead to excess supply in some skills and excess demand in others, and set up pressures to circumvent or break the policy. But it is possible to introduce incomes policies whose function is to reduce nominal wage increases and inflation *without* attempting to tinker with real wages.

Second, we have suggested incomes policy as a temporary adjustment device. In the long run, slow nominal money growth is essential if low

inflation is to be maintained. Some incomes policies have failed because governments hoped that long-term incomes policy could hold down money wages and prices even though nominal money was still growing at a rapid rate. Since real aggregate demand then quickly expands, wages and prices have to rise to reduce aggregate demand to its full employment level again.

Similarly, long-term incomes policies are hard to administer in a world where equilibrium real wages for particular skills are changing over time. Freezing the existing wage structure by awarding everyone an equal cost-of-living wage increase will gradually set up powerful market forces of excess supply and excess demand.

These three important sources of past breakdowns in incomes policy might not apply if the policy were known to be a temporary device to speed up the adjustment of wages to an underlying change in nominal money growth that was widely believed to be permanent.

Tax-based Incomes Policy (TIP)   Some economists have begun to advocate a new form of incomes policy, which would be based not on direct legislation to control wage settlements but on tax incentives. Suppose the government wanted to reduce inflation from 10 per cent to 5 per cent. It could allow firms and workers to reach whatever bargains they liked, subject to the following rule: for each 1 per cent wage increase in excess of the government guide of 5 per cent, firms would have to pay, say, 2 per cent to the government in higher taxes.

If the government then paid out this revenue equally to firms, firms as a whole would not lose. But those firms that paid high wage increases would be net losers and those that managed to hold wages below the average increase would be net gainers. Thus, it is argued, firms would have powerful incentives to try to hold down wage settlements.

As yet this remains untested. In the United States the Carter administration tried unsuccessfully to get Congress to adopt the proposal. In the UK the TIP has been strongly advocated by Professor Richard Layard of the London School of Economics. But since it has not yet been tried out in practice, it is hard to say whether it would be more successful than previous approaches to incomes policy.

Institutional and Constitutional Reform

This approach takes a long run view. It is concerned not with the temporary costs of first getting inflation down, but with how to keep inflation down.

Controlling the Central Bank   The first suggestion is to pass a law permanently restricting the rate of nominal money growth to, say, 4 per cent a year. Why 4 per cent? Because in the long run technical progress and a higher capital stock increase potential output and real income; hence the demand for real money balances increases and the nominal money stock can be expanded a little even if prices remain constant. The exact rate at which the nominal money supply could grow without putting upward pressure on prices in the long run is probably somewhere between 2 and 4 per cent.

The point of this suggestion is to limit the government's freedom to act.[10] Just before elections, governments have a habit of increasing the money supply. With sluggish price and wage adjustment, this buys a temporary output boom near election day, though in the long run the only consequence is higher prices. Strict regulation of the central bank, it is argued, would remove the temptation and prevent spurts of money growth and inflation around election time. It would also increase the credibility of tight monetary policy in the long run. Workers would know that higher wages would *not* be accommodated by higher nominal money, and so their effect would be to reduce aggregate demand and increase unemployment until wages fell back into line with the nominal money supply again.

Controlling the Banking System   In Chapter 24 we argued that the commercial banks have some flexibility in creating deposits and money. Even if the central bank keeps a tight rein on cash (high-powered money), banks may try to get by with lower cash reserves and so create extra deposits, the major component of the money supply. A higher nominal money supply may not be entirely the government's fault. How could government control be increased?

One proposal is to force the banks to have a 100 per cent cash reserve ratio. Banks could

issue chequing accounts only if they had the cash in the vaults to back them. Since the government controls the supply of cash, it would control the money supply exactly. Surely this means there would be a huge drop in the money supply? No. The government would simply print a lot of extra money on a once-off basis. This money would have to be held by the banks in order for them to maintain their deposits at the existing level. Thereafter, the government would have the money supply under control.

This proposal would take banks out of the lending business. It is because banks' assets are not merely cash but also loans and market securities that the corresponding deposit liabilities are not entirely backed by cash. Although this proposal would perfectly control one particular measure of the money supply, new institutions would arise to take over the banks' existing lending business. And the credit that these new institutions provided would start to supplant wider measures of money and would influence both interest rates and consumption and investment behaviour. It would then become important to control these new institutions. This proposal merely redefines the problem under a different name.

Learning to Live with Inflation

We noted earlier that, as higher inflation persisted, most economies gradually learned to live with it. Banks have now begun to pay high nominal interest rates on some types of deposit; firms are beginning to move to inflation accounting; and the government is committed to raising nominal tax bands and nominal transfer payments (unemployment benefit, supplementary benefit, pensions) in line with inflation. What else needs to be done if we are to reduce the costs of inflation?

On the tax front, complicated adjustments would be required to remove the effects of inflation from the taxation of interest income and capital gains. On other fronts, indexation could be widely introduced.

Indexation automatically adjusts nominal contracts for the effects of inflation.

Indexed wages would allow initial settlements to be subsequently corrected for any unantici-

---

[10] We take up this argument again in Chapter 34 in discussing European Monetary Union.

pated inflation that occurred over the life of the contract. Indexed loans would mean that the amount to be repaid would rise with the price level. Lenders would no longer suffer from unexpected inflation and borrowers would no longer gain.

Indexation has already been introduced in countries that have had to live with inflation rates of 30 or 40 per cent for years. And the more that countries such as the UK adjust their institutions to cope with inflation, the more they are moving in this general direction.

Should We Adapt to Inflation? Without indexation and widespread institutional reforms, it is costly to live with high inflation rates. But indexation does not remove the costs of high inflation completely. First, indexation is almost always imperfect. Workers cannot be compensated today for yesterday's inflation. The menu costs of perpetually changing things would be enormous. But compensation at discrete intervals means that real wages are changing during these intervals. Nor can indexation get rid of shoe-leather costs. Until we can invent a way to pay a nominal interest rate on all money, higher inflation will always lead to lower desired real cash balances and more time and effort spent in transacting.

By reducing many but not all of the costs of inflation, indexation means that high inflation is much more likely to continue and even increase. Since fewer people are losing out, there will be less political pressure on the government to do something about it. But at high inflation rates, the menu costs and shoe-leather costs could really become very substantial.

Thus there is no easy solution. Tight monetary and fiscal policies could impose a large loss of output and jobs during the transition to lower inflation. But it would be a once-and-for-all cost, against which should be set the present value of the permanent benefits. Monetarists, who believe prices and wages adjust fairly quickly, believe that even the initial cost might not be too large. More extreme Keynesians believe it could be enormous. Whether incomes policy would speed this transition remains an open question. In practice, it seems most likely that we shall continue with some inflation and with institutions that at least partially offset its worst effects.

Summary

1   In money market equilibrium, the price level must deflate the nominal money supply to make the real money supply equal the demand for real balances. Thus an increase in the nominal money supply, or a fall in real money demand, will increase the price level.

2   The quantity theory of money asserts that changes in prices are caused chiefly by equivalent changes in the nominal money supply. In practice, prices cannot immediately adjust to changes in nominal money, so interest rates or income must alter to change money demand. And in the long run, changes in real income and interest rates can significantly change real money demand and break any simple relation between nominal money and prices.

3   A 1 per cent increase in inflation leads roughly to a 1 per cent increase in nominal interest rates so that real interest rates remain roughly unchanged. Since the nominal interest rate is the opportunity cost of holding money, higher inflation thus reduces the demand for real money balances. The flight from money during hyperinflation is a spectacular example.

4   In the short run, there need be no close relation between the size of the budget deficit and the growth of the nominal money supply. In the long run, persistent use of bond finance to meet large deficits may so increase the government's interest payments that the government must resort to printing money if fiscal action is not taken to cut the deficit.

5   The original Phillips curve showed a trade-off between inflation and unemployment. We now recognize that the short-run Phillips curve is a temporary trade-off showing how unemployment and inflation adjust to shocks to aggregate demand. Adverse supply shocks will lead to higher inflation *and* higher unemployment when wage and price adjustment is sluggish.

6   In the long run the Phillips curve is vertical. If people can completely adjust to inflation, it has no real effects. The economy returns to a given natural rate of unemployment whatever the inflation rate.

7   The height of the short-run Phillips curve depends on underlying money growth and expected inflation. If the government wants to

shift the Phillips curve downwards, it must convince people that inflation will be lower in the future.

8 In the 1970s inflation and unemployment were both high. Inflation was high because of rapid money growth, both to finance large deficits and to accommodate supply shocks. Unemployment was high partly because the natural rate increased and partly because the government was eventually forced to generate a Keynesian recession as it adopted tight fiscal and monetary policies to get inflation under control.

9 Some of the claimed costs of inflation are illusory. Some people forget that their nominal incomes are rising; others fail to see that inflation may be the consequence of a shock that would have reduced real incomes in any case. The true costs of inflation depend on whether it was anticipated and on the extent to which the economy's institutions allow complete inflation-adjustment.

10 Shoe-leather costs and menu costs are unavoidable costs of inflation and are likely to be larger the larger the inflation rate. Failure fully to inflation-adjust the tax system may also impose important costs, even when inflation is anticipated.

11 Unexpected inflation redistributes income and wealth from those who have contracted to receive nominal payments (lenders and workers) to those who have contracted to pay them (firms and borrowers).

12 Uncertainty about future inflation rates imposes costs on people who dislike risk. Uncertainty may be greater when inflation is already high.

13 Incomes policies might temporarily speed the transition to a lower inflation rate and reduce the extent of the Keynesian recession required. But they are unlikely to succeed in the long run. Low money growth is necessary for low inflation in the long run.

14 The longer inflation continues, the more the economy learns to live with it. Moves towards indexation reduce the costs of some inflation effects. But they also increase the likelihood of inflation continuing or increasing, thereby exacerbating the shoe-leather and menu costs which cannot be avoided.

Key Terms

Pure inflation
Quantity theory of money
Fisher hypothesis
Hyperinflation
Flight from money
Nominal and real interest rates
Long-run Phillips curve
Short-run Phillips curve
Stagflation
Credibility
Monetary accommodation
Expected and unexpected inflation
Tax-based incomes policy
Shoe-leather costs of inflation
Menu costs of inflation
Incomes policy
Indexation

Problems

1

1988	M1 GROWTH	INFLATION
	%	%
France	2.4	2.7
Japan	8.4	0.7
Germany	9.8	1.2
UK	18.0	4.9
USA	4.3	4.1
Italy	8.0	5.0

Source: IMF, *World Economy Outlook.*

(*a*) How do you explain the data shown above? (*b*) Is inflation always a monetary phenomenon?

2 Suppose your real income is constant. This year you earn £10 000 and want to borrow £20 000 for ten years to buy a house, paying all the money back at the end. Make a list of your annual incomings and outgoings for each of these years if inflation is zero and the nominal interest rate is 2 per cent a year. Repeat the exercise when inflation is 10 per cent a year and the nominal interest rate is 12 per cent a year. Are the two situations the same?

3 Does your answer to question 2 explain why voters mind about high inflation even when nominal interest rates rise in line with inflation?

4 Looking at data on inflation and unemployment over ten years, could you tell the difference between supply shocks and demand shocks?

5 Name five groups which lose out during inflation. Does it matter whether this inflation was anticipated?

6 How much of the popular dislike of inflation do you think is due to illusion?

7 Common Fallacies Show why the following statements are incorrect. (*a*) Getting inflation down is the only way to cure high unemployment. (*b*) Inflation stops people saving. (*c*) Inflation stops people investing. (*d*) Without a budget deficit, there could be no inflation.

29

Open Economy Macroeconomics

Exports and imports are each about 10 per cent of the size of GNP in the United States, 20 per cent in Japan, and 30 per cent in the UK, France, and West Germany. Even in the United States, the exchange rate, international competitiveness, and the trade deficit were major issues in the 1980s. International considerations will be even more important in more open economies such as the UK, Germany, and Japan.

Open economy macroeconomics is the study of economies in which international transactions play a significant role.

In the early 1980s, President Mitterrand was elected in France on a programme of domestic expansion to reduce high unemployment. The international value of the French franc quickly fell on the foreign exchange market and the French government was forced to abandon its plans for domestic expansion. The large UK trade deficit of the late 1980s led to calls for high interest rates to cut back UK consumption and imports. International considerations have a major role in the formulation of domestic macroeconomic policy in open economies.

In this chapter we show how international transactions affect the domestic economy. We shall see that the effects of monetary and fiscal policy are very different in an open economy from the effects we discussed in a closed economy. The international environment is not merely an afterthought which can conveniently be discussed separately from macroeconomics: in open economies it is intrinsic to the way these economies work. That is why we discuss these issues in Part 4. The wider issues of how the world economy behaves as a system will be examined in Part 5.

To discuss the macroeconomics of a single economy we must first study the international framework in which domestic policies operate. We begin by examining the foreign exchange market in which one national currency can be converted into another.

29-1 The Foreign Exchange Market

Different countries use different national monies or currencies. In the UK, goods, services, and assets are bought and sold in exchange for pounds sterling; in the United States they are bought and sold in exchange for dollars.

The *foreign exchange market* is the international market in which one national currency can be exchanged for another. The price at which the two currencies exchange is called the *exchange rate*.

For UK residents, an exchange rate of $2/£ measures the international value of sterling; the number of units of foreign currency (dollars) that exchange for one unit of the domestic currency (pounds).[1]

As in any market, the equilibrium price depends on supply and demand. If there are only two countries, the UK and the United States, who is bringing a supply of dollars to the foreign exchange market wishing to exchange them into pounds? This demand for pounds comes from two sources. First, with regard to goods produced in Britain for sale in the United States, American consumers pay in dollars but British producers want to be paid in pounds. Second, American residents wishing to buy British assets (shares in ICI or UK Treasury bills) must convert their dollars into pounds

---

[1] With many foreign currencies – US dollars ($), German Deutschmarks (DM), French francs (FF), and Japanese yen (Y) – sterling's *effective exchange rate* is an index of its international value, an average of the $/£, DM/£, FF/£, and Y/£ exchange rates, weighted by the relative importance of each country in Britain's international trading transactions.

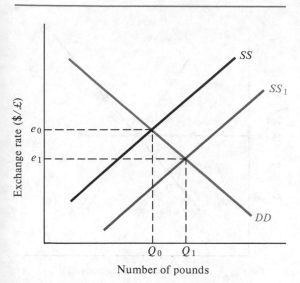

Figure 29-1 THE FOREIGN EXCHANGE
MARKET. The demand schedule *DD* shows the
demand for pounds by Americans wanting to buy
British goods or assets. The supply schedule *SS*
shows the supply of pounds by British residents
wishing to buy American goods or assets. The
equilibrium exchange rate is e_0. If British residents
want more dollars at each exchange rate, the supply
of pounds will shift from *SS* to SS_1 and the
equilibrium international value of the pound will
depreciate from e_0 to e_1.

larger quantity of pounds is demanded at a
lower dollar–sterling exchange rate.

The supply schedule for pounds, *SS*, depends
on the quantity of dollars UK residents require
to pay for UK imports or purchases of dollar
assets. Suppose a holiday in Florida costs $600:
at $2/£ it costs £300, but at $1.50/£ it costs
£400. A lower $/£ exchange rate increases the
price in pounds, and reduces the *quantity* of
Florida holidays demanded by UK residents.
Whether it reduces the number of pounds spent
depends on the elasticity of demand.

In Figure 29-1 we assume that the demand for
Florida holidays and other British imports is
price-elastic. Thus, a rise in the sterling price
reduces both the quantity demanded *and* the
total spending in pounds on such goods and
services. A lower exchange rate reduces the
quantity of pounds supplied to the foreign
exchange market. The supply schedule *SS*
slopes upward. However, if the British demand
for American goods, services, and assets
were price inelastic, a lower exchange rate and
higher sterling price would actually increase
sterling spending on these things, and the
supply schedule of pounds to the foreign
exchange market would slope downwards.[2]

In the figure the equilibrium exchange rate
is e_0 at which the quantity of pounds supplied
and demanded is equal. What would change
this equilibrium rate? If, at each sterling price,
the demand by Americans for British goods or
assets increases, the demand schedule for
pounds, *DD*, will shift to the right, increasing
the equilibrium dollar–sterling exchange rate.
Similarly, if the British demand for goods and
assets denominated in dollars is reduced at each
sterling price, the supply schedule for pounds,
SS, will shift to the left, and the equilibrium
dollar–sterling exchange rate will again increase.

When the dollar–sterling exchange rate
increases we say the pound has *appreciated*,
because the international value of sterling has
risen. Conversely, when the dollar–pound
exchange rate falls we say that the pound has
depreciated, because its international value is
reduced.

before these assets can be purchased. Conversely, a supply of pounds arises from UK
imports of goods produced in the United States,
and from UK residents wishing to purchase
assets in the United States.

Figure 29-1 shows the supply and demand for
pounds in the foreign exchange market. We
begin with the demand. Suppose the UK
produces whisky at £8 a bottle. At $2/£, a bottle
of whisky costs $16, but at $1.50/£ it costs only
$12. Hence at a lower exchange rate, and a
lower dollar price of whisky and other UK
goods, the UK will export a larger quantity of
goods to the United States, since American
consumers will buy more at a lower dollar
price.

If the price in pounds of British goods
remains constant, UK export revenue in pounds
must increase as the exchange rate falls. Since
the export revenue is initially earned in dollars
which must subsequently be converted into
pounds, Figure 29-1 shows that the demand
schedule for pounds, *DD*, slopes downward. A

---

[2] The supply and demand for cars refers to physical quantities
supplied or demanded at each price. However, the supply and
demand schedules for pounds sterling refer to *values* of pounds
supplied and demanded at each exchange rate. That is why
the analysis is a bit more tricky than the analysis of the supply
and demand for physical goods such as cars.

Alternative Exchange Rate Regimes

An *exchange rate regime* is a description of the conditions under which national governments allow exchange rates to be determined.

In Chapter 33 we discuss the different exchange rate regimes that have been adopted to handle international transactions in the world economy. Here we concentrate on the two extreme cases. These cases allow us to grasp the basics of how the macroeconomics of an open economy differs from the macroeconomics of a closed economy.

Fixed Exchange Rates   In a fixed exchange rate regime, national governments agree to maintain the convertibility of their currency at a fixed exchange rate.

A currency is *convertible* if the government acting through the central bank, agrees to buy or sell as much of the currency as people wish to trade at the fixed exchange rate.

Suppose in Figure 29-2 the dollar–pound exchange rate is fixed at e_1. For example, between 1949 and 1967 the dollar–pound exchange rate was fixed at \$2.80/£. In Figure 29-2 the fixed exchange rate e_1 would be the free market equilibrium rate if the supply schedule were *SS* and the demand schedule *DD*. With neither an excess supply of pounds nor an excess demand for pounds, nobody would be wanting to buy or sell pounds to the central bank. The market would clear on its own.

Suppose now that the demand for pounds shifts from *DD* to DD_1.[3] Americans get hooked on whisky and need more pounds to pay for extra imports of whisky from the UK. In a free market, the equilibrium point would now be *B* and the pound would appreciate against the dollar. At the fixed exchange rate e_1 there is an excess demand for pounds equal to *AC*. Since the currency is convertible at this exchange rate, this excess demand is satisfied by people turning up at the Bank of England and demanding *AC* pounds which the Bank is committed to supply on demand.

The Bank prints *AC* additional pounds and sells them in exchange for e_1 times *AC* dollars,

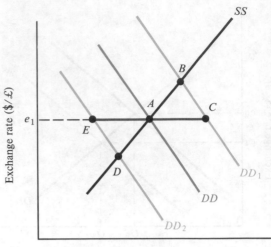

Figure 29-2   CENTRAL BANK INTERVENTION IN THE FOREIGN EXCHANGE MARKET. Suppose the exchange rate is fixed at e_1. When demand for pounds is DD_1, there is an excess demand *AC*. The Bank of England intervenes by supplying *AC* pounds in exchange for dollars, which are added to the UK foreign exchange reserves. When demand is DD_2, the Bank sells off some of the foreign exchange reserves in exchange for pounds. It demands *EA* pounds to offset the excess supply *EA* at the exchange rate e_1. When demand is *DD*, the market clears at the exchange rate e_1 and no intervention by the Bank is required.

which are added to the UK foreign exchange reserves held at the Bank of England.

The *foreign exchange reserves* are the stock of foreign currency held by the domestic central bank.

Now suppose the demand schedule for pounds shifts to the left to the position DD_2. Few foreigners want British goods or assets, and the demand for pounds is correspondingly low. The free market equilibrium exchange rate would lie below e_1 in the absence of any intervention by the central bank. However, the central bank is committed to defending the fixed exchange rate e_1. At this rate, there is an excess supply of pounds *EA*. Because the currency is convertible, the central bank must demand *EA* pounds, which it pays for by selling off a quantity *EA* times e_1 dollars from the foreign exchange reserves. If *EA* equals £1 million and e_1 equals \$2/£, the Bank of England must run down Britain's foreign exchange reserves

---

[3] Although we discuss only shifts in the demand schedule, similar considerations apply when the supply schedule shifts.

by \$2 million to increase the demand for pounds by £1 million and eliminate the excess supply. Whenever the central bank is forced to buy or sell pounds to support the fixed exchange rate, we say that the central bank *intervenes* in the foreign exchange market.

If the demand for pounds fluctuates between DD_1 and DD_2, the Bank of England will be able to sustain the exchange rate e_1 in the long run. When the demand schedule is DD_1 the UK will be adding to its foreign exchange reserves, but when the schedule is DD_2 it will be running down its foreign exchange reserves. In the long run, the UK will neither run out of foreign exchange reserves nor accumulate reserves indefinitely.

However, if the demand for pounds on average is DD_2, on average the Bank will be running down the UK foreign exchange reserves to support the pound at e_1. Under these circumstances, we say that the pound is *overvalued*, or at a higher international value than is warranted by its long-run equilibrium position. As reserves start to run out, the government may try to borrow foreign exchange reserves from the International Monetary Fund (IMF), an international body which exists primarily to lend to countries in short-term difficulties. But at best this is only a temporary solution. Unless the demand for pounds increases in the long run, it will be necessary to *devalue* the pound.

In a fixed exchange rate regime, a *devaluation (revaluation)* is a reduction (increase) in the exchange rate that governments commit themselves to maintain.

Thus, in November 1967 the UK government, after consultations with other governments, devalued the pound from \$2.80/£ to \$2.40/£.

Floating Exchanges Rates　In a floating exchange rate regime, the exchange rate is allowed to attain its free market equilibrium level *without* any government invervention through transactions that increase or reduce the foreign exchange reserves. Thus, in Figure 29-2 the demand schedule shifts from DD_2 to DD to DD_1 would be allowed to move the equilibrium point from D to A to B.

Of course, it is not necessary to adopt the extreme regimes of pure or clean floating on the one hand and perfectly fixed exchange rates on the other hand. *Dirty floating* describes a regime in which intervention is used to offset large and rapid shifts in supply or demand schedules in the short run, but where the exchange rate is gradually allowed to find its equilibrium level in the longer run. Similarly, the European Monetary System (EMS) is a fixed exchange rate regime in which the overvaluation or undervaluation of particular currencies leads quickly to a devaluation or revaluation. We discuss the EMS in detail in Chapter 33.

Although there are many kinds of exchange rate regime, if we understand the implications of the two polar cases – fixed exchange rates and freely floating exchange rates – we shall be well equipped to understand how the intermediate cases would work. Before studying macroeconomics under each of these regimes, we explain the framework of balance of payments accounting.

29-2 The Balance of Payments

The *balance of payments* is a systematic record of all transactions between residents of one country and the rest of the world.

Taking the UK as the domestic country and the United States as the 'rest of the world', all international transactions that give rise to an inflow of pounds to the UK are entered as credits in the UK balance of payments accounts. Outflows of pounds are shown as debits, and are entered with a minus sign. Similarly, inflows of dollars to the United States are credits in the US balance of payments accounts but outflows are debits. Table 29-1 shows the actual UK balance of payments accounts with the rest of the world in 1988.

We begin with the current account.

The *current account* of the balance of payments records international flows of goods and services, and other net income from abroad.

Visible trade refers to exports and imports of goods (cars, food, steel). *Invisible trade* refers to exports and imports of services (banking, shipping, tourism). Together, these make up the *trade balance* or net exports of goods and services. In Chapter 20 we discussed net exports and the definition of GDP in an open economy, and in Chapter 22 we began the analysis of how net exports affect aggregate demand.

However, the trade balance is not identical to the current account on the balance of payments. We must also take account of transfer payments between countries (foreign aid, the budget contribution to the European Community) and of the net flow of property income (interest, profits, dividends) which arises when residents of one country own income-earning assets in another country. In Chapter 20 we showed that the flow of net property income leads to a discrepancy between GDP and GNP.

Table 29-1 combines exports of services with transfer payments and property income received from abroad to give total credits from invisibles as £87.5 billion. Similarly, we combine imports of services with transfer payments and property income paid to foreigners to obtain total debits on invisibles of −£81.3 billion. Combining visibles and invisibles, the UK's current account on the balance of payments was £14.6 billion in deficit in 1988, measuring net exports of goods and services, plus net transfers and property income from abroad.

Now we turn to transactions on the capital account of the balance of payments.

> The *capital account* of the balance of payments records international transactions in financial assets.

Table 29-1 shows that net investment in the UK was −£10.6 billion in 1988. The outflow of money from the UK to buy factories or shares in companies abroad exceeded the inflow of money to the UK as foreigners bought factories or shares in companies in the UK. The second entry on the capital account shows all other net transactions in financial assets. Foreign money flowing into UK bank accounts in sterling or being used to purchase British government bills and bonds exceeded corresponding outflows from the UK to acquire financial assets abroad. Hence we show a net inflow of £17.5 billion. Adding together the items from net investment, and other net transactions in financial assets, we obtain a net inflow of £6.9 billion on the capital account of the UK balance of payments in 1988. The UK capital account was in *surplus* in 1989.

The balancing item is a statistical adjustment, which would be zero if all previous items

Table 29-1 UK balance of payments, 1988 (£ billions)

Visible exports	80.8
Visible imports	−101.6
Invisibles: credits	87.5
debits	−81.3
(1) UK CURRENT ACCOUNT	−14.6
Net investment in the UK	−10.6
Net financial transactions	17.5
(2) UK CAPITAL ACCOUNT	6.9
(3) Balancing item	10.6
(4) UK BALANCE OF PAYMENTS ((1) + (2) + (3))	2.9
(5) Official financing	−2.9

Source: CSO, *Monthly Digest of Statistics.*

had been correctly measured. It reflects a failure to record all transactions in the official statistics. Estimating implicit changes in the value of foreign investments, which the statistics treat as money reinvested abroad, is particularly tricky. Adding together the current account (1), the capital account (2), and the adjustment (3) required to measure (1) and (2) properly, we obtain the UK *balance of payments* in 1988.

The balance of payments shows the net inflow of money to the country when individuals, firms, and the government make the transactions they wish to undertake under existing market conditions. It is in surplus (deficit) when there is a net inflow of money (outflow of money). It takes account of the transactions that individuals wish to make in importing and exporting and in buying and selling foreign assets, and the amount of transactions that governments wish to make in the form of foreign aid (transfer payments to foreigners), military spending (maintaining military bases abroad), and so on.

The final entry in Table 29-1 is *official financing*. This is *always* of equal magnitude and opposite sign to the balance of payments in the line above, so that the sum of all the entries in Table 29-1 is always zero. Official financing measures the international transactions that the government must take to *accommodate* all the other transactions shown in the balance of payments accounts. What is this official financing?

Floating Exchange Rates

Suppose first that the exchange rate is freely floating and there is no government intervention in the foreign exchange market. The government is neither adding to nor running down the foreign exchange reserves. The exchange rate adjusts to equate the supply of pounds and the demand for pounds in the foreign exchange market.

The supply of pounds arises from imports to the UK or purchases of foreign assets by UK residents. It measures the outflows from the UK, the negative items on the balance of payments accounts of the UK. Conversely, the demand for pounds arises from UK exports and purchases of UK assets by foreigners, and measures the inflows to the UK, the positive items on the UK balance of payments accounts. With a freely floating exchange rate, the quantities of pounds supplied and demanded are equal. Hence inflows equal outflows and the balance of payments is exactly zero. There is no government intervention in the foreign exchange market and no official financing.

Since the balance of payments is the sum of the current account and the capital account, under floating exchange rates a current account surplus must be exactly matched by a capital account deficit, or vice versa. What is true for the country as a whole is also true for an individual. Think of your own balance of payments account with all other individuals. If your income exceeds your spending, you run a current account surplus in your transactions with other people. This surplus adds to your assets. You add to your cash balances or your bank account, or buy shares or property. The increase in your asset holdings matches the excess of your income over your spending.

Similarly, for the country as a whole a current account surplus, or net inflow from abroad, must be matched by an increase in the country's holding of foreign assets. Since the government is not adding to the foreign exchange reserves, this must show up in the capital account as a capital account deficit exactly matching the current account surplus. The capital account deficit shows the outflow of money as domestic residents add to their holding of foreign assets. The balance of payments, the sum of the current and capital accounts of the balance of payments, must be zero when there is a freely floating exchange rate.

Fixed Exchange Rates

When there is a fixed exchange rate, the balance of payments need not be zero. When there is a balance of payments deficit, total outflows exceed total inflows on the combined current and capital accounts. How is this deficit financed?

Since there is a balance of payments deficit, the supply of pounds to the foreign exchange market, corresponding to the wish to import or acquire foreign assets, exceeds the demand for pounds, corresponding to the wish to export or the desire of foreigners to acquire domestic assets. Hence the balance of payments deficit is exactly the same as the excess supply of pounds in the foreign exchange market.

To maintain the fixed exchange rate, the central bank has to offset this excess supply of pounds by demanding an equivalent quantity of pounds. The central bank runs down the foreign exchange reserves, selling dollars to buy pounds. In the balance of payments accounts this shows up as 'official financing'. In 1988 the UK had to acquire £2.9 billion of foreign exchange reserves to offset the balance of payments surplus shown as £2.9 billion in the second-last line of Table 29.1. Conversely, when there is a balance of payments deficit, the government is intervening in the foreign exchange market by selling foreign exchange reserves.

Thus we deduce from Table 29.1 that, although the UK officially was pursuing a floating exchange rate regime in 1988, in fact the Bank of England did intervene a bit in the foreign exchange market. On average, it was buying foreign exchange and selling pounds, thus maintaining the exchange rate at a slightly lower level than would have been observed under a completely free float.

Summary

Inclusive of official financing, the balance of payments accounts must sum to zero, just as the foreign exchange market must clear inclusive of central bank intervention using the foreign exchange reserves. A current account surplus must be met either by a capital account deficit or by allowing the foreign exchange reserves to increase. A current account deficit must be met either by a capital account surplus or by running down the foreign exchange reserves. Either way, a current account surplus is matched by an increase in foreign assets held and a current account deficit is matched by a reduction in foreign assets held.

From these consolidated accounts, the balance of payments is the part of the accounts dealing with individual, company, and government transactions *before* official financing and changes in the foreign exchange reserves are taken into account. When the exchange rate is freely floating, intervention is zero, the foreign exchange reserves are constant, and official financing is zero. Since the consolidated accounts inclusive of official financing always sum to zero, the balance of payments must be zero when the exchange rate floats freely.

29-3 The Components of the Balance of Payments

In this section we discuss the determinants of the items on the current and capital accounts of the balance of payments. Then we briefly consider the relative importance of the two accounts in the short run and the long run. First, we introduce the concept of the real exchange rate.

The Real Exchange Rate and International Competitiveness

In 1975, the dollar–sterling exchange rate was \$2.22/£; in 1989 it was only \$1.63/£. Similarly, sterling's effective exchange rate measuring the international value of sterling against all other currencies – an index in which the \$/£ and DM/£ are the most important exchange rates, reflecting the pattern of Britain's international trade – fell from 100 in 1975 to 72 in 1989.

Since a fall in the international value of sterling makes British goods cheaper in foreign currencies and foreign goods more expensive in pounds, this change in the sterling exchange rate tended to increase the quantity of British exports and reduce the quantity of goods imported to Britain. Right?

Not necessarily. Britain had a higher inflation rate during these years than most of its trading partners. Whether British goods became more or less competitive in world markets depends on whether the increase in Britain's competitiveness arising from a fall in the nominal or actual exchange rate was larger than the reduction in Britain's international competitiveness because the domestic price of British goods was rising faster than prices in other countries. Once again, we must distinguish nominal and real variables.

International competitiveness is measured by the real exchange rate.

The *real exchange rate* measures the relative price of goods from different countries when measured in a common currency.

Suppose a shirt can be produced for \$10 in the United States and for £6 in the UK. At the nominal exchange rate of \$2/£, the relative price of UK to US shirts, when measured in a common currency, is 6/5, whether we compare the relative dollar price of shirts (\$12/\$10) or the relative price in pounds (£6/£5). Two things can make UK shirts more competitive with US shirts. An exchange rate depreciation, say from £2/£ to £1.50/£, would change the relative price of UK to US shirts from 6/5 to 9/10, making UK shirts relatively cheaper. Equally, however, at the original nominal exchange rate of \$2/£ a reduction in the domestic price of UK shirts from £6 to £4.50 would also change the relative price of shirts in a common currency from 6/5 to 9/10.

Suppose we measure the real exchange rate by comparing dollar prices of goods produced in the two countries. The shirt example shows that we can define the UK's real exchange rate as

$$\text{Real exchange rate} = \frac{\text{£ price of UK goods}}{\text{\$ price of US goods}} \times (\text{\$/£ exchange rate}) \quad (1)$$

An increase in the real exchange rate, by increasing the price of UK goods relative to US goods when measured in the same currency, makes the UK less competitive relative to the United States. Conversely, a fall in the UK's real exchange rate makes the UK more competitive in international markets.

Table 29-2 shows how this works out in

practice. The first row shows the nominal dollar–sterling exchange rate in 1976, 1982, and 1989. Looking at this rate, we might be tempted to conclude that UK competitiveness relative to the United States had increased between 1976 and 1982. The second and third rows show what happened to the price level in each country over the period. The fourth row calculates an index of the real exchange rate, using the formula of equation (1). For example, to calculate the 1976 value we multiply the price index of UK goods, 59, by the nominal exchange rate, 1.81, and then divide by the US price index, 69. Table 29-2 shows that the real exchange rate for the UK increased from 1.56 to 1.82 over the period. UK goods became significantly less competitive because in a common currency their price increased relative to the price of US goods. The fall in the nominal exchange rate from $1.81/£ to $1.75/£ was not sufficient to offset the much higher increase in the domestic price of UK goods relative to the domestic price of US goods over the period. Nor by 1989 were UK goods more competitive than in 1982. The real exchange rate had risen to $1.90/£.

How much would the nominal exchange rate have had to change to maintain a constant real exchange rate and level of international competitiveness over the period?

> The *purchasing power parity* (PPP) exchange rate path is the path of the nominal exchange rate that would keep the real exchange rate constant over a given period.

Table 29-2 shows that in 1982 UK prices were 2.04 times their 1976 level, whereas US prices were only 1.70 times their 1976 level. Using equation (1), we see that the nominal exchange rate would have to fall to 1.70/2.04 (=0.833)

of its 1976 level to offset the change in relative domestic prices and maintain a constant real exchange rate. Hence in the last row of Table 29-2 we show that the nominal exchange rate would have had to fall to $1.50/£ (=0.833 × $1.81/£) in 1982 if the real exchange rate were to remain at its 1976 level. You can check for yourself that the nominal exchange rate of $1.50/£ would lead to a real exchange rate of 1.56 when the formula of equation (1) is applied to the price data shown for 1982 in Table 29-2.

Similarly, by 1989 the PPP exchange rate was $1.33/£.

The Current Account

Exports   When we introduced the open economy in Chapter 22 we made the simple assumption that export demand for domestic goods and services was given. We now recognize that the demand for UK exports will be influenced chiefly by two things. First, the higher the level of income in the rest of the world, the higher will be the demand for UK exports. Second, the lower the UK's real exchange rate and the higher the level of UK competitiveness in world markets, the higher will be the demand for UK exports.

Although actual exports usually respond quickly to changes in the level of world income or world trade, a reduction in competitiveness is likely to reduce exports only gradually. Why? Because exporters may be unsure whether the decline in competitiveness is temporary or permanent. If they believe it to be temporary, British exports may cut their prices to remain competitive in world markets. Even though this may mean losses in the short run, it may be cheaper in the long run than temporarily withdrawing from those markets and having to spend large sums on advertising and marketing to win back market shares when competitiveness improves again. But if competitiveness fails to improve and the real exchange rate remains high, firms will gradually conclude that the long-run prospects are bleak, and some firms will permanently withdraw from the exporting business.

Imports   For imports we simply tell the same story in reverse. Import demand will be larger the higher is the level of domestic income, the

Table 29-2 Nominal and real exchange rates

	1976	1982	1989
$/£	1.81	1.75	1.63
Prices (1980 = 100)			
UK	59	121	175
US	69	117	150
Real $/£ rate	1.56	1.82	1.90
PPP nominal rate	1.81	1.50	1.33

Source: IMF, International Financial Statistics.

relationship we recognized in Chapter 22 through the marginal propensity to import. But import demand will also be larger the higher is the real exchange rate and the cheaper are foreign goods relative to domestic goods when both are measured in the domestic currency. Again, in practice, imports respond more quickly to changes in domestic income than to changes in the real exchange rate. However, if sustained, a change in the real exchange rate will eventually have significant effects on the level of imports as well as exports.

Other Items on the Current Account Other items include foreign aid and spending on military bases abroad. These are matters of government policy. Also on the current account we include the net flow of interest, dividend, and profit income between countries, which arises because residents of one country hold assets in another. The size of this net flow of income depends on the pattern of international asset-holding and on the level of interest rates, profits, and dividends at home and abroad. In practice, these other items on the current account are usually relatively unimportant.

We now turn to items on the capital account of the balance of payments.

Capital Account Items

These arise through international purchases and sales of assets, and have become increasingly important since 1945 for two reasons. First, computers and telecommunications have made it simple for residents of one country to undertake asset transactions in the financial markets of another. It is almost as easy for a British resident to transact in the financial markets of New York, Frankfurt, Zurich, Tokyo, and Hong Kong as it is in London. Second, the elaborate system of controls, restricting international transactions on the capital account, have gradually been dismantled since 1945.

One important reason for the end of restrictions on capital account flows has been the rise of OPEC. After the sharp oil price rise of 1973, OPEC ran a massive current account surplus and the industrial West a massive current account deficit. The West needed to import expensive oil at a faster rate than

OPEC countries could spend money on imports from the West. With relatively small populations, OPEC countries such as Kuwait could only build so many roads and hospitals requiring inputs from the West.

Since a current account deficit must be matched by a capital account surplus (purchases of domestic assets by foreigners) or by official financing (running down foreign exchange reserves), in practice the West had little option but to meet huge current account deficits by encouraging OPEC to purchase large quantities of assets in the West, thereby providing the capital account inflow to meet the West's current account outflow.

Thus the world's financial markets now have two crucial features. First, capital account restrictions have been almost entirely abolished. Funds can be freely moved from one country to another in search of the highest rate of return. Second, there are billions and billions of pounds that are internationally footloose and capable of being switched between countries and currencies when assets in one currency seem to offer a higher rate of return than assets elsewhere. If the owners of these funds are prepared to transfer them entirely to the currency in which assets seem to offer the highest rate of return, and if there are no obstacles to such transfers, we say that international financial capital is 'perfectly mobile' between countries.

Perfect capital mobility means that an enormous quantity of funds will be transferred from one currency to another whenever the rate of return on assets in one country is higher than the rate of return in another.

Since the stock of international funds held by OPEC, large multinational companies and others is now so large, in principle the movement of these funds from one country to another could lead to capital account flows that would swamp the typical flows of imports and exports we observe on the current account.

Speculation and the Rate of Return *Speculation* is the purchase of an asset for subsequent resale, in the belief that the total return – interest or dividend *plus* the capital gain – will exceed the total return that can be obtained in other assets. In international asset markets, capital gains arising from changes in exchange rates form an important part of the expected rate of return on an asset. We now explain why.

Suppose you have £100 to invest for a year. Suppose UK interest rates are 10 per cent a year but interest rates in the United States are zero. Keeping your funds in pounds, you will have £110 at the end of the year. But what if you convert them into dollars at the beginning of the year, lend in dollars for a year, and then convert the money back into pounds at the end?

Suppose initially the exchange rate is $2/£. Your £100 will buy $200. At a zero interest rate you will still have $200 at the end of the year. But suppose that sterling has depreciated by 10 per cent during the year. At the end of the year the exchange rate is $1.80/£, a fall of $0.20/£ on the original rate of $2/£. Your $200 will convert back to £110 at an exchange rate of $1.80 at the end of the year. Although you get no interest by investing in dollars for a year, you make a capital gain of 10 per cent on holding dollars, whose value relative to pounds increases by 10 per cent during the year.

In this example you end up with £110 whether you lend in dollars or pounds during the year. If the pound had depreciated by more than 10 per cent (the excess of the UK interest rate over the US interest rate), the capital gain on holding dollars would actually outweigh the loss of interest, and the total return on lending in dollars rather than pounds would have been larger. Conversely, if the pound had depreciated against the dollar by less than the interest rate differential, you would have earned a higher total return by keeping your money in pounds. Equation (2) summarizes this important result. It reminds us that the total return on temporarily lending in a foreign currency is the interest rate paid on assets in that currency *plus* any capital gain (or *minus* any capital loss) arising from depreciation (appreciation) of the domestic currency during the period.

$$\begin{matrix} \text{Return on} \\ \text{foreign lending} \end{matrix} = \begin{matrix} \text{foreign interest rate} \\ + \text{ domestic currency} \\ \text{depreciation} \end{matrix} \quad (2)$$

In a world of almost perfect international capital mobility, there will be an enormous capital outflow whenever the total return on foreign lending exceeds the total return on domestic lending, then domestic interest rate. There will be an enormous capital inflow when the total return on domestic lending exceeds the return on lending abroad. And net flows on the capital account of the balance of payments will be small only when the total return on foreign lending is broadly in line with the return on lending or owning assets in the domestic currency.

Equation (2) highlights the importance of current expectations about the level of future exchange rates, for it is these that determine the capital gains or losses that people expect to make through changes in the exchange rate. It also tells us that there will be a crucial difference between a fixed exchange rate regime, in which the government commits itself to intervene to *prevent* exchange rate changes, and floating exchange rate regimes where changes in the exchange rate can become the most important element on total asset returns. For example, between January 1981 and August 1981 the dollar–sterling exchange rate fell from $2.41/£ to $1.82/£, a depreciation of 25 per cent in the value of the pound against the dollar in just seven months, a change considerably more important than the small discrepancy between interest rates in the UK and the United States.

Now that we understand the framework of balance of payments accounting and the determinants of individual components of the balance of payments, we can begin our study of macroeconomics in the open economy.

29-4 Internal and External Balance

In this section, we discuss the relation between the state of the economy – boom or recession – and the external balance or current account on the balance of payments. There is no simple relationship between booms and slumps and current account surpluses or deficits. For example, in the early 1980s Kuwait had a booming domestic economy and a large current account surplus in the aftermath of the second major OPEC oil price rise. On the other hand, the UK had a current account surplus but was in major recession at the time. Brazil and Germany had deficits coupled with recessions, but Mexico had a current account deficit coupled with a booming domestic economy. How are we to make sense of this?

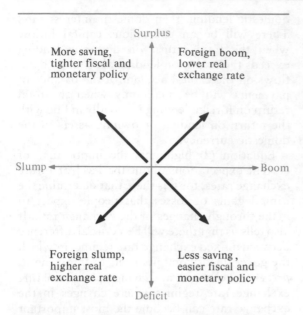

Figure 29-3   INTERNAL AND EXTERNAL BALANCE. With internal and external balance there is neither a boom nor a slump, and the current account just balances. Each quadrant of the diagram identifies shocks that cause departures from internal and external balance. For example, tight fiscal and monetary policy reduce aggregate demand, creating a domestic slump but a current account surplus since import demand is reduced. However, by increasing export demand, a foreign boom leads to both a domestic boom and a current account surplus. Other possible shocks and their consequences are shown.

Figure 29-3 shows the different combinations of boom and recessions and current account surpluses and deficits. We begin by thinking about demand and supply for domestic output. Equation (3) reminds us of the basic equation for the goods market.

$$Y = C + I + G + (X - Z) \qquad (3)$$

Domestic output Y equals aggregate demand, which arises from spending on consumption; investment; goods and services purchased by the government; and net exports, that is the excess of exports X over imports Z. If aggregate demand for domestic output equals the level of potential output, firms produce the full-employment output level and in the labour market demand as much employment as workers wish to supply.

A country is in *internal balance* when aggregate demand is at the full-employment level.

With sluggish wage and price adjustment, a lower level of aggregate demand will lead firms to cut back output and sack workers, creating involuntary unemployment. Only when wages and prices have fallen sufficiently to restore aggregate demand to its full-employment level will internal balance be re-established.

A country is in *external balance* when the current account of the balance of payments just balances.

In the absence of government intervention in the foreign exchange market, the capital account of the balance of payments must also be in balance at this point. In Figure 29-3 the point of internal *and* external balance is the intersection of the two axes, where there is neither a boom nor a slump, and neither a current account surplus nor a deficit.

The combination of internal and external balance is the long-run equilibrium position of the economy. Wage and price adjustment have restored output to its potential level and there is full employment in the labour market. With external balance, not only is the current account in balance, but there is no long-term pressure to change the stock of foreign exchange reserves, nor any permanent flows on the capital account. Foreigners are not acquiring an ever-increasing ownership of domestic assets, nor are domestic residents acquiring ever-larger holdings of foreign assets.

Figure 29-3 shows the shocks that in the short run can move the economy away from internal and external balance. For example, the top left-hand quadrant shows a combination of domestic slump and current account surplus. This can be caused by an increase in desired savings (a downward shift in the consumption function) or by the adoption of tight fiscal and monetary policy. These tend to reduce aggregate demand, which causes both a domestic slump and a reduction in imports. Similarly, an increase in the real exchange rate, a decline in international competitiveness, will reduce export demand and increase import demand. The fall in net exports will cause both a current account deficit and a reduction in aggregate demand, leading to a domestic slump in output and employment, as shown in the bottom left-hand quadrant. The figure explains the shocks that move the economy into other quadrants, causing departures from both internal and external balance.

Indeed, one of the main lessons of Figure 29-3 is that most shocks in an open economy will simultaneously move the economy away from *both* internal and external balance. In studying a closed economy, we examined whether the economy could return to internal balance on its own. We concluded that it could, through price and wage adjustment, which affect the level of the real money stock and aggregate demand; but we saw that when adjustment is sluggish it is possible to use monetary and fiscal policy to speed up the process of adjustment. When the economy is in a slump, expansionary monetary and fiscal policy will hasten the return to full employment.

We now study the same questions in an open economy. Without any policy change, will the economy be able to adjust to any shock and get back to the point of both internal and external balance? And can macroeconomic policy be used to make this transition easier? Since the economy behaves very differently under fixed and floating exchange rate regimes, we shall have to analyse the two regimes separately. We begin by looking at a fixed exchange rate regime.

29-5 Monetary and Fiscal Policy under Fixed Exchange Rates

It is useful first to discuss in greater detail the long-run equilibrium position of internal and external balance, using equation (3). Domestic output Y must be at its full-employment level. Given external balance, net exports $X - Z$ must be zero. Hence monetary and fiscal policy must ensure that domestic demand – sometimes called *domestic absorption* – that is, the desired level of spending on $C + I + G$, must just equal full employment output Y. Given this output level, and given the level of real income in the rest of the world, there is a unique real exchange rate that equates the demand for exports and imports. At a higher real exchange rate, or lower level of international competitiveness, import demand will exceed export demand. At a lower real exchange rate net export demand will be positive. Hence there is only one real exchange rate compatible with internal and external balance.

Under a fixed exchange rate regime, governments are committed to intervention in the foreign exchange market to maintain a given *nominal* exchange rate. Immediately, we reach one important conclusion: under a fixed exchange rate regime, internal and external balance is possible only if the domestic and foreign inflation rates are equal. Otherwise the real exchange rate would be changing in the long run and exports would be changing relative to imports.

The Balance of Payments and the Money Supply

We now highlight one of the key mechanisms through which external balance is restored when the economy is not in long-run equilibrium. Suppose the economy is running a balance of payments deficit. Two things are happening. First, on average, private individuals are withdrawing money from circulation. They need this money to acquire the foreign exchange with which to purchase foreign goods and assets. The domestic money supply is being reduced by exactly the amount of the balance of payments deficit.

Second, the government is intervening in the foreign exchange market. The balance of payments deficit is exactly matched by official financing, as we saw earlier in the chapter. The government is selling foreign exchange reserves, thereby supplying foreign currency to the market. In exchange, the central bank is obtaining pounds sterling which effectively have been withdrawn from circulation.

Thus, under fixed exchange rates, the money supply is not determined exclusively by the original decision of the government about how much money to print. When the economy has a balance of payments deficit, the monetary outflow will be reducing the domestic money supply below the value it would otherwise have attained. Conversely, with a surplus on the balance of payments, the domestic money in circulation will be augmented by the inflow of money from abroad. Exporters will be converting their earnings from foreign currency into pounds and paying this money into the domestic banking system.

Suppose the government does not wish the domestic money supply to be reduced when there is a balance of payments deficit. Can anything be done? The government can try to *sterilize* the domestic money supply.

> *Sterilization* is an open market operation between domestic money and domestic bonds the sole purpose of which is to neutralize the tendency of balance of payments surpluses and deficits to change the domestic money supply.

Thus, if a balance of payments deficit is causing a reduction in the domestic money supply, the government can instruct the central bank to buy domestic bonds in exchange for money, thereby replenishing the domestic money supply. Although the money supply is unchanged, the government now has fewer outstanding bonds and fewer foreign exchange reserves, which were used for official financing of the payments deficit. Thus perfect sterilization essentially involves swapping domestic bonds for foreign exchange reserves.

Adjustment under Fixed Policies

In this section we consider how the economy adjusts to a shock when the government takes no monetary or fiscal action to accommodate the shock. Initially we examine a domestic shock. What happens when there is an increase in the desire to save, and a reduction in desired consumption spending at each output level? With an unchanged money supply and fiscal policy, in a closed economy an initial recession would gradually lead to falls in wages and prices which would increase the real money supply, reduce interest rates, and restore aggregate demand to its full-employment level.

How does the adjustment process differ in an open economy, when the government maintains a fixed nominal exchange rate and when there is almost perfect international capital mobility? Under a fixed exchange rate regime, we can ignore changes in exchange rates.

When desired consumption demand falls, there is a domestic slump. Income falls, and hence import demand falls. There is a current account surplus. However, this is swamped by what happens on the capital account. At the original money supply and price level, the fall in income reduces the demand for money and tends to reduce interest rates. This immediately induces a capital account outflow. Together,

the current and capital accounts are in deficit until monetary outflow reduces the domestic money supply sufficiently to restore interest rates to the level of foreign interest rates, at which point there is no further pressure for outflows on the capital account of the balance of payments.

Gradually, the domestic slump puts downward pressure on wages and prices at home, thereby increasing international competitiveness and net exports $(X - Z)$. Unlike the situation in the closed economy, where falling prices and wages increase aggregate demand by reducing interest rates, in the open economy, with perfect international capital mobility, interest rates are pegged at world levels and falling domestic prices increase aggregate demand by increasing international competitiveness and net exports.

Thus an initial fall in domestic absorption $(C + I + G)$ eventually leads to a sufficient price fall to increase net exports $(X - Z)$ to the point at which domestic absorption plus net exports equals potential output. Internal balance has been reestablished. However, there is now a current account surplus. Induced price changes alone cannot restore both internal and external balance.

In the long run, external balance requires that net exports are zero. Hence full equilibrium can be restored only if domestic absorption returns to its full-employment level. But perfect capital mobility pegs interest rates at world levels. Moreover, the real money supply M/P must equal real money demand $L(Y, r)$, which is fixed by the full-employment income level Y and the level of world interest rates r. Monetary policy cannot affect the real money supply in the long run. Hence the *only* way that the economy can return to internal and external balance is if fiscal policy is used to increase $(C + I + G)$ to offset the reduction in desired consumption. Either government spending must be increased, or tax cuts must be used to boost consumption and investment spending. Unlike the situation in a closed economy, there is no *automatic* mechanism to restore full equilibrium in the long run.

A Shock From Abroad   When the shock comes from abroad, the conclusion is rather different. Suppose that higher foreign income increases the demand for our exports. The current account $(X - Z)$ moves into surplus. By increasing aggregate demand and output, the demand for money is increased and domestic interest rates must rise. This leads to an immediate inflow on the capital account as international investors move in funds to take advantage of higher interest rates. The inflow continues until the balance of payments surplus has sufficiently increased the domestic money supply to restore interest rates to world levels.

With sluggish price adjustment, the monetary inflow increases the domestic real money supply in line with the higher demand for real money balances. Rising interest rates do not choke off the increase in aggregate demand caused by the increase in export demand. In the longer run, higher aggregate demand gradually bids up prices and wages, reducing international competitiveness since the nominal exchange rate is fixed. When international competitiveness has been sufficiently eroded to reduce exports and increase imports to the point at which net exports are zero, both internal and external balance are restored. Induced adjustment of wages and prices *can* eventually cope with shocks from abroad.

Thus far, we have assumed that the government does not respond to shocks by adjusting monetary and fiscal policy. We now examine the effects of changes in these policies under fixed exchange rates and when there is perfect or almost perfect international capital mobility.

Monetary Policy under Fixed Exchange Rates

When price adjustment is sluggish, an increase in the nominal money supply increases the real money supply in the short run, and tends to reduce domestic interest rates. With perfect capital mobility, this leads to a capital account outflow until the domestic money supply has been reduced to its original level and interest rates have returned to world levels. Hence domestic policy is powerless in a fixed exchange rate regime when capital mobility is perfect.

Perfect capital mobility means that the government cannot fix independent targets for both the money supply *and* the exchange rate. Under fixed exchange rates, the government has to accept the domestic money supply that makes domestic and foreign interest rates equal. Later, we shall see that the government

can fix the domestic money supply provided it allows the exchange rate to adjust freely. But it cannot fix both.

This is equivalent to the assertion that sterilization will not work. When attempts to increase the domestic money supply are frustrated by a capital account deficit and a monetary outflow, the government can try to pump yet more money into the economy. With interest rates again below world levels, owners of international funds will want to withdraw yet more money. Since these monetary outflows, and deficits on the balance of payments, require corresponding official financing through reduction in the foreign exchange reserves, the question is essentially who runs out of funds first. The assertion that sterilization won't work hinges on the fact that the volume of international funds that could be withdrawn if interest rates fall below world levels exceeds the government's foreign exchange reserves. The government will have to give up before the speculators.

Fiscal Policy under Fixed Exchange Rates

In a closed economy with sluggish price adjustment, monetary policy can change the real money supply in the short run but not in the long run. In an open economy, we have just seen that capital mobility removes even the short-run power of monetary policy to affect real variables. In contrast, in an open economy fiscal policy is *more* powerful in the short run than in a closed economy.

In a closed economy, fiscal policy leads to two kinds of crowding out. In the short run, a fiscal expansion increases output but bids up interest rates, moderating the output increase. And in the long run, higher demand bids up prices and reduces the real money stock, raising interest rates until consumption and investment demand have fallen to restore aggregate demand to its full-employment level. In an open economy, capital account flows peg interest rates at world levels and prevent induced changes in interest rates.

Hence, in the short run a fiscal expansion has a larger effect in an open economy with a fixed exchange rate. In the longer run, higher aggregate demand bids up prices and wages, reducing competitiveness and net exports. This process will continue until internal balance or full employment is restored. However, as we noted earlier, this will not be a point of external balance. In this example, there will be a current account deficit in the long run. In fact, at a given exchange rate, a given level of world income, and a given level of world interest rates, there is a unique fiscal policy compatible with both internal and external balance in the long run. The domestic price level can adjust to secure the level of competitiveness that makes imports equal exports when the domestic economy is at full employment. Internal balance then requires that potential output Y equals domestic absorption $(C + I + G)$ when interest rates are at world levels. Given private sector demands for consumption and investment, this determines the fiscal policy that the government will have to implement if the economy is to attain both internal and external balance in the long run.

Thus far, we have considered how the economy behaves at a *given* exchange rate. Now we investigate the consequences of changing the exchange rate.

29-6 Devaluation

A *devaluation* (*revaluation*) is a reduction (increase) in the exchange rate which the government commits itself to defend.

The fixed exchange rate system in operation in the 25 years after 1945 was sometimes called the *adjustable peg* system. Although exchange rates were pegged at fixed values, occasional adjustments in these values were allowed. For example, the pound sterling was devalued in 1949 and 1967. But the general idea was to keep exchange rates fixed for long periods if possible. We discuss different types of exchange rate regime more fully in Chapter 33.

In this section we assess the consequences of a devaluation. We distinguish its effects in the short run, the medium run, and the long run. Initially, we assume that the domestic country begins from internal and external balance. This allows us to highlight the effect of the devaluation itself. Then we consider whether devaluation may be the appropriate policy response to a shock that has already moved the economy from its long-run equilibrium position.

The Short-run Effect

When prices and wages adjust slowly, the immediate effect of a devaluation is to increase the domestic price of imports and to reduce the foreign price of the country's exports. Both effects improve international competitiveness. Resources will be drawn into domestic industries such as car production, which can now compete more effectively with imported cars, and will be drawn into export industries, which can now compete more effectively in foreign markets. However, there are two points to note about this short-run impact of devaluation.

First, although devaluation tends to increase the quantity of net exports $(X - Z)$, the initial response may be quite slow. Overnight, there may be a lot of contracts outstanding that were struck at the old exchange rate. Moreover, it may take purchasers some time to adjust to the new prices they face. Similarly, it may take time to build up production capacity in the domestic industries making goods for export or to substitute for goods formerly imported.

Second, and related to this, devaluation may not improve the current account in the short run. The current account of the balance of payments refers to the *value* of exports minus imports. Suppose we measure the current account in pounds. If domestic prices of export goods are unchanged and the quantity of exports has not yet increased very much, export revenues will be only a little higher in the short run. And if import quantities have not yet fallen very much, but import prices in pounds have risen by the amount of the devaluation, the value of imports in pounds may have risen substantially. In *value* terms, the current account may move into deficit in the short run.[4] However, in the longer run, as purchasers and suppliers adjust the quantities of exports and imports, higher export quantities and lower import quantities are likely both to increase the contribution of net exports $(X - Z)$ to aggregate demand and to move the current

---

[4] The famous Marshall–Lerner condition says that a devaluation will improve the current account only if the sum of the price elasticities of demand for imports and exports is more negative than -1. Recall from Chapter 5 that, when demand is elastic, the revenue effect of changes in quantity more than offset the effect of a change in price. In the short run, inelastic demand can make a devaluation worsen the current account.

account of the balance of payments into surplus.[5]

The Medium-run Effect

For convenience, we rewrite equation (3)

$$Y = (C + I + G) + (X - Z) \tag{3}$$

The supply of domestic goods Y equals aggregate demand, which comprises domestic absorption $(C + I + G)$ plus net export demand $(X - Z)$. We have seen that a devaluation increases net export demand $(X - Z)$. What happens next depends crucially on aggregate supply.

If the economy begins with Keynesian unemployment, the economy has the spare resources to produce extra goods and can meet this increase in aggregate demand. Output will increase and unemployment will fall. But if the economy begins at full-employment output, the economy as a whole cannot produce more goods. The higher aggregate demand will quickly bid up prices and wages. With higher domestic prices, the economy's international competitiveness is reduced, and net exports start to fall again. When domestic prices and wages have risen by the same percentage as that by which the exchange rate was initially devalued, the real exchange rate and the level of competitiveness have returned to their original level. If the economy began from internal and external balance, net exports have now returned to zero, and aggregate demand has been restored to the full-employment level.

If for some reason the government intended the devaluation to permanently improve the current account balance, it is necessary that the devaluation should be accompanied by fiscal policy to reduce domestic absorption. Thus, beginning at full employment, a devaluation accompanied by higher taxes will increase the demand for net exports without increasing total aggregate demand. Since there is now no upward pressure on domestic prices, the higher international competitiveness and lower exchange rate can be sustained in the medium run.

The Long-run Effect

One of the themes of modern economics is that it is real variables, not nominal variables, that matter. Can altering the nominal exchange rate permanently change the value of real variables?

Suppose a devaluation has been accompanied by tighter fiscal policy in order to reduce domestic absorption and allow the economy to meet the higher demand for net exports without any direct upward pressure on prices. Although this takes care of demand-side effects on prices, we must also think about supply-side effects. Domestic firms that import raw materials will want to pass on these cost increases in higher prices. And workers who buy imported consumer goods, from food to TV sets, will conclude that the cost of living has increased, and they will demand nominal wage increases to maintain the equilibrium value of their real wages. In turn, these price and wage increases will lead other firms and other workers to react in similar fashion.

Thus, in the absence of any real change in the economy, the eventual effect of a devaluation will be an increase in all other nominal wages and prices in line with the higher import prices, leaving all real variables unchanged. Eventually, a devaluation will have no effect. Using some of the leading computer models of the UK economy, models that try to quantify the forces at work by using econometric techniques to analyse past data, Professors Michael Artis and David Currie conclude that the effects of a sterling devaluation are almost completely offset by a rise in domestic prices and wages by the end of five years.[6]

Table 29-3 shows the effect of the sterling devaluation by 15 per cent in 1967. The first row shows that it took two years before the current account moved from deficit into surplus. As we explained, a devaluation will not improve the value of the current account until quantities of imports and exports have time to respond. In the third row we show the PSBR as a percentage of GDP, as an indicator of fiscal policy. In 1967 UK unemployment was low and the economy was close to full employment. The economy had few spare resources with which

---

[5] Thus we have established that a devaluation may lead first to a deterioration of the current account of the balance of payments but then to an improvement in the current account. Economists sometimes describe this response as the *J-curve*. As time elapses after the devaluation, the current account falls down to the bottom of the *J* but then improves and rises above its initial position.

---

[6] See M. J. Artis and D. A. Currie, 'Monetary Targets and the Exchange Rate', in W. A. Eltis and P. J. N. Sinclair (eds), *The Money Supply and the Exchange Rate*, Oxford University Press, 1981.

Table 29-3 The 1967 sterling devaluation

	1967	1968	1969	1970
Current account (£b)	−0.3	−0.2	0.5	0.8
Balance of payments (£b)	−0.7	−1.4	0.7	1.4
PSBR as % of GDP	5.3	3.4	−1.2	0
$/£	2.8	2.4	2.4	2.4
Real exchange rate (1975 = 100)	109	102	102	103

Source: CSO, Economic Trends.

to produce extra goods for export or import substitution. In 1969 fiscal policy was tightened substantially, reducing domestic absorption and allowing an improvement in net exports. The government (including the nationalized industries) actually ran a surplus in 1969.

The final row of the table shows the real exchange rate, the relative price of UK goods to foreign goods when measured in a common currency. It shows two things. First, instead of using the 15 per cent devaluation to reduce export prices in foreign currencies, UK exporters responded in part by raising prices and profit margins. Only about half the competitive advantage was passed on to foreign purchasers as lower foreign prices for UK goods. Second, even by 1970 we can see competitiveness being eroded. Domestic wages had started to rise as workers asked for cost-of-living wage increases to meet higher import prices. By 1970 the real exchange rate had begun to rise again.

Devaluation and Adjustment We have argued that a devaluation is likely to lead to a temporary but not a permanent increase in competitiveness relative to the position that would have been attained without the devaluation. In the long run, real variables are determined by real forces and changes in one nominal variable merely induce offsetting changes in other nominal variables to restore real variables to their equilibrium values. But devaluation may be the simplest way to change competitiveness quickly. It may be a useful policy when the alternative adjustment mechanism is a domestic slump and a protracted period of gradual wage and price reduction until competitiveness is increased.

Suppose the economy begins at internal and external balance. Suppose there is a real shock, a reduction in foreign demand for our exports. In the short run this leads both to a domestic slump, since the net export component of aggregate demand has fallen, and to a current account deficit, since exports have fallen below the level of imports. Before we think about adjustment, think about what will happen to the economy once long-run equilibrium has been re-established.

If internal and external balance are to be restored, competitiveness must increase. This will boost net exports, and this will both eliminate the current account imbalance and restore aggregate demand to its full-employment level. A higher level of competitiveness essentially means a reduction in domestic real wages. Hence we conclude that, when long-run equilibrium is restored, domestic real wages must be lower than in the long-run equilibrium from which we began. The real shock – a reduction in the demand for our exports – has real consequences, as we should expect.[7]

Now we can think about the adjustment mechanism that secures this real-wage reduction and increase in competitiveness to restore long-run equilibrium. In the absence of a devaluation, the fall in net exports leads to a domestic slump which gradually reduces nominal wages and domestic prices. The fall in domestic prices increases competitiveness since the nominal exchange rate is fixed. The induced increase in net exports helps eliminate the current account deficit and also boosts domestic aggregate demand. You may be thinking that lower domestic prices also stimulate aggregate demand by boosting the real money supply, but it must be remembered that, with a balance of payments deficit in the short run, there is a net monetary outflow which is reducing the nominal money supply at the same time as prices are falling.

Where does the real wage reduction come in?

[7] Alert readers will have noticed already that the economy does not get back to the same long-run equilibrium from which it began. A lower foreign demand for our exports has the consequence of shifting downward the domestic demand schedule for labour. For a given job acceptances schedule, equilibrium in the domestic labour market occurs at a lower real wage and a lower employment level. Try drawing the labour market diagram for yourself.

Even if domestic prices and wages are falling in proportion, we must remember that households spend some of their incomes on imported goods whose prices are *not* being reduced. Imports are becoming relatively more expensive in comparison with domestic prices and wages. That, after all, is what we mean by an increase in domestic competitiveness. And that is why real wages are falling during the adjustment process.

The more slowly domestic nominal wages adjust, the longer will be the adjustment period. Suppose instead the government responds to the fall in export demand by devaluing the exchange rate. Competitiveness improves overnight. And real wages are immediately reduced. At unchanged nominal wages and domestic prices, import prices have risen since the price of foreign goods in foreign currency is unchanged, but these now convert into a larger number of pounds sterling for each imported good.

If workers accept this real wage cut, which we have seen will in any case be required if long run equilibrium is eventually to be restored, then the adjustment process can be completed very quickly. However, workers may resist this reduction in their real wages. They may press for 'cost of living' wage claims to cover the increase in the price of the imported goods they consume. If so, competitiveness will deteriorate again and a domestic slump will be required to persuade workers to accept the real wage cuts required to restore long-run equilibrium.

29-7 The Determination of Floating Exchange Rates

We now turn to freely floating exchange rates in the absence of any government intervention in the foreign exchange market. In this section we explain how the level of the exchange rate is determined. In the next section we use this analysis to investigate the consequences of monetary and fiscal policy in an open economy with floating exchange rates.

Purchasing Power Parity

Our definition of long-run equilibrium requires that the economy is both in internal balance (full employment) and external balance (zero net exports and current account balance).

Import demand depends on the level of domestic output and on the real exchange rate. Export demand depends on the level of foreign output and on the real exchange rate. Hence when both the domestic economy and the rest of the world are at internal balance or potential output, there is only one real exchange rate compatible with external balance at the same time. At any higher real exchange rate the domestic economy will be less competitive. Imports will be higher and exports lower. It will have a current account deficit. Conversely, at any lower real exchange rate, with higher exports and lower imports the domestic economy will have a current account surplus. Only one real exchange rate is compatible with internal and external balance.

For given prices in the rest of the world, one country's real exchange rate can be altered either by a change in its nominal exchange rate or by a change in domestic prices. Under fixed exchange rates, since the nominal exchange rate is fixed, the eventual adjustment of the real exchange rate to its long-run equilibrium level must be achieved entirely through a change in domestic prices relative to prices abroad. But under floating exchange rates the nominal exchange rate can also help in the adjustment process.

Our theory of floating exchange rates in the long run can be summarized very simply. When exchange rates float freely, there is no official intervention in the foreign exchange market and no net monetary transfer between countries since the balance of payments is always zero. Just as in a closed economy, the domestic money supply is determined by the quantity of high powered money issued by the government and by the extent to which the domestic banking system creates domestic bank deposits against this monetary base. In the long run the domestic money supply will determine the domestic price level just as in a closed economy. And in the long run the nominal exchange rate must adjust to achieve the unique real exchange rate required for external and internal balance in long-run equilibrium.

Suppose first that we live in a world without inflation in the long run. We begin in long-run equilibrium with internal and external balance. Suppose there is a once-and-for-all doubling of the domestic money supply and, eventually, a doubling of the domestic price level. Thereafter it remains constant. A once-and-for-all halving of the nominal exchange rate will restore the economy to external balance once all adjustment has been completed. Suppose the exchange rate has fallen from $2/£ to $1/£. Although domestic prices have doubled, the dollar price of British exports in unaffected in the long run. A £10 shirt used to sell for $20 when the exchange rate was $2/£. Now it costs £20 to make the shirt but it still sells for $20 since the exchange rate has fallen to $1/£. Similarly, an American calculator produced for $40 used to sell for £20 in the UK. When the exchange rate has fallen to $1/£ it still costs $40 to produce but now sells for £40 in the UK. The price of imports has doubled because the exchange rate has fallen by 50 per cent. Import prices have risen in line with domestic prices in the UK. Whether we compare the relative price of British and American goods in dollars or in pounds, we conclude that their relative price has not changed in the long run. Competitiveness is unaltered.

How about a world with continuous inflation? Suppose there is no inflation in the United States but that in the UK all nominal variables are increasing at 10 per cent a year. A continuous depreciation of the dollar–sterling exchange rate at 10 per cent a year will preserve the dollar price of British exports (in line with the constant dollar price of American goods) and ensure that the price in pounds of British imports from America rises at 10 per cent a year in line with the price of goods produced in the UK. Again, competitiveness is unaffected.

Earlier in the chapter we defined the *purchasing power parity* (PPP) path of the nominal exchange rate as the path that offsets differential inflation rates across countries and maintains at a constant level the real exchange rate and the level of competitiveness. We can now sum up our theory of how floating exchange rates must be determined in the long run. Since there is only one real exchange rate compatible with internal and external balance, and hence with full long-run equilibrium, in the long run the nominal exchange rate must follow whatever path is required to maintain real competitiveness at this level. In the absence of any real shocks (such as the discovery of large oil reserves, which affect the incentive to import and export even in the long run), the equilibrium level of real com-

petitiveness will remain constant in the long run and the nominal exchange rate will be changing to prevent differences in domestic and foreign inflation rates from altering real competitiveness. The nominal exchange rate will follow the PPP path.

However, in the short run the real exchange rate need not be constant. Goods prices adjust only sluggishly, but floating exchange rates can change by a large magnitude in a short time. In discussing the foreign exchange market and the balance of payments, we noted that the stock of internationally mobile funds is now enormous. If those funds were all to move between currencies on the same day, this massive flow on the capital account could not possibly be offset by the (relatively) small net flows that occur on the current account. And under freely floating exchange rates there is no government intervention and no official financing. The foreign exchange market simply could not clear. But clear it does, day by day. Hence, short-run equilibrium in the foreign exchange market is achieved because the exchange rate is capable of jumping at any instant to the level necessary to *prevent* owners of international funds wishing to make massive transfers between currencies.

To understand this process in greater detail, we must now look at the theory of exchange rate speculation.

Speculation

In discussing the capital account we noted that holders of funds in sterling will compare the interest rate obtained by lending on sterling assets with the expected total return that can be obtained by temporarily lending abroad instead. There are two points to note. First, it is the *total* return that counts. The total return from lending in a foreign currency (dollars) is the interest rate on dollar assets such as US government bonds *plus* the capital gain (loss) from a depreciation (appreciation) of the dollar–sterling exchange rate while the money is lent abroad. Someone who converts £1 into $2 and then converts it back into sterling after the exchange rate has fallen from $2/£ to $1/£ will be able to get £2 for their $2. They will have made a capital gain of 100 per cent (from £1 to £2) by holding their funds in dollars, while the dollar–pound exchange rate fell.

Second, since speculators cannot be certain how exchange rates are going to change over time, it is the *expected* exchange rate changes, and hence the expected capital gains or losses from temporarily lending abroad, that influence decisions today about which currency looks the most attractive currency in which to lend.

Suppose UK interest rates are 2 per cent higher than US interest rates. Why don't holders of funds move all their funds into sterling? What would make them indifferent about which country they lent in? Suppose speculators expect the pound to depreciate by 2 per cent a year against the dollar. People investing in pounds will get 2 per cent extra interest but make a 2 per cent capital loss on the exchange rate change relative to the alternative strategy of lending in dollars. The extra interest just compensates for the expected loss and most speculators won't mind where they hold their funds. Since there are no massive flows between currencies, the foreign exchange market can be in equilibrium. The dollar–sterling exchange rate falls at 2 per cent a year as everyone expected, and investors get the same return on their money in either currency.

What would happen if UK interest rates suddenly rose and were now 4 per cent higher than interest rates in the United States? If people still think that the exchange rate will fall at 2 per cent a year, the capital gain earned by holding dollars rather than pounds is no longer sufficient to compensate for the 4 per cent extra interest that can be earned by lending in pounds. Everyone will try to move into pounds. Almost instantaneously, this will bid up the dollar–pound exchange rate. How high will it rise? Until it has reached such a high level that most people expect the pound then to fall at 4 per cent a year thereafter. Only then will the capital losses expected on funds lent in pounds be sufficient to offset the 4 per cent interest differential, and only then will people stop wanting to get their money into pounds.

Why do speculators believe that a higher value of the pound today makes it more likely that the exchange rate will fall in the future? Because smart speculators figure out that eventually the exchange rate will have to return to its purchasing power parity path, the only path compatible with external balance in the long run. If the exchange rate does not seem to be moving in that direction, eventually

the government is going to have to take some drastic action to restore external balance in the long run.

Thus we can sum up the complete theory of exchange rate determination as follows. In the long run the exchange rate will have to follow the purchasing power parity path which offsets differential inflation rates across countries and allows long-run equilibrium at the unique real exchange rate compatible with external balance. But in the short run the nominal exchange rate can depart significantly from this path and competitiveness can change by a large amount.

In the long run, countries with high inflation rates also have higher nominal interest rates. That is the Fisher relation we discussed in Chapter 28. Hence in the long-run equilibrium when the exchange rate is falling along the PPP path, the speculators are quite happy too. The capital losses on the depreciating exchange rate are just offsetting the high nominal interest rates that can be earned by lending in that currency.

But when a country has higher interest rates in the short run than it is expected to have in the long run, the currency will temporarily be attractive to owners of international funds. To stop them all moving their funds into the currency to take advantage of these high interest rates in the short run, the currency will have to appreciate, perhaps significantly, above its purchasing power parity path. Only then are speculators likely to believe that the exchange rate will fall sufficiently in the near future to provide capital losses that offset the high interest rates that are temporarily on offer. In the short run large movements in the exchange rate may be required to prevent the massive flows on the capital account which would be incompatible with day-to-day equilibrium in the foreign exchange market.

We now show how this model of exchange rate determination can be used to analyse monetary and fiscal policy under freely floating exchange rates.

29-8 Monetary and Fiscal Policy under Floating Exchange Rates

In a closed economy with sluggish wage and price adjustment, we saw that both monetary and fiscal policy have real effects in the short run, although the economy eventually returns to full employment or internal balance. In an open economy with fixed exchange rates, we saw that highly mobile international funds make monetary policy almost powerless in the short run but increase the power of fiscal policy. Under floating exchange rates the converse is true: monetary policy can be a powerful tool in the short run, but the effectiveness of fiscal policy is reduced.

Monetary Policy

Suppose that the foreign price level and the foreign money supply are fixed. The rest of the world has no inflation. Its nominal and real interest rates are constant and equal, perhaps at 2 or 3 per cent per annum. The domestic economy begins in internal and external balance, also with a constant money supply and constant wages and prices. Since there is no domestic inflation, domestic nominal and real interest rates are also 2 or 3 per cent.

In this long-run equilibrium, domestic and foreign interest rates are equal. Unless international speculators expect the exchange rate to remain constant, they will wish to transfer all their funds to the currency they expect to appreciate. But with neither domestic nor foreign inflation, speculators recognize that the nominal exchange rate can remain unchanged for ever. It is at the level that secures the level of competitiveness appropriate to external balance in long-run equilibrium. Hence speculators have no wish to transfer funds between currencies. It is a full long-run equilibrium.

In Figure 29-4 we show this nominal exchange rate as e_1. Suppose that a time t there is a once-and-for-all reduction in the nominal money supply by 50 per cent. Eventually domestic prices and wages will fall by 50 per cent. Thus in the long run it will require an appreciation of the nominal exchange rate, a doubling from e_1 to e_2, for the real exchange rate to be restored to its long-run equilibrium level.

However, domestic prices adjust sluggishly. In the short run, a reduction in the nominal money supply will also reduce the real money supply. Thus the immediate effect is to raise domestic interest rates in order to reduce the demand for money and maintain equilibrium in the domestic money market. Now speculators are keen to invest large amounts in pounds. To choke off a massive inflow of funds on the capital account, the sterling exchange rate must rise *above* its new long-run equilibrium position e_2. We say that the exchange rate must *overshoot* the change eventually required.

When the exchange rate jumps from e_1 to e_3, speculators realize that it will have to fall to get back to its new long-run equilibrium position e_2. The anticipated falls in the exchange rate mean anticipated capital losses for those holding sterling rather than dollars, and these offset the higher sterling interest rate. The exchange rate converges on its new equilibrium position by moving along the path BC as time elapses.

Notice that the path gets steadily flatter over time. Initially the reduction in the nominal money supply caused a large reduction in the real money supply and a big increase in domestic interest rates. But gradually domestic prices and wages start to fall, increasing the real money supply and reducing sterling interest rates. As the interest differential falls, it requires a slower and slower sterling exchange rate depreciation to prevent massive international flows of funds. And of course, the smart speculators had already figured that out in deciding that an initial jump in the exchange rate to e_3 was exactly what was required to keep them happy with the currency in which their funds were held.

So monetary policy can have a powerful effect in the short run. Changes in the real money supply and domestic interest rates not only influence domestic absorption, as in a closed economy, but also induce large changes in the nominal exchange rate and the level of competitiveness, which are only slowly eroded as domestic wages and prices adjust.

Again we emphasize that the government cannot choose independent targets for both the money supply *and* the exchange rate. Under a *fixed* exchange rate, there will be a net monetary flow on the balance of payments until, given domestic prices, the domestic real money supply equals the demand for real balances at the domestic level of real income and world interest rates. Domestic interest rates must match foreign interest rates in order to prevent massive capital flows when interest rates are known to be fixed.

In contrast, under a *floating* exchange rate

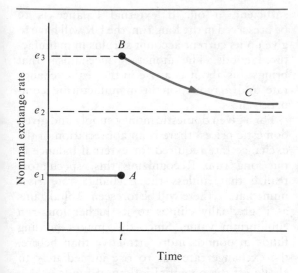

Figure 29-4   EXCHANGE RATE OVERSHOOTING. The economy begins in equilibrium with an exchange rate e_1. When the nominal money supply is halved at time t, speculators realize the exchange rate must eventually double from e_1 to e_2 in order to restore competitiveness once prices have fallen by 50 per cent. Since prices do not change immediately, the effect at t is to reduce the real money supply and increase domestic interest rates above world levels. Only by jumping from A to B, and thereby convincing speculators that subsequent capital losses from exchange rate depreciation will offset higher interest rates, can the exchange rate adjust to maintain equilibrium in the foreign exchange market. As domestic prices fall, the real money supply increases and interest rates fall back to world levels. When full adjustment is complete, the exchange rate has reached e_2. Thus the initial jump from A to B overshoots the long-run change required in the nominal exchange rate.

the balance of payments is exactly zero. Combining currency and capital accounts, there are no international monetary flows. Thus the government can determine the domestic money supply at any level it chooses. But, as Figure 29-4 illustrates, the government must then accept the path for the exchange rate that clears the foreign exchange market and keep the speculators happy. Equally, even without any official financing, the government can peg the exchange rate simply by announcing that it will match foreign interest rates for ever. As foreign interest rates change, the government simply alters the domestic money supply to maintain domestic money market equilibrium at the required interest rate. However we consider the problem, we always reach the same

conclusion: the government must always allow market forces to determine either the money supply *or* the exchange rate.

Fiscal Policy

Whereas the effect of interest rate changes on the exchange rate and competitiveness makes monetary policy a more powerful tool with which to influence aggregate demand under floating exchange rates, the effect of interest rate changes on the exchange rate reduces the short-term effectiveness of fiscal policy.

Suppose the government undertakes a fiscal expansion, say by increasing the level of government spending. This increases aggregate demand and bids up interest rates. The higher interest rate leads to an immediate appreciation of the nominal exchange rate to choke off an inflow of funds, just as in Figure 29-4. In a closed economy, higher interest rates partially crowd out private expenditure by reducing consumption and investment demand. But in an open economy with floating exchange rates, the induced reduction in the demand for net exports further reduces the power of a fiscal expansion to stimulate aggregate demand in the short run.

The Pound in the 1970s and 1980s

Figure 29-5 shows the behaviour of the nominal and real sterling exchange rates since 1975, when most countries had adopted floating exchange rates. We show the exchange rate against a basket of the currencies most important for the UK's international trading transactions.

After 1977 the UK's international competitiveness collapsed. The UK had higher inflation than the rest of the world *and* an *appreciating* exchange rate in the period 1977–81. In part, this collapse of competitiveness showed up in a reduction in net exports. For example, UK imports increased by 11 per cent in 1979. In part, however, UK firms responded to the collapse of competitiveness by cutting prices and making short-term losses, hoping that competitiveness would improve again and the decision to remain in world markets would be vindicated. Thus, profits in manufacturing industry collapsed in the UK in 1980–81 when the real exchange rate was at its peak.

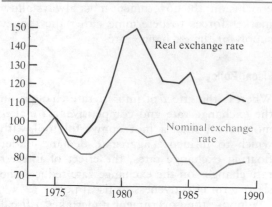

Figure 29-5   UK EXCHANGE RATES, 1975–89
(1975 = 100).   (*Source* CSO, *Economic Trends*.)

Why did the UK's real exchange rate increase so dramatically? We already have part of the answer. A tight monetary policy was introduced to fight inflation. Until domestic prices and wages adjusted, the squeeze in the real money supply meant high interest rates and a sharp appreciation in the nominal exchange rate.

Since 1981, competitiveness has gradually improved as the real exchange rate has fallen. In part, this can be explained by the overshooting story we discussed earlier. The period 1979–81 was a time of sharp appreciation, and subsequently this has been gradually reversed. But it is not the whole story, as we shortly explain.

Finally, note that even by 1989 UK competitiveness was significantly worse than in 1975.

29-9 North Sea Oil

By the late 1970s the UK was beginning to exploit the large reserves of oil that had been discovered in the North Sea. The doubling of oil prices in 1979–80 increased the importance of these reserves. What effect should we expect this to have on the exchange rate?

Let's think first about long-run equilibrium with internal and external balance. External balance means that imports equal exports. The UK was formerly a large oil-importer. This current account deficit was offset by a current account surplus on other trade, primarily trade in manufactured goods. Suppose, for simplicity, that the oil discovery makes the UK self-

sufficient in oil. If external balance is to be preserved in the long run, the UK will have to give up its current account surplus in manufactured goods. The monetary mechanism that brings this about is a rise in the real exchange rate and a reduction in manufacturing competitiveness.

For a given domestic money supply and given domestic prices, there is an appreciation of the exchange rate required for external balance in the long run. Recognizing this, speculators realize that, unless the exchange rate rises immediately, there will be foreseen capital gains as it gradually climbs to its higher long-run equilibrium value. Since this makes holding funds in pounds more attractive than before, the exchange rate has to rise immediately to choke off the potential inflow of funds.

Thus, in Figure 29-5 sterling's real exchange rate rose especially sharply in the period 1979–81 because there was simultaneously a move to tighter monetary policy *and* a sharp increase in the real value of the UK's oil reserves. And in the period 1981–89 there was some improvement in competitiveness, both because of the gradual recovery from overshooting, equivalent to a movement down the path *BC* in Figure 29-4, and because a world slump had reduced the world demand for oil and the real price of oil.

By the mid-1980s, a considerable part of North Sea oil reserves had been extracted. The importance of oil extraction to the UK economy was rapidly diminishing. This had two implica tions. First, the sterling exchange rate was no longer so sensitive to fluctuations in oil prices; it was no longer a petrocurrency. Second, on average we can expect sterling's real exchange rate to be lower in the 1990s than it was in the 1980s.

Summary

1   The exchange rate is the number of units of foreign currency that exchange for a unit of the domestic currency. A fall (rise) in the exchange rate is called a depreciation (appreciation).

2   The demand for the domestic currency arises from exports, and purchases of domestic assets by foreigners; the supply of the domestic currency arises from imports and purchases of foreign assets. Floating exchange rates equate supply and demand in the absence of any government intervention in the foreign exchange market.

3   Under fixed exchange rates, the government meets an excess supply of pounds by running down foreign currency reserves in order to demand pounds. Conversely, any excess demand for pounds at the fixed exchange rate is met by increasing the foreign exchange reserves and supplying pounds to the market.

4   In the balance of payments accounts, monetary inflows are recorded as credits and monetary outflows are recorded as debits. The current account shows the balance on trade in goods and services plus net profits of income earned from assets owned in other currencies. The capital account shows net purchases and sales of assets. The balance of payments is the sum of the current and capital account balances.

5   Under floating exchange rates, a current surplus must be offset by a capital deficit or vice versa. Under fixed exchange rates, a balance of payments surplus or deficit must be matched by an offsetting quantity of official financing. Official financing simply measures government intervention in the foreign exchange market.

6   The real exchange rate adjusts the nominal exchange rate for prices at home and abroad, and measures the relative price of domestic to foreign goods when measured in a common currency. A rise in the real exchange rate reduces the international competitiveness of the domestic economy.

7   An increase in domestic (foreign) income increases the demand for imports (exports). An increase in the real exchange rate reduces the demand for exports, increases the demand for imports, and thus reduces the demand for net exports.

8   Holders of international funds compare the domestic interest rate with the total return that can be obtained by temporarily lending abroad. This return is the sum of the foreign interest rate plus the depreciation of the international value of the domestic currency over the period of the loan. Perfect international capital mobility means that an enormous quantity of funds will shift between currencies when the perceived rate of return differs across currencies.

9   Internal balance occurs when aggregate demand is at the full-employment level. External balance occurs when imports equal exports. Both are necessary for long-run equilibrium.

10   A balance of payments deficit leads to an equivalent reduction of the domestic money supply. A balance of payments surplus increases the domestic money supply by an equal amount.

11   Under fixed exchange rates and perfect capital mobility, monetary policy is almost powerless. Domestic interest rates are pegged at work levels. An increase in the domestic money supply leads to an equivalent balance of payments deficit until the money supply is restored to the level people wish to demand at the given level of world interest rates.

12   In the short run, fiscal policy is a powerful tool under fixed exchange rates. Fiscal expansion no longer bids up domestic interest rates in the short run. Any tendency for interest rates to rise leads to an immediate inflow on the capital account until the money supply is increased enough to maintain interest rates at the world level.

13   A devaluation is a reduction in the fixed exchange rate maintained by the government. With sluggish price adjustment, its immediate effect is to increase competitiveness and aggregate demand. With spare resources, output increases. But at full employment, net exports can increase only if domestic absorption is reduced by tighter fiscal policy.

14   In the long run, devaluation is unlikely to have much effect. Changing one nominal variable merely leads to offsetting changes in other nominal variables. In passing on higher import prices and seeking cost-of-living wage increases, firms and workers will increase domestic prices and wages to offset the competitive advantage of devaluation. But devaluation could speed up the adjustment process when a shock requires an adjustment in competitiveness to restore internal and external balance.

15   Under floating exchange rates, the long-run value of the nominal exchange rate will be determined to secure external balance, given prices at home and abroad. But in the short run it is determined by speculative considerations, and must change to prevent massive flows on the capital account.

16   The exchange rate must begin at a level from which the anticipated convergent path to its long-run equilibrium continuously provides capital gains or losses to offset prevailing interest rate differentials, thus equating the rate of return on lending at home and abroad.

17   Under floating exchange rates, monetary policy is a powerful short-term tool. A reduction in the money supply increases domestic interest rates and leads to a sharp appreciation of the exchange rate, which overshoots its long-run level. The reduction in competitiveness, until domestic prices and wages adjust, can sharply reduce aggregate demand in the short run.

18   Fiscal policy is now a weaker tool in the short run. Fiscal expansion increases interest rates and the exchange rate, crowding out not merely domestic consumption and investment but also net exports.

19   An improvement in the oil-related part of the current account eventually requires an equivalent deterioration in other items on the current account to preserve overall external balance. This is achieved through a rise in the real exchange rate. Anticipating an eventual rise in the exchange rate, speculators move in at once and the exchange rate appreciates immediately.

Key Terms

Open economy macroeconomics
Nominal and real exchange rates
Fixed and floating exchange rates
Intervention and official financing
Convertibility
Foreign exchange reserves
The balance of payments
Current and capital accounts
International competitiveness
Purchasing power parity (PPP)
Perfect capital mobility
Speculation
Internal and external balance
Domestic absorption

Devaluation and revaluation
Appreciation and depreciation
Sterilization
Overshooting

Problems

1   If $1 exchanges for 2 Deutschmarks (DM) and $2 exchange for £1, what is the exchange rate between DM and £? Can the dollar appreciate against the DM but not against the £?

2   A country has a current account surplus of £6 billion but a capital account deficit of £4 billion. (a) Is its balance of payments in deficit or surplus? (b) Are the country's foreign exchange reserves rising or falling? (c) Is the central bank buying or selling domestic currency? Explain.

3   Since 1974 the OPEC countries have run a persistent current account surplus. How is this compatible with the statement that countries must eventually get back to external balance? Does this mean that there is more pressure on deficit countries to restore external balance than there is pressure on the corresponding surplus countries?

4   Rank the following three situations according to the ability of monetary policy to affect real output and employment in the short run: (a) a closed economy; (b) an open economy with fixed exchange rates; (c) an open economy with floating exchange rates. Explain. Assume the same speed of wage and price adjustment in each case.

5   Newsreaders say that 'the pound had a good day' whenever the sterling exchange rate rises on the foreign exchange market. (a) Under what circumstances might an appreciation of the exchange rate be desirable? (b) Undesirable?

6   Common Fallacies Show why each of the following statements is incorrect. (a) Countries with low inflation must be more competitive in the long run. (b) Under floating exchange rates the current and capital accounts have equal magnitude but opposite sign. Hence both must be equally important in determining day-to-day exchange rate changes. (c) UK interest rates are high. This means the pound will appreciate for the next few months.

30

Long-Term Growth and Short-Term Fluctuations

In 1990 real GDP in the UK was nine times its level of 1870. Real income per person quintupled over that period. On average, we are richer than our grandparents but less rich than our grandchildren will be. Table 30-1 shows that these long-term trends were even more pronounced in other countries. Over the same period 1870–1990, real GDP in Japan increased 90-fold and real income per person 25-fold.

We begin by asking three questions about the long-run growth records shown in Table 30-1: What do we mean by long-run economic growth? What factors are responsible for this growth? And what economic policies can be used to change an economy's rate of growth in the long run? In this chapter we discuss mainly the experience of industrialized countries. In Chapter 35 we discuss the growth performance of other nations in the world economy.

We also consider whether growth is a good thing. Are there circumstances in which it might be better to grow more slowly? Can the costs of growth outweigh its benefits?

In the second half of the chapter we emphasize the fact that economies do not grow smoothly. Actual output, income, and employment levels tend to fluctuate around their long-run trend. This phenomenon is called the business cycle. Are these cycles adequately explained by the macroeconomics we have already learned? In part they are, but we introduce some additional considerations to complete the picture. In so doing, we develop a theory of the business cycle.

30-1 Economic Growth

The growth rate of a variable is its percentage increase per annum. To define economic growth we must specify both the variable we

wish to measure and the period over which we wish to measure its rate of change. Table 30-1 is based on real GDP, but we would obtain very similar results if we looked instead at real GNP or national income.

GDP and GNP measure the total output and total income of an economy. We begin by reminding you of some of the problems we raised in Chapter 20 when discussing whether such measures are useful indicators of economic performance. In particular, GDP (and GNP) are very incomplete measures of *economic* output; it is difficult to account for the introduction of new products; and there is no direct relationship between GDP and happiness.

GDP as a Measure of Economic Output

GDP measures the net output or value added of an economy by measuring goods and services purchased with money. It omits output which is not bought and sold and therefore is unmeasured. The two most important omissions are leisure and externalities such as pollutions and congestion.

In most industrial countries, the length of an average work week has fallen by at least ten hours a week since 1900. In choosing to work fewer hours per week, people reveal that the extra leisure is worth at least as much as the extra goods that could have been produced by working harder. But when people decide to swap washing machines and steel for extra leisure, recorded GDP is reduced; hence, GDP understates the true economic output of the economy. Conversely, the output of pollution reduces the net economic welfare that the economy is producing and ideally should be subtracted from GDP. For example, sulphur dioxide emissions from coal-fired power stations

Table 30-1 Real GDP and per capita real GDP, 1870–1990

	REAL GDP		PER CAPITA REAL GDP	
	RATIO OF 1990 TO 1870	ANNUAL GROWTH (%)	RATIO OF 1990 TO 1870	ANNUAL GROWTH (%)
Japan	91.5	3.80	25.3	2.70
USA	59.3	3.34	9.4	1.84
Australia	40.2	3.10	4.0	1.16
Sweden	32.0	2.81	14.3	2.21
W. Germany	18.1	2.41	11.7	2.04
France	14.0	2.19	9.6	1.90
UK	9.0	1.83	5.0	1.33

Source: Angus Maddison, 'Phases of Capitalist Development', in R. C. O. Matthews (ed.), Economic Growth and Resources, vol. 2, Macmillan, 1979; updated from (IMF), International Financial Statistics.

lead to 'acid rain'. In countries such as Germany this is now having a major effect. It is starting to destroy vast acres of German forests. With comprehensive national income accounting, as it was produced this output of acid rain would have been deducted from GDP.

Including leisure in GDP would have increased recorded GDP in both 1870 and 1990. Since the value of leisure has probably increased less quickly than measured output, which increased ninefold in the UK and 90-fold in Japan over the same period, this would tend to reduce the rate of growth of a more comprehensive output measure. Similarly, pollution may actually have increased at a faster rate. Hence it is possible that the growth rates for GDP in Table 30-1 overstate the rate at which economies have been increasing their net output of goods and services with an economic value.

New Products

In 1870 people did not have television sets and motor cars. Although national income statisticians do their best to compare the value of real GDP in different years, the introduction of new products creates a genuine difficulty in trying to make comparisons over time. As each new good is introduced, it is usually possible to figure out roughly what it is worth compared with the good it replaces, because both goods are sold in the market at the same time. We can estimate how much people's real income has been increased by the introduction of a new product that accomplishes the same task more cheaply. But this calculation is more

difficult when the new product allows an activity that had never been possible before.

There is probably only a small error in comparing GDP in 1990 with GDP in 1989. But a succession of small errors can accumulate into something substantial. Thus we have to treat long-term comparisons with some scepticism. Nevertheless, these figures are the best estimates we have.

GDP as a Measure of Happiness

Even with an accurate and comprehensive measure of GDP, two problems remain. First, should we be interested in total GDP or in GDP per capita? In part, this depends on the question we wish to ask. Total GDP gives an indicator of the size of an economy, which may tell us something about its clout in the world economy. However, if we are concerned about the average level of happiness of a typical individual in an economy, it makes more sense to look at GDP per capita. For example, Table 30-1 tells us that, although real GDP grew more quickly in Australia than in France or Germany between 1870 and 1990, in part this was due to very fast population growth, largely through immigration. Germany and France actually had faster growth in GDP per person over the period.

Even so, real GDP per person is a very imperfect indicator of the happiness of the typical individual within a country. When income is shared equally between its citizens, a country's per capita real GDP does tell us what each and every person is getting. But countries such as Brazil have very unequal income distributions. A few people earn a lot and a lot of people earn only a little. It is possible for such countries to have fairly high per capita real income while many of their citizens are really quite badly off.[1]

Finally, we note that, even when GDP is adjusted to measure leisure, pollution, and so on, higher per capita GDP does not necessarily lead to greater happiness. Material goods are not everything. But they do help. Movements in which people return to 'the simple life' have not had much success, and most of the less industrialized countries are trying to increase their GDP as quickly as possible.

A Recent Phenomenon?

Table 30-1 makes one final point. A very small increase in the annual growth rate has substantial results when its impact is cumulated over a long period. Even an annual growth rate of only 1.33 per cent in per capita GDP led to a quintupling of UK per capita real GDP between 1870 and 1990. In 1870, UK per capita income was about £1450 in 1990 prices. If the growth rate had always been 1.33 per cent a year, per capita real income would have had to be about £290 in 1750, £58 in 1630 and only about £12 in 1510. Clearly, this is implausible. In fact, it is only in the last two and a half centuries that per capita levels of real income have been persistently increasing.

In the short run, an economy with Keynesian unemployment and spare resources can increase output by increasing demand and employment. But if potential output is constant, the economy will quickly reach full employment and further growth will cease. In the long run, changes in output caused by fluctuations around potential output are swamped by the effect of persistent growth in potential output itself. If potential output increases at 2 per cent a year, it will increase sevenfold in less than a century. Hence in the long run it is in changes in the level of potential output that we must seek the explanation of economic growth.

---

[1] Since different countries adopt different conventions about exactly which goods and services to measure in GDP, international comparisons of GDP or per capita GDP can never be precise in any case.

30-2 The Production Function

To organize our ideas, we start from the production function, which can be written as

Output = f (capital, labour, land, raw materials, technical knowledge)   (1)

The *production function* shows the maximum output that can be produced using specified quantities of inputs, given the existing technical knowledge.

Equation (1) provides a convenient summary of the things that could change the level of output. In what follows we assume that the economy is always at potential output, the output level produced when there is full employment and all markets clear. Increases in potential output can be traced to increases in inputs of the factors of production – land, labour, capital, raw materials – or to technical advances allowing the existing factors to produce a higher level of output.

In this section we concentrate on changes in total output. Per capita output will increase if total output grows more quickly than population. In the very long run we cannot assume that population growth is independent of per capita output, which will influence both the number of children people wish to have or feel able to afford and the quantity of nutrition and medical care that people on average receive. Nevertheless, we simplify by assuming that the rate of population growth is independent of economic factors over some slightly shorter period. Thus we assume that anything that increases total output will also increase per capita output.

Capital

Productive capital is the stock of machinery, buildings, and inventories with which other factors of production combine to produce output. For a given labour force, an increase in total capital and capital per worker will increase output. However, capital depreciates over time. A certain amount of new investment is required merely to maintain the existing capital stock intact. And with a growing labour force, an even higher quantity of investment is required if capital per worker is to be maintained. With yet faster investment, capital per worker will increase over time, thereby increasing the output each worker can produce. Thus, an increase in capital per worker is one of the principal ways in which output per worker and per capita income is increased.

Labour

Employment may increase for two reasons. First, there may be population growth. Second, a larger fraction of a given population may be in employment. However, labour input depends on the hours worked as well as the number of people working. Even for a given level of employment, an increase in hours worked will increase effective labour input to the production function, and hence increase output.

Since we know that the average work week has fallen substantially over the last 100 years, the increases in per capita real output in Table 30-1 cannot be attributed to increased hours of work. Since 1945, the most significant aspect of the growth of labour input has probably been the steady increase in the number of married women choosing to participate in the labour force. By increasing the labour input obtained from a given population, this tends to increase total and per capita output.

Human Capital   Human capital is the skill and knowledge embodied in the minds and hands of the population. Increasing education, training, and experience allows workers to produce more output from the same level of physical capital. For example, much of West Germany's physical capital was devastated during the Second World War; but the human capital of its surviving labour force had not evaporated between 1939 and 1945. Given these skills, Germany was able to recover rapidly after 1945 and rebuild its physical capital, aided by large loans from the United States through the Marshall Plan. But without the inherited stock of human capital, it is doubtful whether we should ever have heard of the postwar German economic miracle.

Land

Land is especially important in an agricultural economy. If each worker has more land it will be possible to increase agricultural output. Land is less important in highly industrialized economies. For example, Hong Kong has been able to grow rapidly even though it is very overcrowded and land is scarce. Even so, more of a production input is unlikely to reduce the quantity of output that other factors can produce. Increasing the supply of land will allow the economy to produce more output.

Increases in the supply of land are relatively unimportant as a source of growth in modern economies. Indeed, in simple theoretical models we define land as the factor of production whose total supply to the economy is fixed. But in practice the distinction between land and capital is rather blurred. By applying more fertilizer per acre, an input of agricultural capital, the effective quantity of farming land can be increased. With investment in drainage or irrigation, marshes and deserts can be converted into productive land.

Raw Materials

Given the quantity of other inputs, an increase in the input of raw materials will increase the quantity of output that can be produced. When raw materials are scarce and expensive, workers will take time and care not to waste them. With a more abundant supply of raw materials, workers can work more quickly.

It is important to distinguish two kinds of raw material. *Depletable* materials are those that can be used only once. When a barrel of oil has been extracted from the ground and used to fuel a machine, the world has one less barrel of oil reserves in the ground. If the world begins with a finite stock of oil reserves, it will eventually run out of oil though this may not happen for many centuries.

In contrast, *renewable* resources can be replaced. Timber and fish are obvious examples. If harvested in moderation, they will be replaced by nature and can be used as production inputs for ever. However, if over-harvested they may become extinct. When there are only a few whales left in the ocean, they may find it impossible to locate partners with which to breed and the stock of whales will gradually disappear.

Factor Contributions and Scale Economies

The marginal product of a factor tells us how much output will increase when the factor input is increased by one unit but all other inputs are held constant. Microeconomics tells us that marginal products eventually decline as factor input is increased. With two workers already on each machine, another worker does very little to increase total output.

Economies of Scale   Suppose that, instead of increasing one input in isolation, all factor inputs are doubled together. If output exactly doubles, we say there are *constant returns to scale*; if output more (less) than doubles, we say that there are *increasing (decreasing) returns to scale*.

Economies of scale reinforce the growth process. Anything that increases inputs leads to an extra bonus in higher output. And there are sometimes sound engineering reasons to believe that economies of scale will exist. For example, it requires only simple mathematics to show that it takes less than twice the steel input to build an oil tanker of twice the capacity. On the other hand, many developing countries regret the resources they have tied up in huge steel mills which do not produce very efficiently. Bigger is not always better. In practice, economists frequently assume that constant returns to scale is a rough approximation to reality.

Having briefly discussed the different factor inputs, we turn now to the final entry in equation (1), the role of technical knowledge. This is sufficiently important to the process of economic growth that we devote a whole section to it.

30-3 Technical Knowledge

At any given time, a society has a stock of knowledge about ways in which goods can be produced. Some of this knowledge is written down in books and blueprints, but much is reflected in working practices learned by hard experience. Technical advances come through *invention*, the discovery of new knowledge, and *innovation*, the incorporation of new knowledge into actual production techniques.

Inventions

Major inventions can lead to spectacular increases in technical knowledge. The wheel,

the steam engine, and the modern computer are obvious examples. Although we tend to think of industrial processes, technical progress in agriculture has also been dramatic. Industrialized societies began only when productivity improvements in agriculture allowed some of the workforce to be freed to produce industrial goods. Before then, almost everyone had to work the land merely to get enough food for survival. The replacement of animal power by machines, the development of fertilizer, drainage and irrigation, and new hybrid seeds, have all played a large part in improving agricultural production and enabling economic growth.

Embodiment of Knowledge in Capital   To introduce new ideas to actual production, innovation frequently requires investment in new machines. Without investment, bullocks cannot be transformed into tractors even once the knowhow for building tractors has been made available. Major new inventions may thus lead to waves of investment and innovation as these ideas are put into practice. Just as the mid-nineteenth century was truly the age of the train, the interwar years saw the age of the car, and we are now seeing the age of the microchip.

Learning by Doing   Human capital can matter as much as physical capital. Workers get better at doing a particular job as they have more practice. The most famous example is known as the Horndal effect, after a Swedish steelworks built during 1835–36, and maintained in almost exactly the same condition for the next 15 years. Without changes in the machinery or the size of the labour force, output per worker-hour nevertheless rose by 2 per cent a year. Eventually, however, as skills become mastered, further productivity increases become harder and harder to attain.

Research and Development

What determines the amount of invention and innovation? Some new ideas are simply the product of intellectual curiosity or frustration ('There must be a better way to do this!'). But like most activities, the output of new ideas depends to a large extent on the resources devoted to looking for them, which in turn depends on the cost of tying up resources in this way and the prospective benefits from success. Some research activities take place in university departments, usually funded at least in part by the government, but a good deal of research is privately funded through the money firms devote to their research and development (R&D) departments.

The outcome of research is risky. Research workers never know whether or not they will find anything useful. Research is like a risky investment project, since the funds must be committed before the benefits (if any) start to accrue, but there is one important difference. Suppose you spend a lot of money developing a better mousetrap. When you succeed, everyone else copies your new mousetrap; the price is bid down, and you never recoup your initial investment. If we lived in such a world, there would be little incentive ever to undertake R&D.

If the invention becomes widely available when it is discovered, society gets the benefit but the original developer does not: there is an *externality*. Private and social gains do not coincide and the price mechanism does not provide the correct incentives. Society tries to get round this *market failure* in two ways. First, it grants *patents* to private inventors and innovators, legal monopolies for a fixed period of time which allow successful research projects to repay investments in R&D by temporarily charging higher prices than the cost of production alone. Second, the government subsidizes a good deal of basic research in universities, in its own laboratories, and in private industry.

International Comparisons   The government meets nearly half the total cost of R&D in the UK, broadly similar to the fraction met by governments in other industrial countries.[2] And R&D is big business, accounting for 2 per cent of UK GDP in 1990, a slightly lower share of GDP than in other industrialized countries. In most of these countries, defence-related R&D (in which the government is closely involved) is the largest single component of R&D expenditure. We discussed R&D more fully in Chapter 17.

---

[2] HMSO, *Annual Review of Funded R & D.*

30-4 The Limits to Growth and the Costs of Growth

In this section, we ask two simple questions. Can growth continue indefinitely? And is growth always a good thing?

Malthus, Land, and Population

One of the earliest doomsters was the Reverend Thomas Malthus, writing in 1798. Living in a largely agricultural society, Malthus worried about the fixed supply of land. As a growing population tried to work a fixed supply of land, the marginal product of labour would diminish and agricultural output would fail to increase in line with population. The per capita food supply would fall until starvation started to reduce population to the level that could be fed from the given supply of agricultural land.

Some of the poorer developing countries today face this *Malthusian trap*. Agricultural productivity is so low that almost everyone must work on the land if enough food is to be produced. As population grows and agricultural output fails to keep pace, famine sets in and people die. If better fertilizers or irrigation manage to improve agricultural output, population quickly expands as nutrition improves, and people are driven back to starvation levels again.

Yet Malthus's prediction did not prove correct for all countries. Today's rich countries managed to break out of the Malthusian trap. How was this achieved? First, they managed to improve agricultural productivity (without an immediate population increase) so that some workers could be transferred to industrial production. The capital goods thus produced included better ploughs, machinery to pump water and drain fields, and transport to distribute food more effectively. As capital was applied in agriculture, output per worker increased further, allowing yet more workers to be released to industry while maintaining sufficient food production to feed the growing population. Second, the rapid technical progress in agricultural production led to large and persistent productivity increases, reinforcing the effect of moving to more capital-intensive agricultural production.

Thus we conclude that even the existence of a

factor whose supply is largely fixed need not make sustained growth impossible. It is possible to substitute one factor of production for another, and it is possible that continuing technical progress will allow continuing output growth even when one factor is not increasing. Moreover, the price mechanism provides the correct incentives for these processes to occur. With a given supply of land, increasing agricultural production will increase the price of land and the rental that must be paid for land. On the one hand, this provides an incentive to switch to production methods that are less land-intensive (heavy fertilizer usage, battery chickens), and on the other hand it provides an incentive to concentrate on techni-cal progress which will allow the economy either to get by with less land or, effectively, to increase the supply of land. We turn now to a second example in which the same principles apply.

Finite Natural Resources

Even before the first OPEC oil price rise, energy problems had been highlighted in the widely publicized report, *The Limits to Growth*, published by the Club of Rome in 1972. The report argued that many of the world's raw materials were in finite supply and would be completely exhausted within 100 years. Growth would have to stop as the world ran out of depletable resources.

Most economists believe that this argument is incorrect. As resources become scarce their price rises. The OPEC oil price rise has shown how the price mechanism leads the world economy to adapt. Consumers switch from expensive oil-related products; they economize on heating and move to cars with greater fuel efficiency. Producers find it profitable to begin research on substitute sources of energy. At some price of oil it becomes profitable to switch to solar energy, nuclear fuel, or extraction of oil from the vast reserves of shale which are unprofitable to exploit at current oil prices.

Certainly a supply shock can temporarily halt economic growth, as the OPEC shock did in the 1970s. Such a shock could even permanently reduce the level of output below the level that would otherwise have been attained. But after an initial period of adjustment it is likely that economic growth will be resumed albeit from a lower baseline.

The Costs of Economic Growth

A different argument is that economic growth could be sustained but that it is *undesirable* that it should be sustained. It is argued that the benefits of economic growth are outweighed by the costs. Pollution, congestion, and a hectic life-style are too high a price to pay for a rising output of cars, washing machines, and video games.

Since GNP is a very imperfect measure of the net economic value of the goods and services produced by the economy, there is no presump-tion that our objective should be to maximize the growth of measured GNP. We discussed issues such as pollution in Chapter 15. In the absence of any government intervention, a free market economy is likely to produce too much pollution. However, complete elimination of pollution is also wasteful. Society should undertake activities accompanied by pollution up to the point at which the marginal benefit of the goods produced equals the marginal pollution cost imposed on society. We explained how government intervention through pollution taxes or regulation of environmental standards can be used to move the economy towards an efficient allocation of resources in which marginal social costs and benefits are equalized.

The full implementation of such a policy would probably reduce the growth of measured GNP below the rate that is achieved when there is no restriction on activities such as pollution and congestion. And this is the most sensible way in which to approach the problem. It tackles the issue directly. In contrast, the 'zero-growth' solution tackles the problem only indirectly.

> The *zero-growth* proposal argues that, be-cause increases in measured GNP are accom-panied by additional costs of pollution, congestion, and so on, the best solution is to aim for zero growth of measured GNP.

The problem with the zero-growth approach is that it does not distinguish between measured outputs that are accompanied by activities with social costs and measured outputs that give rise to no pollution or congestion. It does not provide the correct incentives. The principle of targeting, one of the important insights of the welfare economics we discussed in Part 3, suggests that it is always more efficient to tackle a problem directly than to adopt an indirect approach which also distorts other aspects of production or consumption. Hence we conclude that, when society believes that there is too much pollution, congestion, environmental damage, or stress, the best solution is to provide incentives that directly reduce these phenomena. Simply restricting overall growth in measured output is a terribly crude alternative which is distinctly second-best.

Of course, some of these difficulties might be removed if economists and statisticians could devise a more comprehensive measure of GNP which included all the 'quality of life' activities (clean air, environmental beauty, etc.) that yield genuine consumption benefits but at present are not captured in measured GNP. Inevitably, voters and commentators tend to judge government performance according to how well the economy is doing on some international league table of published and measurable statistics. A more comprehensive measure of GNP might remove some of the conflicts that governments feel between fostering growth of output as currently measured and encouraging measures to improve the quality of life.

Even so, no matter how complete the statistics, the assessment of the desirable growth rate will always remain a normative question which ultimately hinges on the value judgements of the assessor. Switching resources from consumption, however defined, to investment will nearly always reduce the welfare of people today but allow greater welfare for people tomorrow. The priority attached to satisfying wants of people at different points in time must always remain a value judgement.

30-5 Growth in OECD Countries

The Organization for Economic Cooperation and Development (OECD) is a club of the world's richest 24 countries, ranging from industrial giants like the United States and Japan to smaller economies like New Zealand, Ireland, and Turkey. Table 30-2 shows the long-term growth performance of OECD countries since 1950.

The table shows the sharp productivity slowdown after 1973 in all OECD countries. Several explanations have been put forward to explain this slowdown. Some economists have emphasized the role of increasing pollution control and other regulation of 'economic bads' which, though socially desirable, had the consequence of raising production costs and reducing *measured* output and hence *measured* productivity. Other economists have stressed the increasing power of trade unions and the increasing legal protection they enjoyed in the 1970s. If this explanation is correct, the supply-side reforms of the late 1980s may allow higher productivity growth in the 1990s.

A third explanation may be even more important. 1973 was the year of the first OPEC oil price shock, when real oil prices quadrupled. This had two effects. First, it diverted R & D towards very long-term efforts to find alternative energy-saving technologies. These efforts may take decades to pay off and show up in improvements in actual productivity. Second, the higher energy prices made much of the capital stock economically obsolete overnight. Energy-guzzling factories were simply too expensive to operate and had to be closed down. The world effectively lost a considerable part of its capital stock, and this inevitably reduced output per head. Of course, for a time

Table 30-2 Average annual growth in real output per person employed (%)

	OECD	USA	JAPAN	GERMANY	UK	FRANCE	ITALY	SWEDEN
1950–60	3.12	1.33	7.26	6.76	2.27	3.54	5.17	2.57
1960–73	3.95	2.80	8.45	3.57	2.53	4.63	4.17	3.32
1973–85	1.55	1.27	2.29	1.91	1.13	1.47	1.61	1.58

Source: S. Dowrick and D. Nguyen, 'OECD Comparative Economic Growth 1950–85', *American Economy Review*, 1989.

firms tried to struggle on with their existing factories. In practice, scrapping took a long time, though it was given renewed impetus by the second sharp rise in oil prices in 1980–81. That is why its effects have been drawn out over such a long period.

30-6 Economic Growth and Government Policy

Before discussing specific government policies that might increase the long-run growth rate, we emphasize three points. First, it is the growth of output per person rather than the growth of total output that is likely to be the prime concern. Countries that seek economic and military strength in the world economy may be concerned about their total output and may choose to encourage population growth as a means to increase total output. But in most countries the objective is to increase the growth of output per person and the living standards of the typical individual.

Second, a once-and-for-all improvement in productivity allows only temporary economic growth: sustained growth requires a sustained growth of productivity. Third, although faster growth allows the benefit of higher future output and consumption levels, it may involve a short-run cost. For example, if the economy is at potential output, it will be necessary to reduce current consumption in order to devote a larger part of current resources to the production of new capital goods which allow higher future output and consumption. Whether a faster growth rate is desirable depends on how society trades off present costs against future benefits.

With these qualifications, we now discuss briefly how the government can try to increase the rate of economic growth.

Supply-side Economics   We discussed supply-side economics in detail in Section 27-4. Here we merely note that the purpose of supply-side economics is largely to achieve a once-and-for-all improvement in resource allocation and overall factor productivity. For example, if high marginal tax rates imply that the marginal product of labour (to which profit-maximizing firms equate the pre-tax wage) exceeds the marginal valuation of leisure (to which house-holds equate the after-tax wage), the economy may benefit from a reduction in marginal tax rates. Employment hours will increase and the extra goods produced will more than compensate for the leisure forgone. Not only will social welfare increase, but measured GNP will also increase since there is more employment and output for a given population. But a once-and-for-all tax cut leads to a once-and-for-all increase in output per person in the economy. Thereafter the economy will return to its previous growth rate, unless such policies can affect the rate of innovation itself.

The Role of Capital   The government can influence the ratio of investment to potential output. Microeconomic policies include investment grants and tax concessions which allow firms to deduct the cost of investment from profits before taxable profit levels are assessed. Macroeconomic policies include the mix of monetary and fiscal policy, operating through the level of interest rates, and the extent of current government spending G on goods and services which affects the extent to which private investment is crowded out when aggregate demand is at its full-employment level.

Empirical studies suggest that the real rate of return on capital is about 10 per cent a year for the economy as a whole. Thus if today's investment is increased by 10 per cent of GNP, we expect future GNP to be about 1 per cent higher during the lifetime of the new machinery installed today. Since investment in fixed capital is usually about one-fifth of GNP, this means that the rate of investment would almost have to double merely to add 1 per cent a year to future GNP.

Since it seems unlikely that investment could be increased to this extent, we conclude that policies to increase the rate of investment will increase, but hardly transform, a country's economic growth rate. However, there may be some periods in which new investment has an abnormally high return, namely when there has been a dramatic advance in technical knowledge the benefits of which can be realized only when the new knowledge is embodied in new machinery.

Encouraging Technical Progress   We have seen that advances in knowledge make a key contribution to economic growth. The private returns of R&D are frequently high, and we have seen that advanced economies devote considerable resources to this activity. And the government provides substantial incentives to R&D through support for academic research, the patent system, tax concessions to firms undertaking R&D, and through government-funded research establishments, especially in defence-related fields.

Although it seems likely that additional government support for R&D would increase the rate of technical progress, two qualifications should be borne in mind. First, R&D is a risky business. Spending more on R&D might lead simply to a series of expensive failures which would be a waste of society's scarce resources. Second, invention and discovery is not sufficient; the new knowledge must be successfully incorporated into operational production techniques before society as a whole derives the benefits.

Investing in People We have stressed the importance of human capital. Education, training, learning by doing, and management skills are important sources of productivity growth. In some cases the productivity gains can be quickly realized. However, in other cases, such as education, the benefits are likely to be seen only in the long run. But these benefits may still be substantial. For example, it is well known that the UK invests much less heavily than other European and North American countries in basic education in science and technology. Given the position from which the UK begins, the rate of return on such investment is probably quite high.

This completes our brief examination of long-term economic growth in productive potential and output per person. We turn now to short-term fluctuations around the level of potential output.

30-7 The Business Cycle

In practice, aggregate output and productivity do not grow smoothly. In some years they grow very rapidly but in other years they actually fall.

The *trend path of output* is the smooth path it follows in the long run once the short-term fluctuations are averaged out.

Actual output fluctuates around this hypothetical trend path. British economists used to refer to these short-term fluctuations as the *trade cycle*, but nowadays the American term *business cycle* is generally used.[3]

The *business cycle* is the short-term fluctuation of total output around its trend path.

Figure 30-1 presents a stylized description of the business cycle. The black curve shows the steady growth in trend output over time. But actual output follows the green curve. Point A represents a *slump*, the bottom of a business cycle. At point B the economy has entered the *recovery* phase of the cycle. As recovery proceeds, the output climbs above its trend path, reaching point C, which we call a *boom*. Then the economy enters a *recession* in which output is growing less quickly than trend output, and is possibly even falling. Point E shows the trough, which we call a *slump*, after which recovery begins and the cycle starts

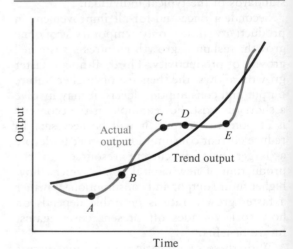

Figure 30-1 THE BUSINESS CYCLE. Trend output flows steadily over time as productive potential increases. Actual output fluctuates around this trend. Point A shows a slump, the trough of a cycle. At B the recovery phase has begun and it continues until the peak of the cycle is reached at C. At C there is a boom. Then a period of recession follows until the next slump is reached at E after which a new cycle begins. It takes roughly five years to move from one point in the cycle to an equivalent point in the next cycle, for example from A to E.

---

[3] The trade cycle did not refer exclusively to *international* trade; the Victorians used 'trade' to mean industry in general and manufacturing in particular.

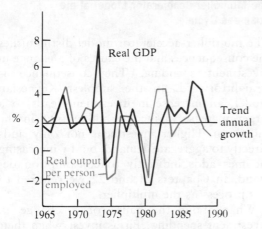

Figure 30-2 GROWTH OF OUTPUT AND
LABOUR PRODUCTIVITY IN THE UK, 1965–89
(% per year). (*Source*: CSO, *Economic Trends*.)

again. Thus, output is growing most quickly
during the recovery and is growing least quickly
(and possibly actually falling) during the
recession.

Figure 30-2 shows the annual percentage
growth of real GDP and of real output per
employed worker in the UK during the period
1965–89. Output and productivity were growing most rapidly in 1964, 1968, 1973, and 1987
and growing least rapidly in 1966, 1974–75, and
1980–81. The figure makes three basic points.
First, the growth of output and productivity is
far from smooth in the short run. Second,
although the economy is not subject to
perfectly regular cycles, there does seem to be
evidence of a pattern of slump, recovery, boom,
and recession, with each complete cycle lasting
around four or five years. Finally, in the short
run there is a close relation between changes
in output and changes in output per person.
These are the facts that we seek to explain in
the rest of this chapter.

We begin by assuming that potential output
grows smoothly as the trend path indicates in
Figure 30-1. Later we shall consider whether
potential output itself can fluctuate significantly in the short run. For the moment, with
trend output assumed to grow smoothly,
deviations of actual output from trend reflect
departures of aggregate demand and actual
output from their full-employment level. Although Figure 30-2 shows that cycles are not
perfectly regular, either in the extent of the

output change between boom and slump or in
the time it takes to move from one cycle to the
next, nevertheless the data show a pattern that
is too regular to be explained away as a pure
fluke. What causes business cycles?

We have studied at length the influences on
aggregate demand. An increase in the demand
for exports, an increase in government spending, or a reduction in interest rates are examples
of changes that will increase aggregate demand
in the short run. Conversely, an increase in tax
rates, a reduction in export demand, or a
reduction in firms' expectations about future
profits can all lead to reductions in aggregate
demand in the short run. It is possible to
argue that the factors on which aggregate
demand depends just happen to fluctuate in
the short run and that the observed fluctuations
in output merely reflect this. However, we
should not wish to call this an *explanation* of
the business cycle: it does not tell us why these
influences on aggregate demand happen to
fluctuate in quite a regular way.

One version of this approach does at least
claim to be a theory. It is known as the *political
business cycle*. The argument is simple. Suppose
voters have short memories and are heavily
influenced by how the economy is doing
immediately prior to the election. Suppose too
that the government understands how to use
monetary and fiscal policy to manipulate
aggregate demand in the short run. To maximize its chances of re-election, the government
adopts a tight monetary and fiscal policy just
after it has been elected, manipulates the
economy into a slump, and then adopts
expansionary monetary and fiscal policy just
before the election is due. Since the economy
has spare resources during the slump, it is
possible to make output grow considerably
faster than its trend growth rate during the
period immediately before the election. The
voters think that the government has got things
under control and votes them in for another
term of office.

This theory provides a reason for fluctuations and also suggests why business cycles tend
to last about five years – that is the period
between elections in countries such as the UK.
And it probably does contain a grain of truth.
On the other hand, it supposes that voters are
pretty naive and do not see what the government is up to. Voters are not always so

short-sighted. For example, in 1983 the Thatcher government was re-elected with a massive majority in the UK not because the economy was temporarily growing very quickly, which it was not, but because voters recognized that the government was taking a much longer-term view and believed that the long-term policies would work. However, it may be true that one reason for the popularity of the Thatcher government was precisely that the electorate recognized the contrast with previous governments, which had placed short-term considerations first; if so, that may tend to support the idea that there has been a political business cycle in the UK in the previous two decades.

Even so, most economists believe that there are more fundamental reasons for the business cycle. We now turn to the most important of these theories.

30-8 Theories of the Business Cycle

If government policy is not the source of the business cycle, in which components of aggregate demand can the cycle originate? Fluctuations in net exports can be important in practice. However, imports fluctuate primarily because of fluctuations in domestic output, and exports fluctuate primarily because of business cycles abroad. International trade helps explain how cycles get transmitted from one country to another, but we really require a theory of domestic business cycle to initiate the process.

The very notion of a cycle suggests sluggish adjustment. If the economy responded immediately to any shock we should expect to see sharp rises and falls in economic activity but not sustained periods of recession or recovery. Since a theory of a domestic cycle must be based on consumption or investment spending, it seems plausible that investment spending is the most likely candidate. Whereas households can in principle adjust their consumption spending relatively quickly, changes in investment spending are likely to take more time. Firms are unlikely to rush into major and irreversible investment projects and new factories cannot be built overnight. Hence we concentrate on investment as the most likely source of the business cycle.

The Multiplier-accelerator Model of the Business Cycle

The multiplier-accelerator model distinguishes the consequences and the causes of a change in investment spending. The consequence is straightforward. In the simplest Keynesian model, an increase in investment leads to a larger increase in income and output in the short run. Higher investment not only adds directly to aggregate demand, but by increasing incomes adds indirectly to consumption demand. In Chapters 21 and 22 we referred to this process as the multiplier.

What about the cause of a change in investment spending? Firms invest when their existing capital stock is smaller than the capital stock they would like to hold. When firms are holding the optimal capital stock, the marginal cost of another unit of capital just equals its marginal benefit, the present-value of future operating profits to which it is expected to give rise over its lifetime. This present value can be increased either by a fall in the interest rate at which the stream of expected future profits is discounted or by an increase in the future profits expected.

In previous chapters we have focused on the role of changing interest rates in changes in investment demand. However, in Chapter 28 we learned how to analyse an economy when inflation is present, and we saw that changes in inflation are the main source of changes in nominal interest rates. In fact, real interest rates don't change very much. The simplest way to calculate the present value of a new capital good is to assess the likely stream of *real* operating profits (by valuing future profits at *constant prices*) and then discount them at the *real* interest rate.[4] Hence in practice changes in interest rates may *not* be the most important source of changes in investment spending. Almost certainly, changes in expectations about future profits are more important. If real interest rates and real wages change only slowly, the most important source of short-term changes in beliefs about future profits is likely to be beliefs about future levels of sales

---

[4] In Chapter 13 we showed that it was wrong to discount at the nominal interest rate, which is high when the market expects inflation in the future, without simultaneously recognizing that inflation will increase the *nominal* value of future profits.

and real output. Other things equal, higher expected future output is likely to raise expected future operating profits and increase the benefit from a marginal addition to the current capital stock. This is the insight of the accelerator model of investment.

> The *accelerator model of investment* assumes that firms guess future output and profits by extrapolating past output growth. Constant output growth leads to a constant level of investment and a constant rate of growth of the desired capital stock. It takes *accelerating* output growth to *increase* the desired level of investment.

Of course, the accelerator is only a useful simplification. A complete model of investment would allow both for the effect of changing output (and other forces) in changing expected future profits and the desired capital stock, and the role of changes in interest rates in altering the present value of these expected future profits, and hence the incentive to invest today. Nevertheless, many empirical studies confirm that the accelerator is a useful simplification.

Precisely how firms respond to changes in output will depend on two things: first, the extent to which firms believe that current output growth will be sustained in the future; second, the cost of quickly adjusting investment plans, capital installation, and the production techniques thus embodied. The more costly it is to adjust *quickly*, the more firms are likely to spread investment over a longer period.

We now show how a simple version of the multiplier-accelerator model can lead to a business cycle. In Table 30-3 we make two specific assumptions, although the argument holds much more generally. First, we assume

that the value of the multiplier is 2. Each unit of extra investment increases income and output by 2 units. Second, we assume that current investment responds to the growth in output *last* period. If last period's income grew by 2 units, we assume that firms will increase current investment by 1 unit. The economy begins in equilibrium with output Y_t equal to 100. Since output is constant, last period's output change was zero. Investment I_t is 10, which we can think of as the amount of investment required to offset depreciation and maintain the capital stock intact.

Suppose in period 2 that some component of aggregate demand increases by 20 units. Output increases from 100 to 120. Since we have assumed that a growth of 2 units in the previous period's output leads to a unit increase in current investment, the table shows that in period 3 there is a 10-unit increase in investment in response to the 20-unit output increase during the previous period. Since the assumed value of the multiplier is 2, the 10-unit *increase* in investment in period 3 leads to a further increase of 20 units in output, which increases from 120 to 140.

In period 4 investment remains at 20 since the output growth in the previous period was 20. Thus output in period 4 remains at 140. But in period 5 investment reverts to its original level of 10, since there was no output growth in the previous period. This fall of 10 units in investment leads to a multiplied fall of 20 units in output in period 5. In turn this induces a further fall of 10 units of investment in period 6 and a further fall of 20 units in output. But since the rate of output change is not accelerating, investment in period 7 remains at its level of period 6. Hence output is stabilized at

Table 30-3 The multiplier-accelerator model of the business cycle

PERIOD t	CHANGE IN LAST PERIOD'S OUTPUT $(Y_{t-1} - Y_{t-2})$	INVESTMENT I_t	OUTPUT Y_t
t = 1	0	10	100
t = 2	0	10	120
t = 3	20	20	140
t = 4	20	20	140
t = 5	0	10	120
t = 6	−20	0	100
t = 7	−20	0	100
t = 8	0	10	120
t = 9	20	20	140

the level of 100 in period 7. With no output change in the previous period, investment in period 8 returns to 10 units again and the multiplier implies that output increases to 120. In period 9 the 20 unit increase in output in the previous period increases investment from 10 to 20 units and the cycle begins all over again.

The insight of the multiplier-accelerator model is that it takes an *accelerating* output growth to keep increasing investment. But this does not happen in Table 30-3. Once output growth settles down to a constant level of 20, investment settles down to a constant rate of 20 per period. Then in the following period, the level of investment must *fall*, since output growth has been reduced. The economy moves into a period of recession, but once the rate of output fall stops accelerating, investment starts to pick up again.

This simple model should not be regarded as the definitive model of the business cycle. If output keeps cycling, surely firms will stop extrapolating past output growth to form assessments of future profits? Firms, like economists, will begin to recognize that there is a business cycle. The less firms' investment decisions respond to change in past output, the less pronounced will be the cycle. Even so, this simple model drives home a simple result which can be derived in more realistic models. When the economy reacts sluggishly, its behaviour is likely to resemble that of a large oil tanker at sea: it takes a long time to get it moving and a long time to slow it down again. Unless the brakes are applied well before the desired level of the capital stock is reached, it is quite likely that the economy will overshoot its desired position. It will have to turn round and come back again.

Ceilings and Floors   The multiplier-accelerator model can generate cycles even without any physical limits on the extent of fluctuations. Cycles are even more likely when we recognize the limits imposed by supply and demand. Aggregate supply provides a *ceiling* in practice. Although it is possible temporarily to meet high aggregate demand by working overtime and running down stocks of finished goods, output cannot expand indefinitely. In itself this tends to slow down growth as the economy reaches a boom. Having overstretched itself, the economy is likely to bounce back off the

ceiling and begin a downturn. Conversely, there is a *floor*, or a limit to the extent to which aggregate demand is likely to fall. Gross investment (including replacement investment) cannot actually become negative unless, for the economy as a whole, machines are being unbolted and sold to foreigners. Thus although falling investment may be an important component of a downswing, investment cannot fall indefinitely, whatever our model of investment behaviour.

Fluctuations in Stockbuilding

Thus far we have emphasized investment in fixed capital. Now we consider inventory investment in working capital. Firms hold stocks of goods even though these have a cost, namely the interest payments on the funds tied up in producing the goods for which no revenue from sales has yet been received. What is the corresponding benefit of holding stocks? If output could be instantly and costlessly varied it would always be possible to meet sales and demand by varying current production. Holding stocks makes sense because it is expensive to adjust production *quickly*. Output expansion may involve heavy overtime payments and costs of recruiting new workers. Cutting output may involve expensive redundancy payments. Holding stocks allows firms to meet short-term fluctuations in demand without incurring the expense of short-run fluctuations in output.

Consider how firms respond to a fall in aggregate demand. We have argued that wages will not respond fully and immediately to allow firms to cut prices and boost aggregate demand to eliminate the short-term fluctuation in the quantity of output demanded. Nor, since output adjustment on a large scale is expensive, do firms immediately react by reducing output substantially and laying off large numbers of workers. In the short run, firms undertake the adjustments that can be made most cheaply. They reduce hours of overtime and possibly even move on to short-time working. If demand has fallen substantially, this still leaves firms producing a larger output than they can sell. Firms build up stocks of unsold finished output.

If aggregate demand remains low, firms gradually reduce their workforce, partly through natural wastage and partly because it becomes cheaper to sack some workers than to meet the interest payments on ever larger volumes of stocks. And as wages gradually fall in response to higher unemployment, prices can be reduced, the real money supply increases, interest rates fall, and aggregate demand picks up again. However, firms are still holding all the extra stocks which they built up when the recession began. Only by increasing output *more slowly* than the increase in aggregate demand can firms eventually sell off these stocks and get back to their long-run equilibrium position.

Hence a fall in aggregate demand will be accompanied by a gradual process of output reduction. And once aggregate demand starts to pick up again, output will increase more slowly until stocks have been sold off and output can return to its full-employment level. Thus changes in stocks help explain why output adjustment is so sluggish; they explain why the economy is likely to spend several years during the phase of recovery or recession.

Now we can make sense of the behaviour of productivity shown in Figure 30-2. The figure shows that output per worker tends to rise during the boom and fall during the slump. In other words, output adjusts more quickly than employment. This is what we would expect, given the adjustment story we have developed. A fall in demand is met initially by cutting hours and increasing stocks. With a shorter work week, output per worker falls. Only as the recession intensifies do firms undertake the costlier process of sacking workers and restoring hours to their normal level. Conversely, a boom is the time when output and overtime are high and productivity per worker peaks.

An Equilibrium Theory of the Business Cycle?

Thus far we have argued that the business cycle reflects fluctuations in aggregate demand when output, employment, and wage adjustment are sluggish in the short run. In particular, our account of the business cycle is completely compatible with the earlier analysis of the sluggishness of wage adjustment in the short run. The view that output fluctuates around the trend level of potential output fits nicely with our account of adjustment in Chapters 25 and 26, which might be succinctly described as Keynesian in the short run but classical or monetarist in the long run.

Nevertheless, not all economists share our assessment of how the economy works. In particular, there is an influential school known as the New Classical economists whose intellectual leader is Professor Robert Lucas of the University of Chicago. Although we discuss competing views of macroeconomics more fully in the next chapter, one implication of the New Classical view should be discussed immediately.

One of the key assumptions of the New Classical school, as the name implies, is that all markets clear almost instantaneously. Effectively, output is almost always at its full-employment level. Since the business cycle indisputably exists, the New Classical economists must explain the cycle not as fluctuations in aggregate demand and output around a trending level of potential output, but as short-run fluctuations in potential output itself.

It is possible to maintain that investment takes time and output adjustment is expensive while simultaneously believing that wages instantly adjust to equate the quantity of labour people wish to supply and the quantity of labour firms temporarily wish to demand. Thus a period of sustained investment, initiated by an upward revision in beliefs about future profits, would gradually increase labour's marginal product, the real wage, and the quantity of labour supplied. What we have diagnosed as a recovery, or a period of abnormally fast output growth, might simply be a period in which the levels of full employment and potential output were growing rapidly. If so, it might be possible to develop an equilibrium theory of the business cycle explaining how potential output itself fluctuates in the short run.[5]

If this view – that business cycles are basically equilibrium fluctuations in potential output – is correct, it has an important policy implication: people are doing the best they can, and there is no reason for government policy to attempt to smooth out the cycle. In contrast, the demand-led approach to the business cycle which we developed above suggests that it may be desirable for governments to reduce fluctuations of actual output around potential output.

The New Classical school does provide one

---

[5] For an accessible introduction to these issues, see the lively exchange between Charles Plosser and Greg Mankiw in the *Journal of Economic Perspectives*, Summer 1989.

important insight. There is no reason why potential output should always grow very smoothly along some trend line. Our discussion of supply-side economics in Chapter 27 suggested that there are forces that can change full employment and potential output even in the short run. The most sophisticated theory of the business cycle might involve short-term Keynesian fluctuations in aggregate demand around a path of potential output which itself was fluctuating. Nevertheless, we believe that the Keynesian component is likely to be important in the short run.

Summary

1   Economic growth is the percentage annual increase in real GNP or per capita real GNP in the long run. It is a very imperfect measure of the rate of increase of economic well-being.

2   Measured GNP omits the value of leisure and the untraded goods and bads which nevertheless may have an important impact on the quality of life. Differences in income distribution make per capita real GNP a very shaky foundation for international comparisons of the welfare of the typical individual in different countries.

3   However measured, significant rates of growth of per capita GNP have been observed only during the last two centuries in what are now called the advanced economies. In other countries persistent growth is even more recent.

4   Aggregate output can be increased either by increasing the inputs of land, labour, capital and raw materials, or by increasing the output obtained from given input quantities. Technical advances are the most important source of productivity gains, although changes in social attitude to work organization may also be important. When economies of scale exist, doubling all inputs will more than double output.

5   An apparently fixed supply of a production input, such as a particular raw material, need not make growth impossible in the long run. As the input becomes more scarce, its price will rise. This leads producers to substitute towards other inputs, increases incentives to discover new supplies, and encourages inventions that economize on the use of that resource.

6   Measured GNP growth is often accompanied by economic bads such as pollution. Rather than aim for zero growth of measured output, it makes more sense to provide incentives to directly reduce the output of activities that society considers economic bads. But the most desirable growth rate will always remain a value judgement, if only because it involves a choice between the welfare of people today and of people in the future.

7   Postwar growth in the UK has been slower than in other advanced countries, but there was a productivity slowdown in most countries during the mid-1970s. Explanations include increasing social concern about the output of economic bads; greater trade union power; the diversion of R&D effort to seek very long-term solutions to the energy crisis; and the economic obsolescence of the capital stock when real energy prices increased dramatically.

8   The government can increase the growth rate by switching resources from consumption to investment in physical capital and in people. It can provide further incentives for R&D and other research aimed at increasing technical knowledge, and it can pursue supply-side policies intended to increase potential output through more efficient resource allocation.

9   The trend path of output is the long-run path after short-term fluctuations have been smoothed out. The business cycle describes fluctuations around this trend. In practice, output and productivity seem to fluctuate in a four- or five-year cycle, though these cycles are not perfectly regular.

10   The political business cycle argues that the government is deliberately manipulating the economy to make things look especially good just before election time. The government may also inadvertently contribute to the business cycle by well-meaning but ill-judged attempts at stabilization policy.

11   Sluggish adjustment is necessary for a theory of cycles but it is not sufficient. We also have to explain why cycles are fairly regular.

12   The multiplier-accelerator model highlights the role of expected future profits in firms' investment decisions and assumes that past output growth is extrapolated to form guesses about future profits. This model is

capable of predicting a cyclical response. However, it assumes that firms are pretty stupid. They continue to extrapolate past output growth without recognizing that such behaviour would itself lead to a cycle that would make such extrapolations invalid.

13 Full capacity working and the impossibility of negative gross investment provide natural ceilings and floors which limit the extent to which output can fluctuate.

14 Fluctuations in stockbuilding are in practice an important source of output fluctuations. However, it is only fluctuations in planned stocks that cause cycles. Fluctuations in unplanned stocks are a symptom of cycles in a world where quick adjustment of production levels is costly.

15 The equilibrium theory of the business cycle interprets fluctuations in actual output exclusively as fluctuations in potential output. It reminds us that potential output need not grow smoothly. But some short-run fluctuations probably reflect Keynesian departures from potential output. Aggregate demand and aggregate supply both contribute to the business cycle.

Key Terms

Economic growth
Production function
Human capital
Economies of scale
Zero growth proposal
Technical knowledge
Invention and innovation
Embodied technical progress
Research and development
Depletable and renewable resources
Trend output path
Business cycle
Political business cycle

Multiplier-accelerator model
Ceilings and floors
Equilibrium business cycle

Problems

1 Explain the distinction between total output and per capita output. Which do you expect to grow more rapidly? Explain. Will this be true in all countries?

2 'Britain produces too many scientists and not enough engineers.' What kind of evidence would you look at in trying to decide whether this statement might be true? Will a free market lead young people to choose the careers that most benefit society as a whole?

3 Explain why the rapid productivity growth of the 1980s might be expected to be (*a*) temporary; (*b*) permanent.

4 Name two economic bads. Suggest feasible ways in which they might be measured. Should they be included in GNP? *Could* they be included?

5 Go back and look at Figure 30-2. Can you say which fluctuations in actual output were caused by changes in aggregate demand and which by changes in aggregate supply? Does this allow you to say anything about the plausibility of the equilibrium business cycle?

6 Does the cyclical behaviour of productivity help you answer question 5?

7 'If firms could forecast future output and profits accurately, there would not be a business cycle.' What truth is there, if any, in this assertion?

8 Common Fallacies Show why each of the following statements is incorrect. (*a*) Among advanced countries, Britain has been bottom of the postwar growth league. This proves that the British economy has been the least successful over this period. (*b*) Higher government spending must be good for growth. (*c*) Higher government spending must be bad for growth. (*d*) Only the Keynesians can explain why output fluctuates.

31

Macroeconomics: Where Do We Stand?

We have come a long way since we began our discussion of macroeconomics in Chapter 20. In the last 11 chapters we have slowly built up an analysis of how the economy works. Within this model we have studied the effects of government policy in both the short run and the long run. In this concluding chapter on macroeconomics we shall use this framework to explore the areas in which controversies still rage. We shall describe the main competing views of macroeconomics and their implications for government policy.

We begin by highlighting the major issues on which there is important disagreement. By major issues we mean issues on which a different view will lead almost inevitably to very different conclusions, whatever the details of the model in which the general approach is applied. We organize our discussion around attitudes to four major issues: the speed with which markets clear, the way in which expectations are formed, whether or not long-run equilibrium is unique, and the relative importance of the short run and the long run.

Against this background we then describe and evaluate the four most prominent schools of macroeconomics thought today: the New Classical economists, the Gradualist Monetarists, the Eclectic Keynesians, and the Extreme Keynesians. We encourage you to view these competing positions not as unrelated and contradictory beliefs, but as the outcome of adopting slightly different positions within the spectrum of views that it is possible to hold.

Thus the purpose of the chapter is to define the spectrum and to indicate where different macroeconomists lie along that range of possible beliefs. In so doing, we shall pull together many of the themes of Part 4.

31-1 The Major Areas of Disagreement

We begin by asking why economists disagree at all. Surely, by looking carefully at the evidence we can say which views are correct and which must be rejected as inconsistent with the facts?

In Chapter 1 we introduced the distinction between positive and normative economics. Positive economics relates to how the world actually works. Normative economics relates to different value judgements about what is desirable. Some disagreements between macroeconomists arise from differing value judgements. Suppose for example everyone agreed that more unemployment today would allow greater output in five years' time. Some people alive today will be dead in five years' time and some people then alive have not yet been born. Choosing between higher unemployment today with more output in the future and lower future output but lower unemployment today involves a choice between the welfare of different groups of people. It is a value judgement on which different people might quite reasonably make different choices. Some disagreements between economists fall into this category. Since they do not arise from differing beliefs about how the world works, they cannot be settled by looking at the facts.

However, many important disagreements are disagreements in the positive economics of how the world actually works. Unlike some of the physical sciences, economists can rarely undertake controlled laboratory experiments. In practice, we have to try to unscramble historical data to make judgements about how the economy works. In Chapter 2 we indicated how econometricians attempt to undertake this task.

Even so, empirical research in economics does not always offer clear-cut answers. Suppose for example we wish to study how the economy works when exchange rates are floating. Since many relevant data, such as GDP, are available only quarterly, we have only 80 separate pieces of data since freely floating exchange rates were adopted in the early 1970s. For some purposes we simply do not have sufficient data to offer more than tentative conclusions. Economists who don't like these tentative conclusions may feel tempted to argue that as yet the case against them remains unproved.

Moreover, we live in a world that is constantly evolving. Even if we had a good estimate of the empirical magnitudes in the demand for money equation in the 1960s, should we expect these to be relevant in the 1990s, when credit cards have been adopted on a wide scale? The truthful answer may be that as yet it is simply too early to say. Only when credit cards have been in widespread use for a long time shall we be able to measure their impact with more confidence. And of course, by then some other factor relevant to the demand for money may have changed.

Taking a different example, much current behaviour is heavily influenced by expectations of the future. The spending decisions of firms and households depend critically on today's expectations of future incomes and profits. But whereas purchases and sales allow us to measure actual spending, we collect no equivalent data on current expectations. Suppose a sharp increase in income and output is *not* preceded by a sharp increase in consumption and investment spending: are we to conclude that nobody had previously expected income and output to rise, or should we conclude that the rise was foreseen but that expected income and profits in fact have little effect on consumption and investment decisions? Different schools of economists can look at the same data and give it different interpretations.

Empirical economists do the best they can. In some cases their research is rather persuasive and their conclusions are widely accepted. Few people dispute that current consumption and the current demand for money are influenced by what is happening to current income. But in other cases empirical research is much less conclusive. Although economists agree about many aspects of positive economics, some disagreements will inevitably remain. We now pick out four disagreements that are not mere quibbles about points of detail. They fundamentally affect one's view of the world and the policy decisions one is likely to support.

Market Clearing

A market clears and is in equilibrium when the quantity sellers wish to supply equals the quantity purchasers wish to demand. Whether, and if so how quickly, all markets clear remains the most important issue in macroeconomics. At the one extreme we have the classical analysis which assumes that all markets clear. The economy is then at full employment and potential output. In these circumstances we have seen that a monetary expansion will increase prices but not output, and a fiscal expansion will crowd out private consumption and investment until aggregate demand is restored to its full-employment level. At the other extreme, Keynesian analysis assumes that markets, especially the labour market, do not clear. With imperfect wage flexibility, a reduction in the aggregate demand for goods and the demand for labour leads to lower output and employment. In such a situation, expansionary fiscal and monetary policy can increase real output.

Do markets clear or not? It is interesting how the onus of proof changes over time. Before Keynes's *General Theory*, most economists took it for granted that markets cleared and tried to explain periods of high unemployment within this framework. In the immediate postwar period, most economists took it for granted that markets did not necessarily clear continuously and sought to interpret macroeconomics within the Keynesian paradigm.

In the 1970s the pendulum swung back again. Many economists argued that, if wage stickiness leads to involuntary unemployment, surely workers will find a way to make wages more flexible, thus avoiding the cost of involuntary unemployment. It became fashionable to say that the Keynesian assumption of wage stickiness could not be given any plausible microeconomic foundation. In the 1980s the pendulum was in motion again. Keynesian economists began to articulate microeconomic foundations for wage stickiness, and fewer economists believed there is a presumption that markets automatically clear. It is for the historians of economic thought to decide whether fluctuations in the mood of the economics profession reflect the elegance of the theoretical underpinnings or the much cruder hypothesis that when measured unemployment becomes very large the market-clearing view becomes less plausible.[1]

In the rest of the chapter, we shall see that differing views about the speed with which markets clear lie at the heart of the different positions adopted by the major schools of modern macroeconomics.

Expectations Formation

Most economists accept that beliefs about the future are an important determinant of behaviour today. For example, consumer spending will depend both on how much today's households wish to spend out of their expected future incomes *and* on how today's households decide what future incomes to expect.

Some important disagreements between economists can be traced to different beliefs about how expectations are formed. For simplicity, we divide the possible approaches to this question into three categories.

Exogenous Expectations   Some economists remain almost completely agnostic on the vital question of how expectations are formed. When analysing the behaviour of the economy, they simply treat expectations as exogenous or given. Expectations are one of the inputs to the analysis. The analysis can display the *consequences* of a change in expectations – for example, an increase in expected future profits might increase firms' investment spending at each level of interest rates – but the analysis does not investigate the *cause* of the change in expectations. In particular, it is unrelated to other parts of the analysis. With given expectations, there is no automatic feedback from rising output to expectations of higher profits in the future.

Thus, at best, economists using exogenous expectations in their analysis give an incom-

plete account of how the economy works. At worst, they completely neglect some inevitable feedbacks from the variables they are analysing to the expectations that were an input to this analysis. On the other hand, since modelling expectations remains a contentious issue, proponents of this approach might argue that the various types of possible feedback on expectations can be explored in an *ad hoc* manner.

Extrapolative Expectations   One simple way to make expectations endogenous, or determined by what is going on elsewhere in the analysis, is to assume that people forecast future profits by extrapolating the behaviour of profits in the recent past, or extrapolate past inflation in order to form expectations of inflation in the near future. Proponents of this approach suggest that it offers a simple rule of thumb and corresponds to what many people seem to do in the real world.

Rational Expectations   Suppose the rate of money growth is steadily increasing and inflation is steadily accelerating. Extrapolating past inflation rates will *persistently* underforecast future inflation. Many economists believe that it is implausible that people will continue to use a forecasting rule that makes the same mistake (underforecasting of future inflation, say) period after period. The hypothesis of rational expectations makes the opposite assumption: on average, people guess the future correctly. They do not use forecasting rules that systematically give too low a forecast or too high a forecast. Any tendency for expectations to be systematically in error will quickly be detected and put right.

This in no way says that everybody gets everything exactly right all the time. We live in a risky world where unforeseeable things are always happening. Expectations will be fulfilled only rarely. Rational expectations says that people make good use of the information that is available today and do not make forecasts that are already knowably incorrect. Only genuinely unforeseeable things cause present forecasts to go wrong. Sometimes people will underpredict and sometimes they will overpredict. But any systematic tendency to do one or other will be noticed and the basis of expectations formation will be amended until guesses are on average correct.

[1] As a matter of logic, a rise in unemployment in no way proves the Keynesian case; it might be entirely attributable to a rise in the natural rate of unemployment.

BOX 31-1

ADJUSTMENT SPEEDS IN DIFFERENT MARKETS

Our macroeconomic model now has four markets – goods, labour, money, and foreign exchange – and four variables – the price of goods, the nominal wage, the interest rate, and the nominal exchange rate – which can respond to excess supply or excess demand in these markets. Which market can adjust most quickly?

Under floating exchange rates, the exchange rate can adjust very quickly. Foreign exchange dealers sit facing banks of computers on which they will transact millions of pounds the minute they think the exchange rate is out of line. A similar story is relevant in the money market. These markets clear almost instantly.

Goods markets adjust more slowly. The prices of goods are not usually set in a daily auction. In practice, most firms quote a price and adjust it only when they perceive significant excess supply or excess demand for their product. A decision to change the price takes time and effort. Moreover, some firms have long-term understandings with regular customers and are reluctant to bombard these customers with frequent price changes.

In the labour market, long-term understandings between a firm and its workforce are even more important. Loyalty and trust can be important and valuable commodities. At best, wage negotiations can take time. At worst they may involve expensive strikes and interruption of production. Wages are likely to be the slowest of the four variables to adjust, and the labour market is likely to be the slowest of the four markets to clear.

Few economists dispute this ordering of the relative adjustment speeds of the four markets. Where economists disagree is how long it takes for equilibrium to be re-established even in the market that is slowest to adjust, the labour market. Some economists think even the labour market adjusts relatively quickly. Others believe it takes a very long time indeed.

We shall see that the differing schools make different assumptions about the way people form expectations. This will help us understand why the schools reach different conclusions about the way in which the economy works.

Is Long-run Equilibrium Unique?

Suppose an economy begins in long-run equilibrium but then experiences a *temporary* shock which drives it to a different position in the short run. What happens when the shock has disappeared? Does the economy, sooner or later, go back to the original equilibrium, or does it settle down in a new, *permanently different*, long-run equilibrium?

The latter case is called *hysteresis*. We introduced it in Chapter 27 when discussing unemployment, but the same argument applies to aggregate supply and potential output. Hysteresis exists when the path an economy follows in the short run affects which long-run equilibrium it eventually reaches. In Chapter 27 we mentioned several possible mechanisms that could give rise to hysteresis.

Suppose an economy faces a temporary fall in aggregate demand. This could lead to the following effects. First, when workers initially lost their jobs, the number of remaining workers still in employment goes down. When demand picks up again, there are fewer insiders than there used to be in long-run equilibrium, and they use their increased scarcity to bid up their own wages, rather than to allow their firms to rehire workers sacked in the slump. For this to work, insiders must have a lot of power in the wage bargaining process. In the new long-run equilibrium, potential output is lower and unemployment higher than in the original long-run equilibrium.

Second, during a recession some unemployed workers may get permanently discouraged from looking for work. A culture of unemployment develops, and labour supply is permanently reduced. Third, firms may scrap capital in a slump, and no longer have the factories when demand picks up again. The new long-run equilibrium has lower potential output, both because there is less capital input and because this in turn will reduce productivity, real wages, and the quantity of labour supplied.

Finally, at low levels of activity, the matching

process between firms and workers may break down. Not only is it not worth unemployed workers looking for work, it is not worth firms trying to find workers. This may become self-sustaining even when demand picks up again.

Whether or not hysteresis is quantitatively an important phenomenon was one of the most controversial issues of the late 1980s. The more economists believe that hysteresis matters, the more they argue that the easiest way to prevent its damaging effects is to prevent the economy from entering a recession in the first place. In contrast, economists who believe that hysteresis is not very important can take a more relaxed attitude to temporary recessions since they believe that these have no long-term consequences.

Short Run and Long Run

Where it is agreed that certain policies have short-run benefits but long-run costs, or vice versa, we have already noted that different groups of economists may adopt differing value judgements about how these gains and losses should be traded off. In part, the differing policy prescriptions offered by different groups of economists can be seen as reflecting differing judgements about the relative importance of the short run and the long run.

In practice, these judgements are closely connected with the three issues on which we have already focused. The more quickly one believes markets clear, the less scope there will be for demand management in the short run and the greater will be the importance attached to supply-side policy aimed at increasing potential output over the longer run. Conversely, the more one believes in the possibility of high levels of Keynesian unemployment in the short run, the more likely one is to judge that the short-run benefits of getting back to full employment are more important than any tendency thus induced to reduce the level of potential output in the long run. Similarly, the more one wishes to focus on very short-run analysis, the more plausible it becomes that expectations can somehow be treated as given in the short run; and the more one wishes to discuss what is happening in the long run, the more important it is likely to be to take account of how expectations are changing over time.

And the more one believes in hysteresis, the more one must look after the short run in order to look after the long run.

Having picked out four major areas of disagreement, we now examine in turn the four major schools of contemporary macroeconomic thought.

31-2 The New Classical Macroeconomics

In the UK the New Classical macroeconomic school is chiefly associated with Professor Patrick Minford of Liverpool University. In the United States, where it was originally developed, it is associated with Professors Robert Lucas and Thomas Sargent.

The New Classical macroeconomics is based on the twin principles of almost instantaneous market clearing and rational expectations. The analysis is *classical* because it assumes that wage and price flexibility restore the economy to its position of full employment and potential output. The analysis is *new* because it assumes that wage and price flexibility is almost instantaneous. At best, monetary and fiscal policy can affect the *composition* of full-employment aggregate demand. Its *level* is necessarily the full-employment level. And this being so, hysteresis is unimportant.

Whereas the classical analysis was sometimes rather vague about the period being analysed – it was whatever period was necessary to allow complete wage and price adjustment and hence the restoration of full employment – the New Classical macroeconomics confronts this question explicitly. Wage and price adjustment is almost instantaneous. Whatever level of unemployment is observed must therefore be the natural rate of unemployment. Unemployment changes over time because microeconomic incentives alter the natural rate itself.

Much of the flavour of this analysis can be understood using the following simple example. Money wages are set at the beginning of each period and are then fixed for the period, since firms and workers cannot forever be arguing about the wage to be paid today. On what basis are wages set? At the level expected to clear the market for labour. Since workers and firms both care about *real* wages this requires that, after forming expectations about the likely level

BOX 31-2

THE GOVERNMENT'S POLICY OPTIONS AND CONSTRAINTS

The following checklist may be useful in working through this chapter.

Aggregate Demand The demand for domestic output. The sum of consumer spending, investment spending by firms, government spending on goods (and services), and net exports.

Demand Management Policies to stabilize aggregate demand close to its full-employment level. The government tries to influence aggregate demand either directly, by changing the government component of aggregate demand, or indirectly. Indirect policies include changes in taxation, which affect private expenditure, and monetary policy. Changes in the money supply and the interest rate affect domestic spending but also influence net exports via their effect on the exchange rate.

Potential Output The level of output that firms wish to supply when there is full employment. It depends both on the level of full employment and on the capital stock with which labour combines to produce output.

Full Employment The level of employment when the labour market is in equilibrium. At the equilibrium real wage, the only people unemployed are the people who do not wish to work at this real wage but are nevertheless part of the labour force.

Supply-side Policies Policies aimed at increasing potential output. These include tax cuts to increase business investment and the capital stock; personal tax cuts; union reform or retraining grants aimed at increasing the effective labour supply at each real wage rate; and less government involvement in the economy in the hope that market forces stimulate effort and enterprise. Reducing inflation is also a kind of supply-side policy if high inflation has real economic costs.

Hysteresis The view that temporary shocks have permanent effects on long-run equilibrium.

---

of prices during the period, firms and workers agree on a money wage that is expected to provide the equilibrium level of real wages during the period.

Suppose prices turn out to be unexpectedly high. Firms will have made a good deal. With money wage, fixed for the period, real wages are unexpectedly low. Firms are likely to expand output temporarily while real wages are low. But at the beginning of the following period, wages are renegotiated in the light of the price expectations then prevailing for the next period, and money wages are then set once again at the level that is expected to produce the equilibrium real wage.

Thus, in each period unexpectedly high prices are accompanied by unexpectedly high output. Conversely, if prices are unexpectedly low, workers will have made a good wage bargain. Real wages will be unexpectedly high and firms will temporarily cut back output. But because of the assumption that, at the start of each period, wages are set at the level expected to clear the market, there is no

tendency for deviations of output and employment from their full-employment levels to persist from one period to the next.

Why does the assumption of rational expectations play an important role in the analysis? Because it implies that the government cannot use fiscal and monetary policy systematically to fool people. Suppose the government switches to a more expansionary monetary policy. This tends to make prices rise, since the economy begins close to full employment. If the initial policy change was not foreseeable, workers will not have foreseen that prices will rise. They will have settled for too low a money wage. Firms will temporarily have cheap labour and will expand output. The unanticipated monetary expansion will have caused an unanticipated rise in output and employment above their full employment or natural rates.

But if everyone has rational expectations they will quickly catch on to what the government is up to. When wages are renegotiated, everyone will know that the money supply is expanding and prices are rising. The money wage settlement will suitably reflect this and, in the absence of any further surprises, real wages will now be at their equilibrium level again.

The New Classical macroeconomics can thus be summed up as follows. It is only the fact that some variables, particularly money wages, must be set in advance that prevents continuous attainment of full employment and potential output. Variables that must be set in advance are set at the levels expected to produce full employment. Only unexpected developments make them temporarily inappropriate and allow output and employment to depart temporarily from their natural rates. But the government cannot use fiscal and monetary policy to make prices unexpectedly high period after period, and thus it cannot hold output systematically above its natural rate. If the government attempted to undertake such a policy, people would quickly see through the policy intentions and start to anticipate the expansion. Thus expansionary policy would already be incorporated in the previous wage claims. It would stop being a surprise. But the combination of expected market clearing and rational expectations means that it is only surprises that can move the economy away from full employment. Essentially, demand management through monetary and fiscal policy is completely impotent.

What remains for the government to do? Only to control the price level and to worry about the supply-side policies aimed at increasing the level of potential output. Supply-side policies include income tax cuts to increase the incentive to work. Tight monetary policy will keep inflation under control. It will increase potential output by reducing shoe-leather and menu costs. It will also reduce the distortions that arise when the tax system is not completely inflation-neutral. Low government spending will prevent large government borrowing from bidding up interest rates and crowding out private investment.

Nor will tight fiscal and monetary policy cause Keynesian unemployment. Wages and prices will quickly fall to boost the real money supply and restore aggregate demand to its full-employment level. If a switch to tighter policy takes people by surprise, at worst it will have only temporary effects on output and unemployment. As soon as wages can be renegotiated they will be reduced to the level

now compatible with full employment. The consequent fall in prices will then boost the real money supply and aggregate demand.

Indeed, this principle can be extended. Since it is only unforeseen surprises that move the economy away from full employment in the short run, the aim of demand management should be to minimize surprises and keep the economy as close to full employment as possible. Policies should be pre-announced precisely so that private individuals can anticipate them and set wages and prices at the full-employment level. In part, this line of argument was reflected in the decision of the Thatcher government to announce the Medium-Term Financial Strategy, setting out target rates of money growth and fiscal deficit for many years ahead.

Is it true that the New Classical economists believe the dramatic rise in European unemployment has almost nothing to do with a fall in aggregate demand? Yes it is. It must all be explained by a rise in the natural rate of unemployment, caused by factors such as those we explored in Chapter 27.

31-3 Gradualist Monetarists

The intellectual leader of this school is Professor Milton Friedman.

We use the term 'monetarist' to mean those economists espousing the classical doctrine that an increase in the money supply leads essentially to an increase in prices rather than to an increase in output. Thus, the New Classical economists might be called extreme monetarists who believe in almost instant monetarism. Whereas the New Classical economists believe in only temporary departures from full employment as a result of unforeseeable shocks which cannot immediately be reflected in wages, the Gradualist monetarists accept that restoration of full employment may take a little longer. Even so, they believe that within a *few* years wage and price adjustment *will* restore full employment. Like the New Classical economists, Gradualist monetarists do not believe that hysteresis is important. When the economy gets gack to full employment after a temporary shock, they believe it is the *same* long-run equilibrium (in real terms) to which it returns.

Thus, this school believes there is some force

in the arguments for wage rigidity that we presented in Chapter 27, but only for a short time. Different members of this school adopt different assumptions about expectations formation. Sluggish adjustment in expectations formation may provide an additional reason for slower adjustment back to full employment.

For the New Classical macroeconomists there is no important distinction between the short run and the long run in the design of fiscal and monetary policy for demand management: the classical long run is relevant almost instantaneously. In contrast, the Gradualist monetarists believe that in the short run a fiscal or monetary stimulus would alter aggregate demand, output, and employment, but that it is neither sensible nor desirable to undertake such policies. The short run must be subordinated to the interests of the long run. Let us examine this argument in more detail.

Since wage and price adjustment takes a few years to complete, it follows from the analysis of Chapters 25 and 26 that expansionary monetary or fiscal policy can increase aggregate demand, output, and employment in the short run. However, the Gradualists offer two reasons why policy should not be used in this way. First, the economy will automatically return to full employment within a few years anyway. In the long run, persistent attempts to expand output beyond its full-employment level will lead simply to inflation. Second, if the objective of policy is not to raise the average level of output and employment (which in any case will be the full-employment level) but rather to react quickly to offset other shocks and reduce fluctuations around full employment, there is a real danger that policy will be counterproductive. By the time the government has diagnosed a downward shock and taken the necessary expansionary action, the economy may already be expanding on its own as wage and price adjustments begin to lead it back towards full employment. If so, government attempts at stabilization policy may exacerbate cycles rather than dampen them.

Thus Milton Friedman has frequently recommended that the government should adopt a low but fixed rate of money growth. Because it is low, it will tend to keep inflation down in the long run. Because it is constant, the government will not be exacerbating the business cycle by intervening too late when corrective action is no longer required.

The term Gradualist derives from the implication of this analysis for a government that inherits a high rate of money growth and inflation and wishes to reduce inflation considerably in the long run. Under the New Classical analysis, immediately slashing the rate of money growth might lead to a very temporary increase in unemployment until existing wages could be renegotiated, but that is all. Since the Gradualists believe that wage adjustment is more sluggish, they believe that a very large reduction in the money supply might lead to quite a large Keynesian slump because a large adjustment in wages and prices would be required. Thus, even though the economy would return to full employment within two or three years, it would make sense to obtain the eventual benefits of lower inflation without incurring the worst of the severe recession in the short run. By reducing the rate of money growth more slowly, the problems of wages and price adjustment could be eased and the recession would be much less severe. Hence the term Gradualist.

Even so, since departures from full employment last a relatively short time, it is on the long-run classical analysis that the Gradualists place the most emphasis. The government's chief responsibility is to increase potential output and full employment by supply-side policies and the reduction of inflation.

31-4 Eclectic Keynesians

Proceeding along the spectrum of opinion, we come next to Eclectic Keynesians, a diverse group of economists that includes Britain's two Nobel prize winners, Professor James Meade and Sir John Hicks. In the United States, it includes Professor James Tobin of Yale University and Professor Robert Solow of MIT, also Nobel prize winners. Counting up Nobel prize winners is, unfortunately, no guide to the current standing of the different camps, since most Nobel prizes are awarded for work undertaken many years ago during the period when most macroeconomists were Keynesians.

Broadly speaking, this group of economists might be summarized as short-run Keynesians and long-run monetarists. They accept the view that the economy will eventually return to full employment, but they believe that wage and price adjustment is fairly sluggish so the process could take many years. In the short run, a fall in aggregate demand can generate a significant recession. Although many economists in this group believe that expectations adjustment is also sluggish, some of them believe in rational expectations and hold that it is not systematic mistakes in expectations formation, but rather the forces for wage rigidity discussed in Chapter 27, that prevent rapid restoration of full employment.

Eclectic Keynesians believe that recessions last a bit longer than the couple of years or so at which a Gradualist monetarist would estimate the time required to restore full employment. And this leads them to draw a different judgement about the relative importance of the short run and the long run. On the one hand, it reduces the danger that attempts at stabilization policy are going to end up making things fluctuate more rather than less. And on the other hand, it increases the need for stabilization policy since recessions can be more severe and more persistent than the Gradualist monetarists believe possible. Thus Eclectic Keynesians believe that the government should accept responsibility for stabilization policy in the short run.

Since Eclectic Keynesians believe the economy will *eventually* return to full employment, they accept that persistent rapid monetary growth must eventually lead to inflation once the full employment position has been reached. And in the very long run, it is only supply-side policies that will generate sustained economic growth by increasing the level of potential output. Thus many economists in this group would argue that the government should not neglect two of the policy prescriptions of the monetarists. Supply-side policies will be important in the long run; and, if high inflation reduces potential output, in the long run the average level of fiscal and monetary policy should be chosen to be compatible with a low inflation rate.

Eclectic Keynesians see no conflict between this stance of policy in the long run and the recommendation that in the short run active stabilization policies should be undertaken. Indeed, some members of this group would go further. Economists like Professors Olivier Blanchard of MIT, Larry Summers of Harvard, Dennis Snower of Birkbeck, Charlie Bean, Richard Layard, and Chris Pissarides of LSE, and Assar Lindbeck of Stockholm stress the importance of hysteresis in practice. They argue that active stabilization is desirable because it prevents short-run difficulties from becoming long-run problems which can be broken down only by supply-side policies.

31-5 Extreme Keynesians

This group of economists is primarily associated with Cambridge University. Its intellectual leaders have been Professors Nicholas Kaldor and Wynne Godley. Extreme Keynesians not only insist that markets fail to clear in the short run; they also believe that markets may not clear in the long run, and that Keynesian unemployment may persist indefinitely unless the government intervenes to boost aggregate demand.

In Chapter 27 we set out the arguments that might be used to explain why wage and price adjustment is sluggish in the short run. We now see that it is only the New Classical economists who totally reject these arguments. All other groups believe that full employment will *not* be completely restored once all groups of firms and workers have had the opportunity to renegotiate wage contracts. Gradualist monetarists believe that full employment will be restored within a further year or two, Extreme Keynesians think it might take half a decade or so, but Extreme Keynesians think even that time span is much too optimistic.

To justify the Extreme Keynesian position, two assumptions are required. First, real wages must *not* fall when there is involuntary unemployment; otherwise, a fall in real wages would eventually eliminate involuntary unemployment by reducing the number of people wishing to work and increasing the number of jobs being offered by firms. Extreme Keynesians refer to their assumption of real wage inflexibility as the *real wage hypothesis*.

Second, there must be no automatic mechanism for aggregate demand to be restored to its original full-employment level. In Chapter 26 we spelled out the mainstream view of how this mechanism works. Keynesian unemployment gradually leads to nominal wage reductions. Since these are quickly passed on as price cuts, their importance is less the fact that they temporarily reduce real wages than the fact that, by reducing both nominal wages and prices, they increase the real money supply, reduce interest rates, and boost private consumption and investment spending. In an open economy, competitiveness is increased both through lower domestic prices at a given exchange rate and through the effect of lower interest rates in leading to a depreciation of the nominal exchange rate. Higher competitiveness boosts net exports and the aggregate demand for domestic output.

How can the Extreme Keynesians deny the validity of this mechanism, even over a period of many years? First, the real-wage hypothesis suggests that workers will be reluctant to take the initial nominal wage cut that starts the process moving. Until prices fall workers won't take wage cuts, but price cuts won't happen until wages fall. Catch 22. Notice the important role of the expectations assumption here. Economists who believe in rational expectations would argue that, even if workers care about maintaining real wages, they can afford to take nominal wage cuts since they should foresee that prices will subsequently be reduced, leaving real wages unaltered. Cambridge economists tend to believe in the oral Cambridge tradition, handed down from Keynes himself, that it is very difficult to say how expectations are formed and that economists should be sceptical of any theory, rational expectations or otherwise, that purports to offer a description of how expectations are revised over time.

Moreover, Cambridge economists tend to argue that *even if* prices and money wages are reduced this will have only a very weak effect in stimulating aggregate demand. First, they dispute that the nominal money supply is effectively under government control. Rather, they believe that, since the major component of the money supply is bank deposits, the level of the money supply depends chiefly on decisions made by the banking system. If a Keynesian slump leads to a reduction both in real output and in prices, it is quite possible that the lower demand for nominal money balances will be met by a reduction in the nominal money supply. Banks will supply fewer bank deposits since the demand for bank deposits has fallen. Hence falling prices may lead not to an increased real money stock

and lower interest rates but to a lower nominal money stock and unchanged interest rates. If so, the forces tending to restore aggregate demand are considerably weakened.

Second, Extreme Keynesians might argue that, even if interest rates did change, this would not have a major effect on aggregate demand. They believe that expected future profits are likely to be a much more significant determinant of investment. If firms expect to make losses, they are unlikely to increase investment, however much the interest rate falls.

What about recognizing the effect in an open economy? Here the analysis seems on the shakiest ground. If a Keynesian slump leads to any reduction in domestic prices and wages, this will tend to increase competitiveness if the nominal exchange rate remains unaltered. Thus, either one has to believe that domestic prices do not fall, or one has to believe that there will be an offsetting appreciation of the nominal exchange rate. Extreme Keynesians might defend this on the grounds that a domestic slump leads to a balance of trade surplus, since, with lower domestic output, import demand is reduced. Extreme Keynesians tend to reject the analysis that we put forward in Chapter 29 where we argued that short-run changes in the exchange rate reflect chiefly international speculation on the capital account of the balance of payments.

Since this group of economists believes that slumps can be severe and extremely protracted, they believe that demand management can be a very powerful tool. The benefits from boosting demand back to its full-employment level are considerably more significant than supply-side policies aimed at increasing the level of potential output itself. If the economy can be a long way from potential output, policies to attain small increases in potential output are almost irrelevant.

Interestingly, many of the extreme Keynesian policy prescriptions can be derived without the real-wage rigidity analysis on which this group have relied for many years. The modern analysis of hysteresis leads to very similar recommendations for policy.

31-6 A Summing Up

We have set out briefly the views of the four competing schools of modern macroeconomics.

Table 31-1 A stylized picture of the competing views

	NEW CLASSICAL	GRADUALIST MONETARIST	ECLECTIC KEYNESIAN	EXTREME KEYNESIAN
Market clearing	Very fast	Quite fast	Quite slow	Very slow
Expectations	Rational – adjust quickly	Adjust more slowly	Could be fast or slow to adjust	Adjust slowly
Long run/ short run	Not much difference since fast adjustment	Long run more important	Don't neglect short run	Short run very important
Full employment	Always close	Never too far away	Could be far away	Could stay away
Hysteresis	No problem	No problem	Might be big problem	Might be big problem
Policy conclusion	Demand management useless; supply side vital	Supply side more important, but avoid wild swings in demand	Demand management important too	Demand management what counts

In each case, we have sought to interpret their views against the four basic criteria that we set out in Section 31-1: the assumption about market clearing, the assumption about expectations formation, the assumption about hysteresis, and the relative priority given to short run and long run when making policy prescriptions. Table 31-1 summarizes our discussion.

By now it should be evident that the competing views of *macroeconomics* rest on differing views about *microeconomics* as well. The economists who are optimistic about market clearing believe that markets work fairly well. Some of these economists – Milton Friedman is a notable example – champion free markets in general and hold that free competition is a good thing. Government should break up monopolies where they exist, and use supply-side policies to help markets function even more efficiently.

In contrast, the economists who are pessimistic about market clearing tend to stress all the things that can inhibit markets from working efficiently. They emphasize the difficulties in acquiring the relevant information to make sensible choices, and the fact that many markets for goods and labour are far from competitive. They do not believe that free unregulated markets are necessarily a good thing. Governments should intervene to help markets function in the social interest.

We discussed these issues at length in our examination of positive and normative microeconomics in Parts 2 and 3. Fortunately, it is not necessary to divide economics arbitrarily into

unconnected areas of analysis. Many of the recent developments in macroeconomics to which we have referred in Part 4 reflect the growing conviction that macroeconomists must pay close attention to what is going on at the micro-level. In Chapter 20 we introduced macroeconomics by saying that sometimes we get a clearer idea of the big picture by surveying the whole scene with the naked eye. But it can be useful to have the occasional squint through binoculars to check that our interpretation of the big picture makes sense.

It is not our intention here to adjudicate between the competing views of macroeconomics, though in fact we should probably place ourselves in the Eclectic Keynesian groups of economists. Rather, our intention in the preceding chapters has been to develop a framework in which the differing positions can be interpreted. In this chapter we have explained how alterations in the basic assumptions, especially the assumption about the speed of adjustment, the time required for restoration of full employment, and the possibility of hysteresis, allow this framework to be used to represent the views of the different schools of modern macroeconomics and to show why they reach differing policy recommendations.

Summary

1   Although there is much about which all economists agree, there remain some important differences of opinion, both in the positive

economics of how the world actually works and in the normative economics of how the government should behave. Although some differences in policy recommendations stem from different positive assessments of how the world works, some differences in policy recommendations are based purely on value judgements.

2   It is desirable that economic theories should be tested against the facts. However, in some cases such tests are unlikely to yield conclusive answers. Some key variables such as expectations are not observable. The world is constantly changing, and it may be impossible to obtain a sufficiently long period of data on the world as it is today to allow definitive empirical tests of the competing theoretical models.

3   In seeking to understand the major schools of macroeconomic thought, it is helpful to bear in mind their attitude to four key issues: the speed with which the labour market clears, the way in which expectations are formed, the possibility of hysteresis, and the relative importance of the short run compared with the long run.

4   The New Classical macroeconomics assumes that market clearing is almost instantaneous. Only predetermined contracts prevent continuous full employment. The additional assumption of rational expectations implies that predetermined variables will have been set at the level reflecting the best guess about their required equilibrium value. Any change that could have been foreseen will already have been reflected in the process that set these variables. Hence, only unforeseeable pure surprises lead to temporary departures from full employment until preset variables can be altered and full employment restored. Since the economy is close to full employment, demand management policies will simply induce offsetting price and wage changes to restore aggregate demand to its full-employment level. Government policy should minimize surprises. Movements in actual output and unemployment are largely explained as movements in the full employment or natural rates. The government should concentrate on keeping inflation down and on promoting supply-side policies to increase the level of full employment and potential output.

5   Gradualist monetarists believe that the restoration of full employment is not immediate but will take only a few years. A violent reduction in the money supply could induce quite a deep albeit temporary recession and should be avoided. Moreover, attempts at demand management might be counterproductive if the economy is already recovering strongly by the time a recession is diagnosed. Hence the government should abandon attempts to 'fine-tune' aggregate demand and concentrate on long-run policies to keep inflation down and promote supply-side policies which increase full employment and potential output.

6   Eclectic Keynesians believe that the automatic restoration of full employment could take many years but that it may happen eventually. Although demand management policies cannot increase output and employment without limit, active stabilization policy is worth undertaking to prevent booms and slumps that could last several years and therefore could be diagnosed relatively easily. In the long run, supply-side policies are still important, but the elimination of large slumps may be important if hysteresis leads to permanent effects on long-run equilibrium.

7   Extreme Keynesians believe that departures from full employment could be even more protracted. Keynesian unemployment will not lead to real-wage reductions and may not lead to lower money wages and prices. Even if it does, an induced contraction of the nominal money supply may prevent any expansion of aggregate demand. In any case, pessimistic expectations may be sufficient to prevent a significant improvement in aggregate demand. In these circumstances the first responsibility of the government is not supply-side policies aimed at increasing a level of potential output that is not being attained, but restoration of the economy to potential output by expansionary fiscal and monetary policy, especially the former. Many of these policy prescriptions would also be valid if hysteresis is very important.

Key Terms

Rational expectations
Extrapolative expectations
Exogenous expectations

New Classical macroeconomics
Gradualist monetarists
Eclectic Keynesians
Extreme Keynesians
Real-wage hypothesis
Hysteresis

Problems

1   Beginning from full employment, the government reduces the level of the money supply. Explain carefully the predictions of the four schools of macroeconomics about what happens (*a*) in the short run and (*b*) in the long run. Does it matter whether the contraction of the money supply had previously been anticipated?

2   How might the four schools of macroeconomics explain why European unemployment increased in the 1980s? If fiscal and monetary policy remain tight during the 1990s, what forecast for unemployment would the four schools offer?

3   As compared with a closed economy, how is the speed of adjustment likely to differ (*a*) in an open economy with a fixed exchange rate? (*b*) in an open economy with a floating exchange rate?

4   Identify each of the following statements with one of the four schools: (*a*) Reducing inflation is easy and will not be accompanied by an increase in unemployment. (*b*) Expansionary monetary and fiscal policy will always increase output unless there is a sudden surge of imports. (*c*) It is always worth incurring a temporary increase in unemployment to obtain a permanent inflation reduction. (*d*) The government can always generate a domestic slump and reduce inflation, but the cost in output forgone could be quite high in the short run.

5   Common Fallacies Show why each of the following statements is incorrect. (*a*) The assumption of rational expectations implies that the economy is always at full employment. (*b*) There is never a trade-off between inflation and unemployment. (*c*) There is always a trade-off between inflation and unemployment. (*d*) Keynesians are people who believe that microeconomics is irrelevant. (*e*) Monetarists believe that the level of the nominal money supply is the main determinant of the level of real output and employment.

5

The World Economy

32

International Trade and Commercial Policy

International trade is a part of daily life. Britons drink French wine, Americans drive Japanese cars, and Russians eat American wheat. If this is unremarkable, why is there a separate branch of economics devoted to international trade? Why is trade between the UK and France different from trade between London and Birmingham?

There are two reasons. First, because international trade crosses national frontiers, governments can monitor this trade and treat it differently. It is hard to tax or regulate goods moving from London to Birmingham but much easier to impose taxes or quota restrictions on goods imported from Taiwan or Japan. Governments have to decide whether or not such policies are desirable.

Second, international trade involves the use of different national currencies. A British buyer of American wine pays in sterling but the American vineyard worker is paid in dollars. International trade involves international payments. We began the study of exchange rates and the balance of payments in Chapter 29, and we examine the system of international payments more fully in the next chapter.

In this chapter we concentrate on trade flows and trade policy. We begin by taking a look at the facts. Who trades with whom and in what commodities? We then examine why international trade takes place. Countries trade with one another because they can buy foreign goods at a lower price than it costs to make the same goods at home.

How can this be possible for all countries? The basis of international trade is *exchange* and *specialization*. International differences in the availability of raw materials, other factors of production such as labour, and technology, lead to international differences in production costs and goods prices. Through international ex-

change, countries supply the world economy with the commodities that they produce relatively cheaply and demand from the world economy the goods that are made relatively cheaply elsewhere.

These benefits from trade are reinforced if there are economies of scale in production. Instead of each country having a lot of small-scale producers, different countries can concentrate on different things and everyone can benefit from the cost reductions that ensue.

We discuss in detail the benefits from international trade and examine whether our analysis can explain the trade flows that actually take place. Although there are many circumstances in which international trade can make countries better off, international trade can also carry costs, especially in the short run. Cheap Japanese cars are great for British consumers but not so good for unemployed car workers in the Midlands.

Because foreign competition may make life difficult for some voters, governments are frequently under pressure to restrict imports. We conclude the chapter by discussing government trade or commercial policy and whether it might be a good idea to restrict imports under some circumstances.

32-1 The Pattern of World Trade

Since every international transaction has both a buyer and a seller, one country's imports must be another country's exports. To get an idea of how much trade takes place, we can count the total value of exports by all countries or the total value of imports. They must be exactly the same. And to count both imports and

Table 32-1 The value of world exports

	1928	1935	1950	1973	1988
World exports (billions of 1980 £)	139	58	89	415	1148
World exports (% of US GNP)	57	27	20	40	53

Source: League of Nations, *Europe's Trade*, Geneva, 1941: IMF, *International Financial Statistics; National Income Accounts of the United States,* 1928–49.

exports would be to count every transaction twice.

Table 32-1 shows the value of world exports for selected years and, as a benchmark, the level of world trade relative to GNP in the world's largest single economy, the United States.

Two facts stand out. First, in real terms world trade has expanded very rapidly since 1950, at an average annual rate of 8 per cent. International trade has been playing an increasingly important part in national economies. Between 1960 and 1989, UK exports as a fraction of GNP rose from 20 per cent to nearly 30 per cent. Details for selected countries are shown in Table 32-2. By 1988, world exports were about 18 per cent of world GNP.

Second, the Great Depression of the 1930s and the Second World War virtually destroyed international trade. It was not until the 1960s that world trade again reached its level of 1928.

As trade has grown, both in absolute terms and relative to the size of national economies, the interdependence of national economies has increased. Like many of the countries shown in Table 32-2, Britain is now a very open economy. Events in other countries affect our daily lives much more than they did 20 years ago. We now look at the facts about who trades with whom.

Table 32-2 Exports as a percentage of GNP

	1960	1989
Belgium	39	70
Germany	19	34
UK	21	27
Italy	14	19
Japan	11	14
USA	5	11

Source: OECD, *Historical Statistics;* OECD, *Economic Outlook.*

World Trade Patterns

In Table 32-3 we show the pattern of trade among three major groups of countries. The industrial or developed countries include Western Europe, North America, Japan, Australia, and New Zealand, the rich countries with the largest share of world trade and world income. The Soviet bloc comprises Russia and the countries of Eastern Europe. The remaining countries are the *less developed countries* (LDCs) – ranging from the very poor, such as China and India, to the nearly rich, such as Brazil and Mexico. We study these in greater detail in Chapter 35.

The entries in Table 32-3 are the percentage of world exports from countries in the left-hand

Table 32-3 World trade patterns 1986 (% of world exports)

EXPORTS FROM	EXPORTS TO			% SHARE OF	
	INDUSTRIAL COUNTRIES	DEVELOPING COUNTRIES	SOVIET BLOC	WORLD TRADE	WORLD INCOME
Industrial countries	53.9	12.7	3.1	69.7	67
Developing countries	13.1	5.1	1.3	19.5	17
Soviet bloc	2.8	2.0	6.0	10.8	14

Source: GATT, International Trade; World Bank, *World Development Report.*

column to the countries in the first three column heads. Thus, for example 53.9 per cent of world exports are from industrial countries to other industrial countries.

What can we learn from Table 32-3? The industrialized countries have about two-thirds of world exports, world income, and world imports. World trade is very much organized around these countries.

The Commodity Composition of World Trade

Table 32-4 shows which goods are being internationally traded. It distinguishes between *primary commodities* (agricultural commodities, minerals, and fuels) and manufactured or processed commodities (chemicals, steel, cars, etc.). Note in particular the sharp declining share of *non-fuel* primary commodities, which fell from 39.3 per cent of world trade in 1955 to only 18.5 per cent in 1984.[1] In contrast, the share of manufactures and of fuels in world trade each rose by about 10 per cent during this

[1] These figures are calculated by subtracting the share of fuels from the share of primary commodities as a whole in Table 32-4.

Table 32-4 The composition of world exports

% share of:	1955	1984
Primary commodities:	50.5	38.3
Food, agricultural goods	22.3	11.0
Fuels	11.2	19.8
Other minerals	3.8	1.8
Manufactures:	49.5	60.0
Road vehicles	3.6	7.5
Engineering goods	21.4	33.9
Textiles and clothing	6.0	5.2

Source: GATT, *International Trade 1984/85, Networks of World Trade 1955–76*, GATT, Geneva.

The increase in the value of fuel exports is due mainly to the dramatic rise in real oil prices after 1973.

For trade in manufactures, engineering goods have become increasingly significant, as have road vehicles. The increased share of engineering goods is one of the significant trends in world trade to which we return when discussing theories of the gains from international trade.

Examples of Trade Patterns

Table 32-5 completes our introduction to the basic facts about world trade. We show the breakdown of exports and imports for selected countries. Although the EC is chiefly an exporter of manufactures, even in 1986 primary commodities accounted for one fifth of exports. And although the EC has to import many raw materials, imports of wholly or partly finished manufactures account for two thirds of EC imports. US trade exhibits the same general pattern.

In marked contrast, almost all Japanese exports are manufactures. Exports of road vehicles alone account for 20 per cent of Japanese exports. Since Japan has to import 99 per cent of its oil, most of its raw materials, and some of its food, primary products form two thirds of all Japanese imports. Although these figures suggest that the Japanese economy is dominated by international trade, it should not be forgotten that Table 32-2 shows that exports are a smaller fraction of GNP in Japan than in many other countries, including the UK. This is explained partly by transport costs. Japan is a long way from most of its trading partners.

Finally, we show the group of Asian LDCs where the balance of commodity trade is similar to Japan though less extreme.

Table 32-5 Export and import composition: selected countries, 1986

	% OF EXPORTS		% OF IMPORTS	
	PRIMARY	MANUFACTURERS	PRIMARY	MANUFACTURERS
EC	21	77	31	66
USA	24	72	22	75
Japan	2	97	65	34
Asian LDCs	13	86	30	69

Source: GATT. *International Trade.*

World Trade: The Facts and the Issues

Tables 32-1 to 32-5 set out the basic facts about world trade. First, world trade has been growing more quickly than world income, and is increasingly important. Second, world trade centres on the industrialized countries. Half of all international trade takes place between these countries and they are also the most important export markets for LDCs. Third, about 40 per cent of world trade is in primary products, the remaining 60 per cent in manufactures.

These facts help explain some of the key issues in world trade that we discuss in Part 5. We introduce three of the most topical issues at once.

Raw Materials Prices   LDCs worry that the industrial countries are exploiting them by buying raw materials at a low price and sending them back, in the form of manufactures, at a much higher price. Producers of coffee, sugar, copper, and many other products would like to be able to copy OPEC and triple the price of their primary products without suffering a significant reduction in the quantities demanded.

Manufactured Exports from LDCs   The LDCs want to make their own manufactured goods and export them to the industrial countries. Brazil, Mexico, and Taiwan already have major manufacturing industries. But exports to industrial countries have led to complaints in industrial countries that jobs are being threatened by competition from cheap foreign labour.

Trade Disputes between the Industrial Countries In some industries, such as motor cars and steel, established producers in the UK, the United States, and even Germany are being undercut by efficient modern producers, especially the Japanese. Should Japanese exports be restricted to prevent massive job losses in Western Europe and North America, or should these countries take advantage of cost reductions in Japan?

These are the kind of issues that we shall be examining. First we need to analyse why international trade takes place at all.

32-2 Comparative Advantage

We start by showing the benefits of trade when there are international differences in the opportunity cost of goods.

The *opportunity cost* of a good is the quantity of *other* goods that must be sacrificed to make one more unit of that good.

Suppose a closed economy with given resources can make video recorders or shirts. The more resources are used to make videos, the less resources can be used to make shirts. The opportunity cost of videos is the quantity of shirt output sacrificed by using resources to make videos instead of shirts.

Opportunity costs tell us about the *relative* costs of producing different goods. We now develop a model in which international differences in relative production costs determine the pattern of international trade. The model demonstrates the law of comparative advantage.

The *law of comparative advantage* states that countries specialize in producing and exporting the goods that they produce at a lower *relative cost* than other countries.[2]

There are many reasons why opportunity costs or relative costs may differ in different countries. We begin with a very simple model in which technology or productivity is the source of the difference. Suppose there are two countries, the United States and the UK, producing two goods, video recorders and shirts. We pretend that labour is the only factor of production and there are constant returns to scale. Table 32-6 shows the assumptions about production costs. It takes 30 hours of American labour to produce one video and 5 hours to produce one shirt. UK labour is less productive. It takes 60 hours of British labour to produce one video and 6 hours to produce one shirt.

Costs and Prices

For simplicity, we assume that there is perfect competition. Hence the price of each good equals its marginal cost. Since there are constant returns to scale, marginal costs equal average costs. Hence prices equal average costs of production. Because labour is the only factor of production in our example, average costs are

---

[2] This law was first formulated by the great English economist David Ricardo (1772–1823), who was a successful stockbroker before retiring at the age of 40 to become a member of Parliament and an economist. Ricardo's arguments have a modern ring to them because he used models, clearly stating their assumptions and implications.

Table 32-6 Production techniques and costs

	USA	UK
Unit labour requirement (hours/output unit)		
Videos	30	60
Shirts	5	6
Wage per hour	$6	£2
Unit labour cost		
Videos	$180	£120
Shirts	$30	£12

given by the value of labour input per unit of output, the unit labour cost.

We assume that American workers earn $6 an hour and British workers £2 an hour. The last two rows of Table 32-6 show the unit labour costs of the two goods in each country. In the absence of international trade, each country produces both goods and these unit labour costs are the domestic prices for which the goods are sold.

Notice that American unit labour requirements are *absolutely* lower for *both* goods than those in the UK. But American labour is *relatively* more productive in videos than in shirts. It takes twice as many labour hours to produce a video in the UK as it does in the United States but only 6/5 times as many hours to produce a shirt. And it is these relative productivity differences that are the basis for international trade.

Allowing International Trade

Suppose the countries are now allowed to trade with each other. In this section we make two key points. First, if each country concentrates on producing the good that it makes relatively cheaply, the two countries together can make more of *both* goods. Trade leads to a pure gain and this additional output can be shared

between the two countries. Second, the free market will provide the right incentives for this beneficial trade to actually take place.

The countries are allowed to trade. Since they use different currencies, a foreign exchange market must be set up and an equilibrium exchange rate established. In Chapter 29 we saw that a country's balance of payments accounts include financial flows on the capital account as well as trade flows on the current account. A current account surplus must be offset by a capital account deficit (including any government transactions using foreign exchange reserves), or vice versa. However, we saw that external balance requires that exports and imports are equal in long-run equilibrium. For simplicity we ignore the capital account and assume that the equilibrium exchange rate is determined to make the value of imports equal to the value of exports, thus ensuring that the trade account is in balance.

Table 32-7 shows the unit labour cost and price of videos and shirts in different currencies and then shows their price in pounds at three possible exchange rates: $2.50/£, $2/£, and $1.50/£. The domestic prices are based on the unit cost data shown in Table 32-6. The price in pounds of UK goods is unaffected by the exchange rate. The more dollars to the pound, the cheaper are both US goods when valued in pounds. At the exchange rate of $2.50 the price in pounds of both US goods is exactly three-fifths their price in pounds when the exchange rate is $1.50/£.

At the exchange rate of $2.50, US videos are cheaper in pounds than British videos but the prices of British and American shirts are exactly the same. If the exchange rate offers more than $2.50 per pound, even US shirts will cost less in pounds. The equilibrium exchange rate *cannot* lie above $2.50, for then everyone would want to buy US goods and nobody would want

Table 32-7 Costs, prices, and the range of equilibrium exchange rates

	DOMESTIC PRICE		COST IN £ AT AN EXCHANGE RATE OF:					
			$2.50/£		$2/£		$1.50/£	
	VIDEOS	SHIRTS	VIDEOS	SHIRTS	VIDEOS	SHIRTS	VIDEOS	SHIRTS
US goods	$180	$30	£72	£12	$90	£15	£120	£20
UK goods	£120	£12	£120	£12	£120	£12	£120	£12

to buy UK goods.[3] A one-way flow in trade and foreign exchange cannot be an equilibrium.

Conversely, at the exchange rate of $1.50/£ US shirts are now more expensive than UK shirts but video prices are the same. If the exchange rate is any lower than $1.50/£ both US goods will be more expensive than UK goods when valued in the same currency. For example, at $1/£, US videos would cost £180 and US shirts would cost £30. Hence at any exchange rate below £1.50/£ there will again be a one way flow of trade and foreign exchange, though it will now be UK not US goods that everyone wants to buy.

The foreign exchange market can be in equilibrium only if the value of UK imports, and hence the demand for dollars with which to purchase them, is equal to the value of UK exports, and hence the supply of dollars as UK exporters convert their revenues back into pounds. Hence the highest possible equilibrium exchange rate is $2.50/£, the exchange rate at which one UK good (shirts) is still just competitive with US shirts; and the lowest possible equilibrium exchange rate is $1.50/£, the exchange rate at which one US good (videos) is still just competitive with UK goods.

Table 32-7 shows one intermediate exchange rate, $2/£. The exact position of the equilibrium exchange rate will depend on the demand for videos and shirts. If the United States is large relative to the UK, US demand for imports of UK shirts will tend to be larger than UK demand for US videos. To balance trade flows, the equilibrium exchange rate will need to be close to $2.50/£, the top of the feasible range, to make the pound price of US videos low and the dollar price of UK shirts high, thereby encouraging the UK to import videos and discouraging the United States from importing shirts.

We can draw this conclusion from our analysis.

Regardless of a country's domestic production costs or *absolute* advantage in producing goods more cheaply, there always exists an exchange rate that will allow that country to produce at least one good more cheaply than

other countries when all goods are valued in a common currency. At the equilibrium exchange rate, the country must have at least one good it can export to pay for its imports.

Production and Trade Patterns

Consider again the range of feasible exchange rates shown in Table 32-7. At $2.50/£ the UK is importing cheaper US videos. In return, the UK must be exporting shirts to the United States. At $2.50/£, the UK can just compete with US shirt producers.

At $2/£, the UK producers now have a competitive edge over US shirt producers. The UK still exports shirts and, although the pound price of US videos has risen, the UK still imports US videos, which remain cheaper than videos produced in the UK. And even at the exchange rate of $1.50/£ the UK must be importing US videos, although they cost just the same in pounds as UK videos. Otherwise the United States would be unable to pay for the shirts it is importing from the UK at a price that now undercuts US producers by a considerable margin.

Thus, for any exchange rate in the feasible range that could balance trade between the United States and the UK, the UK always exports shirts and the United States always exports videos. Trade leads the UK to produce more shirts than it needs for domestic consumption and leads the United States to produce more videos than it needs for domestic consumption. The UK specializes in producing shirts and the United States specializes in producing videos. We now explain why.

Comparative Advantage

This pattern of trade and production illustrates the law of comparative advantage. Countries specialize in producing the goods that they can make *relatively* cheaply. Although we noted that the United States has a lower absolute labour requirement for both goods, the relative cost of videos is lower in the United States, and the relative cost of shirts higher, than in the UK.

In the United States, where videos cost $180 and shirts $30, videos are 6 times the price of shirts. In the UK, where shirts cost £12 and videos £120, videos are 10 times the price of

---

[3] If both US goods are cheaper than British goods when valued in pounds, they must also be cheaper when valued in dollars. We simply multiply all prices in pounds by the *same* exchange rate to get the corresponding dollar prices.

shirts. Making videos costs less relative to shirts in the United States than it does in the UK. The *opportunity cost* of videos is lower in the United States, which must give up 6 shirts to make another video. Conversely, the opportunity cost of shirts is lower in the UK than in the United States. The UK must give up only 1/10 of a video to make another shirt but the United States must give up 1/6 of a video to make another shirt. The law of comparative advantage says that the UK will specialize in shirts, which have a low opportunity cost for UK producers, and the United States will specialize in videos, which have a low opportunity cost for US producers. We discuss comparative advantage further in Box 32-1.

The reason that production and trade patterns depend on *comparative* advantage and *relative* costs is that the level of the equilibrium exchange rate will take care of differences in absolute advantage. Even though US producers have lower unit labour requirements for both goods, a sufficiently low dollar–sterling exchange rate will make US goods exorbitantly expensive in the UK and UK goods outrageously cheap in the United States. Beginning from a high dollar–sterling exchange rate at which no UK goods can compete with US goods, the question is which of the UK goods will first become competitive as the exchange rate falls. The answer is, the good in which the UK has a comparative advantage or lower opportunity costs.

The principle of comparative advantage has many applications in everyday life. Suppose two students share a flat. One is faster both at making the dinner and at vacuuming the carpet. But if tasks are allocated according to absolute advantage, the other student is not helping at all. The jobs will get done most quickly if each student does the task at which he or she is relatively faster.

Many Goods

The principle of comparative advantage continues to hold when there are more than two goods. Table 32-8 shows a whole range of commodities. In the first two rows we show the unit labour requirements for production of each good in the United States and in the UK. In the third row we show the unit labour requirement in the United States relative to the unit labour requirement in the UK.

We have ranked the commodities in order. Beginning at the left, the United States has the largest comparative advantage in producing computers, where its relative unit labour requirement is only 1/6 that of the UK. Next comes cars, where the US relative labour requirement is one-half that in the UK; then TVs, textiles glass, and finally shoes. The comparative advantage of the United States declines as we move to the right in the table.

Conversely, the UK has the largest comparative advantage in producing shoes. This is the good in which UK producers are most efficient relative to those in the United States. As we move to the left in the table, the comparative advantage of the UK declines. Producers in the United States become increasingly efficient relative to producers in the UK.

As it happens, the United States has an absolute advantage in producing computers, cars, TVs, and textiles, but the UK has an absolute advantage in producing glass and shoes. Nevertheless, absolute advantage plays no direct part in the analysis. It is comparative advantage that counts.

Differences in Capital–Labour Ratios

Consider the UK and Hong Kong. The UK has more capital (machinery and buildings) and more labour than Hong Kong, partly because

Table 32-8 Unit labour requirements and comparative advantage: many goods
(Hours of labour input per unit output)

	COMPUTERS	CARS	TVs	TEXTILES	GLASS	SHOES
US goods	200	300	50	5	7	15
UK goods	1200	600	90	8	6	10
US/UK relative unit labour requirement	1/6	1/2	5/9	5/8	7/6	3/2

the UK is a bigger country. But the UK also has *relatively* more capital than Hong Kong. The UK has more capital per worker than Hong Kong.

What is this likely to imply about the relative price of hiring labour and capital in the two countries? With more capital per worker, we should expect the marginal product of labour to be higher in the UK than in Hong Kong. This tends to make real wages higher in the UK than in Hong Kong. Conversely, the number of workers per unit of capital is lower in the UK than in Hong Kong. The marginal product of capital and the rental of capital will tend to be lower in the UK, where machinery is relatively plentiful, than in Hong Kong, where machinery is relatively scarce. We conclude that, because the UK economy is supplied or endowed with more capital relative to labour than the economy of Hong Kong, the cost of using labour relative to capital is likely to be higher in the UK than in Hong Kong.

What does this international difference in the cost of renting factors imply for the relative prices of goods in the two domestic economies? Goods that are made by labour-intensive methods are likely to cost more relative to goods produced by capital-intensive methods in the UK than in Hong Kong. Suppose car production is capital-intensive with sophisticated assembly lines, but textile production is labour-intensive with a lot of fiddly jobs that can only be done by hand. The price of cars relative to textiles is likely to be lower in the UK than in Hong Kong.

We thus reach the following conclusion. A *relatively* abundant supply or endowment of one factor of production tends to make the cost of renting that factor relatively cheap. Goods that use that factor relatively intensively will therefore be relatively cheap. They will be the goods in which the country has a comparative advantage. Thus the UK, which is relatively generously supplied with capital relative to labour, should export capital-intensive cars to Hong Kong. Hong Kong, which is relatively well endowed with labour, should export labour-intensive textiles to the UK. Differences in relative factor supply are an important explanation for comparative advantage and the pattern of international trade.

Figure 32-1 offers some evidence in favour of this analysis. The horizontal axis measures

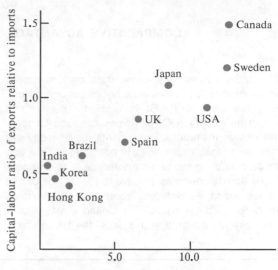

Figure 32-1 CAPITAL–LABOUR RATIOS FOR THE ECONOMY AND FOR EXPORTS RELATIVE TO IMPORTS. (*Source: Changes in the International Pattern of Factor Abundance and the Composition of Trade,* Economic Discussion Paper 8, 1980, US Department of Labour.)

the capital–labour ratio or relative factor endowment of different economies. It is measured in US dollars per worker. The vertical axis shows the capital intensity of exports compared with imports. The number 0.5 means that exports are only half as capital-intensive as imports. The theory says that countries with a relatively high capital endowment on the horizontal axis should tend to export capital-intensive goods and score a high value on the vertical axis. The scatter of points should lie around an upward-sloping line.

Broadly speaking, this prediction is confirmed. In India, with capital worth only $300 per worker, exports are only half as capital-intensive as imports. At the opposite extreme Canada, with over $12 000 of capital per worker, exports goods that are considerably more capital-intensive than its imports.

We now have two explanations for comparative advantage or international differences in relative production costs of different goods. First, there is the Ricardian explanation of international differences in technology: differences in relatively physical productivity and relative unit labour requirements. Second, even

BOX 32-1

COMPARATIVE ADVANTAGE AND THE GAINS FROM TRADE

The table summarizes earlier data on unit labour requirements (ULR) in labour hours per unit output, unit labour cost (ULC) in domestic prices, and opportunity cost (OC) in domestic goods forgone. With lower unit labour requirements, the United States has an *absolute advantage* in both goods. One way to calculate *comparative advantage* is to compare ULRs across countries. Relative to the UK, the United States needs relatively less labour to produce videos than to produce shirts. The United States has a comparative advantage in videos, the UK in shirts.

look at domestic relative prices reflecting opportunity costs.

THE GAINS FROM TRADE

To produce 60 shirts, the UK gives up production of 6 videos. To produce 6 videos, the United States gives up only 36 shirts. Trade and international specialization allow the world economy to have an extra 24 shirts with no loss of videos. Or if the United States produces another 10 videos, giving up 60 shirts, the world economy has an extra 4 videos with no loss of shirts.

	US GOODS			UK GOODS		
	ULR	ULC	OC	ULR	ULC	OC
Videos	30	$180	6 shirts	60	£120	10 shirts
Shirts	5	$ 30	1/6 video	6	£ 12	1/10 video

Alternatively, we can compare opportunity costs, OC. By sacrificing 6 shirts, the United States gets 30 labour hours which make an extra video. More simply, 6 shirts cost $180, the price of 1 video. The opportunity cost of a video is 6 shirts in the United States and 10 shirts in the UK. But the opportunity cost of a shirt in the UK (1/10 of a video) is less than in the United States (1/6 of a video). Hence, again, the United States has a comparative advantage in videos and the UK in shirts. When there are many factor inputs, this method of calculating comparative advantage is simpler. We

These are the *gains from trade*. Only when opportunity costs are the *same* in both countries are there no gains to exploit. Suppose it now takes 10 hours of UK labour to produce a shirt. In both countries videos and shirts exchange in the ratio of 6 shirts per video. No country has a comparative advantage in either good, and there is no gain from trade. We reach the same conclusion using the first method of calculating comparative advantage. The United States uses half as much labour as the UK in producing each good and has no *comparative* advantage.

if countries have access to the same technology and there are no physical differences in productivity, the domestic relative price of goods may differ across countries because the relative cost of renting factor inputs differs across countries. Where a factor is in relatively abundant supply, goods that use that factor relatively intensively are likely to be relatively cheaper than in other countries.

32-3 Intra-industry Trade

The theory we have developed so far suggests that different countries will have a comparative

advantage in different goods and will tend to specialize in producing these goods for the world economy. It explains why the UK exports cars to Hong Kong and imports textiles from Hong Kong. It does not explain why the UK exports cars (Rovers, Jaguars, etc.) to Germany while simultaneously importing cars (Mercedes, Audis, etc.) from Germany. Yet in practice there is a great deal of *intra-industry* trade, or trade in goods made within the same industry.

Of course, a Jaguar is not exactly the same commodity as a Mercedes, nor is Danish Carlsberg exactly the same commodity as Fosters lager. We are now discussing industries each making a wide range of different, and highly substitutable, products which enjoy some brand allegiance.

In analysing intra-industry trade, we must take account of three factors. First, consumers like a wide choice of brands. They don't want to have exactly the same car or radio as everyone else. Second, there are important economies of scale. Instead of each country trying to make small quantities of each brand in each industry, it makes sense for the UK to make Jaguars, West Germany to make Mercedes, and Sweden to make Volvos, and then swap them around through international trade. Third, the tendency to specialize in a particular brand, to which the demand for diversity and the possibility of scale economies gives rise, is limited by transport costs. Intra-industry trade between Germany and Sweden is likely to be larger than intra-industry trade between Germany and Japan.

To measure the importance of intra-industry trade we define an index as zero when trade in a particular commodity is entirely one-way: a country either exports or imports the good, but not both. At the opposite extreme, the index equals 1 when there is a complete two-way trade in a commodity: a country imports as much of the commodity as it exports. Figure 32-2 shows the index for selected commodities traded by the world's largest trading nation, the United States.

At one extreme we have clothing, in which there is little two-way trade. The United States imports clothing but exports very little. Its trade in fuels is largely explained by the principles of comparative advantage we examined in previous sections. At the other extreme we have office equipment (including telecommunications). Here trade is almost completely two-way. As a general principle, the more commodities are undifferentiated goods (fuel, steel), the more we expect comparative advantage based on relative resource abundance to dictate trade patterns. As we move towards finished manufactures, product differentiation becomes dominant and comparative advantage loses some of its overriding role. Intra-industry trade becomes more significant in cars and office equipment.

The more closely markets are integrated, and the lower are the obstacles to trade – in terms both of distance and tariffs – the larger is the

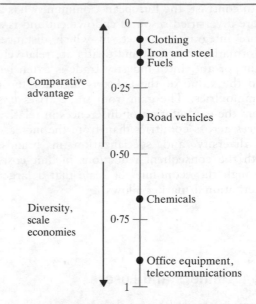

Complete two-way trade

Figure 32-2 US TRADE PATTERNS IN 1984. Comparative advantage leads to specialization. A country imports or exports a good but not both. The value of the index is then zero. Diversity and scale economies lead to different countries specializing in different brands within the same industry. When a country imports as much of a good as it exports, the value of the index is unity. Actual values of the index of US trade in selected commodities are shown.

Table 32-9 Index of intra-industry trade, 1984

	EC	JAPAN
Primary commodities	0.58	0.05
All manufactures	0.80	0.20
Road vehicles	0.70	0.02
Household appliances	0.80	0.04
Textiles	0.91	0.36
Other consumer goods	0.80	0.44
Weighted average	0.83	0.23

Source: GATT, *International Trade, 1984/85.*

extent of intra-industry trade we expect. Table 32-9 compares intra-industry trade indices for the European Community and Japan in 1984.

Japan's trade is substantially one-way. Primary commodities are imported and manufactures are exported. There are very few industries in which Japan is simultaneously importing and exporting. Hence the index of intra-industry trade is low for most goods.

In contrast, the European Community has a more diversified resource endowment and is a more integrated market, in which distance, information barriers, and tariffs are relatively unimportant. Intra-industry trade is extensive and the value of the index is high for most commodities. The gain from trade arises less from the exploitation of differences in relative prices across countries than from the increase in diversity and specialization in brands, with the consequent reductions in unit costs through the economies of scale that a larger international market allows.

32-4 Gainers and Losers

Countries trade because they have a comparative advantage based either on a relative advantage in technology or on relative factor abundance, or because different countries specialize in producing different brands when economies of scale exist. In the latter case the gain from trade is the reduction in average costs that economies of scale allow. Since it takes less factor input to make each output unit, the world economy can produce more goods from its given stock of factor inputs. In the former case, where trade is based on cross-country differences in opportunity costs, we explained in Box 32-1 how trade again allows the world economy to produce more output from any given stock of factor inputs.

These results tell us that the world economy gains when countries first begin international trade: some trade is better than no trade. But they do not tell us that everything that happens in the world economy makes everyone better off. We now give two examples of the conflicts to which international trade gives rise.

Refrigeration

At the end of the nineteenth century, the invention of refrigeration enabled Argentina to become a supplier of frozen meat to the world market. Argentina's exports of meat, non-existent in 1900, had risen to 400,000 tons a year by 1913. The United States, previously a major beef exporter with exports of 150 000 tons in 1900, had virtually stopped exporting beef by 1913.

Who gained and who lost? In Argentina the entire economy was transformed. Cattle grazers and meat exporters attracted resources. Owners of cattle and land gained; other land users lost out because, with higher demand, land rents increased. Argentine consumers found their steaks becoming more expensive as meat was shipped abroad. Although Argentina's GNP increased significantly, the benefits of trade were not equally distributed. Some people in Argentina were worse off.

In Europe and the United States, cheaper beef made consumers better off. But beef producers lost out because beef prices fell. Effects on producers of other commodities were probably small.

Refrigeration opened up the world economy to Argentinian beef producers. As a whole, the world economy gained. In principle, it would have been possible for the gainers to compensate the losers and still have something left over. But in practice, gainers do not often offer compensation to losers. So some people lost out. In this example the major losers were beef producers elsewhere in the world, and other users of land in Argentina.

The UK Car Industry

The second example is the UK car industry. Table 32-10 shows that, as recently as 1971, imports of road vehicles accounted for only 15

Table 32-10 The UK car industry

	1971	1976	1980	1984	1987
Ratio of:					
Imports to home sales	0.15	0.29	0.39	0.51	0.49
Exports to sales of UK producers	0.35	0.43	0.43	0.37	0.34

Source: CSO, Annual Abstracts of Statistics.

per cent of the domestic market while exports of road vehicles were 35 per cent of the sales of UK vehicle manufacturers. Since 1971 exports have become even more important to UK car manufacturers, chiefly because they have rapidly been losing their share of the domestic market to foreign imports from other countries such as Japan. By 1984 imports accounted for 51 per cent of the UK market for road vehicles.

UK car buyers and producers of foreign cars have benefited from the increase in UK imports of cheaper foreign cars. But the Rover Group, the major UK car producer, had a tough time in the 1970s and there were massive redundancies among its workforce. In consequence, the UK government has been under pressure to restrict UK imports of cars to prevent further job losses in the car industry.

Restricting car imports to the UK would help the UK car industry but raise car prices to UK consumers of cars. Should the government heed the wishes of producers or consumers? More generally, how should we decide whether to restrict imports or have free unrestricted trade in all goods? We now develop the general theory of how to analyse the costs and benefits of tariffs or other types of trade restriction. In so doing, we move from *positive economics*, the analysis of the reasons for, and the pattern of, world trade, to *normative economics*, the study of how the government should choose its commercial policy.

Commercial policy is government policy that influences international trade through taxes or subsidies or through direct restrictions on imports and exports.

32-5 The Economics of Tariffs

The most common type of trade restriction is a tariff or import duty. A tariff requires the importer of a good to pay a specified fraction of the world price to the government. With a 20 per cent tariff on cars and a world price of £2000, for example, a car importer would not only have to pay the foreign producer £2000 but would also have to pay the government £400 (0.2 times £2000). The total cost of the car to the importer would be £2400. This is the minimum price at which the importer could afford to sell the car in the domestic market. In general, if t is the tariff rate, expressed as a decimal fraction (e.g. 0.2), the domestic price of imported goods will be $(1 + t)$ times the world price of the imported good.

By raising the domestic price of imports, a tariff helps domestic producers but hurts domestic consumers, as we shall now see.

The Free Trade Equilibrium

Suppose the UK faces a given world price of cars, say £2000 per car. In Figure 32-3 we study the domestic market for cars. The given world price of cars, at which the UK can buy as many cars from foreigners as it wishes, is shown by the solid horizontal green line. Schedules DD and SS represent the demand for cars by UK consumers and the supply of cars by UK producers. We assume that domestic and foreign cars are perfect substitutes. Consumers will buy whichever is cheaper.

At a price of £2000, UK consumers wish to purchase Q_d cars. They want to be at the point G on the demand curve. Domestic firms wish to produce only Q_s cars that this price. The difference between domestic supply Q_s and domestic demand Q_d comes from imports.

Equilibrium with a Tariff

Now the government levies a 20 per cent tariff on imported cars. Car importers have to charge £2400 to cover their costs inclusive of the tariff. The broken horizontal line at this price shows that importers are willing to sell any number of cars in the domestic market at a price of £2400. Thus the effect of the tariff is to raise the domestic tariff-inclusive price above the world price.

What is the effect of the tariff on domestic consumption and production of cars? By raising domestic car prices, the tariff encourages domestic car production. Firms increase production from Q_s to Q'_s. The tariff provides protection for domestic producers by raising the domestic price at which imports becomes competitive. In moving up the supply curve from point C to point E, domestic producers whose marginal costs lie between £2000 and £2400 find that they can now survive because the domestic price of imports has been raised by the tariff.

On the demand side, the price increase moves

Figure 32-3   THE EFFECT
OF A TARIFF.   *DD* and *SS*
show the domestic demand
and supply schedules for
cars. In the absence of a
tariff, domestic consumers
can import cars at a price of
£2000. In free trade
equilibrium, domestic
producers produce at the
point *C* and domestic
consumers consume at the
point *G*. The quantity of
imported cars is *CG*. Q_d is
the total quantity demanded.
Domestic production Q_s is
supplemented by imports
$(Q_d - Q_s)$. A 20 per cent tariff
raises the domestic price of
imports to £2400. Domestic
output is now at the point *E*
and consumers consume at
the point *F*. Imports have
fallen from *CG* to *EF*.

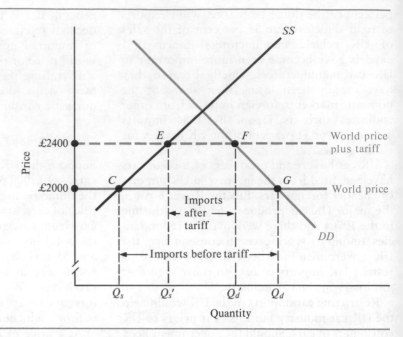

consumers up their demand curve from point
G to point *F*. The quantity of cars demanded
falls from Q_d to Q_d'. From the consumers'
viewpoint, the tariff is like a tax. Consumers
have to pay more for cars.

Figure 32-3 shows the combined effect of the
increase in domestic production and the reduction in domestic consumption: namely a fall in
imports. Imports fall both because domestic
production increases *and* because domestic
consumption is reduced. For any given tariff,
the extent of the reduction in imports will
depend on the slopes of the domestic supply
and demand schedules. The more elastic these
schedules are, the more a given increase in the
domestic tariff-inclusive price will reduce imports. But when both schedules are very
steep, the tariff-induced rise in the domestic
price will have little effect on the quantities
supplied and demanded, and hence little effect
on the quantity of imports.

Costs and Benefits of a Tariff

Figure 32-4 provides a detailed accounting of
the costs and benefits of imposing a tariff. We
have to be careful to distinguish *net costs to
society* from *transfers* between one part of the
economy and another.

We start by noting that, after the tariff has

been imposed, consumers purchase the quantity
Q_d'. Since the price to the consumer has risen
by £400, consumers are spending $(£400 \times Q_d')$
more than it would previously have cost them
to buy the same quantity Q_d' at the world price.
We begin by discussing who gets these extra
payments, which in total are given by the area
LFHJ in Figure 32-4.

Some of the extra consumer payments go to
the government, whose revenue from the tariff
is the rectangle *EIHF*, being the tariff of £400
per imported car times $(Q_d' - Q_s')$ the number
of imported cars. This *transfer*, *EIHF*, from
consumers to the government is *not* a net cost
to society. For example, the government may
use the tariff revenue to reduce income tax
rates.

Increased consumer payments also go in part
to firms as extra profits. Firms receive a higher
domestic price for their output. The supply
curve shows how much firms need to cover the
extra cost of producing Q_s' rather than Q_s.
Hence the area *ECJL* shows the increase in
firms' profits. It measures the extra revenue
from higher prices not required to meet
increased production costs. Thus *ECJL* represents a transfer from consumers to the pure
profits or economic rent earned by firms. It is
not a net cost to society as a whole.

What about the shaded area *A*? This is part of

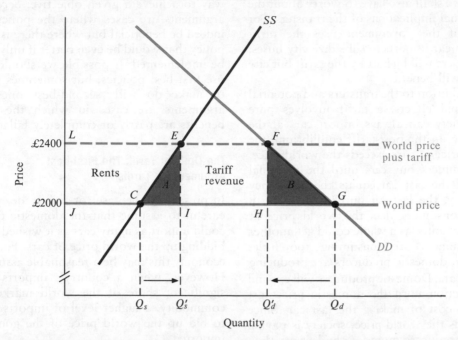

Figure 32-4   THE WELFARE COSTS OF A TARIFF.   The tariff leads both to transfers and to net social losses. The tariff raises the domestic price from £2000 to £2400. *LFHJ* shows extra consumer payments of the Q'_d cars they now buy. But *EFHI* is a transfer to the government and *ECJL* is a transfer to extra profits or economic rents of producers. Areas *A* and *B* are pure waste and net social losses. Triangle *A* is the extra that society spends by producing cars domestically instead of importing them at the world price. Triangle *B* is the excess of consumer benefits over social marginal cost that society sacrifices by reducing its consumption of cars from Q_d to Q'_d.

the area *LFHJ* showing extra consumer payments, but it is neither revenue for the government nor extra profits for firms. It *is* a net cost to society: it is the cost of supporting inefficient domestic firms.

The supply curve *SS* shows the marginal or extra cost of making the last car in the home economy. But society as a whole *could* import cars from the rest of the world in unlimited quantities at the world price £2000. This world price is the true marginal cost of cars to the domestic economy. The triangle *A* shows the resources that society is wasting by producing the quantity $(Q'_s - Q_s)$ domestically when it could have been imported at a lower cost. The resources drawn into domestic car production could have been used more efficiently elsewhere in the economy.

There is a second net loss to society, the triangle labelled *B*. Suppose the tariff was abolished and free trade restored. The equilibrium quantity of cars demanded would increase to Q_d. The triangle *B* shows the excess

of consumer benefits, as measured by the height of the demand curve showing how much consumers are prepared to pay for the last unit demanded, over the marginal costs of expanding from Q'_d to Q_d, as shown by the height of the world price at which imports could then be purchased. Conversely, by imposing the tariff, society incurs a net loss equal to the shaded triangle *B*. It shows the net benefit society has given up by reducing the quantity of cars purchased by consumers.

To sum up, when we begin from free trade equilibrium and then impose a tariff, the subsequent rise in the domestic price leads both to transfers and to pure waste. Money is transferred from consumers to the government and to producers. As a first approximation, the net cost of these transfers to society as a whole is zero. This approximation is exact only if all consumers are identical and share equally in the ownership of firms and in the benefits of whatever the government does with the tariff revenue. In practice this is unlikely to be the case, and we shall also have to worry about the distributional implications of the transfers. For example, if the government uses the tariff revenue on car imports to subsidize city buses, rural car users will be hurt by the tariff but city bus users will benefit.

But in addition to the transfers and potential distributional effects, a tariff involves pure waste. Society can always import cars at the world price. In the post-tariff equilibrium, the domestic price of cars exceeds the world price. Since consumers buy cars until the marginal benefits of the last car equals the price they have to pay, the last car purchased is worth more to consumers than the world price at which the country as a whole could get another car. Consumers are consuming too little. Conversely, domestic producers are producing too many cars. Domestic producers will expand car production until the domestic price just covers the cost of making the last car. Since this exceeds the world price, society is paying domestic producers more for the last car than it would have to pay foreigners for a similar car. Society would do better to use less resources in the car industry and to transfer these resources to an export industry which could earn enough foreign exchange to import cars at the cheaper world price. In Figure 32-4 the two triangles *A* and *B* show the waste arising from domestic overproduction and domestic underconsumption of cars. They are a *deadweight burden* or pure waste. This is the *case for free trade*.

Does this mean that tariffs should never be imposed? We now examine some of the most frequently heard arguments in favour of tariffs.

32-6 Good and Bad Arguments for Tariffs

Table 32-11 lists some of these arguments. We group them under several headings. The *first-best* argument is a case where a tariff is *the* best

way to achieve a given objective. *Second-best* arguments are cases where the policy would indeed be beneficial but where there is another policy that would be even better if only it could be implemented. If possible we should always use first-best policies, but sometimes we have to make do with second-best ones. Non-arguments are cases in which the claimed benefits are partly or completely fallacious.

The Optimal Tariff: The First-best Argument for Tariffs

In presenting the case for free trade, we were careful to assume that the domestic economy could import as many cars as it wished without bidding up the world price of cars. For a small economy this may be a reasonable assumption. However, when a country's imports form a significant share of the world market for a commodity, a higher level of imports is likely to bid up the world price of the good being imported.

In this case, the world price of the last unit imported is *lower* than the true cost of the last import to the domestic economy. The domestic economy should recognize that, in demanding another unit of imports, it raises the price it has to pay on the quantity already being imported. But in a free trade world without tariffs, each individual will think only about the price that he or she pays. Although no single individual bids up the price, collectively the individuals of the domestic economy bid up the price of imports.

Under free trade, each individual buys imports up to the point at which the benefit to that individual equals the world price the individual must pay. Since the collective cost of the last import exceeds its world price, the cost of that import to society exceeds its benefit. There are too many imports. Society will gain by restricting imports until the benefit of the last import equals its cost to society as a whole. When the tariff is set at the level

Table 32-11   Arguments for tariffs

FIRST-BEST	SECOND-BEST	STRATEGIC	NON-ARGUMENTS
Foreign trade monopoly	Way of life, Anti-luxury, Infant industry, Defence, Revenue	Games against foreigners	Cheap foreign labour

required to achieve this, it is called the *optimal tariff*. Only when a country does not bid up the world price of its imports is the cost to society of the last unit imported equal to the world price. Then and only then is the optimal tariff zero. There is no longer any reason to discourage imports. That is the case for free trade under those circumstances.

The optimal tariff is a straightforward application of the principles of efficient resource allocation which we discussed in Part 3. There is another way to see how the optimal tariff works. When a country faces an upward-sloping supply curve for its imports, levying a tariff will reduce the world price of the good by moving foreign suppliers down their supply curve as their output falls. Effectively this is a transfer from foreign suppliers, who lose out, to the importing country, which gains.

Second-best Arguments for Tariffs

We now introduce the principle of targeting.

> The *principle of targeting* says that the most efficient way to attain a given objective is to use a policy that influences that activity directly. Policies that attain the objective but also influence other activities are second-best because they distort these other activities.

The optimal tariff is a first-best application of the principle of targeting precisely because the source of the problem is a divergence between social and private marginal costs in trade itself. That is why a tariff on trade is the most efficient solution. The arguments for tariffs that we now examine are all second-best arguments because the original source of the problem does not directly lie in trade. And the principle of targeting assures us that there are ways to solve these problems at a lower net social cost, without having to incur the deadweight burden or waste triangles such as those shown in Figure 32-4.

Way of Life   Suppose society wishes to preserve inefficient farmers or craft industries. It believes that the old way of life, or sense of community, should be preserved. Therefore it levies tariffs to protect such groups from foreign competition.

But there is a cheaper way to attain this objective. A tariff helps domestic producers but also hurts domestic consumers through higher prices. A production subsidy would still keep farmers in business and, by tackling the problem directly, would avoid hurting consumers. In terms of Figure 32-4, triangle A shows the net social cost of subsidizing domestic producers so they can produce Q'_s rather than Q_s. But a tariff, the second-best solution, also involves the social cost given by the triangle B.

Suppressing Luxuries   Some poor countries believe it is wrong to allow their few rich citizens to buy Rolls-Royces or luxury yachts when society needs its resources to stop people starving. A tariff on imports of luxuries will reduce their consumption but, by raising the domestic price, may also provide an incentive for domestic producers to use scarce resources to produce them. A consumption tax tackles the problem directly, and is a more efficient tool.

Defence   Some countries believe that, in case there is a war, it is important to preserve domestic industries that produce food or jet fighters. Again, a production subsidy rather than an import tariff is the most efficient way to meet this objective.

Infant Industries   One of the most common arguments for a tariff is that a tariff is needed to allow infant industries to get started. Suppose there is *learning by doing*. Only by actually being in business will firms learn how to reduce costs and become as efficient as foreign competitors. A tariff is needed to provide protection to new or infant industries until they have mastered the business and can compete on equal terms with more experienced foreign suppliers.

Society should invest in new industries only if they are socially profitable in the long run. The long-run benefits must outweigh the initial losses during the period when the infant industry is producing at a higher cost than the goods could have been obtained through imports. But in the absence of any divergence between private and social costs or benefits, an industry will be socially profitable only if it is privately profitable.

If the industry is such a good idea in the long run, society should begin by asking why private firms can't borrow the money to see them through the early period when they are losing out to more efficient foreign firms. If the problem is that banks or other lenders are not prepared to risk their money, society should ask whether the industry is such a good idea after all. And if the industry does make sense but there is a problem in the market for lending, the principle of targeting says that the government should intervene by lending money to private firms.

Failing this, a production subsidy during the initial years is still better than a tariff, which also penalizes consumers. And the worst outcome of all is the imposition of a *permanent* tariff, which allows the industry to remain sheltered and less efficient than its foreign competitors long after the benefits of learning-by-doing are supposed to have been achieved. We return shortly to the question of why so many tariffs exist that are justified by the infant industry argument.

Revenue   In the eighteenth century, most government revenue came from tariffs. Administratively, it was the simplest tax to collect. Today this remains true in some developing countries. But in modern economies with sophisticated systems of accounting and administration, it is hard to argue that the administrative costs of raising tax revenue through tariffs are lower than the costs of raising revenue through income taxes or taxes on expenditure. The balance of tax collection should be determined chiefly by the considerations examined in Chapter 16: the extent to which taxes induce distortions, inefficiency, and waste, and the extent to which they bring about the distribution of income and wealth desired by the government. The need to raise revenue is not a justification for tariffs themselves.

Strategic Trade Policy

In Chapter 10 we argued that game theory is a useful tool in analysing strategic conflict between oligopolists. In international trade, strategic rivalry may exist directly, between the giant firms or 'national champions' of different countries, or indirectly, between governments acting on their behalf.

In Chapter 17 we argued that strategic international competition might provide one rationale for domestic industrial policy. We used the example of manufacturers of commercial aircraft. British government subsidies for British Aerospace in its participation in Airbus Industrie not only acts as a pre-commitment which may deter Boeing from trying to force Airbus out of the industry, it may also act as an incentive for the third producer, McDonnell-Douglas, to quit.

Similar considerations arise in trade policy. Levying a tariff on imports, thereby affording protection to domestic producers, may deter foreigners from attempting a price war to force the domestic producers out of the industry, and may prevent foreign producers from entering the industry.

This sounds like a very general and robust argument for tariffs, but it should be viewed with considerable caution. If it is attractive for one country to impose tariffs for this purpose, it may be equally attractive for foreigners to retaliate with tariffs of their own. We then reach an equilibrium in which little trade takes place, domestic giants have huge monopoly power since they no longer face effective competition from foreigners, and all countries suffer.

In fact, this game has the structure of the prisoners' dilemma game we introduced in Chapter 10. All countries may be led to impose tariffs even though all would be better off if they were abolished. This suggests there is a role for international co-operation to agree on, and subsequently enforce, low tariff levels. We take up this theme shortly.

Dumping   Although the preceding discussion relates to tariffs, it can also be applied to trade subsidies. Dumping occurs when foreign producers sell at prices below their marginal production cost, either by making losses or with the assistance of government subsidies. Domestic producers say this is unfair and demand a tariff to protect them from this foreign competition.

If we could be assured the foreigner would supply cheap goods indefinitely, we should say thank you, close down our more expensive industry, and put our resources to work elsewhere. To this extent, dumping is a non-argument for a tariff.

Much more likely, however, the foreign producers, with or without the assistance of their government, are engaged in predatory pricing intended to drive our producers out of the industry. Once the foreigners achieve monopoly power in world markets, they intend to raise prices and cash up.

If so, it may be wise for our government to resist. Even so, for reasons we explained earlier, a production subsidy is the efficient way to insulate our producers from this threat. A tariff has the undesirable side-effect of distorting consumer prices.

Non-arguments for Tariffs

Cheap Foreign Labour　Home producers frequently argue that tariffs are needed to protect them from cheap foreign labour. However, the whole point of trade is to exploit international differences in the relative prices of different goods. If the domestic economy is relatively well endowed with capital, it benefits from trade precisely because its exports of capital-intensive goods allow it to purchase *more* labour-intensive goods from abroad than would have been obtained by diverting domestic resources from the production of capital-intensive goods to production of labour-intensive goods.

As technology and relative factor endowments change over time, countries' comparative advantage alters. In the nineteenth century Britain exported Lancashire textiles all over the world. But textile production is relatively labour-intensive. Once the countries of southeast Asia acquired the technology, it was inevitable that their relatively abundant labour endowment would give them a comparative advantage in producing textiles.

New technology frequently gives a country a temporary comparative advantage in particular products. As time elapses, other countries acquire the technology, and relative factor endowments and relative factor costs become a more important determinant of comparative advantage. Inevitably, the domestic producers who have lost their comparative advantage start complaining about competition from imports using cheap foreign labour.

The basic proof of the gains from trade tells us that in the long run the country as a whole will benefit by facing facts, recognizing that its comparative advantage has changed, and transferring production to the industries in which it

now has a comparative advantage. And our analysis of comparative advantage promises us that there *must* be some industry in which each country has a comparative advantage. In the long run, trying to use tariffs to prop up industries that have lost their comparative advantage – British shipbuilding may be one example – is both futile and expensive.

Of course, in the short run the adjustment may be painful and costly. Workers lose their jobs and must start afresh in industries where they don't have years of experience and acquired skills. But the principle of targeting tells us that, if society wants to provide assistance in the short run, some kind of retraining or relocation sudsidy is more efficient than a tariff.

Why Do We Have Tariffs?

Aside from the optimal tariff argument, there is almost nothing to be said in favour of tariffs. Economists have been arguing against them for well over a century. Why are tariffs still so popular?

Concentrated Benefits, Diffuse Costs　A tariff on a particular commodity helps a particular industry. It is relatively easy for firms and workers in an industry to organize effective political pressure, for they can all agree that this single issue is central to their livelihood, at least in the short run. But if the tariff is imposed, the cost in higher consumer prices is borne by a much larger and more diverse group of people whom it is much harder to organize politically. Hence the politicians are more likely to heed the vociferous, well organized group lobbying *for* tariffs, especially if they are geographically concentrated in an area where, by voting together, they could have a significant effect on the outcome of the next election.

Tariffs versus Subsidies　Even so, why does government assistance frequently take the form of tariffs rather than production subsidies, which we have argued are frequently more appropriate? First, because if the domestic car industry is suffering from imports of Japanese cars, the solution seems to be to do something which will hurt Japan directly. Second, because the government would have to raise taxes to finance a subsidy. For example, British governments in the 1970s were frequently criticized by taxpayers for subsidizing British Leyland. A tariff is politically easier in many cases, not merely because it seems to hurt foreign producers, but because it seems to augment government revenues (raising hopes of an income tax cut), whereas a subsidy seems to deplete government revenues (raising fears of a rise in income tax rates). Although we now know that a tariff hits consumers directly by raising the domestic price of the good, the government may be able to invoke impersonal 'market forces'. Tariffs cause the government less political hassle.

32-7 Tariff Levels: Not So Bad?

In the nineteenth century world trade grew rapidly in part because the leading country, the UK, pursued a vigorous policy of free trade. In contrast, US tariffs averaged about 50 per cent, although they had fallen to around 30 per cent by the early 1920s. As the industrial economies went into the Great Depression of the late 1920s and 1930s, there was increasing pressure to protect domestic jobs by keeping out imports. Tariffs in the United States returned to around 50 per cent, and the UK abandoned the policy of free trade that had been pursued for nearly a century.

Table 32-1 showed that the combination of world recession and increasing tariffs led to a disastrous slump in the volume of world trade, further exacerbated by the Second World War.

GATT

After the war there was a collective determination to see world trade restored. Bodies such as the International Monetary Fund and the World Bank were set up and a large number of countries signed the General Agreement on Tariffs and Trade (GATT), a commitment to reduce tariffs successively and dismantle trade restrictions.

Under successive rounds of GATT, tariffs fell steadily. By 1960 US tariffs were only about one-fifth their level at the outbreak of the Second World War. In the UK the system of wartime quotas on imports had been dismantled by the mid-1950s, after which tariffs were reduced by nearly half in the ensuing 25 years. Europe as a whole has moved towards an enlarged European Community in which tariffs between member countries have been abolished.

Thus, at the start of the 1980s tariff levels throughout the world economy were probably as low as they had ever been. And world trade had seen three decades of rapid growth, arising at least in part from the success of GATT in removing trade restrictions. But the threat of protection had not been abolished for ever. With increasing unemployment in the industrial economies in the early 1980s there has been renewed pressure for tariffs, partly for the reasons we set out in the previous section. The United States imposed a quota on steel imports from Japan and Europe, and the Japanese have agreed to restrict their exports of cars to Europe and the United States.

32-8 Other Commercial Policies

Tariffs are not the only form of commercial policy. In this section we examine three other policy instruments: quotas, non-tariff barriers, and export subsidies.

Quotas

Quotas are restrictions on the maximum quantity of imports. For example, the government might restrict the level of imports of Japanese cars to a maximum of 100 000 cars a year. Although quotas restrict the *quantity* of imports, this does not mean they have no effect on domestic prices of the restricted goods. With a lower supply, the equilibrium price will be higher than under free trade.

Thus quotas are rather like tariffs. The domestic price to the consumer is increased, and it is this higher price that allows inefficient domestic producers to produce a higher output than under free trade. Quotas lead to social waste for exactly the same reasons as tariffs.

Because quotas raise the domestic price of the restricted good, the lucky foreign suppliers who succeed in getting some of their goods sold will make large profits on these sales. In terms of Figure 32-4, the rectangle *EFHI*, which would have accrued to the government as revenue from a tariff, now accrues to foreign suppliers or domestic importers. It represents the difference between domestic and world prices on the goods that are imported, multiplied by the quantity of imports allowed.

If these profits accrue to foreigners they represent a net social cost of quotas over and above the costs of imposing an equivalent tariff. However, the government could always auction off licences to import and so recoup this revenue. Private importers or foreign suppliers would be prepared to bid up to this amount to get their hands on an important licence.

Non-tariff Barriers

These are administrative regulations that discriminate against foreign goods and in favour of home oods. They may take the form of delaying imports at the frontier, ordering civil servants to use goods made at home, or merely a publicity campaign to 'buy British'. Non-tariff barriers may also be more subtle. Contracts can specify standards with which domestic producers are familiar but foreign producers

are not. The 1992 programme aims to end non-tariff barriers inside the European Community. We study it in detail in Chapter 34.

Export Subsidies

So far, we have looked only at restrictions on imports. But countries also use commercial policy to boost exports. This can vary from outright subsidy to cheap credit or exemption from certain domestic taxes.

Figure 32-5 shows the economics of an export subsidy. Suppose the world price of a computer is £5000. Under free trade, domestic consumers would purchase a quantity Q_d at point G on their demand curve, producers would make a quantity Q_s at point E on their supply curve, and a quantity GE would be exported.

To boost the computer industry, the government now imposes a 20 per cent *export subsidy* applying only to computers that are exported. On such goods, domestic producers now earn

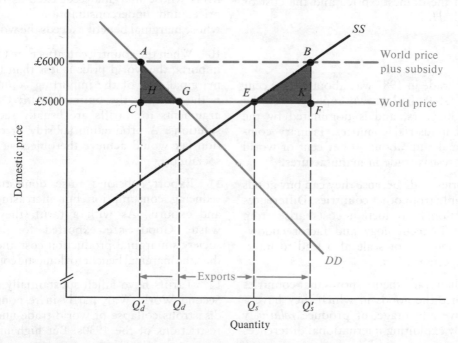

Figure 32-5   AN EXPORT SUBSIDY.   Under free trade, consumers demand Q_d, production is Q_s, and exports are *GE*. With a sudsidy on exports alone, domestic producers will restrict supply to the home market to Q'_d so that home consumers pay £6000, the same as producers can earn by exporting. Total output is Q'_s and exports *AB*. *K* shows the social cost of producing goods whose marginal cost exceeds the world price for which they are sold. *H* shows the social cost of restricting consumption when marginal benefits exceed the world price of the good.

a total of £6000. No firm will sell at home for £5000 when it can sell abroad and get £6000. The supply to the domestic market will be curtailed to Q'_d so that consumers are prepared to pay this price. Total domestic production increases to Q'_s and exports are given by AB.

Although the subsidy increases exports, it does so at the net social cost given by the shaded triangles H and K. Triangle H measures the net social cost of reducing domestic consumption from Q_d to Q'_d. The consumer benefits from the extra consumption would have exceeded the world price or social marginal cost at which the economy would always have obtained computers. Triangle K measures the social cost of increasing output from Q_s to Q'_s even though the marginal domestic cost of using these extra resources exceeds the price being received from the foreigners who buy computers.

Just as with a tariff, an export subsidy is usually a second-best policy. Even if the country did wish to increase its output of computers, it would be cheaper to use a production subsidy, incurring the cost of the triangle K, but avoiding the rise in the domestic price and the cost of the triangle H.

Summary

1   World trade in 1987 was about 18 per cent of world GNP, had grown rapidly over the previous 30 years, and is dominated by the developed industrial countries. Primary commodities make up about 40 per cent of world trade; the rest is trade in manufactures.

2   Countries trade because they can buy goods more cheaply from other countries. Differences in international production costs arise from differences in technology and factor endowments. Economies of scale also lead to international specialization.

3   Ricardian trade theory shows that countries will produce the goods in which they have a comparative advantage, or produce *relatively* cheaply. By exploiting international differences in opportunity costs, trade leads to a pure gain.

4   The extension of trade theory to more than one factor of production emphasizes *relative* factor endowments. Countries tend to produce and export goods that use intensively the factors with which the country is *relatively* well endowed.

5   Intra-industry trade occurs because of scale economies and consumer demand for diversity. The gain from trade is now the extension of the market and the reduction in costs that this enables.

6   If trade is to balance, and the foreign exchange market is to be in equilibrium, each country *must* have a comparative advantage in at least one good. The level of the equilibrium exchange rate copes with international differences in absolute advantage.

7   Although international trade can benefit the world as a whole, some people will lose out unless the gainers offer compensation to the losers.

8   By raising the domestic price, a tariff reduces consumption but increases domestic production. Hence imports fall.

9   A tariff leads to two deadweight losses that are net social costs: overproduction by domestic firms whose marginal cost exceeds the world price, and underconsumption by consumers whose marginal benefit exceeds the world price.

10   When the country can affect the price of its imports, the world price is less than the social marginal cost of the importing country. This is the case for the optimal tariff. Otherwise, arguments for tariffs are usually second-best solutions. A production subsidy or consumption tax would achieve the objective at lower social cost.

11   Export subsidies raise domestic prices, reducing consumption but increasing output and exports. As with a tariff, they involve waste. Goods are exported for less than society's marginal production cost and for less than the marginal benefit to domestic consumers.

12   Tariffs have fallen substantially since the Second World War, partly in response to the disastrous collapse of world trade under tariff restrictions of the 1930s. But high unemployment in the 1980s led to new pressure for tariffs and protection.

13   Trade protection is usually harmful to society. Yet governments frequently adopt it because it is an easy option politically.

Key Terms

Comparative advantage
Absolute advantage
Gains from trade
Factor endowments
Intra-industrial trade
Commercial policy
Import tariff
Export subsidy
Deadweight loss
Optimal tariff
Infant industry tariff argument
Second-best
Principle of targeting
Dumping
GATT
Import quotas
Non-tariff barriers
Protection

Problems

1 (*a*) Why does the composition of EC trade and Japanese trade differ in Table 32-5? (*b*) Which composition of trade in that table do you expect Hong Kong to be most like? Why?

2 'A country with uniformly low productivity can only lose by allowing foreign competition.' Discuss this assertion in detail.

3 'Large countries gain less from world trade than small countries.' True or False? Why?

4 Suppose in Table 32-8 that the United States produces computers, cars, and TVs and the UK produces the other goods. Now a lot of UK labour goes to live in the United States. What will happen to the pattern of trade and specialization?

5 Stereos, wine, transistor radios, steel sheeting: which of these do you think will have a high index of intra-industry trade? Why?

6 Making TVs has economies of scale. Is this a good argument for imposing a tariff on TV imports?

7 To preserve its national heritage, society bans exports of works of art. (*a*) Is this better than an export tax? (*b*) Who gains and who loses from the export ban? (*c*) Will this measure encourage young domestic artists?

8 Common Fallacies Show why the following statements are incorrect. (*a*) British producers are rapidly becoming uncompetitive in every commodity. (*b*) Free trade is always the best policy. (*c*) Buy British and help Britain. (*d*) Tariffs simply transfer money from consumers to producers and the government.

33

The International Monetary System and International Finance

Few areas of economics seem as mysterious to the outsider as the economics of exchange rates and international finance. Indeed they are sometimes mysterious even to insiders. It is said that, in speculating on exchange rate changes, Keynes made three fortunes but lost two.

In the previous chapter we studied the pure theory of international trade. It is known as the 'pure theory' because it discusses questions such as the determination of comparative advantage by examining the real resources – physical quantities of land, labour, and capital – used to make different goods in different countries. But it does not highlight the monetary mechanism through which international payments are made.

In a closed economy, we distinguish between a barter economy, where goods and services are directly swapped for one another, and a monetary economy, in which people sell goods, services, and assets in exchange for money which can then be used to make further purchases of goods, services, and assets. Money serves as a medium of exchange and reduces the transaction costs below the level that would be incurred in a barter economy. In exactly the same way, the international monetary system provides a medium of exchange for international transactions in the world economy. We must now study the operation of this system of international payments in more detail.

When different countries use different domestic money, the exchange rate measures the price at which the two national currencies can be exchanged in the foreign exchange market. We introduced these ideas in Chapter 29. We also pointed out that several different systems of international payments or *exchange rate regimes* were possible. We discussed a fixed exchange rate regime and a regime of freely floating exchange rates.

In Chapter 29 we were chiefly interested in how the adoption of a particular exchange rate regime would affect the operation of domestic monetary and fiscal policies in a particular country. Now we are interested in a different set of questions. What is the implication of a particular exchange rate regime for the world economy as a whole? What are the relative merits of fixed exchange rates and floating exchange rates from the viewpoint of the world economy?

We begin the chapter by briefly reviewing the possible exchange rate regimes. Then we discuss the relative merits of the different regimes. We conclude the chapter by looking at some of the questions raised by the possibility of international economic co-operation and *policy co-ordination*. In Part 4 we discussed only the policy options for a single country acting in isolation. Would the member countries of the world economy be better off if they took deliberate steps to co-ordinate their domestic monetary and fiscal policies? Could this help reduce the world's business cycle? Would it allow the world to reduce inflation without incurring a high cost of additional unemployment in the short run? Is this the purpose of the economic summit meetings which leaders of the advanced economies regularly attend? We try to answer these questions. We also examine the European Monetary System, an example of a tentative step towards international policy co-ordination.

33-1 Alternative Exchange Rate Regimes

In Chapter 29 we explained that the exchange rate is the equilibrium price at which two national currencies are traded in the foreign exchange market. The demand for pounds arises from export earnings in a foreign currency which exporters now wish to convert back into sterling, and from the desire of foreigners to purchase British assets, either financial assets (British government bonds) or physical assets (property in London). Conversely, the supply of pounds to the foreign exchange market arises from the desire of British importers to obtain foreign currency to pay foreign suppliers, and from the desire of British residents to buy foreign assets.

In the absence of government intervention in the foreign exchange market, the equilibrium exchange rate will be determined by these supplies and demands. However, the government may *intervene* in the foreign exchange market. By selling some of its foreign exchange reserves in exchange for the domestic currency, the government can add to the demand for the domestic currency. Conversely, the government can print domestic money and use it in the foreign exchange market to buy foreign currency to add to the foreign exchange reserves. In this way the government can add to the supply of the domestic currency in the foreign exchange market. If you have forgotten the details of how this works, we suggest you go back and read the first part of Chapter 29 before continuing with the discussion of this section.

Different exchange rate regimes are described by the formal or informal conventions that determine the circumstances in which the government intervenes in the foreign exchange market. Table 33-1 summarizes the regimes that we shall be discussing: the gold standard, the adjustable peg, managed floating, and freely floating exchange rates.

The nineteenth century gold standard is an

Table 33-1 Alternative exchange rate regimes

GOVERNMENT INTERVENTION	EXCHANGE RATES	
	FIXED	FLEXIBLE
None or automatic	Gold standard (19th century)	Free float (never?)
Some discretion	Adjustable peg (1960s)	Managed float (1970s and 1980s)

example of an automatic system with fixed exchange rates. A totally free floating exchange rate is an automatic system with flexible exchange rates. The adjustable peg and managed floating systems actually in operation since 1945 have allowed governments some discretion about how to intervene using their foreign exchange reserves. We now consider these regimes in more detail.

33-2 The Gold Standard

There are three distinguishing characteristics of the gold standard. First, the government of each country fixes the price of gold in terms of its domestic currency.

The *par value* of gold is the price of gold in terms of domestic currency. It is fixed by the government.

Second, the government maintains the *convertibility* of the domestic currency into gold. The government will buy or sell as much gold as people wish to transact at the par value. You can always take your pound to the central bank and buy a specified quantity of gold. Third, the government follows a rule that links domestic money creation to the government's holdings of gold. The government can issue pound only by buying gold from the general public. If the public converts its paper money back into gold, the stock of outstanding pounds is automatically reduced again. This is called *100 per cent cover* or *100 per cent gold backing* for the money supply. Each pound in circulation must be backed by an equivalent value of gold in the vaults of the central bank. Unlike the monetary system in operation in most countries today, where the government can simply roll the printing presses and issue extra pounds that are *not* automatically convertible into gold which the government is committed to supply in exchange, under the gold standard the government's ability to increase the money supply was strictly limited by the requirement that it had to hold an equivalent value of gold in the vaults.[1]

---

[1] What we are describing is a pure gold standard. In practice, during the nineteenth and early twentieth centuries central banks tied money creation to gold holdings in many different ways. Sometimes less than 100 per cent cover was used. Governments relied on the fact that not all citizens were likely to wish simultaneously to cash in domestic notes for gold. But the governments were committed to converting notes into gold on demand.

Suppose there are two countries following the three rules of the gold standard: a par value, convertibility, and 100 per cent cover. Specifically, suppose the United States has a par value of $20.67 per ounce of gold and the UK has a par value of £4.25 per ounce of gold. The dollar–pound exchange rate *must* always be $4.86/£. Why? Because this is the ratio of the relative price of gold in the two countries ($20.67/£4.25). At any other exchange rate it would be possible to sell gold in one country in exchange for domestic currency, convert that currency into the other currency in the foreign exchange market, and buy gold with this currency in the other country, making a profit on the whole set of transactions. Since this profit could be made with certainty, everyone would be doing it. In the foreign exchange market, the flow between currencies would be entirely one way. It could not be an equilibrium. The equilibrium exchange rate *must* equal the relative gold prices in the two currencies. This exchange rate is called the *gold parity* rate. At the exchange rate $4.86/£, you can buy one ounce of gold using £4.25 in the UK, or you can convert £4.25 into $20.67 at the gold parity exchange rate of $4.86 and then buy one ounce of gold in the United States. At the gold parity exchange rate, gold effectively costs the same in both currencies.

Balance of Payments Adjustment under the Gold Standard

Suppose we begin from full long-run equilibrium. In each country there is *internal balance* or full employment and there is also *external balance*. Each country has neither a balance of payments surplus nor a balance of payments deficit. Each country also has a constant money supply, a given level of gold in the government vaults, and a given price level.

Beginning from this position, suppose Americans decide to spend more of their incomes on imports of goods produced in the UK. Britain now has a trade surplus since its exports have increased. If domestic prices and wages are sluggish, the UK will also be experiencing an export-led Keynesian boom in the short run since aggregate demand for British output has increased. Conversely, the United States is facing a recession and a balance of payments deficit.

Some private individuals on balance are con-

verting dollars into pounds, there is an excess demand for pounds and an excess supply of dollars in the foreign exchange market at the gold parity exchange rate. However, as the dollar–pound exchange rate starts to rise, it immediately becomes profitable to buy gold in the United States in exchange for dollars and sell it to the Bank of England in exchange for pounds. This acts to reduce the excess supply of dollars relative to pounds.

Thus in effect the central banks in the United States and the UK are automatically required to intervene in the foreign exchange market. A UK balance of payments surplus is matched by an equivalent increase in the Bank of England's gold holdings, the purchase of which provides the extra pounds required to clear the foreign exchange market at the gold parity rate. And in the United States the balance of payments deficit is matched by a reduction in the central bank's gold stock by an equivalent amount.

Hence under the gold standard a country running a balance of payments surplus faces a matching increase in its domestic currency in circulation, the consequence of the excess of receipts from abroad over payments to foreigners, and a matching increase in the government's gold stock which backs the paper domestic money. A country with a deficit is running down its official gold stock and its domestic currency is being correspondingly reduced.

We now see how this provides an automatic international adjustment mechanism. When the demand for UK exports rises, initially there is a Keynesian boom if domestic wages and prices do not immediately adjust to higher aggregate demand for domestic output. With a fixed nominal exchange rate, eventually the boom itself may bid up domestic prices and reduce the international competitiveness of the domestic economy. However, this process is supplemented by the monetary flows taking place. Initially the UK has a balance of payments surplus. This leads to an increase in the stock of pounds in circulation and the stock of gold at the Bank of England. Gradually, the higher domestic money supply puts further upward pressure on domestic prices through the standard mechanism of reducing interest rates and increasing aggregate demand for goods.

As prices rise, the UK gradually becomes less competitive since the nominal exchange rate remains fixed. In turn this gradually eliminates the balance of payments surplus as export demand falls and import demand increases. When UK prices have risen, and UK competitiveness fallen, to the extent required to restore balance of payments equilibrium, international flows of money and gold cease. With the domestic money supply unchanging, there is no further presssure on domestic prices. Internal and external balance have been restored.

Of course, exactly the opposite effects are happening in the United States. With an initial deficit, the American stock of gold and money is falling, thus increasing American interest rates and putting downward pressure on aggregate demand in the United States. Gradually American prices and wages fall and American competitiveness starts to increase. When this has restored the American balance of payments to equilibrium, the process comes to a halt.

Thus the gold standard does provide an automatic mechanism for adjusting imbalances in the trade and payments of different countries in the world economy. However, adjustment is far from instantaneous. Since it occurs because the changes in domestic wages and price change international competitiveness, the speed of adjustment depends on the speed with which domestic prices and wages adjust to the pressures of excess supply or excess demand.

The Gold Standard in Action The gold standard was in operation through most of the nineteenth and early twentieth centuries. In Britain there was an established par value of gold in sterling from the end of the Napoleonic wars in 1816 until 1931, though there were occasional periods, such as the period during and immediately after the First World War, when convertibility was suspended and the system allowed to lapse temporarily.

The gold standard in action was not quite the same as the idealized version described here. Since the money supply was not usually 100 per cent backed by gold, the changes in official gold reserves incurred while defending the parity value of the exchange rate did not necessarily lead to identical changes in domestic money supplies.

The gold standard had one big benefit and one large drawback. By tying the domestic money supply closely, if not perfectly, to the stock of gold, it effectively ruled out persistent money creation of a large scale and ruled out

persistently high inflation rates. However, since the major mechanism by which full employment could be restored was a fall in domestic prices and wages, which might take many years to adjust fully to a large fall in aggregate demand, the period of the gold standard was a period in which individual economies were vulnerable to periods of long and deep recessions.

33-3 The Adjustable Peg and the Dollar Standard

Under the gold standard, nominal exchange rates are fixed indefinitely. We now discuss the adjustable peg system, in which exchange rates are normally fixed but countries are occasionally allowed to alter their exchange rate. This system was in operation for a quarter of a century after the Second World War and became known as the Bretton Woods system after the small town in New Hampshire where the details of the system were first hammered out. The principal architects of the final plan were Harry White, acting for the Americans, and John Maynard Keynes, acting for the British.

Because other countries agreed to fix their exchange rates against the dollar (and hence of course by implication against each other), this system also became known as the *dollar standard*. Each country announced a par value for its currency against the dollar, just as under the gold standard each country had announced par value against gold.

The second rule of the good standard was convertibility. Under the dollar standard, currencies were convertible against dollars rather than gold. At the fixed exchange rate, central banks were committed to buy or sell dollars from their stock of foreign exchange reserves or dollar holdings. They were committed to intervene in the foreign exchange market to defend the fixed exchange rate against the dollar.

The crucial difference between the gold standard and the dollar standard was that there was no longer 100 per cent backing for the domestic currency. Britain's domestic money supply did not have to bear any relation to the stock of dollars held by the Bank of England as foreign exchange reserves. Governments in

BOX 33-1

THE GOLD STANDARD AND INTERNATIONAL CAPITAL FLOWS

In the text we ignored international flows on the capital account of the balance of payments. We treated the balance of trade and the balance of payments as the same thing. This simplification makes the automatic adjustment mechanism of the gold standard seem more successful than it really was in practice. The possibility of international flows on the capital account allowed the adjusted mechanism to be frustrated in two ways.

First, countries with a trade deficit sometimes tried to raise domestic interest rates to encourage an inflow on the capital account of the balance of payments. If the overall balance of payments was thus in balance, there was no net monetary flow between countries, no change in countries' gold stocks, and no pressure on domestic wages and prices to adjust. Thus a trade deficit could persist longer than the idealized account of automatic adjustment suggests.

Second, international capital flows are crucial to understanding Britain's role in the world economy during the nineteenth century. In the first half of the century, Britain's early start during the Industrial Revolution and its worldwide empire allowed Britain to run a huge trade surplus. To maintain an overall payments balance, Britain had a huge outflow on the capital account of the balance of payments, partly because of heavy investment in its colonies. However, investment gradually earns interest and profits. Eventually, Britain's stock of foreign assets became so large that the inflow from interest, profits, and dividends exceeded the rate at which Britain could find new opportunities for foreign investment.

The net inflow of money started to raise domestic prices and wages and make UK producers uncompetitive. Overall payments balance was maintained by a move from surplus to deficit on the trade account to offset the net inflow from financial transactions. The monetary adjustment mechanism of the gold standard suggests that it was probably inevitable that Britain would have a trade deficit in the late nineteenth century. It was not necessarily the result of laziness or decadence, as some Victorians believed at the time.

Britain and other countries could print as much money as they wished.

Why does this matter? Because it inhibits the adjustment mechanism which was built into the gold standard automatically. Under the gold standard, countries with a balance of payments deficit were losing gold and their domestic money supply was falling. Eventually this put downward pressure on the domestic price level and began to increase competitiveness. Under the dollar standard, countries with a balance of payments deficit were still losing money, since residents were paying out to foreigners more than they were taking in from foreigners, but there was nothing to stop the domestic government simply printing more money to restore the domestic money supply to its original level. Thus governments of deficit countries that wished to avoid the initial deflationary pressure that a monetary contraction would imply could simply print extra money. Although this might prevent higher unemployment in the short run, it also prevented the long-run adjustment mechanism from operating through a fall in domestic money and prices, and a rise in domestic competitiveness.

Such behaviour could be justified by an overriding commitment to maintain full employment even in the short run. But such policies were unlikely to be feasible for ever. As the balance of payments deficit persisted, and the government had to use up more and more of its stock of foreign exchange reserves to finance the deficit, eventually the country would begin to run out of foreign exchange reserves. Then the country would have to devalue its exchange rate, moving to a lower par value against the dollar, to attempt permanently to increase competitiveness and remove the underlying imbalance in international payments.

Thus the first objection that can be levelled against an adjustable peg system is that it does not necessarily provide an *automatic* mechanism for resolving imbalances in international payments. Rather, deficit countries tended to stave off the required adjustment until a major crisis had built up, and then undertake a significant exchange rate devaluation. Indeed, since the whole point of the adjustable peg system was that exchange rates should usually be fixed, a series of gradual exchange rate adjustments at frequent intervals was incompatible with the way the system was supposed to operate. Countries that wished to change their exchange rates had to allow important crises to develop, if only to convince their international trading partners that an exchange rate adjustment was now definitely required.

In such circumstances, speculators had a field day. If a country was in balance of payments difficulties there was no danger that its exchange rate would be *raised*. Either the exchange rate would stay the same or there would be a devaluation. Speculators couldn't lose. For example, in 1967 the UK devalued from $2.80 to $2.40. People who converted £1 into $2.80 just before the devaluation could convert it back into £1.17 (=2.80/2.40) as soon as the exchange rate had changed, making 17 per cent on their investment in the space of a few days or weeks. The big loser was the Bank of England, which was giving people $2.80 for each £1 one day, and being forced to buy the same dollars back the next day at $2.40/£.

The dollar standard had a second drawback. Since dollars had become the world's medium of exchange, the United States could never run out of foreign exchange reserves. The US government could always finance an American balance of payments deficit by printing more dollars. As long as the United States ran small balance of payments deficits, the stock of dollars being held by central banks elsewhere in the world – effectively the world's money supply – increased only slowly. And for a time this happened.

However, in the mid-1960s the United States began to run much larger payments deficits with the rest of the world, partly because of heavy military spending in Vietnam. In consequence the world's supply of outstanding dollars increased rapidly. Since other countries now had plenty of foreign exchange reserves, they too could plan to run balance of payments deficits. But one country's deficit must be another's surplus. The world as a whole cannot run a balance of payments deficit. By increasing the world's money supply and its aggregate demand for traded goods at a faster rate than

supply was expanding, this process began to increase the inflation rate throughout the trading world. It provided a mechanism for the international transmission of inflation.

In contrast, under the gold standard national and international money supplies could increase only as quickly as new gold could be supplied. On the one hand this system wasted real resources. Why use scarce workers to dig up gold for use as money when money can be printed at a fraction of the opportunity cost in real resources? But on the other hand, the very difficulty of increasing the gold supply quickly ensured that the world's rate of monetary growth was restricted in the long run.

33-4 Floating Exchange Rates

As we explained in Chapter 29, a regime of *pure* or *clean* floating implies that foreign exchange markets are in continuous equilibrium in the absence of any government intervention via the foreign exchange reserves. The foreign exchange reserves remain constant and there is no external mechanism changing the domestic money supply. Since receipts from foreigners equal payments to foreigners, money is neither flowing into nor out of the country. The balance of payments is exactly in balance.

Before we can evaluate how a floating exchange rate regime acts as a mechanism for international adjustment, we need a theory of how floating exchange rates are determined. It is convenient at this point to review the analysis of Chapter 29.

Purchasing Power Parity

Taking 1974 as 100, by 1988 the price of US goods had risen to 240 but the price of UK goods had risen to 312. If the nominal value of the exchange rate between US dollars and sterling had remained constant, UK international competitiveness would have fallen dramatically compared with that of the United States.

International competitiveness is measured by comparing the relative prices of the goods from different countries when these are measured in a common currency.

Thus, if the nominal $/£ exchange rate had remained constant during 1974–88, the UK would have become 30 per cent less competitive against the United States because UK prices rose 30 per cent more than those in the United States. Suppose, however, that the $/£ exchange rate had fallen 30 per cent over the same period. The $ price of UK exports would then have risen at the same rate as US prices, and the £ price of US exports would have risen at the same rate as UK prices. Competitiveness would have been unaltered.

> The *purchasing power parity* path for the nominal exchange rates is the path that would maintain the level of international competitiveness constant over time. Countries with higher domestic inflation than their competitors would face a *depreciating* nominal exchange rate and countries with lower inflation than their competitors would face an *appreciating* exchange rate.

Under a regime of fixed nominal exchange rates, a single country cannot have higher domestic inflation than its competitors for ever. Gradually it becomes less and less competitive in international trade, and is likely to face an increasing balance of trade deficit and a lower level of aggregate demand since net exports are negative. However, under flexible exchange rates it is *possible* that different countries can maintain different domestic inflation rates indefinitely. If countries with high inflation rates simultaneously face depreciating exchange rates, it is possible that purchasing power parity will be maintained and their international competitiveness will be unaffected.

Thus the crucial question is, *do* exchange rates adjust to maintain purchasing power parity? This question has been the subject of a great deal of research. The short answer seems to be, basically, yes in the long run but not in the short run. We picked the example of the UK and the United States to illustrate this point. Between 1974 and 1988 the nominal exchange rate changed by 25 per cent, from $2.34/£ to $1.78/£. Thus, international competitiveness was almost constant between the beginning and end of the period. Thus the first feature to note about a floating exchange rate regime is that it *can* cope with enormous international discrepancies in domestic rates of inflation and money growth in the long run.

Speculation and Interest Rate Differentials

However, in Chapter 29 we made a second point of equal importance. Floating exchange rates do *not* follow the purchasing power parity path in the short run. Floating exchange rates are determined to clear the foreign exchange market day by day. Demand and supplies of currency arise both from transactions on the current account of the balance of payments – international trade in goods and services – and from transactions on the capital account of the balance of payments – international asset transactions.

We argued that there is now a huge outstanding stock of footloose investment funds which can rapidly be switched from one currency to another in search for the highest expected rate of return in the short run.[2] The rate of return depends both on a comparison of interest rates offered on assets denominated in different currencies *and* on the expected capital gains or loss arising from exchange rate changes during the period the currency is held.

The stock of outstanding funds is now so large that if even one-tenth of it were to move between currencies it would *swamp* supplies and demand for currencies arising that day from trade on the current account. Hence the foreign exchange market would not clear. So the minute funds start to move, *or even threaten to start moving*, the exchange rate is likely to change. For example, a rise in sterling interest rates on offer on government debt in London is likely to lead to an immediate rise in the sterling exchange rate. If the exchange rate rises enough, speculators are likely to conclude that it will have to fall back in the immediate future. The threat of this capital loss on a falling exchange rate will deter some of the speculators who were about to be tempted by higher sterling interest rates to hold more of their funds in London. This keeps the *actual* transactions on the capital account down to manageable proportions and allows the foreign exchange market to clear day by day.

Suppose a government is elected with a commitment to reduce the money supply and

---

[2] Because many of these footloose funds are owned by OPEC countries, they are sometimes called 'petrodollars'.

cut the inflation rate. What happens? If domestic prices and wages are slow to adjust, the initial impact of a reduction in the nominal money supply is a reduction in the real money stock. Interest rates are pushed up and the exchange rate must rise to choke off a potentially massive inflow of funds on the capital account of the balance of payments. Since domestic prices and wages have still not adjusted, international competitiveness is eroded overnight. Over time, high interest rates and the slump in net imports will lead first to a domestic slump, and then to downward pressure on domestic prices and wages. When adjustment has been completed, the domestic economy will have a lower nominal money supply, lower prices and wages, and a higher nominal exchange rate. However, the fall in domestic prices will offset the rise in the nominal exchange rate and international competitiveness will have been restored. The purchasing power parity path of the nominal exchange rate will have been re-established.

We now see that speculation can lead to large departures from the purchasing power parity path in the short run. Interest rates and the exchange rate can change much more quickly than domestic prices and wages can adjust. UK international competitiveness fell by between 50 and 60 per cent between 1976 and January 1981 before it significantly improved again. We have picked these particular dates deliberately. Neither of the end-points may have been a very representative or sustainable value of the exchange rate, but they do show how much competitiveness can change in the short run. Deviations from the purchasing power parity path can be large in the short run and can persist for a long time, even though there is a long-run tendency for the exchange rate to return to its purchasing power parity path and for competitiveness to be restored.[3]

Hence a floating exchange rate regime does not provide continuous short-run insulation from large changes in international competitiveness. A government switching to a tight monetary policy to fight inflation may find that there is a severe Keynesian slump in the short

run. Until prices fall and the real money supply expands again, temporarily high interest rates don't just hit domestic consumption and investment spending; they are also likely to lead to a rapid exchange rate appreciation which reduces international competitiveness in the short run, further reducing aggregate demand through the effect on net exports. Later in this chapter we examine whether a *concerted* move to tight monetary policies in several countries at the same time could reduce the short-run unemployment cost of policies designed to combat inflation in the long run.

A Managed Float

Thus far we have been discussing freely floating exchange rates. Under a free float there is no central bank intervention in the foreign exchange market. The foreign exchange reserves remain constant, the balance of payments is exactly zero, and the net monetary inflow from abroad is also zero.

In practice, exchange rates have rarely been allowed to float absolute freely during the period since 1973 when the Bretton Woods system of the adjustable peg was replaced by a floating exchange rate regime. In the short run, central banks intervene in the foreign exchange market both in an attempt to smooth out fluctuations in the exchange rate and, sometimes, in an effort to nudge the exchange rate in the direction in which the government would like to see it change.

Such intervention may help smooth out day-to-day exchange rate fluctuations, but in the long run it probably makes little difference to the path the exchange rate follows. Central banks have large stocks of foreign exchange reserves which they could dump on the foreign exchange market in an effort to alter the equilibrium exchange rate. But the speculators probably have even larger funds at their disposal. One argument for co-ordinating the central bank intervention in different countries is that, together, the central banks might then have sufficient funds to take on the speculators. Playing the foreign exchanges is not unlike playing poker: if all players are equally good, the player with the most money is very likely to win.

---

[3] For an investigation of this and related questions, see the report of the House of Commons Select Committee on the Treasury and Civil Service, *International Monetary Arrangements*, HMSO, 1983.

33-5 Fixed Versus Floating Exchange Rates

Since 1945 the world has seen both fixed and floating exchange rate regimes. Under the Bretton Woods adjustable peg system, in operation until the early 1970s, exchange rates were usually fixed although there were intermittent devaluations or revaluations of the major currencies. The UK devalued in 1949 and again in 1967. In contrast, West Germany, which on average had a lower inflation rate than most other countries, was periodically forced to revalue the Deutschmark. While fixed exchange rates were never completely fixed before 1973, exchange rates have rarely been allowed to float freely since 1973. Central banks have often intervened quite heavily in the foreign exchange market.

Even so, we have seen both regimes in action and should be able to decide which regime works better. And there are some people who argue that the choice between these two regimes is too restrictive. They would like to return to the nineteenth century gold standard which, as we have seen, automatically linked the money stock to the balance of payments and produced reasonably low inflation on average. In this section we examine the arguments for and against the different exchange rate regimes.

Robustness

We begin by asking how the different regimes can cope with major strains. Strains can be of two kinds, nominal and real. Nominal strains arise when different countries have very different domestic inflation rates. Real strains occur when the world economy suffers a major real shock such as a quadrupling of real oil prices.

It is often claimed that one advantage of an adjustable peg regime is that exchange rates are fixed, and therefore certain, except for occasional realignments. If this argument is to have any merit, countries cannot forever be changing their exchange rate through devaluation and revaluations. A *completely* fixed nominal exchange rate system rules out the possibility of exchange rate changes as a mechanism for adjusting to nominal or real strains.

Countries whose domestic inflation rate is higher than that of their international competitors will gradually become less competitive in international markets. Either they must undertake tight domestic monetary and fiscal policy to get their inflation rate back in line with that in the rest of the world, or they must seek a devaluation of their currency to restore the exchange rate to its purchasing power parity level. And if they persist in having higher domestic inflation than the rest of the world, they will need a series of devaluations at regular intervals to maintain their international competitiveness. In short, unless countries pursue domestic monetary policies that lead to roughly equal inflation rates, a fixed exchange rate system simply cannot cope. Some countries will always be devaluing their exchange rates, and others will be revaluing because their inflation rate is lower than average. If these adjustments are at all frequent the adjustable peg system starts to break down.

This problem is likely to be compounded by the one-way bet that possible exchange rate changes offer speculators. Only in a system where exchange rate changes are rare will speculators not spend most of their time trying to anticipate which will be the next exchange rate to be adjusted. And, in moving vast amounts of funds out of currencies that may possibly be devalued, and into currencies that may possibly be revalued, speculators are likely to increase the inevitability of the exchange rate changes on which they are betting.

How about strains caused by real shocks to the world economy? Just imagine how the OPEC oil price shocks would have hit a fixed exchange rate market regime or an adjustable peg system. Overnight, countries that were heavy oil importers would have faced enormous balance of payments deficits and speculative pressure would have built up as speculators started to bet that these currencies would have to be devalued. Exchange rate adjustments are usually preceded by extensive international consultation between governments and central banks. There is no point in the UK devaluing the pound 10 per cent against the dollar on Monday if the United States simply devalues the dollar by 10 per cent against the pound on Tuesday. Governments and central banks have to try to agree on what exchange rate realignments are required and, having made them, have to try to make them stick. The OPEC oil price shock in 1973–74 would have led to round after round of consultations, tentative exchange rate adjustments, and further consultations to try to determine whether the adjustments already undertaken had been of the correct magnitude to achieve the adjustments required.

History tells us two things. First, the Bretton Woods system of the adjustable peg had to be abandoned in the early 1970s because it could *not* cope with the nominal and real strains in the world economy. Even a series of exchange rate realignments in the early 1970s, such as the revaluation of the Deutschmark, did not remove either current account imbalances or speculative pressures on the capital account. Second, whatever else we may say about floating exchange rates, the system *was* able to cope with the dramatic shocks experienced by the world economy in the 1970s. Believers in floating exchange rates count this a point in their favour.

Volatility

Critics of floating exchange rates point to their extreme volatility. For example, between 1949 and 1967 the dollar–sterling exchange rate was rarely more than 1 cent either side of $2.80/£, and between 1967 and 1972 it was rarely more than 1 cent either side of $2.40/£. The job of the central banks was to intervene in the foreign exchange market to hold exchange rates close to their par values. In contrast, Figure 33-1 shows the volatility of the dollar–sterling exchange rates during the period of floating exchange rates since 1973. Not only has the rate been as high as $2.50 and as low as $1.30, but it has sometimes moved *very* rapidly. Between the first and third quarters of 1981 the dollar sterling exchange rate fell from $2.32/£ to $1.83/£ in less than six months. Such volatility, it is argued, leads to great uncertainty and is likely to reduce the level of international trade and the amount of investment undertaken by firms competing in world markets.

Even a brief glance at Figure 33-1 confirms that the assertion of volatility cannot be disputed. Rather, as economists, we must ask whether volatility is necessarily a bad thing.

First, we should recall that it is the real, or inflation-adjusted, exchange rate that affects international competitiveness. For example, the fall in the dollar–sterling exchange rate in the mid-1970s was largely offsetting higher UK

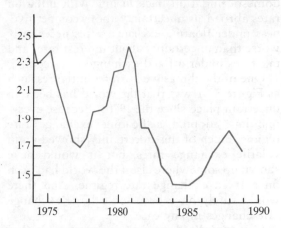

Figure 33-1 THE DOLLAR–STERLING EXCHANGE RATE, 1974–89 ($/£). (*Source*: CSO, *Economic Trends*.)

inflation. Under a fixed exchange rate, competitiveness would have been changing even more quickly. When inflation discrepancies between countries are large and uncertain, pegging the nominal exchange rate throws all the inflation uncertainty on to the level of real competitiveness. The real exchange rate is not necessarily constant or predictable just because the nominal exchange rate has been fixed.

Second, it is not obvious that a system with usually fixed nominal exchange rates but occasionally large changes leads to less uncertainty than a system in which nominal exchange rates change every day. A British firm that signs an import contract with the United States when the exchange rate is $2.80 and suddenly finds it is actually buying the goods after a devaluation to $2.40 will have to pay a much higher price in pounds than it had anticipated. Living in a world where the exchange rate *may* change by 17 per cent in a single day can be just as hair-raising as living in a world where the exchange rate often changes by 1 per cent five days running.

Finally, we must ask what would have happened if the exchange rate had not adjusted so much. If high inflation leads to a large exchange rate depreciation under floating exchange rates, what would have been the government's response if it had been trying to defend a fixed exchange rate? Would it have adopted a tight domestic policy, jacking up interest rates and raising taxes, to try to get domestic inflation back in line with inflation rates abroad? Is uncertainty about competitiveness under floating exchange rates necessarily worse than uncertainty about interest rates and tax rates under a fixed exchange rate regime?

One of the things we learn from figures such as Figure 33-1 was that the world has been an uncertain place since the 1970s. Because everyone has adopted a floating exchange rate regime, much of this uncertainty showed up in volatile exchange rates, but it would have shown up somewhere else if the world had been on a fixed exchange rate regime. And there would surely have been some large exchange rate changes in any case.

Hence it is hard to conclude that the volatility argument goes decisively against floating exchange rates. However, this argument also comes in a more sophisticated form. It is argued that the shocks with which the world international monetary system has to deal are not independent of the exchange rate regime in force. In short, by their very flexibility and robustness, floating exchange rates make shocks more likely. We now turn to the most important version of this argument, which relates to financial discipline.

Financial Discipline

Floating exchange rates allow different countries to pursue different inflation rates indefinitely. In the long run the exchange rates of high-inflation countries will depreciate to maintain purchasing power parity or constant international competitiveness. By the same token, floating exchange rates do nothing to *prevent* individual countries from adopting fast domestic monetary growth and high domestic inflation. Thus, critics of floating exchange rates argue that they do not provide any *financial discipline*.

In contrast, under a fixed exchange rate system countries will become increasingly uncompetitive if they have above-average inflation. Unless they are allowed to devalue, they will eventually have no choice but to adopt more restrictive domestic policies to get their inflation rates back in line with the rest of the world.

Back to Gold?   The most extreme adherents of this viewpoint argues that even the adjustable peg regime does not provide sufficient discipline,

since there is always the possibility of devaluing. The *goldbugs* – those in favour of a return to the gold standard – argue that such a system would have three advantages. First, it would remove from profligate governments the loophole of an exchange rate adjustment. Second, the restoration of 100 per cent gold backing for the domestic money supply would remove the possibility of simply rolling the printing presses. And finally, since high-inflation countries would become uncompetitive and develop a balance of payments deficit, there would be an automatic mechanism for reducing their domestic monetary growth. Money and gold would flow out of deficit countries and into surplus countries.

It cannot be denied that this system would provide financial discipline. On the other hand, one must ask whether the benefits exceed the costs. First, such a system would not be able to use exchange rate changes as a mechanism for adjustment to real shocks. Under the gold standard, countries that were large oil importers could not have depreciated their exchange rate during the mid-1970s. Rather, the OPEC oil price shock would have led to large balance of payments deficits in the oil-importing countries, initiating a period of monetary contraction and domestic recession until the domestic price level had fallen sufficiently to make those countries' non-oil sectors so competitive that they could earn enough foreign exchange to pay for expensive oil imports and achieve overall payments balance. But unless one is very optimistic about the speed with which domestic wages and prices can adjust to a domestic recession, one must conclude that such countries would have faced a severe recession as they tried to adjust. Financial discipline also has its costs.

Second, one must ask, if getting inflation down is such a good thing, why governments don't pursue this objective in any case? Floating exchange rates do not force governments to generate high domestic inflation rates. The financial discipline arguments presuppose that governments must be forced into tight monetary policies against their wishes. While it may be true that many governments pursued policies of easy money in the mid-1970s, in the late 1970s and early 1980s electorates in many countries voted in governments committed to reducing inflation by pursuing tight monetary and fiscal policies. In such circumstances there may be more important reasons for choosing between exchange rate regimes than whether or not they impose additional financial discipline.

Finally, we note that, even if it is desired to tie the government's hands and force it to adopt tight monetary policies, there are almost certainly better ways of doing this than forcing a return to the gold standard. First, it is possible to pass laws requiring the government to balance the budget or to adhere to a low rate of money growth. It is also possible, as in the United States, to divorce the government and the central bank. Officially, American monetary policy is determined not by the President but by the independent Chairman of the Federal Reserve Board. Second, as we remarked earlier, few of the world's scarce resources – labour, capital, and land – are used up in printing paper money. Increasing the world's supply of money under the gold standard requires that labour and capital are used in mining to produce that extra monetary gold. Most people think that labour and capital can be put to better uses.

Freedom From Restrictions on Trade and Payments

In the previous chapter we explained why trade takes place and how international trade allows countries to be better off by exploiting their comparative advantage. Some economists argue that the need to defend a fixed exchange rate is likely to lead countries to impose tariffs or other trade restrictions on goods, and to restrict international capital flows on the balance of payments. If so, some of the benefits of international trade in goods and assets are likely to be lost. Countries will be forced to diversify production instead of concentrating on the goods they produce most efficiently, and owners of wealth will be prevented from lending these funds at the highest possible rate of return.

Is there any factual basis for these arguments, which have a certain theoretical plausibioity? On the question of tariffs and other trade restrictions, the evidence is mixed. In the last chapter we pointed out that GATT, the General Agreement on Tariffs and Trade, accomplished a steady reduction in tariff levels over the last few decades. But most of this progress was made during the Bretton Woods period of an adjustable peg regime. Advocates of floating exchange rates can point out that the world economy got through the difficult period of the mid-1970s under floating exchange rates without the pressures for trade restrictions that might have developed under a fixed exchange rate regime. However, during the world recession of the early 1980s new pressures for protectionism began to develop, less as a response to balance of payments difficulties than as a response to domestic recessions and the belief that import competition is destroying domestic jobs.

When we turn to restrictions on trade in assets the picture is much more clear-cut. Throughout the Bretton Woods period there were extensive controls on transactions on the capital account of the balance of payments. The system simply could not withstand large flows of assets between countries, so they were either prohibited or heavily restricted.

During the 1970s most of these controls were gradually dismantled. By the 1980s most forms of exchange control on transactions in international assets had effectively been abandoned. Some deregulation probably became inevitable after the OPEC oil price shocks. Since the industrial West was running a current account deficit with OPEC countries it had to run a capital account surplus. OPEC countries had to be allowed to invest their enormous wealth in the industrial West if world payments were to balance. Under the Bretton Woods system it is possible that this 'recycling' of oil revenues would have been conducted on an official basis through the International Monetary Fund. Under a system of floating exchange rates, the same effect was achieved simply by dismantling restrictions on transactions in international assets and allowing people to place their funds where they wished.

Unrestricted transactions in international assets allow the world economy to invest in the assets with the highest rate of return, wherever they are located. Potentially this is a great benefit and a big plus for a system of floating exchange rates. If savers in Britain can earn a higher return by lending in Japan, why should they be forced to lend to low-yielding investment projects in the UK merely because the government wishes to defend a fixed exchange rate?

Of course, things can go wrong. The world as a whole benefits from international capital mobility if it allows the high-yielding investment projects to obtain funds more easily. However, if lenders are merely concerned with playing the international casino of betting on exchange rate changes, it is less clear that more worthwhile projects are getting funds more easily, and producers of internationally traded goods may have to live in a world with more volatile exchange rate movements.

Taking all these arguments together, should we go back to a system of fixed exchange rates, possibly with the provision of allowing occasional changes in exchange rate parities? None of the arguments we have discussed offers an absolutely decisive answer. Some of the arguments do seem to learn towards continuing with floating exchange rates, but there may be another option. So long as countries insist on pursuing different policies without regard to the policies being pursued elsewhere, we suspect that a floating exchange rate regime will continue to be the only practical way to reconcile these policies. But it is possible that the world achieve greater exchange rate stability if this were accompanied by a deliberate decision to pay more attention to harmonization of domestic macroeconomic policies in different countries. We conclude this chapter with a brief discussion of international policy co-ordination.

33-6 International Policy Co-ordination

By policy co-ordination, we mean a concerted attempt by a group of countries to formulate policy collectively. At one extreme, this might eventually imply a supranational body to which national sovereignty is subordinated. Clearly, the world economy is a long way from any such arrangement, but Europe is now well on the way towards a monetary union with a single European central bank. At the other extreme, we might mean agreements to brief other governments about one's own policy, and to exchange information. In between lie a spectrum of arrangements which specify some 'rules of the game' subject to which national governments still have a measure of discretion. For example, under Bretton Woods, governments

agreed that exchange rates would usually be fixed, but they retained sovereignty over their domestic monetary and fiscal policies subject only to this constraint. On the other hand, even when floating, sterling has been driven to uncompetitive levels by changes in oil prices, most notably in 1980.

What do governments stand to gain by co-ordinating macroeconomic policy to some extent? Like oligopolists, governments are essentially interdependent, the outcome for each depending on the policies pursued by others. Like oligopolists, they face a tension between the incentive to collude and the incentive to compete. Collusion allows them to 'internalize' the externalities they otherwise impose on one another when each sets policy without regard for its impact on the welfare of others. But there is also an incentive to compete by cheating on collective agreements.

How do these ideas apply in international policy co-ordination? In the previous chapter we applied them to trade policy, arguing that the GATT was a form of co-operation to prevent tariff escalation through retaliation. Now we wish to focus on macroeconomic policy.

The Externality Argument for Co-ordination

The most obvious externality imposed by non-cooperative behaviour is the externality acting through the exchange rate. Suppose a government wants to get inflation down. Essentially, it has two weapons. Demand management can be used to generate a domestic recession, which will put downward pressure on wages and prices. An exchange rate appreciation, in addition to these effects, will reduce prices directly by making imports cheaper. A smart government will wish to use both policy weapons, as for example the Thatcher government did in the UK in 1979–81.

But what works for a country in isolation cannot work for the world as a whole. We cannot all appreciate our exchange rates. A rise in the \$/£ rate is necessarily a fall in the £/\$ rate. Countries that use exchange rate appreciation to reduce their own inflation effectively export inflation abroad. That is the externality they fail to take into account.

In principle, policy co-ordination can solve

this market failure: countries can agree not to use exchange rate policy in this manner. As with other collusive or co-operative agreements, an effective punishment threat is required to prevent individual countries from subsequently cheating on the agreement. If this can be devised, the agreement will be credible, and all countries may benefit.

The Reputation Argument for Co-ordination

Earlier, we discussed the issue of financial discipline. It is of course possible that a government would like to keep inflation under control by tight policies but is unable to resist reflating the economy as the next election draws near. Because everyone knows this will happen, inflation expectations remain high and inflation is hard to control even at the start of the government's period of office.

Such a government might be glad if it could make a binding pre-commitment which ruled out the option to reflate as the next election drew near. We have already portrayed the Thatcher emphasis on 'no U-turn' as an attempt to devise such a pre-commitment, but policy co-ordination may offer an alternative.

Why do people go to Weightwatchers or Alcoholics Anonymous? Because, alone, they are too weak to stick to their resolutions. Joining a club provides peer discipline. Even in everyday language, we say it displays commitment. You look silly if you subsequently pull out.

Policy co-ordination may act in a similar way. Hence it may allow national governments to make credible the promises that would otherwise be incredible. That is the second argument for policy co-ordination.

We now turn to a closer examination of one of the most studied recent examples of co-ordination, the European Monetary System.

33-7 The European Monetary System

In March 1979 the members of the European Community (*including* the UK) founded and joined the European Monetary System (EMS). The most important features of the agreement were as follows.

Table 33-2 ECU composition
(% share of each currency)

Deutschmark (DM)	30.1	Danish krone (DK)	2.4
French franc (FF)	19.0	Irish punt (IP)	1.1
Pound sterling (£)	13.0	Greek drachma (GD)	0.8
Italian lira (IL)	10.2	Portugese escudo	
Dutch guilder (DG)	9.4	(PE)	0.8
Belgian franc (BF)	7.6	Luxembourg franc	
Spanish peseta (SP)	5.3	(LF)	0.3

First, the European Currency Unit (ECU) would be used as a unit of account for certain transactions between governments of the member countries. Table 33-2 shows the shares of the different member currencies in this currency bundle.

Second, member governments would each deposit 20 per cent of their foreign exchange reserves with the European Monetary Co-operation Fund, and receive ECUs in exchange. These funds were to be available for concerted short-term central bank intervention in foreign exchange markets.

It was only the third and most important provision, the Exchange Rate Mechanism (ERM), in which the UK did not initially participate. Under the ERM, each country fixes a nominal exchange rate against each other ERM participant, though collectively the group floats against the rest of the world. Each country participating in the ERM can allow its exchange rate to fluctuate within a band of $\pm 2\frac{1}{4}$ per cent of the parities it has agreed to defend.[4] When the currency hits the edge of a band, *all* central banks in the ERM countries are obliged to intervene to try to defend the parity.

The ERM has two other features. First, realignments are allowed but have to be unanimously agreed by participants of the ERM. In practice, finance ministers have to sneak off in secret on a Friday night to some schloss or chateau and get the agreement hammered out before the foreign exchange markets reopen on Monday morning! Otherwise, speculative pressures on a one-way option for anticipated exchange rate changes would be almost impossible to resist.

---

[4] Italy, an especially high-inflation country in 1979, was allowed a band of ± 6 per cent. By the mid-1980s, it was a matter of honour for Italy not to use this wider band. Spain also joined with a wider band.

Second, members agree to pay attention to a *divergence indicator*. When any individual currency has moved 75 per cent of the amount it can move against the ECU currency bundle before a realignment is required, that government is supposed to take steps to alter its domestic policy to reverse this exchange rate trend.

The EMS in Practice

Table 33-3 shows the realignments of the major ERM currencies. Two facts stand out. First, realignments have largely followed the strategy of restoring purchasing power parity. The relatively high-inflation countries (Italy and France) were allowed nominal exchange rate devaluations. Second, whereas there was a realignment almost every six months between 1979 and 1983, since 1983 realignments have become much less frequent. Since 1987 there has not been a realignment.

Did the EMS exert financial discipline? Were France and Italy forced to live with tight German policies and low German inflation? Not much, initially. When they became uncompetitive at fixed nominal exchange rates, they were soon allowed to devalue to improve competitiveness. Typically, realignments did not *fully* restore purchasing power parity, so some discipline was being exerted. And since 1983 discipline has been much stricter. It is hard to say whether this should be attributed to the EMS biting or to a separate determina-

tion by governments in inflationary countries to squeeze inflation out of the system.

Thus, the EMS was founded when its members had very different inflation rates, but these have gradually been brought into line. The EMS played some role in this. It did not reflect a political will to do this quickly (that is why the divergence indicator had to be couched in such soggy language), nor did it instantly force countries to harmonize policies. But over time, it did have an effect.

One final aspect of the EMS experience should be mentioned. It reduced nominal exchange rate volatility in the short run. Nor have its members experienced the dramatic swings in real competitiveness to which the floating sterling and dollar have been subject over the same period.

Why Did it Work?

We have argued that only part of the success of the EMS should be attributed to rapid policy convergence. Moreover, while the system essentially requires some co-ordination of interest rates and monetary policy, there has been no co-ordinated approach to fiscal policy in member countries.

Could other reasons help explain the survival of the EMS? Two stand out. First, with a band of $\pm 2\frac{1}{4}$ per cent, there were long periods when countries were effectively floating. High-inflation countries had exchange rates that started off near the top of the band and gradually

Table 33-3 EMS realignments, 1979–89*
(Date and percentage realignment)

DATE	DM	FF	DG	IL	BF	DK	LF	IP
Sept. 79	+ 2.0					−2.9		
Nov. 80						−4.8		
Mar. 81				−6.0				
Oct. 81	+ 5.5	−3.0	+ 5.5	−3.0				
Feb. 82					−8.5	−3.0	−8.5	
June 82	+ 4.3	−5.8	+ 4.3	−2.8				
Mar. 83	+ 5.5	−2.5	+ 3.5	−2.5	+1.5	+2.5	+1.5	−3.5
July 85	+ 2.0	+2.0	+ 2.0	−6.0	+2.0	+2.0	+2.0	+2.0
Apr. 86								−8.0
Jan. 87	+ 3.0		+ 3.0		+2.0			
Cumulative	+23.7	−9.1	+19.1	−18.7	−3.3	−6.2	−5.3	−9.5

* DM (Deutschmark), etc., refer to currencies listed in Table 33-2.

depreciated, just as they would have done under floating. When they got near the bottom of the band, people started to talk about the need for a realignment. In part, the EMS was cosmetic.

Second, most countries had foreign exchange controls which prevented large capital account flows. This allowed fixed bilateral parities to survive even when interest rates were out of line. Only occasionally was the prospect of a realignment so imminent that exchange controls had trouble stemming the speculative tide. As part of the 1992 programme of reforms, the major EMS countries committed themselves to remove all foreign exchange controls by June 1990. Greece, Spain, and Portugal have been allowed a little longer, but all controls will disappear before 1992. It remains to be seen whether policy convergence is now sufficient to allow the EMS to survive without exchange controls.

The UK finally joined the ERM in 1990. We discuss this more fully in the next chapter where we look more generally at the process of increasing European integration in the 1990s.

Summary

1   Under the gold standard, each country fixed the par value of its currency against gold, maintained the convertibility of its currency into gold at this price, and linked the domestic money supply to gold stocks at the central bank. It was a fixed exchange rate regime.

2   In the absence of capital flows, countries with a trade deficit faced a payments deficit, a monetary outflow, and a reduction in gold stocks. By inducing a domestic recession which put downward pressure on wages and prices and increased competitiveness, this provided an automatic adjustment mechanism. Similarly, trade surplus countries faced a monetary inflow, higher prices, and an erosion of competitiveness. In practice, this adjustment mechanism was hampered by capital flows. Trade imbalance did not necessarily lead to payments imbalance and the required monetary flows.

3   The postwar Bretton Woods system was an adjustable peg in which fixed exchange rates could occasionally be adjusted. Effectively, it was a dollar standard rather than a gold standard. But the domestic money supply was no longer linked to the stock of foreign exchange reserves, so much of the adjustment mechanism of the gold standard was lost.

4   The purchasing power parity path of the exchange rate is the path that maintains constant competitiveness by offsetting differential inflation across countries. In the long run, floating exchange rates return to the PPP path.

5   In the short run, the level of floating exchange rates is determined largely by speculation. Speculators like high interest rates but dislike expected depreciation of the exchange rate, which implies capital losses while temporarily holding assets in that currency. Exchange rates adjust in the short run to choke off large speculative flows. A sharp exchange rate appreciation increases the chance of a future depreciation. In the short run, exchange rates can depart significantly from their PPP path. Short-run changes in competitiveness can be large if domestic prices change only slowly.

6   Unlike fixed exchange rates, floating exchange rates can cope with permanent differences in domestic inflation rates. High-inflation countries simply face a depreciating exchange rate in the long run. In practice, floating exchange rates also coped with the severe real shocks of the 1970s, such as the oil price shocks. This suggests floating exchange rate regimes are more robust than fixed exchange rate regimes.

7   Critics of floating exchange rates claim they are very volatile in the short run, which discourages international trade and investment. However, they are volatile because the world is uncertain. Under fixed exchange rates the uncertainty would show up somewhere else, possibly in volatile domestic monetary policy to maintain the fixed exchange rate.

8   Fixed exchange rates impose financial discipline by preventing one country from having a permanently higher domestic inflation than the rest of the world. However, there are other ways to prevent governments from adopting rapid rates of domestic money growth.

9   Floating exchange rates are less likely to lead to pressures for restrictions on international trade and capital flows for balance of payments

reasons. Under floating exchange rates the balance of payments is always in balance.

10   Under floating exchange rates, the adoption of a tighter monetary policy in one country alone will lead to a sharp appreciation of its currency as its domestic interest rate is high. This sharp loss of competitiveness will exacerbate the domestic slump. The staggered adoption of tighter monetary policy in different countries may lead to wild fluctuations in their competitiveness in the short run. A concerted move to tighter monetary policies would mean that they all had high interest rates. Exchange rates would not fluctuate so much in the short run.

11   If countries can agree to adopt the same rate of monetary growth, they will tend to have similar domestic inflation rates and it might be possible to move back to a fixed exchange rate regime.

12   There are two general arguments in favour of international policy co-ordination. First, it allows policy-makers to take account of the externalities they impose on each other when policy is set non-cooperatively. Second, it may allow individual governments to commit themselves to policies that would otherwise not be credible. Exchanging information may also prevent simple mistakes about reactions of policy-makers in other countries.

13   The UK is a member of the European Monetary System but did not join its most important feature, the Exchange Rate Mechanism, until 1990. The survival of the ERM and its success in reducing exchange rate volatility arise only partly from greater co-ordination of monetary policy by ERM participants. Foreign exchange controls and relatively wide bands have also been important.

Key Terms

Exchange rate regime
Policy co-ordination
Foreign exchange reserves

Gold standard
Par value of gold
Convertibility
100 per cent gold backing
Adjustable peg regime
Dollar standard
Purchasing power parity (PPP)
International competitiveness
Petrodollars
Exchange rate speculation
Managed or dirty floating
Robustness of an exchange rate regime
Volatility
Financial discipline
Goldbugs
European Monetary System

Problems

1   Reread Box 33-1. During the First World War the gold standard was suspended. Britain also sold off most of its foreign assets to pay for the war. What do you think happened in 1925 when Britain tried to rejoin the gold standard at the old par value of gold?

2   How did the dollar standard differ from the gold standard? Explain the differences in (a) the automatic adjustment mechanism, (b) financial discipline.

3   What would happen in the long run if floating exchange rates did not return to their PPP path? How can speculators make use of the knowledge that PPP will eventually be restored?

4   Suppose the world had been on the adjustable peg dollar standard in the 1970s. What would have been the effect of the OPEC oil price rise of 1973–74? Be as explicit as you can.

5   'There is no more reason to peg exchange rates than to peg the price of motor cars.' Do you agree?

6   Common Fallacies   Show why each of the following statements is incorrect. (a) Floating exchange rates make sure that exports and imports always balance. (b) Since one country's surplus is another country's deficit, it makes no difference to the world economy whether individual countries have a balance of payments equal to zero. (c) Fixed exchange rate regimes prevent world inflation.

34

European Integration in the 1990s

Europe is on the move. The European economy of the 1990s will look very different from the Europe we have known for the last few decades. Some of these developments are of course political. But others are economic, and the economics we have learned in this book is directly useful in thinking about the possible consequences. In this chapter we describe the forces at work, and set out a checklist of what to watch for as the future unfolds.

This chapter is about three things. First, the Single European Act of 1987 committed members of the European Community (EC) to a single market in goods, services, assets, and people by 31 December 1992, a programme now known simply as '1992'. What difference will 1992 make?

Second, in 1988 the Hanover Summit of the EC heads of government established a committee chaired by the President[1] of the European Commission, Jacques Delors, to investigate how European Monetary Union (EMU) could be achieved. The first stages of the Delors Report were accepted by the following EC Summit in Madrid in 1989. In this chapter we discuss what EMU means and what the moves towards it will entail.

The third development is the dramatic reforms, both political and economic, in Eastern Europe. During 1989 the pace of change took everyone by surprise. It is still too early to guarantee that the new liberal climate will survive. However, we can consider the economic issues, that are involved if it does.

---

[1] Each EC country takes it in turn to assume the presidency of the European Community for six months, and hosts a Summit. This should not be confused with the presidency of the European Commission, the body of civil servants sitting in Brussels. The big decisions are taken by national politicians meeting at Summits, at the Council of Ministers, or at more regular meetings of ministers with particular responsibilities. The European Parliament is separately elected and as yet has only a small amount of real power.

34-1 The Single European Act and 1992

The Euorpean Community was established by the original six members in 1957. Its chief features were two: there would be a free trade area inside the Community, and there would be Community-wide programmes financed by fiscal contributions from member-governments. The largest Community programme was the Common Agricultural Policy (CAP), a system of administered high prices for agricultural commodities which has led to the famous wine 'lakes' and butter 'mountains'. A more modest programme was the Structural Funds, designed to provide subsidies for social infrastructure, especially in poorer areas of the Community.

Over the following 30 years, the Community was enlarged. The original six – West Germany, France, Holland, Belgium, Luxembourg, and Italy – were joined by Denmark, Ireland, the UK, Greece, Spain, and Portugal. By 1990, therefore, there were 12 members.

Community enlargement was not accompanied by any change in the fundamental structure of the Community. Member-states continued to set national policies. The dreamers and the Eurocrats were always pressing for closer integration, for example by harmonizing industrial standards or national tax rates, but this was usually thwarted for two reasons. First, since each country had a different way of doing things, it was impossibly cumbersome to negotiate the single set of regulations which would apply to all member-states. Second, of course, it was political dynamite. Nobody wanted to adopt somebody else's procedures and policy.

In the mid-1980s there was a real breakthrough, and it is important to understand why it occurred. We have seen that in most Western countries the 1980s was a decade in which the pendulum swung against big government and extensive regulation of the economy. The emphasis was increasingly on market forces, competition, and deregulation. This new approach influenced not merely the domestic policies adopted in particular countries but also the spirit in which international negotiations were conducted.

Instead of trying to agree on a single set of comprehensive rules, hammered out in Brussels and then rigidly enforced in all member-states of the Community, the logic of competition now led to a different approach. Member-states would agree on some broad outlines for harmonizing policy. Each member-state would then be responsible for deciding in its own way how these should be implemented. And each member-state would recognize the validity of the regulations imposed by other member-states.

Let's look at a specific example. Each country has regulations determining which institutions are allowed to register as a bank or an insurance company, and what conditions they must fulfil. Previously, the differences in national regulations were so great that a bank registered in the UK under UK law did not comply with standards laid down for banks in France, Germany, or Italy. So banks in one country found it almost impossible to compete in other countries. National markets were effectively segmented. Since there are economies of scale in banking, each small national market had only a few banks enjoying significant market power.

Under the new approach, member-states agree on some general principles governing the regulation of banks – minimum standards for capital adequacy (the amount of financial backing needed to undertake particular types of risky business), for external monitoring (to check up that managers are doing their job properly), and so on. Then each government decides how to apply these general criteria and to license banks in its country. Finally, and crucially, if a bank is registered in Germany under German law, it is now allowed to operate in France, the UK, etc.

This new approach has two major advantages. First, it provides a politically acceptable way of moving towards European integration. Individual governments no longer look like they are yielding all political control. Second, it brings competition more directly into the

process. Instead of having to 'pick a winner' or make an all-or-nothing guess about which system of regulation to adopt for everyone, different countries adopt different ways of implementing general principles, *and then the market decides*. Countries that adopt regulatory structures which turn out to be good for business will find their firms getting a bigger share of EC trade. Countries with unfavourable systems (which might have too much regulation but might have too little: business is frightened of anarchy, legal ambiguity, and possible fraud) will lose business. Thus, *competition between forms of regulation* will occur, and Europe is likely to converge on the way of doing things that seems to work best in practice.

Once negotiations had moved to this new basis, progress became rapid. In 1987 the member-states of the EC ratified the Single European Act. The Act set December 1992 as the target for achieving completion of the internal market by harmonizing regulations in the manner described above. Among its main objectives were: (*a*) abolition of all remaining foreign exchange controls on capital flows; (*b*) removal of all non-tariff barriers to trade within the EC (differences in trade-marks, patent laws, and safety standards, which act to segment national markets); (*c*) elimination of the bias in public sector purchasing (defence, etc.) favouring domestic producers; (*d*) removal of frontier controls (delays), subject to retaining necessary safeguards for security, social and health reasons; and (*e*) progress towards harmonization of tax rates.

34-2 The Benefits of 1992

Table 34-1 shows that the completion of the single market will create an economic area larger than the United States or Japan. The potential benefits accruing to member-states can be divided into three categories: more

Table 34-1 The size of the single market

	EC	USA	JAPAN
Population (million)	324	246	123
GDP (billion ECU*)	3856	3993	2205

* 1 ECU is about $1 or £0.6.
Source: European Economy, 1987.

BOX 34-1

PLAYING FOR THE JACKPOT

1992 increases the odds that only one European financial centre will survive to play in the world League. Continental stock markets are trying to challenge London's supremacy, and London is trying to consolidate its head start. Three characteristics are likely to determine where the business gets done: the cost of transacting, the liquidity of the market, and the ease and efficiency of settling up transactions.

In the race towards 1992, London got off to a flying start with Big Bang in 1986. Previously, the market was rigidly separated into *brokers*, who placed orders on behalf of clients, and *jobbers* or marketmakers, who held inventories of stock and quoted prices at which they would buy or sell. Brokers' commissions were strictly regulated and jobbers were tiny family businesses hampered by lack of capital backing. Big Bang abolished fixed commissions, allowed giant financial institutions to become marketmakers, reduced stamp duty, the government tax on transactions, and introduced computerization. As a result, the cost of transacting in London fell up to 30 per cent and London quickly gained business from other continental stock markets.

Paris, Milan, Amsterdam, and Madrid began with a different system. Instead of marketmakers, they used a computerized auctioneer to work out prices that equated demand and supply. But all these exchanges have gradually followed London, introducing a parallel system of marketmaking backed by the large financial institutions. And, like London, they have become more competitive and more efficient.

The pace of change has been slowest in Frankfurt, in part because the structure of German ownership of companies is unique. Whereas in the UK banks make loans to companies, in Germany they take the main equity stake; and German banks are also brokers, with the principal access to German stock markets and fund managers. Only after January 1990 did a system of marketmaking outside the stock exchange begin to emerge. While less overtly competitive than exchanges like London, the German settlement system is easily the cheapest and most efficient in Europe.

What does this all imply? In a pioneering study of European stock markets, Marco Pagano of Naples University and Ailsa Roell of the London School of Economics[1] have calculated the transaction costs and liquidity of different stock markets in Europe. They found that in 1990 London was the most attractive place to undertake wholesale business – large transactions of half a million pounds or more. But Paris was already much cheaper for retail business, the small transactions undertaken by private investors. London may not have it all its own way after 1992.

[1] M. Pagano and A. Roell, 'Trading Systems in European Stock Exchanges: Current Performance and Policy Options', *Economic Policy*, 1990.

---

efficient resource allocation, fuller exploitation of scale economies, and gains from intensified competition.

Gains from Improved Resource Allocation

In Chapter 32 we introduced the principle of comparative advantage and discussed how free trade could lead to a more efficient resource allocation. Opening up trade allows each country to specialize more in the commodities that it makes *relatively* cheaply. Although the EC has for many years operated as a free trade zone without tariff on trade between member-states, the rationale for 1992 is that there still remained non-tariff barriers which continued to segment national markets.

Non-tariff barriers are differences in national regulations or practices which prevent free movement of goods, services, and factors across countries.

Thus, 1992 aims to break down non-tariff barriers and allow countries to exploit their true comparative advantage more fully.

Gains from Scale Economies

When national markets are small and segmented from one another, firms may not be able fully to exploit economies of scale. We know that scale economies are important. In Chapter 32 we explained how these give rise to two-way trade between countries in the same industry. 1992 should intensify this trade in goods, and initiate such trade in some services (such as financial services) where differences in national regulation effectively precluded EC trade in the past.

Gains from Intensified Competition

1992 will intensify competition for two different reasons. First, on average, the degree of regulation around which harmonization is taking place involves a lower degree of regulation for most countries than in the past. For example, in the 1980s the UK pursued deregulation more extensively than many of its continental counterparts. For many continental countries, the 1992 programme embodies a substantial amount of deregulation.

Second, a larger market enables individual firms to enjoy scale economies *without* necessarily having the large market share they would enjoy in a small, segmented national economy. This is a force for competition, which may stimulate greater cost efficiency. In Part 3 we showed how imperfect competition leads to allocative distortions. These should be smaller, the larger the market and the greater the competition.

This argument needs to be qualified in one important regard. For competition to increase, it is important that the size of firms does not increase in proportion to the increase in the size of the market; then the market shares would be unaltered. The late 1980s saw a wave of mergers between European firms as they were getting ready for 1992. Table 34-2 shows the extent of cross-border takeovers arising when domestic firms buy into or sell out to firms based in other countries.

This merger wave has two possible interpre-

tations. The first is that companies are restructuring to get in better shape to exploit comparative advantage and scale economies after 1992. It is the market mechanism at work. The more sinister interpretation is that mergers are simply intended to preserve market power as the size of the market increases. If so, this will frustrate the gains we hope to enjoy through greater competition.

This danger places great responsibility on European merger policy during this transitional phase. Ultimately, power resides with the Competition Directorate of the European Commission in Brussels, which has the power to override national policy. The commissioner in charge of competition policy has a vital role to play in allowing restructuring to take place but not at the expense of a reduction in overall competition.

Thus far we have focused on the market for goods and services. The market for factors is also important. Free capital mobility will allow firms to locate in the areas in which the rate of return is highest. In the long run, this is an important mechanism for increasing efficiency. 1992 will also enhance labour mobility. In principle, this too should increase the overall efficiency of resource allocation within the EC. In practice, its effects are likely to be small.

34-3 Quantifying the Effects of 1992

How large will these gains be in practice? A massive study by the European Commission, popularly known as the Cecchini Report,[2] has

[2] Paolo Cecchini and others, *The European Challenge 1992: The Benefits of a Single Market*. European Commission, 1989.

Table 34-2 Number of cross-border takeovers of UK, French, and German firms

	UK		GERMANY		FRANCE	
	Total	Europe	Total	Europe	Total	Europe
Firms sold						
1987	138	83	269	190	178	127
1988	230	155	360	250	235	170
Firms bought						
1987	427	156	137	85	194	133
1988	767	260	180	109	372	277

Source: J. Franks and C. Mayer, 'Capital Markets and Corporate Governance: A European Comparison', *Economic Policy*, 1990.

estimated that the *once-and-for-all* gains from all the above sources might be between 2.5 and 6.5 per cent of EC GDP. This is useful but modest. Many economists find it hard to square this estimate with the tremendous significance attached to 1992 by politicians and business.

One possible resolution of this puzzle has been provided by Professor Dick Baldwin of Columbia University in New York.[3] Baldwin argues that Europe will enjoy economies of scale in the aggregate which exceed those at the level of individual firms. In the language of Chapter 15, there are *externalities*. When computer firms cluster together in a particular location, the expansion of one firm reduces the costs of *other* firms, for example by expanding the pool of trained staff in the area or by sharing expertise.

If this is so, two things follow. First, the Cecchini Report, by ignoring these external economies of scale, understates the impact effect of 1992. Second, it also ignores the second-round effect. With higher output, there will be more saving. (The marginal propensity to consume is less than one.) At full employment, more saving can be matched by more investment. This extra investment will increase the capital stock, aggregate supply, and potential output. And this will generate more scale economies and yet more saving and investment. Cumulating this effect, Baldwin argues, can lead to an output increase at least twice as large as the Cecchini estimate.

Gainers and Losers

Even if the EC as a whole is a substantial winner, the benefits will not be equally distributed. Who gains (and loses!) is economically important, and may have profound political repercussions on the willingness to proceed further with European integration. This issue is not addressed in the Cecchini Report.

The pioneering study tackling this issue for EC members was undertaken by Professor Damien Neven of INSEAD, the European business school in Fontainebleau.[4] Neven collects data for a larger number of different

industries for each member-state and then views 1992 as a reduction in non-tariff barriers. From Chapter 32, we know this should stimulate two kinds of trade: greater specialization by country, to exploit existing comparative advantage once barriers come down, and more two-way trade in the same industry, to exploit scale economies and larger market size.

From existing trade patterns, Neven deduces which countries still have a comparative advantage in which industries. When non-tariff barriers are removed, the gainers will be exporters who have a comparative advantage they previously could not fully exploit. The losers will be domestic producers who previously were able to keep out imports only because of the hidden protection they enjoyed. Neven concludes that the main winners will be producers of labour-intensive commodities in countries with relatively cheap labour. Table 34-3 shows the unit labour costs (wages adjusted for productivity) in different countries when expressed in common currency. Producers of clothing and footwear in Greece and Portugal will wipe out higher-cost producers of the same goods in northern Europe.

If you understood Chapter 32, you will recognize that, if southern Europe has a comparative advantage in labour-intensive goods, northern Europe must have a comparative advantage in other goods. This is true but not quantitatively very important. Southern markets for these goods will be so small that it will do these northern producers only a little good.

On scale economies, Neven finds that it is Spain, Greece, and Portugal that stand to gain most. At the firm level, producers in France, Germany, the UK, and Benelux have already exploited most of the scale economies. So again, it is the southern countries that stand to gain

---

[3] R. Baldwin, 'The Growth Effects of 1992', *Economic Policy*, 1990.

[4] D. Neven, 'The Distributional Effects of 1992', *Economic Policy*, 1990.

Table 34-3 Hourly labour costs (1984 ECU)

Germany	14.2	UK	9.0
Holland	13.7	Ireland	8.9
Belgium	13.4	Spain	6.1
France	12.4	Greece	4.1
Denmark	12.0	Portugal	2.4
Italy	10.8		

Source: D. Neven, 'EEC Integration towards 1992', *Economic Policy*, 1990.

most. This finding is likely to be overturned only if the Baldwin argument set out above is important. Perhaps the clustering externalities will allow northern Europe finally to compete with the United States and Japan in computers. If so, the north may do well – not at the expense of the south, but because of increased competitiveness in markets outside the EC.

1992 will have important effects on two other groups of European countries. Eastern Europe is considered later in this chapter. We end this section with a brief look at the impact on members of the European Free Trade Association (EFTA): Austria, Finland, Iceland, Norway, and Sweden.

In the long run EFTA countries may become members of the EC, but in the early 1990s the EC will be preoccupied with its own internal restructuring and with its relations with Eastern Europe. How will EFTA countries fare, and would they do better if they could eventually become part of the single market? Professor Victor Norman of the Norwegian School of Economics in Bergen has reached the following conclusions.[5] First, EFTA will not suffer much, relative to the present position, by the completion of the single market, but it would be a substantial winner if it were allowed to participate in the single market. Second, if EFTA does eventually join, EFTA consumers will be major gainers through lower prices and greater efficiency, but some high-cost EFTA producers (e.g. motor vehicles) will suffer.

34-4 European Monetary Union

The objective is European union. That was set by the Solemn Declaration that was subscribed to by all the heads of government at Stuttgart in June 1983 and has been reaffirmed on many occasions since, so there is no argument about what the objective is.... After the single market would come the single currency and after the single currency would come the single economy.

Lord Cockfield, former EC Commissioner
with special responsibility for 1992,
testifying to the UK House of Lords
European Communities Committee, 1989

In this section we consider European Monetary Union (EMU). Proponents of EMU come from one of two standpoints: either, like Lord

[5] V. Norman, 'EFTA and the Internal European Market', *Economic Policy*, 1990.

Cockfield, they see it as the next step along a track whose terminus is nothing short of European union itself; or, more pragmatically, they see it as the logical outcome of the EMS once controls on capital movements have been abolished under the 1992 programme.

A *monetary union* has permanently fixed exchange rates within the union, free capital movements, and a single monetary authority responsible for setting the union's money supply.

Technically, a monetary union need not have a single currency. English and Scottish currency circulates side by side in Edinburgh. What matters is that the exchange rate between them is known with certainty and that a single authority (the Bank of England) is responsible for determining their total quantity. Thus, EMU could involve the separate circulation of Deutschmarks, French francs, Italian lire, and pounds sterling, at fixed exchange rates and with a European central bank; but if we have got to this stage, it is likely to be convenient to have a single currency as well.

In Chapter 33 we argued that in the past the EMS had been sustained partly by exchange controls on capital flows. By insulating national currencies, these allowed different members to pursue different interest rate policies while broadly fixing exchange rates in the short run. Countries could become EMS members without completely sacrificing their autonomy over domestic monetary policy.

1992 committed most EC members to abolish capital controls by June 1990. Only the most recent EC entrants (Spain, Greece, and Portugal) will be given a little breathing space, but their controls too will be gone by 1992. We shall be very close to perfect capital mobility within the EC.

In Chapters 29 and 33 we discussed perfect capital mobility and exchange rate determination. To prevent massive movements of footloose international funds, interest rate differentials across currencies must be offset by expected exchange rate changes. If countries are trying to make fixed exchange rates stick, they have to set domestic interest rates to match foreign interest rates. Individual countries have then surrendered sovereignty over domestic monetary policy. Alternatively, countries can retain the ability to set interest rates for domestic purposes, but then they must float their exchange rate and allow asset market equilibrium to determine the value of the exchange rate.

Hence, whether or not the EC had long-term aims for much greater economic integration, the adoption of the 1992 programme meant that the EMS was at the crossroads. We saw in Chapter 33 that the EMS had been getting steadily tighter during the 1980s; realignments were becoming less frequent and inflation convergence was taking place. Once it was decided to abolish capital controls, *either* exchange rates would have to become looser *or* ERM members would have to pursue almost completely harmonized monetary policies.

ERM members gave a clear answer: they wished to continue the trend to tighter exchange rates, culminating in monetary union, even if that meant they would have to pursue a common monetary policy.

Sterling and UK Membership of the ERM

By early 1990, sterling was still not part of the exchange rate mechanism of the EMS. In the early 1980s, three arguments used to be advanced against full UK membership of the EMS. First, North Sea oil made sterling a petrocurrency; sterling would fluctuate with world oil prices, and this would make it hard to be part of a club for relatively fixed exchange rates. As North Sea oil has run down, however, sterling is now much less sensitive to oil prices, and this argument is basically a dead duck.

Second, it was argued that in the early 1980s only London and Frankfurt were decontrolled financial centres. Since all other ERM countries had foreign exchange controls, money could not flow freely from, say, Frankfurt to Paris. There was in those days no need for harmonizing monetary policy. UK entry would have changed the EMS by creating two decontrolled currencies and the need for explicit co-ordination of monetary policy. But this is now what the whole EMS has decided to adopt under 1992. So this argument too is dead.

Finally, it used to be argued that UK trade was only partly with continental Europe; so even if one accepted the need for more stable exchange rates, this did not necessarily mean stability against EMS members. But Table 34-4

Table 34-4 UK trade patterns since EC membership

	OTHER EC	NORTH AMERICA	REST OF WORLD
% of exports			
1972	32	18	50
1987	49	17	34
% of imports			
1972	36	16	48
1987	54	10	36

Source: HM Treasury, *Economic Progress Report*, 1988.

shows that the trend has been for UK trade to be increasingly with EMS members, and this will be enhanced by 1992, so this argument is also increasingly irrelevant.

Why, then, was the UK reluctant to join the ERM in the late 1980s? Countries such as France and Italy, previously high-inflation countries, had claimed that ERM membership had made their anti-inflation policy more credible; Germany had low inflation, and other countries could not be forever devaluing against the Deutschmark to recoup the competitiveness they had lost through higher inflation. There were three reasons for the reluctance. First, the Thatcher government was proud of having brought UK inflation down on its own, from outside the ERM. However, the appeal of this argument started to wane in 1989–90 when UK inflation rose sharply again.

Second, the Thatcher government had argued for a long time that fiscal policy should be used not for short-term demand management but rather to pursue long-term supply-side reform through steady tax cuts. Hence the UK needed to retain monetary policy as a short-term weapon which could quickly be tightened, as in 1989–90, if inflation started to rise. Joining the ERM and following the common interest rate policy would remove this monetary option, and might force the government to backtrack on some of the things it had said about fiscal policy.

Finally, some of Mrs Thatcher's advisers, notably Sir Alan Walters, believed that the EMS had always been the result of muddled thinking and was unlikely to stand the strains of abolishing capital controls, and felt that it might be better to wait and see what happened.

However, by Autumn 1990 UK inflation was

getting dangerously high. The UK joined the ERM in the hope that financial discipline would be increased and that wage bargainers would recognize that further wage increases would reduce international competitiveness and lead to unemployment in the UK.

The Delors Report

The Delors Committee, commissioned by the 1988 Hanover Summit to propose feasible steps towards EMU, reported in spring 1989 and was discussed at the Madrid Summit of EC heads of government.

It proposed proceeding in three stages. Stage 1 would begin in June 1990 when capital controls would have been abolished by the main EC countries. During Stage 1 the ERM would become progressively tighter, with realignments becoming less and less frequent. *All* EC members would be expected to become full ERM members during Stage 1. The Delors Report was deliberately noncommittal about how long this stage would last.

During Stage 1, negotiations would be undertaken about the Treaty amendments required for eventual establishment of EMU. Stage 2 would be a transitional phase (also of unspecifed length) in which existing EC insitutions would rehearse Community-wide decision-making. One of the most controversial proposals was that precise, though not yet binding, ceilings would be set for the budget deficits of individual member-states. The EC would begin to formulate the common monetary policy. Exchange rate realignments would still be possible, though now only in exceptional circumstances.

Stage 3 would see the completion of EMU. The European Council would have the power to make binding decisions, for example placing limits on the budget deficits of member-states. Exchange rates would be locked for ever, and the new European Central Bank would take on full responsibility for the Common EC monetary policy.

The Delors Committee argued that embarking on this process should be taken as a binding commitment to go all the way to EMU. However, the Madrid Summit only ratified embarking on Stage 1, leaving open the questions of whether and when to proceed to Stage 2.

34-5 The Economics of Monetary Union

Suppose our starting point is the EMS in January 1990. Capital controls are already gone or on the way out. For ERM members, domestic monetary sovereignty has effectively already been given up. What are the extra costs and benefits of proceeding to EMU?

Let's begin with the benefits. A common currency would certainly reduce transaction costs, the time and resources used up in changing money. This is easy to quantify, but in itself it is not a huge saving. Second, we might argue that a EMU would underpin the 1992 reforms: it is the best way to break down the barriers that still segment the markets of member-states.

Third, EMU would bring complete exchange rate certainty. For existing ERM members this is not much of a change. Their exchange rates are already tied together pretty tightly. Business has greater risks to worry about than small exchange rate changes occasionally. For the UK the position was of course rather different, since sterling had fluctuated dramatically against other currencies.

These are probably all big pluses. What about the costs of EMU? First, once all possibility of realignment has been ruled out, what is a country to do if it loses a substantial degree of international competitiveness?

Competitiveness depends not merely on nominal exchange rates but also on relative prices at home and abroad. So it can be changed by changes in domestic prices. An uncompetitive country will suffer a loss of exports and/or experience a recession, and this will gradually bid down nominal wages and prices, restoring its competitiveness. Market forces *will* provide an adjustment mechanism. The problem is that it could take a long time, leaving the unlucky country with a recession in the meantime.

What happens in the monetary union we call the United States? When oil prices fall and Texas has a slump, it does not devalue against the rest of the country. A crucial reason why the United States survives is the existence of a federal, or cross-state, fiscal policy.

In the 1980s, Massachusetts boomed while Texas went bust. At *given* rates of federal income tax and social security levels, people from Massachusetts made extra payments to

Washington (more income tax revenue and less unemployment benefit) and Texans got extra money from Washington (more unemployment benefit and lower income tax payments). Professor Barry Eichengreen of Berkeley[6] has shown that, when the output of a particular state of the United States rose (fell) by a dollar, the automatic transfer payments from the federal government fell (rose) by 40 cents, thus providing a substantial degree of income insurance for individual states.

The EC has no comparable system of federal fiscal transfers. The EC Structural Funds are tiny in comparison, and are intended for long-term infrastructure, not short-term insurance. Over the 1990s, Europe may make progress towards greater economic and political union, involving much greater transfers of power and resources to the federal level; but this remains a contentious issue and was excluded from the Delors Report.

Without both a federal adjustment mechanism to redistribute income towards countries in temporary trouble and the option of exchange rate realignments, member-states will probably wish to retain freedom over their own fiscal policy. A country facing a severe recession because competitiveness has suddenly deteriorated will then have a safety valve: a fiscal expansion to cushion the worse effects until supply-side measures or wage adjustment succeed in restoring competitiveness.

Why did the Delors Report favour ceilings on budget deficits? To build in a credible precommitment that EC monetary policy would fight inflation. Inflation is often the result of fiscal mismanagement. Governments with big deficits and spiralling debt are tempted to create inflation to reduce the real value of outstanding nominal debt.

The Delors solution to this problem was to try to stop governments from getting into fiscal difficulties. But there is another way to block the channel from fiscal problem to pressure for money creation: simply forbid the central bank to print too much money. That is what an independent central bank would mean. Making the European Central Bank independent of political control, and giving it a constitution committing it to price stability, would be just

as good a precommitment as the Delors solution. And it would have the advantage that governments could still run *temporary* budget deficits in times of special difficulty, provided they were prepared to finance them by selling bonds in the world's financial markets.

34-6 Economic Integration and Eastern Europe

For 40 years after 1945, Eastern Europe was under rigid political and economic control from Moscow. These countries had planned economies in which market forces played only a small role. Much of the capital stock was outdated and the planning system led to many fiascos. Coal was mined to make fuel for power stations, electricity was used to make steel, and steel was used to make coal mining machines but no consumer goods: a vicious cycle of inefficiency. Productivity and real wages were low, and there were long queues to buy even the most basic commodities. Table 34-5 documents the basic economic indicators for Eastern Europe in 1988, and compares them with selected countries in the EC. Even in East Germany, the most affluent country, per capita real income was only half that in West Germany. However, unlike many developing countries, Eastern Europe had relatively high standards of education and health provision. Suitably organized, these countries might quickly attain large productivity increases.

1989 took everyone by surprise. Previous

Table 34-5 **Eastern Europe: basic economic indicators, 1988**

	POPULATION (m)	GDP ($b)	GDP PER CAPITA ($)
E. Germany	17	156	9 360
Czechoslovakia	16	118	7 600
Hungary	11	69	6 500
Bulgaria	9	51	5 630
Poland	37	207	5 540
Romania	23	94	4 120
EC	325	4745	14 609
W. Germany	61	1202	19 575
Portugal	10	41	3 987

Source: The AMEX Bank Review, November 1989.

[6] B. Eichengreen, 'One Money for Europe', *Economic Policy*, 1990.

attempts at political and economic reform had quickly been stifled by Soviet tanks. This time, amid perestroika and détente, the pace of change was dramatic. Western observers assumed that Eastern Europe would adopt a form of market socialism, but many countries moved immediately to parties promising the rapid adoption of market-oriented policies like those in the EC.

It is too early to be sure that these ambitions will be realized. However, we conclude this chapter by introducing some of the economic issues that have to be faced if Eastern Europe is to succeed in its current objectives.

The Debt Problem

We discuss the international debt crises more fully in the next chapter. But we must recognize, after years of mismanagement, Eastern Europe has already accumulated substantial debts to Western creditors. The scale of the problem is shown in Table 34-6.

These debts are a substantial burden on Eastern Europe. It is important that this legacy from the past does not get in the way of a difficult period of internal reform. Equally, there is little point in simply propping up the previous economic system. In July 1989 the Paris Summit of the heads of government of the 24 major industrialized countries considered what to do about the two countries, Poland and Hungary, which at that date had already begun the process of reform. The Summit decided that it should be the EC that co-ordinated the world's response to this debt crisis. They agreed on a substantial aid package, linked to continuing efforts at supply-side reform. Similar aid would be extended to other Eastern European countries when they too

had shown a commitment to reform.

Because of its size and its earlier start, Poland has received the most assistance to date. During the reform programme, its major creditors (Western governments) have agreed to defer all debt repayments. And the EC has set up a new European Bank for Reconstruction and Development to finance market-oriented reforms in Eastern Europe.

Such initiatives are not only the beginning of closer co-operation inside Europe. They also act as a useful lever for governments in Eastern Europe. If Western assistance is conditional on continuing reform, this helps Eastern governments persist even when adjustment problems may be severe.

Supply-side Reforms

In the past, production, investment, and employment decisions were made largely by bureaucrats. A larger scale of operation meant greater prestige, even if it used more inputs than it produced outputs. Supply-side reform means allowing the price mechanism to take over the role of allocating resources. This has several aspects.

First, prices need to reflect true scarcity. Previously, prices were held artificially low. This made inflation look good, but such data were meaningless. Consumers couldn't get goods, and factories couldn't buy inputs at these artificial prices. There was chronic excess demand.

Freeing up prices inevitably means that prices rise sharply. During January 1990, the first month of the Polish reform, only some prices were decontrolled, yet measured inflation was 70 per cent in a month, an annual rate of almost 1000 per cent. But this is a one-off phenomenon. Once prices clear the market, they will stop rising. And it is precisely these high prices that are the market mechanism telling suppliers it is now time to increase production.

One of the key issues is what happens to wages at this point. If nominal wages rise with prices, there is no rise in profitability and no signal to suppliers to look for new ways to increase production. Instead, the country settles into spiralling inflation. The reform package looks a failure, and the government may fall.

Alternatively, if nominal wages do not rise nearly as much as prices, measured real wages

Table 34-6   Eastern Europe's debt, 1989

	TOTAL DEBT ($b)	DEBT PER CAPITA ($)	DEBT AS % OF EXPORTS
Bulgaria	9.5	1050	260
Czechoslovakia	6.9	430	95
E. Germany	21.2	1325	120
Hungary	19.7	1875	325
Poland	40.4	1080	532
Yugoslavia	17.6	735	110

Source: HM Treasury, Economic Progress Report, April 1990.

fall. If the government can hold the line long enough, production and productivity will increase, and that is the time to let real wages start rising. In the meantime the government has one good argument: although measured real wages have fallen, standards of living may not have declined. Previously, workers couldn't find goods in the shops: their purchasing power wasn't nearly as large as their apparent real wage. And now they don't have to stand for hours queuing! We shortly examine the macroeconomic policies which can help ensure that the reform package does not degenerate into the high-inflation scenario.

Success does not depend merely on freeing up prices. A supply response to higher prices must take place. Incentives have to work. Bureaucrats who ran state enterprises may not be the best people to rise to this challenge. Hence in many Eastern Europe countries there is now a call for privatization of state enterprises. The aim of privatization is less the need to raise revenue for the government – at present, consumers have little wealth with which to pay – than to put the profit motive up front for those managing the new enterprises.

Trade and Foreign Investment

Eastern Europe needs markets for its output if it is to grow quickly. And the pressure of external competition will be a powerful force for rapid productivity improvement, even if it means unemployment in the short run while painful adjustment is taking place. The most obvious market for their goods is the European Community.

After signing the Single European Act, the EC took a decision to defer community enlargement until 1992 had been digested, and this wish to strengthen relations within the existing Community was reinforced by the beginning of moves towards monetary union. Other countries, such as Turkey and the EFTA countries, had been told there was no possibility of EC entry until well into the 1990s.

Events in Eastern Europe have led to some rethinking within the EC. East Germany is a special case which we discuss more fully below. For the rest of Eastern Europe, it seems probable that these countries can be given some associate member status quite quickly, with free trade access in exchange for continuing commit-

ments to liberalize. Thus, the integration of European trade will reinforce integration arising from official lending and aid described above.

What Eastern Europe still needs is physical capital and management expertise. Some capital goods will be imported from the West, but two other developments may be even more important. First, EC firms (and some from the United States and elsewhere) will invest directly in the East. If Volkswagen can set up factories in Brazil, it can surely do so in East Germany and Poland. Second, there is likely to be a substantial number of *joint ventures*, with Western firms taking a special equity stake, and supplying management expertise and training, in Eastern firms.

Macroeconomic Conditions for Success

If reform programmes are to succeed, they must not allow initial price increases to spill over into hyperinflation. Basically, what is needed is a fairly austere macro policy until the supply side can adjust. Subsidized credit and artificial exchange rates must be abolished; interest rates and exchange rates must find their own level. Then monetary policy must be responsible, and those countries with large fiscal deficits must tackle their fiscal problems.

Every country is different, and no automatic formula can be applied. But it is easy to describe the form of package that seems to have worked most often in developing countries tackling similar difficulties. The currency should become convertible – an end to exchange rate rationing for importers and exporters – and it should be substantially devalued, since domestic prices are about to rise sharply, once and for all. The new lower exchange rate should then be rigidly enforced by macroeconomic policy, thereby providing a nominal anchor. Thereafter, firms and workers know that higher wages and prices will simply price them out of a job.

Initially, foreign exchange controls should be maintained on the capital account (just as in postwar western Europe) in case residents panic and try to get all their money out of the country. As confidence builds up, these controls can be relaxed.

If unemployment rises during the initial period of immense restructuring, aggregate demand management should *not* be increased to take care of unemployment. That would prevent the adjustment from taking place, and would make inflation more of a danger in an already fragile situation.

In short, macroeconomic policy needs to be firm and to be believed to be so. There is no point in half measures when attempting the biggest change in 50 years: 'If you are going to chop off a cat's tail, do it in one stroke, not bit by bit', remarked Gonzalo Sanchez de Losada, the minister responsible for Bolivia's similar reform package during 1986–89.[7]

East Germany

East Germany is a special case, and not just because it is the most affluent and best educated of the Eastern European countries. Germany was forcibly partitioned at the end of the Second World War. The German dream of reunification became a reality in 1990 with the blessing of the original partitioning powers.

This made a difference for several reasons. First, the political risk was smaller. If the Soviet Union ever reverts to Stalinism, Soviet tanks may invade Poland; it is much less likely that they will invade a united Germany. This means that the credibility of *current* government policy, and the incentives for Western firms to invest, is much higher in East Germany than in its Eastern European neighbours.

Second, the EC accepted that a veto on EC enlargement would not apply to East Germany after reunification. Again, this will have incentive and credibility effects.

Third, in July 1990 East and West Germany agreed to German Monetary Union (GMU). With a common currency and the Bundesbank in control of German monetary policy, there was an immediate and very credible guarantee that East Germany will not degenerate into hyperinflation.

There was considerable debate about the exchange rate at which the Deutschmark and the Ostmark should be locked when GMU occurred. Politically, the temptation was to have one-for-one, thus symbolically restoring parity between the two Germanies. Economists pointed out that, when East Germany first broke free of the Soviet Union, the black market exchange rate was between 0.1 and 0.15 Deutschmarks to the Ostmark and that this might be a better indicator of East Germany's competitiveness (or lack of it). Fixing on one-for-one implied a huge *appreciation* of the Ostmark, in the short run a recipe for unemployment in Leipzig and Berlin, but cheap imports of West German consumer goods.

In the event, West German Chancellor Kohl settled for a compromise. East Germans could cash in a small amount of their savings at an exchange rate of one-for-one (a favourable rate for East Germans in terms of the purchasing power over West German consumer goods), but thereafter the exchange rate would be locked at 0.5 Deutschmarks to the Ostmark.[8] East Germany will need substantial productivity gains to become competitive at this exchange rate, but we have argued that there are good grounds for being optimistic. Full economic and political reunification occurred in October 1990.

Summary

1   The Single European Act commits EC governments to completion of the single market by 1992. The framework is a common set of broad outlines for regulation, national implementation, and mutual recognition of firms licensed in other member-states.

2   For many countries this involves substantial deregulation. Together with enlarged market size, this should increase competition unless Euromergers go completely unchecked. The Cecchini Report estimates the total benefit in the range of 2.5–6 per cent of EC GDP. Some economists think the gain will be substantially larger.

3   The main winners will be the southern

---

[7] Reported in J. Sachs and D. Lipton, 'Creating a Market Economy in Eastern Europe: The Case of Poland', *Brookings Papers on Economic Activity*, 1990. Professor Jeff Sachs of Harvard University, who advised both the Bolivian and the Polish governments on how to design their reform package, is also fond of saying, 'You can't jump a chasm in two steps.'

[8] People set up black market foreign exchange stalls in the railway stations in East Germany. When the old government fell, the black market rate was just over 0.1 Ostmark/DM. What should a smart speculator have thought once people began to talk about reunification and GMU? Politically, the eventual exchange rate would have to be a lot closer to 1 Ostmark/DM than its initial level. The touts who poured into East German railway stations were delighted to supply DM to desperate East Germans and made substantial capital gains on the Ostmarks they bought as the black market rate floated upwards.

countries of the EC, who can exploit their relatively cheap labour and still have scope for scale economies. Northern competitors in these industries are likely to lose. More advanced industries in the north may do well if external economies of scale allow them to tackle the heavyweights in the US and Japan.

4   A monetary union means permanently fixed exchange controls, free capital movements, and a common monetary policy. These matter much more than whether or not we go the extra step to a common currency.

5   In abolishing capital controls for 1992, the EMS is already committed to almost complete harmonization of monetary policy. The UK became a full EMS member in 1990.

6   The Delors Report recommended progress to EMU in three stages. Stage 1 began on 1 July 1990 and envisaged exchange rate stability gradually increasing. All EC countries must be full EMS members before the end of Stage 1, and negotiations about the form of EMU will be completed during this phase. Realignments will be possible though discouraged. No date is set for the transition to Stage 2, when the new institutions will begin rehearsing their eventual role, though as yet without formal power. Realignments will be allowed only as a last resort. Stage 3 establishes the European Central Bank to run monetary policy. Exchange rates are fixed for ever. The EC has the power to put ceilings on national budget deficits.

7   In EMU, countries can change their competitiveness through the slow process of domestic wage and price adjustment. In the absence of any federal fiscal system, individual member-states are likely to want to retain control of fiscal policy as a last resort for dealing with crises.

8   To make Europe's tough monetary policy credible, it would be better to make the new central bank independent, and allow governments fiscal freedom provided they are prepared to borrow in bond markets to finance budget deficits.

9   Eastern Europe is embarking on economic reform. It begins with high foreign debt, but Western countries are offering aid and holidays on debt repayment. Tying assistance to con-

tinuing reform helps strengthen the hand of the reformers.

10   Supply-side reform means introducing the profit motive and deregulation, and allowing the price system to work. Because prices have been artificially low, initially there were sharp increases in prices. The challenge for policy is to stop this from turning into hyperinflation. Macroeconomic policy needs to be firm during this dangerous phase.

11   Trade and investment links will quickly develop between Eastern and Western Europe. Productivity growth in the East could be rapid. East Germany has the special advantage of reunification with West Germany. This is likely to keep East German inflation in check after a brief initial period.

Key Terms

The single market
Non-tariff barriers
Monetary union
Federal fiscal system
European Central Bank
European Bank for Reconstruction and Development
German Monetary Union

Problems

1   'Workers have power in the labour market only because their own firms have power in the goods market. In a perfectly competitive firm, attempts to raise wages just drive the firm out of business.' (a) Do you agree? (b) If 1992 increases competition in product markets, what effect will this have on the labour market within the EC?

2   Name three EC countries you think have a comparative advantage in goods that use human capital intensively. Name three countries for which this is not the case.

3   You have been commissioned to write a report on whether London will remain Europe's leading financial centre after 1992. What arguments can you think of? What evidence would you want to collect?

4   Suppose two countries fix their exchange rate for ever, but they have foreign exchange controls preventing private sector capital account flows between them. Is this a monetary union? If not, why not?

5 In the light of your answer to problem 4, are the currencies of different members of a monetary union perfect substitutes? What does this tell you about their interest rates? What does that tell you about the possibility of conducting separate monetary policies?

6 Why might a government trying to pursue an economic programme of liberalization and reform be unable to carry it out?

7 Will German unification make life any more difficult for West Germany? If so, why?

8 Common Fallacies Show why the following statements are incorrect. (*a*) 1992 is a recipe for the rest of Europe to enjoy West German living standards. (*b*) European Monetary Union will severely reduce the monetary sovereignty of individual members of the EMS. (*c*) The European Central Bank must be accountable to politicians, and individual member-states should not be subject to fiscal control for Brussels. That is the recipe for guaranteeing democracy and low inflation.

35

Problems of Developing Countries in the World Economy

In Europe or the United States a drought is bad for the garden; in poor countries it kills people. In this chapter we pay special attention to the poorer countries in the world economy.

We begin by showing how unequally the world's income is divided between the rich industrial countries and the poor, less developed countries (LDCs). We then briefly review the major problems that low-income countries face in trying to develop their economies. However, the theme of Part 5 is the world economy as a whole, not a description of its constituent parts. Therefore two major issues that we discuss are the best way for LDCs to take advantage of the world economy as it currently exists, and the extent to which LDCs actually benefit from participating in the world economy.

In May 1974, the General Assembly of the United Nations passed a resolution calling for a New International Economic Order (NIEO). It called for international co-operation to reduce the widening gap between the developed and the developing countries. The resolution reflected the feeling of many LDCs that the world economy is arranged to benefit the industrial countries and exploit the poorer countries. Since 1974 there has been a lot of talk about restructuring the world economy – but not much action.

We look at the facts behind the movement for an NIEO and the proposals that have been made. Economics cannot give all the answers, but it can be used to analyse the proposed solutions. We begin by showing the enormous degree of inequality between the countries of the world.

35-1 World Income Distribution and the NIEO

In 1987 there were 2.5 billion people in low-income countries, with an average annual income of about £180 per person. In the rest of the world, 2.4 billion people enjoyed an average annual income of about £3400 per person. Although it is hard to make exact comparisons between income data produced in different countries, the basic fact is clear. *Most of the world's people live in poverty beyond the imagination of people in rich Western countries.* And, of course, not everyone in a country gets exactly the average income. Even in some middle-income countries, many people live in great poverty.

Table 35-1 shows data on per capita income, education, life expectancy at birth, and the availability of medical care. The low-income countries are very badly off on every measure.

Progress 1965–87 Nevertheless, the situation of low-income countries has improved since 1965. Table 35-2 shows a marked increase in life expectancy in low-income countries, a clear indication that the quality of life has improved since 1965.

Table 35-2 also shows that per capita income increased in all groups of countries. Although low-income countries achieved real growth, in absolute terms they fell even further behind the rest of the world.

Thus there has been some progress in the past two decades, but the gap between low-income and other countries is wide and in most cases widening. It is this combination of enormous differences in incomes and slow or no progress in reducing the gap that is the driving force behind the NIEO.

The North and the South

The call for an NIEO is often expressed as a difference between north and south. The

Table 35-1 World welfare indicators, by country group

	LOW INCOME	MIDDLE INCOME	RICH INDUSTRIAL
Per capita GNP, 1987 (£)	177	1105	8800
Percentage of age group in secondary school, 1986	35	54	92
Population per nurse, 1984	2150	980	130
Life expectancy at birth, 1987 (years)	61	65	76

Source: World Bank Development Report, 1989.

Table 35-2 World development, 1965–87

COUNTRY GROUP	ANNUAL GROWTH OF PER CAPITA REAL GNP (%)	LIFE EXPECTANCY AT BIRTH		POPULATION PER NURSE	
		1965	1987	1965	1987
Low income	3.1	50	61	5037	2150
Middle income	2.5	52	65	3526	980
Rich industrial	2.3	71	76	425	130

Source: As for Table 35-1.

north–south distinction sees the world divided into the rich north (including the Soviet Union) and the poor south. Those in the south claim the right to a larger share of the world's income, and their claims are on the rich countries of the north whether these countries be capitalist, socialist or communist.[1] The north–south division is essentially the same as the division between the developed or industrialized countries and the LDCs. The LDCs are the countries of the Third World, ranging from the very poor countries of Africa and Asia to the middle-income countries such as Argentina and Yugoslavia.

Although in this chapter we try to understand how LDCs view the problems they face, and although many LDCs see their basic problem as how to get a larger share of the world's existing income and wealth, we should stress at the outset that people living in the industrial north may be interested in the problems of

LDCs not merely out of a concern for fairness and an abhorrence of poverty wherever it occurs. In Chapter 32 we argued that there were many circumstances in which an increase in world trade would benefit everyone concerned. In the long run, even from a purely selfish standpoint, the north has many reasons to be interested in the development of the economies of LDCs.

35-2 Economic Development in Low-income Countries

Why do so many countries have such a low level of per capita real GNP? To get to this position, they must have grown slowly for a long time. In this section we examine the special problems faced by countries with very low incomes.

Population Growth   The growth of per capita real income depends on the growth of total real income relative to the growth of population. In rich countries birth control is widespread; in poor countries much less so. In the absence of state pensions and other benefits, having children is one way people can try to provide

---

[1] For an extensive discussion of the NIEO and what might be done about existing inequalities, see North–South: A Programme for Survival, Report of the Brandt Commission, 1980. The Brandt Commission was a private group headed by former German Chancellor Brandt. The report paints a grim picture of the economic problems of the low-income countries. The second Brandt report, Common Crisis (Pan Books, 1983), is no less pessimistic.

security against their old age when they are no longer able to work. In recent decades the population of low-income countries has been growing at about 2.5 per cent per annum; in rich countries annual population growth is less than 1 per cent per annum. In order merely to maintain per capita living standards, poor countries have to increase total output much faster than rich countries.

A rapidly expanding labour force can allow rapid GNP growth if other factor inputs are expanding at an equal rate. The problem for poor countries is that they cannot expand supplies of land, capital, and natural resources at the same rate as the labour force. Decreasing returns to labour set in.

Resource Scarcity Dubai is generously endowed with oil and has a per capita GNP in excess of the United States or West Germany. Most of the world's low-income countries have not been blessed with natural resources that can profitably be exploited. And having resource deposits is not enough: it takes scarce capital resources to extract mineral deposits.

Financial Capital The rich countries have built up large stocks of physical capital which make their labour forces productive. Poor countries have few spare domestic resources to devote to physical investment. Most domestic resources are required to provide even minimal consumption. Financial loans and aid allow poor countries to buy in machinery and pay foreign construction firms. However, LDCs frequently complain both that financial assistance is inadequate and that multinational firms brought in to assist in economic development actually prevent sustained economic growth by LDCs: they use foreign workers, thus preventing domestic workers from acquiring valuable skills and experience, and they repatriate the profits to their own countries, thus preventing the accumulation of financial capital within LDCs to finance further development.

Social Investment in Infrastructure Developed countries achieve economies of scale and high productivity through specialization, which is assisted by sophisticated networks of transport and communications. Without expensive investment power generation, roads, telephone systems, and urban housing, poor countries have to operate in smaller communities which are unable fully to exploit the possibility of scale economies and specialization.

Human Capital Without resources to devote to investment in health, education, and industrial training, workers in poor countries are often less productive than workers using the same technology in rich countries. Yet without higher productivity, it is hard to generate enough output (surplus to consumption requirements) to increase investment in people as well as in machinery.

Ideology It is easy for people from the north to claim that in LDCs tribal customs and communal living inhibit the development of enterprise and initiative, yet this argument may sometimes have some force. It is easy to forget that the business traditions of the industrial countries and the acceptance of factory working took decades or even centuries to develop. Some LDCs are explicitly searching for alternative development strategies which recognize the culture from which they begin.

Low Productivity Agriculture If agricultural productivity is low, most people must work on the land to produce enough food for the population. Few workers are available for work in other activities. Yet increased agricultural production requires better drainage, irrigation, modern fertilizers and seeds; or better equipment. Until workers can be released from the land, poor countries cannot devote resources to investment to improve agricultural productivity. It is all part of the same vicious circle.

In the rest of this chapter, we discuss the extent to which the world economy can help. However, we do not focus exclusively on the very poorest countries. The group of countries we have classified as LDCs also includes the newly industrialized countries – countries such as Mexico and Brazil which are well on their way to becoming rich countries. In some cases these middle-income countries have developed in the way the poorest countries hope to develop. But together, the LDCs share many grievances about the way the world economy operates. In their view it is stacked in favour of the rich industrial countries, as the resolution of the NIEO makes clear.

35-3 Development Through Trade in Primary Products

In Chapter 32 we analysed the gains from trade when countries specialize in the commodities in which they have a comparative advantage. We saw that relative factor abundance is an important determinant of comparative advantage. In many LDCs, the factor with which they are relatively most abundantly supplied is land. This suggests that LDCs can best take advantage of the world economy by exporting goods that use land relatively intensively. In this section we study LDC exports of primary commodities, both the 'soft' commodities – agricultural products such as coffee, cotton, and sugar – and the 'hard' commodities or minerals, such as copper or aluminium.

Traditionally, the LDCs have indeed sought to secure the gains from trade by exporting primary products to the rest of the world and using the revenue to obtain badly needed machinery and other manufactured imports. As late as 1960, exports of primary commodities accounted for 84 per cent of all LDC exports. Nevertheless, many LDCs have become sceptical of the route to development through specialization in production of primary products. Today, less than half of all LDC exports are primary products. We now explain why.

Long-term Trends in Primary Commodity Prices

Table 35-3 shows that, with the spectacular exception of petroleum, the trend in real prices of primary products has been downwards for the last two decades. This can be attributed both to increased supply and to reduced demand. On the demand side, technical ad-

vances such as artificial rubber and plastics have reduced the price for which many raw materials can be sold in industrial markets.

On the supply side, the problem has been the very success of the LDCs in increasing productivity and output. In going for growth through exports of primary products, LDCs invested in better drainage and irrigation, better seeds, and more fertilizers. Asian agriculture was transformed by the 'green revolution'. And mineral producers developed more capital-intensive mining methods, which again increased productivity and output. In consequence, the concerted effort of LDCs to increase output and obtain more export earnings contributed to the fall in the real price of the commodities that they were trying to sell.

Will these trends in primary product prices continue? Not necessarily. With finite world supplies of some minerals, real prices will eventually have to rise to ration increasingly scarce supplies. But the real price of reproducible commodities such as natural rubber will probably continue to fall as more artificial substitutes are developed.

Price Volatility

A second disadvantage of concentrating on the production of primary products is that their real prices tend to be very volatile. For both soft and hard commodities, a change of more than 40 per cent in the *real* price within a single year is not uncommon. In any particular year, LDCs are uncertain how many imports their exports revenue is going to finance.

Equilibrium prices for primary products tend to be volatile because both the supply and the demand are price-inelastic. On the demand side, people have to have food and industrial raw materials. On the supply side, the crops have already been planted and perishable output has to be marketed whatever the price. Similarly, the supply of metals and minerals tends to be inelastic because it takes many years to develop a new copper mine or aluminium plant. Production output cannot be quickly changed.

Because both supply and demand curves are very steep, a small shift in one curve will lead to a large change in the equilibrium price. Demand curves shift because the industrial economies move through periods of boom and

Table 35-3 **Real price of primary products**
(1950–59 = 100)

	1964–73	1974–83	1984–88
33 nonfuel products	83	78	56
Metals, minerals	102	73	52
Petroleum	61	345	251

Source: World Bank, *Commodity Trade and Price Trends*, 1985; *World Development Report*, 1989.

slump. Harvest failures are the most important source of supply shifts, but there are other sources. A strike by miners in Zambia, one of the world's major copper products, had a significant effect on world copper prices in the late 1970s.

Export Concentration

Fluctuations in the real price of primary products lead to volatile export earnings and fluctuations in GNP in those LDCs that concentrate on producing primary products for the world economy. Table 35-4 shows that a single commodity can account for over half the total exports of some LDCs.

The real price of, say, cocoa is volatile. Its high was more than three times its low in the 1970s. Suppose Ghana faces a 50 per cent drop in cocoa prices: its export earnings fall by over 20 per cent (0.46×0.5), which is catastrophic. Of course, Ghana does very well when cocoa prices soar. But the entire economy of Ghana will be buffeted by changes in the world cocoa market.

The combination of a downward long-run trend in real prices and large short-term fluctuations around this trend has made LDCs reluctant to persist with the route of development through exports of primary products if this means excessive concentration on a single commodity. Each of the countries in Table 35-4 has managed to reduce the export share of its dominant commodity by over 10 per cent since 1969. Diversifying production and exporting into other commodities helps to stabilize export revenue and general macroeconomic performance.

Commodity Stabilization Schemes

By acquiring more economic power, it is possible that primary producers could continue to pursue their natural comparative advantage but within a world economy from which they could more easily benefit. Suppose they got together to organize a stabilization scheme for a particular primary product. By stabilizing the price of the commodity, the scheme would stabilize the export earnings of countries heavily dependent on exports of that particular commodity.

Figure 35-1 shows how the scheme would work. *DD* shows the inelastic demand curve for the commodity. The total supply curve of competitive producers fluctuates between SS_1 and SS_2 depending on the state of the harvest. In a free market, the equilibrium point will oscillate between points A_1 and A_2 on the demand curve. Since demand is inelastic, these oscillations imply major changes in the equilibrium commodity price.

Now suppose a buffer stock is established.

A *buffer stock* is an organization aiming to stabilize a commodity market. It buys when the price is low and sells when the price is high.

Suppose there is a bumper harvest and the supply curve is SS_1. In the absence of intervention, equilibrium would be at A_1. The buffer stock organization can buy a quantity AB, leaving a quantity OQ to be purchased by other buyers at a price P. If the government runs the buffer stock, the country's exports will be Q at the price P.

The buffer stock stores the commodity in warehouses. When there is a harvest failure, the producers' supply curve will be SS_2. Rather than allow free market equilibrium at the point A_2, the buffer stock sells off a quantity CA from the warehouse. Together with new production PC, this implies that again the total quantity exported is Q and the price is P. Thus

Table 35-4 Export concentration and real price variability

	ZAMBIA (copper)	MAURITIUS (sugar)	CHAD (cotton)	LIBERIA (iron)	GHANA (cocoa)
Percentage of total 1982 exports	92%	63%	49%	59%	46%
Ratio of maximum to minimum real price, 1969–83	3.2	5.9	1.8	2.0	3.5

Source: World Bank, Commodity Trade and Price Trends, 1985.

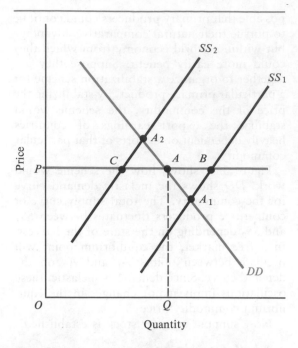

Figure 35-1   COMMODITY PRICE STABILIZATION.   In a free market, fluctuations of the supply curve between SS_1 and SS_2 lead to movements along the demand curve between A_1 and A_2. When the supply curve is SS_1 the buffer stock scheme purchases a quantity AB. The quantity OQ is exported at a price P. When the supply curve is SS_2 the buffer stock scheme sells the quantity CA. Again a total quantity OQ is exported at a price P. Thus commodity prices and export earnings are stabilized.

the activities of the buffer stock organization not only stabilize the commodity price at P but, by stabilizing the quantity of exports at Q, stabilize export earnings.

Although Figure 35-1 illustrates the case in which only the supply schedule fluctuates, fluctuations in the demand schedule may also provide a reason for establishing a buffer stock. The demand schedule for copper tends to fluctuate in line with the business cycle in Europe and North America where copper is a major input to many production processes. Try drawing for yourself a figure like Figure 35-1 to illustrate how a buffer stock might work when demand schedule fluctuates.

At which price should the buffer stock aim to stabilize the market? If the only aim is the elimination of price volatility, the price should be stabilized at the level that implies neither accumulation nor decumulation of buffer stock

holdings in the long run. Suppose in Figure 35-1 that the producers' supply curve fluctuates regularly between SS_1 and SS_2. At the price P shown in the figure, there are as many years in which the buffer stock is purchasing the quantity AB as there are years in which it is selling the equal quantity CA. Stabilizing at a higher price would make AB larger than CA and imply that buffer stocks in the warehouses were growing in the long run.

Such a policy may also make sense. It is simply the policy of restricting supply to the rest of the market, the policy so successfully undertaken by OPEC. OPEC did not even need a warehouse. The separate producing countries simply formed a cartel and agreed to leave the quantity AB in the ground. Since the demand for oil and other primary products is inelastic, restricting the quantity supplied not only raises the commodity price but also raises export earnings of commodity producers. Thus, in principle, effective cartels of producers could not only stabilize the prices of primary products; they could follow the OPEC example and combat the trend of declining real prices by restricting supply.

In recent years there have been attempts b LDCs to organize commodity price stabilization schemes in coffee, cocoa, and tin. Sometimes these have taken a simple form. For example, when there has been a bumper coffee crop in Brazil, the world's largest coffee producer, the Brazilian government has purchased coffee from Brazilian farmers and simply burned it. But none of the LDCs has managed to copy OPEC's example with much success. For many primary commodities, governments have to deal not with a few large oil fields but with a large number of small producers who are much harder to organize.

We discussed cartels in detail in Chapter 10. One problem with the strategy of supply restriction to force up the price is that there is an incentive for individual producers to cheat on the collective agreement. When price is forced above marginal cost, each producer has an incentive to produce more than the agreed output. Yet if all producers cheat, the price will come tumbling down or the buffer stock will be forced to acquire enormous warehouse stocks to keep this production off the market. Even the rich countries of the European Community complain about the cost of warehouse stocks of the famous 'butter mountain'. LDCs simply cannot afford to tie up money in this way.

Since LDCs have been unsuccessful in policing their own attempts to restrict primary commodity supply, and since they cannot afford to stockpile vast quantities when individual producers refuse to cut back output, an important element in the LDC movement for an NIEO is assistance from the rest of the world in establishing effective commodity stabilization schemes. By maintaining higher real prices for primary commodities, these schemes would effectively transfer purchasing power from rich industrial users and consumers to poorer products. But, by also stabilizing real prices, LDCs argue that the benefits would accrue to industrial nations as well as the LDCs that are heavily dependent on exporting these commodities.

35-4 Development Through Industrialization

Many countries have concluded that the route to development lies not through increased specialization in production of primary products but in the expansion of industries that produce manufactures. In this section we discuss the two very different forms that industrial development has taken.

Import Substitution

When world trade collapsed in the 1930s, many LDCs found their export revenues reduced by more than 50 per cent. Not unnaturally, some LDCs resolved never again to be so dependent on the world economy. After the war, they began a policy of import substitution.

Import substitution is a policy of replacing imports by domestic production under the protection of high tariffs or import quotas.

Import substitution reduces world trade and involves suppressing the principle of comparative advantage. LDCs used tariffs and quotas to direct domestic resources away from the primary products in which they had a comparative advantage, into industrial manufacturing where they had a comparative disadvantage.

International trade theory suggests that this policy is likely to be wasteful. Countries are using more domestic resources to make manufactured products than would have been required to make the exports that could have financed imports of the same quantity of manufactures. In a famous and influential study, Ian Little, Tibor Scitovsky, and Maurice Scott tried to measure the quantity of resources being wasted by LDCs pursuing import substitution and concluded that it was large.[2]

Import substitution was pursued partly because LDCs wanted to reduce their specialization in particular primary commodities for the reasons we discussed in the previous section, and partly because these countries associated a developed industrial sector with the high productivity levels observed in the rich industrial countries. Embarking on a strategy of import substitution has one great danger and one possible merit.

The danger is that import substitution may prove a dead end. In the short run, the policy is costly because domestic manufactures are being produced using more resources and at a higher cost than the country's social marginal cost of these goods, namely the world price at which they could be imported. And, although domestic industry may expand quite rapidly behind tariff barriers while imports are being replaced, once import substitution has been completed economic growth may come to an abrupt halt. The country is now specialized in industries in which it has a comparative *disadvantage*, and further expansion can come only from expanding *domestic* demand. That is the danger.

The possible merit is that comparative advantage is a dynamic, not a static, concept. In Chapter 32 we saw that a tariff may help an infant industry even though production subsidies would achieve the same outcome at lower social cost. By developing an industrial sector and learning to use the technology, LDCs may eventually come to have a comparative advantage in some industrial products. Although high-tech projects will continue to be pioneered in the rich countries, which can afford large expenditure on research and development, subsequently many of these production

---

[2] I. M. D. Little, T. Scitovsky, and M. Scott, *Industry and Trade in Some Developing Countries*, Oxford University Press, 1971.

technologies become relatively routine. LDCs may be able to exploit their relative abundance of labour to produce manufactures that are labour-intensive.

Thus import substitution may not be an end in itself. It may be a preliminary phase in which industry gets started, as a prelude to export-led growth.

Export-led growth stresses production and income growth through exports rather than the displacement of imports.

Exports of Manufactures

The real success stories of the last two decades are the countries that have made this transition and are no longer high-tariff countries but rather are successful exporters of manufactures. Instead of withdrawing from the world economy, they are turning it to their advantage. Five countries stand out and are called the NICs (newly industrialized countries). Table 35-5 documents their success.

On average, the NICs grew twice as quickly as the rich industrialized countries during the 1970s. Although Brazil (coffee, soya) and Mexico (petroleum) retain important primary commodity exports, all NICs have significantly increased the share of manufactures in their total exports. As a group, their share of world exports increased from 3 per cent in 1960 to 7 per cent in 1987. These countries now play a larger part in the world economy than countries such as Sweden or Australia.

Should producers of manufactures in the rich industrialized countries worry about competition from producers of manufactures in the NICs? High-tech industries aside, will the NICs wipe out producers of labour-intensive manufactures in Europe, North America, and even Japan? It is sometimes complacently argued that NICs have 'only' 7 per cent of world trade, so this danger is in the distant future. However Japan's share of world trade roughly quintupled between 1950 and 1990, so the possibility of continued expansion of manufacturing production in NICs and other LDCs should be taken seriously.

Although we tend to think of LDCs exporting very labour-intensive low-quality manufactures such as cheap textiles, this stereotype is outdated. It remains true that textiles are the largest single manufactured commodity exported by LDCs, but exports of machinery and consumer durables are growing the most rapidly. LDCs are now major producers of everything from cars to transistors and television sets. How will the industrial countries react to this?

The New Protectionism

The principle of comparative advantage suggests that in the long run the industrial countries and the world as a whole should exploit the gains from this new trade in manufactures. The established industrial economies should reallocate factors to industries in which their comparative advantage now lies, industries such as computers and telecommunications, which use relatively intensively the capital and technical expertise with which the rich countries are relatively well endowed.

However, the adjustment process is costly. Factories have to be closed, outdated plant

Table 35-5 Industry, growth, and trade of the NICs

| | ANNUAL REAL GDP GROWTH | | SHARE OF MANUFACTURES IN EXPORTS | |
	1970–79	1980–87	1960	1987
	%		%	%
Brazil	8.9	3.3	3	45
Mexico	5.4	0.5	12	47
Hong Kong	9.4	5.8	80	92
South Korea	10.0	8.6	14	92
Singapore	8.9	5.4	26	72

Source: World Bank, *World Development Report*; IMF, *International Financial Statistics.*

written off, and workers retrained. In Chapter 32 we explained why politicians may give in to pressure from declining industries to protect them through tariffs and quotas rather than insist that new industries be established. In a world where tariffs among industrial countries have been largely abolished, there is now a re-emergence of protection through quotas, voluntary export restrictions, and non-tariff barriers. Restrictions of trade in textiles and clothing date back to the 1960s. New restrictions have subsequently appeared in cars, steel, and video recorders.

In Chapter 32 we showed how tariffs lead society to waste resources. They also lead to substantial transfers from consumers to producers. Although the new protectionism in the industrial countries is by no means universal; it can be significant in some industries:

> For every $20 000 job in the Swedish shipyards, Swedish taxpayers pay an estimated $50 000 annual subsidy. Protection costs Canadian consumers $500 million a year to provide an additional $135 million of wages in the clothing industry. And when Japanese consumers pay eight times the world price for beef, Japanese farmers are not made eight times better off. It costs them that much more to produce it.[3]

Compared with these costs, subsidized retraining, redundancy benefits, and the closing of plants that are no longer efficient make much more sense. In the long run, protection costs more than subsidizing adjustment as comparative advantage changes.

Nevertheless, the LDCs are justifiably frightened that their strategy of economic development through industrialization and export-led growth through manufactures will be frustrated by protection in their industrial markets. The movement for an NIEO does not want merely an assurance that the rich countries will not impose tariffs and other restrictions on imports from LDCs. It would like the industrial countries to go further: to accelerate imports of manufactures from LDCs by actually imposing tariffs on imports from other industrial countries. At present, the prospects for such discrimination in favour of LDCs seem small.

35-5 Development Through Borrowing

A third route to economic development is by external borrowing, and a third complaint of LDCs about the way the world economy works is that borrowing terms are too tough. LDCs have traditionally been borrowers in world markets, using money borrowed from abroad to finance an excess of imports over exports. By importing capital goods, LDCs have been able to supplement domestic investment financed by domestic savings.

This pattern of external borrowing was reinforced by the OPEC oil price shock. LDCs without oil reserves responded to the increased cost of oil imports not by reducing imports of other commodities, or by reducing their consumption of oil, but by allowing their current account deficits to grow.

Nor was the problem confined to oil importing LDCs. Oil exporters, such as Mexico, responded to higher oil prices and greater oil wealth by embarking on ambitious programmes of investment and importing. When real oil prices fell sharply in the mid-1980s, export revenues collapsed but long-term programmes proved hard to cut back quickly; so the current account deficit became substantial. The rapid accumulation of LDC debts in the 1980s became known as the international debt crisis.

The International Debt Crisis

We remind ourselves of the basic balance of payments arithmetic:

$$\text{Current account deficit} = \text{trade deficit} + \text{debt interest}$$

$$= \text{increase in net foreign debt} \qquad (1)$$

The first line shows the sources of the current account deficit; the second reminds us that it has to be paid for by selling domestic assets to foreigners or by new foreign borrowing.

Table 35-6 shows the dramatic build-up in debt for almost every type of LDC in the 1980s. But the *burden* of the debt is not measured simply by the debt/GNP ratio. Debt hurts only when the real interest rate is positive: only then does a country have to sacrifice real resources to repay the debt in the future. A crucial reason why the 1980s have seen such a debt crisis is that it is the only postwar decade in which real interest rates have been significantly greater than zero. Indeed, for many of the previous

---

[3] World Bank, *World Development Report.*

Table 35-6 LDC debt (% of GNP)

	ALL LDCs	SUB-SAHARAN AFRICA	MIDDLE-INCOME EAST ASIA	LOW-INCOME EAST ASIA	E. EUROPE, MIDDLE EAST N. AFRICA	LATIN AMERICA, CARIBBEAN
1981	23	26	28	8	30	27
1987	42	85	40	16	47	52

Source: World Bank, World Development Report, 1989.

Table 35-7 Debt service (% of net exports), selected LDCs

	1970	1987
Argentina	22	45
Columbia	12	33
Brazil	12	27
Mexico	24	30
Venezuela	3	23
Hungary	—	27
Poland	—	15
Burundi	2	39
Kenya	6	29

Source: as for Table 35-6.

decades real interest rates were actually negative, and debtor countries were actually being subsidized in real terms by creditors.

It is also arguable that the right measure of a country's ability to pay is not its GNP but its export earnings, the foreign currency it earns and which could almost all be used to make debt repayments if imports were drastically reduced. Hence in Table 35-7 we look not at the debt/GNP ratio but the ratio of debt service to exports. Debt service is the flow of interest payments on the existing debt. Table 35-7 shows that for many countries the increase in the ratio of debt service to exports has increased much more sharply than the simple debt/GNP ratio. It explains why debtor countries were hurting so much in the 1980s.

Default and Debt Rescheduling Suppose you are the government of a big debtor country, and the only way to meet the burden of debt interest (and repayment of the original loan) is to plunge your economy into a deep and long recession. This will slash imports and allow export revenue to go to servicing the debt. Politically, you are in big trouble. Voters won't put up with austerity for long.

Do you have any other options? First, you can call in the IMF and the World Bank. Under their *adjustment programmes* you can probably get a short-term loan to pay your other creditors. But these international agencies will insist that you take tough action to get the long-run position under control.

Second, you can go to your creditors – in this case mainly the large private banks of the world's richest economies – and seek a *debt rescheduling*. Basically, this means you still agree to pay back the money with interest, but you negotiate a longer payback period with a lower repayment per period. If you think your economy will expand in the future this may be a good strategy, and you can grow your way out of trouble without too much short-run pain.

If things are even more desperate, you may consider outright default or refusal to repay what you owe. Obviously, this deals with the immediate burden of the debt, but what are the costs? In the most extreme case, governments of the creditors may think about sending in their armies, though this has almost never happened. But governments of creditors might attempt to exert what leverage they could through international negotiations, trade embargoes, and so on. Economists are more interested in a direct market mechanism which might have the same deterrent effect.

When countries borrow in world financial markets, they do not all face the same interest rate. Like individuals, riskier countries face higher interest rates, which build in a *risk premium* to cover the possibility of default. Hence it is possible that countries that default face prohibitive risk premia when they try to borrow in the future. The knowledge that this will happen is then sufficient to deter them from defaulting in the first place.

What has happened in practice? First, there have been very few outright defaults. Second, and somewhat surprisingly, there is very little evidence that, as a country's debt position becomes more risky, the financial markets substantially raise the interest rate on new borrowing. So the deterrent effect may be small. In practice, much of the problem has been met by debt rescheduling. Creditors have preferred to get some money back over a longer period rather than provoke debtors to announce outright default. And, finally, under international pressure from governments, the creditor banks have actually written off much of the debt. This means they acknowledge that it is never going to be repaid even though the debtor has not explicitly announced a complete default. Thus, the late 1980s saw many famous Western banks announcing operating losses as they set off bad debts against their healthy profits from domestic operations.

35-6 Aid

Many of the complaints of the poor south come down to the view that the rich north should provide them with more aid. Such aid can take many forms: subsidized loans, outright gifts of food or machinery, or technical help and the free provision of expert advisers.

The basic issue is a moral or value judgement about equality. Within a country the government usually makes transfer payments to the poor, financed by taxes on the rich, thereby implementing a view of society as a whole that the income distribution thrown up by market forces is unfair and inequitable.

The same value judgement lies at the heart of aid or transfer payments between countries. However, it is complicated by two additional factors. First, within a country with a sense of national identity and social cohesion, it may seem right that the government should be concerned with *all* its citizens. But there is no single government of the world that can accept worldwide responsibility for welfare. Governments of individual countries, and the citizens they represent, may feel much less responsibility for the welfare of people of a different nationality in a distant country, of which they have little knowledge or experience. Second, the issue is complicated by history. Many people of the south feel that the prosperity of

the north was first established during a colonial period when the resources of the south were exploited. Aid seems at least partial compensation. The northern countries do not necessarily share this interpretation of history.

Aid and the Recipient Countries

If aid is to be given, does it matter in what form it is given? Many LDCs believe the single most important contribution the rich countries can make is to provide free access for the LDCs to the markets of the developed countries. 'Trade, not aid' is the slogan. Just as the best service a domestic government can render a 30-year-old redundant steel worker may be to provide retraining which will allow the prospect of a useful working life of another 30 years, LDCs believe that trade rather than handouts is likely to be a more effective and more lasting form of assistance and encouragement.

Critics of existing aid programmes also argue that the donor countries should do more to check up on who is actually benefiting from their transfers. It is argued that too much aid finds its way into the hands of the ruling elite in the recipient countries rather than the poorest people for whom it was intended.

Of course, some people in rich countries like to exaggerate the extent of government corruption in poorer countries. More practically, recipient governments dislike donors telling them what to do, and it is usually necessary to channel aid through recipient governments.

Whenever aid and redistribution are discussed, it is useful to recall the analogy of a leaking bucket, suggested by Arthur Okun.[4] When transfers are made, it is like transferring water in a leaky bucket. Some of the water leaks out (it disappears along the way), but some makes it to the other end and is used for the purpose that was intended. Whether the process is worth while depends on how fast the water leaks and how urgently the water is needed at the other end. And in the meantime, we should be looking for buckets with fewer holes.

---

[4] Arthur Okun's analogy appears in C. D. Campbell (ed.), *Income Redistribution*, American Enterprise Institute, 1976, p. 21.

Aid and Migration

The quickest way to equalize world income distribution would be to permit free migration between countries. Residents of poor countries could go elsewhere in search of higher incomes. And in emigrating, they would increase the capital and land per worker for those who stayed behind.

Nor is this idea entirely fanciful. The massive movements of population from Europe to the Americas and the colonies in the nineteenth and early twentieth centuries represented an income-equalizing movement of this sort. Since the Second World War the major migrations have been temporary, although the steady flow of Mexicans (illegally) across the US border is one major exception. More common has been the use of temporary migrant labour in Europe (especially West Germany) from Yugoslavia, Greece, and Turkey, which countries have all benefited from payments sent home to their families by workers temporarily abroad. Similarly, Egypt, India, and Pakistan receive significant transfer payments from workers temporarily abroad (especially those working in the Persian Gulf). And in 1989–90 we saw substantial westward migration from Eastern Europe as the barriers came tumbling down.

None the less, there is no free and unrestricted immigration to the rich countries today. Indeed, even migrant workers are frequently outlawed. One difference between conditions today and conditions during the massive migrations of the nineteenth century is that there are now extensive systems of welfare and public health in rich countries. Quite apart from any racial or religious arguments, opponents of immigration say that existing residents would end up subsidizing unskilled immigrants who would spend most of their lives receiving public handouts.

The United States grew extremely quickly during the period of large-scale immigration. With economies of scale, it is not clear that existing residents inevitably lose out by admitting immigrants. Although fascinating, the question is largely academic. At present there seems little prospect of the rich countries allowing immigration on a significant scale, least of all from the poorest countries of the world economy.

Summary

1   The call for a New International Economic Order (NIEO) is an attempt by LDCs to get a larger share of the world's income and wealth. It reflects the extreme inequality between the rich north and the poor south. Half the world's population had an annual income of scarcely more than £177 per person in 1987.

2   The south's complaints are that (a) the markets for their primary products are controlled by the north; (b) northern protectionism is hampering their prospects for industrial development; (c) borrowing is too expensive; and (d) simple justice dictates that the north should take practical steps to close the north–south gap.

3   In the world's poorest countries, population growth is faster than the rate at which supplies of other factors can be increased. Hence labour productivity is low and, after provision for consumption, there are few spare resources to increase human and physical capital. It is hard to break out of this vicious circle.

4   The downward trend in real prices, price volatility, and danger of extreme concentration in a single commodity have made LDCs reluctant to pursue development by exploiting a comparative advantage in primary products. Buffer stocks and cartel supply restrictions have proved difficult to organize, with the conspicuous exception of OPEC.

5   LDCs are increasing their export of labour-intensive manufactures. In the last decade their growth performance has been better than that of industrial countries. Although the LDCs are beginning from a small base, their market share could quickly become much more significant. The NICs have already made considerable progress along this route to development.

6   Industrial countries are responding with new moves towards protection from imports of manufactures. Yet they would probably do better by encouraging adjustment towards the industries in which their comparative advantage now lies.

7   LDCs have run large deficits in the last decade, financed chiefly by external borrowing. Larger debts and high interest rates have led to threats of default and an international debt crisis.

8   Trade may help the LDCs more effectively than aid. Migration would help equalize world incomes but there is little prospect of rich countries allowing significant immigration.

Key Terms

New International Economic Order
Less developed countries (LDCs)
Price volatility
Primary commodities
Buffer stocks
Import substitution
Export-led growth
New protectionism
International debt crisis
Debt rescheduling
Migration
Newly industrializing countries (NICs)

Problems

1   Discuss two forces tending to reduce the real price of agricultural produce in the long run.

2   How would a world boom affect a country specializing in producing copper?

3   Why have LDCs been particularly successful in exporting textiles, clothing, and leather footwear?

4   (a) Describe how a buffer stock scheme works. (b) What could go wrong? (c) Why don't private speculators smooth out prices of primary products in any case? (d) Does your answer to (c) help you answer (b)?

5   Can a small LDC gain by a policy of import substitution?

6   How could rich countries best help the poor countries?

7   What are the complaints of the LDCs that have led to their call for an NIEO? Do you think this call will be heeded?

8   Common Fallacies Show why the following statements are incorrect. (a) Aid is all the help LDCs need. (b) Europe's problem is competition from cheap labour in LDCs. (c) LDCs do best by sticking to production of raw materials for the world economy.

Index